Encyclopedia of the
Archaeology of Ancient Egypt

Encyclopedia of the Archaeology of Ancient Egypt

Compiled and edited by
Kathryn A. Bard

with the editing assistance of
Steven Blake Shubert

London and New York

First published 1999
by Routledge
11 New Fetter Lane, London EC4P 4EE

Simultaneously published in the USA and Canada
by Routledge
29 West 35th Street, New York, NY 10001

© 1999 Routledge

Typeset in Times by Routledge
Printed and bound in Great Britain by
T J International Ltd, Padstow, Cornwall

British Library Cataloguing in Publication Data
A catalogue record for this book is available from the British Library

Library of Congress Cataloguing in Publication Data
Encyclopedia of the archaeology of ancient Egypt/edited by Kathryn A. Bard;
with the editing assistance of Steven Blake Shubert.
Includes bibliographical references and index.
1. Egypt – Antiquities – Encyclopedias. I. Bard, Kathryn A.
II. Schubert, Steven Blake.

DT58.E53 1998   98–16350
932′.003–dc21   CIP

ISBN 0-415-18589-0

To my mother, Rosemary Best Bard (1918–1997),
and father, Robert Edward Bard (1918–)
with thanks for all their encouragement,
love, and support

Contents

Illustrations

Illustrations

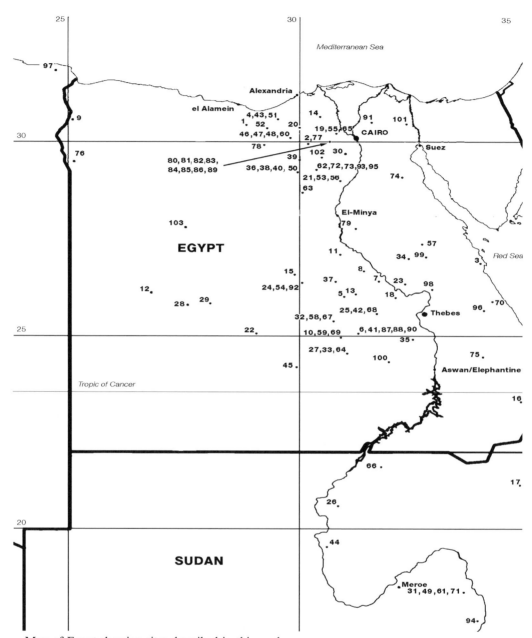

Map of Egypt showing sites described in this work

1 Abu Gurab	7 Akhmim	13 Balabish
2 Abu Roash	8 Antinoopolis	14 Behbeit el-Hagara
3 Abu Sha'ar	9 Apis	15 Beni Hasan
4 Abusir	10 Armant	16 Berenike
5 Abydos	11 Asyut	
6 el-Adaïma	12 el-Badari	

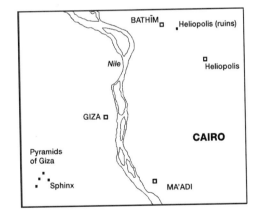

Map of Cairo showing sites described in this work

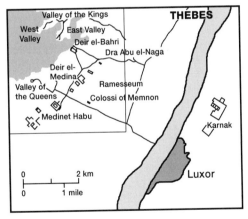

Map of Thebes showing sites described in this work

How to use this Encyclopedia

Structure

The Encyclopedia opens with a map of the region and a chronology which provides a context for the material which follows.

The first section of the Encyclopedia comprises fourteen overview essays. The first offers a general introduction and the remaining essays are guides to developments in the archaeology of the region in specific historical periods.

These are followed by more than 300 entries in alphabetical order. These entries discuss:

a important sites
b thematics on aspects of society or culture
c archaeological practices
d biographies of famous Egyptologists
e buildings
f geographical features

See also references at the end of each entry will lead you to related topics.

There is also a list of further reading following each entry, which includes foreign-language sources as well as references available in English.

Stylistic features

The following stylistic features have been employed in the Encyclopedia:

a metric measurements, such as km, m, cm and so on.
b BC/AD not BCE/ACE.
c Entries are listed by their most familiar place name. Sometimes this is the Greek name for the town, e.g. Hierakonpolis; sometimes it is the modern Arabic name for the (nearby) town, e.g. Nagada. Please use the index for guidance on alternative names.
d transliteration of Egyptian words, for example, *ḥwt*.

Acknowledgments

Work on this book began in 1991 at the instigation of Kennie Lyman, and many friends and colleagues were helpful in its undertaking. I would first like to thank all contributors who wrote their entries in a timely manner, and those who cheerfully volunteered to write several entries, especially Manfred Bietak, Ed Brovarski, Karl Butzer, Rosalie David, Rodolfo Fattovich, Abdel Monem Gomaà, Zahi Hawass, Christian Hölzl, Timothy Kendall, Leonard and Barbara Lesko, Peter Der Manuelian, Bill Peck, Friederike Kampp Seyfried, Steve Sidebotham, Stephen Thompson, Rob Wenke, Bruce Williams, Frank Yurco, and the late I.E.S. Edwards, with whom I had the great privilege to engage in a correspondence that was both educational and enjoyable.

This volume could not have been finished without the editing assistance of Steven Blake Shubert, who, although he came in on the project at a late date, worked with much dedication and a good eye for details. Steven's cheerfulness and reliability are greatly appreciated. Harry C. Broadhead helped Steven with logistical support. A number of professors and former graduate students in the Department of Near Eastern Studies, University of Toronto, where I studied Egyptian archaeology, were supportive and pleased to contribute to this volume.

Richard Fazzini and Donald Redford graciously served as project advisors and also suggested the names of possible contributors. Suggestions for contributors were also provided by Christian and Heike Guksch, Barry Kemp, Leonard and Barbara Lesko, and Bruce Trigger. The late Bernard Bothmer offered encouragement to the project in its early stages. Janet Johnson and Donald Whitcomb were helpful in discussions as the project evolved. Tim Kendall suggested that Nubian sites should also be included in the encyclopedia, and while a number of Nubian sites are missing, some of the major ones that are relevant to the culture of ancient Egypt can be found in this volume. Aslihan Yener and Paul Goldberg were helpful in explaining some of the technical details in the entry on mining at Gebel Zeit.

Translations of several entries were done by Benjamin Clark and Steven Shubert (French), Alexandra O'Brien (German) and Rodolfo Fattovich (Italian).

At Boston University, technical help with computer files was provided by Qadeer Hassan, Sarah Mascia, Ann-Eliza Lewis and Ben Thomas. John Ziemba and Lea Koonce cheerfully sent many faxes for me. My colleagues in the Department of Archaeology and the African Studies Center, Farouk El-Baz in the Center for Remote Sensing, and a number of my students were encouraging and interested in the project.

During my sabbatical leave at the University of Chicago in 1995–96, the project benefitted from discussions with colleagues at the Oriental Institute, and the help of Chuck Jones in the Oriental Institute Archives. My thanks to the Oriental Institute for allowing me to be there as a visiting scholar so that much of this project could be completed.

Diep and Peter Shoemaker provided last-minute help with files, as did Rodolfo Fattovich with a number of entries and contributors. Sidney Kramer was very helpful in getting Routledge involved in the project. At Routledge, Senior Editors Fiona Cairns and Denise Rea were thoughtful, dedicated, and very pleasant to work with via e-mail.

Without the help of these friends and

Acknowledgments

colleagues this volume could not have been completed. The end result, of course, is my own responsibility, and although there are certainly lacunae in the list of entries, I hope it will provide a useful reference and overview to all those interested in the wonderful things of ancient Egypt.

KATHRYN A. BARD

List of abbreviations

ÄA	Ägyptologische Abhandlungen, Wiesbaden
AAR	*African Archaeological Review*
AASOR	*Annual of the American Schools of Oriental Research*
AJA	*American Journal of Archaeology*
ASAE	*Annales du Service des Antiquités de l'Égypte*, Caire
AVDAIK	Archäologische Veröffentlichungen, Deutsches Archäologisches Institut, Abteilung Kairo
BAR	*British Archaeological Reports*, Oxford
BASOR	*Bulletin of the American Schools of Oriental Research*
BdÉ	Bibliothèque d'Étude, Institut français d'archéologie orientale, Caire
Bf	Beiträge zur ägyptischen Bauforschung und Altertumskunde, Kairo, Zurich, Wiesbaden
BES	*Bulletin of the Egyptological Seminar*, New York
BIÉ	*Bulletin de l'Institut d'Égypte*, Caire
BIFAO	*Bulletin de l'Institut français d'archéologie orientale*, Caire
BSFE	*Bulletin de la Société français d'égyptologie*, Paris
CA	*Current Anthropology*
CAJ	*Cambridge Archaeological Journal*
CdÉ	*Chronique d'Égypte*, Bruxelles
CRIPEL	*Cahier de Recherches de l'Institut de Papyrologie et d'Égyptologie de Lille*
DÖAW	*Denkschrift der Österreichischen Akademie der Wissenschaften in Wien, Phil.-hist. Klasse*
FIFAO	*Fouilles de l'Institut français d'archéologie orientale*, Caire
GM	*Göttinger Miszellen*, Göttingen
HÄB	Hildesheimer Ägyptologische Beiträge, Hildesheim
IEJ	*Israel Exploration Journal*, Jerusalem
JAA	*Journal of Anthropological Archaeology*
JAOS	*Journal of the American Oriental Society*
JARCE	*Journal of the American Research Center in Egypt*
JEA	*Journal of Egyptian Archaeology*
JFA	*Journal of Field Archaeology*
JMA	*Journal of Mediterranean Archaeology*
JNES	*Journal of Near Eastern Studies*
JSSEA	*Journal of the Society for the Study of Egyptian Antiquities*
JWP	*Journal of World Prehistory*
LÄ	*Lexikon der Ägyptologie*, ed. W. Helck and W. Westendorf, Wiesbaden
LAAA	*Liverpool Annals of Archaeology and Anthropology*
MÄS	*Müncher Ägyptologische Studien*, Berlin, Munich
MIFAO	*Mémoires piblis par les Membres de l'Institut français d'archéologie orientale du Caire*

List of abbreviations

MDAIK	*Mitteilungen des Deutschen Archäologischen Instituts, Abteilung Kairo*
MMJ	*Metropolitan Museum of Art Journal*
NARCE	*Newsletter of the American Research Center in Egypt*
OIP	Oriental Institute Publications, University of Chicago
RdÉ	*Revue d'Égyptologie*
SAOC	Studies in Ancient Oriental Civilization, Chicago: The Oriental Institute Press
SDAIK	Sanderschrift des Deutschen Arhäologischen Instituts, Abteilung, Kairo, Mainz
WA	*World Archaeology*
ZÄS	Zeitschrift für Ägyptische Sprache und Altertumskunde, Leipzig, Berlin

List of contributors

Barbara Adams
Petrie Museum of Egyptian Archaeology,
  University College London

Matthew Adams
University Museum, University of
  Pennsylvania

Shmuel Aḥituv
Ben Gurion University of the Negev, Israel

David A. Anderson
University of Pittsburgh

Robert Anderson

Wendy Anderson
McGill University

George Armelagos
Emory University

David Aston
Austrian Archaeological Institute, Cairo

John Baines
Oriental Institute, University of Oxford

Barbara E. Barich
University of Rome "La Sapienza"

Farouk El-Baz
Centre for Remote Sensing, Boston University

Robert Bianchi

Manfred Bietak
Institute of Egyptology, University of Vienna

Edward Bleiberg
Brooklyn Museum of Art

Ann Bomann
American Schools of Oriental Research

Douglas Brewer
The Spurlock Museum, University of Illinois

Edwin Brock
Canadian Institute in Egypt

Edward Brovarski
Museum of Fine Arts, Boston

Stanley Burstein
California State University, Los Angeles

Karl W. Butzer
University of Texas, Austin

Georges Castel
Instituit Français d'Archéologie Oriental, Cairo

Alfredo Castiglioni
Centro Ricerche sul Deserto Orientale, Italy

Angelo Castiglioni
Centro Ricerche sul Deserto Orientale, Italy

Sylvie Cauville

Angela E. Close
University of Washington

Eugene Cruz-Uribe
Northern Arizona University

Elvira D'Amicone
Museum of Ancient Egypt, Turin

Rosalie David
Manchester Museum, University of
  Manchester

Leo Depuydt
Brown University

William Dever
University of Arizona

Aidan Dodson
University of Bristol

Anna Maria Donadoni Roveri
Museum of Ancient Egypt, Turin

Peter Dorman
University of Chicago, Luxor

Günter Dreyer
Germany Archaeological Institute, Cairo

Margaret Drower

I. E. S. Edwards†

Dieter Eigner

List of contributors

Josef Eiwanger
Kommission für Allgemeine und Vergleichende
  Archäologie des Deutschen Archäologischen
  Instituts, Bonn

Christopher Ellis

Rodolfo Fattovich
Istituto Universitario Orientale, Naples

Christine Favard-Meeks

Richard A. Fazzini
Brooklyn Museum of art

Erika Feucht
Institute of Egyptology, Heidelberg

Renée Friedman
British Museum, London

Creighton Gabel
Boston University

Luc Gabolde
CNRS.Centre Franco-Egyptien de Karnak

Günther Garbrecht
Technical University of Braunschweig

Achilles Gautier
University of Gent

Jeremy Geller
Hobart and William Smith Colleges, New York

Ogden Goelet
New York University

Jean-Claude Golvin
Centre national de la Recherche Scientifique,
  France

Farouk Gomaà
Institute of Egyptology, University of Tübingen

Darlene Gorzo
University of Toronto

Arvid Göttlicher

Lynda Green
Royal Ontario Museum

Christian Guksch
Kirgisische Staatliche National Universität

M. Nabil El Hadidi
Cairo University Herbarium

Gerhard Haeny

Donald Hansen
New York University

James Harris
University of Michigan

Stephen P. Harvey
Walters Art Gallery, Baltimore

Ali Hassan

Fekri Hassan
Institute of Archaeology, University College
  London

Zahi Hawass

Joyce Haynes
Museum of Fine Arts, Boston

Lisa Heidorn
University of Helsinki

Wolfgang Helck

Stan Hendrickx
University of Leuven

Sharon Herbert
University of Michigan

Anja Herold
Pelizaeus-Museum, Hildesheim

Friedrich W. Hinkel

James Hoffmeier
Wheaton College, Illinois

John S. Holladay, Jr.
University of Toronto

Diane Holmes

Christian Hölzl
Kunsthistorisches Museum, Vienna

Colin Hope
Monash University

Mark Horton

David Jeffreys
Institute of Archaeology, University College
  London

Janet H. Johnson
Oriental Institute, University of Chicago

Michael Jones

Werner Kaiser
German Institute of Arcaeology, Cairo

Friederike Kampp-Seyfried
Institute of Egyptology, Heidelberg

Janice Kamrin

Naguib Kanawati
Australian Centre for Egyptology, Macquarie
  University

Timothy Kendall
Museum of Fine Arts, Boston

Christopher Kirby
Kings College, London

Wojciech Kołataj
Polish Center of Mediterranean Archaeology,
  Cairo

Janusz K. Kozlowski
Institute of Archaeology, Jagellonian
  University

Karla Kroeper
Ägyptisches Museum und Papyrussammlung,
  Berlin

Klaus-Peter Kuhlmann
German Institute of Archaeology, Cairo

Dieter Kurth
Institute of Archaeology, University of
  Hamburg

Peter Lacovara
Emory University

John Larson
Oriental Institute, University of Chicago

Jean-Philippe Lauer
Centre national de la Recherche Scientifique,
  France

Anthony Leahy
University of Birmingham

Christian Leblanc
Louvre Museum, France

Jean Leclant
Cabinet d'Égyptologie, Collège de France

Mark Lehner
Semitic Museum, Harvard University

Albert Leonard, Jr.
University of Arizona

Ronald Leprohon
University of Toronto

Barbara Lesko
Brown University

Leonard Lesko
Brown University

Jadwiga Lipińska
Muzeum Naradowe, Warsaw

Mario Liverani
University of Rome, Italy

Alan B. Lloyd
University College of Swansea

Antonio Loprieno
University of California, Los Angeles

Nancy C. Lovell
University of Alberta

Demetra Makris
University of Toronto

Peter Der Manuelian
Museum of Fine Arts, Boston

Karl Martin
Institute of Archaeology, University of
  Hamburg

Eva Martin-Pardey
Institute of Archaeology, University of
  Hamburg

Valerie Maxfield
University of Southampton

Murray McClellan
Boston University

Mary M. A. McDonald
University of Calgary

Carol Meyer
Oriental Institute, University of Chicago

Béatrix Midant-Reynes
Centre d'Anthropogie, Toulouse, France

Stella Miller
Bryn Mawr College

Anthony Mills

James O. Mills
University of Florida

Bodil Mortensen

Doha Mahmoud Mostafa

James Muhly
American School of Classical Studies, Athens

Greg Mumford
University of Toronto

List of contributors

William Murnane
Institute of Egyptian Art and Archaeology,
  University of Memphis

Paul Nicholson
University of Wales, Cardiff

Edward L. Ochsenschlager
Brooklyn College, The City University of New
  York

David O'Connor
Institute of Fine Arts, New York University

Eliezer D. Oren
Ben Gurion University of the Negev, Israel

Patricia Paice
University of Toronto

David Peacock
University of Southampton

William H. Peck
Detroit Institute of Arts

Peter Piccione
University of Charleston, South Carolina

Rosanna Pirelli
Istituto Universitario Orientale, Naples

Patricia Podzorski
P.A. Hearst Museum of Anthropology,
  University of California, Berkeley

Federico Poole
Istituto Universitario Orientale, Naples

Georges Pouit
Bureau de Recherches Géologiques et Minières
  and Centre National de la Recherche
  Scientifique, Paris

Edgar B. Pusch
Pelizaeus-Museum, Hildesheim

Sarah Quie

John D. Ray
University of Cambridge

Donald Redford
Pennsylvania State University

Carol Redmount
University of California, Berkeley

Jean Revez
Université de Paris-Sorbonne ans Université du
  Québec à Montréal

Janet Richards
Kelsey Museum of Archaeology, University of
  Michigan

Catharine H. Roehrig
Metropolitan Museum, New York

Vincent Rondot
CNRS. Institut de Papyrologie et
  d'Egyptologie, University of Lille

Pamela Russell
Boston University

Abdel Monem Sayed
University of Alexandria

Hans D. Schneider
Rijksmuseum van Oudheden, Leiden

Alan Schulman

Jürgen Seeher
German Institute of Archaeology, Istanbul

Stephan Seidlmayer
Ägyptologisches Seminar, Free University of
  Berlin

Ian Shaw
Institute of Archaeology, University College
  London

Steven Blake Shubert
University of Toronto

Steven Sidebotham
University of Delaware

Mark Smith
Oriental Institute, University of Oxford

Steven Snape
University of Liverpool

Georges Soukiassian
Institut Français d'Archéologie Orientale,
  Cairo

Jeffrey Spencer
British Museum

Denys A. Stocks
University of Manchester

Sally Swain

Tarek Swelim
Cairo, Egypt

Ana Tavares
University College London

Emily Teeter
Oriental Institute, University of Chicago

Aristide Théodoridès†

Stephen E. Thompson

Andreas Tillmann
Bayer. Landesamt für Denkmalpflege,
  Ingolstadt

László Török
Institute of Archaeology, Hungarian Academy
  of Sciences

Joyce Tyldesley
Liverpool University

Eric Uphill
University College London

Dominique Valbelle
Institut de Papyrologie et d'Égyptologie,
  University of Lille *III*

Michel Valloggia
University of Geneva

Charles Van Siclen
Van Siclen Books, San Antonio

William Ward

Thomas von der Way
German Institute of Archaeology, Cairo

Kent R. Weeks
American University in Cairo

Josef Wegner
University Museum, University of
  Pennsylvania

James Weinstein
Cornell University

Fred Wendorf
Southern Methodist University

Robert Wenke
University of Washington

Wilma Wetterstrom
Botanical Museum, Harvard University

Donald Whitcomb
Oriental Institute, University of Chicago

Donald White
University Museum, University of
  Pennsylvania

Terry Wilfong
Kelsey Museum of Archaeology, University of
  Michigan

Toby A. H. Wilkinson
University of Durham

Harco Willems
University of Leiden

Bruce Williams
Oriental Institute, University of Chicago

Elsbeth Williams

Marcia F. Wiseman
Department of Anthropology, University of
  Toronto at Scarborough, and Department of
  Near Eastern and Asian Civilization
  (Egyptian Section), Royal Ontario Museum

Frank J. Yurco
Field Museum of Natural History, Chicago

Chronology of Ancient Egypt

Paleolithic

Lower Paleolithic, *circa* 700/500,000–200,000 BP
Middle Paleolithic, *circa* 200,000–45,000 BP
Upper Paleolithic, *circa* 35,000–21,000 BP
Late Paleolithic, *circa* 21,000–12,000 BP
Epi-paleolithic, *circa* 12,000–8,000 BP

Neolithic, northern Egypt: begins *circa* 5200 BC

Predynastic period:

Ma'adi culture, northern Egypt,
circa 4000–3300/3200 BC
Badarian culture, Middle Egypt,
circa 4500–3800 BC
Nagada culture, southern Egypt:
Nagada I, *circa* 4000–3600 BC
Nagada II, *circa* 3600–3200 BC
Nagada III/Dynasty 0, *circa* 3200–3050 BC

Early Dynastic period:

1st Dynasty, *circa* 3050–2890 BC:
Aḥa
Djer
Djet
Den
Anedjib
Smerkhet
Qa'a

2nd Dynasty, *circa* 2890–2686 BC:
Hotepsekhemwy
Reneb
Nynetjer
Weneg
Peribsen
Khasekhemwy

Old Kingdom:

3rd Dynasty, *circa* 2686–2613 BC:
Nebka
Zoser
Sekhemkhet
Khaba
Huni

4th Dynasty, *circa* 2613–2494 BC:
Seneferu
Khufu
Djedefre
Khafre
Nebka
Menkaure
Shepseskaf

5th Dynasty, *circa* 2494–2345 BC:
Weserkaf
Sahure
Neferirkare
Shepseskare
Neferefre
Nyuserre
Menkauhor
Djedkare-Isesi
Unas

6th Dynasty, *circa* 2345–2181 BC:
Teti
Weserkare
Pepi I
Merenre
Pepi II
Nitocris

First Intermediate Period:

7th–8th Dynasties, *circa* **2181–2125 BC:**
circa 16 kings

9th–10th Dynasties (Heracleopolis),
circa **2160–2025 BC:**
circa 18 kings

11th Dynasty, pre-unification Thebes,
circa **2125–2055 BC:**
Mentuhotep I
Intef I
Intef II
Intef III

Middle Kingdom:

11th Dynasty, unification, *circa* **2055–1985 BC:**
Mentuhotep II
Mentuhotep III
Mentuhotep IV

12th Dynasty, *circa* **1985–1795 BC:**
Amenemhat I
Senusret I
Amenemhat II
Senusret II
Amenemhat III
Amenemhat IV
Queen Sobekneferu

Second Intermediate Period:

13th Dynasty, *circa* **1795–1650 BC:**
circa 65 kings, including:
'Amu-sa-hornedjherjotef
Chendjer
Sobekhotep III
Neferhotep I
Sihathor I
Sihathor II
Sobekhotep IV
Neferhotep III

14th Dynasty, *circa* **1750–1650 BC:**
Possibly up to 76 kings who ruled from Sais in
the Delta and overlapped with the 13th and
15th Dynasties.

15th Dynasty (Hyksos), *circa* **1650–1550 BC:**
Salitis
Khayan
Apophis
Khamudi

16th Dynasty (Hyksos), *circa* **1650–1550 BC:**
circa 17 minor kings/Hyksos vassals who
overlapped with the 15th Dynasty.

17th Dynasty (Thebes), *circa* **1650–1550 BC:**
circa 14 kings, the last four of which were:
Intef VI
Ta'o I
Ta'o II
Kamose

New Kingdom:

18th Dynasty, *circa* **1550–1295 BC:**
Ahmose
Amenhotep I
Tuthmose I
Tuthmose II
Tuthmose III
Hatshepsut
Amenhotep II
Tuthmose IV
Amenhotep III
Amenhotep IV/Akhenaten (Amarna period)
Smenkhkare
Tutankhamen
Ay
Horemheb

Ramesside period:

19th Dynasty, *circa* **1295–1186 BC:**
Ramesses I
Seti I
Ramesses II
Merenptah
Amenmesses
Seti II
Siptah
Queen Tawosret

20th Dynasty, *circa* 1186–1069 BC:
Sethnakht
Ramesses III
Ramesses IV
Ramesses V
Ramesses VI
Ramesses VII
Ramesses VIII
Ramesses IX
Ramesses X
Ramesses XI

Third Intermediate Period:

21st Dynasty (Tanis), *circa* 1069–945 BC:
Smendes
Amenemnisu
Psusennes I
Amenemope
Osorkon the Elder
Siamen
Psusennes II

22nd Dynasty (Libyan), *circa* 945–735 BC:
Sheshonk I
Osorkon I
Sheshonk II
Takelot I
Osorkon II
Takelot II
Sheshonk III
Pami
Sheshonk V

Theban kings, *circa* 818–730 BC:
Pedubast I
Input I
Sheshonk IV(?)
Osorkon III
Takelot III
Rudamen
Iny

23rd Dynasty (Libyan), *circa* 735–710 BC:
Pedubast II
Osorkon IV
Psammous

Local dynasties, *circa* 730 BC:
Thotemhat and Nimlot (Hermopolis)
Peftjauawybast (Heracleopolis)
Input II (Leontopolis)

24th Dynasty, *circa* 727–715 BC:
Tefnakht
Bakenrenef

25th Dynasty (Kushite), *circa* 760–653 BC:
Kashta
Piye
Shabako
Shebitku
Taharka
Tanutameni

Late period:

26th Dynasty (Saite), *circa* 664–525 BC:
Neko I
Psamtik I
Neko II
Psamtik II
Apries
Amasis
Psamtik III

27th Dynasty (Persian), *circa* 525–404 BC:
Cambyses
Darius I
Xerxes I
Artaxerxes I
Darius II
Artaxerxes II

28th Dynasty, *circa* 404–399 BC:
Amyrtaeus

29th Dynasty, *circa* 399–380 BC:
Nepherites I
Hakor
Nepherites II

30th Dynasty, *circa* 380–343 BC:
Nectanebo I
Teos
Nectanebo II

31st Dynasty (Persian), *circa* 343–332 BC:
Artaxerxes III
Arses
Darius III

Ptolemaic period, *circa* 332–32 BC:

Macedonians:
Alexander the Great
Philip Arrhidaeus
Alexander IV

Ptolemaic Dynasty:
Ptolemy I Soter I
Ptolemy II Philadelphus
Ptolemy III Evergetes
Ptolemy IV Philopator
Ptolemy V Epiphanes
Ptolemy VI Philometor
Ptolemy VII Neos Philopator
Ptolemy VIII Evergetes II
Ptolemy IX Soter II

Ptolemy X Alexander I
Ptolemy IX Soter II (again)
Ptolemy XI Alexander II
Ptolemy XII Neos Dionysos
Cleopatra VII Philopator
Ptolemy XIII
Ptolemy XIV Caesarion

Roman period

Begins after the defeat of Cleopatra VII and Mark Antony at the Battle of Actium in 31 BC, when Egypt became a Roman province.

Coptic period

From the defeat of the Roman emperor Maxentius by Constantine I in AD 312, when Christian persercution ended in the Roman empire, to the Arab invasion of Egypt in AD 639.

Introduction

Geographic and chronological scope of Egyptian archaeology

Kemet, the "black land," was the name the ancient Egyptians gave to their state. The "black land" of the fertile floodplain along the lower Nile Valley was differentiated from the barren "red land" of the deserts to either side of the valley. Beginning around 3100–3000 BC, a unified state stretched along the Nile from Aswan at the First Cataract to the Delta coast along the Mediterranean Sea, a distance of over 1,000 km downriver. This was the kingdom of ancient Egypt, ruled by a king and his centralized administration during the periods of political stability known as the Old, Middle and New Kingdoms.

Ancient Egypt was the land of the lower Nile Valley. This is a much smaller region than what comprises the modern country of the Arab Republic of Egypt, which includes the region south of the First Cataract to 22° N, the huge desert to the west of the Nile to the Libyan border, the desert to the east of the Nile bordered by the Red Sea, and the Sinai peninsula to the Israeli border.

Because the Nile flows from south to north, southern Egypt beginning at the First Cataract is called "Upper Egypt," and northern Egypt, including the Cairo region and the Delta, is called "Lower Egypt." The region between Upper and Lower Egypt is sometimes called "Middle Egypt," and consists of the Nile Valley north of the bend in the river at Qena and Nag Hammadi to the region of the Fayum. The main geographic feature of the Fayum is a large lake, now called Birket Qarun, which was much larger when wetter conditions prevailed in the early to middle Holocene (*circa* 12,000 to 5,000 years ago).

The major geographic feature of Egypt is, of course, the Nile River and the fertile floodplains to either side. North of Cairo the main channel of the Nile branches off to form the Delta, a much more humid region than the Nile Valley. In Dynastic times the Delta was much more suitable for cattle pasturage than for large-scale cereal cultivation.

East of the Nile Delta is the Sinai peninsula, now separated from Africa by the Suez Canal and the Gulf of Suez. Mountainous and dry like the Eastern Desert of Egypt, the Sinai provided a land route to southwest Asia. To the west of the Nile is the Western Desert. Within the Western Desert are a number of oases created by springs, where there is evidence of both prehistoric and pharaonic activity. These oases include Siwa, Bahariya, Farafra, Kharga and Dakhla.

To the east of the Nile is the Eastern Desert, also known as the Red Sea Hills because it borders the Red Sea. This is a much more mountainous region than the Western Desert, with some mountains over 1,200 m high. Fresh water is scarce in the Red Sea Hills and along the shore of the Red Sea, and this factor greatly limited human habitation there. The Eastern Desert was the source of many hard stones used for sculpture and other craft goods, and minerals such as copper and gold.

To the south of the First Cataract in the Nile at Aswan is the land known as Nubia. Upper Nubia is now in northern Sudan, and Lower Nubia is the southernmost part of Egypt, between the First and Second Cataracts in the Nile. When the High Dam was built at Aswan in the 1950s, the Nile Valley of Lower Nubia became flooded and formed what is now called Lake Nasser. Six cataracts block navigation in the Nile in Nubia, from Aswan in the north (First Cataract) to the Sixth Cataract located about 100 km downriver from Khartoum, the capital of Sudan at the confluence of the Blue and White Niles. Much of the Nile Valley in Nubia is very narrow, and as a result Nubia did not have the great agricultural potential of pharaonic Egypt.

In terms of the geographic scope of this encyclopedia, not all sites listed as entries are within the limits of what the ancient Egyptians considered the land of Egypt. Pharaonic sites are found at oases in the Western Desert, and in Upper and Lower Nubia, and Roman period sites are located in the Eastern Desert. Much of ancient Nubia's history was closely connected to that of Egypt, culminating in Nubian rule in Egypt under the kings of the 25th Dynasty. Hence, a number of cultures and sites in Nubia are also included in this volume. Although the Sinai peninsula is not a part of ancient Egypt, evidence of Egyptian culture is also found there, especially where the ancient Egyptians mined copper and turquoise, and relevant sites in the Sinai are also listed.

By the beginning of the 1st Dynasty ancient Egyptian civilization had emerged, but this was preceded by a very long sequence of prehistoric cultural development. Perhaps as early as one million years ago there were Paleolithic hunters and gatherers living along the Nile. Farming in the lower Nile Valley did not appear until after *circa* 6000 BC, when domesticated cereals were introduced from southwest Asia. Farming had great economic potential within the floodplain ecology of the Egyptian Nile Valley, and farming villages proliferated along the floodplain. During what is called the Predynastic period, *circa* 4000–3000 BC, these farming village societies became more complex, a development which culminated in the rise of the early Egyptian state.

The chronological scope of this encyclopedia includes Egypt's prehistoric past, which was an important prelude to pharaonic civilization. Indeed, many cultural developments in pharaonic civilization need to be understood from the perspective of their prehistoric origins. Pharaonic civilization spanned thirty-one dynasties, some of which were periods of strong centralized control, followed by periods of political fragmentation and decentralization. During the first millennium BC Egypt was dominated by different foreign powers, but the monuments and written language continued a royal tradition which had developed over two millennia. With Egyptian conversion to Christianity in the fourth century AD, however, the traditions of pharaonic civilization were considered pagan and came to an end. Thus, archaeological sites listed in this book do not include Coptic ones unless they are ancient sites that continued to be occupied during early Christian times.

Archaeological sites and site preservation

Archaeological sites in Egypt have often been named after the (Arabic) names of nearby villages, or what they have been descriptively termed in Arabic by local villagers. Sites are listed in this encyclopedia by their most familiar names, with cross-references in the index. For example, the Predynastic site of Hierakonpolis is listed under its Greek name, and not the modern Kom el-Ahmar or the ancient Egyptian Nekhen, whereas the Predynastic site of Nagada is listed under the name of the nearby village, and not Nubt, the ancient Egyptian name of this town. When appropriate, information about specific sites is given in topical entries, such as the private tombs of the New Kingdom at Saqqara. Very large sites such as

Saqqara contained many tombs and monuments built over three millennia, and could not be discussed adequately in one entry.

Much of the archaeological evidence from ancient Egypt comes from sites located on the edge of the floodplain or slightly beyond in the low desert. Therefore, much of the archaeological evidence is highly specialized, from tombs, temples and mortuary complexes, and not from settlements. Undoubtedly, ancient cities, towns and villages were once located on higher ground on the floodplain, or along levees next to the river. Many earlier sites within the floodplain are now covered by deep alluvial deposits or modern villages, and thus cannot be excavated. Continuous cultivation of the floodplain for five to six thousand years has undoubtedly destroyed many sites, as have shifts in the river and its floodplain. Ancient settlements would also have been located along the edge of the floodplain, and some of these have been excavated in this century, but many have been partially or wholly destroyed as more recent irrigation has extended cultivation beyond the margins of the floodplain. Prehistoric sites located on the low desert above the floodplain are usually deflated, a process in which the desert wind has removed lighter organic materials and deposits, and the heavier artifacts from different periods, mostly potsherds and stone tools, have collapsed onto the desert surface. For a number of reasons, then, settlement patterns and changes in these through time are very incomplete in the archaeological evidence of ancient Egypt.

Because of alluviation, continuous cultivation, geological conditions which destroy sites, and the present dense occupation along the Nile, ancient settlements in Egypt have not been well preserved or are impossible to excavate. Another reason why there is relatively little evidence of settlements in Egypt is probably because of earlier excavators' priorities. Tombs, temples and royal mortuary complexes were simply of greater interest to excavate than settlements which had been disturbed by Egyptian farmers digging for *sebbakh*, organic remains from ancient settlements which is used for fertilizer. Much of Egyptian archaeology, therefore, has been concerned with the clearance, recording and conservation of tombs and temples. Many of the earlier scholars who worked in Egypt were philologists whose interests lay in recording texts, or were trained in fine arts and were attracted to the great art and monumental architecture of pharaonic Egypt. In any case, earlier archaeologists in Egypt did not have the excavation techniques enabling them to understand settlements and their formation processes, with the exception of very well-preserved sites such as Akhenaten's capital at Tell el-Amarna.

Looting has been another factor in the poor preservation of archaeological evidence in Egypt. Looting of tombs occurred throughout pharaonic times. To speed construction, later kings often used stone blocks from the monuments of earlier kings. The most blatant example of this process is the capital city of Tanis in the eastern Nile Delta, where the kings of the 21st Dynasty moved granite monuments block by block from the earlier 19th Dynasty capital of Pi-Ramesses, founded by Ramesses II. Quarried stones from the Old Kingdom pyramids in northern Egypt were used to build monuments in Islamic Cairo. Looting of artifacts accelerated in the nineteenth and twentieth centuries AD as museums and collectors in Europe and North America bought Egyptian antiquities. Unfortunately, looting, though illegal, continues in Egypt today.

Other sources of information

Because archaeological sites in Egypt can only be understood within their cultural context, this encyclopedia includes information about sociopolitical organization, the economy, technology, language, religion and so on. Egyptian culture certainly evolved and changed over three thousand years, and entries about aspects of Egyptian culture are necessarily short, but references are given for where to seek more information. An excellent introduction to the sociopolitical organization of ancient Egypt from Predynastic times through the Dynastic periods is *Ancient Egypt: A Social History* by B.G. Trigger, B.J. Kemp, D. O'Connor and L.B. Lloyd.

With the emergence of the Dynastic state, writing was invented, and the evidence of written texts has greatly added to our knowledge about the culture of ancient Egypt. Ancient Egyptians spoke a language which is today called Egyptian, written in a formal script of hieroglyphs ("sacred writing"), and in a simplified cursive script known as "hieratic." With the invention of writing, Egyptian culture moves from prehistory to history, and in its earliest dynasties ancient Egypt was a literate society. From Early Dynastic times information began to be recorded by and about the state. Unfortunately, many of these early hieroglyphic texts, aside from names, are difficult to decipher.

Writing became more widely used in the Old Kingdom, but most of what has been preserved is from a mortuary context. Beginning in the Middle Kingdom, however, there is much more evidence of writing than just the texts found in tombs. Not only are there accounts and records of a highly organized state bureaucracy, but there are letters, legal documents, literary texts and texts by specialists in fields such as medicine and mathematics. In the New Kingdom an even greater body of textual information recorded on papyri and ostraca has been recovered, as well as what is known from tombs and the many votive artifacts for the mortuary cult. For the first time, numerous cult temples were built of stone, and their walls are covered with reliefs and inscriptions. Following the collapse of the New Kingdom state, writing continued to be an important medium of communication in the Late period, and there are numerous papyri and temple inscriptions from Graeco-Roman times.

Much of the evidence we have for the use of writing in ancient Egypt is fairly specialized, and economic records are much less common in Egypt than in the states of Mesopotamia. Royal inscriptions were not an objective record of events, but were written to glorify pharaoh and his accomplishments, real or exaggerated. Very few people in ancient Egypt ever learned to read or write. Nonetheless, writing inevitably supplements what is known about ancient Egypt from the archaeological evidence, especially concerning ideology and beliefs.

Immediately recognizable in Egyptian civilization are formal styles of art and architecture. This was a material culture promulgated by the crown and emulated by elites in the society. Unfortunately, there is much less information, both archaeological and textual, about the working class in Egypt, most of whom were peasant farmers conscripted periodically to serve in the army and construct royal monuments and temples. Representational evidence, mainly from tombs and temples, but also from artifacts such as ostraca, conveys information about Egyptian workers and farmers, as well as other sociocultural institutions (especially religion and beliefs about the afterlife). Frequently, scenes on the walls of tombs and temples are accompanied by hieroglyphic texts which specify the activities depicted, and in this context the textual and pictorial evidence complement and enhance each other to convey information.

Archaeology is the study of the material remains of past cultures within their excavated contexts, and as such it deals with evidence which is fragmentary and incompletely preserved. But ancient Egypt is rich in different forms of evidence which convey information—archaeological, architectural, textual and pictorial—and a synthesis of all forms of evidence is needed in order to better understand this remarkable civilization in all its complexities.

The study of ancient Egypt

The systematic study of ancient Egypt began with the Napoleonic expedition to Egypt in 1798. Accompanying Napoleon Bonaparte's invading army was a group of *savants*, scholars who recorded ancient Egyptian monuments along with information about the culture of Islamic Egypt and the country's natural history. Systematic excavations in Egypt, however, did not really begin until the late nineteenth century with the work of William Matthew Flinders Petrie. Previous to Petrie's work in Egypt, excavators had mainly been interested in sending ancient art and texts back to museums and collectors in Europe and North America. Petrie, however, was interested in the study of all artifacts that he excavated, and was the first archaeologist to recognize the importance of stylistic seriation of ceramics and other artifacts in a relative chronology of periods, which he called "Sequence Dating."

Egyptian archaeology today is studied in several academic disciplines, and scholars from a number of disciplines have contributed to this encyclopedia. The most prominent of these disciplines is Egyptology, the study of ancient Egypt mainly through the analysis of ancient texts, artifacts and architecture. Egyptian texts are studied by philologists and historians, and later Egyptian history is of interest to biblical and classical scholars. Because ancient Egypt produced so much monumental art and architecture, and private tombs in which the walls are covered with paintings and/or reliefs, art history has also been an important discipline for studying the culture of ancient Egypt. Anthropologically trained archaeologists in the early twentieth century were more interested in ancient Egypt from a theoretical perspective in terms of the rise of civilization. However, beginning in the 1960s a number of archaeologists trained in anthropology began to work in Egypt on the Nubian Salvage campaign, which surveyed, recorded and excavated sites in Lower Nubia before they were flooded by Lake Nasser following the construction of the High Dam at Aswan.

Archaeology in Egypt today is conducted under the auspices of the Supreme Council of Antiquities, formerly the Egyptian Antiquities Organization (EAO), under the Ministry of Culture. Located throughout Egypt are regional offices of the Council, which direct excavations by Egyptian-trained archaeologists and oversee fieldwork conducted by foreign archaeologists. The cordial cooperation of the Supreme Council of Antiquities has made possible the ongoing excavations and current research which are reported here.

KATHRYN A. BARD

Paleolithic cultures, overview

The record of the Egyptian Paleolithic is found in two very different areas, the Nile Valley and the Sahara. The Nile Valley seems to have been used continuously, or almost so, since more than 500,000 years ago. Use of the Sahara, however, was episodic. There were long intervals when it was hyperarid, with no trace of human presence, but there were also at least seven and probably many more periods of significant rainfall and people were present in the Sahara during all of them.

The Nile is a permanent river, and people lived in its valley no matter how dry the adjacent desert. The behavior of the Nile is influenced primarily by the climate in the area of its headwaters in the highlands of East Africa, where, during cold glacial maxima, there was reduced vegetation cover, more frost action and less rainfall. Thus, there was less water in the Nile and the water carried a heavy sediment load, which was deposited on the floodplain until the valley became choked with silt. This process occurred at least three times during the Middle and Late Pleistocene, with intervening episodes of downcutting. In Upper Egypt and Nubia, remnants of these accumulations stand 20–30 m above the modern floodplain and include many Paleolithic sites. The earliest alluvial episode is associated with rare Lower Paleolithic artifacts, the second is late Middle Paleolithic, and the third is Late Paleolithic. Other Paleolithic sites occur near rock outcrops along the margins of the Valley, and there are a few sites in wadi gravels below, between and sometimes within the silt remnants.

The Nile Valley was not luxuriant during the periods of valley filling. The river was much smaller than today and flowed through meandering or braided channels. Large animals were limited to wild cattle, hartebeest, gazelle, hippopotamus and, on the east bank, wild ass. There were, however, other important food resources: ducks and geese were heavily exploited during some periods; fish were used at least from the early Middle Paleolithic; and plant foods, particularly marshland tubers and seeds, were important in the Late Paleolithic.

Lower Paleolithic

Some of the first descriptions (late nineteenth century) of the Paleolithic in Egypt are of handaxes found in the Nile Valley. These characteristic Lower Paleolithic tools tend to be well made, flaked on both faces, pointed at one end and rounded at the other; typologically, they are Late Acheulean. There are no reliable dates for the Egyptian Lower Paleolithic, but elsewhere in Africa, the Late Acheulean is believed to begin around 500,000 years ago, while

Table 1 Correlation of Paleolithic sequence in the Nile Valley

Years B.P.	Nile	Sahara
10,000	?	Early Neolithic
12,500	Late Paleolithic	Hyperarid
22,000	Upper Paleolithic	No known occupation
40,000	Khormusan	—
70,000	Late Middle Paleolithic	Middle Paleolithic
	Early Middle Paleolithic	—
200,000	Final Acheulean	Final Acheulean
300,000	Late Acheulean	Late Acheulean
500,000	Middle Acheulean?	Middle Acheulean?

the earliest Middle Paleolithic is dated to about 230,000 years ago. Most of the Lower Paleolithic sites in Egypt probably fall within this period; a few sites may be older.

Some of the most interesting information on the Lower Paleolithic in the Nile Valley comes from near Wadi Halfa in northern Sudan, where a series of quarries and workshops yielded numerous Acheulean handaxes. Arkin 8, which was embedded in wadi sediments on the western edge of the Valley, may be the largest Acheulean site in this part of Africa. Although the assemblage is crude (perhaps because many of the tools appear to be unfinished), it is classified as Late Acheulean. There are numerous cores (none is prepared), chopping tools and handaxes, the last in a variety of shapes. Other tools include side-scrapers and notches. Late Acheulean sites also occur in the same area on the east bank. The sites were classified as Early, Middle and Late Acheulean on the basis of typology, but there is no stratigraphic evidence to support this.

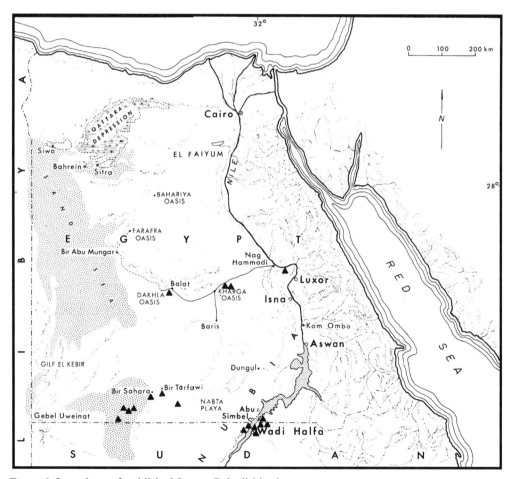

Figure 1 Locations of published Lower Paleolithic sites

Lower Paleolithic sites are also found in the eastern Sahara, in a variety of settings. At Kharga and Dakhla Oases, and Bir Sahara East (about 350 km west of Abu Simbel), they represent camps at the edge of a spring pool, probably from multiple occupations, perhaps over several millennia or more. The sites at Kharga and Dakhla are classified as Late Acheulean. The handaxes at the Bir Sahara East site, however, are small, thin and well-executed. This site is regarded as Final Acheulean. Another setting used in the Saharan Lower Paleolithic was on the edges of ponds and lakes. Two such sites are known at Bir Tarfawi, 10 km east of Bir Sahara East, both of them Late Acheulean. (Middle) Acheulean assemblages were also found stratified in wadi deposits near Bir Safsaf, about 50 km southeast of Bir Tarfawi. Other Acheulean assemblages have been found south of Bir Tarfawi, in an ephemeral lake (playa) and in the large buried channels first discovered by ground-penetrating radar. Some of the latter sites may be very old, possibly Middle Acheulean.

In the Sahara, Lower Paleolithic people used almost every setting where there was water. None of the sites, either in the desert or along the Nile, has yielded sufficient fauna to permit a detailed reconstruction of the environment. There is evidence, however, of considerable local rainfall during several intervals. A characteristic of the Acheulean is that people always used the nearest available raw material. Tools were made for short-term or immediate purposes and were not taken from one area to another, even if the first area had much better raw materials.

Middle Paleolithic

The Middle Paleolithic began in Egypt more than 175,000 years ago, and possibly more than 200,000 years ago; it may have lasted until around 45,000 years ago. It was during the Middle Paleolithic, and probably early in that stage, that the modern form of our species first appeared.

The Egyptian Middle Paleolithic shares the basic elements of the Middle Paleolithic throughout North Africa and Europe. Handaxes are absent or very rare, and most of the tools are made on flakes, often produced with Levallois technology, where a core was prepared in order to produce a flake of a predetermined shape. There are usually quite high frequencies of unretouched Levallois flakes, as well as various kinds of side-scrapers, denticulates and retouched pieces. Some sites also yield high proportions of Upper Paleolithic-type tools, particularly end-scrapers and burins; others contain large, bifacially worked, leaf-shaped pieces (foliates), and there are a few sites with tanged or stemmed (pedunculated) tools.

The Egyptian Middle Paleolithic has been traditionally classified into four major variants: Nubian Middle Stone Age, Mousterian, Aterian and Khormusan. The Khormusan appears to be late and is confined to the Nile Valley. The Aterian is essentially restricted to the Sahara, and it too may be late. Apart from this, there are very few differences between any of the Middle Paleolithic entities, and they may reflect no more than minor differences in behavior; there is no reason to believe that they represent self-conscious social entities.

Middle Paleolithic in the Sahara

The best data on the Egyptian Middle Paleolithic come from Bir Tarfawi and Bir Sahara East. These two basins have a sequence of five Middle Paleolithic wet intervals, with permanent lakes, separated by periods of aridity; in Bir Tarfawi there was also a Middle Paleolithic playa, which may precede the earliest permanent lake.

The wet periods occurred between *circa* 175,000 and 70,000 years ago, and the major permanent lakes probably date to the last interglacial period. The lakes reflect local rainfall, which resulted from the intensification and northward movement of the tropical monsoon. The associated faunal remains indicate that there was perhaps as much as 500 mm of rain a year, and that the lakes existed in a savanna or wooded savanna landscape which supported large animals such as rhinoceros, giant buffalo, giraffe, giant camel, wild ass and various antelopes and gazelles. Fish were present in the lakes, including species that today are found only in the Nile, Chad and Niger basins, evidence that the lakes were occasionally part of a regional drainage system.

There are many Middle Paleolithic sites associated with the lake deposits. They occur in a variety of settings, each with distinctive assemblages of artifacts and apparently used in different ways. The sites were probably used only during the day because of the danger of large predators near the lakes at night. The night camps are likely to have been on the adjacent plateau. The artifacts are made of quartzitic sandstone of various colors and textures. Quarries for these materials lie 3–5 km east of Bir Tarfawi, where outlines of pits and trenches are evident on the surface and the surrounding area is littered with thick flakes and other workshop debris, but almost no cores or tools.

One of the interesting features to emerge from Bir Tarfawi and Bir Sahara East is that almost all of the sites were used repeatedly, and evidence suggests that the same activities took place during every episode of use. It is clear that even during the early part of the Middle Paleolithic, there were well-established patterns of resource exploitation across this landscape; patterns that were maintained over the enormous periods of time represented in this sequence. Neither significant change nor increasing complexity was characteristic of the Middle Paleolithic. Not only did the settlement system and raw material economies continue virtually unchanged for more than 100,000 years, but there was also no marked improvement in the tools. The only evident changes are the appearance of bifacial foliates around 130,000 years ago, and of stemmed tools about 70,000 years ago. Neither of these is likely to have been a local development.

There was a somewhat different raw material economy in the Middle Paleolithic of Kharga Oasis. Most of the Kharga sites were at spring pools, and the tabular flint cobbles preferred as raw material were available in the nearby wadis. The sites contain numerous primary flakes and early stage and Levallois core preparation flakes, but few cores and tools. The sites are classified as Mousterian or Aterian (indicated by pedunculate tools and bifacial foliates), and there is some stratigraphic evidence that the Aterian is the later one. The Kharga night camps were probably at a distance from water, but none is known. The availability of water and related resources and the proximity of suitable stone seem to have been the major features of Middle Paleolithic settlements in the Kharga area.

Middle Paleolithic along the Nile

Three different settings were used by Middle Paleolithic groups along the Nile. From Wadi Halfa at the Second Cataract to beyond the Qena bend in Upper Egypt, there are many quarries and workshops near rock outcrops, usually against the escarpments that border the Valley on each side or in gravel benches between the escarpments and the river. The debris from the quarries is sometimes buried in colluvial sediments, but none of the sites can be tied to the Nilotic sedimentary sequence, and none is dated. The quarries have been classified as Nubian Middle Stone Age (in Lower Nubia) or Mousterian (in Upper Egypt and Lower Nubia).

Middle Paleolithic is also found in the silts of the second of the Middle and Late Pleistocene episodes of valley filling, which coincided with a period of hyperaridity. There is a group of small sites north of Aswan, and another (Site 440, which may be Nubian Middle Stone Age) in a dune at the base of the silts just south of Wadi Halfa. Site 440 had two horizons, both with rich faunas which were mostly wild cattle in the lower level and fish in the upper one. The fish include several large, deep-water species, suggesting the use of boats, traps or other relatively sophisticated fishing techniques. The sites near Aswan are Mousterian. There are five TL (thermoluminescence) dates between 66,000 and 45,000 BP from the deposits of two of the sites; these are the only dates available for the Mousterian in the Nile Valley.

Near the Second Cataract are several Khormusan sites, which seems to be the most recent Middle Paleolithic complex in the Valley. The age of the Khormusan is estimated to be between 45,000 and 55,000 years ago. Some Khormusan sites contain abundant fauna, mostly wild cattle, with a few hartebeest, gazelle and hippopotamus; other sites are rich in fish. The Khormusan stone artifacts are distinctive, with an emphasis on burins, plus occasional side-scrapers, end-scrapers and denticulates, all frequently made on Levallois flakes. No Khormusan workshops or quarries are known.

The third Nilotic setting of the Middle Paleolithic is the wadis along the margin of the Valley. There are massive terraces of wadi gravels in most of the major wadis that enter the Nile on each side; the terraces lie under the silts of the Middle Paleolithic valley filling and therefore precede it. All the wadis are now dry, and therefore reflect intervals of much greater rainfall than today, which probably coincided with the permanent lakes in the Sahara. The very rolled artifacts within the terraces are thus likely to be the same age as the Middle Paleolithic artifacts associated with the lakes at Bir Tarfawi and Bir Sahara East.

There are also occasional clusters of Middle Paleolithic artifacts in or on the older wadi deposits, and some of them appear to be *in situ*. One such site, on the eroded surface of (and probably post-dating) the older wadi terrace near Aswan is the only known Aterian site in the Valley. All of the other sites associated with the older wadi deposits are Mousterian.

Information on the Middle Paleolithic in the Valley is less detailed than that from the Sahara, but it is clear that the workshops and quarries along the Nile functioned very differently from those in the desert. The Nilotic quarries are often surrounded by debris that includes unretouched Levallois flakes, finished tools and cores. This pattern, seen in both Upper Egypt and Nubia, indicates that these sites were also workshops for the final shaping and exploitation of cores and for some tool manufacture (unlike the quarries at Bir Tarfawi, where only initial shaping was done).

The Middle Paleolithic in the Sahara ended when hyperaridity made the desert uninhabitable shortly after 70,000 years ago. In the Nile Valley, however, the Middle Paleolithic persisted throughout the valley filling that seems to have begun at about the same time as local rainfall ceased. About 45,000 years ago or slightly later, the regimen of the river changed again, as the Nile cut a deep channel and the Middle Paleolithic ended.

Upper and Late Paleolithic

Some ten millennia separate the most recent Middle Paleolithic from the earliest Upper Paleolithic known in the Nile Valley. The appearance of the Upper Paleolithic is marked by a major change in stone-working technology. In the Middle Paleolithic, there was a strong preference for wide, flat flakes, often struck from preshaped (Levallois) cores. In the Upper Paleolithic, the emphasis was on the production of long, narrow blades, which made more efficient use of raw material and resulted in blanks that were more consistent in shape and size; the latter may be a major factor in the increased standardization evident in the retouched tools of the Upper Paleolithic.

There are no Upper Paleolithic sites in the Sahara, since the desert was hyperarid. The earliest Upper Paleolithic site known in the Nile Valley is Nazlet Khater-4 in Upper Egypt, a flint mine with several radiocarbon dates of about 33,000 BP. Levallois technology appears to be absent and there are many Upper Paleolithic-type blade cores. The associated tools are retouched blades, denticulates and bifacial adzes, apparently used for quarrying. A bifacial adze was found nearby with a human skeleton, which is of a modern type but retains primitive features (similar to the Mechtoids described below). It is the oldest human skeleton known from Egypt.

The next known Upper Paleolithic sites are Shuwikhat-1, on the east bank near Qena slightly upstream from Nazlet Khater, and Site E71K9, a little farther upstream on the west bank near Esna (Isna). There are TL dates of 24,700 BP ± 2,500 years for Shuwikhat-1 and 21,590 BP ± 1,500 years for E71K9 (the standard errors overlap between 23,000 and 22,000 BP). The artifacts in both sites are large blades, and the tools include numerous denticulates, a variety of well-made burins, retouched pieces and long pointed blades. Endscrapers and perforators are frequent. Both sites had rich fauna, mostly hartebeest and wild cattle, with occasional gazelle, hare and hyena; fish were rare.

About 21,000 years ago, there was another change in the lithic technology. Large blades were replaced by bladelets, some of them microlithic (less than 30 mm long), with steep retouch or backing along one edge. There was also a shift in subsistence to the exploitation of a wider range of resources and more intensive use of the river. These changes mark the beginning of the Late Paleolithic. There are more Late Paleolithic than Middle or Upper Paleolithic sites, and there is more regional variation. The material from Lower Nubia is often different from that of Upper Egypt, and there are local differences within each region. The tempo of change also accelerated, and similar changes in artifacts occurred at about the same time throughout the Valley. Stylistic studies suggest a high degree of interaction along the Valley, with intervals of cultural turmoil and rapid change. The cultural boundary between Lower Nubia and Upper Egypt shifted from time to time, varying from near the First Cataract to near Esna. There may have been other cultural boundaries farther down the Nile, but these cannot be defined since we have almost no information on the Late Paleolithic north of Qena.

A complex series of stone tool industries has been defined for both Lower Nubia and Upper Egypt, each with distinctive features among the tools. Each occurs in several different settings, reflecting seasonality of occupation and showing a variety of activities; they are thought to represent distinct social groups. Most of the sequence records cultural developments through time, rather than changes in population.

However, one stone tool industry, the Sebilian, is so different from what preceded it that population replacement seems likely. For at least six millennia, Late Paleolithic people in both Lower Nubia and Upper Egypt had used bladelets for the production of most retouched tools. Suddenly, about 14,000 years ago, many small Sebilian sites appear, from the Second Cataract to the Qena bend, in which most of the tools are large, wide, flat flakes (struck from Levallois or discoidal cores) retouched into geometric shapes never or rarely seen in earlier sites. Furthermore, Sebilian tools were preferentially made on quartzitic sandstone, diorite and other basement rocks, instead of the Nile chert and agate pebbles preferred by earlier Late Paleolithic groups. Only in Upper Egypt did the Sebilian people use flint, in those areas where there is no sandstone or basement rock.

The closest parallels to the Sebilian are in tropical Africa, and this may represent groups who came from the south, moving along the Nile from central Sudan or beyond. This was a period of climatic change in tropical Africa; temperatures had begun to rise, with accompanying shifts in the distributions of both plants and animals. If this represents an intrusion, it was brief and had almost no effect on later stone tool industries. The Sebilian people were soon replaced by other groups using artifacts that closely resemble the pre-Sebilian complexes in the area. All of these later industries, however, contain geometric microliths, mostly triangles, trapezes or crescents. This may represent new kinds of composite tools or a new weapon, such as the bow and arrow.

The disappearance and reappearance of Levallois technology is a noteworthy feature of the Nilotic Late Paleolithic, and the distribution of this technology illustrates the type of interaction that seems to have gone on throughout this period. Levallois technology, characteristic of the Middle Paleolithic, is not found in the Upper Paleolithic sites of Upper Egypt. Nothing is known about the Upper Paleolithic in Lower Nubia, but Levallois

Table 2 Distribution and chronological range of Late Paleolithic industries in the lower Nile Valley

Lower Nubia	Upper Egypt
Arkinian (10,600 BP)	
	Isnan (12,700 – 11,500 BP)
	Afian (13,500 – 12,300 BP)
Qadan (14,500 – 12,000 BP)	
Sebilian (*ca.* 14,000 BP)	Sebilian (*ca.* 14,000 BP)
Ballanan-Silsilian (16,000 – 15,000 BP)	Ballanan-Silsilian (16,000 – 15,000 BP)
	Idfuan (17,500 – 17,000 BP)
Halfan (19,500 – 18,500 BP)	Kubbaniyan (19,000 – 16,500 BP)
	Industry D (19,100 BP)
	Fakhurian (21,000 – 19,500 BP)

technology reappeared there (if indeed it had disappeared) at the same time as the Late Paleolithic bladelet complexes, around 21,000 years ago. However, the technology was now used differently. In the Middle Paleolithic, it was used to produce the flake blanks that were then retouched into almost all classes of tools; in the Late Paleolithic, it was used to produce only a blank of a particular shape, and this shape varied by industry. The Levallois technique was more important in Lower Nubia throughout the Late Paleolithic, and it may have been reintroduced into Upper Egypt from that direction.

The subsistence economy is one of the most interesting aspects of the Late Paleolithic. Fishing was an important part of the diet at some early Middle Paleolithic sites, but the hunting of large mammals seems to have been more important in the later Middle Paleolithic and Upper Paleolithic. The Late Paleolithic saw a shift away from large mammals to a more diversified subsistence basis. Many Late Paleolithic sites contain large quantities of fish bones, mostly catfish, and it is believed that these were harvested during the seasonal spawn at the beginning of the flood, when more fish could easily have been taken than could be immediately consumed. In some sites there are pits and other features which may have been used for smoking fish. This is the earliest indication in Egypt of the storage of food for future use.

The greater diversity of foods is also evident in the importance of waterfowl and shellfish, which were first eaten in significant quantities during the Late Paleolithic. The most dramatic change in subsistence, however, was in the use of plant foods, particularly those from the marshes and swamps along the edge of the Nile. Tubers and seeds of wetland plants have been recovered from several Late Paleolithic sites in Wadi Kubbaniya, together with the grinding stones presumably used to process them. (Many of the tubers contain toxins which can be removed by grinding and roasting.) Grinding stones occur in many Late Paleolithic sites along the Nile, suggesting that plant foods were an important component of the diet.

The earliest burials known in the Nile Valley are those at Nazlet Khater and Kubbaniya, mentioned above. A group of three slightly younger burials was found at Deir el-Fakhuri, near Esna. All of these skeletons are of fully modern *Homo sapiens sapiens*, but they were very robust, with short wide faces and pronounced alveolar prognathism. They have been compared with a type known as Mechtoid (from the site of Mechta el-Arbi), which are found in Late Paleolithic sites throughout North Africa, and particularly in the Maghreb.

In the Nile Valley there are three Late Paleolithic graveyards, all associated with Qadan assemblages: Jebel Sahaba, a few kilometers north of Wadi Halfa on the east bank of the Nile, with 59 burials; Site 6-B-36, on the west bank almost opposite Wadi Halfa, with 39 burials; and Wadi Tushka, north of Abu Simbel in southern Egypt, with 19 burials. The radiocarbon dates range between 14,000 and 13,000 BP. All of the skeletons are Mechtoid, indicating a long and unbroken history for this type in the Nile Valley.

Several of the Jebel Sahaba skeletons had pieces of stone embedded in their bones; these and other signs of trauma indicate that more than 40 percent of the men, women and children in the graveyard had died by violence, and this may well be the earliest evidence for conflict. The Kubbaniya skeleton also had pieces of stone embedded in his bones and pelvic cavity, suggesting some intergroup competition even before 20,000 years ago. At the Tushka graveyard, skulls of wild cattle were used as markers for several of the graves, suggesting a special attitude toward wild cattle which may anticipate the emphasis on cattle seen several thousand years later in the early Neolithic.

Between 14,000 and 12,000 BP, there were rapid cultural changes in the Nile Valley, some of which may be related to changes in the behavior of the river. Rainfall was increasing in East and Central Africa, and the White Nile, which was previously dry, began to flow again. About 12,500 BP the increased rainfall in the Nile's headwaters resulted in a series of exceptionally high floods in Egypt, followed by downcutting and a change in the river's morphology from numerous small braided channels to the single large channel that is seen today.

Two Late Paleolithic stone tool industries (the Qadan in Lower Nubia and the Isnan in Upper Egypt) survived the onset of these changes, but their subsistence economies must have been seriously affected. Almost nothing is known about the period between 11,500 and 8,500 BP; these sites are either buried in the floodplain or destroyed by cultivation. Our next information relates to 8,500 years ago, when people were still living in small groups in essentially Late Paleolithic ways, with an economy based on fishing, hunting and, to judge by the grinding stones, plant gathering.

See also

climatic history; Dakhla Oasis, prehistoric sites; dating techniques, prehistory; Kharga Oasis, prehistoric sites; Paleolithic tools; Wadi Kubbaniya

Further reading

Close, A.E., ed. 1987. *Prehistory of Arid North Africa: Essays in Honor of Fred Wendorf.* Dallas.

Schild, R., and F. Wendorf. 1981. *The Prehistory of an Egyptian Oasis.* Wroclaw.

Wendorf, F. 1968. *The Prehistory of Nubia.* Dallas.

Wendorf, F., and R. Schild. 1980. *Prehistory of the Eastern Sahara.* New York.

FRED WENDORF
ANGELA E. CLOSE

Epi-paleolithic cultures, overview

The term "Epi-paleolithic" is used in North Africa to refer to artifact assemblages characterized by microlithic tools spanning the interval between the end of the Paleolithic and the beginning of the Neolithic. The term "Neolithic" is often used to refer to the presence of pottery and grinding stones, once believed to be invariably associated with the advent of food production. However, sites in North Africa with no evidence of food production have yielded both pottery and grinding stones. Moreover, evidence for food production, such as bones of domesticated animals and plant remains of domesticated plants, is highly controversial in some of the sites attributed to the Neolithic. In addition, the separation of the Epi-paleolithic from the Final Paleolithic is uncertain because microlithic tools also occur in some sites of the Final Paleolithic. Accordingly, the term Epi-paleolithic is ambiguous, with no definite chronological boundaries, no special mode of adaptation and no distinct tool assemblage. In general, the terms Epi-paleolithic, Terminal Paleolithic or Post-Paleolithic have been used to refer to artifact assemblages (often grouped into "industries"—groups of assemblages from several sites showing overall similarities in the kind and frequency of tool types and manufacturing techniques) dating from *circa* 12,000 to 8,000/6,000 BP (before present in radiocarbon years, i.e. uncalibrated radiocarbon dates).

The Epi-paleolithic assemblages in the Nile Valley include the Arkinian, the Shamarkian, el-Kabian and Qarunian, and span a period from *circa* 12,000–7,500 BP. No Neolithic sites in the Nile Valley date before the sixth millennium BP. By contrast, evidence for domesticated cattle from the tenth millennium BP has been advocated, but not widely accepted. However, it is very likely that domesticated cattle, as well as sheep and goats, were herded in the Western Desert (Eastern Sahara) during the eighth millennium BP.

Tool assemblages from the Western Desert, which are regarded either as early Neolithic or Post-Paleolithic, are characterized by backed and truncated bladelets, denticulates, burins, perforators, end-scrapers, geometric microliths and projectile points. Bone has been reported, but is scarce. Pottery is especially rare in Baharia and Siwa Oases. In the Nile Valley, tool assemblages include end-scrapers, burins, perforators, notches, denticulates, backed bladelets and flakes, (Ouchtata) bladelets, scaled pieces, truncated flakes, geometrics and microburins. Grinding stones are present in the Arkinian assemblage and common in the Qarunian assemblage. Bone tools have also been reported from Qarunian sites and from the site of Catfish Cave, near Korosko in Lower Nubia.

Faunal remains from the Nilotic Epi-paleolithic sites include those of wild cattle, hartebeest and fish. Red-fronted gazelle, addax and hippopotamus were reported from Qarunian sites. Large amounts of fish were recovered from the lower layers at Catfish Cave and from the Qarunian sites in the Fayum depression. Pottery has been reported from Shamarkian sites (*circa* 8,860 BP) and from el-Tarif (*circa* 6,310 BP) in Thebes. The occurrence of pottery in the Sudan dates to *circa* 9,400 BP at the site of Sarurab. In the central Sahara, pottery dates to *circa* 9,400–9,000 BP.

Epi-paleolithic sites apparently reflect a terminal development of cultural changes that were underway as early as 20,000 years ago in response to the advent of arid, cooler conditions. A cooling of as much as 9° C is suggested for East and South Africa then. North Africa would have been subjected to icy blasts in winter from northwesterly winds. Desert dunes advanced some 500 km south of their present limits. By 14,000 BP, conditions began to change as the belt of summer monsoon rains moved northward, coinciding with the retreat of the glaciers in the mountains of East Africa. The rain-fed water pools created mini-oases in many parts of the eastern Sahara. Nile floods also began to rise, and by *circa* 12,500 BP, exceptionally high Nile floods inundated the desert margin beyond the limits of the modern floodplain. Between *circa* 10,000–7,000 BP, mean annual rainfall in the southern part of the Egyptian Sahara was about 200 mm.

The climatic changes during the end of the Pleistocene seem to have triggered a variety of responses, indicated by the emergence of novel stone tool types (especially microlithic tools), bone tools for fishing, grinding stones and pottery. The subsistence base, which included hunting, fowling, plant gathering and fishing, was fairly broad. Fish were apparently exploited more regularly than before. Specialized hunting may have been pursued by some groups, such as the Sebilian. Fishing may have also been the main subsistence activity for other groups (Qarunian). Frequent changes in climatic conditions during the terminal Pleistocene and early Holocene also seem to have led to a fast rate of cultural change, as shown by the relatively quick succession of different industries. Interaction among peoples in the Nile Valley was inevitable. In the Sahara, populations would have had to change or expand their home range frequently, thus facilitating the exchange of ideas and artifacts across a broad belt of Africa.

See also

agriculture, introduction of; Baharia Oasis; climatic history; dating techniques, prehistory; fauna, domesticated; fauna, wild; Fayum, Neolithic and Predynastic sites; Neolithic cultures, overview; Paleolithic cultures, overview; Paleolithic tools; plants, wild; Siwa Oasis, prehistoric sites; Thebes, el-Tarif, prehistoric sites

Further reading

Hassan, F.A. 1980. Prehistoric settlements along the main Nile. In *The Sahara and the Nile*, M.A.J. Williams and H. Faure, eds, 421–50. Rotterdam.
——. 1995. Egypt in the prehistory of Northeast Africa. In *Civilization of the Ancient Near East*, J.M. Sasson, ed., 665–78. New York.
Vermeersch, P.M. 1992. The Upper and Late Palaeolithic of Northern and Eastern Africa. In *New Light on the Northeast African Past*, F. Klees and R. Kuper, eds, 99–154. Köln.
Wetterstrom, W. 1993. Foraging and farming in Egypt: the transition from hunting and gathering to horticulture in the Nile Valley. In *The Archaeology of Africa: Food, Metals and Towns*, T. Shaw, P. Sinclair, B. Andah and A. Okpoko, eds, 165–226. London.

FEKRI A. HASSAN

Neolithic cultures, overview

The "Neolithic" (literally the "New Stone Age") is the common (if imprecise) term widely used to denote the initial appearance in a given region of food-producing—that is, agricultural—economies. For hundreds of millennia before agriculture appeared in Egypt, people lived there by hunting, fishing and gathering the area's rich profusion of natural flora and fauna, but about 7,500 years ago people in several areas of Egypt began cultivating wheat and barley and herding sheep, goats, cattle and pigs. The modest farms and crude hoes and grinding stones (two important new forms of stone tools of the "Neolithic") of these first Egyptian farmers might appear uninteresting and unimportant when compared, for example, to the great pyramids and funerary riches of the pharaohs who followed them, but, as in all other great civilizations of antiquity, Egypt's first states were only possible because agriculture provided vastly greater and more reliable amounts of food than hunting and gathering; all the tombs and temples and great cities of pharaonic Egypt were supported by the primitive annual cultivation of wheat, barley and a few other crops, supplemented by domesticated sheep, goats, cattle, pigs and other animals.

How did this transition to agriculture occur, and precisely when? And most interesting of all, why? Generations of scholars have contemplated these questions, and not only in Egypt; agriculture appeared in many areas of the world at about the same time.

The key element in agriculture is environmental modification. Hunters and gatherers modify the environments of plants and animals in a small way, of course, by making camp fires and so forth, but farmers modify environments in much more intense ways. They plow fields, cut and burn forests, irrigate and weed crops, protect their farm animals from predators, and in many other ways alter the "natural" conditions of plant and animal life. Even in Egypt, where the Nile provided a relatively easy form of agriculture in which seeds could be planted in the wet rich soils left every year by the Nile floods, people still had to weed, build dikes to trap basins of water for irrigation, hand-water some crops, pen cattle, herd sheep and do other simple agricultural tasks.

The essence of domestication is mutualism, the increasing dependence of plants, animals and people on each other, often to the point that plants and animals lose their ability to survive in the wild. Wheat and barley, for example, were altered genetically during the domestication process so that, among other changes, their seeds remain tightly attached to the plant's stem. This would be an extremely maladaptive change if these plants had to live in their natural environment, without human help in seeding these crops. Wild wheat and barley had evolved ways of seeding themselves by means of a brittle grain head that even light wind or the activities of birds and rodents could shatter, spilling the seeds on the ground to germinate the next year's plants. This ability to reproduce without human help has been largely lost as people have manipulated these crops over the millennia. Some of the initial genetic changes were probably accidental, made by people who did not know that by, for example, harvesting wild cereals more intensively by tapping ripe heads and collecting the grains from the shattering grain heads they were removing from the genetic population the seeds with this brittle characteristic. But cereals with this tough non-shattering grain head are far easier to collect with sickles than the brittle wild varieties, and at some point people undoubtedly began intentionally to plant seeds from parent plants with desirable characteristics, just as they began to select for sheep with better wool, cows that produced more milk, and so forth.

Given this sense of what agriculture and domestication are, we can consider how Egypt made the transition to an agricultural society. To begin with, farming in Egypt did not start because some genius observed natural reproduction in plants and animals and then domesticated animals and laid out a farm. The transition from hunting-gathering to agriculture in Egypt took place over centuries and involved plants and animals whose domestication required many millennia of both "natural" and intentional selection. Agricultural economies also require the development of specialized tools. Though vague, the "Neolithic" is not altogether an inappropriate term for early farming, because farming called for an entirely different toolkit from that used in hunting and gathering. Sickles and hoes in particular are important cereal farming tools, and archaeologically one of the most visible signs of changing economies is an increase in the stone mortars and pestles (grinding stones) used by most ancient peoples to make flour from grain.

Perhaps the most infallible marker of the growing importance of agriculture is containers. Hunter-gatherers in different areas of the world used gourds, and occasionally stone and wood bowls (and in Egypt, empty ostrich eggs), but farming requires many cheap containers for food preparation, storage, plant watering and a thousand other uses. Pottery was, of course, the means by which early farmers across the world met this need for containers, and the processes of pottery production were independently invented many times.

It now seems very probable that all the major Egyptian farm crops and some of the domesticated animals were domesticated outside of Egypt, mainly in southwest Asia, and then introduced to Egypt. Various scholars have advanced the hypothesis that agriculture appeared later in Egypt than in southwest Asia because the Nile Valley was so rich in native wild animals and plants that there was a "resistance" to farming, especially since we must assume that early farming was a laborious and not always reliable way of making a living in the preindustrial world. However, there is some evidence that ancient Egyptians were not simply passive recipients of foreign domesticates, for they appear to have domesticated several plants and animals.

The best evidence for this is the result of many years of research by Fred Wendorf, Romauld Schild, Angela Close and their associates, in the Western Desert, the area in modern Egypt's southwest quarter. Their work has given us a detailed picture of the hunter-gatherers who roamed the fringes of the Nile Valley before agriculture appeared. About 11,000 years ago Africa's southern monsoon rain belt shifted northward, so that much more rain fell each year in the southern part of what is now the eastern Saharan Desert. By about 9,500 years ago, people began moving into the areas bordering the Nile Valley, into the rich grasslands that supported great herds of gazelles, wild cattle and other animals. The evidence is sketchy but it seems to suggest that people moved out into these grasslands from the Nile Valley itself, which at this time teemed with huge catfish, hippopotami, waterfowl and many other animal and plant resources. At Kōm Ombo, Wadi Kubbaniya and other southern Egyptian sites, stone tools and other remains have been found that represent sedentary communities of people who relied heavily on animals and plants whose environments they significantly modified. The mortars, sickle blades and other implements found at these sites suggest substantial plant use, but the adaptation appears to have been a mobile one, based on small groups pursuing a diversified hunting-gathering economy. The earliest evidence of forms of subsistence, settlement and technology in northeast Africa that differed significantly from those of the late Pleistocene comes from the desert areas of Bir Kiseiba and Nabta in what is now southwest Egypt. On the basis of evidence from this area, Wendorf, Schild and Close note that both cattle and pottery were known here as early as anywhere else in the world.

Thus, as early as 9,000 years ago, ancient Egyptians seem to have been in the process of domesticating plants and animals and developing the ground stone tools and other implements of an agricultural economy. But these local domesticates appear to have been displaced at some point after about 8,000 years ago, when domesticated strains of wheat and barley were introduced into Egypt, along with domesticated sheep and goats (there is no reliable evidence that the wild ancestors of either sheep (*Ovis orientalis*) or goats (*Capra hircus*) lived in North Africa). We do not know—and may never know—if people using these domesticated plants and animals immigrated to Egypt or whether these domesticates were simply introduced along trade routes that had been in operation for many centuries before farming appeared. Once established, however, the farming communities quickly spread through the Delta and Nile Valley, displacing both those hunter-gatherer groups that might have remained as well as groups that were already highly dependent on local plants and had developed something of an agricultural technology. The growing aridity of the period after about 7000 BC may well have forced people into the Nile Valley from the increasingly barren desert margins, and perhaps they brought with them both domesticated cattle and the ground stone tools that would have been especially productive when combined with southwest Asian domesticated crops and animals. These technological changes and the contrast between non-agricultural and agricultural economies is vividly illustrated in Egypt's Fayum Oasis, which contains some of the earliest and most extensive remains of agriculture in Egypt. Around the ancient shorelines of the lake that used to fill this oasis are the remains of hundreds of camp sites of people who hunted, fished and foraged this rich lacustrine environment between about 9000 and 6000 BC. These camp sites are marked by countless small stone tools, many of them in the form of blades about 10 cm long, and the animal bones found amidst these tool scatters are from the native wild fauna of the region, principally fish, crocodiles, hippopotami, birds and wild forms of cattle. There are no grinding stones, pottery fragments or other evidence that they grew crops, and no evidence that they raised domestic animals.

However, along other, later shorelines of the Fayum lake are the remains of settlements of people who lived partly by farming. In 1925–6, Gertrude Caton Thompson and Ellen Gardner excavated several of these Neolithic sites (later dated to about 5000 BC) on the northern side of the ancient Fayum lake, and near these sites they found many evidences of primitive agriculture. In one area, for example, they found 165 pits, many of them lined with coiled straw "basketry" and some of them containing wheat (emmer wheat, *Triticum dicoccum*) and barley (*Hordeum sp.*). These pits averaged 91–122 cm in diameter and 30–61 cm in depth. Inside some of the silos were agricultural tools, including a beautifully preserved sickle of wood and flint. So well preserved was some of the grain that investigators at the British Museum tried (unsuccessfully) to germinate it. In the sites near these silos are innumerable potsherds, hundreds of limestone grinding stones, sickle blades, and the remains of the domesticated sheep, goats, pigs and other animals that these Fayum people used to complement their grain crops.

These evidences from the Fayum are still among the very earliest signs of agriculture known in Egypt, but no evidence was found by Caton Thompson, or by any of the later researchers in this area, that the people living in the Fayum "invented" agriculture and made the transition to farming there. The wheat, barley, sheep and goats of the Neolithic Fayum appear to be of strains domesticated in southwest Asia, not Egypt, and there seems to have been a period between the hunter-gatherers and the first farmers when the Fayum was not occupied. So where did these Fayum farmers come from, and when? How did they initially take up agriculture?

The answers to these questions, unfortunately, may be lost or deeply buried in the Nile alluvium. Because of the Nile's scouring effects and because of the intensity of occupation and cultivation of the Nile's margins, as well as the thick layer of silt that presumably covers the earliest occupations of the Delta and other areas of the Nile channel, very little is known about early agriculture in Egypt in areas beyond the Fayum and Merimde Beni-salame. If the radiocarbon date of about 4700 BC from samples taken by means of an auger from several meters below ground level (from just above a layer containing pottery) in the far eastern Delta is representative, the earliest agricultural communities in Egypt are far under the groundwater levels, beneath thick layers of silt.

Once domesticated wheat, barley, sheep, goats, pigs and cattle were well established in Egypt, probably at least by 5000 BC, the cultural landscape began changing rapidly. The Fayum agriculturalists, for example, seem never to have made the transition to a fully agricultural way of life based on village communities, perhaps because the productivity of the lake made primitive agriculture a somewhat marginal improvement, but also probably because annual floods made the lake shore a less attractive farming area than the flood basins along the Nile itself.

Although the shift to agriculture quickly resulted in a majority of food being produced from cereals and domesticated animals, Egyptians continued to rely heavily on fish. In fact, fish bones are a common component of nearly every ancient Egyptian archaeological site from the Neolithic period to the recent past. Animals in the Nile and the desert margins also continued to be hunted throughout antiquity, although eventually hunting hippopotami, lions, gazelles and other animals became more of a royal sport than a subsistence activity. Wild fowl, especially ducks and geese, were an important element in ancient Egyptian diets, and early in Egyptian antiquity ducks and geese were penned and kept both for eating and for their eggs (domesticated fowl was not introduced to Egypt until Roman times).

By 4000 BC there were farming communities at el-Badari, Merimde Beni-salame and probably hundreds of other places as well. These early communities seem at first to have been made up of simple round or oval pit-houses made of wood, thatch and mud, but soon rectangular buildings made of mudbrick and sharing common walls—the classic Middle Eastern architectural form—appeared, and within a few centuries most of Egypt's people lived in such communities. This type of farming community has shown great stability and continuity of form and function. The remains of farming communities of 2000 BC greatly resemble those of AD 1000, and even into modern times the Egyptian farming village shows strong resemblances to ancient communities.

If, as seems likely, ancient Neolithic Egyptian communities resembled those that are known from their earliest representatives, they were small clusters of reed huts or, later, mudbrick houses that were probably occupied by members of several extended families, with a total community population of a few hundred at most. The similarity of styles of artifacts suggests cultural connections among these communities but there were probably no political or economic authorities or institutions—that is, no "chiefs" or other hereditary rulers—until after 4000 BC. The natural richness of the Nile Valley would have allowed these Neolithic communities to subsist without much exchange of foodstuffs among them.

As in later Egyptian history, the core of the Neolithic diet was probably bread and beer. Later texts show that beer was, of course, drunk in part for its intoxicating properties, but the beer made in ancient Egypt was also a good nutritional complement to the diet. Beer was made from bread that was crumbled into water, mixed with yeast and perhaps a few other substances, and then simply allowed to ferment; once fermented, it was strained. Thus beer making was an efficient way to use stale bread and surplus grain.

It is difficult to define either a beginning or an ending to the "Neolithic" period, since at least a few Egyptians appear to have been domesticating plants and animals and doing some minor agriculture as early as 10,000 years ago, and in a sense the "Neolithic" economy of mixed grain farming and livestock raising that was well established by 5000 BC was not basically changed until the Romans introduced many new crops and farming techniques 5,000 years later. Research on Egypt's agricultural origins continues, and in the future there is hope that some of the major questions can be resolved. Studies of the DNA of ancient Egyptian cereals may show precisely from what strains of southwest Asian variants they were derived.

Understanding the origins of Egyptian agriculture is just one piece of a much larger puzzle, of course, for at the same time cereals and herd animals were being domesticated in southwest Asia and introduced to North Africa, many other animals and plants were being domesticated in south and southeast Asia, and in North and South America. Certainly the climatic changes that occurred worldwide at the end of the last Ice Age, some 10,000 years ago, may have been directly or indirectly involved in agricultural origins, but in each case a somewhat different combination of climatic change, population growth, evolving tool technologies and other factors seems to have been the basis for this momentous transition in human history.

See also

agriculture, introduction of; el-Badari district Predynastic sites; brewing and baking; Caton Thompson, Gertrude; climatic history; dating techniques, prehistory; fauna, domesticated; fauna, wild; Fayum, Neolithic and Predynastic sites; Merimde Beni-salame; Neolithic and Predynastic stone tools; pottery, prehistoric; Wadi Kubbaniya

Further reading

Butzer, K.W. 1976. *Early Hydraulic Civilization in Egypt*. Chicago.
Caton Thompson, G., and E. Gardner. 1934. *The Desert Fayum*. London.
Eiwanger, J. 1982. Die neolithische Siedlung von Merimde-Benisalame. *MDAIK* 38: 67–82.
Hoffman, M.A. 1991. *Egypt before the Pharaohs*. New York.

Krzyzaniak, L., and M. Kobusiewicz, eds. 1984. *Origins and Early Development of Food-Producting Cultures in North-Eastern Africa*. Poznan.

——. 1989. *Late Prehistory of the Nile Basin and the Sahara*. Poznan.

Wenke, R.J. 1991. The evolution of Egyptian civilization: issues and evidence. *JWP* 5(3): 279–329.

ROBERT J. WENKE

Predynastic period, overview

The Predynastic period dates to the fourth millennium BC, when early farming communities first arose in the Egyptian Nile Valley. By the middle of this millennium social organization in some villages in Upper Egypt was becoming increasingly complex, and by 3000 BC the Early Dynastic state of Egypt had formed, unifing a large territory along the Nile from the northern Delta to Aswan at the First Cataract. During the Predynastic period cereal agriculture, which had been introduced earlier from southwest Asia, was adapted to the floodplain ecology of the lower Nile Valley, with enormous economic potential. By the end of the Predynastic period a simple form of irrigation agriculture may have been practiced which provided the economic base of the Dynastic state.

In the early fourth millennium BC two different cultures emerged: the Ma'adi culture of Lower Egypt and the Nagada culture of Upper Egypt. The Ma'adi culture, named after the site of Ma'adi located south of present-day Cairo, most likely evolved from indigenous Neolithic cultures. Sites with Ma'adi ceramics extend from Buto near the Mediterranean to south of Cairo, and into the Fayum region, but information regarding settlement patterns is fairly incomplete.

The Nagada culture of Upper Egypt is named after the largest known Predynastic site, Nagada. This is a different material culture from that in the north, and the origins of the Nagada culture are probably to be found among indigenous hunter-gatherers and fishermen living along the Nile. Archaeological evidence, mainly from cemeteries, suggests a core area of the Nagada culture that extended from Abydos in the north to Hierakonpolis in the south, but Nagada sites also exist on the east bank in the el-Badari region and in the Fayum. Major centers developed at Abydos, Nagada and Hierakonpolis (Nekhen). By the end of the Predynastic period (Nagada III), sites with Nagada culture ceramics are found in the northern Delta. In Lower Nubia there are numerous A-Group burials which contain many Nagada culture craft goods probably obtained through trade, but the A-Group seems to represent a different culture. Systematic study of the Predynastic began with Flinders Petrie's excavations at Nagada in 1894–5. Relative dating of the Nagada culture has been based on a seriation of grave goods devised by Petrie, which he called "Sequence Dating" (SD). Petrie recognized three periods of the Predynastic: Amratian, Gerzean and Semainean. The Badarian, an earlier phase of the Predynastic, is known from Middle Egypt. More recently, this sequence has been modified by Werner Kaiser into three (slightly different) phases, Nagada I, II and III. Kings of a unified Egypt immediately preceding the 1st Dynasty are placed in what is called "Dynasty 0."

Calibrated radiocarbon dates of two charcoal samples from a Badarian site *circa* the mid-fifth millenium BC, excavated by Diane Holmes, suggest one of the earliest farming villages in the Nile Valley. Calibrated dates published by Fekri Hassan from three early Nagada (I) sites are *circa* 3800 BC, and dates of the Nagada II area of "South Town," the large town excavated by Petrie at Nagada, range from 3600 to 3300 BC. One calibrated date of 3100 BC has been recorded for a Nagada III tomb at Hierakonpolis. A chronology compiled by the late Klaus Baer, based on king lists, places the beginning of the 1st Dynasty at *circa* 3050 BC.

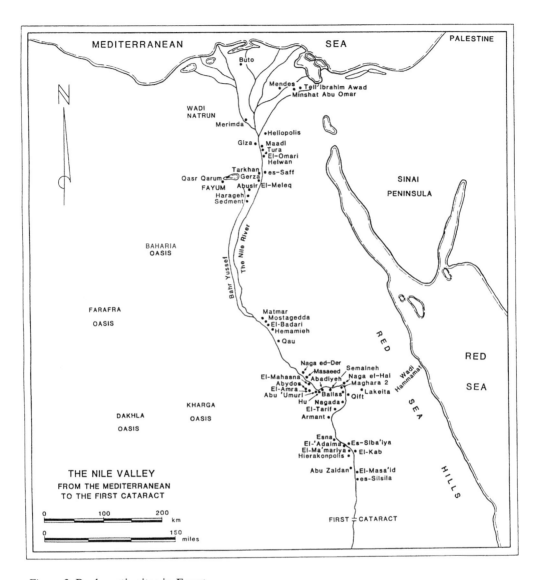

Figure 2 Predynastic sites in Egypt

Archaeological evidence of Predynastic cultures

In Upper Egypt, one of the earliest archaeological surveys was conducted by Henri de Morgan for the Brooklyn Museum in 1906–7 and 1907–8. Surveying between Gebel es-Silsila (65 km north of Aswan) and Esna, de Morgan excavated seven sites with Predynastic and Early Dynastic remains, including settlements as well as cemeteries. Fourteen additional Predynastic sites in the region were reported. More recent investigations have been done by Béatrix Midant-Reynes at one of these sites, el-Adaïma.

Hierakonpolis is certainly the most important Predynastic site in the far south. In the late nineteenth and early twentieth centuries, excavations were conducted there by de Morgan, J.E. Quibell and F.W. Green, and John Garstang. The best known finds from this period are the maceheads of (King) Scorpion and Narmer, and the (Nagada II) "Decorated Tomb," with painted plaster walls. More recent investigations by the late Walter Fairservis and the late Michael Hoffman located over fifty Predynastic sites, including cemeteries, settlements and industrial sites for the production of pottery, beads, stone vases and beer. Hoffman excavated the remains of Predynastic houses, and a large oval courtyard may be the earliest evidence for a (Nagada II) temple complex. A cemetery area (Locality 6) contained large (Nagada III) tombs, up to 22.75 sq m in floor area, which possibly belonged to the late Predynastic rulers of Hierakonpolis.

On the west bank 9 km southwest of Luxor is the Predynastic site of Armant. O.H. Myers excavated a Predynastic village and Predynastic Cemetery 1400–1500 here, with graves from all three Nagada phases. The grave goods from this cemetery were important for Kaiser's revisions of Petrie's Predynastic sequence. In the 1980s Polish archaeologists excavated a Predynastic settlement near this cemetery, but the only evidence of permanent architecture were circular structures built of large limestone slabs.

Located 28 km northwest of Luxor, on the west bank, the three Predynastic cemeteries at Nagada were excavated by Petrie in 1894–5. With over 2,200 graves, these cemeteries, along with the estimated 1,000 burials excavated by Quibell at Ballas, just north of Nagada, form the largest known mortuary area in Predynastic Egypt. The small Cemetery T at Nagada (Nagada II–III) has been considered the burial place of Predynastic chieftains or kings. One well-preserved "royal" tomb with an elaborately niched mudbrick superstructure, excavated by Jacques de Morgan along with small graves with Early Dynastic grave goods, contained mud sealings of (King) Aḥa, who reigned at the beginning of the 1st Dynasty. Two Predynastic settlements, "North Town" and "South Town," were also investigated by Petrie in the Nagada region. In the northern part of South Town Petrie found the remains of a thick mudbrick wall, which appeared to be a type of fortification.

Opposite Nagada are more Predynastic sites. Fernand Debono located a Predynastic village and graves near Lakeita, 33 km southeast of Quft/Qift in the Wadi Hammamat. At Quft in the temple of Isis and Min, Petrie excavated a deposit with Predynastic potsherds, stone tools and maceheads.

About 45 km northwest of Nagada, below the Qena bend of the Nile, a major Predynastic center was located at Hu, known as Diospolis Parva in Graeco-Roman times. In 1898–9, Petrie excavated six "prehistoric" cemeteries in the region, and he noted the remains of prehistoric villages. Cemetery H, near the village of Semaineh, was also where Petrie excavated burials with Nagada III grave goods; hence the term "Semainean" for his latest Predynastic phase.

Site HG, near the village of Halfiah Gibli, was excavated by Kathryn Bard in 1991, but no evidence of permanent architecture was found. This village was associated with the large Predynastic cemetery excavated by Petrie at Abadiya. On the east bank opposite Girga at Naga ed-Deir, a Predynastic cemetery (7000), with over 600 burials, was excavated by Albert Lythgoe in 1903–4. One large burial (7304) contained lapis lazuli beads and a cylinder seal with a (Jemdet Nasr-style) design, imported or emulating an artifact from a contemporaneous culture in southern Mesopotamia. Excavations were resumed in the region in 1910 by the Boston–Harvard Expedition.

Abydos was a major center of Predynastic culture in Upper Egypt. Diana Craig Patch's recent investigations here of cemeteries and settlements show a change in settlement patterns through time, with some nucleation within the region by the end of the Nagada II phase. Predynastic cemeteries recorded in the Abydos region are in three areas, one near the Osiris temple, the others near the villages of el-Amra and el-Mahasna. In 1901, D. Randall-MacIver and A.C. Mace excavated (or estimated) more than 1,000 Predynastic and Early Dynastic burials near the village of el-Amra, from which the term Amratian (= Nagada I) is derived. Excavated at el-Amra was a unique clay model of a rectangular Predynastic house.

The Umm el-Qa'ab at Abydos is where the kings of the 1st Dynasty built their tombs and "funerary enclosures," walled constructions located along the edge of cultivation. Northeast of the royal tombs are smaller and less elaborate tombs (B group) excavated by Petrie, investigated more recently by Kaiser and Günter Dreyer. Several of these tombs have been identified as belonging to three kings of Dynasty 0 and the first king of the 1st Dynasty (Aha). A tomb (U-j) has also been excavated here with over 400 pots imported from Palestine and many bone labels with the earliest known hieroglyphs. This evidence, then, is of a royal cemetery dating to the end of the Predynastic (Nagada IIIa–b/Dynasty 0), possibly of kings whose descendants reigned in the 1st Dynasty.

In Middle Egypt, Predynastic sites are known from the el-Badari district, on the east bank of the Nile. The earliest class of pottery ("Badarian") from sites in this region is thought to be earlier than Petrie's Predynastic classes from Upper Egypt, a chronology demonstrated by Gertrude Caton Thompson's excavation of the stratified midden at Hemamieh. Guy Brunton also thought that the graves he excavated at Deir Tasa, containing stone celts and black incised pottery, represent an early phase of the Badarian. At el-Badari, the remains of small Predynastic settlements and cemeteries were located on spurs above the floodplain. At Hemamieh were the remains of hut and/or storage circles, and at Mostagedda, Brunton excavated several small Predynastic villages, consisting of hut circles and middens. A recent archaeological survey in the el-Badari district by Diane Holmes and Renée Friedman has led to the discovery of two Predynastic sites. The ceramics collected at these sites suggest that in the el-Badari district, the "Badarian" is not a cultural period which entirely preceded the Amratian (Nagada I), but perhaps one which chronologically overlaps the Amratian known farther south.

North of the el-Badari district, no Predynastic sites are known for over 300 km. Archaeological evidence in the Fayum of both Nagada and Ma'adi culture wares now seems to suggest that this region was where peoples of the Predynastic cultures of Upper and Lower Egypt first came into contact. The best known Predynastic site in the Fayum region is the small cemetery at Gerza, from which the term Gerzean (Nagada II) is derived. Excavated by Petrie, this cemetery contained 288 burials with (Upper Egyptian) ceramics which are typically Nagada II. A later Predynastic cemetery with several hundred burials, excavated by Georg Möller, is located at Abusir el-Meleq, about 10 km west of the present Nile. Ma'adi culture ceramics are found at the cemetery of es-Saff on the east bank opposite Gerza, and a site near Qasr Qarun in the southwestern region of the Fayum, excavated by Caton Thompson and E.W. Gardner in the 1930s.

Haraga, southeast of the village of Lahun, was excavated in 1913–14 by Reginald

Engelbach. Two Predynastic cemeteries contained burials with (Upper Egyptian) Nagada II pottery, though some of the pottery from one cemetery (H) resembles Predynastic Lower Egyptian wares. At Sedment, southwest of Haraga, ceramics excavated by Petrie and Brunton included small Black-topped Red Ware jars (Nagada culture, in Cemetery J), but Ma'adi culture ceramics in circular pits (without burials) in another area.

In the Cairo region on the east bank, Predynastic evidence of a material culture different from that of Upper Egypt has been found at two major sites, el-Omari and Ma'adi. At el-Omari, an early Predynastic settlement was excavated by Fernand Debono. To the west was a village, "Omari A," where the dead were interred in houses, including oval structures and round, semi-subterranean ones. A second village had a separate cemetery, where each grave was covered with a mound of stones. Pottery at el-Omari consists of Ma'adi culture ceramics.

Four sites were excavated at Ma'adi by Cairo University archaeologists from 1930 to 1953, including a large settlement of over 40,000 sq m. More recent excavations have been conducted in the eastern part of the settlement by Italian archaeologists. Few grave goods were found in any of the 76 graves next to the Ma'adi settlement. In another cemetery at the mouth of the Wadi Digla ("Ma'adi South"), 468 human burials and 14 animal burials were excavated, consisting of simple oval pits with either a few pots or entirely without grave goods. Ma'adi culture ceramics have also been found at Tura, 2 km south of Ma'adi, and at Heliopolis, now a district of Cairo, in a small early Predynastic cemetery. However, at Tura a large Nagada III/early 1st Dynasty cemetery was also excavated by Hermann Junker, with grave goods of typical Nagada III pots.

Evidence from the recent Ma'adi excavations suggests that through time occupation within the settlement shifted from east to west. There is no evidence of a planned settlement, nor are there any known areas of specialized activity. Houses consisted mainly of wattle and matting, sometimes covered with mud. Pottery from Ma'adi has datable parallels in Upper Egypt from the Nagada I and II phases, and the ceramic evidence suggests an end to occupation at Ma'adi by late Nagada II times (end of Nagada IIc). Most of the pottery excavated at Ma'adi is of a local ware not found in Upper Egypt. Recent investigations suggest that copper ore found throughout the site may have been used for pigment, and not for smelting.

Although archaeological evidence at Ma'adi and Ma'adi-related sites is mainly from settlements, unlike most of the surviving evidence of Nagada culture cemeteries in Upper Egypt, what is known about Ma'adi suggests a material culture very different from that in the south. The cemetery at Ma'adi, with its very simple human burials, is also very different from Predynastic cemeteries in Upper Egypt. Some contact with southwest Asia is demonstrated by the imported coarse-tempered ware at Ma'adi, which may have been a northern Egyptian center for trade with Palestine.

In the northeast Delta, surveys conducted by Dutch and Italian archaeologists in the 1980s have yielded evidence of a number of sites dating to the fourth and third millennia BC, and late Roman times. Excavations at Tell el-Farkha have demonstrated a clear break, with a change in pottery fabrics and stratigraphic evidence of settlement abandonment, between the Predynastic and Early Dynastic occupations. At Tell Ibrahim Awad the stratigraphy shows an uninterrupted sequence from the late Predynastic, with no mudbrick architecture, to the Early Dynastic, with substantial mudbrick architecture. The early pottery is comparable to the straw-tempered ware from Tell el-Fara'in/Buto, farther west in the Delta, but it disappears and is replaced by wares known from Nagada III and Early Dynastic sites in the Delta and the Nile Valley. At Minshat Abu Omar, *circa* 150 km northeast of Cairo, a cemetery with Predynastic/Early Dynastic graves has been excavated by German archaeologists. Similar archaeological evidence is found at other sites in the northeast Delta: Tell el-Ginn, el-Husseiniya, Tell Samara, Gezira Sangaha, Kufur Nigm, Beni Amir, el-Beidha and Bubastis. With the exception of early Nagada culture pottery (Black-topped Red and White Cross-lined classes), all other southern Predynastic classes of pottery are present (Nagada II–III) and continue into the 1st Dynasty.

On the western fringe of the Delta, about 60 km northwest of Cairo, is the large prehistoric site of Merimde Beni-salame. Junker dug here from 1928 to 1939, but most of the excavation notes were lost during the Second World War. Reported by Hassan, radiocarbon dates for Merimde are from the fifth millennium BC. Junker thought that the *circa* 160,000 sq m of settlement was occupied continuously, but it is more likely that there was horizontal movement of the site through time. Merimde burials were without grave goods, and many were of children. In the 1980s, more excavations were conducted at Merimde by Josef Eiwanger, between and to the north of the areas excavated by Junker. Eiwanger has identified five phases of occupation, with a discernible change in the stone tools and ceramics between the first and subsequent phases. Storage pits are known from the four later phases, and emmer wheat and barley were the most abundant plant remains.

At Tell el-Fara'in/Buto in the northern Delta, Thomas von der Way has excavated remains of a settlement from the later fourth millennium BC below levels dating to the third millennium BC. Most of the wares at Tell el-Fara'in were also found at Ma'adi. Above two layers with Lower Egyptian ceramics is a transitional layer with decreasing amounts of these ceramics and, for the first time, Nagada (IId) style pottery. Imported pottery includes Nagada culture classes and a ware known from northern Syria ('Amuq F).

Archaeological evidence clearly demonstrates the existence of two different material cultures with different belief systems in Egypt in the fourth millennium BC: the Nagada culture of Upper Egypt and the Ma'adi culture of Lower Egypt. Evidence in Lower Egypt consists mainly of settlements with very simple burials, in contrast to Upper Egypt, where cemeteries with elaborate burials are found. The rich grave goods in several major cemeteries in Upper Egypt represent the acquired wealth of higher social strata, and these cemeteries were probably associated with centers of craft production. Trade and exchange of finished goods and luxury materials from the Eastern and Western Deserts and Nubia would also have taken place in such centers. In Lower Egypt, however, while excavated settlements permit a broader reconstruction of the prehistoric economy, there is little evidence for any great socioeconomic complexity.

State formation

Archaeological evidence points to the origins of the state which emerged by the 1st Dynasty in the Nagada culture of Upper Egypt, where grave types, pottery and artifacts demonstrate an evolution of form from the Predynastic to the 1st Dynasty. This cannot be demonstrated for the material culture of Lower Egypt, which was eventually displaced by that originating in Upper Egypt.

The highly differentiated burials in later Predynastic cemeteries of Upper Egypt (but not Lower Egypt), where elite burials contained great numbers of grave goods in sometimes exotic materials, such as gold and lapis lazuli, are symbolic of an increasingly hierarchical society. Such burials probably represent the earliest processes of competition and the aggrandizement of local polities in Upper Egypt as economic interaction occurred regionally. Control of the distribution of exotic raw materials and the production of prestigious craft goods would have reinforced the position of chiefs in Predynastic centers, and such goods were important symbols of status.

A motivating factor for Nagada culture expansion into northern Egypt would have been to directly control the lucrative trade with other regions in the eastern Mediterranean. But more importantly, large boats were the key to control and communication on the Nile and large-scale economic exchange. Timber for the construction of such boats (cedars) did not grow in Egypt, but came from Lebanon. Gold was an Upper (not Lower) Egyptian resource, along with various kinds of stone used for carved vessels and beads. Possibly there was first a more or less peaceful(?) movement or migration(s) of Nagada culture peoples from south to north, as suggested by archaeological evidence of Nagada culture in the Fayum region. The final unification of Upper and Lower Egypt under one rule may have been achieved through military conquest(s) in the north, but there is not much evidence for this aside from scenes carved on stylistically late Predynastic palettes. Possibly there was an earlier unification of Upper Egyptian polities, either by a series of alliances or through warfare.

By *circa* 3050 BC the Early Dynastic state had emerged in Egypt. One result of the expansion of Nagada culture throughout northern Egypt would have been a greatly elaborated (state) administration, and by the beginning of the 1st Dynasty this was managed in part by the invention of writing, used on sealings and tags affixed to state goods. The early Egyptian state was a centrally controlled polity ruled by a (god-)king from the newly founded capital of Memphis in the north, near Saqqara. What is truly unique about the early state in Egypt is the integration of rule over an extensive geographic region. There was undoubtedly heightened commercial contact with southwest Asia in the late fourth millennium BC, but the Early Dynastic state in Egypt was unique and indigenous in character.

See also

A-Group culture; Abusir el-Meleq; Abydos, Predynastic sites; agriculture, introduction of; Armant; el-Badari district Predynastic sites; Buto (Tell el-Fara'in); Canaanites; Dakhla Oasis, prehistoric sites; dating techniques, prehistory; Early Dynastic period, overview; Elkab; Fayum, Neolithic and Predynastic sites; Gebelein; Heliopolis, the Predynastic cemetery; Hierakonpolis; kingship; Ma'adi and the Wadi Digla; Mendes, Predynastic and Early Dynastic; Merimde Beni-salame; Minshat Abu Omar; Naga ed-Deir; Nagada (Naqada); Neolithic and Predynastic stone tools; el-Omari; Petrie, Sir William Matthew Flinders; pottery, prehistoric; Quft/Qift (Coptos); representational evidence, Predynastic; Tell el-Farkha; Tura, Predynastic cemeteries; writing, invention and early development

Further reading

Adams, B. 1988. *Predynastic Egypt*. Aylesbury.

Bard, K.A. 1994. The Egyptian Predynastic: a review of the evidence. *JFA* 21: 265–88.

Hassan, F.A. 1984. Radiocarbon chronology of Predynastic settlements, Upper Egypt. *CA* 25: 681–3.

Hendrickx, S. 1995. *Analytical Bibliography of the Prehistory and the Early Dynastic Period of Egypt and Northern Sudan*. Leuven.

Hoffman, M.A. 1991. *Egypt before the Pharaohs*. Austin, TX.

Kaiser, W. 1956. Stand und Probleme der ägyptischen Vorgeschichtsforschung. *ZÄS* 81: 87–109.

——. 1957. Zur inneren Chronologie der Naqadakultur. *Archaeologia Geographica* 6: 69–77.

——. 1990. Zur Entstehung des gesamtägyptischen Staates. *MDÄIK* 46: 287–99.

Petrie, W.M.F. 1939. *The Making of Egypt*. London.

Wenke, R.J. 1991. The evolution of early Egyptian civilization: issues and evidence. *JWP* 5: 279–329.

KATHRYN A. BARD

Early Dynastic period, overview

Also known as the "Archaic", the Early Dynastic period consists of the 1st and 2nd Dynasties (*circa* 3050–2686 BC). What is now known as "Dynasty 0" should probably be placed in this period as well at the end of the Predynastic sequence. Kings of Dynasty 0, who preceded those of the 1st Dynasty, were buried at Abydos and the names of some of these rulers are known from inscriptions. The Early Dynastic state controlled a vast territory along the Nile from the Delta to the First Cataract, over 1,000 km along the floodplain. With the 1st Dynasty, the focus of development shifted from south to north, and the early Egyptian state was a centrally controlled polity ruled by a (god-)king from the Memphis region. With the Early Dynastic state too, there came the emergence of ancient Egyptian civilization.

In Dynasty 0 and the early 1st Dynasty there is evidence of Egyptian expansion into Lower Nubia and a continued Egyptian presence in the northern Sinai and southern Palestine. The Egyptian presence in southern Palestine did not last through the Early Dynastic period, but with Egyptian penetration in Nubia, the indigenous A-Group culture comes to an end later in the 1st Dynasty. With the unification of Egypt into a large territorial state, the crown most likely wanted to control the trade through Nubia of exotic raw materials used to make luxury goods, which resulted in Egyptian military incursions in Lower Nubia. With the display of force by the Egyptians, A-Group peoples may simply have left Lower Nubia and gone elsewhere (to the south or desert regions), and there is no evidence of indigenous peoples living in Lower Nubia until the C-Group culture, beginning in the late Old Kingdom.

In Palestine fortified cities contemporary to the Egyptian 1st Dynasty were built in the north and south. At the site of 'En Besor in southern Palestine, ninety fragments of Egyptian seal impressions have been found associated with a small mudbrick building and ceramics that are mainly Egyptian, including many fragments of bread molds. Made of local clay, the seal impressions are those of officials of four kings of the 1st Dynasty. This evidence suggests state-organized trade directed by Egyptian officials residing at this settlement during most of the 1st Dynasty. Such evidence in southern Palestine is missing during the 2nd Dynasty, however, and active contact may have broken off by then, as the sea trade with Lebanon intensified.

One result of the expansion of the Predynastic Nagada culture from southern Egypt to the north would have been a greatly elaborated (state) administration, and by the beginning of the 1st Dynasty this was managed in part by early writing, used on sealings and tags affixed to state goods. Such evidence also suggests a state taxation system in place in the early Dynasties. Early writing has a royal context and was an innovation of great importance to this state, which used writing for economic/administrative purposes and in royal art.

In the Memphis region graves and tombs are found beginning in the 1st Dynasty, which suggests the founding of the city at this time. Tombs of high officials are found at nearby North Saqqara, and officials and persons of all levels of status were buried at other sites in the Memphis region. Such burial evidence also suggests that the Memphis region was the administrative center of the state. Other towns must have developed or were founded as administrative centers of the state throughout Egypt. Although it has been suggested that ancient Egypt was a civilization without cities, this was certainly not the case. At sites such as Abydos, Hierakonpolis and Buto, there is some archaeological evidence for early towns, but most such towns are probably buried now under alluvium or modern settlements.

Most ancient Egyptians in the Early Dynastic period (and all later periods), however, were farmers who lived in small villages. Cereal agriculture was the economic base of the ancient Egyptian state, and by the Early Dynastic period simple basin irrigation may have been practiced which extended land under cultivation and increased yields. Huge agricultural surpluses were possible in this environment, and when such surpluses were controlled by the state they could support the flowering of Egyptian civilization that is seen in the 1st Dynasty.

Compared with the early cities of southern Mesopotamia, there is much less evidence in Early Dynastic Egypt for cult centers of the gods. Some of the inscribed labels from the 1st Dynasty have scenes with structures that are temples or shrines. Early writing also appears on some of the small votive artifacts that were probably offerings or donations to cult centers. Early Dynastic carved stone vessels were sometimes inscribed, and signs on some of these suggest that they may have come from cult centers. Such evidence points to the existence of cult temples outside of the royal mortuary cult, but there is very little archaeological evidence of this architecture. At Coptos, Abydos and Hierakonpolis, artifacts and deposits from early temples have been excavated, and at Hierakonpolis there is also structural evidence of an early temple consisting of a low oval revetment of sandstone blocks. Recent excavations by the German Archaeological Institute, Cairo (DAI) on Elephantine Island at the First Cataract have revealed the remains of a shrine dating to the Early Dynastic period, a fortress built during the 1st Dynasty and a large fortified wall encompassing the town in the 2nd Dynasty. The shrine is very simple, consisting only of some mudbrick structures less than 8 m wide nestled into a natural niche formed by granite boulders.

Early Egyptian civilization was mainly expressed in monumental architecture of the mortuary cult, especially the royal tombs and funerary enclosures at Abydos and the large tombs of high officials at North Saqqara. Formal art styles, which are characteristically Egyptian, also emerged at the end of the Predynastic period and in the 1st Dynasty. What is characteristically Egyptian in the monumental architecture and commemorative art (such as the Narmer Palette) is reflective of full-time craftsmen and artisans supported by the crown. Artifacts of the highest quality of craftsmanship are found in royal and elite tombs of the period, including many copper tools and vessels. This was probably the result of royal expeditions to copper mines in the Eastern Desert and/or increased trade with copper-mining regions in the Negev/Sinai, and an expanded copper production industry in Egypt.

At North Saqqara, the large tombs of the 1st Dynasty provide evidence of an official class of a large state. These tombs would also have been the most important monuments of the state in the north and thus were symbolic of the centralized state ruled very effectively by the king and his administrators. That huge quantities of craft goods were going out of circulation in the economy and into tombs is indicative of the wealth of this early state, which was shared by a number of officials. Clearly, the mortuary cult was also of great importance to non-royalty and the elements of royal burials were emulated in more modest form in the exclusive cemetery at North Saqqara. Smaller tombs and simple pit graves dating to the 1st Dynasty are found throughout Egypt, which is not only evidence of social stratification but also demonstrates the importance of the mortuary cult for all classes. The simplest burials of this period are pits excavated in the low desert, without coffins and with only a few pots for grave goods.

In the south, Abydos was the most important cult center, where the kings of the 1st Dynasty were buried. From the very beginning of the Dynastic period the institution of kingship was a strong and powerful one, and it would remain so throughout the major historical periods. Nowhere else in the ancient Near East at this early date was kingship so important and central to control of the early state. Although it was previously thought that the kings of the 1st Dynasty were buried at North Saqqara, it is now clear that these tombs belonged to high officials and the Umm el-Qa'ab at Abydos is the burial place of the kings of the 1st Dynasty. Only at Abydos is there a small number of large tombs which correspond to the kings (and one queen) of this dynasty, and only at Abydos are there the remains of the funerary enclosures for all but one of the rulers of this dynasty, as has been demonstrated by David O'Connor's recent excavations. Called "fortresses" by earlier excavators, the funerary enclosures may have been where the cults of each king were practiced by priests and personnel after the burial in the royal tomb, as was the custom at later royal mortuary complexes.

What is clearly evident in the Abydos royal cemetery is the ideology of kingship, as symbolized in the mortuary cult. Through ideology and its symbolic material form in tombs, widely held beliefs concerning death came to reflect the hierarchical social organization of the living and the state controlled by the king. This was a politically motivated transformation of the belief system with direct consequences in the socio-economic system. The king was accorded the most elaborate burial, which was symbolic of his role as mediator between the powers of the netherworld and his deceased subjects, and a belief in an earthly and cosmic order would have provided a certain amount of social cohesiveness for the Early Dynastic state.

All of the 1st Dynasty tombs at Abydos have subsidiary burials in rows around the royal burials, and this is the only time in ancient Egypt when humans were sacrificed for royal burials. Perhaps officials, priests, retainers and women from the royal household were sacrificed to serve their king in the afterlife. The tomb of Djer has the most subsidiary burials—338, but the later royal burials have fewer . In later times, small servant statues may have become more acceptable substitutes.

The Abydos evidence demonstrates the huge expenditure of the state on the mortuary complexes, both tombs and funerary enclosures, of kings of the 1st Dynasty. These kings had control over vast resources: craft goods produced in court workshops, goods and materials imported in huge quantities from abroad, and probably conscripted labor (as well as labor that could be sacrificed for burial with the king). The paramount role of the king is certainly symbolized in these monuments, and the symbols of the royal mortuary cult which evolved at Abydos would become further elaborated in the pyramid complexes of the Old and Middle Kingdoms.

There is much less evidence for the kings of the 2nd Dynasty than those of the 1st Dynasty. Given what is known about the early Old Kingdom in the 3rd Dynasty, the 2nd Dynasty must have been when the economic and political foundations were put in place for the strongly centralized state which developed with truly vast resources. The only 2nd Dynasty monuments at Abydos are two tombs and two funerary enclosures which belonged to the last two kings of this dynasty, Peribsen and Khasekhemwy. Khasekhemwy's tomb consists of one long gallery, divided into 58 rooms with a central burial chamber made of quarried limestone; this is the earliest known large construction in stone. Where the early kings of this dynasty were buried is uncertain, as there is no evidence of their tombs at

Abydos. At Saqqara, two enormous series of underground galleries, each over 100 m long, have been found south of Zoser's Step Pyramid complex, and possibly two kings of this dynasty were buried there. Associated with these galleries are the seal impressions of the first three kings of the 2nd Dynasty (Hetepsekhemwy, Raneb and Nynetjer) and the third king might have been buried in a tomb consisting of galleries now beneath Zoser's complex.

The best preserved funerary enclosure at Abydos belonged to Khasekemwy. Its niched inner walls are still preserved up to 10–11 m in height and enclose an area *circa* 124 × 56 m. In 1988 O'Connor discovered a large mound of sand and gravel covered with mudbrick, approximately square in plan, within this enclosure. This mound was located more or less in the same area as the Step Pyramid of Zoser's complex at Saqqara (3rd Dynasty), which began as a low *mastaba* structure and only in its fourth stage was expanded to a stepped structure. Both complexes, of Khasekemwy and of Zoser, were surrounded by huge niched enclosure walls with only one entrance in the southeast. Zoser's complex was constructed 40–50 years after Khasekemwy's, and very possibly the mound at Abydos is evidence for a "proto-pyramid" structure. Thus at Abydos the evolution of the royal mortuary cult and its monumental form can clearly be seen, which by the 3rd Dynasty came to reflect a new order of royal control over vast resources and labor for the construction of the earliest monument in the world built entirely in stone.

Also recently discovered at Abydos are twelve boat burials, located just outside the northeast outer wall of Khasekhemwy's enclosure. These burials consist of pits which contained wooden hulls of boats 18–21 m long, but only about 50 cm high. Associated pottery is Early Dynastic. Smaller boat burials have also been found with Early Dynastic tombs at Saqqara and Helwan, but their purpose is unknown. Those at Abydos are the earliest evidence of such burials associated with the royal mortuary cult. Later, at Giza in the 4th Dynasty, the most famous boat burials are the two undisturbed boats next to Khufu's pyramid.

In the 2nd Dynasty, high officials of the state continued to be buried at North Saqqara. Near Unas's pyramid (5th Dynasty), James Quibell excavated five large subterranean tombs, the largest of which (Tomb 2302) consists of 27 rooms beneath a mudbrick superstructure. The 2nd Dynasty tombs were designed with rooms for funerary goods that were excavated deep in the bedrock where they were more protected from grave robbing than the earlier storage rooms in the superstructure. Niches placed on the east side of the superstructure (for offerings) in 2nd Dynasty tombs are a design feature that would be found in private tombs throughout the Old Kingdom. Later 2nd Dynasty tombs at Saqqara, which probably belonged to middle level officials, are similar in design to the standard *mastaba* tomb of the Old Kingdom, with a small mudbrick superstructure above a vertical shaft leading to the burial chamber.

Short wooden coffins for contracted burials, which were found only in elite tombs in the 1st Dynasty, are much more common in 2nd Dynasty tombs, such as those at Helwan. At Saqqara, Walter Emery found corpses wrapped in linen bandages soaked in resin, early evidence of some attempt to preserve the actual body before mummification techniques had been worked out. Such measures were necessitated by burial in a coffin, as opposed to Predynastic burials which were naturally dehydrated in warm sand in a pit in the desert. The increased use of wood and resin in middle status burials of the 2nd Dynasty probably also points to greatly increased contact and trade with Lebanon.

The architecture, art and associated beliefs of the early Old Kingdom clearly evolved from forms of the Early Dynastic period. This was a time of consolidation of the enormous gains of unification—which could easily have failed—when a state bureaucracy was successfully organized and expanded to bring the entire country under its control. This was done through taxation, to support the crown and its projects on a grand scale, which included expeditions for goods and materials to the Sinai, Palestine, Lebanon, Lower Nubia and the Eastern Desert. Conscription must also have been practiced, to build the large royal mortuary monuments and to supply soldiers for military expeditions. The use of early writing no doubt facilitated such state organization.

There were obvious rewards to being bureaucrats of the state, as is seen in the early cemeteries on both sides of the river in the Memphis region. Belief in the rewards of a mortuary cult, where huge quantities of goods were going out of circulation in the economy, was a cohesive factor which helped to integrate this society in both the north and south. In the early Dynasties when the crown began to exert enormous control over land, resources and labor, the ideology of the god-king legitimized such control and became increasingly powerful as a unifying belief system.

The flowering of early civilization in Egypt was the result of major transformations in sociopolitical and economic organization, and in the belief system. That this state was successful for a very long time—*circa* 800 years until the end of the Old Kingdom—is in part due to the enormous potential of cereal agriculture on the Nile floodplain, but it is also a result of Egyptian organizational skills and the strongly developed institution of kingship.

See also

A-Group culture; Abydos, Early Dynastic funerary enclosures; Abydos, Umm el-Qa'ab; Buto (Tell el-Fara'in); C-Group culture; Canaanites; Early Dynastic private tombs; Elephantine; Helwan; Hierakonpolis; Kafr Tarkhan (Kafr Ammar); kingship; Memphis; Minshat Abu Omar; Naga ed-Deir; natural resources; representational evidence, Early Dynastic; textual sources, Early Dynastic; Tura, Dynastic burials and quarries; writing, invention and early development

Further reading

Emery, W.B. 1967. *Archaic Egypt*. Harmondsworth.
Helck, W. 1987. *Untersuchungen zur Thinitenzeit*. Wiesbaden.
Hendrickx, S. 1995. *Analytical Bibliography of the Prehistory and the Early Dynastic Period of Egypt and the Northern Sudan*. Leuven.
Kaiser, W. 1967. Die Vorzeit. Reichseinigung und Frühdynastische Zeit. *Ägyptisches Museum Berlin. Staatlichen Museum Preussischer Kulturbesitz*: 9–22.
Kemp, B.J. 1989. *Ancient Egypt: Anatomy of a Civilization*. London.
Spencer, A.J. 1993. *Early Egypt: The Rise of Civilisation in the Nile Valley*. London.
——. 1996. *Aspects of Early Egypt*. London.
van den Brink, E., ed. 1992. *The Nile Delta in Transition: 4th-3rd Millennium* BC. Jerusalem.

KATHRYN A. BARD

Old Kingdom, overview

"Old Kingdom" is the term used by modern scholars to define the first lengthy period of documented centralized government in the history of ancient Egypt. It includes the 3rd through 8th Dynasties (in absolute chronology, *circa* 2665–2140 BC) within the traditional division of Egyptian history which has been adopted by modern Egyptologists. A further issue relates to the time when the end of the Old Kingdom is to be fixed. From a political point of view, the timespan from the 3rd to 8th Dynasties refers to the period of Egyptian history in which the country's residence was in the northern city of Memphis and pharaohs claimed total control over a unified Egypt. From a social point of view, however, beginning with the last decades of the 6th Dynasty and throughout the 7th and 8th Dynasties, Egypt had already developed into a more flexible cultural landscape with numerous local centers of individual initiative as well as administrative power; what modern scholars refer to as the First Intermediate Period.

Sources

While quantitatively rather scarce, our sources for the study of the Old Kingdom display a high degree of variety. The documents closest to historical records in our modern sense are the annals (*gnwt*), records of the natural or political events of particular importance which took place in a specific regnal year. The most important document of this type is the Palermo Stone, a broken piece of diorite from the 5th Dynasty which originally recorded the history of the country back to the first pharaoh, but which is now fragmentary.

Similar to the annals are the king lists, chronicles relating the names of former kings mostly in diachronic succession. These were meant to testify to the contemporary sovereign's legitimate claim to the throne. These texts constituted the basis for Manetho's compilation of the Egyptian dynasties in Hellenistic times. While conveying hardly anything more than names of kings, they nonetheless document the internal Egyptian sense of the historical past. Of historical importance, although highly ideological, are also scenes in the funerary complexes of Old Kingdom kings, such as Sahure or Unas, representing events which took place during their reign.

Far more informative for modern historians are contemporary administrative records. The most important of these are the papyri from the pyramid temple of King Neferirkare (5th Dynasty) at Abusir, compiled under King Djedkare-Isesi, two generations after the establishment of the funerary cult of the king. There are also royal decrees (*wd̠ nzw*), formal decisions by the king on specific matters (as opposed to the laws (*hpw*) which governed general life). Royal decrees exempt the dependants of private funerary estates from state corvées, and communicate promotions or demotions within the bureaucratic hierarchy. Rare royal letters and a few testaments (*jmjt-prw*, literally "what-is in-the house") round out the Old Kingdom administrative records.

The intellectual history of the Old Kingdom is mainly documented by monumental texts. The religious corpus of *Pyramid Texts* are inscribed in the inner chambers of the royal tombs from King Unas of the 5th Dynasty onward. While primarily connected with the funerary ritual of the king, in the richness of their forms and topics the *Pyramid Texts* represent a whole encyclopedia of early Egyptian theology. Autobiographies of the higher officials of the administration are inscribed on the external walls of their rock tombs. Framed as accounts of the services rendered to the king during the tomb-owner's lifetime, these texts are the first examples of the individual concerns, ideas and aspirations of the high officials of the Egyptian administration.

The most impressive source of records for Egyptian society during the Old Kingdom is undoubtedly offered by the architectural and artistic documentation. In the region of the capital at Memphis, the royal funerary complexes in stone architecture around the king's tomb as well as the private tombs of higher administrators document the fixation of formal conventions of stone architecture and the funerary expectations of Egyptian society. They provide an insight into the patterns which governed political effectiveness as well as social cohesion, subsumed under the concept of *ma'at*.

Cultural features: societal centralism versus individual freedom

The main cultural feature of this historical period is the tension between a state structure with a high level of centralization on the one hand and movements toward forms of localism and individualism on the other. A unifying tendency can be observed in the political and religious centers of the country in the Memphite area (Giza, Saqqara, Memphis, Heliopolis, Abusir, etc.) and especially in the earlier periods of the Old Kingdom, during the 3rd–5th Dynasties. A tendency toward individual freedoms is more tangible in the provincial centers in Upper Egypt; this trend characterizes mainly the later phases of the Old Kingdom, achieving a breakthrough during the 6th Dynasty and exploding during the transition to the First Intermediate Period.

The most visible sign of the centralism of Old Kingdom society is represented by the dramatic evolution which affected royal funerary architecture. The funerary complex of King Zoser at Saqqara marks the political change from the Early Dynastic period to the Old Kingdom, in the sense that it conveys a modified picture of the relation between the state and its subjects. Through the use of stone instead of mudbrick and the development of the step pyramid as a superstructure to the shaft containing the king's burial chamber, Zoser's funerary complex indicates the permanent and preeminent role of kingship in Egyptian society. The king of Egypt has now acquired a role as the cultural focus of the country as a whole. His funerary complex is a highly symbolic mirror of the state's ideology rather than a purely religious area for the funerary cult of an individual, however prestigious.

Next to the royal pyramid, Zoser's funerary complex exhibits a series of ceremonial buildings connected in various ways with the country's religious history and identity. The evolution initiated by Zoser and pursued with even greater consistency under his successors of the 3rd and 4th Dynasties shows the fixation of a royal ideology typical of a mature and well-structured society. The final form of the funerary complex as expressed during the 4th Dynasty at Giza and during the 5th Dynasty at Abusir and Saqqara, with its combination of enclosure wall, main pyramid, subsidiary pyramids, mortuary temple, causeway and valley temple, surrounded by fields of the private tombs (*mastaba*s or rock-cut tombs) of administrative officials, becomes in fact the core structure for the development of Egyptian towns, consisting of brick-built private dwellings for the personnel in charge of the construction of the buildings and the maintenance of the cult.

In the domain of private funerary architecture, an explicit sign of centralization in Old Kingdom society is represented by the concentration of the administrative officials' tombs in the Memphite necropolis, especially in Giza (4th Dynasty) and Saqqara (5th Dynasty). These individual *mastaba*s tend to be grouped around the royal funerary complexes; the scenes depicted on their walls suggest the cohesive ideology of Egyptian society (referred to by the term m^3et, or *ma'at*), but perceived from the point of view of the aristocracy rather than of the king (as in the pyramid complex). The ideal of a well-administered social life and an ordered political hierarchy is depicted in the tombs.

A parallel symptom of centralization coming from a different aspect of Egyptian society during the Old Kingdom is represented by the state monopoly in religious affairs. The formula establishing the funerary cult for the individual after his or her death is always presented as a "royal concession" (*htp-dj-nzw*, literally "an offering given by the King"). Similarly, most of the temples known from the Old Kingdom are dedicated either to the royal funerary cult or to the worship of the sun god, itself theologically connected with the king. During the 4th Dynasty, the king adopts compound names with the sun god Re and acquires the title of "son of Re"; the first example is Khufu's successor Djedefre, literally "Re-is-durable." Full-fledged theological discourse is developed around the figure and the role of the king, as is known to us through the *Pyramid Texts*, whereas the metaphysical status of the individual Egyptian remains largely unspecified.

During the 5th Dynasty the pyramid loses the monumentality of earlier periods. With the development of the *Pyramid Texts*, it acquires instead primarily the function of vehicle of theological discourse. Similarly, during the 5th and 6th Dynasties the tombs of the Upper Egyptian nomarchs (provincial governors) not only support the societal *ma'at*, as expressed in the representations of idealized life in the tombs of the residential Memphite cemeteries, but also indicate the individual striving for autonomous self-realization. This movement of intellectual emancipation becomes particularly explicit in the development of the tomb autobiography, the inscriptions on the outer walls of the rock-cut tomb in which the owner recounts his individual achievements in the royal service. These texts convey a focus on values of competitiveness and career which express individual concerns; this individual focus inevitably lessened the elite's total commitment to royal (and societal) expectations. In fact, the intellectual divorce between the royal residence and the powerful nomarchs eventually becomes one of the main causes of that crisis of Old Kingdom society which Egyptologists call the First Intermediate Period.

Administration

The fundamental feature of Old Kingdom administration is a central organization of the country from Memphis under a vizier (*t3jtj z3b t3tj*), who combined judiciary and executive functions. The central administration was active in the areas of archival recording, supervision of the state's building activities, taxation, storage and jurisdiction. From the 5th Dynasty the Nile Valley, but not the Delta, was placed under the control of an "overseer of Upper Egypt," probably residing in Thinis. Both Upper and Lower Egypt were divided into "nomes" (*sp3t*), each governed by a nomarch, represented by a varying array of titles. Traditionally, there were 22 nomes in Upper Egypt and 20 in Lower Egypt. The office of nomarch involved the loyal representation of the king's (i.e. the state's) interest in all areas of economic activity, but from the end of the 5th Dynasty onward, when it began to move away from the royal family and to fall under the control of powerful local clans, this office gradually became the catalyst of the new, less centralistic and more individually oriented culture referred to above.

An important feature of the country's administration during the Old Kingdom was the progressive establishment of pious foundations (similar to the concept of *waqf* in Islamic societies) to ensure the maintenance of the king's mortuary cult in the Memphite pyramid towns, of the king's (or the gods') service in provincial temples, and also of the private funerary cult of selected members of the aristocracy. The personnel of these settlements were exempt from compulsory state corvées. The income from these foundations was assigned to those who maintained the cult, an economic decision which favored the concentration of wealth in private hands. The consequent crisis of the economic system based on the total control by the state of the means of production contributed to the profound revision of political structures at the end of the Old Kingdom and during the First Intermediate Period.

International relations

During the Old Kingdom, Egypt's most important foreign contacts were with the neighboring cultures to the south in Lower Nubia. There, the dissolution of the Nubian A-culture during the Early Dynastic period in Egypt provoked an increased Egyptian attempt on the one hand to create (until the 5th Dynasty) centers of permanent occupation, and on the other hand to control the semi-nomadic chiefdoms by means of incursions and consequent seizure of animals and men. The autobiographical inscriptions in the tombs of Upper Egyptian nomarchs in the 6th Dynasty, particularly that of Harkhuf, and the inscriptions they left behind in Nubia are our most important source of information for these activities. At the end of the Old Kingdom, with the progressive formation in Lower Nubia (called Wawat by the Egyptians) of a new local kingdom, replacing the former smaller units referred to in Egyptian texts (mainly Irtjetj, Irtjet, Zatju) and probably representing the original structure behind the Nubian C-Group of the Middle Kingdom, the Egyptian presence in Nubia changes its patterns and moves to a higher degree of parity, with the contemporary presence of Egyptian imports in Lower Nubian tombs and of organized Nubian contingents (especially of mercenary soldiers) in Egypt.

Farther south, the kingdom of Yam competed with Egypt for control of Lower Nubia. As the autobiographical texts show, Yam was located in Upper Nubia to the south of Wawat. From the 5th Dynasty onward, as documented by the annals of King Sahure on the Palermo Stone, the most important land in this area is coastal Punt. Located along the Red Sea around the Bab el-Mandeb, Punt provided Egypt with myrrh and other valuable commodities. Old Kingdom references to the Western Desert, inhabited by Libyan populations, are scarce and confined to military confrontations, as documented in the autobiography of Harkhuf; however, a 5th Dynasty statue refers to an Egyptian official as "governor of the Farafra Oasis," and in the 6th Dynasty we know of an extensive Egyptian settlement in the Dakhla Oasis.

During the Old Kingdom, inscriptions *in situ* confirm that the Sinai, particularly Wadi Maghara and Serabit el-Khadim, was extensively exploited because of its turquoise. For the

6th Dynasty, we know not only of military campaigns in the southern urbanized portion of Palestine from autobiographies (e.g. Weni) as well as from tomb representations, but also of contacts between Egypt and the Syrian kingdom of Ebla (Tell Mardikh) as early as the 4th–6th Dynasties. But the most intensive relations between Egypt and the Levant during the Old Kingdom were undoubtedly with Byblos on the Phoenician coast. Byblos was the main center for trade in timber and resin, as proven by the presence of Egyptian objects in the local temples throughout the whole period. Contacts with the Aegean region, while made likely by scattered objects from the Old Kingdom in the Aegean world, cannot be established with any degree of certitude.

Intellectual and religious life

The Old Kingdom is the period of the gradual development of structures of religious belief and of patterns of social behavior which remained characteristic for Egypt throughout pharaonic history. During the Old Kingdom, Egyptian culture experiences the need to find a unifying model for three independent dimensions of religious life: (1) the worship of the gods; (2) the representativeness of the king; and (3) the maintenance of the private funerary cult.

The ideology resulting from the blending of these conflicting dimensions is known to us through the *Pyramid Texts*, the corpus of spells and hymns dating to the 5th Dynasty; these have traditionally been taken to present the theological views of the school of thought centered around the cult of the sun god at Heliopolis. In this corpus the dead king is both Osiris, as dynastic ancestor of the reigning king (i.e. Horus), and Re, as the sun god who reappears daily at the eastern horizon, whose son is once more the king of Egypt himself. The description of the dead king's condition in the afterworld thus comes ultimately very close to a presentation of the Egyptian religious world view. As the unifying factor of Egyptian society, the Old Kingdom monarch is at the same time creator and beneficiary of its cohesiveness. If the private funerary cult needs the king as intermediary between the individual and the funerary gods (in the Old Kingdom, especially Anubis), the king also needs Egypt and her people as a stage for the fulfillment of his functions: cosmic as sun god, mythical as Horus, and ritual as the gods' sole priest on earth.

This model of interaction between "royal divinity" (rather than the "divine kingship" frequently displayed by other civilizations of the ancient world) and "kingly society" is best rendered by the Egyptian concept of *ma'at*, a word originally meaning "foundation," which then acquired the sense of "truth, justice," but which should probably be rendered as "Egyptian encyclopedia," in the sense that it summarizes the political and ethical values of Old Kingdom society: social cohesion, performance of the funerary cult, and service to the king.

Fixation of linguistic and artistic canons

After experiments in the Early Dynastic period, a phase still characterized by a high degree of variety in many areas of Egyptian culture, the Old Kingdom is the period during which the canons governing Egyptian civilization throughout its historical development were uniformly fixed. In the area of language, the *Pyramid Texts* and the tomb autobiographies are the main textual sources for the written language of the Old Kingdom, usually called

Old Egyptian. In terms of graphic system, of grammatical structures and of vocabulary, this phase of the history of the Egyptian language represents the basis for the development of the literary language of the Middle Kingdom, which is usually referred to as "Classical Egyptian." The rigid organization and the social values of Old Kingdom society also remain a source of inspiration for later Egyptian literature. Particularly noteworthy in this context are the pseudepigraphic attribution of Middle Kingdom wisdom texts to sages of the Old Kingdom (such as Ptahhotep), the mention of Old Kingdom pharaohs in the narrative literature of the Middle Kingdom (for example, Seneferu, Khufu, Hardjedef and the 5th Dynasty origins of the *Tales of Papyrus Westcar*, or Seneferu in the *Prophecy of Neferti*), and the "classicistic" reference to the great literati of the past (including Old Kingdom figures such as Hardjedef, Imhotep, Ptahhotep in Papyrus Chester Beatty IV) in Ramesside school literature.

The same holds true for artistic conventions. In architecture and sculpture the rules of construction and decoration of temples and tombs and the canon of proportions, which will remain a constant characteristic of Egyptian civilization, are formalized. Here too, the Old Kingdom maintains its paradigmatic function throughout pharaonic history, being the era to which later periods will look back as the most successful compound of the ideological values and the intellectual features of Egyptian culture as a whole.

See also

Abusir; C-Group culture; Dahshur, the Bent Pyramid; Egyptian language and writing; kingship; *ma'at*; Manetho; Memphite private tombs of the Old Kingdom; Meydum; nome structure; Old Kingdom provincial tombs; representational evidence, Old Kingdom private tombs; Saqqara, pyramids of the 3rd Dynasty; Saqqara, pyramids of the 5th and 6th Dynasties; textual sources, Old Kingdom; trade, foreign

Further reading

Kemp, B.J. 1989. *Ancient Egypt: Anatomy of a Civilization.* London.

Posener-Kriéger, P. 1976. *Les archives du temple funéraire de Neferirkarê-Kakaï (Les papyrus d'Abousir). Traduction et commentaire. BdÉ* 65: 1–2. Cairo.

Redford, D.B. 1986. *Pharaonic King-lists, Annals and Day-books: a Contribution to the Study of the Egyptian Sense of History* (SSEA 4). Mississauga.

Smith, W.S. 1971. The Old Kingdom in Egypt and the beginning of the First Intermediate Period. In *The Cambridge Ancient History* I/2A: 145–207. Cambridge.

Stadelmann, R. 1991. *Die ägyptischen Pyramiden: vom Ziegelbau zum Weltwunder* (Kulturgeschichte der Antiken Welt 30). Mainz.

ANTONIO LOPRIENO

First Intermediate Period, overview

The term "First Intermediate Period" has been employed by scholars to mean either the period of the 7th–11th Dynasties or that from the 9th to mid-11th Dynasties. The designation is still useful when referring to the period from the 7th Dynasty to preconquest 11th Dynasty in its entirety, when there was political fragmentation of the centralized state of the Old Kingdom. The designations "late Old Kingdom" and "Heracleopolitan period," referring respectively to the 7th–8th Dynasties and the 9th–10th Dynasties, are more specific.

There is still significant disagreement over the length of the First Intermediate Period. Several years ago consensus seemed to have been reached that the length of the period from the end of the 6th Dynasty to the reunification of Egypt by Nebhepetre Mentuhotep II amounted to approximately 140 years. More recently, a number of scholars have argued that the First Intermediate Period lasted approximately 230 years. This position, which accepts the historical reality of the early Heracleopolitan period (9th Dynasty), is adopted here.

As one scholar has observed, the First Intermediate Period "was the consequence of a cumulative loss of wealth and power on the part of the throne extending over a period of 200 years." In the 5th Dynasty and thereafter, a lesser share of the country's wealth was expended on the king's tomb than in the 4th Dynasty, and other institutions, including the temples of the gods (especially the official sun cult of Re), benefitted from the growing prosperity.

As additional land was brought under cultivation in the course of the later Old Kingdom, both through internal colonization and as a result of a burgeoning population, the bureaucracy that administered the country also increased in size. The king had of necessity to assign tracts of agricultural land from the royal domain to a variety of institutions and individuals for their support. The produce from what had once been crown lands not only served to maintain the royal and divine cults along with their buildings, but also provided the priests and support staff with an income. Further grants of land made to officials of the central administration compensated the latter for their services. Frequently, the tracts of land remained part and parcel of the mortuary endowment of these officials in order that they might continue serving their sovereign in the next world. In turn, the priests and officials subdivided the former crown lands for the benefit of their families and dependents. This exchange of goods and services permitted the state to function and led to a more equitable distribution of wealth, which is reflected in the increased size and complexity of the tombs of officials in the Memphite cemeteries in the later Old Kingdom. However, the revenue owed the royal treasury was increasingly diminished. Ultimately this led to the impoverishment of the monarchy, which could no longer afford to support the infrastructure of government.

In the meantime, the initiative appears to have shifted to the provinces. Provincial administration had originally been divided into different branches of activity, each centrally administered from the capital. With the growing prosperity of the provinces, however, the business of managing a single nome became more complicated and ultimately the entire administration of a nome was given to a single individual who lived in the nome and became firmly entrenched there. The process is first observable in southern Upper Egypt, but in time the new type of provincial administration was extended to central and northern

Upper Egypt. Eventually the office of provincial governor (nomarch) became hereditary. A number of kings attempted to bring these developments under control. Pepi II appears to have made a final attempt to reassert central authority; after his death, however, the temples in many of the provinces also came under the control of the nomarchs, or, vice versa, the chief priests became nomarchs, and the authority and wealth of the provincial governors was greatly enhanced.

The long reign of Pepi II (more than 90 years) ushered in the end of the Old Kingdom. Pepi's immediate successors were his own sons. Already of advanced age at the death of their father, they each ruled for only a few years. The pyramid of the 8th Dynasty king Kakare Ibi at South Saqqara was not much larger than the subsidiary pyramids belonging to the queens of Pepi II, and its size and the lack of the customary associated structures in stone clearly demonstrate the diminution of the king's personal prestige.

With the collapse of the central government, foreign trade languished. Pepi II is the last king mentioned in inscriptions at Byblos. Also after Pepi II there is no evidence of expeditions in the Sinai turquoise mines. One text describes a ship's captain who was engaged at the Gulf of Suez to build a boat for an expedition to Punt, but he and his company of soldiers were killed by local Asiatics, and had to be revenged. Relations with the south also deteriorated. One "caravan leader" was sent out from Aswan with an armed force to punish the tribal chiefs of Lower Nubia. At about the same time there is evidence that Nubians encroached on Egyptian territory, presumably through the desert via Kharga Oasis and then into the Nile Valley. A rock inscription at Khor Dehmit, some 36 km south of the First Cataract, records a punitive expedition against local Nubians dispatched by one of the last kings of the 8th Dynasty. In apparent frustration, the kings of the late Old Kingdom or their officials appear to have resorted to magic to destroy their enemies (especially southern ones). Enemies' names or the names of ethnic/tribal groups were inked on crude clay figurines, which were put in clay jars and ritually buried.

Royal decrees of the late Old Kingdom excavated beneath the ruins of a Roman period mudbrick structure at Quft (ancient Coptos) demonstrate that the Memphite kings of the 8th Dynasty still retained some degree of authority over Upper Egypt, even though this control may have depended to some extent on a dynastic alliance with a prominent Upper Egyptian family from Coptos. Shemai of Coptos married a daughter of one of the kings of the 8th Dynasty and was appointed vizier and overseer of Upper Egypt. At his death, his son Idi became vizier and governor of the 22 nomes of Upper Egypt. The connection between the king at Memphis and Coptos appears to have survived the change of dynasty; Idi himself may have gone on to serve as vizier for the first of a new line of kings from Heracleopolis (9th–10th Dynasties) in the Fayum. At the beginning of the 9th Dynasty a "king's eldest son" named User was the nomarch of the province where Coptos was located, and was buried at Khozam on its southern border.

Little evidence survives regarding the transition between the late Memphite and Heracleopolitan periods. We have only the historian Manetho's statement that the first King Khety was "terrible beyond all before him." Balancing this negative assessment is the fact that the early Heracleopolitan sovereigns were seemingly content to continue the system of provincial administration inherited from their Memphite predecessors. After an initial period of consolidation, however, their successors appear to have made a concerted effort to assert the authority of the crown over the southernmost nomes of Egypt. In a number of places, certainly at Dendera and Naga ed-Deir, the title of nomarch was abolished and the nomes were administered through the local overseers of priests, who were brought under the direct control of an "overseer of Upper Egypt." The resentment caused by such administrative reforms, and the consequent disenfranchisement of the nomarchic families, may help to explain why southern Upper Egypt ultimately rallied to the polity centered at Thebes.

When trouble came, it began in the far south. Here, the narrowness of the cultivated land and a series of disastrously low Nile floods had led to a famine so severe that some resorted to cannibalism, if a local ruler, Ankhtify of Mo'alla, is to be believed. In this desperate time, when refugees fled north and south searching for food, a simple border dispute may have led to open hostilities between Ankhtify and his counterpart in the Theban nome to the north.

Ankhtify was nomarch of Nome III of Upper Egypt, but had previously added Nome II of Upper Egypt to his domain, possibly by force. He also laid claim to the office of "commander of the army of Upper Egypt" from Elephantine to Armant. Armant, however, lay in the Theban nome and when the Thebans, in alliance with the Coptites, besieged the fortress, hostilities began in earnest. Grain became a tool of diplomacy and Ankhtify appears to have used it to purchase the neutrality of the nomes of Dendera and Thinis, and succeeded in isolating Thebes and Coptos politically. Since both sides of the struggle paid lip service to the king in far away Memphis, it is difficult to know what role the latter played in these local squabbles. Ankhtify appears to have prevailed, but soon after his death, the Theban nomarch Intef "the Great" triumphed, bringing the six southernmost nomes under his control as "Great Overlord of Upper Egypt." In the next generation the Theban nomarch Mentuhotep I repudiated the overlordship of Heracleopolis and founded the 11th Dynasty.

From the end of the Old Kingdom, Asiatic pastoralists had been infiltrating the Delta. By the early 10th Dynasty, when the Heracleopolitan rulers were engaged in a struggle with the Thebans for control of Upper Egypt, the Asiatics had occupied much of the Delta and the east bank of the Nile as far south as Beni Hasan in Middle Egypt. Armed bands of Asiatics plunged the entire Delta into chaos, and the Heracleopolitans apparently retained firm control only in the area of Memphis, the Fayum and parts of Middle Egypt. This much is known from the important political testament written by a later Heracleopolitan sovereign for his son and successor, Merikare. While the Heracleopolitans were absorbed with the Asiatic menace, the Theban king (11th Dynasty), Wahankh Intef, seized Nome VIII of Upper Egypt along with the important towns of Abydos, the seat of the Upper Egyptian administration since the Old Kingdom, and Thinis, the provincial capital. In the aftermath of the conquest of Abydos, an uneasy peace prevailed between the two kingdoms. There was at least one attempt by the Heracleopolitans to regain Abydos, but the Thebans successfully fought off the attack.

Meanwhile in the north, a vigorous Heracleopolitan monarch named Khety, like the founder of his line, drove the Asiatics out of Middle Egypt and the Delta, secured Egypt's boundaries and provided the northern kingdom with a new lease on life. In the fourteenth year of the reign of Wahankh Intef's grandson, Mentuhotep II, presumably at the instigation of this King Khety, Thinis rebelled and, supported by a Heracleopolitan army under the command of the nomarch Tefibi of Asyut, threw off the Theban yoke. It was perhaps at this point that the Heracleopolitan and Theban kingdoms adopted the policy of peaceful coexistence, which King Khety urged upon his son in the famous literary work, the *Instruction for Merikare*. Mentuhotep II turned his attention to the oases and Nubia, and the Heracleopolitans were once again able to obtain red granite from the quarries at Aswan.

Both kingdoms, however, were marshaling their resources for the final struggle. The individual stages in that struggle are impossible to document. However, since Mentuhotep II changed his Horus name to *Sm3-t3wy* ("Uniter of the Two Lands") sometime around his thirty-ninth regnal year, it was probably at about that time that the Theban king subdued his Heracleopolitan adversaries and founded the Middle Kingdom.

Although earlier notions of social upheaval and anarchy aimed at overthrowing the established order of society are probably to be rejected, there is evidence to suggest a leveling of social distinctions and a certain redistribution of wealth in the course of the First Intermediate Period. As provincial courts on the royal pattern coalesced around the nomarchs, an increasing number of individuals joined the official class. High-ranking titles, such as "hereditary prince" and "count," which were originally granted only to the most important officers of the royal administration, gradually became cheapened and were claimed by virtually anyone of the least importance. Quite ordinary people now made funerary monuments, usually in the form of simple rectangular tombstones or stelae. Hundreds of these stelae, carved with a funerary prayer, a portrait of the owner and, not uncommonly, a short autobiographical statement, survive. Ordinary people in the Old Kingdom left few monuments, but the hundreds of stelae from the First Intermediate Period attest to the changed circumstances.

The autobiographies on the stelae reveal that the men of the "new middle class" were independent and self-reliant. They were also acquisitive, inclined to the procurement of land, herds and riches of every kind. Frequently, they claimed to be self-made men. At the same time they were civic-minded, and helped to organize the food supplies of their towns, maintained or extended local irrigation systems, set up ferry services and benefitted their fellow citizens in a variety of other ways. They occasionally extended their largesse to other towns and even to neighboring nomes. The texts of the period also attest to a movement of the population from district to district, perhaps in search of a safe haven from the intermittent warfare that later plagued much of Egypt or relief from the recurrent famines. Certain areas may have been depopulated as a result of a series of low Nile floods, and this internal migration was encouraged by the local princes who found themselves in the position of repopulating abandoned settlements. In some cases the newcomers were enticed by the promise of enhanced social status. At the end of the Heracleopolitan period, however, a reaction set in. Epithets at Asyut, Thebes and elsewhere, such as "a spirit of ancient days" or "a prince of the beginning of time," seemingly reflect an effort on the part of the nomarchs and other high officials to assert themselves and lay claim to hereditary prerogatives.

In recent years, the earlier notion of a "Heracleopolitan intellectual movement" has been questioned. Several literary compositions (including the *Eloquent Peasant*) formerly ascribed to the this period have been assigned to the early 12th Dynasty. Attempts have even been made to reassign the great classic of Heracleopolitan literature, the *Instruction for Merikare*, to the later period. According to Gerhart Fecht, the *Instruction* was composed in the metric system of the Old Kingdom, however, and there are affinities between the idiom of the composition and that of Heracleopolitan period and early 11th Dynasty autobiographical texts. The lengthy autobiographical inscriptions in tombs dating to the Heracleopolitan period, especially those of Idi at Kom el-Kuffar, Ankhtify at Mo'alla, and Tefibi and Khety II at Asyut, and the shorter texts on contemporaneous private stelae, exhibit considerable inventiveness and originality, and attest to the literary creativity of the times. In the realm of art and architecture, the Heracleopolitan dynasties played an important role in preserving the traditions of the Old Kingdom and passing them on intact, albeit reinterpreted, to the Middle Kingdom.

See also

Aswan; Asyut; Beni Hasan; Deir el-Bahri, Mentuhotep II complex; Elephantine; funerary texts; Manetho; Middle Kingdom, overview; Naga ed-Deir; Old Kingdom, overview; Punt; Quft/Qift (Coptos); textual sources, Middle Kingdom; Thebes, el-Tarif, *saff*-tombs; trade, foreign

Further reading

Baer, K. 1960. *Rank and Title in the Old Kingdom*. Chicago.
Bell, B. 1971. The Dark Ages in ancient history. *AJA* 75: 1–26.
Fecht, G. 1972. *Der Vorwurf angott in den mahnworten des ipu-wer*. Heidelberg.
Fischer, H.G. 1964. *Inscriptions from the Coptite Nome Dynasties VI-XI* (Analecta Orientalia 40). Rome.
——. 1968. *Dendera in the Third Millennium B.C. down to the Theban Domination of Upper Egypt*. Locust Valley, NY.
Goedicke, H. 1967. *Königliche Dokumente des Alten Reich*. Wiesbaden.
Lichtheim, M. 1973. *Ancient Egyptian Literature* 1: *The Old and Middle Kingdoms*. Berkeley, CA.
——. 1988. *Ancient Egyptian Autobiographies Chiefly of the Middle Kingdom*. Freiburg and Göttingen.
Redford, D.B. 1986. Egypt and Western Asia in the Old Kingdom. *JARCE* 23: 125–43.
Schenkel, W. 1975. Repères chronologiques de l'histoire rédactionnelle des Coffin Texts. *Actes du XXIXe Congrès international des Orientalistes, Égyptologie* 2: 98–103. Paris.

EDWARD BROVARSKI

Middle Kingdom, overview

With his victory over the forces of the northern kingdom of Heracleopolis and the resulting end of the civil war around 2040 BC, the Theban Nebhepetre Mentuhotep II, the fifth king of the 11th Dynasty, became sole ruler of Egypt, taking on the name "Uniter-of-the-Two-Lands." Although he had to wage a few military campaigns against remaining dissidents, he is best remembered for peacetime activities, notably his reorganization of the country and the building of his funerary complex at Deir el-Bahri.

Mentuhotep II's funerary temple at Deir el-Bahri shows various stages of decoration, both pre- and post-reunification. The war is commemorated on the monument, in the numerous scenes of soldiers in the throes of battle. The peacetime reliefs show, for example, the king participating in ritual hunting, the royal family and their attendants at the court and the ubiquitous rows of offering bearers. The design of the funerary temple was original and revolutionary, revealing a vigorous palace, eager for a fresh start.

The funerary temple, along with a great number of other buildings erected in Upper Egypt at the time, demonstrates how the crown held a firmer control over the country's resources. Such building activities presume a confident administration. It was able to support large contingents of craftsmen and workers who were sent to the desert areas in search of the necessary building materials. It also possessed a diligent bureaucracy able to see to the logistical requirements of such expeditions. Mentuhotep II needed able officials to re-establish the central administration. He wisely chose not only from his fellow Thebans, although these naturally formed the bulk of his cabinet, but also from the elite of the now defeated northern realm.

Another change at this time are the inscriptions left in the quarries. Whereas Old Kingdom texts from the mines and quarries—simple excerpts of the royal documents that commissioned the missions—only showed the leaders' names and titles, along with the name of the king who had sent them, the Middle Kingdom officials included autobiographical statements detailing the success of their missions. Long strings of self-praising epithets now occupied major portions of their texts. These epithets had long been known from the autobiographical statements carved on the walls of the Old Kingdom funerary chapels, but their increased use at this time underscores the self-reliance acquired during the troubled times of the civil war.

The two kings who succeeded Mentuhotep II, Sankhare Mentuhotep III and Newtawyre Mentuhotep IV, achieved some success, erecting buildings and sending out large quarrying and mining expeditions, but their reigns brought the history of the 11th Dynasty to an end. Suddenly a new family—the 12th Dynasty—established itself on the throne of Egypt, led by a king who called himself the "Horus Repeating-Births" (i.e. "Renaissance"), the King of Upper and Lower Egypt, He-who-propitiates-the-heart-of-Re, the son of Re, Amenemhat. Who these upstarts were and where they came from cannot be known, although a literary composition states they were from southern Egypt. It is, however, tempting to equate this Amenemhat with the similarly named vizier under King Mentuhotep IV. The obvious surmise is that he skillfully took over the reigns of office after the demise of Mentuhotep IV.

At the beginning of his reign, Amenemhat I was mostly content to follow the lead of his 11th Dynasty predecessors. The capital city remained at Thebes, and the king presumably established his own court there. Construction began on a temple at Karnak to celebrate the growing importance of the god Amen. Amenemhat I's funerary temple was also begun on the west bank of Thebes, in a valley just south of Mentuhotep II's own temple at Deir el-Bahri. Although the complex was never finished, it is clear that Amenemhat I had chosen Thebes as his first burial ground, betraying his own southern origin.

One responsibility the new ruler had to oversee immediately was his relationship with the provincial overlords (known as "nomarchs"). During the civil war, the nomarchs had grown ever more independent from the royal house, and had also encroached upon one another's territories. If the central government was to have any success dealing with these recalcitrant rulers, the king had to forcefully establish his authority over them at the outset of his rule. He accomplished this by personally touring the country and re-establishing the provinces' boundaries, ensuring order by using the old records to settle any disputes. The king also reserved the right to confirm a nomarch's son in place of his father, thus ensuring a properly approved succession of nomarchs devoted to the crown. Furthermore, Amenemhat I installed one of his own representatives in the provinces to ensure the proper accounting of all revenues owed to the crown.

At the same time, Amenemhat I could not simply ignore the nomarchs' claims to a certain independence. Therefore, the latter were allowed to date texts according to their own tenure instead of the king's, have their own courts, collect their own revenues, maintain a small militia, and erect buildings in their domains. This careful compromise between control and latitude over the provincial rulers served the 12th Dynasty in good stead for well over a century.

Some time before his twentieth year on the throne, Amenemhat I suffered an unsuccessful assassination attempt. This may have prompted him to introduce one of his most striking innovations, the institution of coregency. In his twentieth regnal year, Amenemhat I installed his son Senusret (I) on the throne alongside him as an equal Horus-king. In practice, the younger partner assumed the more strenuous activities of kingship, while the older ruler remained in the palace, overseeing the affairs of state. This system worked surprisingly well for the 12th Dynasty, as son succeeded father for nearly 200 years.

The assassination attempt may also have prompted another major decision by Amenemhat I. Toward the end of his reign, the royal residence moved from Thebes to a newly founded city named Amenemhat-It-tawy ("Amenemhat-takes-possession-of-the-Two-Lands"). Although its exact location is unknown, the new residence was probably situated just south of Memphis, possibly at modern-day el-Lisht near the pyramids of Amenemhat I and Senusret I. Perhaps Amenemhat I wished to disassociate himself from the memory of the previous dynasty. The move to the Memphite area also associated the 12th Dynasty with the great ruling families of old, a connection that helped establish them as the legitimate monarchs. According to literary tradition, Amenemhat I died in the thirtieth year of his reign. His demise appears to have been sudden, taking his coregent Senusret I by surprise and possibly hinting at foul play, but the sources do not actually indicate this. If Amenemhat I had indeed been the vizier under King Mentuhotep IV, he must have been of a fairly advanced age after thirty years on the throne. By the time of his accession as sole ruler, Senusret I had already served ten years as coregent and was thus ready to take on the affairs of state. He further consolidated his family's hold on the throne through the skillful use of literature as political propaganda. The so-called *Prophecy of Neferty* recounted how the 12th Dynasty had been foretold by a sage from the great days of King Seneferu (4th

Dynasty). The *Story of Sinuhe* shrewdly wove into the wonderful adventures of its hero Sinuhe long hymns of praise to Senusret I. The humorous *Satire on the Trades*, in which various occupations are unfavourably compared to the comfortable and authoritative life of a scribe, was used to furnish a burgeoning bureaucracy with new recruits.

The central administration itself retained much of the same structure it had acquired since the Old Kingdom. The senior administrator was still the vizier; he had his main office at the capital city, of which he was also mayor, and he was involved with a great many administrative and judicial matters. The major ministries were the Treasury, called the "White House," which was the repository of various goods and commodities; the Granary, which was responsible for supervising the harvesting, recording and subsequent storing of the crops; and the Office of Labor, under the Overseer of all Royal Works, which administered and provided the labor force. Other large departments, such as the Offices of the Fields and of Cattle (whose responsibilities were self-evident), are known for this period. Also attested are the armed forces, which included the army, the navy and a police department.

Senusret I undertook a building program that produced a great number of monuments from Elephantine to the Delta. Included among the projects were a vast court and a kiosk at the temple of Amen at Karnak, perhaps initiated during the coregency period when the 12th Dynasty still resided in Thebes. His reign was also a great period of non-royal activity at the pilgrimage site of Abydos, when vast numbers of cenotaphs were built and furnished with commemorative stelae. The growth in the demand for such stelae at this time demonstrates the stability and security that allowed people to travel the length and breadth of the country to place their stelae at Abydos. The texts on these stelae consist mostly of self-glorifying epithets, demonstrating again the individualism of a self-assertive society. These epithets may, in fact, be the blueprint of the "perfect society," where all members, from the high officials to the lesser bureaucrats, fall in line and simply catalog the road to their own success.

Although the 12th Dynasty is not generally known for militaristic policies, Senusret I managed to strengthen his frontiers with well-aimed military campaigns. His relations with regions to the northeast seem to have been mostly defensive, and at least one campaign is attested against Egypt's Libyan neighbors. In Nubia, Senusret I conducted military campaigns and subsequently built a series of forts between the First and the Second Cataracts, which laid full claim to the area south of Egypt and prepared the way for the eventual full conquest of Lower Nubia later in the 12th Dynasty.

A certain amount of military activity is also demonstrated in the reign of the next king, Amenemhat II, part of whose court annals were recorded on a large stela discovered at Memphis. This document mentions armies sent out "to hack up" parts of Syria, Lebanon and possibly even Cyprus. Although such statements are often interpreted as propaganda, the armies are then described as returning laden with prisoners of war and much booty. In addition, foreigners from southwest Asia and different areas of Nubia are mentioned as coming into Egypt, presenting products from their own countries to the court. Although the Egyptian annals present these offerings as tribute from subject countries, what may have been recorded was the common practice of gift giving between rulers, part of an established ancient Near Eastern tradition wherein rulers acknowledged one another's suzerainty.

The reign of the following king, Senusret II, is best remembered for his pyramid at Lahun, near the entrance of the Fayum oasis. East of the structure was the pyramid town of Lahun, a new settlement built to house the priests and administrators of the royal mortuary cult. The town shows all the earmarks of a planned settlement, with its grid system of well-laid-out streets and town houses, and its hierarchical arrangement of wealthier and poorer sections. The "wealthy neighborhood" was placed on higher ground, to afford it a better view and, presumably, better air. This heavy governmental hand can also be seen in the 12th Dynasty's conscious remodeling of older town sites.

Senusret III, the next king, must be remembered as one of the greatest rulers in Egyptian history. His reign witnessed a major administrative changeover to a highly centralized government and a final conquest of Nubia. Egypt had always coveted the products of Africa to the south and therefore felt a strong need to protect, indeed to control, the trade routes coming from the upper Nile. The conquest itself was accomplished through military campaigns in the King's eighth, tenth, twelfth, sixteenth and nineteenth regnal years. Senusret III was clearly determined to subjugate the area once and for all. The result was the establishment of Nubia as an Egyptian possession, and the territory was actively occupied by an Egyptian population stationed there. Egypt completely controlled the desert region on both sides of the Nile, as well as all river traffic.

Like his earlier 12th Dynasty predecessors, Senusret III now established a second series of forts along the Second Cataract. As with the town of Lahun, these forts reflect the all-pervasive presence of the central administration. The forts themselves were elaborate constructions, with wide mudbrick walls, towers, bastions and other architectural elements to permit an easy defense of the buildings. The interiors of the fortresses were carefully laid out, with a symmetrical grid of streets flanked by housing of different sizes for the various strata of society garrisoned there. Included were cultic places, workshops areas and the ubiquitous granaries, which in some cases reached surprisingly large proportions.

Although the actual title of the commanders of the forts has not yet been identified, the forts seem to have been governed by both military and civil administrators. In fact, the variety of Egyptian officials in the Nubian colonies is noteworthy. Staff from nearly all facets of the central administration are attested in texts found either in the forts themselves or on graffiti engraved in the area. Included are a wide range of palace officials, agents of nearly all the major ministries: the Treasury, the Granary, the Offices of Provisioning, of the Fields, of Cattle and of Labor, and the Ministry of Justice. A great number of military titles are represented as well. All these officials were sent to oversee and protect the newly acquired crown possessions.

The other major event of Senusret III's reign is the almost complete disappearance of the great nomarchical families. The surviving evidence, however, is concerned only with the great families of Middle Egypt; very little is known about the rest of the country at this time. Some of those Middle Egypt overlords even left unfinished tombs behind in their provinces, preferring to be buried near the king at the royal burial grounds. How this change was accomplished is not known, but the most likely explanation is that the King simply refused to confirm the sons of nomarchs in their fathers' positions, and then integrated them into the higher echelons of administration. What has often been interpreted as a fall of the nomarchs may simply have been part of a major administrative change, whereby a loosely knit organization was transformed into a tightly centralized government, focused around the capital city.

The major ministries mentioned above seem to have been little affected by this change, although additional powers may have accrued to them under the new centralization. One new creation was the Office of the Provider of People, which was responsible for registering and assigning the manpower necessary for the various projects at hand. The other major change was the division of the country into three main sectors: the "District of the North," which held sway over the area north of the capital; the "District of the South," which administered Middle Egypt; and the "District of the Head of the South," which was responsible for the nine southernmost nomes. The whole was governed from two major centers: the royal residence in the Memphite area in the north, and Thebes in the south. Each district was administered by a herald, who was in turn assisted by a second herald, under whom were Councils of Functionaries and a large scribal staff. Other officials involved were the *kenbet*-councillors, who were sent to the provinces on government business. At the lowest level, the towns were under the authority of local mayors.

The new centralization seems to have affected more than the political level. The wealth of the country was now concentrated around the royal residence, as well as a few large cities such as Abydos, Thebes and Elephantine. Resources previously circulating in the provinces were now presumably diverted toward the central treasury and subsequently redistributed to the now expanded civil service. Culturally, this is demonstrated by the disappearance of the large provincial cemeteries, which had become too expensive to maintain, and the increase of so-called "middle class burials." The earlier Middle Kingdom burial equipment, with its elaborate wooden models and extensive use of the so-called *Coffin Texts*, was now replaced by amulets and magical tools, which had already been used in everyday life. Also during the late Middle Kingdom a vastly increasing number of commemorative stelae were left at Abydos by middle-rank administrators. That these minor officials could now afford to have such stelae made is another testament to the broadening of powers placed in the hands of a burgeoning bureaucracy.

It was then left to the next ruler, Amenemhat III, to reap the rewards of Senusret III's vigorous policies. His father had left Amenemhat III with what amounted to an Egyptian dependency on his southern border as well as the strongest centralized government since the days of the high Old Kingdom. Amenemhat III was thus able to embark on a full-scale exploitation of mines and quarries. Great numbers of texts are known from the turquoise and copper mines of the Sinai; from the alabaster, limestone and schist quarries of Hatnub, Tura and the Wadi Hammamat, respectively; the granite and diorite quarries of Aswan and Nubia; and the amethyst mines of the Wadi el-Hudi. These activities significantly increased the crown's revenues, which the King could distribute at will to loyal officers. This new wealth created the kind of dependency a highly centralized government needed to sustain itself.

Amenemhat III also embarked on a building program that saw him erecting, or adding to, structures in most major sites in Egypt. His greatest architectural works, however, were in the Fayum. Although the Fayum is well represented in Old Kingdom sources, it is the 12th Dynasty and Amenemhat III in particular who are forever associated with this oasis southwest of the residence city. In the Middle Kingdom, declining flood levels occasioned a lowering of the level of Lake Moeris in the Fayum, exposing a substantial area of land for cultivation and construction. This may have provided the impetus for renewed activity in the Fayum area, and the 12th Dynasty lost no time in exploiting this newly available land.

Both Amenemhat I and Senusret I added to an existing temple of Sobek of Shedyet. Senusret II built his pyramid there, and a literary tradition places a royal residence or rest-house in the Fayum area. Yet it is Amenemhat III—in the guise of King Lamarres, a reworking of his prenomen Ni-ma'at-Re, or King Moeris—who was remembered in later legends as a great builder and the excavator of the lake that took his name. Amenemhat III left a great number of structures in the Fayum: additions to the temple of Sobek of Shedyet; the shrine dedicated to the goddess Renenutet; the colossi at Biahmu, well-known to the classical authors; and his second pyramid at Hawara (his first pyramid at Dahshur had suffered a structural accident, which forced him to abandon it). To the south of the Hawara pyramid was its funerary temple, called a "labyrinth" by the classical authors.

After a long reign, Amenemhat III was succeeded by his son Amenemhat IV, who reigned only briefly and is chiefly remembered for continuing his father's policies. Next came Queen Sobekneferu, daughter of Amenemhat III and wife of Amenemhat IV, who reigned a short three years. With her ended the great dynasty of the Amenemhats and the Senusrets. The Middle Kingdom continued with the 13th Dynasty. In spite of the great number of kings in this dynasty, a few powerful rulers did maintain a strong presence on the throne. Royal building activities continued on a large scale, and the Egyptian throne was still respected in Nubia and Syria. As long as the capital city remained at It-tawy, the new centralized government continued to operate in full force, indicating no breakdown in central authority for some time. Although the period of the 13th Dynasty is obscure because of the paucity of historical records, the impression left is that of a secure nation going about its business as usual, unaware of the troubles ahead.

See also

Abydos, Middle Kingdom cemetery; administrative bureaucracy; Asyut; Beni Hasan; Dahshur, Middle Kingdom pyramids; Deir el-Bahri, Mentuhotep II complex; First Intermediate Period, overview; Gebel Zeit; Hatnub; Hawara; Heracleopolis; Lahun, pyramid complex of Senusret II; Lahun, town; el-Lisht; Mazghuna; natural resources; Nubian forts; Saqqara, pyramids of the 13th Dynasty; Second Intermediate Period, overview; Serabit el-Khadim; textual sources, Middle Kingdom; Thebes, el-Tarif, *saff*-tombs; Tura, Dynastic burials and quarries; Wadi el-Hudi; Wadi Maghara

Further reading

Arnold, D. 1991. Amenemhat I and the early Twelfth Dynasty at Thebes. *MMJ* 26: 5–48.
Bourriau, J. 1991. Patterns of change in burial customs during the Middle Kingdom. In *Middle Kingdom Studies*, S. Quirke, ed., 3–20. New Malden.
Franke, D. 1991. The career of Khnumhotep III of Beni Hasan and the so-called "decline of the nomarchs." In *Middle Kingdom Studies*, S. Quirke, ed., 51–67. New Malden.
Goedicke, H. 1991. Egyptian military actions in "Asia" in the Middle Kingdom. *RdÉ* 42: 89–94.

Leprohon, R.J. 1993. Administrative titles in Nubia in the Middle Kingdom. *JAOS* 113(3): 423–36.

Lichtheim, M. 1988. *Ancient Egyptian Autobiographies Chiefly of the Middle Kingdom. A Study and an Anthology* (Orbis Biblicus et Orientalis 84). Freiburg.

Parkinson, R.B. 1991. *Voices from Ancient Egypt: An Anthology of Middle Kingdom Writings.* Norman, OK.

Quirke, S. 1990. *The Administration of Egypt in the Late Middle Kingdom: The Hieratic Documents.* New Malden.

——. 1991. Royal power in the 13th Dynasty. In *Middle Kingdom Studies*, S. Quirke, ed., 123–39. New Malden.

Weinstein, J.W. 1975. Egyptian relations with Palestine in the Middle Kingdom. *BASOR* 217: 1–16.

RONALD J. LEPROHON

Second Intermediate Period, overview

The "Second Intermediate Period" is the term conventionally used for the period of divided rule in Egypt after the Middle Kingdom. It begins after the end of the 12th Dynasty and ends with the expulsion of the Hyksos from Egypt and the inception of the New Kingdom (18th Dynasty).

Dynastic stability ended with the beginning of the 13th Dynasty. According to Manetho, 60 kings reigned for 153 years, with an average of one king every three years, a definite sign of political instability. There were few or no established criteria for dynastic succession. This seems to have been a period with usurpers on one side, and king-makers and a strong administration on the other. Some of the kings were most probably of Asiatic origin, such as Chendjer, "the Boar." It can be assumed that most of the kings previously held high positions in the court or army. For example, one king was named Mermesha, "the General." Some stability can be observed, however, in the middle of the 13th Dynasty with the reigns of Sobekhotep III, Neferhotep I, Sihathor I and Sobekhotep IV, and for a short time there was some form of dynastic succession.

From the beginning of the 13th Dynasty, mining expeditions to the Sinai and inscriptions in the region of the Second Cataract ended abruptly. The royal mortuary cults of the 12th Dynasty also ended soon afterwards. The 13th Dynasty was very active abroad, however, especially in southwest Asia. A scepter of King Hotepibre was found in a royal tomb at the site of Tell Mardikh (ancient Ebla), in northern Syria. Good relations were fostered with Byblos, whose rulers had probably already accepted the Egyptian title of "governor"(*ḥ3ty-'*) during the 12th Dynasty, as did another Asiatic ruler of Kumidi (in the Beqaa valley in Lebanon). Many Levantine peoples were employed in the Egyptian army or as servants in upper-class households. Some of these foreigners made careers in their positions, especially in the royal household, and consequently rose to positions of power, which explains the foreign names of some kings of this dynasty.

With a lack of dynastic stability, political fragmentation had occurred in Egypt by *circa* 1700 BC and local kingdoms arose in the northeastern Delta. Of special importance was the kingdom ruled by King 'Aasehre Nehesy, with its capital at Avaris (Tell ed-Dab'a). With the 13th Dynasty no longer in control of the whole country, its rulers withdrew to Upper Egypt. Nehesy ruled primarily over peoples of Syro-Palestinian origin, who had settled in large numbers in the northeastern Delta, in special settlements granted by the kings of the late 12th Dynasty. They were probably employed as soldiers, sailors, shipbuilders and workmen. These foreigners introduced the cult of the northern Syrian storm god Ba'al Zephon/Haddad in the region of Avaris, the most important settlement. Nehesy's dynasty in Avaris was probably soon replaced by a local dynasty of Syro-Palestinians, who spoke a West Semitic dialect. Thus, the nucleus of the later Hyksos kingdom was formed. The unstable political situation in the country invited these non-Egyptian rulers to expand their control to Middle Egypt and soon afterwards to Upper Egypt. Facilitating this expansion were an army, ships and foreign connections. An inscription on a stela describes marauding hordes of such soldiers destabilizing the region of Thebes, where one of the last kings of the 13th Dynasty, Neferhotep III, had withdrawn.

By this time the Egyptian garrisons in Lower Nubia were partly abandoned, but some Egyptians remained there and went into the service of the Upper Nubian kingdom of Kush

(Kerma culture), which occupied Lower Nubia *circa* 1650 BC. Egypt was now under the (loose) control of the so-called Hyksos, i.e. "Rulers of the Foreign Countries," an Egyptian term originally used for foreign chiefs and bedouin leaders. This title was officially adopted by the kings of the 15th Dynasty, who emerged from the dynasty in Avaris and probably governed from there. They were crowned in the old capital of Memphis (at least, this is reported by Flavius Josephus about the first king, Salitis). Kings of the contemporaneous 16th Dynasty probably ruled as a sub-dynasty in southern Palestine at Sharuhen (Tell el-'Ajjul). From there the majority of exports, such as olive oil and wine, were shipped to Egypt.

The Hyksos were well connected in the eastern Mediterranean through trade and diplomacy. Besides southern and coastal Palestine and Cyprus, they also had links to the Minoan thalassocracy on Crete, as evidenced by an alabaster lid inscribed with the name of the powerful Hyksos Khayan, found in the palace of Knossos. Hyksos rule was centralized in a "homeland" in the northeastern Delta, from where new settlements of the Syro-Palestinian Middle Bronze Age culture spread. These kings and their followers had mainly West Semitic names. They firmly controlled northern Egypt, where devoted vassals were installed. It does not seem coincidental that the 17th Dynasty in Thebes began at about the same time as the Hyksos dynasty, and perhaps the first king of the Theban dynasty, Nubkheperre Intef VI, had been installed by the Hyksos. The choice of the royal name "Intef" shows that this new dynasty attempted to re-establish a tradition that was rooted in the past glory of the 11th Dynasty, when Thebes became the capital of Egypt and its god Amen was the dominant deity. Once again, at the end of the Second Intermediate Period, Amen became the symbol of Egypt's liberation from the foreigners.

King Seqenenre Ta'o of the 17th Dynasty was probably the first to attempt an uprising against his overlord, 'Aawoserre Apophis, in Avaris. Some diplomatic problems are mentioned in a popular tale found in the Papyrus Sallier I, from the New Kingdom. More conclusive evidence for events is provided by the mummy of King Seqenenre, with deadly injuries on the skull caused specifically by a Syro-Palestinian battleax. After a crown prince named Ahmose (Louvre statue no. E 15682) died prematurely, Seqenenre was succeeded by Kamose, either a son or a half-brother. In his third regnal year, Kamose successfully led a military campaign north to the region of Avaris and set up two victory stelae in the Temple of Amen at Karnak. He was unable to seize Avaris, however, and died soon afterwards. It is therefore tempting to assume that this king died from the injuries he received in a battle near Avaris.

Kamose's successor was a son of Seqenenre also called Ahmose. He was only a child when he came to the throne. In such a situation the king's mother, Ahhotep, was an important figure for the stability of the dynasty and it was many years before Avaris could be attacked again. This probably happened between the fifteenth and eighteenth years of Ahmose's reign. In order to create stability in the dynastic succession, he married his sister Ahmose Nefertary, which had become customary in the late 17th Dynasty. A new official position for the queen, "the God's Wife of Amen," was introduced. According to Egyptian religious fiction, the queen conceived the heir apparent with the god Amen, who took the role of her husband. Thus, the divine origin of the dynasty was created and the institution of sister-marriage guaranteed the exclusivity of the royal family.

Ahmose succeeded in cutting off Avaris from Sile, as described on the reverse of the

Rhind Papyrus (British Museum EA 10.058), and took Avaris. There he built his residence within the Hyksos citadel after the model of Deir el-Ballas. Close connections with the Minoan thalassocracy, most probably with the court of Knossos, are demonstrated by the abundant Minoan-style wall paintings from two or three of the major buildings in the royal residence at Avaris. Avaris served as Ahmose's headquarters during the subsequent campaigns in southern Palestine. He attacked the second major stronghold of the Hyksos at Sharuhen (Tell el-'Ajjul) near Gaza, which he took after a siege of three years. He devoted the following years to destroying the strongholds of the Hyksos and restoring the former Egyptian possessions in Nubia by attacking the kingdom of Kush (Kerma). It seems that Ahmose was not motivated to conquer major areas in southwest Asia or Nubia, but he was determined to rebuild Egypt to its former glory. He resumed the traditional trading relationship with Byblos and took over the trade network of the Hyksos. Goods from Syria, Palestine, Cyprus and the Aegean poured into Egypt and the increasing economic stability of the country after its reunification laid the foundations for the prosperity of the New Kingdom, which was truly founded by Ahmose. It was only later that his successors, Amenhotep I and Tuthmose I, started to conquer territories in Nubia and southwest Asia which had never been held before by Egypt. This was done, however, following the trauma of foreign rule in Egypt and the fear of repetition of such an event. Other major powers in the ancient Near East, such as Mitanni, also arose at this time (Late Bronze Age) and Egypt began to play its part as an emerging superpower.

See also

Aegean peoples; Canaanites; Cypriot peoples; Hyksos; Kerma; Manetho; New Kingdom, overview; Tell ed-Dab'a, Second Intermediate Period; Tell el-Yahudiya

Further reading

Bietak, M. 1996. *Avaris, the Captial of the Hyksos: New Excavation Results.* London.

Hayes, W.C. 1973. Egypt: from the death of Ammenemes III to Seqenenre' II. In *The Cambridge Ancient History* II(1): 42–76. Cambridge.

James, T.G.H. 1973. Egypt: from the expulsion of the Hyksos to Amenophis I. In *The Cambridge Ancient History* II(1): 289–312. Cambridge.

Mazar, B. 1968. The Middle Bronze Age in Palestine. *IEJ* 18: 65–97.

Redford, D.B. 1992. *Egypt, Canaan and Israel in Ancient Times.* Princeton, NJ.

Van Seters, J. 1966. *The Hyksos: A New Investigation.* New Haven, CT.

MANFRED BIETAK

New Kingdom, overview

"New Kingdom" is the term generally given to the five centuries of Egyptian history from *circa* 1550 to 1050 BC. The New Kingdom covers the 17th–20th Dynasties, during which the bounds of Egypt's empire and international influence reached their greatest extent.

Historical summary

The New Kingdom was inaugurated (17th–18th Dynasties) by a family of Theban nobles, probably of Nubian descent, who led the war of liberation against the Asiatic Hyksos ruling in Middle and Lower Egypt. The reigns of Ahmose, Amenhotep I and Queen Hatshepsut represent a period of renewal and consolidation after the expulsion of the Hyksos; Lower Nubia was occupied and annexed and the frontier stood at Karoy, in the region of the fourth Nile cataract. In literature, art and architecture the classic period of the 12th Dynasty was used as a source of inspiration, sometimes to the point of item-by-item imitation.

Following a contretemps of political and ideological nature between Queen Hatshepsut and her nephew Tuthmose III, the latter acceded to full power on his aunt's death and changed the course of history. Casting his action as a pre-emptive strike against the "Hyksos," Tuthmose III launched over seventeen campaigns in two decades against the coastlands of the Levant, which resulted in a repulse of the great empire of Mitanni (in what is now eastern Syria and northern Iraq), and an Egyptian frontier on the Euphrates. Although Amenhotep II, Tuthmose III's son, lost the northern reach of this empire, Mitanni was eventually forced to sue for peace and sign a treaty with Tuthmose IV. Thereafter, a series of diplomatic marriages cemented the alliance between the two empires. The creation of the Egyptian empire resulted in an influx of thousands of Asiatic prisoners of war, merchants and settlers, and an ingress of Asiatic and Aegean products and ideas which transformed Egyptian art and technology.

The reign of Amenhotep III represents the flowering of Egyptian imperial culture. Fifty years of peace found Egypt the unrivalled superpower of the Near East, in receipt of vast amounts of taxes and tribute and the focus of world trade. Amenhotep III was the first king of the empire period who reflected Egypt's dominant position in the boom of gigantic architectural memorials and refined arts. As the "dazzling sun-disc," his chosen sobriquet, he personified to the world a rich and surfeited land.

Amenhotep IV, or Akhenaten as he called himself, son and successor of Amenhotep III, effected a revolution in religion and the arts by espousing the sun disk as sole god and declaring all other gods to have "ceased" (their existence). Along with the new monotheism went a new canon of art characterized by an iconoclastic purging of all traces of polytheism. The better to realize his program, Akhenaten rejected the old royal residences of Memphis and Thebes, and built a new city, Akhetaten ("Horizon-of-the-sun-disc"), in Middle Egypt where he could focus the entire economy of Egypt on the cult of his sole god. The monotheistic program, the personal creation of Akhenaten, could not be maintained by his ephemeral successors, and within fifteen years of his death a reaction set in. The temples to the sun disk were dismantled, the old cults reinstated and Akhenaten declared anathema.

Now discredited, the 18th Dynasty disappeared in the confusion attendant upon an outbreak of plague, and was succeeded by a succession of three unrelated military officers. The last of these, PaRamesses, or Ramesses I, installed his son Seti I as coregent and the 19th Dynasty thus came to power. Seti was bent on coming to grips with the Hittite empire in Anatolia, which had replaced Mitanni as the superpower of Asia and was threatening Egypt's frontier in central Syria. A series of indecisive engagements culminated in the disastrous ambush of Egyptian forces at Qadesh on the Orontes in the fifth year of Seti's successor, Ramesses II; thereafter most of Egypt's territory beyond the Sinai was temporarily lost. But Ramesses fought back doggedly and by his twenty-first year had forced the Hittites, now faced by a hostile Assyria, to sign a peace treaty. Versions of this celebrated pact are extant in the original Hittite, and also in Akkadian and Egyptian translations.

The conclusion of hostilities ushered in a period of peace which saw a burst of international trade and commercial activity all around the Mediterranean. Ramesses II used the highly regimented military and civilian population of Egypt to set on foot a rebuilding program of vast proportions in which virtually all the temples of Egypt were either reconstructed or repaired. Archaeological and textual sources abound for this Ramesside age, and yield intimate glimpses of society at large, its businesses, occupations, entertainments and beliefs. Ramesses II and a few of his sons—his offspring officially numbered over 100—lived on in later legend as the super-king Sesostris, the wise Khaemweset and the blind Pheron. A royal archetype had been established which inspired Egypt and invited imitation for over six centuries.

Following the death of the great Ramesses II, the various branches of his family fell to squabbling over the succession, just at a time when a weakened administration had to face the pressure of ethnic migrations from Libya, Ionia and the Greek islands, seeking to settle in Egypt. The general ineptitude of the last scions of the house prompted a *coup d'état* by one Sethnakht, whose origins are obscure. Thus was established the 20th Dynasty. Sethnakht's son Ramesses III was able to effect a restoration of the country's fortunes: in his fifth year he decisively defeated the Libyan tribe which had settled in Egypt, and in his eighth year a massive invasion of "Sea Peoples" from the Aegean was repulsed. Although the Asiatic principalities of the empire had been devastated by the incursions, Ramesses III by dint of effort extended his frontiers once again to central Syria.

Ramesses III and his eight like-named successors, however, faced numerous problems which in the aggregate spelled doom for the prosperity of the country. The onset of low inundations adversely affected agricultural productivity and granaries stood empty. The violence of the Sea People's invasion had laid waste large parts of Asia Minor and Syria, and many of Egypt's former trading partners no longer existed. Areas producing silver and iron (both absent in Egypt) were shut off from Egyptian traders, and copper and gold-producing regions were showing signs of exhaustion. Inflation hit the marketplace, and strikes by laborers were prevalent. Grave robbing became widespread and proved impossible for the authorities to stop. Gradually the state showed signs of a bifurcation between Middle Egypt and the Delta, where the royal family now resided permanently, and the Thebaid which came increasingly to be treated as the "House of Amen," under the high priests of this deity. When the last of the Ramessides, Ramesses XI, finally passed away and power shifted to the new city of Tanis, the culture, political structure and economy identified as the "New Kingdom" was effectively defunct.

Government

The role of monarch is correctly regarded as the king-pin of the entire structure of government during the New Kingdom. The 18th Dynasty kings harked back to the glorious 12th Dynasty kings, whose heirs they claimed to be. Prominent in the mythology of kingship was the motif of the divine birth of Pharaoh, sired by Amen-Re, King of the Gods. The king became "Son of Amen," the very likeness of the deity on earth, in possession of the kingship as an inheritance from his father. The 18th Dynasty had come to power in war, and the early Tuthmosids were imbued with a military spirit. While they relied on a "citizen" army, they created the institution of the "nursery" where selected children of the future king's own age were brought up with him. From these companions, whose mothers achieved a degree of prominence in the 18th Dynasty, came the future officers and trusted henchmen of Pharaoh. The winning of the empire robbed the Tuthmosids of any military aura and the latter "image" of an 18th Dynasty pharaoh was that of a surfeited voluptuary. By contrast, the 19th Dynasty came from a family of professional army officers and the military was everywhere and at all times in receipt of favors and lofty status.

The personnel of government and administration were dominated by members of a few patrician families who had achieved prominence in the reunification of the country during the late 17th/early 18th Dynasties. These were "the most elite and choicest of the whole land . . . [with] a respectable lineage reaching back over generations" (Amenhotep III). Crisis points in this social system occurred when members of this sort of "family compact" were replaced willy-nilly by parvenus, when a new crop arose on the coat tails of a new regime, or when a gifted individual outside the circle broke in to wrest a high office.

In contrast to the parochial nature of Second Intermediate Period government, the New Kingdom shows a high degree of civilization. Branches of government tended to bifurcate between Upper and Lower Egypt, and to have their "head officers" in Memphis and Thebes, the chief royal residences. Here were located the judicial/executive "councils" (*knbt*) and the office of the vizier. The vizierate, a prime ministerial office, inherited directly from the Second Intermediate Period, was directly responsible to the king for the departments of agriculture, local administration, the judiciary, the workhouses, the state granaries (originally with the chief herald), the palace administration and the royal estates. In addition the vizier presided over the prestigous "Council of Thirty," a quasi-high court. He was not responsible for the treasury, the army or the provincial administration, all the heads of which reported directly to Pharaoh. By the time of Tuthmose III the heads of major departments received the title "king's-scribe," the highest of the "mandarin-ranks" attainable. The middle-ranking civil servants were all scribes, called generically *srw*, "magistrates," drawn from the best of the scribal class and assigned posts and functions all over Egypt. In contrast, the "support staffs" (*smdt*) at the lower end of the bureaucracy were recruited locally and functioned close to home.

In the countryside, power gravitated to the capital from the townships or "nomes," now no longer administrative units. Towns were governed by "mayors" (non-hereditary) or by a scribe and council; in either case, complete control of the local bailiwicks was retained by the vizier. Towns continued to be centered upon the temples of the local municipal gods, but for the purposes of administration had become little more than collection centers for taxes and rents. They could, however, still levy harbor fees on shipping. Tuthmose III began the practice of making an annual progress throughout Egypt to inspect the state of the local governments, but not all his successors followed suit.

Society

Society in the New Kingdom mirrored the hierarchy of the administration. At the apex sat the pharaoh; he, his queen(s) and harims owned large estates throughout Egypt providing produce and riches for a royal privy purse. The chief steward of the king was a very powerful individual, responsible directly to the crown, and usually recruited outside the hereditary nobility. Where the king chose to reside (usually in the Memphite region), there lived also the chief men of government and anyone of any consequence: their roots may have been diverse, but service to the crown necessitated their residence at court. The importance of those who had shared in the wars and the phenomenon of the royal nursery had created a new aristocracy which eclipsed and replaced the old provincial nobility. Now prominent and respectable and endowed with hereditary rights were the scribe, the soldier and the priest. The rural population consisted largely of tenants and sharecroppers, renting land from some of the large landowning institutions, or field hands tied permanently to the soil under a farm manager.

With the creation of the empire came an influx of foreign peoples into Egypt. Prisoners of war constituted the largest single group. These were usually registered, branded and assigned to farms, workhouses or weaving shops. Others were recruited for work in quarries, or on construction sites or as domestics. In the late Ramesside period Canaanite butlers are found in the royal palace. Merchants and their ships frequented the harbors of Memphis and Thebes, and a quarter of the former city was set aside for their residence as a trading post. The commercial and demographic impact of Asia on Egypt resulted in the ingress of numerous foreign words into the Egyptian language.

Economics

Numerous papyri from the New Kingdom provide evidence on taxation and commerce. The yield of the grain harvest (emmer wheat and barley) was estimated yearly by measurement of the fields under cultivation and the nilometer's prediction of the height of the inundation. At harvest time, state and private vessels made the circuit of landing stages to collect a proportion of the yield as grain tax and rent. Other taxes included a quota placed on towns and offices to cover budgetary needs of institutions (usually temples), dues levied on support staffs, a tax imposed on (manufactured) products of labor, and "benevolences" expected from high officers of state. These taxes were imposed on Egypt and its empire alike, but that did not prevent a lively trade between Egypt and the Mediterranean littoral. From Asia, Egypt received oil, wine, cedarwood, boxwood, tin, metalwork, chariotry and weapons; from Cyprus, copper; from Anatolia, silver and (some) iron; and from the Aegean, unguents and spices. In return, Egypt shipped wheat and barley, luxury goods and tropical products from its African sphere of influence.

The climatic changes which brought on a series of diminished inundations in the twelfth century BC, and the foreign invasions of Sea Peoples and Libyans, largely curtailed this trade. The resultant privations and social and political dislocation were catastrophic for the empire. The Ramessides discredited themselves, and political power gravitated to a new regime in a newly created city, Tanis. Thebes and its god Amen lost their royal and imperial status, and Egyptian society lost its *elan vital*. In short, the New Kingdom was dead.

See also

administrative bureaucracy; Aegean peoples; army; Hyksos; kingship; Libyans; nome structure; religion, state; Sea Peoples; taxation and conscription; textual sources, New Kingdom; trade, foreign

Further reading

Brovarski, E., S.K. Doll and R.E. Freed. 1982. *Egypt's Golden Age: The Art of Living in the New Kingdom, 1558–1085 B.C.* Boston.

James, T.G.H. 1984. *Pharaoh's People: Scenes from Life in Imperial Egypt*. London.

Kemp, B.J. 1989. *Ancient Egypt: Anatomy of a Civilization*. London.

Kitchen, K.A. 1982. *Pharaoh Triumphant: The Life and Times of Ramesses II*. Warminster.

Redford, D.B. 1967. *History and Chronology of the Eighteenth Dynasty of Egypt: Seven Studies*. Toronto.

DONALD B. REDFORD

Third Intermediate Period, overview

The "Third Intermediate Period" is nothing more than a generally accepted term used to encompass the 21st–25th Dynasties, which is composed of three distinct cultural periods. Egypt of the 21st Dynasty was, in theory, a unified state whose ruling family was linked through marriage to that of the 20th Dynasty, and in many ways served as an adjunct to the late New Kingdom. From the thirteenth century BC on, large numbers of Libyan tribes had been slowly, but not always peacefully, infiltrating the western Delta, perhaps driven on by famine, drought or simply the desire for a better life. Whatever the origins of these refugees, they were able to adapt to and flourish within native Egyptian culture. So successful were they that by the middle of the tenth century BC, Libyan chieftains were able to ascend to the throne as the 22nd Dynasty, and were seemingly accepted as legitimate pharaohs.

The period of the 22nd–23rd Dynasties, with their chief towns at Tanis and Bubastis, is therefore best described as the "Libyan period." At first these pharaohs were able to impose upon Egypt, by the manipulation of appointments of chief officials throughout the realm, a unity unseen during the 21st Dynasty. As this period wore on, however, the ruling house gradually lost control of parts of the country, so that the last king of Manetho's 23rd Dynasty, Osorkon IV, ruled over little more than the family seat in the eastern Delta. Perhaps first to go was Thebes, which began recognizing its own pharaohs (the "Theban" 23rd Dynasty) during the reign of Osorkon II, and ceased referring to the Tanite kings during the reign of Sheshonk III. At a later point, certainly before Piye's invasion, Sais (24th Dynasty) and Leontopolis ("23rd Dynasty Leontopolis") had also begun recognizing their own monarchs. This plurality was brought to a close by a Kushite (Nubian) invasion, whose leaders were to rule Egypt as the 25th Dynasty. Thus it is clear that Egyptian, Libyan and Kushite cultures all contributed to the art and archaeology of the period.

The Third Intermediate Period is conventionally (and mistakenly) seen as a "Dark Age," since it has left few architectural remains. This view is compounded by the Delta location of the Dynastic capitals, Tanis, Bubastis and Sais, which have either been relatively little explored or survived poorly. The scattered remains of the temple ruins at Tanis and the Festival Hall of Osorkon II at Bubastis testify to the magnificence of the civic buildings which once stood in Delta cities.

Religious buildings

Religious buildings of the 21st Dynasty, in as far as they are preserved, appear to continue the traditions of the New Kingdom. Nowhere is this more apparent than in the Temple of Khonsu at Karnak, which, although principally built during the 20th Dynasty, was added to and finally decorated by Herihor and Pinedjem. Elsewhere scant remains of this date can be found in the Temple of Amen at Tanis; a temple of Isis at Giza; in sacred (?) structures at Tell ed-Dabʿa, known from a block of Siamen; and at Memphis, where only remains of the gateway, also dating to the reign of Siamen, are preserved.

During the Libyan period, further work was carried out on the Amen temple complex at Tanis, particularly during the reigns of Osorkon II and Sheshonk III. The former was also responsible for much remodeling of the temple structures at Bubastis. Elsewhere the best preserved temple is probably the ruinous example at el-Hiba, begun by Sheshonk I and finished by Osorkon I. Blocks which came from smaller shrines have been found at Tell Balala, Kom-el-Hisn, Tell el-Yahudiya and el-Bindaraia. The remains of at least three 22nd Dynasty shrines, one of Sheshonk II and two of Osorkon II, have been found at Karnak. At Karnak too stands the best preserved piece of Libyan architecture, the so-called "Bubastite Portal." More small shrines, of which the most famous is that of the god Osiris Heka-djet (later expanded and remodeled during the 25th Dynasty), were also erected at Karnak by the rulers of the Theban 23rd Dynasty.

Following the Kushite conquest (25th Dynasty), much religious building was undertaken, particularly during the reign of Taharka, whose surviving temples, particularly those at Gebel Barkal, Kawa and Qasr el-Ghueida in Kharga Oasis, are perfect copies of traditional New Kingdom religious temples but on a smaller scale. Also at Karnak, the remains of numerous small shrines attest to a continuation of a style of building made popular by the Theban 23rd Dynasty. Elsewhere, little remains, though blocks from a small temple and shrine at Memphis dating to the reigns of Shabako and Taharka have come to light. At Karnak, Taharka was also responsible for the erection of a large colonnaded portico in front of the Second Pylon, and for the construction of a remarkable building with subterranean cult chambers beside the Sacred Lake.

Secular buildings

The remains of secular buildings are even less well preserved, which is not surprising since most would have been built of mudbrick. The town sites of Medinet Habu and Elephantine have revealed remains of domestic houses extending throughout the entire Third Intermediate Period. With the exception of that of the 21st Dynasty scribe, Butehamen, which clearly had a central colonnaded court, the published buildings have small ground plans, but the remains of staircases indicate that they normally had at least two floors. A growing sense of insecurity during these times led to the building of fortification walls around the towns at Medinet Habu and el-Hiba. Since another fort was erected at the undiscovered site of Per-Sekhemperre, it is likely that many of the towns of this period were so fortified.

Tombs and burial customs

It is through its burials, however, that the archaeology of ancient Egypt is best known, and the Third Intermediate Period stands out as a period of marked change. The isolated royal burial is given up in favor of burial within the sacred precincts of a temple area, most obviously at Tanis and Sais, but this is also noticeable at Thebes, where burials were placed in tombs cut through the New Kingdom mortuary temples. Perhaps more striking, however, is that the idea of spending one's lifetime preparing a "goodly burial" with splendid tomb and furnishings practically vanishes. Apart from the royal burials at Tanis, Memphis, Heracleopolis and Medinet Habu, the concept of a specially constructed tomb is all but abandoned, though some private tomb chapels of this period are known at Tanis, Abydos, and in the Ramesseum area at Thebes, while an extant pyramidion indicates tomb chapels at Bubastis.

Since Thebes provides most of the evidence for burial customs during the Third Intermediate Period, the remainder of this section is based entirely on Theban beliefs. During the 21st Dynasty a practice developed of private interments within usurped earlier tombs, and this practice even extended as high as royal children, as can be seen with the burial of Princess Nauny, interred within the tomb of the 18th Dynasty Queen Meryetamen. At first only single burials were so made, but there quickly developed a system of family vaults, of which the most famous are those of Pinedjem II and his immediate family (which was later used to house the "royal cache" of mummies) and, later, the Montu priest burials, both at Deir el-Bahri. Although there are noticeable changes in style throughout the period, the well-provided Theban went to the grave with little more than coffins, heart scarabs and a complement of 401 *shawabtis* enclosed within a pair of chests. These items were supplemented at different periods by, in the 21st Dynasty, a *Book of Amduat* rolled between the legs, an Osiris figure with funerary papyrus (most often, a *Book of the Dead*) and wax amulets of the Sons of Horus within the body protecting the viscera. During the Libyan period, burial goods included freestanding wooden figures of the Four Sons of Horus, small mummies made of wheat, and a polychrome cartonnage case, which was enclosed within coffins of a much more drab appearance than the ornately decorated ones of the 21st Dynasty. Finally, during the 25th Dynasty, a bead net without face and a figure of the god Ptah-Sokar-Osiris complemented the burial. Throughout the entire Third Intermediate Period the richer burials were also supplemented with wooden stelae and canopic jars, which during the Libyan period were merely symbolic dummies. Specialists can recognize six distinctive funerary phases within the Third Intermediate Period, depending on the styles and types of the grave goods, with distinct changes noticeable at about 1000 BC, at *circa* 950/930 BC, *circa* 850/825 BC, *circa* 750 BC and finally at around 675/650 BC.

Sculpture

Since very little standing architecture remains, it follows that correspondingly little relief sculpture survives. The best of it, however, is to be found at Tanis, particularly in the tombs of Psusennes I and Osorkon II and carved on the temple blocks of Sheshonk III. By contrast, a large number of sculptures in the round can be attributed to the Third Intermediate Period. At Tanis, such objects are fragmentary, generally of small size, and made exclusively out of hard stone. The best known sculptures are probably the stone statuettes found in the Karnak Cachette, a cache of statues intentionally buried at Karnak in the Late period. These tend to show high officials of the realm, and almost all are in cuboid form showing the deceased squatting, or sitting on the floor, in a wrap-around cloak. The seated statue, however, practically disappears at this time. Toward the end of the Libyan period, and certainly during Kushite times, these sculptures show a marked veering away from idealized portraits of eternal youth to a style of portraiture intended to convey an aspect of more maturity, and a harking back to more archaic prototypes. This archaizing tendency began to manifest itself during the eighth century BC before the Kushite conquest, and is most noticeable in royal monuments, particularly in the terse style of the titulary, which harks back to Old and Middle Kingdom models, and in the use of the Blue Crown. However, if there is one type of object for which the Third Intermediate Period should be justly famed, it is for its metal sculptures. The most opulent of these were made of gold, though the usual medium was bronze. These statues exhibit a slenderness of form achieved by an accentuated modeling of the upper torso, a distinctly slim waist and slender thighs. Many of the bronzes, of which the most famous are the Louvre Karomama (reign of Osorkon II) and the statue of Takushet (reign of Piye) in Athens, have their surfaces enriched with gold, silver and electrum inlays.

Minor arts

Within the fields of minor arts, particular mention should be made of the royal jewelry found at Tanis, Memphis and Tell Muqdam, and of the richly painted coffins from Thebes. During the 21st Dynasty, the art of coffin painting reached a peak that has never been equaled. Coffin exteriors of the 21st Dynasty tend to be decorated in rich colors on a yellow ground, while the interiors are on a wine red ground. A reorganization in funerary iconography at the end of the 20th Dynasty led to the adoption of a new repertoire of scenes drawn mainly from Osirian and solar mythology. Also popular were scenes of the Four Sons of Horus, Osiris seated on a double throne, a Hathor cow emerging from the necropolis, and scenes taken from the *Litany of Re.* On the coffin interior, representations of Nut or a *djed* pillar, a hieroglyph symbolizing "stability," are the usual motifs encountered. By the reign of Osorkon I, however, these brightly painted coffins had gone out of fashion and were replaced by new types which were different in shape, construction and style of decoration. These tended to be drab, but the rise of the richly decorated cartonnage case continued the tradition of the earlier coffin painters. These cartonnages are painted most often with numerous winged deities and *djed* symbols on a white ground. These went out of fashion during the early 25th Dynasty, and coffin painting was never again of such a high standard.

See also

Elephantine; funerary texts; Gebel Barkal; Kom el-Hisn; Kushites; Libyans; Manetho; Medinet Habu; Memphis; *shawabtis*, servant figures and models; Tanis (San el-Hagar); Tell Basta; Tell el-Muqdam; Tell el-Yahudiya

Further reading

Aldred, C.A. 1980. *Egyptian Art*, chapters 13–15. London.

Fazzini, R.A. 1988. *Egypt: Dynasty XXII–XXV* (Iconography of Religions XVI.10). Leiden.

Leahy, A. 1985. The Libyan period in Egypt: an essay in interpretation. *Libyan Studies* 16: 51–65.

Kitchen, K. A. 1996. *The Third Intermediate Period in Egypt (1100–650 BC)*, 3rd edn. Warminster.

Ruszczyc, B. 1973. The Egyptian sacred architecture of the Late Period: a study against the background of the epoch. *Archaeologia* (Wroclaw) 24: 12–49.

Wilkinson, A. 1971. *Ancient Egyptian Jewellery*, chapters 8–10. London.

D.A. ASTON

Late and Ptolemaic periods, overview

The Saites took control over the western Delta with the support of the Assyrians, who had driven the Kushite rulers (25th Dynasty) from Egypt by 665 BC. Gradually, Psamtik I of Sais extended his control and by the eighth year of his reign he controlled the entire Delta. He supported men loyal to him for controlling positions in important Nile Valley towns, and he opened negotiations with the Thebans. By the ninth year he had persuaded the high priestesses of the temple of Karnak (the "God's Wife" and the "Divine Votaress of Amen"), who were the last remnants of Kushite control in Thebes, to adopt his daughter Nitocris as their successor. He made no attempt to interfere otherwise with the administrative structure in Thebes, but, with this move, he had become undisputed king of a reunited Upper and Lower Egypt and the founder of the 26th Dynasty. Slowly the powerful old Theban and Middle Egyptian families were replaced by new officials, some but not all of whom came from the Delta. By the time Psamtik I was firmly established as King of Upper and Lower Egypt, his initial dependence on Assyria was abandoned. He made a few gestures in western Asia which might have been construed as offensive by the Assyrians, but they were too busy elsewhere to be able to react. By the end of his long reign, Psamtik and Egypt were firm allies of the Assyrians in their struggle with the Babylonians. Trade contacts continued between Egypt and the Levant and there seems to have been some sort of "agreement" between Egypt and Judah in which the Egyptians encouraged (and sometimes provided ineffective assistance to) the leaders of Judah in their opposition to the Babylonians. Many Jews fleeing from the Babylonians escaped to Egypt.

Since the Egyptians were for the most part unable to exercise any military control in Syro-Palestine, they turned their attention to control of the seas. By participating in the booming international trade across the Mediterranean, Egypt, with its agricultural wealth, was assured access to both "staples" and luxury goods from abroad. By developing a strong navy, using new ships designed specifically for Mediterranean service, they could control movements of men and supplies in times of war. Numerous foreigners now lived in Egypt, many of whom were drawn by commercial potential as trade opened up throughout the Mediterranean. There were military garrisons staffed mainly by non-Egyptians, not only on Egypt's frontiers but also within the country; perhaps these were intended to help establish and maintain control over areas which had only recently been politically independent. The mercenaries were only a part of the growing number of people, mostly but not entirely Greek-speaking, who were moving into the Delta, the center of Egyptian society throughout the Late period. Memphis, at the apex of the Delta, was the administrative capital of the country, a flourishing, sophisticated, "multicultural" city. The development of strong economic and political/diplomatic ties between Egypt and the cities of the Greek mainland and Asia Minor, as a result of immigration, increased trade and development of the Egyptian navy, and had important consequences later.

During the long and prosperous reign of Amasis, the last major Saite king, the new and dynamic culture of Saite Egypt crystallized. While Egypt remained largely a redistributive economy (with the palace, the temples and even high officials serving as the points of collection, storage and distribution), private enterprise was supported and commercial practices were tightened. Administrative corruption (in the temples and elsewhere) was attacked, and excessively wealthy (and powerful) individuals who might threaten the stability of the dynasty were "encouraged" to donate their wealth to the temples. Both public and private building flourished. The 26th Dynasty is a period which clearly exemplifies change within continuity. The Saites took what they felt to be the best of their ancient cultural tradition, modernized it, incorporated important innovations, and produced a culture which not merely "survived" but flourished in a very different, new world.

One of the most important innovations which took place during the Late period was the development of new scripts. Demotic developed in Lower Egypt and is first attested during the reign of Psamtik I. Its use spread south with the Saites and by the reign of Amasis had led to a huge increase in numbers and types of documents, official and private, administrative, economic, religious and legal. The introduction of demotic does not merely indicate a vast increase in the number of documents which the Egyptians wrote. It also coincides with a period of immense creativity in Egyptian literature. On the legal side, the switch to demotic reflects significant changes in the underlying system. Where the law previously emphasized a mechanical process of reciprocity (for example, "I have given you X in exchange for Y"), now volition and intention became important. Changes in the form of so-called "marriage contracts" (actually economic documents whereby a man entails his property for his children) also appear during the reign of Amasis. In some cases, the changes seem to reflect modifications in the legal or social system itself. However, it is impossible to tell whether these changes began in Saite times or whether a conservative legal-documentary system was only slowly coming to reflect a social system which had changed much earlier. Certainly the high legal status of women, which is so striking in contrast to most other ancient societies, is well attested early in Egyptian history.

Egypt became part of the Persian empire in 525 BC, when the Persian king Cambyses captured the capital at Memphis. He was vilified by the classical authors, and the Jewish mercenary community at Elephantine preserved a tradition of the "destruction of all the temples of the Egyptian gods" by Cambyses. But the contemporary records refute Herodotus's specific claim that Cambyses killed the sacred Apis bull and Cambyses's bad repute in later times may have stemmed from the fact that he cut back drastically on the revenue of the temples and antagonized the priesthood. Darius I had been with Cambyses in Egypt and by about 517 BC, when he had control of the empire, he returned to Egypt, where he supervised the digging of a "Suez" canal (begun under the Saite king Neko), connecting Persia by sea with the Egyptian Delta and thus the Mediterranean. He took some pains to behave and have himself portrayed in Egypt as a legitimate and beneficent ruler. Despite Darius's generally sympathetic treatment of captured lands, the end of his reign was marked by further rebellion in the empire and Egypt itself revolted in 486 BC. When Xerxes succeeded Darius in 485 BC, he quickly put down the Egyptian rebellion. Neither he nor any of his successors ever visited Egypt and his treatment of Egypt and the Egyptians was extremely harsh.

Throughout the period of the Persian empire (27th–31st Dynasties) the Persians regarded Egypt as merely one province in its empire, albeit a rich one. Egypt was governed as a satrapy, with the satrap and other senior officials being Persians appointed by the king. The Saite bureaucratic organization of the country was largely retained, with Persians put in most high positions (both in Memphis and in the provinces). Aramaic was the official government language of the Persians.

The records of an Aramaic-speaking colony of Jewish mercenaries stationed on the island of Elephantine, at the First Cataract, provide information about the colony, its relations with its Egyptian neighbors and officials of the Persian government. In some ways the Jewish community maintained its separate identity, keeping their Hebrew names, their own religion and marriage laws, but in other ways the community very much resembled its Egyptian neighbors. Legal scholars have discussed why the Egyptian and Jewish systems of land tenure, including land lease, are so similar.

Some time after 450 BC, during a period of peace and prosperity, Herodotus visited Egypt and wrote his vivid account of Egyptian history and culture. Herodotus, as well as his Egyptian informants, had anti-Persian sentiments. He went to Egypt with the traditional Greek reverence for Egyptian culture and history and he looked at Egypt in terms of general themes (for example, Egypt as the opposite of Greece and the rest of the world). What he recorded was the result of what he looked for and asked about; the deficiencies frequently reflect the attitudes he took with him.

The beginning of the reign of Artaxerxes (464–423 BC) was marked in Egypt by the first of a long series of rebellions by West Delta chieftains, who allied themselves with anyone who was antagonistic to the Persians. Finally, about 404 BC, at the death of Darius II, the Persians were driven out. During the next sixty years (404–343 BC), three different "dynasties," or ruling families, from different cities in the Delta successively wrested power from one another. Major temple construction in the Delta and in Upper Egypt during the longer reigns, especially those of the 30th Dynasty, reflected the relative wealth and security of the country. The number and quality of royal and private monuments, including statuary, also attest to the cultural and economic strength of Egypt under its last native dynasts. Indicative of the role of Egypt in the international commerce of the period is the Delta city of Naukratis, whose Greek residents traded extensively throughout the eastern Mediterranean.

Since the Persian king throughout this period thought of Egypt as just one more rebellious province, and regularly attempted to reconquer it, Egyptian foreign policy consisted of support (sometimes covert or "moral," sometimes formal military aid) for anyone who was opposing the Persian king. This led to a shifting set of alliances between Egypt and the Greek cities, especially Athens and Sparta, and Cyprus, and also led to the stronger Egyptian kings intervening in Syro-Palestine to support those local dynasts who were rebelling against the Persians or could be persuaded to do so. But in reality Egypt was the "Broken Reed" of the Bible, whose support of anti-Persian factions proved unsuccessful in the long run. Egyptian military commanders were frequently Greek and the outcome of several battles was modified by recall (often instigated by the Persians) of some of these leaders to their home cities.

Artaxerxes III Ochus recaptured Egypt in 343 BC, but rebellion continued until its conquest by Alexander in 332 BC. Legend has it that the Egyptians welcomed Alexander as a liberator from the Persians. Alexander had himself crowned king in the appropriate pharaonic manner in Memphis. He went to Siwa Oasis in the Western Desert to consult its oracle, a favorite one in the Greek world, and he was declared the son of Amen/Zeus. He founded Alexandria and established competitive games, drama and a musical festival in the Greek manner. Very soon after he left Egypt in the hands of administrators, who took advantage of his absence to aggrandize themselves. It was not until Ptolemy, one of

Alexander's generals, claimed Egypt as his "prize" after the death of Alexander that Egypt again had a stable, well-run administration, centered in Egypt and designed to promote the wealth and welfare of the country.

Aside from replacing an Egyptian or Persian ruling elite with a Greek/Macedonian one, the major contribution of the early Ptolemies was a quality and unity of leadership over an extended period. It was in their interest to build up Egypt's wealth, and this they did for several generations. The Ptolemies, like the short-lived Egyptian dynasts but unlike the Persians, centered themselves in Egypt, with their capital at Alexandria, although Memphis retained its economic, legal and religious importance. Agriculture remained the foundation of the economy and although some land was worked directly for the crown, most land was worked by private individuals who owned or rented it. There was some agricultural reform, introduction of some new crops, and some new technology and expansion of cultivation, especially in the Fayum, where extensive efforts took place to reclaim potential agricultural land around the lake. This expansion was carried out partly to provide land for soldiers and high government officials and involved creation of several Greek cities and a Greek cultural overlay in the Fayum.

Alexandria became the capital of Hellenistic Egypt, where the Ptolemies and their courtiers resided. But Alexandria catered to a larger world of the eastern Mediterranean, and Memphis retained its economic and cultural importance for Egypt (and grew in importance to the Ptolemies as they came to focus more and more on the core Nile Valley). Alexandria was consciously Greek, rejecting Egyptian culture (and Egyptian natives to the extent that it could). Here was the famous Library of Alexandria and many of the most famous intellects of the Hellenistic (and Roman and Byzantine) world came to study or work and teach in Alexandria. In the early Ptolemaic period, royal patronage of the arts and sciences (including literature) attracted poets, scientists and scholars from all over the Greek world to the Library and Museum. Royal patronage continued through the middle Ptolemaic period and a succession of librarians introduced and organized a program of collecting and interpreting the Greek classical authors. Great advances were made in fields such as geography, mathematics, medicine and physics. By the late Ptolemaic period, Alexandria had become the center for the study of philosophy. At the same time there was growth in the Jewish community in Alexandria and in research in the fields of Jewish and Biblical studies.

However, outside the Fayum and Alexandria life remained much as it had been for centuries, or millennia. Even though the Ptolemaic period was more "monetized" than earlier, and some taxes, license fees and so on had to be paid in silver, Egypt was still heavily a redistributive economy and one of the functions of the palace was to serve as the collection and storage site for domestic and international produce, and as the site from which such goods then circulated through the general economy. Temples and major agricultural estates served as secondary redistribution centers within the system dominated by the palace. Such a system left plenty of room for local markets and local exchange of goods between individuals and it should be noted that such a system was characteristic not only of Late period Egypt, but also of pharaonic Egypt as early as the Old Kingdom. The extensive bureaucracy, ranging from senior central administrators dealing with economic and legal affairs of the entire country to local scribes responsible for collecting and recording taxes, is anticipated already in the New Kingdom. Even the cleruchic system of giving soldiers a small plot of land in return for their military service was a well-established (and relatively cheap) method of tying the loyalties of Egypt's "foreign" soldiers to Egypt, perhaps seen most clearly during the Libyan dynasties (22nd–24th Dynasties).

The Ptolemies developed a growing attachment to, or use of, Egyptian religion, with the development of the royal cult and the cult of Serapis, and royal patronage of traditional Egyptian cults. Myth and ritual remained intact and the temples and priesthood remained major landowners and a major economic force, as they had been throughout Egyptian civilization. Extensive formal royal sponsorship of temple building and rebuilding continued through the Ptolemaic and into the Roman period. Such actions won the Ptolemies the support of the Egyptian priesthood (and the priests, in turn, had great influence over the rest of society). Priests, both those "employed" by temples and those who provided ongoing mortuary services for wealthy Egyptian families, were among the wealthier individuals in Ptolemaic Egypt. They owned some land but gained most of their wealth "in kind" through the age-old practice of reversion of offerings: goods given to the gods, or the deceased, were passed on to the priests, who could consume them or trade them for other goods.

Ptolemy I originally ruled as satrap, then as king. He was succeeded by his son and daughter (the beginning of the royal brother–sister marriages called "Egyptian," but not reflecting Egyptian customs), where the woman was the stronger force. Since Ptolemy had been in Egypt with Alexander, it is generally assumed that he recognized the potential wealth of the country as well as the relative ease of governing it without undue outside interference. However, he also maintained a claim over southern Syria (Coele-Syria) and Cyprus, presumably because of their natural resources, which complemented those of Egypt, and because of Ptolemy's desire to control the Mediterranean and its trade and trade routes. Until 200 BC, control of these regions was contested by the Ptolemies and the Seleucids (in Syria), with the Ptolemies more frequently in the ascendancy. The six so-called "Syrian Wars," fought for control of this region, are the background for one of the best-known Egyptian texts, the Rosetta Stone, instrumental in the decipherment of Egyptian hieroglyphs. The final chapter in the "Syrian Wars" took place in 168 BC when the Seleucid king Antiochus had himself crowned king of Egypt in Memphis. Rome, which had a vested interest in making sure that none of the kings of the eastern Mediterranean gained too much power, stepped in and ordered Antiochus out of Egypt. From this point on, Ptolemaic political history is a story of inept rule, dynastic strife and the growing involvement of Rome, all underlain by growing economic distress resulting from poor management and insufficient control of the enormous bureaucratic machinery.

Educated Greeks in Alexandria and other strongholds of Greek culture looked down on anyone who did not have a Greek education and some Egyptians came to hate their Greek overlords, but, for the most part, Egyptians and Greeks coexisted with a minimum of antipathy. Those problems that did exist (and there were more as the Ptolemaic period progressed) were far more frequently economic than cultural, and were frequently caused by corrupt officials. The resulting discontent and antagonism toward the system, combined with weak central government in the middle Ptolemaic period, or with dynastic strife in the later Ptolemaic period, produced a climate of rebellion, usually Egyptian-led (although sometimes Greek-led) and apparently never ethnically based.

Essentially, Ptolemaic Egypt was home to two separate, vital cultures maintained side by side, which occasionally interacted. The Ptolemies presented themselves to their Egyptian subjects as good Egyptian kings, and to their Greek-speaking subjects as good Greek kings (the ideals of kingship were much the same). In law there were two separate legal systems, Greek when the documents were written in Greek, Egyptian when the documents were written in demotic. In at least some legal matters Egyptian law was more favorable than Greek (especially in the case of women's rights) and people who had a choice (for example, bilingual/bicultural people, especially in families in which there had been intermarriage) would choose to write their documents in Egyptian. In addition, all residents of Egypt, whether Greek-speaking or Egyptian-speaking, were subject to a system of royal law.

Both Greek and Egyptian literary traditions flourished. Extensive papyrus collections of Greek classics have been found even in relatively small, "provincial" towns with a Greek population. However, this period also was one in which major Egyptian literary texts of a number of genres were composed. Traditional genres, such as wisdom texts and narrative stories, were joined by genres with a Greek-flavored sub-stratum; but literary influence worked in both directions. There are examples of Egyptian mythical narrative tales translated into Greek, and some narrative stories about Egyptian kings are preserved only in Greek. The propagandistic value of Late period Egyptian literature and the participation of Egyptian writers in a larger, pan-Near Eastern approach to life have been noted. In art, too, the Egyptians of the Ptolemaic period demonstrated the vitality of their cultural tradition.

Although some authors stress the popularity of animal cults and other signs of "popular," as opposed to formal, religion, the animal cults were not only popular with the masses but were also subsidized by the king (whether "Egyptian," Persian, or "Greek"). At the same time the king was encouraging more standard traditional religion, including the cult of the divine ruler as well as those of old favorites such as Osiris and Isis (whose popularity spread far beyond Egypt). The new cult of Serapis was a very successful attempt by the early Ptolemies to make Egyptian religion appeal to the Greeks.

One of the most visible developments during the Late period is the role of apocalyptic literature in the life and politics of Egypt as well as in much of the rest of the Near East. Egypt has a long tradition of apocalyptic literature, dating back at least to the Middle Kingdom. The kings of Egypt are generally presented in the formal literature as "semi-divine," with links between the people and the gods and partaking a bit of each. In the Late period, the ideal Egyptian king had the same characteristics as earlier kings: he was beneficent to the gods, he carried out the law, he protected his people from foreign invasion and he followed all the proper rituals. But a new element was added: the idea that the length and success of a king's reign directly reflected the extent to which he had acted as a proper king. In the past the Egyptian king had been assumed to be "good"; now it was assumed that the real nature of his leadership could be told from the length of his reign. This same tradition is found in Hebrew texts, such as the Biblical books of Kings, Judges and Chronicles. Conflict between the ideal king (who was merciful, just and powerful, and the guarantor of world order, *ma'at*) and the actual king was resolved by inserting a god or gods above the ruling king in the chain of command. Contemporary wisdom texts argued that wisdom consisted of self-control and pious acceptance of whatever the gods might send. Although man had moral freedom of choice and god endowed man with the capacity for good, and although proper conduct should result in happiness and prosperity, it was recognized that, in reality, this did not always happen. Divine will, unfathomable to man, manifested itself through Fate and Fortune and man must accept what came. Such concepts are also paralleled in non-Egyptian literature, including the Biblical story of Job. It is not to be suggested that either the Egyptian or the West Asian tradition was influencing the other, but rather that similar circumstances may have led to a similarity in world view. This apocalyptic vision appealed to "downtrodden" people, both in Egypt and elsewhere in the Hellenistic world.

To the extent that "foreign" rulers acted as traditional Egyptian pharaohs and allowed themselves to be presented as such to the Egyptians, the pragmatic Egyptians were satisfied and Egyptian civilization adapted to new conditions while remaining essentially Egyptian. Other institutions underwent some change (for example, the increase of foreign trade, the beginning of a monetary economy, the introduction of a mercenary army tied secondarily to the land, the introduction of demotic as the normal written language and the use of foreign languages in the court) without producing fundamental changes in Egypt's institutional structure. Thus, although Egypt in the Late period had been removed from its earlier isolation and forced to be part of a larger world, its Egyptian character, attitude and ideals were not lost.

See also

Alexandria; Assyrians; Egyptian language and writing; Herodotus; Israelites; kingship; Kushites; *ma'at*; Macedonians; Naukratis; Persians; Rosetta Stone; Saqqara, Serapeum and animal necropolis; textual sources, Late period; Third Intermediate Period, overview

Further reading

Bowman, A.K. 1986. *Egypt After the Pharaohs, 332 BC–AD 642*. Berkeley, CA.

Briant, P. 1996. *Histoire de l'empire perse, De Cyrus à Alexandre*. Paris.

Porten, B. 1968. *Archives from Elephantine, The Life of an Ancient Jewish Military Colony*. Berkeley, CA.

Ray, J.D. 1988. Egypt 525–404 B.C. In *The Cambridge Ancient History* 4, 2nd edn, J. Boardman *et al.*, eds, ch. 3. Cambridge.

Samuel, A.E. 1989. *The Shifting Sands of History: Interpretations of Ptolemaic Egypt*. Lanham, MD.

JANET H. JOHNSON

Roman period, overview

The Roman period in Egypt is conventionally defined as extending from the conquest of Egypt by Augustus in 30 BC to the reorganization of the administration of Egypt by Diocletian in the late third century AD. Identification of these three centuries as forming a distinct period in Egyptian history is relatively recent. Nineteenth-century and early twentieth-century scholars tended to treat Roman Egypt as little more than a phase in the history of an entity they called Graeco-Roman Egypt. Contemporary historians of ancient Egypt, however, increasingly recognize the establishment of Roman rule in Egypt as marking a fundamental break with many of the cultural and institutional traditions of Ptolemaic Egypt.

Augustus's triumphal entry into Alexandria in 30 BC was the climax to almost three centuries of growing Roman influence over Ptolemaic Egypt. An embassy sent by Ptolemy II in 273 BC to congratulate Rome on the city's victory over Pyrrhus had begun the process. By the mid-second century BC, however, the initiative had passed to Rome, and Egypt had become a virtual Roman protectorate, whose fortunes varied with the whims of the Senate. Egypt was saved from annexation by the Seleucid king Antiochus IV in 168 BC by Roman intervention, but suffered the loss of Cyrene, on the Libyan coast, and Cyprus a few years later as a result of Senatorial arbitration of the conflicting claims to the throne of Ptolemy VI and his brother Ptolemy VIII. A century later, Roman protection had hardened into domination. Cyrene and Cyprus were both annexed by Rome, and Ptolemy XI, the father of Cleopatra VII, owed his throne to successful bribery of Roman politicians and the support of a Roman army. The attempt by Cleopatra VII to reverse the process of Egypt's decline and regain at least a part of her kingdom's empire in North Africa and the Near East, through cultivation of Julius Caesar and Marc Antony, failed disastrously at the Battle of Actium in 31 BC. With her suicide the following year, three centuries of Macedonian rule in Egypt ended.

Roman annexation of Egypt not only marked the end of Macedonian rule in Egypt. It also meant the end of the history of Egypt as an independent state in antiquity. The emperor Augustus disingenuously claimed in his autobiographical obituary, the *Res Gestae Divi Augusti*, that he had added Egypt to the empire of the Roman people. The reality was different. Egypt had become a province of the Roman empire, but it was a special kind of province. Augustus and his successors ruled Egypt as successors of the Ptolemies and treated Egypt and its great wealth as their personal property, a relationship that was symbolized by the extended ceremonial visits to Egypt made by several reigning emperors during this period. The integration of Egypt into the Roman imperial system meant, however, that it also quickly felt the effects of problems elsewhere in the Roman empire. Thus, Egypt's agricultural wealth drew it into the imperial succession crises of AD 68–70 and 193–7, while the collapse of Roman power in the Near East following the defeat in AD 260 of the emperor Valerian by the Sassanid Persian ruler Shapur I resulted in the temporary subjection of Egypt to Palmyrene rule (AD 269–71).

Rome's interest in Egypt was primarily fiscal. The Ptolemies had been the wealthiest of the Hellenistic kings, and maintaining the economic system that had produced that wealth with its numerous monopolies and taxes was one of the chief priorities of Augustus and his successors. Above all, however, the Roman government was concerned with the successful functioning of Egyptian agriculture and the collection of the grain tax, which was paid in kind and supplied fully one-third of the grain consumed annually in Rome.

To accomplish these goals, Augustus imposed a centralized administration on Egypt that was headed by an equestrian prefect appointed by the emperor and supported by a military force of almost three legions (later reduced to two). Access to Egypt was strictly controlled. Senators were forbidden to enter the country without the permission of the emperor, nor did the Senate exercise jurisdiction in Egypt, where imperial decrees were the ultimate source of new law and policy. The prefect was the official ultimately responsible for the implementation of imperial policy and the resolution of legal disputes. At the local level there was superficial continuity with Ptolemaic Egypt—indeed, even with pharaonic Egypt—since the basis of local administration remained the division of the country into nomes (thirty-six in the time of Augustus). Beneath the surface, however, there was a fundamental redistribution of power. The nome governors, the *strategoi* (generals), who were recruited from the local population and had had both military and civilian functions in the Ptolemaic period, became strictly civilian officials. Henceforth, military authority in Egypt was exercised only by the Roman garrison commanders. The situation was similar with regard to social and cultural life in Roman Egypt.

Roman Egypt was a multi-ethnic society that included not only the native Egyptian population, but also a much smaller immigrant population of Macedonians, Greeks, Jews and other non-Egyptians, most of whom had settled in Egypt during the Ptolemaic period. Under the Ptolemies these various groups had coexisted with relatively little social interaction. This situation had been facilitated by the fact that the vast majority of the Egyptians lived in agricultural villages scattered along the Nile under their own law and officials, while the bulk of the immigrant population was concentrated in the three Greek cities of Egypt—the old Greek colony of Naukratis and the new foundations of Alexandria and Ptolemais—and a number of settlements that had been founded by the Ptolemies on reclaimed land in the Fayum. Although outbreaks of ethnic violence occurred throughout the Ptolemaic period, overall social peace was maintained by two factors: extensive Ptolemaic subsidization of Egyptian religion and the Egyptian priestly elite, and toleration of the usurpation of the privileges of Greek status by Hellenized Jews and Egyptians by the later Ptolemies, who needed the support of such groups to counter their unpopularity with the Greek population of Alexandria. Except for the foundation of a fourth Greek city, Antinoopolis, by the emperor Hadrian in the second century AD, the substitution of Roman for Ptolemaic rule brought little change in the outward organization of Egyptian society. The tone of the society of Roman Egypt, however, was significantly different from that of Ptolemaic Egypt.

The Roman government recognized four principal ethnic groups in Egypt: Romans, Greeks, Jews, and Egyptians. Greek status, however, was limited to the citizens of the four Greek cities. All residents of the Egyptian countryside, whatever their origin, were Egyptians. Change of status was difficult as intermarriage between Greeks and non-Greeks was generally forbidden, as was admission of non-Greeks to the gymnasia, the principal institutional centers of Hellenization. Even the adoption of a Greek name by an Egyptian required the permission of the Roman government of Egypt. The result of these changes was a hardening of the divisions between the various ethnic groups in Egypt. In the cities a rigid social hierarchy emerged with the privileges of citizenship being limited to Romans and Greeks and Egyptians being treated as resident aliens, while Jews occupied an uneasy and unstable intermediate status. In the nome capitals and villages, the descendants of Ptolemaic Greek settlers lost their privileged status. Poor Greeks tended increasingly to disappear into the mass of the rural Egyptian population; wealthy Greeks sought to avoid a similar fate by vigorously cultivating their Greek identity through education and support of Greek cultural institutions such as the gymnasia. At the same time, the combination of the heavy and regressive burden, represented by taxes such as the grain and poll taxes, and a decline in the level of government subsidization of Egyptian religion led to a general worsening of the social and economic situation of the Egyptian priestly elite in particular, and the Egyptian peasantry in general. Clear evidence of this decline in the welfare of the native Egyptian population can be found in the sharp reduction in the number of wealthy native burials, the numerous references in the documentary sources for Roman Egypt to the abandonment of villages and agricultural land, and the growth of banditry.

Roman Egypt was not only ethnically diverse, it was also culturally diverse. Three written languages—Egyptian in its various forms, Greek and Latin—were in common use throughout the period, and speakers of many more languages could be encountered in its more cosmopolitan urban centers, such as Alexandria and Memphis. There was, therefore, no single Roman Egyptian culture, but rather several sub-cultures in Roman Egypt, whose vigor varied with the state of the ethnic groups that produced them. A good example is provided by Judaeo-Greek literature, which had flourished in Ptolemaic and early Roman Egypt, but later disappeared as a result of the decimation of the Egyptian Jewish community following the Jewish uprisings in North Africa and Egypt in AD 115–17. Greek culture, however, flourished in Roman Egypt.

Despite recurrent outbreaks of violence in Alexandria resulting from Rome's refusal to accede to the demands of the Alexandrian Greeks for a city council, it was Roman policy to encourage and support Greek culture in Egypt. The great cultural institutions of Ptolemaic Alexandria, the Museum and the Library, continued to function. The city remained a center for research and education in literature, philosophy and the sciences—particularly medicine and mathematics in all its forms—throughout the period. Alexandria was also a center of the arts, and craft goods made in the city's workshops or reflecting fashions popular there, such as themes drawn from the Egyptian daily life, are found throughout the Roman empire and far beyond its borders. Greek culture in Roman Egypt was not, however, limited to Alexandria. Theaters, schools and gymnasia existed in the Greek settlements and nome capitals of the Fayum and Middle and Upper Egypt, while the papyri document the availability of a wide range of Greek literature to the educated Greek elite of Roman Egypt as a whole. The wide distribution of Greek culture in Egypt is well illustrated by the varied origins of the principal Greek writers of Roman Egypt. So, Alexandria produced the Roman historian Appian and the mathematician and astronomer Ptolemy, Naukratis the grammarian Athenaeus, and Lycopolis the philosopher Plotinus, the founder of Neoplatonism. A firm foundation, therefore, was laid during the first three centuries of the Christian era for the remarkable efflorescence of Greek literature and art that made Byzantine Egypt one of the chief centers of Greek cultural activity in late antiquity.

However, conditions in Roman Egypt were much less favorable for traditional Egyptian culture. The artistic and literary activity that had made the Ptolemaic period one of the great creative periods of ancient Egyptian culture gradually ceased during the Roman period, and the reason is clear. Unlike the Ptolemies, who had needed the support of the temple priesthoods to govern, the Roman emperors, rulers of a vast empire rather than kings of Egypt—no emperor ever underwent a proper Egyptian coronation—did not. Consequently, although Roman building and repair activity is attested at many Egyptian religious sites, including the Great Sphinx at Giza and the Temple of Amon at Karnak, the level of government support for Egyptian religion dropped sharply while government control increased. The temples were put under the direct supervision of the Roman government, which took over the management of their lands and allowed their staffs only an annual allowance for expenses. By the second century AD, Roman control of the temples had been centralized under an equestrian official resident at Alexandria, the High Priest of Egypt. Candidates for the priesthood were required to have all aspects of their candidacy certified by the government, including even their circumcision. The priestly synods that had been so characteristic a feature of Ptolemaic Egypt disappeared, as did the rich burials of the high priests of Memphis and the holders of other major priesthoods. The impact of these changes on Egyptian culture was severe. The priesthood continued to be trained in the old scripts, and hieroglyphic and demotic inscriptions were still being written in late antiquity, but no significant new literary composition can be dated to the Roman period, and even demotic literary papyri cease after the early second century AD. In many respects, therefore, little more remained of traditional Egyptian culture by the early fourth century AD than the great monuments that so impressed the Greek and Roman tourists who covered them with graffiti, and the myth of Egypt as the land of primordial wisdom that dominates accounts of the country in Greek and Latin in late antiquity.

The basic conditions that had governed life in Roman Egypt since the reign of Augustus changed dramatically during the third century AD. The Augustan organization of Egypt gradually broke down during the political and economic upheavals of the middle and late third century AD. This was replaced by Diocletian with a radically different administrative structure in which Egypt was divided into three provinces, each with its own civil governor, while military authority was concentrated in the hands of a single *dux* (military commander). The social structure of Roman Egypt was also transformed by the extension of Roman citizenship to virtually all inhabitants of the country in AD 212 by the *Constitutio Antoniniana*, which obliterated the system of hierarchically ranked ethnic groups on which the previous social structure had been based. This was now replaced by a simpler system in which people were divided economically into rich and poor with different and unequal privileges ascribed to each by law, the division into *honestiores* and *humiliores* that characterized society everywhere in the late Roman empire. The distinction between Greek and Egyptian culture also gradually disappeared everywhere except in the closed world of the temples, as the spread of the new religion of Christianity led to the appearance of a new cultural division of Egypt into pagans and Christians. In Egypt, as elsewhere in late antiquity, pagan culture increasingly came to be identified with a new cosmopolitan form of Greek culture scholars call "Hellenism," while Egyptian Christians used the new Coptic alphabet to create a Christian literature in Egyptian that would be free both of Hellenism and the millennia-old traditions of pharaonic Egypt. By the beginning of the fourth century AD, therefore, the basic pattern of life in Byzantine Egypt had begun to emerge clearly.

See also

Abu Sha'ar; Alexandria; Antinoopolis; Dakhla Oasis, Dynastic and Roman sites; Late and Ptolemaic periods, overview; Macedonians; Marea; Naukratis; Philae; Roman forts in Egypt; Roman ports, Red Sea

Further reading

Bell, H.I. 1948. *Egypt: From Alexander the Great to the Arab Conquest.* Oxford.
——. 1957. *Cults and Creeds in Graeco-Roman Egypt.* Liverpool.
Bowman, A.K. 1986. *Egypt after the Pharaohs: 332 BC–AD 642 from Alexander to the Arab Conquest.* Berkeley, CA.
Friedman, F.D. 1989. *Beyond the Pharaohs: Egypt and the Copts in 2nd to 7th Centuries A.D.* Providence, RI.
Johnson, A.C. 1951. *Egypt and the Roman Empire.* Ann Arbor, MI.
Johnson, J.H., ed. 1992. *Life in a Multi-Cultural Society: Egypt from Cambyses to Constantine and Beyond.* Chicago.
Lewis, N.L. 1983. *Life in Egypt under Roman Rule.* London.
Rowlandson, J. 1996. *Landowners and Tenants in Roman Egypt.* Oxford.

STANLEY M. BURSTEIN

A

A-Group culture

The A-Group is a distinctive culture of Lower Nubia contemporary with the Predynastic (Nagada) culture of Upper Egypt. This culture was first identified by George Reisner, who studied the artifacts collected during the First Archaeological Survey of Nubia (1907–8). Reisner's classification was later revised by Trigger, Adams and Nordström, based on archaeological evidence from the UNESCO salvage campaign in Nubia (1959–65).

A-Group sites have been recorded throughout Lower Nubia (between the First and Second Cataracts). A few sites are known in the Batn el-Hajar region, and near Seddenga in the Abri-Delgo reach (south of the Second Cataract). Recently an A-Group site was discovered at Kerma, near the Third Cataract. A-Group sites include both settlements and cemeteries.

Diagnostic elements of this culture are pottery and graves. The pottery includes several different types of vessels. Black-topped pots, with a polished red slip exterior and a black interior and rim, are common. These pots, though similar to those of the Nagada culture in Upper Egypt, were locally manufactured. Pots with a painted geometric decoration, sometimes imitating basketwork, are particularly distinctive of this culture.

A-Group graves include mainly simple oval pits, and oval pits with a chamber on one side. There is no clear evidence of grave superstructures. At a single site, Tunqala West, tumuli with an offering place of stone and an uninscribed grave stela were recorded.

In A-Group burials, the bodies were laid in a contracted position on the right side, usually with the head to the west. Grave goods were arranged around the body. Seated female figurines are a distinctive type of grave goods found in some A-Group burials. Luxury imported goods, such as beads of Egyptian manufacture, have also been excavated. Poorer graves, with a few simple grave goods or no grave goods, occur as well. These were initially classified by Reisner as another culture which he called the B-Group. At present, "B-Group" graves are considered to be evidence of lower status individuals in the A-Group.

Excavations of A-Group settlements suggest seasonal or temporary camps, sometimes reoccupied for a long time. A few sites have evidence of architecture, such as houses constructed of stone with up to six rooms. Three large (Terminal) A-Group centers were located at Dakka, Qustul and Seyala, where some elaborate burials have been recorded, but the archaeological evidence does not demonstrate the emergence of an early state.

Agriculture was practiced by the A-Group, who cultivated wheat, barley and lentils. Animal husbandry was certainly an important component of their subsistence economy, but evidence for it is scarce.

The chronology of the A-Group is divided into three periods:

1 Early A-Group, contemporary to the Nagada I and early Nagada II phases in Upper Egypt, with sites from Kubbaniya to Seyala;
2 Classic A-Group, contemporary to Nagada IId–IIIa, with sites in Lower Nubia and south of the Second Cataract in the northern Batn el-Hajar region;
3 Terminal A-Group, contemporary to Nagada IIIb, Dynasty 0 and the early 1st Dynasty, with sites in Lower Nubia and northern Upper Nubia.

The dating of the A-Group culture is still debated, however. Based on the evidence of Nagada culture artifacts in Lower Nubian graves, the A-Group arose in the first half of the fourth millennium BC. It is usually assumed that the A-Group disappeared in Lower Nubia during the Egyptian Early Dynastic period (1st–2nd Dynasties), as a consequence of Egyptian military intervention there.

The origins of the A-Group are not yet well understood. Trade contacts with Upper Egypt were an important factor in the social and economic development of the A-Group. In Nagada II times, trade with Upper Egypt greatly increased, as can be inferred from the great number of Nagada culture artifacts in A-Group graves. The occurrence of rock drawings of Nagada II-style boats at Seyala might suggest that this was an important trading center.

In the early 1st Dynasty, Egyptian policy in Nubia changed and raids were made as far south as the Second Cataract. Evidence of this is seen in a rock drawing at Gebel Sheikh Suleiman (near Wadi Halfa) recording a raid against the Nubians by a king of the 1st Dynasty (possibly Djet). A fortified Egyptian settlement was probably founded in the late 2nd Dynasty at Buhen, to the north of the Second Cataract.

Archaeological evidence points to a substantial abandonment of Lower Nubia in Old Kingdom times. Yet the occurrence of A-Group potsherds in the Egyptian town at Buhen dating to the 4th–5th Dynasties suggests that some A-Group peoples were still living in the region then. Moreover, the discovery of a few A-Group sites between the Second and Third Cataracts (between the Batn el-Hajar and Kerma) points to a progressive movement southward in Upper Nubia of A-Group peoples.

See also

Early Dynastic period, overview; Kerma; Predynastic period, overview

Further reading

Adams, W.Y. 1977. *Nubia, Corridor to Africa.* London.

O'Connor, D. 1978. Nubia before the New Kingdom. In *Africa in Antiquity: The Arts of Ancient Nubia and the Sudan* 1: 46–61. New York.

Trigger, B.G. 1976. *Nubia under the Pharaohs.* London.

RODOLFO FATTOVICH

Abu Gurab

Along the edge of the desert plateau at Abu Gurab (29°54′ N, 31°12′ E) and neighboring Abusir, roughly 15 km south of Cairo, lie the sites for the 5th Dynasty pyramids and sun temples. Except for a scattering of Early Dynastic cemeteries between the village of Abusir northward to the Saqqara plateau, no activity previous to the 5th Dynasty has been attested in the immediate vicinity. Queen Khentkaues, the link between the 4th and 5th Dynasties, was buried at Giza, while her husband Weserkaf, the first king of the 5th Dynasty, located his modestly sized pyramid in the northern part of Saqqara, near the northeast corner of the Zoser complex. Nonetheless, Weserkaf was the first king to build a sun temple, naming it "the Fortress of Re" (*Nhn-R'*). This is the first known sun temple and one of only two such structures preserved; the other was built by Nyuserre.

It is unclear why Weserkaf selected the previously unused site of Abu Gurab, approximately 5 km north of his pyramid, but perhaps at the time of the sun temple's construction the administrative capital and royal residence had already relocated in the vicinity of Abusir. Most of what we know about the activities of the new dynasty derives from this region.

According to the Middle Kingdom *Tale of Djedi and the Magicians*, the first three kings of the 5th Dynasty were triplets and the physical progeny of the sun god Re. There appears to be some truth behind this myth: not only were the second and third kings of the dynasty brothers, but these rulers also exhibited an unusually strong devotion to Re, particularly in his aspect as a universal creator deity. The sun temple itself offers proof of their piety, since it represented a new type of temple in many ways. Among other things, these temples were the first known instances of Egyptian monarchs dedicating large-scale stone structures entirely separate from their funerary monuments. No fewer than six kings of the 5th Dynasty are known to have built this kind of temple: Weserkaf, Sahure, Neferirkare, Reneferef or Neferefre, Nyuserre and Menkauhor.

Judging from the numerous references to this type of temple in official titles and other records, the sun temples were among the most important institutions in the land. Their great economic power is reflected in the fact that, according to the Abusir Papyri, offerings sent to the royal mortuary temples were dispensed first through the associated sun temples. Yet it appears that no single Egyptian term for sun temple exists.

Like the classical pyramid complex of the 4th Dynasty, a sun temple can be divided into three major sections according to function. First, there was a small valley temple at the edge of cultivation or an access canal; second, a relatively short causeway led up to the desert from the valley temple; and at the desert plateau stood the third and major part, the sun temple proper. The division of the complex into upper and lower portions was certainly dictated by practical considerations, but it also reflected a separation of the cult place from administrative buildings and the profane world in general. Excavations about the valley temple of Nyuserre's sun temple have revealed that a small village of privately built houses sprang up there over the years, without doubt due to the temple's importance to the local economy.

Because the central portions of the only two sun temples thus far located are so badly preserved, excavators have had to rely on the hieroglyphic signs in the temples' names in order to reconstruct the shape of their characteristic feature, the obelisk. It is only from such textual evidence that we know that squat,

perhaps even truncated, obelisks stood atop a platform and dominated the large rectangular open court of the upper temples. At Nyuserre's sun temple the obelisk mentioned in an inscription from the Zoser complex was constructed out of irregularly shaped stone blocks ingeniously fitted together and may have risen to a height of approximately 35 m. In some cases either a disk or a cross-like appendage may have been affixed to the top of the obelisk.

These first known obelisks in ancient Egypt are somewhat problematic. Although the obelisk and the sun temple have been connected with the "high sand of Heliopolis" and the Heliopolitan sun cult, the evidence does not bear these suppositions out. For one thing, the obelisk at Weserkaf's sun temple appears to have been added much later by Neferirkare, the third king of the dynasty.

The influence of the sun cult is evident in the large court where sacrifices could be made in the bright sunlight, rather than in darkened inner chambers as is so often the case in Egyptian temples. In front of the obelisk was the altar where the presumably burnt offerings were made. The sides of the altar at Nyuserre's temple were formed into four large *hotep* (offering) signs, each oriented roughly toward a cardinal point of the compass, a noteworthy example of the intimate relationship between art, architecture and writing in ancient Egyptian culture.

According to the Palermo Stone, a 5th Dynasty king list, Weserkaf established at his sun temple a daily offering to Re of two oxen and two geese. This largesse may not be an exaggeration, since the two surviving sun temples were both provided with sizable slaughterhouses; two, in the case of the sun temple of Nyuserre, named "Re's Favorite Place" (*Ššp-ib-R'*). The Abusir Papyri show that the slaughterhouses at the sun temples supplied the needs of the associated mortuary temples of the pyramid complexes. Some of the material distributed to the sister institution of Nyuserre's mortuary temple would probably have come from the large covered storehouse containing several magazines that was located adjacent to the sun temple's slaughterhouse.

Art that has survived at the sun temples seems to have been commissioned by Nyuserre. The so-called "Room of the Seasons" in Nyuserre's sun temple, which linked a covered corridor with the obelisk platform, was decorated with a group of reliefs portraying the activities of man and animals through the three Egyptian seasons. Near these were other reliefs which depicted the *Heb-sed* festival, an important ritual of royal renewal. Nyuserre also had part of Weserkaf's sun temple decorated with similar scenes from the same festival, but executed in a smaller scale. Most likely, chapels at both temples were used during the celebration. The reliefs in both places are executed in a fine, wafer-thin style that is characteristic of royal work of the 5th Dynasty.

The area immediately to the south of the enclosure wall of Nyuserre's sun temple has yielded another interesting feature, a large (30 × 10 m) sun boat that was buried in a mudbrick-lined chamber to the south of the temple complex.

Abu Gurab/Abusir after the 5th Dynasty

With the reign of Djedkare Isesi, the eighth king of the 5th Dynasty, royal activity at Abu Gurab and Abusir abruptly ceased. Isesi did not erect a sun temple, and chose to be buried at South Saqqara. The Abusir plateau had become overcrowded by the reign of Menkauhor and the administrative capital may have been shifted back south to Saqqara again. Although there are no Old Kingdom tombs datable later than the 5th Dynasty, a number of loose blocks and stelae found near the *mastaba*s show that Abusir certainly was not abandoned. This is not surprising because the Abusir Papyri reveal that the royal funerary establishments were still in operation as late as the reign of Pepi II (late 6th Dynasty). Although the papyri show that at times a large number of people were employed at these establishments or derived income from their endowments, the Abu Gurab/Abusir region was rarely used as a necropolis after the 5th Dynasty.

In the Middle Kingdom a number of tombs, whose superstructures are nearly all destroyed,

were built near Nyuserre's pyramid at Abusir. A small sanctuary dedicated to the chief goddess of the Memphite region was erected in the southern part of Sahure's mortuary temple during the New Kingdom. It is uncertain how long this cult functioned. Thereafter, except for occasional burials during the Late period, the Abusir plateau seems to have fallen into disuse.

See also

Abusir; Giza, Khufu pyramid sun barks and boat pit; Old Kingdom, overview; pyramids (Old Kingdom), construction of; Saqqara, pyramids of the 5th and 6th Dynasties

Further reading

Hart, G. 1991. *Pharaohs and Pyramids: A Guide through Old Kingdom Egypt*. London.

Stadelmann, R. 1984. Sonnenheiligtum. *LÄ* 5: 1094–9. Wiesbaden.

——. 1985. Das Königtum von Re. In *Die Ägyptischen Pyramiden. Vom Ziegelbau zum Weltwunder* (Kulturgeschichte der Antiken Welt 30), 159–80. Mainz.

OGDEN GOELET

Abu Roash

Abu Roash is a village about 9 km north of the pyramids of Giza (30°02′ N, 31°04′ E). It is chiefly known as the site of the 4th Dynasty pyramid of Djedefre (Redjedef), which was built on an eminence 2 km west of the village, in the white limestone hills west of the Nile. In 1842–3, Richard Lepsius recorded this pyramid and a second one built of mudbricks, situated on the easternmost promontory of the hills. J.S. Perring, who visited Abu Roash five years before Lepsius, also thought the core belonged to a pyramid of "apparent antiquity." Current opinion is skeptical that the mudbrick construction is actually a pyramid, although Swelim identified it as such in his investigation of the site in 1985–6. Perhaps originally this structure was a large *mastaba* tomb. Long stripped of its bricks, this structure now consists of a bare rock core, part of an entrance corridor (sloping from north to south at an angle of 25°), and a rock-cut tomb chamber with a floor measuring 5.5 m square and 5 m in height. The mudbricks were laid over the rock core in accretion layers inclining inward at an angle of 75°–76°.

Apart from the excavation of tombs dating from the 1st–2nd Dynasties and the 4th–5th Dynasties, by A. Klasens for the Leiden Museum of Antiquities in 1957–9, all the major archaeological work at Abu Roash has been conducted under the auspices of the French Institute of Archaeology in Cairo. Émile Chassinat excavated at the stone pyramid complex in 1901–3, followed by Lacau in 1913. In 1995 a combined expedition of the French Institute and the Department of Egyptology of the University of Geneva began joint excavations under the direction of Valloggia at the stone pyramid, which are still in progress. The private tombs, mostly dating from the 1st–2nd Dynasties and the 4th–5th Dynasties, were excavated by P. Montet in 1913–14, and by Fernand Bisson de la Roque in 1922–5. The design of the earliest tombs and the high quality of some of the artifacts found in them demonstrated that their owners were high status individuals, suggesting that Abu Roash was an administrative center long before the time of Djedefre.

Djedefre, who reigned for at least eight years, was a son of Khufu, the builder of the Great Pyramid at Giza. All that remains of the superstructure of his pyramid is a flat-topped edifice, which measures about 98 m square with a height of about 12 m. Its core of rock is surrounded by about ten courses of local stone. All four sides were overlaid with red Aswan granite. When complete, each side of the pyramid at the base measured 106 m (202 cubits) and its height would have been about 67 m (128 cubits). The sides sloped inwards at an angle of approximately 52°. Possibly the granite casing was not intended to be higher than the present level of the core. Many centuries of demolition have resulted in the loss of virtually all the casing stones of the buildings in the complex leaving piles of granite chips, some as high as 5 m.

A perpendicular shaft, measuring 23 m east–west and 10 m north–south, was sunk through the center of the rock to a depth of more than 20 m. At the bottom were the burial chamber and at least one antechamber, probably built of granite, with access from a northern entrance corridor. The chambers may have had corbel roofs or roofs with superimposed relieving compartments, like those in the Great Pyramid. Only some fragments of the king's granite sarcophagus have been found, but enough to suggest that it resembled the oval sarcophagus in the Unfinished Pyramid at Zawiyet el-Aryan.

The entrance corridor, now destroyed, opened low on the north face of the pyramid. Its length was about 49 m, oriented 21′ west of north and with a slope of 26°, increasing to 28°. The flat roof was constructed of slabs of granite and the thick walls of local stone, faced on the inside with granite. The floor was paved with limestone. It was constructed in an open trench which varied in width from 5.5 m to 7.0 m. The corridor was only about 1 m wide, but the trench needed to be wider so that the sarcophagus and massive floor blocks could be transported into the pyramid. This operation required enough space for workmen (and possibly oxen). Failure to make such a provision in the Great Pyramid may explain why Khufu's sarcophagus had to be placed in the superstructure.

At the time of the king's death, work on the mortuary temple on the east side of the pyramid had not advanced beyond the construction of a court with a granite-paved floor. The necessary buildings were hastily constructed of mudbrick overlaid with a thick layer of plaster, undoubtedly painted to simulate stone. Among the few objects found were statues of three sons and two daughters of Djedefre, a painted limestone female sphinx and a small wooden hippopotamus. Outside the pyramid on the south side was a pit for a wooden boat more than 37 m long and 9.5 m deep in the middle. A small subsidiary pyramid stood opposite the southwest corner of the main pyramid. A causeway 1500 m in length and 14 m wide linked the pyramid enclosure with the valley temple next to the floodplain.

Despite its ruined state, the pyramid complex of Djedefre has yielded much of archaeological importance. By their design, the oval sarcophagus and the wide trench for the entrance corridor to the pyramid have helped to establish the date of the Unfinished Pyramid at Zawiyet el-Aryan. The discovery of circular bases and part of the shaft of a round column have shown that free-standing round columns were in use at an earlier date than had been supposed. North of the pyramid is a large enclosure of a kind known from step pyramids but not used with true pyramids until the Middle Kingdom. The mortuary temple had a very different plan from that of any other known temple, and the 1500 m causeway leading from the Wadi Qaren to the pyramid is without parallel. Also important are the many artifacts which have been found in the excavations, including, most notably, three fine quartzite heads from broken life-size statues of the king now in the Louvre and the Cairo Museum.

Near the mouth of the Wadi Qaren are the remains of a Coptic monastery mentioned by the Arab historian Maqrizi (AD 1364–1442) as being one of the most beautiful and best situated monasteries in Egypt. Built on a mound, it provided a fine view of the Nile. Also at the mouth of the wadi are the ruins of a mudbrick fort believed to date from the Middle Kingdom.

See also

Lepsius, Carl Richard; Old Kingdom, overview; pyramids (Old Kingdom), construction of; Zawiyet el-Aryan

Further reading

Edwards, I.E.S. 1994. Chephren's place among the kings of the Fourth Dynasty. In *The Unbroken Reed: Studies in the Culture and Heritage of Ancient Egypt in Honour of A. F. Shore*, C. Eyre, A. Leahy and L.M. Leahy, eds, 97–105. London.

Klasens, A. 1975. Abu Roach. In *LÄ* 1: 24–5. Wiesbaden.

Maragioglio, V., and C. Rinaldi. 1966. *L'Architettura delle Piramidi Menfite* 5: 10–40. Rapallo.

Porter, B., and R.L.B. Moss, revised by J. Málek. 1974. *Topographical Bibliography of Ancient Egyptian Hieroglyphic Texts, Reliefs and Paintings* 3. *Memphis*, 1–10. Oxford.

Valloggia, M. 1995. *Fouilles archéologiques à Abu Rawash (Égypte). Rapport préliminaire de la Campagne 1995*. Geneva, n.s. 43.

I.E.S. EDWARDS

Abu Sha'ar

The late Roman (*circa* late third–sixth centuries AD) fort at Abu Sha'ar or Deir Umm Deheis (27°22′ N, 33°41′ E) on the Red Sea coast is *circa* 20 km north of Hurgada and *circa* 2–3 km east of the main Hurgada–Suez highway. The fort is *circa* 25 m from the Red Sea at high tide. It sits on a natural sand and gravel bank several metres above the mud flats to the west; artificial ditches to the north and south augmented fort defenses. Visitors in the first half of the nineteenth century, including James Burton, J.G. Wilkinson, J.R. Wellsted and Richard Lepsius, erroneously identified the site with the Ptolemaic–Roman emporium of Myos Hormos, as have some subsequent visitors and scholars.

Excavations by the University of Delaware (1987–93) revealed a fort built as part of the overall late third–early fourth centuries AD reorganization of frontier defenses throughout the entire Eastern Roman empire. The fort at Abu Sha'ar is of moderate dimensions with defensive walls enclosing an area *circa* 77.5 m × 64 m. Walls were *circa* 3.5–4 m high (including parapet) and 1.5 m thick (including a 0.5 m wide catwalk). The walls were built of stacked igneous cobbles (from the foot of Gebel Abu Sha'ar, 5.5–6 km west of Abu Sha'ar) with little binding material (mud). The fort had 12–13 quadrilaterally shaped towers of unequal dimensions built

FORT AT ABU SHA'AR

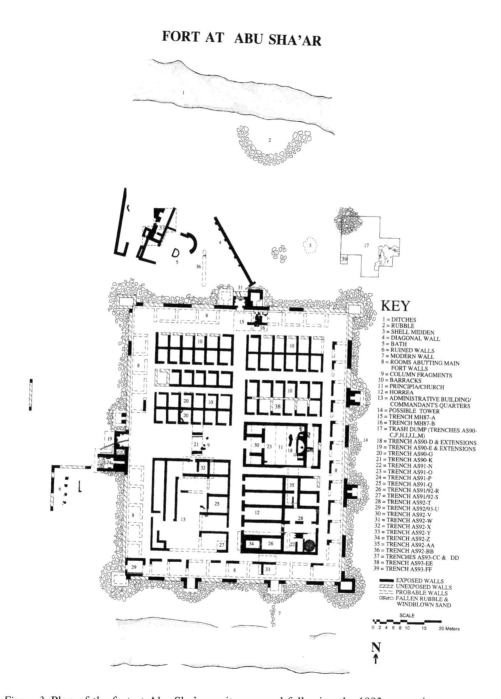

KEY

1 = DITCHES
2 = RUBBLE
3 = SHELL MIDDEN
4 = DIAGONAL WALL
5 = BATH
6 = RUINED WALLS
7 = MODERN WALL
8 = ROOMS ABUTTING MAIN
    FORT WALLS
9 = COLUMN FRAGMENTS
10 = BARRACKS
11 = PRINCIPIA/CHURCH
12 = HORREA
13 = ADMINISTRATIVE BUILDING/
    COMMANDANT'S QUARTERS
14 = POSSIBLE TOWER
15 = TRENCH MH87-A
16 = TRENCH MH87-B
17 = TRASH DUMP (TRENCHES AS90-
    C,F,H,I,J,L,M)
18 = TRENCH AS90-D & EXTENSIONS
19 = TRENCH AS90-E & EXTENSIONS
20 = TRENCH AS90-G
21 = TRENCH AS90-K
22 = TRENCH AS91-N
23 = TRENCH AS91-O
24 = TRENCH AS91-P
25 = TRENCH AS91-Q
26 = TRENCH AS91/92-R
27 = TRENCH AS91/92-S
28 = TRENCH AS92-T
29 = TRENCH AS92/93-U
30 = TRENCH AS92-V
31 = TRENCH AS92-W
32 = TRENCH AS92-X
33 = TRENCH AS92-Y
34 = TRENCH AS92-Z
35 = TRENCH AS92-AA
36 = TRENCH AS92-BB
37 = TRENCHES AS93-CC & DD
38 = TRENCH AS93-EE
39 = TRENCH AS93-FF

▬▬▬ EXPOSED WALLS
▨▨▨ UNEXPOSED WALLS
▭▭▭ PROBABLE WALLS
⌗⌗⌗ FALLEN RUBBLE &
    WINDBLOWN SAND

SCALE
0 2 4 6 8 10   15   20 Meters

N
↑

Figure 3 Plan of the fort at Abu Sha'ar as it appeared following the 1993 excavations

85

of white gypsum blocks atop bases of gray igneous cobbles; the bottom interior portions of the towers were rubble filled. There were two main gates: a smaller one at the center north wall and a larger one at the center west wall. The main (west) gate was originally decorated with an arch and carved, decorated and painted (red and yellow) console blocks and other architectural elements. One or more Latin inscriptions recorded the Roman emperors Galerius, Licinius I, Maximinus II, Constantine I and the Roman governor Aurelius Maximinus (*dux Aegypti Thebaidos utrarumque Libyarum*). An inscription dates fort construction, or possibly "reconstruction," to AD 309–11. The garrison was a portion of the *Ala Nova Maximiana*, a mounted unit (probably dromedary) of approximately 200 men.

Gypsum catapult balls from the towers and fort indicate the presence of artillery. Sling stones suggest another mode of defense. No other weapons have been discovered nor is there evidence of deliberate destruction of the fort; it seems to have been peacefully abandoned by the military some time before the late fourth–early fifth centuries, a trend found elsewhere in the eastern Roman empire at that time. Following a period of abandonment, Christian squatters reoccupied the fort. Parts of the fort interior were used as trash dumps, while other areas were inhabited. The *principia* was converted into a church and the north gate became the principal entrance into the fortified area. Scores of graffiti, Christian crosses and two major ecclesiastical inscriptions in Greek at the north gate attest to the importance of Abu Sha'ar as a pilgrimage center at that time.

A short distance outside the fort northwest of the north gate was a semicircular bath built of kiln-fired bricks covered with waterproof lime mortar. Other rooms of the bath, including a hypocaust, lay immediately to the west. Adjacent to the bath and northeast of the north gate were trash dumps; the former was late fourth–early fifth centuries, the latter fourth century. Immediately outside the north gate was a low diagonal wall of white gypsum *circa* 22 m long; its function remains unknown. The fort interior had 38–9 rooms abutting the inside faces of the main fort walls (average dimensions: 4.4–5.4 × 3.2–3.6 m). These may have served multiple purposes including storage, guardroom facilities and, perhaps, living quarters. On the northern interior side were 54 barracks; 24 larger ones in the northeast quadrant averaged 3.0 × 4.0 m. Thirty others in the northwest quadrant averaged 3.0–3.1 × 3.3–3.4 m. The lower walls were built of igneous cobbles *circa* 0.95 m high, and the upper walls of mudbrick were of approximately the same height, for a total barracks height of *circa* 1.9 m. Roofing was of wood (mainly acacia), matting and bundles of *Juncus arabicus*.

The *principia*/church in the center-east part of the fort was 12.6–12.8 × 22 m, and *circa* 2.4–2.6 m high. It had an apse toward the east end, two rooms flanking the apse, and two rooms behind (east of) the apse which did not lead directly into the main part of the building. There were two column pedestals adjacent to (west of) the apse and there seem to have been wooden dividers separating the nave from the side aisles. Two smaller rooms at the west end flanked the building entrance. Roofing was of wood and bundled *Juncus arabicus*. A military duty roster dating no later than the fourth century, a Christian inscription of the fourth–sixth century, a textile cross embroidery, a 27-line papyrus in Greek from the fifth centuries, and human adult male bones wrapped in cloth were all found inside this building. The latter discovery in front of the apse suggested a cult of a martyr or saint, an especially popular practice in early Coptic religion.

The main entrance of the *principia*/church faced east onto a colonnaded street which led to the main west gate. White gypsum columns (*circa* 46–8 cm in diameter), sat on two parallel socles (stylobates) of gray igneous cobbles. At least two columns with spherical bases also decorated one or both of the stylobates. The street between the stylobates was *circa* 4.6–4.7 m wide. The buildings in the southeastern quadrant included five storage magazines (*horrea*) fronting the main north–south street. East of these in the same block were a kitchen, which included a large circular oven *circa* 3.4 m in diameter made of kiln-fired bricks, small "pantries" and milling (grain, olives) areas.

A road joined the fort at Abu Sha'ar to the main (parent) camp at Luxor via Kainopolis (Qena) on the Nile *circa* 181 km to the southwest. This road, dotted with cairns, signal and route marking towers and installations, including *hydreumata* (fortified water stations), facilitated traffic between Abu Sha'ar and the Nile, supported work crews hauling stone from the quarries at Mons Porphyrites (first–fourth centuries AD) and Mons Claudianus (first–third/early fourth centuries AD) and assisted Christian pilgrims traveling between points in Upper Egypt and holy sites in the Eastern Desert (Abu Sha'ar, monasteries of St Paul and St Anthony), Sinai (such as the Monastery of St Catherine) and the Holy Land itself via Aila (Aqaba). The fort and road also monitored activities of the local bedouin (Nobatae and Blemmyes), and may also have protected commercial activity.

See also

Mons Porphyrites; Roman forts in Egypt; Roman period, overview; Roman ports, Red Sea; Wadi Hammamat

Further reading

Sidebotham, S.E. 1992. A Roman fort on the Red Sea coast. *Minerva* 3(2): 5–8.
——. 1994. Preliminary report on the 1990–1991 seasons of fieldwork at Abu Sha'ar (Red Sea Coast). *JARCE* 31: 133–58, also 159–68 on documents from the site.
Sidebotham, S.E., R.E. Zitterkopf and J.A. Riley. 1991. Survey of the Abu Sha'ar–Nile Road. *AJA* 95(4): 571–622.

STEVEN E. SIDEBOTHAM

Abu Simbel

Abu Simbel (22°21′ N, 31°38′ E) is situated 280 km south of Aswan on the west bank of the Nile and approximately 52 km north of the modern political boundary between Egypt and Sudan. Before the building of the Aswan High Dam (1960–70) and the subsequent flooding of Lake Nasser, there was a relatively rich agricultural zone on the east bank that extended down to the northern end of the Second Cataract region. In antiquity, this was one of the most populated regions in the typically narrow and barren river valley of Lower Nubia.

The site of Abu Simbel is famous for the two rock-cut temples built during the reign of Ramesses II (19th Dynasty), not far from the earlier shrine of Horemheb at Abu Hoda. The site seems to have been previously considered sacred; there are numerous graffiti of the Old and Middle Kingdoms on the cliff face. Several inscriptions in the Small Temple refer to the cliff into which the temples were constructed as the "Holy Mountain."

Although the Great Temple was dedicated to Re-Horakhty (Re-Horus of the Horizon), Amen and Ptah, many images of the deified king himself are also found in this temple. Its ancient name was "The Temple of Ramesses-Mery-Amen" (Ramesses II, Beloved of Amen). The Small Temple was dedicated to both Hathor of Ibshek (the nearby site of Faras) and Queen Nefertari. Twice a year, when the rising sun appeared above the horizon on the east bank, its rays passed through the entrance and halls of the Great Temple to illuminate the statues in the innermost sanctuary.

In 1813, John Lewis Burckhardt stopped at Abu Simbel on his way up the Nile to Dongola, and thus became the first European to visit the site in modern times and record his experiences. Giovanni Belzoni, however, seems to have been the first to enter the Great Temple's halls, when he had the sand cleared from the structure in 1817. Carl Richard Lepsius copied the reliefs on the walls when he visited the site in 1844. Auguste Mariette again cleared the structure of sand in 1869.

These temples were relocated in 1964–8 as part of the UNESCO campaign to rescue the monuments that were eventually to be flooded by the Nile after the completion of the Aswan High Dam. The structures, originally built inside two sandstone cliffs, were cut into blocks and reassembled at a site about 210 m away from the river and some 65 m higher up, atop the cliffs. Sections of the cliff face into which the façades were constructed were also removed and re-erected on an artificial hill built around the relocated temples. The repositioning of the buildings slightly changed the alignment of the Great Temple, so that the sanctuary is now illuminated one day later (22 February and 22 October) than it was originally.

Rock stelae and surrounding area

Rock-cut stelae are located in the cliff face north and south of the entrances of the two temples, and also between them. A number of small inscriptions near the northern and southern ends of the cliff face date to the Middle Kingdom, while one at the northern end is attributed to a "Viceroy of Kush" during the reign of Amenhotep I. Most of the stelae, however, were dedicated by high officials of the Ramesside period.

Although no settlement remains were ever identified in the vicinity of the temples, the statue of Re-Horakhty in the innermost sanctuary of the Great Temple is carved with an inscription mentioning "Horakhty in the midst of the town of the Temple/House of Ramesses-Mery-Amen."

The Great Temple

A gate on the north of an enclosure once led into a forecourt of the Great Temple. Four colossal seated statues of Ramesses II (over 20 m high), wearing the Double Crown of Upper and Lower Egypt, were placed on a terrace on the western side of the court. Smaller standing statues of Queen Nefertari, the queen-mother Muttuya, and some of the royal children, embrace the king's legs. The colossi to the south of the temple entrance have Carian, Ionian Greek and Phoenician graffiti inscribed on the legs. Some of these inscriptions were left by foreign mercenaries during the campaign of Psamtik II against the Kushites in the early sixth century BC.

At the ends of the terrace are two decorated chapels, dedicated to the worship of Re-Horakhty and Thoth (north and south ends, respectively). Stelae are also found carved on the terrace's north and south ends. One large stela records the marriage of Ramesses II to a Hittite princess in the thirty-fourth year of his reign.

The façade behind the statues has the shape of a pylon, topped by a cavetto cornice upon which stand a row of baboons, facing east, with their arms raised in adoration of the rising sun. Over the entrance into the temple is a statue of the sun god Re-Horakhty, a falcon-headed god wearing the solar disk crown. A relief depicts the king offering an image of the goddess of truth (Ma'at) to this god. This sculptural group is a cryptographic writing of the prenomen of Ramesses II, "Userma'atre" (the falcon-headed god Re has by his right leg the hieroglyph showing the head and neck of an animal which is read as *user*, while the goddess by his left leg is Ma'at).

The sides of the terrace along the passage into the temple are carved with the cartouches of the king and with rows of Asiatic and Nubian captives (north and south sides, respectively). The side panels on the innermost thrones are carved with a traditional scene representing the union of Upper and Lower Egypt, depicting two Nile gods binding together the plant emblems of Upper and Lower Egypt (the lotus and the papyrus).

The main hypostyle hall of this temple has two rows of four pillars topped by Hathor heads and decorated with figures of the king and queen giving offerings to various deities. Osiride figures of the king, 10 m in height, are carved against each pillar. Between the third and fourth Osiride figures on the south is the text of a decree which records the building of the Northern Residence (Pi-Ramesses) in the thirty-fourth year of Ramesses II's reign, as well as his marriage to a Hittite princess. The ceiling of the hall is decorated with flying vultures and royal cartouches.

The reliefs along the north and south walls show various military campaigns conducted by Ramesses II in Syria, Libya and Nubia. The north wall shows Ramesses II and his troops at the Battle of Qadesh in 1285 BC, a battle fought against the Hittites in Syria. The Egyptians appear as victors in these scenes, but other inscriptional sources demonstrate that they did not in fact win the battle. Ramesses II is depicted giving offerings to the gods at the top of the opposite wall, while the lower register shows him storming a Syrian fortress in his chariot, accompanied by some of his sons. He also single-handedly tramples and kills Libyan enemies and herds Nubian captives to Egypt.

The entrance and back walls depict the king killing enemies of Egypt and presenting them to various deities, including himself. On the entrance walls, he is accompanied by his *ka* and some of the royal children. Below this scene, on the north side, is a graffito noting that this relief (along with perhaps all the others) was carved by Piay, son of Khanefer, the sculptor of Ramesses-Mery-Amen. Above the door on the back wall, the king is shown either running toward various deities with different ritual objects in his hands or standing before the gods with offerings. The reliefs in the eight side rooms off the main hall include scenes of Ramesses II either making offerings or worshipping gods.

The entrance to the second hypostyle hall was originally flanked by two hawk-headed sphinxes, which are now in the British Museum. The scenes on the walls and pillars of this room, and in the vestibule leading into the sanctuary, are purely religious in character. The deification of Ramesses II during his lifetime is once again apparent in the reliefs of the halls and the sanctuary. The king is shown presenting offerings to himself or performing religious rites before a sacred bark representing his deified person. Representations of the king as a god were sometimes added to scenes after the initial compositions were carved.

The western wall of the vestibule has three doorways. The southern and northern doors lead into two empty and uninscribed rooms. The central door leads into the sanctuary, where the rather poorly carved figures of Ptah, Amen, the deified Ramesses II and Re-Horakhty were placed against the back wall of the sanctuary. The seated quartet were illuminated twice a year by the rays of the rising sun.

On either side of the doorway a figure of the king with arm extended is accompanied by an inscription exhorting the priests: "Enter into the sanctuary thrice purified!" The scenes on the walls show Ramesses worshipping deities. An uninscribed, broken altar stands in the middle of the room in front of the statues.

The Small Temple

Access to the temple of Hathor and Nefertari is gained through a door on the northern side of the enclosure wall surrounding the Great Temple. The plan of this temple mirrors that of the larger temple to its south, but on a smaller scale. The pylon-shaped façade of this temple (about 28 m long) was also originally topped by a cavetto cornice. On each side of the entrance are three niches. A standing statue of Nefertari (over 10 m high) is between two statues of Ramesses II, each of them placed in niches separated by projecting buttresses. The statues are surrounded by small figures of the royal children.

The roof of the hypostyle hall is supported by six pillars, decorated with various royal and divine figures. The pillars are topped with heads of Hathor. On the entrance walls, the king slaughters his enemies before Amen and Horus, with Nefertari looking on. The walls on the north, south and west of the hypostyle hall have reliefs with ritual and offering scenes involving the king and queen and various deities.

Three doorways on the west end of this hall lead into the vestibule. The walls in this room are carved with reliefs depicting the royal couple with the gods. Doorways in the north and south walls lead into two uninscribed chambers. Above the doors are scenes of Nefertari and Ramesses making an offering to the Hathor cow, which stands on a bark in the marshes.

The doorway into the sanctuary is in the middle of the vestibule's west wall. On the back wall of this innermost room is carved the frontal figure of the Hathor cow emerging from the papyrus marshes. The figure of Ramesses II stands protected under its head. Two Hathor pillars stand at either side of this statue group. The walls around this focal point are adorned with the usual scenes of the king and queen accompanied by various deities, including Ramesses II giving offerings to the deified Ramesses II and Nefertari.

See also

Belzoni, Giovanni Baptista; cult temples of the New Kingdom; Late and Ptolemaic periods, overview; Lepsius, Carl Richard; Mariette, François Auguste Ferdinand; New Kingdom, overview

Further reading

El-Achirie, H., and J. Jacquet, with F. Hébert and B. Maurice. 1984. *Le grand temple d'Abou-Simbel* I, 1: *Architecture*. Cairo.
Desroches-Noblecourt, C., and C. Kuentz. 1968. *La petit temple d'Abou-Simbel: Nofretari pour qui se lève le dieu-soleil*, 1 and 2. Cairo.
MacQuitty, W. 1965. *Abu Simbel*. London.
Otto, E. 1972. Abu Simbel. *LÄ* 1: 25–7.
Säve-Söderbergh, T. 1987. *Temples and Tombs of Ancient Nubia*. London.

LISA A. HEIDORN

Abusir

Abusir is a village west of the Nile (29°53′ N, 31°13′ E), about 17.5 km south of the pyramids of Giza. The name of the village is the Arabic rendering of the ancient Egyptian Per-Wesir, which means "House of Osiris." For the greater part of the 5th Dynasty royalty and many high officials were buried in pyramids and *mastaba* tombs in its necropolis on the edge of the desert. In 1838 J.S. Perring cleared the entrances to the pyramids of Sahure, Neferirkare and Nyuserre, the second, third and sixth kings of the dynasty, and surveyed them. Richard Lepsius explored the necropolis in 1843 and numbered the three pyramids XVIII, XXI and XX.

In 1902–8 Ludwig Borchardt, working for the Deutsche Orient-Gesellschaft, resurveyed the same pyramids and also excavated their adjoining temples and causeways with spectacular results, especially in the complex of Sahure. In every building except the pyramid itself, the inner stone walls had been furnished with painted reliefs depicting the king's activities and ritual acts, some undoubtedly traditional. Borchardt estimated that the reliefs in the mortuary temple of Sahure alone had occupied a total of 10,000 m square, of which no more than 150 m square had been preserved, mostly in fragments. A notable survival was a representation of the king hunting, with bow and arrow, antelopes, gazelles and other animals. Perhaps the best known scenes, however, were two located on either side of a doorway in the western corridor. In one the king was witnessing the departure of twelve seafaring ships, probably to a Syrian port, and in the other he and his retinue were present when the ships docked, bearing not only their cargo but also some Asiatic passengers. Besides the wall reliefs, the most conspicuous features in the temple were the polished black basalt floor of the open court and the monolithic granite columns, some representing single palm trees with their leaves tied vertically upward, and others a cluster of papyrus stems bound together.

Much attention had been paid to drainage at the temple. Rainwater on the roof was conducted to the outside through spouts carved with lion heads. On the floor were channels for rainwater cut in the paving which led to holes in the walls. Water which had become ritually unclean ran through 300 m of copper pipes to an outlet at the lower end of the causeway.

Since 1976 an expedition of the Institute of Egyptology, Prague University, under the direction of Miroslav Verner, has excavated an area at Abusir south of the causeway of the pyramid of Nyuserre. They have uncovered several *mastaba*s of the late 5th Dynasty, mostly tombs of members of the royal family, and two pyramids—one belonging to a queen named

Khentkaues (apparently Nyuserre's mother), and the other to the fourth king of the 5th Dynasty, Reneferef (or Neferefre). Another pyramid, which, if it had been finished, would have been the largest at Abusir, was also investigated by the expedition. This pyramid is situated north of the pyramid of Sahure, and it may have been intended for Shepseskare, Reneferef's successor. Reneferef's pyramid, just southwest of the pyramid of Neferirkare, was also unfinished. It was left in a truncated form, like a square *mastaba*, no doubt because of the king's premature death. Among the main features of Reneferef's mortuary temple were a hypostyle hall, with wooden lotus-cluster columns mounted on limestone bases, and two wooden boats, one more than 30 m long, in place of the usual statue niches. A number of broken stone figures, six with heads representing the king, were found in rooms near the hypostyle hall.

One of the best known monuments of Abusir is the *mastaba* of the vizier Ptahshepses, a son-in-law of Nyuserre, and his wife, close to the northeastern corner of the pyramid of Nyuserre. First excavated in 1893 by J. de Morgan, Director of the Egyptian Antiquities Service, it was re-excavated and restored over many years by Z. Žába of Prague University, who was assisted by members of the Antiquities Service. Next to the vizier's tomb are the *mastaba* of his children and a few other tombs dating to later in the dynasty. A graffito by two scribes, who recorded their visit here in the fiftieth year of the reign of Ramesses II, shows that, like the Step Pyramid of Zoser, Ptahshepses's *mastaba* was already a tourist attraction in antiquity.

Six sun temples of kings of the 5th Dynasty are known by name from texts, but only those of Weserkaf and Nyuserre have been found. Both were built at Abu Gurab, a short distance north of the pyramid of Sahure.

At Abusir, alone among the sites of pyramids, written documents have been found which inform about the duties performed by the priesthoods of the pyramids in the necropolis. Known as the Abusir Papyri, the published documents refer to the priests of the pyramid of Neferirkare. They show that records of attendance were kept, and that temple furniture and property were checked by the priests in the course of their tours of duty. Most of these fragmentary papyri were found in the temple of Neferirkare by illicit diggers in 1893. More papyri, as yet unpublished, have since been found by the Prague University expedition in the pyramid complexes of Queen Khentkaues and Reneferef.

See also

Abu Gurab; Memphite private tombs of the Old Kingdom; Old Kingdom, overview; Saqqara, pyramids of the 3rd Dynasty; Saqqara, pyramids of the 5th and 6th Dynasties

Further reading

Edwards, I.E.S. 1993. *The Pyramids of Egypt*, 153–72. Harmondsworth.

Maragioglio, V., and C. Rinaldi. 1977. *L'Architettura delle Piramidi Menfite* 8: 8–57. Rapallo.

Porter, B., and R.L.B. Moss, revised by J. Málek. 1974. *Topographical Bibliography of Ancient Egyptian Hieroglyphic Texts, Reliefs and Paintings* 3: *Memphis*, 314–50. Oxford.

Verner, M. 1994. *Forgotten Pharaohs, Lost Pyramids. Abusir*. Prague.

I.E.S. EDWARDS

Abusir el-Meleq

Near the village of Abusir el-Meleq a late Predynastic cemetery (Nagada IId2–IIIb, *circa* 3250–3050 BC) was discovered on the northeast edge of Gebel Abusir, a desert ridge several kilometers in length running in a northeast–southwest direction along the west bank of the Nile near the entrance to the Fayum (29°15′ N, 31°05′ E). This cemetery, along with the nearby cemeteries of Gerza and Haraga (somewhat earlier in date), and that of Kafr Tarkhan (with somewhat later burials), exemplify the developed and late stages of the Nagada culture in northern Upper Egypt.

The first Predynastic graves were discovered at Abusir el-Meleq by Otto Rubensohn in his 1902–4 expedition, which also revealed priests' graves of the Late period and scattered burials from the 18th Dynasty. Under the auspices of the German Orient-Gesellschaft, Georg Möller excavated the Predynastic cemetery in 1905–6, also exposing several burials of the Hyksos period (15th–16th Dynasties). Ruins of a temple built by Nectanebo (30th Dynasty) were discovered near the village mosque, and it was presumed that this area might represent the location of the Lower Egyptian sanctuary of Osiris.

The late Predynastic cemetery, divided into two sections by a strip of exposed bedrock, covered an area nearly 4 km in length, varying from 100 m to 400 m in width. In the larger section to the north some 700 burials were found; another 150 were in the southern section. The human remains had been placed in graves generally 0.80–1.20 m deep, either long ovals or—more frequently—rectangular in shape. The rectangular graves were usually plastered with mud and fully or partially reinforced with mudbrick. Traces of wood and matting were interpreted as remains of wall coverings or possibly ceilings. Fifteen graves in the southern section had been constructed with a special feature, a grill-like bed of several "beams" of mudbrick, each 0.10–0.25 m high and 0.10–0.20 m wide, laid at intervals transversely across the floor of the graves.

With few exceptions, the deceased had been placed in a contracted position on the left side, facing west with the head to the south. Clay sarcophagi were found in four graves, three of which were child burials. One wooden coffin was found in another grave. Many of the graves had been plundered in antiquity. Wavy-handled jars, apparently containers for ointments, stood near the head, while other vessels (usually storage jars for food for the deceased) had been placed at the feet of the burial. Animal bones indicated frequent offerings of meat. More valuable gifts were generally found near the hands or on the body. Pottery and stone

vessels, as well as large flint knives, had often been rendered unserviceable by piercing or breaking, a procedure which has been variously interpreted as a ceremonial sacrifice of the artifacts themselves, or possibly as a measure against potential grave robbing.

Reflecting the general characteristics of Upper Egypt, the pottery from the graves dates to the later Predynastic period (Nagada IId2–IIId). Red Polished class (P-), Rough class (R-) and Late class (L-) are well represented. The relative abundance of black-polished pottery is noteworthy, while Black-topped Red class (B-) is infrequent. Among the Decorated class (D-) are vessels painted with a net pattern, with wavy handles—thus overlapping with the Wavy-handled class (W-)—as well as vessels painted in imitation of stone. Other Decorated class pots have motifs of ships, animals and landscapes. Occasionally potmarks are found. Certain vessel forms, including lug-handled bottles painted with vertical stripes and a bowl with knob decorations, suggest the influence of the Early Bronze Age in Palestine.

Some ninety-five relatively small stone vessels were recovered from the graves. Characteristic are jars with pierced lug handles and bowls made of colorful rock of volcanic origin. Two theriomorphic vessels and one tripartite vase are unusual. Vessels of alabaster appear to have been more common here than in Upper Egypt.

Other small vessels were made of ivory, shell, horn, faïence and copper. There were also copper chisels or adzes, a fragment of a dagger, a few pins and beads, as well as bracelets. One bracelet was cast with a snake in high relief; another had crocodiles. Artifacts in bone and ivory, some of which are decorated, include spoons, pins, cosmetic sticks and combs, one of which had a handle in the form of a bird. Most of the palettes, in slate and other stones, are decorated. Some are shaped like animals or have birds' heads on one end, but simple geometric forms are unusual.

Flint blades, 3–10 cm long, were often found in the graves, frequently in pairs. Smaller obsidian blades were also relatively common, and a total of fifteen large, ripple-flaked flint knives were recovered, all broken in the same manner. One grave contained three transverse "arrowheads" of flint.

Six pear-shaped stone maceheads were recorded, one with a bull's head in relief. Other small finds include various articles of jewelry: bracelets or armbands of shell, ivory, leather and horn, and many beads of stone, copper, shell and faïence. A few small carved animal figurines (dogs, lions and a hippopotamus) were also excavated. An ivory cylinder seal carved with three rows of animals (dogs, a crocodile, antelopes, jackals, a scorpion, snake and vultures) was found in Grave 1035. Of local manufacture, this cylinder seal is a type of artifact that originated in Mesopotamia, as did its orientalizing motifs.

When we consider the northern location of the Abusir el-Meleq cemetery, not only are the occurrences of the cylinder seal and the several vessels of Palestinian influence significant, but also two types of skeletons have been distinguished in the anthropological study. An "Upper Egyptian" type occurs, but there is also a more robust "Lower Egyptian" type, which may represent the descendants of the Predynastic Ma'adi culture of Lower Egypt. In the fourth millennium BC, Abusir el-Meleq must have played some role in the colonization of Lower Egypt by peoples of the Upper Egyptian Nagada culture, which resulted in the subsequent disappearance of the Lower Egyptian Ma'adi culture. The site may have been an outlying post regulating the routes of communication to trade colonies in the Delta, such as Buto and Minshat Abu Omar.

Figure 4 Design on carved ivory seal, Abusir el-Meleq, Grave 1035

See also

Buto (Tell el-Fara'in); Fayum, Neolithic and Predynastic sites; Hyksos; Kafr Tarkhan (Kafr Ammar); Ma'adi and the Wadi Digla; Minshat Abu Omar; Nagada (Naqada); pottery, prehistoric; Predynastic period, overview

Further reading

Kaiser, W. 1990. Zur Entstehung des gesamtägyptischen Staates. *MDAIK* 46: 287–99.

Möller, G., and A. Scharff. 1926. *Die Archaeologischen Ergebnisse des Vorgeschichtlichen Gräberfeldes von Abusir el-Meleq.* Leipzig.

Müller, F.W.K. 1915. *Das Vorgeschichtliche Gräberfeld von Abusir el-Meleq, Band II. Die Anthropologischen Ergebnisse.* Leipzig.

JÜRGEN SEEHER

Abydos, Early Dynastic funerary enclosures

The rulers of the 1st Dynasty and the last two of the 2nd Dynasty were buried at Abydos (26°11′ N, 31°55′ E). Some scholars have argued that the true tombs were at Saqqara, and the Abydos ones were cenotaphs or dummy burials, but this is unlikely: the enclosures described here do not occur at Saqqara. Clustered together far back from the inhabited floodplain, the large subterranean tombs of Abydos had modest superstructures; 1.96 km due north were the public manifestations of the royal funerary cult, large mudbrick enclosures easily visible to the local population.

Corresponding to the burials, ten enclosures must have been built; eight have been located (one in 1997 by a ground-penetrating radar survey). The specific owners of some are unknown, but others are identified by inscriptions (Djer, Djet and the queen-mother Merneith of the 1st Dynasty; Peribsen and Khasekhemwy of the 2nd Dynasty). Eventually, the enclosures formed three irregular rows. The earliest may have clustered around that of Aḥa (not yet identified), the founder of the dynasty. Later enclosures lay northwest, while the last two (2nd Dynasty) were southwest of the earliest cluster.

The features of a generic enclosure can only be tentatively reconstructed, since data on individual ones are very incomplete. The area each occupied varied. Some, on average, covered 2560 m², others 5100 m². At the extremes, one was only 1740 m², while Khasekhemwy's was 10,395 m². Most were rectangular in plan, usually with the average ratio of 1:1.8; one was 1:4, another 1:2.4. Three (and presumably all 1st Dynasty enclosures, like the royal tombs) were surrounded by subsidiary graves for attendants dispatched at the time of the royal funeral. Aḥa's subsidiary graves were perhaps adjacent to his enclosure, rather than surrounding, and 2nd Dynasty enclosures had none.

Externally, the enclosures were impressive. As much as 11 m high, their walls were plastered and whitewashed. A low bench ran around the footings of 1st Dynasty walls, while Khasekhemwy's enclosure had a unique perimeter wall, lower than the main one.

The eastern (actually northeastern) aspect of each enclosure was especially significant, perhaps because it faced the rising sun, already a symbol of rebirth after death, as later. On the northeast face, the simple niching typical of the enclosures was regularly interspersed with deeper, more complex niches, and the entrance was near the east corner. Highest ranking subsidiary graves clustered near this entrance. In 1st Dynasty enclosures the entrance was architecturally elaborate, and in 2nd Dynasty ones it provided access to a substantial chapel within the enclosure.

Internally, these chapels display complex ritual paths, and presumably housed the deceased king's statue. Offerings were made there, as evidenced by the masses of discarded offering pottery and broken jar sealings (many inscribed). However, no cult seems to have continued beyond a successor's reign, and ritual activity might have been short-lived.

Each enclosure's northwest wall also had an entrance, near the north corner. Simple in plan,

these were soon bricked up after each 1st Dynasty enclosure was completed. Second Dynasty entrances were larger, more complex architecturally and apparently kept open. This development may relate to a substantial mound-like feature, traces of which occurred in the west quadrant of Khasekhemwy's enclosure, relatively close to the northwest wall entrance. Otherwise, virtually nothing is known about structures, other than chapels, within each enclosure.

Nested among the enclosures were twelve large boat graves, their total number confirmed by investigations in 1997. Arranged in a row, each grave parallel to the others, they average 27 m in length. Each consists of a shallow trench cut in the desert surface, in which a shallow wooden hull was placed and surrounded by a mudbrick casing, rising *circa* 50 cm above the desert surface. Plastered and whitewashed, the resulting superstructures, schematically shaped as boats with prominent "prows" and "sterns," must have resembled a moored fleet, and were even supplied with rough stone "anchors." To which of the four adjacent enclosures these boat graves belonged is uncertain. Although single boat graves are occasionally found with contemporary elite, non-royal tombs, the Abydos ones are unique in number, proximity, size and, to some extent, form. Presumably, each boat was believed to be used by the deceased king when he traversed the sky and the netherworld, as described in later funerary texts (*Pyramid Texts*).

The Abydos royal tombs are adjacent to those of pre-1st Dynasty rulers who may also have had enclosures, near the later ones. Like the tombs, these enclosures were likely quite small, and recognizable traces have not yet been found. An enclosure at Hierakonpolis, dating to Khasekhemwy's reign, is about half the size of this king's enclosure at Abydos. Like the latter, it had an outer perimeter wall and massive main walls, but it is square (ratio 1:1.20), not rectangular in plan, has only one entrance (northeast wall, near the east corner), and a centrally, rather than peripherally, located chapel. Its purpose is unknown. Perhaps Khasekhemwy originally planned to be buried at Hierakonpolis, although no tomb for him is known there.

Within the early town at Hierakonpolis were two large, mudbrick enclosures very reminiscent of the Abydos ones in plan, but housing temples rather than royal funerary chapels. However, one was at least built (or rebuilt?) in part in the Old Kingdom, and the other, of which only the gateway (northwest wall) survives, has also been identified as a palace.

Prior to Peribsen, 2nd Dynasty kings were buried at Saqqara. Their supposed tombs differ in plan from those of Peribsen and Khase-khemwy at Abydos, and no associated enclo-sures have been demonstrated. However, the first version of Zoser's Step Pyramid complex at Saqqara seems modelled on Khasekhemwy's Abydos enclosure (including the possible mound), although the Saqqara complex is about three times the size and in stone. This development, like the boat graves (also asso-ciated with later pyramids), indicates that the Abydos enclosures were the ultimate origin of the pyramid's complex.

See also

Abydos, Umm el-Qa'ab; funerary texts; Hierakonpolis; Saqqara, North, Early Dynastic tombs; Saqqara, pyramids of the 3rd Dynasty

Further reading

Dreyer, G. 1991. Zur Rekonstruktion der Oberbauten der Königsgraber der 1. Dynastie in Abydos. *MDAIK* 47: 43–7.

Kemp, B. 1967. The Egyptian 1st Dynasty royal cemetery. *Antiquity* 41: 22–32.

O'Connor, D. 1989. New funerary enclosures (Talbezirke) of the Early Dynastic Period at Abydos. *JARCE* 26: 51–86.

—— 1991. Boat graves and pyramid origins. *Expedition* 33: 5–17.

—— 1992. The status of early Egyptian temples: an alternate theory. In *The Followers of Horus: Studies Dedicated to Michael Allen Hoffman*, R. Friedman and B. Adams, eds, 83–98. Oxford.

DAVID O'CONNOR

Abydos, Middle Kingdom cemetery

The Northern Cemetery was the principal burial ground for non-royal individuals at Abydos during the Middle Kingdom, and continued in use through the Graeco-Roman period. Its exact limits are as yet unknown, but it covers a minimum of 50 ha. During the Middle Kingdom, this area served local elites, as well as members of the middle and lower classes. Royal activity in the Abydene necropo-lis shifted to South Abydos during this period. Based on the evidence of ceramic assemblages in the cemetery, the area around the Early Dynastic royal funerary enclosures was pre-served as an exclusive sacred space until the 11th Dynasty, a period of some 700 years. Early in the Middle Kingdom, the central govern-ment appears to have officially granted private access to this previously restricted burial ground: the orthography of a 13th Dynasty royal stela of Neferhotep I recording such an action indicates that it might actually be a copy of an earlier Middle Kingdom royal decree.

Excavators and opportunists have been working in the Northern Cemetery for almost two centuries, beginning with the collecting activities of the entrepreneurs d'Athanasi and Anastasi and the wide ranging excavations of Auguste Mariette in 1858. These early explora-tions shared a focus on surface remains and museum-worthy objects, unearthing a substan-tial number of Middle Kingdom funerary and votive stelae. An era of more systematic exploration began with the work of Flinders Petrie in 1899, followed by several excavators working for various institutions, most notably Thomas Peet and John Garstang. This period of research ended with the work of Henri Frankfort in 1925–6. Although much informa-tion was gathered on non-royal burial practices during the Middle Kingdom, no detailed comprehensive map was developed, and the excavators rarely published the entirety of their findings. The goal of the multidisciplinary Pennsylvania–Yale Expedition, which has excavated in the Northern Cemetery area since 1966, has been to build a comprehensive map and provide as complete a record as possible of mortuary remains at the site, including for the first time information on the health status of individuals buried in the cemetery.

The earliest Middle Kingdom graves occurred in the northeastern part of the cemetery, perhaps because of its proximity to the town's Osiris temple. The choice of space might also reflect a more pragmatic concern with favorable subsurface conditions, characterized in this area by an extremely compact sand and gravel matrix; this type of matrix permitted the excavation of deep and regular burial shafts. As this portion of the cemetery filled up, burials spread in a southwesterly direction around the 2nd Dynasty funerary enclosure of Khasekhemwy toward the cliffs, but during the Middle Kingdom never encroached on the wadi separating the Northern Cemetery from the Middle Cemetery, which was preserved as a processional way out to Umm el-Qa'ab. It is unclear whether or not there were rock-cut tombs in the cliffs at Abydos, the usual venue for provincial elite graves, making it possible that a more differentiated population than usual shared this low desert cemetery.

There were two basic grave types in the Northern Cemetery during the Middle Kingdom, reflecting the socioeconomic status of the deceased and his or her family: shaft graves and surface graves. Shaft graves occurred most often at Abydos in pairs, although excavators have documented rows of eight or more. These shafts were oriented to river north, and were typically associated with some form of mudbrick surface architecture serving as a funerary chapel, often bearing a limestone stela inscribed with standard offering formulae and the name and title of the deceased. The size and elaboration of these chapels ranged from large mudbrick *mastaba*s with interior chambers down to very small vaulted structures less than 30 cm in

height. The shafts themselves were of highly variable depth, ranging from 1 to 10 m. Burial chambers opened from either the northern or southern ends of the shaft; often several chambers were present at different depths, each typically containing one individual in a simple wooden coffin. Grave goods could include pottery, cosmetic items and jewelry in a variety of materials ranging from faïence to semiprecious stones to gold. Shaft graves with multiple chambers were most likely family tombs used over time. Frequently, more than one chapel was constructed on the surface to serve the different occupants of the grave.

Burials were also deposited in surface graves: shallow pits dug into the desert surface, either with or without a wooden coffin. Surface graves are documented throughout the cemetery, dispersed among the shaft graves, and like them are oriented to river north. Most of these graves do not seem to possess any surface architecture, but some appear to be associated with very small chapels, or surface scatters of offering pottery which suggest the idea if not the reality of a "chapel." A range of grave goods and raw materials similar to those found in shaft chambers also occurred in surface graves; in fact, some of the wealthiest graves in terms of raw materials recorded by Petrie were surface graves.

The Northern Cemetery is one of the largest known cemeteries from the Middle Kingdom that provides data on the mortuary practices of non-elites. These data include evidence for a middle class during this period, which may not have been entirely dependent upon the government for the accumulation of wealth, as is illustrated by the modest shaft graves and stelae of individuals bearing no bureaucratic titles. The cemetery remains document shared mortuary beliefs and shared use of a mortuary landscape by elites and non-elites, and in the broader context of Abydos as a whole, by royalty as well. Additionally, current archaeological research in the Northern Cemetery focuses on the physical anthropology of the skeletal remains, allowing scholars to suggest links between the health status and socioeconomic level of individuals buried here, and contributing to our knowledge of disease in ancient Egypt. Work in the settlement area has suggested a partial explanation for the under-representation of infants and small children in the cemetery context in the form of sub-floor burials in the settlement itself. Simultaneously, the Northern Cemetery also illustrates one of the most formidable challenges facing archaeologists in Egypt: coping with the effects of long term plundering and with the fragmentary records of earlier work at the site to produce a coherent picture of ancient activity.

See also

Egyptians, physical anthropology of; Middle Kingdom, overview

Further reading

Buikstra, J., B. Baker and D. Cook. 1993. What diseases plagued ancient Egyptians? A century of controversy considered. In *Biological Anthropology and the Study of Ancient Egypt*, V. Davies, ed. London.

O'Connor, D. 1985. The cenotaphs of the Middle Kingdom at Abydos. In *Melanges Gamal Eddin Mokhtar*, P. Posener-Krieger, ed., 162–77. Cairo.

Richards, J. 1989. Understanding the mortuary remains at Abydos. *NARCE* 142: 5–8.

Simpson, W.K. 1974. *The Terrace of the Great God at Abydos: The Offering Chapels of Dynasties 12 and 13* (Publications of the Pennsylvania–Yale Expedition to Egypt, 5). New Haven, CT and Philadelphia.

JANET RICHARDS

Abydos, North

The ancient settlement at Abydos (Kom es-Sultan) is adjacent to the modern village of Beni Mansur on the west bank of the Nile in Sohag governorate, Upper Egypt (26°11′ N, 31°55′ E). Often identified with the Osiris-Khenty-amentiu Temple enclosure, the site is presently defined by a series of large mudbrick enclosure walls of various dates, as well as by a limestone pylon foundation and a mass of limestone debris, which marks the site of a large stone temple dated by Flinders Petrie to the 30th Dynasty. Auguste Mariette excavated a large area of late houses in the western corner of the site, which produced a great number of demotic inscriptions (on ostraca). Surface features visible in 1899 were mapped by John Garstang. In 1902–3, Petrie excavated a large area of the cultic zone of the site, revealing a series of superimposed cult structures ranging in date from the late Old Kingdom through the Late period. No further excavation took place until test excavations were conducted in 1979 by David O'Connor, co-director (with William Kelly Simpson) of the Pennsylvania–Yale Expedition. Based on the results of this work, a major new research program was initiated as the Abydos Settlement Site Project of the Pennsylvania–Yale Expedition in 1991, under the field direction of Matthew Adams.

The site is located at the transition from the alluvium to the low desert, at the mouth of the desert wadi which extends to the southwest past the Early Dynastic royal tombs at Umm el-Qa'ab. The town site is bounded on the southwest by the slope to the low desert in which is situated Abydos's North Cemetery. On the north and east, the site most likely extends under the modern village of Beni Mansur into the present alluvium. To the southeast the site may have been bordered, at least in later antiquity, by a substantial lake or harbor, since a large depression is shown on early maps of the site. Gaston Maspero noted the presence of stone masonry, which he interpreted to be the remains of a quay, although this area is now completely covered by village houses.

The site was originally a classic "tell," a mound built up of superimposed layers of construction and occupation debris, which may have been as much as 12 m or more in height. Except in the western corner of the site, where large late mudbrick walls protected the underlying deposits (Kom es-Sultan proper), much of the component material of the tell has been removed by digging for organic material (*sebbakh*) used by the farmers for fertilizer.

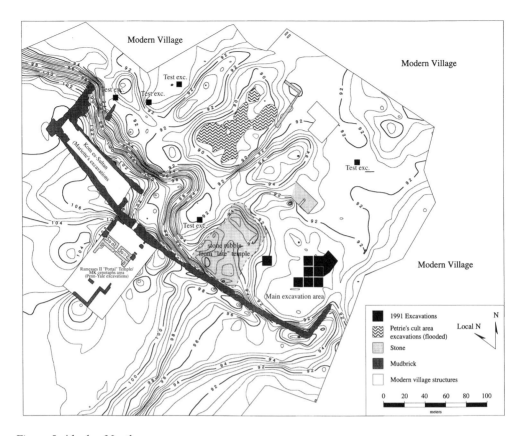

Figure 5 Abydos North

Southeast of Petrie's excavations, almost all deposits post-dating the late third millennium BC appear to have been destroyed, and Old Kingdom and First Intermediate Period levels lay immediately under the modern surface.

Due to the destruction of later strata, the best evidence at present for the nature of the site in ancient times comes from the later third millennium BC. At this time, the cultic core of the site consisted of the Temple of Khenty-amentiu (only later Osiris-Khenty-amentiu), with a number of subsidiary chapels, all situated within a series of enclosure walls. Around these to the west and south were shifting zones of houses, workshops and some open areas. Whether the non-cultic components of the town in this period were inside the enclosure wall system is as yet unclear.

Petrie's excavations concentrated primarily on the cultic zone of the site and have been re-analyzed by Barry Kemp. The complex sequence of superimposed cult structures can be divided into three main building levels: an earlier one of the Old Kingdom, one of the New Kingdom, and the latest one of the Late period. Below the Old Kingdom level, Petrie was able to define only traces of earlier mudbrick structures, which, as published, do not form a comprehensible plan. None of the structures in this area is likely to represent the actual temple of Osiris-Khenty-amentiu. Where evidence is preserved, they appear to have been royal "*ka*" chapels, subsidiary buildings common at major temple sites, as argued by O'Connor and Edward Brovarski, *contra* Kemp. Given the importance of the Osiris cult, especially from the Middle Kingdom onward, a major temple building should be expected in the vicinity, the latest incarnation of which is likely to be seen in the nearby stone remains. The main temple in earlier periods may have been located in the same approximate area.

Petrie's excavations also revealed a substantial zone of houses to the west and southwest of the cult buildings, which spanned the period from late Predynastic times (Nagada III) to at least the 2nd Dynasty. Occupation here probably continued much later, but the evidence has been destroyed by *sebbakh* digging. During a temporary phase of abandonment of this part of the site, though still in the Early Dynastic period, a number of simple pit graves and brick-lined chamber tombs were dug into the occupational debris; these were Petrie's Cemetery M. These were covered by renewed Early Dynastic occupation.

A major portion of the work of the Abydos Settlement Site Project in 1991 focused on the largely unexplored area to the southeast of Petrie's excavations and the Late period temple remains. Excavation revealed substantial zones of residential and industrial activity, dating to the Old Kingdom and First Intermediate Period. The residential area consisted of a number of mudbrick houses, courtyards and a narrow street, situated adjacent to a large building. The plans of three houses are relatively complete, consisting of between seven and ten mostly small rooms. All the houses had long histories of use and were subject to many minor and some major modifications over time, illustrating functional changes which likely relate in part to the evolving composition and needs of the family groups which occupied them. The function of the large building against which some of the houses were built is as yet unclear, but it may have been a large house similar to the Lahun "mansions," a notion supported by the entirely domestic character of the material excavated from within it.

Much evidence was recovered relating to the organization of life in this ancient "neighborhood." All the houses had evidence of bread baking and cooking, and the faunal and botanical remains reveal the patterns of food consumption. The residents appear to have been farmers, while at the same time they seem to have obtained meat through some sort of system of redistribution, perhaps through the local temple or a town market. Most ceramics from this portion of the site were locally made, but in the Old Kingdom imports were common from as far away as Memphis, while in the First Intermediate Period such long-distance imports were absent. At the same time, evidence suggests that Abydos's residents had access in both periods to other exchange networks, such as those which brought to the site exotic raw materials such as hematite and quartzite; the latter was commonly used for household querns and other grinding stones. The most common tools were made of chipped stone and bone, which appear to have been locally produced. These patterns suggest that, although Abydos was not unaffected by the political and other changes which characterized the end of the Old Kingdom and First Intermediate Period, the basic parameters of life in the town were locally and regionally oriented, a pattern which existed continuously through both periods.

The nearby industrial area was for faïence production. A number of pit kilns were found, which were used, reused and renewed over a long period. Evidence was found for the manufacture of beads and amulets, probably for local funerary use. This is the oldest and most complete faïence workshop yet found in Egypt. There is at present little evidence for any institutional sponsorship, and this site may represent an independent group of craftsmen servicing the needs of the local population.

Textual evidence reveals the presence at Abydos, in the Old Kingdom and First Intermediate Period, of high officials such as the "Overseer of Upper Egypt" and illustrates the connections between the royal court and local Abydos elites. This suggests the political importance of Abydos in these periods. However, the vast majority of the residents of Abydos would have been non-elite persons, who would have been connected with each other and with local elites and institutions through complex social, economic and political ties. The aim of the Abydos Settlement Site Project is to examine the spatial organization and the full range of activities represented at the site, in order to build a comprehensive picture of the structure of life in the ancient community and its context in the Nile Valley.

See also

faïence technology and production; Lahun, town

Further reading

Adams, M.D. 1992. Community and societal organization in early historic Egypt: introductory report on 1991–92 fieldwork conducted at the Abydos Settlement Site. *NARCE* 158/159: 1–10.

Brovarski, E. 1994. Abydos in the Old Kingdom and First Intermediate Period II. In *For His Ka: Essays Offered in Memory of Klaus Baer*, D.P. Silverman, ed., 15–44. Chicago.

Kemp, B.J. 1968. The Osiris Temple at Abydos. *MDAIK* 23: 138–55.

——. 1975. Abydos. In *LÄ* 1: 28–41.

Petrie, W.M.F. 1902. *Abydos I, II*. London.

MATTHEW D. ADAMS

Abydos, North, *ka* chapels and cenotaphs

To the east of the vast cemetery fields of North Abydos was a long-lived town and temple site, where "*ka* chapels" and "cenotaphs" are important archaeological features, better attested here than at most sites. *Ka* chapels (*ḥwt k3*) date from the Old and Middle Kingdoms and earlier. Originally, the term referred to royal mortuary complexes and elite tombs, even to the inaccessible statue chamber (*serdab*) within the latter. By the 6th Dynasty "*ka* chapels" could be relatively small buildings, separate from the tomb, and built in the precincts of provincial (and central?) temples.

Built for both royalty and different strata of the elite, *ka* chapels are rarely explicitly referred to in the New Kingdom or later, yet the concept remained important: the New Kingdom royal mortuary temples at Thebes, as well as other enormous "Mansions of Millions of Years" at Abydos and Memphis, are demonstrably "*ka* temples": in effect, *ka* chapels on a grand scale.

Ka chapels were like miniaturized temples and tombs. Usually they were serviced by *ka* priests—like tombs—but sometimes by other priests (*w3b*), as was typical of temples. They were endowed with estates to provide offerings for the *ka*, and support for the priests, administrators and personnel of the cult. Although they had both political and social meaning, their fundamental purpose was cultic.

Each individual was born with a *ka*, a separate entity dwelling in the body and providing it life. Each *ka* was individual, but also, according to Lanny Bell, the manifestation of a primeval ancestral *ka* moving from one generation to another of each family line. After death, the *ka* remained essential for the deceased's eternal well-being. It was regularly persuaded by ritual to descend from a celestial realm and re-imbue both mummy and the tomb's *ka* statue with life. Thus, the mortuary cult was enabled to effectively provide endless regeneration and nourishment to the dead.

Ka chapels attached to temples provided deceased individuals with additional revitalization and nourishment, via their own cults and also the temple cult. Moreover, through his *ka* statue the deceased could witness and "participate in" special processional rituals emanating from the temple and important for regional, cosmological and individual revitalization. Sociologically, such chapels enabled the living elite to express status by venerating and renovating the *ka* chapels of distinguished ancestors.

Royal *ka* chapels had a special dimension. Each king was vitalized by his own *ka*, and that of the "*ka* of kingship," providing the superhuman faculties needed by Pharaoh in order to rule. Royal *ka*s then had a unique nature, whether celebrated in modest chapels such as that of Pepi II at Bubastis, or great temples like that of Ramesses III (6870 m²).

North Abydos provides uniquely rich data on royal *ka* chapels. The few that have been excavated elsewhere were for Teti and Pepi II

(Bubastis), Pepi I and perhaps Pepi II (Hierakonpolis), Nebhepetre Mentuhotep II (Dendera), and perhaps Amenemhat I (Ezbet Rushdi). Ramesses I had a *ka* chapel at Abydos, but near the vast "*ka* temple" of his son Seti I.

At Abydos, Flinders Petrie excavated a series of royal *ka* chapels, each superimposed upon the other, and extending from the Old into the New Kingdoms, or later. Some prefer to identify these as being—or incorporating— the Osiris temple in a mode unusual for most known (and mostly later) temples. However, a largely unexcavated Late period temple south of the chapels may well overlie the ruins of the earlier temples, dedicated originally to Khentyamenty, a local deity, and subsequently to "Osiris of Abydos," a funerary god of national significance.

On this assumption, four probable royal *ka* chapels of the Old Kingdom are identifiable. Two have tripartite sanctuaries preceded by roofed halls and an open court. The circuitous route traversing each is not unusual in pre-New Kingdom cult structures. Markedly rectangular in form, the chapels occupied $450\,m^2$ (building L) and $151.50\,m^2$ (K); their owners are not identified, and a statuette of Khufu found in one may not be contemporary. The other two royal chapels were square in outline; the better preserved (building H; $384.40\,m^2$) had a court with side chambers, and rear chambers (sanctuaries?). It was associated with Pepi II, who may have had a similar structure at Hierakonpolis.

These early chapels were razed and replaced by others in the 12th and 13th Dynasties. They were poorly preserved, but included the inscriptionally identified *ka* chapel of King Sankhare Mentuhotep of the 11th Dynasty. Above them in turn, several New Kingdom structures, probably *ka* chapels, were built. Plans were fragmentary, but they seem usually to have been square in outline. The earliest, built by Amenhotep I for his own and his father Ahmose's *ka*, had a colonnaded courtyard, a columned hall and a centrally placed rear sanctuary (building C; $422.90\,m^2$). The latest identifiable *ka* chapel was for Ramesses IV. Later, perhaps when these chapels were in ruins,

Amasis of the 26th Dynasty built a substantial stone chapel (all earlier ones were mainly of mudbrick), perhaps for his *ka*. Square in outline ($1734\,m^2$), it was oriented east–west, whereas all earlier royal *ka* chapels at Abydos ran north–south.

Private, non-royal *ka* chapels, well documented textually, have rarely been excavated; none is identified at Abydos, but one is known at Elephantine and three or possibly four at Dakhla Oasis in the late Old Kingdom. The latter are arranged in a row; each has a substantial single chamber for a statue at the rear of a hall or court. They are reminiscent of the later private "cenotaphs" of North Abydos.

Of these, some were cleared but not recognized in the nineteenth century, and a selection were re-excavated in 1967–9 and 1977, providing detailed plans and elevations. Many stelae, recovered in the area during the nineteenth century, evidently came from such "cenotaphs," and a few were found *in situ* in the recent excavations (Pennsylvania–Yale–Institute of Fine Arts, New York University Expedition). The excavated "cenotaphs" stood on a high desert scarp overlooking the temple; others probably extended down to the entrance of a shallow wadi. The latter linked the Osiris temple to the Early Dynastic royal tombs 2 km back in the desert; the great annual festival of Osiris passed along this route in the Middle Kingdom, the period to which the "cenotaphs" belonged, as abundant associated ceramics show.

"Cenotaph" is an inaccurate term invented by Egyptologists. It implies a dummy tomb, but in reality the Abydos "cenotaphs" are chapels without tombs, false or otherwise. On the stelae, the "cenotaphs" are often called *maḥat* (a standing or erected structure), a term applied also to tombs and even pyramids. If any were also called "*ka* chapel" the term should have occurred on the stelae, but does not. Yet in form and function the "cenotaphs" or *maḥat*s seem identical with "*ka* chapels." Perhaps proximity to a temple made the difference; the Abydos "cenotaphs" lay outside the temple precincts while some textually identified "*ka* chapels" were within them.

The excavated cenotaphs, a fraction of the original whole, present a complicated yet structured picture. All were built of mudbrick. Individually, most had a single chamber, which would have contained a statue or statuette and had stelae set on its internal wall faces. The chamber was at the rear of a low walled court, or preceded by one. Small ones tended to have no court; others, some with a court, were relatively large but consisted of a solid cube of mudbrick. Stelae were probably set in their upper external faces.

The excavated area is dominated by three conspicuously large cenotaphs (averaging 145 m^2) set side by side in a row; their owners must have been of high status although even larger cenotaphs probably occurred elsewhere in North Abydos. Presumably, they originally had a clear view of a processional route located to the east, but gradually other relatively large cenotaphs (the largest is 55 m^2) were scattered across the intervening area and smaller ones clustered around them in increasingly dense fashion. Eventually, movement among them would have been very difficult, or impossible.

Large or small, all cenotaphs face east, toward the Osiris temple and the processional way. The stelae inscriptions show that those commemorated in the chapels (many of whom probably lived, died and were buried elsewhere) expected, via their *ka* statues, to receive food offerings originally proferred to the deity. Inscriptionally attested *ka* chapels, in contrast, sometimes have their own endowments; but perhaps all products were first offered to the deity, and then at the *ka* chapels and cenotaphs. Through their statues, the cenotaph "owners" also expected to inhale the revitalizing incense offered the god in its temple, and to witness and (notionally, not actually) participate in the great annual festival. Indeed, some small cenotaphs had their entrance blocked by a stela pierced by a window (one was found *in situ* in 1969) through which the statuette could "see," and a large cenotaph's entrance was blocked off by a mudbrick well into which perhaps a similar stela had been inserted. These examples are very reminiscent of Old Kingdom tomb *serdabs*, also called "*ka* chapels."

The cenotaphs attest to a striking social diversity amongst those permitted this privilege. They vary from very large to tiny examples, the latter supplied nevertheless with ostraca-like stelae, limestone flakes painted or inscribed with the owner's name and a prayer. The better stelae, although not assignable to any excavated cenotaph, show that relatives, subordinate officials and servants associated themselves with the cenotaphs of higher ranking persons, and such individuals were probably responsible for the smaller chapels which enfold the larger. One of the latter kind belonged specifically to a "butler," presumably of the owner of a grander chapel nearby.

After the Middle Kingdom, the situation in the cenotaph zone is less clear, because of extensive disturbance and destruction. It continued, however, to be an important cultic area. High-ranking New Kingdom officials had mudbrick structures set up (as "cenotaphs"?), and for the first time royalty became directly interested in the area. The entrance to the wadi processional route was flanked by two small, beautifully decorated chapels of Tuthmose III, currently being excavated by Mary Ann Pouls, while later Ramesses II built a large stone temple directly over some of the earlier cenotaphs. It is possible that these were three royal *maḥat*s.

See also

mortuary beliefs; Old Kingdom, overview

Further reading

Kemp, B.J. 1989. *Ancient Egypt: Anatomy of a Civilization*, 64–83. London.

——. 1995. How religious were the ancient Egyptians? *CAJ* 5(1): 25–54.

O'Connor, D. 1985. The "cenotaphs" of the Middle Kingdom at Abydos. In *Mélanges Gamal Eddin Mokhtar*, 161–78. Cairo.

Seidlmayer, S. 1996. Town and state in the early Old Kingdom. A view from Elephantine. In *Aspects of Ancient Egypt*, J. Spencer, ed., 108–27. London.

Simpson, W.K. 1974. *The Terrace of the Great God at Abydos: the Offering Chapels of*

Dynasties 12 and 13. New Haven, CT and Philadelphia.

DAVID O'CONNOR

Abydos, Osiris temple of Seti I

Beside the modern village of el-'Araba el-Madfuna (26°11' N, 31°55' E) are the impressive remains of a unique Egyptian temple constructed by Seti I (19th Dynasty). The temple contains seven sanctuaries set in a row, each dedicated to a different deity, the southernmost one honoring Seti I himself. This dedication underscores the building's role as a funerary shrine for Seti I. This is confirmed by the name of the temple: "The house of millions of years of the King Men-Ma'at-Re [Seti I], who is contented at Abydos." Actually buried in the Valley of the Kings at Thebes, Seti I was following a longstanding Egyptian royal tradition in building a secondary funerary complex at Abydos, the cult center of the Egyptian god Osiris. The temple's raised relief decoration carved under Seti I on fine white limestone evokes a traditional, classical style. Many of the delicate reliefs also retain their original painted details, forming some of the finest bas-reliefs preserved from ancient Egypt.

The aftermath of the Amarna period, with Seti I restoring the worship of the traditional Egyptian gods, may explain the combined dedication of the temple to (from south to north) Ptah, Re-Horakhty, Amen-Re, Osiris, Isis and Horus. The unusual L-shaped plan of the temple is caused by a southeast wing appended to the main rectilinear temple. This wing contains rooms dedicated to Memphite funerary deities, such as Sokar and Nefertum, further emphasizing the national and funerary focus of the temple. In addition, a selective list of legitimate pharaohs is provided in the "kings' gallery" to the south of the sanctuaries in the passageway leading to a butchering room. The names of Akhenaten, Smenkhkare and Tutankhamen are omitted from the list, as if to erase their reigns from recorded history.

The temple is set within a large enclosure wall (*circa* 220 × 350 m) with a large mudbrick pylon facing the desert, from which a processional way probably led to the royal tombs at Umm el-Qa'ab. Access to the temple was from the east, up ramps that led into two large courtyards, one after the other. The temple was left unfinished at the death of Seti I and most of the front section of the temple was finished in sunk relief during the reign of Seti I's son Ramesses II. The southeast interior wall of the first court contains a representation of Ramesses II fighting the Hittites at Qadesh. The names of Merenptah, Ramesses III and Ramesses IV are also preserved on these front courts. To the east of these courts lies a large storehouse or set of magazines, such as were also found at the Ramesseum. In the center of these is a podium with pillars which would have served as a reception center for incoming or outgoing goods.

With seven sanctuaries, the temple's plan is exceptionally broad. Access to the sanctuaries was through two transverse hypostyle halls, the first with two rows of columns and the second with three. In the first hypostyle hall the names of Seti I have been overwritten by Ramesses II. The seven sanctuaries are mostly decorated with scenes from the daily cult ritual showing the king entering the shrine, offering and anointing the god's statue and bark and then departing while sweeping away his footprints as he goes. Six of these shrines have a false door depicted on their western wall through which the deity was thought to enter the temple. The exception is the shrine to Osiris; here an actual door leads to a unique suite of rooms at the back of the temple in which the Mysteries of Osiris were celebrated. The highlight of these ceremonies was the erection of the *djed* pillar, symbolizing the resurrection of Osiris.

Immediately behind the chambers dedicated to the Osiris cult is another unique feature, a subterranean structure known as the "Osireion." The Osireion is built in the shape of an 18th Dynasty tomb in the Valley of the Kings. It is entered from the north through a long passage decorated with scenes from the *Book of Gates* and offering scenes. Taking a 90° turn, the passage leads into the structure from the west, along the main axis of the temple, through two transverse halls decorated with mythological scenes, including some from the *Book of the Dead*. The center of the structure is a large (30.5 × 20 m) hall built of red granite with ten piers set in two rows. In imitation of the primeval hill of creation, two platforms (for sarcophagus and canopic chest?) were surrounded by a water-filled moat. The final transverse hall contains reliefs of Shu, god of the atmosphere, supporting the sky goddess Nut. Deliberately built to recall earlier structures, the Osireion is nevertheless an integral part of the Seti temple complex. Merenptah, Seti I's grandson, added reliefs to the Osireion.

Graffiti indicate that the Osireion was visited by pilgrims from the 21st Dynasty until the Roman period. During the later periods of ancient Egyptian history, foreign visitors also left graffiti in the Seti temple in languages such as Aramaic, Phoenician, Carian, Greek and Cypriot. In the Ptolemaic period, Serapis was worshipped in the temple, but was replaced by Bes in the Roman period. Strabo (17.I.42) calls the Osireion the "Memnonium," perhaps from the name Men-Ma'at-Re (Seti I), and indicates that Abydos was only a small settlement in the first century AD. The Bes oracle was suppressed by the emperor Constantine II in AD 359 and again by the Copts under St Moses in the fifth century AD. A Christian convent established in the back of the Seti I temple did not last long and the temple site was soon abandoned. The site was not rediscovered until 1718, when it was visited by the Jesuit Père Claude Sicard. The temple was cleared in the mid-nineteenth century under the direction of the French archaeologist Auguste Mariette.

See also

cult temples of the New Kingdom; Mariette, François Auguste Ferdinand; Thebes, royal funerary temples

Further reading

Calverley, A.M., and M.F. Broome. 1933–58. *The Temple of King Sethos I at Abydos*. 4 vols. London and Chicago.

David, R. 1981. *A Guide to Religious Ritual at Abydos*. Warminster.

Otto, E. 1968. *Egyptian Art and the Cults of Osiris and Amon*. London.

STEVEN BLAKE SHUBERT

Abydos, Predynastic sites

The region encompassed by this discussion stretches approximately 20 km north and south of Abydos (26°11′ N, 31°55′ E), about two-thirds of the Dynastic Thinite nome. A number of early excavations focused on Predynastic sites, particularly cemeteries, dating to the fourth millennium BC. In 1900, David Randall MacIver and Arthur Mace excavated the important Predynastic cemetery at el-Amra, with hundreds of shallow graves from all Predynastic phases. Other important early excavations were conducted at the cemeteries of Naga ed-Deir, el-Mahasna, Mesheikh, Beit Allam and the numerous cemeteries at Abydos itself (Cemeteries B, C, D, E, G, U, X and Φ). More recently, excavations of the cemeteries at Deir el-Nawahid and es-Salmani have increased our knowledge of Predynastic burial practices and social organization.

Several settlement sites within the region have also been investigated. In the early 1900s, while excavating Predynastic and Dynastic tombs at Abydos, T. Eric Peet discovered and excavated the remains of a late Predynastic settlement. At the same time, John Garstang identified an important settlement at el-Mahasna, which was continuously occupied throughout all Predynastic phases. In 1982–3 Diana Craig Patch conducted a large-scale regional survey of the low desert plain in the Abydos region in order to locate all preserved Predynastic sites, both settlements and cemeteries. Patch was then able to reconstruct the regional spatial arrangement of Predynastic villages and towns. Settlements were evenly spaced, approximately 1–2 km apart along the low desert margin. However, there appears to

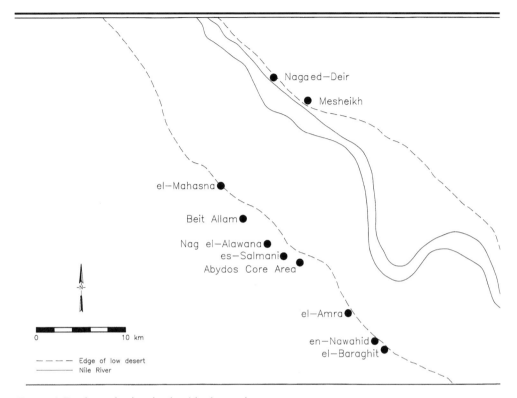

Figure 6 Predynastic sites in the Abydos region

be a somewhat greater spacing between the Abydos core area and sites immediately north and south, which may suggest that an artificial "spacing" was maintained between the larger zones of settlement and the smaller ones.

The majority of the settlements appeared to be uniform in size, 1.5–2.0 ha (Nag el-Alawana, en-Nawahid and el-Baraghit). Most of these sites represent small farming villages, especially in the earlier phases of the Predynastic period. Over time some nucleation and abandonment of settlements occurred, and later in the fourth millennium BC populations were concentrated at Abydos, el-Mahasna and Thinis. Except for el-Mahasna, the increase in settlement size is only evident in the increased size of the cemeteries at Abydos and Naga ed-Deir. The abandonment of the other settlements may not have been entirely the result of populations nucleating in the larger settlements, but rather a result of settlement patterns shifting from low

desert locations to locations within the flood-plain itself, where, because of overlying flood deposits, these settlements have not been located. Unfortunately, the actual settlement of Thinis, later an important nome capital, has never been located.

By late Predynastic times the larger settlements had specialized areas of activities. El-Mahasna, which may have covered up to 15 ha, had beer-brewing facilities, which Garstang identified as pottery kilns. From 1909 to 1912, while working in the cemeteries in the Abydos core, T. Eric Peet excavated the remains of a large Predynastic settlement just outside the wall of the New Kingdom temple of Seti I. The settlement consisted of a layer of dark debris, possibly the remains of Predynastic houses, within which were thousands of flint tools and flakes, as well as potsherds dating the site to the late Predynastic. In the center of the site was a large concentration of small stone drills and borers associated with unworked pieces of semiprecious stones and the debris from working these materials. Stone beads were manufactured here, providing evidence of craft specialization. Also in this settlement was a kiln structure consisting of large ceramic vats supported by baked brick structures, now thought to be a large-scale brewing facility.

See also

brewing and baking; Naga ed-Deir; nome structure; Predynastic period, overview

Further reading

Patch, D.C. 1991. "The Origin and Early Development of Urbanism in Ancient Egypt: A Regional Study." Ph.D. dissertation, University of Pennsylvania.

Peet, T.E. 1914. *Cemeteries of Abydos II, 1911–12.* London.

Randall MacIver, D., and A.C. Mace. 1902. *El-Amrah and Abydos, 1899–1901.* London.

DAVID A. ANDERSON

Abydos, South

To the south of the main center of the ancient town of Abydos (26°11′ N, 31°55′ E) is an extensive area of low desert, generally referred to as South Abydos. This part of Abydos was developed primarily as a zone for the construction of a series of royal cult foundations during the Middle and New Kingdoms. Two relatively well preserved cult complexes have been identified at South Abydos. These are the complex of Senusret III of the 12th Dynasty, and that of Ahmose of the 18th Dynasty. There is an additional unfinished complex, apparently of the 12th Dynasty, and evidence of other royal cult establishments in the area. Besides the cult structures themselves, extensive areas of settlement, responsible for maintenance and operation of the cults, lie along the desert edge.

Mortuary complex of Senusret III

Archaeological work at the Senusret III complex was first conducted by the Egypt Exploration Society (EES) between 1899 and 1902. In 1899 the Senusret III mortuary temple was located by David Randall MacIver, who excavated most of the temple and mapped the standing architecture. His fieldwork was followed in 1901 by that of Arthur Weigall, who excavated and mapped the great enclosure around the subterranean tomb, as well as the associated superstructures (*mastaba*s) and other subsidiary buildings. Weigall also initiated excavations which led to the discovery of the tomb entrance. The tomb's interior was cleared and a plan was made by Charles Currelly in 1902.

Subsequent to the EES work, no work was conducted at the site until the excavations by the Pennsylvania–Yale expedition to Abydos in 1994. This work concentrated firstly on a re-examination of the mortuary temple and its surroundings, and secondly on excavation of the Middle Kingdom town site to the south of the temple.

The Senusret III complex is focused on a large subterranean tomb built at the base of the desert cliffs. The stone-lined tomb, approximately 170 m in length, contains a burial chamber with a concealed sarcophagus and canopic chest, in which the deceased's viscera were placed. Built within a large T-shaped mudbrick enclosure, the burial chamber lies behind an elaborate blocking system. Associated with the tomb enclosure are a series of structures, including a complex of storerooms and a raised mudbrick platform, which may be connected with cultic activities. Four *mastaba*s are associated with the tomb enclosure, including two dummy ones on the south side which were filled with limestone chippings from the construction of the subterranean tomb. On the north side of the enclosure are two *mastaba*s with elaborate interiors. These tombs probably date to the 13th Dynasty. As with the Senusret III tomb itself, these *mastaba*s are fronted by mudbrick platforms, possibly for structures for offering cults.

Approximately 750 m from the tomb enclosure of Senusret III, located on the edge of the low desert, is a large mortuary temple. In form this temple consists of a large rectangular mudbrick structure, fronted by a pylon gateway and surrounded by a mudbrick-paved street and enclosure wall. The central third of this temple consisted of a limestone court where the actual cult building was located. It stood on a raised platform and was fronted by a columned forecourt. The temple interior was decorated with reliefs very similar to those of earlier Old and Middle Kingdom royal mortuary temples. Additional reliefs, however, suggest scenes specifically connected with Abydos and the cult of Osiris. Life-size alabaster statues stood within the cult building, while red quartzite ones decorated the forecourt. Flanking this court were two wings, one with three houses for temple personnel and the other with storerooms and areas for preparing offerings. Outside the temple, but directly adjacent to it to the south, are areas of extensive industrial debris. These appear to have been used primarily for baking and brewing associated with the temple.

Approximately 300 m to the south of the Senusret III mortuary temple are the remains of a large planned settlement founded during the late 12th Dynasty. This town may have been established in connection with the Senusret III complex or another 12th Dynasty royal cult. The town was continuously occupied until the end of the 13th Dynasty, when it appears to have been abandoned. At least partial reuse of this town occurred during the 18th Dynasty.

In function and organization the mortuary complex of Senusret III at Abydos closely parallels other Middle Kingdom establishments for the maintenance of royal cults. Its greatest similarities are with the royal pyramid complexes in the Memphis and Fayum regions. The combination of burial place with attached cult area, separate valley temple and associated settlements is also seen in other Middle Kingdom royal cult complexes, such as at Lahun, el-Lisht and Dahshur.

The Senusret III complex has been interpreted as a royal cenotaph, a symbolic tomb built at Abydos to connect the deceased king with the god Osiris. Expression of the relationship between the dead king and Osiris appears

to have been a fundamental element of this complex. However, there are no indications that it was constructed as a cenotaph. The complex was a fully functional royal mortuary establishment, which maintained an offering cult like those associated with pyramid complexes. Senusret III may have been buried either in this tomb or in his pyramid at Dahshur.

JOSEF WEGNER

Early 18th Dynasty monuments

About 1 km south of Senusret III's complex at Abydos, a series of monuments was constructed in the early 18th Dynasty by King Ahmose for the veneration of the king as an aspect of the god Osiris, and in honor of female members of his family. Mudbricks impressed with the phrase "Nebpehtyre [Ahmose], beloved of Osiris" are found in all cult structures of the complex, which was probably begun after Ahmose's Hyksos campaigns. The king's Abydos monuments are the most significant ones known from his reign, and are thus important for the development of New Kingdom architectural traditions.

Although Émile Amélineau appears to have sampled the area in 1896, the pyramid and pyramid temple of Ahmose were first systematically identified and investigated by Arthur Mace for the EES in 1899–1900. Looking for interior chambers, Mace also attempted unsuccessfully to tunnel inside the pyramid. Working for the EES in 1902, Charles Currelly discovered the terraced temple of Ahmose, a small cemetery next to the pyramid, the shrine of the king's grandmother, Tetisheri, a subterranean tomb, and the "Ahmose town." The settlement area was further excavated in 1966 by the Egyptian Antiquities Organization (EAO). In 1993, the University of Pennsylvania–Yale University–Institute of Fine Arts, New York University Expedition to Abydos (Stephen Harvey, field director) undertook an intensive program of mapping, surface collection and excavation of the Ahmose monuments, resulting in the discovery of thousands of additional fragments of limestone relief from the pyramid temple, as well as the location of an additional structure constructed for Queen Ahmose-Nefertary.

Ahmose's complex consists of a series of structures 1.4 km long aligned on a northeast–southwest axis across the low desert. Close to the edge of the modern cultivation is a sandy mound about 80 × 80 m and 10 m high, known locally as Kom Sheikh Mohammed. The mound conceals the remains of a large pyramid, with a loose core of sand and stone debris. According to Mace's account, the pyramid was originally cased with limestone blocks, with an angle of inclination of about 63°. Associated with the pyramid is a mudbrick and limestone temple, 48 × 57 m, dominated by a central pillared court and fronted by a wide mudbrick pylon. Subsidiary annexes on either side of the court were perhaps intended for storage and priests' houses. A smaller chapel, 19 m wide, was partially excavated in 1993 and may be associated with Queen Ahmose-Nefertary.

Since the pyramid and temple were both thoroughly razed in antiquity, their reconstruction can only be incomplete. Reliefs appear to have consisted of scenes relating to (1) the royal mortuary cult, especially scenes of the offering table ritual, and (2) an extensive battle narrative, which, on the basis of fragments, may be identified as Ahmose's triumph over an Asiatic enemy (probably the Hyksos). Fragments of the battle narrative include the earliest detailed representations of horses and chariots in Egyptian art, as well as depictions of elaborate royal ships. Substantial remains of a 6 m high mudbrick ramp behind the rear wall of the pyramid temple most likely derive from the dismantling of the pyramid's limestone casing for reuse elsewhere.

On either side of the pyramid were domestic and industrial zones for personnel of the royal cult. To the west of the pyramid, a series of orthogonally planned houses in mudbrick probably served as a residence for officials and workers. Burials found by Currelly immediately east of the pyramid may be part of this community's cemetery. Also to the east of the pyramid was an industrial area, where large volumes of construction debris and evidence of bakeries have been recently excavated.

Ahmose and Ahmose-Nefertary constructed a mudbrick memorial shrine in honor of Queen Tetisheri, as described in the text of a monumental stela now in Cairo (CG 34002). The stela was found in the shrine, about 450 m to the southwest of Ahmose's pyramid temple. Most likely built in pyramidal form, the shrine is approximately 21 × 23 m in area. About 500 m to the south of the Tetisheri shrine is a subterranean rock-cut tomb consisting of a mudbrick-lined shaft at the level of the desert surface leading to a winding passage and a central hall supported by eighteen pillars. However, it is uncertain whether this tomb was intended for use as an actual or symbolic burial.

At the base of the high cliffs, 1.15 km to the southwest of the pyramid, Ahmose constructed terraced foundations for another cult structure, which may have remained unfinished. A lower terrace wall, 104 m long, was built of mudbrick, while the upper terrace had a retaining wall of rough limestone. Deposits of miniature ceramic and stone model vessels, as well as a series of model wooden boats and oars were discovered along the upper terrace. At the southeastern end of the terraces a series of rooms and passages of unknown function were constructed in mudbrick; no traces of structures have been located atop the terraces.

Both textual and archaeological evidence attest to the 250-year history of the Ahmose cult at Abydos. Titles of priests of Ahmose are known throughout the later 18th Dynasty and up to the time of Ramesses II, which accords well with the latest inscription found at the site, a cartouche of Merenptah (19th Dynasty). A stela from Abydos provides evidence of an oracle of Ahmose in the Ramesside era. The cult came to an end with the destruction of the temple complex in Ramesside times.

See also

Dahshur, Middle Kingdom pyramids; Hyksos; Lahun, pyramid complex of Senusret II; Lahun, town; el-Lisht; Middle Kingdom, overview; New Kingdom, overview

Further reading

Arnold, D. 1991. *Building in Egypt*. New York.
Ayrton, E.R., C.T. Currelly and A.E.P. Weigall. 1904. *Abydos Part III*. London.
Harvey, S. 1994. The monuments of Ahmose at Abydos. *Egyptian Archaeology* 4: 3–5.
Simpson, W.K. 1974. *The Terrace of the Great God at Abydos*. Pennsylvania–Yale Expedition to Abydos. New Haven, CT.

STEPHEN P. HARVEY

Abydos, Umm el-Qa'ab

The Predynastic/Early Dynastic royal cemetery at Umm el-Qa'ab is located about 1.5 km from cultivated land in the low desert (26°11′ N, 31°55′ E). To the east is a large wadi ending near the ancient settlement at Abydos known as Kom es-Sultan, next to the great funerary enclosures of the 1st and 2nd Dynasties.

The cemetery seems to have developed from north to south and consists of three parts:

1 Predynastic Cemetery U in the north;
2 Cemetery B with royal tombs of Dynasty 0 and the early 1st Dynasty in the middle;
3 the tomb complexes of six kings and one queen of the 1st Dynasty and two kings of the 2nd Dynasty in the south.

The cemeteries were first excavated by É. Amélineau in 1895–8. Flinders Petrie continued the excavation of Cemetery B and the later complexes in 1899–1900. Some parts of the cemetery were investigated again in 1911–12 by E. Peet and É. Naville. Since 1973 the German Institute of Archaeology (DAI) has been re-examining the entire cemetery. To date, parts of Cemetery U, Cemetery B and the complexes of Den (Dewen) and Qa'a have been re-excavated, and more limited investigations have been conducted at the subsidiary tombs of Djer and the complexes of Djet (Wadj) and Khasekhemwy. The complex of Den is being reconstructed.

From the very beginning, these tombs have been plundered many times and most of the 1st Dynasty tombs show traces of immense fires.

The finds from the early excavations were in part sold (by Amélineau) and distributed to many collections. The most important ones are in Berlin, Brussels, Cairo, Chateaudun, Chicago (Oriental Institute), London (University College, British Museum), New York (Metropolitan Museum), Oxford, Paris (Louvre) and Philadelphia (University Museum). The artifacts found by the German mission are stored at Abydos.

Cemetery U

Cemetery U covers an area of *circa* 100 × 200 m on a slightly elevated plateau between Cemetery B and the "*heka-reshu*" hill (where Petrie found New Kingdom *shawabti*s inscribed with this name). Amélineau reports excavating *circa* 150–60 graves of different types here (in four days!); 32 small graves were excavated by Peet in 1911. Both excavators published only a few details without a general plan.

During the clearance of the desert surface by the DAI, about 400 grave pits and hundreds of small empty offering pits (New Kingdom and later) were mapped. By 1993 about 120 tombs had been excavated, mostly in the central and southern part but a few at the northwestern edge. Ceramics are those of the Predynastic (Nagada) culture of Upper Egypt, which were first described and classified by Petrie and later revised in Nagada culture sub-periods by Werner Kaiser.

In Nagada I–IIa times Cemetery U seems to have been fairly undifferentiated, although there are a few somewhat rich burials. Thus far the Nagada IIb–c sub-period is under-represented (there are almost no D-class pots), but in Nagada IId2 the cemetery had obviously developed into an elite one, with large tombs which were probably those of chieftains (and their kin). The multiple-chamber tombs (Nagada IIIa) and the larger single-chamber tombs (Nagada IIIa–IIIb/Dynasty 0) belonged, in all likelihood, to a sequence of rulers succeeded by the kings of Dynasty 0, who were buried in Cemetery B.

Of particular importance is the large tomb, U-j, discovered in 1988. According to calibrated

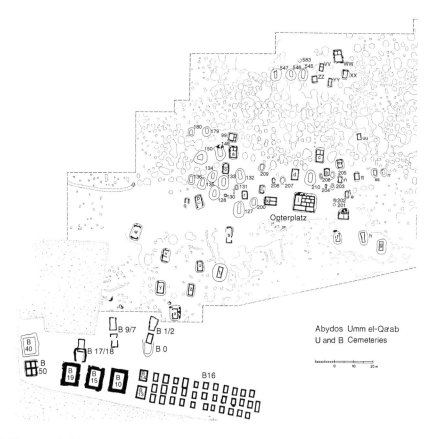

Figure 7 Umm el-Qa'ab, Abydos, Cemeteries U and B (1992)

radiocarbon samples, it dates to *circa* 150 years before King Aḥa (beginning of the 1st Dynasty). The tomb is divided into twelve chambers and measures 9.1 × 7.3 m.

Although robbed and perhaps partly excavated earlier, Tomb U-j still contained much funerary equipment, including many ivory and bone artifacts, about 150 small labels with short inscriptions, large amounts of different kinds of Egyptian pottery, and more than 200 imported (wine) jars, probably from Palestine. In the burial chamber there were traces of a wooden shrine on the floor, and in the northeastern corner a complete crook-style scepter of ivory was found, leaving no doubt that the owner of the tomb was a ruler.

The small labels, incised with numbers or one to four hieroglyphic signs, show writing was at a developed stage. In all likelihood, the numbers indicate sizes of pieces of cloth and the signs presumably give the provenance of different goods. At least some of the inscriptions are readable (with phonetic values), mentioning administrative institutions, royal (agricultural) estates, or localities such as Buto and Bubastis in the Delta. Many of the W-class pots are also "inscribed" with one or two large signs in black ink. The most frequent sign is a scorpion, sometimes together with a plant. This is likely to be read as the "(agricultural) estate of Scorpion." Because of the high frequency of pots with this toponym, it can probably be concluded that a king named Scorpion was buried in the tomb.

Cemetery B

Cemetery B is the location of three double-

Figure 8 Inscribed labels from Tomb U-j, Umm el-Qa'ab, Abydos (2:1).

chamber tombs of Dynasty 0 (B1/2, B7/9, B17/18) and two tomb complexes of the early 1st Dynasty (B10/15/19+16, B40/50). The area to the northwest of these tombs is still covered by debris and has never been cleared.

Petrie's attribution of the tombs to Kings Horus Ro (B1/2), Ka (B7), Narmer(?) (B10), Sma(?) (B15) and Aḥa(?) (B19) was widely accepted until Kaiser re-examined the information in Petrie's report. Since a King "Sma" never existed, Kaiser concluded that the three large chambers (B10/15/19) together with the rows of subsidiary chambers (B16) should in fact be ascribed to King Aḥa, whereas the groups of double chambers were most likely those of his predecessors: Narmer (B17/18), Ka (B7/9) and perhaps, as Petrie had suggested, another king, Ro (B1/2). During the excavations by the DAI, Kaiser's reassessment was fully confirmed and the tomb's development became much clearer.

The relative sequence of the double chamber tombs is clearly demonstrated by their sizes and positions (following the general north–south development). Evidence of inscribed pots from

B1/2 and B7 indicates that these two tombs belonged to (Kings) Irj-Hor (Petrie's Ro) and Ka. Scattered seal impressions and different artifacts with inscriptions found around B17/18 are evidence that this tomb belonged to Narmer. These kings were the last rulers of Dynasty 0.

The inscribed material found nearby, as well as the similarities of construction and size of the large chambers (*circa* 7.5 × 4.5 m, and 3.6 m deep), leave no doubt that the whole complex of chambers belongs to Aḥa. It seems, however, to have been built in three stages.

In B10/15/19 there are traces of large wooden shrines. Relatively few tomb goods were found in B15 and B19, which had been robbed and were later set on fire. Human remains were collected around the subsidiary chambers of B16. Most of the bones were of young males about twenty years of age, who must have been killed when the king was buried. Near the long easternmost chamber, bones of at least seven young lions were found.

B40, a large pit similar in size to B10/15/19 but without a mudbrick lining, was discovered in 1985. Although there were remains of a wooden roof construction, the tomb was found empty and without any evidence of use. According to its size and its position between the complexes of Aḥa and Djer, B40 may be ascribed to Athotis I, the ephemeral successor of Aḥa.

The little complex of four small chambers (B50) to the south of B40 was probably intended for the subsidiary burials. B40 was probably regarded as not suitable, and the king (and his wife?) were buried in the southern chambers of B50, where there are traces of wooden coffins.

Tomb complexes of the 1st–2nd Dynasties

The seven tomb complexes of Kings Djer, Djet, Den, Adjib, Smerkhet and Qa'a, and Queen Meret-Neith of the 1st Dynasty, generally have the same plan. This consists of a large burial chamber surrounded by storerooms and many subsidiary burial chambers for servants (men, women, dwarves) and dogs.

The burial chambers all contained a large wooden shrine. The earliest known use of stone on a large scale is seen in the burial chamber of Den's tomb, where the floor was originally paved with slabs of red and black granite. From the time of Den there is a staircase leading into this chamber, which was blocked off after the burial. In the earlier tombs the storerooms are inside the burial chamber (Djer, Djet); in the later tombs they are attached to the walls on the outside or very close to it (Den).

From Djer to Den, the subsidiary burial chambers are arranged in separate rows around the royal burial chamber; only in the complexes of Smerkhet and Qa'a are they attached to it. The largest of these tomb complexes, belonging to Djer, contained over 200 subsidiary chambers. Except for one high official (of Qa'a), the subsidiary burials seem to be those of persons of lower rank (all in wooden coffins). In all probability they were killed to serve the king in his afterlife, but this custom ceased at the end of the 1st Dynasty. The two 2nd Dynasty tombs here, belonging to Kings Peribsen and Khasekhemwy, contained no subsidiary burials.

No remains of superstructures have been found, but it is likely that the royal burial chambers were covered by a mound of sand.

At each tomb complex there were two large stelae with the owner's name. The most famous one, the stela of Djet, was found by Amélineau and is now in the Louvre. There were also small stelae for the occupants of the subsidiary chambers, including those of the dogs (Den). None of these stelae, however, were found *in situ*.

Apart from an arm with bracelets made of precious stones, which was found having been hidden by robbers behind the staircase in Djer's tomb, and two fragmentary skeletons in Khasekhemwy's tomb, no other remains of the royal burials were discovered. Some of the subsidiary burials and storerooms, however, were found more or less undisturbed.

Khasekhemwy's large tomb has the new feature of a limestone-lined burial chamber, built below the floor level. This tomb has a completely different design from the other royal tombs at this site, and is similar to the gallery tombs of the 2nd Dynasty at Saqqara with an increased number of storerooms.

Important evidence of writing has been found in the tomb of Qa'a. Seal impressions of Hetepsekhemwy, the first king of the 2nd Dynasty, indicate that he completed Qa'a's burial and there was no break between the dynasties. Impressions of another seal found here, probably used by the administration of the cemetery, lists the names of all the kings buried at Umm el-Qa'ab, from Narmer to Qa'a. About thirty ivory labels with inscriptions referring to deliveries of oil were also found near this tomb.

Umm el-Qa'ab as a cult center

Beginning in the Middle Kingdom, the site gained new importance because of its association with the cult of Osiris, who was believed to have been buried here. It thus became the most sacred site in Egypt, and during the New Kingdom and Late period thousands of pilgrims left large amounts of offering pots, mostly small bowls called *qa'ab* in Arabic (hence the modern name of Umm el-Qa'ab). Amélineau estimated a total of about eight million pots.

There is evidence that the tombs were already excavated during the 12th Dynasty, probably in order to identify the burial place of Osiris. In Qa'a's tomb, some Middle Kingdom pots were found on the floor of the burial chamber, and a staircase had been built over the remaining lower part of the portcullis. In Den's tomb the entrance to the burial chamber is also partly restored in large (unburned) mudbricks, and the whole staircase shows traces of a secondary whitewash. The conversion of Djer's tomb into a cenotaph of Osiris may have taken place at the same time. A bier for Osiris (with an erased inscription) was found in this tomb by Amélineau.

See also

Abydos, Early Dynastic funerary enclosures; Abydos, Predynastic sites; Nagada (Naqada); Petrie, Sir William Matthew Flinders; pottery, prehistoric; Predynastic period, overview;

Figure 9 Tomb of King Qa'a, Umm el-Qa'ab, Abydos

Saqqara North, Early Dynastic tombs; writing, invention and early development

Further reading

Amélineau, É. 1895–1904. *Les Nouvelles Fouilles d'Abydos* 1–3. Paris.
——. 1899. *Le Tombeau d'Osiris*. Paris.
Dreyer, G. 1991. Zur Rekonstruktion der Oberbauten der Königsgräber der 1. Dynastie in Abydos. *MDAIK* 52: 11–81.
——. 1992. Recent discoveries at Abydos Cemetery U. In *The Nile Delta in Transition: 4th.–3rd. Millennium* BC, E.C.M. van den Brink, ed., 293–9. Tel Aviv.
——. 1993. Umm el-Qaab, 5./6. Vorbericht. *MDAIK* 49: 23–62.
——. 1996. Umm el-Qaab, 7./8. Vorbericht. *MDAIK* 51: 11–81.
Kaiser, W. 1964. Einige Bemerkungen zur ägyptischen Frühzeit III. *ZÄS* 91: 86–125.
——. 1981. Zu den Königsgräbern der 1. Dynastie in Umm el-Qaab. *MDAIK* 37: 247–54.
Kaiser, W., and G. Dreyer. 1982. Umm el-Qaab, 2. Vorbericht. *MDAIK* 38: 211–69.
Naville, É. 1914. *Cemeteries of Abydos* 1. London.
Peet, T.E. 1914. *Cemeteries of Abydos* 2. London.
Petrie, W.M.F. 1900–1. *The Royal Tombs of the First Dynasty*, 1–2. London.
——. 1902. *Abydos* 1. London.

GÜNTER DREYER

el-Adaïma

The Predynastic site of el-Adaïma is situated on the west bank of the Nile, about 8 km south of Esna (25°14' N, 32°35' E). It includes a very plundered cemetery and a settlement consisting of artifacts scattered over the surface for about 1 km along the edge of cultivated land. The whole site covers about 40 ha.

The site was discovered at the beginning of the century by Henri de Morgan, who excavated a part of the settlement and the plundered tombs. Most of the associated finds are now in the Brooklyn Museum. In 1973 Fernand Debono, working for the French Institute of Archaeology in Cairo, excavated thirty badly plundered tombs in an area of the cemetery which, by 1988, had been destroyed by extending the land under cultivation.

Excavations of what remained of the site were begun in 1989, under the direction of Béatrix Midant-Reynes for the French Institute. A surface collection was first conducted, followed by several field seasons of excavation. This revealed a complex development of the settlement, which gradually shifted in location from the desert to the valley during the course of the Predynastic and Early Dynastic periods (fourth and early third millennia BC).

The settlement is divided to the north and south by a large east–west depression which has been identified as a clay quarry, but its date remains unknown. On the northern side, terraces of gravel and silt show evidence of much disturbance by illicit digging for organic remains of the ancient settlement (*sebbakh*), used by local farmers for fertilizer. The southern side consists of a thick layer of sand, which slopes down to the south.

Excavations in the northern part of the site revealed occupation features of trenches and holes which were cut into the gravel terrace. The trenches, perpendicular or parallel to each other, were arranged in three areas which were associated with 73 mud holes. The diameter of these holes varied from 13 to 145 cm (averaging *circa* 45 cm); they varied from 2 to 19 cm in depth (averaging *circa* 8 cm). The trenches are probably the remains of reed fences plastered with mud and occasionally reinforced with wooden posts, as found at other Predynastic sites. More enigmatic are the holes, which could sometimes be interpreted as postholes, but most of them are too large and not deep enough for postholes.

Paleobotanical material was recovered by flotation from the filling of the holes, including seeds of wheat (*Triticum monococcum*) and barley (*Hordeum sativum*). Evidence for two kinds of activities is found here: storage of grain, and pounding/grinding grain. The absence of large grinding stones at the site and the presence of an elongated, rod-shaped, granite hammerstone in one of these holes suggest the latter function.

Based on the potsherds found in the filling of the trenches and holes, these structures date to the early/middle Predynastic period (end of Nagada I to the middle of Nagada II). The very mixed material on the surface is later, however, but never later than the 1st Dynasty.

The excavation in the southern part of the site revealed the existence of an undisturbed domestic area of special interest. Features such as hearths, storage jars and large grinding stones of granite and limestone contrast with badly eroded dwellings, the remains of which consisted of consolidated sand mixed with sherds. Numerous postholes and small wooden posts suggest light houses of timbers and reed. At least two occupational phases have been identified. There is also evidence here of four newborn infants, a skull of a young adult and five animal skeletons. One of the newborn remains was associated with a small pot and a Nile shell (*Etheria elliptica*), which was probably used as a spoon. The skull of the young adult had been deposited with offerings of animal bones. (Headless skeletons have been found buried in the cemetery at el-Adaïma, and the buried skull may be ritually connected to such burial practices.) The skeletons of four dogs and one pig were found in pits which had been dug in the completely virgin soil apart from the other settlement remains.

In the cemetery, 130 graves have been excavated out of an estimated 1,500. Seventeen of the excavated burials were intact, but others were completely destroyed. Most of the burials, however, had been disturbed during Predynastic times and some observations about the human remains and the funerary offerings were possible.

Concerning mortuary practices, two kinds of burials can be distinguished: single burials (82) and multiple burials (21). The single burials included those with grave goods (up to thirty vessels), and those without (two undisturbed burials). The multiple burials included double burials (two out of seventeen were intact) and

burials with three skeletons (three, all disturbed). One burial contained five skeletons associated with a large hearth; this burial had been badly plundered, so that the hearth ashes were mixed with broken human bones. A few cases of infectious disease have been identified from the human remains, which is an interesting occurrence in this pre-urban period.

The multi-component character of the site of el-Adaïma, with its functionally specific activity areas and domestic units, makes it an important site for data on Egyptian prehistory, the paleo-environment and subsistence strategies. With a contemporaneous cemetery and settlement, comparisons of the different data can be made. Even though it is partially disturbed, the site offers information of special relevance to those interested in town planning, daily life and mortuary practices. The stone tool industry and the ceramics also provide samples for comparison with other late prehistoric sites in Egypt and abroad.

See also

Neolithic and Predynastic stone tools; pottery, prehistoric; Predynastic period, overview

Further reading

Crubezy, E., ed. 1992. *Paléo-ethnologie funéraire et Paléo-Biologie. Archéo-Nil* 2.
Midant-Reynes, B. 1992. *Préhistoire de l'Égypte. Des premiers hommes aux premiers pharaons.* Paris.
Needler, W. 1984. *Predynastic and Archaic Egypt in The Brooklyn Museum.* Brooklyn, NY.

BÉATRIX MIDANT-REYNES

administrative bureaucracy

A fully developed administrative bureaucracy is one of the most characteristic features of ancient Egyptian civilization. Whereas the king was the religious and political embodiment of the state, the administration represented the state in practical terms for its citizens. Legislation was a royal prerogative. There is no clear evidence that the king ever delegated it to any other person. Officials of the administration had the power, the right and the duty to execute plans, wills and orders of the king and to put law into effect. They served the king, who theoretically had the power and the right of appointment and removal in all departments of public service, in temple administration and in the army. The Egyptian administration was highly centralized as far as its hierarchy was concerned. The delegation of executive power was strictly authoritarian: from the top downward, from the king to the highest officials of the state and from them to their subordinates. The head of the civil administration was the vizier, who acted as the king's deputy.

The importance of the administrative bureaucracy is underlined by the fact that the vast majority of individuals known from pharaonic Egypt are persons belonging to that bureaucracy. From the Middle Kingdom onward, "scribe" was the general term applied to them. From as early as the Old Kingdom, there are statues which represent officials as a scribe squatting on the earth, a papyrus roll on his lap with a brush in his hand to write on it. Their social status and their privileges are mentioned in literary texts from the Middle and New Kingdoms, although these texts do overestimate or exaggerate the advantages of being a member of the bureaucracy. For example, scribes are said not to pay taxes, a statement that is certainly not correct.

The Egyptian administration is mainly known from the titularies of its officials. The value of this huge amount of data, however, is restricted. Titles reflect the organizational structure of the administration; they reflect the position of the title holder within the administration, and they define his position in society. They are evidence of the department to which officials belonged, and they show their level of responsibility or authority within that department's hierarchy. Information about their functions and responsibilities generally must be drawn from other sources, such as administrative documents, biographies and other texts.

The so-called *Duties of the Vizier* is the only text known from ancient Egypt that clearly describes the function of an Egyptian official. Copies of this text are found in tombs of the Theban necropolis dating to the New Kingdom; the best preserved one is that in the tomb of Rekhmire, the vizier under Tuthmose III and Amenhotep II. There can be no doubt that the text goes back to the Middle Kingdom.

The first titles of officials are known from the 1st Dynasty. These titles prove the existence of a certain kind of administration, but they do not prove the existence of a fully developed administrative bureaucracy. By the beginning of the Old Kingdom, however, the development of the administrative bureaucracy must have reached an advanced stage. Huge building projects, such as the construction of pyramids for the reigning king, were possible only with the help of a bureaucratic system to put all necessary means (men and materials) at the king's disposal.

The first preserved text dealing with administrative matters, the inscription of Metjen from the beginning of the 4th Dynasty, clearly shows that registration of land property, its owner and size, was done by representatives of the state administration. Land was the basis of all economic life and its registration was the basis for taxation. A fully developed bureaucratic system is to be seen in the Coptos Decrees issued by King Pepi II at the end of the 6th Dynasty. The complexity of the administrative system is illustrated by these decrees exempting the temple of Min at Coptos and its staff from taxation and temporary labor for the State. They mention different offices and branches of the administration, all of which are involved in tax collection and levying the corvée. They show how different bureaus had to cooperate and control each other. On one side, there are the offices of the central administration represented by the vizier and his deputy in Upper Egypt, the overseer of Upper Egypt; they gave the directives. On the other side, there are the regional officials, the nomarchs and their staff. To fulfill their duties, the assistance was needed of offices concerned with registration and of document departments, where land and people were registered.

Land, and people attached to the land, are the basic economic resources of the country. Their registration and control was the basic element of administrative work throughout Egyptian history. This was the starting point for its organization. The administration was responsible for seeing that a certain amount of Egypt's production and productivity could be used for and by the king, i.e. the state. It was necessary to take field measurements every year, due to the different heights of the Nile inundation, and to calculate the resulting assessments of revenues. Transfer of property, such as possessions or servants, had to be testified by local officials, according to documents from the late Middle Kingdom. It was important to register the right owner, even in the case of servants, who could replace their master when he was asked for corvée labor. Agricultural products, with or without processing, form the basis for payment of governmental employees at every level: officers, people serving in the army, workers working on the king's tomb and other important projects or in workshops, and so on. Those people forced to do temporary work for the state had to be "paid" as well. Goods were used, as well as gold, for trade with foreign countries. This trade was not done by private merchants, but by the king's agents.

A great deal of Egypt's economic production was controlled by the government; the importance of private production was restricted to local markets. The main workshops and dockyards were supervised by the treasury or attached to other institutions, such as the temples, which played an important role as administrative and economic institutions during the New Kingdom. The workshops of the temple of Amen-Re at Karnak, supervised by the treasury department of the temple, are well known from documents of that period. A representation in a Theban tomb shows craftsmen of the Karnak temple producing chariots and weapons.

Temples were administrative institutions normally belonging to the local level of administration. Institutionally, they always were independent from the local or regional civil administration. At certain times, however, a nomarch could be both head of the civil administration and at the same time head of the temple administration as "overseer of priests." Priests acted as the king's representatives when they performed the daily ritual in the temple. Temple endowments constituted the material basis for the daily cult. Such endowments included agricultural land and other types of real estate given by the king to the god. In temple workshops, different kinds of articles were manufactured. Both agricultural and manufactured products could be used as payment for priests and other temple functionaries. Temples were economically self-sufficient institutions run by the high priest, who was a technocrat rather than a theologian. According to the growth of endowments, a growth of temple administration can be seen during the New Kingdom. Great temples, like that at Karnak, became the wealthiest property holders in Egypt beside the king. They had fully developed administrations similar to that of the state, with their own departments of treasury, granary and work. It seems that the right to collect taxes was delegated to them by the central government as well.

Expeditions to mining areas, quarries or building projects for national welfare were normally organized by the national department of work. In the New Kingdom, they were sometimes delegated to administrative institutions of local level or to the army. These projects comprised building the king's tomb, temples, fortifications, dams and channels, which were used not only for transportation but also, from the end of the third millennium BC, for irrigation.

As well as a technical staff with special training and experience, there were clerks attached to each project to control the workers. They had to register their presence or absence; even the reason why they were absent was sometimes written down. They registered the distribution of tools and material to avoid abuse, supervised the work and saw to the provisioning of the labor force. The best information about these procedures is from Ramesside documents discovered at Deir el-Medina, where lived the community of workmen who were responsible for the king's tomb in the Valley of the Kings in Western Thebes.

In the Old and Middle Kingdoms there was usually only one officer under the king, the vizier, who exercised supreme authority in the country in most of the departments. During the Middle Kingdom the office of the treasurer became one of the most important offices, even being equal to the vizier in some respects. Under the Hyksos kings (15th Dynasty), the treasurer replaced the vizier as head of the administration. Later, during the New Kingdom, the office of treasurer lost some of its prominence and the office of vizier was divided. At least from the times of Tuthmose III, there were regularly two viziers, one for Upper Egypt and one for Lower Egypt and the northern part of the Nile Valley. Each of these viziers was subordinate to the king only, and had his own bureaucracy at his disposal. At the end of the New Kingdom, the high priest of Karnak seems to have taken over the responsibilities of the Upper Egyptian vizier.

The authority of the vizier was normally restricted to Egypt itself. He was responsible for what the Egyptians called the "House of the King," an expression which was used to designate Egypt, or the central administration of the country. As an exception to this rule, it seems probable that in the Middle Kingdom, Nubia was under direct control of the vizier. In the New Kingdom an independent administration, similar to the adminsitration in Egypt, was installed in Nubia under a viceroy, the "King's son of Kush." The viceroy of Nubia was responsible directly to the king. His position within the administration and his function as head of the executive power can be compared to that of the vizier in the mother country.

In the Old Kingdom and first half of the Middle Kingdom, military affairs were an administrative duty organized by persons belonging to the civil administration. There was no difference in the titles held by persons responsible for military campaigns and those responsible for non-military campaigns, such as trade and mining expeditions. Members of the civil bureaucracy, such as nomarchs but also overseers of priests, led military contingents on such campaigns. In the second half of the Middle Kingdom a standing army came into existence, and the situation was changed. The army was an independent part of the state, not controlled by the civil administration or the vizier. A separate military administration was created, headed by the "great overseer of the army."

The principles of Egyptian administrative bureaucracy were established during the Old Kingdom. During the long history of Egyptian administration the main principles did not really change. Of course new titles and offices were created, sometimes replacing older ones. Certain functions were transferred from one office to another. But the overall administrative system remained in use until the end of pharaonic times, when under Ptolemaic rule a new system was introduced and Greek became the language used for administrative purposes.

See also

army; Deir el-Medina; kingship; law; nome structure; taxation and conscription; trade, foreign

Further reading

Boorn, G.P.F. van den. 1988. *The Duties of the Vizier* (Studies in Egyptology). London.

Eyre, C. 1987. Work and the organisation of work in the New Kingdom. In *Labor in the Ancient Near East*, M.A. Powell, ed., 167–221. New Haven, CT.

Quirke, S. 1990. *The Administration of Egypt in the Late Middle Kingdom*. New Malden.

Strudwick, N. 1985. *The Administration of Egypt in the Old Kingdom* (Studies in Egyptology). London.

EVA MARTIN-PARDEY

Aegean peoples

The Aegean area, which includes the Greek mainland and nearby islands to the south and east, was home during the third and second millennia BC to two main groups of people, the Minoans and the Mycenaeans. The Minoans, based on the island of Crete, enjoyed a prosperous economy dependent on a redistribution system centered on palatial complexes at sites such as Knossos, Phaistos, Mallia and Chania. In the mid-second millennium BC, the Mycenaeans of the Greek mainland gained ascendancy in the Aegean, extending their influence from imposing citadels at Mycenae, Tiryns and elsewhere to sites farther afield on the coast of Asia Minor, Rhodes, and as far east as Cyprus and the Levant. Both the Minoans and the Mycenaeans looked to the sea for transportation and trading opportunities. It is not surprising that during their marine voyages they came into contact with Egypt, the dominant power of the eastern Mediterranean at the time.

It seems likely that there was contact in both directions; that is, Aegean peoples traveled and traded in Egypt, and Egyptians ventured into the Aegean. Evidence for this contact is documented through archaeological finds of pottery and other artifacts, through depictions of Aegean gift-bearers in Theban tombs, and through texts and inscriptions.

Aegean pottery has been found at several sites in the Nile Valley and also at Marsa Matruh on the western coast of Egypt. Minoan pottery appears in Egyptian Middle Kingdom contexts, but none is yet known from before the 12th Dynasty. (Middle) Minoan sherds from settlement debris have been found at Haraga and Lahun, a planned town in the Fayum for the workmen at the pyramid complex of Senusret II. The types of Minoan pottery are varied and do not suggest the existence of a specialized trade. However, the types of Mycenaean pottery, which is more abundant in Egypt, are generally restricted to closed shapes and are usually found in tombs. The two-handled spouted vessel, the stirrup jar, is particularly popular in 18th Dynasty contexts and suggests an active trade in perfumed oil.

A rich deposit of Mycenaean pottery of almost 2,000 sherds and a half dozen vessels have been recovered in trash dumps near Akhenaten's palace at Tell el-Amarna. Such a large deposit in a settlement context is unique in Egypt. Stirrup jars are present, but more common is the flask. A few open vessels, such as cups, are also represented. Other sites with Mycenaean pottery include Memphis, Gurob, Sedment, Abydos, Thebes, Luxor and Aswan.

The appearance of Aegean pottery in datable Egyptian contexts has been very important for establishing a chronology for Minoan and Mycenaean pottery styles and for Bronze Age sites in Greece. As the understanding of Egyptian chronology is refined and as more reliance is placed on Aegean radiocarbon dates, many scholars are now attempting to establish new synchronisms. Examinations of radiocarbon dates for the eruption of the volcano on the island of Thera (Late Minoan IA period), conventionally assigned to *circa* 1500 BC, suggest that this event actually occurred *circa* 1625 BC. This new high chronology for the pottery periods of the Aegean Bronze Age is now accepted by many scholars.

Carved stone bowls were an early item of exchange between Crete and Egypt. Egyptian bowls of Early Dynastic and Old Kingdom date have been found on Crete and were probably instrumental for the beginnings of the Minoan stone vessel industry. A (Middle) Minoan stone bowl was found at Lahun.

It has long been held that the artifacts from the (Late Helladic I) shaft graves at Mycenae demonstrate strong Egyptian influence; the gold funerary masks, an inlaid "Nilotic" scene on a dagger, and a wooden box decorated with dogs are cited most commonly. The idea that Mycenaean chiefs were employed in Egypt as Hyksos mercenaries has not been given much credence, although a new higher dating of the shaft graves may revive the possibility.

Of New Kingdom date are several clearly identifiable Egyptian imports in the Aegean. In addition to Egyptian, or perhaps in some cases "Egyptianizing" scarabs, tombs in Crete have produced several Egyptian alabaster vases, including one with the cartouche of Tuthmose III. Fragments of faïence plaques inscribed with the cartouche of Amenhotep III are known from Mycenae. These plaques may be the result of an official diplomatic exchange between the pharaoh of Egypt and the ruler of Mycenae, whose power in the Mediterranean was gaining ground at the time.

Excavations conducted by Manfred Bietak at Tell ed-Dab'a in the eastern Nile Delta have yielded fragments of wall paintings which seem to be of Minoan inspiration. The site is identified as Avaris, the Hyksos capital.

A number of early 18th Dynasty tombs of royal officials and noblemen in Thebes portray male offering-bearers which seem to be from the Aegean because of their costumes and the nature of the gifts they bring. The earliest representations come from the tomb of Senmut (TT 71). The men wear short loincloths with a decorated waistband of the type seen on Minoan wall paintings. The men's hair hangs down in long locks, another Minoan trait. Among the typically Aegean artifacts carried by these men are vessels of Vapheio cup shape and a three- or four-handled jar. Perhaps the best known representations of Aegeans in Egyptian wall painting are those from the tomb of Rekhmire (TT 100), a vizier of Tuthmose III. In this tomb, the figures carry other typically Aegean artifacts including conical and animal rhytons.

The well-known "Miniature Fresco" from Akrotiri, Thera is sometimes mentioned as evidence for Egyptian or North African links with the Cyclades because elements of the scene look foreign to the Aegean: in particular, a riverscape reminiscent of the Nile and a group of dark-skinned, curly-haired warriors. Until more is known about the subject matter of Aegean wall painting, this tie remains tenuous.

The depictions of the Aegeans in Theban tombs are associated with the term "Keftiu," which appears in some of the hieroglyphic texts accompanying the paintings. The term occurs rarely in Egyptian documents, but appears with greatest frequency in the early 18th Dynasty. The identification of Keftiu with Crete seems secure, although attempts have been made to associate the name with Syria, Phoenicia and Cyprus. "Isles in the midst of the sea [great green]" is another term which first appears in

the 18th Dynasty and may refer to the Aegean area, perhaps Mycenaean Greece in particular.

An important inscription for the study of relations between Egypt and the Aegean appears on a statue base at the funerary temple of Amenhotep III at Kom el-Hetan. The base was erected with at least four other bases, each of which is carved with a series of toponyms. The place-names on the other bases refer to areas of Syro-Palestine and Mesopotamia, while those on the fifth base seem to refer to the Aegean. The list strongly suggests an Egyptian awareness of the leading centers of the Aegean, and may even reflect a specific itinerary, perhaps for a diplomatic mission.

Groups from the Aegean have also been connected with the notorious "Sea Peoples," who wrought havoc at the end of the New Kingdom in Egypt and probably played a role in the general collapse of the other great Late Bronze societies of the eastern Mediterranean. Carved reliefs and texts from the funerary temple of Ramesses III at Medinet Habu document the Sea Peoples' raids on Egypt. Aegean peoples, perhaps Mycenaean refugees, may have joined ranks with these marauding bands, which seem to have settled eventually in areas as far apart as Palestine and Sardinia.

The archaeological evidence suggests that Aegean contacts with Egypt increased over time. As the two regions grew more complex socially and economically, their ties grew closer. Initial contact with Crete was sporadic, and involved the exchange of pottery and stone vessels. Much of this trade may have been indirect, through the hands of other merchants of the eastern Mediterranean, whether from Cyprus, Syria or other Levantine centers. Later, items of greater prestige were exchanged between the two areas. Egypt may have been the Aegean's source for many valuable, exotic raw materials such as gold, alabaster, amethyst, carnelian, spices, ebony and ostrich eggshell.

Around 1450 BC, Minoan primacy gave way to a strong Mycenaean presence in the Aegean and eastern Mediterranean, at about the same time that Tuthmose III re-established Egyptian dominance in Syro-Palestine. This change is reflected in the evidence from Egypt, where

Mycenaean pottery becomes more common; little Minoan pottery is found after the Second Intermediate Period. The Mycenaean vessels, usually found in tombs, are of a type that suggests there was a specialized trade in perfumed olive oil.

Trade mechanisms of the ancient Mediterranean are currently a major topic of study, and the evidence from Egypt and the Aegean offers fruitful data for testing hypotheses about the roles of private entrepreneurs and governing states in organizing commerce. Theban tomb paintings and the faïence plaques from Mycenae suggest that exchanges also occurred on a diplomatic level, and that political alliances or at least reciprocal acknowledgment of spheres of influence may have come about. The fact that there is very little Minoan pottery in Egypt at the time of the Theban tomb paintings has suggested to some that commercial activities and diplomatic exchanges were separate phenomena.

An illustrated papyrus, from Tell el-Amarna and now in the British Museum, provides evidence for another kind of contact between the Aegean and Egypt. It seems to depict Mycenaean soldiers fighting on the side of the pharaoh, either as mercenaries or allies. The papyrus, thought to be connected with the cult of Akhenaten, shows two rows of warriors wearing short, spotted (perhaps ox-hide) tunics and what appear to be boar's tusk helmets. This pictorial evidence, combined with the large concentration of Mycenaean pottery at Tell el-Amarna, could suggest that a group of Aegeans actually resided at the royal city.

Contact between the Aegean and Egypt came to an end not long after the raids of the Sea Peoples, around 1200 BC. For a couple of centuries, Greece turned inward with little overseas contact. When international exchange began again, in the tenth century BC, the ties were primarily with the Levant. By the seventh century BC contact with Egypt was once more securely established, as is demonstrated by the important Greek mercantile settlements at Naukratis and Tell Defenna.

See also

Sea Peoples; Tell el-Amarna, city; trade, foreign

Further reading

Cline, E. 1987. Amenhotep III and the Aegean: a reassessment of Egypto-Aegean relations in the 14th Century B.C. *Orientalia* 56: 1–36.

Helck, W. 1979. *Die Beziehungen Ägyptens und Vorderasiens zur Ägäis bis ins 7. Jahrhundert v. Chr.* Darmstadt.

Kemp, B.J., and R. Merrillees. 1980. *Minoan Pottery in Second Millennium Egypt.* Mainz.

Manning, S. 1988. The Bronze Age eruption of Thera: absolute dating, Aegean chronology and Mediterranean cultural interrelations. *JMA* 1: 17–82.

Merrillees, R. 1972. Aegean Bronze Age relations with Egypt. *AJA* 76: 281–94.

Muhly, J.D. 1991. Egypt, the Aegean and Late Bronze Age chronology in the eastern Mediterranean: a review article. *JMA* 4: 235–47.

Parkinson, R., and L. Schofield. 1993. Mycenaeans meet the Egyptians at last. *The Art Newspaper* 24: 10.

Strange, J. 1980. *Caphtor/Keftiu: A New Investigation* (Acta Theologica Danica 14). Leiden.

Wachsmann, S. 1987. *Aegeans in Theban Tombs* (Orientalia Lovaniensia Analecta 20). Leuven.

Warren, P., and V. Hankey. 1989. *Aegean Bronze Age Chronology.* Bristol.

PAMELA RUSSELL

agriculture, introduction of

The earliest evidence of agriculture in Egypt dates to about 5000 BC and consists of traces of crops and livestock found at modest camps in the Fayum Depression and the Delta. From these humble beginnings, farming and village life quickly developed and became well-established by roughly 4100 BC in Lower Egypt and by 3800 BC in Upper Egypt.

The shift from hunting and gathering to food production was one of the most important changes in human history, and has accordingly been the focus of intensive research. Unfortunately, because Egypt has a very meager archaeological record from this period, probably less is known of the transition here than in other regions.

There are very few sites from the crucial period of 5000 to 4000 BC when farming was developing in Egypt, and almost none from the sixth millennium BC when farming was apparently first introduced. There are very few early farming villages and even fewer sites showing the transitional stages between foraging and farming. In addition, there is no archaeological record of Egypt's last hunter-gatherers. The last forager sites date to 800–1,000 years before the first farmers.

It is likely that much of the archaeological record has been buried under Nile sediments or destroyed through millennia of farming and village life. Indeed, all of the known early farming sites are located in marginal areas, primarily the desert. As a result, the archaeological record is not only meager but also skewed. However, the trends and patterns these sites reveal are probably representative.

The crops and their origins

The transition to farming in Egypt did not entail an independent origin of agriculture. Rather, Egyptians adopted a complex of crops, including emmer wheat, barley, peas, lentils and flax, that were domesticated in southwest Asia between 9000 and 7000 BC. Over time other domesticates were added to the economy, including some indigenous African crops, but the Near Eastern complex remained the core of Egypt's highly productive system of agriculture through pharaonic times.

Emmer wheat (*Triticum dicoccum* Schübl.), one of several wheats domesticated in southwest Asia, is now nearly forgotten as a food except in a few remote areas, but is cultivated by breeders for genetic material. Emmer is considered a "primitive" wheat because the grain is tightly encased in a hull. Upon threshing the grains do not separate freely from the hulls. The cereal head breaks into spikelets which must be pounded and then winnowed or sieved to separate the grains from the hulls. In contrast, in the more highly evolved wheats, such as durum (*Triticum durum* Desf.), the grains fall cleanly away during threshing. Perhaps because durum was easier to process, it became a major cereal in the ancient world. In Egypt, however, emmer remained virtually the only wheat until Roman rule established durum as the main cereal crop. Although there are rare finds of durum, it played no role in the Predynastic or Dynastic economy. Why durum was ignored in Egypt, while it flourished elsewhere, is a mystery.

In pharaonic Egypt, emmer was used primarily to make bread and sometimes beer, the staples of the Egyptian diet. The only evidence for Neolithic uses are a few coarse loaves of bread found in graves and settlements.

Two other wheats have been mistakenly associated with ancient Egypt. Einkorn (*Triticum monococcum* L.), a primitive wheat, has been misidentified in a few cereal finds. Spelt (*Triticum spelta* L.), a hulled wheat popular in northern Europe, is often cited as an Egyptian cereal but there is no evidence that it was ever grown in Egypt. The confusion may stem from a careless translation of the German term for hulled wheats.

Several types of barley were domesticated in the ancient Near East. Egyptians raised mainly hulled, six-row barley (*Hordeum vulgare* L.), which is well adapted to the hot, dry low lands of the Near East, but two-row types (*Hordeum distichon* L.) have also occasionally been found. Barley has a shorter growing season than wheat and a higher tolerance for poor, dry soils and saline conditions. In pharaonic Egypt, barley was used primarily for making beer but was also sometimes made into bread and used as fodder. Neolithic Egyptians may well have brewed beer and could also have used barley as a porridge or in soups, stews and breads.

Field peas (*Pisum sativum* L.) and lentils (*Lens culinaris* Medik-) were grown through pharaonic times, as evidenced by archaeological remains, but they are rarely mentioned in texts and never appear in tomb art or as offerings. Both lentils and peas are used primarily in soups and stews, and were probably prepared this way by Neolithic Egyptians.

Flax (*Linum usitatissimum* L.) was cultivated for its long stem fibers, which were woven into linen, and for the seeds which were pressed for oil, used in cooking and lighting. There are specimens of flax fibers from early farming villages but no clear evidence that the seeds were used as oil, although it is unlikely that the seeds were ignored.

While Egypt's crops were Asian, the farming techniques were African. Ecological conditions in the Nile Valley were strikingly different from those in southwest Asia where crops were planted in the fall *before* the winter rains. In Egypt seeds were sown in October *after* the flood waters drained, a technique practiced in some other African river basins as well.

By chance, the Near Eastern crops and Nile floods were perfectly matched. In contrast, the indigenous African cereals were not suitable for the Egyptian Nile Valley as they were summer crops. Sorghum was not cultivated in Egypt until Graeco-Roman times or later, when water-lifting techniques made it possible to irrigate fields located on high levees in the summer.

The Near Eastern crops probably came to Egypt from the Levant across the Sinai. The oldest agricultural sites are in the north and the shortest route from the Levant is across the Sinai. It is not clear how crops were introduced, but trade seems more probable than migration. The one known Delta Neolithic site, Merimde Beni-salame, bears no resemblance to sites in the Levant, but pottery from its oldest levels is similar to contemporary Levantine pottery, suggesting contacts across the Sinai. Various artifacts from the Fayum and Merimde also are similar, suggesting contacts among Neolithic communities as well.

The archaeological record

The scant archaeological record suggests that crops were first cultivated casually by people who were still essentially hunter-gatherers. The earliest sites are little more than hunter-gatherer camps with scatters of debris and hearths, and sometimes small pits, but no evidence of permanent structures. Within a relatively short time, however, settlements appeared with signs of more substantial occupation including structures such as pens, wind-breaks and storage facilities, particularly granaries, and in some cases dwellings. At the same time, the evidence for hunting diminished, while signs of herding increased. The Fayum sites, the oldest known sites with remains of domesticates, span a period of 5200–4500 BC. Except for the presence of crude pottery and traces of livestock and crops, the sites could be mistaken for forager camps. Situated along the shores of what was once a large freshwater lake, teeming with aquatic resources, the sites were primarily seasonal camps used by people who hunted, gathered and raised small quantities of crops and livestock.

The evidence for the Fayum crops came from a remarkable chance discovery of a basket-lined storage pit on a ridge above one of the sites which led to another 164 granaries nearby, each about 1 m wide. Traces of emmer wheat, six-row and two-row hulled barley and flax were found in seven pits while wild plants were found in others. Radiocarbon dates derived from charred grain in two of the pits averaged 5145±155 BC.

Over the course of its lifespan, the Fayum Neolithic culture changed little. There was no shift to real farming villages, as occurred in the Nile Valley. Why the Fayum cultures remained unchanged is not known, but some scholars speculate that the conditions of the Fayum Depression did not encourage full reliance on farming.

At Merimde Beni-salame, located on the western edge of the Delta, successive occupations (*circa* 5000–4100 BC) showed a rapid shift to a sedentary farming village. The oldest phase is similar to the Fayum sites, with a small, sparse occupation and few signs of farming except the domesticates: small quantities of emmer wheat, hulled six-row barley, lentils, peas, flax, and a possible free-threshing wheat. But with the second phase, Merimde became a substantial permanent settlement with storage facilities.

By the late fifth millennium BC, the same

shift to a farming economy was occurring elsewhere in northern Egypt. Near Helwan, the oldest of the el-Omari sites, dated by a single radiocarbon date to 4110±260 BC, showed many of the same features as found in Merimde's final phases, with extensive storage facilities as well as domesticates, including six-row barley, emmer and flax.

Farming appears to have gradually moved south up the Nile; the earliest evidence in Upper Egypt is from the Matmar-Badari district. The oldest phase here, the Badarian (4400–4000 BC), showed scant traces of settlement, comparable to Merimde's Phase I, along with remains of emmer wheat, six-row barley and flax capsules. The succeeding Nagada I phase (4000–3600 BC) showed more substantial settlements with a shift from underground storage pits to large, above-ground facilities. In addition to the plants in Badarian levels, lentils, vetchling (*Lathyrus sativus*), another Near Eastern crop, and fruits of sycamore fig were found, although they were probably not new at this time. They may have been missed by the small samples from earlier levels.

Farther south in the Armant-Gurna area, farming appeared slightly later, *circa* 4000 BC. Eleven sites, dated to roughly 4000–3600 BC, followed a pattern similar to the other early Nile Valley farming settlements. While the earliest occupation left few traces, succeeding occupations were more substantial with evidence of permanent settlement. Plant remains included emmer wheat, six-row barley, lentils and wild plants.

Moving farther south to the Nagada region, the earliest evidence for farming is again later, roughly 3900 BC, but by this point farming seems to be well-established. While these settlements, which date to the Nagada I phase, are modest hamlets, there is ample evidence of a farming economy, including abundant remains of emmer wheat, six-row hulled barley and flax, a large number of field weeds, and very little evidence of hunting or reliance on wild foods.

How farming traveled up the Nile valley is unknown, but it appears to have been a transfer of ideas and domesticates, moving gradually from north to south, rather than migrations of people. The regional variation seen in lithics, architecture and settlement plans suggests that these were all unique regions with their own histories. Migrants, on the other hand, would probably have established settlements that were similar. However, there was trade and communication between regions, as evidenced by similarities in ceramics. It is clear that Near Eastern crops were introduced some time before 5000 BC from the Levant and adopted by hunter-gatherers. There remains much to learn about the transformation to full-fledged farming economies throughout the Nile Valley.

See also

el-Badari district Predynastic sites; brewing and baking; Fayum, Neolithic and Predynastic sites; Helwan; Nagada (Naqada); Neolithic and Predynastic stone tools; Neolithic cultures, overview; el-Omari; plants, wild; pottery, prehistoric; Predynastic period, overview; subsistence and diet in Dynastic Egypt; Thebes, el-Tarif, prehistoric sites

Further reading

Caton Thompson, G., and E.W. Gardner. 1934. *The Desert Fayum*. London.

Eiwanger, J. 1984. *Merimde Benisalame I: Die Funde der Urgeschichte* (AVDAIK 47). Mainz.

Hassan, F.A. 1985. A radiocarbon chronology of Neolithic and Predynastic sites in Upper Egypt and the Delta. *AAR* 3: 95–116.

Wetterstrom, W. 1993. Foraging and farming in Egypt: the transition from hunting and gathering to horticulture in the Nile Valley. In *The Archaeology of Africa: Food, Metal and Towns*, P. Sinclair, T. Shaw, B. Andah and A. Okpoko, eds, 165–226. London.

WILMA WETTERSTROM

Akhmim

Akhmim, the ancient Ipu or Khent-Min, called "Khemmis" by the Greeks and "Khemin" by the Copts, is an ancient town on the Nile's east bank, opposite Sohag (26°34′ N, 31° 45′ E). The chief deity of Akhmim is the fertility god Min who, possessing powers of regeneration, is an important national god venerated throughout ancient Egyptian history. The claim of the cosmographer Leo Africanus (fifteenth–sixteenth centuries AD) that Akhmim was the oldest town in all Egypt is highly uncertain, but archaeological evidence proves that the town was already important during the Predynastic period and remained so throughout the centuries to the present day. Most of what we know about ancient Akhmim comes from the town's cemeteries.

Two cemeteries dating to the Old Kingdom, el-Hawawish on the east bank of the Nile and el-Hagarsa on the west bank, have been systematically excavated and recorded by the Australian Centre for Egyptology. El-Hawawish contains 884 rock-cut tombs, making it one of the most extensive Old Kingdom provincial cemeteries. Although most of its tombs are undecorated, many of these once possessed inscribed stone stelae now located, with other artifacts such as statues and coffins, in museums throughout the world. About sixty tombs have retained most or part of their scenes and inscriptions; they enable the study of the development of art, architecture, administration and other fields in this province through at least ten successive generations, or some 400 years in the latter part of the Old Kingdom.

One of the earliest governors of the province, Memi (late 5th Dynasty), decorated the walls of his tomb with twenty-four engaged statues, representing the tomb owner and occasionally his wife, cut into the native rock. In order to protect the valuable possessions, which were no doubt buried with a rich man like Memi, a brilliant architectural scheme was designed. A long sloping passage leads down to a burial chamber which has the appearance of a true and final burial place. However, in the corner is cut a vertical shaft, originally filled and concealed, which descends for an additional 7 m leading to a second, identical burial chamber where Memi was actually interred. Despite the architectural ingenuity, this tomb's fate was no better than that of the great majority of others throughout Egypt.

As Governor of the South, Hem-Min (tomb M43) was probably the most powerful man in Upper Egypt at the end of the 5th or the beginning of the 6th Dynasty (*circa* 2350 BC); at Akhmim, he was positioned in the center of the area under his jurisdiction. Hem-Min had an ambitious design for a single-roomed chapel (20.2 × 9.2 m), with a ceiling 3.9 m high that was to be carried on two rows of five pillars each. As his chapel was excavated into the heart of the mountain, the quality of the rock deteriorated, preventing him from leaving standing pillars. Large areas of rock from the ceiling then collapsed, totally spoiling the appearance of this magnificent chapel. The decoration was subsequently finished on a much reduced scale depicting three long registers of offering bearers, spear fishing, an offering table and dancing. Although incomplete and fragmentary, these scenes show great artistic merit, particularly in regard to the detail depicted in fish, birds, baskets and so on.

One of the most remarkable features of the governing family at Akhmim is their extraordinary love of art. A governor named Shepsipu-Min left a surprising inscription in the tomb (G95) of his father and predecessor, Nehewet, stating that he was the artist who decorated the tomb. There is no reason to doubt his claim, but no other man in such a position in ancient Egypt claimed to be an artist, and the paintings in Nehewet's tomb certainly corroborate his son's artistic talent.

The following generations of governors were perhaps not so gifted artistically, but in order to maintain the same high standard they employed probably one of the most exceptional artists of the time, Seni. He decorated two tombs, those of Kheni (H24) and Tjeti-iker (H26), belonging to father and son. Unlike most Egyptian artists who remained anonymous, Seni left the following inscription in the tomb of Tjeti-iker: "the painter Seni says: it was I who decorated the tomb of the Count Kheni, and it was I also who decorated this tomb, I being alone."

The scenes in the two tombs are similar and, luckily, wherever part of a scene was damaged in one tomb, it was preserved in the other. Thus between the two tombs, we have a complete record of the work of one of the most talented Egyptian artists of the Old Kingdom. While following the general traditions of Egyptian art, in which the artist drew what he knew rather than what he saw, such as a frontal eye on a profile face and a frontal shoulder on a profile body, Seni did not lack originality. For example, in his treatment of a hand holding a spear in the spear-fishing scene, the foreshortening of the fingers is both unusual and very successful. All the scenes are painted on mud plaster, and these depict various aspects of the daily life of the owner, including those in which he participated and those he watched and enjoyed. Fishing, fowling, harvesting, various workshop activities, sports and entertainments are represented. Although occasionally depicted in other Upper Egyptian cemeteries, watching bull-fighting seems to be a particularly favored form of entertainment at Akhmim.

The importance of a tomb should not only be judged by its richness and size; some of the poorer, smaller tombs are equally informative. One of the later tombs of the cemetery, belonging to Rehu (BA17), is small and exhibits neither grand architecture nor a high style of art. However, dating to the very end of the Old Kingdom, the biographical inscription of the owner is of inestimable value for the understanding of this dark and little-known period. The inscriptions, as well as the scenes, were cheaply and hastily painted on mud plaster and reflect the poor workmanship of the time, but the information presented about war, famine and difficult conditions is of great value.

From the same period as the tombs of el-Hawawish, those of el-Hagarsa are generally smaller and belong to officials of lesser status. The discovery there of two tombs, one belonging to an Overseer of the Army named Wahi and the second belonging to a Treasurer of the King of Lower Egypt named Hefefi, throws important new light on the last years of the Old Kingdom, before its collapse around 2200 BC. The undisturbed burial chamber of Hefefi contained six mummies in coffins belonging to one family, men and women, forming three

generations, including two children, four and seven years old. Complete medical and DNA examinations currently in progress are adding to our information on family relationships in ancient Egypt and on the results of the probable civil war which erupted at that time between the northern and southern parts of Upper Egypt. Akhmim was apparently at the borderline between the two warring factions.

With the exception of a stela belonging to a provincial governor named Intef, nothing is known about Akhmim in the Middle Kingdom. More is known from the New Kingdom; King Ay (the successor of Tutankhamen) originated from Akhmim. As a proud native of this town, Ay restored its temples and erected a new rock-cut temple for Min at el-Salamuni following the end of the Amarna period and the return to polytheistic religion. Most of his building projects were assigned to his architect, Nakht-Min, another citizen of Akhmim. Yuya and Tuya, the parents of Queen Tiye (wife of Amenhotep III) are also known to have come from Akhmim. Excavations in the town of Akhmim by the Egyptian Antiquities Organization have uncovered a temple built by Ramesses II. Large statues of the king and of his daughter-wife, Merytamen, were found and part of the layout of the temple has been discerned. Whether this was the famous temple, the so-called "Birba" referred to by the Arab historians, remains uncertain.

Of particular interest is the recently investigated large tomb of Sennedjem at Awlad Azzaz. The owner was overseer of tutors, possibly of Tutankhamen, whose cartouches occur in a number of places in the tomb. The human figures are depicted in the Amarna style, but modifications to the original reliefs show an attempt to eliminate the Amarna features. Although fragmentary, the scenes in this tomb include important themes like Tutankhamen in his chariot and a representation of the "window of appearances." The tomb casts some new and important light on the leading personages in Egypt during the tumultuous closing years of the 18th Dynasty.

Akhmim seems to have maintained its importance during the Late period and throughout the Ptolemaic dominance of Egypt, when the town was called "Panopolis," i.e. the city of Pan, the Greek god who was identified with Min. In the earlier centuries AD, Christianity was introduced in Egypt, resulting in conflict with the old pagan traditions in certain centers like Akhmim. During the Roman period the Egyptian Christians (Copts) were persecuted, with this movement reaching its peak under the Roman emperor Diocletian. Many Christians escaped to the surrounding mountains, living in ancient tombs after replastering

Figure 10 The mummy of Hefefi (from el-Hagarsa) in its wooden coffin

the walls to cover what they considered to be scenes of pagan idolatry. Shortly afterwards, however, Christianity became the official religion of the Empire and many monasteries were built at Akhmim. The most important of these is the "white monastery," also called the monastery of St Shenute, which was constructed in the fourth century AD, reusing many decorated stones from ancient Egyptian temples.

Akhmim is an important archaeological site which preserves valuable information on Egyptian history during the pharaonic, classical, Coptic, Islamic and more recent periods. While its cemeteries at the edges of the desert have now received scholarly attention, the original settlement itself remains, as the majority of others in Egypt, mostly buried under the modern town.

See also

Old Kingdom provincial tombs; representational evidence, Old Kingdom private tombs

Further reading

Kanawati, N. 1980–92. *The Rock Tombs of el-Hawawish: The Cemetery of Akhmim*, 10 vols. Sydney.
——. 1992. *Akhmim in the Old Kingdom 1: Chronology and Administration*. Sydney.
Kanawati, N., *et al.* 1993–5. *The Tombs of el-Hagarsa*, 3 vols. Sydney.
McNally, S. 1993. *Excavations in Akhmim, Egypt: Continuity and Change in City Life from Late Antiquity to the Present*. Oxford.

NAGUIB KANAWATI

el-Alamein, Marina

The coastal region between Alexandria and Marsa Matruh has been little investigated by archaeologists. One of the few known sites from this region is Marina, located 6 km east of el-Alamein (30°50′ N, 28°57′ E).

The ruins of the ancient town were accidentally discovered during building construction, and in 1986 the Egyptian Antiquities Organization (EAO) began salvage excavations at the site. Shortly afterwards the Polish Center of Archaeology in Cairo, headed by Wiktor A. Daszewski, began systematic excavations in the western part of the site and conducted a survey and documentation of all the monuments.

The ancient site is located between the slope of an ancient beach and a lagoon, separated from the open sea by a narrow strip of sand and the modern Alexandria–Marsa Matruh highway. It extends over an area 1 km in length east–west. In the lower (northern) part of the site near the sea is the town where several buildings were partly cleared of sand by the EAO. The upper part of the site was extensively used as a cemetery.

Fieldwork by the Polish Mission was concentrated in the cemetery, where a series of important discoveries were made. Some well preserved tombs were uncovered, of four different types:

1 Trenches hewn in the bedrock and covered with limestone slabs.
2 Tombs cut in the bedrock with superstructures in the shape of step pyramids.
3 Tombs of cubic structures built on the rock surface with two or four loculi, frequently surmounted by funerary monuments, such as a column or sarcophagus. Investigation of the remains of Tomb 1C determined that the loculus was covered by a structure imitating a huge sarcophagus. Parallels to this type of tomb are found in Turkey and Cyrenaica. Another tomb (1F) contained two loculi and was surmounted by a huge pillar decorated with two capitals in the so-called "Nabatean" style. The upper (smaller) capital stood on a short base which rested on the lower (larger) capital.
4 Hypogea consisting of superstructures with monumental entrances which lead to vaulted staircases with burial chambers hewn in the bedrock. Large vertical shafts provided the burial chambers with air and light. The chambers were designed with rock-cut benches, loculi and stone altars on the floor.

These four groups of tombs can be dated from the late second century BC (Groups 1 and 2) to the late first century AD (Group 4). The tombs of Group 3 can be assigned to the early first century AD. Both Alexandrian and local traditions are seen in these tombs.

The Polish excavations yielded a vast collection of finds, including lamps, glass vessels and pottery from Cyprus, the Aegean, Asia Minor and Italy. Several sculptures were also found. Among the most remarkable discoveries were a lead coffin in Tomb 1GH and mummies in one of the side chambers of Tomb 6. Like the well-known Fayum examples, the mummies from Marina have portraits painted on wooden panels.

In 1988 the joint Polish–Egyptian Preservation Mission initiated a restoration program. Three monuments in the necropolis (Tombs 1, 1B, 1C), toppled by an earthquake, were restored. Several other excavated tombs were reinforced and repaired.

Figure 11 El-Alamein, Marina, monument and superstructure of Tomb 1

In the area of the town a series of buildings, both private and public, were excavated by the EAO. Several large houses (Nos. 1, 2, 9) located in the central part of the site were found surprisingly well preserved. They were designed with rooms usually grouped around one or two peristyle courtyards. Each house was provided with vaulted underground cisterns and a well-developed system of aqueducts. Fragments of architectural decoration, such as moldings, cornices, capitals and so on, were found in the debris. In some cases, painted plastering was still preserved on the walls.

In the central part of the site, a *tholos*-shaped bath was investigated by the EAO. Some recently discovered structures located close to the lagoon (Nos. 12, 13, 14) seem to have served as storehouses. The finds from these excavations were also plentiful, and included various lamps, coins, statues and pots.

Based on these finds, the chronology indicates that most of the excavated structures date to the first–third centuries AD. The ancient town must have been a very prosperous community. A wide range of imported pottery, particularly amphorae, suggests flourishing trade relations with the entire Mediterranean.

The settlement at Marina was probably destroyed by an earthquake in the late third century AD, but was partially inhabited again in the fifth–sixth centuries AD. A small basilica church (No. 15) uncovered in the eastern sector by the EAO is the best evidence of this occupation. No traces of any later (Islamic) occupation were found.

See also

Alexandria; Apis; Marea; Marsa Matruh; Taposiris Magna

ALI HASSAN

Alexandria

The Mediterranean port city of Alexandria was established by Alexander the Great in 332 BC at the northwestern edge of the Nile Delta

(31°12′ N, 29°53′ E), in the Egyptian nome of Western Harpoon. The city's location was strategic, on a rocky strip separating Lake Mareotis from the Mediterranean Sea, opposite the small islet of Pharos just off the coast; it lay at the crossroads between Europe, the Near East and Africa. The small Egyptian settlement of Ra-kedet, or Rakhotis in Greek, already existed at the site.

The plan of the new city was the work of the royal architect Deinocrates of Rhodes; it resembled a *chlamys*, a Greek cloak, spread along the sandy coast. It was 30 stadia long (5 km) and 7–8 wide (1.5 km). The city developed along a regular grid of wide streets set at right angles. The main street, sometimes referred to as the processional road or *platea*, ran lengthwise from east to west, being an extension of the road to Canopus to the east. Two main crossroads running north–south divided the city into three equal parts and may have separated the city's three main nationalities: Greeks, Jews and Egyptians. The districts, whose borders remain unknown, were given the names of the first letters of the Greek alphabet. Other local names in use included Rhakotis (for the Egyptian quarter), Brucheion (for the royal quarter), Copron Mons, Neapolis and Necropolis. Walls encircled the city. To the east and west of the fortifications were gardens and necropoli.

Potable water was supplied to Alexandria by a canal from the westernmost branch of the Nile. The island of Pharos was connected to the mainland by a pier-bridge (about 1 km long), called the "Heptastadion." On the island a lighthouse was constructed, presumably by Sostratos of Knidos; the tall tower was to become a symbol of the city. The royal district (Brucheion), together with the port and necropolis of the rulers (Ptolemaion), was located on the coast in the vicinity of Cape Lochias, at the end of the eastern of the two chief crosswise streets. Thanks to the underwater investigations carried out in 1996 by the French, the ancient coastline of the eastern port and Cape Lochias have been surveyed and mapped. The city ports lay on either side of the Heptastadion. The eastern or Great Port extended up to Cape Timonium. In the western port, called Eunos-

tos, the canal from the Nile and Lake Mareotis emptied into the port basin, called Kibotos.

Nothing is known of the location and appearance of the city's main buildings, the commercial stores, docks, agora, museum (library), gymnasium, theater, royal necropolis with the tomb of Alexander, and numerous temples. The location of the lighthouse, Serapeum, Caesareum, stadium, hippodrome, temples of Serapis and Isis, and the Thesmophorium are known. Even the numerous tombs constantly being discovered on the outskirts of the city do not have their aboveground structures preserved (except for some unrecorded ruins in the Wardian district).

This picture of the city is known from the ancient sources: Strabo (VXI1, 8), Diodorus (XVI1, 52, 5), Achilles Tatius, Ammianus Marcellinus, Pseudo-Callisthenes and numerous other texts concern life in the city, its appearance and historical events. In the first three centuries of its existence, that is, until the fall of the Ptolemies, Alexandria's location near the wealth of Egypt and its qualities as a modern city and port made the capital with its population of one million people one of the leading cities in the part of the eastern Mediterranean dominated by the Greeks.

The Roman period was a time of repeated destructions and gradual decline. This started in 32 BC with the conquest of Alexandria by Julius Caesar, the burning of the fleet, part of the port district and probably the library. The defeat of Cleopatra VII and Antony by Octavian made the city and country dependent on Rome. The rebellion in AD 116 of the Alexandrian Jews was overcome by Trajan and ended in the destruction of the western, Jewish district of the city. Presumably as a result, the chief eastern cross-street became a peripheral tract and the western one gained new importance as the central crossroad within a reduced city area.

Alexandria remained a favorite with Roman emperors throughout the second century AD, as indicated by honorific and foundation inscriptions discovered there (Antoninus Pius erected the Gates of the Sun and Moon, Hadrian a palace and the town walls). An incident with

Caracalla in AD 218 seems not to have led to any damages to the city's architecture, contrary to what followed the repressions of Aurelian in AD 273, when the city dared to take the side of Queen Zenobia of Palmyra.

Archaeological evidence of destruction in the third century AD is more extensive than just in the royal quarter (Brucheion), which is mentioned in texts. Diocletian squashed another rebellion of the inhabitants in the last years of the third century AD. Commemorating the event is the gigantic column, known mistakenly as Pompey's Pillar, set up in the Serapeum. The great imperial foundations of the early fourth century, such as the complex of imperial baths begun presumably by Constantine the Great, excavated in the city center, are not mentioned anywhere in the written sources.

Even though the Apostles did not have a hand in establishing Christianity in Egypt, tradition has it that St Mark the Evangelist was buried in a martyr's chapel located in close proximity to the eastern harbor. Of the church built on the spot in the fifth century AD, only four capitals remain. Christianity in the first two centuries was gnostic in character and played a secondary role. It got rid of pagan elements only after the time of Septimius Severus, and then developed quickly.

In the late fourth century AD, particularly during the times of Theodosius I when Theophilus was the patriarch, religious fanaticism led to destructive anti-pagan repressions. The Serapeum went up in flames (AD 389), the temple of Dionysos and the theater were destroyed, and other temples were transformed into churches (St Michael's church in the temple of Saturn, a cathedral in the Caesareum, St John the Evangelist's church in the Serapeum). Statues were broken into pieces and libraries burned. Even so, in homogeneous ceramic deposits of the fifth century AD there are votive figurines of Isis, Harpokrates and the Dioskuroi next to ampullae of St Menas and Christian lamps.

Earthquakes in AD 365, 447 and 535 completed the destruction of the city. The sinking of the area by about 3 m, probably as a result of the earthquake in AD 365, flooded many of the structures located directly on the coast. A rising water table necessitated changes in the infrastructure (sewerage and underground aqueducts) and a raising of the foundation levels. Pauperized and disintegrated, the Alexandrian community could not face up to the invasion and long-standing siege of the Persians under Chosroes II in AD 619 and the Arabs of Caliph Omar in AD 642. After the invasions and earthquake of AD 792 the city's decline continued, and churches were rebuilt into mosques.

The first large-scale, systematic excavations at Alexandria were conducted in 1866 by Mahmud Bey (el-Falaki) on an order from Khedive Ismail of Egypt. The results were published together with a reconstructed plan of the ancient city showing the course of the walls, canals and streets discovered in trenches and verified by data in the textual sources. The street network is from the Roman period. Later excavations helped fill in the plan, but never undermined its accuracy.

Mahmud Bey drew another map of the city showing the plan before the Arab walls were dismantled in 1892, before the boulevard was constructed along the bay in 1902–5 and before the Ramleh railway and stations were built in the first half of the twentieth century. The map (1:5000) was published in 1902. All the ruins and deposits of ancient rubble were marked on this map, as well as the current names of streets, the more important architectural structures and building lots. Modern archaeology uses Arab names or arbitrary designations from Mahmud Bey's plan to determine locations. Bartocci's map, in *Alexandrea ad Aegyptum* (1922) is the model for combining the topography of the ancient city with that of the modern one.

The establishment of the Graeco-Roman Museum in 1893, with Giuseppe Botti as director, was important for the city's history for several reasons. In creating its own collection, the museum made an effort to stop the dispersion and destruction of the archaeological finds. It also conducted more systematic observations and salvage excavations wherever and whenever possible. Finally, it created the possibility of publishing the results of archaeological research in the *Bulletin de la Société archéologique d'Alexandrie* (*BSAA*) and in the *Rapport sur la marche et la service du Musée Greco-Romain d'Alexandrie.*

Evaristo Breccia, who succeeded Botti in the post of director of the Museum, published *Alexandrea ad Aegyptum* (1922), a compendium of knowledge on the ancient city. The next museum director, Achille Adriani, restored and preserved the ruins of the Alabaster Tomb and saved a set of frescoes depicting oxen turning a water wheel, from a tomb in the Mafrousa necropolis, to name just two of his achievements. Alan Rowe extended the explorations in the Serapeum and A.J.B. Wace excavated on Hospital Hill in Mazarita and on the outskirts of the Kom el-Dikka fort (his results were published only in part). Postwar directors of the museum, Riad, Hanna and el-Gheriany, in cooperation with the Alexandrian University, carried out investigations in different areas of the city, particularly in the cemeteries of Hadra, Mustapha Pasha and Gabbari, and published a selection of their finds.

A mission from the Polish Center of Mediterranean Archaeology of Warsaw University has worked on the site of the dismantled Kom el-Dikka fort since 1959. Kazimierz Michalowski's idea of creating a special park displaying the discovered ruins in their urban context, after proper restoration procedures, is being implemented with the permission of Egyptian authorities. Polish excavations have confirmed Mahmud Bey's plan, adding a cross-street through the insula (between streets R4 and R5). Public buildings were constructed in the eastern part of the insula, after the destructions of the third century AD. An imperial bath complex with subsidiary structures and service areas was discovered in the vicinity of a small theater of the fourth–seventh centuries AD,

Figure 12 General view of the 1979 excavations at Kom el-Dikka

which was rebuilt repeatedly, resulting in a total change of form (added dome) and function (*bouleuterion, ecclesiasterion*). A large cistern building also belongs to this complex. In the first–third centuries AD the area was covered with houses of the *villa urbana* type, and then later by less affluent houses, workshops and stores (fourth–seventh centuries AD).

Excavations have established stratigraphic sequences, confirmed periods of destruction, reconstructed the architecture and investigated the ancient water supply. Newly discovered ruins of early Roman date demonstrate how the city developed and verify data from the written sources. Stratigraphic investigations have added to studies on pottery, workshop influences, trade and imports. The plan of the Ptolemaic streets and the ruins of this period, however, will probably remain unknown. On the basis of the Hellenistic features of the Roman plan, we can assume it repeats the Ptolemaic network. It would also appear that the coastal part of the city (north of street L1) had a greater concentration of public buildings, while the southern districts were reserved for domestic and industrial areas, thus explaining the dearth of monuments there. Modern archaeology in Alexandria is often, however, a tedious penetration of secondary deposits and rubbish layers of considerable depth, only to reach rising ground water below.

See also

Late and Ptolemaic periods, overview; Macedonians; Roman period, overview

Further reading

el-Abbadi, M. 1990. *Life and Fate of the Ancient Library of Alexandria*. Paris.
Bernand, A. 1995. *Alexandrie des Ptolemées*. Paris.
Fraser, P.M. 1972. *Ptolemaic Alexandria*. 3 vols. Oxford.
La Riche, W. 1996. *Alexandria: The Sunken City*. London.
Steen, G.L., ed. 1993. *Alexandria: The Site and the History*. New York.
Tkaczow, B. 1993. *Topography of Ancient Alexandria*. Warsaw.

WOJCIECH KOŁATAJ

Amarna Letters

The Amarna Letters, inscribed on clay tablets in the cuneiform writing of Babylonia, were discovered in 1887 at the site of Tell el-Amarna by a group of peasants. The circumstances of discovery led to the loss of perhaps 150–200 tablets; the surviving tablets (*circa* 360) were sold to different individuals and institutions, and are presently kept in various collections, mostly in the Berlin (*circa* 200), British (*circa* 100) and Cairo (*circa* 50) museums. The discovery provided a stimulus for excavations at the site, but only a score of additional tablets were found.

After pioneering works by Winckler, Sayce, Scheil and others, a complete edition of the Amarna Letters was published in 1907 by J.A. Knudtzon (a volume of notes and indexes was added in 1915). Knudtzon's work was supplemented in 1987 by that of A.F. Rainey. More recently a definitive translation has been produced by W.L. Moran (French in 1987, English in 1992), but Knudtzon's is still the basic transcription of the letters.

The Amarna tablets clearly belonged to the archive of a royal office dealing with foreign affairs; hence the use of the cuneiform writing and the Babylonian language, the "diplomatic" medium of the time. Most of the tablets are letters, sent to and received from foreign correspondents in western Asia. Because of selective archival procedures, the incoming Asiatic letters were regularly kept, while the outgoing Egyptian ones constitute a small minority (just a dozen) in the extant collection. In addition to the letters, some lists of gifts were also part of the diplomatic exchange. A few Babylonian literary texts (Adapa, Sargon's "King of Battle") and school texts (Egypto-Babylonian vocabularies) were used for scribal training.

The chronology of the archive is basically coincident with the period of Akhetaten (18th

Dynasty), to the early years of Tutankhamen. Some letters, addressed to Amenhotep III, were brought to Amarna some time after they were received in Egypt. A precise chronology of the letters is not easily constructed; the cuneiform letters bear no date, and only a few hieratic ink datations have been added. Even the cuneiform renderings of Egyptian names (of pharaohs and courtiers alike) are not always clear. The historical synchronisms with events known from Egyptian and Hittite historical texts are well ascertained in basic outline, but some doubts are still left (connected with the identity of the pharaoh's widow writing to Suppiluliuma, the Hittite (Hatti) king, and with the problem of coregencies).

A minority of the letters (about forty) came from the independent "great kings" of western Asia: Hatti, Arzawa, Mitanni, Assyria, Babylonia and Alashiya. Most of the letters came from the "small kings" of Syria and Palestine. Inner Syria was independent of Egypt, and its letters have a political and military content. The coast of Syria and all of Palestine were Egyptian dependencies, and their letters have an administrative content. The dossier of Rib-Adda, the king of Byblos, belongs to this group, but is worthy of special mention because of its size (by far the largest in the archive, with about seventy letters) and character. Important lots were written by Abdi-Ashirta and Aziru of Amurru, by Aitagama of Qadesh, by Abi-Milki of Tyre, by Lab'aya of Shechem and by Abdi-Hepa of Jerusalem.

Only the few letters written in Babylonia are in "good" middle Babylonian dialect. The rest are written by scribes of different mother tongues, and show many peculiarities belonging to (or influenced by) their native language. The scribes' mother tongues were many and varied: northwest Semitic "Canaanite" in Phoenicia and Palestine, Hurrian in northern Mesopotamia and inner Syria, Hittite in Anatolia, and Egyptian in the outgoing letters. The letters have been studied in order to reconstruct the Canaanite dialect, on the basis of the glosses (words in the local language, written in the Babylonian syllabary) and of the morphological and syntactical deviance in the verbal system.

The Amarna Letters provide a detailed picture of the international relations at the time of the 18th Dynasty. It has become customary to label the "Amarna age" as the period covered by the letters, throughout the entire Near East. If compared to the celebrative inscriptions of the time, the letters help in understanding how both groups of texts make use of biased and opposed interpretive patterns. The official inscriptions celebrate the central position of Egypt and the higher status of Pharaoh, and view the foreign rulers as inferior, vanquished and submissive or destined to submit, offering their goods and women as a tribute in exchange for survival. The same relationships are described in the letters in a different way: as a network of reciprocal performances among peers. The so-called "great kings" (those of Egypt, Hatti, Mitanni, Babylonia and Assyria) address each other as "brothers," exchange messages and greetings, bargain on the value of gifts and counter-gifts, ask and lend specialized personnel, and negotiate for dynastic marriages.

Such a reciprocal arrangement is largely fictional and ceremonial in character. In reality Egypt had a higher and stronger position, both in economic terms and cultural prestige. This is shown by the self-humiliating tone used by Asiatic kings in asking for the Egyptian gold, and by the fact that Pharaoh is always receiving and never providing women. As to the military balance, the memory is still alive of the victorious wars led by the Tuthmoside kings in Syria. But the situation is changing with the intervention of Suppiluliuma, who, after subduing Mitanni and his vassals in Syria, takes possession of some former vassals of Egypt as well (Amurru, Qadesh, Ugarit). The Egyptian army does not seem to have been quick or strong enough to resist the Hittite advance. However, it is not certain whether this failure is to be imputed to a lack of decision and interest by the Amarna court (because of its religious engagements, or because of inner feuds), or simply to Hittite superiority.

Formerly, a "catastrophical" view prevailed in reconstructions of the Egyptian political and military control of Syro-Palestine. The letters of the local kinglets insistently call upon help against their enemies, lamenting the surrounding insecurity. They ask for food and troops in order to ensure the protection of their cities and lament the disinterest of Pharaoh. The situation was interpreted as a general crisis of the Egyptian presence and control, a crisis often credited to Akhenaten's engagement with his religious reforms. In recent years, it has become clear that the Egyptian control went basically unchallenged; the local kinglets were simply trying to present their own enemies as enemies of Egypt as well, in order to get some help. The Egyptian messages are part of a seasonal routine of tribute-collecting by Egyptian officials with a small armed corps. The local letters both assert the vassals' submission and try to gain additional benefits from the Egyptian presence. The local kingdoms kept their rulers, and kept fighting each other. The Egyptian administration was basically disinterested in what happened, provided that tribute was regularly delivered. No general collapse of the Egyptian "empire" in Syro-Palestine can be detected in the Amarna Letters, although the northern area of the region was lost to the Hittites.

Syro-Palestine was divided into three provinces, each containing an administrative center with an Egyptian governor, garrison and storehouses. These were located in Sumura (for the northern or Amurru province, eventually lost to the Hittites), Kumidi (for the inner province of Ube, i.e. the Beqaa and Damascus area) and Gaza (for the southern province of Canaan). Some areas, like the Yarimuta agricultural land and a few coastal cities, were under direct Egyptian exploitation. The inner steppe and highlands, inhabited by nomads and refugees, were largely outside any control (by the Egyptians and the local kinglets alike), but this was a normal state of affairs in the region.

See also

Canaanites; New Kingdom, overview; Tell el-Amarna, city

Further reading

Heintz, J.G. 1982. *Index documentaire d'El-Amarna*. Wiesbaden.

Liverani, M. 1990. *Prestige and Interest: International Relations in the Near East ca. 1600–1100 B.C.*. Padova.

Moran, W.L. 1992. *The Amarna Letters*. Baltimore.

Rainey, A.F. 1978. *El Amarna Tablets 359–379*. Kevelaer-Neukirchen-Vluyn.

MARIO LIVERANI

anthropology and Egyptology

Egyptology as a discipline began in the early nineteenth century. It has always been an independent field of research dealing with a particular culture area, from the Predynastic period until AD 395, the date of the last known hieroglyphic inscription. (Coptic studies deal with the Christian era and culture in Egypt.) Anthropology, on the other hand, consists of four fields: physical or biological anthropology, anthropological linguistics, archaeology, and sociocultural anthropology. It thus aims to study human cultures of all times and places, individually or from a comparative view, synchronically or diachronically.

The methods and theories applied by anthropology are, of course, applicable to the study of ancient Egyptian culture. Indeed, since the beginning of modern scientific research in Egypt physical anthropologists have been part of excavation teams. Linguistics, in the form of historical linguistics within the European tradition, has dealt with texts in Old, Middle and Late Egyptian and the language that evolved in the Late, Ptolemaic and Roman periods, often within the wider framework set for Afro-Asiatic languages. It is only since the mid-1970s that modern linguistic theory has been taken into account by Egyptologists specializing in the language of the Dynastic period.

For the most part, interdisciplinary work in archaeology and sociocultural anthropology has not been a concern of Egyptological studies. One reason that has been given for this is the extensive labor going into the editing, translating and interpretation of hieroglyphic texts from all phases of ancient Egyptian culture. The predominance of funerary data has also made many Egyptologists concentrate on the religious aspects of culture.

The cultural analysis of ancient Egypt, however, has always required Egyptologists to use concepts that carry meanings reflecting the cultural tradition from which they arose (for example, the concepts of English *kingdom*, German *Reich* or French *empire*, which are used to describe ancient Egyptian sociopolitical organization during Dynastic times; these concepts superimpose fields of meaning that restrict an understanding of the archaeological and textual evidence). Similarly, anthropology is dependent on applying scientifically defined concepts: for example, terms that describe forms of sociopolitical organization, such as tribe, chiefdom, state; the functioning of the economy, such as trade, market, center and periphery, distribution, reciprocity, taxes, selling, buying, bartering; the social structure, such as class, aristocracy, official, patron–client, title, status, rank, prestige; and the belief system, such as state religion, beliefs, gods and priests.

Anthropology and Egyptology are both sciences of culture and therefore have similar concerns. As such, both fields of inquiry are dependent on an acceptable vocabulary to communicate their results. Furthermore, most of the terms noted above are fairly general; this means that their semantic field contains by implication further assumptions which color our view of the culture described. The anthropologist Clifford Geertz has made a useful distinction between experience-distant (or etic) concepts which reflect our scientific tradition and experience-near (or emic) concepts which are from the vocabulary of the cultures we study. It is useful to integrate indigenous concepts from ancient Egypt, such as "pharaoh" or "*ma'at*" (referring to the correct order of the universe), into our critical discourse in order to balance possible misunderstandings that could arise from our own concepts of culture.

From the beginning of Egyptological studies, understanding of ancient Egypt and its textual evidence was biased. This is not different today, but in current ethno-archaeological research, this insight is consciously highlighted and integrated into interpretations. It has recently been argued that we might "read" archaeological sites like a "text" and that the archaeologist produces a new "text" with his/her site report; proposed by Ian Hodder, this view is controversial, but it does have interesting aspects and consequences for archaeological research.

Apart from the concepts, with their denotations and connotations, it is the permanent application of analogies within a comparative perspective that helps make the past and/or a different civilization accessible. A reasonable argument against analogies may be made by stating that they only demonstrate our ignorance of the operative principles in cultures. However, the integration of new information, usually by induction, very much relies on comparing it to what we already know. It is here that analogies allow us to develop new hypotheses about culture processes.

Two kinds of analogies need to be distinguished: there are direct historical analogies which use knowledge from a different time period in the same geographical area to understand the period in question, such as when we draw on folklore studies of contemporary funerary behavior in rural modern Egypt to understand funerary texts from ancient Egypt. There are also indirect or unconnected analogies. These apply knowledge of other cultures and ones from different times to the interpretation of archaeological and cultural data, such as when analogies are made about the processes of state formation in Mesopotamia and in ancient Egypt (different region/same time), or by treating the economic behavior of people in the markets of East Africa under colonial rule as reflecting a kind of economic behavior that ancient Egyptians may have shown (different region/different time).

A further differentiation, however, is necessary. Cultural artifacts, such as tools, may be compared and their development traced, i.e.

using substantive analogies in which similarities of components are compared. In her book *The Fellahin of Upper Egypt*, Winifred S. Blackman included a chapter on ancient Egyptian analogies in order to show the cultural continuities in peasant life. Similarly, folklorist H.A. Winkler in his *Ägyptische Volkskunde* traced direct historical continuities, but he was also able to show that changes in the material culture were extreme, due to the influence of the Graeco-Roman occupation in Egypt.

Facets of cultural systems, such as the function of monumental architecture in Egyptian and Mesoamerican cultures, may also be compared. Here, systems with similar form (structure) probably show a number of other properties in common and therefore make the comparison helpful in postulating evidence only available in one dataset for the other: these analogies are called structural analogies.

An important example of this kind of structural analogy is Michael Hoffman's comparison of trade and the acquisition of sumptuous and prestige goods by the chiefs at Hierakonpolis during Predynastic times, using the concept of chiefdoms as understood by cultural anthropologists. Hoffman cites the Melanesian *kula* system, a form of economic exchange with strong social and ritual aspects, as described by Bronislaw Malinowski, to help explain the archaeological evidence from Predynastic Hierakonpolis.

It is not possible to provide any evidence of direct archaeological or ethnohistorical links between the Nile Valley and areas farther south, beyond a postulated common substratum resulting from the early movements of pastoralists following climatic shifts around 2500 BC. Thus, all references to African political systems, especially from East Africa, and references to similarities visible in symbolism and performance in ethnographies and ancient Egyptian texts (e.g. referring to divine kingship, as described by Henri Frankfort), should be treated as structural analogies. In such cases, however, the cults and rituals referred to are mostly from the early phases of ancient Egyptian history, where such practices are only fragmentarily recorded using an elusive writing system and unconnected symbols.

Because most of their research is text-aided, Egyptologists have not often applied anthropological knowledge, methods or theories. The beginning of scientific Egyptology, which dates to 1822 with Jean-François Champollion's publication of his decipherment of hieroglyphic texts, and the early achievements of Egyptologists were very much based on archaeological research, which supplied huge amounts of new data and texts. Even Adolf Erman's influential *Ägypten und ägyptisches Leben im Altertum* or Eduard Meyer's history of ancient Egypt, though reflecting the *Zeitgeist*, did not integrate the then available anthropological knowledge about other cultures.

It was only just before the turn of the century that a diffusionist perspective was introduced into Egyptology by Flinders Petrie with his concept of the "New Race," to explain artifacts from the First Intermediate Period. This interpretation was soon discarded. But apart from this example, Egyptologists did not take account of the theoretical trends in anthropology until well after the Second World War. Consequently, a positivistic view dominated Egyptology, resulting in the excavation of huge areas and cemeteries, and epigraphic surveys and the publication of texts.

However, the diffusionist argument had gripped anthropology mainly as an antidote to the theory of evolution that had dominated the field during the second half of the nineteenth century. Thus the physical anthropologist Grafton Elliot Smith, who was embroiled in a scientific dispute with Flinders Petrie following Smith's book *The Ancient Egyptians and the Origins of Civilization*, proclaimed an extreme diffusionism by arguing that nothing was invented more than once. Outside Egyptology scholars, such as James G. Frazer (*The Golden Bough: A Study in Magic and Religion*), Oswald Spengler (*Der Untergang des Abendlandes – Umrisse einer Morphologie der Weltgeschichte*) and many others, used knowledge about ancient Egypt as a source for their universal histories. How easily the evidence may be misread, however, is exemplified in the important study on *Oriental Despotism* by Karl Wittfogel, who made statements about the hydraulic aspects of ancient Egyptian society that are not valid when archaeological and textual sources are consulted.

It is conspicuous that there was hardly any attempt from cultural anthropology to comment on ancient Egypt. The exceptions are few: the most famous is Leslie White's 1948 paper, "Ikhnaton: the Great Man vs. the Culture Process," in which he argued for the importance of cultural traditions which channeled Akhenaten's creative possibilities, thereby reducing his status as an independently innovative individual. There have been some attempts by comparative anthropologists and Egyptologists to comment on kinship and on brother–sister marriages, integrating data mainly contained in papyri from the Late and Ptolemaic periods. In the field of economics, discussions emerged that resulted in a renewed debate about substantivism and formalism, i.e. as to whether contemporary economic theory is applicable to ancient Egypt or whether the Egyptian economic system was based on redistribution.

Since the 1960s there has been increased participation in Egypt of archaeologists, especially those in the international endeavors to save monuments and sites in Nubia that were to be flooded by Lake Nasser after the construction of the Aswan High Dam. As a result, the influx of ideas from anthropological archaeology can be seen. During the last 25–30 years, work on many Predynastic sites in Upper and Lower Egypt has often been conducted within the paradigm of processual archaeology. Processual theory integrates cultural evolutionism and a materialistic perspective using ecological data to explain culture change due mainly to outside influences. In studies of ancient Egypt, it has led to numerous publications about the evolution of culture, institutions and sociopolitical organization, and the emergence and collapse of complex societies. These have been followed by attempts to apply suggestions from post-processual archaeology, i.e. the view that culture change very much depends on internal social relations and conflicts, and that material objects reflect the ideologies in the social system

in question. Questions of power, social relations, religious symbolism, the emergence of kingship and of an Egyptian state have been addressed and led—with the help of analogies and post-modern culture interpretations from sociology and philosophy—to new hypotheses and interpretations of ancient Egyptian society. Out of all this, an eclectic approach is slowly emerging that integrates processual as well as post-processual perspectives, anthropological archaeology and, most importantly, text-based Egyptology. Prominent examples are Trigger's and Assmann's papers on monumental discourse.

Ancient Egypt's *long durée* of over 3,000 years not only allows anthropologically minded archaeologists and Egyptologists to study the functioning and historical development of a fascinating cultural system, but it also offers tremendous insights into an ancient culture, its sociopolitical system, symbolism and ideology. Studies of ancient Egypt benefit from the rare combination of archaeological remains, superb and rich textual evidence and dedicated scholars who put it all together.

See also

Champollion, Jean-François; Egyptian (language), decipherment of; Egyptians, physical anthropology of; Egyptology, history of; *ma'at*; Petrie, Sir William Matthew Flinders; Predynastic period, overview; Rosetta Stone

Further reading

Assmann, J. 1987. Sepulkrale Selbstthematisierung im Alten Ägypten. In *Selbstthematisierung und Selbstzeugnis: Bekenntnis und Geständnis*, A. Hahn and W. Kapp, eds, 208–32. Frankfurt.

——. 1989. *Maât, L'Égypte pharaonique et l'idée de justice sociale*. Paris.

Bard, K.A. 1992. Toward an interpretation of the role of ideology in the evolution of complex society in Egypt. *JAA* 11: 1–24.

Butzer, K.W. 1976. *Early Hydraulic Civilization in Egypt*. Chicago.

Fortes, M., and E.E. Evans-Pritchard. 1940. *African Political Systems*. London.

Frankfort, H. 1948. *Kingship and the Gods; A Study of Ancient Near Eastern Religion as the Integration of Society and Nature*. Chicago.

Geertz, C. 1975. On the nature of anthropological understanding. *American Scientist* 63: 47–53.

Harris, M. 1968. *The Rise of Anthropological Theory*. New York.

Hassan, F.A. 1988. The Predynastic of Egypt. *JWP* 2: 135–85.

Hoffman, M.A. 1991. *Egypt before the Pharaohs*. Austin, TX.

Janssen, J. 1978. The early state in ancient Egypt. In *The Early State*, H.J.M. Claessen and P. Skalník, eds, 213–34. The Hague.

——. 1982. Gift-giving in ancient Egypt as an economic feature. *JEA* 68: 253–8.

Kemp, B.J. 1989. *Ancient Egypt: Anatomy of a Civilization*. London.

Malinowski, B. 1922. *Argonauts of the Western Pacific*. London.

McGuire, R.H. 1983. Breaking down cultural complexity: inequality and heterogeneity. *Advances in Archaeological Method and Theory* 6: 91–142.

O'Connor, D. 1974. Political systems and archaeological data in Egypt: 2600–1780 B.C. *WA* 6: 15–38.

Schenkel, W. 1978. *Die Bewässerungsrevolution im Alten Ägypten*. Mainz.

Tainter, J.A. 1988. *The Collapse of Complex Societies*. Cambridge.

Trigger, B.G. 1990. Monumental architecture: a thermodynamic explanation of symbolic behaviour. *WA* 22: 119–32.

Wenke, R.J. 1991. The evolution of early Egyptian civilization: issues and evidence. *JWP* 5: 279–329.

CHRISTIAN E. GUKSCH

Antinoopolis

Antinoopolis is an ancient city on the east bank of the Nile in Middle Egypt (27°49′ N, 30°53′ E), founded by the Roman Emperor Hadrian on 30 October AD 130. The site, now called Sheikh 'Ibada, is completely destroyed. It was called Antinoë, Antenon, Adrianopolis and Besantinopolis. Medieval Arabic sources refer to it by the name Besa, or Tisa, sometimes as Atsa or Itsa, but most commonly it is referred to by the name Ansina. The geographer Idrisi (d. 1165) relates that during the lifetime of the Prophet Moses, Ansina was the city from whence Pharaoh's magicians came. Hence, it was named in Arabic Medinet el-Sahharah (City of the Magicians).

During his visit to Egypt, the Roman emperor Hadrian was accompanied by his favorite friend, the athlete Antinous of Bithynia. On the journey up the Nile, learning that some great catastrophe threatened his master the emperor, Antinous sacrificed his life and drowned himself in the river as an offering. However, the details of his death are obscure. Hadrian, being overwhelmed with grief over the loss of Antinous, decided to commemorate him by building a great city in his name. Thus, Antinoopolis was founded. The location of the new city was close to where Antinous had drowned. This was south of the then deserted ancient Egyptian town of Besa, almost opposite Hermopolis Magna (the modern village of el-Ashmunein).

The city of Antinoopolis was inhabited mainly by Greeks, who were encouraged to move to the new city; the first settlers called themselves the "New Greeks." At Antinoopolis, the citizens enjoyed certain privileges that they did not have in their native towns; these included the right to intermarry with Egyptians. Newborn children could become citizens of the new city. They were also exempted from a 10 percent sales tax on property and slaves and on imported goods, as well as being exempt from payment of the poll tax. These privileges were intended to encourage people to settle in the city. Later, the emperor Antoninus Pius encouraged veteran settlement through a system of land allotment. The emperor Severus Alexander undertook great architectural projects and developed the entire northern district of the city.

Antinoopolis soon became an important commercial center, especially because of its location along the Via Hadriana, the road which lead to the port of Berenike (the modern Baranis) on the Red Sea. It continued to flourish as an urban complex until at least the tenth century AD, for the nineteenth-century historian 'Ali Mubarak states that the historian Eusebius (d. 912) wrote that the inhabitants of Antinoopolis were associated with the clergymen of Jerusalem. However, by the twelfth century the site was described as extensive ruins. In that respect, the traveler Ibn Jubayr states that the city's great enclosure wall was completely destroyed by Sultan Salah al-Din (Saladin), some time in the period or during AD 1176–83. He adds that orders were given to every sailing boat on the Nile to transfer at least one block of stone downstream to Cairo.

Edmé François Jomard, who accompanied Napoleon Bonaparte's expedition to Egypt in 1798, provided an excellent survey of the site in the monumental volumes of the *Description de l'Égypte*. In 1822, Gardner Wilkinson said that all the good marble, limestone and granite that were used in the buildings of Antinoopolis had then been removed to build a bridge at the town of Reramoon. However, other sources mention that this systematic destruction was intended to build sugar factories in that region of Egypt. This must have left the city in an even more devastated state of ruin because only a decade later, the Italian antiquarian Giovanni Belzoni visited the site and wrote that the ruins of Antinoopolis did not surprise or impress him at all.

Between 1896 and 1912, the archaeologist Albert Jean Gayet undertook excavations at the site, which led to the discovery of an ancient Egyptian temple of Ramesses II as well as a number of cemeteries outside the city. In 1914, other excavations were undertaken by Johnson, who was mainly searching for papyri. In the 1930s the Italian archaeologist Evaristo Breccia directed excavations at Antinoopolis, to be followed in the 1960s by further Italian excavations by the Institute of Papyrology of Florence in collaboration with the University of Rome.

Our knowledge of the physical layout of Antinoopolis is based on Jomard's survey in the *Description de l'Égypte*. The site was trapezoidal in plan. A double enclosure wall surrounded the city on three sides, only leaving the river side open. A natural valley of extraordinary size ran across the city along its east–west axis; this was created by torrential waters flowing down from the desert hills into the Nile. The city was laid out on a grid plan, with orthogonal streets intersecting at right angles to each other. The two major streets, the *cardo* and *decumanus major*, were adorned by many Doric columns of medium height, and statues. The *cardo* started near a theater on the south and ended by a shrine on the north, and was adorned by 772 columns along its length (1622 m). The *decumanus major* (1014 m) led from a triumphal arch on the west to a gate on the east. It too was adorned by columns, 572 in number. Archaeological evidence shows that the *decumanus minor* was never colonnaded.

The streets formed two main intersections. These were marked by four thick granite Corinthian columns that were raised on high platforms and were surmounted by statues. The intersection formed by the *cardo* and the *decumanus major* bore statues of Antinous above its columns. The intersection formed by the *cardo* and the *decumanus minor* had statues of the Roman Emperor Alexander Severus surmounting its columns; these were added in AD 233, commemorating his victory over the Persians.

The main streets of Antinoopolis were 16 m wide. The columns adorning them formed shaded walkways, 2 m wide, on both sides of the street. A triumphal arch, intended to be viewed from the Nile, acted as the principal portal of Antinoopolis. It was composed of a triple-arched passageway of two stories, which was divided by tall Doric pilasters and had a decorated entablature with triglyphs. In front of the arch stood two large pedestals which probably supported monumental statues of Antinous. The area between the triumphal arch and the Nile was a vast open court which was formed by great hypostyle halls on both its north and south sides, each having forty columns with Corinthian capitals. The columns displayed a variety of stones, such as granite, porphyry and limestone.

Along the *decumanus major* stood the main public bath of the city, which is the largest surviving building at Antinoopolis. Its façade on the main street consisted of eight pillars, four flanking each side of the entrance. It had a large circular basin made of marble. A wall ran along the central part of the interior of the bath, which according to Jomard was to separate the two sexes. At the eastern extremity of the *decumanus major* was an eastern portal. Further to the east was a path in the bed of a small wadi, or valley, which led outside the city walls into the desert plain toward the hippodrome, where chariot races were held. The hippodrome (307 m long and 77 m wide) was in the usual shape of a rectangle terminating at one end in a semicircle. The façade of the hippodrome had walls that inclined at an angle, which reminded Jomard of pylons of an ancient Egyptian temple.

A theater originally stood at the southern extremity of the *cardo*. It was semicircular in plan, and was built of white marble and had a very large orchestra, which was adorned by Ionic columns. The theater had two large monumental gates. On the south side was a simple wall with a passageway through it. A monumental portal was situated on the northern side of the theater. This portal was known by local people as *Abu'l Qurun*, meaning "the Father of Horns." Jomard explained that the capitals of its Corinthian columns had long protruding corners which were noticed at a far distance, and resembled horns. The whole portal gave the effect of a Roman temple front.

The principal buildings of Antinoopolis were oriented toward the main intersection, where the statues of Antinous were located. The triumphal arch, the hippodrome and the theater were all focused toward the intersection of the *cardo* and the *decumanus major*, which must have been a great social center. There would have been a constant awareness of Antinous in the city. In addition to the central intersection, Antinous was likely honored by a massive square monument at the northern end of the *cardo*.

Unfortunately, the severe destruction of Antinoopolis does not allow for much further analysis. The major monuments of theater, shrine, triumphal arch and hippodrome have been identified, as well as the public baths. However, we know almost nothing about the private houses and the administrative buildings. The excavations of the site did not help much in understanding the urban fabric, as they focused on retrieving objects, textiles, and most especially, papyri. Hadrian founded the city of Antinoopolis to be the only Roman city in Egypt, a memorial to Antinous, and a symbol of Hadrian's own power. Thus, Antinoopolis was a Roman foundation, governed by Greek culture, on Egyptian soil.

See also

el-Ashmunein; Berenike Panchrysos; Roman period, overview

Further reading

Bell, H.I. 1940. Antinoopolis: a Hadrianic foundation in Egypt. *Journal of Roman Studies* 30: 133–47.

Coquin, R.-G., S.J. Maurice Martin, S. Donadoni and P. Grossman. 1991. Antinopoolis. In *The Coptic Encyclopedia* 1, Aziz S. Atiya, ed., 144–6. New York.

Donadoni, Sergio. 1973. Antinooupolis. In *LÄ* 1(3): 324–5.

Thompson, David L. 1981. The Lost City of Antinoos. *Archaeology* 34(1): 44–50.

TAREK SWELIM

Apis

Apis, now the modern village of Zawiet Umm el-Rakham (31°34′ N, 25°09′ E), was known in pharaonic times as Hut-Ka (House of the Bull). It was a minor coastal settlement situated at the northeastern fringe of the Marmaric region, some 25 km west of Marsa Matruh (ancient Paraitonion). Despite inadequate anchorage beneath the lee of a projecting headland (Ras

Umm el-Rakham), the Graeco-Roman town is mentioned by a number of the classical authors, starting with Herodotus (*circa* 430 BC). While worship of the bull god that gave the town its name can be locally documented for the 30th Dynasty, little else is known of the town's history prior to the fourth century BC. The author of the *Periplus of Scylax of Caryanda* indicates that by the mid-fourth century BC Egyptian control extended as far west as Apis.

The potsherd-littered plain between the coastal road and the sea is still largely unexcavated, but its appearance suggests that the later town followed the normal layout for Roman period settlements on this coast. The Egyptian Antiquities Organization (EAO) has recently cleared a number of rock-cut tombs, some of which have been provisionally assigned to the 26th Dynasty. Bits of clothing or shrouds still survive from the burials, which were placed in lead coffins and provided with pottery and glass vessels. An uninscribed but heavily built rectangular building of cut stone, with interior rooms of probable post-pharaonic date, has been partly cleared in the ancient town north of the coastal road. Some tombs are known to exist in the face of the low line of hills that parallel the sea to the south.

The most important archaeological evidence at Apis is its Ramesside fortress, located a short distance south of the coastal road. The walled compound, originally surveyed by Alan Rowe soon after the Second World War and subsequently excavated in a few random places by Labib Habachi in the 1950s, is a rectangular enclosure, measuring *circa* 80 × 100 m. It was laid out with its four corners at the four cardinal points of the compass. Traces of a thick mudbrick outer wall are only visible on the northeast side. At the east corner was the entrance, now a poorly preserved stone gateway, to the west of which was a stone-lined passageway.

A small stone temple, *circa* 20 × 12 m, was erected against the northwest wall of the fortress. A ramp leads to a pillared courtyard behind which are two transverse chambers, leading to three sanctuaries. Apart from one pillar inscribed with one of the names of Ramesses II, the temple is uninscribed and lacks decoration.

In the vicinity of the stone passageway, Rowe recovered three detached, inscribed door jambs, hailing Ptah, "Lord of Ankhtaui." An inscription on one jamb is of "...the real (royal) scribe, his beloved, the chief of the troops, and Overseer of the Foreign Lands, Nebre, justified." In the group of storerooms west of the temple, Habachi subsequently found additional door jamb fragments, which perhaps belonged to separate chapels, along with fragments of votive stelae. One of the door jambs refers to Ramesses II "destroying Libya." The stelae continue the same theme, repeating the pharaoh's name and depicting captive Libyans. On one stela Ramesses II prepares to smite a prisoner, while Amen-Re offers a sword. The stela was given to the temple by the standard-bearer Amenmessu, who is shown kneeling in a lower register. On another stela Ramesses II offers a bouquet of flowers to the goddess Sekhmet. The lower register shows the dedicant, "the royal scribe and the great chief of the army, Panehesi," kneeling with uplifted arms to adore the goddess and to wish the king numerous jubilees (*heb-sed*).

The entrance and stone passageway were inscribed with the names of the pharaoh and fragmentary texts describing his prowess. Badly preserved relief scenes depict Ramesses II descending from his chariot to smite his enemies. Habachi suggests that the temple was erected to the triad of Memphite gods, and, following Rowe, that the fortress served as the westernmost one in a chain of fortresses erected by Ramesses II to provide an early warning system against an attack by Libyans, and perhaps also their Sea People allies.

See also

Libyans; Marsa Matruh; New Kingdom, overview; Sea Peoples

Further reading

Habachi, L. 1980. The military posts of

Ramesses II on the coastal road and the western part of the Delta. *BIFAO* 80: 13–30.

Helck, W., and E. Otto, eds. 1986. Umm er-Raham. In *LÄ* 6: 846.

DONALD WHITE

Armant

The site of Armant, known as Hermonthis in Graeco-Roman times, is located on the west bank of the Nile about 9 km southwest of Luxor (25°37′ N, 32°32′ E). O.H. Myers excavated there in the late 1920s and early 1930s with the financial backing of Sir Robert Mond. Several areas were excavated with Predynastic, Dynastic and Coptic burials. Two cult centers, the Great Temple of Armant and the Bucheum, were also investigated.

Predynastic evidence

The main Predynastic cemetery at Armant was in Area 1400–1500, on the low desert fringe beyond the present-day edge of cultivation. Some Predynastic graves were also located in Area 1300 and near two Middle Kingdom tombs (1213 and 1214). Of the numerous Predynastic cemeteries excavated in Upper Egypt in the first half of this century, Cemetery 1400–1500 is the best documented one, and Werner Kaiser has developed a seriation system for Predynastic pottery based on this sequence of graves.

To the east of Cemetery 1400–1500, Area 1300 contained twenty-seven burials. The larger burials in this area are all Dynastic, with a few Predynastic graves located closer to the edge of cultivation. To the east of Area 1300, two large brick-lined tombs (1207, 1208), dating to the end of the Predynastic sequence (Nagada IIIb), were excavated in Area 1200. These tombs have areas of 24.00 m² and 30.45 m², and are divided into several chambers, but it is unknown whether they were built for one individual or several. They are quite unlike other Predynastic burials at Armant, in scale, energy expenditure and quantities of grave goods.

Myers also excavated a Predynastic settlement in Area 1000, about 2 km from Cemetery 1400–1500 at the edge of cultivation. Although the cemetery next to this settlement was destroyed by later graves, pottery in Area 1000 suggests that it was earlier in date than Cemetery 1400–1500. In 1984 this settlement was investigated by Polish archaeologists. The recent excavations at this site, called MA 21/83, uncovered various features: postholes for a rectangular structure, a series of pits (for ovens, storage and unknown purposes), hearths, and circular structures built of large limestone slabs. Most of the ceramics at this site were of a chaff-tempered ware (known as Rough class), but a red-polished class and grey and brown classes were also found.

The burials in Cemetery 1400–1500 were usually single inhumations in pits *circa* 1 m deep. Mummification was not practiced until Dynastic times, and skeletons were always in a flexed position, usually resting on the left side. Matting was sometimes found over and/or under the skeleton, or lining the sides of the grave pits, but there was a recognizable decline in the use of matting in the later burials. In a few instances corpses were covered with linen instead of matting. Several graves had traces of wood, either as a grave lining or a coffin, and two graves (1466, 1511) contained a wooden bed. Five graves had recesses cut next to the burial pit, presumably for additional grave goods.

Burials in Cemetery 1400–1500 may have been oriented to the river: where the river is straight burials were aligned north–south, but they were erratic in orientation where it bends. Body orientation with the head to the south to southwest facing west, was by far the most common, as Flinders Petrie also observed at the main Predynastic cemetery at Nagada.

Armant, however, was not a major Predynastic center like Nagada and Ballas. Cemetery 1400–1500 numbered around 200 graves and was 170 × 75 m in area. Burials exhibit spatial patterning that shifts through time. The early graves (Nagada Ic and IIa), which are small rough ovals (commonly less that 1 m² in area), are distributed throughout the southern part of the cemetery in a somewhat crowded pattern. This pattern changes in Nagada IIb, when larger rectangular graves are distributed farther north, in less dense concentrations, while smaller Nagada IIb oval graves tend to be more closely spaced among those of Nagada Ic and IIa. With a shift to larger rectangular graves (Nagada IIc, 1–3 m^2 in area), there is a northward movement in the cemetery, and graves are widely spaced. In Nagada IId1 and IId2 the graves are farther north still, and very widely scattered. Finally, the latest graves (Nagada IIIa1 and IIIa2) are clustered in the far north of the cemetery.

Pottery was the most common type of grave goods found in the Predynastic burials at Armant. Even the poorest burials which contained no other grave goods usually included one or two pots. Slate palettes were found in graves of all phases. The earliest palettes at Armant (Nagada Ic) are shaped as rhombs, sometimes with two amorphous animal heads or horns at the top. Fish- and turtle-shaped varieties appear in the middle Predynastic phase (Nagada II), and circular and rectangular examples were found in a late grave (Nagada IIIb). Palettes were more common at Armant in the earlier graves (Nagada Ic and IIa), but this could be the result of the earlier graves being much less robbed than the later ones. Small grinding pebbles were sometimes found along with the palettes, and pigments to be ground on the palettes for cosmetics, such as galena, malachite and red ocher, were placed in some of the graves.

Next to pottery, beads were the most common grave goods. Materials for beads varied, from one bead of lapis lazuli (from Afghanistan) to simple beads of fired clay. Steatite beads were the most common, but carnelian was also frequent. Stones from the Eastern and Western Deserts, such as chalcedony, quartz and garnet, were used for beads, as were faïence and imported materials, such as malachite, amber, bitumen, resin and Red Sea coral. Ostrich eggshell was also used for beads. Other jewelry included bracelets or armlets in shell, and an ivory finger ring. Whole shells, both riverine and marine (Red Sea), were found in a number of burials.

Chipped stone tools, such as points, flakes and blades, and cores from tool manufacture were found in some of the graves. Other stone artifacts in graves included polishing and grinding stones, and a hammer stone.

Other craft goods were found in the Predynastic burials at Armant, including combs, tag-like objects, points and a vessel carved in ivory. Some of the more unusual grave goods included a carved ivory "gaming set" with two stone balls, two carved stone hippopotami and three clay "hands." Baskets were preserved in several graves.

Numerous stone vessels or fragments were found in the two brick-lined tombs (1207 and 1208). These were made of alabaster, diorite, limestone, marble, porcelainite, rose quartz, slate and steatite. Copper was rare at Armant: four axes of the metal were found in one tomb (1207), and two bracelets were in a grave (1547).

Analyses of the Predynastic burials at Armant show a trend to greater numbers of pots and larger grave pits through time. Larger graves are probably a function of larger numbers of grave goods (mainly pots), and indirectly, greater energy expenditure on burial. The burials do not seem to be greatly differentiated except into two basic hierarchies (of poorer and richer graves, based on numbers of pots and relative grave size).

Dynastic evidence

In the west forecourt of the Great Temple in the town of Armant, Myers excavated a sondage (deep sounding) and found potsherds and fragments of stone vessels dating to the Early Dynastic period. A second sondage with artifacts from the Old Kingdom and First Intermediate Period was excavated in what Myers thought was the ancient town. Although the sondages demonstrated earlier archaeological evidence, blocks of the earliest temple at Armant date to the 11th Dynasty. Construction of this temple continued in the 12th Dynasty, and there is an offering table with the name of a 13th Dynasty king (Sobekhotep).

Kings of the early 18th Dynasty left their inscriptions, but most of the temple was constructed during Tuthmose III's reign. There is evidence that many inscriptions with the name of Amen were deleted during Akhenaten's reign. In the 19th Dynasty Ramesses II gave two colossi to the temple and his son Merenptah is associated with some statues of Osiris.

During the Ptolemaic period the older temple was dismantled and blocks were used for the foundation of a great new temple, but one New Kingdom pylon was left standing. Cleopatra VII built a "House of Births" (*mammisi*) to commemorate the birth of her son Caesarion (by Julius Caesar). During the Roman period construction continued on this temple, and Antoninus Pius built a "gateway" in the second century AD. Traces of a Roman bath were recorded by Myers, and a large town wall was built in later Roman times. Unfortunately, many building stones from the Graeco-Roman temple were used for the construction of house foundations and a sugar factory in the nineteenth century AD.

The Bucheum, another temple northwest of the town of Armant, was also investigated by Myers. This is where the Buchis bulls, believed to be representatives of the god Re, were mummified and buried. Offering tables and stelae with inscriptions recording events in a bull's life were found in this temple. To the east of the Bucheum was a Roman village with a large walk-in well. Northwest of this village was the Baqaria, a long vaulted passage with twenty-eight tombs for the mothers of Buchis bulls. Human burials in the area of the Bucheum were mostly from the Roman period, but Myers states that Ptolemaic priests were buried in a cemetery east of the Bucheum.

Although Armant was never a major city in ancient Egypt, there is evidence of continuous occupation from Predynastic times to the present. During the Coptic period it was the seat of a bishopric and a large church was built. Muslim burials cover many (unexcavated) parts of the ancient temple.

See also

cult temples of the New Kingdom; Late and Ptolemaic periods, overview; New Kingdom, overview; Predynastic period, overview; Roman period, overview

Further reading

Ginter, B., J. Kozlowski and M. Pawlikowski. 1987. Investigations into sites MA 6/83 and MA 21/83 in the region of Qurna-Armant in Upper Egypt. *MDAIK* 43: 45–66.

Mond, R., and O.H. Myers. 1934. *The Bucheum I, II, III*. London.

——. 1937. *The Cemeteries of Armant I*. London.

——. 1940. *The Temples of Armant: A Preliminary Survey*. London.

KATHRYN A. BARD

army

In the Old and Middle Kingdoms, the concept of an "army," as it is understood today, namely the organized military establishment of the state, did not exist. Regardless of its size, any body of fighting men was referred to as an "army" (*mš'*) and military terminology was restricted to the designations "general" (*imy-r mš' wr*), "military officer" (*imy-r mš'*) and "soldier" (*w'w*). A number of *ad hoc* military titles are recorded, but the rank of their incumbents cannot be determined. In short, there was no real table of organization. When the occasional pictorial depictions of armed warriors are accompanied by descriptive captions, they are simply labelled "retainers" (literally, "followers," *šmśw*). The sole preserved Old Kingdom narrative in which the raising and use of "the army" is recounted is the tomb biography of Weni, the governor of Upper Egypt under the 6th Dynasty King Pepi I. Weni describes how he sent orders to the local provincial rulers to call up the levies of their own subordinates, and these in turn summoned their subordinates down through every level of the local administration.

This same situation appears to have continued through the Middle Kingdom. The military forces of the state were those supplied by the provincial magnates when needed. Consequently, Egypt had a real "army" only when a strong, charismatic ruler occupied the throne. Most of the battles fought during the Old and Middle Kingdoms, for which we have any evidence, were infantry battles on land. By the end of the turbulent Second Intermediate Period, when Egypt was under the rule of the Asiatic Hyksos, the "rulers of foreign countries," a new dimension was added to the existing practice of warfare. This was the use of the horse, which had been introduced into Egypt from southwest Asia along with the war chariot which it pulled. Henceforth, after the defeat and expulsion of the Hyksos, the Egyptian army of the New Kingdom was comprised of two arms of service: the infantry and the mounted troops.

At the outset of the 18th Dynasty, chariotry is first mentioned in narrative texts where it appears to have been an organic part of the infantry. Military ranks and titles are attested which are peculiar to the chariot, but not to the chariotry. In the middle of the reign of Amenhotep III, however, the army seems to have undergone a reorganization into the two arms of infantry and chariotry, and from then on until the end of the New Kingdom, each arm had its own table of organization and chain of command.

The entire army was still called the *mš'*, but this same term was also used as the designation for the largest self-contained infantry unit, the division, with its attachment of chariotry troops. Within each arm there were two distinct military hierarchies, that of the front-line combat troops and that of the rear-echelon administrative troops, the military scribes. The smallest formally organized infantry combat unit was the ten-man squad, commanded by a squad leader. Five of these made up a company whose commander was the "leader of fifty." The fifty-man company was the standard tactical line unit, and all higher units comprised a number of these companies. Thus, the strength of the next highest unit, the regiment (*s3*), varied between 400 and 500 men, i.e. 8–10 companies. It was commanded by an officer called the "standard-bearer" (*t3i sryt*) whose

immediate subordinate was the adjutant (*idnw*). Two or more regiments, but no fewer than five, could comprise, *ad hoc*, a brigade (*pdt*) under the command of a brigadier (*hry pdt*). Two brigades, with a maximum strength of 2,500 men each, formed an army division (*mš'*) commanded by a general (*imy-r mš'*). Both the brigadier and the standard-bearer had a second-in-command, known respectively as the "army adjutant" (*idnw n p3 mš'*) and the "regimental adjutant" (*idnw n p3 s3*). The highest ranking officer within the military scribal hierarchy, the "scribe of the infantry" (*sš mnfyt*), was immediately subordinate to the brigade commander. Beneath him stood the "scribe of elite troops" (*sš nfrw*), the "scribes of the assemblage of the army" (*sš shn n p3 mš'*) and "of the distribution of the army" (*sš dni n p3 mš'*), all three of whom were superior in rank to the army adjutant. Immediately below the rank of regimental adjutant was the "scribe of the regiment" (*sš n p3 s3*).

At the head of the table of organization for the combat ranks of the chariotry stood the brigade commander of the chariotry, who led a squadron of fifty vehicles. The squadron contained five troops, each of ten chariots and commanded by a "standard-bearer of chariot warriors" (*t3i sryt n snni.w*). Each individual chariot had a two-man crew, the "charioteer" (*kdn*) and the chariot warrior. In addition to these, there are two other chariot ranks known to exist, the "runner" (*phrr*) and the "tkm-bearer" (*t3i tkm*), but their exact function within the chariot is unclear; the former may have been the foot soldier who is occasionally depicted in the pictorial representations running beside the chariot.

All units down to the regiment had names. Those of the individual army divisions consisted of the name of a god, certainly the patron deity of the division, which was then compounded with either an epithet or a pious wish. The names of the brigades seem to have consisted of the term "brigade" plus a geographic designation, presumably either the place from which the brigade originated or else where it served. The names of the individual regiments, regardless of whether they served solely on land or whether they functioned as naval infantry (ḥnyt), were, without exception, composed of the name of the king under whom they served. This royal name, in turn, was compounded with a descriptive epithet.

After the New Kingdom, Egypt was ruled by successive dynasties of foreigners, Libyans, Kushites, Saites, Persians and, finally, the Graeco-Macedonians. While the earlier pharaonic military ranks were occasionally still used, the earlier table of organization was now supplanted by that of Egypt's new rulers.

See also

chariots; ships

Further reading

Schulman, A.R. 1964. *Military Rank, Title and Organization in the Egyptian New Kingdom* (MÄS 6). Berlin.

Shaw, I. 1991. *Egyptian Warfare and Weapons.* Aylesbury.

Spalinger, A.J. 1982. *Aspects of the Military Documents of the Ancient Egyptians.* New Haven, CT.

ALAN SCHULMAN

el-Ashmunein

El-Ashmunein is the modern name of a large village in Middle Egypt, on the site of which are located the archaeological remains of the pharaonic city of Khmunw, known in the Graeco-Roman period as Hermopolis Magna. The ancient site is normally referred to by the names Ashmunein or Hermopolis Magna, although the former is preferable in view of its descent from the original Khmunw. This term means "City of the Eight," a description linked to an ancient local myth surrounding eight creator-gods (*ogdoad*). The ruins of the ancient city (27°47′ N, 30°48′ E) lie in the cultivated land to the west of the Nile, approximately 40 km south of the important modern town of Minya. The site is marked by a stratified archaeological mound (1 × 1.5 km) formed from crumbling mudbrick buildings. The southern part of this area is covered by the modern houses of el-Ashmunein; a part of the northern limit of the mound lies beneath a separate village, called el-Idara. Between the two villages is the accessible portion of the site (some 850 × 1000 m), in which archaeological work has been concentrated.

Early attention was devoted to the search for papyrus documents in the mudbrick remains of the Roman town, and to the recording or excavation of certain stone-built monuments. Some of the latter were always visible, particularly the columns of the portico of a temple at the north end of the site. This temple was erected *circa* 370 BC and inscribed at a slightly later date with the name of Philip Arrhidaeus. The portico was built as the façade of a great temple, dedicated to the local god Thoth. The portico was quarried away by 1826, but had been drawn by the French antiquarians accompanying Napoleon's expedition, and by other early travelers.

A German expedition, directed by Günther Roeder, worked at el-Ashmunein from 1929 until 1939. Important discoveries included a limestone gateway from a temple of the Middle Kingdom, inscribed for Amenemhat II, remains of two colossal statues of Ramesses II at the southern end of the site, and a temple entrance pylon of the same king, to which additions had been made in the 30th Dynasty. The foundations of this pylon had been constructed of reused masonry blocks, brought from the temples built by King Akhenaten at the site of his capital city, located not far away at Tell el-Amarna on the other side of the Nile. Some 1,500 blocks were recovered, many of them still bearing high-quality reliefs from their original use under Akhenaten.

The German expedition searched for the two major streets of the Roman town, the names of which were known from Greek papyri to be "Antinoe Street" and "The Dromos of Hermes." The papyri made it clear that these streets crossed in the center of the city, with Antinoe Street running east–west and the Dromos of Hermes from south to north. The

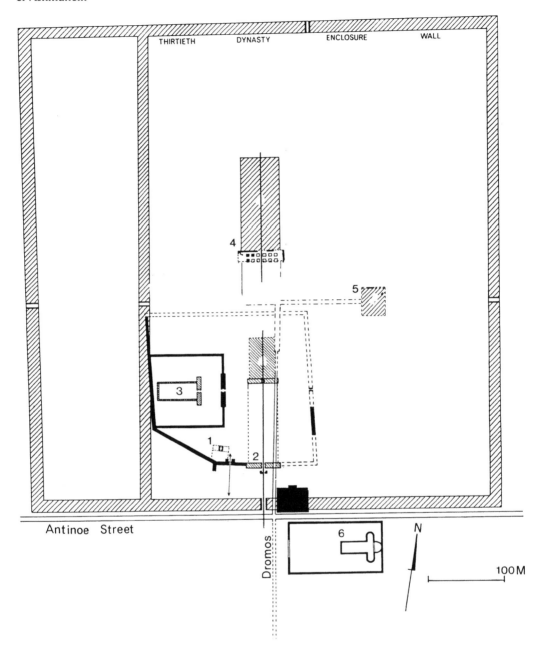

Figure 13 Plan of the major monuments in the central city at el-Ashmunein
1 gate of Amenemhat II
2 New Kingdom temple
3 subsidiary temple dedicated to Amen and Thoth
4 30th Dynasty temple
5 subsidiary chapel, later enlarged under Domitian
6 Greek-style temple to King Ptolemy III and Queen Berenike

position of Antinoe Street was correctly identified and the ruins of several Roman monumental buildings beside it were studied by Roeder. The location of the second street of the city, the Dromos of Hermes, was not discovered until 1982, when parts of it were revealed in excavations carried out by the British Museum. Fragments of columns and capitals from the great tetrastylon, a group of four huge limestone columns at the street crossing, were also identified in the British Museum work. These probably supported statues of the Emperor, but no traces of the sculptures remain.

The excavations of the German expedition produced important information on the layout of the town, such as the extent of the great mudbrick enclosure wall (*temenos*) around the temple area. This sacred region lay in the heart of the city, surrounded by areas of domestic settlement. In the latter, the German test trenches revealed something of the distribution of settlements at different periods, identifyingv areas of New Kingdom, Late period and Roman occupation. One large building with red granite columns and corinthian capitals was mistakenly identified with the Roman market, or agora. Subsequent work has shown this building to be a Christian cathedral of the fifth century AD, built on the site of a classical temple to King Ptolemy III and Queen Berenike. The true identity of these buildings was discovered by Makramallah, Megaw and Wace during excavations for the University of Alexandria in 1945–50.

The results achieved by the German expedition provided a valuable foundation for the planning of the British Museum excavations, which took place each year between 1980 and 1990. The British Museum expedition investigated both the temples and settlements of el-Ashmunein. The position of a major New Kingdom temple was identified between 1981 and 1985 in the region north of the pylon of Ramesses II, found previously by Roeder. This temple had been enlarged by different rulers from the 18th–20th Dynasties, including Amenhotep III, Horemheb, Ramesses II and Ramesses III. The discovery of a broken stela,

dated to year 15 of King Osorkon III, showed that additions continued to be made to the building in later periods.

Several colossal quartzite statues of baboons, one of the sacred animals of Thoth, were carved for the New Kingdom temple under Amenhotep III. Fragments of these sculptures were found by Professor A.M. Abu-Bakr in 1946, cached under the foundations of the 30th Dynasty temple, a structure founded by King Nectanebo I to replace the older temple of the New Kingdom. Two of the baboon statues were reconstructed in the 1950s, and placed on modern plinths at the northern end of the site.

The whole sacred complex was rebuilt in the 30th Dynasty, and surrounded by a brick enclosure wall with a perimeter in excess of 2,000 m. The inscription of Nectanebo I on a stela from the site, recording the foundation of temples, probably refers to this building. To the east of this temple lay a subsidiary chapel, probably constructed at the same time, but later redecorated and enlarged under the Emperor Domitian.

Another major monument in the central part of the city is a temple to the west of the axis of the main shrine, dedicated to the gods Amen and Thoth. Although decorated under the kings Merenptah and Seti II, construction of this temple certainly began in the reign of Ramesses II, a colossal statue of whom once stood at its entrance. At the south end of the site, close to the modern village of el-Ashmunein, a separate small temple of Ramesses II was excavated by Professor Abu-Bakr in 1946. It had been restored under the Emperor Nero, and in the fifth century AD its front courtyard was overbuilt by a small church, recently studied by Grossman and Bailey.

The enlarged temple enclosure of the 30th Dynasty was built over areas that had previously contained domestic settlements, which surrounded the sacred area on all sides. Late Roman deposits cover the surface in many areas, but the level immediately below these varies from Late period to New Kingdom or even Middle Kingdom in different parts of the site. Work on the excavation of the domestic areas includes certain test-trenches dug by the

German expedition in 1929–31 and detailed study at selected points carried out in 1985–90 by the British Museum. This work revealed mudbrick houses, in three levels dating between 900 and 650 BC. Another area, not far north of the subsidiary temple of Amen, contained a group of burials dating to about 2000 BC, some of the earliest remains so far discovered at el-Ashmunein. The burials were very poor, with few grave goods apart from flint tools and pottery, and they were contained in small vaulted graves of mudbrick construction.

See also

Karnak, Akhenaten temples; New Kingdom, overview; Roman period, overview; Tell el-Amarna, city; Tuna el-Gebel

Further reading

Bailey, D.M. 1991. *Excavations at El-Ashmunein* 4. London.

Roeder, G. 1959. *Hermopolis 1929–1939*. Hildesheim.

Spencer, A.J. 1983–1993. *Excavations at El-Ashmunein* 1–3. London.

Wace, A.J.B., and A.H.S. Megaw. 1959. *Hermopolis Magna, El-Ashmunein: The Ptolemaic Sanctuary and the Basilica*. Alexandria.

A.J. SPENCER

Assyrians

Assyria was a Bronze Age and Iron Age state located in what is today northern Iraq. The earliest evidence of a relationship between Egypt and Assyria is in the early New Kingdom, in years 24, 33 and 40 of the reign of Tuthmose III (18th Dynasty). These accounts attest to attempts by Assyria to gain Egyptian support against the expanding kingdom of Mitanni, located in the upper Euphrates region. Egypt at that time was fighting Mitanni in Syria. This Egyptian–Assyrian relationship, which largely manifested itself in the sending

of gifts (Assyria sent lapis lazuli and characteristic "Assyrian" vessels), possibly appears again seventy years later in a cuneiform letter found in Egypt at the site of Tell el-Amarna. In this text, deliveries of Egyptian gold are mentioned taking place during the reign of an Assyrian king, Assur-nadin-ahhe (I or II?). According to this king, Assur was a Mitannian province, unable to free itself until the last years of the reign of the Egyptian king Akhenaten. Then the king of the Mitanni, Tushratta, was murdered and succession problems followed. The then ruler of Assyria, Assur-uballit I, recommended diplomatic relations with Egypt, and there are two more letters to Akhenaten concerning this. However, in a letter of protest from Burnaburiash, king of Babylonia, dating to *circa* 1325 BC, an opposing claim to sovereignty over Assyria, based on historical grounds, was expressed.

In the following 600 years there is no information about relations between Egypt and Assyria. This changes, however, with the advances of King Tiglath-pileser III of Assyria (745–727 BC) against the small city-states of Syro-Palestine, a situation which also involved Egypt. In 731 BC the Assyrian king took Damascus and made subjects of the rulers in Palestine. On the border with Egypt, he set up a buffer zone controlled by a bedouin sheikh.

From the Old Testament (II Kings, 17:3–4) we know that the king of Judah, Hosea, conspired with a King "So" of Egypt (possibly the Libyan ruler Osorkon IV, resident in Bubastis and ruler of the eastern Delta) for a change in the succession to the Assyrian throne. In this way Shalmaneser V came to the Assyrian throne. Also at this time, Egyptian scribes appear to have been present in the Assyrian court.

The death of Shalmaneser V in 722 BC led to revolts in the Assyrian provinces and a loss of power in Palestine, a movement again supported by Egypt. Cuneiform texts mention an Egyptian general named Re'e. The next Assyrian king, Sargon II (721–705 BC), suppressed the revolts and defeated the Egyptian army. Osorkon IV then commenced diplomatic relations with Sargon II, a trading treaty was made and Osorkon sent horses to the Assyrian king.

In these years there was great political change in Egypt. Bocchoris, the prince of Sais in the Delta, advanced upstream into the Nile Valley until he was halted in 714 BC by Shabako, the Kushite ruler of the 25th Dynasty then in control of Upper Egypt. The latter king then embarked upon a policy of appeasement with Assyria. A request for help against Assyria from Jamani, the prince of Ashdod (in Palestine), was refused by Shabako. Thus abandoned by Egypt, Jamani was attacked by Sargon II's army. However, under the next Assyrian king, Sennacherib (704–681 BC), revolts again broke out in Syro-Palestine. An Egyptian army came to help, but it was defeated in 701 BC. Sennacherib then took Jerusalem, despite the advances of another Egyptian army, which Shabako's successor, Shebitku, had sent.

In 690 BC, Taharka (25th Dynasty) succeeded to the Egyptian throne. Sennacherib was murdered in Assyria in 681 BC and a struggle over succession broke out between the princes, which was won by Essarhaddon (680–669 BC). He too had to suppress revolts in Syro-Palestine, especially in Sidon on the Mediterranean coast. Due to the constant Egyptian support of rebels, the Assyrian king decided on the elimination of this adversary. His first attack at Sile, at the border fortifications of the eastern Delta, failed in 674 BC. However, in 671 BC the Assyrian army gave the border forts a wide berth and instead advanced through the desert, battling their way through the Wadi Tumilat in the eastern Delta to Memphis. After the capture of the city, doctors, officials and artisans were taken to Assyria, along with fifty-five royal statues, several of which have been found at the Assyrian royal palace at Kouyundjik. While Taharka held Upper Egypt, Lower Egypt was organized as an Assyrian territory. The city of Memphis received an Assyrian name and its leaders were controlled by Assyrian governors.

A counterattack by Taharka in 669 BC led to a recapture of Memphis and a responding Assyrian expedition was abandoned on the death of Essarhaddon. In 667 BC his son and successor, Assurbanipal (668–626 BC), sent his army against Taharka. The Kushite troops were defeated in Lower Egypt at Kar-banite (now known as Saft el-Henne) and the Assyrians pursued them into Upper Egypt. Nevertheless, the Kushite king held the Assyrians at Thebes. Then the local princes in the Delta rebelled but, lacking organization, their efforts were fruitless. Among these rebels was a certain Neko of Sais, who was re-established in his rule and became a vassal of Assyria. Under the Assyrian name of Nabu-sezibanni, his son received the rule of the city of Athribis.

Taharka's successor, Tanutamen, came to the throne in 664 BC and began his reign with a renewed attack on the Assyrians in Egypt. He even succeeded in recapturing Memphis. Thus Neko of Sais fell, as he chose to remain loyal to the Assyrians, and his rule was taken over by his son, Psamtik. However, the other local princes remained on the side of the Assyrians and so Tanutamen's advance was checked. Assurbanipal now involved himself in the dispute, expelling Tanutamen from Upper Egypt and then plundering Thebes. The Assyrian king took much Theban booty, including two obelisks.

In 652 BC a struggle began between the two Assyrian royal brothers, Assurbanipal and Shamash-shum-ukin, who was ruling in Babylon. This proved to be the beginning of the end of Assyrian power. Psamtik, previously a loyal Assyrian vassal, allied himself with Shamash-shum-ukin, along with Gyges of Lydia in Asia Minor, who sent his Ionian and Carian soldiers, mentioned by Herodotus as "bronze men." With their help Psamtik conquered the Delta princes, followed in 656/655 BC by conquest of the Theban region, previously considered part of Tanutamen's kingdom. Egypt was unified once more and Assyria's control ended with little bloodshed, since the Assyrian troops were preoccupied with their internal dispute.

It is striking that there are no monuments from the time of Assyrian rule in Egypt, nor did those who fought against this control, such as Tanutamen or Montuemhet, the ruler of Thebes, mention their Assyrian overlords in texts. Only in later Egyptian texts did the Assyrians emerge as sworn enemies. This suggests that Assyrian rule in Egypt was seen as an abnormal period and was therefore dealt with in a customary Egyptian fashion, by concealment.

In 629 BC the Babylonian king, Nabopolassar, drove the Assyrians out of Babylon, and two years later Assurbanipal died. However, in 616 BC Nabopolassar and his army were defeated by Assyrian and Egyptian troops at Balikh on the Euphrates River. Seeking to maintain the balance of power in the region, Psamtik I had sided with the Assyrians. Nevertheless, the Assyrian kingdom quickly collapsed.

In 614 BC the Medes captured Assur, the Assyrian capital, and in 612 BC the Medes and Babylonians took Nineveh, another major Assyrian city. The remnants of the Assyrian army retreated to Harran in northern Mesopotamia under their last king, Assur-uballit II, who had become ruler after Assurbanipal's son Sin-shar-ishkun was burned to death in his palace at Nineveh, an occurrence remembered by the Greeks in the story of Sardanapalus. In 610 BC both Assyria and Egypt had to give up Harran. That same year Psamtik I died and his son, Neko II, came to the throne. He immediately gave up the Euphrates front, but was nevertheless unable to retake Harran. Assur-uballit II stood alone against the Babylonian and Egyptian troops now involved in Neko II's organization of Syro-Palestine as Egyptian territories. In 606 BC the Egyptians were in an advantageous position: they had recaptured Kummuh, south of Carchemish, and had broken through the Babylonians' line of defense at Qurumati. However, in 605 BC the Babylonian crown prince, Nebuchadnezzar, took command of the army and from the west stormed Carchemish, the center point of the Egyptians' Euphrates front. The Egyptian army, including many Greek mercenaries, was annihilated, having been intercepted near Hamath in Syria. All of Syro-Palestine fell into the hands of the Babylonians. For Egypt, the fall of the kingdom of Assyria merely meant replacement of the Egyptian–Assyrian stalemate with an Egyptian–Babylonian one.

See also

Amarna Letters; Late and Ptolemaic periods, overview; New Kingdom, overview; Tell el-Amarna, city; Third Intermediate Period, overview

WOLFGANG HELCK

Aswan

Aswan is a town on the east bank of the Nile at the northern end of the First Cataract (24°05′ N, 32°54′ E). In Greek it was called Syene and in Egyptian Swnw. At Aswan, the course of the Nile is interrupted by an outcrop of the magmatic basement-complex, imposing a natural borderline. Breaking through this barrier, the river divides into numerous branches; rapids and shoals make navigation dangerous, even impossible, for a distance of about 6 km. Here, in the ethnic borderland between the Egyptian and Nubian peoples, the southern frontier of pharaonic Egypt was established in Early Dynastic times; the region of Aswan, or Nome I of Upper Egypt, was always regarded as the starting point of Egypt. Situated where the overland routes bypassing the Cataract start and where the loading and unloading was done, Aswan occupied a key position controlling the trade in African luxury items. Further, desert trails linked Aswan to the great western caravan routes via the well-stations Kurkur, Dungul and Selima, while the Wadi Abu Aggag and the Khor Abu-Subeira provided an eastward connection to the tracks leading to Berenike at the shore of the Red Sea.

The Aswan region itself offered a unique array of colorful hard rocks, all of them highly valued as material for monumental buildings and for the sculptural arts. Taking advantage of the convenient location for river transport, large-scale quarrying was therefore conducted at Aswan throughout pharaonic history. Finally, the area held an important religious significance. Since the Nile entered Egypt here, it seemed appropriate to locate the sources of its all-sustaining inundation in the dramatic river scenery of the cataract. Thus, the cult of the local deities became closely linked to the life-cycle of the Nile.

Starting in Predynastic times, an unbroken series of sites and monuments offers the opportunity to trace the history of the area. The oldest and, throughout antiquity, most important town of the region was situated on Elephantine Island. Opposite the island, on the plain of the east bank, where the portage road circumventing the Cataract ended, a harbor and marketplace should have existed very early. Attested for the first time in the Ramesside period under the name of Swnw (for which, viewing the circumstances, the etymology as "marketplace" seems virtually certain), the town was of some importance in Persian times (late sixth to fifth centuries BC).

The extant monuments date only from Ptolemaic and Roman times, when Aswan enjoyed some importance as a garrison and a base for military operations against Lower Nubia. Most conspicuous nowadays is the temple dedicated by Ptolemy III and Ptolemy IV to the goddess Isis "who fights in front of the army," a theological device conceived well in accord with the military character of the town. Situated in the southeastern part of the modern city, the building consists of a hypostyle hall supported by two pillars, giving access to three parallel sanctuaries in the rear part. The relief decoration showing the usual array of ritual scenes remained confined to the main doorways and the back wall of the central sanctuary. The enclosure wall, pylon and forecourt, which should have been present, as well as eventual ancillary structures, are covered by the modern settlement. In the immediate vicinity another temple, erected by Trajan, is known from decorated blocks reused in the medieval town wall. Also in the southern part of the modern city, nearer to the river, a second temple erected by Ptolemy IV was discovered at the beginning of the twentieth century. Additions to its architecture by Tiberius, Claudius and Trajan, as well as inscribed votive altars, attest to its use down to the early third century AD. Unfortunately, this building has since vanished completely.

While all the earlier monuments are found concentrated in the southern part of the site, in Roman times it appears that the town expanded northward. From the distribution of these remains, the area of the town can be roughly estimated as about 12 ha in the Ptolemaic period, growing in Roman times to about 16 ha. Near the river, some 300 m north of the temple of Isis, badly decayed remains are still visible of a chapel dedicated by Domitian, possibly to Khnum. Relatively well preserved is the *pronaos* (front porch) with a four-columned façade and an engaged portal, while the *naos*, consisting of antechamber and sanctuary, is lost today nearly to the foundations. From the neighborhood, the discovery of pillars, columns and capitals is reported, which might have belonged to a basilica erected under Antoninus Pius.

South of Aswan, remains of an enormous fortification wall are still visible. It connected, over a distance of some 7.5 km, the loading-place of Aswan to the plain of Shellal. Clearly, the wall served to protect the portage road bypassing the unnavigable stretch of the Cataract against eventual bedouin raids. Recent fieldwork by Jaritz has revealed its construction: 5 m thick at the base, built in filled casemate masonry, the wall reached a height of about 10 m, towering above a sloping *glacis* on its outer face, while a wide track runs along its inner (western) side. The date of this building is still doubtful. Remains of three Roman watchtowers, discovered along the road, attest to its use down to that period.

Originally, the cemetery of the ancient Egyptian metropolis of Elephantine was situated immediately west of the settlement on the island itself. When rock-cut tombs became fashionable in the 6th Dynasty, however, a separate necropolis for the burials of the elite was founded on the west bank, some 1.5 km downstream of Elephantine. Here, halfway up the slope of a prominent sandstone hill called Qubbet el-Hawa (Hill of the Wind), the tombs were laid out in three horizontal rows overlooking the valley.

Tombs dating from the late 6th Dynasty (Pepi II) form the first and most numerous

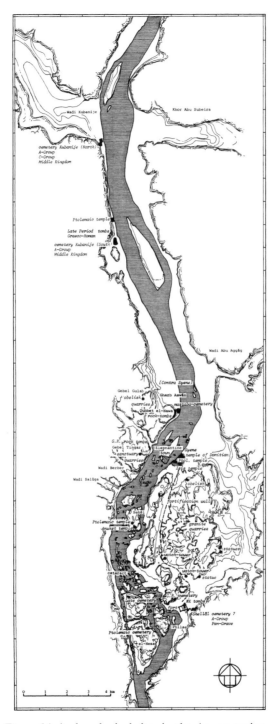

Figure 14 Archaeological sites in the Aswan region

phase of occupation, which extends well into the First Intermediate Period. In the most sumptuous tombs, an open causeway leads up from the river to a narrow courtyard extending in front of the tomb. The entrance to the chapel, set centrally in the façade and sometimes flanked by miniature obelisks, opens into a broad rectangular hall hewn out of the living rock. Its ceiling is usually supported by up to three rows of rough pillars or columns, while the offering place in the middle of the rear wall is regularly marked by a false door. Decoration is sparse and distinctly provincial in style. Even in the richest tombs, decoration is confined mainly to doorways, the false door and a few tableaux on the walls or the faces of the pillars. Quite an unusual feature in the burial customs of this cemetery is the habit to furnish the dead with scores of offering jars inscribed with hieratic labels naming, sometimes in combination, contents, addressee or donor. The tomb owners, the aristocracy of ancient Elephantine and their subordinate personnel, served the king as troop commanders and caravan leaders, organizing and conducting far-ranging trading, quarrying and military expeditions.

Only recently, a necropolis of *mastaba* tombs was discovered on the riverbank at the foot of the Qubbet el-Hawa, extending northward into the plain of modern Gharb Aswan. The single excavated 6th Dynasty mudbrick *mastaba* closely resembles the tombs known at Elephantine. The geographical extent of this cemetery, as well as its chronological range, still remain to be determined. Equally, it is not yet clear whether this cemetery was used by the inhabitants of Elephantine, or whether it possibly belonged to an ancient settlement in the plain north of the Qubbet el-Hawa. In Roman times, at least, the settlement and military post known from the documents as Contra Syene must have been situated here. While archaeological traces of this settlement are missing, a few badly decayed tomb chambers cut into the foot of the Qubbet el-Hawa could date from this time.

At the beginning of the 12th Dynasty, Senusret I appointed a new line of local governors at Elephantine. These officials, who controlled the civil, military and religious administration of the region, commissioned a series of great rock-cut tombs. As in the Old Kingdom, a pillared hall, now oriented longitudinally, is entered via the causeway and forecourt. From the hall, a narrow corridor leads deep into the rock, giving access to a small square chapel holding the shrine for the cultic statue of the owner. A series of Middle Kingdom corridor tombs of lesser status is known to have been situated on a narrow terrace above the rows of the rock-cut chapels.

Later tombs are conspicuously few. While two tombs of the 18th Dynasty are interspersed among the earlier ones, a tomb of a 19th Dynasty high priest of Khnum, named Kakemu, is to be found isolated on a hillock a little northward. Though badly defaced since its discovery, the tomb, comprising entrance pylon, forecourt, pillared hall and a burial apartment entered *via* a sloping passage, is rightly famous for its painted decoration, especially the ornaments on the ceiling of the hall. While still later tomb constructions are absent, the existing ones were used for secondary and intrusive burials throughout the Late period.

South of Aswan, the main settlement area was located on the east bank, in the wide plain of Shellal at the upper end of the cataract. Mainly in its southern part, a series of cemeteries was excavated by Reisner in 1907–8, comprising numerous burials of the Nubian A-Group, a small cemetery of the Nubian Pan-Grave Culture dating from the Second Intermediate Period, as well as a series of shaft tombs of the New Kingdom. In the northern part, a burial ground of Graeco-Roman date was discovered. The early settlements themselves were not excavated, but the trenches of the fort, where the *Legio I Maximiana* was garrisoned during the late Roman empire, could be identified in the plain.

More cemeteries of Graeco-Roman date were discovered on the islands of the Cataract, most importantly an extensive cemetery of rock-cut chambers on el-Hesa containing the interments of the priests of Isis of Philae from Ptolemaic times. In addition, a group of similar but badly plundered rock-cut tombs dating from the first century AD is known on the west bank opposite Elephantine.

Excavations in the vicinity of the temple of Isis in Aswan revealed a few stone sarcophagi remarkable for bearing name-labels in Aramaic. There are no convincing reasons, however, to link this find with the group of Aramaic-speaking Jewish mercenaries stationed at Elephantine during Persian rule, which is known so well from the Aramaic papyri discovered there.

Apart from the large temples at Elephantine, Aswan and Philae, a number of lesser sanctuaries are known from the region. At Sehel, halfway up the eastern slope of Husseintagug, a rocky hill in the southeastern part of the island, the site of a temple of the goddess Anuket, the principal deity of Sehel, is marked by a narrow terrace and a broad niche cut into the face of the hill. Sandstone slabs decorated with offering scenes attest two sides of a small shrine or an altar dedicated by Sobekhotep III of the 13th Dynasty to Anuket, while only a series of architectural fragments remains of a chapel erected by Amenhotep II. A truly enormous number of dedicatory rock-inscriptions on the boulders opposite and around the place bears witness to the importance of this sanctuary from the latter part of the Middle Kingdom. Another much later temple at Sehel is known from decorated blocks bearing the cartouches of Ptolemy IV, mostly found reused in the modern village north of Husseintagug.

On top of the mountains of the Western Desert, at the Gebel Tingar, a small chapel was installed in the New Kingdom, protected by a huge solitary block of silicified sandstone. As in the temples of Anuket at Sehel and Satet at Elephantine, it is evident here that the sacred place originated in a conspicuous natural site. A rough enclosure wall of piled rubble and some cuttings in the floor for the foundations of the shrine are the only remains of the architecture of the former chapel. Scores of dedicatory rock inscriptions on the faces of the natural boulders, however, attest to its celebrity throughout the New Kingdom. Apart from the civil and religious authorities of the region, the personnel of the nearby quarries figure prominently among the devotees of this cult. A

similar situation may be assumed for a chapel of Amen located in the quarries east of Aswan, which is mentioned in the time of Tuthmose III in a list of offering endowments.

The most characteristic feature of the region of Aswan is its extensive quarries. Traces of the quarrying activities are abundant. The most impressive relics are an unfinished New Kingdom obelisk measuring a gigantic 42 m in length, which is lying immediately south of Aswan, and several unfinished colossal statues left behind in the southeastern part of the quarry. Lesser quarries, mostly of Roman date, are known on several of the islands of the Cataract, as well as at several places on both riverbanks north of Aswan.

Thanks to the geographical situation with suitable rock-faces abounding, the Aswan area can boast of the most important concentration of rock inscriptions and rock drawings known in Egypt. The rock drawings, depicting mostly animals but also stylized human figures, occur most often at the mouth of wadis and at natural shelters along the riverbanks. A few of them, especially those depicting ships, are clearly Predynastic; others are recognizably pharaonic, but most of them are probably late Roman or medieval although exact dating remains a problem.

The rock inscriptions, on the other hand, start in the 4th Dynasty and continue throughout pharaonic times, though the bulk derive from the Middle and New Kingdoms. Inscriptions of private persons are found most often, especially during the New Kingdom, in connection with important shrines: the temple of Anuket at Sehel, the temples at Elephantine and the chapel at the Gebel Tingar. They display the devotion to the local deities, commemorating a visit to their sanctuaries. Other inscriptions, particularly those of the Middle Kingdom, were engraved at conspicuous places alongside important roads, the riverbanks and, above all, the roads connecting Aswan and the harbor at Shellal. They were commissioned by people who were sent to Aswan or Nubia to carry out quarrying, trading or administrative tasks for the crown.

Normally in the Middle Kingdom, the texts state only the name, titles and family relations of the owner. In the New Kingdom, short formal prayers to the king and/or the local gods become frequent. Narrative texts detailing the objectives of the sojourn at Aswan are rare, though forthcoming. Often, the inscriptions accompany relief figures of the persons mentioned and the gods addressed in the prayers, some of which are beautifully carved. Various kings, on the other hand, left a series of important historical texts. Sixth Dynasty royal visits to the area to receive homage by the native headmen are recorded in several inscriptions. In the Middle and New Kingdoms, a series of stelae was carved in the boundary area commemorating military expeditions against Nubia, while a group of texts on the eastern face of Sehel island relates to the clearing out of navigation channels.

Another remarkable text is the so-called "famine stela" located on top of Bibitagug hill at Sehel. This document, composed in the Ptolemaic era but fictitiously dated back to the 3rd Dynasty, recounts how the king donated the land of the Dodekaschoinos from Aswan to Takompso near Quban in Lower Nubia to (the temple of) the god Khnum for bringing about relief after a seven-year period of famine; a fake, the stela was evidently made up to support proprietary claims of the priesthood of the temple of Khnum at Elephantine.

Numbering over a thousand, this unique collection of texts provides invaluable historical information regarding the civil and religious administration of the region, as well as Egyptian–Nubian relations. Furthermore, the texts provide important aid in dating and/or interpreting the archaeological and geographical contexts in which they occur. Thanks to the rich and varied archaeological as well as epigraphic record, a unique reconstruction of the conditions and of the organization of provincial life is possible for the area of Aswan. In particular, the interplay between natural and cultural factors, and between local and nationwide interests, can be studied here in an exemplary manner.

See also

A-Group culture; C-Group culture; Elephantine; Nubian forts; Nubian towns and temples; obelisks; Philae; quarrying; Reisner, George Andrew

Further reading

Jaritz, H. 1993. The investigation of the ancient wall extending from Aswan to Philae. *MDAIK* 49: 107–32.

Jaritz, H., and M. Rodziewicz. 1996. Syene: investigations of the urban remains. *MDAIK* 52: 233–49.

Kamil, J. 1993. *Aswan and Abu Simbel: History and Guide.* Cairo.

Klemm, D., and R. Klemm. 1992. *Steine und Steinbrüche im alten Ägypten.* Berlin.

STEPHAN SEIDLMAYER

Asyut

Asyut, the capital of Nome XIII of Upper Egypt, lies on the west bank of the Nile (27°11′ N, 31°10′ E) approximately halfway between Minya and Qena, at the beginning of a caravan route leading to Kharga Oasis, and from there on to Darfur in western Sudan. The modern toponym "Asyut" derives from its ancient Egyptian name Z3wt or Z3wty, meaning "the Guard." The town must have already existed in the Old Kingdom, as its first mention goes back to the *Pyramid Texts*. The archaeological record, however, begins in the 9th/10th Dynasties with three tombs of the governors (nomarchs) of Asyut, who were possibly related to the kings of Heracleopolis and were their allies in the campaigns against the rising Theban power. The *savants* accompanying Napoleon's expedition to Egypt devoted special attention to the site, a fortunate circumstance since some of the tombs later suffered heavy destruction. In spite of their shortcomings, the plans and drawings published in the *Description de l'Égypte* are our only source for the texts and reliefs of some of the tomb façades.

The oldest rock-cut tomb (no. 5) belongs to Kheti I. The doorway gave access to a roughly square chamber with two pillars, the back wall of which has an unusual plan: instead of being straight, it is divided into three angled sections. The biographical text relates Kheti's achievements, including the digging a canal for his city. It contains no reference yet to strife with the Thebans, although it does allude to the mustering of troops. In this tomb the temple of the main deity of Asyut, the jackal-god Wepwawet, "Lord of Asyut," is mentioned for the first time. The façade of Tomb 3, which belonged to Kheti I's successor Itibi (possibly his son), was decorated in the same manner. The one chamber of this tomb is innovative in plan, being longer than it is wide, and it is divided into two distinct sections by the two pillars. Itibi's victories against the "Head of the South" (tp-Šm3w, i.e. Thebes) are mentioned in his biographical inscription. The texts referring to these wars, however, were later plastered over and replaced by another, painted text. The niches in the back wall and additions on the façade belong to a later reuse of the tomb.

Itibi's son and successor, Kheti II, was a contemporary of King Merikare of the 10th Dynasty. His tomb (no. 4) also consists of a single chamber, but with four pillars instead of two. Its façade is destroyed, but the chamber contains well-known reliefs depicting the police troops of Asyut and a biographical text of Kheti II, who was also involved in the wars against Thebes. The fact that he is the last of this line of nomarchs of Asyut is evidence that the nome must have eventually fallen under the control of the Thebans in their northward push to reunify Egypt. All three of the Asyut nomarchs bear, along with their administrative titles, the title of high priest of the town gods, Wepwawet and Anubis.

Three nomarchs of Asyut in the Middle Kingdom, all called Hapidjefa, are known from their tombs there. The best preserved burial is that of Hapidjefa I, who lived during the reign of Senusret I. This consists of a forecourt, now destroyed, which led to a passageway, a hall with side rooms and, through another passageway, an inner hall and a chapel flanked by two small side rooms. The inscriptions provide many details of his administrative and priestly duties and titles. Unfortunately, the texts in the tombs of Hapidjefa II and III are badly damaged. The tomb of the latter featured a pillared hall, a second hall, a vaulted passage and a wide narrow room which gave access to three chapels. It contained a later hoard of over 600 stelae, mostly consisting of votive stelae to Wepwawet; some were dedicated to Amen-Re, Hathor, Osiris, Ptah and Thoth. The tomb had also been used to store demotic papyri and mummies of *canidae*, presumably sacred animals worshipped as manifestations of the jackal-god Wepwawet.

The vestiges of tombs of contemporaries of the Asyut nomarchs, dating from the 9th/10th to 12th Dynasties, have also been recorded. Numerous Middle Kingdom coffins inscribed with *Coffin Texts* come from Asyut, although their exact provenance is not known.

At the end of the Second Intermediate Period, the town is mentioned in Kamose's account of his campaigns, as the king halted here for the flood season during his war against the Hyksos. In the New Kingdom, Hatia, the "scribe of the registrar" (*sš n wḥmw*) and "magistrate" (*ḳnbty*) of Asyut is represented in the Theban tomb of Rekhmire (TT 100, reign of Tuthmose III) bringing the tribute of his city. This indicates that Asyut belonged to the southern administrative district, falling under the authority of the Vizier of the South.

Stone blocks from a temple of the Aten (worshipped by the heretical King Akhenaten) were found under a house in Asyut, but they must have been brought there from elsewhere. A block found in the same location, with an inscription of a speech of "Wepwawet of the South" in favor of Ramesses II (19th Dynasty), may have belonged to a temple of this deity. Papyrus Harris I states that Ramesses III (20th Dynasty) restored the temple of Wepwawet in Asyut, and erected two funerary temples for himself within the precinct of the main temple. The papyrus also states that the king gave the Wepwawet temple four slaves, while he presented his funerary temples with 157 slaves and later 122 slaves.

In the Late and Graeco-Roman periods, some tombs at Asyut were reused. A demotic papyrus from the time of the Persian King

Cambyses (27th Dynasty) provides an indication of the temple's location: it lay west of an imaginary line drawn between the southern quarter and the city proper.

See also

First Intermediate Period, overview; funerary texts; Napoleon Bonaparte and the Napoleonic expedition

Further reading

Beinlich, H. 1975. Assiut. In *LÄ*: 489–95.

Brunner, H. 1937. *Die Texte aus den Gräbern der Herakleopolitenzeit von Siut.* (Ägyptologische Forschungen 5). Glückstadt.

Griffith, F.L. 1889. *The Inscriptions of Siût and Dêr Rifeh.* London.

Porter, B., and R. Moss. 1934. *Topographical Bibliography of Ancient Egyptian Hieroglyphic Texts, Reliefs, and Paintings* 4: *Lower and Middle Egypt*, 261–70. Oxford.

FEDERICO POOLE

B

el-Badari district Predynastic sites

The el-Badari district (26°50′–27°10′ N, 31°16–31°31 E) lies on the east bank of the Nile near the modern city of Asyut. Most of what is known concerning Predynastic culture of the region is based on the work of Guy Brunton, who conducted extensive fieldwork in the area in the 1920s and early 1930s, and Gertrude Caton Thompson's meticulous excavation in 1924–5 of a site known as North Spur Hemamieh (usually referred to as Hemamieh).

For Brunton, the el-Badari district consisted of the 16 km stretch of low desert between the modern villages of el-Etmania (Qau el-Kebir) and Naga Wissa. He then continued working northward in two sectors he called "Mostagedda" and "Matmar." However, these two sectors are now regarded as merely an extension of the el-Badari district and this region is defined as the area between and including two large wadis, Wadi el-Asyuti and Qau Bay, approximately 60 km long.

Between 1922 and 1931, Brunton excavated over 100 Predynastic sites, both cemeteries and settlements, in his three sectors of the el-Badari region. His colleague, Caton Thompson, chose to conduct a more careful excavation at the small village locality of Hemamieh, about 3 km to the north of the modern village of el-Hemamieh in a stretch of low desert Brunton had dismissed as being too narrow for a cemetery. The work of both Caton Thompson and Brunton left many fundamental aspects of the Predynastic culture of the region unresolved, and in 1989 and 1992 a small team, led by Diane L. Holmes of the Institute of Archaeology, University College London, conducted new investigations.

The known Predynastic sites all occur in the low desert between the cultivation and the limestone plateau. In the el-Badari region this strip of desert is very narrow, seldom exceeding a few hundred meters in width. The sites are generally shallow, with deposits approximately 0.5–2.0 m in depth. The majority are multiperiod localities with later Predynastic and Dynastic graves dug into earlier village levels. The habitation deposits consist of loose sandy sediments mixed with ash, charcoal, vegetable matter and animal bone. Potsherds and lithics are abundant, but evidence of any habitation structures is rare. Because the sites tend to be palimpsests of different phases, the Predynastic culture of the el-Badari region is perhaps best described by period rather than by considering individual sites.

During his first field season, Brunton encountered a "new" kind of pottery that was thin-walled and had a rippled or combed exterior. Brunton concluded that this pottery was early and represented a culture preceding the other Predynastic cultures then known. His conclusion was vindicated by the work of Caton Thompson at Hemamieh. She peeled off the sediments of this small settlement in 6 inch (15 cm) layers. As she went down, she encountered ceramics belonging to the familiar Predynastic classes (from the Nagada I/Amratian and Nagada II/Gerzean phases). Then in the lowest levels she found examples of the rippled pottery along with other types that Brunton found in the graves he was excavating. They named this culture with the rippled pottery "Badarian."

The Badarian is significant as it remains the oldest known agricultural tradition in the Nile

Valley of Upper Egypt (though preliminary reports indicate there may be a partly contemporaneous early phase of the "Nagadian" culture in the Armant area. The people of the Badarian culture planted wheat and barley and kept cattle, sheep and goats, but it is unknown to what extent they were dependent on these resources. They also caught fish from the Nile and hunted gazelle. Little indication was found of the kind of structures they inhabited except at one locality (site no. 2000/3500 near Deir Tasa), where the stumps of several wooden posts were found which may represent the remains of a light hut or shelter. The only other features Brunton reported for any Badarian settlements are a number of deep pits, which Brunton assumed were granaries.

Aside from the numerous Badarian settlements (over fifty), Brunton cleared a large number of Badarian burials (about 750 spread over forty-five localities). The graves consisted of shallow, roughly oval-shaped pits with the body generally placed in the position and orientation that was to become characteristic of burials throughout the Predynastic period in Upper Egypt (i.e. in a contracted position, lying on the left side, with head to the south facing west). The Badarian grave goods were relatively simple. The deceased was usually wrapped in matting or animal skins and placed on a reed mat. Buried with the body were often items of personal adornment, such as necklaces of marine shells or stone beads. Other artifacts in the grave usually included a single pot, and sometimes a slate palette or a few flint tools.

Although the Badarian was recognized as "early," it was a long time before any absolute dates could be assigned. In the early 1970s a series of thermoluminescence (TL) determinations were obtained for eight potsherds from Caton Thompson's Hemamieh excavations, but they only substantiated the relative sequence already known and did not provide realistic absolute dates. Five new radiocarbon dates have now been obtained from samples recovered during recent excavations at Hemamieh and Site 3400 (near Deir Tasa), and these show that the Badarian clearly falls into the 4000–4500 BC range.

Only in the Gurna-Armant region are there other Predynastic sites in Upper Egypt dating to earlier than 4000 BC (sites MA 6/83 and MA 21/83). However, these are not Badarian sites. Rather, the excavators assign them to their "Nagadian" culture. Although there are some similarities in the pottery between the Armant and el-Badari regions, they are not sufficient to support the notion of the Badarian culture extending as far south as Armant. While some scholars have tried to claim a Badarian affiliation for a number of sites outside the el-Badari region, their evidence, usually comprising just a few sherds with rippled decoration, may merely indicate trade with the el-Badari region.

When Brunton began working near Deir Tasa, he thought he was finding evidence of an even earlier culture, which he named "Tasian." Few people assessing his results in detail have accepted the Tasian. Brunton did not excavate his sites stratigraphically and he did not find any site yielding what he claimed were "Tasian" finds without there also being Badarian evidence. Any artifacts that Brunton considered to be characteristic of the Tasian should be regarded as part of Badarian material culture. The incised flaring-mouthed beakers that Brunton thought were typical of the Tasian, however, may represent a non-local import, possibly from a people inhabiting the Eastern Desert or perhaps northern Sudan.

Many of the Badarian sites also show evidence of later Predynastic use, both as settlements and as cemeteries. However, while Brunton dated the graves in terms of Flinders Petrie's Sequence Dating system, he did not always provide an indication of the relative chronological position of the post-Badarian Predynastic settlements. Nevertheless, in general, Brunton concluded that most of the later graves were Gerzean (Nagada II) in date while the settlements were mainly Amratian (Nagada I).

One of the intriguing results of the recent fieldwork conducted by Holmes, however, was the paucity of pottery and other objects that could be assigned to the Nagada I phase. The Predynastic sites surveyed had readily identifiable Badarian and/or Nagada II ceramic classes, but only very rarely was a sherd encountered that could be considered Nagada I. While this paucity of Nagada I material is not yet fully understood, it is unlikely to reflect a break in occupation between the Badarian and the Nagada II phase in the el-Badari region. Both Caton Thompson's and Holmes's excavations at Hemamieh indicate that the site was occupied more or less continuously throughout the Predynastic period, from the Badarian to late Nagada II. What the Hemamieh sequence and the results of the 1989 and 1992 surveys seem to suggest, however, is that during the Nagada I phase (*circa* 3900–3500 BC) the material culture of the el-Badari region was of a different appearance from contemporary assemblages elsewhere in Upper Egypt. In 1956, Werner Kaiser suggested that the Badarian of the el-Badari region was largely contemporary with the Nagada I phase represented in other parts of the Nile Valley. While more data are needed, this suggestion may turn out to be partly true. The results of the recent field investigations suggest that perhaps after 4000 BC, the Badarian developed into an "evolved Badarian" or "transitional Badarian/Nagada I," still essentially Badarian in character but with some Nagada I elements. This "evolved Badarian" then gave way to a clear Nagada II phase with both the settlements and the cemeteries yielding artifact types familiar from Nagada II sites throughout Upper Egypt, although the flint artifacts seem to reflect a local tradition which has been termed the "Mostagedda industry."

Evidence for habitation structures dating to the post-Badarian Predynastic comes from Hemamieh and a series of sites to the north of Sheikh 'Esa. At Hemamieh, Caton Thompson found nine "hut circles," which she dated to the Amratian (Nagada I). These were small mud constructions, 1–2 m in diameter, some of which had at least some sort of wattle-and-daub superstructure. Only the larger ones, however, could have served as any kind of human shelter, and they all may have been storerooms or shelters for young animals.

At the series of settlement localities near Sheikh 'Esa, Brunton uncovered several roughly circular, mud-plastered floors (at localities 3000/3, 3000/9 and 3000/11). These floors were about 3 m in diameter and were bounded by low mud walls or sills. Parts of wooden stakes, which would have supported the superstructure of these huts, were also found at locality 3000/3. In addition, the remains of a roughly rectangular hut or shelter (approximately 1.6 × 2.1 m) were found at locality 3000/12. Although Brunton assigned these localities to the Amratian (Nagada I), recent results suggest that they are in fact Nagada II.

During the Nagada III phase, the desert seems to have been used only for burials. The settlements were presumably in the area of cultivation. One locality (3000/3), however, has a two-chambered, rectangular mudbrick structure (approximately 3.6 × 2.0 m). Brunton was uncertain of its age, though it is probably Nagada III or 1st Dynasty. Although its function has not been established, it was possibly an early temple, as it was overlain by the remains of two Dynastic temples.

While a rich variety of Predynastic sites has been found in the el-Badari region, the sites are disappearing rapidly due to modern developments, especially extensive land reclamation projects.

See also

Armant; Caton Thompson, Gertrude; Nagada (Naqada); Neolithic and Predynastic stone tools; Neolithic cultures, overview; pottery, prehistoric; Predynastic period, overview; Thebes, el-Tarif, prehistoric sites

Further reading

Brunton, G. 1937. *Mostagedda and the Tasian Culture*. London.

Brunton, G., and G. Caton Thompson. 1928. *The Badarian Civilisation*. London.

Holmes, D.L. 1988. The Predynastic lithic industries of Badari, Middle Egypt: new perspectives and inter-regional relations. *WA* 20: 70–86.

Holmes, D.L., and R.F. Friedman. 1994. Survey and test excavations in the Badari region, Middle Egypt. *Proceedings of the Prehistoric Society* 60: 105–42.

DIANE L. HOLMES

Baharia Oasis

Baharia Oasis is located about 400 km south of the Mediterranean coast and 225 km west of the Nile Valley (27°40′–28°30′ N, 28°35′–28°10′ E). Through desert tracks the oasis is connected with Siwa Oasis, the Fayum, Farafra Oasis in the Western Desert, and el-Minya and el-Mahasna in the Nile Valley.

Baharia Oasis is located in a depression 42 km wide (east–west) and 18 km long (north–south). The floor of the depression is about 100 to 175 m below the surface of the desert plateau. Today the cultivated area, fed mostly by springs and wells, is still very limited. The majority of the depression is barren with scattered desert vegetation.

Archaeological investigation of el-Heiz, in a small depression south of the main depression, shows that the area was occupied in early to mid-Holocene times by small groups of people who lived in close proximity to ephermal lakes (playas). The sites range from 20–2000 m², but they are generally in the range of 20–80 m². Artifacts in the sites include fragments of grinding stones, bifacial and unifacial arrowheads, thin large bifacial tools, bifacial double-pointed points (perforators?), side-scrapers, end-scrapers, burins, and notches and denticulates. Ostrich eggshell pieces (some perforated) and stone balls are present. With the exception of the bifacial tools, the stone tool industry (which may be called "Khomanian" after a spring in the oasis, Ain Khoman) fits in the same tradition of the Late Paleolithic assemblages from Dishna in the Nile Valley, assigned to the Isnan Industry (dated to *circa* 12,300 BP, "before present" in radiocarbon years).

The small sites were associated with a sequence of dune sands intercalated with playa sediments. The playa deposits belong to a moist episode well recorded in the Western Desert from *circa* 6,900 to 6,100 BP, postdating an interval of severe aridity *circa* 7,000 BP, and followed by another episode of aridity *circa* 6,000 BP.

See also

dating techniques, prehistory; Paleolithic cultures, overview; Paleolithic tools; Siwa Oasis, prehistoric sites

FEKRI A. HASSAN

Balabish

The site of Balabish consists of several cemeteries on the east bank of the Nile (26°12′ N, 32°08′ E), about 22 km downriver from Nag Hammadi. It was excavated by G.A. Wainwright and Thomas Whittemore in 1915, but had been excavated earlier by the Department of Antiquities and was plundered in antiquity. Cemeteries here date to the Middle and New Kingdoms, and the Coptic period. There may also have been a Predynastic cemetery in the vicinity. Some very small tombs were probably of Late period date, but the archaeologists found Coptic potsherds on the slopes outside the tombs mixed with artifacts of the Late period, suggesting that the tombs had been cleared out and used by a colony of Coptic hermits. The New Kingdom cemetery still contained some artifacts, including an inscribed limestone *shawabti*, and an inscribed heart scarab in slate. Egyptian pottery was found in this cemetery along with imported wares from southwest Asia, one-handled juglets (*bilbil*s), and two-handled "pilgrim flasks," some of which contained "ointment."

Most notable at Balabish, however, was the excavation of a Pan-grave cemetery. The Pan-graves belonged to people of a different material culture from the Egyptians. They entered Upper Egypt in small numbers between the Middle and New Kingdoms. Unlike the shallow Pan-graves that Petrie excavated at Hu, the Balabish Pan-graves were deep (about 1.5 m). Most of the Pan-graves were round or oval in shape, and there was no evidence of superstructures. Twenty-one round graves and thirteen oval graves with contracted burials were excavated with typical Pan-grave goods, but fifteen rectangular graves with extended burials and Pan-grave goods were also found scattered among the others and extending into the area of the New Kingdom cemetery. Graves were oriented north or northwest, following the course of the Nile at Balabish. Two deposits of pots containing "ointment" were found in small holes, but without burials.

Unlike Egyptian burials, the Pan-grave burials at Balabish contained a large number of leather goods, especially leather garments, sometimes with beads sewn in the seams, and leather wrist guards used by archers, in both decorated and plain styles. Leather sandals of a different syle from Egyptian ones of the New Kingdom were found in six graves. Beads were made of imported Red Sea shells and ostrich eggshells, but carnelian and glazed blue beads were also common. In one grave was a typical Pan-grave bracelet of flat, rectangular shell beads strung together. Pottery was also typically Pan-grave; the most common classes found in burials were bowls of the Black-topped Red class and "hatched ware" made of Nile clay.

See also

Hu/Hiw (Diospolis Parva); Pan-grave culture

Further reading

Wainwright, G.A. 1920. *Balabish*. London.

KATHRYN A. BARD

Behbeit el-Hagara

Near the modern village of Behbeit el-Hagara (31°02′ N, 31°17′ E) in the Delta province of Gharbia are the ruins of a temple dedicated to the Osirian family. The temple is located to the north of Samanoud, the ancient capital of Nome XII of Lower Egypt. The Arabic name of Behbeit is derived from the ancient Egyptian toponym Per-hebite(t). The site was erroneously identified with the Isis temple (at Busiris) that Herodotus described (Book II, 59) when European travelers visited Behbeit in the early eighteenth century. Confusion between Behbeit and Busiris lasted for some time. Since the Behbeit temple had a short existence, the question as to whether it is the "Iseum" quoted in Roman sources remains to be confirmed.

The history of the site is poorly known. Although inscriptions were copied from blocks on the surface 100 years ago, archaeological investigations have been minimal. The only excavations were by the Montet Mission in the late 1940s and early 1950s, when blocks in the southeast corner of the temple were excavated. Consequently, there is not much historical information about the cults even though the names of the builders of the temple (Nectanebo II, Ptolemy II, Ptolemy III) are known.

From the New Kingdom onward texts mention the name of the site, Per-hebite(t), or the name of the temple, Hebit, but this evidence is problematic since both names also occur in other parts of Egypt. The earliest textual reference to Per-hebite(t) is from the reign of Amenhotep III. One isolated block of granite inscribed in the Ramesside period (19th–20th Dynasties) is not convincing evidence for a temple dating to this period, as reused blocks taken from Ramesside sites are well known at post-Ramesside sites in the Delta (especially Tanis). Later textual evidence that cult statues of the last kings of the 26th Dynasty were located here strongly suggests that a temple was also built here by these kings.

According to a text of the Third Intermediate Period, Set-wah-ikhet is the other name of Behbeit. Rites at this time included the fabrication of clay statues of the god Osiris-Khenty-imentet. Three centuries later, an inscription on the base of a cult statue belonging to the last king of the 30th Dynasty (Nectanebo II), the temple or a part of it was given another name, Netjeri.

Unfortunately, a plan cannot really be made until the site is properly excavated. Within the mudbrick walls, which have survived on three sides, granite blocks of various sizes are found toppled across the surface in high mounds. The temple was destroyed in ancient times, either by

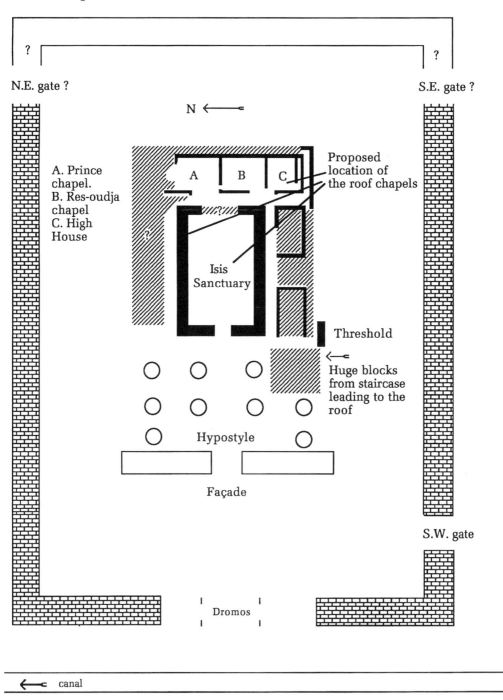

Figure 15 Tentative plan of the Behbeit el-Hagara temple

an earthquake or the collapse of the whole building under its own weight. This occurred some time after the second century BC, as evidenced by the reuse of a Behbeit block in a temple in Rome dedicated to Isis and Serapis, either at the time of its founding in 43 BC, or when it was renovated under Domitian (AD 81–96). After the Behbeit temple's destruction, the site was used as a quarry by the local inhabitants.

According to a tentative reconstruction, a ceremonial way was lined with Nectanebo II's sphinxes. This led to a stone entranceway and hypostyle hall, added onto the main temple by Ptolemy III. Reliefs on the outer façade of the entrance give prominence to Osiris, and in the registers the king makes offerings to three aspects of this god. In the accompanying inscriptions, Isis is the main enactor of the cult rites: "Isis, Lady of Hebit who deposits offerings to her brother Osiris and who protects the great god within the [*Hemag*-]chapel."

Many fragments of red granite columns, which probably belonged to the hypostyle, have been found in the area between the mudbrick enclosure walls and the temple proper. Accounts of eighteenth century travelers describe how these columns were sawed by the local inhabitants to make millstones and it is now difficult to reconstruct this area. On the south side of the hall, huge blocks of black granite form parts of a staircase which probably led to chapels on the roof of the main sanctuary.

To the east of the hypostyle is the façade of the sanctuary of Isis. Reliefs here are about Isis and the kingship, which is inherited through her. In the lower register the king is presented to the goddess by the deities Horus-*Behedety*, Nekhbet and possibly Rayt. In the upper register Isis guarantees the king domination over foreign countries.

The sanctuary of Isis, with its huge blocks of dark gray granite, is the most impressive part of the temple. Carved in high relief, the scenes here are mostly devoted to the cult of Isis. On the eastern wall is a very fragmentary hymn to Isis, one of the earliest known. Three chapels to Osiris are located to the east of the sanctuary, but it is not known if there was direct access to the chapels from the sanctuary or if it was closed off. The chapels are devoted to the rebirth of Osiris-Andjety as a young child and his transformation into a falcon.

The "Prince" chapel (*Hwt-Ser*) and an adjacent room(?) are to the northeast of the sanctuary. This reconstitution, however, is based only on what remains of the lower register of the axial walls. According to religious tradition, the great Prince (*Ser*) from Andjet becomes a divine falcon in Behbeit. Possibly this was where the deified king Osiris-Nectanebo II achieved his transformation into the divine falcon.

The chapel (*Res-oudja*) is representative, through its gods, of major religious centers in the Delta, such as Bubastis, Busiris, Mendes and Sais. The third and southernmost chapel, the "High House," has reliefs of gods (Anubis, Sobek, Thoth and Akhet) assuring the protection of Osiris. Possibly there were additional chapels on the temple roof: some of the blocks found on the surface came from roof constructions which would have been accessible by the staircase in the hypostyle hall.

According to the temple inscriptions, it was built by Nectanebo II, but the decoration could not be completed. Apart from one or two exceptions, the cartouches of this king appear only on blocks belonging to a chapel dedicated to Osiris-Hemag, where the scenes are partly unfinished. The inscriptions were completed sixty years later by Ptolemy II, while Ptolemy III extended the building to the west.

See also

Busiris (Abu Sir Bana); Herodotus; Late and Ptolemaic periods, overview; Mendes, Dynastic evidence; Tanis (San el-Hagar); Tell Basta

Further reading

Favard-Meeks, C. 1991. *Le temple de Behbeit el-Hagara*. Hamburg.

Montet, P. 1949. Les divinités du temple de Behbeit el-Hagar. *Kêmi* 10: 43–8.

CHRISTINE FAVARD-MEEKS

Belzoni, Giovanni Baptista

Trained in hydraulic engineering, Giovanni Belzoni (1778–1823) left his native Italy in 1803 to escape political unrest. He immigrated to England and supported himself for a while as a strongman in the Sadlers Wells theater, where he was billed as the "Paduan Giant," due to his immense size (6'7", 200 cm) and strength. He married Sarah (1783–1870), who accompanied him on subsequent travels.

In hope of selling his invention of a water wheel to Egypt's ruler, Mohammed Ali, he traveled to Egypt in 1816, where he met the British Consul-General and antiquities collector, Henry Salt, who seized upon the idea of using this professional "strongman" to wrest colossal statues from monuments and maneuver them onto boats for shipment to England. The most challenging of these was the 7.5 ton bust of Ramesses II from his mortuary temple (the Ramesseum) on the west bank at Thebes. The attempt was ingenious and successful, and this and many other large sculptures reached the British Museum safely.

Having met its discoverer, Johann Ludwig Burchardt, Belzoni was eager to visit the rock-cut temple of Abu Simbel in Nubia, and once there found the entrance. By removing part of a sand dune, he was able to copy some of the wall scenes and collect, after first drawing them on a scale plan, portable artifacts for his employer, Salt.

Returning to Luxor, Belzoni was the first westerner to investigate the Valley of the Kings, finding four royal tombs in twelve days. The last of these was the extensive and richly decorated tomb of Seti I, whose brilliantly colored scenes appeared freshly painted. This was to be Belzoni's greatest discovery, and one he took pains to preserve for posterity by making wax casts of the walls and a complete record in watercolors.

In 1818, Belzoni opened Khafre's pyramid at Giza, by way of its original hidden entrance. Upon returning to Luxor, he found agents of the French Consul threatening reprisals and claiming territory among the monuments, so he left to search for the Ptolemaic Red Sea port of Berenike. This arduous desert journey was followed by a return upriver to Philae in the company of William Bankes, who desired one of its obelisks for his estate at Kingston Lacey in Dorset, England.

After accomplishing this feat, Belzoni returned to Luxor to retrieve Seti I's magnificent alabaster sarcophagus and the wax impressions. While in Alexandria awaiting departure for England, Belzoni made a solo exploration of the Fayum and the oases of Baharia and Farafra in search of Alexander's temple of Zeus-Amen, but for political reasons he was prevented from traveling to Siwa, its actual location.

Back in London after a ten-year absence, Belzoni was hailed in 1820 by the *Times* as the "celebrated traveller." Before the year was out, he published a two-volume book on his extraordinary career in Egypt: *Narrative of the Operations and Recent Discoveries within the Pyramids, Temples, and Excavations, in Egypt and Nubia; and a Journey to the Coast of the Red Sea in Search of the Ancient Berenice and Another to the Oases of Jupiter Ammon* (London, 1820). A folio of plates was available with this publication and it was a huge success, going into a second English edition and translated into Italian, French and German. In May 1821, Belzoni mounted a very popular exhibition of Seti I's reproduced tomb (its two best halls), a model of Abu Simbel and the cross-section of Khafre's pyramid, along with his own antiquities, papyri and mummies. This won him fame, but by early 1822 the intrepid explorer was restless and returned to Africa to search for the sources of the river Niger, only to die of dysentery and be buried in a now lost grave in Benin.

While castigated by some for his "rampageous methods" of opening tombs, Belzoni exhibited respect and intelligent appreciation for the art he uncovered and his copies have preserved information of walls now defaced. Through exhibition and publication, Belzoni helped in large measure to educate the early nineteenth-century public about the culture of ancient Egypt. Today his legacy is apparent in the many important sculptures which enhance the collection of the British Museum, thanks to his efforts.

See also

Abu Simbel; Siwa Oasis, Late period and Graeco-Roman sites

Further reading

Dawson, W.R., and E.P. Uphill. 1995. *Who Was Who in Egyptology*, 3rd edn, M.L. Briebrier. London.

Fagan, B.M. 1975. *The Rape of the Nile*. New York.

Mayes, S. 1959. *The Great Belzoni*. London.

BARBARA S. LESKO

Beni Hasan

The ancient cemetery at Beni Hasan (27°56′ N, 30°53′ E) is on the east bank of the Nile, some 23 km south of Minya, in Nome XVI of Upper Egypt, the Oryx nome. The whole area was a necropolis for civil and military officials, dating from the Old Kingdom to the 30th Dynasty, with a gap in the New Kingdom. The most important group of tombs is the Middle Kingdom cemetery of the nomarchs (governors) and their officials, north of the modern town. To the south of the tombs is a temple built by Hatshepsut, known as the "Speos Artemidos," dedicated to a local lion goddess.

The tombs were visited and described during the nineteenth century by Nestor l'Hôte, Bonomi and Saint-Ferriol, and published in the first half of that century by Ippolio Rosellini and Jean-François Champollion. The most complete study of the larger tombs was conducted for the Egypt Exploration Fund by George W. Fraser and Percy E. Newberry, who published four volumes (1893–1900). Smaller pit burials in the hillside below the large tombs were later excavated by John Garstang.

Of the thirty-nine rock-cut tombs, oriented approximately east–west, only twelve have inscriptions. Some of them are unfinished; others, which are very small and crudely made, were not described by Newberry, who simply published their plans. All the tombs are preceded by a small, rock-cut court. The mouth of the tomb shaft lies in the floor of the main room.

The rock-cut tombs can be divided into three groups. The first type is composed of a simple square room, sometimes with a slightly vaulted roof. The second type consists of a rectangular room whose roof is supported by one or two rows of lotus-bud columns, each pair of which is surmounted by an architrave. Of this group, Tomb 18, although unfinished, is worthy of mention. It consists of a hall with a vaulted roof supported by four rows of three lotus-bud columns. The third tomb type has a more complex plan, consisting of (a) an open court, (b) a rectangular portico with a vaulted roof supported by two columns surmounted by an architrave, (c) a square main chamber with two rows of two columns with longitudinal architraves, and (d) a shrine with the statue of the deceased and, in some instances, of his relatives. In this tomb type, the portico columns are eight-sided, while the columns of the main chamber are sixteen-sided.

Tomb paintings include scenes of daily life, offering scenes, representations of the deceased and his relatives, and the pilgrimage to Abydos. More unusual are detailed scenes of battles and hunting in the desert, and scenes of athletic games and dancing, which depict motion. Worthy of mention are the scenes in the main chamber of Baqet III's tomb (no. 15), and those in Kheti's tomb (no. 17). Both were nomarchs of the Oryx nome, with the title of "Great Chief of the Oryx Nome in its entirety." A similar freedom and originality also characterize the paintings of the smaller, simpler tombs. In the tomb of Khnumhotep II (no. 3) is a well-known scene of a caravan of Asiatics.

Notable inscriptions include some of the nomarchs' autobiographies (especially that of Khnumhotep II), which give historical information about the nome during the 12th Dynasty. From these inscriptions we learn that King Amenemhat I redefined the boundaries of each town and the nome borders, dividing it into two parts. It was the king himself who appointed the nomarch to administer the district.

See also

Canaanites; Middle Kingdom, overview; representational evidence, Middle Kingdom private tombs

Further reading

Garstang, J. 1907. *The Burial Customs of Ancient Egypt as Illustrated by Tombs of the Middle Kingdom*. London.

Junge, F. 1975. Beni Hassan. *LÄ* 1: 695–8.

Montet, P. 1909. Notes sur les tombeaux de Béni Hassan. *BIFAO* 9: 1–36.

Newberry, P.E. 1893–1900. *Beni Hasan*, 4 vols. London.

Porter, B., and R.L.B. Moss. 1934. *Topographical Bibliography of Ancient Egyptian Texts, Reliefs, and Paintings* 4, 141–63. Oxford.

ROSANNA PIRELLI

Berenike

The third century BC–sixth century AD Red Sea port of Berenike (also Berenice, modern Medinet el-Haras; 23°55′ N, 35°28′ E) is about 820 km south of Clysma-Cleopatris-Arsinoë-Qolzoum (near Suez), and about 260 km east of Aswan. Pliny the Elder (in *Natural History* 6.33.168) claims that Ptolemy II Philadelphus (283–246 BC) founded the emporium and named it after his mother. The foundation of Berenike was part of a broader plan by Ptolemy II and his immediate successors of Eastern Desert road and Red Sea port construction. The latest ancient reference to activity at Berenike is in the *Martyrium Arethae*, which records in AD 524/5 a Roman proposal to support militarily the Aksumites, whose kingdom was in northern Ethiopia/Eritrea, in a war against the Himyarites (in southern Arabia).

The bulk of the literary references relate to Berenike's role in the Red Sea–Indian Ocean

trade and its connection by trans-desert roads to the Nile at Apollinopolis Magna (Edfu) in Ptolemaic times, and to Coptos (Quft/Qift) from the early Roman period onward (e.g. Strabo, *Geography*; Pliny the Elder, *Natural History*; *Periplus of the Erythrian Sea*). The late first century BC to first century AD Nicanor archive of ostraca seems to deal more with trade between the Nile and Berenike and Myos Hormos, and less with transit trade from the Nile to other Red Sea/Indian Ocean emporia passing through Berenike and Myos Hormos. Berenike appears on several ancient maps and in various itineraries, including those of Claudius Ptolemy (*Geography*), the *Tabula Peutingeriana*, the *Itinerarium Antoniniana* and the *Ravenna Cosmography*.

Berenike lent its name to the region governed by a Roman military official as early as AD 11. The territory, in all likelihood, spanned the region in Upper Egypt somewhere between the Nile and the Red Sea. The area was under civilian administration by the reign of Hadrian, but seems to have reverted to military control some time thereafter.

The Portuguese explorer Joam de Castro knew of Berenike and came close to discovering it in 1541. In the eighteenth century, J.B. Bourguignon d'Anville also knew about the site, but failed to locate the ancient remains. The first modern explorer to visit the ruins was Giovanni Belzoni in 1818. Thereafter, numerous European travelers visited, commented upon and collected artifacts from the site. In 1826 J.G. Wilkinson drew the first plan of the ancient remains and he and several other visitors, including Belzoni, J.R. Wellsted, Golénischeff and Bent, either "cleared" the Serapis temple or otherwise commented upon the ruins. Early twentieth-century visitors such as Daressy and Murray add little to the earlier accounts.

Excavations conducted since 1994 by the University of Delaware and Leiden University have demonstrated activity at the port between the third century BC and late fifth/early sixth century AD. The Ptolemaic town seems to have been farther north and west of the Roman emporium due to silting of the harbor by local wadi water run-off, which more than offset an estimated 1–2 m rise in sea level since Hellenistic times. Built mainly of locally available materials (coral heads, gypsum ashlars, sandbricks, field cobbles and boulders from nearby mountains, and occasionally courses of timber: acacia, mangrove, teak and pine), the edifices reflect a basically utilitarian function. Some buildings had walls or floors revetted in marble or covered with tapestries.

On the eastern and southeastern parts of the site excavations have identified warehouses, a food preparation area and, possibly, a temple. The center of the site immediately north of the Serapis temple has large, probably public, structures of unknown function. Farther west a building contained fragments of at least two nearly life-size bronze statues, other artifacts of a religious nature, over 100 wooden bowls, a small gypsum sphinx built into the lower wall, and two inscriptions. One of these is in Greek, the other is in Greek-Palmyrene, which indicates the presence of Palmyrene auxiliary troops (from Syria).

West and northwest of town was the main industrial area (for brick-making, metal and perhaps glass production). North of the town was a massive Roman trash dump, which seems to overlay earlier Ptolemaic structures.

Archaeological evidence reveals much about the trade and the inhabitants. Indian fine, coarse and shipping wares, a first century AD Tamil-Brahmi (south Indian) graffito, over 1,200 peppercorns, coconuts, sorghum, rice, Job's tears and teak wood attest to contacts with the Indian Ocean basin throughout the Roman occupation of Berenike. A garbled Ethiopic/South Arabian/North Arabian inscription of *circa* AD 400 indicates contacts with one or more of those lands. Roman pottery comes from as far west as Spain, Italy, North Africa and the eastern Mediterranean, including the Aegean, Asia Minor and Syro-Palestine. Numerous ostraca of the early Roman period relate to activities at the port. Elephants for military use were the main commodity imported to Berenike in the early Ptolemaic period aboard specially constructed ships called *elephantagoi*. In Roman times, imports to and exports from Berenike were mainly consumer goods.

Pig bones suggest the presence of a more Romanized Mediterranean population in the early Roman period. The dearth of pig bones and presence of large quantities of goat, sheep and camel byproducts in one part of the city in late antiquity, and large numbers of fish bones in other parts of the city at that time, suggest that at least two different cultural groups lived there contemporaneously. Ceramics of a Nubian/desert origin found in conjunction with the extensive goat, sheep and camel fauna suggest a desert-dwelling population, perhaps including the Blemmyes, whose presence in the region is attested in late antique sources (Ammianus Marcellinus; Priscus, *History*; Olympiodorus, *History*; Procopius, *History of the Wars*; *Martyrium Arethae*). Small decorated artifacts (jewelry, textiles, wood carvings) suggest a degree of wealth among some of the port's inhabitants.

An elaborate road network joined Berenike to the small and large forts in the Wadi Kalalat (perhaps the source of much of Berenike's drinking water), the settlements at Shenshef, Hitan Rayan and the first station (at Vetus Hydreuma/Wadi Abu Greiya) on the road leading to the Nile. These routes are marked by cairns, graves, cemeteries and the occasional building. Although there are scattered sites between Berenike and Aswan (at el-Ileiga, Abraq, Bir Abu Hashim and the amethyst mining settlements at Wadi el-Hudi), there is no solid evidence for a road linking Berenike directly with Aswan in antiquity. Ras (Cape) Banas to the north somewhat protected Berenike from the strong north winds and ships may have been hauled across it to avoid long trips around the peninsula. The reason for the port's decline and abandonment is uncertain, but in the early Islamic period it was superseded by Aydhab/Suakin el-Qadim to the south.

See also

Quft/Qift (Coptos); Roman forts in Egypt; Roman period, overview; Roman ports, Red Sea; Wadi el-Hudi

Further reading

Blockley, R.C. 1983. *The Fragmentary Classicising Historians of the Later Roman Empire. Eunapius, Olympiodorus, Priscus, and Malchus* 2: *Text, Translation, and Historiographical Notes.* Liverpool.

Daressy, G. 1922. Bérénice et el Abraq. *ASAE* 22: 169–84.

Meredith, D. 1957. Berenice Troglodytica. *JEA* 43: 56–70.

Ruffing, K. 1993. Das Nikanor-Archiv und der römische Süd- und Osthandel. *Münstersche Beiträge zur antiken Handelsgeschichte* 12(2): 1–26.

Sidebotham, S.E., and W.Z. Wendrich. 1996. Berenike: Roman Egypt's maritime gateway to Arabia and India. *Egyptian Archaeology* 8: 15–18.

——, eds. 1998. *Berenike 1996: Report of the 1996 Excavations at Berenike (Egyptian Red Sea Coast) and the Survey of the Eastern Desert.* Leiden.

Sidebotham, S.E., and R.E. Zitterkopf. 1995. Routes through the Eastern Desert of Egypt. *Expedition* 37(2): 39–52.

STEVEN E. SIDEBOTHAM

Berenike Panchrysos

Berenike Panchrysos is an ancient town in the Nubian Desert which was located in February, 1989, by an expedition to the Wadi Allaqi led by Alfredo and Angelo Castiglioni and Giancarlo Negro. Subsequent excavations were conducted there in 1990, 1991, 1993, 1994, and 1997. The site is situated at 21°56′.93 N, 35°08′.88 E, and is *circa* 550 m^2 above sea level.

Mentioned in the *Naturalis Historia* of Pliny the Elder, who located the town between Berenike Trogloditica and Berenike Epi-Dire, Berenike Panchrysos is so named because gold quartz is abundant in the region. Called Deraheib (i.e. buildings) by the local Beja peoples, it was given the name Allaqi after the Arab invasion of the Nubian Desert. The Moorish explorer and geographer Ibn Sa'id

al-Andalusi (AD 1206–86) wrote: "the mountainous region of Allaqi is famous for gold of the highest quality, which is mined in the Wadi."

The same gold mines, called "Ma'din ad-Dahab," were also mentioned by the Arab geographer and astronomer al-Khwarezmi, who in AD 830 located the town with great precision at 21°45′ N, which is only 20 km from its actual position. The Egyptian historian al-Maqrizi (AD 1364–1442) later wrote that "it was still possible to see traces of the Greeks (ar-Rum Ptolemaic people) in the mines." This suggests a lengthy period of mining activities after the Graeco-Roman period.

In his *Géographie ancienne abrégée*, published in Paris in 1768, the French geographer d'Anville located Berenike Panchrysos in the vicinity of "a mountain with mines where the Ptolemaic people extracted much gold. The mountains are called by Arab geographers Alaki or Ollaki." D'Anville, however, erroneously located the town on the map which accompanied his volume, and placed the Allaqi "Gebel" (mountain) close to the Red Sea. But these mountains, which are rich in gold-bearing quartz, are located in the heart of the Nubian Desert, 250 km due west of the Red Sea (even though they are on the same latitude indicated by the French geographer). Subsequently, the site was visited by Linant de Bellefonds in 1832, but he did not understand its importance.

During the recent excavations at Berenike Panchrysos, two Ptolemaic coins were discovered (one of which dates to Ptolemy Soter I). There was also much evidence of smelting, which, according to Marco Tizzoni, is similar to what has been found on the island of Kithnos (on the Peloponesian coast in Greece), dating to the Hellenistic period. Also discovered were a small faïence head of the god Bes and a miniature bronze statue of Harpocrates, from the Graeco-Roman period.

Among the numerous potsherds found at the site some can be dated to the 15th Dynasty as well as the end of the 30th Dynasty. The town was a major center of the Beja kingdom (known to the Romans as the "Blemmyes," nomadic peoples living in the Red Sea Hills to the east of the Nile). In *circa* AD 425 Olympiodorus visited the emerald mines in the Eastern Desert, with the permission of the Blemmye king, and wrote that the Blemmyes had built four towns in the Nile Valley, the southernmost one of which was Kasr Ibrim. However, the king of the Blemmyes himself did not actually live on the river but in the desert interior. Excavations conducted by Sir Leonard Woolley at Karanog, a town in Nubia near Kasr Ibrim, uncovered a fortress which is architecturally identical to the largest fortress at Berenike Panchrysos. If Kasr Ibrim and Karanog were centers of the Blemmyes in the Nile Valley, then Berenike Panchrysos may have been their capital in the desert. Ibn Sa'id al-Andalusi wrote that "the city of Allaqi was the royal city of the Beja king." However, by AD 861 it had been conquered by the Arabs. Its wealth and power was such that the sultan of Allaqi was even able to declare his independence from the caliph of Baghdad. In fact, jointly ruled by the Beja and Hadareb Muslims, the town in the tenth century boasted a standing army of 3,000 horsemen and 30,000 Beja tribesmen mounted on camels. Only further excavations can give a more complete picture. One fact, however, remains certain: for centuries Berenike Panchrysos was the most important gold mining center of the ancient world.

Today at the site of Berenike Panchrysos two imposing fortresses and numerous houses can be seen, stretching more than 2 km along a bend in the Wadi Allaqi. The main group of houses are located on a north–south axis about 400 m long. They are slightly elevated above the bottom of the wadi to provide protection from infrequent flash floods.

On the east–west axis, the average length of these houses is *circa* 150 m. Some buildings are more carefully constructed with rough schist slabs in mortar. Others have walls of skillfully laid, loose stone. The houses extend along a main road *circa* 6 m wide, which is flanked by at least two narrower parallel streets: the eastern

Figure 16 The town of Berenike Panchrysos

one runs along the foot of the hills and the western one is aligned in the direction of the wadi. The principal road is intersected by secondary streets, which enclose a central square and the various quarters of the town. This suggests that the town was planned and laid out before any construction was undertaken.

The main fortress has massive walls more than 25 m in length. It is constructed with schist slabs, which in some sections are 6 m high, revealing the original elevation of three stories. The very low entrance of the fortress is located at the foot of a semi-cylindrical, partly ruined tower. Inside, a series of arches lead to small, well-preserved rooms. A second fortress is 50 m to the south; it is also a rectangular construction and resembles a Roman *praesidium*, similar to those built along the desert caravan routes. In the interior of this fortress a ramp made of rough stones leads to the battlements. Con-

structed along the walls around the courtyards are rooms with arches in different styles.

The mines are located in the hills surrounding the town. Excavated galleries and shafts reveal that gold-bearing veins of quartz were worked for many centuries.

See also

metallurgy; Roman forts in Egypt; Wadi Hammamat

Further reading

Adams, W.Y. 1977. *Nubia: Corridor to Africa*. London.
——. 1994. Castle-houses of late medieval Nubia. *Archéologie du Nil Moyen* 6: 11–47.
——. Castiglioni, A.A. and J. Verioutter. 1995. L'Eldorado dei fardoni. Milan 1998. *Das Goldland der Pharaonen*. Mainz.

Figure 17 The main fortress, Berenike Panchrysos

Emery, W.B. 1965. *Egypt in Nubia*. London.

Kirwan, L.P. 1982. Nubia and Nubian origins. *Geographical Journal* 140: 43–52.

O'Connor D. 1983. New Kingdom and Third Intermediate Period. In *Ancient Egypt: A Social History*, B.G. Trigger, B.J. Kemp, D. O'Connor and A.B. Lloyd, 183–278. Cambridge.

Sadr, K. 1987. The territorial expanse of the Pan-Grave culture. *Archéologie du Nil Moyen* 2: 265–91.

Vantini, G. 1975. *Oriental Sources Concerning Nubia*. Warsaw.

Vercoutter, J. 1959. The gold of Kush. *Kush* 7: 120–53.

ALFREDO CASTIGLIONI
ANGELO CASTIGLIONI

Bir Umm Fawakhir

Bir Umm Fawakhir (26°02′ N, 33°36′ E) lies in the central Eastern Desert about halfway between the Nile at Quft (Coptos) and the Red Sea at Quseir. The site is a large Coptic/ Byzantine gold-mining town datable to the late fifth through sixth centuries AD by Greek wine jar labels and by the pottery.

There is evidence of pre-Coptic activity at the site, perhaps as early as the Turin Papyrus, which may reasonably be interpreted as a 20th Dynasty map showing the route to the stone quarries in the Wadi Hammamat and beyond to a "Mountain of Gold" and a "Mountain of Silver." Nineteenth-century travelers reported a Ptolemy III temple dedicated to Min; it has been destroyed by mining activity, but a piece of a column with cartouches survives near the modern rest house. Although Bir Umm Fawakhir has long been called Roman, remains from that period are actually quite sparse. The Roman caravan route to the Red Sea certainly passed by the wells at Bir Umm Fawakhir, as indicated by one of about sixty signal towers marking the ancient road. A nearby cave preserves some Greek graffiti of the first–third centuries AD, and one in South Arabic. A few Roman sherds and faïence fragments have been

recovered, and the small granite quarries are probably Roman as well. The sixty-odd ostraca published by Guéraud pertain to Roman military activity in the area, but the ostraca may actually have been recovered from the Wadi el-Sid mines.

Bir Umm Fawakhir and its immediate vicinity are on the Precambrian Fawakhir granite. The granite is economically valuable as quarry stone, as the aquifer for wells, and above all for the gold mines. The metal occurs in quartz veins in the granite. In antiquity the ore was mined by surface trenches or shafts cut into the mountain sides. The quartz was crushed with small granite blocks into chunks that in turn were ground to powder on concave grinding stones with an upper hand stone or in rotary querns. Both rotary and concave grinding stones are abundant on site, though generally reused for building or loose on the surface. The powdered ore was probably washed at Bir Umm Fawakhir but carried to the Nile valley for final purification.

The archaeological remains at Bir Umm Fawakhir consist of a main settlement in a long narrow wadi whose steep cliffs limit the site like town walls, and whose sandy bottom serves as the main street. More than 200 houses and outbuildings line both sides of the main street. The ancient population of the main settlement is estimated at a little over 1,000. Although the buildings are constructed of rough granite cobbles chinked with small stones and sherds, the ruins are sufficiently well preserved that doors, benches, wall niches, and a few other built-in features such as troughs or cists can still be seen. Almost all of the buildings appear to be domestic in nature. The basic house unit consists of two or three rooms, though several of these units may be built together into agglomerated houses of as many as twenty-two rooms. There are also many detached square or rounded one-room outbuildings; whether they were used for storage, kitchens, animal shelters, workshops, latrines or for some other purpose is not yet known.

The cemeteries, all looted, lie on ridges overlooking the site. The graves are either cists built of stone slabs or natural clefts in the

Figure 18 Bir Umm Fawakhir main settlement, southeast end

granite; they are so short that the bodies must have been flexed. Rough granite cobbles were piled on top, and a considerable amount of Coptic/Byzantine pottery is scattered around the cairns. Crosses stamped on dishes indicate a Christianized population.

A guardpost is situated on one of the highest peaks where it commands a view of the main settlement, all three roads leading to the wells, and some of the mines and quarries. Apart from the guardpost, however, no defensive structures at all have been found, which is somewhat surprising in a desert where security was often a concern. Nor have any churches, warehouses, animal stables or administrative buildings been located; they may have lain closer to the modern road where wadi wash is heaviest. In addition to the main settlement, there are at least 14 other outlying clusters of ruins, one with over sixty buildings. All have the same kind of construction and layout as the main settlement, and the same type of pottery.

Bir Umm Fawakhir is the only ancient gold-mining community in Egypt, and one of only a few within the Byzantine Empire, to have been intensively investigated. It is one of the few cases where not only the layout of an entire ancient community, but also peripheral features such as industrial areas, roads, paths, wells, cemeteries and outlying clusters of ruins, can be seen. Older accounts of Byzantine Egypt say that the Eastern Desert was virtually abandoned to nomadic tribesmen. The lack of defenses at Bir Umm Fawakhir as well as the growing number of archaeologically investigated desert sites such as Abu Sha'ar, Berenike, Bir Nakheil, Khasm el-Menih and Mons Porphyrites suggest that the Byzantine government not only ruled the desert, but maintained sizable operations there.

See also

Abu Sha'ar; Berenike Panchrysos; Mons

Porphyrites; Roman forts in Egypt; Wadi Hammamat

Further reading

Guéraud, O. 1942. Ostraca grecs et latins de l'Wâdi Fawâkhir. *BIFAO* 41: 141–96.

Meyer, C. 1995a. Gold, granite, and water: The Bir Umm Fawakhir Survey 1992. *AASOR*.

——. 1995b. A Byzantine gold-mining town in the Eastern Desert of Egypt: Bir Umm Fawakhir, 1992–1993. *Journal of Roman Archaeology* 8: 192–224.

CAROL MEYER

Breasted, James Henry

James Henry Breasted, American Egyptologist, Orientalist and historian, was born in Rockford, Illinois on 27 August 1865, the second child and elder son of Charles and Harriet Garrison Breasted. In the summer of 1873, the Breasted family moved to Downers Grove, Illinois, where James grew up and attended a small rural school. In 1880, he began to take classes sporadically at North-Western (now North Central) College in Naperville, Illinois, where he eventually received a Bachelor of Arts degree in 1890. In the meantime, Breasted worked as a clerk in local drugstores and entered the Chicago College of Pharmacy in 1882, whence he graduated in 1886. He then was employed as a professional pharmacist and acquired much knowledge about drugs, which was to prove useful in later life when he was dealing with ancient Egyptian medical texts.

In 1887, Breasted began the study of Hebrew at the Congregational Institute (now Chicago Theological Seminary) in Chicago, Illinois, and subsequently was enrolled at Yale University in New Haven, Connecticut in 1890–1, where he was awarded a Master of Arts degree *in absentia* in 1892. With the encouragement of William Rainey Harper, then Professor of Hebrew at Yale University, Breasted went to Berlin in 1891 to study Egyptology with Professor Adolf Erman, who himself had been a student of

Richard Lepsius. Breasted became the first American to earn a Ph.D. in Egyptology (University of Berlin, 15 August 1894) and the first to receive an appointment to teach the subject in an American university (University of Chicago). He was associated with the University of Chicago for the rest of his life, serving as Director of the Haskell Oriental Museum (1901–35) and Professor of Egyptology and Oriental History (1905–35). His first appointment at the University of Chicago began with a six-month leave of absence, during which time he was scheduled to do exploration work in Egypt.

On 22 October 1894, Breasted married Frances Hart, a 21-year-old American student whom he had met in Berlin. The Breasteds went on to have two sons, Charles and James, Jr, and a daughter, Astrid. The newlyweds spent a working honeymoon in Egypt during the winter of 1894–5, and Breasted acquired several thousand Egyptian antiquities for the new Haskell Oriental Museum (since 1931, the Oriental Institute Museum) at the University of Chicago.

During the next twenty-five years, the publication of a series of textbooks and technical works established James Henry Breasted as one of the senior Orientalists in the United States. From 1900 to 1904, he collected data for the great Berlin *Wörterbuch der Ägyptischen Sprache*, and the German academies in Berlin, Leipzig, Munich and Göttingen asked him to copy and arrange hieroglyphic inscriptions in their collections. During the same period he began work on the most important ancient Egyptian historical texts, including many unpublished ones, with the intention of producing a sourcebook of English translations for the benefit of historians in general; the accumulated 10,000 manuscript pages of translations and commentary were published in five volumes as *Ancient Records of Egypt: Historical Documents from the Earliest Times to the Persian Conquest*. This major corpus of primary source material enabled the ancient Egyptians to speak for themselves and served as the basis for Breasted's popular book, *A History of Egypt from the Earliest Times down to the Persian Conquest*, in which he drew his conclusions from his translations of the ancient texts.

Breasted's wife Frances died in 1934. On 7 June 1935, Breasted married Imogen Hart Richmond, the divorced younger sister of his late wife. James Henry Breasted died of a streptococcic infection in New York City on 2 December 1935. He is best remembered as the founder of the Oriental Institute as a research center for the study of the ancient Near East at the University of Chicago. Breasted's vision established three related types of research at the Oriental Institute: archaeological field work and excavation; salvage and epigraphic recording of standing monuments for publication; and the preparation of basic reference works, such as dictionaries and grammatical studies.

See also

Egyptology, history of; Lepsius, Carl Richard; Reisner, George Andrew

Further reading

Breasted, C. 1943. *Pioneer to the Past: The Story of James Henry Breasted, Archaeologist.* New York.

Breasted, J.H. 1905. *A History of Egypt from the Earliest Times down to the Persian Conquest.* New York.

——. 1906–7. *Ancient Records of Egypt: Historical Documents from the Earliest Times to the Persian Conquest.* Chicago.

JOHN LARSON

brewing and baking

In tomb scenes, bread and beer are represented as essentials for the sustenance and pleasure of the dead. In daily life they were the staples for Egyptians of all classes. They also played an important economic role in this moneyless society. Bread and beer (or their ingredients) were collected as taxes and given to workers as wages.

These two foods share fundamental ingredients and some steps in production, and were made in the same or adjacent facilities. They often appear together in tomb scenes. For example, in the 5th Dynasty tomb of Ti, steps common to brewing and baking are shown in a central register, above which are steps specific to brewing, and below, steps in baking. A detailed model of a combined bakery and brewery was included in the 11th Dynasty tomb equipment of Meket-Re. Beer dregs and breweries of Predynastic date are known from several Upper Egyptian sites. Actual remains of a leavened bread from el-Badari and both wheat and barley bread from el-Omari also date to late prehistoric times.

Emmer wheat (*Triticum dicoccum*) and barley (*Hordeum vulgare*) are by far the most common grains of ancient Egypt, while other varieties of these species and some millets have also been identified. During Dynastic times, flour was prepared by pounding threshed grain in stone mortars, then grinding it between a portable, flat-bottomed or rounded hand-stone, and a corresponding inclined stone embedded in a bin to catch the flour. Such quern emplacements have been found *in situ* at, for example, Lahun and Tell el-Amarna. Grinding stones are not uncommon finds at Egyptian sites having a domestic component. Grit from grinding flour inevitably was baked into bread, and the considerable tooth wear suffered by ancient Egyptians is attributed to this. Sieves made of rushes were used for cribbling flour, and also for straining beer mash.

The simplest Egyptian bread was made from flour mixed with water and salt, shaped into a flat, round loaf and baked either on a stone griddle, on the floor or interior wall of a clay bread oven, or in ashes. In appearance and production, it resembles the modern Egyptian *'aish baladi* (pita bread).

A sourdough method was employed for leavened bread. Remnants of a previous batch of dough or barm (a yeasty froth evolved during brewing) from a batch of beer was mixed with new dough and allowed to ferment, or "sour," overnight. Attempts to verify deliberate addition of domesticated yeasts to bread or beer are inconclusive prior to 1500 BC, but a yeast, *Saccharomyces winlocki*, is known from that time. The hieroglyph for bread (*t*) resembles a round, risen loaf, similar to the modern Egyptian *'aish shemsi*.

Some loaves were braided or coiled, and triangular, pyramidal and zooform shapes are known. Sometimes cavities were made in a loaf for a portion of food. Bread was also baked in clay pots or molds, some of which were greased and reused, while others were crudely modeled around conical wooden forms and broken to free the loaf after baking. Large quantities of broken molds are often found in ancient villages. Some breads or cakes were made from a dough to which milk, eggs or butter had been added, and then baked with, for example, cumin, nuts, honey, dates or other fruits.

Beer has been called ancient Egypt's "national drink." It was nutritious and highly caloric, containing protein, B vitamins and live yeast. It was brewed in the same manner as modern *bouza*: lightly baked bread is crumbled into water, then malted (sprouted) cereal, the remainder of an old batch of beer or yeast, and flavoring agents are added. The mash is gently heated for several hours and then allowed to ferment for a day or more, growing stronger until it spoils by about the fifth day. In Dynastic times dates, which enhance the supply of simple sugars for fermentation, were the favored additive. Tomb scenes show that the final product was either eaten unfiltered as a thin gruel or sieved and consumed as a beverage, which was sipped through a straw placed in the clear level between floating barm and sediment. There are words for many varieties and qualities of beer, but *ḥnḳt* was the generic term.

Breweries are virtually unknown archaeologically from the Dynastic period, but several Predynastic ones have been identified at Hierakonpolis (*circa* 3500–3400 BC; Nagada Ib–IIa). They consist of a series of deep, conical vats with a dark, sugary residue in which wheat and barley, and fragments of dates and grape pips, were found. Similar features at Ballas and Mahasna, and what were previously published as grain-parching kilns at Abydos, are now recognized as breweries. The Egyptian evidence for brewing is the world's earliest.

See also

agriculture, introduction of; subsistence and diet in Dynastic Egypt; taxation and conscription; wine making

Further reading

Darby, W.J., P. Ghaliounghi and L. Grivetti. 1977. *Food: The Gift of Osiris* 2. London.
Geller, J.R. 1993. Bread and beer in fourth-millennium Egypt. *Food and Foodways: Explorations in the History and Culture of Human Nourishment* 5(3): 255–67.
Wilson, H. 1988. *Egyptian Food and Drink*. Aylesbury.

JEREMY GELLER

Busiris (Abu Sir Bana)

Busiris is the Greek name of several pharaonic towns in Egypt (nine are known at present), where a cult center of the god Osiris existed. One of these towns, famous for its prehistoric finds, was at Abusir el-Melek (ancient Busir Quredis) in Middle Egypt, halfway between Beni Suef and the pyramid of Meydum. Another, now called Abusir, was located just north of Saqqara (about 11 km south of Cairo); it is best known for its 5th Dynasty pyramids and the tombs of the families of high officials. Another Busiris, also known as Taposiris Magna (about 45 km west of Alexandria), was an important town in the Ptolemaic period with a temple and an animal necropolis.

The most famous Busiris is identified with modern Abu Sir Bana (30°55′ N, 31°14′ E) in the middle of the Nile Delta on the left bank of the Damietta branch, about 5.5 km south of Samannud. The pharaonic name of the town was Djedu, derived from the symbol of the god Osiris, the *djed*-pillar (a hieroglyphic sign symbolizing "stability"). The first reference to this town appears in the *Pyramid Texts*. From the Old Kingdom until the Late period, Djedu served as the capital of Nome IX of Lower Egypt, named Andjet after the original deity of the town. Beginning in the Old Kingdom, however, Osiris became the principal deity of the town and it was later known as *Per-Wsirj* (*neb Djedu*), the "Temple of Osiris (lord of *Djedu*)." From this later town name were derived the Assyrian name Pushiru, the Greek Busiris, the Coptic Busir and the Arabic Abu Sir.

Like Abydos, the other center of worship of Osiris in Upper Egypt, Busiris played a very important role in ancient Egyptian religion. It was believed to be the place where Osiris was born and where his tomb was located. In some periods his temple at Busiris was a place of pilgrimage. Besides Osiris, other deities, such as Isis, Horus, Shu, Anubis and Sobek, were also worshipped at Busiris and Herodotus (Book II 95, 61) mentions a large temple of Isis there.

Not much is known about the early history of the town, but it played a role in the events of the Third Intermediate Period. When Piye (25th Dynasty) attacked Egypt, a Libyan prince ruled in Busiris. A few monuments of the Old and Middle Kingdoms, and also of the Late period, have been found at Abu Sir Bana, but the site has not been excavated. Artifacts, such as false doors and offering tables, have been found at Kom el-Akhdar, about 2 km south of Abu Sir, and this may have been the cemetery of the pharaonic town.

Regarding the other five towns named Busiris, we can only state that one was located near Quft (ancient Coptos) in Upper Egypt; another was near el-Ashmunein (Hermopolis Magna), but the exact locations of both are not known. The third Busiris was in the Fayum province, near the village of Itsa, now known as Abu Sir Difinnu. The fourth Busiris was east of Alexandria, and may be the old Taposiris Parva. The fifth and last town known with the name Busiris was situated 5 km south of Abu Sir Bana (the famous Busiris); its name is now Bana Abu Sir. Nothing, however, is known about the history of these five towns in pharaonic times.

See also

Abusir; Abusir el-Meleq; el-Ashmunein; Herodotus; Marea; pantheon; Quft/Qift (Coptos); Taposiris Magna

Further reading

Fischer, H.G. 1977. Some early monuments from Busiris in the Egyptian Delta. *MMJ*: 157–76.

Gomaà, F. 1987. Die Besiedlung Ägyptens während des Mittleren Reiches II. Unterägypten und die angrenzenden Gebiete. *Beiheft zum Tübinger Atlas des Vorderen Orients* 66(2): 137–42, 145.

FAROUK GOMAÀ

Buto (Tell el-Fara'in)

The ancient site of Buto, today called Tell el-Fara'in (Mound of the Pharaohs) is located in the northern Delta, about 15 km east of the Rosetta branch of the Nile and 30 km south of the present coastline (31°12′ N, 30°45′ E). It consists of a mound about 1 km^2. Visible structures on the surface are the temple precinct, two settlement mounds up to 20 m above the cultivated fields, and a cemetery. Two modern villages, Sekhmawy and Mohammed el-Baz, and a Muslim cemetery are on its edges.

The first test excavations were conducted at the site in 1904. During the 1960s excavations were conducted by the Egypt Exploration Society (EES), mainly in Graeco-Roman period strata in the temple area, but also on the southern settlement mound, in Late period strata. Since 1982 excavations have been conducted by the Universities of Alexandria and Tanta, and the Egyptian Antiquities Organization (EAO), in the temple and in parts of the cemetery dating from the Late to Roman periods. Since 1983 investigations were also conducted by the German Archaeological Institute, Cairo and the Geographical Department of the University of Marburg (Germany). The most recent fieldwork included an archaeolgical survey of the site and its surroundings, and excavations at the western, lower edge of the tell, north and south of the village of Sekhmawy.

Using a pumping system, the German excavations reached remains of the earliest

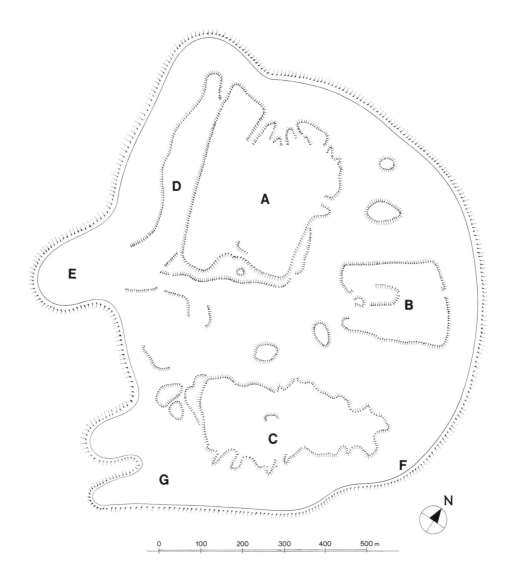

Figure 19 Buto, mound at Tell el-Fara'in

A ancient settlement mound
B temple precinct
C ancient settlement mound
D Graeco-Roman period cemetery
E modern village of Sekhmawy
F modern village of Mohammed el-Baz
G Muslim cemetery

settlement, which are below the water table. On the western side of the site a sequence of seven main layers from four different periods of use were found:

1 Layers I–II: the Predynastic of Lower Egypt (second half of the fourth millennium BC).
2 Layers III–V: late Predynastic/Dynasty 0 (Nagada III phase)/Early Dynastic (end of the fourth millennium BC and first centuries of the third millennium BC).
3 Layer VI: early Old Kingdom (27th–26th centuries BC).
4 Layer VII: Late period (7th–4th centuries BC).

Written traditions

The hieroglyphic spelling "House of Uto" (pr-w3dyt), the name for the temple of the cobra goddess Uto, was the name of the town since Ramesside times (thirteenth century BC) and later became the Greek form Buto, while before that the names Pe and Dep were used. An even older name of the site, already in use in the fourth millennium BC, is that of the heron god Djebaut, who was worshipped there along with Horus (mainly connected with the Pe) and Uto (mainly connected with the Dep). Stressing the duality of the country, Buto symbolized the capital of Lower Egypt in rituals and myths, with Hierakonpolis its counterpart in Upper Egypt.

It seems doubtful whether a prehistoric "kingdom" ever existed at Buto. The town, which was later in Nome VI of Lower Egypt (with Sais as the capital), must have lost political importance already in the Old Kingdom, and there is no textual evidence for it in the Middle Kingdom. It is first mentioned again in the 18th Dynasty, and in the Ptolemaic period it was capital of the "Phthenotes" nome, "The Land of Uto."

Settlement

Geological investigations demonstrated a huge underlying sand formation that accumulated during late Pleistocene and/or the early to mid-Holocene. Only below the western edge of the tell there is a gentle descent in the sand, where the oldest areas of occupation have been detected (Layers I–II). An area of about $200 \, m^2$, with a thickness of nearly 2 m, has been excavated here, which dates to the middle to late fourth millennium BC (equivalent to Nagada IIb–IId phases of the Predynastic culture in Upper Egypt). However, evidence of structures, mainly from houses of wattle and daub, and artifacts, especially pottery and flint tools (but also copper ones), shows that the settlement belonged to a different, distinctly Lower Egyptian Predynastic culture known first from the settlement at Ma'adi (south of Cairo). This culture is now being found at other sites in the Delta, its apex, and in the Fayum. Due to the slightly different material cultures and chronologies, it is termed the "Buto-Ma'adi" culture.

Although divided into two layers (I–II), based on the excavated artifacts and stratigraphy, the earliest settlement at Buto exhibits cultural homogeneity. Pottery, about one-half of which is burnished, has a variety of decorations, including small oblique strokes or slashes and dots aligned horizontally below the rim. Indented rims have their origin in the Chalcolithic of southern Palestine. Only Layer I yielded potsherds with a decoration of whitish horizontal stripes, unknown at other sites in Egypt, but assumed to be inspired by a technique ("reserved spiral decoration") used in northern Syria. Typical of Layer II is pottery with a rocker stamp decoration (in most cases forming patterns of pointed triangles), also found at other sites in the Delta but not at Ma'adi.

The stone tool industry is one of blades; the most frequent tool is a small twisted blade, which also has its origin in the Chalcolithic of Palestine. Copper, although found in very small quantities, was imported from Palestine (the Araba in southern Jordan), as was that at Ma'adi. Some artifacts were probably influenced by contacts with the Uruk culture of southern Mesopotamia or its colonies in northern Syria: more than a dozen finger-like clay objects, including a large one with a thick hollow at one end—similar to the clay cones found in southwest Asia which were used to make mosaic patterns in temple walls—were found. The local architecture at Buto to which these clay artifacts must have been applied is still missing.

The lowest phase of Layer III at Buto is called "transitional," since it shows a remarkable change of artifacts from the Lower Egyptian Predynastic to the Upper Egyptian Nagada culture, which is interpreted as gradual cultural assimilation. Recognized at Buto for the first time in Egyptian archaeology, this shift dates to *circa* 3300–3200 BC (Nagada IId phase). In the following stratigraphic phases an increasing use of mudbrick is found in buildings of the late Predynastic/Dynasty 0 (Nagada III, in Layer III), and the beginning of the first Dynasty (in Layer IV), which were used at least in part for cultic activities. A building in Layer V, uncovered over an area of 25 × 10 m, has a complex arrangement of rooms with walls still standing up to 60 cm, and evidence of plaster and colored decoration. Destroyed by fire, it contained few artifacts. While ceramic analysis excludes a date later than the 2nd Dynasty, a seal impression might date to Zoser's reign (3rd Dynasty).

From the 3rd–4th Dynasties, excavations yielded only scattered remains in Layer VI. Strangely, surveys conducted with augers have not revealed evidence of a Middle or New Kingdom settlement, but only intensifying activities not earlier than the late second millennium BC.

From the Late period, excavations have yielded a domestic area and buildings with walls of considerable size, 2 m or greater in thickness, thought to have been platforms. They date between the late eighth and the first half of the sixth centuries BC. Overlying evidence of industrial activities, a pottery sequence in a nearby area indicates continuing occupation through the fifth and fourth centuries BC.

The EES excavations in the 1960s unearthed two complexes with public baths to the north and south of the temple area and nearby industrial areas. On the so-called Kom ed-Dahab, a building was unearthed which contained a Ptolemaic occupation sequence, but which may have been built in the Late period. Surface potsherds indicate extensive occupation at Buto in Graeco-Roman times, but these are much reduced in area by the fourth century AD, with occupation probably ceasing by the sixth century.

Temple

The temple precinct has a mudbrick enclosure

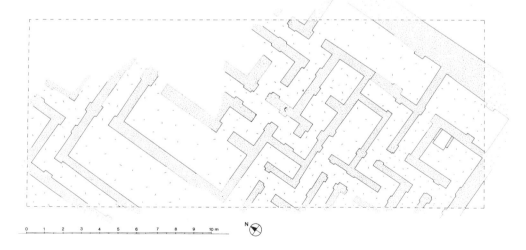

Figure 20 Remains of an Early Dynasty mudbrick building in Layer V at Buto (Tell el-Fara'in)

wall, *circa* 300×200 m in area, with walls 17–25 m in width still standing more than 10 m high. It is thought to have been built during the Late period. The main entrance is on the west, with an approach between the two settlement mounds, but there is also a smaller entrance on the east. Structures inside the temple enclosure include a double staircase leading to two wells, which might have served as a nilometer, most likely built in Ptolemaic times with older material. There is also a stone pavement and some of the lowest parts of an inner enclosure wall of stone probably belonged to a temple built during the 26th Dynasty. From an earlier (Ramesside?) and larger temple with a columned hall are traces of a mudbrick platform. These structures, however, cover only the western part of the enclosure; the eastern, rear part of the temple is still unexplored.

Mentioned for the last time in the "Satrap stela," dating to the beginning of the Ptolemaic period, the temple must have gone out of use and was dismantled in early Roman times, as indicated by archaeological evidence. Work in the temple area, however, has not yet established a clear stratigraphy. Scattered stone artifacts (mostly not *in situ*) include a stela of Tuthmose III, several large statues of Ramesses II (mainly with deities, including a lion-headed Uto), a black granite head of a lion goddess (most likely Ramesside), some stone blocks from Ramesses II and kings of the 26th Dynasty, a stela of a king from the Third Intermediate Period, a statue of King Nepherites of the 29th Dynasty, statues of a hawk and two small sphinxes (one with the name of King Hakor of the 29th Dynasty), and a statue of a priest of Uto of the Late period.

Cemetery

A cemetery, which has been tentatively dated from the late first millennium BC to the late Roman period, covers a considerable area in the western part of the northern settlement mound. It was partly excavated by Egyptian archaeologists.

Regional investigations

Remains of a marshy area, dated to the fifth and fourth millennia BC, were located only a few kilometers north of the site. About 4 km southwest of Buto at least one more settlement of the Buto-Ma'adi culture was detected by augering. It is not located on a sub-surface mound of sand, contradicting the opinion of S. Passarge and K.W. Butzer that prehistoric Delta settlements could only have been established on sand islands or "turtle backs."

See also

Fayum, Neolithic and Predynastic sites; Hierakonpolis; Ma'adi and the Wadi Digla; Merimde Beni-salame; Neolithic and Predynastic stone tools; pottery, prehistoric; Predynastic period, overview

Further reading

Charlesworth, D. 1970. The Tell el-Farâ'în excavation, 1969. *JEA* 56: 19–28.

Seton-Williams, M.V. 1969. The Tell el-Farâ'în Expedition, 1968. *JEA* 55: 5–22.

Way, T. von der. 1992. Excavation at Tell el-Farâ'în/Buto in 1987–1989. In *The Nile Delta in Transition: 4th to 3rd millennium B.C.*, E.C.M. van den Brink, ed., 1–10. Jerusalem.

——. 1993. *Untersuchungen zur Spätvor- und Frühgeschichte Unterägyptens*. Heidelberg.

——. 1997. *Tell el-Fara'in-Buto* I (AVDAIK 83). Mainz.

Wunderlich, J., and W. Andres. 1991. Late Pleistocene and Holocene evolution of the western Nile Delta and implications for its future development. In *Von der Nordsee bis zum Indischen Ozean*, H. Brückner and U. Radtke, eds, 105–20. Stuttgart.

THOMAS VON DER WAY

C

C-Group culture

Archaeological evidence of the C-Group culture, a people of uncertain origin who inhabited Lower Nubia from *circa* 2200 BC to *circa* 1500 BC, was initially encountered south of Aswan in 1907. Archaeologists have established that the C-Group occupation began around the time of the 6th Dynasty (in Egypt) and continued up to the 18th Dynasty. The five periods of C-Group development (Stages Ia, Ib, IIa, IIb and III), based on changing grave construction as well as on pottery types, constitute the Middle Nubian phase of Lower Nubian history. At various intervals during this time span, Lower Nubia was also occupied by other groups, including the Kerma and Pan-grave peoples.

Dozens of C-Group cemeteries and a few settlements have been located along both banks of the Nile from Shellal to Saras, near Semna in Lower Nubia. These sites are in a region where fertile land was scarce. Where it existed, the floodplain was narrow and settlement location tended to correspond to the available tracts of arable land. The rarity of C-Group settlements has been attributed to the small size of their scattered villages and the concealment of ancient villages under modern ones.

Uncertainty about the nature of C-Group subsistence has resulted because excavated food remains are lacking. Nevertheless, it is usually assumed that C-Group communities, like earlier Lower Nubian Neolithic populations, practiced a form of agriculture that was totally dependent on the annual flooding. Barley, wheat and various legumes may have been cultivated, whereas wild dates and other fruits were collected. Settlement excavations suggest that by the time of the First Intermediate Period, C-Group populations were probably semi-sedentary agriculturalists who were engaged in hunting and fishing, and whose domestic animals included cattle and goats. The claim that C-Group peoples were pastoralists has been challenged by archaeologists who insist that it would have been impossible to graze large herds of cattle in Lower Nubia because of the poor environment. Faunal remains from an early occupation site at Seyala were dominated by the bones of sheep.

In the earliest cemeteries, contracted bodies were placed in graves marked by small, well-built, stone circles filled with gravel. Pottery, including locally produced black-incised bowls containing offerings, was placed against the east wall of the tumulus. In addition to Egyptian storage jars, which indicate that foodstuffs were probably being imported from Egypt, copper mirrors, seal amulets, and scarabs have also been recovered from early (Ia) cemeteries. Most archaeologists have assumed that these foreign goods were obtained through trade. According to Old Kingdom texts, however, Egyptian goods were presented to C-Group leaders as gifts. Other possible sources of foreign craft goods may have been tolls levied against the transport of Egyptian trade goods through Lower Nubian territories and payment earned by Lower Nubian mercenaries, especially during the First Intermediate Period. Still, the true extent of Egyptian involvement with the lands south of Aswan at this time remains a matter of conjecture.

The primary motive for the Middle Kingdom Egyptian incursion into Nubia was access to luxury materials from the south. During this period (IIa), many C-Group peoples lived near fortresses built by the Egyptians at Kuban, Aniba and elsewhere. In C-Group settlements, two varieties of circular, or almost square, semi-subterranean houses were constructed. One type consisted of many rooms, including granaries; the other was simply one large room. Houses were not located close together or arranged in a formal plan, and none appeared to be substantially more elaborate than the others. C-Group villages of Stage IIa were small, and the evidence suggests that both types of houses were inhabited by extended families. Although there may have been differences in status between members of some communities, there were not marked economic differences.

The stone circles that surrounded Middle Kingdom C-Group graves tended to be larger and not as well built as those of Stage Ia. Offerings contained in pottery bowls were deposited against the north wall of the tumulus. Apart from the water jars and occasional metal objects that were placed in the burial pit along with the contracted bodies, very few Egyptian artifacts have been recovered from these graves. Exchange with Egyptians is assumed to have been minimal. Like the settlement evidence, Stage IIa burials indicate no differences in wealth between cemeteries or individual burials.

By about 1800 BC, crowded, fortified villages (C-Group IIb) appeared at several locations, including Wadi es-Sebua and Amada. Three kinds of graves are known from this period, including a new, large, high-status type. Mudbrick offering chapels were built against the east wall of some of the largest tumuli, and grave pits varied in both size and construction. Those that contained extended bodies and had barrel vaults of mudbrick, stone slabs or wood may have been the burials of rulers. Like Stage IIa burials, those of Stage IIb sometimes contained black-incised or red-incised handmade bowls, as well as pitchers of chaff-tempered ware on which figures or geometrical designs were incised. Imported, or at least Egyptian-style, pottery increased throughout the period until it became the dominant type used in the latest C-Group (III) burials.

The final C-Group occupation of Nubia was probably contemporary with an Egyptian expansion south as far as the Fourth Cataract in the early New Kingdom. Some C-Group (III) graves, in which the burial pits were protected by loosely placed, standing slabs of stone, appear to be those of Pan-grave peoples, whose earliest remains in Lower Nubia are seemingly contemporary with later C-Group (IIb) remains. The subsequent apparent "Egyptianization" of both the C-Group and Pan-grave elements in the population was followed by the disappearance of all traces of Lower Nubians by the end of the New Kingdom. The meaning of this disappearance of (Middle) Nubian culture remains unresolved. Like other questions concerning the C-Group, attempts to explain its significance will require further study of the excavated evidence from burials and settlements.

See also

Nubian forts; Pan-grave culture

Further reading

Adams, W.Y. 1984. *Nubia: Corridor to Africa*. London.

Bietak, M. 1968. *Studien zur Chronologie der nubischen C-Gruppe*. DÖAW 57. Vienna.

Trigger, B.G. 1976. *Nubia Under the Pharaohs*. Boulder, CO.

WENDY ANDERSON

Canaanites

Greater Canaan stretched from south of Gaza to as far north as Ugarit (an important port and commercial city in the eastern Mediterranean). Canaanites were the peoples who lived in this region during the Bronze Age (third and second millennia BC). Because of Canaan's geographical position, Canaanites had much contact with Egyptians, and there is both archaeological and textual evidence of this.

The name "Canaanites" first appears in a cuneiform text written in Akkadian from the archives excavated at the site of Mari (in Syria) dating to the nineteenth–eighteenth centuries BC. In Egyptian texts, the term for Canaanites is encountered for the first time in the 18th Dynasty in the Karnak and Memphis annals of Amenhotep II. The name "Canaan" appears frequently in the Amarna Letters, as well as in texts in Ugaritic. Because of the Hurrian element in the population of Canaan, the common name used by Egyptians in the New Kingdom was *H3rw* (Khuru), which replaced earlier names (*D3hy* or Djahy, and *Rtnw* or Retjenu). The name *Kn^cn* in Egyptian texts might sometimes refer to Gaza, the capital of the Egyptian province in Canaan in the New Kingdom.

Early Dynastic period

Canaanite relations with Egypt go back to the Predynastic period, corresponding roughly to the Palestinian Chalcolithic period (fourth millennium BC). However, with the unification of Egypt clear evidence for these relations emerges from prehistory. Evidence for military activities in Canaan by Egyptian kings of the Early Dynastic period is also found in the annals of the Palermo Stone, and in other early inscriptions.

Egyptian economic activity in Canaan in the Early Dynastic period is attested by stamped clay sealings and bullae found in southern Israel. A *serekh* (royal name) of King Hor-aha (1st Dynasty) was excavated at an Egyptian commercial station at 'En-Besor in the western Negev. This was the northernmost station on the road from Egypt to Canaan along the coast of northern Sinai. Egyptian kings and high officials of the 1st Dynasty imported decorated jars from Canaan that may have contained scented oils. This trade began in the Predynastic period.

Old Kingdom and First Intermediate Period

With the emergence of the Old Kingdom there is much evidence for Egyptian–Canaanite relations, from Egyptian texts as well as from Egyptian artifacts found in Palestine and the Lebanon. Egypt was, and is, very poor in high quality woods for construction, shipbuilding, furniture and other craft goods. However, in the forests of Lebanon a variety of coniferous trees grew which yielded high quality timber. The annals of Old Kingdom kings and other documents record ships, palace doors and flag-masts made from ash and a wood known in texts as *meru*, which are Lebanese woods. Cedar, juniper, fir and cypress from the Lebanon were used in Egyptian coffins, Khufu's solar bark at Giza, and beams in some pyramids.

The need for wood brought Egypt into close contact with Byblos, a seaport on the Lebanese coast. Beginning in the Early Dynastic period, Egyptian artifacts, such as a fragment from a vessel bearing the name of King Khasekhemwy (2nd Dynasty), are known from Byblos. An inscription on a broken alabaster bowl found at Byblos, dating to the 2nd or 3rd Dynasty, mentions "the scribe of the royal tree-fellers." Old Kingdom artifacts, such as statues, statuettes and inscribed vessels, have also been found at Byblos. Some of them bear the names of kings of the 4th, 5th and 6th Dynasties. Evidence is also found at Abusir in the reliefs of Sahure's pyramid complex, which depict Syrian bears, Canaanite jars, a captive Canaanite and a ship with Canaanite men, women and children on its deck.

With the collapse of the Old Kingdom, Egyptian artifacts almost disappear from Canaan: evidence for the cessation of regular trade. The *Admonitions of Ipuwer*, a text that describes conditions during the First Intermediate Period, laments the cessation of trade with Byblos and the infiltration of "archers" (i.e. Asiatics) into Egypt. Possibly some Canaanites came into the eastern Delta at this time when there were no forces to stop them.

Middle Kingdom and Second Intermediate Period

New attitudes toward Asiatics are seen in the Middle Kingdom. The *Prophecy of Neferty* describes the policy of Amenemhat I (12th Dynasty), who fortified the border between Egypt and the Sinai by building the "Wall of the Ruler" to repel the Asiatics (the Sinaitic tribes and Canaanites). The *Tale of Sinuhe* describes an Egyptian fugitive and courtier of Senusret I who settled in the land of Qedem, perhaps in the hinterland of Lebanon. A ruler of Retjenu, the Egyptian name for part of Syria, welcomed Sinuhe and wanted to benefit from his knowledge of Egyptian.

The most important documents testifying to Egyptian interests in Canaan are the *Execration Texts*, which date to the 12th Dynasty. These texts are found in two groups: on bowls from the reign of Amenemhat II or Senusret III now in Berlin, and on figurines which date to the first half of the eighteenth century BC, now mostly in Brussels. Both groups of texts enumerate Egypt's potential enemies, in Egypt, Asia and Nubia. The Brussels figurines have much more detailed information than the Berlin bowls, listing more toponyms (both towns and regions) and their rulers, and names of tribes.

A tomb painting at Beni Hasan in Middle Egypt describes a caravan from the land of Shut (in trans-Jordan?). The caravan consists of whole families with their donkeys laden with merchandise.

Many Egyptian artifacts, scarabs and seals of Middle Kingdom date have been found at various sites in greater Canaan, including four stelae of a nomarch (governor) of the Hare nome in Middle Egypt from Megiddo. Canaanite exports to Egypt, especially olive oil and wine, can be interpreted as taxes or as commerce. There is evidence for cattle from Retjenu in Egypt, and many Canaanite vessels have been found in Egypt, such as the so-called Tell el-Yahudiya Ware.

Along the eastern Mediterranean coast, strong Egyptian connections with Ugarit are demonstrated by the Egyptian artifacts found there. These include a statue of a daughter of Amenemhat II, who was the half-sister and wife of Senusret II, and two stone sphinxes of Amenemhat III. High officials at Byblos were given honorary titles written in Egyptian.

Although almost all relations between Egypt and Canaan ceased during the First Intermediate Period, this was not the case in the Second Intermediate Period. Hyksos rulers established themselves as kings who ruled in northern Egypt and at least in southern Canaan (15th–16th Dynasties). They took Egyptian royal titles and accession names, but some of their scarabs have typical Canaanite names.

Excavations at Tell ed-Dab'a, the site of the Hyksos capital and stronghold of Avaris in the eastern Delta, have revealed architecture and pottery which are typical of the MB II culture in Canaan. Hyksos burial customs are unique, especially the burial of equids. The most common evidence for this period are the many scarabs unearthed at sites in Egypt and Israel.

New Kingdom

The New Kingdom began with the annihilation of the Hyksos in northern Egypt, and continued military activities destroyed Hyksos strongholds in Canaan. Egypt's army pushed northward and built an empire and Egyptian garrisons were stationed at key points, with Egyptian administrators and couriers traveling throughout the empire. Egypt was exposed to Canaanite culture, religion and language, and Canaanite words and phrases were used by knowledgeable Egyptians. Canaanites went to Egypt as couriers or merchants. Others were brought there as enslaved prisoners of war.

With the arrival of Tuthmose III in Canaan in his first regnal year, Egyptian–Canaanite relations intensified. He established a policy of taking members of Canaan's ruling class as hostages to Egypt, where they were educated with Egyptians. Such Egyptianized Canaanites were enlisted in the Egyptian administration.

Canaanite commodities flowed into Egypt, as taxes imposed on the rulers of Canaanite city-states or as merchandise. These commodities included foodstuffs, raw materials, artifacts and slaves, both male and female. A Canaanite merchant's ship anchored in the Memphis harbor is depicted in the tomb of Ken-Amen at Thebes (from the reign of Amenhotep III).

Egyptian presence in Canaan is attested by many small artifacts, such as scarabs and vessels. Monuments were also erected in Canaan by Egyptian monarchs and administrators. For example, a fragment of a stela of Tuthmose III, or Amenhotep II, mentioning a defeat of the army of the kingdom of Mitanni (in northern Syria), was found at Tell Kinroth overlooking the Sea of Galilee.

During the 19th Dynasty the Egyptian capital was moved to the northeast Delta in order to govern the empire in Asia more effectively. With the transfer of the capital to Pi-Ramesses, Canaanites and Egyptians were brought into closer contact, and Canaanites migrated to the Delta. Ships of Canaanite merchants sailed up the Nile to the harbor at Memphis, where there was a temple for their god Ba'al (Papyrus Sallier V). Canaanite deities, such as Ba'al, Resheph, Horon, Qud-shu, 'Anat and Astarte, became familiar in Egypt and were worshipped there. Canaanite as well as other Semitic words infiltrated the Egyptian language. Most of these loan words are technical terms which came to Egypt with new technologies and materials.

Egyptianization of Canaanites from Gaza, the seat of the Egyptian administration of Canaan, is disclosed through the Egyptian names of some Gaza couriers whose fathers' names are still Canaanite (in Papyrus Anastasi III). However, only a very limited segment of the society had any contact with Egyptians there. Egyptian military activity in Canaan during the 19th Dynasty is attested not only in inscriptions in Egypt, but also in Egyptian monuments in Canaan. Stelae of Seti I, Ramesses II and Merenptah have all been found there.

In the early 20th Dynasty, an important event in the reign of Ramesses III was the invasion of the "Sea Peoples." Among the migrating peoples were those who were later known as the Philistines. Ramesses III defeated the invaders' fleet in the Nile estuaries, and their army was defeated somewhere along the Canaanite coast. The Philistines, however, settled in what became known as Philistia, stretching from the north bank of the Yarkon River (Tel Aviv) to the fringes of the Sinai coast. A related group, the Tjeker (or Tjekel), settled at the port city of Dor, at the foot of Mt Carmel.

Egyptian artifacts dating to the 20th Dynasty are found throughout Canaan, including ones inscribed with the names of Ramesses III and Ramesses IV. The decline of Egyptian prestige in the Levant at this time, however, is best described by the text of the Egyptian official Wenamen, who was unsuccessfully sent to Byblos to acquire wood for Amen's sacred bark during the reign of Ramesses XI, at the end of the 20th Dynasty. Instead, Wenamen was humiliated by rulers who were no longer threatened by Egyptian power in southwest Asia.

See also

Beni Hasan; Hyksos; Israelites; Levantine peoples (Iron Age); Medinet Habu; Sea Peoples; Tell ed-Dab'a, Second Intermediate Period; Tell el-Maskhuta; Tell el-Yahudiya

Further reading

Ben-Tor, A. 1982. The relations between Egypt and the land of Canaan during the third millennium B.C. *Journal of Jewish Studies* 23: 3–18.

Helck, W. 1971. *Die Beziehungen Ägyptens zu Vorderasien im 3. und 2. Jahrtausend v. Chr.* Wiesbaden.

Hoch, J.E. 1994. *Semitic Words in Egyptian Texts of the New Kingdom and Third Intermediate Period*. Princeton, NJ.

Redford, D.B. 1992. *Egypt, Canaan, and Israel in Ancient Times*. Princeton, NJ.

Stadelmann, R. 1967. *Syrisch-Palästinensische Gottheiten in Ägypten*. Leiden.

Wright, M. 1988. Contacts between Egypt and Syro-Palestine during the Old Kingdom. *Biblical Archaeologist* 51: 143–61.

SHMUEL AḤITUV

Carnarvon, George Edward Stanhope Molyneux Herbert, Earl of

George Edward Stanhope Molyneux Herbert, fifth Earl of Carnarvon, was born in 1866 and succeeded to the earldom in 1890. He was an

189

early automobile enthusiast, and was badly injured in a crash in Germany in 1901. His convalescence was long, and in 1903 he first visited Egypt, a favorite destination for invalids. There he was bitten by the bug of Egyptology and, with his large private means and socio-political connections, was able to obtain a permit to excavate at western Thebes. His first excavation season revealed little more than a mummified cat, but the next year he found the tomb of Tetiky (TT 15) and a tomb (Carter's no. 9) containing a tablet bearing a copy of Kamose's account of the war against the Hyksos.

Needing expert help, in 1908 he obtained the services of Howard Carter, who was to work for him for the rest of the Earl's life. Together they made a number of significant discoveries, culminating in the discovery of the tomb of Tutankhamen in 1922. Carnarvon was also a major collector of Egyptian antiquities, deriving both from his own excavations and the market. Apart from a few which remain at Highclere, the family seat in Berkshire, England, the bulk of his artifacts now reside in the Metropolitan Museum of Art, New York.

The Earl died in 1923 as a result of complications stemming from a mosquito bite in the Valley of the Kings: the lesion was nicked while shaving, became infected and led to blood poisoning. His demise was attributed by the popular press to "Tutankhamen's Curse," a non-existent incantation probably invented by Arthur Weigall, a former Egyptologist who was covering the excavation of the tomb of Tutankhamen for a London newspaper.

See also

Carter, Howard; Thebes, Valley of the Kings; Tutankhamen, tomb of

Further reading

Carter, H., and A.C. Mace. 1923. *The Tomb of Tut-ankh-Amen I*. London.
James, T.G.H. 1992. *Howard Carter: the Path to Tutankhamun*. London.

Reeves, N., and J.H. Taylor. 1992. *Howard Carter before Tutankhamun*. London.

AIDAN DODSON

Carter, Howard

Howard Carter was born in 1874 into an artistic family. His first Egyptological employment was at the age of seventeen, when he inked in tracings made at Beni Hasan by Percy Newberry; shortly afterwards he was taken out to that site as an artist. He subsequently became the principal copyist in the 1893–9 campaign to record the temple of Queen Hatshepsut at Deir el-Bahri. His drawings of these reliefs are some of the best of their kind.

In 1899, he was appointed Antiquities Service Inspector General for Upper Egypt, and spent the next four years excavating and restoring the monuments in his care, in particular those of Thebes. During that period he found the cenotaph of Nebhepetre Mentuhotep II and the sepulchers of Hatshepsut, Tuthmose II and Tuthmose IV. He also cleared a number of tombs of debris, in particular that of Merenptah.

In 1904 he was moved to Lower Egypt, but resigned as a result of difficulties following a fracas with French tourists at Saqqara in 1905. He spent the following months as a freelance painter and dealer in antiquities, the latter helped by his excellent eye, and a good relationship with the common Egyptian: unlike many of his fellow Europeans, he felt that his home was in Egypt. In 1908 he was engaged by Lord Carnarvon to direct the excavations that the latter had begun the previous year in western Thebes.

This work revealed an extensive early 18th Dynasty tomb (Carter's no. 37) and the valley building of Hatshepsut's temple complex, along with many other significant finds. After spending 1912–13 carrying out largely abortive work at Sakha (ancient Xoïs) and Balamun in the Delta, Carter returned to Thebes. In 1914, he discovered an early 18th Dynasty royal tomb that was probably the resting place of Ahmose-

Nefertiry, wife of Ahmose I, and in 1915, Carnarvon, having obtained the concession for the Valley of the Kings, cleared parts of the tomb of Amenhotep III.

Carter spent the years of the First World War in Egypt. In 1916 he found the tomb intended for Hatshepsut as regent, hidden in a remote southern wadi, and then in 1917 he started proper excavations in the Valley of the Kings. For the next five years, careful investigations were made in the various parts of the valley that Carter felt might conceal tombs. Apart from material related to the burial of Merenptah (19th Dynasty), and various small finds such as ostraca, *shawabtis* and other broken items, little was found. With his patron becoming disheartened at the lack of major discoveries, the 1922 season threatened to be the last.

Soon after its beginning, in November 1922, the tomb of Tutankhamen was revealed, leading to ten years of clearance, recording and restoration work, frequently hindered by the abrasive relationship between Carter and the Egyptian Antiquities Service, and also by the death of Carnarvon in 1923. Although a popular account of the excavation was published rapidly, Carter was never able to start proper work on the final publication, and died from Hodgkin's disease in 1939.

See also

Beni Hasan; Carnarvon, George Edward Stanhope Molyneux Herbert, Earl of; Deir el-Bahri, Hatshepsut temple; Deir el-Bahri, Mentuhotep II complex; *shawabtis*, servant figures and models; Thebes, Valley of the Kings

Further reading

James, T.G.H. 1992. *Howard Carter: The Path to Tutankhamun.* London.
Reeves, N., and J.H. Taylor. 1992. *Howard Carter before Tutankhamun.* London.

AIDAN DODSON

Caton Thompson, Gertrude

Gertrude Caton Thompson (1888–1985) was an English prehistorian who conducted pioneering excavations in Egypt, Africa and Arabia between the two world wars. She was the first archaeologist working in Egypt to appreciate the importance of prehistoric settlement sites, in contrast to the cemeteries so enthusiastically excavated by her contemporaries, and in 1924 began the first stratigraphically controlled excavation of a Predynastic village site. This was North Spur Hemamieh in the el-Badari district, which remains unique for its clear Badarian–Nagada I–II sequence. She also recognized the value of geological data in archaeology. Thus, starting with her next project in the Fayum region, she began working with the geologist Elinor Gardner. Their Fayum investigations led to the discovery of two Neolithic cultures: the Fayum A and B. Although, Caton Thompson thought the Fayum B was a degenerate culture that came after the Fayum A, more recent work has shown that it represents an Epi-paleolithic tradition preceding the Fayum A Neolithic.

After spending much of 1929 excavating among the famous ruins of Zimbabwe in southern Africa, Caton Thompson returned to Egypt to explore the prehistory of Kharga Oasis, where she located and excavated sites ranging from Lower Paleolithic to Neolithic in date.

For her final field project in 1937–8, she went to the Hadhramaut in southern Arabia, where she conducted the first systematic excavations ever to be undertaken in the region, uncovering the Moon temple, and shrines and tombs of Hureidha of the fifth–fourth centuries BC. Though this marked the end of her field investigations, Caton Thompson's career in archaeology continued with writing, giving lectures and attending conferences. She was very much involved in founding the British Institute of History and Archaeology in East Africa.

See also

el-Badari district Predynastic sites; Epi-paleolithic cultures, overview; Fayum, Neolithic and

Predynastic sites; Kharga Oasis, prehistoric sites; Neolithic cultures, overview; Paleolithic cultures, overview; Predynastic period, overview

Further reading

Caton Thompson, G. 1983. *Mixed Memoirs*. Gateshead.

DIANE L. HOLMES

Champollion, Jean-François

The decipherer of the Egyptian hieroglyphs, Jean-François Champollion (1790–1832) was probably one of the most brilliant scholars of all time. A child prodigy, Champollion was educated at Figéac, his birthplace in southeast France, and later at nearby Grenoble. While still a child, he learned about the Rosetta Stone from a meeting with the great mathematician Jean-Joseph Fourier, who had been a member of the Napoleonic expedition which discovered it; the young boy, who was a genius at languages, vowed to decipher it. To this end he had, by his mid-teens, studied Greek, Latin, Arabic, Hebrew, Syriac, Sanskrit and Coptic.

By age eighteen, Champollion had published the geographical section of a projected encyclopedic book, *Egypt under the Pharaohs*, and compiled a Coptic dictionary. For this he was made a faculty member at Grenoble's local college. Champollion's interests, however, were wide and included politics. His democratic and anti-clerical views resulted in his being banished from Grenoble, and he eventually sought refuge with his elder brother in Paris. From 1807–9 he attended the Collège de France and continued to work on his goal. He recognized the shorthand nature of the demotic writing on the Rosetta Stone, and equated some demotic signs with Coptic. Because of the shortness of the hieroglyphic section of the Rosetta Stone and because of the late date of the text, scholars could not be sure that the equivalences they were able to make between the Greek signs and the seemingly alphabetic hieroglyphs, such as in the royal names, were not a late, Greek-influenced phenomenon. (This was later explained by Champollion in his famous letter of 1822, *Lettre à M. Dacier relative à l'alphabet des hiéroglyphes phonétiques*.) More texts from earlier periods were clearly needed for study.

Fortunately, Champollion received copies of a much earlier inscription of Ramesses II from Abu Simbel, which assured him that the alphabetic characteristics went back to pharaonic times. Thus able to proceed, he soon presented his detailed monograph (*Précis du système hiéroglyphique*). Two trips to Italy to study and purchase Egyptian collections were followed by his appointment as conservator at the Louvre. In 1828 Champollion and his student Niccolo Rosellini journeyed throughout Egypt to gather more antiquities and copies of inscriptions. Not long after his return, Champollion received the first Chair of Egyptology at the Collège de France. Unfortunately, his career and life were cut short at age forty-two by a stroke.

His devoted brother succeeded in the posthumous publication of his Egyptian grammar in 1836, and also labored to bring out the accompanying dictionary. Because these publications appeared so long after his initial achievement, and because Champollion had spent so much time collecting primary source material, his rivals and detractors prevailed until in 1837 the distinguished German professor Richard Lepsius agreed in print with his philological arguments. Then Champollion was finally given the credit he deserved for correctly deciphering the ancient Egyptian language.

See also

Egyptian (language), decipherment of; Egyptian language and writing; Lepsius, Carl Richard; Napoleon Bonaparte and the Napoleonic expedition; Rosetta Stone; textual sources, Late period

Further reading

Dawson, W.R., and E.P. Uphill. 1995. *Who Was

Who in Egyptology, 3rd edn, M.L. Bierbrier. London.

Griffith, F.L. 1923. The decipherment of the hieroglyphs. *JEA* 37: 38–46.

BARBARA S. LESKO

chariots

While the wheel was known in Egypt prior to the New Kingdom, the chariot does not make its appearance in Egyptian records until the beginning of the 18th Dynasty. Wheeled vehicles are first attested in Mesopotamia as early as the end of the fourth millennium BC at Uruk. More widely known there in the succeeding millennium and a half, it has long been assumed that the horse and chariot were subsequently introduced to Anatolia, Syria and Palestine prior to their arrival in Egypt with the Hyksos. In fact, as early as Flinders Petrie at the beginning of the twentieth century, it was suggested that the Hyksos were able to so easily overwhelm Egypt because they possessed the chariot and composite bow, which the Egyptians did not have. This understanding, although frequently noted in the secondary literature, does not have strong archaeological support.

After three decades of excavations at Tell ed-Dab'a, almost certainly the Hyksos capital of Avaris, no traces of chariots have been found; only some horse teeth from the late Hyksos period (17th Dynasty) have been discovered. From the beginning of the wars of liberation against the Hyksos comes the stela of King Kamose of Thebes in which the monarch brags that he will take away the *ti nt ḥtry* of the Hyksos monarch. While this expression has been translated as "chariotry," the hieroglyphic determinative for chariot is not written. As Alan Schulman has shown, the context of Kamose's boast does not support this interpretation. Consequently, the first certain reference to a chariot in Egyptian literature is found in the tomb biography of Ahmose Si Abena, a naval officer from El-kab, who mentions following on foot the chariot of King Ahmose in his campaign against Avaris. Thanks to an important discovery of painted fragments from a funerary structure of King Ahmose at Abydos by Stephen Harvey in the early 1990s, evidence now exists showing horses and a fallen warrior in Asiatic attire. These fragments apparently depict the war of liberation against the Hyksos by Ahmose and indicate that chariotry was involved in a military setting. From the early 18th through the 20th Dynasties, chariots are regularly depicted in Egyptian tombs, temples and even on scarabs.

The earliest occurring and most common word for chariot is *wrr(y)t*, which is found in the Ahmose text mentioned above from the outset of the 18th Dynasty, and throughout the New Kingdom. Unlike the word for horse, *ssm(t)*, whose etymology is Semitic (*sûs* (Hebrew) or *sisu* (Akkadian)), *wrr(y)t* does not derive from a Semitic root. However, by the middle of the 18th Dynasty, the common Semitic term for chariot, *mrkbt*, is found in Egyptian texts, but it never supersedes *wrr(y)t*. The term *ḥtry*, meaning "chariotry" as a distinct military unit, does not occur until the time of Amenhotep III. Prior to this time, *ḥtry* applied to a yoke or span of draught animals, oxen or horses, and hence "chariot."

First and foremost, the chariot is a vehicle for more speedily delivering the rider to a desired location. Since chariots (and horses) were costly, their use was limited to royalty, aristocracy and the military elite. As a means of transportation, the chariot enjoyed limited use in Egypt since boating on the Nile was the primary means of long-distance transportation north and south. The Egyptian chariot was light enough that even a single man could carry one, and they could be placed on boats for transport.

The chariot was closely linked with the military, although Schulman has argued it had less strategic value than is commonly thought. Essentially, a chariot provides a moving platform from which an archer could shoot at the enemy. The term for "chariot warrior" was *snny* and the charioteer was *kṯn*. The Egyptian chariot is invariably portrayed as a military vehicle, always equipped with a bow case (even during the Amarna period). In the 19th and

20th Dynasties, a case for holding javelins is secured to the body of the chariot. The tombs of Amenmose and Kenamen in the Theban necropolis display all the equipment a charioteer would use; these include the bow, quiver, sword, whip and helmet.

Hunting was a favorite sport of Egyptian royalty and nobility; both are represented pursuing desert game while riding in their chariots. The horses are shown in the same rearing stance that is found in military scenes where the king attacks his enemies. The kings of the 18th Dynasty, especially Amenhotep II (Sphinx Stela) and Amenhotep III (Hunt Scarab) were especially proud of their hunting accomplishments. The sportsman motif, where the king is shown hunting on a chariot, is popular throughout the New Kingdom. It occurs on artifacts from the tomb of Tutankhamen. It also appears in the 19th Dynasty and is last seen in the reliefs of Ramesses III at his funerary temple of Medinet Habu.

Chariot processional scenes were popular from the latter half of the 18th Dynasty onward. The triumphant pharaoh is sometimes depicted alone returning from the battlefield. The displaying of prisoners of war is also common throughout the New Kingdom. In other cases, the king's entourage is portrayed, including members of the royal family and ranking officials. Unique to the Amarna scenes is the queen riding her chariot after the king or actually accompanying Akhenaten in his chariot, sometimes with princesses as well. The Amarna processional scenes show the royal party going to or returning from cultic observances in a temple.

The chariot can be divided into three parts: (1) the body, (2) the yoke, saddles and harness, and (3) the bridle. Information about these components can be gleaned from the numerous painted scenes and reliefs. In addition, a number of chariots have actually survived, including six from the tomb of Tutankhamen, a body that belonged to Tuthmose IV and the chariot of Yuya, all of which are on display in the Cairo Museum, as well as one in the Museum in Florence, Italy. From the 18th Dynasty a number of tombs (for example,

Puyemre, Menkheperresenb and Hepu) contain workshop scenes showing artisans making chariots. They are shown preparing, shaping and carving wood, as well as tanning and cutting leather.

Wood and leather are the primary materials for constructing chariots; only a minimal amount of metal was used. Analysis of a chariot in the Florence museum shows that the body, yoke, wheel hub and saddle yokes were made of elm which most likely came from the Lebanon–Syria area. Birch was the wood found in the axle, wheel and floor. The pole was made of willow, while the wheel spokes were of plum. None of these trees is indigenous to Egypt. The closest source of birch is eastern Anatolia. Consequently, a complex international trade system was required to supply the various types of wood for making chariots in Egypt. Local leather was used for the bridle and harness. The floor of the chariot was made of rawhide thongs that were secured on a frame, arranged like the strings on a tennis racket. Thus the floor could adequately sustain the weight of the occupants while being extremely light. Leather straps were also wrapped around the wheel to help hold it together.

When chariots first appeared in the 18th Dynasty, they employed four spokes in the wheel. The transition to the six-spoked wheel, which became standard during the second half of the 18th Dynasty, was reached after brief experimentation with the eight-spoked wheel which is found during the reigns of Tuthmose III and Tuthmose IV. Except for a few anomalies, such as a chariot scene of Akhenaten where an eight-spoked wheel is found, the six-spoked wheel prevailed into the Third Intermediate Period. It has been suggested that the reason for the move from four to six spokes was because of the addition of the chariot warrior to the chariot during the time of Tuthmose III. A stronger wheel was necessary to support the added weight.

The bodies of chariots, especially those of royalty, could be decorated with gold foil, making the vehicle splendid indeed. The chariot may not have originated in Egypt, but during the New Kingdom, Egypt mastered its use and construction. Consequently, even in later periods Egyptian chariots were in demand in the Levant. During the 21st Dynasty, King Solomon of Israel was a middleman in the trade of Egyptian chariots and horses to Syria and Anatolia (I Kings 10:28–9).

See also

army; Hyksos; Tell ed-Dab'a, Second Intermediate Period

Further reading

Harvey, S. 1994. Monuments of Ahmose at Abydos. *Egyptian Archaeology* 4: 3–5.
Hoffmeier, J.K. 1976. The evolving chariot wheel in the 18th Dynasty. *JARCE* 13: 43–5.
Littauer, M.A., and J.H. Crouwel. 1985. *Chariots and Related Equipment from the Tomb of Tut'ankhamun* (Tutankhamun tomb series 8). Oxford.
Schulman, A.R. 1979. Chariots, chariotry and the Hyksos. *JSSEA* 10: 105–53.

JAMES K. HOFFMEIER

climate

The climate of Egypt is quite arid. Although there are cool spells during the winter months, temperatures normally are mild. During the summer half-year the heat is oppressive, with daily maxima in the southern part of the country reaching 42° to 50°C (108°–122°F), barely mitigated by the northerly breezes experienced in Cairo.

The Mediterranean coastline receives the most rain, some 100–200 mm (4–8 inches) on average, exclusively in mid-winter. Rainfall decreases rapidly inland, to 25 mm (1 inch) near Cairo, with most of the interior receiving only a few millimeters every generation or two. The aridity exceeds that of any part of the New World except for the desert of northern Chile. The Egyptian deserts, as a result, are largely lifeless and the few stream valleys remain totally inactive for centuries at a time. Although cool fronts blow in from the Mediterranean Sea several times each winter or spring, humidities are so low that they only raise dust. The Red Sea Hills, along the eastern spine of the country, differ because of their topographic relief (1000–1500 m) and northeasterly winter winds that blow across the warm waters of the Red Sea. Fog or low clouds form over the higher mountains, especially in the far southeast, bringing moisture that supports more vegetation. Upper lows from the westerlies occasionally drift toward the Red Sea, setting off scattered but sometimes intense showers in the hill country. As a result, the valleys of the Red Sea Hills have well-defined courses that may actually flood for some distance every century or so.

The available weather stations record practically no rain of tropical origin, even in Nubia. However, on very rare occasions, light summer showers may stray across the border from Sudan, bringing a few sprinkles. But in statistical terms, monsoon influences are limited to south of that border. It is uncertain whether the Gebel Uweinat and Gilf Kebir highlands in the southwest receive an occasional summer shower, or whether the rare rains received there come during the spring months, when low pressure cells embedded in the higher atmosphere cross the Sahara to produce March or April showers in northern Ethiopia.

See also

climatic history

Further reading:

Griffiths, J.F., and K.H. Soliman. 1970. The northern desert. In *Climates of Africa*, J.F. Griffiths, ed., 75–131. Amsterdam.

KARL W. BUTZER

climatic history

During Pleistocene times (two million to 10,000 years ago), Egypt remained arid despite periodic amelioration of its perpetual drought. At times of glacial cooling in high latitudes, evaporation was lower in the subtropics, but rainfall was not demonstrably greater in the Saharan lowlands. For the period 25,000 to 10,000 years ago, the oases had a water supply as meager as they have today. To the west, only the towering Tibesti Mountains on the Chad–Libya border, with peaks rising above 3000 m, show evidence of some spring activation. To the east, there were more frequent rains and sporadic stream activity about 17,500 to 12,000 years ago; but an annual rainfall of 25–50 mm in the Red Sea Hills would adequately explain the silty or sandy alluvial deposits in question.

Evidence for late prehistoric climates in Egypt comes from (a) the desert margins of the Nile Valley and the Fayum Depression, and (b) widely scattered, shallow basins in the Western Desert that once harbored perennial or ephemeral bodies of water, on a scale similar to the surviving desert oases.

Although common and well developed, wadi deposits in the Eastern Desert are difficult to date, except when interfingered with Nile flood silts. On the Kom Ombo Plain (Upper Egypt) and along the eastern margins of the valley in Nubia, one phase of wadi activation began before 11,000 BP (uncalibrated radiocarbon dates "before present") and terminated by 8,000 BP; snail proliferations and root impressions suggest more vegetation. The wadis were again active from before 6,000 to about 4,600 BP. Both episodes overlapped with times of higher Nile floods and accelerated siltation, but wadi beds were swept across the margins of the Nile alluvium when it was dry, and in turn were overlapped by fresh Nile mud while the wadis were inactive. In other words, sporadic wadi flooding came during the winter or spring months, when the Nile was low.

Despite more frequent activation of the Eastern Desert wadis, the climate of the Red Sea hill country remained arid. More indicative of a modest qualitative change is a reddish paleosol that developed on the older of these wadi deposits during a millennium or more after 8,500 BP. This fossil soil led to oxidation, partial leaching of calcium carbonate, and clay mineral formation to a depth of 30–100 cm that suggests more sustained moisture, some sort of plant cover, and less torrential rains that did not favor erosion.

Other informative relationships have been identified from the Fayum Depression, which is connected to the Nile floodplain. During periods of higher Niles, this deep basin was filled by a lake. Two lacustrine episodes are identified from late prehistoric times, one dated about 8,900–7,100 BP, the other 6,500–5,500 BP. During the first lake phase, fine lakefloor and lakeshore sediments were deposited, interrupted by two episodes when waves undercut by encroaching drift sand at the shore; the absence of drift sand for much of the time suggests that dunes were mainly fixed by vegetation. The sediments of the second lake phase point to an even more stable desert surface, until about 4250 BC (calibrated) when the lake shore was again briefly invaded by tongues of drift sands that prograded into the lake, where they were reworked by wave action into massive, so-called deltaic beds. Subsequently the lake retreated to an intermediate level, while a modest organic soil formed. Stream activity then cut channels into the surface sediments, prior to a third lacustrine phase (beginning about 4000 BC) that culminated in Middle Kingdom times, with repeated flooding and wave destruction of the workers' settlements near the Qasr el-Sagha temple. Three episodes of unusually high Nile floods are dated between 2000 and 1700 BC, but the nature of desert climate at the time is uncertain. The Fayum record is reasonably compatible with that from Kom Ombo and Nubia, suggesting that the desert surface in northern Egypt had some sort of vegetation cover for most, but not all, of the time between 8,500 BP and perhaps 3800 BC (early Predynastic times).

The best information on late prehistoric climate comes from many sites in the Western Desert where sheets of water developed seasonally, or during a run of wet years, on flat shallow surfaces known as playas or pans. Most features of this kind simply collected surface runoff from large areas after heavy showers, although a subsurface sandsheet might additionally serve to store water for more protracted periods. The Egyptian playas accumulated water-borne silt and clay as well as eolian sand, carried in by running water or blown in directly. They tend to lack evidence of mollusca, diatoms and other "pond" organisms that require more persistent waters, and most probably alternated between conditions of stagnant, open water and vegetated marsh, deteriorating to alkali flats on occasion. Analogs can now be observed in parts of Nevada, although on a much larger scale than in prehistoric Egypt.

Contrary to some efforts to generalize late prehistoric wet phases in the eastern Sahara, there are distinctive regional patterns. First, with the exception of Bir Kiseiba, where playa lakes appear before 9,500 BP (at a comparable date to Selima Oasis in northern Sudan), more abundant water is first evident at Kharga and Dakhla around 8,800 BP, and Nabta Playa by 8,200 BP. Second, the first moisture peak at about 8,000 BP is inconspicuous in the Gilf Kebir, Dakhla and Fezzan, but prominent in Selima, Kiseiba, Nabta, Kharga and the north Tibesti foothills. Third, a playa lake phase at about 6,900–5,800 BP at Nabta is unique except at Selima in the Sudan. Fourth, the second moisture peak at 5,700–5,000 BP is prominent in Kharga, Dakhla, the Gilf Kebir and Libya, totally missing at Nabta and Kiseiba, and weak at Selima. Fifth, there is evidence for lingering moisture or tree growth in the Gilf Kebir, northern Tibesti and Libya, and possibly in the Eastern Desert *circa* 4,900–3,700 BP, but nowhere else.

The lack of synchronic parallelism is best explained by different anomalies in the westerlies and the monsoonal circulation. Summer rains appear to have primarily affected Kiseiba, Nabta, Kharga and the Tibesti, peaking about 8,000 BP and remaining unimportant here after 5,800 BP. Winter or spring rains of the westerly type appear to have been dominant in the Gilf Kebir and Lower Nubia, and were responsible for the rainfall maximum 5,700–5,000 BP, and its sporadic aftereffects to 3,700 BP, without, however, effecting the southernmost playa sites at Kiseiba and Nabta. This presumes some

measure of overlap between summer and winter rains in the southern part of the Egyptian Sahara about 7,500–5,800 BP. Given such a complex picture, it is inappropriate to label and date "wet" and "dry" phases as if they had some general validity across the eastern Sahara, and even more so to categorize archaeological components with reference to such a scheme.

A second problem in the Western Desert is that there now are large numbers of radiocarbon dates, but "geological" and "archaeological" dates are difficult to separate, creating a circularity of reasoning in regard to the interrelationships between paleoenvironment and settlement: sites are commonly dated by clusters of age assays on materials that also date sediments, and dispersed dates on geological phenomena such as playa beds typically lead to searches for some surface artifact scatters, that may or may not be contemporary. Systematic study of good stratigraphic sequences, such as in the Gilf Kebir, has yielded comparatively little direct archaeological association with the critical sedimentary units, while the model sequence at Selima Oasis lacks settlement evidence entirely, reflecting deep lakes or thick cover sands. Furthermore, plotting all radiocarbon dates from the Egyptian Western Desert together suggests above-average settlement density for the period 7,100–6,600 BP, when climate was relatively dry in most areas, and a low density 6,200–5,800 BP, when it was mainly wetter. The large number of radiocarbon dates from the Western Desert creates an illusion that the archaeology and prehistoric settlement ecology are firmly established. In fact, given the time spans and distances involved, research is still in an exploratory phase.

Questions of cultural contacts and possible desert emigration that interest the archaeologist of the late prehistoric Nile Valley require focused research in specific adjacent areas, employing extensive survey techniques and interdisciplinary coordination, to establish not only dating frameworks but also the microecology of land use on both lowlands and uplands. At the moment the database is adequate for little more than the recognition of stone tool technologies and broad, ecological scenarios. Perhaps most promising for collateral development with the Nile Valley Predynastic are the "Peasant Neolithic" and related sites of the Kharga, Dakhla and Farafra oases, where radiocarbon dates cluster around 5,700–5,000 BP (circa 4500–3800 BC). The Mediterranean coastal plain remains unexplored, however.

One of the salient features to emerge from recent research is that, since circa 5,000 BP (3800 BC), the Egyptian deserts have been about as bleak as they are today. There is little tangible evidence of playa beds during this time range, but delayed artesian flow to the "mound springs" of Dakhla and Kharga may have continued in diminished volume through the 6th Dynasty.

Other evidence sheds light on minor rainfall anomalies during the historical period. Tamarisk trees that colonize small sand dunes, accumulating around oases with a high water table, leave a residue of organic debris. Tamarisks are deeply rooted and tolerate brackish sources of deep ground moisture, while the needle litter spread over now-buried dune surfaces can be dated. In the northern foothills of Tibesti, there were two such generations of vegetated dunes, dating to 1600–350 BC and AD 90–650. A higher water table over such long intervals implies a trend to slightly greater rainfall, and since some of these trees are found on higher ground, there may have been partial dependence on more direct rainfall. In Siwa Oasis in northern Egypt, vegetated eolian mounds are dated to 2450–1880 BC, 1210–1100 BC, and 70 BC–AD 560. These weak anomalies appear to be associated with winter or spring rains in the westerlies.

Brief intervals of expanded human settlement in favored areas can be compared with such undramatic historical evidence. They can be verified in the Gilf Kebir, Kharga and Dakhla oases, and in the Red Sea watersheds of the Eastern Desert circa 2700 BC and again circa 2300 BC. The abundant 6th Dynasty archaeological record from Dakhla is noteworthy, and C-Group-related sites are found around Dungul Oasis, west of the Nubian Nile, dating to circa 2000 BC. Such potential relationships merit closer attention, as do the Libyan attacks on the western Nile Delta and subsequent immigration beginning circa 1210 BC. For now, this must remain an agenda for future fieldwork.

See also

C-Group culture; Dakhla Oasis, prehistoric sites; Epi-paleolithic cultures, overview; Fayum, Neolithic and Predynastic sites; Kharga Oasis, prehistoric sites; Nile, flood history; Paleolithic cultures, overview; Siwa Oasis, prehistoric sites

Further reading

Brooks, I.A. 1989. Early Holocene basinal sediments of the Dakhla Oasis region, south central Egypt. Quaternary Research 32: 139–52.

Butzer, K.W. 1995. Environmental change in the Near East and human impact on the land. In Civilizations of the Ancient Near East, J.M. Sasson, ed., 123–52. New York.

——. 1998. Late Quaternary problems of the Egyptian Nile Valley. Paléorient 23(2):151–73.

Hassan, F.A., and G.T. Gross. 1987. Resources and subsistence during the early Holocene at Siwa Oasis, northern Egypt. In Prehistory of Arid North Africa, A.E. Close, ed., 85–104. Dallas.

Kozlowski, J.K., and B. Ginter. 1989. The Fayum Neolithic in the light of new discoveries. In Late Prehistory of the Nile Basin and the Sahara, L. Krzyzaniak and M. Kobusiewicz, eds, 157–80. Poznan.

Kröpelin, S. 1987. Palaeoclimatic evidence from early to mid-Holocene playas in the Gilf Kebir (Southwest Egypt). Palaeoecology of Africa 18: 189–208.

Pachur, H.J., H.P. Röper, S. Kröpelin and M. Goschin. 1987. Late Quaternary hydrography of the Eastern Sahara. Berliner Geowissenschaftliche Abhandlungen, A. 75(2): 331–84.

Wendorf, F., and R. Schild, eds. 1980. Prehistory of the Eastern Sahara. New York.

KARL W. BUTZER

cult temples, construction techniques

The process of building an Egyptian stone temple can be deduced and reconstructed on the basis of the physical remains, particularly unfinished buildings, as well as with the aid of some preserved texts, documents and tomb paintings relating to various aspects of the work. The ready availability of many types of stone in the Nile valley made the construction of mortuary monuments (tombs, pyramids and cenotaphs) and religious structures (shrines, chapels and temples) possible almost from the beginning of the pharaonic period. The process of temple construction can be divided into five distinct phases: (1) planning the structure; (2) preparation of the site and foundation; (3) quarrying and delivery of stone; (4) positioning of the stone; and finally, (5) the final dressing of the stone and decoration.

(1) During the initial planning of any temple structure, careful consideration was given to its intended purpose and function. The site of a temple may have been dictated by a traditional reverence for a hallowed location of great antiquity or for the simple and practical considerations of terrain. Sanctified or venerated areas included places identified with cosmological events such as the emergence of the primal hill from the waters of chaos, or associations from the earliest times with a natural shrine, a grotto or cave, such as one which has been found on Elephantine Island. On such revered locations, temples grew from simple structures to elaborate complexes by the work of successive kings and dynasties. The practical considerations of location often dictated the building of temples on the edge of the cultivation at the limit of the inundation, adjacent to a necropolis, or in some configuration with existing structures, perhaps within an established complex.

The working plan for the structure was developed by an architect, builder or overseer of the works, along strict canonical lines. There is evidence that architectural drawings in ink on papyrus, prepared wooden panels or flat stone surfaces were made, but only a few general examples of temple planning and other architectural projects have been preserved and no detailed construction drawings exist. Typically, line drawings of single columns, layout sketches for precincts or elevations of small structures such as shrines are all that have been found. The amount of detail committed to working plans can only be conjectured.

(2) Once a suitable plan had been decided and marked, the emplacement for the foundation had to be prepared. For much of Egyptian history this consisted of a series of foundation trenches and pits, each designed to level a wall, a single column or a row of columns. This trench technique was particularly adaptable to the tradition in which successive rulers added to and embellished their predecessors' structures. Sand was put into the bottom of the trenches and pits to serve as the leveling surface on which the foundation blocks of the structure were positioned, but in some instances the amount of sand used is so minimal that it must have only been considered a ritual element and not a practical device by which stone could be moved and leveled.

A network of foundations was constructed to support the entire structure. The foundation could be aligned and squared by sighting on surveyor's marks made on plaster swatches on the mudbrick precinct walls. The eventual positions of walls, columns and other features were often marked by incision on the top surface of each course of the foundation. In some instances where a temple structure has been dismantled, the plan is still preserved on the upper surface of the stone, even to details of door closures and decorative moldings. The depth and effectiveness of this substructure was not consistent throughout Egyptian history. The foundation of the Ramesside Hypostyle Hall in the Amen temple at Karnak was eventually found to be inadequate to support the weight of the columns, especially after subsoil water had further weakened it.

A much more lasting foundation method was developed late in Egyptian history, probably during the 25th Dynasty. This was accomplished by the excavation of a foundation pit for the whole temple structure, which was then delimited and lined with mudbrick walls and filled with sand. On this well-prepared bedding several courses of large foundation stones were laid to create a solid and stable platform to receive the architectural elements of the temple. As an example of this construction technique, the foundation for the four 26th Dynasty *naoi* or shrines at Mendes in the eastern Nile Delta was massive in size and depth and overcompensated for the weight it had to accommodate several times over.

Each step in the building of a temple was accompanied by prescribed prayers and rituals. Illustrated on the north wall of the sanctuary of the small temple at Medinet Habu and in other temples, such as at Dendera or Edfu, are a series of acts carried out by the king: "The Stretching of the Cord" (measuring the ground plan), "Scattering the Gypsum" (marking the plan with white gypsum chips), "Hacking the Earth" (excavating the trenches). These are followed by the king molding a brick, offering wine, and making an offering to Amen. The founding of the temple was consecrated with the ceremony of laying down a symbolic foundation deposit. This usually consisted of model tools and implements, ritual dishes, plaques and model bricks bearing the name of the founder and, in some instances, a ceremonial meat offering. These were placed in pits under the cornerstones and thresholds and at intervals along the sides of the planned building.

(3) It is presumed that the actual process of quarrying the stone proceeded at the same time as the preparation of the site and the foundation. Stone was only roughly shaped at the quarry, with more accurate shaping and finishing done on the building site. Stone was transported up and down the Nile Valley on the river; as well, the annual inundation further facilitated transportation of materials by boat or raft. Some modern hypotheses credit the ancient Egyptians with the use of ingenious systems employed in the transportation and lifting of stone for which there is no historical evidence; the explanation is usually to be found in massive manpower and the use of available materials. Such illustrations on tomb walls as

are preserved indicate that even massive stone blocks and sculpture were moved on wooden sleds, without benefit of wheels or rollers, but with the use of some sort of liquid to help reduce friction. The use of block and tackle or the pulley in any form is not indicated.

Stone for construction was often not produced to a standard module but was instead cut, fit and joined in a manner that utilized the material in the varied sizes in which it had been delivered from the quarry. There were exceptions, such as in the reign of Akhenaten, when considerable construction was ordered in a short time and use was made of a standard block size (*talatat*) based on the Egyptian cubit measure. Often material was reused from earlier, dismantled buildings as interior fill in walls and other structures. In some of the large pylons in the Amen Precinct at Karnak there have been found reused blocks ranging from the small modular units of Akhenaten to large wall and roof slabs from shrines. This common practice of reusing material has enabled archaeologists to recover evidence of buildings no longer in existence, but still preserved in parts as fill.

(4) At the completion of the foundation, the first course of blocks for walls, thresholds, columns and any other features received their rough dressing and were put into place. Mortar or cement was generally only used to repair broken corners or ill-fitting junctures, and to act as a lubricant for the movement of stone on stone. The use of beams and bars to lever stones into place is attested by sharp depressions cut into the upper surface of courses exactly at the point where it would have been necessary to provide purchase as the block of the next course was placed.

The entire structure was then packed with a rubble and mudbrick fill to create a platform defined by the first course of the exterior walls. Material for the second course of walls, columns and other features was brought into place with the aid of temporary ramps, also of rubble and mudbrick, positioned and given its final dressing. The packing process was repeated, again filling the entire structure with material which would extend the level platform to the height of the second course. The ramps were augmented and lengthened at the addition of each course and the level of the interior fill heightened so that, by the time the roofing blocks were to be positioned, they could be moved across the top of the structure, as had been the other blocks, over the composite platform of stone and packing. It is difficult to visualize an Egyptian temple completely filled from floor level to roof with brick and rubble, but this seems to have been the most practical and economical building method in a country where wood was scarce and rarely used for ramps or scaffolding.

(5) When the construction phase was complete the filling process was reversed; the rubble fill was removed slowly so that the same material which had served as a platform for moving blocks could also function as a temporary floor, reducible in height, on which the finishing masons, relief sculptors and painters could work. Thus, the final dressing of the stone for walls and columns was done in place. This can be seen most clearly in the first court of the Amen Temple at Karnak where unfinished columns, completely erected, still await the final dressing and carving away of excess stone. In other instances this process is demonstrated by the presence of decoration which is carefully finished at the top of walls or columns but done with less care at the bottom, suggesting some acceleration of the process in finishing the building.

The Egyptian temple was finished with carved and painted decoration on the interior and exterior walls, presenting a colorful effect far from the modern impression given by the predominant color of sandstone seen today. There are enough preserved traces of original painted decoration to suggest the intended appearance of temples, particularly where walls were protected by later over-plastering, as they were at the temple of Medinet Habu. Colorful glazed tile decoration was also employed in the embellishment of some temple structures in some periods. It should be noted that not all temples were finished completely in stone before being decorated. Some temple structures were only completed in unbaked mudbrick,

which was plastered and painted to resemble the more substantial parts made of stone. In the Precinct of Mut at Karnak the remains of two major pylons exist only in mudbrick, attesting to this practice. It might be said that much of Egyptian monumental architecture was a combination of careful stone work and a cosmetic concealment of inferior materials. Since the final appearance and total impression of a temple was based on the finishing of the structure in plaster and paint, it was important that the surface appearance was maintained.

See also

Karnak, precinct of Mut; Karnak, temple of Amen-Re; Medinet Habu; quarrying; sculpture (stone), production techniques

Further reading

Arnold, D. 1991. *Building in Egypt: Pharaonic Stone Masonry.* London.
Baldwin Smith, E. 1938. *Egyptian Architecture as Cultural Expression.* New York.
Cernival, J.-L. de. 1964. *Living Architecture: Egyptian.* London.
Golvin, J.-C., and J.-C. Goyon. 1987. *Les batisseurs de Karnak.* Paris.

WILLIAM H. PECK

cult temples of the New Kingdom

The temple in ancient Egypt was essentially the mansion or dwelling of a deity, and as such it was expected to fulfill all the functions of a domicile. The dressing and toilet of the god along with regular provision of sustenance (the offerings) were of prime concern in the layout and appointments of Egyptian temples. But other considerations such as the housing of guest gods and the *ex-votos* of devotees, the deities' promenades and journeys, the banking and disbursement of the god's income, the instruction and admonition of the masses, all weighed heavily in dictating the physical arrangements of the god's house, especially in the New Kingdom.

The most successful architectural solution to all these demands was realized in the processional temple of early 18th Dynasty origin. The roots of this temple lie in the earlier cult temples of the Middle Kingdom; these are self-contained, enclosed units, in which the cella provided the focal point for a surrounding complex of ancillary rooms. It was the contribution of the deviser of the processional temple to front this basic complex with three "screening" elements: a hypostyle hall, a peristyle and a pylon built along the elongated axis of the core temple. These elements essentially distanced the deity from the outside world, since the pylon-pierced cross walls permitted the creation of a cordoned-off security area: the common folk were not permitted beyond the first court. The hypostyle and inner ambulations provided considerable space in which to house the ever increasing number of *ex-voto* statues of private individuals, beneficiaries and supporters of the god, who were in return allowed to partake of the divine offerings in perpetuity. Side doors of the outer courts could be used as law courts and places for public business, and it has been suggested that the balcony over the front gate between the pylons was used by choirs.

The elongation of the central axis of the New Kingdom temple principally highlighted the processional way of the god, and turned this aspect of the cult from a simple promenade into a parade. Since the journey was made in a sacred bark borne upon the shoulders of the priests, it was necessary to set aside a room in the environs of the cella (where the god "dwelt" in the form of a statue in the *naos*) for the purpose of housing the bark. Thus, in the classically designed processional temple, a "bark shrine" equipped with a stone block on which the bark sat when not in use was placed in advance of the cella. The placing of the cult statue in the bark, and the latter's progress through antechambers, hypostyle, peristyle and pylon to the *dromos* leading to the landing stage and canal, was rationalized as the creator-god's primordial act of creation. The cella, a low-roofed room built on the highest point in the temple, became the mound of creation on which the deity at the dawn of time had performed his act of creation in semidarkness. Thereafter, the deity emerges in his bark upon the surface of the Primeval Ocean (Nun), through the semi-twilight of the archetypal marsh (the hypostyle), into the half light of the lagoon where the reeds draw back (the peristyle), and finally dawning in full light of day between the two mountains of the east (the pylon). The lotus and papyriform columns of the fore-halls enhanced this imagery.

After some early experimentation, it became an accepted pattern to decorate temple wall surfaces which the masses could see with themes which would admonish and chasten them within the ambit of the aims of the political hierarchy. Thus, the fronts of pylons and the exterior façades of the side walls of the forecourts were often (although not always) reserved for relief scenes depicting Pharaoh's triumphs over foreign lands and his policing action against recalcitrants and terrorists. The "head-smiting" scene, showing the king about to crush the skulls of a clutch of foreign rebels, became a favorite theme for the decoration of the exterior face of the first pylon, and in later times gave rise to an instruction manual on how to draw the scene expertly. The side walls and those in the first court, where the masses were allowed, often recounted specific military successes, albeit larded with a high-flown rhetoric in the case of the accompanying text.

At the point where further access was restricted to priests and nobility, the character of the relief scenes changes. Here cultic themes dominated the repertoire, including (and especially) the offering scene showing the king as celebrant, processional scenes, temple foundation scenes, a simple coronation scene showing the king kneeling before the god, introduction scenes (ancillary gods leading the king into the presence of the principal deity), and sometimes detailed portrayals of particular festivals. Here and there along the *dromos* and longitudinal axis stood stelae, those within view of the public being usually "triumph" texts recounting the prowess of the king and his mighty deeds in peace and war. Closer to the cella were stelae inscribed with texts intended for the god: hymns, records of bequests, supplications, memorials and so on. The walls of storage chambers were also decorated, usually with offering scenes, but the reliefs and inscriptions do not often betray the contents of the store; in fact it is generally difficult to elicit specific room use from the reliefs in a chamber. In addition to "official" reliefs and inscriptions, one might also encounter "unofficial" private graffiti within the restricted sectors of the temple: priests might carve self-laudatory texts giving their pedigrees, prayers and supplications, oracles which had issued in their favor, or even their contracts within the temple. Such texts, together with the ubiquitous visitors' scribblings, usually date from periods when the temple was suffering from hard times and security was lax.

The main temple at a site was often surrounded within its *temenos* by a number of ancillary installations. Most temples had a sacred lake close at hand for purification and libations. The houses of the high-priest and his associate priests nestled close to the main shrine, as did special structures designed as treasuries. To accommodate the processionals of the sacred bark, way-stations would be built at intervals along the route, consisting of peripheral one-room shrines with a block to receive the bark. Shrines for "guest" gods (usually smaller versions of the main temple) could be included within the principal enclosure.

The pattern of the processional temple described above was adopted *mutatis mutandis* for most of the township deities (nome gods) in Upper Egypt. In Lower Egypt it is attested at several sites (for example, Buto, Mendes, Bubastis, Heliopolis and (probably) Saft el-Henneh), but the inferior record of excavation in the Delta continues to deprive us of much-needed evidence. The prevalence in the north of cults in which an animal was revered as principal divine avatar dictated slightly different arrangements from those demanded by the procession. The cow at Atfih, the Apis and Mnevis bulls at Memphis and Heliopolis respectively, the cat at Bubastis, the lion at Leontopolis and the ram at Mendes all required well-appointed "stalls" as well as cellae, and a place to rest after death. Thus there grew up separate structures to house the animal in life, and a burying-ground (subterranean toward the close of the New Kingdom) with stone sarcophagi to receive the mummified animal remains. At Heliopolis, the special requirements of sun worship created a type of temple in which large, simple courts open to the sky dominated the plan. It may well have been this feature of the solar cult which impressed itself on the heretic pharaoh Akhenaten when he designed his vast shrines at Karnak and Amarna, dedicated to the Sun-disc.

The strength of the monarchy throughout the New Kingdom is reflected in the size and nature of the royal funerary temple. At Thebes and Memphis there grew up a series of these structures, called in the jargon of the times "The-Temple-of-Millions-of-Years of King so-and-so"; at Abydos a sequence of cenotaphs or "resting-places" where, in company with the ancestors, the royal spirits might consort with Osiris. At West Thebes, by the middle of the 18th Dynasty the layout of the processional temple had been adopted *in toto*, save that now it was a king that was the owner and occupant rather than a member of the pantheon. On the south side of the first court, and abutting onto it, was a small palace which communicated with the temple by means of a balcony ("Window of Appearances"). The palace housed the king and his entourage during those few weeks every year when the court took up residence at Thebes—the king normally dwelt in Memphis or Pi-Ramesses—in order to participate in one of the local festivals. Ostensibly serving the royal tombs in the Valley of the Kings, the New Kingdom funerary temples functioned within the overall administration of the greater Amen temple on the east bank.

Of lesser cult temples we know scarcely more than the names. Shrines of the "protected images" (divine barks and their occupants) are mentioned in New Kingdom texts; and minor manifestations of major deities sometimes spawned small cult centers in and around more important towns. These were small affairs, modestly appointed and commensurate with the penury of the lower classes that frequented them. Natural phenomena—trees, hilltops, wild animals—might also find themselves the object of a spontaneous cult, likewise with rudimentary installations for carrying on divine service.

See also

Karnak, Akhenaten temples; Karnak, temple of Amen-Re; Luxor, temple of; religion, state; representational evidence, New Kingdom temples; Thebes, royal funerary temples

Further reading

Barguet, P. 1962. *Le Temple d'Amon-rê à Karnak*. Cairo.

Finnestad, R.B. 1985. *Image of the World and Symbol of the Creator*. Wiesbaden.

Helck, W., ed. 1987. *Tempel und Kult*. Wiesbaden.

Spencer, P. 1984. *The Egyptian Temple: A Lexicographical Study*. London.

DONALD B. REDFORD

cult temples prior to the New Kingdom

The building history of Egyptian temples may be divided into a pre-formal and a formal stage, following the work of Barry Kemp and others. Pre-formal characterizes the earliest known Egyptian shrines developed in the Predynastic era and continuing largely until the Middle Kingdom, with even a few New Kingdom examples attested. Formal denotes the standard, processional, royally sponsored temples that began to be built throughout Egypt by the Middle Kingdom, though they achieved fullest development only in the 18th Dynasty of the New Kingdom.

The earliest cult temples were mainly the creation of individual Egyptian communities, starting in the Predynastic era. They followed local traditions, including a wide variety of shapes, forms, architecture and decoration. For instance, at Elephantine, a cleft between two large granite boulders served as the focus point of early religious belief. From the artifacts recovered, not even the name of the resident deities can be identified. At Medamud, a grove of trees surrounded by an irregular polygonal wall was the earliest attested shrine. Elsewhere, other styles are found.

Early Dynastic decoration, labels and other materials sometimes illustrate what local shrines of that era looked like. There is a general pattern of an enclosed courtyard, an offering stand and a sanctuary, all built of mudbrick, or of reed and mud plaster. A large image of the deity may dominate the sanctuary, even projecting above the roofline. Such was the actual shrine at Coptos in the Late Predynastic to Early Dynastic eras. Two immense colossal statues of the god Min, already in his identifiable hieratic pose, stood in the sanctuary area. They must have dominated the shrine and projected above it. Their antiquity is extreme, as Narmer scratched on them his name (*serekh*) amidst the already carved older graffiti on the legs of the figures. Another echo of the archaic Min shrine is seen in later depictions of the deity in the shape of a conical peaked booth, with a totem symbol atop. Again, the deity is much larger than the booth, perhaps recalling the archaic images. Small finds from early shrines add further to the types of buildings depicted. Many show a round-topped reed-constructed shrine, with the divine image within. A Field Museum (Chicago) late Nagada I chaff-tempered-class jar has scratched onto its side a rectangular building of reeds, with flagpoles and flags at each end. Early versions of shrines also are found in the famed *ḥeb-sed* court of Zoser's funerary complex at Saqqara.

The Nagada II buff-painted pottery is another source of early divine totem emblems. Pots showing boats with cabins often depict an attached pole with an image fixed atop it. The repertoire of totems include the familiar stylized thunderbolt of Min, jackals or other canines, symbolizing Asyut's Wepwawet, and Abydos's Khenty-Imentyw. A group of three hills symbolizes Thebes, taken from three mountains that still dominate the eastern horizon at the site. A stylized woman's head with bovine ears is an early icon of Hathor of Dendera and Bat, a deity of Nome VII of Upper Egypt. An elephant perhaps symbolizes Elephantine. Many of these totems can be identified with later deities because they appear as fixed imagery for the respective deity.

Even after Egypt's political unification in the 1st Dynasty, very sparse royal activity is attested at the provincial cult centers. It seems that whatever these early governments could muster was concentrated at the capital, Memphis, and at Heliopolis, its suburb devoted to the solar cult of Re. Heliopolis too had a pre-formal cult symbol, but one subsequently adopted by the formal religion. The shrine was open to the sky, in a courtyard with a tall, raised stone (*menhir*) at one end, called the *ben-ben* stone. This *ben-ben* was regularized by the 5th Dynasty into the short squat obelisk of the Abusir and Abu Gurab solar temples. The *ben-ben* underwent further development, becoming the obelisk of Middle and New Kingdom Egypt. At Heliopolis, an obelisk built by Senusret I of the 12th Dynasty still marks the temple site. The solar temples of Abusir and Abu Gurab received extensive royal patronage during the 5th Dynasty through the influence of Re's cult on the royal persona. The temples had reliefs, depicting scenes of the seasonal spirits and activities, temple foundation ceremonies, and events of the king's reign, especially the jubilee (*heb-sed*) ceremony. These reliefs were carved in a corridor that flanked the open-air court and opened onto the *ben-ben*. The solar temples represent the earliest royally sponsored formal temples; temples to Re ever afterward retained the open-air court style.

The meager royal resources devoted to the other cults echoes in the finds excavated from them. At Elephantine Island, German archaeologists found a plaque of faïence dedicated by Pepi I of the 6th Dynasty. At Dendera, a text in the much later Ptolemaic and Roman temple commemorates an early dedication by Pepi I.

At Coptos (Quft), exemption decrees were issued by the 6th and 8th Dynasty pharaohs in favor of the temples of Min and Isis. This royal patronage to Coptos stemmed from Pepi I's marriage to two daughters of the nomarch of Coptos, and similar ties of the nomarch to the 8th Dynasty rulers. The exemption decrees illuminate another aspect of royal policy toward local shrines. The early Egyptian temples were not automatically tax-exempt. Only by a special decree of pharaoh could they achieve tax-exempt status.

Zoser's funerary temple complex at Saqqara illustrates another aspect of early cult temples. At the celebration of the king's jubilee (*heb-sed*), the nomes (provinces) were expected to send their divine images to Memphis, where they were enshrined at the *heb-sed* site. The gods had to approve a king's rejuvenation and rededication at the ceremony, thus their presence was required. The chapels of the gods of Upper Egypt and Lower Egypt respectively flank the *heb-sed* court of Zoser. Another example of royal patronage to shrines is mentioned in the Royal Annals of the 1st to 5th Dynasties. Occasionally a regnal year is named after a divine cult image fashioned and dedicated that year. Local deities were also depicted on statuary created for the royal funerary temples in the 4th and 5th Dynasties.

Certain special shrines received much attention from the early monarchy. One was Hierakonpolis (Nekhen), an early Predynastic center. Its deity, Horus, was the god in whom pharaoh was incarnate. The ancient shrine at Nekhen was pre-formal, a raised oval structure with a simple building atop it; this came to symbolize Nekhen in the hieroglyphic script. Khasekhemwy of the 2nd Dynasty dedicated a granite gateway and statues of himself, and archaic kings from Scorpion to Narmer dedicated palettes and maceheads and other artifacts displayed in this ancient shrine. Fortunately for later archaeology, when a formal shrine was built at Nekhen by Tuthmose III of the New Kingdom, all the early, archaic dedications to the shrine were collected and placed in a sealed deposit, where J.E. Quibell excavated them early in the twentieth century.

Another early shrine that received special royal attention was Buto in the central Delta, symbolizing the kings of Lower Egypt; the deep antiquity of this town has also been attested.

Abydos received much early royal attention as the burial place of the earliest Dynastic kings. The cult temple in the town was originally dedicated to a jackal deity, named Khenty-Imentyw. A small mudbrick walled structure was probably built in the 1st or 2nd Dynasty; already it displayed a court and chapel structure. Minor royal dedications were made to it, including a small ivory statuette of Khufu. From excavated evidence it seems clear that early provincial shrines, aside from those affiliated with the monarchy and the royal capital, received little or no royal patronage right through the late Old Kingdom. The pre-formal temples continued to function as they had from time immemorial, operated by their local community; these temples were not even normally tax-exempt.

During the 11th and 12th Dynasties in the Middle Kingdom, the pharaohs began to build formal, royally patronized temples in many of the provincial capitals and towns. Evidence for such activity is attested at many sites, including Thebes, Medamud, Armant, Tod, Dendera, Abydos, Hermopolis, throughout the Fayum, Memphis, Heliopolis and in the Delta. All these sites have Middle Kingdom ruins or reused blocks from later structures. At Thebes, the Middle Kingdom pharaohs founded the temple of Amen at Karnak, and built the earliest court and sanctuary. The Theban nome became specially favored as their home base. At Elephantine, the pre-formal religion continued, with a substantial shrine dedicated to Pepi-nakht-Ḥeqa-ib, an Old Kingdom nomarch who had been deified. Within it, the local notables dedicated their own statues. This tradition of local notables dedicating statues in temples continued into the New Kingdom. The statues often asked for prayers from passers-by for a particular deity, and invoked blessings on those who heeded.

Another cult eventually developed around the person of Imhotep, architect of King Zoser, to whom an early instruction is attributed.

Several other wise men are commemorated in the collection of stories, *Khufu and the Magicians*. These tales mention a temple of Thoth in which was a secret chamber. The few formal shrines of Middle Kingdom date that survive in good condition indicate that the standard type of formal architecture for temples, with gateway, court, pillared hall (hypostyle) and sanctuary, was developed in this era. The best-preserved example is at Medinet Madi in the Fayum region. Also, the great religious festivals with their processions of deities' images may have started in this period. The earliest known bark resting shrine, that of Senusret I, occurs at Karnak, where it was retrieved from a later building.

Finally, from the Middle Kingdom era come two stories that echo the earlier, pre-formal religion inasmuch as deities reveal themselves to private individuals with the goal of receiving cult offerings. The first tale, *The Shipwrecked Sailor*, concerns a bejeweled serpent deity living on a magical isle who reveals himself to be the Lord of Punt. The second tale, the *Story of the Herdsman*, concerns a revelation of Hathor to a herdsman working in the Delta marshes. A case of more formal involvement of divine figures with royalty is the final tale in the cycle of stories, *Khufu and the Magicians*. In it, Re fathers three sons by the wife of a priest of Re, who are then delivered by Isis, Khnum, Meskhenet and Ḥeqat, who present themselves as midwives and assistants in the human guise of a porter and dancers. This tale in its basic aspects foreshadows the divine birth accounts of the New Kingdom, and it may be the origin of the genre.

The Middle Kingdom stands at the transition from pre-formal to formal religion in the cult temples, but it still has strong echoes of the earlier, pre-formal religion. Even in the New Kingdom, shrines like that of Ptah at Deir el-Medina, located in a cleft in the mountain, or the veneration of the peak over the Valley of the Kings, and the various shrines of Amen related to mountain peaks, such as Gebel Barkal or the Roaring Crag at Gebel el-Teir in Middle Egypt, basically echo the pre-formal early religion.

See also

Elephantine; Hierakonpolis; Karnak, temple of Amen-Re; Medamud; obelisks; pottery, prehistoric; Quft/Qift (Coptos); representational evidence, Early Dynastic; Saqqara, pyramids of the 3rd Dynasty; Tod

Further reading

Arnold, D. 1996. Hypostyle halls of the Old and Middle Kingdom? In *Studies in Honor of William Kelly Simpson* 1, P.D. Manuelian, ed., 39–54. Boston.
Badawy, A. 1954–66. *History of Egyptian Architecture*, 3 vols. Berkeley, CA.
Kemp, B.J. 1989. *Ancient Egypt: Anatomy of a Civilization*. New York.
O'Connor, D. 1992. The status of early Egyptian temples. In *The Followers of Horus: Studies Dedicated to Michael Allen Hoffman*, 83–98. Oxford.

FRANK J. YURCO

Cypriot peoples

The island of Cyprus, situated some 400 km to the northeast of the Nile Delta, has served over the millennia as a crucial link between Egypt and the Mediterranean. The island supplied Egypt with such commodities as copper and wood, and was itself a consumer of Egyptian products. Moreover, given the prevailing counter-clockwise winds of the eastern Mediterranean, Cyprus was an important landfall for ships sailing from the Delta to more westerly ports.

The earliest secure evidence for contact between Egypt and Cyprus can be dated to the later part of the Second Intermediate Period (13th–17th Dynasties). Cypriot pottery (White Painted Pendant Line and Cross Line styles, and of White Painted VI, Base Ring I and Red Lustrous fabrics) has been found in Egypt and Nubia in Second Intermediate Period contexts, at Tarkhan, Sidmant, Dishasha, Abydos, el-Shalla, Deir Rifa and Aniba. Further evidence

for contact between the two regions is demonstrated by Tell el-Yahudiya pottery, which was imitated in Cyprus. This pottery was first identified at the Hyksos site in the Nile Delta, but is now understood as a set of related wares produced in both Egypt and Palestine during the Second Intermediate Period.

There seems to have been no dramatic break in the importation of Cypriot material into Egypt following the expulsion of the Hyksos. Cypriot pottery continued to be brought into Egypt in some quantity throughout the 18th Dynasty. White Slip bowls and Base Ring juglets (*bilbils*) were especially popular imports, and it has been suggested that the latter may have served as containers for opium. Such juglets have been recovered from many 18th Dynasty tombs throughout Egypt and are by far the most common type of Cypriot ceramics found in the Nile Valley.

In Cyprus, the earliest securely dated contexts to yield Egyptian material belong to a period roughly equivalent to the reigns of Amenhotep I to Tuthmose II (early 18th Dynasty). This material consists of alabaster, faïence and glass vessels as well as scarabs and jewelry. The existence of a scarab of Senusret I (12th Dynasty) found on the surface of the Late Bronze Age site of Enkomi raises the possibility that contact between Egypt and Cyprus may have begun as early as the Middle Kingdom. However, the presence of a faïence scepter head with the cartouche of King Horemheb (end 18th Dynasty) found in an early twelfth century BC context at Hala Sultan Teke and the discovery of a scarab of Amenhotep III in an eleventh century BC grave at Palaepaphos-Skales suggest that many of the Egyptian artifacts in Cyprus may have been imported into the island considerably after the time of their manufacture.

It is often impossible to determine whether a particular example of Egyptian material found in Cyprus had been manufactured in Egypt or was an Egyptianizing object produced in the Levant. Similarly, it is impossible to tell whether the Cypriot pottery found in Egypt or the Egyptian material found in Cyprus had been transmitted between the two areas directly, or whether Levantine traders were responsible for this exchange.

A majority of scholars agree that the kingdom of "Alashiya" referred to in Egyptian, Hittite, Ugaritic and Mesopotamian texts of the eighteenth to twelfth centuries BC most likely was Cyprus. If the association of Cyprus and Alashiya is correct, then the evidence for trade between Cyprus and 18th Dynasty Egypt that survives in the material record can, in part, be attributed to the system of royal gift exchange documented in the Amarna Letters. Some of these letters (EA 33–40) record large quantities of copper being shipped by the king of Alashiya in exchange for ebony, gold, linen and other items from the pharaoh. The mid-fourteenth century BC Ulu Burun shipwreck, which was carrying several tons of copper ingots as well as Cypriot pottery when it sank off the southern coast of Turkey, may well have been part of this gift exchange network. On the other hand, the eclectic nature of the Ulu Burun cargo cautions against interpreting Late Bronze Age trade in the eastern Mediterranean in terms of nationalized merchant fleets. Much of this trade was likely to have been conducted by independent shippers with multinational crews. The mixed Cypriot, Minoan, Palestinian and local Libyan ceramics recovered in Egypt on an islet at Marsa Matruh may indicate that this small, fourteenth century BC entrepôt and revictualing station had been utilized by such multinational shippers.

The importation of fine-ware Cypriot pottery into Egypt was dramatically reduced at the end of the 18th Dynasty. Some scholars have argued that Cypriot trade with Egypt had been controlled by the Levantine city of Ras Shamra, and that the reduction of Cypriot imports into Egypt after the Amarna period (reign of Amenhotep IV/Akhenaten) resulted from the Hittite conquest of that city. More recent scholarship, however, has shown that the majority of New Kingdom Egyptian material found in Cyprus is 19th Dynasty (LCIIC to LCIIA:1 periods on Cyprus). The reduced importation of hand-made Cypriot fine-wares into 19th Dynasty Egypt may thus represent the growing popularity in Egypt for wheel-made Mycenaean pottery—perhaps transmitted via Cyprus—rather than reflecting a politically motivated trade embargo.

It would appear that there was virtually no direct or indirect exchange between Cyprus and Egypt for nearly two centuries after the end of the 19th Dynasty. The 18th or 19th Dynasty artifacts which occasionally appear in Cypriot contexts of the twelfth or eleventh centuries BC are probably best understood as heirlooms, or may represent a Levantine trade in Egyptian antiquities. In the poorly preserved conclusion of the Egyptian text of a late 20th Dynasty shipwrecked official named Wenamen, an interpreter was needed to appeal for help from the queen of Alashiya. This suggests that the network of royal gift exchange had broken down by the close of the twelfth century BC.

In the ninth century BC Egyptian and Egyptianizing artifacts, primarily scarabs and faïence figurines, are once again found in some quantities in Cypriot contexts, such as at the Phoenician temple of Astarte at Kition. However, since virtually no Cypriot material of this date has been reported from Egypt, it is likely that this early Iron Age material was brought to the island by Phoenician and other Levantine traders. Such intermediaries were also probably responsible for the continued importation of Egyptian material into Cyprus during the subsequent eighth and seventh centuries BC, when the island came under the domination of the Assyrian empire.

After the fall of the Assyrian capital of Nineveh in 612 BC, a resurgent Egypt began to move against Cyprus. The first century BC historian Diodorus (I.68.1) records a successful naval expedition by "Hopre" (King Waḥibre of the 26th Dynasty, more commonly known as Apries) against Cyprus and Phoenicia. Herodotus (II.182.2) claims that Hophra's successor Ahmose II (Amasis) was the first to take Cyprus and subject it to tribute. When in the reign of Ahmose II Cyprus was conquered, and for how long it remained under Egyptian hegemony, is difficult to determine. Some scholars have attempted to link stylistic developments of Cypriot statuary to the political fortunes of the island in the sixth century BC, and have suggested that the cessation of the so-called Cypro-Egyptian style of sculpture around 545 BC was a result of the island coming under Persian domination. More recent studies have stressed the fact that Egyptianizing motifs can be found on local Cypriot statuary from *circa* 650 to 450 BC, and that these Egyptianizing features reflect local social or ethnic factors rather than political developments. It is thus most likely that Cyprus remained in Egyptian hands until the Persian campaign (under Cambyses) against Egypt in 526 BC.

With the destruction of the Persian empire by Alexander the Great, Cyprus once again came under the control of an Egyptian power, the Macedonian dynasty of the Ptolemies. Contested among the successors of Alexander in the first two decades after his death, Cyprus was in full Ptolemaic control by the end of the fourth century BC and would remain an integral part of that kingdom until the middle of the first century BC. Administered by a high-ranking governor—on occasion a brother of the king—Cyprus served as a staging ground for Ptolemaic military operations in the Aegean as well as a resource for supplying Egypt with wood and other materials.

When the Ptolemaic kingdom fell to the Romans after the Battle of Actium in 31 BC, Egypt and Cyprus were administered separately. Trade between Cyprus and Egypt continued uninterruptedly, however, as the exchange of fine-ware (*terra sigillata*) and transport amphorae demonstrate. The conquest of Egypt by the Arabs, which began in AD 640, marked the end of a millennium of close contact between Cyprus and Graeco-Roman Egypt.

See also

Hyksos; Late and Ptolemaic periods, overview; New Kingdom, overview; Roman period, overview; Tell el-Yahudiya; Third Intermediate Period, overview

Further reading

Åström, P. 1984. Aegyptiaca at Hala Sultan Tekke. *Opuscula Atheniensia* 15: 17–24.

Bagnall, R.S. 1976. *The Administration of the Ptolemaic Possessions outside Egypt*. Leiden.

Clerc, G., V. Karageorghis, E. Lagarce and J. Leclant. 1976. *Fouilles de Kition 2: Objets égyptiens et égyptisants*. Nicosia.

Clerc, G. 1983. Appendix I. Aegyptiaca de Palaepaphos-Skales. In *Palaepaphos-Skales, An Iron Age Cemetery in Cyprus*, V. Karageorghis, ed., 375–95. Ausgrabungen in Alt Paphos auf Cypern 3.

Cline, E. 1994. *Sailing the Wine-Dark Sea: International Trade and the Late Bronze Age Aegean*. Oxford.

Courtois, J.-C. 1990. Aegyptiaca de Kouklia-Palaepaphos. *Report of the Department of Antiquities, Cyprus*: 69–74.

Jacobsson, I. 1994. *Aegyptiaca from Late Bronze Age Cyprus* (Studies in Mediterranean Archaeology 112). Göteborg.

Merrillees, R.S. 1968. *The Cypriot Bronze Age Pottery Found in Egypt*. Studies in Mediterranean Archaeology 18. Göteborg.

——. 1987. *Alashia Revisited* (Cahiers de la Revue biblique 22). Paris.

Peltenberg, E.J. 1986. Ramesside Egypt and Cyprus. In *Acts of the International Archaeological Symposium "Cyprus between the Orient and the Occident," Nicosia, 8–14 September, 1985*, V. Karageorghis, ed., 149–79. Nicosia.

Reyes, A.T. 1994. Cyprus and Egypt. In *Archaic Cyprus. A Study of the Textual and Archaeological Evidence*, 149–79. Nicosia.

MURRAY MCCLELLAN

D

Dahshur, the Bent Pyramid

The site of Dahshur is 26 km south of the Giza pyramids on the west bank of the Nile, about 4.5 km from the river (29°48' N, 31°14' E). Two of the four pyramids of Seneferu, the first king of the 4th Dynasty, are located here. The more southerly of the two has been variously called the Bent, Rhomboidal, Blunt, False or Double-Sloping Pyramid. The other pyramid, 2 km to the north, is known as the Red or Northern Stone Pyramid.

The ancient name of the Bent Pyramid was "The Southern Pyramid Seneferu Gleams." Its base is 183.5 m square, and its original height was 105.07 m (the present height is 101.15 m). This site was visited by Richard Pococke in 1743. In 1750, when Robert Wood, James Dawkins and the Italian artist Giovanni Borra surveyed the pyramid, the northern corridor was blocked up 64.8 m from the entrance. It was cleared by J.S. Perring in 1839, and he also unblocked the upper entrance corridor leading from the western face of the pyramid. In his survey of 1843, Richard Lepsius catalogued it under number LVI. Later investigators, working for the Egyptian Antiquities Service, were Gustave Jéquier in 1924, Abdel Salam Hussein in 1946–9 and Ahmed Fakhry (assisted by Ricke) in 1951–2 and 1955. In 1961, Maragioglio and Rinaldi published a report on the whole complex.

The pyramid is unique among the pyramids of the Old Kingdom. Externally its superstructure has two angles of incline, and internally there are two corbel-vaulted chambers with separate passageways, one from the north face to the lower chamber, and the other from the west face to the upper chamber. No other pyramid has preserved so much of its outer casing.

The first plan was to build a pyramid with a base measurement of 156 m square and a slope of 60°. Cracks developed when the pyramid reached a height of either 34 m (the height of the western entrance) or 49.07 m (the height of the change of angle). The base was subsequently enlarged to 188.6 m square and the slope was reduced to 43°31'13". More cracks appeared, and at a perpendicular height of 49.07 m the slope was further reduced to 43°21'. The instability of the pyramid has been ascribed to its builders having overestimated the carrying properties of the clay foundation. In the lower part of the pyramid they employed the same technique of laying the stones on inwardly inclined beds as had been used in earlier pyramids. The stones in the upper part are smaller and poorer in quality than those in the lower part, and they are laid in flat or nearly flat beds.

The lower corridor, which is about 78.6 m long, 1.06 m wide and 1.1 m high, opens from the northern face of the pyramid at a height of 11.8 m above the level of its base. It has a gradient of 28°22', which diminishes slightly as it descends to an antechamber. The lower chamber, a corbel-roofed room built in a pit hollowed perpendicularly downward through the rock from ground level, measures 6.25 m north–south, 5.0 m east–west, and is 17.3 m high. The reason for the many layers of stone blocks which were laid on the floor of this chamber is obscure, unless perhaps it was thought that they would increase the stability of the building. On floor level, opposite the entrance to the chamber, a passage 3 m long leads to the base of a high and narrow shaft or chimney, the purpose of which is also unknown.

The entrance to the corridor leading to the upper chamber is at a height of 33.22 m above the base of the pyramid and is 13.7 m south of the center of the west face. The downward sloping corridor is about 67.5 m long, 1.05 m wide and 1.09 m high. For the last 20 m it is horizontal. Near each end of the horizontal section there is a limestone portcullis, which slid on its edge obliquely from a cavity in a side wall. After sealing the western portcullis on the inside, the workmen must have left the corridor by a passage hewn through about 18.8 m of core masonry to an opening in the south side of the roof of the lower chamber.

Over the floor of the upper chamber, as in the lower chamber, a layer of stone blocks at least 5 m deep had been superimposed. When this layer was removed in 1946, a framework of thick cedar poles, stretching from wall to wall, was revealed. The purpose of the framework may have been to counter inward pressure on the walls after the discovery of cracks in the stonework.

In addition to the pyramid, remnants of other standard elements of an Old Kingdom pyramid complex have survived. The flat-roofed mortuary temple housed a low alabaster altar, flanked by two round-topped stelae, each with a carved figure of the seated king. Also carved on the stelae were the king's names and titles placed within a frame, which was surmounted by the royal falcon wearing the White Crown of Upper Egypt.

A subsidiary pyramid, which lies 55 m south of the Bent Pyramid, has an entrance corridor with two antithetical gradients of unequal length. The first descends, and after a very short horizontal section with a portcullis, there is a longer ascending one. Four limestone plugs were stored in the inner end of this corridor, but when they were released only the two front blocks slid down into the corridor. On the east side of this pyramid were two stelae. The position of the subsidiary pyramid, due south of the main pyramid, suggests that it fulfilled the same function as the South *Mastaba* (Tomb) in Zoser's Step Pyramid complex.

A causeway 704 m long ran from a temple near the valley to the east corner of the northern stone enclosure wall of the pyramid.

The so-called valley temple, which was discovered in 1951–2, contrasts strongly not only with the mortuary temple of this complex but also with all the other known valley buildings of the Old Kingdom. Perhaps its function has not yet been properly recognized. Two monumental stelae of the same kind as those at the mortuary temple and the subsidiary pyramid were erected outside the front wall of the forecourt, one at each end, facing south. Colossal statues of the king were attached to niches at the back of some—and possibly all—of six shrines in the temple. Painted reliefs must have decorated the walls of many of the rooms of this temple.

See also

Dahshur, the Northern Stone Pyramid; Lepsius, Carl Richard; Meydum; Old Kingdom, overview; Saqqara, pyramids of the 3rd Dynasty; Seila/Silah

Further reading

Fakhry, A. 1959, 1961. *The Monuments of Seneferu at Dahshur* I, II (1 & 2). Cairo.

Maragioglio, V., and C. Rinaldi. 1964. *L'Architettura delle Piramidi Menfite* 3: 54–123. Rapallo.

Porter, B., and R.L.B. Moss, revised by J. Málek. 1974. *Topographical Bibliography of Ancient Egyptian Hieroglyphic Texts, Reliefs and Paintings* 3: *Memphis*, 877–8. Oxford.

I.E.S. EDWARDS

Dahshur, Middle Kingdom pyramids

The cemetery of Dahshur extends for *circa* 3 km north–south on the Western Desert plateau about 40 km south of Cairo and 1 km west of the modern village of Menshiet Dahshur (29°48′ N, 31°14′ E). Up to ten pyramid complexes have been identified at Dahshur, which was one of the favored cemetery sites of the Old and Middle Kingdoms. Besides the Bent Pyramid and the Northern Stone Pyramid of King Seneferu, the necropolis also includes the 12th Dynasty pyramid complexes of Amenemhat II, Senusret III and Amenemhat III. In addition, several small pyramidal structures which probably date to the 13th Dynasty are found in a stretch of the desert plateau at the southern end of the cemetery.

All three of the 12th Dynasty pyramid complexes were excavated in 1894–5 by Jacques de Morgan, who not only succeeded in entering the burial chambers, but was also fortunate to find some of the finest jewelry of the period in tombs of princesses located in the western court of the complex of Amenemhat II (Iti and Khnemt, Itiwert), and north of the pyramid of Senusret III (Sithathor, Mereret). In addition, in the northern court of the pyramid complex of Amenemhat III he found the more or less intact tombs of the 13th Dynasty King Awibre Hor and Princess Nebhotepti-khred.

After de Morgan, no systematic excavations of the Middle Kingdom pyramids were carried out until 1976, when the German Archaeological Institute (DAI) began working at the pyramid complex of Amenemhat III. This fieldwork, which continued until 1983, demonstrated that de Morgan's excavations were far from exhaustive. In 1990 the Metropolitan Museum of Art began excavating at the pyramid complex of Senusret III.

Pyramid complex of Amenemhat II

This pyramid complex was originally surrounded by a mudbrick wall, *circa* 93 × 225 m, which enclosed a court oriented east–west. In the center of its eastern wall was the entrance to a causeway, which led to the valley temple (unexcavated) at the edge of the cultivation. The greater part of the western half of the court was occupied by the pyramid, which has been entirely removed. Like the pyramid of Senusret I, it consisted of a stone core with radial retaining walls and was covered with a casing of Tura limestone.

The corridor leading to the burial chamber opened from the north side of the pyramid.

Two granite slabs (portcullises) built into the horizontal passage at the lower end of the corridor blocked the entrance into the small burial chamber, where a quartzite sarcophagus was found sunk into the floor along the western wall. A narrow shaft in the floor gives access to another chamber beneath the horizontal passage. Its purpose is not known, but it may have been intended for another burial.

The temple on the east side of the pyramid, as well as two buildings of unknown purpose at the eastern end of the court, are completely destroyed.

Pyramid complex of Senusret III

Senusret III did not follow the building traditions of his predecessors earlier in the 12th Dynasty, but adopted a new plan for his pyramid, which shows the strong influence of Zoser's Step Pyramid complex at Saqqara. The most obvious borrowed features are the north–south orientation of the precinct, its paneled enclosure wall with the entrance near the southeast corner, and the position of the pyramid to the north of the center of the complex. The rounded door jambs in the burial apartment also reflect traditions of the 3rd Dynasty, and the sarcophagus is carved with paneled decorations resembling the enclosure wall of the Step Pyramid complex.

The whole complex, which measures 192 × 299 m, is divided into three courts. A narrow court of unknown purpose in the north may be compared to the northern magazine of Zoser's complex. The pyramid was in the central court, with a small mortuary temple on its eastern side and a northern chapel. Nine *mastaba*-like buildings surrounded the pyramid to the south, east and north. The southern court is divided by a mudbrick wall into western and eastern parts. The western part was accessible through a doorway in the southern enclosure wall. A row of shafts are found there but without any evidence of a building. Recent excavations in the larger eastern part did not produce the long expected evidence of a "southern tomb" (as in Zoser's Step Pyramid), but instead revealed the foundations of a temple-like building.

Fragments of its relief decoration, as well as many statue fragments, suggest its use for the cult of the royal statues. A door in the eastern enclosure wall gave access to the southeastern court from the causeway leading up from the valley temple, which has not been located. The pavement of the causeway seems to have continued into the court and through the eastern end of the temple-like building, where it turned north and continued into the mortuary temple.

The pyramid, which originally measured 105 m at the base and was about 60 m high, occupied the greater part of the central court. It consisted of a mudbrick core which was covered by a casing of fine white Tura limestone. On its northern side stood a small northern chapel, although the entrance to the burial chambers was shifted to the western court. Like the northern chapel, the remains of the mortuary temple on the eastern side have been entirely removed. Apart from the foundations, which suggest a building of *circa* 20 m square , only a few fragments of the temple architecture and relief decoration were found. The dimensions of the foundations, however, indicate that the pyramid temple differed considerably from the earlier examples and probably had been reduced to an offering chapel.

The arrangement of the burial apartment followed the traditional plan of the Old Kingdom, with antechamber, *serdab* (statue chamber) and burial chamber. Along the western wall of the burial chamber, with its curved ceiling, is a granite sarcophagus. In the southern wall a niche was provided to hold the canopic chest (for the preserved viscera).

Close to the northeast corner of the pyramid is a shaft which leads to a group of twelve tombs built for female members of the royal family. In two of these tombs de Morgan found some extraordinary pieces of jewelry, now in the Cairo Museum.

Pyramid complex of Amenemhat III

Amenemhat III's pyramid complex at Dahshur was built during the first half of his reign. Yet before the interior rooms were finished, the pyramid was abandoned after a settling process caused considerable damage to the corridors and chambers. Subsequently, Amenemhat III built a new pyramid complex at Hawara, where he was buried.

With its east–west orientation, Amenemhat III's pyramid complex at Dahshur follows the plan of the royal monuments before Senusret III. At the edge of the desert, the remains of a valley temple have been excavated. From there a long causeway led up to the mortuary temple, which is entirely destroyed. South of the causeway the foundations of a palace-like building, which was probably used during the construction of the pyramid, were found. Beyond its northern wall the causeway was flanked by houses of priests.

The pyramid was built of mudbricks and covered by a casing of Tura limestone. It measures 105 m at the base line and was originally 75 m high. Its capstone of black basalt was found in the debris to the east of the pyramid. Apart from the corridors and chambers intended for the burial of the king, the pyramid design also included a similar but smaller arrangement of rooms for the interment of two queens, one of whom was named Aat. Both apartments were connected by a long corridor. A third arrangement of corridors and small chambers or niches seems to have been planned for the king's *ka* burial. The entrance to the royal burial apartments was found near the southern end of the east side of the pyramid. A separate entrance on the west side gave access to the burial chambers of the two queens. Each burial chamber contains a granite sarcophagus. Two of them (belonging to the king and Queen Aat) are elaborately carved with a paneled decoration imitating the enclosure wall of the Step Pyramid complex.

The pyramid was surrounded by two mudbrick enclosures; the inner one was paneled. In the northern outer court, ten shafts were excavated by de Morgan. These were probably intended for members of the royal family, but were not used. Only in the two easternmost shafts did de Morgan find the burials of King Awibre Hor (13th Dynasty) and Princess Nebhotepti-khred.

Pyramids of the 13th Dynasty

Several additional small pyramidal structures are known from the Dahshur region, but most of them have never been excavated. They all seem to have belonged to ephemeral kings of the 13th Dynasty, who probably did not even live long enough to see their funerary complexes finished.

See also

Dahshur, the Bent Pyramid; Dahshur, the Northern Stone Pyramid; Hawara; el-Lisht; Middle Kingdom, overview; Saqqara, pyramids of the 3rd Dynasty; Second Intermediate Period, overview

Further reading

Arnold, D. 1987. Der Pyramidenbezirk des Königs Amenemhet III. In *Dahschur 1: Die Pyramide*. Mainz.

——. 1994. *Lexikon der ägyptischen Baukunst*. Zurich.

Morgan, J. de. 1895. *Fouilles à Dahchour. Mai–juin 1894*. Vienna.

—— 1903. *Fouilles à Dahchour. 1894–1895*. Vienna.

CHRISTIAN HÖLZL

Dahshur, the Northern Stone Pyramid

The Northern Stone Pyramid is one of two pyramids at Dahshur (29°48′ N, 31°14; E) built by Seneferu, the first king of the 4th Dynasty. At its base the pyramid is 220 m square, and its original height was 104 m. Its angle of incline is 43°22′. Like the southern pyramid built by Seneferu at this site (known as the "Bent Pyramid"), the Northern Stone Pyramid (also known as the Red Pyramid) bore the name "Seneferu Gleams," but without the adjective "Southern."

Using a quadrant, Robert Wood, James Dawkins and Giovanni Borra were the first travelers to survey this pyramid, both internally and externally, in November 1750. They were, however, unable to reach the burial chamber because its entrance was high above the floor level of the antechamber, and there was nothing to which they could attach their rope ladder. J.S. Perring, who went to Dahshur in September 1839, was able to survey the whole pyramid, and in 1843 Richard Lepsius gave it the catalog number XLIX. In 1980 the German Institute of Archaeology (DAI) in Cairo, under the direction of Rainer Stadelmann, began the exploration of the whole pyramid complex. Their discoveries include a foundation block at the northwest corner of the pyramid, dated in the year of the 15th census of cattle in Seneferu's reign (perhaps his twenty-ninth year) as the year in which work on the pyramid began. Also found by the Germans were the capstone of the pyramid and pieces of wall reliefs from the mortuary temple.

From the entrance on the north face, 3.8 m east of the center and about 28.55 m above ground level, a corridor, 1.04 m wide and 1.16 m high, slopes down at an angle of about 27°56′ for 62.63 m to ground level, where it becomes horizontal for 7.43 m. Immediately beyond this are two chambers almost in line. Both chambers are 12.31 m high and 3.65 m wide, and have almost the same length (8.37 m, 8.34 m). Each chamber has a corbel roof with eleven overlapping courses on the east and west sides. The burial chamber, oriented with its main axis east–west, is approached through a passage with its entrance in the south wall of the second chamber at a height of 7.8 m above the floor of the chamber. Its length is 8.35 m and its width is 4.18 m. The roof of the burial chamber is corbelled on the north and south sides.

In 1950 incomplete remains of a male skeleton were found in the burial chamber and the possibility that they are the remains of Seneferu cannot be dismissed, if only because discoveries at Meydum show that corpses at this time were buried with the flesh removed. Moreover, this pyramid is likely to have been his tomb because it was almost certainly the last of Seneferu's three pyramids to be built. The first was the Meydum pyramid in its stepped forms, and the second was the Bent Pyramid at Dahshur. Dated blocks from the true pyramid at Meydum record the 13th, 18th and possibly the 23rd censuses of cattle, and blocks in the Dahshur were dated in the time of the 15th census and later. Work was thus progressing concurrently on the final forms of the Meydum pyramid and the Dahshur pyramids, both of which were built with blocks laid in flat courses.

Each of the Dahshur pyramids had its own group of priests, living in separate communities but having a close administrative relationship. In the 5th Dynasty a priest named Duare, whose tomb lay near the Bent Pyramid, held, among other high offices, the position of "Overseer of the Two Pyramids of Seneferu." A stela found in 1905 in the vicinity of this pyramid preserves a decree of Pepi I of the 6th Dynasty dating to the twenty-first year of his reign. This decree grants immunity from certain duties and taxes to the priest of the "Two Pyramids [named] 'Seneferu Gleams'."

See also

Dahshur, the Bent Pyramid; Dahshur, Middle Kingdom pyramids; Lepsius, Carl Richard; Meydum; Middle Kingdom, overview; Old Kingdom, overview

Further reading

Edwards, I.E.S. 1991. *The Pyramids of Egypt*, 89–97. Harmondsworth.

Maragioglio, V., and C. Rinaldi. 1964. *L'Architettura delle Piramidi Menfite* 3: 124–45. Rapallo.

Porter, B., and R.L.B. Moss, revised by J. Málek. 1974. *Topographical Bibliography of Ancient Egyptian Hieroglyphic Texts, Reliefs and Paintings* 3: *Memphis*, 876. Oxford.

Stadelmann, R. 1985. *Die ägyptischen Pyramiden*, 100–6. Mainz.

I.E.S. EDWARDS

Dakhla Oasis, Balat

The village of Balat (25°34' N, 29°16' E), built at the eastern entrance to the Dakhla Oasis, is situated at the junction of two caravan routes. The desert track of Darb el-Tawil coming from Manfalut, to the north of Assyut, connects there with the Darb el-Ghabari. This second track connected Dakhla with Kharga Oasis, leading to the great Darb el-Arbain route, which took the caravans south to Darfur and the Kordofan. The village of Balat has given its name to an archaeological concession of about 700 ha, joining together the urban settlement (40 ha) at Ain Asil, and a cemetery at Qila' el-Dabba, ranging chronologically from the Old Kingdom to the Second Intermediate Period, with a late reoccupation in the Roman Period. The importance of this site is found in the exceptional situation of an Egyptian settlement far from the Nile Valley, and in the fact that this concession offers the unique opportunity to study an urban system of the Old Kingdom *in situ*.

The urban remains of Ain Asil were uncovered during the winter of 1947, as a result of strong sandstorms. The credit for this discovery belongs to Ahmed Fakhry, who immediately was able to draw a correlation between the site and the necropolis 1.5 km away, at Qila' el-Dabba. Some brief archaeological borings, between 1968 and 1970, preceded two excavations in 1971 and 1972. The excavation concession to the site was taken over by the Institut français d'archeologie orientale (IFAO) in Cairo; since 1977, this institution has carried out annual investigations in the oasis.

At Ain Asil, the remains of three phases of the urban settlement have been distinguished, dating between the late 5th/early 6th Dynasties and the First Intermediate Period. Excavation in the southern part of the site revealed the presence of four pottery workshops. Subsequently, the extension of these investigations led to the clearing of an administrative district, perhaps including the governorate of the oasis. The funerary chapels of three governors of the oasis were located. Each has the same basic plan. A wooden porch with two columns leading from a common courtyard formed the entrance. Beyond this, another courtyard led to a *naos* flanked by two oblong rooms. A stela was discovered *in situ* in the central building. It contains a copy of a royal decree of Pepi II, which mentions the establishment of a "dwelling of vital strength" (*ḥwt-k3*), explicitly confirming the purpose of these constructions, which were surrounded by bakeries. To the east of the chapels was a large administrative complex, built around a courtyard with a porch. It contained a batch of clay tablets inscribed in hieratic, along with fragments of a jar, inscribed with the name of Medunefer, Governor of the Oasis in the reign of Pepi II. The *mastaba* (mudbrick tomb) of this dignitary has been located in the necropolis.

At Qilaʿ el-Dabba, the Old Kingdom cemetery includes a field of *mastaba*s surrounded by a large number of smaller secondary burials. The excavation of a sample of these tombs dating to the 6th Dynasty and the First Intermediate Period showed three different types of substructure plans:

1 The simplest burial places are oval subterranean chambers, without any structure. These tombs can be entered by a flight of stairs or a shaft, blocked after the interment.
2 Other burials are in tombs dug into the rock and covered by mudbrick vaults, to which access is provided by a descending staircase.
3 In other places the burial chamber, dug in a trench, takes on the shape of a rectangular room, covered by a Nubian vault topped by rows of arched mudbricks. Access is possible by a descending ramp or a shaft.

In their superstructure, the first two types of tombs sometimes have preserved signs of a small enclosure, back to back with a large mudbrick structure, intended to shelter a funeral stela. The third tomb type, usually having a courtyard with its limits defined by low walls, includes a vaulted chapel built inside a small mudbrick *mastaba*. The deceased, laid out either north–south or west–east in the small burials, may be lying on or wrapped in mats or put in a wooden coffin. In the 6th Dynasty the funeral equipment consisted of alabaster perfume vases, toilet instruments (copper razors and mirrors), tools (adze blades), ornaments and stamp seals. The burials of the First Intermediate Period usually just show a few provisions put in ceramic jars.

Four *mastaba*s for the Governors of the Oasis (*ḥk3 wḥ3t*) were known to Ahmed Fakhry; later work by the IFAO has revealed two more. These funerary establishments, numbered I to V from south to north in the necropolis, date to the 6th Dynasty from the reigns of Pepi I and Pepi II. The sequence of these *mastaba*s is as follows:

Kom (mound) of *Mastaba* I (really two tombs):
a *mastaba* of Decheru
    (prior to the reign of Pepi I?)
b *mastaba* of Ima-Pepi/Ima-Meryre
    (reign of Pepi I)
Mastaba II: *mastaba* of Ima-Pepi II
(reign of Pepi II)
Mastaba III: *mastaba* of Khentika
(reign of Pepi II)
Mastaba IV: *mastaba* of Khentikaupepi
(6th Dynasty)
Mastaba V: *mastaba* of Medunefer
(reign of Pepi II)

In superstructure, these dwellings have a quadrilateral shape, defined by mudbrick precinct walls. This surface area is divided into two open courtyards, next to the mudbrick superstructure. The enclosure gate leads into a forecourt, which is usually used for small secondary burial places. An interior courtyard provided space for rituals with obelisk-stelae, offering basins and funeral stelae. The chapels of the *mastaba* can be recognized by their traditional niched palace façade decoration.

Excavation of four of these *mastaba*s (Ib, II, III and V) revealed important differences in construction. Two distinct architectural programs are attested; the building technique of the substructures varies from a complex with several burial chambers (type I) to a single sepulcher (type II). In the first case (type I, *mastaba*s Ib and III), the substructures were entirely built in the open air by carrying out a vast excavation; at the bottom, retaining walls were built to create the structure. The burial

Figure 21 Qila' el-Dabba, Balat, Dakhla Oasis: *mastaba* tomb of Ima-Pepi I, courtyard

chamber and access to it were built inside the space confined by this protective wall. Once these foundation works were completed, earth mounds covered these substructures. From then on, access was only through the burial shafts. The second building technique (type II, *mastabas* II and V) used a more economical method requiring less displacement of the soil. One or even two rectangular shafts were dug in the clay soil. These shafts were linked to each other by tunnels at their lowest level. The tomb chamber, with one antechamber and two storerooms, was then built in stone and mudbrick within these galleries.

The dimensions and fittings of Old Kingdom *mastabas* generally diminish between the reigns of Pepi I and Pepi II. Such is the case at Balat as well, notably in comparing the tombs of Ima-Pepi I (Pepi I) and Medunefer (Pepi II). The absence of a *serdab* (statue chamber) in the Balat tombs follows the practice of Old Kingdom private tombs after the second half of the

6th Dynasty. Furthermore, the evidence of an onomastic alternation between Ima-Pepi and Ima-Meryre points to a contemporary of Pepi I as the owner of *mastaba* Ib. The mention of the first jubilee (*heb-sed*) of Neferkare (one of the names of Pepi II) on an alabaster vase from Medunefer's tomb places *mastaba* V in the reign of Pepi II. A limestone group statue of Ima-Pepi I and his wife Lady Isut was deposited in the burial chamber of their tomb. Also notable is the *in situ* discovery of one of the oldest renderings of the *Coffin Texts* (aside from Gardiner's Papyrus IV) appearing on the coffin of Governor Medunefer, a contemporary of Pepi II. One should also mention the polychrome funeral scenes, painted on the walls of Khentika's burial chamber (*Mastaba* III), and the variety of the stone vessels from Ima-Pepi II's *mastaba* (*Mastaba* II).

Overall, the above data indicate that Balat was an important Old Kingdom administrative site. This evidence makes it possible to estimate the intensity of the exchange between the

Figure 22 Qila' el-Dabba, Balat, Dakhla Oasis: *mastaba* tomb of Ima-Pepi I, substructures

central government in Memphis and a remote administrative district such as Dakhla. It is evident not only that such a situation survived the hazards of the First Intermediate Period, but that Balat existed as the center of an administrative district through the Middle Kingdom and into the Second Intermediate Period. Evidence of this has been found in the excavations undertaken in the southern part of the necropolis, with the discovery of a decorated tomb inscribed from the period of the Intef nomarchs of Thebes.

See also

Memphite private tombs of the Old Kingdom; Old Kingdom provincial tombs

Further reading

Minault-Gout, A., and P. Deleuze. 1992. *Balat*

II. Le mastaba d'Ima-Pépi (Fouilles de l'IFAO 32). Cairo.

Pantalacci, L. 1985. Un décret de Pépi II en faveur des gouverneurs de l'oasis de Dakhla. *BIFAO* 85: 245–54.

——. 1989. Les chapelles des gouverneurs de l'oasis et leurs dépendances. *BSFE* 114: 64–82.

Soukiassian, G., M. Wuttmann and D. Schaad. 1990. La ville d'Ayn Asil à Dakhla: État des recherches. *BIFAO* 90: 347–58.

Valloggia, M. 1986. *Balat I. Le mastaba de Medou-Nefer* (Fouilles de l'IFAO 31, 1–2). Cairo.

——. 1998. Balat IV. *Le monument funéraire d' Ima-Pepy/Ima-Meryrê* (Fouilles de l'IFAO 38, 1–2). Cairo

MICHEL VALLOGGIA

Dakhla Oasis, Dynastic and Roman sites

The Dakhla Oasis is the largest of Egypt's great western oases. The present Oasis basin, some 75 km east–west and a maximum of 25 km north–south, has been continuously inhabited throughout the historical period. The area lies some 600 km southwest of Cairo and is centered on 25°30′ N and 29°00′ E. The Oasis floor is a rich clay plain, lacustrine in origin, interrupted in places by outcrops of the Nubia sandstone formation. Abrupt northern and eastern boundaries are formed by a Cretaceous limestone escarpment, up to 500 m high. As of 1992, there was an expanding population of 70,000 living in small communities. The capital, Mut, is centrally situated at the southernmost point of the Oasis. The economic foundation of the Dakhla Oasis community is in agriculture; there are no mineral or other resources. The climate is hyperarid and all agricultural and domestic water needs are supplied by artesian pressure from subterranean aquefers through springs and wells.

The Dakhla Oasis first came into modern European knowledge with the arrival of the British explorer Sir Archibald Edmondstone in 1819. The first extensive description of the archaeological remains in Dakhla was made by H.E. Winlock of New York's Metropolitan Museum of Art, from a journey made there in 1908, when he noted and recorded the standing ruins of the Oasis. Little further notice was taken of the region until the late 1960s, when Dr Ahmed Fakhry discovered the large Old Kingdom town and *mastaba* tombs in the vicinity of Balat. Since 1977, the Institut français d'archéologie orientale has been engaged in the major excavations of the Balat complex. Since 1978, the Dakhleh Oasis Project has been making a regional study of the entire Oasis as a microcosm of eastern Saharan cultural and environmental evolution since the mid-Pleistocene.

The earliest indications of ancient Egyptians having been in contact with the Dakhla Oasis region are a few finds of Early Dynastic period ceramics, some in isolation, some from Sheikh Muftah sites. The occurrences do not, however, really indicate more than just a casual or occasional contact. It is not until late in the Old Kingdom that there is evidence of major activity by the pharaonic Egyptians in the Oasis.

At the Oasis entry point of the direct route from the Nile, in the vicinity of present-day Balat, there is a large settlement site, Ain Asil, which dates to the late Old Kingdom and the First Intermediate Period. Also in the vicinity are extensive burial grounds which include five substantial *mastaba* tombs of the Egyptian governors of the oasis during the reigns of Pepi II and his immediate predecessors.

The Ain Asil town was not, however, the only settlement of the period in the Dakhla Oasis. There are archaeological traces and eroded remains of some twenty other Old Kingdom sites scattered across the Oasis. There is a concentration of these sites in western Dakhla, in the vicinity of el-Qasr. Several cemeteries attest to the strength of the Egyptian cultural content of the settlements, while habitation sites, albeit terribly eroded, show the settled and essentially domestic nature of the occupation. One of the settlements in western Dakhla is nearly as extensive in area as Ain Asil, although not so well preserved. It is important because it interfingers with a site of the Sheikh Muftah culture and is indicative of the relationship between the indigenous Dakhlans and the migrant pharaonic Egyptians. Apparently, this was a peaceful relationship with evidence for trade in lithic tools and ceramics. That there was close and frequent contact with the Nile Valley can be seen in a variety of small objects that were imported from the Nile Valley, but might best be exemplified by the ceramics of the period in the Oasis. The shapes and manufacturing technology allow them to be precisely placed with the range of ceramics from the Nile Valley sites, while clay analysis shows that all were locally manufactured in the Dakhla Oasis. This is supported by the discovery of a number of sites where pottery kilns are present.

The evidence is not strong for the remaining two millennia of pharaonic history in the

Dakhla Oasis, although it does seem that there was always some Egyptian population there. There are a number of small sites, variously dated, that give support to this; but the best information comes from sites at 'Ein Tirghi, a cemetery with dated material from the Second Intermediate Period onward, and from the cemeteries at Ain Asil, which seem to include material from the Old Kingdom down into the 18th Dynasty. Mut el-Kharab is a large temple enclosure, apparently a cult center of Seth, where potsherds from virtually all major periods, from the Old Kingdom down to the Byzantine, have been recovered from surface inspection. The site at Mut is merely the religious center of what must have been the most extensive town in the ancient Oasis, but which has been lost under the modern settlement. Inscriptional evidence from stelae gives datings of the 22nd and 25th Dynasties. Although the extensive ruins on the surface are primarily Roman in date, Egyptian Antiquities Organization excavations have recently uncovered massive walls of an earlier period.

The evidence from the Oasis is vital to our understanding of its function within the Egyptian sphere. Apart from very occasional references to administration of the oases, there is virtually no information from the Nile Valley. From the Oasis itself there are stelae from the temple at Mut, and also administrative documents from Ain Asil that show that the community was officially seen as part of "Egypt." Certainly, there was always an Egyptian population in the Oasis, but perhaps it was an area of banishment, or served some other similar kind of function for the rulers in the Nile Valley.

It is only from the decades just before the birth of Christ that the Dakhla Oasis becomes fully occupied. From the first five centuries AD there are almost 250 sites: isolated farmsteads, three large towns, major irrigation works, industrial sites, over twenty temples, cemeteries and all the range of settlement that one might expect to see in a self-sufficient agricultural community. With the increase in economic importance of Egypt within the Roman world, Dakhla must have been seen as a potentially rich source of produce and migration of farmers was encouraged. It seems that finally whatever available farmland was present was actually utilized and the Dakhla population produced more than its subsistence requirements.

Texts, recovered in the excavations at Kellis, together with organic finds in the debris of farmhouses and houses, as well as remnants on the surface in various places across the Oasis, give us a clear picture of the agriculture of the period. Cereals were a major crop, of course, but there was also oil and wine production, and a variety of vegetables and herbs, fruits, including figs, dates, peaches and pomegranates, and honey all were being produced. Domestic animals included pigeons, chickens, pigs, goats, sheep, cattle, donkeys, camels and dogs. In the region of Deir el-Haggar there are massive aqueducts leading northwards out of spring mounds toward field system which closely resemble those still in use in the Oasis. A scene in the tomb of Pady-Osiris at el-Muzzawaka shows some of the products of the Oasis, including dates, barley, grapes, olives, dom-palm nuts and flowers. Housing for migrant farmers was constructed to a set pattern: two vaulted rooms at ground level and a pigeon loft above, all enclosed within a surrounding wall. These "colombarium" farmhouses occur singly and in villages of up to half a dozen. There are three large towns of the period in the Oasis: Trimithis, now called Amheida, Mouthis, the capital, now called Mut, and Kellis, now called Ismant el-Kharab.

Two main types of temple were built during the Graeco-Roman period in the Oasis. The first is of mudbrick construction and consists of three or four axially placed rooms, and is generally only about 25 m in length. Entered through a pylon at the east end, the rooms are successively smaller, ending in the sanctuary, where there is a brick altar. None of these temples preserves any decoration intact, although one, which has been badly ruined, bears a considerable number of fragments of painted plaster in the debris. The second type of temple, of which there are at least seven, is built of local sandstone and generally bears carved decoration. Again, these temples are not large, being less than 30 m long. Arranged axially, they have a more complicated architectural plan, with side chambers, stairways to roof areas, *temenos* enclosure walls and the usual pharaonic temple appearance. Decoration is carved relief, which was originally painted in the normal fashion. The attribution of some of these temples is more secure than others. That at Deir el-Haggar is dedicated to the Theban deities, Amen, Khonsu and Mut, and was built during the second half of the first century AD. There is a temple dedicated to Thoth of Hermopolis at Trimithis. The major shrine of Seth at Mouthis was probably built on the site of an earlier, pharaonic temple. At Kellis the main temple is dedicated principally to Tutu and there is a smaller shrine dedicated to Neith and Tapsais. The easternmost one is at 'Ein Birbiyeh, where the building decoration can be dated to the reigns of Augustus and Hadrian, and the dedication is to Amen-Nakht and his consort, Hathor.

The decline of this high point in the Dakhla Oasis coincides with a natural phenomenon and historical trends in the Roman world. Several sites across the Oasis were apparently abandoned as the result of the incursion of heavy sanding conditions, which may in turn have been the result of environmental change elsewhere. Both the temples at Deir el-Haggar and 'Ein Birbiyeh were filled with sand before any deliberate damage was done to them; in other words, while they were probably still functioning as temples. Ismant el-Kharab, a large town, is full of domestic buildings which were abandoned as the result of their filling up with wind-blown sand. The sand of the Western Desert is inexorable and, where present, will fill wells and cover fields, removing at a stroke the livelihood of the inhabitants. The date for this geological event was probably early in the fifth century AD. Also at the beginning of the fifth century, the Roman Empire was splitting into its eastern and western parts and one consequence of this was a weakening of the solidarity of that great economic unit. Some of the population moved back to the Nile Valley, where they had always maintained strong ties;

others remained and eked a subsistence living out of the harsh climate as best they were able. It took several centuries to rebuild the Oasis economy to the strength it had during the first four centuries AD.

See also

Kharga Oasis, Late period and Graeco-Roman sites

Further reading

Giddy, L.L. 1987. *Egyptian Oases*. Warminister.
Mills, A.J. 1985. The Dakhleh Oasis Project. In *Mélanges Gamal Eddin Mokhtar* (BdÉ 97/2): 125–34. Cairo.
Osing, J., *et al.* 1982. *Denkmäler der Oase Dachla aus dem Nachlass von Ahmed Fakhry*. Mainz.
Wagner, G. 1987. *Les Oasis d'Égypte*. Cairo.

ANTHONY J. MILLS

Dakhla Oasis, Ismant el-Kharab

The Romano-Byzantine town site of Ismant el-Kharab (Ismant "the Ruined," or "Kellis" in Greek) in the Dakhla Oasis lies 2.5 km east of the modern village of Ismant (25°32' N, 29°04' E). The well-preserved mudbrick ruins drew the site to the attention of early travelers in the nineteenth century and archaeologists in the twentieth century. None left more than short descriptions of certain structures, although Herbert Winlock, who visited the site in 1908, took valuable photographs of painted reliefs that are now destroyed.

In 1981 the study of the site by the Dakhleh Oasis Project commenced. A detailed plan of the surface remains has been prepared and excavations began in 1986. The site appears to have been occupied only during the first–fourth centuries AD.

The ancient town is built upon a natural terrace of Nubian clay, which stands 4–6 m

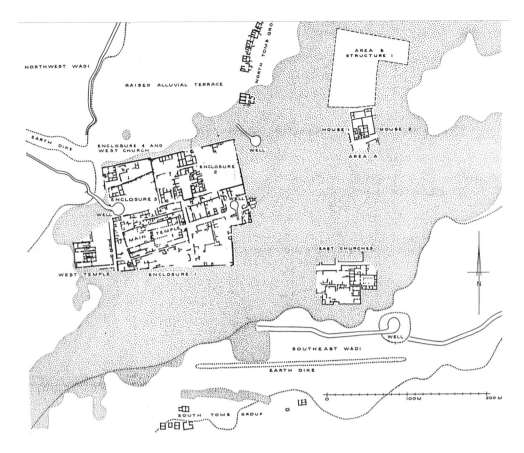

Figure 23 Plan of excavated remains at Ismant el-Kharab, Dakhla Oasis

above the floors of two wadis on its northwest and southeast, and covers an area approximately 1050 × 650 m. The area is clearly defined by the remains of mudbrick buildings and a cover of artifacts, especially potsherds. A dense scatter of chert containing some tools of the Middle Paleolithic surrounds the site, but there is no evidence of occupation during that period.

The earliest structure is the Main Temple, situated within a large enclosure in the western part of the site. A processional route leads through the enclosure to the temple *temenos*, which is entered through two undecorated stone gateways on its east, and then along a mudbrick colonnade to a portico and the temple itself. This small sandstone structure, which is poorly preserved, was dedicated to the protective deity

Tutu (in Greek, Tithoes), son of the goddess Neith. It is the only surviving temple dedicated to this god. A double doorway, originally decorated with offering scenes, gives access to a small courtyard and to the temple, which comprises three rooms and a two-roomed contra-temple at the rear. A painted and gilded cult relief representing Tutu and a goddess was the focal point of either the main sanctuary or the contra-temple. The temple may have been begun during the first century AD, as an inscription of the Roman emperor Nero (AD 54–138) has been found there, as have fragments of demotic papyri, possibly also of that period. It appears to have been extended and decorated from the reigns of Hadrian (AD 117–38) to Pertinax (AD 193). Vestiges of temple furnishings include fragments of small and large anthropomorphic sculptures in stone and plaster, some of which attest to figures of Isis and Serapis, stone altars and pieces from elaborately decorated, gilded and painted wooden shrines.

Within the *temenos* are also four mudbrick shrines; two of these flank the temple and two flank the main east gate. The two-roomed shrine to the south of the Main Temple, Shrine I, is larger than the temple and originally stood to 5 m in height. In its inner room elaborate painted reliefs are preserved on the walls and on the remains of the barrel-vaulted roof; these provide evidence of its use as a *mammisi* (house of births). A classical dado of alternately colored panels, with floral sprays and birds at the center, was topped by four registers in pharaonic style depicting priests and gods in procession before Tutu, who is accompanied by the goddesses Neith and Tapshay. The latter is described as "Mistress of the City." These two goddesses were also worshipped in a small sandstone temple located at the extreme west of the site, set within its own enclosure, which is probably to be ascribed the same date as the Main Temple. Access to this temple, the West Temple, from the Main Temple, was gained via a stone gateway in the rear of the *temenos* wall. In addition to the classical paintings in Shrine I, there are others on the walls of the court to the east of the Main Temple and in each of the other three mudbrick structures. One room of the structure on the south of the gateway has three layers of plaster; the latest one preserves an elaborate painted coffer motif with birds and fruit, and the earliest has black ink graffiti representing Tutu, Seth, Bes and a winged vulture.

The temple of Tutu appears to have continued in use throughout the life of the city, with additions and modifications to its plan. The portico, with its baked-brick columns fronted by sandstone plinths, two bearing dedicatory inscriptions in Greek, was probably added in the third century AD. Three large enclosures were added to the north of the temple enclosure, possibly containing administrative buildings and storage facilities, though at what date is unknown. In the most northerly are the

remains of a small church adjacent to the remains of two monumental, classical-style tombs. The architecture of the latter is unique within Egypt and is paralleled only by monuments in Libya; they resemble buildings depicted on first century BC coins from North Africa and second century AD Roman coins from Alexandria. One of the tombs contained the remains of eleven burials with grave goods consisting of pottery, glass, a basket and a bed, and numerous floral bouquets. Five gold rings were also found. The burials may be ascribed to the third century AD, although the tombs themselves are earlier. The small church and a seven-roomed building immediately to its south date to the fourth century AD.

Three large building complexes on a north–south alignment are the main feature of the northern part of the site, Area B. The south complex contains 216 rooms, courts and corridors, some preserved to second floor level. Several of the rooms preserve traces of polychrome wall paintings in classical style. Excavation has revealed part of a large peristyle court against the south wall of this structure, which stood some 5 m in height. Its columns of baked brick were plastered and painted and the lower 2 m of the walls received classical painted decoration of panel motifs separated by pilasters. The ceiling was originally decorated with a variety of coffer designs which incorporated figurative motifs. Jar sealing dockets inscribed in Greek from the fill in the foundations of the room indicate a date for its construction at the latest in the second century AD. There is evidence of four major phases of use. Constructed as a formal hall within what was probably the center of administration, it was eventually used for domestic purposes, including the stabling of animals, during the fourth century AD.

Immediately to the north is an agglutinative series of buildings, which may have been for domestic use, and to their north is a complex of a more formal nature. Here the buildings are of differing size and complexity. One comprises a court surrounded by ten rooms which are lime-plastered and several bear polychrome geometric and floral motifs. There are also three buildings with pigeon lofts.

To the west of Area B is a line of mausolea which face east. They consist of an entrance chamber leading to one or more inner rooms, all of which were vaulted. Several also have porticos. The two on the south are the largest and most elaborate, with three inner chambers (the central one is stone lined) and white-plastered exteriors ornamented with pilasters and niches. The central rear chamber of the southernmost mausoleum once bore painted funerary scenes, which were photographed by Winlock but are now destroyed. This monument was cleared by Bernard Moritz in 1900. A similar group of mausolea lies to the south of the site. Both groups appear to have been family vaults. Approximately 0.5 km to the northwest of the site are a series of low hills which contain an extensive cemetery. These have yielded multiple burials in single-chamber tombs, a few of which have painted and gilded carton-nage mummy cases; grave goods are rare. These burials date to the first–second centuries AD. On the southeast of the site there is another cemetery with single burials in pit graves, some with mudbrick superstructures. They are oriented east–west; grave goods are largely absent. This cemetery seems to have been in use during the third–fourth centuries AD.

The east and central parts of the site are residential sectors. Ceramics on the surface of the former, Area C, indicate that it may have been occupied from the second century AD onward. The survey of the latter, Area A, shows it to contain single-story houses with courtyards built in blocks, many of which are preserved to roof level. These blocks are separated by open areas and lanes, at least one of which was roofed with a barrel vault. One group of three houses within this sector, located immediately to the south of Area B, has been excavated. They contain barrel-vaulted, rectangular rooms and larger square rooms, which were either open or had flat roofs. Niches, open shelves and cupboards, some originally closed by wooden doors, are set in the walls and some rooms had a palm-rib shelf. Most of the wooden doors, door frames and roof beams were removed when the site was abandoned, but large quantities of artifacts were left behind. These include fragments of household furniture, utensils (mostly pottery), clothing, jewelry, coins and, most significantly, documents in Coptic, Greek and occasionally Syriac, written on wooden boards, papyrus and, rarely, parchment. Four intact wooden codices have been found and in one house alone approximately 3,000 fragments of inscribed papyrus were discovered. Much of this was at floor level and clearly represents part of a family archive.

Among this material are private letters, and economic and literary texts. Kellis emerges as the center of a regional economy which was agriculturally based. It traded with nearby villages and towns elsewhere in the oasis and had contacts with those in Kharga Oasis and several in the Nile Valley. While there are references among the texts to what may be orthodox Christianity, references to one of its main rivals, Manichaeism, occur more frequently. A unique bilingual board inscribed in Coptic and Syriac documents the efforts made by the Manichaean proselytizers to translate their sacred literature into the vernacular. Dated contracts written in Greek cover the period AD 304–81; the coins and ceramics confirm a fourth century AD occupation of these houses. A fourth house with similar architectural features and of similar date has been partly excavated due east of the entrance to the Main Temple enclosure.

In the south of Area A there is a wide east–west street which runs from the southeast corner of the Main Temple enclosure on the west, past the remains of a bath house (with a central heating system), and ends at a complex of two churches with associated buildings. These, the East Churches, are located on the northeast edge of the site. The larger of the two is a two-aisled basilica with a painted cupola in the apse and four chambers along its south wall; it is preserved to a maximum height of 3.8 m. The smaller one has a single chamber with an elaborately decorated apse. The coins and ceramics excavated in the large church date to the early to late fourth century AD. It is, therefore, one of the earliest surviving purposely built churches in Egypt.

Available evidence all points to an abandonment of the site at the end of the fourth century AD. The reasons for this are uncertain. Possible contributing factors may have been overexploitation of the local water supply and an increase in sand dune activity in this part of the Oasis. All structures examined reveal a fill predominantly of windblown sand with pockets of building collapse and no trace of subsequent occupation in antiquity.

See also

Dakhla Oasis, Dynastic and Roman sites

Further reading

Hope, C.A. 1985. Dakhleh Oasis Project: report on the 1986 excavations at Ismant el-Gharab. *JSSEA* 15: 114–25.

——. 1986. Dakhleh Oasis Project: report on the 1987 excavations at Ismant el-Gharab. *JSSEA* 16: 74–91.

——. 1987. Dakhleh Oasis Project: Ismant el-Kharab 1988–1990. *JSSEA* 17: 157–76.

——. 1988. Three seasons of excavations at Ismant el-Gharab in Dakhleh Oasis, Egypt. *JMA* 1: 160–78.

Hope, C.A., O.E. Kaper, G.E. Bowen and S.F. Patten. 1989. Dakhleh Oasis Project: Ismant el-Kharab 1991–2. *JSSEA* 19: 1–26.

Mills, A.J. 1982. Dakhleh Oasis Project: report on the fourth season of survey. October 1981–January 1982. *JSSEA* 12: 93–101.

Winlock, H.E. 1934. *Ed Dakhleh Oasis. Journal of a Camel Trip Made in 1908.* New York.

Worp, K.A. 1995. *Greek Papyri from Kellis* 1. Oxford.

COLIN A. HOPE

Dakhla Oasis, prehistoric sites

Dakhla Oasis (centered on 25°30′ N, 29°00′ E) is located in the Egyptian Western Desert, halfway between the Nile Valley and the Libyan border, at roughly the latitude of Luxor. The largest of several Western Desert oases, Dakhla is a depression 70 km long (east–west) by 20 km wide. The oasis, bounded on the north by a 300 m high plateau, is divisible into three zones north to south. The piedmont zone slopes southward from the base of the plateau to the central lowland, which is marked by a discontinuous belt of cultivation fed by artesian wells (the only water available today in this hyperarid area). South again, the third zone, with fossil spring terraces and spring mounds, old playas (ancient lakes) and sandstone ridging, slopes upward to the desert plain beyond.

Aside from the mention of a few stone tools in a 1936 publication by H.E. Winlock, the study of Dakhla prehistory began only in the 1970s. In 1972 members of the Combined Prehistoric Expedition (CPE), led by Fred Wendorf of Southern Methodist University and Polish archaeologist Romuald Schild, visited Dakhla as part of an archaeological reconnaissance of the southern half of the Western Desert. While in Dakhla they excavated two Pleistocene spring vents in the eastern lowlands. Then in 1978, the Dakhleh Oasis Project (DOP), with Canadian archaeologist A.J. Mills as field director, began its investigation of human adaptations to changing environmental conditions within the oasis throughout prehistoric and historic times. The DOP divides the prehistoric sequence into Pleistocene and Holocene portions, with M.R. Kleindienst responsible for the former, and M.M.A. McDonald for the latter portion.

Dakhla Pleistocene prehistory begins with the appearance of the first hominids in the area over a quarter of a million years ago and persists until the end of the last Ice Age, about 10,000 BC. Holocene prehistory runs from that date to about 2200 BC, when immigrants from the Nile Valley brought elements of late Old Kingdom civilization to Dakhla.

A problem shared by Pleistocene and Holocene prehistorians in Dakhla and elsewhere in the Western Desert is that sites are usually severely deflated. In these arid areas, the wind over time removes all but the most consolidated of deposits, plus most organic material including food remains and datable remains such as charcoal. Often all that remains are surface scatters of stone tools and occasional hearth stones.

The problem is particularly severe at sites of Pleistocene age, where the sometimes extensive scatters can be redistributed or mixed with later material. Accordingly, the focus in Dakhla, with some exceptions, has been less on finding localized "sites" than on mapping the distribution of artifacts across the landscape, relating this to geomorphic units, changing paleoclimates and potential resources. The Pleistocene geomorphological sequence, defined by DOP geographer I.A. Brookes, includes erosional episodes which left three gravel-bearing pediment remnants in the piedmont zone, labeled, from oldest to youngest, P-I, P-II and P-III. A sequence of lacustrine laminated sediments falls between P-II and P-III in time, while several episodes of artesian spring activity, within and just south of the central lowlands, have left behind extensive sheets of water-deposited sediments, as well as spring mounds or vents at points where the water surfaced. Kleindienst has been running a series of archaeological survey transects north–south across these geomorphic regions and into the desert beyond, sampling lithic artifact distributions on each, in order to determine human land-use patterns and changes in those patterns through the Pleistocene. In the absence of chronometric dates, artifacts are dated from their association with units of the geomorphic sequence, and through comparisons with archaeological sequences elsewhere in this part of Africa, notably that worked out by Gertrude Caton Thompson for nearby Kharga Oasis.

So far, several Pleistocene cultural units have been identified from analysis of the stone tools. They can be classified as either Early Stone Age (ESA), traditionally characterized by the Acheulian handax or biface, or Middle Stone Age (MSA), with its Levallois or specialized core preparation technique. The earliest materials identified so far in Dakhla are a few distinctive handaxes found on P-II gravel surfaces and the flanks of a spring mound. The handaxes are large, usually of quartzite rather than flint, and worked around their entire circumference. Typologically they are "Upper Acheulian," and might be 400,000 years old.

The next well-defined unit, called the "Balat," also features bifacial tools, but of a very different kind. Mostly of chert, they are small (less than 160 mm long, mean *circa* 100 mm), with thick unworked butts and trimming confined to the tip and one or both side edges. There is little evidence for the use of the Levallois technique or core preparation. It is Balat unit material that the CPE excavated in 1972, recovering hundreds of bifaces and other tools at two spring mounds. While Balat unit artifacts are commonly found on pediment surfaces and elsewhere in the oasis, the only other *in situ* finds are from river gravels of probable P-II age. The Balat, on analogy with East African material, might be very late Early Stone Age or, more likely, a transitional ESA/ MSA industry, and appears to be well over 100,000 years old.

For the Middle Stone Age, several units have been defined, distinguishable in part by the size of artifacts and by site locations within the oasis. Present as well are two specialized groupings of stone tools, the "Aterian" or "Dakhla unit," and the "Khargan." As before, the evidence is largely from surface scatters, but now specialized sites/workshops, living sites and lookout points can sometimes be detected. A "large-size" MSA unit, featuring specialized cores averaging 90 mm in length, and long, lanceolate bifacial tools is, on analogy with the Khargan sequence, early MSA. A probably younger "medium-size" MSA unit (mean artifact sizes 70–75 mm) is, like the large-size unit, found mostly on P-II and other northern gravel surfaces.

The Aterian is a distinctive North African stone tool industry featuring tanged implements of various kinds as well as bifacial lanceolates and specialized cores. In Dakhla, the Aterian or Dakhla unit is divisible into at least two variants, based in part on artifact size. The larger variant, featuring implements up to 150 mm long, has been found on the piedmont, associated with post P-II sediments and P-III gravels, and on an occupation site in the desert well south of the oasis. Similar material occurs at Adrar Bous, 2,100 km to the west in the central Sahara. The smaller variant, with flakes ranging to 110 mm, occurs as knapping sites on P-II gravels and as scatters in central and southern Dakhla Oasis. It resembles the Aterian of Kharga Oasis, and may be less than 50,000 years old. A still smaller MSA unit, found in Dakhla on younger surfaces and spring deposits, and perhaps the equivalent of Caton Thompson's "Khargan," has yielded a date of 23,000 BP (years before present) at Dungul Oasis in southern Egypt.

One intriguing finding at Dakhla Oasis is the still somewhat fragmentary evidence for continued occupation of the oasis throughout the late Pleistocene; studies elsewhere in the area have suggested abandonment of the desert in the hyperarid period 50,000–12,000 BP.

The last three prehistoric cultural units identified in Dakhla Oasis are of Holocene age. These sites are also severely deflated but, due to late prehistoric cultural innovations, more categories of evidence are now available, including grinding equipment, small finds of stone and shell, stone shelters, pottery and rock art. Also, fragmentary *in situ* deposits yield such organic material as bone, plant remains and charcoal for radiocarbon dating. Moreover, the climate can be reconstructed with some accuracy: generally, the Sahara was more humid than it is today through the Holocene, until about 3000 BC.

The three Holocene prehistoric cultural units in Dakhla are the "Masara," dated 7200–6500 BC, the "Bashendi," 5700–3250 BC and the "Sheikh Muftah," which begins during the Bashendi and survives to overlap with the Old Kingdom occupation in the oasis.

"Masara" is the local name for a cultural unit elsewhere called the "Epi-paleolithic." Epi-paleolithic sites, scattered from the Nile Valley westward across the Sahara, tend to be little more than sparse clusters of lithics, the products of small, highly mobile groups of hunter-gatherers. Similar small sites are found in Dakhla as well, where they are labeled "Masara A." In Dakhla, however, the picture is complicated by the presence of contemporaneous sites

of another kind. "Masara C" sites, in addition to lithic artifacts, feature clusters of stone rings, anywhere from 2–20 per site. These stone rings, 3–4 m in diameter, oval or bi-lobed, are interpreted as bases of hut structures. They suggest somewhat more settled groups than at other Epi-paleolithic sites, an impression reinforced by the evidence for a wide variety of activities performed at these sites, from storage to bead making, and by their reliance on inferior but locally abundant lithic raw material. While Masara A sites are found across the oasis and even atop the northern plateau, Masara C sites are confined to one well-watered spot on the sandstone ridging in the southeastern corner of the oasis, an area that was also heavily settled by later Bashendi groups. The Dakhla Masara C sites seem unique within the eastern Sahara for that time: it is another 500 years before the next group of relatively settled sites appears, at Nabta Playa in southern Egypt.

The next Dakhla cultural unit, the Bashendi, is divisible into two phases, A and B, on the basis of site location, artifact inventories, subsistence and age. While Bashendi sites occur throughout the oasis, the fullest record comes from the large basin and ridges in the southeastern corner of Dakhla in the vicinity of the Masara C sites. Bashendi phase A sites consist of extensive scatters of hearths and artifacts eroding out of playa silts in the basin floor. Artifacts include fine bifacial knives, a variety of arrowheads (including hollow-based, leaf-shaped and tanged forms), grinding stones, abundant ostrich eggshell beads, lip-plugs of barite and rare pottery. While the assumption was that these were the campsites of pastoral nomads, in fact, all animal bones identified so far are of wild species. Radiocarbon dates are from 5700 to 5000 BC.

One anomalous kind of site dates to the very end of the Bashendi A sequence. A group of stone ring sites, one consisting of 200 structures, occurs on the ridge adjacent to the large basin. In addition to hunting, people on these sites seem to have herded goats. Phase B campsites are found on the basin edge, above silt level. Characteristic artifacts include, besides knives and arrowheads, (side-blow) flakes, planes, small polished axes, amazonite beads, and marine shell pendants and bracelets. Faunal remains, mostly of cattle and goat, suggest a heavy reliance on domesticated animals. Phase B spans a millennium, starting at 4550 BC.

Many of the characteristic artifacts of both phases A and B, including knives, arrowheads and many of the small finds, are shared with Neolithic and Predynastic sites in the Nile Valley, from Khartoum to the Delta, and also with Neolithic sites far to the west across the Sahara. Interestingly, though, the Dakhla occurrences are older than dated examples from either of the other two regions.

Sites of the third Holocene unit, the Sheikh Muftah, are located much closer to the oasis central lowlands, where they are often obscured by later cultural material. There is still no evidence of permanent settlement, although pottery is abundant and copper was used. The unit survived to overlap with the Old Kingdom presence in the oasis after 2200 BC.

The picture emerging from the study of Dakhla prehistory is not so much that of an oasis isolated within a vast desert, as one with at least occasional far-flung contacts: with neighboring oases and the Nile Valley, with sites westward across the Sahara and with sub-Saharan Africa. Apparently large enough to support life even during a hyperarid period when the rest of the eastern Sahara was deserted, Dakhla Oasis seems to have served sometimes as a node on communication lines crossing the desert, sometimes as a meeting point for desert-adapted cultural traditions, and occasionally, as in mid-Holocene times, as a center for cultural innovation. In this last role, as cultural innovator, the Dakhla Bashendi unit, through its contact with the Nile Valley, appears to have contributed to the early stages of the development of Egyptian Neolithic and Predynastic cultures.

See also

Caton Thompson, Gertrude; climatic history; Kharga Oasis, prehistoric sites; Neolithic cul-tures, overview; Paleolithic cultures, overview; Paleolithic tools

Further reading

Brookes, I.A. 1989. Early Holocene basinal sediments of the Dakhleh Oasis region, South Central Egypt. *Quaternary Research* 32: 139–52.

Kleindienst, M.R. In press. Pleistocene archaeology and geoarchaeology of the Dakhleh Oasis status report. In *Reports from the Survey of Dakhleh Oasis, Western Desert of Egypt, 1977–1987* 1, C.S. Churcher and A.J. Mills, eds. Oxford.

McDonald, M.M.A. 1991a. Origins of the Neolithic in the Nile Valley as seen from Dakhleh Oasis in the Egyptian Western Desert. *Sahara* 4: 41–52.

——. 1991b. Technological organization and sedentism in the Epipalaeolithic of Dakhleh Oasis, Egypt. *African Archaeological Review* 9: 81–109.

MARY M.A. MCDONALD

dating, pharaonic

The chronology of pharaonic Egypt is based on a sequence of thirty-one dynasties, or ruling families, as defined by Manetho, an Egyptian priest who compiled a history of Egypt in the third century BC. While modern study has shown that Manetho's work is incorrect at many points, his basic dynastic structure with the appropriate changes is still used today. Manetho's dynasties and lists of kings echo those of earlier times. The earliest king-list we now possess is the fragmentary Palermo Stone which, in its original state, named the kings of Egypt up to the 5th Dynasty and important events that took place during their reigns. Another king-list is found on a fragmentary papyrus in Turin, originally a catalog of Egyptian kings up to the later 19th Dynasty with the regnal years of each. Other king-lists were drawn up for various reasons. The best known is the long roster of kings receiving offerings inscribed in the Abydos temples of Seti I and Ramesses II. Other lengthy lists come from private tombs, again for cultic purposes or as footnotes to long genealogies of high officials. Scores of shorter sequences of kings are found in tomb inscriptions and administrative documents.

The sum result is that, except for the more obscure periods of Egyptian history, we have a workable list of families of kings for the entire thirty-one dynasties of pharaonic history. Thousands of religious, administrative and private documents dated to a specific year of a given king have helped fill in the lengths of reigns. While this element in the dynastic structure is still far from perfect, the chronological skeleton is there. The next step is to translate the dynasties, the lengths of royal reigns and the multitude of documents dated to these reigns into an absolute chronology in terms of dates BC.

The background for such an absolute chronology is the Egyptian calendrical system. As any society must, the Egyptians kept track of units of time—days, years, seasons and the like—for the requirements of both religion and administration. For this, they created what at first sight appears to be a conflicting pair of calendars, lunar and civil. That these were never in synchronism presented no problem since the two calendars served different purposes.

The most obvious method of gauging time, dating back to prehistoric times, was the simple observation of the seasons created by the annual phases of the Nile River. A period of inundation of the valley was followed by a growing season, in turn followed by a dry period when the Nile was low. But the onset of the inundation which began the agricultural year could occur at any time within a period of several weeks. The length of time from inundation to inundation therefore fluctuated, and any given agricultural year could be longer or shorter than the one before and after. Such a time frame was sufficient for agricultural purposes, but for nothing else.

The more precise measurement of time required for religious festivals was accomplished by observing the phases of the moon, also a very early development. This lunar calendar was divided according to the three agricultural seasons, each of which lasted approximately four lunar months. The resulting twelve-month lunar year averaged 354 days, as each lunar month is 29 or 30 days long. The names of the agricultural seasons—inundation, growing, dry—were retained and the months were named after the most important feast that took place in each. But this lunar year was also tied to the sidereal year in which the heliacal rising of the star Sirius, or Sothis, played a major role. Each year for a period of seventy days, Sirius is hidden by sunlight. The day when the star can again be seen in the eastern horizon just before sunrise is its heliacal rising, called "the coming forth of Sirius" by the Egyptians. New Year's Day in the lunar calendar was the first day of the lunar month following the annual heliacal rising of the star.

It seems likely that the reappearance of Sirius was chosen as the herald of the New Year because this event took place about the time the inundation of the Nile began each year. Since the length of the lunar year was shorter than the sidereal year of 365.25 days, a thirteenth lunar month was added every three or four years which kept the two in general synchronism with each other and with the agricultural seasons. Such a method of reckoning time served the needs of religion, though it was too flexible for administrative requirements.

To fill the latter need, a civil calendar with a fixed length of 365 days was introduced shortly after Egypt was first united under a central government. Various theories suggest the 365 days arose from the average length of a series of lunar years, or the average length of a series of agricultural years, or simply the period between heliacal risings of Sirius. Whatever its origin, the civil calendar adopted the three seasons and the twelve months of the lunar year, each month now fixed at thirty days. Five extra, or epagomenal, days were added at the end of the year to fill out the 365-day total. This provided a calendar that was perfectly regular and without the fluctuations of the lunar calendar.

Dates were recorded as "Year 2, month 3 of Inundation, day 16 (of King *X*)." It did not trouble the Egyptians that this "month 3 of

Inundation" could occur during the dry season of the natural year for they understood this simply as "month 3 of season 1." In the civil calendar, the three "seasons" were only traditional names for three segments of the civil year which, from its inception, had nothing to do with agriculture. The civil calendar became the medium by which all documents and events were dated and provided a simple and uniform method for keeping administrative records.

It must be emphasized that while the civil calendar of fixed length and the lunar calendar of variable length were used concurrently, they were not opposed or in competition with each other, but were used for entirely different purposes. The lunar calendar established religious events such as feast days and sacrifices. The civil calendar was for the ordering and recording of daily life. Judaism and Islam still use both a lunar and a civil calendar for the same reasons.

From our viewpoint, there is a major flaw in the civil calendar. Its 365-day year fell just short of the sidereal year of 365.25 days. This means that every four years the civil calendar fell one more day behind the sidereal year. Dubbed by modern scholars "the wandering year," the civil year regularly progressed backward so that its first day eventually fell on every day of the sidereal year. The resulting period of 1,460 years (365 × 4) is called the "Sothic Cycle," that is, the length of time between concurrences of New Year's Day in both the civil and sidereal years. But this is a modern measurement of time, unknown to the Egyptians who always knew their civil year did not correspond to either the lunar year or the annual appearance of Sirius. Since this was not a problem to them, they never took steps to bring the two calendars into synchronism.

It does present a problem to modern historians, for the documents they must use are dated by the civil calendar with its slightly shorter years, whereas our own absolute chronology of Egypt must be expressed in terms of the sidereal year if that chronology is to make sense to us. Synchronizing the Egyptian calendars is therefore a primary task of present-day scholarship. One important help in creating

that absolute chronology are the rare instances in which the Egyptians recorded a heliacal rising of Sirius on a particular day of the civil calendar. There are only five such references known in all of Egyptian history, the first in the 12th Dynasty, the last in the Roman period. Using somewhat complicated astronomical arguments, modern scholars are able to use these as fixed chronological points. For example, a heliacal rising noted for the seventh year of Senusret III of the 12th Dynasty can be placed *circa* 1872 BC; another for the ninth year of Amenhotep I of the 18th Dynasty indicates *circa* 1541 BC. Adding the substantial information from king-lists, dated documents, and other material, a chronology can be worked out for the 12th and 18th Dynasties, then for the Middle and New Kingdoms to which these dynasties belong, and finally the dynasties before and after those kingdoms. The result is only an approximate chronology in terms of years BC, not a precise one. As there are so many variables involved, it is doubtful that precision can ever be achieved.

A dynastic chronology such as that of Egypt depends heavily on two factors: the lengths of the reigns of individual kings and the number and length of coregencies. In themselves, individual discrepancies may seem relatively unimportant: Merenptah ruled ten years rather than the traditional nineteen; the coregency between Tuthmose III and Amenhotep II lasted from none at all to three years, according to different scholars. But when such minor differences occur frequently over three thousand years of history, their collective impact is a serious obstacle to reliable absolute dates.

Even the astronomical testimony—records of lunar months, heliacal risings of Sirius, and the like—is plagued with variables. There is, for example, the *arcus visionis*, the angle between Sirius and the sun when the star is first observed in its heliacal rising. Modern studies have fixed this angle at 7.5°, but variations in the *arcus visionis* change the chronological calculations based on it and we have no way of determining what this angle was for any ancient observation.

Another variable is the point in Egypt where

an ancient observation took place. Memphis, Thebes and Elephantine have been defended as the site of a "national observatory" where official sightings of lunar phases and heliacal risings were made. The problem here is that a heliacal rising, for example, is observed one day earlier for every degree of latitude as one moves south along the Nile. Translating this into absolute dates, the heliacal rising recorded in the ninth year of Amenhotep I would have occurred around 1521 BC, 1523 BC or 1519 BC, depending on whether the observation was made at Memphis, Thebes or Elephantine.

The alternative is to see the whole matter in terms of the ancient setting. We have no reason to suppose that the Egyptians expected the new year or the new month of the lunar calendar to begin simultaneously throughout the country. To them, it was a matter of a few days at most and it did not really matter if the same religious festival was celebrated a few days earlier at Elephantine than at Memphis. What did matter was that any religious festival should occur on the proper day of the lunar year. This suggests that astronomical observations were made in each locality which kept its own lunar calendar. The lunar month or new year thus began at this or that town when the appropriate observations were made locally, allowing each district to adhere to the strict pattern of festivals and ceremonies required by religion. The civil calendar, which had none of the drawbacks of the lunar calendar, could be used throughout the country. It had a uniform meaning everywhere that never changed. A date such as "Year 2, month 3 of Inundation, day 16 (of King *X*)" meant exactly the same day—the 76th day of the king's second regnal year—whether it was used to date a document at Memphis, Thebes or Elephantine.

In spite of all the problems involved, with a judicious use of all the sources noted above it is possible to present an absolute chronology, though one with a margin for error that expands the farther one moves back in time. The earliest fixed date in Egyptian history on which all agree is 664 BC, the beginning of the 26th Dynasty. Moving back from that year, through historical synchronisms with Assyrian

chronology, the beginning of the 22nd Dynasty fell in the period 947 to 940 BC, so there is already a small margin for error. The beginning of the 19th Dynasty is calculated as anywhere from 1320 to 1295 BC, the margin for error now a quarter-century. This remains about the same for the beginning of the 18th Dynasty, said to be from 1570 to 1540 BC.

It is with the beginning of the 12th Dynasty that a really serious discrepancy in current chronological studies begins; the dates currently defended range from 1994 to 1938 BC. This much larger margin for error results from very different interpretations of the astronomical evidence, in particular, the location of an assumed national observatory where "official" observations of the heliacal rising of Sirius were recorded. This six-decade margin for error remains fairly constant back through the Old Kingdom, but looms larger for the earliest dynasties; dates from 3100 to 2950 BC are currently proposed for the unification of Egypt at the beginning of the 1st Dynasty.

See also

dating techniques, prehistory; Manetho; overviews (all periods)

Further reading

Aström, P., ed. 1987. *High, Middle or Low: Acts of an International Colloquium in Absolute Chronology held at the University of Rothenburg 20th–22nd August 1987.* Göteborg.

Bierbrier, M.L. 1975. *The Late Middle Kingdom in Egypt.* Warminster.

Kitchen, K.A. 1973. *The Third Intermediate Period in Egypt (1100–650 B.C.).* Warminster.

Krauss, R. 1985. Sothis- und Monddaten. *Studien zur astronomischen und technischen Chronologie altägyptens* (HÄB 20). Hildesheim.

Neugebauer, O. 1975. *A History of Ancient Mathematical Astronomy*, 2. Berlin.

Parker, R.A. 1950. *The Calendars of Ancient Egypt* (SAOC 26). Chicago.

——. 1976. The Sothic dating of the Twelfth

and Eighteenth Dynasties. In *Studies in Honor of George H. Hughes* (SAOC 34), J. Johnson and E.F. Wente, eds, 177–89. Chicago.

Redford, D.B. 1986. *Pharaonic King-lists, Annals and Day-books: A Contribution to the Study of the Egyptian Sense of History* (SSEA 4). Mississauga.

Ward, W.A. 1992. The Present Status of Egyptian Chronology. *BASOR* 288: 53–66.

Wente, E.F., and C. van Siclen. 1976. A chronology of the New Kingdom. In *Studies in Honor of George H. Hughes* (SAOC 34), J. Johnson and E.F. Wente, eds, 217–61. Chicago.

WILLIAM A. WARD

dating techniques, prehistory

Before the advent of chronometric dating methods, archaeologists of prehistoric sites in Egypt relied on a relative chronology based on the sequence of riverine terraces bordering the Nile. This sequence was first established at the beginning of this century by geologists K.S. Sandford and W.J. Arkell, who correlated Nile terraces with circum-Mediterranean marine terraces. Today this approach has been abandoned in favor of a relative chronology based on lithostratigraphic units belonging to successive stages in the evolution of the Egyptian landscape.

So far, radiocarbon dating has been the most widely used chronometric technique. Recently, thermoluminescence, optical, electron spin resonance, amino acid racemization and uranium series dating techniques have been applied to a series of sites predating the range of radiocarbon age determination (approximately 60,000–40,000 years ago).

Radiocarbon dating has been extensively used for sites ranging from Middle Paleolithic to Predynastic sites (as well as Dynastic sites). Carbon-14 is a carbon isotope formed from nitrogen in the atmosphere. Plants and animals receive Carbon-14 during their lifetimes. Carbon-14 begins to decay after the death of organisms. Until the 1970s, age determination was based on measurement of the radiation resulting from the decay of Carbon-14, which required relatively large samples of organic materials (usually charcoal). Today, the concentrations of Carbon-14 in very small samples can be measured directly using accelerator mass spectrometry (AMS).

Thermoluminescence dating (TL) can be used on a number of materials, but has a much wider range of error than radiocarbon dating. The method is based on a measurement of the emission of light upon heating the sample. The amount of TL is proportional to the amount of radiation the material was exposed to after a certain event, such as the firing of clay. Optical (stimulated) dating (OSL) is based on the luminescence resulting from the eviction of electrons from traps in the material by the action of light.

Electron spin resonance dating also depends on the nuclear radiation that has been experienced by a sample. However, in this method the electrons are not excited. Their signal is detected by their response to high-frequency electromagnetic radiation. The method is suitable for tooth enamel, mollusk shells, calcite and quartz.

Amino-acid racemization dating depends on changes in the molecular structure of amino acids, the building blocks of protein. The changes hypothetically occur at a constant rate and produce mirror images of amino acids. The ratio of isomers of aspartic acid (one of the amino acids) can be used for dating samples a few thousand to several million years old. The technique is of limited use and is subject to errors due to the susceptibility of racemization to temperature.

Uranium series dating is based essentially on the decay of thorium-230 into a series of uranium radio-isotopes. Calcite samples can provide age estimates in the range of 5,000–350,000 years.

Thermoluminescence, optical, electron spin resonance, amino-acid racemization and uranium series dating techniques have been used to date Lower and Middle Paleolithic sites and climatic events. Middle Paleolithic sites range from 175,000–70,000 years ago. Using a combination of radiocarbon dating and TL dating, late Quaternary sites in the Nile Valley and the Western Desert have been dated and assigned to arid climatic conditions from 65,000–12,500 BP (before present in radiocarbon years). Upper Paleolithic sites in Egypt date from 33,000–30,000 BP, Late Paleolithic sites date from 20,000–12,000 BP, and Epi-paleolithic sites date from *circa* 11,000–7,000 BP.

Neolithic and Predynastic sites (excluding Nagada III sites) in the Nile Valley date from 5,900–4,600 BP. Since radiocarbon years do not correspond to calendric years, radiocarbon dates may be calibrated using measurements on samples dated both by tree-ring and radiocarbon dating techniques to obtain calendric years (BC).

See also

Epi-paleolithic cultures, overview; Neolithic cultures, overview; Paleolithic cultures, overview; Predynastic period, overview

Further reading

Hassan, F.A. 1985. Radiocarbon chronology of Neolithic and Predynastic sites in Upper Egypt and the Delta. *African Archaeological Review* 3: 95–116.

Sandford, K.S. 1934. *Paleolithic Man and the Nile Valley in Upper and Middle Egypt.* Chicago.

Wendorf, F. 1992. The impact of radiocarbon dating on North African archaeology. In *Radiocarbon Dating after Four Decades: An Interdisciplinary Perspective*, R.E. Taylor, A. Long and R.S. Kra, eds, 309–23. New York.

Wendorf, F., and R. Schild. 1992. The Middle Paleolithic of North Africa: a status report. In *New Light on the Northeast African Past*, F. Klees and R. Kuper, eds, 39–80. Köln.

Wendorf, F., R. Schild and R. Said. 1970. Problems of dating the Late Paleolithic age in Egypt. In *Radiocarbon Variations and Absolute Chronology*, I.U. Olsson, ed., 57–79. Stockholm.

FEKRI A. HASSAN

Deir el-Bahri, Hatshepsut temple

Queen Hatshepsut of the 18th Dynasty built her "Temple of Millions of Years" in the rock semicircle of Deir el-Bahri (25°44′ N, 31°36′ E) north of the funerary temple of the 11th Dynasty King Nebhepetre Mentuhotep II, located on the west bank of the Nile opposite the modern town of Luxor. The ancient Egyptians called Hatshepsut's temple "Djeser-Djeserw," meaning "Holy of Holies." The Arabic name of the site, Deir el-Bahri, meaning "The Northern Monastery," derives from the structure built there by monks during the Christian period. The temple of Hatshepsut is the only great temple complex of the early 18th Dynasty that can be reconstructed in its plan and decoration.

Hatshepsut's temple extends approximately on an east–west axis, which appears as the prolongation of that of the temple of Karnak on the east bank of the Nile. In addition to the main temple, there is a badly preserved valley temple connected to the main temple by a 1 km alley formed by fifty pairs of sphinxes. Midway from the lower terrace an intermediate station for the divine bark was built (called *Kha-akhet*). The main temple consists of three successive terraces, fronted by porticoes. It ends on the upper terrace with a double sanctuary cut into the rock. The whole temple is built of limestone, except for the architrave of the Northern Portico of the middle terrace. The violet sandstone of this architrave is the same as that used by Nebhepetre Mentuhotep II in his Deir el-Bahri temple.

The temple was first explored by Richard Pococke in 1737, then by Jollois and Devilliers, members of the Napoleonic expedition, in 1798. A mission of the Egypt Exploration Fund (EEF), directed by Édouard Naville, worked at Deir el-Bahri in 1893–1904. The results of the EEF excavation and architectural studies were published in seven volumes which are still one of the basic reference sources on the temple. From 1911 to 1931 the American Mission of the Metropolitan Museum of Art in New York worked at Deir el-Bahri, under the direction of H.E. Winlock, who went on with the excavation, analyzed the building phases and studied the statuary. Some restoration work was conducted in those years by Baraize.

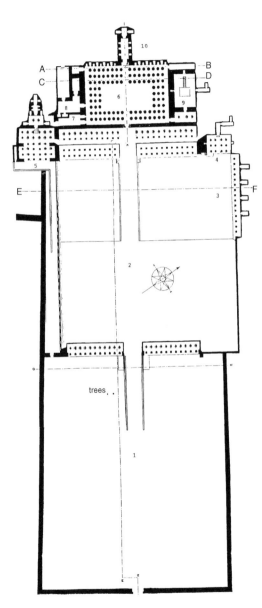

Figure 24 Plan of Queen Hatshepsut's temple, Deir el-Bahri

In 1961 a mission of the Polish Center of Mediterranean Archaeology of Warsaw University in Cairo undertook a new extensive study, a consolidation of the architectural structures and a restoration of the wall bas-reliefs. In the 1990s two Polish missions alternate seasons at Deir el-Bahri: an Epigraphic Mission of Warsaw University directed by J. Karkowski, and a Polish-Egyptian Restoration Mission, directed by F. Pawlicky.

The temple was built between year 7 and year 20 of Hatshepsut. The basic religious and architectural conception of the temple was clearly formulated from the beginning. Some changes in the plan, however, are recoverable from the analysis of the architectural elements. The sequence of these changes is not certain: (a) an outer hypostyle hall was added to the Hathor shrine with a consequent change of the inclination of its ramp and lowering of the pavement of the middle colonnade; (b) the original plan of the solar court was changed and the size of the altar was increased; (c) some details of the foundations bear witness to further changes on the upper terrace.

Tuthmose III had almost all of the names of Hatshepsut erased and substituted by those of Tuthmose II, or more rarely by those of Tuthmose I. At the same time, the statues and Osiride pillars of Hatshepsut were destroyed. Tuthmose III also replaced the coronation text of Hatshepsut with one dedicated to Tuthmose I. During the reign of Akhenaten, the names of the non-Amarna gods were erased; the divine names were restored during the reign of Horemheb and some of the scenes were redrawn. Ramesses II restored the temple and engraved a restoration formula in many places of the temple. Finally, in the Ptolemaic period, a completely new chapel was cut in the rock, beyond the sanctuary, in front of which a portico was added. This new sanctuary was dedicated to Imhotep/Asclepius.

The lower terrace measures 120 × 75 m; it is not paved. Pairs of sphinxes were probably set up along the axial way. The terrace is enclosed by a wall with a gate about 2 m wide at the center of its eastern side. On the outer side of the entrance, two quadrangular holes housed persea trees. The ascending ramp to the middle terrace has a rounded top balustrade, decorated at the base by the figure of a recumbent lion. In front of the ramp two T-shaped basins housed papyrus and flowers. The two porticoes at the western end of the terrace are symmetrical, and are about 25 m wide. Their roofs lie on two rows of eleven elements. The outer row is composed by eleven "semi-pillars," i.e. "D-shaped" columns which are shaped as square pillars in the façade and, on their inner side, reproduce the protodoric columns of the second row. The walls of the porticoes are decorated with bas-reliefs representing the transportation of two obelisks in the southwest portico, and hunting and fishing in the northwest one.

The middle terrace measures about 90 × 75 m. It is paved from the porticos to the end of the ramp, the balustrades of which are decorated with the coils of a snake. Three pairs of sphinxes were probably set along the axial way. The porticoes are slightly wider (about 26 m) than those of the lower terrace. Their roofs lie on two rows of eleven square pillars. The walls of both of the porticoes are decorated with the most famous reliefs of the temple: in the southwest one, the expedition to the land of Punt; in the northwest one the scenes of the divine birth of Hatshepsut and her pilgrimage to the sanctuaries of northern and southern Egypt, accompanied by her father Tuthmose I.

The Hathor Shrine on the southwest corner of the terrace is a chapel dedicated to the goddess Hathor, situated as an independent temple, with a ramp of its own which ran along the southern retaining wall of the lower terrace. It is composed of an outer hypostyle hall, an inner hypostyle hall, a vestibule and a double sanctuary. The roof of the first hypostyle hall was supported by eight square pillars and eight protodoric columns; the inner sides of the axial pillars are decorated with large Hathor sistra. The inner hypostyle hall has sixteen cylindrical columns with Hathor capitals. The most meaningful scenes represented on the walls of the Hathor shrine are connected with coronation rituals, including the cow goddess Hathor licking the hands of the queen (hypostyle halls); the goddess Weret-hekau giving the queen the

menat necklace (hall of the two columns); the cow goddess Hathor suckling the queen represented as the god Amen (outer and inner sanctuary).

The Anubis Shrine in the northwest corner of the middle terrace serves as a counterpart of the Hathor chapel; a narrow ramp with steps connects it with the northern portico. It consists of a hypostyle hall with twelve protodoric columns, followed by a narrow room on the axis, a second perpendicular room (oriented south–north) and a small niche. Cult and offering scenes are represented on its walls. On the southern wall of the hypostyle hall, the god Anubis accompanies the queen into the shrine.

The structure of the third terrace is different from the others. The ramp leads directly to the porticoes, each composed of an inner row of twelve protodoric columns and an outer row of twelve pillars with Osiride figures of the queen. Their walls are very damaged and their study is still in progress; the northwest portico is decorated with the coronation text and scenes. A granite doorway between the porticoes opens onto a peristyle enclosed by three rows of protodoric columns on the south, west and north sides and two rows on the east side. The walls are decorated as follows: on the east and north walls, bark processions of the Beautiful Festival of the Valley and the Festival of Opet; on the south wall, coronation rituals; the back wall (west) has five smaller and four higher niches on each side of the axial passage to the sanctuary. They presumably contained kneeling and standing statues of the queen. Two groups of rooms are built beyond the southern and northern walls of the court, the funerary complex preceded by the so-called "royal palace" and the solar complex. The southern rooms, at the east end of the southern wall of the court, have been interpreted by R. Stadelmann as the royal palace, having a "window of appearance" immediately west of the entrance. The second doorway in the southern walls lets into a vestibule with three protodoric columns, which in turn leads to the funerary chapels dedicated to Tuthmose I (north) and Hatshepsut (south). Their walls are decorated with offering scenes and chapters of the *Book of the*

Dead. A monumental stela completed the back wall of each chapel.

The solar complex is composed of three elements: (1) a vestibule with three protodoric columns with access from the east end of the northern wall of the court; (2) the actual solar court (oriented east–west) with an altar in the open air; and (3) the Upper Anubis shrine, which opens on the northern wall of the court. Two niches are present in the court, one in the southern wall, the other in the western wall, just opposite the ramp leading to the altar. The scenes and texts are: the gods Re-horakhty and Amen accompanying the Queen into the court (inside of the left jamb of the entrance); the "Text of the Baboons," "Cosmographic Text" and beginning of the *Book of the Night* (eastern wall of the altar court); various scenes of offering and of daily rituals (Upper Anubis shrine and in niches) Rehorakhty giving the symbol of life (*ankh*) to the Queen; and Hatshepsut as the (*Inmutef*) priest making offering to her own sacred image (western niche of the solar court).

The sanctuary is composed of two rooms, one after the other, on the main axis of the temple. The first is a bark station, as is demonstrated by the main scenes of the long walls, in which the bark of Amen receives offering from Hatshepsut and Tuthmose III accompanied by Queen Ahmose and the two princesses Nefrura and Nefrubity. The inner sanctuary contained the cult image of Amen, probably housed in the ebony shrine presently in the Cairo Museum. A window cut in the tympanum of the western wall of the bark sanctuary allowed the sun's rays to reach the statue of the god.

As all the other temples on the west bank of the Nile, Djeser-Djeserw is usually seen as the funerary temple of Hatshepsut. According to Haeny, however, some elements indicate that these sanctuaries were also used for the cult of the living king. At Deir el-Bahri, this double aspect is reflected in the structure of the temple, which is organized on two main axes: an east–west one connected with the voyage of the god Amen-Re, paralleled with the daily voyage of the sun god; and a south–north one connected with the life cycle of the pharaoh (coronation, death, rebirth). These two aspects were closely connected, however, as is borne out by an analysis of the scenes carved on the walls of the temple, where a preponderant role was certainly played by the rituals celebrated during the Beautiful Festival of the Valley. On that occasion the bark of Amen, coming from Karnak, visited the west bank and rested in the temple. During the festival, the queen was ritually enthroned, "Osirified" and in the end united with Amen-Re on the solar altar.

See also

cult temples of the New Kingdom; Punt; representational evidence, New Kingdom temples; Thebes, royal funerary temples; Thebes, Senenmut monuments

Further reading

Haeny, G. 1982. La fonction religieuse des "Chateaux de millions d'années." In *L'Égyptologie en 1979: axes prioritaires de recherches* 1. Paris.

Naville, É. 1894–1908. *The Temple of Deir el-Bahari*, 7 vols. (Memoirs 12–14, 16, 19, 27 and 29). London.

Pirelli, R. 1994. Some consideration on the temple of Queen Hatshepsut at Deir el Bahari. *Annali dell'Istituto Universitario Orientale, Napoli* 54: 455–63.

Stadelmann, R. 1979. Totentempel und Millionenjahrhaus in Theben. *MDAIK* 35: 303–21.

ROSANNA PIRELLI

Deir el-Bahri, Meket-Re tomb

Meket-Re held the titles of Chancellor and Steward of the Royal Palace in the reign of Nebhetepre Mentuhotep II in the 11th Dynasty. He chose to have his large, terraced, tomb (TT 280) prepared in the valley south of Deir el-Bahri in the Theban necropolis. It was excavated by Georges Daressy in 1895 and again by

Sir Robert Mond in 1902, but it was not until a later clearing operation carried out by the Metropolitan Museum of Art under Ambrose Lansing and Herbert Winlock in 1920 that the most sensational finds connected with this tomb came to light.

Meket-Re's tomb is approached by a wide and steep avenue 80 m long. At the top of this inclined ramp is a long portico of nine columns with two corridors cut into the rock behind it. One of the corridors is centered on the portico while the other is to the left and was probably prepared at a later time for Meket-Re's son. Little was preserved of the decoration of this rich tomb and the original intention of the Metropolitan Museum expedition was to clear the approach and chambers so that the tomb could be accurately mapped and planned. Work was proceeding on the tomb until 17 March 1920, when one of the workmen employed in the clearance noticed that small chips of stone were slipping into a crack in the rock. When the supervisors were able to bring flashlights to illuminate the cavity, one of the great archaeological discoveries in Egypt was recognized.

The find consisted of a small chamber which had previously escaped notice and still contained the complete set of tomb models prepared for the owner. During the Middle Kingdom, when Meket-Re lived, one of the funerary practices current was to furnish the tomb with models of activities such as cattle raising, baking and brewing, carpentry, weaving and other aspects of daily life. Generally such models were made of wood, coated with gesso or plaster, and painted. Their quality could vary considerably according to the rank and wealth of the tomb owner, but the detailed information they furnish on aspects of the crafts and trades in ancient Egypt is great.

The small chamber in Meket-Re's tomb took three days of hard work to clear. Although most of the twenty-four models found were in good condition, some had been damaged by falling fragments of stone within the chamber. On the whole, they were remarkably preserved and no similarly complete complement of high quality models has been found. These included three

models which were properly associated with the burial in the tomb. Of these, two were large images of single female offering bearers, beautifully painted and posed with baskets of food and drink on their heads. The third, a model of a group, depicted a priest carrying his censer and libation vessel followed by three offering bearers, a combination of figures known from the furnishings of other tombs. The remainder of the twenty-four models were all miniature tableaux of daily life, included in the tomb furnishings for the magical purpose of providing the spirit or soul with necessities in the afterlife.

The largest of these was a scene of cattle counting in which the tomb owner is found seated on a columned porch, accompanied by his son. Clerks and stewards count and manage the count. Herdsman prod and chastise the brightly colored cattle, all together capturing the activity of the estate and the accounting to the master. The counting is actually only one part of the cattle production cycle portrayed in the models. Two others, the cattle barn and the butcher shop, show in detail the steps in the feeding and the ultimate slaughter with such telling details as the preparation of blood pudding and the hanging of meat cuts to dry.

Two of the models have to do with the storage and processing of grain. The activities of the granary include not only the men who are measuring and storing the grain, but also the scribes who are keeping the accounts on papyrus rolls and tally boards. The grain as it is prepared for consumption is shown in a composite model which includes the processes of both baking and brewing. The grain is ground and made into cakes, and mash is prepared. Vats of fermenting mash stand to the side and some of it is poured into jars. In the bakery the grain is cracked and ground, dough is worked and cakes fashioned which are then put into ovens.

The weaving shop illustrates the whole procedure from the preparation of flax and spinning of thread to the weaving of cloth on horizontal looms. The carpentry shop is equally detailed including the process of squaring timbers and ripping planks, as well as the cutting of mortises in furniture. Included in the shop was a tool chest, with a complete set of carpenter tools in miniature. Two garden models represent the most important aspect of any richly appointed house or dwelling. Rather than depicting interior rooms for activities such as sleeping, a choice was made to illustrate the center of life for the well-to-do Egyptian, the walled garden with pool. Wood and plaster fruit trees surround a copper-lined pool which could have held real water.

No fewer than half of the models in the tomb were of boats, underlining the importance of the river to the ancient Egyptians. Winlock, who published the models, described four of the vessels as large traveling boats, either rigged with full sail for sailing with the wind or with mast lowered for rowing with the current. Smaller vessels ("yachts") were probably intended for short trips, and there is one skiff of the type used for hunting and fishing. In addition, two models of kitchen tenders illustrate the necessity for separating that activity from the master's vessel for his comfort. Two papyrus or reed boats are represented with a drag net stretched between them, complete with model fish being caught. The amount of detail in these boat models provides a great deal of information on the construction, rigging, handling and use of ancient Egyptian boats.

Half of the models were retained by the Egyptian Museum in Cairo and half were given to the Metropolitan Museum of Art and are now in New York. In both museums they are among the most interesting, detailed and vivid reminders of daily life in Egypt as it was almost four thousand years ago.

See also

mortuary beliefs; *shawabti*s, servant figures and models; ships; tomb furnishings

Further reading

Winlock, H.E. 1942. *Excavations at Deir el Bahri 1911–1931*. New York.
——. 1955. *Models of Daily Life in Ancient Egypt from the Tomb of Meket-Re' at Thebes*. Cambridge, MA.

WILLIAM H. PECK

Deir el-Bahri, Mentuhotep II complex

Nebhepetre Mentuhotep II (11th Dynasty) was the first Theban king to build his temple at Deir el-Bahri (25°44′ N, 31°36′ E), south of the later temples of Queen Hatshepsut and Tuthmose III. This is also the first and only Middle Kingdom monument whose history, architecture, texts and decoration are well known. Like the other two temple complexes at Deir el-Bahri, it lies on an east–west axis and has a valley temple, monumental ramp, large enclosure wall and main temple. The temple consists of a quadrangular, three-level structure with pillared porticoes, followed by a peristyle court and a rock-cut sanctuary.

The first investigations of the temple were conducted by Baron Dufferin and collaborators in 1858–9, and again in 1869. They discovered numerous monuments, including the tomb of Queen Tem, a seated statue of Amen-Re and a granite altar of the king. In 1868 Howard Carter chanced upon the royal "cenotaph" of Bab el-Hosan, within the enclosure wall, which he excavated in 1900–1. Édouard Naville worked in the temple from 1903 to 1907 and published three volumes for the Egypt Exploration Fund. He also formulated the hypothesis that the original temple was surmounted by a pyramidal building. In the early 1920s Herbert Winlock, director of the Metropolitan Museum of Art expedition, studied the tombs of the princesses, and the large forecourt. The most recent study was by Dieter Arnold, who directed an expedition for the German Archaeological Institute, Cairo, from 1966 to 1971. Arnold's work suggests a new reconstruction of the temple and a new interpretation of the whole complex.

Construction of the temple began in the first decade of Mentuhotep II's reign, and probably continued until the end of his life. The main building phase, however, was from regnal years 30–39. Sandstone was used for the foundations, columns, architraves and walls of the inner part of the temple; limestone was used for the walls of the outer part. According to Arnold, there are four main phases of construction:

1 An eastern enclosure wall was built, presumably for a project that was later abandoned, dating to the period of reunification of Egypt under Mentuhotep II, when the king's Horus name was "S'ankhibtawy."
2 A large enclosure wall, replacing the old one, the "cenotaph" of Bab el-Hosan and the tombs and statue chapels of the princesses were built when Mentuhotep II used another Horus name, Netery-Hedjet.
3 Most of the structures of the temple were built in this phase (corresponding to the period of the later Horus name of Mentuhotep, Smatawy), including the terrace, central structure surrounded by an ambulatory, hypostyle hall, the long ramp with the king's tomb and the statue chapel.
4 In this last phase, the ramp and the lower pillared hall were completed, and the sanctuary of Amen-Re was built.

A mudbrick-paved ramp, 960 m long and flanked by limestone walls, led from the valley temple (not discovered) to the enclosure wall (which originally followed the curve of the valley and was successively changed to a rectangular shape), where a pylon gateway gave access to the large court in front of the temple proper. A seated statue of Mentuhotep II was on each side of the entrance. Within the court, a subterranean structure (Bab el-Hosan) is cut into the rock. It contained the sandstone statue of the seated king, painted with black skin and wearing the Red Crown of Lower Egypt, and a wooden coffin. Boat models were found in another pit below this structure, which has been variously interpreted as a cenotaph or a ritual burying place for the statues of the king, connected with the jubilee (*heb-sed*) ceremony.

In front of the lower pillared portico, where circular depressions are still visible, were the remains of fifty-five tamarisk trees and eight sycamores, which flanked the ramp leading to the upper level of the temple. Standing statues of the king were found here by Winlock. The ramp divides the lower portico into two asymmetrical halves, the northern of which is wider (28.58 m, with two rows of 13 square pillars) than the southern one (23.75 m, with two rows of 11 square pillars). On the east wall of the northern half were reliefs of the bark procession of Amen-Re.

The ramp led to an upper level, with pillared porticoes on the north, east and south sides, whose walls were decorated with scenes of battles, hunting and fishing. These walls enclosed an ambulatory around a central square nucleus, which rose about 11 m above the ambulatory in a stepped shape. The roof of the ambulatory was supported by three rows of eight-sided columns (on its north, east and south sides) and two rows of columns (on its west side). The inner walls of the ambulatory were decorated with cult scenes. Six earlier limestone chapels were incorporated in the west wall of the ambulatory, and were dedicated to the royal wives. The chapels, which housed statues of the royal wives, were decorated with scenes of them with the king, and offering scenes. Their tombs were behind the chapels.

To the west of the ambulatory was a peristyle court with two rows of eight-sided columns on its east side and one row on its north and south sides; its walls were decorated with butchering scenes. From the middle of the court a descending east–west ramp, 150 m long, was cut into the rock. Covered with sandstone, this has a vaulted roof and three niches in its walls contained wooden models of boats, granaries and bread. The ramp leads to the burial chamber, which is covered with granite slabs and has an alabaster shrine for the royal coffin. Unfortunately, the tomb was robbed and very few fragments of tomb goods were still on the floor. To the south of the ramp entrance, a square limestone altar was found.

A gate in the middle of the west wall of the peristyle court gave access to the oldest known hypostyle hall, consisting of eighty columns. Its walls were decorated with offering scenes. Two sandstone false doors were erected on the south and north sides of the west wall, in the middle of which was a rock-cut sanctuary for a standing statue of the king, and, according to Arnold, a third false door (not found). In the southwest corner of the hall was the rock-cut tomb of the chief royal wife, Tem. It contained only the remains of an alabaster coffin.

In the last building phase, the four western-most columns of the hypostyle on each side of the temple axis were incorporated into a newly built Amen-Re sanctuary in which the royal cult was, for the first time, connected with that of the god. In the sanctuary was a high offering table with a ramp on its east side. The sanctuary walls were decorated with various cult and ceremonial scenes. Artifacts found nearby include a sandstone statue base of Mentuhotep II's and a limestone seated statue of the god Amen.

The great innovations that Mentuhotep II introduced in the building of his temple complex at Deir el-Bahri resulted in an original structure which expressed a sophisticated conceptual framework. According to Arnold, this 11th Dynasty temple is the missing link between the royal *ka* chapels of the Old Kingdom and the royal funerary temples of the New Kingdom. In the design of this temple, the king respected both Memphite traditions and the Upper Egyptian tradition of a rock-cut tomb with a pillared portico in the façade.

Around this funerary structure, however, Mentuhotep II created a network of royal and divine cults, which was a new conception for the royal cult center. Added to this is the concept of the mound-shaped temple, which, according to Arnold, recalls the cult centers of Montu (here in his aspect as Montu-Re). The king himself is represented with a falcon head and double feather, the emblem of the god Montu. The sanctuary of Amen-Re also shows for the first time a clear link between the cult of the royal statue and that of the "new" god (Amen-Re).

Beginning with Amenemhat I's reign (early 12th Dynasty), the Amen-Re sanctuary in the Mentuhotep II temple became one of the settings for the ceremonies of the "Beautiful Feast of the Valley," but it was not until the reign of Senusret III that the temple was

enriched with other monuments: a large granite stela and six standing statues of the king, which were found by Naville. Naville also discovered fragments of several artifacts (for example, a limestone slab and a wooden shrine) inscribed with the names of various kings of the 13th–17th Dynasties, which demonstrate that the temple remained in use throughout the Second Intermediate Period.

From the beginning of the 18th Dynasty, the site of Deir el-Bahri became one of the most important seats of the cult of Amen-Re in connection with the cult of the king. Amen-hotep I built a mudbrick sanctuary in this area and erected statues in the forecourt, probably flanking the ramp leading up to the temple. In Queen Hatshepsut's reign, the religious center was moved to the north, where she built her great temple. Under Tuthmose III, who built his own temple and a new shrine of Hathor near the terrace of Mentuhotep II's temple, the Middle Kingdom sanctuary was again brought into the ritual circuit and many statues dedicated to Hathor were found here. During the Amarna period (Akhenaten's reign) many of the sculptures in this complex were destroyed. The temple was restored during the Ramesside period (19th–20th Dynasties), as is demonstrated by inscriptions of Ramesses II and Siptah and many *ex-votos* dedicated to Amen-Re and Hathor. From the end of the 19th Dynasty and the beginning of the 20th, however, the ceremonial use of Mentuhotep II's temple came to an end. It was used as a quarry and limestone and sandstone blocks were removed to construct new buildings. Most of the columns fell and very little of the temple was preserved before its ruins were covered by debris of the Coptic era and desert sand.

See also

Abydos, North, *ka* chapels and cenotaphs; First Intermediate Period, overview; kingship; Middle Kingdom, overview; Thebes, royal funerary temples

Further reading

Arnold, D. 1974. *Der Tempel des Königs Mentuhotep von Deir el-Bahari*. Mainz.

Naville, É. 1907–13. *The XIth Dynasty Temple at Deir el-Bahari*, 3 vols. London.

Winlock, H.E. 1942. *Excavations at Deir el Bahri 1911–1931*. New York.

ROSANNA PIRELLI

Deir el-Bahri, royal mummy cache

The Deir el-Bahri cache, Theban Tomb (TT) 320, was the larger of two caches of royal mummies discovered near the end of the nineteenth century in the Theban necropolis, opposite modern Luxor. TT 320 is located in the northern corner of a small bay in the cliffs just south of Deir el-Bahri. The date of its original excavation and the history of its reuse are currently being debated, but certain facts are undisputed. From inscriptions we know that tomb robbery was a serious problem at Thebes by the end of the 20th Dynasty. Inscriptions also indicate that for about thirty-five years, from year 5 of Siamen (21st Dynasty) to years 10–13 of Sheshonk I (22nd Dynasty), TT 320 served as a crypt for the family of the High Priest of Amen, Pinudjem II, and for some of his ancestors whose original tombs may have been robbed. During most of this period, the tomb was also used periodically for the reburial of some of the most famous kings of the New Kingdom, their relatives and valued retainers. Inscriptions on the wrappings and coffins of the royal mummies record that some had been moved several times before finding their way into the cache.

The choice of TT 320 as a secure hiding place for the royal mummies was an inspired one. Its entrance is a wide shaft, approximately 10 m deep, excavated into an alcove at the level where a talus slope meets the base of the high cliffs. The shaft was easily filled and camouflaged to resemble its surroundings. After it was finally sealed about 935 BC, it lay undetected for more than 2,800 years. It was rediscovered in the summer of 1871 by members of the Abd er-Rassul family from the nearby village of Sheikh Abd el-Qurna.

During the next ten years, the tomb was entered about three times and some of the more portable and marketable objects, including papyri, *shawabti*s, heart scarabs and canopic jars, were removed and sold on the antiquities market. Most of the pieces came from the 21st Dynasty burials and when funerary objects naming the high priests of Amen and their relatives began appearing in Europe in 1874, Gaston Maspero suspected that one or more tombs belonging to this powerful Theban family had been found by modern tomb-robbers. In January of 1881, after succeeding August Mariette as Director of the Egyptian Antiquities Service, Maspero had gathered enough information to initiate an official inquiry. Late in June, when Maspero was out of Egypt, the tomb's location was revealed to local authorities in Upper Egypt.

In Maspero's absence, Émile Brugsch, one of his assistants at the Bulaq Museum (precursor of the present Egyptian Museum), was sent to investigate. When he entered the tomb, Brugsch was astonished to find, lying along a lengthy corridor and in a side chamber, the mummies and fragmentary burial equipment of pharaohs and royal relatives from the 17th–20th Dynasties. The 21st Dynasty burials that Brugsch had expected to find lay in a large chamber at the end of the tomb. For security reasons, Brugsch felt compelled to clear the tomb as quickly as possible. As a result, the mummies and funerary equipment were removed in a mere forty-eight hours. No complete inventory of the tomb's contents was ever made, either during the clearance or later. The most complete contemporary descriptions of the cache were written by Maspero, who never saw the objects *in situ*, although he visited the tomb with Brugsch early in 1882.

As far as it is possible to reconstruct, the disposition of burials in the tomb was some-what confused. This was partly because of the modern robbers, but also because most of the mummies and equipment had been salvaged in ancient times from pillaged tombs. The names of forty-five individuals were preserved in inscriptions on the funerary furniture, but only forty mummies were present. These were enclosed in a variety of coffins, not necessarily their own. For example, the mummy of Queen Ahmose-Inhapy (18th Dynasty) was found in the coffin of the royal nurse Rai (18th Dynasty), whose mummy was discovered in the coffin of a man named Paheripedjet (21st Dynasty), whose mummy was not in the cache. Among the mummies were those identified as Seqenenre Ta'o II of the 17th Dynasty, who appears to have died in the wars against the Hyksos; Ahmose, first king of the 18th Dynasty, and his immediate successors Amenhotep I, Tuthmose I, Tuthmose II and Tuthmose III; Ramesses I, Seti I and Ramesses II, the first three rulers of the 19th Dynasty; and Ramesses III and Ramesses IX of the 20th Dynasty. The majority were identified in inscriptions written on their wrappings and coffins by officials of the 21st and 22nd Dynasties who were attempting to protect them from further desecration. However, a number of the bodies had been rewrapped in ancient times and the identities of several have been questioned on forensic grounds.

Two suggestions have been made concerning the origin of TT 320: either that it was excavated for Ahmose-Inhapy or another queen of the 18th Dynasty and modified in the 21st Dynasty; or that it was entirely excavated in the 21st Dynasty. Only the discovery of foundation deposits will conclusively identify the intended owner; however, the dimensions and plan of the first half of the tomb (as recorded by Maspero and Brugsch) suggest that it was excavated early in the 18th Dynasty and expanded in the 21st Dynasty. The placement of the mummies within the tomb, as far as we know it, indicates that, in the 21st Dynasty, TT 320 was intended as a crypt for the family of the high priests of Amen, but that it gradually became viewed as a secure cache for some of the displaced royal mummies of the New Kingdom.

See also

Maspero, Sir Gaston Camille Charles; mum-mies, scientific study of; mummification; Thebes, Valley of the Kings

Further reading

Dewachter, M. 1975. Contribution à l'histoire de la cachette royale de Deir el-Bahari. *BSFE* 74: 19–32.

Niwinski, A. 1984. The Bab el-Gusus tomb and the royal cache in Deir el-Bahri. *JEA* 70: 73–81.

Reeves, C.N. 1990. *Valley of the Kings: The Decline of a Royal Necropolis*. London.

CATHARINE H. ROEHRIG

Deir el-Bahri, Tuthmose III temple

Discovered by Polish archaeologists working on behalf of the Egyptian Antiquities Organization in 1962, the Deir el-Bahri temple of Tuthmose III lies immediately south of the temple of Hatshepsut (25°44′ N, 31°36′ E). The excavations brought to light the ruined building and thousands of broken polychrome wall reliefs, originating from the temple decoration. Royal and private statues were found, dating from the New Kingdom, along with hieratic graffiti left by the Ramesside pilgrims on the columns and walls, hieratic and Coptic ostraca, and a large collection of stone-cutting tools. The latter served in dismantling the temple and recutting its building materials for reuse. This happened at the very end of New Kingdom.

The temple was probably founded in the middle of the Tuthmose III's reign and was named "Holy of Monuments" (Djeser-menu). Later, in the last decade of that reign, under the supervision of Vizier Rekhmire, it was rede-signed and renamed "Holy Horizon" (Djeser-akhet). In general, the building followed the earlier terraced temples at Deir el-Bahri, having three levels joined by ramps flanked with porticoes. The upper level, a platform partly cut into the cliff and partly constructed, supported the main body of the edifice. This consisted of a large (26 × 38 m) hypostyle hall, and a row of smaller shrines behind it. A granite doorway led to the bark shrine. The hypostyle hall had an unusual inner arrangement, with a double row of eight polygonal, 32-sided columns in its center, situated transversally to the main axis. From all sides this central "kiosk" was surrounded by seventy-six smaller, 16-sided columns. The roof of the side colonnades was lower, with mullion windows filling the space between two levels of the roof. This hall can be considered as one of few predecessors of later ones with a raised central aisle.

The main god of the temple was Amen-Re in two forms: Amen-Re and Amen-Re-Kamutef. Hathor had a special chapel with an inner speos in which the famous cow statue was discovered by Édouard Naville in 1904. Both the richly decorated shrine and the statue are displayed in the Egyptian Museum in Cairo. The chapel was located behind the northern side of the Nebhepetre Mentuhotep II temple, below the Tuthmose III temple platform.

The entire interior of the temple was decorated with finely carved polychrome reliefs depicting various offering scenes and the procession of the sacred bark of Amen during the Beautiful Feast of the Valley. During the demolition of the building, probably after it was damaged by a rock slide, all the walls were dismantled. Before recutting of the stone blocks was finished the stonecutters left the site, which was then buried deep in the ever-growing mound of rocky debris. The monks of the neighboring Coptic monastery used the site as a burial ground and dump.

Some of the wall blocks cracked during the demolition and were left as useless; the rest of the building material was reshaped, and in the process its decoration was hacked out. The flakes were left behind, creating a gigantic jigsaw puzzle for the team of Polish archaeologists, who have been working since 1978 to reconstruct on paper the original decoration of most of the temple walls. The actual reconstruction of the beautifully painted reliefs was undertaken by professional restorers. Two of the completely preserved wall blocks—one with the image of black-faced Amen-Re-Kamutef and one with the head of Tuthmose III—are displayed in the Luxor Museum. A small museum is planned in the building at the site in which the Tuthmoside material is stored. A restored wall of the sanctuary will be a major exhibit there.

See also

cult temples, construction techniques; cult temples of the New Kingdom; New Kingdom, overview; representational evidence, New Kingdom temples

Further reading

Lipinska, J. 1977. *The Temple of Tuthmosis III, Architecture* (Deir el-Bahari II). Warsaw.
——. 1984. *The Temple of Tuthmosis III, Statuary and Votive Monuments* (Deir el-Bahari IV). Warsaw.
——. 1996. Exquisite details: Thutmose III relief fragments. KMT 7(2): 46–51.

JADWIGA LIPINSKA

Deir el-Ballas

The ancient settlement of Deir el-Ballas is located on the west bank of the Nile in northern Upper Egypt, next to the modern village of Deir el-Gharbi, also known as ed-Deir (26°03′N, 32°45′E). The area had been noted by early travelers as a pottery production center for a type of marl-ware water jar known as a *ballas*. During excavations at Nagada and Ballas, a brief investigation of the site was undertaken for the Egypt Exploration Fund by Flinders Petrie and J.E. Quibell. At Quibell's suggestion, George Reisner, who had been appointed head of an expedition from the University of California at Berkeley, began working at Deir el-Ballas in 1900, with the Hearst Expedition.

The Hearst Expedition uncovered a large royal palace, a settlement and a series of cemeteries dating to the late Second Intermediate Period and early 18th Dynasty. The ancient settlement at Deir el-Ballas is situated in a natural amphitheater formed in the limestone cliffs bordering the high desert to the west. The two ends of this bay circumscribe the area of settlement which ran along the desert edge of the cultivation for a distance of approximately 2 km. The terrain is a low gravel plain dissected by wadi beds. The site can be divided into six main areas as defined by topographic features. From north to south they are: the North End, the North Hill, the North Wadi, the Central Wadi, the South Hill and the South Wadi. Occupation stretched back only a few hundred meters from the edge of the cultivation; however, the settlement may have originally extended under the present edge of the modern town and surrounding agricultural lands.

Situated at the approximate center of the bay are the remains of the largest and most prominent structure at the site. The importance of this building was immediately recognized by Reisner and it was termed the "North Palace." It is a large mudbrick structure surrounded by a large enclosure wall, approximately 300 × 150 m. The eastern end of the enclosure ran under the modern cultivation and has never been traced. A smaller walled court, roughly 60 m square, is appended to the northwest corner of the main enclosure. Both these enclosures cover an area of at least 45,000 m square.

The North Palace was positioned at the center of the large enclosure and was laid out as a series of courts with a long entrance corridor. The whole complex was grouped around an elevated platform constructed on casemate foundations which consisted of long mudbrick chambers filled in with rubble and capped by a mudbrick pavement. Some of these casemates are preserved to a height of approximately 5 m, and since traces of pavement were found above them, this must have been their original height. Presumably, this core of casemates supported the raised private apartments of the palace.

As with other royal residences, the North Palace was decorated with wall paintings. In this case little of any figural decoration remained except for fragments of a platoon of men carrying battleaxes. The Hearst Expedition also discovered fragments of gold leaf and faïence tiles, which appear to have embellished the structure.

To the west of the small enclosure were three large houses (*circa* 5 × 10–20 m). The interiors had been decorated with wall paintings, only traces of which remained. These dwellings were fairly lavish and must be related to some significant function of the palace. Another nearby structure consisted of a large rectangular court, *circa* 25 m^2, surrounded by smaller rooms along with two grain silos within the court and a large semicircular oven on the northern side of the building which probably had been a bakery built to serve the palace.

Many of the private houses excavated by Reisner's expedition were poorly recorded; however, it is clear from the recent surveys that a substantial part of the ancient settlement has survived unexcavated and a significant amount of information is still recoverable, even in the areas previously exposed.

To the south of the central wadi is a low rise which was designated as the "South Hill." On the northern side of this hill a group of small, roughly built, contiguous-walled dwellings were uncovered by the original expedition. The plan of this group suggests a workmen's village, comparable to the initial stage of the Deir el-Medina village. Traces of about thirty-five individual structures were uncovered by the Hearst Expedition. The houses vary in size and plan, but basically there are three-room units with a large court and two smaller rooms opening onto it. The courts were sometimes paved with mudbrick and contained hearths and mangers for animals. The individual buildings varied in size, approximately 5–15 m^2.

Near this area, on the east side of the hill by the village, the recent expedition discovered scattered traces of small rectangular structures roughly built and partially cut into the hillside. Varying in size and plan, they generally appear to be about 20 × 10 m, and occasionally have short flights of stairs. The design of these buildings resembles the chapels of the workmen's village at Tell el-Amarna, which consisted of one or more courts connected with a short flight of steps and a niche for the placement of votive artifacts. The layout and positioning of these shrines also corresponds to the chapels associated with the Tell el-Amarna workmen's village.

At the southern end of the site in the South Wadi, Reisner excavated a number of very large structures. They were among the most lavish in the site and some had columned halls, grain silos, mangers and associated outbuildings.

Farther east of the wadi was another group of buildings which did not appear to be of the same character. Here there are traces of structures forming a very orderly arrangement and of unusually large size (*circa* 60 × 40 m). They appear to be tightly grouped in an orderly pattern, and bordered by long narrow structures (*circa* 70+ × 10 m). This layout suggests an administrative complex analogous to that found in the central city at Tell el-Amarna.

The southernmost structure was termed the "South Palace" by the Hearst Expedition. In reality, the structure does not appear to be a palace at all. It sits atop a high hill that marks the southern end of the site and consists of a large rectangular platform built on casemates, measuring 100 × 44 m. The top tier reaches a height of 25 m above the plain and commands a view of the Nile and surrounding territory. A broad stairway runs 5.5 m from the top of the platform to the lower level of the building. Atop the platform must have been an additional structure, and large quantities of mudbrick rubble and gypsum plaster rise several meters above the top of the upper casemates. Its design and location suggest that it must have served as an observation post.

From the stratigraphy uncovered here and noted elsewhere at the site, it was evident, as indicated by the records of the Hearst Expedition, that the site had a single period of occupation with some possible "squatter" reoccupation after a period of abandonment in the early 18th Dynasty.

The site seems to have been occupied for only a very brief period of time. A lintel of Sekhenenre Ta'o II (*circa* 1591–1576 BC) was discovered reused in the modern village, which probably came from the North Palace. The ceramic material likewise seems to be of exclusively late Second Intermediate Period

types. Jar sealings of Ahmose and votive models of ships and weapons were found in a level of post-abandonment debris in the North Palace. Graves which cut through the workmen's village date to the early 18th Dynasty, suggesting that this part of the site was also vacated at this date.

The archaeological evidence, including the inscribed material, indicates that Deir el-Ballas functioned as a "campaign palace" for the Theban pharaohs during the Hyksos expulsion. This would also explain its rather rapid abandonment in the early 18th Dynasty after the reunification of Egypt. Recent fieldwork at the Hyksos capital in the Delta by Manfred Bietak and the Austrian Archaeological Institute at the site of Ezbet Helmi have uncovered two large structures remarkably similar to the North and South Palaces at Deir el-Ballas and they have now been ascribed to this period.

See also

Deir el-Medina; New Kingdom, overview; Reisner, George Andrew; Second Intermediate Period, overview; Tell ed-Dab'a, Second Intermediate Period; Tell el-Amarna, city

Further reading

Lacovara, P. 1990. *Deir el-Ballas: Preliminary Report on the Deir el-Ballas Expedition 1980–1986*. Winona Lake, IN.
——. 1997. *The New Kingdom Royal City.* London.

PETER LACOVARA

Deir el-Bersha

Near and partly under the modern village of Deir el-Bersha (27°45′ N, 30°54′ E), this site is mainly known for its rock-cut tombs of the Middle Kingdom. Located on the east bank of the Nile, the site is opposite the town of Mallawi. Due east of the village is the Wadi Deir en-Nakhla. Rock-cut tombs of the Old Kingdom are on the southern side of the wadi, near its mouth, and the Middle Kingdom tombs are higher up on the north side. North of the later tombs are the remains of a Coptic hermitage.

The Middle Kingdom tombs are mainly those of the governors (nomarchs) of the Hare nome, who resided in Hermopolis (modern el-Ashmunein). The owners of the earlier Old Kingdom tombs, however, were not nomarchs, for these tombs were located at Sheikh Sa'id.

On the desert plain east of the village is an extensive Middle Kingdom cemetery with simple tombs of mudbrick. Some tombs in this area, however, were fairly large, as demonstrated by a recently discovered mudbrick superstructure (*mastaba*) with false doors and reliefs. The rock-cut tombs must have been beautifully decorated, although they were somewhat smaller than the contemporary ones at Beni Hasan. Unfortunately, most are now badly damaged by quarrying in the New Kingdom and Late period.

The quarries were excavated over an extensive area, from deep in the wadi to its mouth. Some features of the quarries are still visible, such as transport roads and the remains of workers' huts. Limestone columns and sarcophagi for ibises and baboons, used at Tuna el-Gebel, were produced here.

After the initial publication of the Middle Kingdom texts and reliefs, extensive excavation took place around the turn of the century. Currently, an American–Dutch mission is investigating these tombs and the quarries.

See also

Beni Hasan; Middle Kingdom, overview; Old Kingdom provincial tombs; Tuna el-Gebel

Further reading

Newberry, P.E., and F.L. Griffith. 1894. *El-Bersheh* (2 vols). London.

Terrace, E.L.B. 1968. *Egyptian Paintings of the Middle Kingdom*. New York.

Silverman, D., et al. 1992. *Bersheh Reports I. Joint Expedition of the Museum of Fine Arts, Boston, University Museum, University of Pennsylvania, State University of Leiden*. Boston.

HARCO WILLEMS

Deir el-Medina

This is a site in western Thebes (25°44′ N, 32°36′ E) consisting of the village and tombs of the workmen who carved and decorated the royal New Kingdom tombs in the Valley of the Kings and Valley of the Queens. The village was laid out probably during the reign of Amenhotep I, as he and his queen Ahmose-Nefertari became its divine patrons during its later history. The site lies between the two royal valleys and behind Gurnet Murai, the first range of hills of the Theban west-bank mountain. The village was situated in this locale for security and control by the royal necropolis authorities. Starting with Tuthmose I, special precautions were taken to protect the locale and the work on the royal tomb, as Ineni's autobiography records. The village was walled and guarded, and its houses were laid out along a central street, as block units of several rooms each. Houses of the village foremen and scribe were larger, and were situated at the entrance and exit of the surrounding wall.

All of the villagers' needs were provided by the royal government, from grains to meat, fish, vegetables, water and firewood, as they were not expected to perform any agricultural labor. The workmen received their pay in grain and commodities on a monthly basis, and all their tools and other equipment were government-supplied also. Damaged and worn tools were collected for replacement by the scribe and foremen. The workers spent eight days of the ten-day Egyptian week camped near their work site in the Valley of the Kings, while work on the king's tomb was in progress. The scribe, appointed by the vizier, kept a daily record of attendance at the work site, and also of absences. Absences were permitted for illness, for certain religious holidays and for certain family problems or celebrations. In addition, they also received days off during major religious festivals, such as the Opet Feast of Amen in Thebes.

The working day on the tomb occupied roughly the daylight hours, and in deeper stages of the work, candles were issued. For work purposes, the crew was divided into a right and left side, each with its own foreman and assistant. Each crew worked its respective side of the tomb walls. The workers included quarrymen, plasterers, and the more skilled outline draftsmen and painters. These artisans laid out the drawings of the scenes and their accompanying inscriptions, which the painters then finished. Each workman was responsible for his government-issued tools. Every "weekend" and for holidays, the workmen returned to the village, where their families resided. The village personnel included a carpenter and a physician.

During their free time, villagers were able to make coffins and other funerary objects for sale to outside people, thus supplementing their incomes. They also could work on their own family tombs, located in the hills just above the village. Outside the village, there were several shrines to deities, some built by them, others built by the government. The more prosperous villagers owned various small properties around the village. All this meant that the village functioned as a somewhat specialized economic unit. Because of their pay and supplemental income, some villagers had private property concerns. Like any other village or town, Deir el-Medina had its own local court to adjudicate local legal matters. The court was constituted of the village heads, foremen and highest ranked workmen. The court sat on an *ad hoc* basis and could hear local disputes over property and exchanges, and also register deeds of conveyance of property and hear complaints about the conduct of individuals. When more serious cases arose, involving theft from a tomb, shrine or other government property, the court referred the case to the vizier's court sitting in the city of Thebes.

Additionally, if a particularly sensitive case arose, such as a workman accusing a foreman, or foreman's relative, of theft, appeal could be made to the oracle. The oracle consisted of the statues of the village's founders, that on festival occasions were paraded around the village by bearers of the divine barks in which the image rested. The queries were framed in "yes" or "no" format, and evidently, movements of the bark's bearers were interpreted as responses by the deity. Thus the oracle served as a valuable release mechanism for tensions that might arise in the village. No one, not even a foreman or scribe, could contest an oracular decision, though some individuals tried by consulting other oracles; the force of religion backed the oracular decisions.

During Akhenaten's reign, the village was closed and transferred to Akhetaten (Tell el-Amarna), the new capital. Horemheb refounded the village at Deir el-Medina for the work on his own sizable tomb in the Valley of the Kings. The Ramesside pharaohs who followed enlarged the village, as they added tombs in the Valley of the Queens to the workload of the village. During Seti I's reign, the long reign of Ramesses II, and on into Merenptah's reign, the village operated smoothly and efficiently under competent, honest scribes and foremen. The recently rediscovered K.V. 5, the tomb of Ramesses II's sons, exhibits their excellent work. Troubles began after Merenptah's reign, when Amenmesses usurped the throne from Seti II, the intended successor. He removed the last vizier appointed by Merenptah and installed his own man. Soon after the start of work on Amenmesses' tomb (KV 10), a village crisis erupted. An orphaned boy, Pa-neb, began to threaten his father-by-adoption, Neferhotep. When Neferhotep filed a complaint to the vizier, Pa-neb filed a counter-complaint, and was successful. Emboldened, Pa-neb continued with his threats, and probably murdered Neferhotep. Next, Pa-neb took five of Neferhotep's servants, and handed them over to Seti II's new vizier as a bribe to secure the foreman's post and was again successful.

Under Pa-neb's tenure, the village endured a turbulent period. There was a series of court cases arising from crimes committed during the war between Amenmesses and Seti II. Worse yet, Pa-neb began to pilfer stone from the king's tomb and to divert workmen to build his own family tomb near the village. Pa-neb also misappropriated workmen in other ways, for example, employing them to feed his ox. Next he started to persecute the members of the family of Neferhotep, the slain foreman. When Seti II died and was buried, Pa-neb entered the royal tomb after it had been sealed; he also began to rob tombs of some of the village workmen. Then he began to rape the wives of certain workmen, while his son raped their daughters. All these deeds were recorded by Amennakht, Neferhotep's brother. So long as the bribe-taking vizier, Pareemhab, was in office, Amennakht dared not file the complaint. Siptah, who succeeded Seti II, appointed a new vizier, Hori, a grandson of Ramesses II. Under this respected vizier, Amennakht filed the complaint; Hori brought Pa-neb and his son to trial. Pa-neb and his son were demoted and sent to labor for the rest of their days in the quarries of the Wadi Hammamat.

Under Queen Tawosret and the early 20th Dynasty rulers Sethnakht and Ramesses III, the village returned to smooth, tranquil life, and the work quality on the royal tombs improved markedly. Ramesses III kept the workmen busy with his own tomb, and with others for his queen and for several sons in the Valley of the Queens. Later in Ramesses III's reign, another crisis struck the village; Ramesses III had difficulty supplying grain to the village on the monthly schedule. Desperate, the villagers appealed to their officials, laid down their tools and went on strike. Though discouraged, they marched out of the village, and went down to the administrative headquarters, demanding to see the vizier. Finally, the vizier heard their appeal, and promised to release some grain stored in the funerary temples to them, and they returned to work. Under Ramesses IV, the royal administration gave up trying to support the village, and turned over its administration to the High Priest of Amen in Thebes. Ramesses IV doubled the size of the work force, as he ambitiously tried to speed up work on his tomb, but his reign was short. Later in the mid-20th Dynasty, the workmen's labor was halted because of marauding Libyans in the vicinity.

Under Ramesses VI–VIII, grain prices rose sharply. With the attending hardship, some people on the west bank now turned to tomb-robbing, starting with the tombs of the nobility. Under Ramesses IX, the mayor of the east bank at Thebes received a report from two scribes on the west bank of the robbery of a royal tomb. Outraged, he filed a complaint before the vizier, and the vizier thereupon appointed a commission to investigate the claims. A late Middle Kingdom tomb of a king was indeed found violated. A gang of robbers was apprehended and confessions were wrung from them under duress. They admitted robbing the Middle Kingdom tomb and the commission found the other royal tombs unviolated. They noted that most private tombs had been violated, and their mummies lay strewn over the hills.

Under Ramesses XI, a rebellion erupted in Thebes and the rebels drove out the High Priest of Amen, who fled. Pharaoh called upon the Viceroy of Nubia with his army to restore order, and the viceroy, Panehsy, complied. The High Priest was restored, and trials of all sorts were instituted. During the rebellion, priests had left their temples, stripping their valuables, and the Deir el-Medina villagers had turned to robbing tombs. Now caught with the stolen goods, the village of Deir el-Medina was shut down. The authorities transferred its people to Ramesses III's funerary temple enclosure at Medinet Habu. Work on the tomb of Ramesses XI ground to a halt. The Deir el-Medina village had seen its final days; its people eventually merged into the west bank Theban populace.

See also

law; New Kingdom, overview; Tell el-Amarna, city; Thebes, Valley of the Kings; Thebes, Valley of the Queens

Further reading

Bierbrier, M.L. 1984. *The Tomb Builders of the Pharaohs*. New York.

Černý, J. 1973. *Community of Workmen at*

Thebes in the Ramesside Period (BdÉ 50). Cairo.

Lesko, L.H., ed. 1994. *Pharaoh's Workers: The Villagers of Deir el Medina.* Ithaca, NY.

Ventura, R. 1986. *Living in a City of the Dead* (Orbis Biblicus et Orientalis 69). Göttingen.

FRANK J. YURCO

demography

The only hard data to estimate population, when written sources are unavailable, are the surface areas of contemporary settlements. Beyond that one can suggest models, based on explicit assumptions. "Reconstructions" over time are therefore no more than interpretations that may serve a heuristic purpose when overviewing the historical ensemble of change. For Dynastic Egypt even the information on settlement sizes is sparse, because of the sprawl of modern towns, and the tendency of traditional archaeology to excavate monumental buildings rather than to test residential areas. Furthermore, nineteenth-century excavators simply stripped away younger occupation traces from such monuments without making any records.

For Early Dynastic to Old Kingdom times, the following settlement areas are available (excluding temple enclosures): Memphis, 31 ha; Hierakonpolis, 5 ha; Elkab, 9 ha; Kom el-Hisn, over 6 ha; Elephantine, 1.6 ha; Abydos, over 1 ha. For the Middle Kingdom, there are Elephantine, 3.5 ha, and Lahun, 12 ha. For the New Kingdom, the northern capital was either Pi-Ramesses (Tell ed-Dab'a), 350 ha, or Tanis, 105 ha, while the southern capital, Luxor, exceeded 280 ha. The short-lived capital at Tell el-Amarna expanded across 380 ha, but had a very low density. Other New Kingdom towns were either intermediate in size (Hermopolis, 100 ha; Memphis, more than 79 ha), or much smaller, e.g. Tell el-Yahudiya with 13.7 ha. During the Late period and Graeco-Roman times, the largest provincial centers were in the order of 85–170 ha, intermediate provincial towns, 25–65 ha, and smaller provincial capitals, 8–15 ha.

Converting such spatial dimensions into population numbers involves difficult assumptions. In 1882, six Upper Egyptian cities had a population density of 3,000 persons per hectare (after adjusting for a 16 percent undercount), with relatively tightly packed, two-story or three-story buildings. That is probably applicable to most New Kingdom and Late period cities, but Old Kingdom towns such as Hierakonpolis had spacious courtyards or gardens, and were mainly single-storied. Here, a density of 200 per hectare seems generous. On this basis, cautious estimates can be offered for town populations at different times.

For the Old Kingdom, Memphis by this method would have had 6,000 inhabitants, with perhaps 1,000–2,000 in the larger provincial towns, and as few as 250 in their smaller counterparts. With some forty provinces (nomes), and assuming that half of these had capitals with an average population of 1,500, it can be posited that only 35,000–40,000 people lived in places with more than 1,000 inhabitants. By standards of Early Bronze Age Palestine, this was a decidedly rural society.

That picture had changed by New Kingdom times, with close to 85,000 in Luxor, perhaps 100,000 in Pi-Ramesses, but a maximum of only 31,000 in Tanis, its successor. Since the size and role of these capitals varied over time, the combined population of the northern and southern metropoles is best assessed at no more than 125,000. Major provincial centers may have had 15,000–30,000 inhabitants, with perhaps fifteen places in that category, making about 300,000. Data for another perhaps twenty-five smaller provincial capitals are sparse, but 125,000 can serve as a working figure, to estimate an urban population of up to 550,000 for the early Ramesside period (19th Dynasty).

For the later periods, there may have been ten large provincial cities with 25,000 to 50,000 people, another fifteen with 7,500–25,000, and at least twenty-five with 2,500–5,000 or so. That would total 600,000–650,000, plus the estimate of over 300,000 for the capital, Alexandria (first century BC), by Diodorus (17.52.6), making close to one million urban Egyptians. Possibly based on actual data, Diodorus (1.31.8) also gives a figure of seven million for the total population. That figure, and the size classes of provincial towns estimated here, closely approximate those of the adjusted census of 1882, if the new, hegemonic entrepôt of Alexandria is omitted, to leave Cairo as the single primate city: 7.65 million for Egypt, with 880,000 people in towns over 15,000. During the first century BC, an estimate for towns over 15,000 would be in the order of 800,000. Diodorus's seven million figure therefore seems reasonable.

Assuming a similar urban ratio, early Ramesside total population would have been roughly half that of the first century BC, i.e. about 3.5 million. A range of 3.0–3.5 million for *circa* 1250 BC gives a reasonable order of magnitude. Estimating Old Kingdom population is far more difficult, because of the limited nucleated settlement. Herodotus (2.177) gives 20,000 inhabited places for the sixth century BC, remarkably close to the 18,000 of 1882. That serves as a caution in regard to inferring national population size from the paltry urban sum. An estimate must balance the labor forces necessary to build the pyramids with the inference of the Hekanakht letters (*circa* 2002 BC) that half of the floodplain was either in pasture or fallow. Something in the order of 1.5 million is no more than an educated guess.

The hypothetical progression, in the absence of adequate data for the Middle Kingdom, posits three successive peaks of perhaps 1.5 million *circa* 2500 BC, 3.0–3.5 million *circa* 1250 BC, and close to 7.0 million *circa* 50 BC. Major population growth must be assumed in Egypt during the centuries prior to the mid-1st Dynasty; toward the end of the 2nd Dynasty, the population seems to have dipped, perhaps reflecting a 30 percent decline in flood volume. Demographic retraction can be assumed during (a) the political chaos of the First Intermediate Period, (b) the high flood disasters of the late 12th and 13th Dynasties, followed by the political impotence of the Hyksos period (15th–16th Dynasties), and (c) the collapse of the New Kingdom and its aftermath. A potential factor to estimate decline is suggested by medieval Islamic trends. In the Fayum the number of villages and towns increased from 66 in 1094, to 156 *circa* 1250, and 164 in 1290, then fell to 144 *circa* 1320, even before the Black Death, and 97 as reported *circa* 1375. This particular proxy suggests a decline of 41 percent in response to mismanagement and epidemic, similar to the 38 percent decrease in cultivated area. A comparable decline of 35–40 percent can be suggested *circa* 2950–2750, 2350–2100, 1800–1600 and 1150–950 BC.

See also

Abydos, North; Alexandria; Canaanites; Elephantine; Elkab; Hierakonpolis; Hyksos; Kom el-Hisn; Memphis; nome structure; subsistence and diet in Dynastic Egypt; Tanis (San el-Hagar); Tell ed-Dab'a, Second Intermediate Period; Tell el-Amarna, city; Tell el-Yahudiya

Further reading

Baer, G. 1968. Urbanization in Egypt, 1820–1907. In *The Beginning of Modernization in the Middle East*, W.R. Polk and R.L. Chambers, eds, 155–69. Chicago.

Butzer, K.W. 1976. *Early Hydraulic Civilization in Egypt*. Chicago.

——. 1980. Civilizations: organisms or systems? *American Scientist* 68: 44–58.

——. 1984. Siedlungsgeographie (Settlement Geography). *LÄ* 5: 924–33.

Church, R.L., and T.L. Bell. 1988. An analysis of ancient Egyptian settlement patterns using location-allocation covering models. *Annals, Association of American Geographers* 78: 701–14.

Hassan, F.A. 1990. Population ecology and civilization in ancient Egypt. In *Historical Ecology*, C. Crumley, ed., 155–81. Santa Fe, NM.

Kemp, B.J. 1989. *Ancient Egypt: Anatomy of a Civilization*. London.

Whitmore, T.M., B.L. Turner, D.L. Johnson, R.W. Kates and T.R. Gottschang. 1990. Long-term population change. In *The Earth* as Transformed by Human Action, B.L. Turner, ed., 25–40. Cambridge.

KARL W. BUTZER

Dendera

Situated on the west bank of the Nile, the metropolis of Dendera (Tentyris in Greek) was an important administrative and religious site from the Predynastic period onward (26°08′ N, 32°40′ E). Its most famous remains today, however, date to the last stage of its history in the Graeco-Roman period16

The site consists of a mudbrick *temenos* wall (280 m on each side), which encloses the temple area and is surrounded by several cemeteries. An archaeological survey of the site was undertaken in 1897–8 by Flinders Petrie and Charles Rosher. From 1915 to 1918 systematic excavations were undertaken by Clarence Fischer for the University Museum, Philadelphia. Exploration of the First Intermediate Period cemetery also revealed Predynastic remains, Graeco-Roman tombs and some tombs of the 17th Dynasty. The area west of the great 6th Dynasty *mastaba* tombs (notably that of Idu) has not been excavated. The finds were studied by H.G. Fischer and A.R. Slater.

Documentation of the Graeco-Roman period rests principally on the accidental discoveries made within the temple enclosure of cult artifacts, statues and stelae, now in the Cairo Museum, the Louvre (silver vases) and the British Museum (bronze plaques). A cemetery of sacred cows and Osiris figurines and the New Kingdom and Late period cemeteries have yet to be discovered. The French Archaeological Institute in Cairo has made a topographical survey of the enclosure and the necropolis.

Texts carved in the crypt recount that the temple's foundation charter was written in Predynastic times, and was later found during Khufu's reign (4th Dynasty) in a chest in the royal palace at Memphis. The temple was restored during the reign of Pepi I (6th Dynasty) and was renovated by Tuthmose III (18th Dynasty). The festivals at Dendera con-

form to those in a decree of Amenemhat I (12th Dynasty). In fact, traces of construction attributable to these kings, with the exception of Khufu, have been found in the enclosure. The earliest monuments still *in situ* in the temple enclosure date to the reign of Nectanebo I (30th Dynasty). Evidence of earlier construction is provided by reused blocks inscribed with the names of the following kings: Mentuhotep II, Amenemhat I and Senusret I of the Middle Kingdom; Ahmose, Amenhotep I, Tuthmose III, Amenhotep II, Tuthmose IV, Amenhotep III, Ramesses II and Ramesses III of the New Kingdom; and Shabako and Shebitku of the 25th Dynasty.

The monuments within the temple enclosure at Dendera are summarized below in chronological order:

1 the chapel of Mentuhotep II, now in the atrium of the Cairo Museum, with only the foundations in place at Dendera.

2 the *mammisi* (birth house) with the sanctuary of Nectanebo I. The vestibule lists the names of Ptolemy IX Soter II, Ptolemy X Alexander and Ptolemy XII. A gateway was built by Ptolemy VIII Euergetes II.

3 the chapel of Thoth erected by a scribe of Amen-Re in the reign of Ptolemy I.

4 the bark chapel of Ptolemy VIII Euergetes II built in 122–116 BC.

5 the small temple of Isis with a wall of Nectanebo I, added to by Ptolemy VI Philometer and Ptolemy X Alexander, with reused blocks of Amenemhat I and Ramesses II. A gateway has the name of Augustus.

6 the temple of Hathor. Construction was begun on July 16 54 BC with temple services beginning in February, 29 BC. The foundation of the *pronaos* (porch) was begun in the reign of Tiberius and the walls were decorated with the names of Caligula, Claudius and Nero.

7 north gate from the reigns of Domitian and Trajan.

8 Roman *mammisi* from the reigns of Trajan and Marcus Aurelius.

9 wells, sacred lake.

Figure 25 The temple at Dendera

10   sanitarium.
11   Roman cisterns.
12   Coptic basilica.

The Hathor temple inscriptions were studied by Dümichen (1865–75), Mariette (*circa* 1879), and Heinrich Brugsch (*circa* 1880); systematic publication of the inscriptions was undertaken by Émile Chassinat, followed by François Daumas (1934–87) and is being continued by Sylvie Cauville. The *mammisi* were studied and published by François Daumas (1959). The publication of the temple of Isis is in progress and will be followed by that of the north gate and the monuments situated outside the enclosure wall (i.e. the temple of Ptolemy VI Philopater and the gateway of Horus). Architectural studies are being undertaken by Zignani of the Hathor temple and by Boutros of the basilica.

A structure whose axis is aligned with the heliacal rising of the star Sirius was constructed during the reign of Ramesses II, therefore preceding the building of Ptolemy XII by some 1,200 years. Astronomical research has demonstrated that the famous Dendera zodiac relief was conceived during the summer of 50 BC; it reveals that Egyptian priests had a more advanced knowledge of astronomy than had previously been known. The decoration of the Osiris chapels took place over three years, from 50–48 BC, and their inauguration took place on December 28, 47 BC (the 26th day of Khoiak), the day of a zenithal full moon, a conjunction that takes place only once every 1,480 years.

The temple of Hathor does not differ appreciably from the plan of the Edfu temple, the most complete cultic monument of the Graeco-Roman period. This plan consists of a sanctuary, chapels and great liturgical halls alongside cult rooms to store the equipment and offerings necessary for the daily ritual or various festivals. The architectural originality of the temple of Hathor resides in the majestic crypts contrived in the thickness of the walls and on three levels. The underground crypts served as a sort of foundation for the temple. Inside these hidden spaces were stored about 160 statues, which ranged from 22.5 to 210.0 cm in height. The oldest statues, made of wood, were buried in an almost inacessible crypt.

The gods worshipped at Dendera are organized into two triads, one with Hathor and another with Isis. Hathor is the feminine conception of the royal and solar power. Isis is the wife and mother, who reigns in her own temple in the southern part of the enclosure. Horus is the father of Harsomtous, to whom Hathor gives birth in the *mammisi*. Osiris is evidently the posthumous father of Harsiesis, whom Isis looks after. Hathor, the queen of the temple, is honored under diverse aspects easily identifiable by her names and epithets and by the iconographic depictions. Several divine entities were developed by the priests to express all the subtlety of their theology. Thus, there coexist four forms of Hathor and three forms of Harsomtous.

Around these two triads are arranged deities used as representations of religious themes and ideas or as representations of places. These include (1) aspects of the goddess Hathor as both a vengeful goddess and a protectress (Bastet, Sekhmet, Mut and Tefnut); (2) deities of the Delta (Wadjet, Hathor Nebethetepet and Iousaas); and (3) deities of Memphis or Heliopolis (Re-Horakhty and Ptah). Re-Horakhty is the father of Hathor and the texts state that he created Dendera as a replacement for Heliopolis; the Egyptian term for Dendera (Iwnet) is the feminine form of the term for Heliopolis (Iwnw).

Each part of the temple has a mythological context, which guarantees the permanence of the divine presence. The *mammisi* celebrate the divine birth of the next generation nine months after the "sacred marriage" between Hathor of Dendera and Horus of Edfu. The bark chapel built beside the sacred lake was the location of the famous navigation festival in which the return of Hathor from Nubia was celebrated. The six Osiris chapels on the roof of the Hathor temple were used for the celebration of the resurrection of Osiris in the month of Khoiak, serving as images of the divine tomb for the rest of the year. Numerous festivals from the national calendar were also celebrated, such as the first day of the new year. From the evidence of the reliefs, the festivals honoring the most important local deities, Hathor and Harsomtous, had the most numerous and most elaborate ritual ceremonies.

See also

Edfu; Late and Ptolemaic periods, overview; pantheon

Further reading

Aubourg, É. 1995. La date de conception du Zodiaque du temple d'Hathor à Dendera. *BIFAO* 95: 1–10.

Cauville, S. 1990. *Dendera*. Cairo.

——. 1992. Le temple d'Isis à Dendera. *Bulletin de la Société français d'égyptologie* 123: 31–48.

——. 1997a. *Les chapelles osiriennes*, 5 vols. Cairo.

——. 1997b. *Le Zodiaque d'Osiris*. Louvain.

Daumas, F. 1958. *Les mammisis des temples égyptiens*. Paris.

Fischer, H.R. 1968. *Dendera in the Third Millennium*. New York.

Slater, A.R. 1974. *The Archaeology of Dendereh in the First Intermediate Period*. Ann Arbor, MI.

SYLVIE CAUVILLE

Denon, Dominique Vivant, Baron de

Art connoisseur, artist, writer and diplomat for France under Louis XV and XVI, Vivant Denon (1747–1825) achieved early literary and social success even though he was born in the provinces, at Givry. Despite his name being proscribed, he survived the French revolution to serve illustriously under Napoleon Bonaparte, to whom he was introduced by Josephine. Selected to accompany Napoleon's Egyptian campaign, Denon became its most energetic and illustrious recorder.

Overseeing careful measurements of monuments and copying inscriptions as well as sketching, Denon may well be considered as the first scientific Egyptologist, while Napoleon, through his vision, was the founder of the field. Recording went on in the Delta and Upper Egypt, often in the harshest of conditions and even under enemy fire as the French General Desaix pursued the Mameluke troops upriver. Denon's drawings are the only surviving records of some monuments, such as the lovely temple of Amenhotep III on Elephantine Island at Aswan, which was torn down in 1822.

Denon acquired many Egyptian antiquities and later wrote an account of his sojourn on the Nile, *A Journey to Lower and Upper Egypt* (1802), published in two volumes with 141 plates. One hundred and fifty plates were published from his drawings in the multi-volume opus of the Napoleonic expedition (*Description de l'Égypte*), but his own book, which appeared first, instigated the profound effect of Napoleon's expedition on European scholarship and popular appreciation. Translated into English and German, the book has had some forty editions.

Appointed Director General of Museums by Napoleon in 1804, Denon accompanied Napoleon's campaigns in Austria, Spain and Poland, not only sketching on the battlefields but also advising on the choice of artistic spoils from vanquished cities. Thus he had a major role in forming the Louvre collections and making Paris a major artistic capital.

See also

Napoleon Bonaparte and the Napoleonic expedition

Further reading

Dawson, W.R., and E.P. Uphill. 1995. *Who Was Who in Egyptology,* 3rd edn, M.L. Bierbrier. London.
Nowinski, J. 1970. *Baron Dominique Vivant Denon (1745–1825): Hedonist and Scholar in a Period of Transition.* Rutherford, NJ.

BARBARA S. LESKO

domestic architecture, evidence from tomb scenes

The results of archaeological excavations in ancient settlements are our primary source of information about domestic architecture in ancient Egypt. Generally this information is limited to the ground plans of houses. Further information can be obtained from the study of models and representations of houses in tomb scenes.

Middle Kingdom models

Two types of models are known: (1) the so-called "soul houses," made of fired clay, originally painted, and (2) models made of painted wood. Both types are part of the funerary equipment of the Middle Kingdom.

Soul houses were usually the only funerary equipment for simple pit-graves in Middle Kingdom cemeteries, mainly in Middle Egypt. They were placed on the surface of the grave in the open air where they functioned as an offering table, replacing one of stone. This is clearly indicated by the addition of a spout to release libations and by the food offerings modeled in clay on the surface, found even on full three-dimensional house models. The idea that the soul house should give shelter to the soul of the deceased is no longer considered valid. In fact, only a few of the known specimens include the representation of a house or parts of one.

Miniature architectural elements, such as a false door, columned portico or canopied seat for the statue of the deceased, are modeled in the rear of the basin-shaped offering table and are a substitute for a rock-cut funerary chapel. As in the real tombs of this period, elements of domestic architecture were incorporated; in some cases these include the more or less complete representation of a house. In such soul houses, the portico of the tomb is transformed into the portico of a Middle Kingdom house, as known from the site of Lahun. Inner rooms are sometimes represented in detail by partition walls. Doors and windows are indicated by openings or incisions suggesting wooden lattices. Some ceramic models show a group of three openings in the front wall, comparable to those in a wooden model from the tomb of Meket-Re at Deir el-Bahri (see below). The rim of the offering table forms the enclosure wall of the court in front of the house. In the court are models of trees, wooden canopy poles, water jars and other household furnishings, which are combined with the models of funerary offerings: still the most important symbolic elements.

A prominent feature in almost all models is the stairway leading up to the roof along one of the side walls of the court. The roof is surrounded by a parapet and in this space are various structures, from simple protective walls to what appears to be a full upper story. Roof ventilators shaped like half-domes, which give air to the rooms below, are represented in most of the models. The increased number of columns on the upper floor, as well as the recessed upper portico, indicate a light structure of wood which could not be represented more appropriately in the coarse clay of the models.

Wooden models had the function of providing the deceased with material goods in his afterlife and were deposited in more elaborate rock-cut tombs near the burial or in separate chambers. Granaries and different crafts, including their architectural setting, are represented in many models, but models with an actual residence are rare. In a model of grazing cattle from a tomb at Deir el-Bersha, a somewhat simplified house is suggested by a tower-like structure. Misinterpretation of evidence

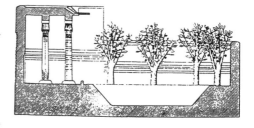

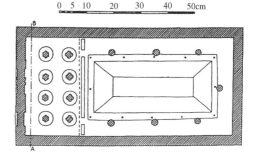

Figure 26 Wooden model of house and garden from the tomb of Meket-Re at Deir el-Bahri (from H.E. Winlock)

such as this has led to the notion of a multi-storied town house.

The only other evidence of domestic architecture is found in two almost identical models from the tomb of Meket-Re. While emphasis is given to an enclosed court of a garden with a pool surrounded by sycamore trees, the house itself is rendered in a very reduced manner by a portico with a double row of columns and a rear wall. On both sides of this wall two doors and one window are indicated by carved and painted designs. Archaeological evidence from Lahun and other Middle Kingdom sites shows that these openings represent the tripartite core of a Middle Kingdom house, consisting of a central room flanked by a bedroom and another side room.

The roof construction of the model's portico is rendered in minute detail. Three water spouts seem to be inappropriate elements, as hyperarid climatic conditions had been established in Upper Egypt since the Old Kingdom. Possibly the spouts served a symbolic function in keeping the pool supplied with water. The model of a small pavilion of Meket-Re is also provided with spouts, and another possibility is that the roofs were kept wet for cooling purposes.

The purpose of Meket-Re's model court was to provide him with the pleasant environment of garden and pool and the cool shade of the portico. An exact representation of his residence seemed unnecessary, as he now resided in his tomb, his "house of eternity."

Tomb scenes

Possibly the same explanation can be used to demonstrate why domestic architecture is rarely represented in tomb scenes. Only nineteen examples are known from the Theban necropolis, dating to the 18th and 19th Dynasties. In the tombs at Tell el-Amarna there are many representations of architecture, but they generally depict the royal palace or the royal domain. Only the Tell el-Amarna tombs of Meri-Re II and Mahu include their own houses in their tomb scenes.

Houses in tomb scenes are only the background for scenes showing the tomb owner engaged in various activities or funerary rites. Often they are a component of a garden or country estate. They are rendered in plan or elevation, or a combination of both, but section drawings in the modern sense are not known. Tomb paintings do not show an actual house in its exact dimensions, but the artists took liberties to choose certain typical elements which they thought appropriate to convey the idea of a house.

The large painting of Djehuty-Nefer's house from one of his two Theban tombs (TT 104) has been misinterpreted as a section drawing of a

multi-storied town house. In fact, it shows the modified plan of a high official's house, with the private apartments omitted and the elements rearranged by the artist. Egyptian artists used what could be called a "collapsed side view," where the vertical elevation of each room is fitted within the plan, also depicted vertically. Thus the plan, elevation, decoration and other furnishings were all included in one representation. Considering these conventions, Djehuty-Nefer's house was really a one-story structure with a court, reception hall, central hall, common rooms and private quarters. This type of house is well known from Tell el-Amarna, and Djehuty-Nefer's tomb painting demonstrates that it already existed in the early 18th Dynasty.

In Djehuty-Nefer's other tomb (TT 80), a house is depicted reduced to elementary features. The upper part with the large window might represent a loggia on the roof, as is also indicated by the receding step in the façade on the left side. In another Theban tomb scene (TT 334), the simplified plan of a house is represented. Clearly shown are the three zones of the plan, each with increasing privacy: (1) reception hall, (2) central hall and (3) private rooms. The positions of the doors correspond to archaeological evidence: the reception hall precedes a central hall with an axial door, behind which are private apartments.

The house depicted in the tomb of Mosi (TT 254) might have two stories, although it is obvious from the large number of small windows in the bottom row, representing the clerestory windows of the central hall, and from the presence of two entrance doors, that the artist wanted to show as many openings as possible. The top of the walls is protected against intruders by a fence of palm fronds, as is still used in Egypt today. Such a precaution would not be necessary on top of a two-story house. The trees in front of the house are protected by round brick structures with numerous openings for ventilation, a device which is also still used in Egypt.

The house depicted in TT 96 has a combination of two elevations, one with two windows and one with two doors. The upper

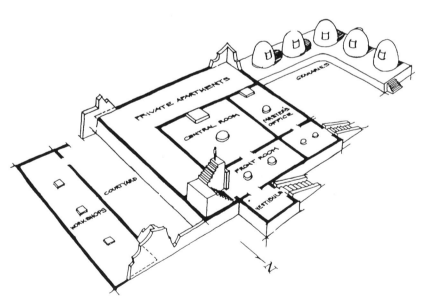

Figure 27 Representation of Djehuty-Nefer's house in his tomb in western Thebes (TT 104) and its interpretation (from H.A. Assad)

representation shows a chapel consisting of three identical rooms. The buildings are part of a vast estate with gardens and trees.

The same technique of representing two elevations in one seems to be applied in a scene from TT 23. What at first glance appears to be a two-story house is probably the representation of two elevations of a one-story house, according to the arrangement of trees and the broken line behind the female figure.

Two roof ventilators, consisting of rectangular openings in the flat house roof with slanting covers, are depicted in TT 90. The same device (*malkaf*, in Arabic) is still used today in Egypt to catch the cool northern breeze. Similar devices are shown above the royal bedroom in representations of the royal palace in tombs at Tell el-Amarna.

Models and tomb scenes help to corroborate archaeological evidence and broaden our information about domestic architecture. From such evidence additional information is obtained on the size and shape of windows, columns, decoration and devices to cool the house interior (porticoes, roof ventilators, position of windows). In tomb scenes trees and gardens are invariably linked to the house. Models give us information about the importance of roof space as a place of rest and recreation, and were accordingly equipped with protective walls, canopies and loggias. The question of a full second story or even higher elevations must remain open, however.

See also

Deir el-Bahri, Meket-Re tomb; Deir el-Bersha; Lahun, town; Tell el-Amarna, city; Tell el-Amarna, nobles' tombs

Further reading

Assaad, H.A. 1983. The house of Thutnefer and Egyptian architectural drawings. *The Ancient World* VI (1–4): 3–20.

Badawy, A. 1966. *A History of Egyptian Architecture: The First Intermediate Period, the Middle Kingdom, and the Second Intermediate Period*: 12–19. Berkeley, CA.

——. 1968. *A History of Egyptian Architecture: The Empire (the New Kingdom)*: 15–35. Berkeley, CA.

Roik, E. 1988. *Das altägyptische Wohnhaus und seine Darstellung im Flachbild*. Frankfurt.

Winlock, H.E. 1955. *Models of Daily Life in Ancient Egypt*. Cambridge, MA.

DIETER EIGNER

Dorginarti

Dorginarti was an island fortress located at the northern end of the Second Cataract in Sudanese Nubia (21°51′ N, 31°14′ E), a site excavated by the Oriental Institute of the University of Chicago in 1964, as part of the High Dam Campaign led by UNESCO.

The original construction of the fortress and its main phases of occupation were originally thought to date to the Middle Kingdom or New Kingdom phases represented at other fortresses in Lower Nubia, though the archaeological materials uncovered at the site were different from those expected. A recent study demonstrates that Dorginarti's pottery and small artifacts are similar to types found in Egyptian and Sudanese contexts, ranging in date from the Third Intermediate Period through the 27th Dynasty in Egypt. Therefore, the fortress was probably occupied between the mid-seventh century BC and the end of the fifth century BC. Its original occupation may have begun a century earlier.

During this period Lower Nubia was thought to have been unpopulated, due to low Nile floods and its position as a buffer zone between two hostile kingdoms. However, the textual and archaeological records show that there were adequate Nile floods in the first half of the first millennium BC; also, the evident prosperity of the 25th and 26th Dynasties argues against consistently low Niles. Therefore, if there was a decline in the occupation of Lower Nubia, this would have been caused by the lessening of trade and diplomatic activity as a result of strained relations between Egypt and Kush with the rise of Saite power in Egypt (26th Dynasty).

Dorginarti

Evidence indicates that there was activity in Lower Nubia during at least parts of this period. Pottery and artifacts dating to the first half of the first millennium BC have recently been identified at sites between the First and Third Cataracts, and beyond. There is also evidence that the area was resettled earlier in the Meroitic period (after *circa* 270 BC) than has previously been thought. Therefore, the supposed gap in the occupation of Lower Nubia during the first millennium BC has closed considerably, and the existence of a first millennium BC fortress on Dorginarti is not an anomaly.

The fortress

The fortress interior was divided into three main areas. Buildings were also constructed outside the fort walls in the bay at the southwestern corner, as well as to the south of the northwestern corner buttress. The West Sector contained garrison quarters, storage facilities, workshops and the main fortress gateway, which led out to a roadway. A north–south wall divided the western half from both the Central Sector's "Official's Residence" and the East Sector's storage areas and River Gate.

The main building of the Central Sector, called the "Official's Residence," underwent two major building phases before the latest (Level II) construction. In an earlier (Level III) building, a number of Ramesside blocks (19th–20th Dynasties) were reused for door sills, jambs and lintels. They may have been procured from across the river at Buhen, where building activity by both Ramesses I and Ramesses IV is attested in inscriptions.

Stratigraphy shows that there was a period of abandonment after a fire in the central sector and before the construction of the latest fortification, consisting of retaining walls of a square, buttressed platform with corner towers. At a later time, some of the bays in the outer faces were partly filled with stone.

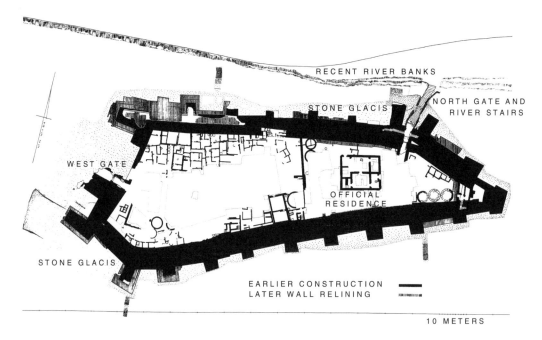

Figure 28 Plan of the Nubian fort at Dorginarti, Levels III and IV

Material remains

The garrison soldiers and staff who lived in the fort left behind ceramic vessels and small artifacts of East Greek, Levantine and Egyptian manufacture. Also, handmade pots of Sudanese tradition and stone arrowheads excavated here indicate that there were also soldiers or staff from regions south of Egypt.

Most of the pottery and small artifacts from Dorginarti resemble remains from sites in Egypt dating to the late-Kushite and Saite periods (*circa* 700–525 BC), and the Persian period (*circa* 525–400 BC). Also, numerous crucible fragments with deposits on the interiors, as well as the remains of two tuyères and two fragments from possible pot-bellows, resemble the metallurgical evidence from Saite fortresses in the Delta and (late Iron II) fortresses in southern Palestine. The original levels of the fortress (IV and III) were occupied some time in the late eighth and seventh centuries BC.

The pottery types that were found in association with the later Level II terrace can perhaps all be dated to the second half of the sixth and the fifth centuries BC. East Greek and Phoenician amphorae fragments were brought into the fortress either at the end of the Saite period or during the Persian period. The Phoenician amphorae fragments are particularly numerous.

Conclusion

Throughout earlier pharaonic periods, Egypt sent trade, diplomatic and military expeditions to the south, along both the river and the Western Desert routes of Lower and Upper Nubia. The merchandise, gifts, booty and tribute which they acquired were hauled down the Nile and along the desert routes from Nubia or from elsewhere in Sudan and Ethiopia. These goods included gold, copper, semi-precious and quarried stones, and cattle, all of which could be acquired along the Nile or in the deserts and highlands to the east and west of the river. Other goods, such as ivory, rare woods, gum, incense, ostrich feathers and eggs, animal skins and wild animals, including leopards, monkeys and giraffes, were most likely obtained through intermediary traders coming from areas farther south.

During the Kushite, Saite and Persian periods, trade goods from Africa (as well as from Kushite people) also appeared in the Near Eastern world beyond Egypt. Archaeological and textual evidence shows that movements of populations and goods were occurring not only along the Nile River between Egypt and Kush, but also along other land and sea routes. The Phoenicians were utilizing the Red Sea during this period, and Egyptian and Persian interest in a canal between the Red Sea and the Nile may reflect a lucrative sea trade from coastal Ethiopia, Sudan and the Arabian peninsula.

The Egyptians and Persians (as well as the Kushites) undoubtedly sought to win control of the Lower Nubian routes in order to secure the safe conduct of trade and diplomatic expeditions, and to tap the profits of the trade in African luxury materials. The fortress on the island of Dorginarti was undoubtedly only one of the military outposts on the riverine route between Elephantine and the Kushite region.

See also

Late and Ptolemaic periods, overview; Nubian forts; Punt; Third Intermediate Period, overview

Further reading

Heidorn, L.A. 1991. The Saite and Persian Period forts at Dorginarti. In *Egypt in Africa: Nubia from Prehistory to Islam*, W.V. Davies, ed., 205–19. London.
——. 1992. The fortress of Dorginarti and Lower Nubia during the seventh to fifth centuries B.C. Ph.D. dissertation, University of Chicago.

LISA A. HEIDORN

Dynastic stone tools

In the early days of Egyptian archaeology, about one hundred years ago, a detailed investigation of lithic technology, raw material procurement and the importance of stone tools for ancient Egyptian daily life was never conducted, and there are only some preliminary and very superficial reports about Early Dynastic flint-working. Unfortunately, most of this material was from tombs, which always contain only the best-fashioned tools and stone blanks, so that the deceased could live well in the afterlife. However, due to an increasing interest in settlements, archaeological activities in Egypt have changed during the last two decades. Some very interesting lithic material has now been excavated in well-stratified sites, ranging in date from the late Predynastic period to the 25th Dynasty.

For the late Predynastic and Early Dynastic periods, lithic assemblages from three settlements are important: Tell el-Fara'in (Buto) and Tell Ibrahim Awad in the Delta, and Elephantine (Aswan) at the Nubian border. Also of great importance for this early period are the rich flint tools from Hemaka's tomb at North Saqqara (1st Dynasty). For the Old Kingdom, the lithic artifacts from Giza and Ain Asil are good examples. For the Middle Kingdom and Second Intermediate Period, there are assemblages from Tell ed-Dab'a in the Delta and the Nubian fortress of Mirgissa. Undoubtedly, the best example of New Kingdom flaked tools is the vast material from Qantir/Pi-Ramesses in the Delta, excavated in the city's industrial area.

Given the large corpus of information, some clear patterns of development are now recognizable. One of the most exciting observations is of the different stages of raw material extraction and tool preparation, and flint mines are known for all Dynastic periods. Studies of the flint working technologies have also been conducted, and a clear development can be demonstrated in which the tools became rougher and coarser, from late Predynastic times (Nagada III) to the late New Kingdom.

Beginning with the 1st Dynasty, only well-fashioned stone blanks and finished tools were brought into the settlements. Necessary for this were organized mining activities and also an effectively organized trade of the blanks and tools, produced in or near the settlements of the quarriers and professional flint-knappers.

It is first important to identify rich and usable flint deposits which were not too far from settlements. Fortunately, some ninety years ago the German geologist Blankenhorn conducted an extensive geological survey of the Nile Valley and his results are still useful. From his information, the main deposits of good workable flint have all been located in wadis near the Nile Valley. The most southerly flint source is the mountains near Thebes West, which belong to a geological formation of the Eocene (Libyan stage). Rich layers of very homogeneous flint nodules of the highest quality can be found here. Some small quarries in Thebes West date to the Old and Middle Kingdoms, but the most extensive mining activity took place when Thebes was the New Kingdom capital. Numerous tombs were excavated then, which also resulted in a high output of flint, providing material not only for the local settlements but also for more distant regions, such as the Nile Delta and Nubia.

Early in this century, two more extensive flint sources of the best quality were found about 100 km south of Cairo, in two tributary wadis on the eastern fringe of the Valley. A short survey in 1981 demonstrated that on top of the high terraces of Wadi Sojoor and Wadi el-Sheikh, which both belong to an Eocene formation (lower Mokattam stage), there are vast dumps from extensive quarrying. Analysis of the stone tools indicates that the Wadi Sojoor deposits were mostly mined during Early Dynastic and Old Kingdom times. Archaeological evidence from the Wadi el-Sheikh points to mining in late Predynastic/Early Dynastic times, and then later during the New Kingdom, when freshly mined flint was traded in the settlements. However, the most extensive quarrying was during the Middle Kingdom, when finished blades and knifes were sent to Tell ed-Dab'a in the Delta.

Only one quarry to the northwest of Cairo, in the Cretaceous formation of Abu Roasch, is

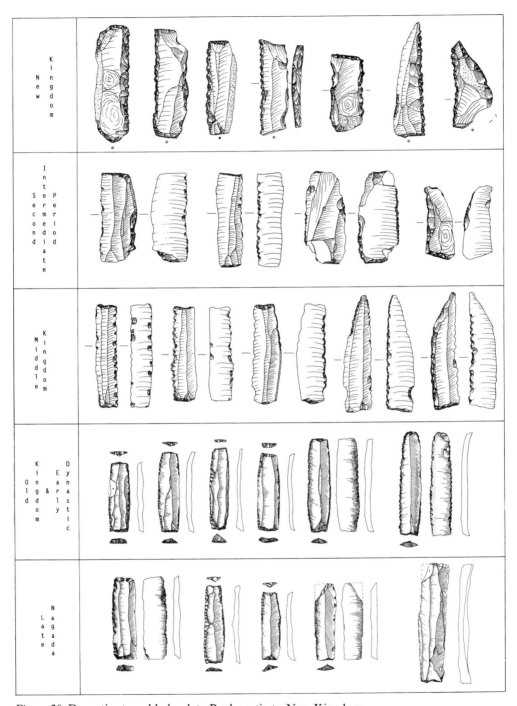

Figure 29 Dynastic stone blades, late Predynastic to New Kingdom

lacking in evidence of ancient activity, because it was heavily mined for gunflint in the nineteenth and twentieth centuries. This quarry must have supplied much flint to the Delta because artifacts made of this characteristic material have been found there in large quantities, from late Predynastic times onward.

Stone tool technology in Dynastic times had its roots in late Predynastic flint manufacturing, especially that of the Nagada culture. Very high-quality tools were produced then, especially the thin ripple-flaked knifes found in elite, (late) Nagada culture burials. Bifacially worked knifes were manufactured until the New Kingdom, but their form changed and the quality of flaking declined. There were also tool types which were used mainly in domestic contexts (scrapers, burins, borers and hafted blades for cutting meat).

Huge blades, up to 20 cm long and 3 cm wide, have been found in an Early Dynastic context. These are the so-called "razor blades," but their

Table 3 Chronology of tool production in the Near East

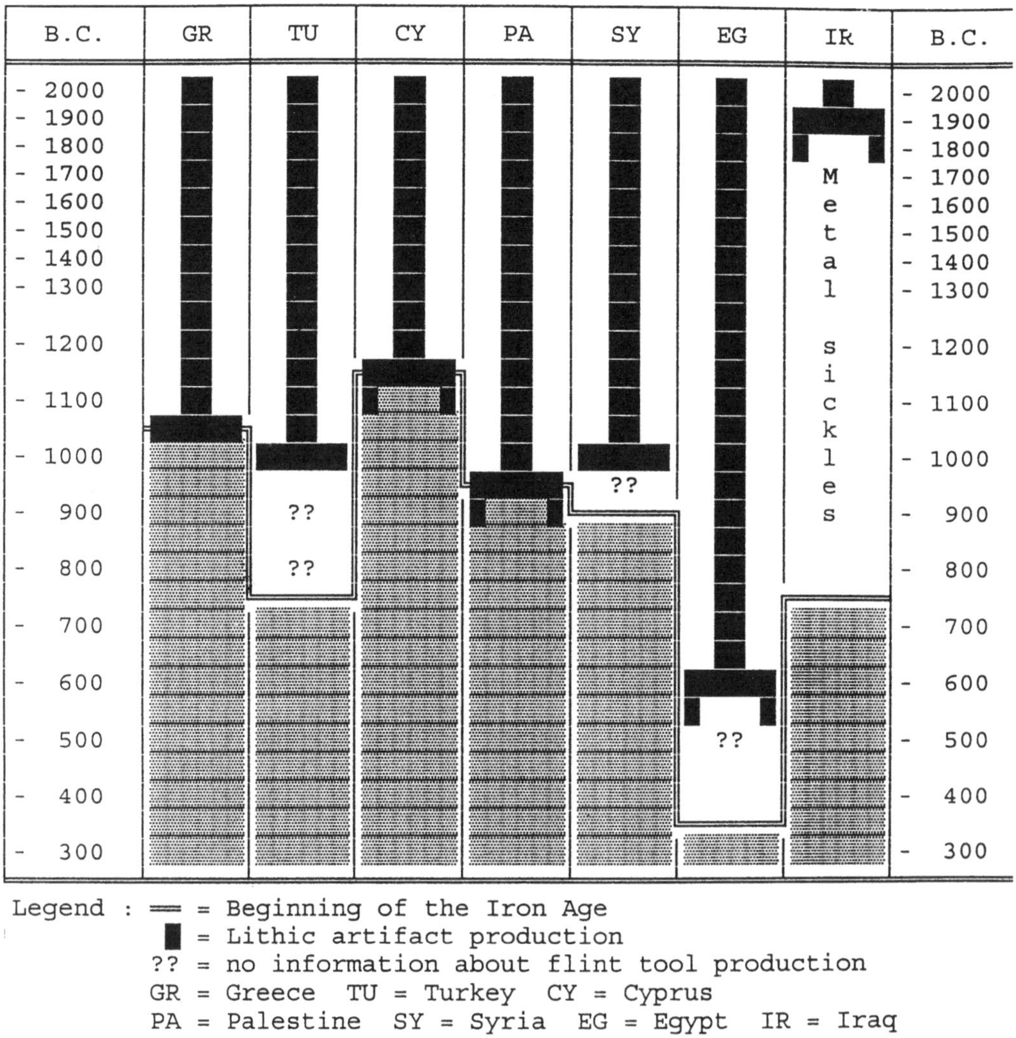
B.C.
GR
TU
CY
PA
SY
EG
IR
B.C.
- 2000
- 1900
- 1800
- 1700
- 1600
- 1500
- 1400
- 1300
- 1200
- 1100
- 1000
- 900
- 800
- 700
- 600
- 500
- 400
- 300
??
??
??
??
Metal sickles
Legend : = Beginning of the Iron Age
= Lithic artifact production
?? = no information about flint tool production
GR = Greece TU = Turkey CY = Cyprus
PA = Palestine SY = Syria EG = Egypt IR = Iraq

real use is unknown. Undoubtedly, this blade technology originated in Palestine, where this technology is first found. All other tools, up to the late Middle Kingdom, were made of smaller blades, which tend to get broader and thicker through time, especially the different sickle blades. Beginning in the Second Intermediate Period, the cutting edge of the sickle blade, which earlier had been retouched only during resharpening, was heavily denticulated, pointing again to a Palestinian origin. Also at this time the type of flint used for tools changed and the Egyptian tradition of core flaking tradition ended. In New Kingdom times the stone blanks were increasingly replaced by flakes or blades, and the tools became more coarse.

The bifacially worked flint knifes and sickle blades described above are the two most important tool groups of Dynastic Egypt, showing a stylistic and functional development through time. Their manufacture until the 25th Dynasty can be best explained by their high degree of usefulness and low production costs. Examples in Dynastic Egypt of borers, burins, axes and arrowheads, however, are rare.

Why stone tools were used for such a long time in ancient Egypt needs some explanation. In contrast to its rich chert resources, Egypt has only very small deposits of copper and virtually no tin (for bronze production). This also explains why ancient Egypt was not able to play a leading role in metallurgical technologies like its neighbors, especially Palestine, which has large deposits of copper. In exchange for metal from Palestine and later from Cyprus, Egypt traded gold and cereals, both of which were abundantly available in Egypt. Egypt therefore had to import nearly all its copper and tin, which greatly limited its distribution to most of the population. Copper/bronze was limited in quantity and very expensive, and most metal in Egypt was needed for weapons used by the army. The remaining metal would have been distributed among elites.

The use of stone tools finally ended in Egypt when iron processing began because this metal was much cheaper than bronze, and it was also harder. However, this occurred in Egypt several hundred years later than in the neighboring countries.

See also

Buto (Tell el-Fara'in); Elephantine; metallurgy; natural resources; Neolithic and Predynastic stone tools; Qantir/Pi-Ramesses; Saqqara, North, Early Dynastic tombs; Tell ed-Dab'a, Second Intermediate Period

Further reading

Kromer, K. 1978. Siedlungsfunde aus dem frühen alten Reich in Giseh. Österreichische Ausgrabungen 1971–1975. *DÖAW* 136.

Midant-Reynes, B. 1985. L'industrie lithique en Égypte: a propos des fouilles de 'Ain-Asil (Oasis de Dakhla). *BSFE* 102: 27–43.

Miller, R. 1983. Lithic technology in East Karnak, Egypt. *JSSEA* 13: 228–36.

Rosen, S.A. 1983. The Canaanean blade and the Early Bronze Age. *IEJ* 33: 15–29.

Schmidt, K. 1992. Tell Ibrahim Awad: preliminary report on the lithic industries. In *The Nile Delta in Transition; 4th–3rd Millennium B.C.*, E.C.M. van den Brink, ed., 79–96. Jerusalem.

Tillmann, A. 1986. Ein Steinartefaktinventar des Neuen Reiches aus Qantir/Piramesse (Ein Vorbericht). *Archäologisches Korrespondenzblatt* 16: 149–55.

Weisgerber, G. 1987. The ancient chert mines at Wadi el-Sheikh (Egypt). In *The Human Uses of Flint and Chert*, G. Sieveking and M.H. Newcomer, eds, 165–71. Brighton.

ANDREAS TILLMANN

E

Early Dynastic private tombs

Private tombs of the 1st and 2nd Dynasties are the most important source of evidence for Early Dynastic society because excavations of contemporary settlements are limited. Cemeteries with Early Dynastic graves are distributed throughout Egypt, mostly at desert-edge locations, although increasing archaeological activity in the Delta has revealed new sites, such as Minshat Abu Omar. Non-royal Early Dynastic cemeteries usually contain a wide range of burials, from the high status tombs of local officials to the simple graves of the ordinary people. Exceptions are the cemeteries of court retainers surrounding the royal tombs and funerary palaces at Abydos (which clearly form a special class), and the exclusively elite cemeteries in the Memphite region, which served the highest state officials. The most important elite cemetery is at North Saqqara, which contains an uninterrupted sequence of burials spanning the 1st Dynasty, as well as a large number of 2nd and 3rd Dynasty tombs. On the opposite bank of the Nile, the vast Early Dynastic cemetery at Helwan, containing over 10,000 tombs, served as the main burial ground for the officials and inhabitants of Memphis.

Within the Early Dynastic period a clear sequence of development in tomb architecture is seen. The main factor affecting the design of a tomb was the wealth of its owner. Modifications and innovations were introduced first in royal and elite burials, and were subsequently adopted by the other sectors of the population. From the beginning of the 1st Dynasty, elite tombs were characterized by a large mudbrick superstructure called a *mastaba*, with exterior walls decorated with recessed niches. This style of architecture, known as "palace façade," is thought to have imitated the external appearance of the royal palace. The façade of the tomb superstructure was plastered, and the niches were painted with elaborate patterns, imitating woven mats. During the early 1st Dynasty, the burial chamber was a shallow pit roofed with wood. It was surrounded by mudbrick storerooms, which housed some of the grave goods. Further storerooms were located in the superstructure, which was divided up by cross-walls. Access to the burial chamber must have been difficult, and the superstructure could not have been completed until after the interment. Later, during the reign of Den, an entrance stairway to the burial chamber, starting outside the superstructure, was introduced. The resulting threat to security was addressed by blocking the stairs at intervals with large limestone slabs (portcullis).

Toward the end of the 1st Dynasty, tomb design underwent major changes, including the adoption of an L-shaped plan for the entrance stairway. Tomb robbing probably inspired the tendency to dig tombs more deeply. The focus of the tomb shifted toward the substructure, and the storerooms adjoining the burial chamber housed all the grave goods. Consequently, the above-ground *mastaba* was built as a solid mass of mudbrick and rubble. The niched exterior largely disappeared, to be replaced by plain walls with an offering niche, called a "false door," at either end of the east façade. The southern niche was the more important one, and later became the focus of the mortuary cult.

From the beginning of the 2nd Dynasty, tombs in the Memphite necropolis, where the limestone strata are near the surface, were hewn in the rock. Access was by a stairway, and the tomb was covered by a mudbrick *mastaba*.

Outside the Memphite region, where the geology was less favorable for rock-cut tombs, the older, partially excavated mudbrick constructions continued to be built. In the 2nd Dynasty the tomb appears to have been conceived as a house for the deceased, and the burial chamber was divided by mudbrick walls into a suite of rooms. The coffin was placed on a raised platform in the "bedroom" and some tombs were even provided with a replica lavatory. Later in the 2nd Dynasty a longitudinal layout was gradually adopted for tombs, with subsidiary chambers, often in pairs, opening off the central corridor.

Burials of lower-ranking officials and members of local elites (represented, for example, at Naga ed-Deir in Upper Egypt) generally followed the same sequence of development, though tombs were smaller. With fewer grave goods, there was never any need for a hollow superstructure divided into storerooms.

Royal retainers and craftsmen were generally buried in simple mudbrick-lined rectangular pits, covered with a low, vaulted superstructure. A false door at the southern end of the eastern face was introduced in the middle of the 1st Dynasty. In the 2nd Dynasty, simple shaft tombs (a vertical shaft leading to a single, rock-cut chamber) were the norm for lower status officials.

The graves of the vast majority of the population showed little change from the Predynastic period. The body might be wrapped in a cloth or animal skin, or simply placed directly in a rectangular or oval pit, cut in the surface gravel. Some pits were divided into two chambers, a larger one for the actual burial and a smaller one for pottery. After the pit had been roofed with a mat or wooden planks, the excavated gravel was heaped up in a mound to cover the grave. Toward the end of the 1st Dynasty, pits lined with mudbricks became increasingly common, but otherwise, the simplest graves changed little throughout the Early Dynastic period.

Although the basic design of tombs varied little between different regions of the country, the local geology had some effect on construction techniques. Thus the availability of good-quality limestone in the Memphite area encouraged the early use of stone. Some of the 1st Dynasty tombs at Helwan show extensive use of stone for portcullis blocks, roofing slabs and the lining of the burial chamber.

Early Dynastic tombs were furnished with a wide variety of grave goods. The sumptuous burial equipment of the elite tombs at North Saqqara included numerous stone vessels. Some tombs had stone vessels which had probably been deliberately smashed, as part of the funerary ritual. Many artifacts from the North Saqqara tombs appear to have been produced in the same royal workshops which supplied the king's tomb. They include fine wooden furniture, games, jewelry, chests of linen garments, copper vessels and tools, and flint tools. The most important supplies were of food and drink, to provide sustenance for the tomb owner in the afterlife. The provisions commonly included large joints of meat, loaves of bread, jars of cheese and rows of so-called "wine jars." Some high status burials were provided with a funerary meal, laid out on ceramic and stone plates next to the coffin. Poorer graves merely contained some jars of provisions and a few additional offerings, such as toilet implements or the occasional stone vessel.

Some 1st Dynasty elite tombs also included the burial of a wooden boat, placed in a shallow trench next to the tomb and covered with a layer of mudbricks. Boat burials have been found at Abu Roash, North Saqqara and Helwan, and suggest that beliefs about the afterlife already incorporated the notion of a celestial journey.

First Dynasty tombs of courtiers, particularly at Abydos, were often marked by a limestone stela with the name, and sometimes the titles, of the deceased. In the 2nd Dynasty a feature of many officials' burials at Helwan was a "ceiling stela." This stela showed the name, titles and a representation of the tomb owner. Some of the earliest examples of the well-known offering formula are preserved on such stelae.

Irrespective of status, the deceased was buried in a contracted position. The orientation of the body varied and probably depended upon the direction from which offerings would be brought. Although true mummification had not yet been developed in the Early Dynastic period, attempts were made to preserve the body, or at least its appearance. In some 2nd Dynasty burials at North Saqqara the features of the deceased were carefully modeled in linen bandages, soaked in a resinous substance. Wooden coffins are attested from the early 1st Dynasty in high status burials, but by the 2nd Dynasty they had been adopted by all classes.

See also

Abydos, Early Dynastic funerary enclosures; Abydos, Umm el-Qa'ab; Early Dynastic period, overview; Helwan; Kafr Tarkhan (Kafr Ammar); Minshat Abu Omar; Naga ed-Deir; Saqqara, North, Early Dynastic tombs; Tura, Dynastic burials and quarries

Further reading

Emery, W.B. 1961. *Archaic Egypt*. Harmondsworth.

Reisner, G.A. 1936. *The Development of the Egyptian Tomb down to the Accession of Cheops*. Cambridge, MA.

Saad, Z.Y. 1969. *The Excavations at Helwan: Art and Civilization in the First and Second Egyptian Dynasties*. Norman, OK.

Spencer, A.J. 1993. *Early Egypt: The Rise of Civilisation in the Nile Valley*. London.

TOBY A. H. WILKINSON

Edfu

The town of Edfu (24°59′ N, 32°52′ E) is located on the west bank of the Nile River, between Luxor to the north and Aswan to the south (about 100 km from each). In Graeco-Roman times it was called Apollinopolis Magna, the local god Horus being identified with the Greek god Apollo. The modern Arabic name Edfu is a direct descendant of the ancient Egyptian name Djeba, (Etbo, in Coptic). Edfu was an important regional center since the Old Kingdom. This is partly due to the large area of fertile land belonging to the town, and partly to the fact that Edfu was situated near the former frontier between Egypt and Nubia. Edfu was a starting point for desert routes leading to the Kharga Oasis in the west, and to the mines of the Eastern Desert and the Red Sea coast in the east.

No remains go back beyond the 5th Dynasty, but at least toward the end of the Old Kingdom, Edfu was the capital of Nome II of Upper Egypt. The most ancient Edfu cemetery, comprising the *mastaba*s of the Old Kingdom as well as later tombs, covers the area southwest of the precinct of the great temple of Horus. One of the *mastaba*s belonged to Isi who was the "great chief of the Nome (of Edfu)" early in the 6th Dynasty. Later, in the Middle Kingdom, Isi became a local saint and was worshipped under the title "living god." Before the beginning of the New Kingdom, the necropolis was transferred to Hager Edfu, a place about 4 km to the west, and finally in the Late period to Nag' el-Hassaya, 12 km to the south, the whole area being called Behedet. Some ruins of the ancient town rise at a distance of about 150 m west of the great temple of Horus. They form an artificial hill (in Arabic, *tell*) consisting of the usual debris of a permanently inhabited human settlement. In this western part of Tell Edfu, excavations were carried out in the first decades of the twentieth century. A resumption of the excavations would likely achieve good results, but would encounter difficulties because the eastern part of the ancient town lies under the modern habitations of Edfu. There are, however, plans to evacuate the people living near the eastern enclosure wall in order to be able to start excavations in this area.

Close to the eastern tower of the pylon (the monumental gate) of the great temple the remains of another pylon have been unearthed. It dates from the Ramesside period and, though having a different orientation, it perhaps formed part of one of the predecessors of the extant great temple of Edfu. This temple precinct was comprised of many buildings, first of all the main temple within its own enclosure wall made of stone, and further subsidiary temples, smaller chapels, workshops, store-houses and dwellings. Most of them have been destroyed completely or lie beneath the houses of the present town. This is also true of the sacred lake and the slaughterhouse, which were located east of the great temple. South of the temple are the ruins of the so-called *mammisi*, or birthhouse, a temple in which the birth of the god Harsomtus was celebrated. The scanty architectural remains east of the *mammisi* probably belong to the temple of the sacred falcon. The most important building at Edfu is the temple of the god Horus Behedeti, lord of Edfu. Its excellent state of preservation is partly due to the fact that most of it was buried under sand before about 1860. In that year the French Egyptologist Auguste Mariette ordered it to be cleared of the sand, rubbish and mudbrick houses that had been built against its enclosure wall, in the court and even on its spacious roof.

The most sacred part of the Horus temple is the granite shrine (*naos*) which gave shelter to the main statue of Horus Behedeti, located near the rear wall of the sanctuary. Eight chapels open off the corridor that leads around the sanctuary; probably most of them lodged the statues of the major gods and goddesses of Egypt, who formed the divine following of Horus Behedeti; others were used for special religious rites. In front of the sanctuary there is an antechamber. East of the antechamber, a small sacrificial court gives access to the *w'bt*, or "pure place," where the statues of the deities were anointed and dressed, where they received their crowns and amulets before leaving the interior of the temple and gaining its roof, on the occasion of special festivals. To the west of the antechamber is a small room dedicated to the god Min. The next main chamber toward the exit is the hall of the offering tables; on each side of it there is an approach to one of the staircases leading to the temple roof. Next follows the inner hypostyle hall, the roof of which is supported by twelve columns with rich floral capitals. The adjoining side chambers to the east served as access to the inner passage round the temple and as a treasury for precious metals and stones. The adjacent chambers to the west are the so-called "laboratory" for the sacred oils and ointments, and the "Nile-chamber" where the sacred water was poured into a basin after it had been brought from the nilometer, situated outside the girdle-wall. The main fabric of the temple ends with the outer hypostyle hall; the twelve columns inside are the highest of the whole temple (12.5 m). In the eastern part of its façade the library has been installed in a small chamber; two catalogs are inscribed on the walls giving the titles of the books (scrolls) that were preserved in two niches. The small chamber in the western part of the façade was dedicated to the consecration of the priest who performed the religious rites on behalf of the king. The main entrance of the *pronaos* opens to a large court, surrounded on three sides by a covered colonnade of thirty-two columns. To the south the court is limited by the mighty pylon, the towers of which are more than 35 m high. The girdle-wall having a height of about 10 m abuts against the towers of the pylon (*circa* 137 × 47 m).

A lengthy inscription on the outer face of the girdle-wall (a text-band *circa* 300 m in length) gives details concerning the names and functions of the different halls and chambers of the temple. This inscription not only gives an account of the entire building, but also relates the history of its construction. The temple was begun on August 23, 237 BC by Ptolemy III and completed on December 5, 57 BC under the rule of Ptolemy XII.

The inscriptions of the temple of Edfu were published by Émile Chassinat in eight volumes, amounting to about 3,000 pages altogether. They contain an enormous amount of information on many different subjects. For instance, one long sequence of texts and ritual scenes accurately lists the estates of the temple, which extended over 180 km between Aswan and Thebes. On the walls of the "laboratory" we can read the exact prescriptions for making the sacred oils and ointments. The jambs of some of the doorways bear inscriptions that reveal the moral obligations of the priesthood. Many texts on the inner face of the girdle-wall treat the creation of the world which emerged from the primeval waters at the very spot that would become Edfu; the world and all the things and creatures on it were the emanation of "Horus Behedeti, the great god, the lord of the Sky," forming a part of his body. About 2,000 ritual scenes show the king offering to the gods in order to obtain from them what Egypt needed for the maintenace of life. Other texts deal with the daily ritual, festivals and the complex theology of Edfu.

The lords of Edfu were Horus Behedeti, his divine consort Hathor of Dendera and their son Harsomtus. Besides them many other deities were venerated, for instance Isis, Nephthys and Osiris, Re, Ptah, Khonsu, Min, Khnum and Mehit, and there was even a cult for the royal ancestors. In Egypt many Horus-gods were worshipped. The specific Horus of Edfu was Horus-Re, often represented as a winged sun-disk or as a winged scarab. Being the divine archetype of terrestrial kingship, he defended Egypt against all kinds of foes. The embodiment of his enemies was the god Seth, and many scenes in the temple of Edfu show Horus killing Seth, the latter appearing in the shape of a crocodile, a hippopotamus or a donkey.

The daily ritual in the temple started with a morning song that was sung in front of the sanctuary. In several stanzas all the members of the god's body are woken, as well as his insignia, his throne and finally even the halls, chambers and columns of the temple. Then the sanctuary and the shrine were opened. Incense and fresh water were offered to Horus, religious rites were performed and the god received his offering meal. The ritual was repeated twice in the course of the day, probably in an abbreviated form. In the evening the doors of the shrine were closed and sealed. On festival days the religious ritual was more extensive.

One of the most important festivals commemorated the victory of Horus over Seth. Here, an analogy is drawn between this victory and the annual coming north of the sun until the summer solstice. Each year on the occasion of the Festival of Behedet, Hathor traveled from Dendera to Edfu. This feast lasted for fourteen days; during that period Horus and Hathor visited the tombs of the ancestor-gods situated in the necropolis of Behedet and performed all the necessary rites before these gods who were believed to guarantee the annual regeneration of the world. Two other important festivals were the yearly coronation of the sacred falcon and the festival of the New Year, when the statues of the deities were carried out of the interior of the temple up to the roof in order to expose them to the vivifying rays of the sun god Re.

See also

Dendera; Late and Ptolemaic periods, overview; Mariette, François Auguste Ferdinand; pantheon

Further reading

Alliot, M. 1949–54. *Le culte d'Horus à Edfou au temps des Ptolémées* (BdÉ 20). Cairo.

Cauville, S. 1987. *Essai sur la théologie du temple d'Horus à Edfou* (BdÉ 102). Cairo.

Fairman, H.W. 1974. *The Triumph of Horus: An Ancient Egyptian Sacred Drama*. Berkeley, CA.

Kurth, D. 1994. *Inschriften aus dem Tempel des Horus von Edfu*. Zürich.

——. 1998. *Die Inschriften des Tempels von Edfu*. Wiesbaden.

Vernus, P. 1986. Tell Edfu. In *LÄ* 6: 323–31.

DIETER KURTH

Egyptian (language), decipherment of

Few triumphs of human ingenuity capture the imagination as much as the decipherment of hieroglyphic writing in 1822. The decipherment came in the wake of Napoleon's expedition to Egypt (1798–1801). While working on a fort near Rosetta in 1799, soldiers found a stone slab inscribed with three scripts: Greek at the bottom and two undeciphered scripts, hieroglyphic proper and demotic, at the top and in the center. From its discovery to the watershed developments of 1822, the Rosetta Stone formed the focus of all efforts at decipherment, even if it did not provide the final clues. Yet as the beacon of incentive, it has appropriately become the symbol of the decipherment.

The process leading to the decipherment is complex. With hindsight, occasional correct insights can be isolated, but many are lucky guesses. Many others are mixed with false views. Above all, a plausible assumption is not proof. Three scholars whose contributions deserve mention with respect to the decipherment of Egyptian are Silvestre de Sacy, Johan Åkerblad and Thomas Young.

Three definitions of the decipherment are possible. In the broadest sense, the decipherment involves the recovery of: (1) the Egyptian *language* (Old Egyptian, Middle Egyptian, Late Egyptian, Demotic and Coptic); (2) three *scripts* (hieroglyphic proper and two cursive derivatives, hieratic and demotic); and (3) the *system* of hieroglyphic writing. In this sense, the decipherment is still ongoing.

In another definition, the decipherment involves (3) only: recovering the hieroglyphic script as a system of putting language into writing. Two steps can be distinguished in this second definition. The second of these two steps is the pivotal insight by Jean-François Champollion on the morning of September 14 1822. This second step by itself is the decipherment in the third, narrowest, sense.

Champollion was in two respects well prepared for the task of decipherment. He had a thorough knowledge of Coptic, a language which was generally thought to be later Egyptian. By 1821, he was also convinced of what had been suspected before, that the three hieroglyphic scripts were basically the same. Finding the key to one would result in the decipherment of all three.

Decipherment of the alphabet (spring and summer 1822)

When one faces an unknown language in an unknown script, one first looks for words of which both meaning and sound are known to obtain a sense of how the script represents the language. But this may seem like putting the cart before the horse. Yet hieroglyphic inscriptions

do, in fact, contain such words, the names of Greek and Roman kings and emperors who had ruled over Egypt and were known from classical sources. Since names such as Alexander, Cleopatra and Caesar could not be translated, it was reasonable to assume that hieroglyphic writing would present them roughly as pronounced in Greek. Foreign names could therefore offer a point of departure.

In comparing what seemed to be the names of Ptolemy and Cleopatra, Champollion observed that the first hieroglyph in Ptolemy was the same as the fifth in Cleopatra and could therefore be identified as the hieroglyph expressing the sound "p." Then he noted that the fourth hieroglyph in Ptolemy was the same as the second in Cleopatra. By repeating this matching procedure with several names, Champollion reconstructed a fairly complete alphabet, first in demotic and a little later also in hieroglyphic proper.

In retrospect, the recovery of the alphabet was possible due to the coincidence of three facts: (1) hieroglyphic texts contained names known from non-hieroglyphic sources; (2) these names were spelled phonetically or alphabetically; and (3) the alphabet played a crucial role in hieroglyphic writing of all times. These three facts are independent from one another.

The alphabet had now been deciphered. This discovery was communicated to the French Academy in the famous "Letter to M. Dacier," which is often referred to as the Magna Carta of the decipherment. However, it contains only the first step of two steps. After all, the Egyptian alphabet might have been used only to spell foreign names. The crucial second step, which constitutes the decipherment in its narrowest definition, followed in 1822.

Mixed character of the hieroglyphic script

Champollion had not had access to many texts from before the Ptolemaic period when, on the morning of September 14 1822, he received copies of inscriptions from the famous rock temple at Abu Simbel, built in the thirteenth century BC. In one of the cartouches, he saw the royal name ☉𓅓𓏥. The sign 𓏭, depicting a folded cloth, represented *s* in his alphabet. This gave "?-?-s-s." Turning his attention to the sun disk at the beginning, he had the good fortune of thinking of the Coptic word for "sun": *re*. This provisionally gave "Re-?-s-s." Next, "Ramesses" came to mind, a royal name often mentioned in Greek sources. If ☉𓄟𓏭 was Ramesses, what about 𓄟, a sign now known to depict three animal skins tied together? Tentatively proceeding on this path, Champollion recalled two things. First, on the basis of relative location, it had been established that the group 𓄟𓏭 occurs on the Rosetta Stone in the word for "birthday." Second, in Coptic, "birthday" is "day of *mise*," that is, "day of giving birth." On the basis of these two observations, combined with the knowledge that 𓏭 is *s*, 𓄟𓏭 could be identified with the two sounds *ms*. It was then only logical to identify 𓄟 with *m*. However, 𓄟 is a biliteral sound sign for *m + s*. Hieroglyphs representing sequences of two consonants were discovered only in 1837, after Champollion's death, by Richard Lepsius. But in the meantime, Champollion's erroneous assumption that hieroglyphs like 𓄟 and 𓄜 were homonyms posed no significant obstacle to reading texts because the value of the signs representing two consonants is often specified by other hieroglyphs referring to one consonant, a phenomenon known as phonetic complementation. In other words, it does not make much difference whether one reads 𓄟𓏭 as *m + s = ms* or as *ms + s = ms*. However, the many homon;yms result in an improbably high number of alphabetic signs. Which alphabet has about 130 signs? This problem was used as an argument against Champollion's system. Lepsius's discovery of biliteral sound signs and the principle of phonetic complementation did much to remove any lingering doubts about the validity of Champollion's decipherment.

On September 14 1822, Champollion became certain not only that his alphabet was valid for all of Egyptian history and that Egyptian was related to Coptic, but above all that the hieroglyphic script was a *mixed* system. It consists of both meaning signs and phonograms. This may have been suspected before, but providing positive proof by means of concrete and indisputable examples is another matter. The name "Ramesses" remains an excellent illustration. The first part is written with the *meaning* sign ☉. The second part is written with the *sound* signs 𓄟 and 𓏭.

This discovery was only the beginning of the decipherment in the broad sense. Champollion proceeded quickly. His alphabet allowed him to identify the sounds of many words in any text. Since many Egyptian words are preserved in Coptic, he could rely on his knowledge of this stage of the language to match sound sequences with Coptic words, often successfully. He read hieroglyphic texts in Coptic fashion, as it were, and even transcribed them in Coptic characters. This path could obviously be followed only with words written mainly with *sound* signs. But for words written with meaning signs and determinatives, there was help of another kind. Meaning signs and determinatives depict what they mean. One can derive the rough *meaning* of a word from the picture with which it is written. But what about the *sounds*? If the word happened to be preserved in Coptic and one happened to have chosen the correct Coptic word, one was lucky. There was otherwise no way of establishing the sounds of a word positively until a variant writing containing sound signs emerged. Such variant writings are often found in the earliest hieroglyphic texts, many of which were discovered only decades later.

When the sounds of a word were not known with certainty, Champollion used the sounds of the Coptic word with the same meaning. For example, the sign 𓈅 represents desert hills and is used to write the word for "foreign land." Champollion used the sounds of the Coptic word for "earth, land" to transcribe 𓈅 "foreign land," namely *kah*. Now we know that 𓈅 "foreign land" is to be read as *khaset*. Likewise, Champollion did not read 𓉐 "house" as *pr*, because no spelling such as 𓉐 (𓊪 = *p*, 𓂋 = *r*) was known to him. Instead, he used the Coptic word, which sounds somewhat like *ay* in the English "way." Champollion therefore deciphered quite a few words in meaning only.

Because of the precipitation of insights, September 14 1822 is the pivotal date in the decipherment of hieroglyphic writing. It is now regarded as the birthday of modern Egyptology.

See also

Champollion, Jean-François; Egyptian language and writing; Napoleon Bonaparte and the Napoleonic expedition; Rosetta Stone

Further reading

Champollion, J.-F. 1928. *Précis du système hiéroglyphique des anciens égyptiens*, 2nd edn. Paris.
Depuydt, L. 1994. On the nature of the hieroglyphic script. *ZÄS* 121: 17–36.
Griffith, F.L. 1951. The decipherment of the hieroglyphs. *JEA* 37: 38–46.
Hartleben, Hermine. 1906. *Champollion: Sein Leben und sein Werk*, 2 vols. Berlin. See especially chapter 7.
Schenkel, W. 1983. Schrift. In *LÄ* 5: 728–32.
Sottas, H. 1922. *Lettre à M. Dacier par M. Champollion le Jeune*, centenary edition. Paris.

LEO DEPUYDT

Egyptian language and writing

Egyptian belongs to the phylum of languages known as Afroasiatic, or variously as Lisramic, Erythraic or Hamito-Semitic. The other language groups in this phylum are Semitic (e.g. Akkadian, Hebrew, Ugaritic), Berber (Kabyle, Tuareg), Cushitic (Agaw, Bedja, Somali), Chadic (Hausa) and Omotic. The Afroasiatic languages display a prevalence for consonantalism over vocalism; the ratio between consonants and vowels is higher in the Afroasiatic languages than in other known languages.

In Afroasiatic languages, word-roots play a major role. Roots consist of from two to six consonants (three being the most common number), and words are derived from these roots through changes of various sorts. For example, the Afroasiatic languages use an *n* prefix to form reflexive stems, an *s* prefix to form causative stems, and an *m* prefix to form instrumental nouns. There is also a certain amount of shared vocabulary among the Afroasiatic languages, although the extent to which this is to be explained as borrowing among the languages is disputed. Two genders are distinguished: masculine, which is unmarked, and feminine, which shows a *t* ending. The ending *w* is used to indicate plurals and occurs at the end of masculine nouns and before the ending in feminine nouns (*wt*). Among the pronouns, the consonant *k* is used as the second masculine singular suffix pronoun, *i* as the first person singular suffix, and *n* as the first person plural suffix. The use of *ink* (Hebrew *'ānōkî*, Berber *inok*) as the first person independent pronoun is common in Afroasiatic languages.

There are features found in Egyptian which are paralleled in some, but not all, of the Afroasiatic languages. For example, Egyptian and Berber form an indirect genitive (i.e. "of" construction) through use of the morpheme *n*. Egyptian shares with the Semitic languages the possibility to form adjectives (called *nisbe* adjectives) from nouns or prepositions. A characteristic common to Egyptian (in its earliest stages) and African languages is the formation of passive forms through duplicating the final consonant of a root.

The Egyptian language can be divided into five main stages: (1) Old Egyptian, (2) Middle Egyptian, (3) Late Egyptian, (4) Demotic and (5) Coptic. Old Egyptian, which was the language of the Old Kingdom (3rd–6th Dynasties), can be further subdivided into archaic Egyptian, the language of the earliest hieroglyphic documents and the inscription in the tomb of Metjen, and the language of the *Pyramid Texts*, which shows a somewhat earlier stage of development than the language of the later Old Kingdom tomb biographies. Middle Egyptian was used during the First Intermediate Period and Middle Kingdom. Toward the end of this period one begins to observe features typical of the next stage of the language, Late Egyptian, in Middle Egyptian texts. Although Middle Egyptian was no longer used as the spoken language of Egypt after the

Middle Kingdom, it continued to be used in literary, monumental and religious inscriptions and texts throughout the rest of Egyptian history, until the use of hieroglyphs died out around the end of the fourth century AD. The latest attested hieroglyphic inscription is found on a temple at Philae and dates to AD 394. Old and Middle Egyptian are very similar to one another, and are often grouped together as Classical Egyptian or Older Egyptian.

Late Egyptian, the next phase of the language, shows considerable differences from Middle Egyptian. The verbal system of Classical Egyptian was primarily synthetic, employing inflected forms rather than auxiliaries (i.e. "I go" is a synthetic form; "I am going," using the auxiliary verb "to be," is an analytic form). In Late Egyptian we find that synthetic forms have been almost completely replaced by the use of analytic constructions. At the same time, Egyptian shifts from having been primarily a verb–subject–object language to one that is almost exclusively subject–verb–object. The resulting tense system of Late Egyptian is more defined than that of Classical Egyptian, which seems to have begun primarily as a system expressing aspectual (i.e. completed versus incomplete) and modal (indicative versus subjunctive) oppositions. Also, Late Egyptian shows the opposition of gender, number and definiteness in nouns through the use of articles which precede the noun, while Classical Egyptian did not mark nouns as defined/undefined, and indicated gender and number through the use of suffixes.

Late Egyptian has been divided by scholars into groups based on the genre of texts available. Non-literary Late Egyptian is defined as the language of the private letters and documents from Upper Egypt dating to the 20th Dynasty, and is thought to correspond closely to the spoken language of the time. Literary Late Egyptian is evinced in such texts as the *Late Egyptian Miscellanies*, as well as the language found in the later Ramesside monumental inscriptions. Literary Late Egyptian exhibits certain distinctive characteristics which separate it from its non-literary counterpart. Examples of such differences include the facts that literary Late Egyptian uses prepositions more frequently, and that it continues to use certain Middle Egyptian narrative tenses not found in the non-literary language.

Demotic, the next phase of Egyptian, describes both a language and its script. Demotic documents first occur during the 26th Dynasty, beginning in 664 BC, and are attested until AD 450, the last example of demotic known being graffiti in the temple at Philae. Demotic shows a number of similarities with Late Egyptian, as well as a few differences. For example, the Late Egyptian continuative $iw.f\ ḥr\ sḏm$ is no longer used in demotic; it is replaced by the use of strings of identical narrative verb forms.

The last stage of Egyptian is Coptic. By the first or second century AD, an alphabet made up of Greek and demotic characters was being used to transliterate terms in Egyptian magical and astrological texts. By the third century AD, this alphabet was standardized and consisted of the Greek alphabet augmented by six characters adapted from the demotic script which were used to represent sounds not found in Greek. The introduction of Coptic seems to coincide with the introduction of Christianity into Egypt; the impetus which gave rise to its use was the desire to provide translations of the Christian scriptures to the Egyptian converts. Coptic continued in use as a spoken language until the fifteenth century. It is still used as a liturgical language in the Egyptian Coptic Church.

The first three stages of Egyptian could be written using the hieroglyphic script. The use of hieroglyphs (Egyptian: *tit*) is first attested around 3000 BC. The hieroglyphic script consisted of three main types of signs. Logograms were signs used to represent a word by depicting the object itself, or through depicting a quality or property associated with it (i.e. scribe's kit for *sš*, scribe). Phonograms were derived from logograms and were used to represent the sounds of the language. There were three types of phonograms: those representing a single consonant, sometimes called alphabetic signs; those representing two consonants; and those representing three consonants. (Vowels were not written in Egyptian until the introduction of

Coptic.) Signs representing two or three consonants were frequently accompanied by alphabetic signs, called phonetic complements, which represented one or more of the letters in the multiliteral sign. This practice led to redundancy in hieroglyphic orthography. The third type of sign is known as a determinative. Determinatives derive their name from the fact that these signs occur at the ends of words and serve to determine, or help to clarify, the meaning of the word. Determinatives have no phonetic value. These three classes of hieroglyphs are not mutually exclusive; it is possible for a sign to function in all three.

The main principle of Egyptian writing is the rebus. Pictures of objects are used to represent not only the objects themselves, but also the consonants which make up the name of the object. For example, a word for "house" in Egyptian is *pr*. The hieroglyphic sign for this word is a schematic plan of a house. This sign is also used to write the word for "go out," *pri*. The addition of the determinative of walking legs helps to distinguish which *pr* is meant.

Hieroglyphic texts could be written in either columns or lines, and read from either right to left, or left to right. The signs usually faced the direction of the beginning of a text, so that signs in a text read from right to left faced right. There are examples of retrograde texts, in which the signs face the end rather than the beginning of a text. There were several different styles of hieroglyphs, the usage of which was determined primarily by the medium in which the scribe worked and the nature of the text. Elaborately carved hieroglyphs executed in minute detail were reserved for monumental inscriptions in temples and tombs. On stone stelae could be found incised, or occasionally in raised relief, hieroglyphs which lacked internal markings. A "semi-cursive" type of hieroglyphic script was first used on papyrus where it served to indicate the heading of hieratic accounts. This style of hieroglyphs, usually written in columns, was later used to record religious texts such as the *Book of the Dead*.

Roughly contemporaneous with the occurrence of hieroglyphs, examples of texts written in hieratic, an extremely cursive form of hieroglyphs written with ligatures, are found. The earliest datable hieratic inscription is the Horus name of King Scorpion found on jars at Tarkhan. Hieratic was written using a brush and black, or occasionally red, ink (red being used to delimit sections or as punctuation); it is found mainly on such materials as papyrus, ostraca, leather and linen. There are, however, examples of hieratic incised in stone. Hieratic was always read from right to left. Originally, hieratic was written in columns, but beginning in the 12th Dynasty this practice was abandoned in favor of horizontal lines.

There are two main styles of hieratic: an elegant script used in literary works, court decisions, school texts and final copies of administrative texts, and a more cursive script, used mainly in such texts as personal letters, dictated material, the first drafts of reports and so on. From this cursive hieratic script developed a script known as abnormal hieratic, first attested at Thebes during the 21st–22nd Dynasties. This script was used to record administrative texts such as cadasters, tax lists, accounts and personnel lists. Abnormal hieratic was used for about five hundred years, the last such text being dated to the reign of Amasis in the Saite period (26th Dynasty).

Another descendant of cursive hieratic is the demotic script, first attested in Lower Egypt during the reign of Psamtik I, around 650 BC. By the end of the Saite period, demotic had completely replaced abnormal hieratic throughout Egypt. Demotic is an even more cursive script which frequently employs ligatures and abbreviations, making it often difficult to read. It is no longer closely related to the hieroglyphic script and, unlike most hieratic, cannot be easily transcribed into hieroglyphs. Demotic was originally used to record legal and administrative texts, but from the Ptolemaic period on literary texts are also found in this script.

See also

Amarna Letters; Egyptian (language), decipherment of; writing, invention and early development; writing, reading and schooling

Further reading

Allen, J. 1992. Egyptian language and writing. In *The Anchor Bible Dictionary* 4, D. Freedman, ed., 188–93. New York.

Davies, W. 1987. *Egyptian Hieroglyphs.* Berkeley, CA.

Diakonof, I. 1965. *Semito-Hamitic Languages.* Moscow.

Emmel, S. 1992. Coptic language. In *The Anchor Bible Dictionary* 4, D. Freedman, ed., 180–8. New York.

Hodge, C. 1971. *Afroasiatic: A Survey.* Paris.

Loprieno, A. 1995. *Ancient Egyptian: A Linguistic Introduction.* Cambridge.

STEPHEN E. THOMPSON

Egyptians, physical anthropology of

Physical anthropology is the study of the biological features of ancient and modern humans, including health, nutrition, mortality, genetics and physical variability in the past and present, and of humans' primate relatives and fossil ancestors. These studies are all informed by modern evolutionary theory and take their place in anthropology rather than biology because they consider the biocultural context within which human evolution, adaptation and variation occur. Historically, however, physical anthropology focused on the physical variation observed among living peoples and assumed that a fixed number of definitive physical "types" lay behind this variation. These fundamental types were identified as the different "races" of humankind and were thought to be recognizable also in the fossil or skeletal record. The racial origins of the ancient Egyptians thus were assumed to be found in their skeletal remains, and were expected to help determine whether Dynastic Egyptian civilization resulted from the diffusion of ideas and materials from elsewhere, migration of people who brought with them their culture, or *in situ* development of the culture without reliance on external factors. Two opposing theories for the origins of the

Dynastic Egyptians dominated scholarly debate for over a century: whether the ancient Egyptians were Black Africans (historically referred to as Negroid), originating biologically and culturally in Saharo-tropical Africa, or whether they originated as a "Dynastic Race" in the Mediterranean or western Asian regions (people historically categorized as White, or Caucasoid).

Contemporary physical anthropologists recognize, however, that race is not a useful biological concept when applied to humans. Although many people believe that they can distinguish "races" on the basis of skin color, more of the variation in human genetic make-up can be attributed to differences within these so-called races than between them. Furthermore, the observable and unobservable (to the eye) physical variation is so great and complex that there are no criteria that can satisfactorily segregate all individuals into one race or another. The movement in historic times of genes throughout different populations of the world and the sharing of genes through interbreeding ensures that different populations around the world are becoming more alike. Unlike the classic typological approach, which interprets variation in physical form as resulting only from the admixture of races, contemporary approaches to understanding variation also take into account genetic and physiological adaptations to local and regional environmental factors, such as the intensity of ultraviolet radiation or ambient temperature and humidity. Conceptually, biological affinity expresses a continuum of relationship that reflects genetic mixing (gene flow) from different local and regional areas in antiquity in addition to the influences of other evolutionary factors, such as natural selection and genetic drift. Modern studies of the origins of the ancient Egyptians are thus concerned not with identifying racial archetypes, but with investigating the affinities of different chronological or geographical groups, that is, who they are most closely related to in terms of biogeography. Degrees of biological affinity are thought to be expressed as patterns of similarity or difference among local populations or among skeletal samples that are believed to be representative of an ancient population. An underlying assumption is that the degree of similarity in a set of biological characteristics is proportional to the degree of genetic relatedness, but the selection of comparisons must be informed by archaeological, documentary or other data.

When attempting to explain observed physical variation among the ancient inhabitants of the Nile Valley and Delta, all evolutionary forces, as well as their interactions, must be considered. Migrations are thought generally to be explained by environmental factors such as climate change or by an imbalance between population size and the habitat's carrying capacity. It has been suggested, for example, that extensive mid-Holocene droughts in the Sahara may have led to the movement of people into the Nile Valley. The Sahara may have isolated much of Egypt from some more southerly populations, but gene flow along the Nile would have increased population heterogeneity over time, and warfare and political alliances throughout the region undoubtedly also had an impact. Migrations as individual phenomena, involving families or other small units, also may have been important. Population movement, replacement and admixture are all probable events in Egyptian history and prehistory, but their respective likelihood varies in different settings. The physical variability within Egypt as a "state," for example, probably increased with unification as differences between northern and southern populations decreased due to immigration, trade and other contacts.

While genetic mixing as a result of migration makes populations more alike, genetic differences among populations can become amplified if they are separated by geographic or cultural barriers. For example, if a small population, such as a religious enclave or an extended royal family, has marriage rules that require marriage within the group, then there will be less mixing with other populations and a phenomenon called "genetic drift" will lead to an increased biological distance, or a weaker biological affinity, between this group and others. The significance of genetic drift for our understanding of the biological affinities of the ancient Egyptians is that it provides an alter-

native to migration or invasion as an explanation for genetic differences among some groups. An example can be found in a comparison of the people buried in three cemeteries at Predynastic Nagada. Recent analyses of morphological characters of the teeth and skull suggest that the individuals buried in what archaeologists have identified as a higher status cemetery are distinguishable from the individuals buried in the other cemeteries. The people buried in the higher status cemetery probably formed a distinct socioeconomic group and tended to mate within the group instead of with outsiders, a practice well documented for a variety of social caste and class systems throughout history. The amount of the difference is too small to be compatible with the alternative explanation, that a foreign people moved into the area to rule the local inhabitants.

The logical way in which to determine the genetic relatedness of past populations would be to examine genetic material itself. Until recently, however, this has not been possible and most studies of past biological affinities are based upon skeletal remains. The recovery of ancient DNA (aDNA) from archaeological bone and preserved soft tissues was demonstrated in the late 1980s, but a number of analytical difficulties have so far prevented the routine application of the technique. Although researchers are refining methods of extraction and analysis, aDNA studies are dogged by problems of contamination from human handling of material during and after excavation as well as from fungi, bacteria and other agents that invade bone when it is buried. An additional problem is that embalming practices and the use of preservatives on skeletal and mummified tissues may not only contaminate the material but may lead to damage of the DNA, making it more difficult to analyze.

The utility of a DNA analysis for examining the biological origins and relationships of the ancient Egyptians will be most widely accepted after being demonstrated on a few individuals who are thought, from archaeological or inscriptional evidence, to be related. A tomb group in which all evidence points to a family interred together, or a documented royal lineage, suggest logical tests of DNA analysis of ancient Egyptian tissues. The extraction and analysis of DNA from archaeological remains is costly and complex, however, so it is not practical at present to analyze aDNA from a large number of individuals. Therefore, since the majority of extant Egyptian mummies are individuals of royal or noble status and hence are not entirely representative of ancient Egyptian populations, skeletal collections, which are relatively large and may more accurately represent local populations, will undoubtedly continue to serve as study material.

An underlying assumption of skeletal and dental studies is that observed physical characteristics represent the combined effects of the individual's genetic make-up and the environment, and thus characteristics that are not much influenced by the environment must be identified if one hopes to use those traits to infer genetic relationships. Many studies have relied on comparisons of measurements of size and shape to determine relationships, and, while some of the earliest metrical studies of Egyptian biological data are significantly flawed, recent investigations have employed published standards for obtaining precise and accurate measurements and have utilized historically and geographically relevant population comparisons. Alternatively, nonmetric characteristics, particularly of the teeth and the bones of the skull, are used to examine biological affinities.

There is now a sufficient body of evidence from modern studies of skeletal remains to indicate that the ancient Egyptians, especially southern Egyptians, exhibited physical characteristics that are within the range of variation for ancient and modern indigenous peoples of the Sahara and tropical Africa. The distribution of population characteristics seems to follow a clinal pattern from south to north, which may be explained by natural selection as well as gene flow between neighboring populations. In general, the inhabitants of Upper Egypt and Nubia had the greatest biological affinity to people of the Sahara and more southerly areas.

In contrast, reliable interpretations of the biological affinities of the people of Lower Egypt are currently hampered by a lack of well preserved skeletal material, largely due to agricultural and settlement encroachment on archaeological sites as well as the high water table, which interferes with excavation and preservation of archaic and earlier levels. Examinations of the biological relatedness of skeletal populations of Lower Egypt to those of other areas are needed, however, because they should determine whether the archaeological evidence for Egyptian contact with Syro-Palestine during the late Predynastic/Early Dynastic can be ascribed to trade relations or actual population movements. The archaeological and inscriptional evidence for contact suggests that gene flow between these areas was very likely. The biological affinity between peoples of Upper Egypt and the Sinai is also an important research question since archaeological evidence suggests a connection, presumably via the Red Sea. Migration into the Nile Valley from the Eastern Desert is also a subject for examination.

Any interpretations of the biological affinities of the ancient Egyptians must be placed in the context of hypotheses informed by archaeological, linguistic, geographic or other data. In such contexts, the physical anthropological evidence indicates that early Nile Valley populations can be identified as part of an African lineage, but exhibiting local variation. This variation represents the short and long term effects of evolutionary forces, such as gene flow, genetic drift and natural selection, influenced by culture and geography.

See also

mummies, scientific study of; mummification; paleopathology

Further reading

Brace, C.L., D.P. Tracer, L.A. Yaroch, J. Robb, K. Brandt and A.R. Nelson. 1993. Clines and clusters versus "race": A test in ancient Egypt and the case of a death on the Nile. *Yearbook of Physical Anthropology* 36: 1–31.

Johnson, A.L., and N.C. Lovell. 1994. Biological differentiation at Predynastic Naqada, Egypt: An analysis of dental morphological traits. *American Journal of Physical Anthropology* 93: 427–33.

Keita, S.O.Y. 1993. Studies and comments on ancient Egyptian biological relationships. *History in Africa* 20: 129–54.

Lewontin, R. 1972. The apportionment of human diversity. In *Evolutionary Biology* 6, T. Dobzhansky *et al.*, eds, 381–98. New York.

Prowse, T.L., and N.C. Lovell. 1996. Concordance of cranial and dental morphological traits and evidence for endogamy in ancient Egypt. *American Journal of Physical Anthropology* 101: 237–46.

NANCY C. LOVELL

Egyptology, history of

The study of ancient Egypt can be said to have begun with the Egyptians themselves. There is ample evidence that during the three millennia history of the country they often looked back on their ancestors' accomplishments with a mixture of awe and respect. Tuthmose IV, in response to a prophetic dream, cleared the great Sphinx at Giza of the encroaching sands. This was certainly one of the first recorded examples of excavation for the recovery of a monument, even though his motives were not those of modern archaeology. We know that Khaemwaset, one of the sons of Ramesses II, was much concerned with the identification and preservation of the ancient monuments as well. Graffiti of later periods on some monuments inform us of the veneration the Egyptians paid to the work of their ancestors which had been created in earlier times.

The ancient Greeks and Romans were interested in the history and antiquities of Egypt and their historians wrote concerning the great age of the country and the artistic and architectural accomplishments of the people. The writings of Herodotus, an East Greek historian who lived in the fifth century BC, and Diodorus Siculus, of the first century AD, give us much of the information we have for our understanding of the fascination Egypt held for the classical world. Antiquities and monuments, particularly obelisks, were avidly collected by Roman emperors and officials and were carted off wholesale to decorate circuses and other public places. Authentic Egyptian objects collected and transported to Rome were supplemented by local imitations in "Egyptian" style.

After about AD 400 the ancient Egyptian language was no longer generally understood and the only contact Europeans had with Egypt thereafter was through pilgrims, merchants and crusaders. The Greek and Roman authors remained the only available source of information on the ancient civilization of Egypt and the accounts found in them were admittedly somewhat biased descriptions of a culture their authors had found remarkable and mysterious. Since the ancient Egyptian language could no longer be read, fabulous interpretations of the hieroglyphic inscriptions abounded. Athanasius Kircher, a seventeenth-century Jesuit polymath who wrote extensively on Egypt, was able to derive a lengthy prayer from the signs which simply spelled out the name of a Roman emperor, basing his "translation" on the mistaken notion that each sign stood for a complete idea. An understanding of the principles underlying the language was not achieved for another two hundred years, but the seventeenth century saw the arrival of the first serious European scholars in Egypt.

To name only a select few of these pioneers who must serve as examples of others, the Roman Pietro della Valle traveled in the East, collecting Egyptian antiquities including mummies; John Greaves, an astronomy professor at Oxford, was one of the first to attempt a scientific measurement of the pyramids; and Jean de Thévenot, a Parisian traveler, opened a *mastaba* tomb at Saqqara and, like many others of his time, published an account of his travels and adventures. Egypt was a constant source of interest to Europeans which never completely failed, so it is an error to speak of a revival of interest in Egyptian history; however, the intense modern concern for the antiquities of Egypt could be said to have begun in the eighteenth century. The French were well represented by Benoit de Mallet, consul in Alexandria for Louis XIV, and Claude Sicard, Superior of the Jesuit mission in Cairo. Educated travelers such as Frederick Ludwig Norden, a Danish naval officer traveling on an official commission of exploration, and Richard Pococke, an English clergyman, were typical of many who visited Egypt independently at mid-century, recorded their observations and published them with generous illustrations of the monuments and sites. Norden and Pococke were later to be members of the Egyptian Club of London, one of the first organized groups for the study of Egyptian antiquities.

Along with Pococke and Norden, other travelers and explorers such as James Bruce and Claude-Étienne Savary helped to spur an interest in the ancient history and culture of Egypt among Europeans of their time. With all of this interest, the real birth of the specialized study of Egyptian antiquity must be dated to the Napoleonic expedition of 1798–1801. Napoleon Bonaparte invaded Egypt at the head of a French army, determined to secure the country as a colony and to obtain control of the most direct route to the Far East. Attached to the army, Napoleon established a corps of scholars, artists, engineers and scientists for the purpose of studying the "unspoiled" country in every aspect. The first accurate maps of the country and measured plans and illustrations of the ancient architecture were made. Lengthy inscriptions, at that time yet to be deciphered, were copied and the monuments were measured, drawn and engraved. The vast amount of information contained in the multi-volume *Description de l'Égypte* on both ancient and modern considerations helped to lay the groundwork for any further study of the country.

One of the best-known results of the Napoleonic campaign was the discovery of the so-called "Rosetta Stone." In the preparation of fortifications near the Rosetta mouth of the Nile, French soldiers found part of an inscribed slab with an inscription, preserved in three different forms of script – in ancient Greek,

which was still well understood, and in two forms of ancient Egyptian, which could not be read. This "bilingual" inscription provided part of the material which made it possible for Jean-François Champollion to decipher the ancient language. He based his study on the tentative work of other scholars including Silvestre de Sacy, Johan Åkerblad and Thomas Young, and he further proved that the hieroglyphic signs were not simply symbols but were based in a complicated system in which they functioned phonetically as well as ideologically.

The first quarter of the nineteenth century was primarily a period of treasure hunting and collecting on a grand scale. Consular agents, adventurers and entrepreneurs, including Henry Salt, Bernardino Drovetti, Giovanni Belzoni and William Banks, searched the country for antiquities of all kinds. During this time the Egyptian collections of the British Museum in London, the Musée du Louvre in Paris and the Museo Egizio in Turin were developed. At the same time expeditions to Egypt led by Champollion, Ippolito Rosellini and Richard Lepsius began the important work of further documenting the existing monuments with publications which are still of great importance today. Independent students and scholars such as Gardner Wilkinson and Robert Hay contributed to knowledge by copying inscriptions and decoration as well as by excavation. The work of the early explorers and pioneer Egyptologists from Belzoni to Hay often provides us with information on monuments which have become seriously damaged or no longer exist.

The archaeological situation was somewhat regularized in 1858 when Said Pasha, the Khedive of Egypt, appointed the first Conservator of Egyptian Monuments. Auguste Mariette, a French scholar, had gone to Egypt in 1854 as an agent for the Musée du Louvre to collect Coptic manuscripts. At Saqqara he recognized landmarks which indicated to him the possible location of the Serapeum, described in antiquity by Strabo. He abandoned his commission and started an excavation which continued for four years and revealed the ancient complex where the sacred Apis bulls had been buried. Mariette was largely responsible for the creation of an antiquities service, the regulation of excavation, the founding of the first national museum in which antiquities could be preserved, and for a general reduction in the wholesale destruction of the monuments. With Mariette a tradition was established in which the direction of the antiquities service in Egypt was headed by a French scholar.

The latter half of the nineteenth century was a period of great development in the science of Egyptology. Mariette's work and foundations were carried on by his successor, Gaston Maspero, who was appointed in 1881. Maspero consolidated the Department of Antiquities, further regularized excavation and insisted on the proper publication of results. His tenure was a long and productive one in which the monuments of ancient Egypt were further protected. He was joined in the field by excavators such as Édouard Naville and William Matthew Flinders Petrie. Petrie was one of the first to recognize that archaeological knowledge had to be based on attention to the smallest detail.

The English Egypt Exploration Fund was organized in 1882 with the aim of excavating principally in the Delta, but eventually expanded its activities to include even Nubia. Naville and Petrie, two men of remarkably different interests and temperaments, were the first excavators in its long history. The rich potential for research and acquisition of Egyptian antiquities was quickly recognized and appreciated by European and American museums and universities, but excavation in Egypt at the end of the nineteenth century was mainly under the control of the Egyptian Antiquities department.

By the turn of the twentieth century, national institutes of Egyptian archaeology came into being. Among American Egyptologists, George A. Reisner was among the first to work in a scientific manner. From 1905 he conducted work throughout Egypt and Nubia with the Harvard University–Boston Museum of Fine Arts expedition. James Henry Breasted, the first American to hold an appointment as a professor of Egyptology, was instrumental in founding the Oriental Institute at the University of Chicago in 1919. One of its most important objectives was the recording of inscriptions and decoration on monuments in Egypt, already recognized to be in danger of destruction from nature and man.

One of the best-known moments in the history of Egyptology was the discovery in 1922 of the tomb of the pharaoh Tutankhamen in the Valley of the Kings at Thebes. Howard Carter, English Egyptologist, and his patron, the Earl of Carnarvon, after years of seemingly fruitless search, found the nearly intact burial of a minor king of the 18th Dynasty. The treasure of burial goods preserved has provided considerable information on the arts and crafts of the king's pivotal time in Egyptian history. By contrast, French archaeologists under the leadership of Pierre Montet discovered a group of royal tombs of the 21st and 22nd Dynasties at Tanis (San el-Hagar) in the eastern Nile Delta. Due to the world situation in the late 1930s, the finds at Tanis did not receive the worldwide attention that had been accorded to Tutankhamen.

The present state of Egyptology may be suggested by the existence of the International Association of Egyptologists, through which scholarship is exchanged, by a number of national institutes for the study and advancement of the science, and by the growing attention being paid to other disciplines through which the aims of Egyptology may be furthered in a scientific manner.

See also

anthropology and Egyptology; Egyptian (language), decipherment of; Lepsius, Carl Richard; Mariette, François Auguste Ferdinand; Maspero, Sir Gaston Camille Charles; Napoleon Bonaparte and the Napoleonic expedition; Petrie, Sir William Matthew Flinders; Rosetta Stone; Tanis (San el-Hagar); Tutankhamen, tomb of

Further reading:

Bierbrier, M.L. 1995. *Who Was Who in Egyptology*, 3rd edn. London.

Greener, L. 1966. *The Discovery of Egypt.* London.

Wilson, J.A. 1964. *Signs and Wonders Upon Pharaoh.* Chicago.

WILLIAM H. PECK

Elephantine

During most of pharaonic times Egypt's southern border was located at the town of Elephantine. It occupied an island in the Nile (24°05′ N, 32°53′ E), at the northern entrance to the First Cataract opposite modern Aswan, of which it was the ancient forerunner.

All that remains of the ancient town (then called Abu) is a mound *circa* 350 m wide and up to 15 m high. The first excavations were undertaken at the beginning of this century, mainly to search for papyri rather than to investigate the remains of the town. The current program of comprehensive exploration of the entire town site, begun in 1969, continues to uncover increasingly detailed evidence of 4,000 years of the town's history, unparalleled to date at any other ancient Egyptian settlement.

The earliest traces of the settlement identified so far date to the middle of the fourth millennium BC. They were found on the eastern of two granite ridges that then comprised the habitable area of the island. This 'east isle'

preserves the remains of the sanctuary of the "Lady of the Town," the antelope goddess Satet. Dating to around 3200 BC, the earliest sanctuary was a modest mudbrick construction between three tall granite boulders.

It is unclear whether the inhabitants of the early settlement at Elephantine were Egyptianized Nubians whose culture had expanded northwards of the First Cataract, or if the site was already an Egyptian outpost. The ethnic identity of the earliest inhabitants is probably irrelevant to the significance of the settlement, which, because of its location at the northern end of the unnavigable cataract area, functioned as a center for trade with the south. The chief landing place then may have been located at the sheltered bay directly north of the east isle. The pharaonic name of the town, which means "ivory", as well as "elephant," might well hint at what was traded by the southerners with the Predynastic Egyptians.

With the unification of the Egyptian state *circa* 3100–3000 BC, the town's function as a trading center became linked with state control. In the course of the 1st Dynasty, a fortress was built on the highest point of the east isle's shore, and it seems that it housed a non-local, i.e. Egyptian, occupying force. A little later the whole settlement was surrounded by a mudbrick wall, which enclosed the entire south part of the east isle. This implies that from the first an area was reserved for an increase in

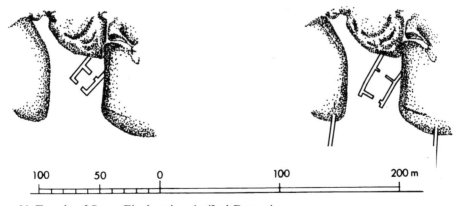

Figure 30 Temple of Satet, Elephantine: 1st/2nd Dynasties

population resulting from the dissolution of smaller settlements in the region and/or further immigration from the north. In the 2nd Dynasty the remaining part of the east isle was included within the fortification walls, which were maintained for the next 600–700 years, throughout the Old Kingdom. At the same time the walls of the 1st Dynasty fortress gradually disappeared beneath the increasingly densely populated settlement, and the whole town began to take on the appearance of a fortification. In hieroglyphic texts from the Old Kingdom and down into the Middle Kingdom, the sign for "fortress" was included in the writing of Abu.

In the town, administrative buildings, residences and various industrial areas are distin-guished by architectural remains and artifacts. Toward the end of the 3rd Dynasty a large complex was built on the west isle. Its most notable feature was a small step pyramid, similar to others at some contemporary important sites in Middle and Upper Egypt, such as Nagada and Abydos (Sinki). Like the 1st Dynasty fortress, the complex was a project of the central authority. The pyramid seems to have represented the fictive presence of the king, and was a symbolic means of reinforcing state control implicit in Elephantine's role in the collection and distribution of goods. Possibly a statue cult was associated with the pyramid. The entire complex was short-lived. It fell into neglect and the area began to be developed for other purposes. In the late 4th Dynasty craft

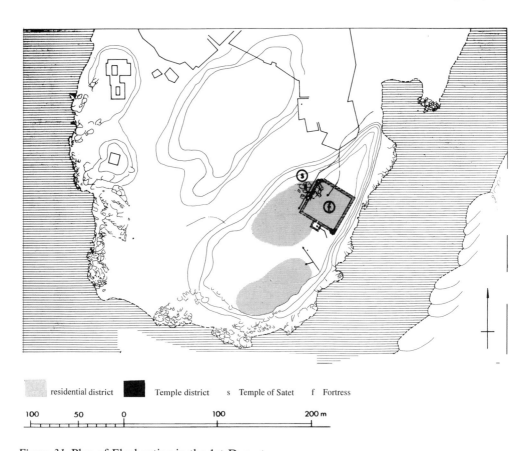

residential district　　■ Temple district　s Temple of Satet　f Fortress

100　　50　　0　　100　　200 m

Figure 31 Plan of Elephantine in the 1st Dynasty

workshops were located there, and in the 5th Dynasty the town cemetery expanded into the area.

Throughout the Old Kingdom the temple of the goddess of the town, Satet, was repeatedly rebuilt on its original site. It remained essentially a modest mudbrick structure with a forecourt. A granite sanctuary for the goddess's statue survives from a rebuilding ordered by Pepi I in the early 6th Dynasty. Numerous votive offerings, both royal and private, have been recovered from these early levels. Rock inscriptions document visits by later 6th Dynasty kings. By this time at the latest, the ram-headed god Khnum of the cataract region possessed a cult place within Satet's temple.

The collapse of the central authority in the First Intermediate Period further increased the significance of Elephantine within Upper Egypt. Kings of the 11th Dynasty, who resided in Thebes, rebuilt the Satet temple several times and for the first time stone was used for some elements. Around 2000 BC the first ruler of the reunified kingdom of Upper and Lower Egypt, Nebhepetre Mentuhotep II, built an entirely new sanctuary and added an installation for the celebration of the Nile flood, which, according to ancient Egyptian belief, began at Elephantine.

Already in the late Old Kingdom the settlement was expanding beyond the earlier fortifications. With the strengthening of the unified Egyptian state under Mentuhotep II and the 12th Dynasty, town growth at Elephantine gained momentum. Senusret I advanced from there to the Second Cataract and subjected the whole of Lower Nubia to Egyptian rule. For the first time, Elephantine lost its function as a border town and instead became an important administrative and economic center for trade to the south, beyond the First Cataract. Presumably, the enlarged town continued to be surrounded by a wall, but the archaeological evidence does not yet demonstrate this.

When the new Satet temple was only 100 years old, Senusret I replaced it with a richly decorated stone structure connected to a courtyard, built for the inhabitants of the town to celebrate the Nile Festival. Also at this time,

Khnum acquired a temple of his own in the elevated town center.

During the 11th Dynasty a third cult center had sprung up to the northwest of the Satet temple, for the worship of Heqaib. He was a mayor (nomarch) of the town, who had apparently manifested such exemplary leadership in the difficult times of the late Old Kingdom that after his death he became revered as the local saint. His original, modest cult chapel was first rebuilt in the 11th Dynasty and then again at the beginning of the 12th Dynasty. For the next few centuries the governors of the town followed suit and set up their own memorial chapels there, in addition to their rock-cut tombs at the site of Qubbet el-Hawa. Numerous other officials dedicated stelae and statues in the Heqaib sanctuary.

For a time during the Second Intermediate Period, after the second collapse of the central government, Egypt's southern border was again at Elephantine, until the kings of the early 18th Dynasty reconquered Nubia and extended the border as far south as the Fourth Cataract. Elephantine flourished once again and Queen Hatshepsut and Tuthmose III built large new temples to both Satet and Khnum. In the interim, the cult of Khnum, who was worshipped throughout Egypt, had eclipsed Satet at Elephantine. In the 18th Dynasty, but primarily in the 19th and 20th Dynasties, his temple was further enlarged. Along the processional way from the harbor to the temples of the town, Amenhotep III erected a way-station, apparently in connection with the rebuilding of the installations for the Nile Festival.

The temples and associated economic institutions grew to occupy nearly one-third of the area of the town. It is thus probably no coincidence that Syene, the ancient name for Aswan on the mainland, first appears in texts of this period. Scattered houses and industrial areas may have expanded farther into the farmland to the north of the town. An indication that this development occurred is the way-station built by Ramesses II outside the town to the northwest.

With the beginning of the Third Intermediate Period, when there were repeated internal

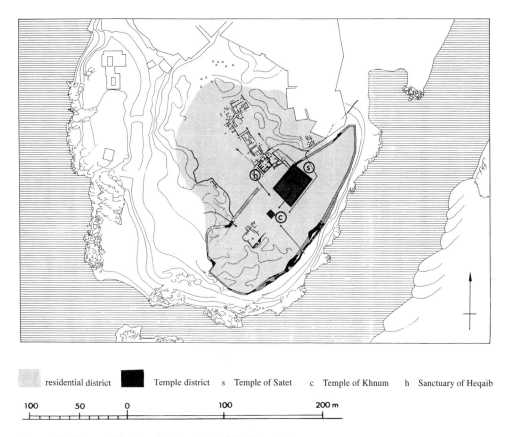

residential district   ■ Temple district   s   Temple of Satet   c   Temple of Khnum   h   Sanctuary of Heqaib

| 100 | 50 | 0 | 100 | 200 m |

Figure 32 Plan of Elephantine in the Middle Kingdom

conflicts in Egypt and Nubia became independent, the strategic aspect of this town once again came to the fore. Stelae are the only monuments to attest the kings of this period and of the Kushite 25th Dynasty at Elephantine. With the 26th Dynasty construction was resumed on the town's temples. A nilometer was added to Khnum's temple to measure the height of the flood waters. Shortly before the dynasty ended with the Persian conquest of Egypt, Amasis added a colonnade to the Satet temple.

During the Persian occupation of Egypt Elephantine served as a bulwark against threats not only from the south. The occupying force utilized by the Persians in Elephantine consisted at least in part of members of the pre-existing Aramean and Jewish colony. Its members already possessed a temple to Yahweh before the Persians' arrival. Apparently the enlargement of Khnum's temple in the 30th Dynasty resulted in its loss with scarcely a trace. The ruins of a number of non-Egyptian-type houses survived from which important papyri relating to early Judaism could be salvaged.

Under the kings of the 30th Dynasty, another era of prosperity began for Elephantine which continued under the Ptolemies and then, beginning in 30 BC, under the Romans. Nectanebo I (30th Dynasty) added to the New Kingdom temple to Khnum. His second successor, Nectanebo II, began a large new building but only managed to complete the sanctuary and a small forecourt. The Ptolemies, especially Ptolemy VI and VIII, resumed construction on this temple, which was finally completed under the Roman emperor Augustus when a large river terrace was built. Considerably smaller, but also well appointed with a river terrace and nilometer, was the new temple complex of Satet (begun by Ptolemy VI), part of which had to be relinquished to serve as a cemetery for the sacred rams of the Khnum temple.

In the Roman period the river bank between the two temple terraces was built up and also the area to the north of Satet's nilometer. A monumental staircase with a sanctuary to the Nile was constructed at the town harbor. The exact locations of two other temples within the sacred precinct are still unclear. Altogether the

temples and their dependencies ultimately covered almost half the area of the town. In the residential areas there are well-preserved remains of houses from the Ptolemaic and early Roman periods. These are two storey structures crowded together. Because of the loss of the sites uppermost levels, only the cellars have survived from a few houses of the later Roman period.

Because the temple town came to occupy over nearly half the ancient site in Graeco-Roman times, the daily life of trade and administration apparently shifted to Aswan on the east bank of the river. With the triumph of Christianity in the early fourth century AD Aswan overtook Elephantine for good. Elephantine forfeited its role as a fortress. In the

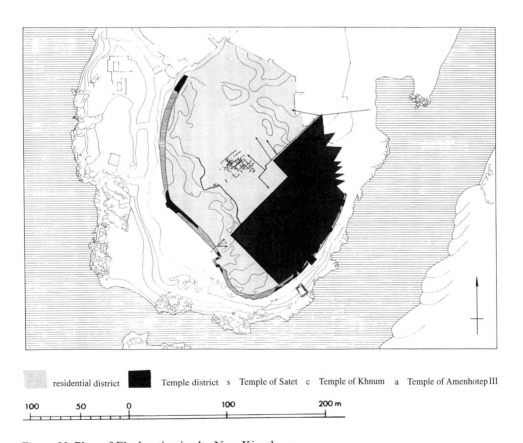

residential district　　Temple district　s Temple of Satet　c Temple of Khnum　a Temple of Amenhotep III

100　　　50　　　0　　　　　　100　　　　　200 m

Figure 33 Plan of Elephantine in the New Kingdom

Elephantine

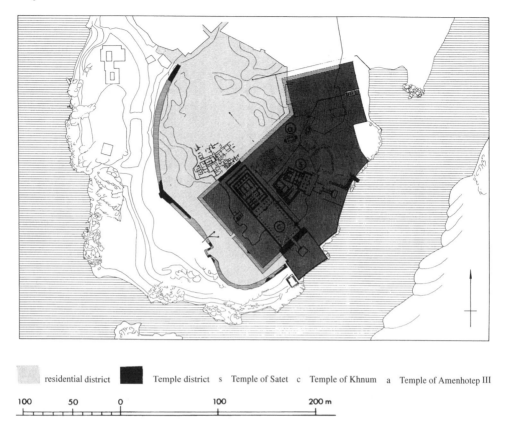

residential district ▮ Temple district s Temple of Satet c Temple of Khnum a Temple of Amenhotep III

100   50   0   100   200 m

Figure 34 Plan of Elephantine in the Graeco-Roman period

fifth century a company (cohort) of soldiers, stationed on the island to strengthen border defenses against attacks by marauding tribes from the Eastern Desert, built a fortified camp in the great court of the Khnum temple.

It is likely that the work of dismantling the temples for building material had begun by this time and in the following centuries, it led to the loss of virtually all but the foundations of the main temples and the total disappearance of smaller structures. Arabic sources from the early Middle Ages describe a monastery and two churches on Elephantine. The plan of a small early sixth-century church in the courtyard of the temple of Khnum could be recovered. The scattered remains of an important, slightly later basilica, found scattered in the town's residential area suggests it once

stood there. With the increasing influence of Islam in Egypt from the seventh century, the last Christian phase of the town's history was comparatively short-lived. It probably ended not much later than the thirteenth or fourteenth century.

See also

A-Group culture; Aswan; Early Dynastic period, overview; Late and Ptolemaic periods, overview; Middle Kingdom, overview; New Kingdom, overview; Nubian forts; Old Kingdom, overview; Predynastic period, overview; Roman period, overview; Third Intermediate Period, overview

Further reading

Kaiser, W., *et al*. 1997. Stadt und Tempel von Elephantine. 23./24. Bericht. MDAIK 53: 5.117–193.

WERNER KAISER

Elkab

The site of Elkab (25°07′ N, 32°48′ E) is situated on the east bank of the Nile, about halfway between Luxor and Aswan. The name "Elkab" is probably a corruption of "Nekheb," the ancient Egyptian name of the capital of Nome III of Upper Egypt, known as "Eleitheiaspolis" in Graeco-Roman times. The ancient town is close to the Nile and at the mouth of the Wadi Hellal, which opens into the valley to form a vast semicircle.

The site is very extensive and contains ruined temples, cemeteries and rock-cut tombs. Today the most impressive ancient feature is a vast mudbrick enclosure wall (35 in the plan). Several monuments, as well as an important collection of rock inscriptions and drawings, are also found a few kilometers east of Elkab in the desert.

The principal deities worshipped at Elkab were Nekhbet and Sobek. During the Old Kingdom Nekhbet's cult was situated in the desert, where the goddess had a sanctuary. Later the cult moved into the Nile Valley and it finally predominated over those of other deities.

Recorded information about Elkab dates back to the eighteenth century, but the first major description of the site was made in 1799 by a member of the Napoleonic expedition, Saint-Genis. Later in the nineteenth century Elkab, and especially its New Kingdom rock-cut tombs, became very popular with tourists. At the end of the nineteenth and during the early twentieth centuries, excavations at Elkab were conducted by the English archaeologists J.E. Quibell, A.H. Sayce and E. Somers Clarke. From 1937 to the present, a Belgian expedition has been excavating at the site.

The history of human occupation at Elkab is a very long one. A number of handaxes and other flint tools, found isolated on the hills surrounding the Wadi Hellal, testify to human presence during Lower and Middle Paleolithic times. Much better documented, however, is the Epi-paleolithic culture known as the "Elkabian," which was discovered within the great enclosure wall in 1968 (23). This microlithic stone tool industry dates to the seventh millennium BC and belongs to a population of hunters and gatherers which frequented the site in the interval between the high summer floods and the winter activity of the Wadi Hellal.

Predynastic remains dating to the fourth millennium BC have been found at several locations. A late Predynastiac cemetery consisting of about 100 tombs (Nagada III phase) was excavated in 1977–9 in the northeast area of the great wall (24). Scattered sherds, however, indicate that the earlier phases of the Nagada culture, and probably even the earliest one (Badarian), are also represented at Elkab.

A large number of rock drawings occurs on two isolated rocks in the Wadi Hellal. Less extensive groups can be found at various locations along the wadi. Some of the drawings may predate the Predynastic period, but on stylistic grounds the majority can be attributed to the Nagada I and II phases. The drawings consist of a large number of animals, but the typical Nagada II-style boats are also present.

The Early Dynastic period (1st–2nd Dynasties) at Elkab is represented by a cemetery, consisting mainly of small *mastaba* tombs (with mudbrick superstructures), excavated by Quibell, within the northern area of the great wall (25–6) In the same area, he also found a few blocks of granite (27), now lost, which belonged to a building erected by Khasekhemwy of the 2nd Dynasty. A number of circular constructions immediately west of the temples (19), excavated in 1955, have also been dated to this period because Early Dynastic artifacts have been found there, but it is unlikely that these are Early Dynastic.

A curved double wall (17), connecting the enclosure wall of the temple with the great wall of Elkab, has been interpreted by some scholars, without substantial proof, as the remains of a very ancient, circular city wall.

Although nothing can be stated with certainty about its date or function, two charcoal samples from it have recently been radio-carbon-dated to the First Intermediate Period or early Middle Kingdom. The area enclosed by the double wall (18) was completely ransacked by the excavation of *sebbakh* (organic debris from the ancient settlement used for fertilizer by farmers), but potsherds and flint tools found on the surface seem to indicate that it was inhabited beginning in the Old Kingdom. Houses were probably located north of the curved wall. Until the middle of the nineteenth century, the entire area, including the great wall facing the Nile, was still covered by a *tell* (a mound formed through many years of human occupation). It has since disappeared, but the sides of the great wall are still remarkably well preserved in this area.

Old Kingdom stairway tombs and *mastaba*s of mudbrick were excavated by Quibell and Sayce (28–34). Two large *mastaba*s (31–2), identified as those of Kameni and Neferche-mem, were originally attributed to the 4th Dynasty, although this date is not certain. In 1986 a decorated rock-cut tomb, belonging to the priest Sawka, was discovered in the south-western part of the hill containing the necro-polis, north of the great wall. More undecorated rock-cut tombs, two of which were undisturbed, were recently discovered in the same area; all of these tombs probably belonged to priests of the 6th Dynasty. In 1996 excava-tions began at an important mudbrick *mastaba* with a niched façade, which probably dates to the 3rd or early 4th Dynasties, located on top of the hill.

The most abundant information relating to the Old Kingdom, however, comes from over 600 rock inscriptions on the isolated rocks in the Wadi Hellal. These inscriptions, relate to the 6th Dynasty priests of Elkab, who also performed duties in the temple of Nekhbet. This temple was probably located at the site of the later temple of Amenhotep III (18th Dynasty), where there are concentrations of Old Kingdom sherds. The names of the priests and their affiliations are often included in the inscriptions, facilitating the study of genealogies

and the phyle system, in which the priests were organized to serve on a rotating basis (phyles). From the genealogies it is also clear that the rock-cut tombs excavated in from 1986 onward belonged to a number of these priests. The rock inscriptions also mention the existence at Elkab of funerary cults of Pepi I and Merenre I.

Dating from the end of the First Intermedi-ate Period and the beginning of the Middle Kingdom is a large cemetery (38–41, 44), now bisected by the eastern part of the great wall at Elkab. The cemetery was definitely plundered, and remains largely unexcavated. Tombs are arranged in a planned pattern, and those that have been excavated consist of a chamber on the desert surface behind which is a vaulted mudbrick burial pit.

Remains of Middle Kingdom monuments at Elkab are scarce. One block belonging to an 11th Dynasty building was found in the temple of Nekhbet (2). Blocks which were originally from a temple-stand for the sacred bark, built on the occasion of the first *ḥeb-sed* (jubilee) of Sobekhotep III of the 13th Dynasty, have also been found.

Decorated tombs dating to the Second Intermediate Period and early 18th Dynasty are found in the necropolis north of the great wall. The oldest of these tombs are the 13th Dynasty tomb of Sobeknakht and the 17th Dynasty tomb of Renseneb. The most important tombs are those of Ahmose, son of Abana, and Ahmose Pennekhbet, descendants of Ahmose, the first king of the 18th Dynasty. Both tombs contain biographical accounts of Ahmose, who drove the Hyksos out of Egypt, and his successors. The most beautiful tombs, however, are those of Pahery and Renni, dating to the reign of Tuthmose III. Pahery's tomb is parti-cularly well-known for its agricultural scenes.

Several temples were built at Elkab in the New Kingdom. A temple of Tuthmose III, to the north of Elkab, was seen almost intact by members of the Napoleonic expedition but was destroyed in 1828. Temples were also built in the desert to the east of the town. The most famous of these is the small but well-preserved temple of Amenhotep III, dedicated to Hathor and Nekhbet. Another small temple, now known as "el-Hammam," was built by Setau, Viceroy of Kush during the reign of Ramesses II (19th Dynasty). It was probably dedicated to the deities Re-Horakhty, Hathor, Amen and Ramesses II. Both Amenhotep III's temple and the el-Hammam monument were restored during the Ptolemaic period and enlarged with porticos.

The two most important temples at Elkab were built side by side. The principal temple was dedicated to Nekhbet (2), while the second one was dedicated to Sobek and Thoth (1). Only the temples' foundations and the lowest layer of wall blocks survive today, although a number of columns and part of the wall of the western temple were still standing at the beginning of the nineteenth century. A causeway (5) linked the temple of Nekhbet with a quay (16), but their dates are uncertain. Quibell and Somers Clarke began excavations in the temple area, but it was not until the 1930s that the temples were excavated in their entirety by the Belgian Egyptologist Jean Capart. Although earlier temples already existed at the same site, construction of the temple of Nekhbet was especially active during the 18th Dynasty. Most of the pharaohs of this dynasty added to the building, but Tuthmose III and Amenhotep II were particularly active. The present form of the temple of Nekhbet was built during the 26th–30th Dynasties, in part with blocks from older constructions (such as those from the 11th Dynasty chapel). The temple of Sobek and Thoth in its present form dates to the reign of Ramesses II.

Near the two main temples at Elkab are the foundations of four small temples (6–9), which cannot be dated with any certainty. One of these temples (6) may have been a *mammisi* (house of births). The sacred lake (4), which originally was square in area, probably dates to the 30th Dynasty. A massive covered stairway was excavated in this area in 1968, but revealed no inscriptions. Surrounding the temple precinct was a mudbrick wall (14), of unknown date.

The massive mudbrick enclosure wall (35), which is preserved to a height of 11 m in some places, surrounds an area approximately 530 × 600 m. The southern corner of this wall has either disappeared due to Nile erosion, or was never built in order to allow easy access to the Nile harbor. Built against the wall are three large ramps, each of which is situated near a gate, which lead to the top of the wall. Such ramps are not found on any of the large mudbricks walls at Elkab considered to be temple enclosures. Several radiocarbon dates now confirm that the enclosure wall dates to the Late period, probably to the 30th Dynasty. Textual evidence suggests that the wall was built under the instructions of Nectanebo II (or perhaps the original order had already been given by Nectanebo I), in order to create a stronghold which could eventually be used as a refuge against the Persian threat. The rarity of evidence for occupation at this time, however, seems to indicate that the enterprise was abandoned, perhaps because of the death of Nectanebo II or because of Alexander the Great's conquest of Egypt. A small temple built by Nectanebo I or Nectanebo II (37), now completely ruined, is found outside the great wall, within the axis of the eastern gate.

The best preserved monument at Elkab dating to the Ptolemaic period is located in the desert, where a New Kingdom rock-cut temple was transformed into a sanctuary (hemispeos) dedicated to the lion goddess Chesemtet. This was principally the work of Ptolemy VIII and Ptolemy IX.

From the fourth century BC onward, a village settlement developed within the great wall, mainly along both sides and in front of the mudbrick temple wall (12, 20). Excavations from 1968–81 uncovered a number of houses in this village, some of which could be identified as those of potters. The discovery of two caches of coins suggests that the village may have been deserted during the fourth century AD, for unknown reasons.

During the Graeco-Roman period earlier tombs in the rock-cut necropolis north of the town were extensively reused and some small undecorated tombs were added. Only one decorated tomb is known from the Ptolemaic period. Throughout this necropolis are many horizontal niches, which were intended for the burial of crocodiles, the sacred animal of the

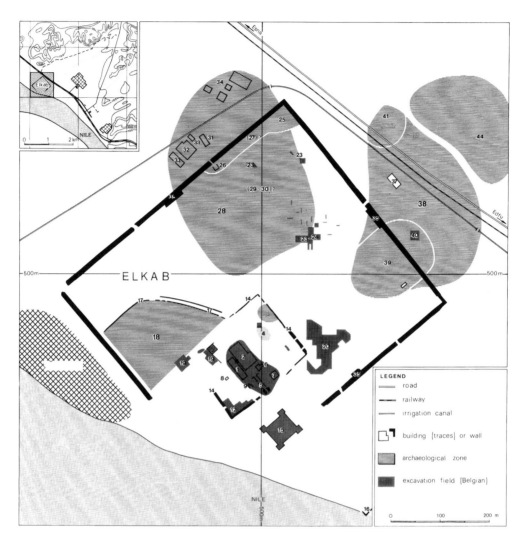

Figure 35 The enclosure wall of Elkab and its immediate surroundings
Source: Map and site numbers after Depuydt *et al.*, 1989, p. 2.

god Sobek. During the late Roman period, a small fort was built close to the river (15), using many blocks from earlier temples. Few remains at Elkab are known after the Roman period. A small Coptic monastery is situated next to the Ptolemaic sanctuary of Chesemtet, but no Islamic settlement developed at the site.

See also

Epi-paleolithic cultures, overview; Late and Ptolemaic periods, overview; New Kingdom, overview; Old Kingdom, overview; Paleolithic cultures, overview; pottery, prehistoric; Predynastic period, overview

Further reading

Bingen, J., and W. Clarysse. 1989. *Elkab* 3: *Les ostraca grecs*. Brussels.

Depuydt, F., S. Hendrickx and D. Huyge. 1989. *Elkab* 4: *Topographie*. Brussels.

Derchain, P. 1971. *Elkab* 1: *Les monuments réligieux à l'entrée de l'Ouady Hellal*. Brussels.

Hendrickx, S. 1994. *Elkab* 5. *The Naqada III Cemetery*. Brussels.

Vermeersch, P.M. 1978. *Elkab* 2. *L'Elkabien, épipaléolithique de la vallée du Nil égyptien*. Brussels–Leuven.

STAN HENDRICKX

Emery, Walter Bryan

Born in Liverpool, Bryan Emery (1903–72) later attributed his early enthusiasm for ancient Egypt to the novels of H. Rider Haggard, which he read as a child. In his teens he was apprenticed to a firm of engineers, but when he was eighteen he studied Egyptology under Professor T.E. Peet at the University of Liverpool. In 1923–4 a field season with the Egypt Exploration Society (EES) at Tell el-Amarna gave him his first experience of archaeological surveying. Then in 1924 Sir Robert Mond put him in charge of the restoration of private tombs in western Thebes, and in the following year, with 400 workmen, he cleared and rebuilt the tomb chapel of the vizier Ramose (no. 55), one of the finest in the necropolis. Still working for Mond in 1927, he discovered the cemetery of the Buchis bulls (the "Bucheum") at Armant. However, after one season at that site under Henri Frankfort, the Egyptian government appointed him to direct the Archaeological Survey of Nubia in the area north of Adindan, which was threatened by submersion due to the construction of the Aswan Dam.

For two seasons Emery surveyed Lower Nubia on foot, assisted by his wife Molly, L.P. (now Sir Laurence) Kirwan and five Egyptian assistants. In 1931 he excavated the great mounds of Ballana and Qustul, previously thought to be natural hills. They proved to be the undisturbed tombs of the "X-group" kings, rulers who controlled Lower Nubia after the collapse of the state of Meroe. These kings were buried with their barbaric furniture and finery, their horses and camels, and human sacrifices: their women and servants.

In 1935 Emery was appointed by the Egyptian Antiquities Service to excavate the Early Dynastic cemetery of North Saqqara, begun by Cecil Firth. He found that the superstructures of the great *mastaba* tombs of the 1st Dynasty contained storerooms crammed with funerary artifacts, revealing for the first time the masterly craftsmanship of this dynasty. The Second World War interrupted his work here; he served with the British Army in the Western Desert. For a time after the war, he was an attaché in the British Embassy in Cairo, but he longed to return to Egyptology.

In 1951 his opportunity came: he was appointed to the chair of Egyptology at University College London. His teaching load was to be light, and he was expected to spend part of each winter excavating in Egypt. As Field Director of the Egypt Exploration Society (EES) he excavated at Saqqara for five more years. The volumes of his publication of what he believed to be the royal tombs of the 1st Dynasty are remarkable for the isometric drawings of the brickwork, which gave a new dimension to early architecture. (Though these tombs contained sealings with royal names of the 1st Dynasty, many archaeologists now believe that they are the burials of high officials, while the kings themselves were buried at Abydos.)

Unable to work in Egypt in 1956 at the time of the Suez crisis, Emery persuaded the EES to let him return to Sudan. At Buhen near the Second Cataract he excavated the elaborate mudbrick fortifications of the Middle Kingdom town. He worked here for eight seasons; his meticulous plans of the walls and ramparts are a unique record of Egyptian military architecture. Meanwhile, the Egyptian government had decided to construct the High Dam at Aswan, which was to engulf all of Lower Nubia, including Buhen. Emery was appointed advisor to the committee of UNESCO concerned with the recording and rescue of the ancient monuments and sites threatened by the rising water of Lake Nasser. He himself saw to the removal of the temple of Hatshepsut at Buhen to the Khartoum Museum.

Emery was then able to return to North Saqqara. His work centered on the *mastaba* field of the 3rd Dynasty, where he hoped to find the tomb of Imhotep, the architect of the Step Pyramid who was later deified. In this he was not successful, but he came across a vast network of catacombs of the Late period containing mummified baboons and ibises. Further investigations in this area yielded demotic and Aramaic papyri, Carian inscriptions and temple furniture, and the catacombs of the sacred cows, mothers of the Apis bulls.

However, Emery had taxed his strength too far. On March 7 1971, he collapsed on the dig and died two days later. He is buried in Cairo.

See also

Abydos, Umm el-Qa'ab; Armant; Early Dynastic period, overview; Nubian forts; Saqqara, North, Early Dynastic tombs; Saqqara, pyramids of the 3rd Dynasty; Saqqara, Serapeum and animal necropolis

Further reading

Emery, W.B. 1938. *The Royal Tombs of Ballana and Qustul*. Cairo.

——. 1949. *Excavations at Saqqara. Great Tombs of the First Dynasty* 1. Cairo.

——. 1954. *Excavations at Saqqara. Great Tombs of the First Dynasty* 2. London.

——. 1958. *Excavations at Saqqara. Great Tombs of the First Dynasty*. London.

——. 1965. *Egypt in Nubia*. London.

——. 1979. *The Fortress of Buhen: the Archaeological Report*, with H.S. Smith. London.

——. 1981. *Archaic Egypt*. Harmondsworth.

Smith, H.S. 1971. Walter Bryan Emery. *JEA* 57: 190–201.

MARGARET S. DROWER

Esna

The town of Esna (25°18′ N, 32°33′ E), Latopolis in Greek, is situated on the west bank of the Nile River, about 60 km south of Luxor. Approaching its temple, a visitor perceives the roof first because the temple still stands on the original ground level, whereas the modern town rises 9 m higher, on top of the remains of the ancient town and its descendants which have grown up around the temple in the course of the last 2,000 years.

There is no evidence for the town of Esna and its temple before the Middle Kingdom, but from this time onward we have source materials up to the end of ancient Egyptian history. In Graeco-Roman times the temple in the town was only one of several temples and shrines belonging to the district of Esna. These other religious structures all were destroyed between the Middle Ages and the nineteenth century. Even the temple in the town of Esna has only partially survived. The extant part of it is but the outer hypostyle hall (*pronaos*); the main building (*naos*) once placed behind it has almost wholly disappeared. The *pronaos* of the temple of Esna is impressive, with the beautiful capitals of twenty-four columns supporting the ceiling. The decoration comprises about 230 scenes that most often show the king giving offerings to the deities, but also killing their foes or even dancing for them. Furthermore, there are interesting astronomical representations on the ceiling.

The rear wall of the *pronaos*, once the façade of the temple (naos), received its decoration under the Ptolemies, specifically under the common rule of Ptolemies VI and VIII and their sister Cleopatra II. The inscriptions and reliefs of the three other walls date from Roman times; on them we read the names of most of the emperors between Claudius and Decius. The inscriptions have been copied, studied and translated by the French scholar Serge Sauneron.

The principal deity of the temple was Khnum, a god mostly depicted as a ram-headed man, but also shown in the shape of a crocodile. Khnum was the creator of the world and the begetter of life who formed all living beings on his potter's wheel. The goddesses Nebet-uu and Menhit were his divine consorts. Heka was Khnum's eldest son and successor to the throne. Next to Khnum, the principal deity was Neith, a warlike goddess often represented as a woman holding bow and arrows in her hands. Her sons were Shemanefer and Tithoes, the former appearing as a crocodile, the latter as a lion. Neith almost always wears the crown of Lower Egypt; in fact her cult had been transplanted to Esna from Sais, the center of Neith's veneration in the Delta.

Both Khnum and Neith are described in the texts as the sole creator of the world, combining male and female capacities; each of them is "the father of the fathers and the mother of the mothers." But in other contexts Khnum is called "the father" and Neith "the mother"; they become the parents of the sun god Re, the latter being reborn as Khnum-Re. Here one must keep in mind that the ancient Egyptians' thinking did not define, but was open to an infinite number of aspects which did not exclude each other. For instance, the omnipotent Khnum, when he was conceived as sun god, had to die periodically.

The inscriptions on the columns (dated AD 81–161) give abundant information about the local festivals of Esna. The first of these was celebrated on the first day of the month of Phamenoth; it commemorated Khnum's creation of the world, beginning with the separation of heaven and earth and with the installation of Khnum's creative potter's wheel (even in the womb of the female beings). The second feast (13 Epiphi) referred to Neith's coming into existence in the primeval waters at the very beginning of the world, when she uttered seven sentences which at once materialized and started to organize the world. Another important festival (19 and 20 Epiphi) recalled the mythical events of a rebellion against the old sun god, when Khnum "seized the staff" in order to defeat his enemies with it. The festival took place in two temples situated a few kilometers to the north of the town, where the victorious god appeared in a special form and was called "Khnum, the lord of the fields" and also "Khnum-Shu," the son of Re who fought for his father.

Many texts are (religious) poetry, such as the hymns to the principal deities, the litanies of the morning-songs or the description of the world before creation. The reading and understanding of the Esna texts is difficult because the system of hieroglyphic writing employed in this temple is extremely complicated, but also fascinating; in this field of research, much work needs to be done. The most intricate texts are two hymns to Khnum written for the most part only with the hieroglyphs of the ram and the crocodile.

See also

Egyptian language and writing; Late and Ptolemaic periods, overview; pantheon; Roman period, overview

Further reading

Downes, D. 1974. *The Excavations at Esna, 1905–1906*. Warminster.

Kurth, D. 1984. Esna 400; 405. *Mélanges Adolphe Gutbub*, 135–44.

Sauneron, S. 1959–1982. *Le Temple d'Esna*, 8 vols. Cairo.

——. 1977. Esna. In *LÄ 2: 30–3*.

DIETER KURTH

F

faïence technology and production

Faïence, more properly called Egyptian faïence to distinguish it from certain tin-glazed pottery made at Faenze in Italy, has been called the first high-technology ceramic. It is a non-clay ceramic whose body is composed of silica in the form of crushed quartz or sand with small amounts of lime (perhaps naturally present in the sand) and alkali, added either as plant ash or natron. This body material lacked the plasticity of clay, and so was more difficult to form. For this reason some shapes were first roughly formed by hand or in molds and then had the details "carved" into them by abrasion once dry. In this way faïence technology shared some features in common with stone working, as well as with the pyrotechnical industries such as glass and metal working.

The quartz body of the faïence, especially if coated with a still finer layer of brilliant white quartz, was probably preferred above glazed stone since it gave a bright, sparkling, optical effect, whereas glazed stones such as steatite gave a comparatively dull one. This body was coated with a soda–lime–silica glaze, frequently bright blue in color. The ancient Egyptians knew the material as *ṯḥnt*, a word derived from "shining" or "dazzling" perhaps in reference to the use of the material to imitate precious stones, such as lapis lazuli or turquoise.

The glaze could be produced by several techniques. In the "efflorescence technique" the glazing material—copper, alkali salts and plant ashes—are mixed among the body constituents. The body is then shaped either by hand modeling, molding or occasionally wheel throwing and the soluble salts in the mixture gradually effloresce on the surface as the piece dries. Firing fuses this efflorescence to give the glassy surface characteristic of faïence. With this technique the thickness of glaze varies considerably, and may be poor. It has been suggested that the ground copper or other metals, which were added as coloring materials, may have been byproducts of metallurgy. The "cementation technique" involved embedding the shaped artifact in glazing powder. During the firing the body is glazed by a chemical combination at the surface of the object with the glazing powder in contact with it. This method is more time-consuming than efflorescence, but can give a very high quality, uniform glaze. The object is easily removed from the surrounding glazing powder after firing. In "application glazing," the glaze was applied to the object as a powder or slurry before firing. The firing then melted and fused this layer. Unlike pottery glazing, which employs a preliminary or biscuit firing, the glaze is added directly to the unfired body. The glaze is often of uneven thickness and may retain marks from supports used to separate pieces in the kiln. Faïence firing temperatures are still a matter of some debate, though most authorities agree on a temperature between 800 and 1000°C.

Small faïence objects are known from the Predynastic period onward, though it was once thought that faïence actually declined in the Early Dynastic and Old Kingdom. Recent excavations, notably those at Abusir, have shown that this is not the case; faïence was in use for many architectural purposes, such as inlays, in addition to its use for amulets and for the well known tiles of the Zoser complex at Saqqara. Efflorescence was the commonest glazing method at this time, and forming was done using molds along with modeling and abrasion of partly dried pieces. Details of the body could also be built up using a slurry of the body paste. Vessels were occasionally formed around a core of vegetable material and mud, which was later removed.

With the Middle Kingdom, the core-forming technique became common, though cementation glazing and application of the glaze as a liquid are also evidenced. These factors may have helped to accelerate faïence production. Animal figurines are popular during this period and, like vessels, those of spherical form, such as hedgehogs, were often made around a core or ball of straw. The rich burial of an overseer of faïence workers known from Lisht and dating to the 13th Dynasty may attest to the importance of specialist faïence craftsmen at this time. Another production site is known at Kerma in Sudan.

Faïence enjoys a particularly innovative phase during the New Kingdom with the introduction of new colors and color combinations to give polychrome effects. Efflorescence, cementation and application are all in use during this period and glass is introduced into some faïence glazes to help deepen them, and perhaps also to give a greater range of colors. Such colorful pieces are known from many of the palaces of the New Kingdom such as Malkata, Qantir and Tel el-Amarna; at Amarna there is evidence of production. Mold-making of rings and amulets is particularly well attested at Amarna by the numerous fired clay molds which are found there; ring manufacture was facilitated by an extensive glassy phase in the fired faïence. It has been suggested that throwing of faïence was first attempted during the New Kingdom. The making of vessels can be especially sophisticated in this period with very delicate pieces, such as chalices, being produced. Egyptian faïence is exported to Cyprus and elsewhere at this time.

By the Third Intermediate Period faïence is commonly used for votive objects, as well as for the numerous *shawabtis* of the period. Henceforward throwing becomes more common. It is during this period, probably around the 22nd Dynasty, that a very shiny variety known as glassy faïence first appears, perhaps supple-menting glass production which seems to decline somewhat after the 21st Dynasty. Efflorescence and liquid application of glaze are the most common methods of glazing. With the resurgence of Egyptian culture in the 26th Dynasty comes a new bright green faïence, commonly used for *shawabtis*, votive items and vessels. Matte faïence is popular at this time. The Ptolemaic and Roman industry is still not fully documented, though factory sites are known from Memphis. A type of hemispherical bowl, perhaps made at Memphis and/or Alexandria, and vases with secondary painted decoration are both common finds.

See also

glass; jewelry; Kerma; el-Lisht; *shawabtis*, servant figures and models; Tell el-Amarna, city

Further reading

Friedman, F. D. (ed.). 1998. *Gifts of the Nile: Ancient Egyptian Faïence*. London.

Kaczmarczyk, A. and R.E.M. Hedges. 1983. *Ancient Egyptian Faience*. Warminster.

Nicholson, P.T. 1993. *Egyptian Faience and Glass*. Princes Risborough.

Tite, M.S., I.C. Freestone and M. Bimson. 1983. Egyptian faience: an investigation of the methods of production. *Archaeometry* 25(1): 17–27.

Vandiver, P., and W.D. Kingery. 1987. Egyptian faience: the first high-tech ceramic. In *Ceramics and Civilisation* 3, W.D. Kingery, ed., 19–34. Columbus, OH.

PAUL T. NICHOLSON

Farafra Oasis

Farafra Oasis is the smallest of the northern Egyptian oases, lying at the center of a depression 10,000 km^2 in area (26°40′–27°30′ N, 27°30′–28°40′ E). It is mentioned in texts as early as the 5th Dynasty, and its name, "T3-ihw" (Land of the Cows), is associated with the goddess Hathor.

Because of possible attacks by tribes from regions farther west in the Sahara, Farafra's location was strategic for the ancient Egyptians. During the reign of Merenptah (19th Dynasty), such an attack was made by armed Libyans. According to the Karnak inscriptions, the Libyans followed an ancient road which directly connected Fezzan in southern Libya with Farafra, lying at about the same latitude. This route had the advantage of avoiding the military posts constructed by Ramesses II on the Mediterranean coast.

Pharaonic remains in Farafra are unknown, however, and the oldest monuments are from the Roman period. These consist of groups of rock-cut tombs at Ain Jallow and Ain Bishoi, in the vicinity of Qasr Farafra, in the center of the oasis. The exact dates of these tombs are not known, however, and they were also reused by Copts.

As in the other oases of the Western Desert, Farafra's major period of prosperity was between the first century BC and the second/third centuries AD, after which the Oasis became increasingly isolated. The el-Khadra spring, not far from Ain el-Wadi, was an important rest stop for caravans traveling from Farafra to Asyut in the Nile Valley. Near the spring are the foundations of an ancient house dating to the Roman period, and on the surface around the spring are many potsherds. A few Roman coins have also been found here. The ruins of a Roman building are also found in the Wadi Hinnes, which begins at the spring.

The Oasis was visited in 1819 by Frédéric Cailliaud, who described the fortress of Farafra and the village around it, and also recorded information about the geology of the depression. Other information was recorded by John Gardner Wilkinson, who visited Farafra in 1825, and the German geologist-explorer Rohlfs in 1876. Of these early travelers, Rohlfs's information is the most extensive, and included his criticism of the inhabitants of the Oasis.

Despite the long-term occupation of Farafra Oasis, knowledge of its prehistory has been scarce. Research of the University of Rome began in 1987 and has continued in annual field seasons. Fieldwork has focused on an archaeological survey to determine as much as

possible the type of exploitation of the region in prehistoric times.

During the Holocene in Farafra Oasis there have been periods of intense humidity when playas (ponds) formed and left beach fossils. Fekri A. Hassan has reconstructed at least three phases of humidity beginning with a moist phase of the Early Holocene, 9,300–8,800 or 8,600–7,100 BP (uncalibrated radiocarbon dates in years "before present"), and two moist intervals of the late Middle Holocene, 5,900–5,000 BP, and 4,800–4,600/4,500 BP.

From 1987 to 1991, fieldwork focused on specific areas of the depression, at Qasr Farafra, the center of the oasis, Ain Dalla and Rajih. Fieldwork was also conducted in another area about 15 km from the center of the oasis where the remains of campsites are located, at Ain Kifrein, Ain e-Raml and Abu Kasseb.

Ain e-Raml was investigated intensively during 1987 and 1988. Excavations were preceded by a topographic survey of an area approximately 200 m^2. *In situ* materials were excavated in an area of about 5 m^2. Stratigraphy here was thin (not more than 10–15 cm), but hearths were present. A charcoal sample collected from one of these hearths has been dated to 9650 ±190 BP (calibrated radiocarbon date, years "before present"). The most common stone tools are flakes and blades. Ceramics are found here as well, but they are difficult to evaluate given the amount of surface weathering.

Other important sites were found about 130 km northwest of Qasr Farafra, around the small oasis of Ain Dalla. Abundant materials were collected on the surface in an area of saline formation (*sebkhas*). These showed certain peculiarities for the Farafra region in specific lithic types and in the raw material, a very shiny dark brown chert. Ceramics have not been found in this area. A radiocarbon date of 7000 ± 410 BP has been obtained from an ostrich eggshell sample collected from one of the stone tool concentrations.

In 1988 and 1989, the Rajih–Bir Murr region was investigated. It is located about 80 km east of Qasr Farafra and represents an additional zone of prehistoric occupation. Situated on the eastern side of the depression, it is a very marginal zone and is separated from the center of the Oasis by a dune formation. Rajih is connected to a caravan route beginning at Siwa Oasis which led through Farafra to Asyut in the Nile Valley. The presence here of thin-walled ceramics with impressed designs, not found elsewhere in Farafra Oasis, is important.

In 1990 and 1991, fieldwork concentrated on a systematic exploration of Bahr Playa/Wadi el-Obeyid, a unique and important site found almost at the top of a plateau, Quss Abu Said, which overlooks Qasr Farafra to the northwest. The area is located on one of the pediments of a rectangular-shaped plateau named Abu Said, surrounded by a steep escarpment cut into the Farafra limestone. Artifacts were found here scattered over a surface of about 12 km. The site consists of numerous concentrations of artifacts, and represents an ideal sample for studying the continuity of occupation during the Holocene. Five areas have been recognized including stone tool workshops, hearths and probable hut foundations. Most of the evidence seems to belong to the climatic phase of the Middle Holocene, characterized by a general increase of aridity. Stone tools demonstrate skillful blades and flakes (small saws, sickle knives, axes, gouges and drills). Some of the stone tools, particularly the axes and perforators (drills), can be compared to products found in the el-Badari district of Middle Egypt and the Nagada region in Upper Egypt. Grinding stones are also abundant.

Archaeological research in Farafra Oasis is aimed at reconstructing prehistoric subsistence practices, especially the development of agricultural or pastoral activities by late Paleolithic hunters and gatherers. Consequently, archaeological evidence here tends to be interpreted according to a similar pattern of development in the other oases of the Western Desert, and also suggests how agricultural activities could have been transmitted to the Nile Valley from the oases.

See also

Baharia Oasis; dating techniques, prehistory; Epi-paleolithic cultures, overview; Neolithic and Predynastic stone tools; Neolithic cultures, overview; Paleolithic tools; Predynastic period, overview; Siwa Oasis, prehistoric sites

Further reading

Barich, B.E. 1993. Culture and environment between the Sahara and the Nile in the Early and Mid-Holocene. In *Environmental Change and Human Culture in the Nile Basin and Northeast Africa until the Second Millennium B.C.*, L. Krzyzaniak, M. Kobusiewicz and J. Alexander, eds, 171–83. Poznan.

Barich, B.E., F.A. Hassan and A.M. Mahmoud. 1991. From settlement to site: formation and transformation of archaeological traces. *Scienze dell'antichita'* 5: 33–62.

BARBARA E. BARICH

fauna, domesticated

Domestication can be defined as a micro-evolutionary process during which animals are removed from their community in the wild and forced to reproduce and live under man's control for the latter's benefit. As a result, the animals involved acquire domestic traits, that is, characteristics which are rarely or not found in wild animals. These changes affect the animal at the various levels of its organization: size, skeleton and horns, skin and coat, pigmentation, metabolic system, reproduction, behavior and so on. Such changes would begin to appear within 50–100 generations, and a few centuries would normally suffice to produce a recognizable primitive domestic breed. Domestic traits are not due to mutations caused or made operative by the manmade environment, but result mainly from the profound alteration of the selective processes to which the animals are exposed. Individuals highly sensitive to stress induced by abnormal conditions (restriction of free movement, crowding, presence of man) do not develop or reproduce well, or are removed by man, while animals with reduced changes for survival in the wild receive protection. Sexual selection changes since the limited mating choices allow animals with less "sex appeal" to contribute differently to the gene pool of the next generation, and the removal or castration of older dominant males allows younger ones to be involved similarly. In these ways and others, "natural" selection is replaced by "artificial" selection, which in a first phase would be "unconscious" since the people involved aim mainly at maintaining or increasing the number of their animals. Conscious artificial selection resulting in highly selected, advanced breeds occurs in complex societies.

Biological, archaeo(zoo)logical and historical evidence indicates that domestic animals have a monophyletic origin; in other words, each of them has but one principal wild ancestor. This monophyletic origin does not imply that a single ancestor cannot give rise to quite different domesticate types, as would be the case of humpless cattle and zebu (humped) cattle, both of which would derive from the wild bovid *Bos primigenius*. Most domestic animals have been labeled as separate species, but they are not genetically isolated from their wild parents, with whom they produce fertile offspring.

No agreement has yet been reached regarding the technical (Latin) nomenclature for domestic animals. "Domestic cattle," for example, occurs in the literature as *Bos taurus*, *Bos "taurus," "Bos taurus," Bos primigenius taurus, Bos primigenius* f. taurus, *Bos indicus* (if with hump) and so on. In what follows, the most commonly used names will be given, as well as the ones proposed by Herwart Bohlken and applied by the Kiel school and followers.

Reconstruction of the older history of domestic animals relies mainly on bone finds from archaeological deposits, which are studied by archaeozoologists, and evidence of the visual arts. The water buffalo (*Bubalus bubalis/Bubalis arnee* f. bubalis) is not included here, since this animal would have reached the Nile Valley only in medieval times.

Domestic donkey (*Equus asinus/Equus africanus* f. asinus)

Until recently scholars accepted that the wild donkey (*Equus africanus*) was confined to North Africa, but various finds now suggest that this equid also occurred formerly in Asian regions adjacent to Africa. As a result, the view that the donkey was domesticated in Egypt from the subspecies found in the Eastern Desert (*E. a. africanus*) has lost part of its foundation. Bones from the Predynastic site of Ma'adi near Cairo (*circa* 3600 BC) are attributable with reasonable certitude to domestic donkeys. The ancient Egyptian donkey was a fairly large animal. The pictorial record shows it generally as grey and often with a dark stripe along the length of the back and a short stripe across the shoulders. Donkeys occurred in appreciable numbers as beasts of burden, traveling widely in the desert before the dromedary was adopted. They also treaded seeds in the field and were used for threshing. Elites traveled in a sedan between a couple of donkeys, but whether the animals were used for riding is not shown in the pictorial record.

Domestic cat (*Felis catus/Felis silvestris* f. catus)

The available evidence supports the view that the origin of our domestic cat is in ancient Egypt, but the timing and motives of the process are not very clear. The African wild cat, formerly known as *Felis libyca*, would be the ancestor and it is now considered to belong to the same, widely distributed species as the European wild cat (*F. silvestris*) and its Asian relatives (formerly *F. ocreata*), hence *F. silvestris libyca*. The latter appears to be less shy and individualistic than the European wild cat and would be easily tameable. According to various scholars, domestication of the cat began when wild cats were attracted by rodents living on the reserves of early food-producing communities, and were adopted to destroy pests. However, since pet-keeping is a universal human habit, little need exists for such a scenario. The few Predynastic finds of cats include one buried with a gazelle in a human grave at Mostagedda (Badarian period). This may indicate a close association of people and cats (not necessarily domesticated) long before the Middle Kingdom, when cats are found in tomb paintings.

During New Kingdom times, the paintings portray them as pets of the well-to-do, but none of the individuals shows visible domestic traits.

From the eighteenth century BC onward the deification of the cat began, leading to the cult of various cat goddesses, especially that of Bastet, and to the practice of mummifying cats and the creation of cat cemeteries, such as the one at Bubastis. These mummified cats are larger than their extant wild relatives. This has been interpreted as an indication that their domestication was incomplete, on the assumption that domestication leads inevitably to size decline, a notion that is debatable for small animals. Moreover, some Old Kingdom finds from Elephantine are of small cats, and finds in a late grave near Balat (Dakhla Oasis) have a reduced cranial capacity with respect to the African wild cat, as one would expect for primitive domestic cats. Therefore, domestication of the cat may have already been a fact during Old Kingdom times. The large size of most finds studied would indicate optimal living conditions, especially in later times when the animal had acquired special status.

Domestic goose (*Anser anser domestica/ Anser anser* f. *domestica*)

Some scholars think that the goose was domesticated some 6,000 years ago in southwest Asia, but other domestication centers may have existed in Europe. Food sacrifices in ancient Egypt frequently included geese, and each year impressive numbers of the various geese coming to winter along the Nile were captured and fattened for sacrifice. Domestication of the gray goose (*Anser anser*) had begun already during the Old Kingdom, probably to increase the supply and to obtain more tender meat. Gray goose appears to have been a native species in Egypt, but today it rarely winters there; therefore, it has been wrongly assumed that the Egyptians domesticated the Nile goose (*Alopochen aegyptiacus*). Pictorial evidence from the 5th Dynasty shows geese with the typical white feathers of domestic animals, as well as goslings. Osteological evidence comes from Elephantine (Ptolemaic period) and from Tell el-Maskhuta in the Wadi Tumilat (Late period), where the remains of dwarf geese were excavated as well as large geese which probably exceed modern large breeds in size.

Dog (*Canis familiaris/Canis lupus* f. *familiaris*)

How and why wolves have been domesticated and the earliest dates for this are not clear. The earliest generally accepted finds would come from the Mesolithic site of Star Carr in England (*circa* 7500 BC). Until recently, it was accepted that dogs had been introduced in Egypt, as wolves were not supposed to occur there. However, it has been claimed that the Egyptian wolf-jackal (*Canis aureus lupaster*) is a wolf; therefore, it is not excluded but unlikely that the domestication of local wolves was attempted in Egypt.

Neolithic and Predynastic sites contain appreciable numbers of dog bones, and a drawing from Predynastic Nagada shows the type of dog called *tesem* in Dynastic times: a medium-sized greyhound with upright ears and curled-up tail. A dog figurine from Predynastic Hierakonpolis is of a lop-eared canid. Representations of dogs from the Old Kingdom show *tesem* dogs, sometimes with drooping ears, and an absurdly tightly rolled tail. These representations are probably highly idealized. In the Middle Kingdom greyhounds are depicted with upright, half upright, or lop ears, and curled-up as well as sickle tails. Hunting dogs of the New Kingdom were more robustly built with hanging ears and a medium, long-haired uncurled tail. The skeletal finds, mostly from dog cemeteries of later periods, are mainly of medium-sized, somewhat slender dogs adapted to a dry and hot climate, which one can classify as pariah dogs, i.e. the common canid type found around preindustrial settlements in various parts of the Old World. Other finds are derived from dwarf dogs: spitz-like animals and robust larger dogs among which was a mastiff-like animal perhaps imported from southwest Asia. Brachymelic dogs (dachshund-type) are already documented by bones from a 5th Dynasty context and are represented during the Middle Kingdom. They most likely were mutations of the *tesem* and/or pariah dogs. It is impossible to relate the various types described to present-day breeds.

Domestic cattle (*Bos taurus/Bos primigenius* f. taurus)

The oldest evidence in Eurasia for domestic cattle has been found in Thessaly and Macedonia (*circa* 6500 BC). Some 1,000 years later cattle are also known in southwest Asia, where they may have been introduced or were domesticated from the local aurochs. Aurochs are also found along the Mediterranean coast of North Africa, and Upper Palaeolithic people hunted this large bovid regularly along the Nile as far south as the Second Cataract. Large bovid remains from early Neolithic sites in the Western Desert have been attributed to primitive, large domestic cattle. The oldest finds, from the eighth millennium BC, suggest that cattle were domesticated independently in Africa, probably by people utilizing the Western Desert in the early Holocene humid period and coming from the Egyptian Nile Valley, where they may have already established a sophisticated form of cultural control over aurochs. Ancient Egyptian cattle may derive from this putative early domesticate, but cattle were also introduced from southwest Asia. Because of their significance in husbandry, agriculture and religion, cattle are well documented in ancient Egyptian art.

Male as well as female cattle were used for plowing, threshing, transport and so on, and for their meat. Milk production was modest, but milk cows resembling those of early twentieth-century European milk breeds may have existed. There is a milking scene on the sarcophagus of Princess Kawit of the 11th Dynasty. Castration was practiced already during the Old Kingdom to obtain more powerful animals, and to increase meat and fat production. During the New Kingdom impressive results of forced fattening are known.

The oldest and most typical breed, already known from Predynastic sites, is the longhorn,

formerly called *Bos africanus*. The shoulder height of these animals (cows, bulls and bullocks) probably varied between 120 and 150 cm, and the size and form of the horns show much individual and sexual variation. A mutation within this breed produced hornless animals, which were sometimes kept in separate herds. Zebu cattle were introduced from southwest Asia during the 18th Dynasty.

The second important cattle group in ancient Egypt consisted of small, short-horned animals, imported mainly from Syro-Palestine. Such cattle were perhaps already present at the Predynastic site of Ma'adi, but they were not yet very common during the Old Kingdom. Small hornless cattle may also have been depicted in tomb scenes, but their relation to the shorthorn group is not clear. Animals with artificially deformed horns, as can still be found in the herds of the Nilotic tribes in southern Sudan, are also depicted, as well as animals with sawed-off horns. A 12th Dynasty papyrus from Lahun constitutes the oldest known written veterinary document; the best preserved part gives an account of cattle diseases and their cures.

Domestic sheep (*Ovis aries/Ovis ammon* f. aries)

Sheep, which do not occur wild in Africa, were domesticated in southwest Asia around 7500 BC and later introduced in Egypt, probably together with the goat. In Neolithic and Predynastic sites the animal is already well attested. A Predynastic representation from Abydos shows the typical breed of the Old Kingdom, known formerly as *Ovis longipes palaeoaegypticus*: the slender high-legged, thin-tailed hair sheep, with screw horns directed outward. The ears are upright, but later they droop. The males often have a neck mane. The horns exhibit a marked individual and sexual dimorphism, and hornless animals have been found. Osteometric data suggest this ovine had a shoulder height of 65–75 cm.

Sheep were not used as sacrificial animals, and the pictorial record depicts them treading seeds in the field and even threshing. During the Middle Kingdom a wool sheep was introduced from Asia, which eventually replaced the hair sheep. The horns of the wool sheep are spiral, but show considerable variation, and hornless animals occur. In size the animals were comparable to their screw-horned cousins. This new sheep, which provides wool, caused a decline of the goat, as the latter was essentially only a meat provider. Whether the Middle Kingdom wool sheep were fat-tailed cannot be deduced from the pictorial record. A Late period mummified sheep has a fat-tail tapering to its point, and a still later figurine shows a sheep with a fat-tail that does not taper. One can tentatively interpret both fat-tailed sheep as more advanced Asian breeds, introduced later in Egypt. Sheep fat may have been an important source of fat whenever pig was unacceptable. The wool sheep is also known as the "amen" sheep, since the rams are associated with the god Amen. The screw-horned ram embodied the god Khnum, but after its disappearance the screw-horned he-goat replaced the latter as a symbol. Representations of rams with the amen's horns and equipped with a beard and he-goat screw-horns are also known; they have been wrongly interpreted as natural four-horned rams.

Domestic goat (*Capra hircus/Capra aegagrus* f. hircus)

Domestication of the goat took place in southwest Asia at about the same time as that of the sheep. The wild or bezoar goat (*Capra aegagrus*) does not live in Africa; therefore, domestic goats were introduced in Egypt, probably together with domestic sheep. Goats occur in Neolithic sites, and such finds from Predynastic Ma'adi and representations of the same period are attributable to screw-horned goats, which were the prevailing type until late times. Both sexes are short-haired, but he-goats are characterized by a beard, vaulted forehead, and long horns directed slightly outward and backwards (with a double torsion clockwise in the left horn, counter-clockwise in the right horn); sometimes a short upright mane hangs over the forehead. Females have smaller horns, a

straight profile and often no beard. The ears are drawn upright in prehistoric drawings, hanging in those of the Old Kingdom, and generally again standing up in later representations. Appreciable variation can be seen, however, as evidenced by hornless males and females, as well as animals with scimitar horns and others interpreted as caprines with much less tightly twisted horns. The height at the shoulders would have varied between 59 and 75 cm, but smaller animals have been found. Goats were sometimes fattened as sacrificial animals, but apparently were mainly meat providers for the lower classes. The use of goat milk is not documented. Several tomb scenes illustrate the deleterious effect of goats on the vegetation.

Domestic pig (*Sus domestica/Sus scrofa* f. domestica)

The oldest domestic pig finds come from southwest Asia (*circa* 7000 BC), but wild boar (*Sus scrofa*) occurred until recently in the Egyptian Delta and possibly farther south; therefore, local domestication of the animal is theoretically possible. The typical Egyptian pig was a high-legged, slender, often hairy animal with long snout, prick ears, high dorsal bristles and a short curled tail, resembling its wild ancestor. Pig bones occur frequently in Predynastic refuse, and the pictorial record suggests the animal was still important during the early Old Kingdom. Later it tends to disappear from the pictorial record, but bones from settlements and graves indicate pork was still on the menu. During the New Kingdom, the pig figures more frequently among the animals depicted, sometimes treading seeds in the soil, or even helping with threshing. As to the importance of pig in the diet during the New Kingdom, the data are contradictory, but certainly indicative of the fact that avoidance of pig and pork was not a general rule. The pig was the sole animal raised for consumption only. It was mostly herded, but pigs were also fattened in temple compounds and sties. Such fatting pigs of advanced type found during the Graeco-Roman period probably derive from the original herd pig.

Domestic horse (*Equus caballus/Equus przewalskii* f. caballus)

The earliest well-documented domestic horses (*circa* 3500 BC) were excavated in the Ukraine, but domestication may have taken place at an earlier date more to the east in the Central Eurasian steppes. Horses would have reached Egypt with the chariots of the Hyksos, as suggested by the second stela of Kamose (end 17th Dynasty). The oldest finds of horse bones are from the Buhen fortress near the Second Cataract and from Tell ed-Dab'a in the eastern Delta, both dating to the Second Intermediate Period. These and later finds pertain to animals with a shoulder height varying between 136 and 150 cm and correspond to the so-called "oriental" type, common in the ancient Near East.

Horse riding developed only in late times, and horses were mainly used to draw chariots. Differences in the pictorial record have been interpreted as evidence for a long-bodied, slender breed and a short-bodied, more robust breed, which subsequently became more prominent, but these differences may reflect artistic conventions.

Mule and hinny

Crosses of domestic donkeys and domestic horses became possible as soon as the latter were introduced in Egypt, together with the knowledge of this feasibility. Texts and bone finds indicate that the Hittites practiced crossing of these equids. Such crosses combine the strength of the horse with the more placid temperament of the donkey, and are especially useful in mountainous terrain. A mule is a cross of a male donkey and a female horse, and looks rather like a donkey, with long ears but a tail like that of a horse. A hinny results from the reciprocal cross. It is generally small and slender, and looks like a horse except for the stripes and the tail, which are inherited from the donkey. Bones attributed to mules have been excavated in the vicinity of the Ramsesside palace of Pi-Ramesses near Qantir. Together with donkeys, they were probably used as pack animals in the army, and a mule may be represented in a scene of a tent camp, from the tomb of Horemheb at Thebes (end 18th Dynasty). A few scenes depict hinnies replacing horses drawing chariots; these animals have been erroneously identified as onagers (*Equus hemionus*) or an unusual type of horse.

Domestic fowl (*Gallus gallus domesticus/Gallus gallus* f. domesticus)

Domestic fowl is derived from the red jungle fowl (*Gallus gallus*) found in southeast Asia, and was domesticated around 4500 BC in the Indus Valley. Recently an earlier domestication center has been proposed in southern China, but the evidence is equivocal. Domestic fowl reached Asia Minor by 1500 BC, and Egyptians became acquainted with it through the Asiatic campaigns of Tuthmose III (18th Dynasty). This king received a gift or tribute of four "birds which give birth daily," i.e. which lay eggs daily. The oldest drawing, of a rooster, has been found on a sherd in the Valley of the Kings. A rooster and two hens/chickens, on a 19th Dynasty silver plate from Tell Basta near Zagazig in the Delta, represent the only other evidence from the New Kingdom. With the Persian period (27th–31st Dynasties), the number of representations increases, but it is not clear whether intensive husbandry of domestic fowl started during this period or later. In late times incubators were used to hatch eggs.

Dromedary (*Camelus dromedarius/Camelus ferus* f. bactriana)

Dromedary and camel were domesticated in southwest Asia at least 5,000 years ago, but it is not clear whether these domesticates have separate wild ancestors or not. Originating in the Arabian peninsula, the dromedary could have reached Egypt quite early across the Bab el-Mandeb. The few contested camelid figurines and the few bone finds suggest that dromedaries were known to the ancient Egyptians but not adopted. Later in the first millennium BC, dromedaries and perhaps camels were brought to the Delta and the Nile Valley. Under Ptolemy

I, a black camel was exhibited in the theater of Alexandria. In the same period, or perhaps already during the Persian period, the dromedary was finally adopted.

Semi-domesticated animals

Past definitions did not always take into account the fact that domestication is not only a cultural phenomenon but also a biological process bringing about inevitable and rather rapid changes in the animals involved. Some scholars have argued that animals may have been domesticated in the past without acquiring domestic traits. The proposed cases of forgotten or episodic domestications, however, can be interpreted as the result of various forms of cultural control not reducible to domestication, such as highly selective culling of game, corralling of game (more or less comparable with modern game ranching), raising of captured game animals, taming of such animals and so on. In Egyptian palaces, wild animals such as lions (*Felis leo*), elephants, probably of African origin (*Loxodonta africana*), and others were kept in captivity as symbols of prestige or as curiosities. Others, such as the vervet monkey (*Cercopithecus aethiops*), dorcas gazelle (*Gazella dorcas*) or leopard (*Panthera pardus*), were pets of elites. Moreover, several game species were fattened in captivity for sacrificial purposes, including various aquatic birds, oryx (*Oryx dammah*), dorcas gazelle, Nubian ibex (*Capra ibex nubiana*), addax (*Addax nasosulcatus*), hartebeest (*Alcelaphus buselaphus*), Barbary sheep (*Ammotragus lervia*) and, strangely enough, during the Old Kingdom, the striped hyena (*Hyaena hyaena*). Some of these animals have been labeled "semi-domestic" and, moreover, described as forgotten domesticates. The pictorial evidence, however, documents that little or no effort was made to make the animals reproduce in captivity, which is a basic condition for domestication, and restocking was essentially done by capture, often of young animals. Also, none of the supposed domesticates shows visible domestic traits or behavior. There is no reliable proof, then, for serious attempts to domesticate sacrificial animals, and

it is advisable not to use the ill-defined term "semi-domestic."

See also

fauna, wild; Neolithic cultures, overview

Further reading

Boessneck, J. 1988. *Die Tierwelt des Alten Ägypten*. Munich.
Clutton-Brock, J. 1981. *Domesticated Animals from Early Times*. London.
Darby, W.J., P. Ghaliongui and L. Grivetti. 1977. *Food: The Gifts of Osiris*. London.
Gautier, A. 1990. *La domestication. Et l'homme créa ses animaux*. Paris.

ACHILLES GAUTIER

fauna, wild

The indigenous Egyptian fauna was first documented by the prehistoric inhabitants of the Nile Valley and neighboring desert regions. Representations of elephant, giraffe, hartebeest, oryx, addax, wild cattle, hippopotamus, lion, ibex, gazelle, ass, Barbary sheep, leopards and other wild cats are recorded in the rock art found throughout the Nile Valley and the surrounding Eastern and Western Deserts. These early animal representations were pecked, etched and painted on stone surfaces along wadis, on cliffs and atop mountain escarpments.

Inferences based on the prehistoric representations and further augmented by geological, climatological and paleontological studies suggest that the environment of Egypt was more moist during some periods in the past than it is today, and that the faunal resources available to prehistoric Egyptians were more diverse. Today, nearly fifty species of indigenous mammals can be found in Egypt, but the former presence of elephants and giraffe (animals indicative of savanna regions) suggests that environmental conditions of the past were much more conducive to a varied large mammal fauna. The Nile (and its earlier forms) apparently provided an environmentally rich haven and a migration route from Africa for numerous species even through periods of hyperaridity. The river(s) also supported a rich and varied fish fauna and attracted a myriad of migratory birds in search of food and breeding areas.

That prehistoric Egyptians made use of the indigenous animals of the Nile Valley and desert for subsistence as well as for the raw materials needed for tool manufacture (e.g. projectile points, fish hooks, sinew, hides and so on) is well attested through archaeological investigations. The frequency of skeletal remains recovered from prehistoric sites indicates that Egypt's Paleolithic and early Neolithic (*circa* 4800 BC) inhabitants were successful terrestrial predators. Work conducted on ancient Egypt's wild terrestrial fauna is unfortunately uneven with respect to regional coverage. It is difficult, therefore, to draw definite conclusions concerning human–animal relationships for earlier cultures than the Late Paleolithic. One can safely state, however, that the Nile Valley was a stable, conservative environment, while the neighboring desert regions were considerably more unstable and subject to appreciable climatic change and fluctuations in faunal composition.

In Late Paleolithic times the deserts and valley harbored an essentially modern fauna, although by Dynastic times several species had already become extinct in Egypt. Human activities along the Nile caused the extirpation of many of these animals, while climatic change (enhanced perhaps by overgrazing of livestock) was the major cause in the desert regions. By 20,000 BC there appear to have been two well-developed strategies for acquiring animal proteins: hunting mammals and fishing. Bones of gazelle, wild cow and hartebeest are the most common large game animals recovered in many prehistoric sites. The pursuit of these animals was, however, not always the most efficient means of obtaining animal protein. Compared to hunting quadrupeds, fishing provided an abundant source of animal protein and often involved less effort than the capture of large mammals. Although little archaeological evidence has been recovered relating directly to the

technological development of Paleolithic fishing, evidence from the skeletal remains of fish recovered from archaeological sites suggests that certain taxa were targets of an efficient seasonal fishing strategy.

Wendorf, Schild and Close suggest that occupation of settlements shifted seasonally in the Wadi Kubbaniya region of Upper Egypt (*circa* 16,000–10,500 BC). Their findings also imply that fishing was more important at certain types of settlements. Fish bones occurred at all sites they investigated, but represent an important part of the faunal assemblage at only one type of site, i.e. dune sites. The preponderance of fish remains at dune sites and the seasonal occupation of dunes was reasonably explained by the physiographic setting of dune areas near seasonal ponds created by the annual Nile flooding.

Further insights concerning the role of fish in prehistoric Egypt come from research at Lake Qarun in the Fayum depression. Faunal remains collected by a number of researchers provide ample evidence that Late Paleolithic and Neolithic groups in the Fayum relied heavily on the lake's piscine resources. Fish accounted for 74 percent of the Paleolithic and 71 percent of the Neolithic skeletal remains recovered from these sites. Again, this activity was thought to be seasonal in nature. During Predynastic times, fishing continued to be an important source of protein. Evidence from Hierakonpolis (Nekhen) indicates that with the onset of a more settled lifestyle, fishing became a year-round activity. During Dynastic times, fishing for both pleasure and sustenance is depicted in tomb scenes at Saqqara, Beni Hasan and Thebes. Salted and dried fish were prepared for export, and fish were given as rations (wages) to state employees. Numerous market scenes also depict the sale and barter of fish.

It is interesting to point out that fish resources and wild terrestrial resources followed a different trajectory from Paleolithic through Dynastic times. As the ancient Egyptians became more settled and later developed an agriculturally based society and finally statehood, wild terrestrial animals became increasingly less utilized, both in terms of species diversity and in actual numbers. On the other hand, fish increased in importance both in diversity and in numbers utilized, in particular, those species that display a predictable seasonal behavior, such as migrating mullets.

The Egyptian Nile also offered an excellent haven for migrating birds, and thousands of ducks, waders and many other groups can be found wintering in Egypt. Approximately seventy-five avian taxa have been identified in Egyptian art, and over 450 taxa have been identified as living in Egypt. Ancient fowling was undertaken with the use of large (and small) nets which encased a given tree or habitat, trapping the birds within. Small clap-nets, arrows and boomerangs were also used to hunt birds. Fowling was almost always associated with fishing: both were depicted as occupations of the Delta marshes.

During Dynastic times, elites hunted and tamed many large and often dangerous wild species. Lions as well as other species of great cats were a favorite companion of kings and nobles, and are often shown accompanying the king at the hunt. Hunting particularly dangerous animals, such as the hippopotamus and the lion, became a royal prerogative, but one that also held symbolic significance. Artistic scenes depicting the king (or noble) harpooning a hippopotamus, for example, are thought to represent the ruler's triumph over chaos. Hippopotamus ivory, incidentally, is harder than elephant ivory and provided the raw material for many ornaments and utilitarian objects.

There is evidence from the Dynastic period that large numbers of wild animals were held captive in what could be described as a royal menagerie. One such example was that of Amenhotep III, who had animals enclosed and roaming freely within a 300 × 600 m fenced area. The captive animals served a variety of religious and secular purposes, including "the hunt."

See also

Beni Hasan; Epi-paleolithic cultures, overview; fauna, domesticated; Hierakonpolis; Neolithic cultures, overview; Paleolithic cultures, overview; Predynastic period, overview; representational evidence, Middle Kingdom private tombs; representational evidence, New Kingdom private tombs; representational evidence, Old Kingdom private tombs; Wadi Kubbaniya

Further reading

Brewer, D.J., and R. Friedman. 1989. *Fish and Fishing in Ancient Egypt*. Warminster.

Brewer, D.J., D. Redford and S. Redford. 1994. *Domestic Plants and Animals: The Egyptian Originals*. Warminster.

Butzer, K.W. 1976. *Early Hydraulic Civilization in Egypt*. Chicago.

Janssen, R., and J. Janssen. 1989. *Egyptian Household Animals*. Aylesbury.

Wendorf, F., R. Schild and A. Close. 1980. *Loaves and Fishes: The Prehistory of Wadi Kubbaniya*. Dallas.

DOUGLAS J. BREWER

Fayum, Graeco-Roman sites

Hundreds of Graeco-Roman sites in the Fayum are known from archaeological remains, textual references or both. The majority were towns founded under Ptolemy II as part of a reclamation project around the Birket el-Qarun (Lake Moeris), and some of these settlements grew to great prosperity in the Roman period. The Roman practice of settling retired military veterans in the Fayum increased and diversified the population in the region during the first and second centuries AD. Religious activity in the Fayum was dominated by the cults of local crocodile gods; temples to these divinities were prominent features of the towns of the region. The fortunes of these towns were dependent on political, geographical and economic factors; many were abandoned by the fourth century AD. Those sites that were not abandoned usually include later churches and monasteries, and even Islamic remains.

Graeco-Roman sites in the Fayum were known to early European travelers in Egypt, who sometimes published accounts of their trips. The Fayum was included in the itinerary of the Napoleonic expedition and was also the subject of a more systematic survey in 1843 by Richard Lepsius. The *sebbakh*-digging in the ruins of Graeco-Roman sites for decomposed mudbrick to be used as fertilizer resulted in two major groups of papyrus finds in the 1870s and 1880s, and a general awareness of the archaeological potential of the Fayum region. The earliest systematic attempt to investigate the archaeology of the Graeco-Roman Fayum were the 1895–1901 surveys of B.P. Grenfell, D.G. Hogarth and A.S. Hunt for the Egypt Exploration Fund; although their objective was to uncover papyri, Grenfell and Hunt preserved valuable archaeological information and identified many of sites with their ancient names.

More recent excavations have tended to concentrate on individual sites, most often those associated with papyrus finds. Fayum Graeco-Roman settlement sites are among the best preserved in Egypt and large numbers of Greek, Demotic and Coptic papyri, ostraca and inscriptions (along with texts in Latin and Egyptian in both hieroglyphic and hieratic scripts) come from the Fayum, making this region one of the best documented in Egypt. Textual and artifactual remains from these sites graphically illustrate the complex combination of cultural elements in the society of the Graeco-Roman Fayum. Roman period cemeteries in the Fayum have yielded hundreds of the paintings known as "Fayum mummy portraits." Many came from illegal digging at a necropolis near modern Rubayyat. Flinders Petrie's 1888–9 excavations of the Roman period necropolis north of the Hawara pyramid also yielded numerous examples of these portraits. A few of the better published of the Graeco-Roman sites in the Fayum are described below.

Dimai (Soknopaiou Nesos)

A Graeco-Roman town site on the northern edge of the Fayum, north of the Birket el-Qarun (29°27 N, 30°40′ E), Soknopaiou Nesos was founded in the third century BC, probably under Ptolemy II Philadelphus. The town's Greek name means "Island of Soknopaios," the latter being the Egyptian name of the local crocodile god, "Sobek, lord of the Island" (*Sbk nb P3-jw*), and may refer to the appearance of the town like an island in the midst of cultivation. In addition to extensive remains of mudbrick houses and public buildings, the site also includes a temple complex, containing two temples to the crocodile god Soknopaios surrounded by a high wall. Occupation of the site seems constant until the middle of the third century AD, when the documentary evidence breaks off and the town seems to have been abandoned.

The ruins of Dimai were known to early European travelers in Egypt and the site was briefly surveyed by Lepsius in 1843; the mining of the mudbrick structures for *sebbakh* in the 1870s led to the discovery of papyri at the site. After a major papyrus find at Dimai in 1887 (the "second Fayum find"), two separate officially sanctioned "excavations" were carried out by local antiquities dealers in 1890–1 and 1894, during which more papyri were said to have been found on the floors of the houses. The site was briefly examined by Grenfell and Hunt in 1900–1 during their general survey of the Fayum and further investigated by F. Zucker and W. Schubart in 1908–9. Portions of Dimai were formally excavated by the University of Michigan Archaeological Expedition in 1931–2 under Enoch E. Peterson, as a complement to the more extensive work being done by the Michigan team at Karanis. The Michigan excavations were only partially published and more recent work at the site has been sporadic and unsystematic. Beginning in late 1996, material from the University of Michigan Dimai excavation has been made available online through the auspices of the Kelsey Museum of Archaeology; a final publication of the archaeological remains from the Michigan excavation of Dimai is planned.

The settlement of Dimai originally covered an area of about 23 ha. Like most Graeco-Roman sites in the Fayum, the central part of the town at Dimai was heavily destroyed by *sebbakh*-diggers and the better preserved portions of the town are on the outskirts. The houses on the outer edge are turned inward, accessible from within the town only, thus forming a sort of wall around Dimai. One of the main access points into the town was through a gateway at the south of the site; from this gateway a stone-paved road led to the temple complex in the north of the town. This complex covered an area of about 1.1 ha and was surrounded by a mudbrick wall that may have originally been as high as 15 m. Within the enclosure were two temples: a mudbrick and stone structure still partially preserved and an almost completely destroyed stone building to the north. The remainder of the site is filled with smaller buildings, mostly houses that are very typical of their region and time: multi-level mudbrick structures consisting of rooms around a central courtyard, grouped in *insulae* along streets. Fragmentary wall-paintings are known from some of these houses as well. Within the houses, excavators found pottery, fragmentary furniture, agricultural equipment, coins and papyri and ostraca in Demotic and Greek. Patterns of use indicate that, as with other Graeco-Roman Fayum towns, the court-yards of the Dimai houses were used as stables and also for milling and cooking. The excava-tors observed as many as four distinct levels of occupation in the areas surveyed. The only non-residential structure known at Dimai, outside of the temple complex, was the structure designated II 201 by the Michigan expedition. This was an unusually large structure made of large mudbricks that yielded very little in the way of domestic artifacts; its function is still unclear.

Kom Aushim (Karanis)

A town in the northeastern Fayum, west of the Birket el-Qarun (29°27′ N, 30°54′ E), Karanis is one of the most important Graeco-Roman sites in the region. Although not the largest, Karanis is the best-preserved and most extensively excavated town in the Fayum, and has yielded a very large amount of artifactual and textual material with archaeological context. Karanis was founded in the mid-third century BC, as part of the Fayum development of Ptolemy II Philadelphus. The town prospered throughout the Ptolemaic period, expanding northward from its original site. The first century AD was a time of great building activity at Karanis, and the following centuries of Roman rule were a time of expansion and economic growth for the town. Karanis managed to survive the general abandonment of many Fayum sites in the fourth century AD, and much of the material from the site comes from this period. Dated written documentation from the site breaks off in the fifth century AD, as do the excavated coins, but the pottery from the site suggests continued (or renewed) habitation of the site well into the sixth and possibly seventh centuries before it was completely abandoned.

In 1924, F.W. Kelsey of the University of Michigan chose Karanis as an archaeological site that could be excavated as a complement to Michigan's large collection of Greek papyri. The University of Michigan excavations of Karanis lasted from 1924 through 1935, under the direction of J.L. Starkey in 1924–6 and E.E. Peterson in 1926–35. The Michigan excavations resulted in the recovery of thousands of buildings and papyri, and also huge amounts of artifactual material, much of which came to the Kelsey Museum of Archaeology in the division of finds. Further excavation of Karanis was carried out under the auspices of the University of Cairo from 1966 through 1975; these excavations uncovered Roman baths, residential structures, coin hoards and papyri, and examined a nearby village and cemetery. Unexcavated portions of Karanis were surveyed magnetically by A. G. Hussain around 1983, revealing the presence of still further structures. More recently, the site of Karanis is now home to the Kom Oshim Museum, where artifacts from the Michigan and Cairo excavations are displayed, under the direction of S. Ghaboor. Material from the University of Michigan excavations has received renewed attention in the past few decades, resulting in publication of corpora of objects and a major exhibition at the Kelsey Museum of Archaeology in 1983.

The sheer mass of material available from Karanis has proven to be an obstacle to the full publication and interpretation of the site. The difficulties of integrating the many different kinds of evidence from Karanis have led to concentration on very specific aspects of the site, resulting in preliminary reports on architecture and topography, as well as corpora of objects and texts. The excavators' preliminary reports were very much colored by their preconceptions of the site; their chronological scheme of stratigraphic levels and their general "construction" of Karanis as a typical small farming town have pervaded subsequent work on the site, but are badly in need of reconsideration. The publications of the ceramics, glass, coins, lamps, papyri and textiles from Karanis present the most extensive sequences of such objects with archaeological context from Roman Egypt, but none of these publications is complete and all require revision and updating. With a few exceptions, the subsequent Cairo excavations of Karanis remain completely unpublished.

Kom Darb Gerza (Philadelphia)

A Graeco-Roman town site on the eastern edge of the Fayum (29°27′ N, 31°05′ E), Philadelphia served as an important link between the Nile and the Fayum. Founded by Ptolemy II Philadelphus and named after an epithet of his sister Arsinoe, Philadelphia was an important administrative center in the Fayum through much of the Ptolemaic period and continued as such into the Roman period. Part of the reason for the importance and prosperity of the town must be its geographical location: Philadelphia lay on a major route between the Nile and the Fayum region and much of the trade between the Nile Valley and the Fayum passed through it. The town eventually came to occupy an area of about 24 ha, mostly made up of mudbrick dwellings laid out in regular blocks. Philadelphia was home to a number of temples, and a large pottery works lay just to the southwest of the town. A contemporary cemetery lay to the east of Philadelphia; the town may have also been connected to the cemeteries to the west at Rubayyat (source of a large find of Fayum mummy portraits). In common with many of its Fayum neighbors, Philadelphia appears to have gone into decline

in the fourth century AD and was ultimately abandoned by the fifth century.

Although known to earlier travelers and apparently noted in the Fayum survey of Grenfell and Hunt, the only formal excavation of Philadelphia was the 1908–9 excavations by F. Zucker and P. Viereck on behalf of the Berlin Museum. This excavation uncovered much of the town plan, in addition to remains of houses and their contents, as well as a large number of papyri, ostraca and wax tablets, mostly Greek. Prior and subsequent illegal digging at the site brought to light many finds of papyri, perhaps the most extensive being the Ptolemaic archive of Zenon discovered in the winter of 1914–15. A visit by Ludwig Borchardt in 1924 revealed much damage at the site and little, if any, formal excavation has been carried out there since.

Papyri finds span the entire history of the site and include a number of important "archives" or, more properly, related groups of documents. Best-known (and most extensive) is the third century BC Zenon archive, which contains papyri in Greek and Demotic. Certain documents from the Zenon archive are of special interest to the archaeologist, since they describe the building, decoration and repair of the large house of Zenon's employer Diotimos and give a useful insight into the construction of an elite dwelling in the early Ptolemaic period. The early first century AD archive of the tax-collector Nemesion was discovered some time in 1920–1, and includes a copy of the famous letter of Emperor Claudius concerning the Jews of Alexandria. The archive of Roman military officer Flavius Abinnaeus originated in Dionysias, but was brought to Philadelphia some time after 351, when Abinnaeus retired there, and is of great significance for its glimpse of the career of a military officer in the fourth century AD.

Medinet Madi (Narmouthis, Ibion)

A town and temple site on the southwestern edge of the Fayum (29°12′ N, 30°38′ E) with prehistoric, pharaonic and Graeco-Roman, Byzantine and Islamic period remains, Medinet Madi is perhaps best known as the site of the Graeco-Roman town of Narmouthis. The site of Medinet Madi consists of two main areas, an eastern and western kom, that have yielded a great variety of architectural and artifactual remains. Medinet Madi is the most consistently and extensively excavated of the Graeco-Roman Fayum sites, having been continuously excavated under the same director for the past thirty years.

In addition to the temple and tomb remains, Medinet Madi has preserved the extensive remains of a settlement site. Most of the excavated houses are from the Ptolemaic and Roman periods. Architecturally, the urban areas of Medinet Madi are similar to other contemporary sites in the Fayum, and excavation of the houses and other structures has yielded a large amount of artifactual evidence for life in the town. These finds have been supplemented by extensive finds of Demotic and Greek texts. Urban activity at the site continued long after the introduction of Christianity and even after the Muslim conquest of Egypt; Coptic and Arabic textual material attests to habitation that extends as late as the ninth century AD. Although not from an excavated context, Manichaean codices in Coptic from as early as the fourth century AD point to the existence of religious minorities at Medinet Madi under Christianity. At some time around or after the fourth century, activity at the site seems to have shifted south and southeast of the earlier settlement, where much of the Byzantine and Islamic period remains have been found. Medinet Madi contained at least seven churches, one built entirely of mudbrick. It is likely that the town at Medinet Madi remained mostly Christian after the Muslim conquest in the seventh century; no mosques or other evidence of substantial Muslim population have been found. The reason for the apparent abandonment of the site in the Fatimid period is uncertain.

Like most Fayum sites, Medinet Madi suffered from the sebbakh-digging and antiquities-hunting common in the region in the second half of the nineteenth century. Medinet Madi was one of the few major Graeco-Roman sites not investigated by B.P. Grenfell and A.S. Hunt in their survey of the Fayum; the earliest published scholarly investigation of the site was undertaken by Jouguet in 1900–1. This survey appears to have attracted further illegal digging at Medinet Madi. The next controlled excavation of the site was carried out in 1909–10 by Zucker and Schubart, who investigated the Graeco-Roman houses and uncovered a number of Greek papyri. The Zucker–Schubart excavation was likewise followed by intermittent illegal digging at the site; one of the most important discoveries made in the course of this looting of the site was a group of Coptic papyrus codices containing Manichaean texts, found around 1929. Large-scale excavation of Medinet Madi began under Achille Vogliano in 1934 for the University of Milan and continued through 1939. A University of Milan team, under the direction of Edda Bresciani, reopened large-scale excavation and investigation of the site in 1966. This Italian expedition to Medinet Madi has continued under the same director through the present day, although the sponsoring institution is now the University of Pisa. Several reports on this excavation have appeared to date, in addition to numerous articles.

See also

Hawara; Roman period, overview

Further reading

Doxiades, E. 1995. *The Mysterious Fayum Portraits: Faces from Ancient Egypt*. London.

Grenfell, B.P., A.S. Hunt, D.G. Hogarth and J.G. Milne. 1900. *Fayûm Towns and their Papyri*. London.

Lane, M.E. 1985. *A Guide to the Antiquities of the Fayyum*. Cairo.

Minnen, P. van. 1994. House-to-house enquiries: an interdisciplinary approach to Roman Karanis. *Zeitschrift für Papyrologie und Epigraphik* 100: 227–51.

——. 1995. Deserted villages: two Late Antique town sites in Egypt. *Bulletin of the American Society of Papyrologists* 32: 41–56.

Montserrat, D. 1996. "No Papyrus and No Portraits": Hogarth, Grenfell and the First

Season in the Fayum, 1895–6. *Bulletin of the American Society of Papyrologists* 33: 133–76.

Rathbone, D. 1996. Towards a historical topography of the Fayum. In *Archaeological Research in Roman Egypt: The Proceedings of the Seventeenth Classical Colloquium of the Department of Greek and Roman Antiquities, British Museum*, D.M. Bailey, ed., *Journal of Roman Archaeology Supplement* 19: 50–6. Ann Arbor, MI.

Wilfong, T.G. 1996. *A Select Bibliography of the Archaeology of Karanis and the Graeco-Roman Fayum*. Electronic resource available on the World Wide Web at http://www.umich.edu/~kelseydb/Excavation/KaranisBib.html.

TERRY G. WILFONG

Fayum, Neolithic and Predynastic sites

The Fayum Depression encloses the only large freshwater lake in Egypt. To the ancient Egyptians, the Fayum lake was a holy place, sacred to the crocodile god Sobek, whose material manifestations swarmed the lake's beaches. The strong religious significance of the lake (whose Arabic name is Birket el-Qarun, but which was known in ancient Egyptian as "She-resy" (Southern Lake), and later divided into "She-resy" and "Mer-wer" (Great Lake)) was paralleled in several periods with considerable economic and political importance. For prehistorians the Fayum is particularly important because it provides the earliest extensive evidence about how cereal farming—the economic foundation of all Egyptian civilization—was introduced and practiced in Egypt.

Beginning at least 10,000 years ago, the Fayum lake was fed by a branch of the Nile, so the lake rose and fell annually with the river, and when the Nile crested in late spring, floods covered a large area of the Fayum Depression. As the floods receded in summer and autumn, the lake bottom would have been exposed, and these areas of shore and shallows would have been rich in plant and animal life. This annual flood cycle continued for thousands of years but, beginning probably in the 12th Dynasty, at about 1990 BC, the water-flow into the lake was artificially restricted, apparently in order to reclaim land for farming. Land reclamation over the centuries eventually reduced the lake to less than 20 percent of its original extent. In the early 1990s water run-off from agricultural fields has increased the size of the lake slightly and made it so saline that most aquatic animal species disappeared.

Traces of human activity in the areas around the Fayum region go back hundreds of thousands of years, but the earliest substantial and well-preserved occupations date to about 10,000 years ago, when hunter-gatherers began intensive exploitation of the rich interface of land and lake. There is some evidence that the depression that the lake eventually filled, as well as the natural channel that connected the main Nile and the Fayum, were the result of geological processes that occurred at the end of the last Ice Age, about 10,000 years ago. In any case, for most of the past 10,000 years the areas even a few kilometers away from the lake's shoreline were extremely arid and would have provided only a few animal, mineral and plant resources. However, ground-water near the lake was high enough to support swamps and forests, and the plants and animals of these areas, in combination with those of the lake itself, constituted lush and open niches for the hunter-gatherers who lived in Egypt after the end of the Ice Age.

These areas were first colonized about 10,000 years ago, and many of these occupations, which are marked by great numbers of small chert blades and other tools (known as the "Qarunian Industry"), can still be found around the lake's perimeter. These sites clearly indicate at least part of the economy of these first inhabitants of the Fayum, for they contain the bones of fish, gazelle, hartebeest, hippopotamus and other animals. These early Fayum groups seem to have combined various resources in a reliable mix of hunting, fishing and foraging; they do not appear to have been in the process of domesticating plants or animals, or using these domesticates in any form of agriculture. Few or no grinding stones are found on these sites, and the meager plant remains from them that have been analyzed are mainly reeds and other marsh and swamp plants; the animals all appear to be wild species. The conformation of the land at some points along the shore of the ancient Fayum lake was such that very likely large schools of fish were trapped in natural basins as flood levels receded, and these fish would have been easily caught. In fact, the typical site of this period is located on a small hillock close to what would have been in ancient times the lake's shoreline, and is marked by thousands of small stone blade tools and the bones of countless Nile catfish and other fish.

People living at about the same time as these Qarunian people, but hundreds of kilometers away, in the oases in what are now Egypt's southwestern deserts, do appear to have been in the process of domesticating cattle and, perhaps, some plants. On the basis of evidence from Bir Kiseiba and Nabta in southwest Egypt, Fred Wendorf and Romauld Schild have suggested that both cattle and pottery seem to have been known in the Sahara as early as anywhere else in the world. The Fayum's Qarunian peoples appear to have been culturally related to these people at Bir Kiseiba and Nabta, but, perhaps, the unique and rich resources of the lacustrine/terrestrial interface in the Fayum allowed a continuation of the hunting-fishing-gathering way of life at a time when other groups in Egypt were beginning the transition to agriculture.

About 7,500 years ago, the Fayum hunter-fisher-gatherers were replaced, displaced or "converted" (the evidence is still uncertain) to "Neolithic" cultures, the members of which lived at least in part on farming: specifically, on domesticated wheat, barley, sheep, goats and cattle. There is a gap in radiocarbon dates between about 6500 and 5500 BC that suggests that the Fayum may have been abandoned for a century or more between the Qarunian hunter-fisher-gatherers and the first farmers.

In fact, it is somewhat imprecise to call even the Neolithic Fayum peoples "farmers," because although people in the Fayum after about 5500 BC were clearly raising domesticated sheep and cattle and farming wheat and barley, they also continued to rely heavily on fishing and hunting, and probably wild plant collecting. Sites in the Fayum that date to the period between about 5500 and 4500 BC are found in heavy concentrations on most of the perimeter of the lake. There is no question that these people cultivated wheat and barley. In the 1920s, archaeologist Gertrude Caton Thompson found silos full of wheat and barley that also contained sickles and other tools of these early cultivators. So well preserved were these cereals that scientists at the British Museum tried to germinate them, but without success. Except for a few possible traces of poles for huts, no dwellings of the Fayum Neolithic have been found, and it seems likely that these people lived in reed huts. Even these huts may have been temporary dwellings, lived in for only part of the year, for at even the largest Fayum Neolithic sites one finds thousands of hearths and massive quantities of stone tools, pottery fragments and animal remains, but none of the superimposed debris of successive occupational areas that comprise most Neolithic sites elsewhere.

The Neolithic peoples of the Fayum may have relied on a form of agriculture that involved frequently shifting fields and settlements in order to exploit the rich lake bottom that would have been exposed by the annual flood. Because the Nile levels and thus the lake levels fluctuated greatly each year, the location of wheat and barley fields would also have had to be somewhat different each year.

One of the most intriguing aspects of the Fayum Neolithic is its origins, because the Fayum and a few other nearby sites, such as Merimde Beni-salame, are the oldest known developed agricultural economies to appear in Egypt. Wheat and barley seem to be native mainly to upland areas of southwest Asia and were domesticated there at least a thousand years before they were used in the Fayum, so it seems likely that domesticated cereals and cereal farming techniques were introduced into Egypt, and thus into the Fayum, from southwest Asia. Domesticated sheep and goats, and possibly some species of cattle, also seem to have been introduced to Egypt from Asia.

Despite the apparent introduction into Egypt of southwest Asian domesticates, scholars disagree about from where the Fayum Neolithic peoples and their cultures came. Some argue for origins in the Near East, and more specifically in the Jordan Valley. Others have argued for a northwest African origin, a Sudanese origin or a Saharan origin. The stone tools used by the Neolithic peoples of the Fayum show very distinctive styles, such as a form of a projectile point or "arrowhead," and similar projectile points are found in many Saharan and Upper Egyptian sites, but not in the Sinai or Syro-Palestine; so, perhaps the people of the Fayum originally came from that area and simply incorporated in their economies the cereals and cereal cultivating techniques introduced from southwest Asia.

After at least a thousand years of dense occupation, between about 5500 and 4500 BC, the Fayum seems to have been abandoned some time after 4500 BC, and only a few small sites can be reliably dated to the period of about 4000 BC. These appear to have been seasonal hunting and fishing camps. It seems likely that, once a way of life based on farming wheat and barley and raising sheep, goats and cattle became well established not just in the Fayum but in the main Nile Valley, the Fayum would have been considered a marginal place to farm. The main Nile Valley would have been much more reliable for farming, as the fertility-renewing silts deposited in the main Nile channel would have been greater than those in the Fayum lake, and also the farmlands created by the annual floods would have been more predictable and larger in the main Nile channel than those along the shallows of the Fayum lake. Moreover, by 4000 BC the Egyptian economy was not simply a matter of farming the best available lands: towns and villages along the Nile were already in regular communication, and at least some products were being exchanged via boat traffic. Thus the Fayum would have been somewhat isolated from the evolving social and economic world of the Nile.

The Fayum seems to have been nearly abandoned during this formative epoch.

Closer to the Nile Valley but still in the Fayum region is the site of Gerza (29°27′ N, 31°12′ E), where a small Predynastic cemetery was excavated by Flinders Petrie in 1910. Out of the 288 burials, 249 were intact; nine Early Dynastic graves were found on higher ground, but they had been robbed. From the name of the site Petrie derived the term "Gerzean," the middle phase (*circa* 3600–3200 BC) of his seriation of Predynastic artifacts (Sequence Dating). The contracted burials in this cemetery were typical of the Nagada (II) culture of Upper Egypt, and contained Nagada culture grave goods. Pottery consisted of typical Nagada culture wares, including Wavy-handled class and Decorated class. Other Nagada culture artifacts, such as cosmetic palettes, stone vessels and beads in many materials, including gold and lapis lazuli, were found in these burials. Unrelated to the earlier Fayum Neolithic culture, the cemetery at Gerza seems to be an early intrusion of the Nagada culture in northern Egypt. Petrie found glumes of wheat in many of the pots he excavated, and the Gerza site may represent a village in which agriculture was becoming more important for subsistence—and exchange of craft goods—than it had been earlier.

See also

agriculture, introduction of; Caton Thompson, Gertrude; climatic history; fauna, domesticated; fauna, wild; Merimde Beni-salame; Neolithic and Predynastic stone tools; pottery, prehistoric

Further reading

Butzer, K.W. 1976. *Early Hydraulic Civilization in Egypt*. Chicago.

Caton Thompson, G., and E. Gardner. 1934. *The Desert Fayum*. London.

Ginter, G., J.K. Kozlowski, M. Pawlikowski and J. Sliwa. 1982. El-Tarif und Qasr el-Sagha. Forschungen zur Siedlungsgeschichte des Neolithikums, der Frühdynastischen

Epoche und des Mittleren Reiches. *MDAIK* 38: 97–129.

Hassan, F.A. 1986. Desert environment and origins of agriculture in Egypt. *Norwegian Archaeological Review* 19: 63–76.

Kozlowski, J.K., ed. 1980. *Qasr el-Sagha*. Warsaw.

Kozlowski, J.K., and B. Ginter. 1989. The Fayum Neolithic in the light of new discoveries. In *Late Prehistory of the Nile Basin and the Sahara*, L. Krzyzaniak and M. Kobusiewicz, eds, 158–79. Poznan.

Petrie, W.M.F., G.A. Wainwright and E. MacKay. 1912. *The Labyrinth, Gerza and Mazghuneh*. London.

Wendorf, F., and R. Schild, eds. 1976. *Prehistory of the Nile Valley*. New York.

Wenke, R.J., J. Long and P. Buck. 1988. The Epipaleolithic and Neolithic subsistence and settlement in the Fayyum Oasis of Egypt. *JFA* 15(1): 29–51.

ROBERT J. WENKE

First Intermediate Period, private tombs

During the 6th Dynasty there was a gradual decline in the size and elaborateness of tombs of all classes in the Memphite cemeteries. This was probably the result of a decrease in the resources of every class of officials. By the end of the Old Kingdom large, stone *mastaba* superstructures with multiple decorated rooms were a thing of the past. But even in this period of decentralized political control, famine and warfare, the mortuary cult was important enough in the Egyptian belief system that burial practices, though impoverished and transformed, continued in some form.

The necropolis around the pyramid of Pepi II at South Saqqara provides eloquent testimony to the state of affairs in the capital at the end of that king's long reign (90+ years) and immediately following. It contains tombs of many different levels of officials, but only the highest state officials, the viziers, could still afford to build tombs with stone-lined chapels. Even these were severely restricted in their number of rooms, and only one shows traces of significant decoration with carved reliefs.

The tomb of a middle ranking official named Degem is representative of a type of tomb peculiar to South Saqqara in this period. The tomb's superstructure was a mudbrick *mastaba*, 8.25 × 5.50 m and 2.50 m high. In the center of the east face a small limestone false door inscribed for Degem marked the offering place. Beneath the superstructure, a mudbrick-lined shaft led to a stone-lined burial chamber, which was roofed over with a barrel vault of two courses of mudbrick. Its interior was painted with an offering list and representations of food and funerary equipment necessary for Degem's afterlife. Two false doors painted in the style of an elaborately niched palace façade occupied the middle of each lateral wall. At the back, next to a niche for a canopic box (for the preserved viscera of the deceased), were paintings of piles of grain and five round-topped granaries preceded by a columned portico. The chamber was just large enough to contain a wooden coffin.

Dwarf *mastaba*s on the same pattern as that of Degem contained the burials of poorer individuals. These are rarely more than 3–4 × 2 m in area. A small mudbrick chamber for the body was located at the base of a shallow shaft beneath the *mastaba*.

Other contemporaries of Degem were buried in communal tombs. These consisted of a number of shafts and burial chambers covered by mudbrick barrel vaults, grouped beneath a superstructure of square or rectangular mudbrick retaining walls filled with rubble. Arrangements for the mortuary cult were usually modest, but a few tombs had stone-lined niche-chapels built against the east face. The decoration of these chapels was confined to a false door at the rear and simple offering scenes on the side walls, while an offering stone formed the floor of the chapel.

By the Heracleopolitan period (9th–10th Dynasties), niche-chapels set into the east face of small mudbrick or rubble filled *mastaba*s had become the preferred type of burial place, as, for example, in a cemetery to the north of the Teti pyramid at Saqqara. These sometimes included scenes of daily life on the side walls. The body, enclosed in a wooden coffin, occupied a rock-cut chamber to one side of the shaft below. At Heracleopolis, the coffin might be placed directly on the floor of the niche chapel, which also had a square cavity in the floor for a canopic box. The niche chapel was then sealed with a large stone and covered with earth.

At South Saqqara, a more modest type of communal tomb consisted of a series of contiguous vaulted chambers built of mudbrick in a shallow trench in the ground. In place of shafts, the undecorated chambers opened onto a common corridor on the north side.

Communal tombs are also found in Upper Egypt. Throughout the First Intermediate Period in the provinces, however, important individuals continued to erect large *mastaba*s of a more traditional type, such as those at Edfu, Dendera and Khozam. In plan, the Dendera *mastaba*s of the First Intermediate Period follow the traditions of the later 6th Dynasty, with a long interior chamber perpendicular to the entrance corridor. These chambers were sometimes vaulted to better protect a number of rectangular stelae, each with a standing figure of the owner and a short funerary prayer, mounted at the top of a long row of niches in the rear wall. An inscribed architrave with seated figures of the owner and his wife approached by offering bearers spanned the entrance of a number of tombs, while a frieze with a line of biographical text often ran along the façade near the top. An inner offering chamber contained the false door.

Rock-cut tombs with inscriptions and reliefs likewise continued to be made for provincial governors (nomarchs) and other high officials throughout the First Intermediate Period. Increasingly, the long axis becomes perpendicular to the façade, as is the rule in the Middle Kingdom. Otherwise, Old Kingdom traditions of tomb design remained influential until the end of the period. The traditional façade, reminiscent of a *mastaba*, with its sloping side and inscribed lintel and drum, is still found but

carved in rock. Exceptionally, the façade of the tomb contained a biographical inscription, such as in the tomb of Pepynakht Heqaib at Aswan. A false door in the west wall remained the focal point of the mortuary cult until the latter part of this period.

However, even the most important of the rock-cut tombs are now commonly one--chambered affairs and generally both smaller in size and less ambitious in layout than those of the Old Kingdom. Columned porticoes rarely appear, while the rows of pillars which divided the offering room had disappeared at most places by the end of the 6th Dynasty, except at Aswan. The rock-cut statues which were such a distinctive feature of Old Kingdom provincial tombs are also absent. Sporadically, statue chambers appear, such as at Deir el-Gebrawi. Usually no attempt was made to decorate the entire chapel.

In rock-cut tombs and stelae of the late Old Kingdom, a clear attempt to carry on the artistic traditions of the capital at Memphis is evident. Nevertheless, scenes are less well spaced and subjects intermingle with little apparent connection. A deterioration of technical skill is also apparent, and late Old Kingdom work is often executed in a poor sunk relief. Increasingly, paint is the preferred medium. The figures are more attenuated than before with short upper bodies, overly long limbs, narrow shoulders and waists, and disproportionately small heads. Together these features constitute what has been called the "First Intermediate Period style." Clear evidence of this style, however, is found already in the late 6th Dynasty at Deir el-Gebrawi and Meir.

The hundreds of lesser rock-cut tombs of the First Intermediate Period which dot the cliffs on both sides of the Nile in Upper Egypt, like the tombs of the nomarchs and other high officials, normally consist of a forecourt and a large square or rectangular offering chamber. In the smaller tombs the walls were roughly hewn and decoration was restricted to small limestone stelae. The burial places were commonly situated under the floor of the offering chamber at the bottom of a vertical shaft or sloping passage. Alternatively, burial niches or tunnels might be cut in the chapel walls.

At the beginning of the Heracleopolitan period, there is evidence of more prosperity in the rock-cut tombs and stelae in Middle and Upper Egypt (Aswan, Thebes, Coptos, Dendera, el-Qasr wa es-Saiyad, Thinis, Hagarsa), where a revival of traditional forms is seen. Raised relief is once more in evidence and is competent in execution. The proportions of the figures, whether in paint or relief, are again in accord with the Old Kingdom canons. This revival is presumably due to the renewed influence of models from the capital, where the Heracleopolitan rulers of the 9th Dynasty had fallen heir to the Memphite workshops. It did not last long, except in the north and in Middle Egypt.

In the southernmost nomes of Upper Egypt, far from the sophisticated influence of the capital, a vigorous school of tomb painting developed just prior to the outbreak of the war between Thebes and Heracleopolis, fought for the domination of Upper Egypt. At this time an ambitious nomarch of the Hierakonpolite nome named Ankhtify had brought Edfu under his sway and exerted some control over Aswan and the southern part of the Theban nome. His short hegemony perhaps helps to explain the close resemblance in the decoration between Ankhtify's tomb at Mo'alla, the tomb of (General) Iti at Gebelein, and the tomb of the nomarch Setka at Aswan. Scenes in all three tombs contain figures that are thin, tall and awkward, and unpleasant combinations of harsh, bright colors are found. The depiction of Nubian bowmen in the three tombs is notable, since these are the first representations in Egyptian art of peoples with black skins. At Ankhtify's death the southernmost nomes came under Theban control, and the traditions of the southern school of painters were passed on to the artists of the new royal house and went on to influence the art of the Middle Kingdom.

Given the striking similarities in decoration, it is perhaps surprising that the plans of the three tombs are completely dissimilar. Most interesting architecturally, Iti's tomb is two generations earlier than the Theban *saff*-tombs

of the kings named Intef (early 11th Dynasty), with which it shares certain design features. Like the latter, it was preceded by a large forecourt whose rear wall formed an imposing façade, pierced by a series of doorways leading to a transverse corridor.

Three tombs of the late Heracleopolitan period (10th Dynasty) form an important link between Old and Middle Kingdom traditions. Situated in the rocky promontory overlooking the modern city of Asyut, they belonged to nomarchs of the Lycopolite nome. The tombs of Tefibi (Iti-ibi) and Khety II (Tombs 3 and 4) date to the reigns of King Merikare of the 10th Dynasty and his father, the author of a well-known literary text, the *Instruction for Merikare*. Tomb 5 belonged to Khety I, who was probably the father of Tefibi.

The three tombs are vast, and are certainly among the largest rock-cut tombs in Upper Egypt. Tefibi's tomb, for example, measures *circa* 19 × 31 m. A new treatment of the façade is evident in the tombs of Tefibi and Khety II. In the center of a vertical area of dressed stone, the frame of the doorway projected a few centimeters and was inscribed with lines of hieroglyphic texts, which included suitable threats, at the entrance, on the lintel and jambs, to visitors with malicious intent. Important and lengthy historical texts which narrate episodes in the war against the Thebans were carved on the north wall east of the pillars in both Tefibi's and Khety II's chapels. The sunk reliefs of Khety II's chapel are neatly and surely carved in accordance with the precepts of the Old Kingdom canon.

The transition to the classical Middle Kingdom type of tomb was not complete in the Asyut tombs, however. The architraves continue to run transversely to the longitudinal axis, as in tombs of the Old Kingdom and First Intermediate Period, even though that axis is perpendicular to the façade in Tombs 3 and 4, as in tombs of the later period. In addition, the supports of the ceiling are square pillars, not columns with floral capitals, and the roof is flat. Moreover, in the only tomb where it is possible to tell, the focus of the funerary cult is still a false door and not a statue shrine in the form of a deep niche cut in the middle of the rear wall.

See also

Aswan; Asyut; First Intermediate Period, overview; Gebelein; Naga ed-Deir; Old Kingdom provincial tombs; Thebes, el-Tarif, *saff*-tombs

Further reading

Badawy, A. 1966. *A History of Egyptian Architecture: The First Intermediate Period, the Middle Kingdom, and the Second Intermediate Period.* Berkeley, CA.

Fischer, H.G. 1964. *Inscriptions from the Coptite Nome: Dynasties VI–XI,* Analecta Orientalia 40. Rome.

——. 1968. *Dendera in the Third Millennium B.C. down to the Theban Domination of Upper Egypt.* Locust Valley, NY.

Lopez, J. 1975. Rapport préliminaire sur les fouilles d'Hérakléopolis (1968). *Oriens Antiquus* 14: 57–78.

Spanel, D.B. 1989. The Herakleopolitan Tombs of Kheti I, *Jt(.j)jb(.j),* and Kheti II at Asyut. *Orientalia* 58: 301–14.

Vandier, J. 1950. *Mo'alla: la tombe d'Ankhtifi et la tombe de Sébekhotep* (BdÉ 18). Cairo.

EDWARD BROVARSKI

First Intermediate Period, royal tombs

Most of the kings of the First Intermediate Period are ephemeral figures known only from king lists, small finds or casual mention in the tombs of their contemporaries. Few of them have left monuments of any kind. It is clear, however, that the successors of Pepi II (6th Dynasty) continued to build pyramids.

The pyramid of a son and successor of Pepi II, Neferkare II Pepi III, which was named "Neferkare is established and alive," is known only from the decorated false door of his mother, Queen Ankh-nes-pepi, found at South Saqqara (29°40′ N, 31°13′ E) by Gustave Jequier. The royal tomb itself may still lie undiscovered beneath the desert sands.

The pyramid of an 8th Dynasty king, Kakare Ibi, was uncovered by Jequier at South Saqqara in 1929. The pyramid lies about midway between the pyramid temple and valley temple of Pepi II, south of the covered causeway that connected these temples. The core of the pyramid consisted of two concentric walls of more or less regular small stones bonded with a mortar of Nile mud, filled with rubble and cased with limestone from the quarry site of Tura across the river. Except for the foundations, the superstructure had entirely disappeared, but the pyramid measured $31.5\,\mathrm{m}^2$ at the base and perhaps originally 24–28 m in height. By contrast, Pepi II's pyramid measured about $78.5\,\mathrm{m}^2$ at the base and 52.5 m in height. Ibi's monument was in fact not much larger than the pyramids of the queens of Pepi II, which it also resembles in its interior plan. The entrance corridor, opening approximately in the middle of the north face, descends at an angle of 25° directly to the burial chamber. The entrance corridor, burial chamber, and a long narrow storeroom entered from the east end of the latter were all lined with fine white limestone. Except for the north and south walls opposite the ends of the sarcophagus, which were decorated with carved paneling of a niched, palace-façade design, vertical columns of *Pyramid Texts* completely covered the walls of the burial chamber, as in the pyramids of the kings and certain queens of the 6th Dynasty. Most of the texts reproduced on the walls had previously been known, but a number of new spells also occur. The sarcophagus, carved from a huge block of red granite, filled the entire far end of the room and was encased in its walls. The interior was never hollowed out, and it is questionable whether Ibi was ever buried in his pyramid.

Methods of construction analogous to those apparent in Ibi's pyramid were utilized in building the pyramids of the 5th–6th Dynasties. Such methods were cheap and efficient, and allowed the resources of the royal builders to be expended instead on an elaborate program of wall decoration. In Ibi's case, however, a pyramid temple in stone was never built, undoubtedly due to the premature death of the king who reigned for a brief four years and two months, according to the Turin Canon of Kings (king list). Instead, a structure with mudbrick walls, erected on the east side of the pyramid, sufficed for the royal mortuary services. An axial room against the face of the pyramid held a stone basin for libations set in the ground and an emplacement for a false door, which was never found. The modest scale and plan of Ibi's pyramid and temple constitute eloquent testimony to the reduced prestige and economic power of the Memphite pharaohs at the end of the Old Kingdom.

One royal tomb of the First Intermediate Period stands at Dara (27°18 N, 30°52′ E) on the edge of the Western Desert 12 km west of Manfalut in Middle Egypt. It is a large square structure constructed of mudbrick, measuring 130 m along each side, but preserved to a height of only 4 m. There is considerable disagreement over whether the structure is a destroyed pyramid or a square *mastaba*. The vaulted entrance tunnel opens in the center of the north face. A sloping corridor with two level stretches and arches at intervals descends to the door of the burial chamber. The burial chamber was built entirely of limestone, and its entrance was framed by a semicircular (torus) molding. In its floor was a square depression for a canopic chest.

The Dara monument is ascribed to an otherwise unknown king on the basis of a fragment of relief found in a mudbrick *mastaba* south of the pyramid which showed part of an offering scene and a cartouche with the name Khui. King Khui's name does not appear in any surviving king list, and he has been variously assigned by scholars to the late Old Kingdom and First Intermediate Period (6th–8th Dynasties), or as late as the 10th Dynasty.

The corridor to the burial chamber was paved with limestone, some of it reused blocks taken from tombs of earlier periods. From the style of one false door recovered from the corridor, which has a crossbar that extends above all the jambs and niches and an offering scene that completely fills the space between the outer jambs, at least some of the reused material is probably as late as the 9th Dynasty, and the Dara monument also at least as late. Since the kings of the 9th Dynasty are relatively well attested, it is possible that King Khui was one of the lesser known kings of the early 10th Dynasty who retained control only of the Fayum and its immediate vicinity. In this event, the choice of the site for the royal tomb, at Dara in Upper Egyptian Nome XIII (Lycopolite), very near the entrance to the Bahr Yusuf channel of the Nile, may not be without significance. Heracleopolis itself lay only about 200 km downstream on that ancient branch of the Nile, and Dara thus lay in the very heartland of the Heracleopolitan kingdom. At only a slightly later date, the nomarchs of Asyut (Lycopolis) were the friends and supporters of the Heracleopolitan kings Khety and Merikare, and the Lycopolite nome formed a buffer state, warding off the attacks of the Theban kings of the 11th Dynasty.

Another pyramid known from textual evidence is named "Merikare is flourishing of places." It probably stood close by Teti's pyramid at Saqqara, since this is the region where the English archaeologist C.M. Firth discovered a number of false doors and coffins of priests and officials who held office in Merikare's pyramid cult, both in the "Street of Tombs" alongside the northern enclosure wall of the Teti pyramid and just in front of its pyramid temple within the enclosure of the later Ptolemaic Serapeum. Ahmed Fakhry suggested that it might be the ruined pyramid situated some 100 m northeast of Teti's pyramid where blocks of white limestone still litter the surface.

In 1930 Firth excavated the site (for the Egyptian Antiquities Service), and determined that the pyramid must have measured about 52 m on each side. Firth cleared its descending passage and measured the internal chambers of the pyramid. In the burial chamber he found the remains of a destroyed, hard gray stone sarcophagus. The two red granite portcullises (blocks) in the descending passage being down, he supposed that the burial had actually taken place. No inscribed artifacts identifying the owner of the pyramid were found, however, and one scholar has recently argued that the pyramid in fact belongs to King Menkauhor of the 5th Dynasty.

See also

First Intermediate Period, overview; funerary texts; Saqqara, pyramids of the 5th–6th Dynasties

Further reading

Beinlich, H. 1974. Dara. In *LÄ* 1: 990–1.

Edwards, I.E.S. 1985. *The Pyramids of Egypt*. Harmondsworth.

Gomaà, F. 1980. *Ägypten wahrend der ersten Zwischenzeit*. Wiesbaden.

Spencer, A.J. 1979. *Brick Architecture in Ancient Egypt*. Warminster.

Málek, J. 1994. King Merykare and his pyramid. In *Hommages à Jean Leclant* 4, C. Berger, G. Clerc and N. Grimal, eds, 203–14. Cairo.

Maragioglio, V., and C. Rinaldi. 1975. *L'Architettura delle Piramidi Menfite* 8. Rapallo.

Weill, R. 1958. *Dara, Campagnes de 1946–1948*. Cairo.

EDWARD BROVARSKI

funerary texts

Of the various classes of ancient Egyptian literature, the body of texts employed in the ritual and cult associated with the dead, to ensure the everlasting existence of the deceased in the realm of the divine order, is both rich and enigmatic. Other than bureaucratic/inventory inscriptions, this body of texts is one of the earliest.

Funerary texts begin with the inscriptions on stelae set into the walls of Early Dynastic tomb superstructures (*mastabas*) listing the offerings to be presented to the deceased throughout eternity. From this developed the so-called "offering formula," introduced by the phrase "an offering which the king gives" (*ḥtp di niswt*). This phrase embodies the basic needs and desires of every deceased individual for the provision of a burial in a tomb with an adequate supply of food, drink, clothing and equipment, as well as freedom of movement and membership in the community of the other world. The providers of these necessities were the deities associated with the realm of the dead, through the intercession of the king, Anubis and Khenty-Amentiu (later Osiris), the ruler of the realm of the dead. Developing from the offering stelae, the texts and decoration became increasing elaborate, from a carved "false door" in tombs, to the depictions on the walls of offering chambers of *mastabas* of Old Kingdom officials.

The deceased was believed to be an effective force partaking in the realm of the divine spirits. There are many instances of texts in which the deceased claims to possess the status of an "effective spirit" (*akh iqr*). The priest responsible for reciting the appropriate texts in the funerary ritual is said to "spiritualize" (*sakh*) the dead.

The concept of making available the necessities of eternal life in a very literal and mundane sense also necessitated giving the deceased a physical focus, as a preserved corpse, statue or depiction in painting or relief, which the spirit could inhabit. A series of ritual spells developed, referred to as the "Opening of the Mouth," which were performed on the physical likeness of the deceased to magically impart the powers of movement and use of the body. These texts became particularly prevalent in the New Kingdom, but excerpts occur earlier in various contexts.

A special body of texts, known today as the *Pyramid Texts*, came to be adopted during the late Old Kingdom for use in the royal burial cult. They were inscribed on the walls of the inner chambers (antechamber and burial chamber) of the pyramids of kings beginning with Unas, at the end of the 5th Dynasty, to the end of the Old Kingdom. Consisting of a body of over 759 spells or utterances for the welfare and eternal deification of the king, these texts vary in length and subject matter. Some are written as the speech of the king, but others are utterances of various gods. Some texts are of narrative nature, often describing divine attributes of the king, while others are obvious incantations by priests reciting different aspects of the funerary cult.

Following the collapse of centralized authority at the end of the 6th Dynasty, the exclusive use of the *Pyramid Texts* as a royal body of funerary literature seems to have declined. With the re-imposition of a powerful centralized state in the Middle Kingdom, pyramids were again used for burials in the royal cemeteries at Thebes, el-Lisht, South Saqqara, Dahshur and the eastern Fayum (Lahun and Hawara). Where the burial chambers of these pyramids are accessible, however, there are no examples of funerary texts inscribed on the walls or on the sarcophagi. Examples are known of contemporary private tombs, such as that of Si-Iset at Dahshur and Senusretankh at el-Lisht, with *Pyramid Texts* inscribed on the walls of their burial chambers. This lack of funerary texts in royal tombs of the Middle Kingdom is not adequately explained, nor is the lack of funerary texts in burial chambers of the kings of the Old Kingdom prior to Unas.

When the use of *Pyramids Texts* declined in royal burials, a series of funerary texts developed in the context of non-royal burials. These were usually inscribed on wooden coffins and sarcophagi, hence their modern name of *Coffin Texts*. The texts were composed as a series of spells, usually written in vertical columns. Certain spells found earlier in the *Pyramid Texts* continued to be used, but a wider variety of spells developed. In many cases the spells varied in writing and basic composition from region to region, suggesting that there may have been different traditions of funerary beliefs in various religious centers during the Middle Kingdom or earlier.

A characteristic of the *Coffin Texts*, which differentiates them from their antecedents, is an increase in the mention of the god Osiris, including myths of Osiris as the resurrected king of the dead and descriptions of his realm. Earlier Egyptologists regarded this emphasis on Osiris as an apparent decline in the strength of the cult of the sun god Re and it has even been cited as evidence of a so-called "democratization" of the afterlife. Such simplistic views are now largely denied as different understandings of the development of and meaning of Egyptian religious literature have been adopted.

In the New Kingdom the sets of spells and rituals formulated in the *Pyramid Texts* and *Coffin Texts* are often referred to as the *Book of the Dead*, anciently known as the *Spells of the Coming Forth by Day*. Although most commonly known from the numerous examples on papyri accompanied by illustrations or vignettes, this series of spells, which numbered 189 in the New Kingdom versions, was also inscribed on tomb walls and coffins, usually as excerpts. These spells deal with various concepts already set forth in earlier funerary literature, and elaborate and add new concepts. Major themes include overcoming obstacles (including a judgment of the dead), making transformations into various divine forms, having freedom of movement and being protected against various dangers. The goal was an eternal, blissful existence in the paradisiacal "Field of Reeds" in the realm of Osiris, which was an idealized form of the best of this life. There are also spells that are hymns of praise to various deities, especially the sun god and Osiris. To a certain extent, this body of literature was for the use of the non-royal funerary cults, although certain excerpts are found in royal mortuary contexts. Changes in the order and composition of this corpus occurred in the 26th Dynasty, and continued well into Graeco-Roman times in a much more ordered form.

During the New Kingdom an elaborate series of compositions developed for the use of royal burials that took as their central theme the journey of the sun god at sunset through the dark regions of the underworld ruled by Osiris, during which the inimical forces were overcome and renewal was achieved at sunrise. Beginning with the reigns of the Tuthmosid kings of the 18th Dynasty, a composition referred to by Egyptologists as the *Book of Imyduat* (or *Amduat*, "that which is in the underworld") formed an important part of the decoration of the burial chamber of the tombs in the Valley of the Kings. Later this composition was found in the corridors of royal tombs. The actual title of the composition, as stated in the opening text, is the *Writings of the Hidden Chamber*. This probably alludes to the actual burial chamber in the tomb where the texts first appeared, and that part of the underworld where the resurrection of Osiris and the rebirth or revitalization of the sun god Re took place. The king, as both an embodiment of the sun god and of Osiris, the ruler of the realm of the dead, was linked to the concepts of renewal of life associated with these two gods.

A somewhat similar composition, which first makes its appearance in the royal tomb of Horemheb at the end of the 18th Dynasty, is referred to by Egyptologists as the *Book of Gates*, although its ancient title is unknown. The modern name is derived from the characteristic representations of gateways and doors that separate each of the twelve sections of the composition. Only a few completed copies of this book are known. The first complete representation of the *Book of Gates* is found on the anthropoid sarcophagus of Seti I (early 19th Dynasty), which was discovered by Giovanni Belzoni in 1817 and is now displayed in the Sir John Soane Museum in London. Only two other complete renditions of this book in the context of a royal funerary cult in the New Kingdom have been found. One is in the first corridor of the Osireion, a cenotaph constructed by Seti I behind his temple at Abydos, but with decoration from the reign of his grandson Merenptah. The third complete version is in the upper corridors and first pillared hall of a tomb in the Valley of the Kings (KV 9), begun by Ramesses V and completed by Ramesses VI. Only excerpts of the *Book of Gates* are found in the remainder of the kings' tombs of the 19th and 20th Dynasties, up to and including that of Ramesses VII (KV 1).

About one-third of the series of "books" describing the sun god's night passage though the realm of the dead has been called the *Book of Caverns*, a modern name for a composition that makes its first full appearance on the entrance corridor of Seti I's cenotaph at Abydos. It is not found on the walls of the tombs in the Valley of the Kings prior to the 20th Dynasty, and although it appears in the tomb of Ramesses IV (KV 2), its complete form is not seen until the reign of Ramesses VI. Excerpts are also found on the walls of the tombs of Ramesses VII (KV 1) and Ramesses IX (KV 6). Differing in form from the previous two books, the *Book of Caverns* has only six sections (rather than twelve), and lacks the linearity of composition in the progress of the sun god. As in the other books, this deity is depicted in the form of a ram-headed man, but is not shown in a bark, except in the closing vignette, where the scarab-shaped form of the god is in a bark being drawn to his rebirth at dawn on the eastern horizon.

Beginning with the tomb of Tuthmose III (KV 34), a series of texts extolling the sun god in his seventy-five forms comprises the core of a composition called the *Litany of Re*. This text is not found again until the 19th Dynasty, when it reappears in the first two corridors of the tomb of Seti I (KV 17). It continues in use in an expanded form through the reign of Ramesses IV, while a shortened version includes an introductory vignette depicting a disk containing two representations of the sun god as a scarab and a ram-headed male deity, flanked by a crocodile and a snake. While most scholars suggest that this represents the sun god dispersing the forces of darkness and evil as he enters the realm of the dead, there is reason to think that the flanking reptiles personify guardian spirits. The expanded texts accompanying this composition equate the deceased king with two divine entities that may be identified with Re and Osiris.

The 19th and 20th Dynasties continued to be innovative in the production of royal funerary texts. Such compositions as the *Book of the Earth*, the *Book of Aker*, the *Book of the Day* and the *Book of the Night* dealt with various aspects of the journey and revivification of the sun god. Through the process of identification and power inherent in the depiction of scenes and texts describing the divine realm, the dead king, as both the embodiment of Osiris and Re, shared in the revivification of these gods. By inscribing the walls of the tomb and the surfaces of the stone sarcophagus with these texts, the tomb and its owner were transformed into the realm of the divine. Through both its shape and its decoration, the tomb became a model of the underworld, and the interment of the dead king was carried out to echo the progress of the sun god in the realm of the dead where both he and the deceased king underwent eternal renewal.

See also

Abydos, North, *ka* chapels and cenotaphs; Dahshur, Middle Kingdom pyramids; Hawara; Lahun, pyramid complex of Senusret II; el-Lisht; Memphite private tombs of the Old Kingdom; mortuary beliefs; mythology; pantheon; representational evidence, New Kingdom royal tombs; representational evidence, papyri and ostraca; Saqqara, pyramids of the 13th Dynasty; Thebes, Valley of the Kings

Further reading

Faulkner, R.O. 1969. *The Ancient Egyptian Pyramid Texts.* Oxford.

——. 1978. *The Ancient Egyptian Coffin Texts.* Warminster.

——. 1985. *The Ancient Egyptian Book of the Dead.* London.

Hornung, E. 1992. *Die Unterweltsbucher der Aegypter.* Zurich.

EDWIN C. BROCK

G

Gebel Barkal

Gebel Barkal, on the western edge of modern Karima, Sudan, is an isolated sandstone butte 1 km from the right (northwest) bank of the Nile and about 20 km downstream from the Fourth Cataract in Upper Nubia (18°32′ N, 31°49′ E). Triangular in outline, the mountain is about 1 km in circumference, rises 102 m from present ground level, and faces the river with a sheer cliff 93.06 m high. Marking the location of the ancient city of Napata, it is bounded on the southeast by a huge cult precinct and on the west by an ancient cemetery, including royal pyramids. Described in the early nineteenth century by George Waddington and Barnard Hanbury, Frédéric Cailliaud, Louis Linant de Bellefonds, George Hoskins, John Lowell, Richard Lepsius and John Gardner Wilkinson, among others, the site was briefly excavated in 1897 by E. Wallis Budge for the British Museum and in 1907 by James Breasted for the University of Chicago. The first major excavations were undertaken by George Reisner and his Harvard University–Museum of Fine Arts (MFA) Boston expedition from 1916 to 1920. These investigations have been followed more recently by an expedition of the University of Rome, under F. Sergio Donadoni (1972 to present), by a renewed expedition of the MFA under Timothy Kendall (1986 to present) and, from 1996, by an expedition of the Fundacion Clos, Barcelona, in the Barkal cemetery.

From at least the 18th Dynasty, Gebel Barkal was identified as a sacred hill. The Egyptians declared it the chief Nubian residence of the Theban god Amen, and for this reason they called it "The Pure Mountain" (P3 Dw-w'b) and "Thrones [or Throne] of the Two Lands"

(Nswt [or Nst]-T3wy): or the source of Amen's most ancient epithet (Lord of the Thrones of the Two Lands). The name "Napata" (Npt) is thought to have been derived from the word *ipt* (sanctuary, forbidden place), and the god worshipped here, by the 19th Dynasty, would come to be called "Amen of Napata," or, by Meroitic times, "Amanapa."

The Egyptians, and perhaps the earlier Nubians as well, attached religious significance to the mountain because of the unusual free-standing pinnacle on its southwestern corner. Viewed from different angles, this statue-like, natural rock formation appeared to them variously as (a) a uraeus (sacred cobra) wearing the White Crown of Upper Egypt, (b) a uraeus wearing a sun disk, and (c) an erect phallus, evocative of the procreative forms of Amen/Re-Atum. The mountain came to be seen not only as a primeval source of creation, but also as the original home of the sun god's uraeus (the "Eye of Re") and the king's uraeus, and thus an important source of kingship.

Pottery of the Neolithic, Pre-Kerma and Kerma periods has been found on or beside the mountain, indicating that the site probably had been continuously occupied long before the Egyptians conquered Upper Nubia in the early 18th Dynasty. A cave site on the western cliff of Gebel Barkal was apparently frequently visited in pre-18th Dynasty times as a source of the fine white clayey material kaolinite. The earliest evidence of Egyptian settlement and building activity is from the reign of Tuthmose III. His stela at Gebel Barkal, dated to his 47th regnal year, is the first to mention Gebel Barkal by name and to refer to an existing native settlement and a newly built Egyptian fort called "Repelling the Foreigners." The fragmentary stela describes a miracle by which the

Egyptians identified the mountain with Amen, although there is reason to believe that the Egyptians may have identified a ram-headed local Nubian god as an alternate form of their own supreme god and to have simply taken over a pre-existing sacred place.

Tuthmose III built the first Amen sanctuary (labeled B 500-sub by Reisner) at Gebel Barkal. The stela at Amada of Amenhotep II is the first to record a town here called Napata, from whose "walls" a Syrian chief was said to have been hung. Temple building activity continued under Tuthmose IV, who added temples B 700-sub, B 600-sub and B 300-sub. During the Amarna period (reign of Amenhotep IV/Akhenaten), the name of Amen was methodically erased from local monuments, revealing that the king even attempted to eradicate the local cult in Nubia. It was restored, however, under Tutankhamen and Horemheb, who erected the nucleus of temple B 500. This temple was greatly enlarged in the 19th Dynasty by Seti I and Ramesses II, with the addition to it of a hypostyle hall (B 502), probably of 72 columns. After Ramesses II's reign all evidence for building activity ceases, and the temples appear to have fallen into ruin and disuse until the advent of the earliest Napatan monarchy (circa 850–800 BC).

The Amen cult and sanctuary at Gebel Barkal were revived by the native Nubian kings buried at nearby el-Kurru. Why they became adherents to the Egyptian cult of Amen remains unclear, but one theory suggests that their conversion may have been brought about by expatriate Theban priests, fleeing persecutions caused by civil disturbances in Upper Egypt at the end of the 22nd Dynasty. The earliest Napatan temple (B 800-sub) was of mudbrick with stone columns, and this can almost certainly be attributed to Alara (circa 785–760 BC), the first Napatan king known by name. Its stone extension, as well as the lowest level of the adjacent Napatan palace (B 1200), can be attributed to his successor, Kashta (circa 760–747 BC), the first Kushite king to reign also in Egypt. His son Piye (circa 747–716 BC) refurbished the old Egyptian temple B 500, first encasing it in new masonry and adding new

rooms, then later restoring the hypostyle hall (B 502) with 46 columns and adding a new outer court (B 501). He also refurbished B 800 in stone. These parallel Amen temples are presumed to have been dedicated to Amen of Napata and Amen of Karnak, respectively, since each god was said to have conferred upon the Kushite kings a half part of their kingship. Piye's son and third successor, Taharka (circa 690–664 BC), added temples B 200 and 300, dedicated to the goddesses Hathor, Mut, Tefnut and Sekhmet, who were all aspects of the "Eye of Re," manifested in Gebel Barkal's uraeiform pinnacle beneath which the temples were built. He also placed a statue and inscription, covered with gold sheet, on the summit of the pinnacle.

Tanutamei (circa 664–553 BC), the last Kushite ruler of Egypt, contributed a kiosk (B 502) inside B 500. His successor Atlanersa (circa 653–643 BC) started construction on the smaller temple B 700, but died before it was completed, leaving the work to be finished by his heir Senkamenisken (circa 643–623 BC). This temple seems to have been dedicated to the Osirian aspects of Amen, as well as to the Nubian god Dedwen, and all deceased kings; its bark stand is now in the MFA, Boston. B 800 and 1200 were again restored during the reign of Anlamani (circa 623–600 BC); the latter was completed by Aspelta (circa 600–580 BC). Shortly afterward the temples and palace were burned, and the many royal statues in B 500 were pulled down and vandalized. This, and contemporary damage noted at other Napatan sites, is almost certainly to be attributed to the invasion of Nubia by the army of Psamtik II (26th Dynasty) in 593 BC.

Although this destruction may have been a primary cause of the move of the Kushite court to Meroe, the Gebel Barkal sanctuary seems to have been restored during the sixth century BC. Unfortunately, no royal names can yet be connected with this restoration. In the early fourth century BC Harsiotef again restored B 800, B900 and the palace B 1200, and Nastasen restored Taharka's pinnacle monument, adding his own name to it. Both Harsiotef and Nastasen also set up stelae at Gebel Barkal detailing their works at the site, works that can no longer be

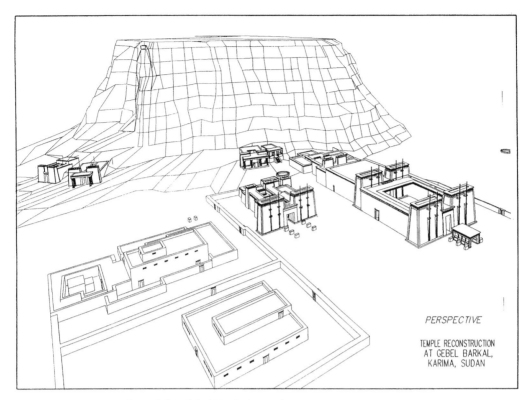

Figure 36 Reconstruction of the Gebel Barkal temples
Courtesy of the Museum of Fine Arts, Boston, Sudan Mission; plan by William Riseman.

traced in the archaeological remains. Following a probable final restoration of B 1200 by Amenislo (*circa* 260–250 BC) , a new palace (B 100) was erected about 75 m in front of the former during the second century BC.

The rock ledges of Hillet el-Arab, immediately southwest of Gebel Barkal, were evidently used continuously as a burial place beginning in the New Kingdom; they are honeycombed with rock-cut tombs and are presently being excavated by a joint Sudanese and Italian Mission under Irene Vincentelli-Liverani. The desert area immediately west of Gebel Barkal was also a cemetery, probably as early as the 25th Dynasty, and a ruined royal tomb, recently discovered by the archaeological mission of the Fondacion Clos, apparently belongs to the mid-sixth century BC. Again, in the early third century BC, a king, perhaps Arnekhameni,

selected the site for his pyramid tomb and those of his several queens. While his immediate successors preferred to build their tombs at Meroe, more royalty erected their pyramids at Gebel Barkal during the second and first centuries BC.

Prior to the second century BC, the Gebel Barkal sanctuary seems to have been centered primarily in an arc around the pinnacle, with its western extremity marked by B 200 and its eastern by B 1700, the yet unexcavated temple bakeries. Later, however, when Meroe was the capital of the Kushite state, there was a massive new development of the area northeast of B 1700. Several new temples were built (B 1800–2400), which have not yet been excavated, as well as a large new palace (B 1500), which replaced B 100. B 500 was extensively restored, and a new kiosk (B 551) was added in front of B

501. All of this construction probably dates to the reigns of Amenishakheto, Natakameni and Amenitore, a program very likely undertaken as a result of the reported destruction of Napata at the hands of the Roman general Petronius about 24 BC.

Throughout most of the history of Kush, Gebel Barkal remained the most important religious center of the kingdom, and was for many centuries the primary center for coronations and kingship ritual. After the decline of the Meroitic kingdom (*circa* AD 350), the site became a Christian village and cemetery.

See also

Kerma; el-Kurru; Kushites; Meroe, cemeteries; Meroe, city; Meroitic culture; New Kingdom, overview; Nuri; Reisner, George Andrew; Sanam; Third Intermediate Period, overview

Further reading

Dunham, D. 1970. *The Barkal Temples.* Boston.
Kendall, T. 1991. The Napatan palace at Gebel Barkal: a first look at B 1200. In *Egypt and Africa: Nubia from Prehistory to Islam*, W.V. Davies, ed., 302–13. London.
——. 1997. Excavations at Gebel Barkal, 1996: report of the Museum of Fine Arts, Boston, Sudan Mission. *Kush* 17: in press.
Reisner, G.A. 1931. Inscribed monuments from Gebel Barkal. *ZÄS*: 76–100.
Robisek, C. 1989. *Das Bildprogramm des Mut-Tempels am Gebel Barkal.* Vienna.

TIMOTHY KENDALL

Gebel el-Haridi

The limestone headland at Gebel el-Haridi in Upper Egypt (26°46′ N, 31°34′ E) contains archaeological remains from the end of the 6th Dynasty of the Old Kingdom through to the late Roman period prior to the Arab conquest in AD 642. These remains illustrate a wide variety of occupation and employment on the site: the Haridi headland was used as a necropolis for rock-cut tombs, for large-scale quarrying of stone, for the squatter occupation of Christian hermits, and for the site of an enclosed mudbrick settlement.

Gebel el-Haridi lies 350 km south of modern Cairo within Sagulta, Sohag province in Upper Egypt. The site is physically defined as a projecting headland promontory which forms part of the Ma'aza limestone plateau. It is about 11 km in length projecting toward the east bank of the Nile, just below the modern village of el-Nawawra and receding away from the river just to the north of el-Galawiya. This headland comprises steep limestone cliffs, averaging about 120 m in height, lying above a steep deposition of Nile silt, interspersed with rock rubble, which runs a further 100 m down to the valley floor into the east bank of the Nile. The character of the site has been greatly affected by the construction in 1933 of the el-Isawiya canal which truncated the base of the slope, divorcing it from the edge of the Nile.

One of the earliest references in Western sources to the site is to be found in the writings of Richard Pococke (1763), who mentions a grotto of the "famous serpent named Heredy." The site was later noted by members of the Napoleonic expedition (1798), who observed ancient quarries and caves and a mutilated figure in a toga 2.58 m high. Robert Hay (1832–3) undertook important epigraphic work and was followed by John Gardner Wilkinson (1855), who noted an Old Kingdom tomb. Wilheim Spiegelberg published a royal quarry inscription of Ptolemy XII (formerly called XIII) in 1913. A large rock-cut inscription of Ramesses III was published by Labib Habachi in 1974.

The importance of the site in antiquity may be reflected in its position as a frontier between two political districts called nomes, these being Nome IX of Upper Egypt (Min-standard) with its capital at Akhmim, and Nome X of Upper Egypt (plumed serpent-standard) with its capital at Qau el-Kebir. The tradition of Haridi as a nome border may stem originally from Ptolemy the Geographer's placement of a town known as "Passalon" in the area of Haridi, between Antaeopolis and Akhmim, although it also

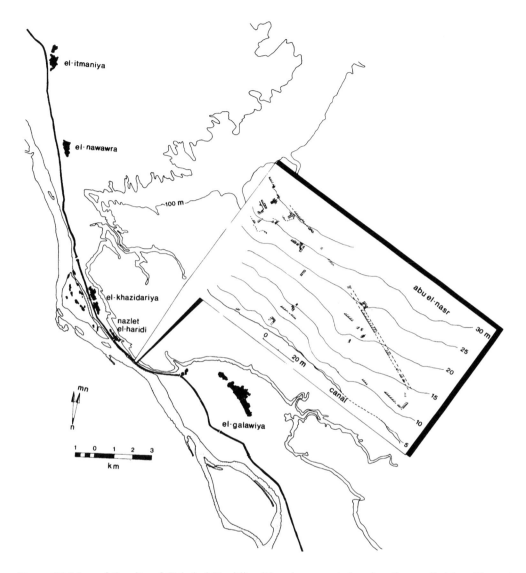

Figure 37 Map of the site of Gebel el-Haridi, with enlargement showing the mudbrick settlement
on the lower slopes of Abu el-Nasr (possibly a fortified monastery)
Courtesy of the European Exploration Society

finds proof in the archaeological record on the site.

The earliest archaeological features on the site are tombs cut into a rocky mantle near the top of the slope at the south end of the Haridi in an area known locally as Gebel Abu el-Nasr. These tombs were badly quarried-out in later times, although the outer chamber of one contained two mutilated rock-cut sculptures, perhaps the tomb owner and his wife, and the remains of a raised relief figure before two vertical bands of heiroglyphic text. This text indicated that the tomb owner was an [*Imy-r wp(w)t*] *ḥtpt-nṯr m prwy* ([Overseer of the apportionments] of the god's offerings in the two houses), a title known from tombs at Deir el-Gebrawi and Kom el-Ahmar (Sawaris) to be associated with the governor of a nome. This Old Kingdom tomb at Haridi supports the possibility that the town of Tahta on the opposite side of the river (identified with ancient Hesopis) may have been the site of an important Old Kingdom town.

Next to this tomb are the remains of a tomb with painted plaster decoration showing a scene of birds being caught in a clap-net; the scene shows a man signaling for the net to be closed as a row of men tug on a rope. The untidy composition and the clumsy variation in scale of the scene's figures is contrary to the rigid conventions of classical Egyptian art; the tomb may therefore belong to the First Intermediate Period when rigid canons of decoration were abandoned. The ceiling of the tomb is also decorated: four pointed stars are interspersed among unidentified yellow-colored figures. This decoration is highly unusual and it is possible that it represents an astronomical scene. Such scenes are not known on tomb ceilings before the mid-18th Dynasty.

The above-mentioned tombs are located on the lower of two main terraces that contained other much smaller tombs consisting of tiny entrance chambers with sloping ramps leading into the inner burial chamber. Over sixteen of these have been noted on the upper terrace. Farther down the slope are more scattered rock-cut tombs, the most impressive of which comprises a large, square entrance chamber (2.15 × 2.45 m) with a round-topped niche in the north wall and three sloping ramps leading to burial chambers just big enough to take a coffin. This may date to the First Intermediate Period.

Nestor L'Hôte recorded a New Kingdom tomb at Haridi containing a hymn to the sun, although this has yet to be found in the recent archaeological survey. However, at the north end of Haridi, near the village of el-Khazindariya, is a rock-cut inscription of Ramesses III (7 m high and 10.5 m broad), lying 120 m up the cliff. It shows the king between the gods Seth and Anti, hawk-headed but in human form. Seth and Anti were joined together (syncre-

tized) to form Anty, the patron deity of Antaeopolis. This shows that the inscription lay within the area of Nome X of Upper Egypt. The inscription may be related to a series of underground quarries, cut deep into the limestone hillside, that lie nearby. Wilkinson's mention of the inscribed cartouches of Apries at Haridi may indicate that quarrying at the site also took place under that king in the 26th Dynasty.

The excavation of the Old Kingdom tomb uncovered a coin of Ptolemy VI, indicating that the quarrying-out of the tombs took place during or later than the reign of that king. Quarrying on a larger scale took place under the Ptolemies in at least three substantial underground quarries at the site, all of which contained royal inscriptions. Only one of these is legible enough to identify the king as Ptolemy XII in his 11th year (70/71 BC). The inscription shows the king offering a *ma'at* figure to the gods Min, Horus, Isis, Horus the Younger and Triphis. Beneath the relief is a demotic text recording a dedication made by the Strategen (administrator of a nome) Psais to the gods of Panopolis, indicating that this region was within Nome IX of Upper Egypt. The other two royal inscriptions similarly show the king offering to a series of gods with demotic text beneath the scene.

Evidence of Roman occupation is found in two groups of mudbrick ruins at Abu el-Nasr. The first covers the lower slopes of the mountain down to the river and, although eroded and partially covered by landslide material, appears to represent an enclosed settlement with lookout towers. Within this enclosure are the remains of terraced buildings, some with buttress supports and barrel-vaulted cellars. A rock-cut knoll at the base of the site contains rock-cut tomb chambers with horizontal wall niches for the corpses. Pottery dates the possible extent of use of the site to between the second and fourth centuries AD, or perhaps a little later. It is possible that the enclosed settlement was for a monastic commune. Many of the tombs and quarries on the upper part of the slope, as well as natural caves, had been plastered with gypsum (some with examples of graffiti), and contained food bins and refuse pits, indicative of the squatter occupation associated with Coptic hermits.

To the south of this site and at the top of the slope, in front of the underground quarry of Ptolemy XII, were a series of terraced buildings, one of which was preserved to over 2.5 m in height. African red slipware pottery found on the surface of this area dates from the fifth century AD. One explanation for these structures is that they may represent the resettlement of the community from the lower slope enclosure to a better defended position at the top of the mountain to escape marauding bedouin tribes which increasingly threatened valley settlements in late antiquity.

The site itself is named after an important Muslim holy man or "sheikh" named Haridi. At least since the sixteenth century, the tomb of this sheikh and his son Hassan has been a focal point of pilgrimage; a legend has grown of a serpent, representing Sheikh Haridi, who has the power to heal the sick. Visitors to the site up to the present have observed the belief in this fabled snake among the local village communities.

Gebel es-Sheikh el-Haridi was occupied or exploited from the twenty-third century BC until the sixth century AD. In microcosm, the site illustrates the changing nature of man's presence in a segment of the Nile Valley through a passage of 3,000 years. This continuity of use of the site can be partly explained by its proximity to the river, its resources of quality limestone and its geographical prominence in the local landscape. The latter made Gebel es-Sheikh el-Haridi an appropriate frontier between two important nomes. Today the site lies at the frontier of the governates of Sohag and Asyut, reflecting its ancient role and illustrating the continuity of Egypt with its past.

See also

Akhmim; nome structure; Qau el-Kebir (Antaeopolis), Dynastic sites; quarrying

Further reading

Habachi, L. 1974. Three large rock-stelae carved by Ramesses III near quarries. *JARCE* 11: 69–75.

Kirby, C.J., and S. Ikram. 1992. Land of the plumed serpent. *Egyptian Archaeology* 2: 35–36.

——. 1994. Haridi's high society. *Egyptian Archaeology* 4: 32–3.

CHRISTOPHER J. KIRBY

Gebel el-Silsila

Gebel el-Silsila (24°39′ N, 32°54′ E) is the Arabic name given to a district stretching over both banks of the Nile, roughly 145 km south of Luxor and 65 km north of Aswan. The river is at its narrowest here, flanked on either side by large hills of sandstone. For more than a kilometer, its channel runs between steep rocky banks a mere 395 m apart. The name Gebel el-Silsila means "Mountain of the Chain." According to an Arab tradition, a chain was once fastened across the Nile at this point in order to render navigation more difficult. In the pharaonic period, the district was called "Kheny" or "Khenu," an appellation of uncertain significance, which probably denoted originally a town or settlement on the east bank. The adjacent stretch of the river was called "the Pure Water," and this came to be used by extension to designate the district itself. During Graeco-Roman times the area was called "the Quarry" as well. Its chief divinity was the crocodile god Sobek.

The archaeological remains and written records at Gebel el-Silsila extend from prehistoric times to the Coptic period. The earliest evidence of human activity there is provided by Paleolithic surface sites and industries. Remains of a Predynastic cemetery have been discovered on the east bank. There are also numerous rock drawings on both sides of the river of roughly the same date, depicting people, boats, and various animals and birds.

Remains from the Old Kingdom are relatively sparse. They consist chiefly of hieratic graffiti left by visitors to the west bank, one of which preserves the cartouche of the 6th

Dynasty monarch Pepi I. Further graffiti are attested for the early Middle Kingdom, inscribed by travelers and caravan leaders who passed by the site on their journeys. Virtually all of these are to be found on the west bank of the Nile. Only a single hieroglyphic graffito of Middle Kingdom or possibly First Intermediate period date has been discovered on the east bank, the earliest piece of writing extant on that side of the river.

During the New Kingdom, Gebel el-Silsila began to be exploited as a quarry for sandstone, and soon became the Egyptians' single most important source for this material. The local stone was easily extracted and available in large quantities not far from the river, upon which it could be transported with ease to any destination in the country. From the mid-18th Dynasty to the Roman period, many of the chief temples of Egypt were built of sandstone blocks obtained from this site. Perhaps as a consequence of its newly gained prominence, the area was increasingly regarded as a locus of divine immanence; from the 18th Dynasty onward, both kings and high officials caused shrines and other religious monuments to be erected there.

Among the earliest of these is a series of funerary chapels cut into the cliffs overlooking the west bank of the river. There are thirty-two in all, of which only eighteen can be dated precisely. These were executed at the behest of important officials, most of whom served under Hatshepsut or Tuthmose III. A typical specimen consists of a single chamber entered through a doorway, the lintel of which records the names of the monarch whom the chapel owner served, the jambs being inscribed with offering formulae. The walls of the chamber are decorated with scenes in painted relief; at the rear is a niche containing a life-size seated figure of the owner and, occasionally, statues of one or more relatives. In many cases, the owners of these chapels are known to have been buried elsewhere (at Thebes). They must have served, therefore, as cenotaphs designed to commemorate those for whom they were made and ensure their provision with funerary offerings in the presence of the local divinities. The latest

such chapel was inscribed in the reign of Amenhotep III. Contemporary with it are a pair of stelae and three small shrines on the east bank. The latter vary in size from 2 to 3 m³. Their decoration is now almost completely destroyed. Also on the east bank is a large stela dated in the reign of Amenhotep IV, recording a decree which was issued by that ruler in respect of various quarrying activities.

Perhaps the single most important monument at Gebel el-Silsila is the speos, or rock temple, of Horemheb. This is carved into the cliff face on the west bank near the northern end of the site, only a few meters from the water's edge. The edifice consists of a covered gallery with four pillars at the front. Inside, the gallery opens into a small sanctuary with a niche at the back containing seated statues of seven divinities: Amen, Mut, Khonsu, Sobek, Thoeris, Thoth, and the deified Horemheb himself. The remaining walls of this sanctuary are covered with representations of other gods and goddesses, a total of seventy-five in all.

Remains of another temple built by the same ruler stood some 350 m to the north of this speos until relatively recently. These comprised inscribed blocks, fragments of columns, the top portion of a stela with a depiction of the king presenting offerings to Osiris and Isis, and a part of a mud-brick temenos wall which originally enclosed the edifice. The remains have now disappeared, except for a small number of fragments, destroyed by modern quarrying activity.

Subsequent monarchs added to the decoration of the speos of Horemheb, among them Ramesses II, Merenptah, Seti II and Ramesses III. They are depicted on its walls in company with sundry wives, princes, viziers and lesser officials. Texts and representations commemorating these persons cover the exterior as well as the interior surfaces of the building.

In general, the kings of the 19th and 20th Dynasties appear to have taken a more active interest in Gebel el-Silsila than their predecessors did. Some 750 m to the south of the speos of Horemheb, three royal shrines stand side by side. These were built by Seti I, Ramesses II and Merenptah. Each has the form of a large niche cut into the cliff face, flanked by a papyrus column on either side and surmounted by a cavetto cornice. The rear wall of each niche is inscribed with a copy of the same text, a royal ordinance making provision for the endowment of a twice-yearly festival in honor of Hapi, the god of the Nile inundation. A further copy of this text is preserved on a large stela set up by Ramesses III not far away.

A number of other stelae of Ramesside date have been found on the west bank of Gebel el-Silsila. On the east bank, traces of a temple of Ramesses II have been discovered, as well as a stela dated in year 6 of Seti I's reign. The inscription on the latter concerns the provisioning of an expedition of 1,000 men who were sent to the region to quarry stone.

Among post-New Kingdom records may be mentioned a large stela erected by Sheshonk I, the founder of the 22nd Dynasty. This stands roughly 100 m to the south of the speos of Horemheb and records a royal decree authorizing the opening of a quarry to obtain stone for various building projects in the temple of Amen at Karnak. On the east bank, in a prominent place overlooking the river, are two large cartouches inscribed with the prenomen and nomen of the 26th Dynasty king Apries.

Visually, the most striking remains at Gebel el-Silsila are the massive quarries of Graeco-Roman date on the east bank. These are of the open variety, and provide ample evidence of the techniques used for extracting sandstone from them. Near the surface, a block of suitable dimensions was marked out with paint or some other material. Then the vertical faces were chiseled away from the surrounding stone. Finally, the block was separated from its bed by means of wedges driven in horizontally. Using the same method, the ancient quarrymen could remove block after block, layer after layer of stone until the quarry floor was reached. The skill and precision with which the blocks were removed are apparent when one looks at a typical quarry wall. In many cases, the impression is given that the sandstone has simply been sliced away in huge sheets.

The walls of these quarries are inscribed with numerous graffiti, the majority in Demotic or Greek. Some graffiti record only the name of the writer and his patronym. Others incorporate a short formula requesting that the good name of the writer endure in the presence of the local gods. In a few instances, there are more elaborate prayers and dedications. Yet other texts record the local height of the Nile inundation in a given year, or provide details about particular quarrying expeditions. The graffiti show clearly that, as in earlier times, Gebel el-Silsila was still regarded not merely as a source of building material, but as a sacred place as well. Each individual quarry was under the protection of a particular god or goddess. Among such divine patrons one encounters Montu, Min, Khnum, Hathor, Amen and Horus of Edfu. A number of graffiti in the quarry sacred to the last-named make reference to a deity called Pakhimesen, "He of the uplifting of the harpoon." This is evidently a local form of Horus. Apart from such writings, the walls of the Graeco-Roman period quarries at East Silsila are inscribed with a large number of designs of diverse sorts: harpoons, offering tables, vases, stars, temple pylons, obelisks and other architectural elements, boats, parts of plants or trees, as well as a number of unidentifiable objects. These can occur both singly and in groups. They appear to be quarry markings, but their precise function is uncertain.

On the west bank, written records of Graeco-Roman date are not common. Only a small number of Demotic graffiti have been discovered there, two of them on or in the speos of Horemheb. The most curious record from this period on that side of the river is a tablet inscribed upon an outcrop of rock to the south of the three New Kingdom royal shrines, depicting a tree, a figure mounted on a horse, and a second figure standing in front of them, accompanied by a Greek dedication.

Coptic graffiti have been discovered at Gebel el-Silsila on both sides of the river. In addition, there are various archaeological remains to which it is difficult to assign a definite date. These include a series of small covered stone quarries on the east bank, situated to the north of the larger ones described above; two nilometers, or scales designed for measuring the height of the river when it was in flood; and sundry large-scale pieces of sculpture in a damaged or unfinished state, among them a falcon and several criosphinxes.

The site, on either river bank, is for all practical purposes unexcavated. Only minor sondages have been conducted there. Virtually all that is known of its history is derived from what can be seen upon the surface. The great pioneers of Egyptian epigraphy, Jean-François Champollion, Ippolito Rosellini, John Gardner Wilkinson and Richard Lepsius, all visited Gebel el-Silsila during the first half of the nineteenth century and made copies of inscriptions that they saw there. Further recording was done by other Egyptologists later on in the same century, notably Francis Llewellyn Griffith and Flinders Petrie in 1886–7. In 1910 Arthur Weigall published what is still, even today, the most detailed description of the site. Friedrich Preisigke and Wilhelm Spiegelberg edited a large number of Demotic and Greek graffiti from the Graeco-Roman period quarries at East Silsila in 1915, basing their work upon copies made earlier by Georges Legrain.

Thereafter, sporadic visits to the site were made by other scholars. In the early 1950s, the Egypt Exploration Society decided to undertake the task of making a comprehensive epigraphic record of Gebel el-Silsila and its monuments. This work was entrusted to Ricardo A. Caminos, who accomplished it successfully in nine campaigns from 1955 to 1982. The first part of this record, dealing with the New Kingdom funerary chapels on the west bank of the Nile, was published in 1963, the joint work of Caminos and T.G.H. James. Succeeding volumes are being prepared for publication.

See also

cult temples, construction techniques; Late and Ptolemaic periods, overview; New Kingdom, overview; quarrying; Roman period, overview

Further reading

Caminos, R.A. 1955. Surveying Gebel es-Silsilah. *JEA* 41: 51–5.
——. 1977. Gebel es-Silsile. *LÄ* 2: 441–7.
——. 1987. Epigraphy in the field. In *Problems and Priorities in Egyptian Archaeology*, J. Assmann, G. Burkard and V. Davies, eds, 57–67. London.
Caminos, R.A., and T.G.H. James. 1963. *Gebel es-Silsilah 1: The Shrines* (Archaeological Survey of Egypt Memoir 31). London.
Preisigke, F., and W. Spielberg. 1915. *Ägyptische und griechische Inschriften aus den Steinbrüchen des Gebel Silsile (Oberägypten)*. Strassburg (Strasbourg).
Weigall, A.E.P. 1910. *A Guide to the Antiquities of Upper Egypt from Abydos to the Sudan Frontier*, 356–73. London.

MARK SMITH

Gebel Zeit

The mountain range of Gebel Zeit is situated on the Red Sea coast, 50 km south of Ras Gharib. Thirty km long (north–south), 5 km wide and 457 m at its highest point, it is a highly visible range (27°59′ N, 33°26′ E–27°57′ N, 33°28′ E). The Wadi Kabrit forms a wide, deep valley running down the length of the formation and separates the jagged red granite that rises sharply out of the sea from the sedimentary rock that slopes shallowly westward.

From the 12th Dynasty to the late New Kingdom, mining took place in the only two areas of the Gebel Zeit that contain a limestone formation with a pervasive network of hydrothermal veins, full of the highly prized mineral galena. Investigations by the French Institute in Cairo (IFAO) have revealed a mining complex comprising two large, complementary sites. The first, designated "Site 1," contains several mines, a settlement and a sanctuary. The second, "Site 2," comprises a large cluster of mines 4 km to the south, and is the main area from which ore was extracted.

Site 1

The settlement and the sanctuary are situated in the sedimentary rock of the upper part of the site, 230 m above sea level. Narrow terraces,

5–10 m wide, are found here along 200 m of a small valley. In antiquity, the valley was entirely filled by debris taken from the mines and the inhabited section.

In the early stages of development, galleries opened by the miners were turned into rock shelters. During periods of abandonment the inhabited spaces collapsed, and when they were later occupied a terraced structure formed, re-establishing the original slope of the rock. The top level, which dates to the New Kingdom, is a wide terrace resting upon its accumulated predecessors. At this point the rock is no longer visible, and the manmade terrace is as high as the mountain ridge. However, in spite of the later occupation levels above, some of the older mining galleries remained accessible in the later periods.

The sanctuaries of the different periods are not isolated, but instead were placed in the middle of the settlement, constructed in a sequence parallel to the terraced dwellings. The earliest one, dating to the Middle Kingdom, was built in a natural cave. The next one was built above it, and likewise the next, until in the New Kingdom the sanctuary was a circular construction of dry stone masonry erected on the uppermost terrace. A stratigraphic probe has identified the different levels, but only the New Kingdom level has been completely excavated.

The New Kingdom sanctuary is formed by a wall made of local limestone and evaporites that forms an enclosure in a partial circle, set against the rock. Approximately 6.5 m in diameter, the wall is preserved to a height of 0.8 m, but the volume of the collapsed stone indicates an original height of *circa* 1.2 m. Large, regular blocks form the wall's foundation, on which stones of various sizes are piled.

Inside this sanctuary is a group of four posts joined by cross-beams, which are the frame of a small rectangular space (1.3 × 0.8 m), perhaps the main place of worship. There are also two upright stones, each presumably marking the place where expedition members would build a low, temporary structure.

Artifacts were found in two locations. In the cracks between the stones of the outside wall, which was periodically repaired, clusters of artifacts, presumably votive offerings, were hidden for safekeeping. A New Kingdom hiding place, in the northeast corner of the sanctuary, demonstrates the other method of storing artifacts: stelae and statuettes of the gods were carefully put away at the end of each expedition.

During periods of abandonment, both robbing and rock slides disturbed the stratified remains. Periodically repairs were done, the site was cleaned and structural reinforcements were made. During such activities scattered artifacts were collected, which explains why older artifacts, preserved or salvaged, were discovered in groups with more recent ones.

The three main gods honored in the sanctuary are the traditional patrons of mines and desert roads: Hathor, "mistress of galena" (*nbt msdmt*), Horus, "lord of the deserts" (*nb ḥ3swt*), with whom she was associated; and Min of Coptos. Ptah was also worshipped. Devotion to these gods is indicated by stelae, statuettes and other artifacts, such as the castanets shaped like cupped hands used in the festivals of Hathor.

Some votive figurines of a more original type, undoubtedly linked to the goddess Hathor, were also found. Examples consist of ceramic figurines of women dressed in linen and wearing beads and scarabs. They are modeled with the woman holding her arms down along her body; this type is also known from cemeteries in Upper Egypt, from the end of the Middle Kingdom to the 18th Dynasty. At Gebel Zeit these figurines have two different styles of headdresses: (1) a ceramic wig, in three sections, found on the earlier figurines (Middle Kingdom/Second Intermediate Period); and (2) a later style in which linen strands pass through holes in the disk-shaped top of the head and are attached to balls of clay and beads, introduced in the Second Intermediate Period and also known in the 18th Dynasty. A second type of figurine, of a woman, standing or kneeling, with a child in her arms or on her back, was also found at Gebel Zeit.

The most remarkable feature of the site is a specialized activity area, with cooking hearths and debris of local calcite from a stone vessel workshop, in a former mining gallery north of the sanctuary. Its opening was protected by walls and remained accessible for a long time, even as the terraces outside were built above it.

Three main levels were observed here. The lowest one, where the original mining gallery was transformed into a living space, dates from either the end of the Second Intermediate Period or the beginning of the 18th Dynasty. Associated with this level was a pot filled with pieces of galena. In the second level were four jars and four amphorae, placed upright against the rock wall. One of them is stamped with the cartouches of Tuthmose III. In the uppermost level, which cave-ins had disturbed, were a group of 18th Dynasty amphorae, jars and containers, some with their contents preserved (lentils, dried plants, wicks). Also in this level were some baskets, a cane, two pillows and a collection of tools made of basaltic rock. The occupants must have made fairly frequent expeditions to the site, since they stored these things with the intent to use them upon their return.

Numerous artifacts from the layers of the terraces also provide information about life in this settlement. Goat skins, gazelle bones, fish bones and the remains of edible shellfish indicate that the inhabitants hunted and fished on the sea coast. A few grains preserved on the stalk suggest that they perhaps also grew some food here. Local resources, such as calcite and sea shells (for tools), were used as much as possible. Imported materials were also recycled: sherds from broken pots were reshaped into tools, and old cloth was made into rope or wicks.

Site 2

Site 2, the main mining site, is located to the south of Site 1. It is an area 1.8 km long (north–south) and 0.5 km wide, with a vertical range of 150 m. Six hundred distinct features were catalogued here, including mining galleries, work stations and various facilities.

The ancient mines were located along three principal linear deposits of ore, which begin close together in the south and spread vertically farther north. One group of mines follows the ridge of the mountain range. A middle plateau is the location of a second group of mines. A third group of mines is located at the bottom of the mountain range. Heaped at the entrances to the mines are enormous quantities of debris, particularly in the wider, flatter, middle deposits.

Although the location of the mines suggests systematic extraction, the veins are irregular with various branches, and change in thickness and depth. Mines range from trenches and open pits at the surface, to multiple galleries and shafts underground which cut through hard rock. Some of the mining galleries are enormous, and were exploited over a long period of time on different expeditions. Others are quite small. A brief description of one of the large mining galleries will serve to illustrate the whole system of mining.

Mine 399 is 25 m deep and about 100 m long. There are narrow veins of usable galena, surrounded by a thick matrix, which fill a linear network of natural fissures with branches patterned like the veins of a leaf. In proportion to the volume of extracted rock, the solid, extremely hard, limestone mass was breached in very few places, and then only to reach branches of veins containing the mineral. The size of the passages and some of the exploited galleries (only 0.4–0.5 m in diameter) shows that the miners made the effort to break such hard rock only when necessary.

The veins of this mine are fairly straight, and are spaced vertically over two levels (Figure 38, c–d and e–f). Shafts and platforms, with shelters reinforced against falling rocks, allowed the miners to move about and extract minerals and debris. Two vertical shafts provide the only access to chambers 1 and 2.

An almost perfectly vertical shaft (from chambers 3 and 12) leads to the lower network (chambers 4–7). Ore was taken from station 13, to 12, to platform 11. In a similar way, it passed from station 16, through 15, to 13, or starting in the bottom of the mine, from 26, through 20, to 17. Two large rope nets were used to transport ore out of the deepest shafts.

The miners used rough picks made of basaltic rock to excavate the veins and pockets of mineral. They also must have used copper or bronze chisels, as indicated by green traces on

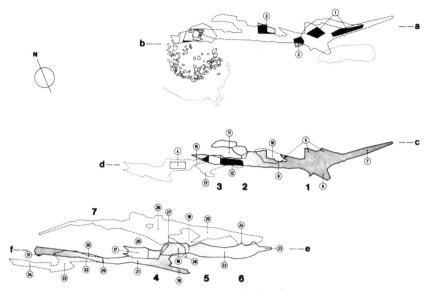

Figure 38 Gebel Zeit, plan of Mine 399: the three main levels

the walls and on some stone hammers. The narrowness of the galleries must have limited the miners to working one at a time in any given spot and only small teams of about ten miners could have worked in the mine. Toward the end of operations in Mine 399, if one person were working in chamber 7, five or six miners would have been able to move the extracted ore out of the mine.

Daylight was only sufficient in the upper chambers (1–3), and lamps were needed below this. Ventilation was adequate only down to chamber 4, and the lack of ventilation in the lower galleries must have made work there very difficult.

The galena here appears to be a pure metal, dark gray in color and shiny. It is encased in a matrix colored black and white inside and reddish-brown outside. Once extracted from the mine, the ore was processed nearby. Stone hammers and grinders were used to break the matrix and free the mineral in areas which are roughly circular and covered in fine gravel. There was no further processing of ore on site. The pieces of galena found in a vase in the storeroom at Site 1 are nuggets of metal with the matrix mostly, but not completely, removed.

In this form they were taken to the Nile Valley, to make black eye-paint.

The archaeological evidence from the two sites, especially the deep stratigraphy of Site 1 and the large number of mines at Site 2, seems to indicate that the area was visited many times by small mining parties in close succession. The oldest certain evidence of an expedition is from the reign of Amenemhat III. The next well represented period of activity is, paradoxically, during the Second Intermediate Period. Evidence from this period includes Pan-grave ceramics and Tell el-Yahudiya-style pots and stelae, some of which mention little-known kings. The greatest period of use was during the New Kingdom, and inscriptions of all the kings of the late 18th Dynasty, from Amenhotep III to Horemheb, are found here.

The Theban area appears to have been the general point of departure of expeditions sent during the Second Intermediate Period and the 18th Dynasty. More specifically, Coptos (modern Quft) is indicated by the copious evidence of Min worship and by artifacts such as the stela erected by Minemhat, a nomarch of Coptos during the 17th Dynasty.

See also

metallurgy; Middle Kingdom, overview; natural resources; New Kingdom, overview; Pangrave culture; Quft/Qift (Coptos); Second Intermediate Period, overview; Tell el-Yahudiya

Further reading

Castel, G., and G. Soukiassian. 1985. Dépôt de stèles dans le sanctuaire du Nouvel Empire au Gebel Zeit, *BIFAO* 85: 285–93.

Castel, G., G. Soukiassian, G. Pouit, *et al.* 1989. *Gebel el-Zeit* 1: *Les mines de galène (Égypte, IIème millénaire av. J.-C.)*. Fouilles de l'Institut français d'archéologie orientale 35. Cairo.

GEORGES CASTEL
GEORGES SOUKIASSIAN
G. POUIT

Gebelein

Gebelein is the name of an archaeological site in Upper Egypt which in Arabic means "the two mountains." At present, the site is known as Naga el-Gherira. The ancient Egyptian name of the town is "Inr.tj" (the two rocks), and in Graeco-Roman times it was known as Aphroditopolis, or Pathiris, taken from the Egyptian "Per Hathor," meaning "House [Temple] of Hathor." It was the seat of the cult of the goddess Hathor, sometimes identified with the Greek goddess Aphrodite.

Gebelein is located 29 km to the south of Thebes, on the west bank of the Nile, and was included in Nome IV of Upper Egypt (25°29′ N, 32°29′ E). The site consists of two hills, with a cemetery, only partially investigated, located on the northern hill. The temple of Hathor is located on the southern hill close to the Nile, where a man-made cave was excavated in a "T" plan, consisting of a hall and sanctuary. In late pharaonic times the temple was fortified with a mudbrick wall. The ancient town, now covered by the modern settlement, was located on the western slopes of the southern hill and the plain to the north.

The site was already recorded in the *Description de l'Égypte*, published in the early nineteenth century after the Napoleonic expedition to Egypt. After some clandestine excavations demonstrated the site's relevance, French archaeologist Gaston Maspero began investigations in 1884. Eugène Grébaut and Georges Daressy worked there in 1891, followed by Jacques de Morgan and Georges Foucart in 1893. G.W. Fraser and M.W. Blackden excavated at Gebelein for the Egypt Exploration Fund in 1893, and Jacques de Morgan returned there in 1900. Louis Lortet and Claude Gaillard worked at this site as well in 1908–9. Artifacts from these excavations are presently in museums in Cairo, Berlin and Lyons.

Systematic excavations at the site were conducted by the Egyptian Museum, Turin, in 1910, 1911, 1914 and 1920 under the direction of Ernesto Schiaparelli. Schiaparelli's successor, Giulio Farina, worked at the site in 1930, 1935 and 1937. Investigations are presently being conducted to accurately map the site.

The Italian excavations included the remains of the temple of Hathor, with a large mudbrick wall which contained bricks with the cartouches of the High Priest Menkhepere, son of (King) Pinedjem of Thebes (21st Dynasty). One of the more remarkable finds was a royal stela of the 2nd–3rd Dynasties in a style similar to the reliefs of (King) Zoser from Heliopolis. Many fragments of wall reliefs dating to the reign of Nebhepetre Mentuhotep II of the 11th Dynasty were also excavated. Evidence from the New Kingdom included a foundation deposit of Tuthmose III, and stelae and stela fragments, usually dedicated to Hathor. Earlier excavations uncovered the remains of a temple dating to late Ptolemaic times (Ptolemy VII?).

About 400 Demotic and Greek ostraca were found in the settlement area. They record a garrison of mercenaries settled at this site in the second–first centuries BC. The texts are similar to others written on papyrus that were bought from antiquities dealers and are presently scattered in different collections. Other texts in Greek and Coptic, written on skins and dating to the late fifth and early sixth centuries AD, record people known as "Blemmyes" settled at this site or on the island to the east of it. The Blemmyes were nomadic peoples of the Eastern Desert in late antiquity.

The cemetery, located on the eastern slopes of the northern hill and on the plain to the north, dates from the Predynastic period to the end of the Middle Kingdom. Except for a few skeletons probably placed in a (late) 12th Dynasty tomb during Ptolemaic times, there is no evidence of later burials.

Excavations conducted in the cemetery before those of Schiaparelli, by Maspero and others, uncovered Predynastic graves, both oval and rectangular, with typical Predynastic pottery of the Nagada culture of Upper Egypt (Black-topped Red class). Loret and Gaillard collected some remarkable figurines, including one of a bearded man, and Predynastic stone tools and palettes, which are now exhibited in Lyons. Also excavated in the cemetery were rectangular sarcophagi with inscriptions and painted scenes, dating to the First Intermediate Period. A remarkable group of sarcophagi from a clandestine excavation was bought by John Burckhardt for the Berlin Museum. The sarcophagi came from a family tomb consisting of five rock-cut rooms, each with a sarcophagus. Small wooden models, of ships, a granary and women carrying offerings, pottery, bows and sticks, were also found in this tomb.

Excavations of the Turin Museum were conducted in the area of the Predynastic burials, on the plain near the northern hill. The graves consisted of simple holes with contracted burials; grave goods were mainly pots of Black-topped Red class. The later (Dynastic) burials were located along the slope of the hill where rock-cut tombs with a corridor or a shaft and two or more small, roughly hewn chambers were excavated. Some tombs had a *mastaba* superstructure with two or more chambers excavated in the bedrock. The most elaborate tombs had a superstructure with a transverse portico of mudbrick pillars, and chapels partly excavated in the bedrock leading to the funerary chambers.

Many artifacts from the Gebelein cemetery are exhibited in the Turin Museum. One of the more remarkable finds is a unique cloth from a Predynastic grave painted with ships and dancing figures. The painted designs are comparable to the well known wall paintings from Tomb 100 at Hierakonpolis.

Papyri with administrative texts were found in a Gebelein tomb dating to the late 4th Dynasty. They are similar to texts discovered near the 5th Dynasty pyramid of Neferirkare at Abusir (presently in the Cairo Museum). Three burials with rich grave goods were found in an undisturbed tomb dating to the 5th Dynasty. Provincial officials were also buried in these tombs, including Iti, an "Overseer of the Desert Expeditions" at the end of the 6th Dynasty, and Ini, a nomarch (governor) during the 10th Dynasty, possibly of Nubian origin. Painted scenes of rituals and daily life were found on the pillars and walls of a tomb belonging to another Iti, dating to the 11th Dynasty. These paintings exhibit a provincial style of the First Intermediate Period. From the end of the 12th Dynasty is a sarcophagus of a man named Iqer inscribed with funerary texts.

Stelae of Nubian mercenaries dating to the First and Second Intermediate Periods, and C-Group or Pan-grave artifacts were also found in the Gebelein region. They appeared on the antiquities market at the beginning of this century and are now in several museums, including the Turin Museum.

See also

Abusir; First Intermediate Period, overview; Hierakonpolis; Pan-grave culture; pottery, prehistoric; Predynastic period, overview; textual sources, Old Kingdom

Further reading

D'Amicone, E. 1988. L'area archeologica di Gebelein. In *La cività degli Egizi* II, A.M. Donadoni, ed., 38–43. Milan.

Fisher, H.G. 1961. The Nubian mercenaries of Gebelein during the First Intermediate Period. *Kush* 9: 44–80.

Porter, B., and R.L.B. Moss. 1937. *Topographical Bibliography of Ancient Egyptian Hieroglyphic Texts, Reliefs, Paintings* 5: 162–4. Oxford.

Wildung, D. 1977. Gebelein. *LÄ* 2: 447–9.

A.M. DONADONI ROVERI

Giza, Hetepheres tomb

Queen Hetepheres I was the wife of King Seneferu and mother of King Khufu, builder of the Great Pyramid at Giza. Her historical and archaeological significance is due to the discovery of her tomb, the only partially intact royal burial known from the Old Kingdom.

In 1925, three years after the opening of the tomb of King Tutankhamen at Thebes, an Egyptian photographer of the Harvard University–Museum of Fine Arts, Boston Expedition at Giza was taking photographs east of the Great Pyramid when he discovered a plaster fill area in the limestone bedrock. The plaster was removed to reveal a sealed shaft over one hundred feet (30.5 m) deep and filled with limestone blocks. A small burial chamber at the bottom of the shaft held a large stone sarcophagus surrounded by thousands of fragments of pottery vessels, stone and copper dishes and vases, scattered inlays and bits of gold leaf. The expedition diary for Sunday, March 8, 1925 records the following events at the bottom of the newly discovered tomb shaft:

At 11:00 am Rowe first looked through the wide hole made by this clearing, using reflected sunlight from above. The others in the pit looked in afterwards. Towards the east side of the chamber (which was wider S–N than E–W) stood a perfect and large alabaster sarcophagus, of good stone and cutting. No inscription was visible upon this. Upon the sarcophagus a number of wooden(?) staves or maces with heads of gold or(?) in some cases of copper or bronze lay side by side. Decayed wood from these had trickled over the lid of the sarcophagus. All these were sheathed in gold. Beyond, to the east, on the floor was a good deal of gold in strips which seemed to bear some embossed design. Upon the sarcophagus also is what seems to be a mat(?) of gold lacery wherein the name Snefru is clearly legible from the door besides the vulture of the title *Nebty*. This *may* belong to a bed or canopy of which the "staves" above are parts. The whole space west of the coffin and to the south is packed with the deposit of *royal* furniture. There are a great number of vessels of the rarer stones,—a large alabaster bowl is very prominent towards the south-west corner; near the centre of this space are a fine copper or bronze ewer and basin; two golden head-rest supports stand beyond these. There is a great deal of gold (much of it in strips) laid out all over the area. Immediately upon having ascertained the character of the discovery Rowe sent a code cablegram to Dr. Reisner announcing the simple facts about it.

It took George Reisner, leader of the Museum Expedition, and his team nearly two years to clear out the small room. Great care had to be taken to photograph and plan the position of every fragment. Because of their methodical and painstaking approach, the expedition was eventually able to reconstruct the ancient gilded and inlaid furniture placed in the tomb. The wood had long ago crumbled to dust. Nevertheless, by studying the pattern in which the various gilding layers and inlays had fallen from the wood, the excavators could determine the size and shape of each piece, and check it against tomb reliefs and wall paintings showing similar kinds of furniture.

The recording process involved (1) drawing the objects to scale as they lay on the floor; (2) photographing the area; (3) removing the objects one by one, while referring to the drawings and photographs; and (4) repeating the process with the next underlying layer of objects. The entire project took 280 days, required 1,057 photographs and filled 1,701 pages of notebook records. Reisner was able to identify the tomb's owner because the inlaid gold hieroglyphs originally set into the back of the carrying chair lay in order on the floor of the tomb. They spelled out the name and titles of the wife of King Seneferu and mother of King Khufu, Hetepheres.

Figure 39 Tomb of Queen Hetepheres at Giza: detail of the butterfly-pattern bracelets as
discovered lying in her jewelry box in 1926
Courtesy of the Museum of Fine Arts, Boston

After the tomb was completely cleared, the sarcophagus could finally be opened. To the excavators' surprise, however, it was found to be empty. Reisner theorized that Hetepheres had originally been buried elsewhere and that the tomb had later been robbed. He suggested that her burial was moved to a secret tomb beside the pyramid of her son, King Khufu, to safeguard the rest of the burial and cover up a court scandal. More recent scholarship, however, has suggested that the Giza tomb Reisner discovered was indeed the original burial place of the queen. Because of a change in the ancient architectural layout of the Great Pyramid complex, a super-structure was never built over the shaft leading to the tomb. The body of the queen might then have been robbed during the funeral rites, as often happened in ancient Egypt.

After all the objects were removed from the tomb, special wooden replicas of the furniture were made to match the dimensions of the ancient gold foil casings. Because of the importance of this discovery, all the material was kept by the Cairo Museum except for some of the pottery and a few of the bracelets, which came to Boston. The original gold coverings and inlays were then placed around the new wooden cores to restore the furniture to its original shape. The queen's carrying chair, bed, curtain box, chair and canopy are significant as examples of the earliest and most elaborate furniture ever discovered in the ancient world.

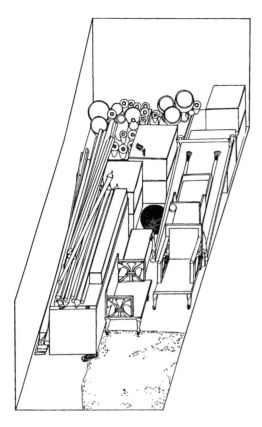

Figure 40 Drawing of the reconstructed contents of the tomb of Queen Hetepheres at Giza

See also

Old Kingdom, overview; Reisner, George Andrew; tomb furnishings

Further reading

Lehner, M. 1985. *The Pyramid Tomb of Hetepheres and the Satellite Pyramid of Khufu.* Mainz.

Reisner, G.A., and W.S. Smith. 1955. *A History of the Giza Necropolis 2: The Tomb of Hetep-heres the Mother of Cheops.* Cambridge, MA.

Seipel, W. 1977. Hetepheres I. *LÄ* 2: 1172–3.

PETER DER MANUELIAN

Giza, Khafre pyramid complex

The pyramid complex of Khafre, the second to be built at Giza (29°59′ N, 31°08′ E), is located to the south of Khufu's monument. Khafre named his pyramid "Khafre is Great." Originally it was 143.2 m high and each side measured 215 m at the base, with a slope of 53°7′.

The pyramid has two entrances on the northern face. The first opens into the pyramid about 11 m above ground level. The other entrance is cut into the bedrock floor. The upper entrance may have been for workmen during pyramid construction, but the existence of two entrances may also reflect a change in plan. Both entrances lead to a horizontal passage with two chambers, one of which still contains a sarcophagus.

The complex is identified with Khafre from inscriptions on granite casing blocks from the western entrance of the valley temple. Reliefs from this complex were discovered at el-Lisht, where they were used as fill for the pyramid of Amenemhat I (12th Dynasty). Some of Khafre's statues were found smashed in the valley temple, suggesting that the complex was partially destroyed during the First Intermediate Period. The cult of the king was revived in the 26th Dynasty, a time when Khufu was worshipped as a god.

The architectural components of the Khafre complex are: (1) an enclosure wall, (2) mortuary temple, (3) boat pits, (4) subsidiary pyramid, (5) *serdab*, (6) the so-called "workmen barracks," (7) causeway, (8) valley temple and (9) the Great Sphinx and its temple. The pyramid was encased in Tura limestone and surrounded by an enclosure wall about 2 m high. A court is located on four sides between the pyramid and the enclosure wall. Tombs of the officials and nobles are to the south of the causeway.

A series of round holes *circa* 40 cm in diameter were cut about 5 m apart in the bedrock around the pyramid, about 9.5 m from the base line. These are thought to be connected with the surveying and laying out of the base of the pyramid.

Khafre's mortuary temple, one of the best preserved examples from the Old Kingdom, was excavated by the German archaeologist Uvo Hölscher in 1909–10. Made of local limestone, its outer walls are faced with granite and the inner walls with Tura limestone. The floor is partially paved with alabaster. Granite beams supported the limestone ceiling. The temple contains a large pillared hall with three recesses. To the north and south are two long narrow rooms built into the thick masonry around the pillared hall that run east–west. Another wide hall (*pr-wrw*) to the west contained statues of the king on one side and pair statues of the king and queen on the other. This hall leads to an open courtyard. From the west side of the courtyard are five passages, which lead into the surrounding corridor and then into five long east–west rooms. Three of these rooms are thought to have contained statues of Khafre, with a statue of Khufu as the god Re in the fourth one. In the fifth room was a statue of the goddess Hathor. Another set of five long rooms, located behind the five statue chambers, contained cult objects for the statues. Some scholars think that there was a platform with a stela and altar in the space between the western wall of the temple and the east side of the pyramid.

As in the pyramid complex of Khufu, five boat pits were found associated with Khafre's pyramid. Two on the north side of the mortuary temple are oriented east–west. Three more boat pits are to the south of the temple: two of these are oriented east–west and the third is north–south. All of the boat pits are cut in the bedrock and there is evidence that two were roofed with limestone slabs.

A single subsidiary pyramid lies to the south, on the north–south axis of the main pyramid, but very little remains of its superstructure. In the center of the pyramid's north side a series of steps lead down from the entrance to a short corridor which opens into the burial chamber. Fragments of stoppers or bases from jars, two carnelian necklaces, ox bones and pieces of wood were found inside this chamber. These finds seem to support its identification as a queen's tomb and the wooden fragments were probably the remains of a coffin.

To the west of the subsidiary pyramid, 4 m from its east–west axis, is an undisturbed sealed

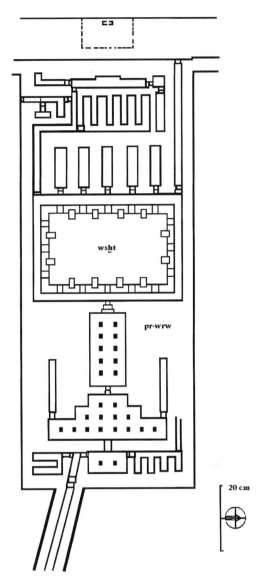

Figure 41 Mortuary temple of Khafre's pyramid complex

passage (*serdab*) without a superstructure. The passage consists of a descending corridor about 80 cm square with an entrance that was sealed by three limestone blocks. At the end of the descending corridor is a niche within which were dismantled pieces of a small wooden artifact that had been tied with a string. After careful restoration, the artifact appeared to be a frame for a box or shrine, 74 × 63 × 186 cm. Some scholars think that this underground passage is associated with the subsidiary pyramid. Others believe that it housed a wooden shrine for a statue of the king's *ka*.

To the west of Khafre's pyramid Flinders Petrie excavated the remains of structures, which he thought were ninety-one rooms for the workmen who built the pyramid. Artifacts associated with these rooms included Old Kingdom potsherds, large pieces of quartzite, damaged blocks of granite and fragments of alabaster and diorite. Evidence from recent excavations at this site, which did not reveal any settlement debris, indicates that it was a storage area and royal workshop. Artifacts included several small broken statuettes of the king and some smaller royal figurines.

The causeway of Khafre's pyramid complex has substantial remains and its foundation can be traced for most of its length. Some of the side walls, about 3 m thick and built of large slabs of Tura limestone, still stand to a height of four courses. From the mortuary temple to the valley temple, the causeway is oriented 106°17′ to the east of magnetic north. It is 494.6 m long and 5 m wide. No decoration has been found outside or inside the walls of the causeway and whether it was roofed or painted is unknown.

The valley temple of Khafre's pyramid complex was discovered in 1853 by the French Egyptologist Auguste Mariette, who cleared the interior. Hölscher cleared the front of this temple in 1909–10. It is made of local limestone and cased with granite, with huge pillars of red granite and floors of alabaster on the interior. The temple faces east with two doorways. A short passage from the entrance leads to a long north–south antechamber, where a famous diorite statue of Khafre was found upside down in a pit in the floor. Another passage leads to a large T-shaped hall, which was paved with alabaster. Against the western wall of the room are twenty-three sockets for statue bases, originally for seated statues of the king. Statue fragments were found scattered throughout the temple. Three double storerooms, each with two

levels, open to the south of the T-shaped hall. These rooms were probably for storing funerary and cult artifacts.

It is unlikely that Khafre's valley temple was used for mummification. The holes in its roof are not for the poles of the washing tent, as some scholars have thought, but are associated with the temple's construction. The ground plan, wall reliefs, cult artifacts and statues found in the valley temple do not indicate any association with the mummification process nor with its ritual. In recent excavations of a platform in front of Khafre's valley temple evidence was found for the tent used for purification of the king's body. To the northeast of this was a mudbrick platform, possibly where

Figure 42 Diorite statue of Khafre found in the valley temple

members of the royal family viewed the dead king. Two ramps, each about 19 m in length, were excavated in front of the north and south entrances of the temple. Underneath each ramp was a tunnel, which may have contained symbolic royal boats.

The Great Sphinx, which is associated with Khafre's pyramid complex, is unique in ancient Egypt and is considered to be the first colossal royal statue. The sphinx is a composite of a lion with the head of a king wearing the cloth headdress (*nms*) and a long curled "false" beard, symbols of kingship. The Great Sphinx rests on the lowest part of the Giza plateau to the east of the three major pyramids of the 4th Dynasty. Because of its location near Khafre's pyramid complex and the similarity of the Sphinx Temple to Khafre's valley temple, it has traditionally been dated to the reign of this king.

The recent conservation project of the Great Sphinx has revealed many parts of its core and permitted close examination of its composition. The sphinx was indeed an element of the master plan of Khafre's pyramid complex and was not located haphazardly where there was leftover quarry rock, as some scholars have suggested. The architect ordered the workers to cut and remove the rock from around the chosen site in a U-shaped ditch, leaving a standing rock core which became the sphinx. The stone that was removed may have been used in building the pyramid and temples.

The Sphinx Temple is located to the north of Khafre's valley temple: the two temples are aligned and separated by a narrow passage. The main axis of the Sphinx Temple runs east–west, and there are two entrances on the north and south. By the New Kingdom, many of the casing stones of the Great Sphinx had fallen and the lion body was damaged. Evidence for Tuthmose IV's restoration of the Great Sphinx is preserved in the so-called "Dream Stela" that he erected between its two paws. According to this text, the sphinx was buried up to its neck in sand. Tuthmose IV cleared the sand away from the monument, and as a result he succeeded to the throne. He also built mudbrick walls around the sphinx to protect it from wind and sand. In addition, the king had the fallen stones restored

and he may have commissioned further repairs. Evidence of a statue base of Osiris, also dating to the New Kingdom, suggests that the four large masonry constructions attached to the northern and southern sides of the sphinx were chapels for Osiris and other deities.

Another conservation campaign was undertaken during the 26th Dynasty. The Great Sphinx may also have been painted at this time. More restoration was done in the Roman period when a layer of protective brick-sized stones was added to the paws and the two sides of the sphinx.

Modern excavations around the sphinx began in the nineteenth and twentieth centuries. Most important was the campaign of the French engineer Émile Baraize from 1925 to 1936. Archaeological surveys by Goyon have revealed the existence of harbors for the Giza pyramids, and the 1980 excavations by Hawass in front of the Sphinx Temple uncovered evidence for the harbor of Khafre's pyramid complex. The most recent restoration campaign began in 1989, and an international effort is now needed to face the challenge of conserving the monument.

See also

Abu Roash; el-Lisht; Old Kingdom, overview; pyramids (Old Kingdom), construction of

Further reading

Edwards, I.E.S. 1993. *The Pyramids of Egypt*. Harmondsworth.

Hawass, Z. 1990. *The Pyramids of Ancient Egypt*. Pittsburgh, PA.

——. 1995. The program of the funerary cult of Khufu, Khafre and Menkaure during the 4th Dynasty. In *Kingship in Ancient Egypt*, D. O'Connor and D. Silverman, eds. Leiden.

Hawass, Z., and M. Lehner. 1994. The Great Sphinx at Giza: who built it and why? *Archaeology* 47(5): 30–41.

ZAHI HAWASS

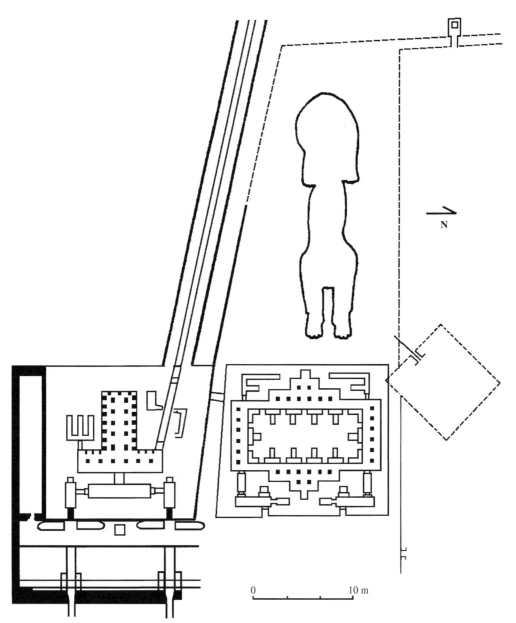

Figure 43 Valley temple and Sphinx Temple of Khafre's pyramid complex

Giza, Khufu pyramid complex

Khufu was the son of Seneferu, the first king of the 4th Dynasty. Khufu ruled for about twenty-three years, and his pyramid at Giza (29°59′ N, 31°08′ E) is the largest ever built. Its design established the standard architectural components of the royal pyramid complex for the rest of the Old Kingdom.

Known today as the "Great Pyramid," the monument was originally named "Akhet-Khufu" (Horizon of Khufu). Investigations of the structure began in 1647 with John Greaves's work, *Pyramidographia*. Edmé François Jomard, a scientist attached to the Napoleonic expedition, did one of the many subsequent surveys/measurements. Measurements were also taken by Howard Vyse and J.S. Perring in 1837–8. The most important survey of the site—which set the standards for accuracy—was conducted by Flinders Petrie in 1880–2. Petrie's measurements were so accurate that they can still be used today. After Petrie others also examined the Great Pyramid's dimensions, including Cole, Borchardt, Lauer, Goyon, Maragioglio, Rinaldi, Fakhry, Edwards,

Lehner, Stadelmann, Arnold and Hawass. Although much information has been amassed, there are still many unanswered questions about this pyramid.

Khufu's pyramid is accurately oriented to true north and is a nearly perfect square at its base, covering an area of 5.5 ha. Modern survey indicates that there is only a 2.5 cm difference between the level of the north side of the base and that of the south side. How the ancient builders achieved such accuracy has only been demonstrated recently. Around the bases of the pyramids of Khufu and Khafre are a series of holes, each about the size of a dinner plate. Regularly spaced along lines running parallel to the sides of these pyramids, the holes must have held stakes for a line used as a reference for the builders as they constructed the pyramid base. There are also trenches which must have been used for channeling water to the base area and draining it during the leveling operations.

The original entrance to the Great Pyramid was a passageway sloping down to an unfinished room cut in the bedrock. Subsequently, there were plans to enlarge the monument, and the subterranean chamber was abandoned.

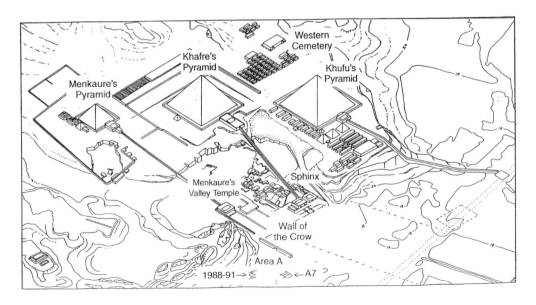

Figure 44 The Giza pyramids

First, the so-called Queen's Chamber was constructed in the lower courses of the pyramid, but it also remained unfinished. Then the King's Chamber, considered to be the final burial place of the king, was constructed in granite higher up in the pyramid. Five "relieving" chambers, thought to have been designed to relieve the weight of the stones above the burial chamber, were built. The only hieroglyphs left by the ancient builders were found on blocks in these chambers. These texts are the names of the work gangs, which included the king's name. For example, "Friends of the Khufu Gang" is the translation of one text which was painted in red to identify blocks assigned to a particular gang.

On the north and south sides of the King's Chamber are the so-called "air shafts." These may have been a symbolic exit and entrance for the king's *ka*, which was believed to travel on the sun bark by day and return at night for the trip through the underworld. During work to create a ventilation system to preserve the Great Pyramid, a robot was sent through one of the air shafts. Sixty-five meters inside the pyramid, the robot was forced to stop by what appears to be a stone door with two copper handles. Further investigation is needed.

The pyramid was surrounded on all four sides by an enclosure wall. Remains of this wall are visible today, especially on the eastern and northern sides. Between the wall and the pyramid was a court paved with large slabs of limestone, some of which are still in place.

Very little remains of the pyramid's mortuary temple. In the Middle Kingdom it served as a quarry. A shaft, which was either a Saite tomb (26th Dynasty) or a well of the Roman period, was dug in the center of the western part of the temple and completely destroyed the plan of that area. Most of the temple consisted of a large court, oriented north–south. To the west was a pillared recess and a door which led to the most sacred area of the temple, a hall with five niches. An altar flanked by two stelae with the names and titles of the king stood on a platform next to the pyramid. The eastern entrance of the mortuary temple led to the causeway, at the end of which was the valley temple.

In 1989, the Sphinx Emergency Sewage Project was inaugurated in the village of Nazlet el-Samman in order to drain waste water away from the Giza monuments. The trenches for this project provided an unprecedented opportunity to examine buried levels, and remains of the causeway of Khufu's pyramid complex were discovered in five locations. From the mortuary temple the causeway is aligned 14° north of due east. It descends across the gradual slope of the desert plateau for 280 m and then reaches the vertical edge of the escarpment overlooking the Nile Valley. From the escarpment to the valley temple the causeway continues in a straight line, but at an angle more north of east than in the western part. Its total length is 750 m, and the distance from the east face of the Great Pyramid to the valley temple is 810 m.

The location of the valley temple of the Great Pyramid has been a matter of speculation ever since the early nineteenth century. Sewage

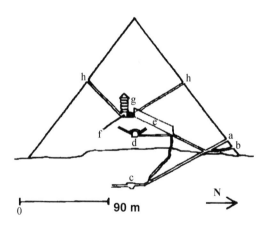

a entrance leading to newly opened corridor
b Mamun's entrance
c first burial chamber
d second (queen's) chamber
e grand gallery
f third (Khufu's) chamber
g five relieving chambers
h airshafts

Figure 45 Cross-section plan of Khufu's pyramid tomb at Giza

trenches excavated in Abdel-Hamid al-Wastani Street of the town revealed that at this point the causeway turns 32° to the north of the original direction, continuing 125 m to the valley temple. Black-green basalt paving stones were found here about 4.5 m below the present ground level.

The basalt pavement was neither continuous nor complete. Removal of blocks in antiquity had reduced the area of the original pavement, although some of the apparent gaps may be where there were once interior walls. At the southern edge of the basalt blocks, excavations revealed part of a mudbrick wall, possibly as much as 8.0 m wide, although its south side is not defined. North of this wall, the basalt blocks extend 56 m in the trench thus excavated. These remains are certainly those of Khufu's valley temple.

The three small pyramids to the east of Khufu's pyramid are generally thought to belong to his queens. Each originally had a small chapel on its east side, and a boat pit. The southernmost pyramid, usually assigned to Queen Henutsen, is the best preserved, but it does not have a boat pit. The central pyramid belongs to Queen Merities and the northern one is that of Hetepheres I, Khufu's mother.

On the west side of Khufu's pyramid are tombs of officials which date from year 5 of his reign to the end of the Old Kingdom. On the east side of the pyramid are tombs of nobles and members of the royal family, built beginning in Khufu's twelfth regnal year.

North of the causeway are underground corridors cut in the bedrock that have the same plan and cross-section dimensions as the passages of the Great Pyramid. Petrie believed that the pyramid builders used these "trial passages" as a model for those inside the Great Pyramid. Another possibility is that Khufu's architect intended these passages to be the substructure of the king's satellite or ritual pyramid, which was never built due to changes in construction plans.

Just south of the Great Pyramid, Hermann Junker found a rock-cut passage, which he thought was planned as a queen's pyramid, but was abandoned when the three queens' pyr-

amids were built to the east. During construction of Khufu's pyramid the area to the south was probably free of structures because it was covered by the supply ramp, which extended farther south to the quarry. Another subsidiary pyramid, with a base of 20 m square, was found southeast of the pyramid, but very little remains of it.

Five boats pits are known from Khufu's pyramid complex. In 1954, two of these were discovered by Kamal El-Mallakh to the south of the pyramid, oriented east–west and parallel to its southern face. A full-size, dismantled wooden boat was found in the southeastern pit. The boat, over 43 m long and with five oars on each side, is now restored and exhibited in a museum in the same location. Waseda University is now engaged in a project to reexamine and conserve a second boat discovered in the southwestern pit in 1987.

The other three boat pits are located to the east of the pyramid, cut in the bedrock of the plateau. Two lie to the north and south of the mortuary temple, and the third one is parallel to the causeway, several meters in front of the entrance to the mortuary temple. Some scholars believe the two boats on the south side of the pyramid were used as funerary boats. A white stain found on the gangplank of the reassembled boat and on the rope from the pit might indicate that the boat was actually used on the Nile. These marks, however, may be the result of humidity in the boat pit, rather than water. The five boat burials may have been purely symbolic, associated with the cults of the king as Horus and as the son of Re, and possibly with the cult of Hathor, who was one of the triad of deities worshipped at Giza.

South of the site of the valley temple, an Old Kingdom settlement of unusually large size was discovered beneath the houses of Nazlet el-Samman. A continuous horizon of mudbrick buildings, which contained large quantities of Old Kingdom pottery, was traced 3 km to the south. Part of this settlement was probably the pyramid city which housed the personnel who maintained the cult of the king and the gods. A limestone and basalt wall was also discovered in the modern village during the construction of an apartment building. This wall has been identified as part of the harbor of Khufu's pyramid complex.

See also

Old Kingdom, overview; pyramids (Old Kingdom), construction of; Reisner, George Andrew

Further reading

Edwards, I.E.S. 1993. *The Pyramids of Egypt.* Harmondsworth.

Hawass, Z. 1990. *The Pyramids of Ancient Egypt.* Pittsburgh, PA.

——. 1996. The discovery of the satellite pyramid of Khufu (GI-d). In *Studies in Honor of William Kelly Simpson*, P.D. Manuelian, ed., 379–98. Boston.

Lehner, M. 1985. The development of the Giza Necropolis: The Khufu Project. *MDAIK* 41: 109–43.

ZAHI HAWASS

Giza, Khufu pyramid sun barks and boat pit

In 1954, a 44 m long boat was discovered beneath forty blocks of limestone, which sealed a rock-cut chamber over 30 m long on the south side of the Great Pyramid (of Khufu) at Giza. The ceiling stones of the chamber had been sealed with a gypsum mortar, which filled the spaces between the blocks. This suggested that the cavity was hermetically sealed. Another sign of the tight seal was the emission of the smell of cedarwood from the disassembled boat when the first ceiling block was removed.

Once assembled, the boat was housed in the Boat Museum, built next to the Great Pyramid. Unfortunately, a few years after opening the museum to the public in 1982, the boat shrank by about 0.5 m, and it was feared that such deterioration may have been caused by changing environmental conditions.

Near the opened pit of the excavated boat was another set of 40 blocks, and it was believed that a second disassembled boat had been buried there. It was hoped that an investigation of the environment of this chamber would lead to a better understanding of how best to preserve the ancient wood. In addition, sampling the air inside the pit might reveal important data on the atmosphere of the earth 4,600 years ago.

A nondestructive investigation of the contents of the second covered chamber was conducted in 1987 using remote sensing methods and techniques, which included:

1 geophysical surveying of the site using a ground-penetrating radar to establish the shape of the chamber and the profile of its contents;
2 drilling a 9 cm hole using dry rotary drill motion through the limestone ceiling stones, with the drilling and other operations sealed by an air lock to separate the air inside from that outside;
3 sampling the air in the cavity at different levels;
4 measuring pressure, temperature and relative humidity inside the chamber;
5 photographing the interior with a high resolution, black-and-white video camera using a fiber-optic "cold" light and a 35 mm still camera using color film; and
6 sealing the drilled hole with a material similar to that used by the ancient Egyptian builders, to return the environment to its original state.

Photography of the interior revealed a disassembled boat. Much like the one that was discovered in 1954, the second boat chamber contained stacks of wood with pieces of the cabin arranged on top. The second boat appeared to be smaller than the first, with four small pointed oars on top. Bronze hooks were visible, and appeared similar to those that hinged the cabin doors in the first boat.

Seventy liters of air were collected from 18 cm, 94 cm and 145 cm below the ceiling for analysis by specialists of the National Oceanic and Atmospheric Administration (NOAA) in

Boulder, Colorado. Results of the analyses indicated that the air pressure inside the chamber was identical to that outside. Further chemical analyses of the air samples and radiocarbon dating of the carbon dioxide indicated a mixture between ancient air (2,000 years old) and a modern counterpart.

Three attempts were made to capture organic particles from the air for biologists to identify any microorganisms. These samples were completely free of microbial contaminants. This may have been because the air was pumped from nearly 1 m above the contents of the chamber, whereas bacteria or other organisms may have settled to the bottom of the chamber or on the upper surface of the wood. This project established without a doubt the applicability of advanced remote sensing technology to the study of the material remains of ancient Egypt.

See also

Giza, Khufu pyramid complex; ships

Further reading

El-Baz, F. 1988. Finding a pharaoh's funeral bark. *National Geographic* 173(4): 513–33.

El-Baz, F., B. Moores and C.P. Petrone. 1989. Remote sensing of an archaeological site in Egypt. *American Scientist* 77(1): 60–6.

Jenkins, N. 1980. *The Boat Beneath the Pyramid: King Cheops' Royal Ship*. London.

FAROUK EL-BAZ

Giza, Menkaure pyramid complex

Menkaure was the son of Khafre and Khamerenebti I and the next to last king of the 4th Dynasty. He was the builder of the smallest of the three pyramids at Giza. The pyramid, named "Menkaure is Divine," was constructed of local limestone with a facing of fine limestone from the Tura quarries, like the other Giza pyramids. However, the lowest sixteen courses were encased in granite, but the blocks left unfinished. The pyramid was first entered in modern times by Howard Vyse in 1837. Vyse discovered an elaborate paneled sarcophagus that was lost off the coast of Spain while he was attempting to ship it back to England.

The pyramid itself is preserved to a height of 66 m with a base approximately 103 m square and a slope of 51°. The burial chamber is reached by a descending passage partially encased in granite. The passage appears to have been altered in conjunction with an expansion of the original design of the pyramid. The burial chamber that held the sarcophagus has a vaulted ceiling and is entirely made of granite. Three small "queen's pyramids" are situated to the south side of the pyramid and, like the other monuments, they were never finished. It has been suggested that the largest and most complete of these belonged to Menkaure's principal wife, Khamerenebti II.

The temples associated with the pyramid of Menkaure were excavated by George Reisner for the Harvard University–Museum of Fine Arts, Boston Expedition beginning in 1908. Reisner perceived a number of building stages in the remains. He ascribed the initial construction of the temples to Menkaure; the final completion of the structures, in mudbrick rather than stone, was attributed to Menkaure's son and successor, Shepseskaf, and later alterations within the temple enclosures were connected with a change in cultic practices, an intrusive settlement and plunder.

Reisner's excavations of the pyramid complex yielded a tremendous quantity of sculpture, which had originally been placed in the associated mortuary and valley temples. Unfortunately, most of the statues had been ritually buried or moved as the temple fell into disuse, so determining the original decorative program of the temples is difficult. In addition, it appears there was some iconographical change in the design of some of the images.

One of the most impressive examples of Old Kingdom royal sculpture is the colossal alabaster (calcite) statue of Menkaure in the Museum of Fine Arts, Boston. The statue was

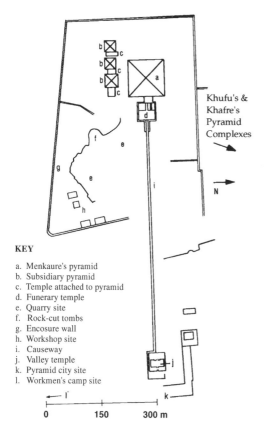

KEY

a. Menkaure's pyramid
b. Subsidiary pyramid
c. Temple attached to pyramid
d. Funerary temple
e. Quarry site
f. Rock-cut tombs
g. Encosure wall
h. Workshop site
i. Causeway
j. Valley temple
k. Pyramid city site
l. Workmen's camp site

0   150   300 m

Figure 46 Plan of King Menkaure's pyramid
          complex at Giza
Drawing by Z. Hawass

polished, inscribed and painted. Inlaid eyes and a wooden arm indicate that wooden statues were also used in the temples, but did not survive.

In addition to the sculpture, Reisner also discovered a large cache of stone vessels deposited in some of the storerooms of

Figure 47 Alabaster statue of King Menkaure
Courtesy of the Museum of Fine Arts, Boston

re-assembled from fragments discovered by Reisner in Menkaure's mortuary temple in 1907. The restored sculpture depicts the king seated on a block throne wearing a *nemes* headcloth surmounted by a *uraeus* (the royal cobra) and dressed in a royal kilt. This must have been the principal cult statue for the pyramid temple. Life-size and smaller seated statues of the king were found in the valley temple as well as a pair statue of the king and his queen and a series of triads depicting Menkaure and the goddess Hathor in association with the nome gods of the more important districts. The sculpture was left in varying states of completeness, some being only roughed out while others had been

Menkaure's valley temple. While many of the vessels had been smashed and broken when they were placed in the magazines, it was possible to reconstruct over 500 individual pieces. The vessels were made from a variety of hard and soft stones and included a number of unfinished specimens. Reisner assumed that the majority of the vessels dated to the reign of Menkaure; however, many are of types that belong to the Early Dynastic period (1st–2nd Dynasties) and not to the Old Kingdom. Of the few inscribed vessels, none mentions Menkaure, while two mention Hotep-sekhemwy, one of which is over an erased inscription of Reneb (kings of the 2nd Dynasty). Two vessels are inscribed with the name of Seneferu (4th Dynasty). As with Zoser's step pyramid complex at Saqqara, it would appear that many of the vessels were taken from earlier tombs and temples and re-deposited in the Menkaure temple. In addition to these, equipment for the "opening of the mouth" ceremony, (*hes*) vases and other temple furniture was recovered. Throughout the later Old Kingdom and early First Intermediate Period, settlement gradually encroached on the valley temple and many of the statues were buried in caches beneath the temple floor.

An inscription around the entrance to the pyramid records the day and month of the king's death, but it seems to be a restoration inscription added at a later date. Recent clearance around the base of the pyramid turned up an unfinished statue of the Ramesside period (19th–20th Dynasties) that may have been made from one of the granite casing blocks. The burial was restored in the Saite period (26th Dynasty) and the remains of a wooden coffin of that date were discovered by Vyse inside the sarcophagus.

Herodotus (Book II, 129–33) recorded that Mycerinus (Menkaure) ruled with justice and moderation, in contrast to his predecessors, but the gods ruled that Egypt should suffer and he was given only six years to live. The king, however, was said to have doubled his allotment by not sleeping and filling his days and nights with feasting and music. The tale was the subject of a poem written by Matthew Arnold in 1849.

See also

Herodotus; mortuary beliefs; Old Kingdom, overview; Reisner, George Andrew; Saqqara, pyramids of the 3rd Dynasty

Further reading

Reisner, G.A. 1931. *Mycerinus: The Temples of the Third Pyramid at Giza*. Cambridge, MA.

PETER LACOVARA

Giza, workmen's community

Although the Giza necropolis (29°59′ N, 31°08′ E) is one of the best excavated and studied of the royal pyramid sites, the social organization of the labor force at the site has only recently been examined archaeologically. Flinders Petrie thought that a series of long galleries he excavated to the west of Khafre's pyramid were a "barracks" for the pyramid workers, but re-examination of the site in 1988–9 by Zahi Hawass in cooperation with Mark Lehner confirmed that this area was not a settlement.

In Menkaure's pyramid complex, in the central open court and in the area due east of the valley temple, remains of Old Kingdom houses were excavated by George Reisner. Selim Hassan also excavated parts of the ancient town here. Houses were made of mudbrick and some had wooden roofs, but the settlement must have been for the personnel who maintained the cult of the dead king.

Industrial complex southeast of the Menkaure pyramid

About 73 m south of the causeway of Menkaure's pyramid complex, a complex of stone rubble walls was excavated by Abdel-Aziz Saleh. The principal structure is a long thick wall that runs through an industrial complex of square buildings and open courtyards with hearths where alabaster and copper were worked. Saleh also found ceramic kilns and facilities which may have been used for levigating clays, as Lehner has suggested. Altogether fifteen buildings were found here, but they probably were not houses since there are not enough to accommodate a work force of any size. However, these remains are an example of what is expected to be found on a much greater scale in the areas to the south of where stone was quarried and south of the necropolis.

South Field

From 1971 to 1975 the Austrian archaeologist Karl Kromer conducted excavations at a large mound in the South Field at Giza. In the mound were bone, ash, potsherds, flint, stone bowls and mudbrick seals of Khufu and Khafre. Kromer concluded that this was a dump with the remains of a settlement of specialized artisans. Karl Butzer, who carefully analyzed Kromer's data, has stated that the artifacts found here are typical of settlements and can be assigned to five distinct strata.

Recent excavations

Recent excavations at Giza in three major areas southeast of the Great Sphinx and south of the great stone boundary wall have revealed the following:

1 a city at the foot of the Giza Plateau;
2 an industrial area;
3 tombs of workmen and their overseers.

The major part of the settlement associated with the Giza pyramids spreads out along the eastern base of the plateau, an area now under the modern city. The industrial area is west of the ancient (and modern) town in the area of low desert south of the Great Sphinx and the boundary wall.

The major settlement

The village of Nazlet es-Samman is located at the foot of the Giza Plateau, preventing excavation here. However, borings and an excavated trench for a sewer project in the modern town have unearthed foundations and potsherds which offer tantalizing evidence that the area was densely inhabited in ancient times.

The total length of the ancient settlement is 3 km, extending south from the recently discovered valley temple of Khufu's pyramid complex. Remains of the settlement have been consistently recorded at levels 3–6 m below the modern ground level. All cores taken within a 3 sq km area east of the Giza pyramids suggest a continuous spread of remains of an early settlement.

With the excavation of sewage trenches, a more comprehensive assessment of the archaeological material was made possible than through coring. Evidence indicated a continuous horizon of mudbrick buildings associated with layers of ash and other rubbish, including large quantities of Old Kingdom potsherds. Thousands of potsherds from all types of pots, including cooking pots, bread molds, beer jars and trays for sifting grain, were excavated. Many red burnished bowls were found, which seems to disprove the theory that such vessels were reserved only for the upper classes. Also found was a finer class of pottery, probably used as food containers, which were imported from southern Egypt. Animal bones with butcher marks still on them are informative about the ancient Egyptian diet, which consisted mostly of beef and sheep, but also pork. The excavations also revealed the microscopic remains of pollen.

These discoveries will also help in locating the workers' camps. The layout of the tombs of the overseers and their workmen suggests that there were two workers' communities, one village for the artisans who decorated the tombs and cut the stones, and possibly a camp for the temporary workmen who transported the stones.

Estimates of the size of the work force employed to build the large 4th Dynasty pyramids vary considerably. Herodotus stated that 100,000 men were employed to build the pyramid of Khufu for a three-month period each year over 20 years, but this estimate could not be accurate. The size of the recently discovered settlement could house about 30,000 workers and artisans. Other workers must have lived in the Memphite region and returned to their homes after work.

Industrial area

This area is in the low desert south of the Great Sphinx and the stone boundary wall, just to the west of the modern village. Excavations began here in 1988–9 in cooperation with M. Lehner. Two Old Kingdom bakeries were found which may have produced bread for the pyramid work force. Bread and beer were the staples of ancient Egyptian laborers.

A large cache of the Old Kingdom bread molds was discovered here. They are exactly like those shown in many baking scenes on the walls of Old Kingdom tomb chapels, such as the tomb of Ti at Saqqara. The most common type of bread mold is a large bell-shaped vessel with thick walls, some weighing as much as 12 kg. In tomb scenes, such pots were set into holes in baking pits, filled with dough from large vats, then covered with another bread pot placed upside down. The bakers covered the pits with hot coals and ash and the dough expanded and baked inside the pots.

Cereals identified from flotation samples taken from the bakeries suggest that the bread was made of barley, resulting in dark loaves that were heavy and dense. Hearths were found in the southeast corners of the bakery rooms to heat the bread molds before the dough was poured into them. This was done by placing them in a tall stack with the interiors open down toward the fire on a flat hearth. The bakery rooms gradually filled with ash, which homogenized from being turned over in the baking pits, until the ash was so deep it reached the brim of the vats.

The word *pr-sn'* was found inscribed on an artifact in the dump associated with the bakeries, suggesting that government workshops were established at Giza to feed the workmen. This word indicates a royal institution for food production, including bakeries. During the Old Kingdom, bakeries were part of a larger establishment that included grain silos and beer brewing. Bakeries and breweries were found together because lightly baked bread dough was used in the mash for beer and it is possible that some beer went back into the dough.

Another building found in the industrial area could have been used for storing grain. On some seal impressions associated with this building is the term "*wabet* (*w'bt*) of Menkaure." A *wabet* is a mortuary workshop, where the body was prepared for burial, but also where funerary offerings were stored and grave goods manufactured. It may refer to the overall royal administrative unit responsible for equipping the burial, including the storage of offerings.

Tombs of the workmen and overseers

This area is located just west of the industrial area and higher on the slope of the Giza Plateau. Thus far, excavations have revealed over 300 tombs. Many of them are small-scale copies of the grand designs used for the royal pyramids and the great stone *mastaba* tombs of the nobles. This small southern cemetery includes miniature stepped mudbrick tombs reminiscent of the step pyramids. Some round tombs that are vaulted or domed are surrounded by a small enclosure wall. Small *mastaba* structures and beehive-shaped tombs are also found. Construction materials included mudbrick and pieces of limestone, basalt and granite, probably saved from the construction of pyramids and temples.

Behind and to the west of a large tomb that belonged to an "Overseer of Tomb Builders," family burial shafts, painted false doors and the meager graves of the workmen who labored under the overseer were excavated. Titles such as "Inspector of Royal Tombs" and "Building Director," found inscribed on these tombs, identify some of the officials in this cemetery. Women who were buried in this cemetery bore titles such as "Priestess of Hathor," the goddess and protector of the workers.

Many workers were buried on their sides in contracted positions. Some of their skeletons reveal signs of lower back stress. One skeleton showed evidence of cancer in the cranium and ribs. Another burial contained the remains of a pregnant female dwarf. Several fine statues were found, including those of a woman on her knees grinding grain or pigment, a smiling artisan and a "reserve" (portrait) head. Protected by the arid climate and sand, these statues still retain their delicate color and minute details.

Figure 48 Tombs of Giza artisans

Larger and finer tombs built of limestone have been found higher up the slope of the escarpment. To the north of one of these tombs is a *serdab* (statue chamber) cut in the limestone which contained four well preserved statues.

The pottery from this cemetery dates to the 4th–5th Dynasties. Beer jars, bread molds, molds shaped like the *hotep*-sign, flower pots, plates and other pottery used in daily life have all been excavated.

The workmen's camps, the industrial area and the cemetery were separated from the pyramids by a large stone boundary wall, 10 m high, 12 m wide at the base and nearly 200 m long. A tall central gate allowed the workers to pass through daily.

See also

brewing and baking; Deir el-Medina; Giza, Khafre pyramid complex; Giza, Khufu pyramid complex; Giza, Menkaure pyramid complex; Herodotus; Old Kingdom, overview; paleopathology; pyramids (Old Kingdom) construction of; subsistence and diet in Dynastic Egypt

Further reading

Hawass, Z. 1996. The workmen's community at Giza. In *Haus und Palast in Alten Ägypten*, M. Bietak, ed., 53–67. Vienna.

Hawass, Z., and M. Lehner. 1997. Builders of the pyramids. *Archaeology* 50(1): 31–9.

Lehner, M. 1985. A contextual approach to the Giza pyramids. *Archiv für Orientforschung* 32: 136–58.

Saleh, A.-A. 1974. Excavations around the Mycerinus pyramid complex. *MDAIK* 30: 131–54.

ZAHI HAWASS

glass

Glass, a mixture of silica, alkali and lime, appears in Egypt as an apparently fully developed industry around 1500 BC. Despite the early development of faïence, the earliest reliably dated Egyptian glass suggests that the industry may have been imported into Egypt, particularly as a result of the campaigns of Tuthmose III. Examples of glass predating the New Kingdom are extremely rare and for the most part uncertain. The words most commonly used by scribes for glass are *mekku* and *ehlipakku*, both of non-Egyptian origin although Egyptian words for "precious stones" are also used, perhaps referring to its use as a substitute for such material.

Glass may have been imported into Egypt at the earliest phase of the industry but it is likely that by the late 18th Dynasty some glass was being produced from local materials at sites such as Tell el-Amarna. It has been suggested that glass making may have been a royal monopoly; although this is open to debate, it is clear that the material was costly and rare, as evidenced by the making of wooden vessels in imitation of glass. The materials—sand for silica and perhaps lime and plant ash (or later natron) for the alkali—were readily available in Egypt, so local development is not unreasonable. The number of workshops at Amarna tend to reinforce such a view. In fact, recent work suggests that by late 18th Dynasty Egypt may actually have been exporting glass. It is *possible* that the glass ingots from the Ulu Burun shipwreck off the Turkish coast were actually made in Egypt, rather than bound for it.

The first stage in ancient glass making was to "frit" the ingredients, a process which involved heating the raw materials together at a temperature between 700° and 850°C until they formed a mass resembling partly melted sugar. Constant raking of the mixture prevented the formation of semi-liquids and also kept the ingredients in constant contact with one another. This process, a solid state reaction, leaves a dry sodium silicate, and allowed the subsequent melting of glass at a relatively low temperature without significant generation of gas bubbles. On cooling, a solidified mass was left whose lower part comprised unmelted sediment, the middle a crystallized glass and the upper a vesicular mass. The upper and lower parts were chipped away and the remaining portion crushed into a fine glass powder. This powder could then be melted at a higher temperature, up to 1000°C, to produce molten glass which would be relatively free of gas bubbles. The molten glass could then be shaped. The glass would not be clear but greenish or brownish from impurities in the sand, and a decolorizer or a coloring agent would be added to the mixture depending upon the type of glass required.

Glass was worked in a number of different ways. Perhaps the most impressive was hot working to produce vessels such as unguent vases and kohl tubes. To produce such vessels, a core of the desired body shape was first fashioned around a stick which would form a convenient handle and around which the neck of the vessel could eventually be added. The core, made from dung/vegetable matter mixed with clay and sand, would be coated in glass of the intended body color, usually blue, and any excess removed. The decoration could then be added to this body. This was done by taking pre-formed rods of colored glass and softening them so that they could be trailed around the still soft body of the vessel. These trails might then be pulled to give a feathering effect or simply left as swags. Once the decoration was arranged correctly the vessel would be rolled on a flat surface, a process known as marvering, impressing the colored decoration into the body. A neck and foot would then be added to the vessel separately and the completed item allowed to cool slowly in order to gradually release the stresses in the glass. The core would then be removed in pieces via the neck and the whole vessel given a final smoothing using pumice or cloth.

Glass could also be formed in molds, as for example in the case of the few *shawabti* (servant) figurines which have been discovered, or in making other pieces of sculpture such pieces were then given a final working by hand. Vessels, most commonly open forms such as bowls, might also be molded, although they are not especially numerous during the New Kingdom when glass making is at its peak. Cold working of glass is also known, not only as retouching on small items of sculpture but also in the making of more substantial items, such as two of the headrests from the tomb of Tutankhamen. Because of the conchoidal fracture of glass, such cold working demands considerable skill, even if the rough shape has already been cast.

After the New Kingdom, glassmaking declined and until recently was thought to have all but disappeared in Egypt after the 21st Dynasty, not to return until the 26th. However, recent work suggests that it may have lingered on; a 27th Dynasty shrine door shows the same coloring as 18th Dynasty glass, including red, which is a difficult color to produce and whose secret, once lost, would not have been easily recovered.

After the Late period, Egypt comes within the Hellenistic tradition and the forms of vessels produced in Egypt are often so similar to those made elsewhere in the Mediterranean and imported that it is difficult to separate them. The core-formed vessels, however, are less accomplished and the colors vary from those of the New Kingdom. In Ptolemaic and Roman times Alexandria became a center of glass working and trading. Glassblowing, which was probably discovered on the Syrian coast in the late first century BC, gradually spread to Egypt in Roman times where it was practiced alongside the more traditional core forming and cold cutting. The techniques were sometimes combined in the production of cameo vessels, the most famous of which is the Portland Vase, possibly an Alexandrian product, although Italy is favored by many as its place of manufacture.

See also

faïence; Qantir/Pi-Ramesses; Tell el-Amarna, city

Further reading

Bimson, M., and I.C. Freestone. 1988. Some Egyptian glasses dated by royal inscriptions. *Journal of Glass Studies* 30: 11–15.

Cooney, J.D. 1976. *Catalogue of Egyptian Antiquities in the British Museum 4: Glass.* London.

Nicholson, P.T. 1993. *Egyptian Faience and Glass.* Princes Risborough.

Nicholson, P.T., and J. Henderson. 1999. Glass. In *Ancient Egyptian Materials and Technology*, P.T. Nicholson and I. Shaw, eds. Cambridge.

Riefstahl, E. 1968. *Ancient Egyptian Glass and Glazes in the Brooklyn Museum.* New York.

PAUL T. NICHOLSON

Gurob

Medinet Gurob (Arabic for "Town of the Raven") is situated on the desert edge, approximately 4 km west of the point where the Bahr Yusef channel begins to turn northwest to enter the Fayum (29°12′ N, 30°57′ E). The site includes the remains of a New Kingdom town and burials dating to the late Predynastic/ Dynasty 0, Early Dynastic, Old Kingdom, First Intermediate Period, New Kingdom and Ptolemaic period (where burials from each period form at least fourteen distinct cemeteries/burial groupings). The ancient name for the town, "Mer-wer" (Mr-wr), meaning "great channel" or "great canal," was undoubtedly derived from the channel next to which the town was constructed, either the Bahr Yusef or a branch. It has been suggested that Mer-wer was a workers' village, although the founding of the town is undoubtedly the result of the royal harim having been established there.

The first excavations at Medinet Gurob were conducted by Flinders Petrie, in 1888–9 and 1889–90 in archaeological expeditions to the Fayum region. He concentrated on the remains of the town site (private dwellings and the temple of Tuthmose III), the New Kingdom cemetery southwest of the town and the New Kingdom

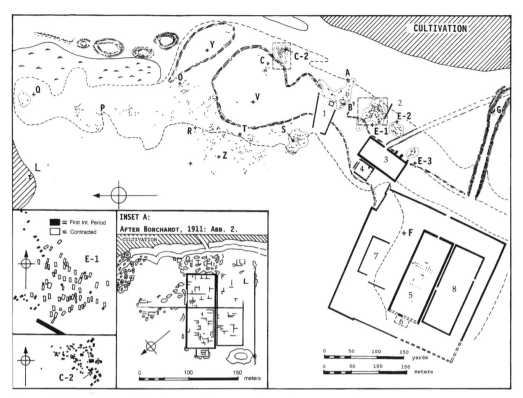

Figure 49 Gurob, New Kingdom settlement and northern cemeteries
Source: adapted from W.M.F. Petrie, 1891, pl. 25, and G. Brunton and R. Engelbach, 1927, p. 1.

and Ptolemaic cemeteries north of the town. A schematic plan of the town was published in the excavation report of his second season.

In 1901 J.E. Quibell published an undisturbed tomb (containing two burials) found by Danios Pasha at Hawaret el-Gurob. Some artifacts found in the tomb bore the names of Amenhotep III and Queen Tiye, while a wooden statuette of a girl was inscribed on its base with the name "T3m3." That same year, M.E. Chassinat published artifacts that had been plundered from the tomb of a woman named "Twty" in the vicinity of Gurob. Some artifacts bore the names of Amenhotep III, Queen Tiye and Amenhotep IV.

Further excavations at Gurob were undertaken by C.T. Currelly and W.L.S. Loat in 1903–4. South of the town they discovered the remains of a New Kingdom village and five

cemeteries: a late Predynastic (Nagada III/ Dynasty 0) cemetery, three New Kingdom cemeteries (one for infant burials) and a 19th Dynasty animal cemetery. In addition, Loat found a small mudbrick shrine dedicated to Tuthmose III, adjoining the northwest wall of the central enclosure. In his report Loat published a plan of the shrine and mapped the animal cemetery.

In 1905, Ludwig Borchardt acquired an ebony head of a queen (possibly Tiye) and later traveled to Gurob to locate the site where the head had been found. He examined the architectural remains within the town enclosures and in his publication of the head included a sketch plan of the site. Borchardt concluded that the central enclosure contained the remnants of a palace. In 1920, Guy Brunton and Reginald Engelbach conducted the last excavations at Gurob, focusing on a comprehensive survey of the cemeteries. The excavation report included a site plan of burials and the town, with associated architectural features.

Two Nagada III/Dynasty 0 cemeteries provide the earliest evidence of activity at Gurob. Loat discovered fifty graves on a small hill, approximately 1 km south of the town. The graves were oblong in shape, varying in depth from 60 to 90 cm. Brunton and Engelbach excavated sixteen graves (around "Point O") in which the bodies were contracted, lying on the left side with the head to the south. Loat originally dated the southern cemetery to the prehistoric period, but Brunton and Engelbach later redated it to the "Protodynastic" (now called Nagada III/Dynasty 0) based on the ceramic evidence. An earlier Predynastic cemetery may have existed (Point A) where debris contained fragments of alabaster dishes of an earlier type.

Brunton and Engelbach surveyed 151 graves dating to the Old Kingdom, the majority of which are in two groups (Points C and C-2). They found other graves from this period (Points A, B, E-1, E-2, E-3, L and S), all of which are mixed with later burials (either First Intermediate Period or New Kingdom). All of these burials are low-status ones. The graves were irregularly cut, varying in depth from 50 to 200 cm. Some were lined with mudbrick; others had arched roofs. Most bodies were contracted, usually on the left side with the head to the north or northeast. This area also yielded traces of mudbrick walls, possibly the remnants of an Old Kingdom settlement.

The First Intermediate Period is represented by the remainder of the burials (Points A, B, E-1, E-2 and E-3), which were dated through the ceramic assemblage. More than half of the bodies within these burials lay on the side, a practice primarily discontinued by the 12th Dynasty. In addition, the coffins were of the narrow pre-12th Dynasty type.

No evidence of activity during the Middle Kingdom exists at Gurob. The main regional settlement at that time was at Lahun. Brunton and Engelbach have tentatively dated the structure at the northeast corner of the town,

thought to be a fort, to the Second Intermediate Period, as graves originally thought to be of that date were found in a nearby cemetery. They later redated the graves to the First Intermediate Period. Behind the fort are the remains of a small, square structure on top of which was evidence of kilns and glass production dating to the New Kingdom. Brunton and Engelbach note the presence of lime kilns in this area; numerous examples occur in the Graeco-Roman period.

The main town was surrounded by a large, square enclosure wall, within which were three smaller enclosures: the north enclosure, the central enclosure and the south enclosure. The re-entrant angle at the northeast corner of the town enclosure would indicate that this wall is later than either the fort or the workshop.

The central enclosure contained a large limestone temple dedicated to the crocodile god Sobek. Its construction date has been firmly established: mudbricks, a stone slab and a limestone lintel slab, all bearing the name and titles of Tuthmose III, have been uncovered within the complex. The mudbrick shrine adjoining its northwest wall was constructed during the Ramesside period (19th–20th Dynasties), but also contained many stela fragments (originally fixed on the walls as votives) with the name of Tuthmose III.

There is evidence of two other temples at Gurob built during the Ramesside period. A temple called "Mansion of Ramesseum" is mentioned in the Wilbour Papyrus and on a sheet of papyrus found at Gurob dating to the reign of Ramesses II. The name of the second temple, "House of Osiris-Ma'at-Re, Beloved of Amen [Wsr-M3'.t-R' mry Imn], East of W3st in Mer-wer," is inscribed on a piece of wood from Gurob dating to the reign of Ramesses III.

The north enclosure may have contained the town's earliest occupation phase and was inhabited until the end of the 18th Dynasty. Later an external northern domestic area (less than 0.5 km north of the main town) was built over late 18th/early 19th Dynasty shaft tombs. The south enclosure was inhabited until the reign of Ramesses II, at which time the temple of Tuthmose III was dismantled and, according to Petrie, houses were built on top of what remained of its foundation. The area outside the internal enclosures contains only scant traces of walls.

Barry Kemp disagrees with Petrie's two-phase interpretation (i.e. that the initial temple was dismantled, and housing was then built on top of remains of the foundation) and argues that the town architecturally is of one period. Kemp also supports Borchardt's conclusion that the architectural remains within the central enclosure are not those of a temple but of a palace (a large harim palace). He identifies the structures within the north and south enclosures as storerooms and service buildings for the palace.

The proportion of foreign settlers to native Egyptians resident at Mer-wer has been questioned. In addition to the burial of personal items under the floors of houses (interpreted by Petrie as a foreign burial custom), his excavations yielded Cypriot and Mycenaean pottery and examples of foreign elements in names. Aegean ceramics were imported in the 18th Dynasty, however, and are not necessarily evidence of foreign residents. Angela Thomas maintains that artifacts found at Gurob were predominately Egyptian, and although textual evidence firmly indicates that foreigners were resident at Gurob during the 19th–20th Dynasties (most notably in the employ of the harim), they certainly constituted a minority of the population.

The main New Kingdom cemetery, northeast of the town, dates from the early 18th Dynasty to the Ramesside period. Lower and middle status individuals were buried there. Graves consisted of oval or rectangular pits, 125–150 cm deep, with no superstructures. In the simplest burials the body was wrapped in reeds or matting, or laid upon a layer of reeds. In some cases, mudbricks were placed around or over the body, or the body was placed in a coffin of either mudbrick, wood or pottery. Brunton and Engelbach do not report finding any canopic jars, indicating that bodies were not mummified. Loat excavated a New Kingdom cemetery of infants where bodies were placed in oval ceramic jars and buried in small pits.

The remainder of the New Kingdom graves lie to the south and west of the town enclosure.

One cemetery, first uncovered by Loat, dated to the late 18th Dynasty and the early Ramesside period. Brunton and Engelbach later excavated ten graves in this cemetery, some of which were shaft tombs, with pottery and anthropoid coffins. The graves apparently belonged to officials and professional people.

Brunton and Engelbach surveyed another area to the west of the town which contained approximately 500 shaft tombs belonging to officials and other important people. Included in this group is the tomb of Pi-Ramessu, who may be the son of Seti I and an elder brother of Ramesses II. About 600 m south of this cemetery, Loat excavated a 19th Dynasty cemetery with animal burials, none of which was mummified. Oxen and goats were buried in shallow, irregular pits, usually containing more than one animal (although only one species was included per pit). Fish (primarily Nile perch) were also buried here in carefully dug pits, often for a single fish; perhaps this was the focus of a local cult. Multiple fish burials demonstrated a purposeful arrangement. Ashes of halfa grass were used as a preservative and several fish were found wrapped in cloth.

The Ptolemaic period is represented at Gurob by a cemetery that Petrie describes as lying on a rise of the desert to the north of the town. The grave pits were about 2.4 m deep and sometimes contained as many as twelve coffins of unpainted wood, widening at the shoulder and tapering at the feet (the only decoration was a carved wooden head). The lids had very deep sides while the cases were shallow trays. A large collection of Greek and Demotic texts was discovered among the burials there. From the reign of Ptolemy Philadelphus, inscribed papyri were substituted for cloth in the manufacture of cartonnage mummy cases and many texts were inadvertently preserved in this way. Petrie's collection includes private letters, accounts and wills dating to 250–200 BC, and fragments of classical works. The texts provide some of the earliest examples of Greek cursive writing. Two additional Ptolemaic burials are associated with the shrine of Tuthmose III. Petrie suggests that a Ptolemaic town may have existed in what is now cultivated land.

Gurob

Tuthmose III is undoubtedly responsible for the founding of the town of Mer-wer (the bulk of scarabs found at the site date from from his reign), and its terminal date of occupation can now be fixed as late as Ramesses V (20th Dynasty). A cadastral survey dating to his reign lists several land holding institutions at Mer-wer, but it was probably abandoned shortly thereafter.

See also

Lahun, town; New Kingdom, overview

Further reading

Brunton, G., and R. Engelbach. 1927. *Gurob*. London.
Petrie, W.M.F. 1890. *Kahun, Gurob, and Hawara*. London.
——. 1891. *Ilahun, Kahun and Gurob*. London.
Thomas, A.P. 1981. *Gurob: A New Kingdom Town*. Warminster.

DARLENE GORZO

H

Hatnub

Hatnub is the ancient name for the site of a group of travertine (Egyptian alabaster) quarries located 18 km southeast of Tell el-Amarna, on the eastern side of the Nile in Middle Egypt (27°33′ N, 31°00′ E). The inscriptions, graffiti and archaeological remains at the site indicate that it was intermittently exploited by the Egyptians for a period of about 3,000 years, from at least as early as the reign of Khufu (4th Dynasty) until the Roman period.

Hatnub (the name meaning "mansion of gold") was regularly mentioned in ancient texts as the principal source of travertine (*shes*), but for a long time it was assumed to have been located in the desert to the east of modern Asyut. It was not until December 1891 that the site itself was rediscovered by the English Egyptologists Percy Newberry and Howard Carter. The archaeological remains at the site comprise three basic quarrying zones, which were labeled P, R and T by Flinders Petrie when he included the site in his general map of the Tell el-Amarna region. A slightly more detailed survey of Hatnub was conducted by Paul Timme as part of a survey of the area in 1911, prior to excavations at Tell el-Amarna by the German Egyptologist Ludwig Borchardt. More recently, between 1985 and 1994, the site was mapped in considerable detail, including the recording of surface remains and the excavation of two structures in the quarry workers' settlement.

The largest quarry (P), described by Petrie as "an open circular pit with vertical sides, about 200 feet [61.0 m] across and 50 feet [15.2 m] deep," is still surrounded by huge spoil heaps of travertine chips. It lay in a slight depression and was entered via a sloping passage from the north. The area surrounding Quarry P was peppered with the small dry stone huts that housed the quarry workers, with a particularly dense area of occupation on top of the spoil heaps immediately to the southwest of the quarry. Some huts were built in wadis and basins, so as to take advantage of the shelter provided by the terrain; others were positioned on the crests of ridges and beside prominent cairns, presumably acting as guardposts against attack from the surrounding desert.

The inscriptions and graffiti at Quarries P and R were first recorded by Marcus Blackden and Willoughby Fraser, and were later more exhaustively published by Rudolf Anthes, who listed fifteen inscriptions and fifty-two graffiti, printing facsimiles of each as well as providing copies and translations. Virtually all of the texts were inscribed or incised on the walls of Quarry P, where the large-scale incised cartouches of Khufu provide the earliest date for the site. Fraser mentions two inscriptions and twenty-eight painted graffiti on the walls of the smaller Quarry R, but only three of the graffiti are now legible; the rest are visible only as depictions of men and offering tables.

The epigraphic evidence from Hatnub itself has been supplemented by a number of inscriptions in tombs or cenotaphs describing quarrying expeditions to Hatnub. The "auto-biography" of Weni from his tomb chapel (or cenotaph) at Abydos, for instance, describes the quarrying of a very large travertine offering stone on behalf of the 6th Dynasty king Merenre, which is perhaps corroborated by inscription VI at Hatnub, dating to the same reign. The 12th Dynasty tomb of Djehuty-hotep at Deir el-Bersha includes a depiction of the transportation of a colossal travertine statue from Hatnub, dragged along on a sled by lines of men pulling on ropes.

The texts at Hatnub provide much useful information concerning the size of the work teams and the professions of the expedition members. These texts, and similar inscriptions at other quarrying and mining sites, such as the Sinai turquoise mines, suggest that there was a complex hierarchy of quarry workers, involving as many as twenty-five different types of government officials, eleven varieties of local mining supervisors and numerous categories of skilled and unskilled workers.

An inscription from the reign of the 6th Dynasty king Pepi II describes an expedition to Hatnub led by a ship's captain named Nefer-khas: "I have sailed down with 1,000 people behind me; 80 people journeyed northward so that they came to the road into the quarry. I went down there and afterwards I provided a ship. I brought them back from there by water and kept alive the troops." About 300 years later, in the reign of the 12th Dynasty pharaoh Senusret III, a "chief workman" named Senus-ret left a more concise message: "I came here in order to bring alabaster, together with 1,080 quarry men, 360 artists and...necropolis workers."

Since there was only one inscription of the New Kingdom at Hatnub, it used to be thought that the quarry had fallen into disuse after the Middle Kingdom, but the 1985–94 survey revealed substantial archaeological remains of New Kingdom quarrying expeditions, as well as ceramics showing that there was still limited activity at the site as late as the Roman period. The numbers of rooms in the structures at Hatnub suggest that the gangs of workmen in the Old and Middle Kingdoms may have been organized in multiples of three. In the New Kingdom settlement, on the other hand, there are only single-room shelters, perhaps indicating that the basic method of organization had changed over time.

Hatnub is linked with the Nile Valley by a long ancient dry-stone road, marked at intervals with cairns and still clearly visible for much

of its route. At its northwestern end, in the el-Amarna plain, the first traces are in the vicinity of Kom el-Nana, but it must originally have extended farther to the west, presumably terminating in some form of harbor, the remains of which would now be buried beneath the modern cultivation. To the east of Kom el-Nana, the road ascends the scarp face of the Eastern Desert and passes southeastward across undulating terrain. At two points along its route it had to be transformed into a causeway in order to bridge the larger wadis that interrupted its progress. The upper surface of one of these embankments, only about 200 m from Quarry P, still shows occasional traces of the parallel trackways left by gangs of workmen dragging large blocks of travertine.

There are also traces of the religious life of the quarry workers, in the form of votive sets of model steps carved into the rock surface at the foot of a cairn on the highest point in the area. Scattered throughout the settlement at Hatnub are a number of small structures approached by stone-lined paths, probably to be identified as shrines. The most impressive of these is a small hemispherical roofed building with a long approach path and a square entrance, too small to shelter a man but large enough for offerings to have been inserted. It is perhaps significant in this regard that several of the quarry inscriptions mention priests as members of the expeditions.

See also

Deir el-Bersha; natural resources; quarrying; Serabit el-Khadim; Wadi el-Hudi; Wadi Maghara

Further reading

Badawy, A. 1963. The transport of the colossus of Djehutihetep. *Mitteilungen des Instituts für Orientforschung* 8: 325–32.

James, T.G.H. 1991. The discovery and identification of the alabaster quarries of Hatnub. *CRIPEL* 13: 79–84.

Shaw, I. 1994. Pharaonic quarrying and mining:

settlement and procurement in Egypt's marginal areas. *Antiquity* 68/258: 108–19.

IAN SHAW

Hawara

Hawara is about 10 km southeast of Medinet el-Fayum at the entrance to the Fayum (29°17′ N, 30°54′ E) and is the site of the pyramid complexes of Amenemhat III and Princess Neferuptah. Surrounding the pyramid complex of Amenemhat III is a cemetery which was used from the late Middle Kingdom to the Roman period.

Amenemhat III's complex covers an area approximately 160 × 385 m and is by far the largest and most elaborate funerary monument of the Middle Kingdom. Like the pyramid complex of his father, Senusret III, at Dahshur, Amenemhat III's complex also shows the strong influence of building traditions which had their origin in Zoser's Step Pyramid complex (3rd Dynasty) at Saqqara. Unlike the first pyramid complex of Amenemhat III at Dahshur and most of the other royal funerary complexes of the Middle Kingdom, the precinct at Hawara was oriented north–south. A paneled mudbrick enclosure wall, of which only the foundations remain, probably surrounded the complex. A similar motif was used to decorate the king's granite sarcophagus, which was found in the burial chamber.

The complex consists of a mudbrick pyramid covered with casing stones of Tura limestone which occupied the northern part of the enclosure. To the south stood a large temple which has been described by several classical authors (e.g. Herodotus Book II, 148), known as the "labyrinth." The only major excavations conducted at the site were in 1888–9 by Flinders Petrie, who demonstrated that the whole complex had suffered great damage from stone-robbing, Roman building activities and the excavation of a canal. The area of the labyrinth, which, according to Herodotus (II, 148), even "surpasses the pyramids" in size, was completely ransacked. Unfortunately, the descriptions of the building and the few scattered architec-tural fragments found in the area do not provide enough information for a reconstruc-tion of this unique monument.

The pyramid, which was originally *circa* 60 m high, has been stripped of its casing stones, leaving only a mudbrick mound *circa* 20–25 m high. Petrie succeeded in opening the pyramid entrance on the south side and entered the burial chamber, which contained provisions for two burials. Judging from inscribed objects found in the antechamber, it seems that the daughter of Amenemhat III, Princess Nefer-uptah, was at least temporarily buried beside her father before her own tomb was completed.

The corridors and funerary apartments of the Hawara pyramid show some innovations which became standard features in later pyr-amids of the 13th Dynasty. For the first time in a royal tomb there are sliding porticullises made of quartzite, which block the corridors leading to the burial chamber. In addition, a new T-shaped plan was adopted for the burial apart-ment, with the burial chamber cut from a single block of quartzite. This innovation, as well as additional protective measures, such as the elaborate construction of the ceiling, were probably developed subsequent to the problems experienced at Dahshur.

The tomb of Neferuptah is located *circa* 2 km southeast of her father's pyramid. It was excavated in 1956 by Farag and Iskander. Its pyramid-shaped superstructure had almost entirely disappeared, but seven limestone slabs which covered the burial chamber were still in place. Though filled with ground water, the burial chamber proved to be undisturbed by tomb-robbers and still contained the sarcopha-gus and funerary equipment of the princess.

See also

Dahshur, Middle Kingdom pyramids; Herodotus; Middle Kingdom, overview; Saq-qara, pyramids of the 3rd Dynasty

Further reading

Farag, N., and Z. Iskander. 1971. *The Discovery of Neferwptah*. Cairo.

Petrie, W.M.F. 1890. *Kahun, Gurob, and Hawara*. London.

Petrie, W.M.F., G.A. Wainwright and E. Mackay. 1912. *The Labyrinth, Gerzeh, and Mazghuneh*. London.

CHRISTIAN HÖLZL

Heliopolis, the Predynastic cemetery

Heliopolis was the main cult center of the sungod Re. Today it is part of modern Cairo, and little has been excavated there except a Predynastic cemetery. The cemetery was situated on a desert plain about 20 km east of the present Nile (approximately 30°19′ N, 31°5′ E).

The cemetery was found in 1950 during construction of a building complex. It was subsequently investigated by Fernand Debono, an archaeologist living in Egypt. Forty-five human burials and eleven animal burials were excavated. Fieldwork was continued in 1951 by the Desert Institute and about 100 human burials and three animal burials were excavated, but remain unpublished. The cemetery was not completely excavated, but it is estimated that the total number of burials was around 200. The small number of burials indicates that this was the cemetery of a small village. Unfortunately, no trace of the village has been found.

All of the graves are simple and consist of round to oval pits of various sizes and depths. Only a few were lined with reed mats or wood. Wood from a collapsed roof construction was found in four graves. Most of the burials were in a partially contracted position, lying on the right side with the head to the south, facing east. About half of them had been wrapped in either reed mats or animal skins, and sometimes both.

Other than pots, grave goods are rare: twenty-one graves had none. In some graves only one pot was placed either in front or behind the head. When more pots were present (up to ten) they were always located next to the upper part of the body, and at least one red pot of a different ware was placed close to the head. Other grave goods include a few simple flint knives, roughly carved palettes, some copper and two stone vessels. Child burials either had no pots or only one in front of the face, but one child's grave contained thirty shells (*Ancillaria*) on a string. The copper and shells represent long-distance imports.

Burial differentiation in this cemetery by age and sex seems to reflect a society with a simple social structure. Fetuses and small children were buried elsewhere, probably in the settlement, as was the case at the Lower Egyptian Predynastic sites of Ma'adi and Merimde Benisalame. Older children seem to have been buried together in one row oriented east–west in the western part of the Heliopolis cemetery. Burials without grave goods in the southeastern corner of the cemetery were mainly those of women. Two of the burials with a number of pots belonged to males. Some small pits arranged in two clusters contained only pots.

The burials produced little evidence of ritual behavior, but the presence of several hearths suggests that funerary meals had taken place. Traces of burning were found in some graves, possibly indicating that the funerary meal was before the burial was finished. Evidence of many broken pots may indicate that they were ritually broken at the funeral.

The animal burials in this cemetery were unusual. The goat burials were oriented like those of the humans, lying on the right side, with the head to the south, facing east. The dog burials, however, did not have a standardized orientation. All the goats were buried with several pots, while the dog burials had no grave goods. One dog and one goat had been wrapped in matting.

Together with the animal burials in one of the Ma'adi cemeteries (Wadi Digla), those at Heliopolis are the earliest ones found in northern Egypt. Possibly the dogs were buried to magically guard the cemetery: these burials were found at the cemetery's edge. The goats were probably buried for religious reasons.

The Heliopolis cemetery is closely related to those associated with the settlement at Ma'adi. The pottery tradition is clearly the same, as are most of the pottery forms. Stone vases similar to the two from the Heliopolis graves are found in the Ma'adi settlement. Because of similarity in the orientation of the burials and the dominance of black pottery, the Heliopolis cemetery is most comparable to the earliest burials in the Wadi Digla (phase II), south of the Ma'adi settlement. Compared to the relative chronology of the Upper Egyptian Predynastic Nagada culture, the Heliopolis cemetery can be dated to the first half of the fourth millennium BC (Nagada I and early Nagada II phases).

See also

Ma'adi and the Wadi Digla; Merimde Beni-salame; Predynastic period, overview

Further reading:

Debono, F., and B. Mortensen. 1988. *The Predynastic Cemetery at Heliopolis*. Mainz.

BODIL MORTENSEN

Helwan

The name "Helwan" for the important Early Dynastic cemetery on the east bank of the Nile (29°51' N, 31°22 E), opposite Saqqara and 21 km south of Cairo, is something of a misnomer since the main tomb groups are really closest to Ma'sara and Ezbet el-Walda, some distance north of Helwan el-Beled and Helwan el-Hammamat. Due to its concentrations of natural springs, the area was important as a spa from at least the seventh century AD and possibly in Dynastic times.

An extensive series of Epi-paleolithic and Neolithic settlements, collectively known today as el-Omari, was explored from 1943 to 1951 around the mouth of the Wadi Hof, north of Helwan el-Hammamat. The subsistence of the Neolithic Lower Egyptian culture was probably based on seasonal vegetation in the wadi rather than in the Nile Valley, which at that time was over 3 km from the floodplain. Culturally, the settlement shows affinities with Merimde Beni-salame in the western Delta and Ma'adi to the north.

The paleofan of the Wadi Hof intruded 3 km or more into the floodplain in antiquity. The lower slopes were intensively used for burials during the 1st–2nd Dynasties and then sporadically thereafter, in the Middle Kingdom, Late period and Coptic times, when the monasteries of Deir Shahran and Gregorius (Abu Qarqura) were founded. A little to the north the imposing cliffs near Ma'sara and Tura were quarried for the quality building stone used to case the Old Kingdom pyramids of the Memphite royal necropolis, and there were also alabaster (calcite) quarries in the Wadi Hof and the Wadi Garawi to the south. In modern times the hot springs led to the area being developed in the late nineteenth century, and it is now a sprawling satellite of Cairo.

The most important groups of Early Dynastic tombs were discovered by Z.Y. Saad in the 1940s and 1950s and stretch for some 3 km along the east bank. Only the first six of ten seasons of excavation have been published in full. The nucleus of the necropolis features medium-sized tombs (*mastaba*s) as well as others resembling those at Abydos, and thousands of subsidiary or later simple cyst burials. The density and average size of burial decreases south of this (H1–2 and later seasons), and to the north at Ezbet Kamil Sidqi, where more work was subsequently done by the Egyptian Antiquities Organization (EAO). In general, the cemetery seems to complement the elite *mastaba* tombs and smaller burial sites at North Saqqara, although superstructures, when found by Saad, were far less well preserved than at Saqqara and have now suffered greatly by erosion.

One of the main features of the site is the variety of tomb types. Tombs could be approached from any of the four cardinal points, although the larger *mastaba*s with niched (palace façade) decoration were usually approached from the west (the direction of the river). In the northeastern area are two grave pits, one of which is very large (653H5). Both are entered from the north and both are reminiscent of the unconventional late 2nd

Dynasty tomb of Khasekhemwy at Abydos. As at Saqqara, several tombs have attendant boat burials, and although none has the funerary temples or "model estates" featured at Saqqara, there are examples of model granaries. One pit (679H5) appears not to be a grave at all but a sunken enclosure for four imitation grain silos. Several tombs show the use of large limestone slabs for revetting the sides of the burial chamber, as well as for doorways and portcullises, although this construction is probably due to the fact that the ground here is a loose gravel matrix and not limestone bedrock as at Saqqara. Many tombs had a carved funerary offering scene inserted above the doorway. A few were accompanied by animal burials, such as dogs, and in two cases by donkey burials grouped in threes, as at Tarkhan. One human burial was covered by a large carapace of a Nile turtle.

Grave goods include a standard repertoire of uninscribed pottery and stone vessels, model boats, metal, flint and chert implements, body decoration and amulets of shell, ivory and so on, and occasional cylinder seals. A number of royal names, ranging from Neithotep and Narmer to Qa'a, are found on sealings, jars and tags.

The most easterly tomb in the main central group is 287H6, a very large unfinished(?) *mastaba* of the late 3rd Dynasty which faces east, with a square shaft incorporating reused stone slabs that lined earlier tombs. Curiously, one of the most westerly tombs is an isolated one of the 11th–12th Dynasties, prepared for Sokar-Hotep but apparently never used. The tomb inscriptions mention the necropolis of Heliopolis, which led Saad to follow Junker's suggestion that the Helwan tombs actually belonged to the late Predynastic/Early Dynastic city of Heliopolis (ancient Iunu), which lies over 30 km to the north. Most recent studies of the Early Dynastic period, however, implicitly accept that the cemetery's main affinities were with Memphis.

The sweet water and sulphur springs from which Helwan takes its name, which means "sweet places" in Arabic, seem to be important for therapeutic purposes from the seventh century AD, when Marwan, the governor of

Egypt, built a hospice and the monastic complex of Gregorius. Remnants of an extensive monastic community were also found by Saad to the east of the Early Dynastic cemetery, apparently known to him as "Deir Shahran," although this is also the alternative name of the monastery of Deir [Anba] Barsum el-'Aryan (Barsum the Naked) near the Ma'sara railway station farther north. In the Late period this whole area was probably called Ainu "springs", which suggests that they were always a feature of the district, if not exploited until later. The area was, in fact, an eastern enclave of the city of Memphis. This arrangement was probably originally necessary to exercise quarrying rights in the Old Kingdom.

Étienne Drioton's suggestion that Helwan was the site of Pi-Hapi, the temple to the god of the Nile, has been superseded by the consensus that Pi-Hapi was farther north at Athar el-Nabi.

See also

Early Dynastic period, overview; Early Dynastic private tombs; Ma'adi and the Wadi Digla; Merimde Beni-salame; el-Omari; Saqqara, North, Early Dynastic tombs; Tura, Dynastic burials and quarries

Further reading

Debono, F., and B. Mortensen. 1990. *El Omari*. Mainz.
Saad, Z.Y. 1969. *The Excavations at Helwan*. Norman, OK.
Woods, W. 1987. The Archaic stone tombs at Helwan. *JEA* 73: 59–70.

DAVID JEFFREYS

Heracleopolis

Heracleopolis is the Greek name of the town known in Dynastic times as Neni-nesu, which means "town of the king's child." It became the capital of Nome XX of Upper Egypt during the Old Kingdom. Its Coptic name is Hnes, and in modern Arabic it is known as Ihnasya el-

Medina. The town is located on the right bank of the Bahr Yusuf channel of the Nile (29°05′ N, 30°56′ E), approximately 15 km west of Beni Suef. The Greek name comes from the identification of Herishef, the principal deity of the town, with Heracles. Herishef, literally "he who is upon his lake," was a ram-headed god, known to the Greeks as Arsaphes. He is pictured standing and wearing an elaborate (*atef*) headdress and holding a scepter. One of his most common epithets is "the king of the two lands," or "lord of the two territories."

Herishef's temple and its sacred lake are located at Heracleopolis. The temple is considered the ancient town's most important monument. Most of its buildings were founded by Ramesses II (19th Dynasty), but some must have existed prior to his reign since there are many blocks with the names of kings of the Middle Kingdom. Some even bear the name of Queen Sobekneferu (12th Dynasty).

The temple's excavations, which were begun by Édouard Naville in 1891 and were continued by Flinders Petrie in 1904, have yielded a number of limestone blocks with decorations and inscriptions, as well as columns and other fragments. The temple was called "the house of Herishef" and it is mentioned in the great Harris Papyrus, which recounts the donations made by Ramesses III (20th Dynasty) to various Egyptian temples. From an inscription of Sheshonk I (22nd Dynasty), we learn that the daily sacrifice in the temple was one ox.

According to an inscription on a statue now in the Louvre, important repairs were made to the temple during the Saite period (26th Dynasty). The temple of Herishef was not the only monument built on this site, however. At least one other temple was located there, but with the exception of a gateway, known as the Kom el-Aqareb, in the southern part of the site, this temple has disappeared. Many columns and blocks are scattered over the vast mounds of ruins, and some standing columns, which belong to a Roman or Byzantine edifice, can also be found on the settlement's eastern side.

Heracleopolis was an important center in two different periods. After the end of the Old Kingdom, an attempt to restore dynastic rule was made by the rulers of Heracleopolis, during what is known as the Heracleopolitan period (9th–10th Dynasties). According to Manetho, Heracleopolis became the capital of Egypt during these two dynasties and the town played an important role in the events of that obscure period. Evidence for this also comes from an autobiographical inscription in the tomb of a vassal prince at Asyut. From this inscription we know that a war which lasted several years broke out between the Heracleopolitans and the Theban kings. It ended when the Theban king, Mentuhotep II, finally reunified Egypt.

Heracleopolis once again became an important center after *circa* 950 BC, during the reign of Sheshonk I. What is interesting from a historical standpoint is that Sheshonk I, who was the first Libyan king and founder of the 22nd Dynasty, was also the local ruler of Heracleopolis, but the town never became the capital of Egypt. Heracleopolis was inherited by a junior member of the family who wore the priestly robes of the High Priest of Herishef. Later, when the Kushite (Nubian) King Piye attacked Egypt (25th Dynasty), a Libyan king named Peftauemauy-baset took Heracleopolis as his residence. During the reign of Psamtik I, Heracleopolis returned to its former status as provincial capital. A family of shipmasters lived in Heracleopolis at the beginning of the Saite period, and it was Psamtik I who conferred upon them the privilege of controlling the Nile traffic for the length of the river from Elephantine to the customs post at Memphis.

During the Graeco-Roman period Heracleopolis was the capital of the Heracleopolitan nome. Ihnasya was an important town in Byzantine and early Islamic Egypt, but was badly damaged in the thirteenth century. Today the ancient town and its temples are deserted. The ruins are now covered by modern Ihnasya, and small villages and farms.

In addition to its political role, Heracleopolis also played an important religious role in ancient Egyptian history. Like many other Egyptian cities, Heracleopolis claimed for itself the grave of the god Osiris, which was supposedly located at a place called "Naref." The god's right leg was generally believed to be preserved there as a relic. By the end of the Old Kingdom, Osiris was already the dominant god in Heracleopolis, as demonstrated in *The Tale of the Eloquent Peasant*, which dates to the early Middle Kingdom. Osiris was thought to be one aspect of Re in Heracleopolis, and, according to myth, he and his son Horus had their coronations there. The main deity of the town, Herishef, was also identified with Osiris-from-Naref. According to several texts from the Ptolemaic period, the high priest of Heracleopolis held the title "King of Upper Egypt" (*nsw*). Ptolemaic texts from the temples at Edfu and Dendera provide further information about the cult center at Heracleopolis, describing a battle between Horus and Seth which took place in the environs of the city.

Besides Herishef and Osiris, there were other deities who were also worshipped at Heracleopolis, including Hor-em-akht, Atum, Hor-sema-taui, Hathor and Bai. In the Late period, the demon Neheb-kau had his own cult there. Strabo (XVIII, 821) reports on the cult of the shrew, the town's sacred animal.

The cemetery of the pharaonic and Graeco-Roman settlements of Heracleopolis is located at Sidmant el-Gabel, west of the Bahr Yusuf channel and about 6.5 km northwest of the old town. Tombs were built there for important officials, especially those of the New Kingdom, including Sen-nefer of the 18th Dynasty and Prince Pi-Ramessu and the viziers Pa-Rahotep and Rahotep of the 19th Dynasty. Another cemetery was discovered within the boundaries of the ancient town. In 1966–9 and 1976–7, Spanish archaeologists excavated a cemetery dating to the First Intermediate Period or possibly the beginning of the Middle Kingdom.

See also

Asyut; First Intermediate Period, overview; Manetho; pantheon; textual sources, New Kingdom; Third Intermediate Period, overview

Further reading

Gomaà, F. 1977. Herakleopolis Magna. *LÄ* 2: 1124–7.

Gomaà, F., R. Müller-Wollermann and W. Schenkel. 1991. Mittelägypten zwischen Samalut und dem Gabal Abu Sir. *Beiheft zum Tübinger Atlas des Vorderen Orients* 69: 78–88, 215–20.

Lopez, J. 1975. Rapport préliminaire sur les fouilles de Hérakléopolis. *Oriens Antiquus* 14: 57–78.

Mokhtar, G. 1983. *Ihnâsya el-Medina (Herakleopolis Magna)*. London.

FAROUK GOMAÀ

Herodotus

The Greek historian Herodotus was born in the 480s BC at Halicarnassus in southwestern Asia Minor and was probably dead by 425 BC. He was the author of a *History* in nine books that discussed the Persian invasions of Greece culminating in the defeat of the expedition of Xerxes in 479 BC. This work marks the foundation of the European historical tradition as well as forming one of the masterpieces of Greek literature. The first part of the *History* is devoted to the description of the rise of the Persian Empire under Cyrus, Cambyses and Darius I, including the conquest of Egypt in 525 BC. The latter event gave Herodotus an excuse to incorporate a long account of Egypt and its history which occupies the whole of Book II and the early part of Book III; references to things Egyptian occur not infrequently elsewhere in his narrative. While this account of Egypt draws to some degree on earlier work such as that of Hecataeus, it is largely the product of Herodotus' own inquiries, probably conducted largely during a visit to the country itself some time around 450 BC.

Herodotus' discussion of Egypt falls into two main sections: Book II, chapters 1–98, is devoted to the physical context (geology, geography, botany and zoology) and to a survey of Egyptian culture which embraces such topics as diet, clothing, technology, personal hygiene, medicine and particularly religion. The second section (Book II, chapter 99–Book III, chapters 43 and 61–6) is devoted mainly to history. This falls into two parts: chapters 99–142 of Book II cover the period from Menes, the alleged first human king of Egypt, to the reign of Sethos (Seti); the second section runs from Book II, chapter 147 (the reign of Psamtik I) down to, and including, the reign of Cambyses.

As a whole, Herodotus' discussion of Egypt is the earliest surviving consecutive account of pharaonic Egypt in any literary tradition; it has exercised an enormous influence on all subsequent discussions of the country in classical antiquity and later. Its accuracy has been the subject of much debate. There is indubitably an element of impressionism in his descriptions, and we certainly cannot expect from him the precision of a modern historical or scientific writer. Nevertheless, his observations on many aspects of Egyptian culture, despite occasional infelicities, have stood the test of scrutiny surprisingly well. The historical narrative, on the other hand, is uneven: the first section is largely made up of unofficial and often sensationalist Egyptian stories seriously contaminated by Greek material and is important to the modern scholar largely for providing access to the fifth century BC stratum in such traditions. The second section, based predominantly on Greek sources, is much more valuable. While retaining a good measure of folklore and being very much defined by Greek foci of interest, it still provides us with our only consecutive account of Egyptian history between 664 and 525 BC and, for all its faults, it continues to provide the bedrock on which all modern work on the period is based.

See also

Late and Ptolemaic periods, overview; Naukratis; Persians

Further reading

Lloyd, A.B. 1975–1980. *Herodotus, Book II*, 3 vols. Leiden.

Spiegelberg, W. 1927. *The Credibility of Herodotus' Account of Egypt*, trans. by A.M. Blackman. Oxford.

Wilson, J.A. 1970. *Herodotus in Egypt* (Scholae Adriani de Buck Memoriae Dicatae 5). Leiden.

ALAN B. LLOYD

Hierakonpolis

Hierakonpolis is the Greek name for the ancient site of Nekhen, which became the focus of an autonomous district at the end of the Ptolemaic period. The modern name of the site is Kom el-Ahmar, named after the red mound of potsherds in the low desert. Adjacent to the village of Kom el-Gemuwia, the site is located on the west bank of the Nile 17 km northwest of Edfu (25°05′ N, 32°47′ E). Its ancient name, Nekhen, was also the name of Nome III of Upper Egypt, although Nekheb, opposite Hierakonpolis on the east bank of the Nile, was the nome capital by the time of Senusret I (12th Dynasty). Hierakonpolis was the Predynastic capital of Upper Egypt, and possibly the southern limit of Egypt in late Predynastic times. The patron deity was Horus the Falcon, represented wearing the White Crown of Upper Egypt. The site owes it fame to the legendary prehistoric conquest of Lower Egypt and subsequent unification by the "Followers of Horus."

The Hierakonpolis region covers an area of about 144 km^2, and on the floodplain comprises the town enclosure of Nekhen, with its temple, and two outliers to the north and east. In the desert beyond the floodplain are settlements, kilns, cemeteries, tombs and petroglyphs. At the mouth of the Wadi Abul Suffian (Great Wadi) stands the imposing 3,705 m^2, recessed, mudbrick "Fort" structure, dated to King Khasekhemwy (2nd Dynasty) by an inscribed granite jamb. The most extensive settlements and cemeteries in the desert are Predynastic, including three deflated stone mounds, but there are Old Kingdom (Pepynenankh), Middle Kingdom (Horemkhauef), New Kingdom (Djehuty, Hormosi) and Roman tombs. Recent corings beneath Nekhen have revealed Predynastic occupation at a depth of 3.5 m below the 1st Dynasty level, and an earlier foundation for the city than was previously supposed. The main expansion of the town was in the Early Dynastic period and Old Kingdom, when the 320 m^2 enclosure wall was built. New Kingdom (Akhenaten, Seti I, Ramesses II, Ramesses IX) and Late period inscriptions were found in the temple, and the town site was leveled in the Ptolemaic period. Pockets of mixed Ptolemaic, New Kingdom and Early Dynastic sherds are found just beneath the present surface.

In the early 1880s, French scholars first investigated the New Kingdom tombs in the Burg el-Hamman (Pigeon Hill), about 2 km up the Great Wadi. From 1898–1900, James E. Quibell and Frederick W. Green excavated on behalf of the British Egyptian Research Account. Quibell's first season of work concentrated in the New Kingdom temple enclosure of Tuthmose III in the southern corner of the town enclosure. This area had obviously been sacred for a considerable time; within it were a circular revetted structure of sandstone blocks enclosing an artificial mound, limestone columns, and patches of sandstone pavement, which seem to date to the Early Dynastic period. In the Old Kingdom or early Middle Kingdom, a 30 m wide mudbrick building with five rooms was erected in the northwest of the temple enclosure. Life-size copper statues of the 6th Dynasty king Pepi I and his son Merenre were found in one of the chambers along with a red polished pottery lion and a slate statuette of Khasekhemwy. In another chamber was a gold falcon head with a headdress of a double plume and inlaid obsidian eyes, together with small stone vases, maceheads and a faïence W35 sign or sceptre. These cult objects had been cached either during the political disunity at the end of the Old Kingdom, or during rebuilding in the Middle Kingdom, but there is scant evidence for Middle Kingdom activity at the site except for a few royal inscriptions (Intef, Senusret I, Sobekhotep).

Other caches located in the temple area, notably the so-called "Main Deposit," confirmed the site's importance through the late Predynastic and Early Dynastic ceremonial objects found within them. These include the decorated maceheads of the (Dynasty 0) kings Scorpion and Narmer, the Narmer Palette, a stela, stone vases and a limestone statuette of Khasekhemwy, and the "Two Dog" decorated palette. Small votive statuettes in faïence, pottery and stone, of humans and animals, have also been found along with the mass of decorated and sculpted ivories, one inscribed for Narmer and another for King Den (1st Dynasty).

John Garstang of Liverpool University worked at Hierakonpolis with Harold Jones in 1905–6, in the temple and town of Nekhen and the Predynastic cemetery (Nagada IIc–IIIc) around and beneath the Fort. Henri de Morgan also excavated in the Fort cemetery and in the settlement across the wadi for the Brooklyn Museum in 1907–8. The British excavator Guy Brunton surveyed the desert-edge settlements in 1927, and Ambrose Lansing excavated more of the Fort cemetery and various other sites for the Metropolitan Museum in 1934. Werner Kaiser and Karl Butzer surveyed and mapped the desert in 1958.

Modern inter-disciplinary research began in 1967, led by the late Walter A. Fairservis, who concentrated on the excavation of the town site in a north–south traverse (in 1967, 1969, 1981 and 1987). An overall plan of the Early Dynastic structures was produced, and excavations followed the line of a building complex which leads from a large, mudbrick, niched façade gateway he discovered in 1969.

After an interruption of fieldwork for political reasons, the expedition resumed in 1978 under the direction of the late Michael A. Hoffman until 1990. Hoffman was not only responsible for important discoveries at Hierakonpolis, but also for new attitudes in settlement archaeology in the Nile Valley. Hoffman instigated the first topographical map of the region, undertook detailed survey and site identification, and related excavation to the geomorphological work of Hany Hamroush. In 1978, working in the large, desert-edge Predynastic settlement (Locality Hk29), he discovered a semi-subterranean, rectangular house, 4.0 × 3.5 m, with one calibrated radiocarbon date of 3435 ± 121 BC. Set in a complex of outbuildings with evidence of consecutive building phases, the house had lower walls of mudbrick, probably once surmounted by wattle and daub. Nearby is a kiln consisting of eight depressions with ceramic supports for large pots, possibly similar to a vat site for brewing wheat-based beer excavated by Jeremy Geller in 1988 northeast of the Fort (Locality Hk24A). The Fort cemetery seems to lack an elite section, although a large ceramic coffin with a decorated lid was found there in 1980.

Green undertook excavations in 1899, both in the town site of Nekhen, where he established the stratigraphy which has been confirmed by Fairservis and Hoffman, and in a desert-edge (Nagada II) cemetery (Locality 33). There he found five large rectangular tombs, similar to those in the elite cemetery T at Nagada, one of which (Tomb 100) had unique painted decoration on the walls. Shells from the tomb yielded a (calibrated) date of 3685 BC. Five sickle-shaped boats and a high-prowed black boat are depicted in a desert landscape with scenes of human and animal figures. Some of the poses, such as the "master of animals," were borrowed from the ancient Near East, and others, such as the king smiting the enemy, became classic Egyptian royal motifs.

Excavation has taken place (1980, 1982, 1985, 1997) in a large cemetery, 400 m in length, located in the Wadi Abul Suffian (Locality Hk6). Notable here are two large oval graves (Tombs 6 and 9), and Tomb 3, a large rectangular grave (2.50 × 1.80 m in area, and 1.80 m deep), with transitional (Nagada Ib–IIa) pottery. So far, no later Predynastic (Nagada IIc–d) graves have been located, but there are Nagada II surface finds.

In 1985, work in a section of the Predynastic town nearer the cultivation (Locality Hk29A) revealed a complex identified as a temple; associated ceramics date its use to Nagada IIb–IId. It consists of a large, parabolic-shaped courtyard, paved four or five times with smoothed clay. At the south end, to which the floor sloped up, was a deep hole with rocks inside which perhaps supported a free-standing pole, possibly surmounted by the totem of a god, or a ceremonial macehead. On the north side, postholes mark a gateway, while others connect with a brick wall and various out-buildings; this part may be associated with a Nagada IIIa reuse and re-paving. It is possible

that the 40 cm of sand found over the last courtyard floor was deliberately placed there in late Nagada III (Dynasty 0) times to create a mound similar to that in Nekhen. Opposite the gateway are four large postholes (1.7 m deep) which form the monumental façade of a 13 m wide structure, possibly the original "Great House" (*Per Wer*, i.e. temple) of Upper Egypt. There are traces of an unusual, sinusoidal mudbrick wall to the east. Artifacts included a significant mass of potsherds, with imported Palestinian types, and debris from the production of beads, stone vases and bifacial chert tools. Analysis of the faunal remains shows that adult cattle, sheep and goats were killed, while the heads were probably used elsewhere for ritual purposes. Large and dangerous aquatic Nile fauna, such as perch, turtle and crocodile, were caught for use in the complex.

Three important Nagada III tombs, all looted, have been excavated in the Great Wadi cemetery (Locality Hk6). At the east end, Tomb 1 is a large, mudbrick-lined, rectangular tomb (6.5 × 3.5 m in area, and 2.5 m deep), with one calibrated radiocarbon date of 2980 ±141 BC. It had been surmounted by a wood and reed building and surrounded by a picket fence. Near Tomb 1 is a rock overhang with graffiti chiefly of the early New Kingdom, including a glyph of a boat with a bull above it. Beside Tomb 1 on the west is Tomb 10 (4.70 × 1.90 m in area, and 1.90 m deep), which contained similar potsherds (Nagada IIIb) and a mud sealing with the hieroglyphic signs for "town" and "god." Some distance to the southeast is the slightly earlier Tomb 11 (5.0 × 2.40 m in area, and 1.75 m deep). Its grave goods included a wooden bed with carved bull's feet which had been thrown out by looters; beads and amulets in gold, silver, carnelian, garnet, copper, turquoise and lapis lazuli; ivory carvings; and stone and ceramic models of animals and humans. Pottery from Tomb 11 included types copying Palestinian imports and others similar to those found in the Main Deposit and at Locality Hk29A.

At the west of the cemetery, near the Predynastic tombs, a large rectangular tomb cut into the sandstone bedrock was cleared by Lansing in 1934 (No. 2; 6.25 × 2.1 m in area, and 3.5 m deep). Near its base is a small side chamber, originally sealed with two stones. Potsherds from the interior and surround excavated in 1980 suggest a Nagada III date. West of Tomb 2 were animal graves. Tomb 7 contained three cattle: a bull, cow and calf. Tomb 12 contained six baboons. Elephant, hippopotamus and crocodile bones were also found on this side of the cemetery.

Petroglyphs have been found in the desert at various places in addition to Locality Hk6. On the southeast side of the Great Wadi (Locality Hk61) are prehistoric depictions of boats, ungulates, elephants, a giraffe and a water carrier. The sandstone hill (Locality Hk64), which was altered by tomb tunneling in the Roman period, is notable for numerous petroglyphs of ostriches and boats, sometimes superimposed. Renée Friedman's excavations here in 1987 and 1996 revealed evidence dating to the Predynastic, Early Dynastic, Old Kingdom and Second Intermediate Period. The successive old Kingdom/Nubian A "camps" on this lookout post and an inscription in a pit with ostrich feathers are part of the ritual celebration of the yearly return of the goddess Hathor from Nubia.

See also

brewing and baking; dating techniques, prehistory; Early Dynastic period, overview; Neolithic and Predynastic stone tools; pottery, prehistoric; Predynastic period, overview; representational evidence, Predynastic

Further reading

Adams, B. 1995. *Ancient Nekhen: Garstang in the City of Hierakonpolis* (Egyptian Studies Association 3). Surrey.

Fairservis, W. 1986. *Excavations of the Archaic Remains East of the Niched Gate Season of 1981* (Hierakonpolis Project Occasional Papers in Anthropology 3). Poughkeepsie, NY.

Friedman, R.F. 1996. The Ceremonial Centre at Hierakonpolis: Locality 29A. In *Aspects of Early Egypt*, Proceedings of a Colloquium held at the British Museum in 1993, A.J. Spencer, ed., 16–35. London.

Hoffman, M.A., *et al.* 1982. *The Predynastic of Hierakonpolis. An Interim Report.* Egyptian Studies Association 1. Cairo.

Quibell, J.E., and F.W. Green 1900–2. *Hierakonpolis*, 1 and 2. Egyptian Research Account IV and V. London.

BARBARA ADAMS

Hu/Hiw (Diospolis Parva)

Hu (or Hiw), known as Diospolis Parva in Graeco-Roman times, is the name of a modern village 10 km southeast of Nag Hammadi (26°01′ N, 32°17′ E). In 1898–9 Flinders Petrie excavated a number of cemeteries from Hu to Semaineh, 16 km east of Hu. These included five Predynastic cemeteries, nine Dynastic cemeteries and two Roman period cemeteries. The Dynastic cemeteries have grave goods which Petrie assigned to the late Old Kingdom, 12th Dynasty, 18th Dynasty, and the First and Second Intermediate Periods. Petrie also excavated a Roman fort, which had been converted from a Ptolemaic temple, but inscribed blocks from the temple are still visible today. According to Petrie, round bastions were added to the mudbrick wall of the temple when the garrison of Diospolis Parva lived there in the second century AD.

In his excavations of Cemetery X, about 0.5 km southwest of the Roman fort, Petrie was the first to identify burials of what he called "Pan-graves." These were shallow, circular or oval graves with reused artifacts of Middle Kingdom date, such as cosmetic (*kohl*) vases and Egyptian pottery of the Second Intermediate Period, but also artifacts that were distinctly non-Egyptian. The latter included bracelets made of flat, rectangular shell beads threaded together in strips. Pan-grave pottery was also different from Egyptian pottery. These included bowls and cups of a handmade black ware with diagonal lines or "basket" patterns incised around the rim, and fine Black-topped Red class cups with everted rims that would later be known as "Kerma Ware" (from the kingdom of Kerma located near the Third Cataract in Upper Nubia). Stacked deposits of animal skulls, cut away at the back leaving only the frontal bones and horns and painted with red ocher and black carbon, were also excavated. The largest of these deposits contained the skulls of 138 goats, 5 oxen, 5 calves and 1 sheep, stacked in rows facing west, along with a pair of copper tweezers.

Petrie correctly concluded that the Pan-graves belonged to (foreign) people who came into Egypt after the fall of the Middle Kingdom. Pan-grave pottery and Kerma Ware were also excavated by Petrie at another cemetery (YS) to the west of Cemetery X, where they were found in rectangular (Egyptian-style) graves with mainly Egyptian pottery and artifacts. The YS burials could either represent increasingly "Egyptianized" burials of Pan-grave people who were becoming assimilated in Egyptian society, or Egyptians who had some contact with the local Pan-grave people.

In Petrie's 1901 publication of these excavations he also published his seriation system, which he called "Sequence Dating," based on the relative sequence of Predynastic grave goods.

Predynastic evidence

In 1989 Kathryn Bard did a reconnaissance survey for Predynastic settlements in the vicinity of Petrie's excavated Predynastic cemeteries, and in 1991 two Predynastic settlements, HG (Halfiah Gibli) and SH (Semaineh), were excavated. HG and SH are situated on spurs of the low desert above the floodplain, and to the south of the el-Ranan canal. HG is the settlement associated with the cemetery that Petrie called Abadiya.

During the 1989 and 1991 fieldwork, some observations were also made about the later (Dynastic) archaeological evidence. In the 1980s Egyptian Antiquities Organization archaeologists from the Qena office had excavated an Old Kingdom cemetery with rectangular grave pits (unpublished) near housing for workers at the Nag Hammadi aluminum factory. In 1991 a previously undeveloped area in the aluminum factory had been bulldozed for a water purification plant, and a number of whole offering bowls and beer jars from Old Kingdom tombs, as well as a ceramic offering stand, were collected there.

Excavations in 1991 began at Site SH, which was thought to be a late Predynastic settlement because of the Nagada III grave goods excavated there by Petrie. Petrie named his latest Predynastic period "Semainean" after the modern village next to this cemetery. One calibrated radiocarbon date of *circa* 3780–3530 BC (OxA-2184) had been obtained on a charcoal sample from a test pit excavated in 1989. The test pit from which the sample (OxA-2184) was obtained was near what is now thought to be an early (Nagada I–IIa?) cemetery area, excavated by Petrie to the southwest of the site. Indicative of an early Predynastic date for this cemetery area, a White Cross-lined class sherd (Nagada Ic to IIa in date) was excavated in another test pit in this cemetery in 1989, and a fragment of a ceramic anthropomorphic figurine was found in a grave pit in 1991. Although he did not differentiate two cemeteries, Petrie excavated another cemetery area (H) on a small spur east of the village site, and this area is probably where the mainly Nagada III grave goods were found. Excavations at SH in 1991 revealed a site with a great mixture of ceramics, predominantly dating to the Old Kingdom but mixed with a few Predynastic and New Kingdom sherds. No evidence of domestic structures was found at SH, and the site is deflated. Large chunks of vitrified clay were found on the surface of SH and were thought to be the remains of a pottery kiln(s), but no kiln structures were found during the excavations. The ceramics consisted mostly of sherds of very gritty-tempered Old Kingdom bread molds, and SH may have been a kiln site for the production of Old Kingdom bread molds. A calibrated radiocarbon date of *circa* 2860–2460 BC (OxA-2185) obtained from a charcoal sample from this feature would place it firmly in the Old Kingdom.

Excavations at Site HG in 1991 did not reveal any evidence of houses or any other structures, and it is presumed that cultivation in the 1950s and 1960s on the main spur destroyed any such features. When Petrie visited this site in 1898 he stated that it was "entirely plundered," and the settlement was probably constructed of more ephemeral (organic) materials.

Ceramics consisted of wares belonging to the Predynastic Nagada culture of Upper Egypt. Large quantities of chaff-tempered ware (Rough-class) were intermixed with smaller quantities of polished red, black and Black-topped Red class. The Rough-class represents large and smaller storage jars, and cooking vessels and bowls, while the finely polished classes represent a better quality material, possibly for serving food. Sherds of Predynastic bread molds were also identified. These ceramics probably date to late Nagada I and early Nagada II, but with the possibility that there may be a small later (mid-Nagada II) component. A pot-stand, consisting of a pinched ring of clay, tapered at the top, and a loop handle of Nile clay, imitating imported (Palestinian) pots, were also excavated at HG.

Stone tools consisted of sickle blades (some with polish), some bifacial tools, flakes and grinding stone fragments. No projectile points or other hunting/fishing tools were found, and there were relatively few scrapers. Numerous grinders and grinding stone fragments were also found on the surface of HG; the stone tools were those of an agricultural village. Evidence was also found for the major Predynastic (and Dynastic) cereal crops, emmer wheat and barley, in the form of carbonized grains and segments of cereal heads, confirming the agricultural subsistence base.

To the east of the spur on which the main Predynastic settlement at HG is located is a smaller spur where two excavation units revealed numerous pits with much wood charcoal and ash, but very few other botanical remains. Burned and fire-cracked rocks and cobbles were also found, as well as a number of heat-treated flakes and tools of flint. Much debris from all stages of stone tool manufacture was also excavated, and it is thought that this was an industrial area for flint working (by heat treating).

Other evidence on this spur also suggests stone working. A small carnelian bead, an unfinished agate bead and an unworked green stone, identified as green feldspar, were recovered in the excavations. Green feldspar was used for beads beginning in Predynastic times, as were agate and carnelian. Also excavated was a small ground stone palette of hard sandstone, slightly trapezoidal in shape with rounded corners. Its size (6.0 × 4.1 cm) suggests domestic use, as it is not of the larger, more elaborate types found in elite Predynastic burials. An end fragment of a large rhomboid slate palette (late Nagada I, early Nagada II) was also excavated along with a polishing stone. Large mammal bones also found here may have been the raw material for bone tools and toilet articles.

Analysis of the materials found at HG suggests a widespread exchange network in which even a relatively small farming village was engaged. Agate is found locally in wadi deposits, but the green feldspar and carnelian come from the Eastern Desert. Grinding stones collected on the surface of HG consisted of igneous and metamorphic rocks from the Eastern Desert and Aswan. Two small lumps of copper were recovered, and the nearest copper mines are also in the Eastern Desert. A (pierced?) cowrie shell from the Red Sea was also found.

Complex economic interaction is also suggested by another artifact excavated at HG: a fragment of a mud-sealing. The sealing was created when a mud lump was impressed over three loops of string tied around a jar (or some kind of container). The existence of such a sealing suggests the exchange of valued goods in a regional or long-distance, and not local, exchange network. Such economic evidence from the settlement at HG would also correlate with grave goods excavated by Petrie in sometimes exotic materials, such as lapis lazuli and gold, from the nearby Cemetery B (Abadiya).

See also

agriculture, introduction of; Kerma; Neolithic and Predynastic stone tools; Pan-grave culture; Petrie, Sir William Matthew Flinders; pottery, prehistoric; Predynastic period, overview

Further reading

Bard, K.A. 1992. Preliminary report: The 1991 Boston University excavations at Halfiah Gibli and Semaineh, Upper Egypt. *NARCE* 158/159: 11–15.

Petrie, W.M.F. 1901. *Diospolis Parva. The Cemeteries of Abadiyeh and Hiw.* London.

KATHRYN A. BARD
SALLY SWAIN

Hyksos

"Hyksos" is the Greek rendering of the Egyptian term *ḥḳꜣ ḫꜣstwt* (rulers of the foreign countries). Originally, this was a term for foreign rulers or chieftains, especially those in southwest Asia. It later became the official title of the foreign kings who ruled Egypt for about 108 years during the Second Intermediate Period. Manetho placed these kings in the 15th–16th Dynasties. Following Manetho, the account by the historian Flavius Josephus describes the Hyksos as invaders who ruthlessly burned Egyptian cities and razed temples; Egyptians were massacred or enslaved. Written about 1,600 years after the Hyksos rule in Egypt, Josephus's history is suspect, and for a long time the origins and development of Hyksos rule were controversial. Fortunately, recent archaeological investigations at Tell ed-Dab'a, the Hyksos capital of Avaris, and in the Wadi Tumilat have contributed considerably toward a better understanding of this obscure period.

In the late Middle Kingdom, especially during the 13th Dynasty, there is evidence at Tell ed-Dab'a of increasing settlement by peoples from Syro-Palestine called Amorites or Canaanites. In the northeastern Nile Delta soldiers, sailors, shipbuilders and workers from the Levant were settled by the Egyptian crown in order to create a base for foreign trade and economic and military activities. According to papyri found at Lahun and archaeological evidence in the vicinity of Lisht, a similar community existed near the Middle Kingdom capital of *Ity-tꜣwy*. While Asiatics at the royal residence had more influence in the 13th Dynasty court, the Asiatic community at Avaris seems to have been responsible for the creation of Hyksos rule in Egypt. After the rise of a small independent kingdom in the northeastern Delta ruled by a local Egyptian dynasty of former officials or military officers, with a capital at Avaris, a local dynasty of Asiatic origin gained control and created the nucleus of the later Hyksos kingdom. With an army, ships and perhaps kinsmen in the royal residence, they were able to establish loose control over Egypt by intimidation or force. Evidence for this comes from a stela of King Neferhotep III (late 13th Dynasty) that mentions hordes of foreigners roaming around Thebes.

The first Hyksos king, Salitis, was crowned in Memphis, but, according to Manethonian tradition, he used Avaris as a power base. There is also inscriptional evidence for Hyksos strongholds at Nefrusi in Middle Egypt and at Gebelein, south of Luxor. From Egyptian texts, especially two stelae of King Kamose and the Carnarvon Tablet, and also later sources such as the Papyrus Sallier I, we may conclude that other dynasties were contemporaneous with the Hyksos of the 15th Dynasty, and were bound as vassals to their overlords in Avaris. Among these contemporaneous dynasties were the 17th Dynasty in Thebes and local chieftains in Middle Egypt. It seems increasingly likely that kings of the Manethonian 16th Dynasty, also Hyksos, resided at Sharuhen (Tell el-'Ajjul) and controlled a small kingdom in southern Palestine. Perhaps the 16th Dynasty can even be considered a sub-dynasty of the 15th Dynasty. Other minor dynasties of Hyksos were located in coastal strongholds and in northern Palestine, such as at the site of Kabri. The rest of Palestine was politically independent and perhaps even in conflict with the Hyksos, as may be evidenced by the enormous fortifications at major town sites in Palestine during the late phase of this period.

The Hyksos were able to make Avaris into one of the major trading centers in the eastern Mediterranean. They continued to worship the northern Syrian storm god, Ba'al Zephon/

Hadad, whose cult had been introduced earlier in Avaris by their ancestors. This foreign god was identified by the Egyptians of the 14th Dynasty with the Egyptian god Seth. Thus the cult of Seth of Avaris was created around 1700 BC, and continued to have an Asiatic identity until the Ramesside period (19th–20th Dynasties).

The economic strength of the Hyksos dynasty rested primarily on the Avaris–Sharuhen connection. Southern Palestine was exploited for its olive oil and wine, which were exported to Egypt in huge quantities. These products were also shipped to other places in the eastern Mediterranean, as demonstrated by the results of neutron activation analysis of their ceramic containers done at the MASCA laboratory, University of Pennsylvania. Other trade connections existed, especially with Cyprus.

The rulers of the 15th Dynasty, however, are elusive. Unfortunately, an important papyrus with a king list, written in the 19th Dynasty and now in Turin, reveals only the name of the last ruler, Khamudi, and the duration of the Hyksos dynasty, 108 (?) years. It is also difficult to correlate the corrupted kings' names from the Manethonian tradition with names preserved on monuments of the 15th Dynasty.

There are numerous scarabs with the prenomen Ma'aibre, and others with the name Sheshy, probably the same king. (Sheshy is probably only a diminutive of another name.) The widespread distribution of these scarabs, from Kerma in Upper Nubia to the southern coast of the Levant, suggests an important ruler of the Hyksos. However, no major monument of this king is known.

Recently the name of a major Hyksos ruler was revealed on a limestone door jamb from the Hyksos citadel at Tell ed-Dab'a. Inscribed on this block is the official title of a Hyksos king and the West Semitic name, "Seker Her" (Sikru Haddu, a theophoric name connected with the Syrian storm god Hadad).

To judge from the number of inscriptions of Khayan, this Hyksos king must have been of special importance. A lid of an alabaster ointment jar inscribed with Khayan's name was found in the palace at Knossos on Crete. A fragment of another ointment jar inscribed with his name was found at Boghazköy (Hattusas), the capital of the growing Hittite empire. Both artifacts were probably diplomatic gifts to the two most important courts in the eastern Mediterranean at that time. The origin of a basalt lion inscribed with this king's name, purchased in Bagdad, is uncertain.

Khayan continued to usurp royal statues of the Middle Kingdom, as did some of the ephemeral kings of the 13th Dynasty. Many statues were brought to Avaris to furnish temples and royal buildings. The stela of a son of Khayan has been found at Tell ed-Dab'a. He can probably be identified with the Hyksos king Iannas, known from the Manethonian king lists.

According to the Turin papyrus, King 'Aawoserre Apophis reigned for about forty years toward the end of the Hyksos dynasty. Two other prenomens of this king are also preserved. During his reign Egyptian science continued to flourish: the Rhind Papyrus (British Museum: EA 10.1057, 10.058), a mathematical treatise, was written in the 33rd year of Apophis's reign. Egyptian literature was also copied then.

Apophis was a contemporary of the Upper Egyptian king Kamose, who launched an attack against his overlord and advanced to Avaris. An attempt by the Hyksos to persuade the king of Kush (Kerma culture, Sudan) to occupy Upper Egypt while Kamose's army was engaged in the Delta failed when the courier carrying the letter was stopped by Kamose's troops. Kamose, however, was unable to take Avaris. He withdrew and died most probably in the same year. His successor, Ahmose, was far too young (about five years old) to continue the campaign of his predecessor.

When Ahmose became an adult he attacked the Hyksos. Between his 15th and 18th regnal years he seized Memphis and then besieged Avaris, probably for a long time. According to Josephus, the Egyptians despaired of taking Avaris and the Hyksos were able to negotiate a retreat with their people to Palestine. We do not know if this is historically accurate, but at Avaris there is no evidence of a layer over the entire town created by conflagration. Only in the area of the citadel, where a sophisticated defense system was recently discovered, is there evidence of some kind of destruction. Ahmose pursued the Hyksos into southern Palestine and after three years of siege he destroyed the second largest stronghold of the Hyksos, Sharuhen (Tell el-'Ajjul), 7 km south of Gaza.

In retrospect, the Hyksos as a foreign dynasty in Egypt were unpopular. Queen Hatshepsut's *Speos Artemidos* inscription near Beni Hasan states that they ruled "without Re" and that she rebuilt the shrines which were neglected and had fallen into disrepair during their dynasty. In later traditions (Manetho, Josephus), the recollection of their presence in Egypt was even worse.

One explanation for the bad reputation of the Hyksos is provided by the large number of Middle Kingdom statues, especially private ones, found in the Levant and on Crete. Such statues have also been found at Kerma, the capital of the Nubian kingdom of Kush. The Hyksos plundered Egyptian temples and tombs and profitably used these craft goods in trade. Most of the usurped royal statues were removed to Avaris and later everything was moved to Pi-Ramesses, the capital of the 19th Dynasty. In the 21st–22nd Dynasties, the statues were moved again to the new capital at Tanis. Such large-scale appropriation of earlier statues would explain why no court art was created by the Hyksos.

A major accomplishment of the Hyksos was their trade network in the eastern Mediterranean. They also introduced the horse and chariot in Egypt and new technologies in ceramic production and metal working, especially in the production of weapons. Their lasting impact on Egypt was perhaps an indirect one. By pursuing the Hyksos to their last stronghold in southern Palestine, the Egyptians soon became involved on a large scale in the politics of the ancient Near East, and thus became one of the major powers in the Late Bronze Age.

See also

Canaanites; chariots; Cypriot peoples; fauna, domesticated; Gebelein; Kerma; Lahun, town; Manetho; New Kingdom, overview; Second Intermediate Period, overview; Tell ed-Dab'a, Second Intermediate Period; Wadi Tumilat

Further reading

Bietak, M. 1980. Hyksos. In *LÄ* 3: 93–103.
——. 1996. *Avaris, The Captial of the Hyksos: New Excavation Results.* London.
Hayes, W.C. 1973. Egypt: from the death of Ammenemes III to Seqenenre' II. In *The Cambridge Ancient History* 2(1): 42–76. Cambridge.
Mazar, B. 1968. The Middle Bronze Age in Palestine. *IEJ* 18: 65–97.
Redford, D.B. 1992. *Egypt, Canaan and Israel in Ancient Times.* Princeton, NJ.
Van Seters, J. 1966. *The Hyksos: A New Investigation.* New Haven, CT.

MANFRED BIETAK

I

irrigation

Like the lower Mississippi and middle Niger rivers, the Egyptian Nile has a "convex" floodplain, subdivided into gently undulating basins that flood and drain naturally. Higher ground is provided by the levees that border the channel and also delineate abandoned river arms or secondary channels that diverge from the main river. As a first step to irrigation control, breaches in the main levees can be artificially opened or closed to facilitate or prolong flooding. As a second step, such ridges of higher ground can be reinforced or raised with earthen embankments. As a third step, water can be selectively directed to particular sectors by cutting canals directly from the river. Finally, particularly large basins that are difficult to manage can be subdivided by transverse dikes, in the form of earthen dams. In other words, artificial irrigation along the Egyptian Nile served to enhance the inherent qualities of the natural flood basins in the interest of greater water control.

Functional examples of basin irrigation were documented in Egypt during the 1880s, prior to the construction of barrages and high-lying canal systems that increasingly changed the topography. Since inauguration of the High Dam at Aswan, most of the Nile silt is deposited in Lake Nasser and water is fed in measured increments to each irrigation unit, with the result that fertility is not renewed and salinization has become a problem. Traditional basin flooding deposited a fresh increment of organic silt in the basins on an annual basis, precluding the need for manure or nitrogen-building crops except in gardens used for double cropping. Salt was not a problem because the basins were naturally flushed out as the flood ebbed. The system was therefore sustainable.

There is no direct archaeological evidence for irrigation except for representational art and inscriptions, such as the inscribed rocks of the nilometer at Elephantine. The earliest allusion to irrigation is a carved macehead of the Scorpion King (Dynasty 0, *circa* 3100 BC), shown with hoe in hand, ceremonially opening a canal, as he is offered the traditional basket and broom used to move earth. Included are figures of two workmen with hoes next to the canal, and a schematic vignette of a parcel of irrigated land, with four panels of long lots, apparently divided by three parallel canals. The last is as significant as the symbolic role of the king in inaugurating the irrigation season, because it implies the presence of canal grids somewhere in Egypt. Old Kingdom records mention canal digging and basin creation, on royal initiative. Middle Kingdom reliefs occasionally show men carrying two containers of water attached to a shoulder yoke, presumably to water gardens requiring special attention. The first representation of lifting devices come from the Amarna period, namely, the bucket-and-lever "sweep" or *shaduf*, introduced from Mesopotamia. Such *shaduf*s are shown raising water from a canal, to tend to ornamental trees in a garden, in one case next to a large pool. *Shaduf*s can only raise water 1–2 m, one bucket at a time, and can be set up in a series to draw water out of the low-water Nile channel, but they are suitable for only small-scale water distribution. The much more ingenious, animal-powered, chain-and-bucket waterwheel (*saqiya*) first came into use during Ptolemaic times, after its introduction from southwest Asia. It alone could lift water continuously, as much as 7.5 m, to irrigate large areas. Its introduction coincides with the appearance of the first summer grain, sorghum, presumably because the *saqiya* was indispensable for growing two crops per year on the same plot.

Basin irrigation operated on a local scale, according to natural units with a few such interfingering basins. Although larger canals may have been built for navigation purposes during the New Kingdom, traditional (pre-barrage) canals of the nineteenth century were short, shallow and not interconnected, probably because they would silt up rapidly. Water allocation in one set of basins had no bearing on the amount of water received in the next downstream set, so that each operated independently of the other. During the nineteenth century, village headmen were responsible for mobilizing labor for maintenance and for controlling levee breaks, and Roman period records tell of canal cleaning in the Fayum at the behest of a public surveyor, by collaborative corvée labor supervised by a local official. Indeed, there is no record of any Dynastic title for an official responsible for irrigation as such, at either the national or provincial level. There never was an integrated system of basin or canal management, or water allocation. This differed from Mesopotamia, where control could be applied on the arterial canal at the head of a radial system. Radial canals were introduced in the Fayum under the Ptolemies, as a royal project, but even here there is no record of centralized management.

Egyptian irrigation closely imitated the natural pulses of energy typical of a seasonal, tropical river. Its management defied centralization and was handled on a community basis. Unlike in the Karl Wittfogel model, irrigation never involved a managerial bureaucracy, nor did it become an instrument of authoritarian control.

See also

Nile, modern hydrology; subsistence and diet in Dynastic Egypt

Further reading

Butzer, K.W. 1976. *Early Hydraulic Civilization in Egypt*. Chicago.

——. 1984. Schaduf. *LÄ* 5: 520–1.

——. 1996. Irrigation, raised fields and state management: Wittfogel redux? *Antiquity* 70: 200–4.

Dunham, D. 1938. The biographical inscriptions of Nekhebu in Boston and Cairo. *JEA* 24: 1–8.

Harlan, J.R., and J. Pasquereau. 1969. Décrue agriculture in Mali. *Economic Botany* 23: 70–4.

Westerman, W.L. 1925. Dike corvée in Roman Egypt. *Aegyptus* 6: 121–9.

Willcocks, W., and J.I. Craig. 1913. *Egyptian Irrigation*. London.

KARL W. BUTZER

Israelites

The term "Israelites" here refers principally to the peoples and states of ancient Israel and Judah, from their emergence in Canaan just before 1200 BC, until the end of the Judean monarchy in 586 BC. Only the periods when Israel's history may have been affected by Egypt will be discussed.

Patriarchal era

In Biblical tradition, the prehistory of Israel includes an episode when the Patriarchs, or ancestors of later Israel, migrated from Canaan into Egypt in a time of famine. In this account Joseph, Jacob's son, rose to power in the Egyptian court, only to fall out of favor later. This story supposedly has its setting in the Hyksos period, when Asiatics ruled briefly in northern Egypt, and in its aftermath. Archaeological and textual studies, however, have cast doubts on the historicity of the entire Patriarchal narrative.

The exodus

The Biblical tradition continues by picking up the story at a time when the proto-Israelites were enslaved in Egypt. They were then miraculously delivered from Pharaoh's armies by Moses, the founder of Israelite religion, who led them on a forty-year odyssey through the Sinai Desert to the borders of the promised land. Reckoning on the basis of internal Biblical chronology, these events would fall in the fifteenth century BC, and thus they might be connected with the expulsion of the Hyksos in the early 18th Dynasty. Again, however, recent archaeological discoveries in Israel and the West Bank have shown that the majority of the proto-Israelites had probably never been in Egypt. They were displaced Canaanites who had fled the Late Bronze Age city-states and had colonized the sparsely settled hill country frontiers of central Palestine. There was no military conquest of Canaan, only a socio-economic revolution. Furthermore, the emergence of early Israel must be placed not in the fifteenth century BC, but shortly before and after 1200 BC. Thus the Biblical story of the exodus and conquest of Canaan has little basis in fact. The Egyptian elements in the Biblical story—the Joseph saga, a few Egyptian names like Moses, references to the "store cities of Pithom and Ramesses" in the Delta—can all be shown to be literary devices. They are most easily accounted for in the Saite Dynasty (26th Dynasty) or Persian period (27th–31st Dynasties), precisely when the Biblical tradition was being edited into its final form.

In summary, the patriarchal and exodus/conquest narratives in the Bible may rest on genuine oral traditions, or even on distant memories of a few actual historical events, of the Hyksos and Ramesside (19th–20th Dynasties) eras. Later tradition, however, has set Israelite prehistory into a supposed Egyptian context that greatly exaggerates any real role that Egypt could have played in the formulation of the Israelite people and state. The best documented and most significant connection remains the well known "Israel" Stela of Merenptah (19th Dynasty), which simply demonstrates that an ethnic group in Canaan calling itself "Israel" was known to the Egyptians at that time. Yet this inscription is aware of nothing else about ancient Israel: no long sojourn in Egypt, and no exodus from Egypt.

Solomonic era

The period of the Judges, *circa* twelfth–eleventh centuries BC, was a period when Israel was completely isolated from Egypt, locked in struggle with local Canaanite and newly arrived Philistine peoples. During the reign of Solomon (*circa* 960–920 BC), however, at the end of the United Monarchy, two Biblical stories reintroduce Egypt. I Kings 9:15–17 recounts that an Egyptian pharaoh—in this case, possibly Siamen of the 21st Dynasty—partially destroyed the city of Gezer, then ceded it to Solomon as a dowry accompanying an Egyptian princess offered in marriage to the Israelite king. The latter element seems fanciful; but modern excavations at Gezer have revealed a mid-tenth century BC destruction layer, followed immediately by new fortifications of a distinctly Israelite type.

According to Biblical tradition (I Kings 14:25, 26), in the fifth year after Solomon's death, *circa* 918 BC, Pharaoh "Shishak"—clearly Sheshonk of the 22nd Dynasty—conducted a raid on Palestine. Biblical historians and Palestinian archaeologists have quite plausibly identified some twenty destruction layers in Israel with Sheshonk's raid. A fragment of a victory stela was actually found at Megiddo in northern Palestine (although churned up in later fills). Following this, there was virtually no Egyptian influence in Israel or Judah for 200 years, throughout most of the Divided Monarchy. Egyptian amulets (*wadjet* eyes or Bes figures) are found in tombs of the eighth–seventh centuries BC, but these are of minor significance.

Assyrian and Babylonian periods

Although the expansion of the Neo-Assyrian empire to the borders of Egypt in the eighth century BC might have drawn Egypt into Asia to stem the advance, it did not. In II Kings 17:4, King Hoshea of Israel is said to have approached the "King of Egypt" for help (probably Tefnakht of the 24th Dynasty), but that is the only evidence we have.

By the time of the Neo-Babylonian advance, however, Egypt had to intervene in Asia. Thus by the time of the famous Battle of Carchemish in 609 BC, Egypt had allied itself with the last of the Assyrians, partly as a power-broker to check the rise of the Babylonians to power. Pharaoh Neko II (*circa* 610–595 BC) intervened in the battle, marching through Palestine on his way to the Euphrates, during which King Josiah of Judah was killed. Having lost the battle, Neko deposed Josiah's son Jehoahaz and deported him to Egypt (II Kings 23:31–5). Following that, Egypt dominated Judah for several years, during which the Babylonians rose to power under Nebuchadnezzar. Neko attempted to intervene once again at the second Battle of Carchemish in 605 BC, but the Egyptian forces were dealt a resounding defeat.

Egyptian influence on Hebrew literature

Biblical scholars have suggested that Egyptian influence can be discerned in several strands of the literary tradition in the Hebrew Bible. The story of Joseph, which is cited above, has been compared with the Egyptian *Tale of the Two Brothers*. Proverbs 22:17–24 may have been modeled partly upon the *Instruction of Amenmope*. Other traces of direct borrowing, however, are rare. Only a generalized Egyptian influence can be seen, for instance in some of the "wisdom literature" (i.e. portions of Proverbs, Job and Ecclesiastes); but the genre of "wisdom" literature was, in any case, very widespread in the ancient Near East.

See also

Assyrians; Canaanites; Hyksos; Late and Ptolemaic periods, overview; Levantine peoples (Iron Age); New Kingdom, overview; Persians; Second Intermediate Period, overview

Further reading

Dever, W.G. 1990. *Recent Archaeological Discoveries and Biblical Research*. Seattle, WA.

Finkelstein, I. 1988. *The Archaeology of the Israelite Settlement*. Jerusalem.

Herrmann, S. 1973. *Israel in Egypt*. London.

Kitchen, K. 1977. *The Bible in its World*. Exeter.

Redford, D.B. 1992. *Egypt, Canaan and Israel in Ancient Times*. Princeton, NJ.

Shanks, H., ed. 1988. *Ancient Israel: A Short History from Abraham to the Roman Destruction of the Temple*. Washington, DC.

WILLIAM G. DEVER

J

jewelry

Jewelry was an important component of burials in ancient Egypt in Predynastic and Dynastic times. Unfortunately, much ancient jewelry, especially in precious metals, has been lost to grave-robbers, and what is found today in museums is only a small fraction of what was actually produced. In spite of continuous grave-robbing, the jewelry that has been excavated in burials is a major source of information about symbolism in the mortuary cult, and tomb scenes and statues are also informative about the use of jewelry in daily life.

Beginning in Predynastic times (fourth millennium BC), men and women wore simple jewelry or amulets to protect themselves from illness, accidents, dangerous animals, evil spirits or dangers in nature. Amulets come in different shapes. At Naga ed-Deir, oryx and bull-shaped amulets made of gold foil wrapped around a core were found in an Early Dynastic grave. A beetle amulet with an inlaid emblem of the goddess Neith was found in the same grave. Beetle amulets reappear in the tombs of queens of the Old Kingdom. Amulets shaped like hieroglyphs, which are symbols of protection and good wishes, have been found in the 12th Dynasty burials of princesses at Lahun and Dahshur.

Predynastic figurines of women are shown wearing strings of beads around the neck and ankles. Complete necklaces, bracelets, girdles, rings and a circlet have been found in graves as early as the Badarian period. Early Predynastic (Nagada I) beads are made of gold, silver, copper and faïence. Beads of amethyst, calcite, carnelian, chalcedony, garnet, green feldspar, jasper (brown, green, red, yellow), obsidian and rock crystal appear in Nagada II times. Malachite and steatite were introduced later.

Bracelets developed from Predynastic bangles made of ivory or bone. During the Old Kingdom more elaborate silver or gold bangles with inlays, or strands of beads joined together by spacers, appear. Bands of beads were also worn around the upper arm.

"Dog" collars (choker necklaces) were worn by women only from the 4th Dynasty through the 6th Dynasty. More popular were broad collars, worn from the end of the 3rd Dynasty or the beginning of the 4th Dynasty through the Late period. These collars are made of strings of simple beads or flower-shaped beads (and sometimes ones shaped like hieroglyphs), which are held apart by spacers or sheets of gold, silver or copper foil. The famous statues of Rahotep and Nofret (early 4th Dynasty) in the Cairo Museum are painted with a broad collar around Nofret's neck and an amulet hanging on a string around Rahotep's neck. Broad collars were first worn only by women, but beginning in the 5th Dynasty men are also shown wearing them. Sometimes these collars have counter-weights hanging down the back.

The statue of Nofret is also painted with a diadem of rosettes, similar to actual diadems made of gold with inlays found at Giza. Diadems from the 12th Dynasty tombs of the princesses at Dahshur and Lahun have floral elements made of cloisonné work and gold wire. Some of these diadems are mounted with the royal uraeus (cobra) or vulture. Later headdresses worn by minor wives of Tuthmose III (18th Dynasty) were influenced by jewelry from Mitanni (a kingdom in Syria and northern Mesopotamia). They consist of circlets decorated with gazelles' heads or even the head of a stag with large antlers.

Rosettes or tubes of gold were sometimes strung in the hair (wigs) by noblewomen. Carnelian rings worn in the hair came into fashion for commoners in the New Kingdom.

From the Early Dynastic period through the Middle Kingdom, kings wore bead "aprons" hanging from elaborately decorated belts with inlaid clasps and attached animal tails. On the Narmer Palette (Dynasty 0), the king is depicted with an apron covering his loins. Pendants on this apron are decorated with an image (of the goddess Bat?) and strings of beads. Bead aprons could also be worn by women. The earliest known example is from the 12th Dynasty tomb of the Lady Senebtisi at Lisht; other examples are known from the Middle Kingdom, including those of the princesses buried at Dahshur.

Broad belts are also made of beads fastened with gold or gilded buckles with inlays. Girdles made of cowrie shells were worn by women around the hips. Because of the shell's resemblance to a partly closed eye such adornment may have had symbolic value to ward off the evil eye from a woman's womb.

On the Narmer Palette, a sandal bearer following the king is shown wearing a pectoral necklace in the shape of a *naos* (shrine) hanging from a string. Pectoral necklaces belonging to the princesses buried at Lahun and Dahshur are some of the finest examples of jewelry from ancient Egypt. On these pectorals are scenes symbolic of royal power, crafted in gold with inlays of carnelian, lapis lazuli and turquoise. Some of these pectorals show evidence of wear, but others appear not to have been worn and were made only for use in the afterlife. Beginning in the New Kingdom pectorals are decorated with scenes to protect the deceased, both males and females, and to help them survive the journey and trials of the afterlife. Examples in precious metals and stones have been found in royal tombs (Tutankhamen's in Thebes, and those of Sheshonk and Osorkon of the 22nd Dynasty in Tanis). Cheaper pectorals made of faïence or stone were placed in the mummy wrappings of anyone who could afford them. Such pectorals were often designed with the image of the rising sun, a symbol of

resurrection, or with different gods who would protect the deceased.

During the Old Kingdom only women wore anklets, but in the Middle Kingdom they became fashionable for men as well. During the New Kingdom, anklets are found only on goddesses.

Only a few examples of earrings date to the Middle Kingdom, but they become much more common in the early 18th Dynasty. Possibly earrings were introduced from southwest Asia during the Second Intermediate Period. In the New Kingdom earrings were worn by both men and women. Early earrings are simple rings, but later a greater variety is seen: hoops, earplugs, rings with or without pendants, and large disks and elaborate hangings decorated with symbolic scenes.

Finger rings are rare until the Middle Kingdom. Among the treasures of the 12th Dynasty princesses are rings with scarabs made of different materials or with plain or inscribed bezels. Finger rings become increasingly elaborate in the New Kingdom and Late period, and some were even designed with simple scenes.

Most of the jewelry that has survived has been found in tombs. Jewelry worn during an individual's lifetime was placed in the tomb to be used in the afterlife. In addition, he/she was furnished with funerary jewelry to which magical properties were ascribed to safeguard his/her well-being in the afterlife. A pendant depicted on a Middle Kingdom coffin is described as one "for the hereafter." Jewelry and amulets, which show no signs of wear and were usually placed between the mummy wrappings, are often of less skillful workmanship. The materials used are fragile and of inferior quality, such as a core of clay or wood covered with gold foil. On the royal mummies, ornaments of the royal deities spread their protective wings across the king's chest. The best known example of such jewelry is from the mummy of Tutankhamen, found with all its ornaments intact within the wrappings.

Tomb scenes and sculpture show that men, women and children all wore jewelry. During the Old Kingdom workers were rewarded with jewelry. The king bestowed his followers with the "gold of honor" or the "gold of valor" and officials of the New Kingdom mention such gifts with pride in their tombs. The royal reward of jewelry is a favorite scene in tombs of the Amarna period (late 18th Dynasty) and it appears on stelae from Horbeit dating to the reign of Ramesses II. In the Amarna period scenes Akhenaten, accompanied by his wife and daughters, leans out of a ceremonial window ("window of appearances") and hands gold necklaces down to the honored individual. Royal gifts to honor subjects include broad collars and strings of golden lens-shaped beads. Amulets shaped like a fly or lion are usually interpreted as rewards for bravery, although fly amulets were also included in the treasures of Queen Ahhotep (beginning of the 18th Dynasty) and three queens of Tuthmose III.

Large quantities of jewelry were also produced for the gods and stored in temple treasuries. During temple ceremonies, the jewelry was placed on statues of the gods. The text accompanying a scene of Tuthmose III presenting an ornament to the god Amen describes "the jewelry which had protected the members of the god" (i.e. the king). Such a text clearly demonstrates the magical power which was still attributed to jewelry in the New Kingdom.

Color in jewelry certainly had symbolic meaning. Blue was used to ward off the evil eye, and green was the color of growth and regeneration.

Tomb reliefs and paintings depict scenes of jewelers at work. The earliest such scene is in the 4th Dynasty tomb of Nebemakhet (Giza). Scenes of beads being drilled and strung are found in some tombs as are scenes of metal working. First the metal is weighed and distributed to workers, then it is melted over a charcoal fire while workers make use of blow pipes or bellows. The metal is then either poured into molds or beaten into foil for gilding. The thinnest gold leaf that has been found in jewelry from ancient Egypt is only 0.001 mm thick.

In cloisonné work, stones were first cut before being fixed with an adhesive into patterned forms made of fine gold strips soldered upright onto a flat shape. The back of the cloisonné ornament was then chased or incised with the same design. Stones used for inlays include carnelian, turquoise and lapis lazuli, but colored glass and faïence were also substituted for more precious materials. Gold wire was hammered into a round shape or was drawn and twisted into ornaments. Beginning in the Middle Kingdom granulation was practiced: tiny gold beads were arranged in patterns and soldered onto a gold ornament.

Metal amulets and figures of gods were cast in the lost wax method. First a wax model was covered with clay to make a mold, which was left to dry and harden. Then the wax was melted out and replaced by the molten metal. When the metal had cooled the clay mold was destroyed.

Most metals and stones used in jewelry came from regions outside the Nile Valley. The king had a monopoly on mining and he equipped expeditions to mine precious stones and minerals. Major gold mines were located in the Nubian Desert to the east of the Nile, and during the Middle Kingdom when Egypt gained control of Lower Nubia the production of gold jewelry increased. Silver was more expensive than gold during the Old and Middle Kingdoms because no mines are found in the Eastern or Western Deserts, but it lost its value in the New Kingdom when Egypt had an empire in Nubia and southwest Asia and sources were more accessible.

See also

faïence; metallurgy; natural resources; stone vessels and bead making; Tutankhamen, tomb of

Further reading

Aldred, C. 1971. *Jewels of the Pharaohs*. London.

Feucht, E. 1975. Schmuck. In *Das Alte Ägypten, Proplyäen Kunstgeschichte* 18, C. Vanderslyeyen, ed., 384–493. Berlin.

ERIKA FEUCHT

K

Kafr Tarkhan (Kafr Ammar)

The site of Kafr Tarkhan lies approximately 59 km south of Cairo, on the west bank of the Nile in the low desert, and was named after a nearby village (29°30′ N, 31°13′ E). The site was excavated in 1911–12 and 1912–13 by Flinders Petrie with the assistance of his wife Hilda, three of his students (Rex Engelbach, Ernest Mackay and Gerald Wainwright) and, for a short time, a young archaeologist named T.E. Lawrence.

Kafr Tarkhan comprises a strip of low desert, about 1.6 km long, which has been utilized as a cemetery from late Predynastic to Roman times. Burials date to the late Predynastic and the 1st, 3rd–5th, 10th–11th and 23rd–25th Dynasties, and the Graeco-Roman period. There is also a poorly preserved mudbrick temple which dates to the 23rd–25th Dynasties. For the later periods the site was called Kafr Ammar (after a nearby railway station) to avoid confusion with the earlier finds from the same area.

The most archaeologically important burials, and by far the most numerous, date from the late Predynastic to the late 1st Dynasty. Spanning the period of the "unification" of Egypt, the Kafr Tarkhan data form a highly important link in the construction of a relative chronological framework with which to assess the evolution of late prehistoric culture into that of the early historical, Dynastic periods. This fact was recognized by Petrie, and the Kafr Tarkhan material allowed him to continue his relative chronology (of Sequence Dates, S.D.) to the beginning of the 3rd Dynasty (S.D. 86).

Another highly important aspect of the Kafr Tarkhan material is the inscriptional evidence, found incised or inked on pottery, or as impressed seals on the mud stoppers on pots.

This evidence aided Kaiser and Dreyer in formulating a sequence for the development of the "royal" name within the *serekh* design. The *serekh* is the earliest format of the king's name, which is in hieroglyphs within a niched, "palace façade" design, usually surmounted by the Horus falcon, the symbol of the kingship. This analysis has led to the discovery of a previously unknown possible king, called "Horus Crocodile." This king may have ruled in the Fayum/ Kafr Tarkhan region just prior to the beginning of the 1st Dynasty and was possibly a rival to Kings Irj-Hor and Ka of the "Thinite" dynasty at Abydos (Dynasty 0).

The burials at Kafr Tarkhan are dispersed over a wide area, which Petrie named the "hill" cemeteries, lying predominantly on small hillocks to the west of the cultivation. They are divided, almost centrally, by a small shallow wadi running east–west, which Petrie named the "valley" cemetery. One thousand and fifty-four "valley" burials and 305 "hill" burials were mapped. Along with Abydos, and the later discovered vast cemetery of Helwan, Kafr Tarkhan was one of the largest cemeteries of this period anywhere in Egypt.

Most of the graves at Kafr Tarkhan were simple oval or rectangular holes in the sand in which the body was placed in a contracted position, usually with the head to the south, lying on the left side, facing west (as was the custom for Predynastic burials in Upper Egypt). Less commonly, burials were placed with the head to the north, lying on the left side and facing east. The body was usually covered with a linen shroud or a woven mat; in a few cases the body was placed in a well-made coffin of reeds or basketry, and rarely in large pottery vessels.

The "richer," higher status individuals were buried in larger graves with a greater number and variety of grave goods. In some cases the graves had roofs and linings of wood or mudbrick. In a very few cases tombs were constructed with rectangular mudbrick super-structures (*mastaba*s) over the graves which served as permanent markers of the burial.

A great variety of artifacts for personal and domestic use were found in the burials at Kafr Tarkhan. These included pots containing wine, grain and other foodstuffs; stone vessels of various materials (but predominantly calcite); slate palettes with rubbing stones; ivory cos-metic spoons with carved zoomorphic designs on bowls and handles; ivory *kohl* (eye-paint) sticks; and bracelets and beads of various materials. Tools included copper chisels, knives, adzes and spearheads. Baskets and even wood-en beds with ivory feet modelled into bull's legs were found in some burials. The quality of preservation at Kafr Tarkhan in places was so good that some of the oldest intact garments in Egypt were discovered here and are now on display in the Petrie Museum, London.

The highest status burials at Kafr Tarkhan were the *mastaba* tombs in two locations: at the southern end of the "hill" cemeteries and at the western end of the "valley" cemetery. The four large or "great" *mastaba*s located in relative isolation in the "hill" cemetery were dated by Petrie to his S.D. 80–1 (Kaiser's Nagada IIIc2–IIIc3). These structures included features such as niched, mudbrick "palace façade" superstructures, multiple-room tombs, stair-ways, enclosure walls and a few subsidiary burials. The scale and form of many of these features are comparable to other large *mastaba* tombs of the late Predynastic/Early Dynastic periods at such important sites as Abydos, Saqqara, Nagada and Giza.

In the "valley" cemetery, Petrie found seven small mudbrick *mastaba*s, dating to S.D. 77–8 (Kaiser's Nagada IIIa2–IIIc1). All seven had offering chapels, usually in the northeast corner. These chapels were partially filled and/or surrounded by stacks of pottery, indicating the importance of mortuary offerings. At Kafr Tarkhan the *mastaba* tombs definitely display the greatest investment of labor and materials. They not only reflected the status of the deceased, but the *mastaba* structures also facilitated the required rituals associated with the deceased.

Spatially discrete areas, possibly used by subgroups within the society for status distinc-tions, are clearly visible at Kafr Tarkhan. In both cemetery areas the *mastaba*s are grouped relatively closely together. The westernmost area of the "valley" cemetery also exhibits a repeated clustering of larger graves, with more grave goods and a greater percentage of the rarer artifacts, such as coffins, stone vessels, incised rectangular palettes, beads and ivory *kohl* sticks. Another example of such symbolic use of space is Predynastic Cemetery T at Nagada.

See also

Abydos, Umm el-Qa'ab; Early Dynastic period, overview; Hu/Hiw (Diospolis Parva); Nagada (Naqada); Petrie, Sir William Matthew Flinders; pottery, prehistoric; Predynastic per-iod, overview; writing, invention and early development

Further reading

Dreyer, G. 1992. Horus Krokodil, ein Gegenkönig der Dynastie 0. In *The Followers of Horus*, B. Adams and R. Friedman, eds, 259–64. Oxford.

Ellis, C. 1992. A statistical analysis of Protodynastic burials in the "Valley" Cemetery of Kafr Tarkhan. In *The Nile Delta in Transition: 4th–3rd Millennium B.C.*, E.C.M. van den Brink, ed., 241–58. Jerusalem.

Petrie, W.M.F. 1914. *Tarkhan II*. London.

——. 1953. *Ceremonial Slate Palettes and Corpus of Protodynastic Pottery*. London.

Petrie, W.M.F., *et al.* 1913. *Tarkhan I and Memphis V*. London.

——. 1915. *Heliopolis Kafr Ammar and Shurafa*. London.

C.J. ELLIS

Karnak, Akhenaten temples

Akhenaten, second son and successor of Amenhotep III, instituted a revolution in art and religion that thrust the sun god to the fore as sole god and celebrated his creation in a colorful, expressionistic style of art. Born and brought up in Thebes, Akhenaten spent the first five years of his reign in this southern city, and there evidence is found of the first stage in the development of the new monotheism. The new god was solar in aspect, "the living Sun-disc," and the king favored the simple type of sun shrine characteristic of the Heliopolitan center of solar worship, which featured open courts on a central axis. To expedite the work the king chose a smaller size masonry block than was normal, 52 × 26 × 24 cm, which a single man could shoulder and transport. These blocks, called in the local dialect of Luxor *talatat* (probably from the Italian *tagliata*, "cut masonry"), were quarried in the tens of thousands at Gebel el-Silsila, *circa* 100 km south of Thebes, where the best local sandstone was to be had. A country-wide work project was authorized to accomplish this task, and personnel and funds were diverted from temples all over Egypt. Extreme haste attended the construction, as the king wished to celebrate a jubilee as soon as possible; the laying of the blocks and their decoration display a casualness uncharacteristic of ancient Egyptian architecture.

Despite the anathema Akhenaten's memory suffered at the hands of later generations, and the wholesale destruction wrought on his buildings, thousands of *talatat* have survived. Easily and conveniently recyclable, these small blocks were removed from the dismembered walls of the sun temples and reused as fill or foundation material in later walls and pylons erected in the 19th Dynasty. They are found in Horemheb's Pylons II and IX at the Theban temple of Amen at Karnak, as foundation blocks beneath the hypostyle hall of the Amen temple, and in Ramesses II's pylon and outbuildings in the Luxor temple. Some survived to be used as late as the reign of Nectanebo I, and not a few drifted far afield, such as those which have turned up in Ptolemaic constructions at Medamud. They first attracted scholarly attention about the middle of the nineteenth century, when *talatat* with relief in the startling new style and texts mentioning Akhenaten and the sun-disc turned up around the badly ruined Pylon IX. By the end of WWI a sizable collection of *talatat* had been amassed by Legrain and Pillet, Inspectors of the Department of Antiquities; but it was only in the 1920s that new blocks began to emerge by the thousands. Henri Chevier, Inspector of Antiquities at Karnak from 1925 to 1952, in the course of a program to shore up and restore the ruins, had occasion to replace the flooring in the hypostyle hall and to "gut" parts of Pylon II with an eye to inserting concrete coring. In both places thousands of decorated *talatat* came to light, and many more which had not sat in wall-surfaces and so had received no relief decoration. In the 1960s one of Chevier's successors, Ramadan Saad, undertook methodically to remove the *talatat* from the core of the west wing of Pylon IX, a project pursued with great success after 1967 by the newly formed Centre Franco-Égyptien for the restoration of Karnak, under the direction of Jean Lauffray. Thousands of decorated *talatat* were recovered here, many with bright paint still intact. The total number of *talatat* recovered from the mid-nineteenth century to the present numbers 80,000–90,000.

Intensive scientific study of the *talatat* was slow to develop. In 1966 Ray Winfield Smith, a retired foreign service officer of the US government, conceived of the notion of applying computer science to the problem of reconstructing the *talatat*. With the assistance of IBM Cairo, Smith set up a project staffed by a dozen young Egyptologists. All the *talatat* then known, both those in Egypt and those in foreign collections, were photographed to scale and described in meticulous detail. By 1968 contact prints of the *talatat* began to be matched together in collages, and a "jig-saw puzzle" of relief-scenes began to take shape. By 1972, when the first volume of results was published, over 800 scenes had been matched. The Centre Franco-Égyptien experienced equal success in matching *talatat* from the Pylon IX into scenes, especially when their careful recovery of *talatat* from superimposed beds in that structure revealed a salient fact. In dismantling Akhenaten's constructions, Horemheb's men had immediately deposited the blocks in the new pylon and foundations, so that scenes often lay in their new locations in reverse order, as it were, and could be reconstituted on the spot. This fact had unfortunately eluded Henri Chevier. In 1975 the Akhenaten Temple Project initiated excavations in East Karnak at a spot where the municipal canal had uncovered two fallen colossi of Akhenaten in 1925. Work has continued at East Karnak until the present day.

From an examination of the reliefs alone (specifically the captions accompanying the sundiscs), it soon became apparent that Akhenaten had erected four major structures at Karnak during the first five years of his reign. Of these the major building, to judge by the frequency of references in the *talatat*, was the *Gm-p3-itn* (literally, "The Sun-disc is Found"[?]); slightly smaller on the same criteria were the *Tni-mnw-n-itn* ("Exalted are the monuments of the Sun-disc") and *Rwd-mnw-n-itn* ("Sturdy are the movements of the Sun disc"). The smallest appears to have been the *Hwt-bnbn* ("Mansion of the *benben*-stone"). A *Ḥwt-itn* ("Mansion of the Sun-disc") mentioned in tombs on the west bank has not as yet turned up in the *talatat* scenes. The order in which these buildings were erected is not clear, except that *Ḥwt-bnbn* appears to have been the last. *Gm-p3-itn* was built in anticipation of the jubilee (end of the third or beginning of the fourth regnal year), so that perhaps a point late in the second regnal year represents the inception of *talatat* construction. Prior to this the king erected a gate (blocks now secreted as core material in the Pylon X) decorated in traditional relief, somewhere on the south side of Karnak.

Only one of the four structures named above has been located and partly excavated. The *Gm-p3-itn*, 210 m wide and of (at present) unknown length, was built to the east of Karnak on ground that had not been occupied for centuries. Its longer axis ran east–west, with its

south side aligned with the central east–west axis of the Amen temple. From the center of its western side a columned corridor 4 m wide led from the temple westward to communicate with the 18th Dynasty royal palace which lay just north of Pylons IV, V and VI of the Amen temple. The *Gm-p3-itn* was surrounded by an outer wall of mudbrick laid in undulating courses and, at a distance of 5 m, an inner stone wall 2 m thick constructed of *talatat*. The vast court thus enclosed was lined on the north, west and south sides by a continuous colonnade of rectangular piers, each 2 × 1.80 m, set at intervals of 2 m, and supported by the *talatat* wall. In front of this colonnade and parallel to it ran a stylobate 5 m wide, to support the colossal statues which, on the south side and southern half of the west side, adorned the inner faces of the piers. Probably before each statue stood a granite offering table bearing the names of the king, queen and the sun-disc. On the north side the excavated fragments suggest the presence of life-size, free-standing statues of red quartzite and occasionally granite, at intervals of 7–8 m. Most seem to have depicted the king with arms crossed in "Osiride"-fashion, but some fragments suggest double statues of the king and queen. The inner faces of the piers on the north side, not obscured by statues, were decorated in sunk relief showing the king with one arm outstretched and caressed by the rays of the sun-disc.

The inner face of the stone *talatat* wall, protected by the colonnade in front, was the location of the painted relief scenes. Especially on the south and west sides, sufficient fragments of relief were recovered in the excavation to enable identification of scene types. In the *Gm-p3-itn* the consistent theme was the celebration of the jubilee, or *heb-sed*. In the entrance corridor coming from the palace were to be found scenes showing the approach of the royal party, outrunners, courtiers kissing the earth, men dragging bulls, payment of rations and so on. Turning right along the inner face of the west wall as far as the southwest corner and then east along the south wall, one encountered the ritual of "the days of the White Crown," when the king made offerings in the regalia of

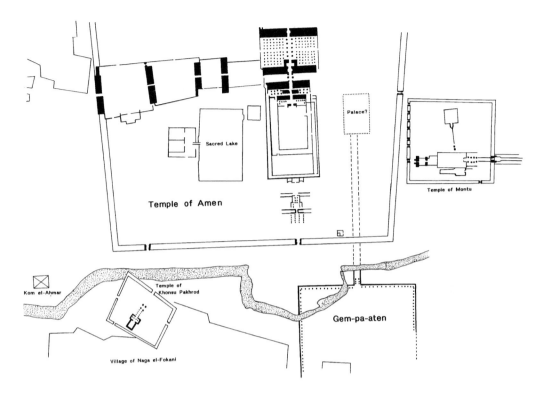

Figure 50 Location of Akhenaten's *Gm-p3-itn* temple at East Karnak

the King of Upper Egypt, and was duly crowned as southern monarch. Here a repeating motif, *circa* 12 m long, showed the events of a single day: emergence from the palace, procession in palanquin to the temple, sacrifices in open-roofed kiosks to the sun-disc, recessional to the palace and feasting in the palace. At least four repetitions of the sequence can be identified along the south wall proceeding from the southwest corner, and at a point *circa* 180 m to the east on the south wall the fragments suggest the motif is still present. Too little is preserved on the north side of the court to make any final statement, but it is likely that the same sequence was followed, with the king wearing the Red Crown and the regalia of Lower Egypt.

The location and ground plan of the three remaining buildings, and even their purpose, remain in doubt. The *benben*-stone, commemorated in the *Ḥwt-bnbn*, is shaped like an obelisk

in the hieroglyphic writing of Akhenaten's inscriptions; one wonders whether this points to the unique obelisk (now in St John Lateran, Rome) which once stood east of the temple of Amen. The *Ḥwt-bnbn* as reconstructed in the *talatat* scenes featured tall graceful pylons and their cross walls. What comes as a surprise is the identity of the celebrant of the offering to the sun-disc (the only scene type found in *Ḥwt-bnbn*): Nefertiti appears (sometimes with one, rarely two daughters) to the total exclusion of her husband! The locations of *Tni-mnw* and *Rwd-mnw* are unknown, although it may be argued that they lay on the south side of Karnak. Their relief decoration is much more varied than that of *Gm-p3-itn*, showing scenes taken from life: offering bringers, domestic apartments, scenes of agriculture and animal husbandry, the proffering of taxes, appointment and rewarding of officers, and the like.

In the light of Akhenaten's hatred of Amen, chief of the pantheon, what use was made during Akhenaten's first five years of the Karnak temple? Several scenes of rewarding and feasting show those officials being honored squatting before the façade of the palace, with a head-smiting scene in the background. This can only be the large relief of Akhenaten which decorated the reveals of the gate of Pylon III at Karnak, and lay just south of the royal palace. Whether a large colonnade decorated with figures of Nefertiti once stood on the site of the present Pylon II must remain moot; it remains a possibility that some parts of the Amen temple remained in operation, at least until the celebration of the jubilee. Thereafter, we find the high priest of Amen, Maya, sent to the quarries (year 4), and the writing of the name "Amen" obliterated intentionally throughout Karnak and the whole Theban area. On the eve of Akhenaten's abandonment of Thebes for Amarna the king changed his name from "Amenhotep" to "Akhenaten," and had every cartouche modified accordingly. After this *hejira*, work stopped on his Theban buildings: none of the later changes in nomenclature or art style appears at Thebes.

The phenomenal number of *talatat* with relief scenes recovered from Karnak and Luxor offers us two unique opportunities: first, to view the astounding revolution in art and religion authored by the monotheist king in its initial experimental stage; and second, to view the oldest festival of ancient Egypt, the royal jubilee, in the fullest and most detailed set of reliefs which ever recorded it.

See also

cult temples of the New Kingdom; cult temples, construction techniques; Gebel el-Silsila; representational evidence, New Kingdom temples; Tell el-Amarna, cult temples

Further reading

Gohary, J. 1992. *Akhenaten's Sed-festival at Karnak*. London.

Redford, D.B. 1988. *Akhenaten Temple Project 2: Rwd-mnw and the Inscriptions*. Toronto.

Roeder, G., and R. Hanke. 1969–1979. *Amarna-Reliefs aus Hermopolis*. Hildesheim.

Smith, R.W., and D.B. Redford. 1977. *The Akhenaten Temple Project 1: The Initial Discoveries*. Warminster.

DONALD B. REDFORD

Karnak, precinct of Montu

The Montu precinct is the most significant architectural complex on the archaeological site north of the temple of Amen-Re at Karnak (25°43′ N, 32°40′ E). It includes other monuments besides the Montu temple. In 1940 the French Archaeological Institute in Cairo (IFAO) began excavations and studies in this area, which are still ongoing. The extant brick girdle wall and its monumental gate were probably built by Ptolemy III, replacing a previous wall tentatively dated to the time of Nectanebo I and II. However, we know for sure that a girdle wall, although with different eastern and western limits, existed in the time of Amenhotep III, the founder of the main temple. In its current state, the Montu precinct encloses the following identified structures: (1) the Montu temple; (2) a temple of Ma'at; (3) a temple of Harpre; (4) a sacred lake; (5) a "high temple"; and (6) six chapels dedicated by the Divine Votaresses of Amen. A *dromos* (7) leading to a quay on a canal (no longer extant), completes the complex.

The so-called "temple of Montu," largely destroyed today, was founded by Amenhotep III. Like other temples of this king at Luxor and Soleb, it is built on a podium. Its masonry included blocks belonging to various dismantled monuments bearing the names of Amenhotep I (a copy of the "White Chapel" of Senusret I), Hatshepsut–Tuthmose III, Amenhotep II (a peristyle chapel for the sacred bark of Amen) and Tuthmose IV. The plan was modified twice during the building process. At first, the project consisted of a square building with two rows of columns in the façade and an

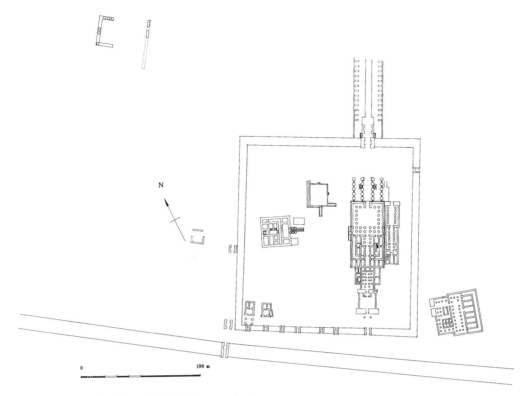

Figure 51 Karnak, plan of the Montu precinct

entry ramp facing north. However, before the surface of the walls was completely smoothed the temple was extended to the south, where the rear wall was opened and a range of supplementary rooms were added. The façade was modified with the addition of a peristyle court that incorporated the previous ramp into the new extended foundation. A new ramp flanked by obelisks led to the portal opening onto the peristyle court.

No significant modification is known up to the reign of Taharka, except restorations after the Amarna period (including the erection of a copy of the "Restoration Stela" of Tutankhamen), a stela of Seti I, inscriptions of Ramesses II, Merenptah, Amenmesses, Pinedjem and Nimrod. We know that the eastern part of the temple collapsed at the end of the New Kingdom, and it is most probable that reconstruction of the temple was undertaken by Taharka,

who is also responsible for a great portico on the main façade (very similar to those of East Karnak and the Khonsu temple). The portico was dismantled and rebuilt by the first Ptolemies, who also rebuilt the gate of the temple proper and that of the enclosure wall.

Among the numerous finds, the statuary is of particular interest, including statues of Amenhotep II and Amenhotep III in the *heb-sed* (jubilee) garment; two quartzite statues of Amenhotep III holding the sacred pole of Amen (found shattered to pieces and buried in two adjoining heaps beneath a chapel in the middle of the *dromos*), and two human-handed sphinxes of the same king presenting an offering table. Very little of the decoration on the walls remains. It should be mentioned that the Ptolemies recarved the walls of the hypostyle hall, the bark sanctuary and architraves in the name of Amenhotep III.

The temple of Ma'at, the only one extant dedicated to this deity, leans on the rear side of the Montu temple. Largely destroyed today, it still preserves inscriptions of some of the viziers of Ramesses III and XI. Scattered reliefs and stelae belonging to the reign of Amenhotep III indicate that a previous Ma'at temple existed at that time in the same area. The door in the wall of the precinct opening to this temple was rebuilt by the Nectanebos, reusing a previous Kushite door. The trials of the perpetrators of the great tomb robberies at the end of the Ramesside period took place in the temple of Ma'at.

The temple of Harpre is built along the east side of the Montu temple. The oldest part (i.e. the sanctuary on the south side) may date back to the 21st Dynasty. Nepherites and Hakor (29th Dynasty) built a hypostyle hall with Hathor capitals. A geographical procession formed part of the decoration of the hypostyle hall. An open court and a pylon were added to the north façade during the 30th Dynasty. The question of the identification of this temple as a *mammisi* or birthhouse has been proposed and rejected by various scholars. A subsidiary building, in front of the pylon, is known as the "eastern secondary temple" and may be related to the cult of the bull of Montu.

The sacred lake, on the west side of the Montu temple, may have been dug by Amenhotep III and restored by Montuemhat, as can be inferred from his biographical inscription in Mut temple. A "high temple," built on a massive brick structure, was erected by Nectanebo II as a "pure storehouse" for the offerings.

Six doors in the south wall of the Montu precinct lead to six chapels dedicated by Divine Votaresses of Amen to different forms of Osiris. From west to east they are: (a) chapel of Nitocris (Psamtik I); (b) Amenirdis (Shabako or Shabataka); (c) and (d) unattributed; (e) Karomama (Takelot II); (f) reign of Taharka. These chapels may not have been included in the precinct until the girdle wall was built under Nectanebo I and II, as there are other chapels of the same type outside of the precinct.

The *dromos* is a stone-paved road leading from the gate of the precinct to a quay on a canal which lay north of the site. The quay may be dated to the reign of Psamtik I, as his name is found on the masonry. The temple *dromos* is flanked by sphinxes, now badly damaged. It was probably part of the original temple plan of Amenhotep III, as indicated by the discovery of two quartzite statues of the king carrying the sacred pole of Amen found broken and buried under a chapel in the middle of its length. They probably once stood in a chapel on the same site.

Outside of the temple precinct, a number of buildings have been located in the vicinity. A limestone gate of Hatshepsut and Tuthmose III (formerly attributed to Tuthmose I), usurped by Amenhotep II and completed by Seti I, is on the west side of the west wall of the precinct. It probably led to a palace complex of Hatshepsut situated farther north, only known from textual sources. Only two brick walls remain of the chapel dedicated to Osiris by Shepenwepet II (Taharka), the site where Auguste Mariette discovered the splendid statue of goddess Taweret (CG 39145). Farther west, a door of Ptolemy IV marks the entrance to a small temple of Thoth, now in ruins. In the northwest of the area, a columned building consecrated to the Theban triad by Nitocris has suffered greatly since the time of its discovery. To the east of the Montu precinct, the remains of a building of Tuthmose I have been excavated. Known by quarry marks as a "Treasury," it consisted of a bark station of Amen, storerooms and workshops.

The oldest remains on the site of North Karnak date back to the end of the Middle Kingdom (13th Dynasty) and belong to urban settlements identified at different parts of the site, consisting of mudbrick houses, granaries and workshops. The chronology of monumental constructions on the site is as follows: the oldest building known today is the Treasury of Tuthmose I, which is most probably a modification of a sanctuary of Ahmose; then, reused blocks of Amenhotep I, Hatshepsut and Amenhotep II in the Montu temple (although there is no evidence that they belong to buildings once erected on the spot), and the limestone door of Hatshepsut and Tuthmose III; then, the temple of Amenhotep III itself.

It should be pointed out that all the above mentioned monuments (or parts of monuments), including the temple of Amenhotep III, are dedicated to Amen-Re of Thebes, even if rare mentions of Montu have been found on the site (mainly epithets describing various kings as "beloved of Montu"). The dedicatory inscription of the main temple attributes the sanctuary to "Amen-Re, Lord of the Thrones of the Two Lands, Pre-eminent in Ipet-Sut," an attribution which is confirmed by the text of the "Petrie Stela," and various minor monuments such as the obelisks, the two quartzite statues of Amenhotep III and other pieces of statuary. The first dedicatory inscription to Montu known to us appears on the stela erected by Seti I in the court of the temple. It is from the reign of Taharka, however, that we have a comprehensive documentation in the decoration of the portico, stating that Montu is the main god of the temple. The scenes on the Ptolemaic gate of the precinct confirm this rank for Montu, paralleled however by the expected presence of Amen-Re. In this matter, the dedicatory inscription carved under the Ptolemies in the central bark station of the Montu temple is eloquent: while attributing to Amenhotep III the foundation of the monument, the text clearly dedicates the temple to "Montu, Lord of Thebes."

Thus, the area of North Karnak appears to have been originally a dependency of the temple of Amen-Re and was only progressively and partially devoted to Montu. The cult of this divinity of the Theban nome, which predates that of Amen, was developed during the Late period in the framework of the theology of the "four Theban Montu," at Medamud, Armant, Tod and North Karnak. In Graeco-Roman times, Montu was identified with Apollo and the temple was designated as an Apolloneion. The Demotic documentation reveals that this area was called "the House of the Cow" while Greek papyri call it Chrysopolis.

See also

Armant; cult temples, construction techniques; cult temples of the New Kingdom; cult temples, Medamud; New Kingdom, overview; Tod

Further reading

Gabolde, L., and V. Rondot. 1993. Une catastrophe antique dans le temple de Montou à Karnak-Nord. *BIFAO* 93: 245–64.
——. 1996. Le temple de Montou n'était pas un temple à Montou. *BSFE* 136: 27–42.
——. 1996. *BIFAO* 96: 177–215.
Jacquet, J. 1970. *BIFAO* 69: 267–81.
Jacquet, J and Jacquet-Gordon, H. 1983, 1988, 1994 *Le trésor de Thoutmosis I. La décoration, Karnak-Nord* 6: Cairo. (*FIFAO* 32).
Robichon, Cl. and Christophe, L.A. 1951. *Karnak-Nord* III, *FIFAO* XXIII. Cairo.
Robichon, Cl., Barguet, P. and Leclant, J. 1954. *Karnak-Nord* IV, *FIFAO* XXV. Cairo.
Siclen, C.C. van, III. 1986. Amenhotep II's barque chapel for Amun at North Karnak. *BIFAO* 86: 353–9.
Sourouzian, H. 1997. *BIFAD* 97: 239–45.
Varile, A. 1943 *Karnak* I, *FIFAO* XIX, Cairo.

VINCENT RONDOT
LUC GABOLDE

Karnak, precinct of Mut

The precinct of Mut at Karnak, the goddess's main cult center, lies on the east bank of the Nile about 325 m south of the precinct of Amen (25°43′ N, 32°40′ E). During the New Kingdom, Mut, Amen and their son Khonsu became the pre-eminent divine family triad of Thebes. The Mut Temple proper is oriented toward the Amen precinct and is surrounded on three sides by a sacred lake called "Isheru."

Recent excavations indicate that much—and possibly all—of the present precinct was settlement until some time in the Second Intermediate Period. The earliest reference to "Mut, Mistress of Isheru," a common epithet, occurs on a statue of the 17th Dynasty in the British

Museum (EA 69536), suggesting that by then the site was dedicated to her. Inscriptional evidence also links the site to Mut in the early 18th Dynasty reign of Amenhotep I. The earliest, securely dated *in situ* Mut Temple remains are no later than the reigns of Tuthmose III and Hatshepsut.

While the Mut precinct was noted by the Napoleonic expedition, the Royal Prussian Expedition and individual early explorers, the first major excavations took place in 1895–7, led by Margaret Benson and Janet Gourlay, who concentrated on the interior of the Mut Temple. In the 1920s Maurice Pillet directed the Egyptian Antiquities Organization's excavation and partial restoration of two other temples: Temple A in the northeast corner, and Temple C (built by Ramesses III of the 20th Dynasty) west of the sacred lake, which was later recorded and published by the Epigraphic Survey of the University of Chicago. In 1975 the French Institute of Archaeology in Cairo cleared and recorded the site's main entrance. In 1976, the Brooklyn Museum of Art, under

the auspices of the American Research Center in Egypt, began a systematic investigation of the site, assisted since 1978 by the Detroit Institute of Arts. By 1995 this expedition had conducted excavations in various areas to elucidate the site's history and the interrelationships of its buildings.

Under Hatshepsut and Tuthmose III, the precinct seems to have consisted of the Mut Temple and the sacred lake and to have extended no farther north than the temple's present first pylon. Parts of the west and north walls of this precinct have been uncovered, including a gate bearing Tuthmose III's name and a Seti I restoration inscription. The eastern and southern boundaries of this precinct are as yet undefined, although its southern limit was probably just south of the sacred lake.

The Mut Temple was enlarged later in the 18th Dynasty, when the Tuthmoside building was completely enclosed by new construction. The ruler responsible for this work cannot be identified, but was probably Amenhotep III, even if, as some argue, none of the hundreds of

Figure 52 Karnak, precinct of Mut

Sekhmet statues at the site that bear his name was brought to the precinct until the 19th Dynasty or later. Amenhotep III may also have enlarged Temple A, which lay outside the precinct and may have originally been built earlier in the dynasty. None of its standing walls, however, predates the 19th Dynasty.

The Mut Temple's present second pylon, of mudbrick, dates no later than the 19th Dynasty and may have replaced an earlier mudbrick precinct or temple wall. Its eastern half was rebuilt in stone late in the Ptolemaic period. The temple's first pylon, also of mudbrick, has a stone gateway built no later than the 19th Dynasty and displays at least one major repair. This pylon, too, may replace an earlier northern precinct wall. Also in the 19th Dynasty, Ramesses II rebuilt Temple A, although it remained outside the precinct. Before it he erected two colossal statues (at least one usurped from Amenhotep III) and two alabaster stelae recarved from parts of a shrine of Amenhotep II brought from the Amen precinct. One of these stelae appears to describe the renewal of Temple A and indicates that it was then dedicated to Amen.

Extensive building at the precinct occurred during the 25th Dynasty. Some of this work took place during the reign of Taharka and also commemorates the extremely important official, Montuemhat. A significant part of the Mut Temple was rebuilt, and the present Ptolemaic porches probably represent a rebuilding of the 25th Dynasty originals. Temple A was even more extensively renovated during the 25th Dynasty, by which time it functioned, at least in part, as a *mammisi* (birth house) celebrating the birth of Amen's and Mut's divine child with whom the king could be identified. Structure B, a "pure magazine" east of the Mut Temple, whose present form dates to the 30th Dynasty, was probably originally built at this time as well.

During the 25th Dynasty there also seems to have been an expansion of the Mut precinct to encompass Temple A and an area north of the Mut Temple, and a processional way was created from Taharka's newly constructed west gateway to Temple A. Taharka's north precinct wall is buried beneath the present enclosure wall, but part of the west wall and the gateway survive.

In the 25th and 26th Dynasties a proliferation of small chapels began that continued into the Ptolemaic period. These include at least two chapels dedicated by Montuemhat; a magical healing chapel dedicated by Horwedja, the "Great Seer of Heliopolis"; a chapel in Temple A related to Divine Votaresses (high priestesses of Amen); a small Ptolemy VI chapel in the Mut Temple; and Chapel D, just inside the Taharka gateway, built by Ptolemies VI and VIII. Chapel D is dedicated to Mut and Sekhmet, and perhaps to the Ptolemies' ancestor cult as well.

The massive enclosure walls built by Nectanebo II of the 30th Dynasty gave the precinct its present shape and size, incorporating not only Temple C (which appears to have been used in the 25th Dynasty as a source of building stone), but also a large area south of the sacred lake that has yet to be explored.

Besides the works already mentioned, the Ptolemaic period was a time of considerable activity in the Mut precinct. The small Contra Temple abutting the south wall of the Mut Temple was at least redecorated, if not rebuilt. The Mut Temple and Temple A were again partially rebuilt and some of their decoration was recarved, and the present main gateway to the precinct (the "Propylon") was constructed. The Ptolemaic texts on this gateway and other buildings at the site are major sources for understanding the goddess and her cult.

Inscriptional evidence commemorates early Roman period construction by Augustus and Tiberius that may be represented by the present wall around the Mut Temple. However, during the late Ptolemaic and early Roman periods habitations were built within the precinct, between the 30th Dynasty walls and the older precinct walls. When precisely the precinct ceased to function as a religious center is unclear, but by the fourth century AD, houses had been built against and inside the site's temples.

See also

cult temples of the New Kingdom; Karnak,

precinct of Montu; Karnak, temple of Amen-Re; pantheon

Further reading

Fazzini, R. Report on the 1983 Season of Excavation at the Precinct of the Goddess Mut. *ASAE* 70: 287–307.

Fazzini, R., and W. Peck. 1981. The Precinct of Mut during Dynasty XXV and early Dynasty XXVI: A Growing Picture. *JSSEA* 11: 115–26.

Goyon, J.-C. 1985. Inscriptions tardives du temple de Mout à Karnak. *JARCE* 20: 47–61.

Porter, B., and R. Moss. 1972. *Topographical Bibliography of Ancient Egyptian Hieroglyphic Texts, Reliefs, and Paintings* 2: *Theban Temples*, 2nd edn, 255–75. Oxford.

RICHARD A. FAZZINI

Karnak, temple of Amen-Re

The development of the temple of Amen-Re at Karnak (25°43′ N, 32°40′ E) can only be understood as a function of its extraordinary religious significance for the ancient Egyptians. The Thebans considered Karnak as the place of "the majestic rising of the first time," where the creator god Amen-Re made the first mound of earth rise from Nun, the primordial ocean. The qualities of Amen, the ancient, local god of Thebes, and Re, the sun god of ancient Egypt's great spiritual center and legendary capital in the north, Heliopolis, were combined in the entity Amen-Re.

Both transcendent and immanent, Amen-Re was believed to be all things at once. Having brought about his own existence at the beginning of time, he was called the "Kamutef" (bull of his own mother), and he presided over the creation of all things. Amen-Re was also the "king of the gods," sometimes termed the "unique one." His name, Amen, means the "hidden one."

It was believed that the world he had created could survive only as long as the observance of his cult in the temple of Karnak fully maintained his original powers as the supreme god. In the rituals there Amen was called upon to perpetuate and repeat his action of "the first time," thereby insuring the continued cohesion of the world. This was a victory, achieved again and again over the indestructible forces of chaos. It guaranteed the everlasting survival of the basic principle incarnate in the goddess Ma'at, which comprised the concepts of order, truth and justice.

The extraordinary role played by the temple of Amen-Re is linked to its two major functions. Karnak was unique: first, as the divine temple and principal earthly residence of the highest god, and second, as the Dynastic temple and source of legitimacy for all the kings of Egypt. The temple of Amen-Re thus played a considerable part in the spiritual, political and economic affairs of Egypt. It was in this temple that the high priests recognized a king as the "beloved son of Amen." The coronation and jubilees (*heb-sed*) also took place there. The true intermediary between god and man, the king was the only "priest" in title: the other members of the priesthood were simply "servants of Amen." The "first prophet of Amen" (high priest) was witness to all important decrees of the kingdom. Staffed by more than 80,000 under Ramesses III, the temple was also the administrative center of enormous holdings of agricultural land.

The relationship between god and king was founded on a principle of exchange: the sovereign made offerings, and Amen continued or renewed his beneficence. Each of the monuments built at Karnak is intended as a son's grateful gesture to his divine father. The act of making the offering was more essentially valuable than the finished work *per se*. That is why, during the temple's many centuries of existence, kings did not hesitate to tear down the works of their predecessors. Much use was made of old blocks, usurped and placed in new buildings dedicated to Amen.

As a result, the long architectural history of Karnak is difficult to delineate. The order in which the halls, courts and pylons were built is problematic, as stone blocks were quarried and inscribed in different periods but became intermingled in rebuilt constructions. Old stones were reused in the foundations and walls of more recent monuments. Consequently, the restoration of Karnak by periods is like an immense jigsaw puzzle, requiring great care and patience.

Amen and his temple no doubt owe their particular good fortune to the fact that the city of Thebes (Ouaset) twice became the capital of the unified kingdom of Upper and Lower Egypt. Although no trace survives at Karnak of the 11th Dynasty monuments, the continuous evolution of the temple can be followed beginning with the reign of Senusret I (12th Dynasty). This king used large limestone blocks to build the central sanctuary and its subsidiary halls, which would be the heart of the temple throughout its long history.

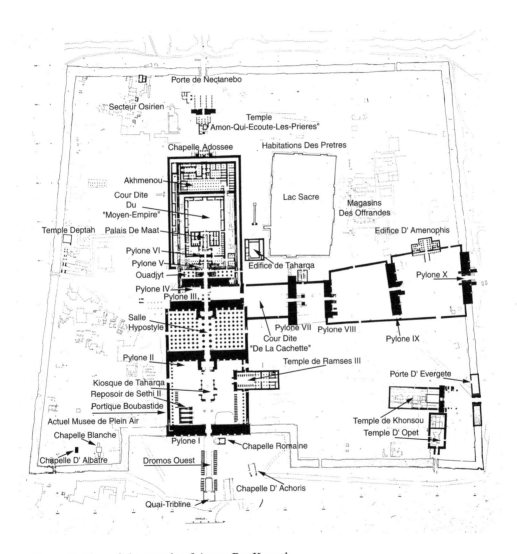

Figure 53 Plan of the temple of Amen-Re, Karnak

Subsequently, Karnak's role increased significantly, especially during the 18th Dynasty when Thebes was the capital of a reunified Egypt. Around Senusret I's complex of buildings, the temple developed along two perpendicular axes. Along the east–west axis, symbolically the direction of the sun's path, are the main halls and courts, and most of the obelisks. Along the other axis, which is the direction of the flow of the Nile (south–north), is a great processional walk, essentially a sequence of courts and pylons. At the intersection of these two axes is the entrance to the house of the god.

The temple complex's main stages of development are as follows.

18th Dynasty

(1) To the original temple, Amenhotep I added a court with a pylon (a large gateway; VI in the numbering system employed by archaeologists) at its entrance. In the middle of this court was the famous "alabaster chapel," the first known shrine of the image of the sun bark, which played a central role in all ceremonies.

(2) Tuthmose I built an enclosure wall and, to the west, two pylons (IV and V) forming the sides of a jubilee hall (the *wadjit*, "hall of columns"). In front of the west façade of the temple he erected the first pair of obelisks.

(3) Tuthmose II created a great "festival court" in the open area in front of the temple, and placed two more obelisks there.

(4) Queen Hatshepsut made some major changes. She demolished Amenhotep I's works in the heart of the temple and replaced them with offering halls and a second sun bark shrine, which together were called the "Palace of Ma'at." On the western side, she removed the roof of the *wadjit* hall, which became a court where she placed two enormous obelisks. A new jubilee complex was then undertaken, east of the temple. Finally, along the north–south axis, she constructed a pylon (VIII). It was also during her reign that sandstone blocks systematically replaced the limestone ones used earlier.

(5) Tuthmose III, wishing to destroy the queen's work, restored the *wadjit* hall's roof, which then hid her obelisks from the ground view. Before the temple's west façade he erected a pair of his own obelisks. The vast jubilee complex of the *akhmenu* ("sacred images" of the gods) was constructed to the east and a second, tall stone enclosure wall was built around the whole temple. He also built Pylon VII on the north–south axis and erected its two obelisks.

(6) Tuthmose IV gave the festival court a portico to the east of the *akhmenu* complex, in which he erected a single obelisk, the largest of all Egyptian monoliths. It is placed on the central axis of the temple, at the extreme east, and makes an end point for the plan.

(7) Amenhotep III destroyed the festival court of Tuthmose II and in its place built Pylon III with the reused blocks of many earlier buildings. Most of the blocks on display now in the open-air museum at Karnak were found during the excavation of this edifice. Along the north–south axis, Amenhotep III began to build the southernmost pylon (X), and in front of its facade he erected immense royal colossi.

(8) The reign of Amenhotep IV/Akhenaten was marked by the construction of a large, separate complex of temples to the east, near Tuthmose IV's obelisk. These temples were dedicated to the worship of the Aten. They were made with small modular blocks of stone, known today as *talatat*, which allowed very rapid construction.

(9) At the end of the dynasty the temples in Akhenaten's complex were systematically destroyed by Horemheb, who reused thousands of *talatat* for the foundations and filling of his own buildings. Horemheb erected Pylon II to the west of the one built by Amenhotep III. He also built all of Pylon IX and finished Pylon X.

19th Dynasty

(1) Seti I began the great Hypostyle Hall between Pylons II and III; it was later completed by Ramesses II. The latter king also laid out the plan of the great western causeway and quay (when the temple was approached by water), and, in the complex's eastern part, built

the temple named "Amen-who-hears-prayers," enclosing Tuthmose IV's obelisk in its sanctuary. Farther east along the central axis a monumental gateway was erected, with two obelisks at its entrance.

(2) Seti II built a triple shrine for the barks of Amen, Mut and Khonsu west of the temple.

20th Dynasty

In the western court, Ramesses III built a triple bark shrine which is of such enormous size that it appears to be a temple. He also undertook the construction of the temple of Khonsu.

Third Intermediate Period

(1) During the 22nd Dynasty the last festival court was laid out. It was bounded on the north and south by a colonnade, and on the west by Pylon I.

(2) The most remarkable subsequent works are those of Taharka (25th Dynasty), the Kushite (Nubian) king who built the large sacred lake with a temple, the so-called "lake edifice," at its northwest corner. He also built columned pavilions leading to the eastern and western entrances of the temple, and in front of the temple of Khonsu. The small pylon of the temple of Opet was also begun during the 25th Dynasty.

Late period

Nectanebo I (30th Dynasty) gave the temple a huge enclosure wall made of horizonally curved courses of mudbrick (thought to resemble the primeval waters of Nun). He began, but left unfinished, two stone piers for Pylon I, and he built secondary gates outside the enclosure wall to the north, east and west.

Ptolemaic period

The large gate of Ptolemy III Evergetes was built in front of the entrance of the temple of Khonsu and at the back of the temple of Opet. During this period extensive repairs were made to the bases of walls that were damaged where ground water had percolated up, through capillary action. The foundations of the Hypostyle walls were repaired, and the eastern and western gateways were entirely redone. Likewise, all the inner rooms of the temple show signs of repair, during which many of their statues and offerings were removed. They were buried, level by level, in the famous "Karnak cachette," where they were discovered at the beginning of this century during Georges Legrain's spectacular excavations.

Roman period

Few buildings were undertaken during the Roman period. For example, there is a modest, baked-brick chapel for the cult of the Emperor to the west of Pylon I, near the temple's main entrance.

During the time of Constantine I (*circa* AD 330), Karnak's decline, apparently already complete, was punctuated by the removal of the two largest surviving obelisks (Tuthmose IV's huge obelisk and one in front of Pylon VII). The final abandonment of the religion of Amen is also indicated by the establishment of a Roman camp around the temple of Luxor. After this only a few monks' cells and some modest mudbrick buildings occupied Karnak. During the centuries of abandonment, many limestone blocks from temple walls disappeared into the lime kilns of the inhabitants.

Having vanished from memory, Karnak was not identified as the ancient cult center until the eighteenth century. Its true scientific rediscovery would not come until Napoleon's expedition in 1799. The pioneering work in the nineteenth century of Jean-François Champollion, Richard Lepsius, Auguste Mariette and Gaston Maspero, and, in the twentieth century, the work of Paul Barguet, the Office of the Directorship of Works at Karnak, and later the Franco-Egyptian Center for the Study and Restoration of the Temples of Karnak, have all made possible this broad outline of development of the most important complex of temples in ancient Egypt.

See also

Champollion, Jean-François; Late and Ptolemaic periods, overview; Lepsius, Carl Richard; Luxor, temple of; *ma'at*; Mariette, François Auguste Ferdinand; Maspero, Sir Gaston Camille Charles; Middle Kingdom, overview; Napoleon Bonaparte and the Napoleonic expedition; New Kingdom, overview; Thebes, royal funerary temples; Third Intermediate Period, overview

Further reading

The research of the Centre Franco-Égyptien, which was created in 1967, is published in *Les Cahiers de Karnak*, at first within *Kemi*, vols 19 (Paris 1967–8), 20 (1970) and 21 (1971), and then as independent volumes: *Karnak V*, Cairo 1975; *Karnak VI*, Cairo 1980; *Karnak VII*, Paris 1982; *Karnak VIII*, Paris 1987; *Karnak IX*, Paris 1993.

Albouy, M., H. Boccon-Gibod, J.-C. Golvin, J.-C. Goyon and P. Martinez. 1989. *Karnak: le temple d'Amon restitué à l'ordinateur*. Paris.

Aufrère, S., J.-C Golvin and J.-C. Goyon. 1991. *L'Égypte restituée* 1. Paris.

Golvin, J.-C., and J.-C. Goyon. 1987. *Les Bâtisseurs de Karnak*. Paris.

JEAN-CLAUDE GOLVIN

Kerma

This site is notable for two well preserved mudbrick ruins termed "Deffufa" in the local dialect. These were noted by earlier travelers, but it was not until the excavations of the Harvard University–Museum of Fine Arts, Boston Expedition to the Sudan under the direction of G.A. Reisner in 1913–16 that the nature of the site was revealed. Much more has been added to our understanding of Kerma and its development from the ongoing fieldwork of Charles Bonnet and the Expedition of the University of Geneva.

For much of the third and second millennia BC, the most important state in the Nile Valley aside from Egypt was the Kingdom of Kush, centered in the area of the Third Cataract, which seems to be the principal rival of the Egyptians for control of Nubia. In all likelihood, their state was centered at the site of Kerma, in the Dongola Reach. Unlike much of Nubia, in this region there is a broad floodplain that allowed rich agricultural production, thereby enabling the growth and maintenance of a very large population and accumulation of surplus wealth.

The town itself was situated on the east bank of the Nile. It is roughly circular in plan and built along an east–west axis. The central portion covers an area of about 0.5 km in diameter and is surrounded by a dry moat and ramparts. Outliers of the settlement have been found to the southwest and may have consisted of cultic buildings and temple workshops. Other remains close to the river may have included port facilities. At the center of the town was a vast mudbrick temple known as the Lower or Western Deffufa, measuring over 50×25 m and preserved to a height of almost 20 m. It was surrounded by a series of workshops and storerooms. Nearby was a large circular structure over 15 m in diameter, of post and thatch construction, that may have served as an audience hall. Perpendicular to the main axis of the town and to the Deffufa, a large palace was recently discovered that combined both Egyptian and local architectural features.

About 3 km north-northeast of the center of the ancient town, on the desert edge, lies the associated cemeteries. Over 1 km in length from north to south, the necropolis is estimated to contain over 30,000 separate burials. It was divided by Reisner into Cemetery N, the northernmost of the cemeteries, Cemetery M, the central portion of the necropolis, and the large tumulus burials of the so-called "Egyptian" or South Cemetery. Included in the last are the isolated "B cemetery" graves, which are intermediate between the M cemetery and the earliest tumulus burials of the South Cemetery.

In accordance with Nubian tradition, the deceased was not mummified but was placed in a contracted position, occasionally on a bed, under a large mound. At Kerma these mounds were decorated with geometric patterns in black and white pebbles and were sometimes adorned with painted skulls of gazelles, goats or cattle. Grave goods were placed with the deceased, including sacrificed animals and humans. Offerings could also be left outside the graves and eventually small chapels were built to contain them. These evolved into large cult chapels, including the monumental Upper or Eastern Deffufa.

The chronology of these burials has confounded scholars since Reisner's excavations there. Reisner himself had reservations about the historical position he hypothesized for the culture, and admitted that he was at a loss to date the site by ceramics in the traditional way because the exact dating of Egyptian pottery of the 11th–18th Dynasties had not yet been worked out. Without pottery to serve as a dating tool, Reisner was led astray by imported Egyptian statues and inscribed monuments. This problem was further compounded by flawed anatomical analysis provided by D.E. Derry, who postulated a racial difference between the populations buried in the southern ("Egyptian") cemetery and those to the north. Based on these false clues, Reisner surmised that a garrison was installed at Kerma by Amenemhat I or II (12th Dynasty) to act as a trading post and to safeguard the string of fortresses to the north along the Second Cataract; later Hepdjefa, nomarch of Asyut, was made governor of the colony, "went native" and was buried there in Nubian style.

Reisner's evolutionary scheme has been revised and the sequence he proposed, beginning with the great burial tumulus, K III and ending with the group K XVI–K XX, has been reversed, with K III being the last of the great tumuli. These are certainly the graves of the Kerma kings, datable to the end of the Second Intermediate Period in Egypt. Likewise, the M and N cemeteries are earlier, not later, and date to as early as the First Intermediate Period. Bonnet has also discovered a pre-Kerma phase that may date to the Old Kingdom and be related to the Nubian A-Group.

Recent excavations, notably at Sai, Mirgissa and Kerma itself, have markedly improved our knowledge of the Kerma culture. Based on results of the excavations at Sai, Brigitte Gratien has proposed a new chronology for the Kerma culture subdividing it into four main phases: KA (Archaic Kerma), dating to the First Intermediate Period and early Middle Kingdom; KM (Middle or Formative Pre-Classic Kerma), coeval with the Middle Kingdom; KC (Classic Kerma), the high point of the culture equivalent to the Second Intermediate Period; and KR (Recent Kerma or Post-Classic Kerma), belonging to the period of the Egyptian reconquest of Nubia in the early New Kingdom. During the earliest periods of development, there are great similarities between the Kerma culture and contemporary C-Group and "Pan-grave" Nubians. Through time, however, a growing differentiation in material culture can be seen between these groups.

During the Second Intermediate Period, the Kerma state extended its sphere of influence into southern Egypt and, according to Egyptian sources, made an alliance with the Hyksos in the north to divide and conquer Egypt. Eventually, the Kerma threat was removed after a series of campaigns by the pharaohs of the early 18th Dynasty. Bonnet has discovered remains beneath the modern town that appear to date to this later period. Napatan and Meroitic remains discovered by the Swiss expedition attest to the continued importance of the site to later Nubian cultures.

See also

A-Group culture; C-Group culture; Kushites; Pan-grave culture; Reisner, George Andrew

Further reading

Bonnet, C. 1990. *Kerma: Royaume de Nubie.* Geneva.

Gratien, B. 1978. *Les Cultures Kerma: Essai de Classification.* Lille.

Reisner, G.A. 1923a. *Excavations at Kerma I–III* (Harvard African Studies 5). Cambridge, MA.

——. 1923b. *Excavations at Kerma IV–V* (Harvard African Studies 6). Cambridge, MA.

PETER LACOVARA

Kharga Oasis, Late period and Graeco-Roman sites

Kharga Oasis is located in the Western Desert (24°–26°N, 29°26′E) within the great Libyan depression. The oasis consists of a series of spring-fed areas about 100 km in length. Ancient Egyptian terms used for this area were the hieroglyphic *wḥ3.t* (oasis), *wḥ3.t rsy.t* (southern oasis), and perhaps *knmt* (though the last probably refers to both Kharga and Dakhla Oases). In Graeco-Roman times it was referred to as "e prote Auasis" (Strabo), "Oasis Megale" (Ptolemy), and the Latin "Oasis Major." In Arabic terminology, Kharga also had the names "Biris" and "Bihit" (perhaps deriving from Coptic). In modern times it is known as Kharga or Wadi Gadeed (New Valley).

Numerous prehistoric peoples lived in and around Kharga Oasis. There is, however, little archaeological evidence surviving in Kharga until the Third Intermediate Period, although major archaeological sites from the Old Kingdom are found in Dakhla Oasis to the west. The important archaeological sites in Kharga all date from the Late period. In the 6th Dynasty the royal agent Harkhuf used the desert route through Kharga in order to travel south to Nubia. In the New Kingdom, the oasis was known to export a fine variety of wines to the Nile Valley. The area is also known as a place of exile (for example, by the Christian heretic Nestorius, or as discussed in the New Kingdom literary work, *Tale of Woe*).

The principal importance of Kharga Oasis throughout history remains its sweet water wells, which supplied the numerous desert caravan routes that intersected and went through the region. All of the major sites in Kharga are located at sources of water along desert routes to wadis leading up to the desert escarpment. The ancient city of Hibis at the northern end of the oasis clearly developed due to its water sources. Although Dakhla Oasis was the capital of the western oases during Old and Middle Kingdom times, in the Late period the sites around Kharga rose in importance as a result of the conscious attempt to better control the desert areas.

The Egyptian Antiquities Organization (EAO) has been conducting numerous excavations throughout the oasis, but most of these are unpublished. Except for Hibis Temple and Bagawat, all of the sites described here are not well known and are in need of major archaeological excavations.

ed-Deir

Located 26 km northeast of Kharga City, the Roman period fortress of ed-Deir sits at the opening of the major wadi leading from the oasis up to the desert plateau. The fort served to control the desert caravan route to the Nile Valley which passed by the site. The impressive ruins feature 10–12 m high mudbrick walls with round towers at the four corners. To the north of the site are several Roman period tombs and the unexcavated remains of a town site.

Hibis Temple

Located just to the north of Kharga City, Hibis Temple is the largest temple in the oasis and the only relatively intact structure in Egypt that survives from the Saite and Persian periods. Temple construction began in the Saite period (26th Dynasty), probably during the reign of Psamtik II, with additions by Darius I, Hakor, Nectanebo I and II, Ptolemy IV(?) and at least one Roman emperor. Several blocks found at the site indicate that an earlier temple dating to the New Kingdom also stood on the site.

Hibis Temple is dedicated to the syncretistic deity, "Amen of Hibis" and "Amen-Re of Karnak who dwells in Hibis." The architecture and religious inscriptions are closely related to temples of New Kingdom and Ptolemaic date from Thebes.

The site was excavated in 1909–11 by the Metropolitan Museum of Art. Epigraphic work, begun in 1985 by Eugene Cruz-Uribe, continues at the present. The EAO recently excavated the area between the two front gates, revealing an open courtyard surrounded by columns. The ancient town of Hibis, which surrounds the temple on the south, west and north, has never been excavated because it lies under modern cultivation.

Bagawat

Just north of Hibis Temple, surmounting a large hill, are the impressive ruins of a Coptic cemetery known as Bagawat. The site contains several hundred mudbrick tombs as well as the remains of a basilica. The tombs date from the late third/early fourth through tenth centuries AD, and are mainly single tombs consisting of a vaulted structure (cupola) over a sunken burial pit. Several family tombs are known. Most of the tombs are undecorated, but several have biblical scenes painted on the ceilings. The site was excavated mainly by Ahmed Fakhry for the EAO.

Nadura

Located about 2 km southeast of Hibis is the Roman period temple of Nadura. The dating of the temple is based upon the presence of the cartouches of Antoninus Pius (AD 138–61). The temple site and surrounding structures (including mudbrick houses and vaulted granaries) are mostly unexcavated. There is much debate concerning the deity of the temple. Suggestions include Amen-Re, Mut and the Dioscuri (the Graeco-Roman cult of the Twins, Castor and Pollux).

Qasr el-Ghuieta

The most archaeologically unknown area in Kharga Oasis is the hilltop site of Qasr el-Ghuieta. Located 17 km south of Hibis, the town site is mostly unexcavated. A temple (ancient Perwesekh) has been cleared within the 8–10 m mudbrick walls of the town. The earliest part of the temple probably dates to the 25th or 26th Dynasty, with later work done by Darius I and Ptolemies III, IV and X. The temple is dedicated to the triad of Amen of Perwesekh, Mut and Khonsu.

The excavated area in front of the temple has some stone buildings, probably administrative rooms, which appear to have suffered fire damage during the sacking of the city, probably in AD 450 by the Eastern Desert tribe known as the Blemmyes. The remainder of the town within the walls consists of numerous archaeological strata 5–8 m deep. The EAO recently excavated part of the town southeast of the wall, and cleared a number of rooms and passages with recorded finds of pots, bronze artifacts and ostraca in Demotic and Greek.

Qasr Zaiyan

Twenty-seven km south of Hibis is the mudbrick enclosure of Zaiyan (ancient Tchonemuris). The sanctuary of the temple is the only stone portion of the edifice except for the lintels of the two gates and the floor. The only dated inscription is from the reign of Antoninus Pius (AD 140), but the lintel of the inner gate is Ptolemaic in style. The inscriptions in the sanctuary are at the latest Ptolemaic in date, but may be earlier. The temple is dedicated to Amen of Hibis, Mut and Khonsu.

The EAO recently completed clearing out most of the temple precinct, revealing a large granary and associated administrative rooms. At the lowest layers of mudbrick are remains of painted plaster covering the inner walls.

Qasr Dush

At the far southern end of the oasis, 104 km south of Hibis and 17 km southeast of Baris, is the site of Qasr Dush (ancient Kysis). The large temple here is axial in plan with an inner and outer sanctuary, columned hall and two pylons. Hieroglyphic inscriptions indicate the temple is dedicated to Osiris, although the Greek inscriptions suggest it is a temple of Serapis and Isis. Surrounding the temple are the ruins of a large town. The site has a number of inscriptions dating to the reigns of the Roman emperors Domitian, Hadrian and Antoninus Pius.

The site is currently under excavation by the French Institute of Archaeology, Cairo, which has built a small excavation house there. Recently they discovered a cache of gold and other items during the excavations.

See also

Dakhla Oasis, Dynastic and Roman sites; Late and Ptolemaic periods, overview; pantheon; Roman period, overview

Further reading

Cruz-Uribe, E. 1988. *Hibis Temple Project* 1: *Translations, Commentary, Discussions and Sign List*. San Antonio, TX. Volumes in preparation.

Fakhry, A. 1951. *The Necropolis of El Bagawat in Kharga Oasis*. Cairo.

Giddy, L. 1987. *Egyptian Oases, Bahariya, Dakhla, Farafra and Khargha During Pharaonic Times*. Warminster.

Metropolitan Museum of Art Egyptian Expedition. *The Temple of Hibis in el-Khargeh Oasis*. New York. 1941, Part 1: H. Winlock, *The Excavations*. 1938, Part 2: H.E. White and J. Oliver, *Greek Inscriptions*. 1953, Part 3: N. deGaris Davies, *The Decorations*.

Porter, B., and R. Moss. 1952. *Topographical Bibliography* 7, *Nubia, the Deserts and Outside Egypt*, 277–95. Oxford.

Redde, M., *et al.* 1990. Quinze années de recherches français à Douch. Vers un premier bilan. *BIFAO* 90: 281–301.

EUGENE CRUZ-URIBE

Kharga Oasis, prehistoric sites

Kharga Oasis, situated about 200 km west of the Nile Valley, is the easternmost of the five major oases of the Western Desert. It is an elongated depression, approximately 185 km long and 20–80 km wide, lying with its principal axis in a north–south direction. On the east and north it is bounded by steep escarpments capped with Eocene limestone, and on the west by an irregular escarpment which lacks this limestone cap. The oasis is open to the south and southwest, where the floor of the depression, generally some 300–400 m below the top of the adjacent Libyan Plateau, rises gradually to meet the sandstone floor of the Sahara.

Kharga appears in several memoirs of seventeenth- eighteenth- and nineteenth-century travelers interested primarily in pharaonic and Graeco-Roman antiquities. Laying the foundations for prehistoric research were early geological investigations by A.K. von Zittel, a member of Gerhard Rohlfs' expedition to the Western Desert in 1873–4, Captain H.G. Lyons, whose stratigraphic observations were presented to the Geological Society of London in 1883–4, and John Ball, director in 1898 of the first systematic survey of Kharga. Early references to the prehistoric stone tools of Kharga appear in the work of H.J.L. Beadnell, a colleague of John Ball, and in H.E. Winlock's account of his 1908 round trip by camel between Kharga and Dakhla Oases.

The first systematic investigation into the prehistory of Kharga was conducted from 1930 to 1933 by Gertrude Caton Thompson and E.W. Gardner. Caton Thompson not only defined the archaeological sequence of stone tool industries but, with the aid of Gardner placed these cultural remains into a broader geological and paleoenvironmental context. Unfortunately, relative dating was made complex by the absence of site stratigraphy, and Caton Thompson's sequence, therefore, is based on the comparison of characteristic artifacts from known assemblages.

Prehistoric research in Kharga Oasis was resumed in 1976 with the Combined Prehistoric Expedition (CPE) led by Fred Wendorf and Romuald Schild. In 1983 Fekri Hassan and Diane Holmes contributed additional data on the Khargan Neolithic. A short survey undertaken by the Western Desert Expedition (WDE) in 1982–3 contributed an important assessment of prehistoric settlement patterns in Kharga. Since 1992, members of the Dakhleh Oasis Project (DOP) have been engaged in reassessing

Caton Thompson's classic sequence, and in obtaining Uranium-series (U-series) dates on associated wadi tufas from Kharga.

The earliest cultural material found in the oasis is described by Caton Thompson as "typically evolved Acheulian" (Lower Paleolithic). Although none of the sites with Upper Acheulian tools can be dated directly, preliminary U-series dates on associated tufas suggest an age of over 400,000 years BP (before present). Well-made handaxes (lanceolate and pear-shaped) are the dominant tool-type. Other tools, such as choppers and flakes, are present, but in low frequencies. Levallois elements are rare, indicating that this technique (where a core is intentionally prepared in order to produce a "specialized" flake of predetermined shape) does not yet play an important technological role. It appears likely that Caton Thompson's "Acheulio-Levalloisian" material, found only at Refuf Pass, is a natural admixture of Upper Acheulian and "Lower Levalloisian" artifacts.

The presence of wadi tufas overlying Acheulian deposits, and floral evidence including remains of plants such as fig, suggest that the climate of the oasis during the late Acheulian was considerably wetter than today. Favored site locations appear to be near wadi courses in the vicinity of the Libyan Plateau, or adjacent to spring vents on the depression floor.

Although the dating is inadequate, it is generally accepted that the Acheulian was replaced by the specialized flake industries of the Middle Paleolithic by at least 220,000 years ago. A period of hyperaridity which followed the late Acheulian wet phase was succeeded by multi-staged, Middle Paleolithic wet periods, interrupted by drier intervals. Caton Thompson believed that there were at least two stages of renewed spring activity at Kharga.

In Caton Thompson's (relative) sequence, there are five Middle Paleolithic taxonomic units at Kharga: "Lower Levalloisian" (earliest), "Upper Levalloisian," "Levalloiso-Khargan," Khargan and Aterian (latest). More recent evidence, however, suggests that the Khargan postdates the Aterian.

Only two of the ten "Levalloisian" sites reported by Caton Thompson are found in spring mound deposits on the floor of the depression. The remaining eight are situated in four different scarp areas. Thirty-five additional components, mostly from the Libyan Plateau, were reported by the WDE.

The Aterian is considered a typologically late, Levallois-based industry, characterized by very thin, carefully shaped cores (triangular or discoidal), which produce correspondingly thin flakes, many with finely faceted butts. Stemmed (pedunculated) implements, primarily points, and finely flaked, leaf-shaped pieces (bifacial foliates) are characteristic tools.

According to the WDE, Middle Paleolithic settlement is oriented to the exploitation of a wide range of habitats. Of the forty-two Middle Paleolithic sites identified, however, 72 percent are associated with deposits of ephemeral lakes (called "playas"), 26 percent occur along wadi courses, and 2 percent are near spring vents.

In view of the fact that none of Caton Thompson's "Levalloiso-Khargan" assemblages is in a secure context, the integrity of this cultural unit is considered doubtful. The validity of the Khargan itself has been questioned by some, primarily because of the random, *ad hoc* appearance of much of the retouch, which could be the product of natural agencies. Also, the industry as a whole is so morphologically variable that it defies rigid typological classification. However, since neither ambiguous retouch nor highly variable morphology invalidates the distinct technological traits present, others believe the Khargan to be a valid archaeological designation. Among tools which permit formal classification, scrapers (particularly end and nosed varieties) and borers are common.

The restricted distribution of Khargan material, both at Kharga and in the Western Desert as a whole, appears to reflect the increasingly arid conditions which followed the Aterian wet phase. At Kharga, all known sites are in the scarp deposits of the Bulaq Pass.

Caton Thompson claims that her term "Epi-Levalloisian" denotes all those regional, Levallois-related industries which are believed to fall "anachronistically" within the time-span of

30,000 to 10,000 years (represented in the circum-Mediterranean by the blade industries of the Upper Paleolithic). This term, however, seems to be a theoretical construct of Caton Thompson's to bridge the gap between these apparently late, Levallois-derived industries and succeeding microlithic assemblages.

To date, there is no known lithic sequence in any of the oases, and only one from the Nile Valley, which documents a transition from the (Levallois-based) Middle Paleolithic to the blade-producing technologies which characterize the Upper Paleolithic in the lower Nile Valley. In fact, with only two exceptions, there is an almost total gap in the Egyptian archaeological record between 40,000 and 20,000 BP. Climatic conditions improved around 10,000 BP, and with the onset of the Holocene wet period there is renewed evidence of increased human habitation in the Western Desert. At Kharga, there is renewed artesian spring discharge and playa formation.

Archaeological assemblages of the early Holocene display considerable regional diversity. They are all characterized by blade and bladelet technologies, and by an emphasis on microlithic tool production. Grinding stones and ostrich eggshell beads are commonly found in these early Holocene sites. Caton Thompson classified such material as "Bedouin Microlithic," found at eight localities in Kharga (two on the depression floor and six at silt pans on top of the eastern escarpment). An additional twenty-one "Terminal Paleolithic" (Epi-paleolithic) components have been reported by the WDE.

Following the "Bedouin Microlithic," Caton Thompson defined the "Peasant Neolithic," which she regarded as the equivalent of the Predynastic culture in Upper Egypt, a conjecture wholly supported by radiocarbon dates obtained by the CPE. The "Peasant Neolithic" at Kharga, therefore, marks the latest period of prehistory.

Caton Thompson found Neolithic material associated with spring mounds and also at the chert-mining quarries on the eastern escarpment of the Libyan Plateau. Holmes has reported a single radiocarbon date of around 7,220 BP for the Umm ed-Dabadib area which has yielded fourteen Neolithic surface scatters. The lithic industry is reported to be very similar to that recovered by Caton Thompson.

Six Neolithic sites have been reported at Kharga by the CPE. Sites E-76-7 and E-76-7a at truncated spring vents in the airport area are the most notable. Site E-76-7 is the earliest, with one radiocarbon date of around 5,450 BP. This site consisted of a large concentration of lithic artifacts, a few bones and ostrich eggshell. Only one (upper) grinding stone was in evidence. Several potsherds were found nearby, as well as a hearth. Both Sites E-76-7 and E-76-7a have yielded fragments of a large bovid which has been identified tentatively as domesticated. The Neolithic industry reported by the CPE is characterized by a technology limited to unprepared cores, and by a stress on working tabular chert into bifacial tools such as foliates and large oval hoes. The major elements among the flaked tools are denticulates and perforators. Rare sherds of undecorated, coarse-tempered pottery are present.

The WDE has reported only nine Neolithic sites, the majority of which suggest ephemeral, task-specific occupations. They appear to be very unlike those reported by Caton Thompson or the CPE.

Data from playas elsewhere in the Western Desert suggest a complex pattern of alternating wet and dry intervals throughout the Holocene. The combined floral and faunal evidence, however, indicates that these wet phases were drier than earlier ones, and that the Western Desert was a semi-arid grassland. This paleoenvironmental situation is reflected in the Epipalaeolithic and Neolithic settlement patterns in Kharga Oasis. According to the WDE findings, most sites of these periods are associated with playas; a few are associated with springs on the depression floor. In contrast to earlier settlement evidence, none of these sites is associated with wadis.

The scarcity of *in situ* cultural material as opposed to deflated surface concentrations, the absence of radiometric techniques for much of the early time range involved in the prehistoric record, and the lack of datable material from sites which are amenable to radiocarbon analyses all continue to plague prehistoric research in Kharga Oasis. That we are able to reconstruct any part of it, even in a fragmentary way, is a tribute to the pioneering efforts of Caton Thompson and Gardner, and to the skill and patience of those who have followed in their tracks.

See also

climatic history; dating techniques, prehistory; Neolithic and Predynastic stone tools; Paleolithic cultures, overview; Paleolithic tools; Predynastic period, overview

Further reading

Caton Thompson, G. 1952. *Kharga Oasis in Prehistory.* London.

Churcher, C.S., and A.J. Mills, eds. In press. *Reports from the Survey of Dakhleh Oasis, Western Desert of Egypt, 1977–1987.* Oxford.

Clark, J.D. 1987. The cultures of the Middle Palaeolithic/Middle Stone Age. In *The Cambridge History of Africa* 1: *From the Earliest Times to c. 500 BC,* J.D. Clark, ed., 248–341. Cambridge.

Simmons, A.H., and R.D. Mandel. 1986. *Prehistoric Occupation of a Marginal Environment.* Oxford.

Wendorf, F., and R. Schild. 1980. *Prehistory of the Eastern Sahara.* New York.

MARCIA F. WISEMAN

kingship

The king (pharaoh) was the absolute authority, the ruler for life, and the intermediary between the gods and mankind. Menes is traditionally considered to be the first king of Egypt. However, in the king list inscribed on the Palermo Stone, dating to the 5th Dynasty, Menes is preceded by kings who are shown wearing the double crown symbolizing rulership over all Egypt. The existence of such earlier rulers (the so-called Dynasty 0) is increasingly supported by the excavations of Günter Dreyer in cemetery U at Abydos, the work of Werner Kaiser in the Delta, and the late Michael Hoffman at Hierakonpolis. The tradition of Egyptian kingship continued into the Ptolemaic period and in part, the Roman era, during which time the Roman emperors adopted the traditional iconography and titulary of the Egyptian king.

Names and titles

The most common form of reference to the king is "his majesty" (*hemef*) or "king" (*nesw*). The term "pharaoh" is applied to the king from the New Kingdom onward, when the appellation of the palace (*per-aa,* "the great house") was transferred from the residence to the king himself, much as the term "Sublime Porte" was used to refer to the Ottoman Sultan and his residence. Each king had a formalized titulary which, from the 5th Dynasty onward, consisted of five great names (Horus name; "Two Ladies"; Golden Horus; prenomen; nomen), each of which associated the ruler with specific attributes and deities. In the earliest period, the king bore the Horus name, which might be enclosed in a rectangular format thought to resemble a niched gateway, called the *serekh.* This name was probably assumed upon accession and served to associate the king with the god Horus. In the reign of Den (1st Dynasty) the title "He of the Sedge and the Bee" (*nesw bit*), translated as "King of Upper and Lower Egypt," was added. Under Andjib (1st Dynasty), the title "Two Ladies" (*nebty*), another reference to the duality of the cosmos and land, was added to the titulary. Although the names of rulers of the 1st–2nd Dynasties were placed in an oval cartouche by later historians, it was Seneferu of the 4rd Dynasty, or perhaps his predecessor Huni, who initiated this innovation. The "Golden Horus Name" of the rulers of the 1st–4th Dynasties is known only from the Palermo Stone, at which time it became an element in the titulary. The last major modification occurred under Neferirkare (5th Dynasty) when the prenomen, the formal throne name taken at accession and written in a cartouche, was added before the epithet "Son of Re."

Representation of the king

Most frequently the king is shown in human form, idealized as if in the prime of life. He is distinguished from commoners by a bull tail which trails from his kilt, the royal sporran, headgear and scepters. The most common forms of headgear are the White and Red Crowns, known from Predynastic times, the striped headcloth (*nemes*), the Blue Crown (18th Dynasty), the *atef* and *hemhem*, all of which may also be worn by various gods. The characteristic scepters are the crook (the hieroglyph for "to rule") and the flail, which may allude to agriculture and the ability of the king to provide for his people. The king was also portrayed in symbolic form, in particular as a sphinx, and he was likened to a lion, panther or bull.

Succession

The living king was associated with the god Horus; his predecessor was associated with Horus's father, Osiris, the main deity of the afterlife. According to this mythic succession, each king was considered to be the son of his predecessor, regardless of actual filiation. Therefore, the Egyptians considered the line of kings to be unbroken from the beginning of time. Once raised to kingship, the king served for his or her entire lifetime. The well-being of the king and the symbolic renewal of the ability to rule for a period beyond thirty years was ensured by the *heb-sed* festival, celebrated in the thirtieth year of rule and usually every third year thereafter.

Generally, the eldest son of the primary wife ("queen") of the previous king succeeded his father. However, the succession in the reign of Ramesses II, confused by a myriad of male offspring, indicates that strict primogeniture was not always followed. The idea that the inheritance of the throne was passed through the matrilineal line (the "heiress theory") is disproved by the fact that the chief wives of Tuthmose III, Amenhotep II and Amenhotep III were not themselves of royal blood, yet their sons acceded to the throne. The important role of royal daughters in the succession of the 18th Dynasty may be due to the lack of sons among the chief queens of this dynasty, through whom the royal legitimacy was passed, rather than being a reflection of any matrilineal tradition. From the 12th Dynasty onward, coregencies were instituted whenever there was a possible cause of instability surrounding the succession.

Potentially disputed succession was confirmed by oracle (Tuthmose III), by a claim of divine birth (kings of the 5th Dynasty in the Papyrus Westcar; Hatshepsut; Amenhotep III; Ramesses II), or by military intervention (Psamtik I and Amasis of the 26th Dynasty). In cases where there were no surviving heirs, the king could be elected from among the highest echelon of the administration (Ramesses I), or from the military (Horemheb), who traditionally married into the extended royal family. Little is known about the actual coronation ceremony, although at least one ruler (Hatshepsut) was crowned in the temple of Ma'at at Karnak. Representations of the coronation reflect divine assistance and approval, for the gods Horus, Seth, Atum, Amen and Thoth, as well as other gods, are shown placing or steadying the crown on the king's head.

Role and duties

The king was an absolute ruler. He was the final authority over economic matters. In theory, the land and its inhabitants were his personal property, although the existence of land grants and tax exemptions indicate the truer state of affairs. The king was assisted in the administration by one or two viziers who stood over a multi-level bureaucracy. The king served as the highest appeal court in the land, and, in theory, every commoner had access to the king to personally plead a case. The king was the supreme commander of the armed forces and many kings led Egyptian troops in battle.

The king was the highest priest in the land. All cult actions, regardless of the actual officiant, were enacted in the king's name. He was the intermediary between the gods and mankind who, through the maintenance of *ma'at* (justice) and through offerings to the gods, ensured the unending cycle of the sun's rising and setting, birth and rebirth, and justice in everyday affairs. On temple walls scenes of offering rituals are usually narrated by inscriptions that elucidate the relationship between the king and the god. In such scenes, the god pronounces the gift of basic attributes (life, health) which allow the king to live. The king's action of offering is phrased in the infinitive, making the dedication simultaneous with the action of the donation. The final element of the inscriptions is conventionally translated "may he make given life." This serves as an acknowledgment which, in the 18th Dynasty, is understood as "he [the king] acts for him [the god] who has given life." The grammatical construction of this formula was modified in the Ramesside period (19th–20th Dynasties) to mean "May he [the god] make life for the donor [on account of the king's offering]." This reinterpretation indicates that the action of the king was thought to influence a future action of the god, thereby creating a cycle of giving and receiving, which is absent in offering inscriptions of the earlier and post-Ramesside periods.

Jan Assmann has suggested that the power of the king declined in the Ramesside period. This conclusion is based on the assertion that the population increasingly believed that all aspects of the future, including judgment in the afterlife, were directed not by acting in accordance with the precepts of the traditional moral code (*ma'at*), which was ensured and protected by the king, but rather by the arbitrary will of the gods. According to Assmann, the influence of the Ramesside king, based on his role as the intermediary between the gods and mankind, was eroded as mankind looked directly to the gods for salvation. This assertion may be countered by the greater incidence of the ritual of the presentation of the goddess Ma'at shown in temples of the Ramesside period, which indicates a close association of the king, the gods and Ma'at, and also by continuing references to Ma'at in Late Egyptian and Demotic texts. In summary, although there was political instability in the Ramesside period, there is little evidence to suggest that the theological power of the king waned.

Divinity of the king

The king may be considered to be a mortal who was associated with deities and hence possessed a dual nature. The royal epithets "the good god" and "the great god," both known from the Old Kingdom onward, are characteristic of the divine element of the king's nature. Texts and representations in the royal tombs of the New Kingdom closely identify the king with the sun god Re, as they journeyed through the darkness of night. However, this must be balanced against the deification of some kings after their death (Senusret I, Amenhotep I), during their lifetime (Amenhotep III, Tutankhamen, Seti I, Ramesses II and perhaps Akhenaten), or during the celebration of certain festivals (the New Year, *Opet*), which suggests that under ordinary circumstances, the king was not considered to be divine. This mortality of the king is stressed by the title "Son of Re," which was assumed by kings from the 5th Dynasty onward. Erik Hornung has suggested that rather than being a diminution of the pharaoh's divine status, the phrase sought to define the king's relationship with the gods.

See also

Abydos, Umm el-Qa'ab; administrative bureaucracy; Hierakonpolis; law; *ma'at*; religion, state; taxation and conscription

Further reading

Assmann, J. 1984. *Ägypten: Theologie und Frömmigkeit einer frühen Hochkultur.* Stuttgart.

Hornung, E. 1982. *Conceptions of God in Ancient Egypt: The One and the Many*, Ithaca, NY.

Murnane, W.J. 1977. *Ancient Egyptian Coregencies.* Chicago.

O'Connor, D., and D. Silverman, eds. 1995. *Ancient Egyptian Kingship*. Leiden.

Robins, G. 1983. A critical examination of the theory that the right to the throne of ancient Egypt passed through the female line in the 18th Dynasty. *GM* 62: 67–77.

Teeter, E. 1997. *The Presentation of Maat: Ritual and Legitimacy in Ancient Egypt* (SAOC 57). Chicago.

EMILY TEETER

Kom Abu Bello

Kom Abu Bello is a small village on the western edge of the Delta, approximately 70 km northwest of Cairo (30°26′ N, 30°49′ E). It is situated where the route leading from the Wadi el-Natrun approaches the Rosetta branch of the Nile. The famous prehistoric site of Merimde Beni-salame lies to the south, and Kom el-Hisn is to the north.

In pharaonic times the site was known as "Mefket," which is the (ancient) Egyptian word for both turquoise and the goddess Hathor, who was worshipped here. During the Graeco-Roman period the site was known as "Terenuthis," which was derived from the pharaonic words *ta Rennouti* (land of the goddess Renenutet). The site was also known as "Terenouti" in Coptic. The modern name of the village, Tarana, is derived from the ancient name of the city. The name Kom Abu Bello refers specifically to the northwestern part of the site, where the Graeco-Roman cemetery is located. This name is probably derived from the name of the temple of the Greek god Apollo, the remains of which were found at the northern edge of the site.

Very little remains of the site today, as it has been explored and excavated for over a century, beginning with F.L. Griffith, who found the temple of Hathor, "Mistress of *Mefket*," in 1887–8. In 1935, a portion of the site was excavated during a one-month project, conducted by the University of Michigan under the direction of E. Peterson. The majority of the excavations took place from 1969 to 1974 when a salvage archaeology project was undertaken, necessitated by the construction of the Nasser Canal.

In 1969–70, Shafik Farid conducted work at the southern end of the site, where Old, Middle and New Kingdom tombs were discovered. From 1970 to 1972 the Egyptian Antiquities Organization (EAO) continued excavations under Abdou el-Hafiz Abdou el-Aal, assisted by Zahi Hawass. Ahmed el-Sawi, assisted by Hawass, directed the work from 1972 to 1975, and Hawass was director of excavations in 1975–6. The 1969–1974 excavations covered a 5 km^2 area, extending from the Kafr Daoud bridge on the north to the edge of the contemporary village of Tarana on the south.

In the pharaonic cemetery the majority of Old Kingdom tombs date to the 6th Dynasty. New Kingdom burials were placed in ceramic coffins with large faces characteristic of this period. Most of the site is covered by the large cemetery of Graeco-Roman and Coptic date, which extends from the Tarana Bridge, just north of the Middle Kingdom cemetery, to the remains of the temple of Apollo, some 2 km to the north, and on the west from the area known as "Tomb of the Ruler" to the railroad tracks running along the edge of modern Tarana. Approximately one-fourth of the original cemetery is covered by the contemporary village of Nasr Moustafa, lying to the north of Tarana just across the railroad tracks. The site is one of the richest in Egypt for the Graeco-Roman and early Coptic periods (*circa* 300 BC to AD 500), when it was an important center of trade for wine and salt from the Wadi el-Natrun.

Mudbrick tombs were found in the cemetery. The superstructure of many of the tombs was rectangular or square, with a barrel-vaulted roof. Some tombs had superstructures shaped like a truncated pyramid. Most of the tombs rested on mudbrick platforms. Stelae depicting the dead were placed inside tomb niches and became known as "Terenuthis stelae." Over 450 stelae, which date from the second–fourth centuries AD, have been recovered. The most common motif on the stelae is the deceased standing between two Egyptian-style columns with Greek pediments. Below him is a short text in either Greek or Egyptian (demotic).

Offerings to the deceased consisted of wine, lettuce and grapes, which were placed on offering tables in the tombs. Lamps were also lit for the dead and one stela even shows a party with music, from which we can infer that such events were frequent at Terenuthis. Hunting and fishing seem to have been the most common occupations, but potters, vintners, jewelers and artisans who carved the funerary stelae were also found in the town. Personal artifacts from the tombs indicate that there was active commerce in wine and salt with the Wadi el-Natrun, only 24 km away.

A cattle cemetery, associated with the cult of Hathor, has also been discovered. In a cemetery dedicated to the Greek goddess Aphrodite, dating to the second century AD, many faïence statuettes of the goddess were found in niches in the tombs. Statues and statuettes of Egyptian deities, such as Anubis, Isis, Taweret and Bes, were also discovered at the site. They are made of faïence and inscribed with hieroglyphic formulae. Statuettes of Greek deities, such as Harpocrates and Hermes, were also found.

Many ceramic lamps were excavated, with impressed designs of olive branches, Nile fish, the frog goddess Heket and Serapis. Other artifacts, such as ivory combs, necklaces, gold and silver rings, gold earrings, bracelets, hair clips and amulets, were also recovered. A great deal of pottery dating from the end of the pharaonic period through the Coptic period was likewise recovered. Many of the vessels were painted in various colors. Amphorae were also found. Pots in the burials were placed around the head of the deceased.

A small section of the settlement of Terenuthis was excavated. The remains of dwellings were uncovered on the east side of the Nasser Canal, immediately southwest of the excavated cemetery and east of the Middle Kingdom cemetery.

Remains of the Apollo temple are located at the northern edge of the site, 0.5 km north of the "High Place," at the point through which the Nasser Canal was cut. The temple was completely destroyed, however, and it was not possible to trace its foundations. Immediately

to the south of the temple area, two limestone fragments were found bearing the name of Psamtik II. A short distance farther south were two Roman baths, with remains of the characteristic *tepidarium* and *frigidarium*, and a well approximately 10 m deep where water was obtained for the baths. Blocks were also found from the temple of Hathor, decorated in low raised relief, which date to the reign of Ptolemy I Soter.

Unfortunately, a major part of the ancient city is now covered by the modern town of Tarana and by the surrounding cultivation to the west and south. Evidence for the town consists of mudbrick walls and potsherds on the surface in the area immediately west of Tarana at the place called "Baltous," between Tarana and the railroad track.

The data from Kom Abu Bello have been important for reconstructing the history, culture, religion and social relations in Egypt in a critical period of transition from pharaonic times into the Coptic era.

See also

Late and Ptolemaic periods, overview; Roman period, overview; wine making

Further reading

Hawass, Z. 1979. Preliminary report on the excavations at Kom Abou Bellou. *Studien zur altägyptischen Kultur* 7: 76–87.

Porter, B., and R.L.B. Moss. 1934. *Topographical Bibliography of Ancient Egyptian Hieroglyphic Texts: Reliefs and Paintings* 4. Oxford.

ZAHI HAWASS

Kom el-Hisn

Kom el-Hisn (30°48′ N, 30°36′ E) is one of the more important and ancient settlements in the western Nile Delta. The name of the site—literally "Hill of the Fort" in Arabic—is probably a reference to the rectangular mudbrick temple enclosure that was still well preserved a century ago but few traces of which remain today. A large *gezira*, or sand and gravel mound, which in ancient times contained burials from communities at Kom el-Hisn, is today the most visible aspect of the site. Several small mudbrick villages overlie parts of Kom el-Hisn, and much of the rest of the site has long since been converted to agricultural fields. Only the central area of the Old Kingdom and part of the Middle Kingdom community are relatively well preserved, but these are steadily being diminished by agricultural expansion.

Kom el-Hisn today lies about 90 km from the present coastline. In antiquity the site would have been near a branch (now shifted to the east) of the Nile, and the coastline may have been less than 50 km from the sea. Kom el-Hisn would also have been very near the desert edge, to the west, and it is likely to have been directly on the route to the Libyan frontier. The site has been visited and described by numerous people since 1884, and the most recent investigations of the site, by American archaeologists under the direction of Robert J. Wenke, have involved excavations of Old and Middle Kingdom areas and re-analysis of a stone tomb.

Much of what we know about Kom el-Hisn comes from texts. The site is thought to have been the ancient locality named "Im3w" (i.e. the plural form of a type of tree), mentioned in texts since the 5th Dynasty. Middle Kingdom inscriptions from Kom el-Hisn identify Hathor as the principal deity of the locality then, and remains of her temple, dating from the 19th and 22nd Dynasties, have been found. Kom el-Hisn is situated in Nome III of Lower Egypt, the same nome in which Egyptian texts list the locality "Estate of the Cattle" (*ḥwt-iḥwt*). Not yet located precisely, the "Estate of the Cattle" was originally one of the oldest state foundations in Egypt. Artifacts of the 1st Dynasty (a seal found in the tomb of Queen Merneith at Abydos and impressions on jar lids from the reign of King Den, in Tomb 6 at Abu Roash) date the "Estate of the Cattle" to this early period.

Various Ramesside statues were found on the site's surface, as well as large earthen temple walls that have now largely been removed by local farmers. The stone tomb of a man named Hesew-wer, dated to the First Intermediate Period, is located on the main mound of the site, around which at lower elevations are the irregular areas of Old and Middle Kingdom occupation. The last occupation of the site in many areas appears to have been in the Old Kingdom, but other large areas were occupied from the First Intermediate Period into the Late period. The German Egyptologist Hermann Junker found flint artifacts on the surface that he dated to the 1st and 2nd Dynasties, but no substantial remains of this period have yet been located at the site.

The best documented period of Kom el-Hisn's occupation is that of the Old Kingdom. Radiocarbon dates as well as artifact styles and epigraphic finds indicate that most of the area recently excavated was a large community in the 4th–6th Dynasties, but that some areas of the site were occupied into at least the early Middle Kingdom, to about 1800 BC. Most areas of Kom el-Hisn comprise three distinct superimposed building levels, which constitute up to 2.4 m of deposits.

Sterile levels were reached in only about 22 sqm of the site. Studies indicate that Old Kingdom Kom el-Hisn's environment was, as it is today, well watered and heavily vegetated. However, Kom el-Hisn's environs were probably more heavily forested than today, after centuries of agricultural expansion. Geomorphological investigations suggest that Kom el-Hisn's occupations rest on a point bar deposit associated with an extinct water course, possibly a major stream connected to a major Nile distributary.

Most of the main occupational mound is composed of Old Kingdom mudbrick buildings whose upper wall remnants constitute the site's surface: intact walls are usually found at less than 20 cm depth. Many of the buildings and rooms are small structures that contain hearths, storage features, smoke-blackened pottery, burned organic materials, and many other traces of domestic activities. In general, none of the buildings so far revealed exhibits evidence of vastly different construction cost or use. Nor do there appear to be major differences in construction or contents of buildings when comparing the three different building phases.

Although Kom el-Hisn's floral and faunal remains generally resemble those from other early pharaonic sites, they differ sharply in two potentially important ways: Kom el-Hisn contains far fewer cattle bones and cereal remains than comparable sites. The low frequency of cattle bones is surprising in that the use of cattle dung as fuel was the primary source of Kom el-Hisn's plant remains. Plant remains are mainly fodder crops (such as clover), as well as the weeds commonly found in fodder crops, and the wastes of cleaning grain. The Kom el-Hisn cattle were perhaps fed in pens, rather than free-browsing, based on the kinds and proportions of plant remains in their dung. Only a few pieces of sheep/goat dung were found in the Kom el-Hisn samples; and since such pellets are commonly preserved in domestic hearth fires, their absence supports the inference that cattle dung was the primary fuel.

Given this botanical evidence, the low frequency of cattle bones in the samples may, somewhat paradoxically, support the possibility that Kom el-Hisn was a specialized cattle-rearing center that sent most of its herds to Memphis and other cult and settlement centers. This interpretation is not contradicted by the artifact assemblage: nothing in the samples would be out of place in a relatively simple peasant agricultural community except, perhaps, the inscribed mud sealings, which probably reflect direct economic ties with the central government.

The Kom el-Hisn ceramics are extremely similar in styles and forms to Old Kingdom ones from other sites in the Delta and from elsewhere in Egypt. Many vessels were crude containers ("beer jars" and "bread molds"); another common form is a round-bottom carinated bowl in a medium-fine clay. Only a few potsherds made of fine clay with very little organic tempering (Nile Silt A) were found; all of them are fragments of the "Meydum" bowls well known at other Old Kingdom sites. Vessels made from marl clays thought to be from Upper Egypt (Qena) comprise a tiny fraction of the overall assemblage.

Kom el-Hisn's lithic artifacts also generally fit this simple agricultural pattern. The hundreds of fragments of ground stone tools found reflect the considerable importance of stone tools in Old Kingdom agriculture. By far the most common retouched tools were "sickle blades." Many of these appear to have been broken, either through use or intentionally, to fit sickle hafts, and well developed sheen formed by cutting grasses is visible on many of them. The very low frequencies of cores and debitage may indicate that these blades were not made locally, although lithic workshops may well have been concentrated in areas of the site that have not yet been excavated. The raw material for these lithics is common along much of Egypt's desert margins.

Many fragments of clay sealings have been found at the site, but only about twenty-one have decipherable inscriptions. Sealings were used from at least Early Dynastic times through the pharaonic era, often as sealings on pottery vessels containing commodities, but also on documents and small containers and boxes. The presence of these sealings at Kom el-Hisn no doubt reflects at least some direct ties with the central government. No commodities, however, are named in these sealings and most of the names are ambiguous.

Thousands of graves at Kom el-Hisn were excavated in the 1940s in the sand-gravel mound and in adjacent areas. Most of these burials appear to have been post-Old Kingdom in age, but their contents were never fully described and their present whereabouts in unknown. The more recent excavations at Kom el-Hisn were in occupational areas, and the several burials we have found appear to be intrusive from post-Old Kingdom periods.

In general, the evidence seems most consistent with the supposition that Kom el-Hisn was a specialized government-sponsored, cattle-raising settlement or transport station on the routes to Libya. There is almost no evidence of local craft production. Artifact styles are impressively similar to those at Old Kingdom sites all over Egypt, from Giza to the Dakhla Oasis, implying strong cultural ties to the Old Kingdom state. The inscribed clay sealings probably reflect direct import or export of commodities to government stores. The radical difference between Kom el-Hisn and other sites in cattle bone frequencies, as well as the evidence that cattle dung was a main source of fuel, may reflect cattle raising and export as a primary economic activity. The relatively minor differences in construction costs and contents of the buildings and apparently restricted range of economic activities and social classes at Kom el-Hisn are consistent with a community primarily made up of herdsmen, subsistence farmers, and a few administrators.

See also

Dynastic stone tools; Old Kingdom, overview; pottery, Early Dynastic to Second Intermediate Period; subsistence and diet in Dynastic Egypt

Further reading

Hamada, A., and S. Farid. 1950. Excavations at Kom el-Hisn 1945. *ASAE* 50: 367–99.

Moens, M.F., and W. Wetterstrom. 1988. The agricultural economy of an Old Kingdom town in Egypt's Western Delta: insights from the plant remains. *JNES* 31: 159–73.

Wenke, R.J. 1988. Old Kingdom community organization in the Western Egyptian Delta. *Norwegian Archaeological Review* 19(1): 15–33.

Wenke, R.J. and D. Brewer. 1996. The Archaic-Old Kingdom Delta: the evidence from Mendes and Kom el-Hisn. In *House and Palace in Ancient Egypt*, M. Bietak, ed., 265–85. Vienna.

Wenke, R.J., and R. Redding. 1986. Excavations at Kom el-Hisn, 1986. *NARCE* 135: 11–17.

Wenke, R.J., R. Redding, P. Buck, M. Kobusiewicz and K. Kroeper. 1988. Kom el-Hisn: excavations of an Old Kingdom West Delta community. *JARCE* 25: 5–34.

ROBERT J. WENKE

Kom Ombo

Kōm Ombo is the name of an industrial town 46 km north of Aswan on the east bank of the Nile where an important temple of Ptolemaic–Roman date is located (24°27′ N, 32°56′ E). The town's modern designation preserves its ancient pharaonic name, translated as "the district where original creation occurred" (*nebit* in hieroglyphs, *imba* in Demotic). The temple has been investigated by French scholars and recently an Egyptian team has begun excavations to the south of the enclosure wall.

The site appears to have been occupied in prehistoric times, based on the evidence of lithic material excavated in the area. Early historical epochs of the site are imperfectly understood, despite mentions of the town in inscriptions dating to both the Middle and New Kingdoms. The only excavated evidence of these periods consists of isolated blocks of stone, ostensibly from one or more temples, inscribed with the cartouches of a Senusret, as well as with the names of Amenhotep I, Hatshepsut, Tuthmose III and Ramesses II.

During the Ptolemaic period Kom Ombo became an important administrative center of Nome I of Upper Egypt, in part because it commands the heights overlooking the river from which troops could guarantee the security of Egypt's southern frontier. At this time the present temple was begun by one of the Ptolemaic kings whose cartouches are, unfortunately, imperfectly preserved. By the time of Ptolemy VI Philometor (180–164 BC and again 163–145 BC) the walls of the temple were being decorated and inscribed in his name. Thereafter construction at the site continued well into the reign of the Roman emperor Macrinus (AD 217–18).

The present temple is magnificently situated on elevated rock, but the Nile has more recently changed its course and many of the temple's outer buildings have been washed away or seriously denuded. These include the so-called *mammisi* (birth house), which was begun during the reign of Ptolemy VIII Evergetes II (170–163 BC and again 143–116 BC), and parts of the mudbrick enclosure wall. The construction of the modern quay where tour boats moor has reduced the danger of further erosion of the river bank. Past damage has been compounded by the recent earthquake.

Despite these problems, the temple of Kom Ombo still preserves several distinctive features. Foremost among these is its ground plan, which reveals that the temple is really divided into two halves down its central axis. Such a "double temple" is rare in Egyptian architecture. The northern half of the temple is dedicated to the god Harwer ("Horus the Elder") and his consort Tasentnefert ("the beautiful sister"), who is identified with the goddess Tefnut, and their offspring, the child god, Panebtawy ("the lord of the two lands"). Panebtawy shares some of the characteristics of Sobek, to whom the southern half of the temple is dedicated. Sobek, the crocodile god, is likewise a member of a triad of deities comprising his consort, Hathor, and their offspring, Khonsu. A careful examination of the temple inscriptions and their location reveals that primacy is accorded to Harwer. This is particularly evident in the arrangement of the hieroglyphs on the outer hypostyle hall's double architrave, beneath which are twin entrances leading to each parallel half of the temple. Passing through the outer, central and inner vestibules, one eventually comes to the sanctuary, divided in half by a hollow central wall, perhaps to give access to the now destroyed roof from which astronomical observations could be made. Some scholars maintain, however, that this passage was intended to hide a priest who would be the voice of an oracle in the name of either deity. Within each sanctuary is a black granite stone, incorrectly called an altar. These were originally the stands on which rested the sacred barks of Harwer and Sobek, which were used in processions. A series of underground crypts, of uncertain function but possibly used to store valuable ritual objects, and a suite of symmetrically arranged rooms are found at the rear of the temple.

The temple itself is surrounded on three sides by a corridor formed by extending the outer walls of the first hypostyle hall. This is again another unusual feature of the temple's architectural design, and one which is without

parallel in other temples of Ptolemaic and Roman date.

Other structures include a small chapel dedicated exclusively to the god Sobek in the northwest of the temple precinct, bounded by the enclosure wall. To the west of this structure is a curious pit, cut into the living rock and lined with blocks of stone. This feature has sometimes been identified as a cistern, but some scholars, citing the analogy of the precinct of the Apis Bull at Memphis, have suggested that it was a sacred precinct where a living crocodile, the manifestation of the god Sobek, was housed.

In the southeast is the lateral gateway of the temple's enclosure wall. This gateway was built by Ptolemy XII (80–57 BC and again 55 BC) and is now the principal entry to the temple. In the vicinity of this gateway and almost abutting the enclosure wall is a small chapel to the goddess Hathor. The chapel has been converted into a museum which houses a selection of mummified crocodiles excavated in the vicinity of the temple.

In addition to the innovative design of the ground plan, the decoration of the temple contains some very unusual scenes and embellishments. The columns of the first hypostyle hall still preserve abundant traces of their original paint. Furthermore, some of these representations, including those of Harwer, were once embellished with inlays, mostly notably in the eyes. This same technique of inlaying the eyes is found again on the figures of colossal scale which adorn the exterior rear wall of the temple proper.

Some of the temple reliefs are extraordinarily crafted and reveal a sensitivity to spacial concerns that is indebted to advances already exploited in the reliefs of the temple of Seti I (19th Dynasty) at Abydos. One noteworthy example is a scene on the west wall of the inner hypostyle hall where Ptolemy VIII Evergetes II is shown with his wife, Cleopatra II, and his daughter, Cleopatra III. The queens, each wearing the characteristically tightly fitting sheaths and holding floral scepters, form the left hand side of a balanced composition. The contours of their floral crowns are harmoniously balanced by the placement of their cartouches above their heads. Next comes Ptolemy VIII Evergetes II, who holds in his near hand a scepter shaped like the hieroglyph *w3s* and extends his far hand toward Harwer in a gesture of adoration. Ptolemy here wears a festive, gossamer garment which reveals the contours of his legs beneath. Delicate as these touches are, they should not obscure the fact that the overlapping of the attributes held by Harwer in the far right of the composition recalls the arrangement of the attributes held by Seti I and the deities he adores at Abydos. The three notched palm fronds held by the near hand of Harwer twist in space and go beneath his outstretched far arm, which offers the scimitar to Ptolemy VIII Evergetes II. This generation of space is a masterful evocation of pharaonic artistic tenets.

The west wall of the Kom Ombo temple also contains a rare, cultic relief, placed on the central axis of the temple, which is dated by its accompanying inscriptions to the reign of the Roman emperor Trajan (AD 98–117). A winged sun-disc hovers over images of the *wadjet* eye (a protective symbol) and an array of beneficent animal-form deities. The center of the relief contains a hollowed-out shrine, flanked by depictions of ears, while images of Sobek, left, and Harwer, right, serve as vigilant sentinels. In the lowest register are representations of bound prisoners. It has been suggested that this relief was created to meet the religious needs of lower status individuals who were unable to gain access to the temple proper. They would make their supplications to an image of Ma'at, the goddess of truth, which was originally placed within the niche. The depicted ears were there to guarantee that she would indeed hearken to their prayers, and in so doing would assist them in triumphing over adversity (in the form of the bound prisoners below). The entire scene may have been framed by a system of shutters which could be opened as needed by specially appointed priests, who may also have employed a balustrade to keep the petitioners at some distance from the relief and the image of Ma'at.

A second relief on the northeastern interior wall of the corridor has generated a great deal of discussion, particularly since the upper courses of the wall have been destroyed and with them whatever inscriptions may have originally accompanied this scene. Depicted in this relief are objects, grouped into three registers, which are readily identifiable as an assortment of instruments—forceps/tweezers/tongs, probes/awls, spatulas/spoons, and the like—as well as a variety of vessels and containers. Many scholars have identified these objects as instruments used by physicians performing surgery and dispensing different medications. Practicing physicians together with scholars specializing in the medical history of ancient Egypt, however, dismiss this notion, and there is no good evidence that the temple of Kom Ombo functioned as a medical center in pharaonic times. Others have suggested that these implements are tools belonging to a craftsmen's workshop, probably of metalsmiths, a highly justified conclusion considering that artisans were attached to temples.

One of the peculiar features of the site of Kom Ombo is the devotion of its inhabitants to animal cults. This is evident not only in some of the inscriptions carved on the walls of the temple, in which the generations of Egypt's deities are equated in general with the family tree of Sobek, but also in the fact that several different species of mummified animals have been found interred in the vicinity of the temple. In addition to the crocodile mummies mentioned above, these include mummified ibis and falcons, as well as serpents. The popularity of such cults among Egyptians during the Ptolemaic and Roman periods has been explained as a reaction against their foreign overlords. It was a well-known fact that the Greeks, and particularly the Romans, were appalled by Egyptian deities with animal forms, which is quite clear from the text of a biting satire by the Roman author Juvenal. Possibly the more repugnant this practice was to the Greeks and Romans, the more it was embraced by the native Egyptians as a symbol of their nationalism.

In time the inhabitants of the Kom Ombo region converted to Christianity, and archaeologists have excavated evidence of an early

Coptic church here. Little remains of this church aside from column fragments and their bases.

See also

Late and Ptolemaic periods, overview; pantheon; religion, state; Roman period, overview

Further reading

Ghalioungui, P., and Z. Dawakhly. 1965. *Health and Healing in Ancient Egypt*. Cairo.

Gutbub, A. 1978. Éléments ptolemaïques préfigurant le relief culturel de Kom Ombo. In *Das ptolemäischen Ägypten. Akten des Internationalen Symposions 27. 29. September 1976 in Berlin*, H. Maehler and V.M. Strocka, eds, 165–76. Mainz.

Porter, B., and R.L.B. Moss. 1970. *Topographical Bibliography of Ancient Egyptian Hieroglyphic Texts* 6: 179–203. Oxford.

ROBERT S. BIANCHI

el-Kurru

El-Kurru (18°25′ N, 31°46′ E) lies on the west bank of the Nile, 15 km downstream from Karima, Sudan, and the site of Gebel Barkal, and 35 km downstream from the terminus of the Fourth Cataract in Upper Nubia. Its ancient name is unknown, but Francis Lloyd Griffith proposed to equate it with the Egyptian "Karoy," the name of a place at the southern limit of the Egyptian empire during the New Kingdom.

The archaeological interest of the site was noted in the nineteenth century by, among others Frédéric Cailliaud and Carl Richard Lepsius, who had observed its two standing pyramids and the ruins of other small tombs. Excavations were first conducted there by George Reisner and the Harvard University–Museum of Fine Arts, Boston Expedition between February and May 1919. Reisner found that the two large pyramids were those of a late Kushite king and queen of the fourth century BC, whose names were not preserved. The smaller ruined tombs belonged to four of the five kings of the 25th Dynasty: Piye (*circa* 747–716 BC), Shabako (*circa* 716–704 BC), Shebitku (*circa* 704–690 BC) and Tanutameni (*circa* 664–553 BC), as well as their major and minor queens, and sixteen ancestors, whose names were not preserved. There was also a cemetery of horse burials belonging to the four kings of the 25th Dynasty.

Until recently the site was known exclusively for its cemetery, which was the only part ever published by Reisner and his assistant, Dows Dunham. Reisner's unpublished excavation diaries in the Museum of Fine Arts, Boston, however, indicate that for several days he probed the area of the modern village and identified remains of an important ancient walled town, thus accounting for the cemetery. El-Kurru can now be presumed to be the earliest royal seat of the Kushite Napatan dynasty. A small late Meroitic cemetery, called esh-Sheikheil (and designated Ku. 700 by Reisner) was also identified about 800 m north of the royal cemetery. It was partly excavated and the material, still unpublished, is now in both the Museum of Fine Arts, Boston, and the University Museum, Philadelphia (by exchange with the Museum of Fine Arts, 1991).

The ancient town site at el-Kurru was identified by Reisner within and at the border of the modern village. Its remains consisted of a section of an early rubble-filled wall with a rounded bastion (Ku. 1200) and an apparent later wall (Ku. 1300) with a large central gateway. Ku. 1300, which seemed to mark the edge of cultivation, was traced by Reisner for over 200 m. Ancient house remains were noted immediately inside it, as was a large rock-cut well or cistern (Ku. 1400), 6 × 4.5 m in area and 5 m deep at water level, with a descending stairway. Reisner thought that this feature provided the main water supply for the community at the time of Ku. 1300. Unfortunately, no precise maps or plans of these features were ever produced. They do suggest, however, that el-Kurru was the earliest residence of the Napatan dynasty and that, prior to the ascendancy of Gebel Barkal (Napata) and Sanam, probably in the later eighth century BC, it had been the major trans-shipment point on the north bank of the Nile between the Bayuda desert road (to and from the Fifth Cataract region) and the Meheila road (to and from the Third Cataract region) across the Nubian Desert.

The royal cemetery at el-Kurru offers the only evidence yet available for the origin of the Napatan dynasty (later to become Egypt's 25th Dynasty). Unfortunately, the evidence for dating the sixteen ancestor tombs remains problematic. Radiocarbon dates from the earliest tomb (Ku. Tum. 1) range from the New Kingdom to the late ninth century BC. Stone, faïence and ceramic vessels from the earliest tombs seem to belong to both the New Kingdom and the Third Intermediate Period. The fragmentary nature of the skeletal material and the chaotic mixing of the tomb contents from plundering has rendered the sex of the occupants debatable. Although Reisner dated the earliest tombs to the early ninth century BC, the chronology of the cemetery has recently become the subject of a heated scholarly debate.

The early tombs consisted of rock-cut pits or side-chambers, sealed by stone superstructures, now almost entirely quarried away. These tombs occupied the highest and best points in the original cemetery, which was bounded on either side by a wadi. The earliest tombs (Ku. Tum. 1, 5, 4, 2, in chronological order), which Reisner called "tumuli," had round ground plans and probably took the form of typical Nubian C-Group graves. From rough stone to cut stone masonry, they rapidly advanced in form. Tumulus Ku. Tum. 6 had an offering chapel on its east side, and it and its near duplicate (Ku. 19) both had horseshoe-shaped enclosure walls. The remaining ten tombs in the series, which were square in plan, were all built lower down a slope in a single line from northeast to southwest (Ku. 14, 13, 11, 10, 9, 23, 21, 8, 20, 7, in that order). Of these, Ku. 21 and 20, the only ones built without chapels, were smaller tombs that had apparently belonged to minor queens or family members of the king buried in Ku. 8, whom Reisner

identified with Kashta (*circa* 760–747 BC). Reisner called these square tombs "*mastabas*," which he believed metamorphosed into small pyramids at the advent of the 25th Dynasty. Recent evaluation of the evidence by Timothy Kendall, however, suggests that even the earliest square tombs had probably been small pyramids or step pyramids built on *mastaba* bases.

Reisner recognized six different tomb types among the ancestral tombs and equated these with as many human "generations." He thus envisioned six probable rulers prior to Piye, the first king with whom a tomb (Ku. 17) could be identified by textual evidence. Recently, this traditional theory of the ancestral generations has come under critical review by both Kendall and László Török. Essentially agreeing with Reisner and Dunham, Kendall has proposed, on the basis of tomb evolution, and analyses of artifacts and the human remains, that the ancestral tombs probably belonged to seven individual rulers and their chief wives prior to Piye. Since during the earliest historical period at Napata rulers were succeeded by brothers or first cousins, he suggests that the seven rulers probably belonged to no more than four generations, thus giving a mid-ninth century BC date for the founding of the cemetery. Török, on the other hand, has proposed to view the ancestral tomb sequence as a succession of exclusively kings' tombs. In this manner, he suggests that the founding of the cemetery occurred shortly after the end of the New Kingdom.

Within the tomb sequence at el-Kurru there is a dramatic evolution from Nubian to Egyptian burial customs. Initially the dead were buried in a contracted position on beds, oriented northwest to southeast. Through time, however, the bodies were buried extended in coffins, oriented east–west, and burials were increasingly Egyptian in style. By the reign of Piye, mummification was certainly being practiced; the royal mummies of the 25th Dynasty were shrouded with bead nets, placed in nested coffins, and these rested on raised benches that supported funerary beds. The bodies were also accompanied by canopic jars, for preservation of the viscera, and *shawabti*s (servant figurines).

With Piye the royal tombs ceased being simple pit chambers capped by masonry superstructures. Piye's tomb was a novel type, consisting of a partly rock-cut, partly masonry-built vaulted chamber, surmounted by a pyramid but accessible by stairway. The stairway allowed the pyramid to be built over the open tomb while its owner was still alive. After the burial the stairway was sealed by the construction of the funerary chapel. Shabako's tomb (Ku. 15) was constructed in the same manner, but with two connected vaulted chambers at the bottom of the stairway rather than one, a custom which continued in Shebitko's tomb (Ku. 18) and Tanutameni's (Ku. 16). The tombs of the chief queens (Ku. 3, 4, 5, 6) were built in the same way, but their pyramids were slightly smaller in size. The kings' pyramids ranged from 8 to 11 m in base length, while the great queens' tombs ranged from 6.5 to 7 m in base length.

With Piye, the tombs of chief queens were placed on a new ridge immediately to the southwest of the ancestral field. The kings, however, continued to be buried in the original field. Minor queens for the first time were provided with smaller tombs in separate cemeteries far to the northeast but still precisely in line with the original cemetery. The minor queens of Piye, Shabako and Shebitko were buried in separate cemeteries: Ku. 50, Ku. 60, Ku. 70, respectively. All but one tomb (Ku. 53) were single-chamber tombs with no preserved superstructures.

At el-Kurru Reisner found a cemetery of twenty-four horse graves (Ku. 201–224), in which individual horses were buried standing up, facing southeast. These had belonged to the four kings of the 25th Dynasty, who had interred these animals in groups of four or eight. Two smaller circular graves (Ku. 225, 226) were also found here; one contained a dog skeleton.

See also

Gebel Barkal; Kushites; Nuri; Reisner, George Andrew; Sanam; Third Intermediate Period, overview

Further reading

Dunham, D. 1950. *The Royal Cemeteries of Kush* 1: *El-Kurru*. Boston.

Kendall, T. 1998. The origin of the Napatan state: el-Kurru and the evidence for the royal ancestors. In *Meroitica* 16, S. Wenig and P. Andrassy, eds.

——. 1998. A response to Laszlo Török's "Long Chronology" of el-Kurru. In *Meroitica* 16, S. Wenig and P. Andrassy, eds.

Török, L. 1995. The birth of an ancient African kingdom: Kush and her myth of the state in the first millennium B.C. *CRIPEL*, Suppl. 4: 29–55.

TIMOTHY KENDALL

Kushites

The name "Kas" first appeared at the beginning of the Middle Kingdom, in the 18th year of the reign of Senusret I, when the Egyptians, having set out to conquer Nubia, ventured above the First Cataract and went as far south as the Second Cataract. Early in 1830, at the Second Cataract site of Buhen, Jean-François Champollion and Italian Egyptologist Niccolo Rosellini discovered a great stela on which the Theban god of war, Montu, is depicted presenting the king a row of bound prisoners with the names of ten places in Nubia. From this, "Kas" has been located just above the Second Cataract.

The name of the region eventually became established as "Kush," which already appears in another account of the same Egyptian victory in Nubia. Ameni, the nomarch (governor) of Beni Hasan in Middle Egypt, states that he went upriver to the south in a boat with the king, who "went beyond Kush and to the end of the earth." Less than a century later, Senusret III claimed to have established a frontier at Semna, in the mid-Second Cataract, "in order to stop all Nubians ["Nehesyw"], even their beasts, from passing it on their way north, whether they come by land or water."

Kush and Nehesyw remained mere names for a long time. In 1913, the American archaeologist

George Reisner began excavations at Kerma, just upstream from the Third Cataract. His attention had been captured there by two *deffufas*, enormous mudbrick buildings. Not far from the Nile, the one on the west side was a compact mass of mudbricks. The one on the east side at the edge of the desert was a vast mudbrick temple, in the midst of a large necropolis of burial mounds composed of rings of white gravel around large circles of black stones. Reisner's excavations at Kerma, especially in the cemetery, yielded a rich collection of material, above all pottery of original design. Burial in the larger tumuli was entirely in the Nubian manner: the unmummified body rested on a bed, with women, children and retainers in the same tomb. But at Kerma, Reisner also discovered Egyptian artifacts such as statues and fragments of hieroglyphic inscriptions, which led him to believe that the Egyptians had set up a sort of commercial outpost. Artifacts collected from the western *deffufa* suggested a center of commerce, not administration.

If Kerma really had been an Egyptian outpost, it was dangerously isolated far south of the Second Cataract and there were no significant relay stations. Thus, Reisner's interpretation of the site was unlikely. Gradually the idea of a close relation between the name of Kush and the site of Kerma began to seem tenable to Egyptologists. This hypothesis was demonstrated in 1977 when the Swiss archaeologist Charles Bonnet uncovered the vestiges of a vast city with mud buildings similar to ones still found in the Saharan region of West Africa. The western *deffufa* was shown to be a mudbrick temple, vaguely in the shape of an Egyptian one. The site was organized like a capital city, most likely the capital of Kush, the second oldest African state (after Egypt) and a rival worthy of its great neighbor.

Due to a total lack of written records, the state of Kush arose under conditions that remain obscure. Between about 2300 and 1560 BC it developed in complexity, the nature of which can only be inferred from archaeological evidence. The state's power probably extended far to the south, but investigations are just beginning in the region below the Fourth Cataract, where a series of long basins watered by the Nile are found. The large size of Kerma, which is in the northern part of Kush, helps to explain why, throughout the Middle Kingdom, the Egyptians remained behind their border fortresses at Semna-Kumma, above which is the extensive barrier in the river of the Batn el-Hagar ("belly of stone"). Downstream from this point, all along the rapids of the Nile's Second Cataract and as far north as Kuban in the heart of Lower Nubia, the Egyptians constructed a series of forts within sight of each other, a kind of Maginot Line in the desert. From these fortresses, they could guard the Nile's lines of communication and, if necessary, control local nomadic raiders. Above all, they could completely block the dangerous, looming rival of Kush.

Archaeological expeditions conducted in Nubia in the 1960s, notably at the forts of Buhen and Mirgissa, removed sand from the huge mudbrick constructions, uncovering towers, bastions and stepped walls commanding steep slopes, and well protected slits at the best angles for Egyptian archers. Unfortunately, all of these fortifications are now under the high waters of Lake Nasser.

At Kerma, research and discovery continue, in spite of the systematic campaign of destruction accomplished by the New Kingdom Egyptians, who expanded their empire southward, destroying their powerful neighbor. After the Middle Kingdom, during the troubled Second Intermediate Period, the Egyptians were obliged to abandon their forts in Nubia and withdrew to a point north of Elephantine (Aswan). However, the Theban kings of the 17th Dynasty finally reapplied the old aggressive policy toward Nubia. A stela from the time of King Kamose, found at Karnak in 1950, describes an overture made by the Asiatic (Hyksos) king, who controlled northern Egypt, to the prince of Kush, with the idea of pressing on the Thebans from both the north and south. The Thebans thwarted the plan by capturing the messenger after a breathless race on the oasis route. Kamose was able to advance to Toshka, in Lower Nubia, but it was his successor, Ahmose, the founder of the 18th Dynasty, who finally attacked the Nubians after having first destroyed the Hyksos power in the north.

Ahmose rebuilt the fortress of Buhen and perhaps advanced to the island of Sai in the forbidding region of the Second Cataract. The third king of the 18th Dynasty, Tuthmose I, defeated Kerma and put an end to Kush's independence. Moving across the rocks at Tombos in the southern end of the Third Cataract, he conquered Kerma and the fertile Dongola basin in one stroke, and reached the Fourth Cataract. At Napata, he instituted the cult of the Theban god Amen at the foot of what would become the sacred mountain, Gebel Barkal. An inscription was found bearing his name at Kurgus, above the Fourth Cataract and south of Abu Hamed. In arriving at that point, the Egyptians had reached the vast Sudanese steppes, the boundary with sub-Saharan Africa. In the second year of his reign Tuthmose I was able to engrave a grandiose victory stela at Tombos, proclaiming that his empire stretched from Kush to the Euphrates River. The great independent African kingdom was finished and Egypt's colonial dominion would last until the end of the New Kingdom. Occasional revolts by "base Kush" are reported, especially at the beginning of the reigns of various pharaohs, but they were quickly crushed.

All along the river, the Egyptians pursued a program of construction. In each of their settlements there are temples marking the triumph of their power over the defeated Kush. One example is Amenhotep II's temple of Soleb; another is the renowned complex that Ramesses II built at Abu Simbel. At Soleb, the names of those subjugated by Egypt provide a list of African peoples. Although the northernmost ones have been identified, a long series of these names remains unknown.

The heyday of Egyptian colonialism ended with the 20th Dynasty. The regions of Kush became independent and indigenous rulers returned to power, most prominently around Napata, near the sacred mountain of Gebel Barkal. Near Napata, the cemetery of el-Kurru contains the burials of a series of princes, still anonymous, buried first in indigenous-style tumuli and then later in Egyptian-style masonry *mastaba*s (rectangular superstructures). The first names that are known here are Alara (Alul) and his successor Kashta, whose very name, meaning "the Kushite," is politicized.

From this point on, Kush became a dominant power, whose history is divided into two periods: the "Napatan" period, after the name of the ancient capital; then, beginning in the sixth century BC, the "Meroitic" period, named for Meroe, the new capital, which would survive until the fourth century AD. For 1,200 years Kush dominated a long stretch of the middle Nile, an area of fertile basins, savannas and vast deserts. Our knowledge of this kingdom is primarily archaeological. The early history is relatively well known because it overlaps the late history of pharaonic Egypt. Kashta advanced as far north as Elephantine. His son Piye (whose name was read as "Piankhy" until recently) conquered Egypt around 730 BC. He left a splendid stela in Egyptian hieroglyphs in which Egypt is described as being divided by petty polities. After conquering its coalition of princes, Piye presented himself as a faithful worshipper of the Egyptian gods and demanded that his troops respect their temples and watch over the celebration of the festivals. But Piye had withdrawn quickly to Upper Nubia, and his name is rarely found in Egypt. Various monuments near Napata bear his name, and he insisted that his remains be put in the cemetery at el-Kurru. Not far from his relatively modest tomb, his favorite horses were buried standing, in carefully excavated ditches with a deep hole for each leg.

The Egyptian 25th Dynasty, which is commonly called "Ethiopian," or more recently "Kushite," begins with Piye's brother Shabaka, the most important ruler of the line of kings that ends with Tanutamen. For about half a century, Egypt and Nubia were united to make a great African power that effectively opposed the Assyrians' attempted conquest of the Nile Valley. It was a double monarchy: its symbol is the double *uraeus* (the sacred cobra, an Egyptian symbol of kingship along with the sacred vulture). In the general impression they created, and in their dress and poses, the 25th Dynasty rulers copied styles and symbols of the earlier Egyptian pharaohs, whose successors, or even descendants, they claimed to be. Their monuments in Egypt and Nubia were designed in pharaonic style and inscribed in Egyptian (hieroglyphs). On the other hand, the reliefs and statues depict a people with the distinct physical features of the herdsmen of the Upper Nile: brachycephalic heads with large noses, pronounced cheekbones, thick lips and strong chins. The kings are also depicted wearing some new ornaments. A kind of skullcap, with a flap covering the temple, goes down tightly to the nape of the neck; a thick, knotted band holds two more flaps that hang down behind the shoulders. The heads of rams, sacred to the god Amen, decorate earrings and pendants.

Amen, the god most prominently associated with the Dynasty, was worshipped in four major sanctuaries in Nubia: at Napata, Tore (probably Sanam), Kawa and Pnubs (Tabo, on Argo Island). In each of these centers, Kushite princesses were consecrated as musicians of the god and the Kushite kings are frequently depicted with mothers, wives, sisters and female cousins. This is not the case in reliefs of this period in Egypt, although the Kushite pharaohs at Thebes were attended by the divine "votaresses," princesses sworn to virginity as exclusive wives of Amen. Endowed with royal powers, the Kushite princesses were a kind of parallel dynasty, succeeding one another from aunt to niece.

The most numerous Kushite buildings are unquestionably those of Taharka. At Napata he is represented by several temples. Many other sites in Nubia bear his name, particularly at Kawa and also at Sedeinga, where his presence remains unexplained. In the heart of the Second Cataract, in the temple that he built in the fortress of Semna, Taharka dedicated a bark stand to the deified Middle Kingdom king, Senusret II. The island of Philae, at the border of Egypt and Nubia, was also an object of his attention. However, his monuments are the most numerous at Karnak. There, in the immense complex of temples, he erected colon-nades at each of the four points of the compass; he also restored several gates and built some small chapels, in many of which Osiris is depicted in multiple forms. His name can be read in the oases of the Western Desert and even as far north as the Delta, at Tanis.

The Kushite dynasty was dominated by the great conflict between the Nile Valley and Assyria. Shabaka apparently wished to maintain good relations with the Assyrians, but as he heard the increasingly urgent cries for help from the princes and cities of Syro-Palestine, especially Jerusalem, he decided to intervene. Taharka's name resonates in the Old Testament (Isaiah 37:9, II Kings 19:9). The Assyrian king Assurhaddon (681–669 BC) tried to subjugate Egypt, but it was only his successor, Assurbanipal, who conquered it, with the sack of Thebes in 663 BC. In spite of the favorable auguries related on Tanutamen's "Dream Stela," this king, who succeeded Taharka, was unable to permanently recapture Egypt and fled back to his kingdom of Kush. Nevertheless, the names of Kushite rulers can be seen for several more years in Upper Egypt, especially in Taharka's inscription on the shrine of the bark of Amen, borne in a procession in the 14th year of Psamtik I's reign (26th Dynasty). It was not until 591 BC that the Egyptians under Psamtik II, with the aid of Greek and Carian mercenaries, were able to lead a great expedition against Kush, as far south as Napata. After this, the reliefs of the Kushite rulers, depicted with their characteristic attribute, the double *uraeus*, were systematically destroyed throughout Egypt.

At the same time, in the view of the 26th Dynasty (Saite) pharaohs of the Delta, the balance of power was definitively shifting toward the eastern Mediterranean and southwest Asia. The kingdom of Kush, first Napatan and then Meroitic, being cut off from the Lower Nile Valley, returned to its origins and became more and more African.

The first two successors of Tanutamen are mere names to us: Taharka's son Atlanersa (653–643 BC), and his son Senkamenisken (643–623 BC), substantial fragments of whose statues were found at Gebel Barkal. The latter's two sons and successors, Anlameni (623–593 BC), then Aspelta (593–568 BC), are better known. At Kawa, a stela of Anlemeni tells of the king's journey through a series of provinces in which he built temples, and also mentions his campaign against an unidentified people (perhaps the Blemmyes, nomadic peoples of the Eastern Desert). Anlameni's brother and successor Aspelta (593–568 BC) left two great texts: one describes the enthronement or coronation where some chiefs decided to consult Amen of Napata to choose the king; the other, which concerns the prerogatives of princesses, is a transcription of the ceremony of one's investiture as a priestess. The "Excommunication Stela," on which the king's names have been chiseled out, is sometimes, perhaps doubtfully, attributed to Aspelta. The stela's text remains partially obscure, but it explains that the members of a family who had plotted a murder were excluded from the Napatan temple of Amen. Aspelta was a contemporary of Psamtik II, who ordered the invasion of Kush: the date of the resulting conflict, 591 BC, is one of the very rare dates, and perhaps the only one in more than a millennium of history, that has been definitely established by a concurrence of events.

From that point on, the Kushites wished to distance themselves as much as possible from their powerful northern neighbor. Perhaps the Egyptian raid, the importance of which was long underestimated, was the reason the capital was transferred from Napata to Meroe, much farther south. Certainly Napata remained the religious capital of the kingdom: the rulers continued to have themselves buried in the nearby cemetery of Nuri until the end of the fourth century BC.

In 525 BC, the Persians threatened the Kushite kingdom, but Cambyses's expedition against them ended in failure. The transfer of the capital can also be explained by economic and climatic conditions: the steppes around Meroe offered a much larger agricultural area than the basins near Napata. The relative abundance of trees and bushes at Meroe meant that firewood was available for processing the iron ore contained within the Nubian sandstone. Also, commerce must have been busy: Meroe was an enviable crossroads of the caravan routes between the Red Sea, the Upper Nile and what is today the country of Chad.

Concerning the many obscure centuries, historians must rely solely on the royal tombs excavated earlier in this century by George Reisner. His attempt to make the list of kings' names correspond to the discovered pyramids produced uncertain results, which have already undergone numerous corrections and may need to be modified further. The last ruler buried at Nuri was Nastasen, a little before 300 BC. After him, the remains of the kings and princes were buried at Meroe; their pyramids constitute a flowering of Sudanese architecture. However, the fact that several rulers returned to be buried at Napata has led a few historians to believe that there were two different northern Nubian dynasties, parallel to that of their Meroitic cousins: the first immediately after Nastasen's reign and the second in the first century AD.

See also

Abu Simbel; Assyrians; Gebel Barkal; Hyksos; Karnak, temple of Amen-Re; Kerma; el-Kurru; Late and Ptolemaic periods, overview; Meroe, cemeteries; Meroe, city; Meroe, the "Sun Temple"; Meroitic culture; Middle Kingdom, overview; New Kingdom, overview; Nubian forts; Nubian towns and temples; Nuri; Persians; Philae; Reisner, George Andrew; Second Intermediate Period, overview; Tanis (San el-Hagar)

Further reading

Adams, W.Y. 1977. *Nubia, Corridor to Africa*. London.

Bonnet, C. 1986. *Kerma, territoire et métropole*. Cairo.

——. 1990. *Kerma, royaume de Nubie*. Geneva.

Davies, W.V., ed. 1991. *Egypt and Africa, Nubia from Prehistory to Islam*. London.

Dunham, D. 1950–63. The *Royal Cemeteries of Kush*, 5 vols. Cambridge, MA.

Hintze, F., K.-H. Priese, S. Wenig, C. Onasch, G. Buschendorf, and U. Hintze. 1971.

Musawwarat es-Sufra, Der Löwentempel. Berlin.

Hochfield, S., and E. Riefstahl, eds. 1978. *Africa in Antiquity, The Arts of Ancient Nubia and the Sudan,* 2 vols. Brooklyn.

Leclant, J. 1981. The empire of Kush: Napata and Meroe. In *General History of Africa* 2, G. Mokhtar, ed., 278–97. Berkeley, CA.

Macadam, M.F.L. 1949–55. *The Temples of Kawa,* 4 vols. Oxford.

O'Connor, D. 1994. *Ancient Nubia, Egypt's Rival in Africa.* Philadelphia.

Reisner, G.A. 1923. *Excavations at Kerma.* Cambridge, MA.

Török, L. 1988. *Late Antique Nubia.* Budapest.

Vercoutter, J., J. Leclant, F. M. Snowden and J. Desanges. 1976. *L'Image du Noir dans l'art occidental* 1: *Des Pharaons à la chute de l'Empire romain.* Fribourg.

JEAN LECLANT

L

Lahun, pyramid complex of Senusret II

The pyramid complex of Senusret II, which was built at the entrance to the Fayum about 70 km south of Dahshur (29°14′ N, 30°58′ E), has not been investigated in recent times and the only information is from Flinders Petrie's excavations conducted in 1889–90, 1914 and 1920–1. Although the whole complex, which consists of a valley temple, causeway(?), mortuary temple, pyramid and northern chapel, generally follows the early 12th Dynasty plan of his predecessors' pyramids, there are major innovations which reflect the strong influence of the cult of Osiris.

Similar in construction to the pyramids of Senusret I or Amenemhat II, the core of this pyramid consists of a system of gridded walls of mudbrick and stone built above a 12 m high rock nucleus. The spaces between the walls were filled with mudbricks and the whole core was covered by a thick casing of Tura limestone. The entrance to the burial chambers, however, was transferred from the north side to the south, probably as a protective measure from tomb robbers. Here a vertical shaft was found underneath the floor slab of the tomb of a princess (No. 10), which leads to a horizontal passage running north. From a small chamber at the northern end a short corridor opens toward the west and leads into the burial chamber, which is not aligned beneath the center of the pyramid but to the southeast. The burial apartment which is surrounded by a corridor may reflect the idea of a tomb of Osiris. The row of trees planted along the outer enclosure wall, where pits were found on the east, south and west sides, probably also has its origin in Osirian traditions.

The remains of a valley temple were found at the edge of the pyramid town of Kahun, about 1 km east of the pyramid. From here a causeway once led to the pyramid complex. A few remains of the mortuary temple are in the eastern court, which seems to have been considerably reduced in size from those of the earlier 12th Dynasty pyramids. No plan of this building is available, but columns found in the Ramesside temple of Ihnasya, inscribed with the name of Senusret II, seem to have come from this site and probably formed part of an open court.

A small subsidiary pyramid (*circa* 26 m square) in the northeastern corner of the pyramid's outer court, as well as eight *mastaba* superstructures farther west, remain enigmatic since there is no evidence of shafts or burial chambers in any of them. Fragments of wall paintings, an altar and a statue found in the debris of the subsidiary pyramid seem to indicate the existence of a northern chapel.

See also

Dahshur, Middle Kingdom pyramids; Hawara; Lahun, town; el-Lisht; Middle Kingdom, overview

Further reading

Petrie, W.M.F. 1891. *Illahun, Kahun, and Gurob*. London.

Brunton, G. 1920. *Lahun 1: The Treasure*. London.

Petrie, W.M.F., G. Brunton and M.A. Murray. 1923. *Lahun 2*. London.

CHRISTIAN HÖLZL

Lahun, town

The Middle Kingdom town now known as el-Lahun (29°13′ N, 30°59′ E) was built *circa* 1895 BC to house the workmen engaged in building the nearby pyramid and temples of King Senusret II. In addition to the workforce and their families, the town accommodated the officials and overseers who supervised the work, the priests and other personnel employed in the king's pyramid temple where his mortuary cult was performed after his burial, and an associated community of doctors, scribes, craftsmen and tradesmen. The site was discovered and excavated by Flinders Petrie, who began work there in 1889. Petrie asked an old man in the nearby village what the ancient town was called and was told "Medinet Kahun." Today the town is sometimes referred to as "Kahun" to differentiate it from the site of Senusret II's pyramid at el-Lahun. In antiquity both the town and the adjoining pyramid temple were known as "Hetep-Senusret" (Senusret is satisfied).

Lahun lies in the Fayum region southwest of Cairo. This area owes its remarkable fertility to local springs of water and the Bahr Yusef, a channel through which the waters of the Nile flow into the lake known today as Birket el-Qarun (Lake Moeris in antiquity). The area has always provided excellent hunting and fishing, and in antiquity, kings and courtiers visited it regularly to enjoy these pastimes. The kings of the 12th Dynasty chose to build there and to be buried in pyramids on the edge of the desert, which brought unprecedented activity and prosperity to the area.

In 1888–9, Petrie began his excavations of several sites in the area at the northern and southern ends of the great dike of the Fayum mouth. These included the Lahun pyramid and its surrounding cemetery; two temples, the smaller one adjoining the pyramid on the east and the other lying *circa* 800 m away on the edge of the desert; the town of Lahun, to the north of the larger temple; and, at the southern end of the dike, the New Kingdom town of Gurob or Medinet Gurob.

The discovery and excavation of Lahun town were important for several reasons. It was the first time that an archaeologist had uncovered a complete plan of an Egyptian town. Specially built to house the workforce, it had been laid out by one architect on a regular plan. Petrie claimed that there had been two periods of occupation, the first for about 100 years from the 12th to 13th Dynasties, and then a brief reoccupation of part of the site in the 18th Dynasty. However, this interpretation of the evidence is now disputed: there may have been a continuous but dwindling occupation from the earlier to the later periods.

Second, the site appears to have been deserted in some haste, and Petrie discovered that many of the houses were still standing and contained property left behind by their owners. These artifacts provide a unique insight into the contemporary living conditions. Artifacts from Lahun include domestic wares, workmen's tools, agricultural and weaving equipment, toys and games, jewelry and toilet equipment. Some artifacts have been preserved here which would have been considered too mundane to be included among tomb goods.

Third, in addition to these artifacts of everyday use, the collection of papyri discovered in the town provides a written record of civil and domestic life, and includes details of legal, medical and veterinary practices. Of particular importance are the lists and records which throw light on the working conditions of the pyramid builders, and the Kahun Medical Papyrus, which is the earliest known document on gynecology in the world. It includes details of tests to ascertain sterility, pregnancy and the sex of unborn children, as well as gynaecological prescriptions and contraceptive measures. Finally, because of the wealth of tools and equipment found among the artifacts at Lahun, there is an unparalleled opportunity to study the technological developments of the period, such as important advances in metal-working techniques.

Petrie excavated approximately two-thirds of the site over a two-year period. The town was surrounded by a massive mudbrick wall, and was divided internally by a wall into two areas, east and west, which were both of the same Middle Kingdom date. In the larger, eastern section there was an "acropolis" which probably had temporary quarters where the king stayed when he was inspecting progress on the construction of his pyramid. There were also five large houses which accommodated the officials who were in charge of the royal works. In the western area of this section were rows of workmen's houses. All the streets had channels down the middle to take away waste water and occasional rain. Altogether, Petrie cleared over 2,000 chambers, and in his records of these excavations he describes his working methods in some detail.

The houses, also built of mudbrick, were usually arranged so that several rooms were grouped together with one outer door opening onto the street. They were one storey in elevation, with stairs leading to the roof. Some were vaulted with a barrel roof of mudbrick, but more often they were made with beams of wood on which poles were placed. Bundles of straw or reeds were lashed to the poles and mud plaster was then applied to the inside and outside surfaces.

The walls of the rooms were also smoothly plastered with mud (Petrie found two plasterers' floats at the site). Walls were sometimes painted in red, yellow and white, and the best room was often decorated with a dado. In the larger rooms, columns were used to support the roof, and most doorways had wooden thresholds. There was evidence that rats had tunneled through holes in virtually all the houses.

The artifacts from Lahun were ultimately distributed among various museums, but the largest proportion of this material was divided more or less equally between what is now in the Petrie Museum at University College London, and the Manchester University Museum. Artifacts from Lahun include domestic items such as ceramic dishes, scoops, brushes and a grinder, and wooden furniture (including stools and boxes). A fire-stick, which worked on the bow-drill principle, was the first such tool found in Egypt. The unique collection of tools found here included building tools (a mudbrick mold and plasterers' floats), stone-working tools and carpenters' tools. Petrie discovered a metal caster's shop with some of its original contents, and it was a noticeable feature of the site that stone and flint tools continued to be used along with metal tools. There were also agricultural implements (the town produced its own food), fishing equipment and a set of tools for textile production. Unlike tomb equipment, which was often intended for religious or ceremonial purposes, the artifacts from Lahun were for domestic use or were used in craft production and trade.

In the houses there were also craft goods belonging to women, including jewelry and cosmetic equipment. Toys and games have also survived: there were game boards, balls, tops, tipcats and small mud toys, presumably made by children. However, Petrie also found evidence of a more sophisticated toy-making industry. Wooden dolls and quantities of hair prepared for insertion into holes in their heads were found in one house, which probably belonged to a doll-maker. Some of the artifacts from Lahun have no parallels elsewhere, since they were regarded as humble, everyday objects which were never placed in tombs.

There is also evidence relating to the religious practices of the inhabitants. These include some unusual stone stands in the form of human figures, which were probably used for making offerings in the houses, and a set of equipment—including magic wands and a well-preserved face mask representing the household god Bes—which may have been owned by a local magician.

In recent times, the artifacts from Lahun have been intensively re-examined, including neutron activation analysis of pottery and metals, and studies of the textile tools and botanical specimens. The theory originally proposed by Petrie, that some of the town's inhabitants were not of Egyptian origin, has also been reconsidered. Petrie excavated sherds at the site which he described as "foreign," and more specifically as "Greek." This identification was originally treated with skepticism by classical scholars, but with the subsequent discovery of Minoan civilization it was possible to determine that some of the Lahun sherds, which had patterns incorporating swirls and spirals, were indeed examples of the Kamares

Ware found on Crete. However, not all these "Minoan" sherds at Lahun were true imports; some were identified stylistically as local Egyptian imitations. It is uncertain if even the true imports were brought to Lahun by immigrants or arrived there through trade connections.

At Lahun Petrie also discovered weights and measures, some of which were of non-Egyptian origin, and he believed that these had been introduced by foreign traders and merchants. Some of the religious practices found there may not be Egyptian; the stone offering stands placed in the houses are unusual in style and the burial of infants in boxes found near the houses was not an Egyptian custom. A copper torque found in a house at Lahun may also indicate foreign associations. Very few examples of these neck ornaments have been found in Egypt, although they were worn for over five centuries in southwest Asia and were produced at Byblos on the Syrian coast.

Perhaps the papyri discovered at Lahun provide the strongest evidence for the presence of foreigners in the town. In the legal documents, they are mentioned as servants in households, and some are also identified in the lists of temple personnel, as participants in a festival in the temple of Senusret II. The word *aamu* (loosely translated as "Asiatic") was placed after the individual's name to indicate his foreign origin. Some *aamu* are mentioned in the military or police units, and they must have existed at Lahun in sufficient numbers to warrant positions of "officer in charge of Asiatic troops" and "scribe of Asiatics."

Petrie's hypothesis was that foreigners were first brought to Egypt as captives to work on public projects, following Egypt's military engagements with other peoples in the 11th Dynasty. Some of Lahun's inhabitants may have been their descendants, but others probably came as traders or itinerant craftsmen; they may have originated from several homelands, including Syria, Palestine, the Aegean islands and Cyprus.

There are also different theories regarding the end of the Middle Kingdom occupation at Lahun. This may have been caused by declining local economic conditions or by foreign infiltration and harassment. Some evidence suggests that the evacuation of the site was sudden and unplanned: the inhabitants left behind a quantity and range of personal possessions, which may have been the result of a natural disaster or even an epidemic. The evacuation, however, may have been gradual and partial so that by the New Kingdom only a token number of houses in the western quarter remained occupied. The suggestion that the workforce departed to another place once their construction of the pyramid was completed is untenable since they would surely have taken their tools with them, and the length of the Middle Kingdom occupation at Lahun (*circa* 100 years) would have exceeded the period required for construction of a pyramid.

New studies of the artifacts and current excavations at the site by Nicholas Millet of the Royal Ontario Museum, Toronto, will undoubtedly continue to reveal more information about the daily existence of this community and its wider historical significance.

See also

Aegean peoples; Lahun, pyramid complex of Senusret II; Middle Kingdom, overview; Petrie, Sir William Matthew Flinders; textual sources, Middle Kingdom; towns, planned

Further reading

David, R. 1996. *The Pyramid Builders of Ancient Egypt*, 2nd revised edn. London.

Kemp, B.J. 1977. The early development of the town in Egypt. *Antiquity* 51: 185–200.

Petrie, W.M.F. 1890. *Kahun, Gurob and Hawara*. London.

——. 1891. *Illahun, Kahun and Gurob*. London.

A.R. DAVID

Late period private tombs

Private tombs of the Late period are known in more than forty cemeteries in Egypt. At many of these sites, however, there is only evidence of scattered funerary artifacts, stelae and fragments of inscribed blocks. In some cases the dating is uncertain and the remains could also date to the Graeco-Roman period. In most cemeteries, Late period tombs have no distinctive character and follow local traditions (rock-cut tombs, *mastabas* or small shaft-tombs, sometimes with superstructures, and vaulted mudbrick structures in the Delta). Some cemeteries consist only of simple pit-graves. It was also customary to usurp and adapt older tombs, where many burials of the Late period were frequently stacked into the existing chambers.

At Abydos several cemeteries of the Late period are known, mainly with tombs of modest size. These tombs consist of a *mastaba* (superstructure) with a shaft leading to undecorated rock-cut chambers which sometimes contain multiple burials. At one cemetery there are small, steep mudbrick pyramids, with the burial in a subterranean chamber. At el-Amra, near Abydos, shaft-tombs with mudbrick superstructures in the shape of a small temple or shrine were traditional from the 18th Dynasty until the end of the Late period.

At Heliopolis, besides some simple shaft-tombs, tombs were discovered with burial chambers constructed of limestone blocks in pits. These tombs are similar to the large shaft-tombs at Saqqara (see below), but are much smaller in size. They often contained multiple burials of families.

In Baharia Oasis, several rock-cut tombs were made for a family of governors and priests during the Saite period (26th Dynasty). The subterranean chambers, with religious scenes painted on plastered walls, are reached by a shaft and consist of a pillared central hall flanked by smaller side rooms. Superstructures are not preserved, but probably existed. A similar tomb of the same period, consisting of two sunken courts with small side chambers, is located in Siwa Oasis. These Oases' tombs seem to be patterned after a type of tomb found in the Theban necropolis during the Late period.

It was indeed in the cemeteries of the two capitals, Thebes and Memphis, where new concepts for the tomb developed during the Late period. In western Thebes the tradition of the "classical" Theban rock-cut tomb came to an end after the collapse of the New Kingdom. No individual private tombs seem to exist for the 21st Dynasty, and many coffins were stacked into caches, mostly in older tombs. The elaborate decoration of the coffins, with an extensive iconographic repertory, took over some of the religious functions of the earlier decorated tomb chambers.

During the 22nd–23rd Dynasties a new type of tomb appeared in western Thebes, although it had a long tradition in other places, such as el-Amra. This tomb consisted of a mudbrick superstructure shaped like a small temple, where the funerary cult took place, with one or more shafts leading to the burial chambers cut in the bedrock. Placed on the plain and not on the slopes of the desert hills, this "new" tomb type was the prelude to future developments.

During the Kushite and Saite periods (25th and 26th Dynasties) a Late period necropolis *par excellence* developed in western Thebes in the valley named el-Asasif. Passing through this valley are the causeways to the mortuary temples of Queen Hatshepsut, Nebhepetre Mentuhotep II and Tuthmose III (at Deir el-Bahri). In the Late period, the causeways of the two kings' temples were no longer in use and the area was used by high officials of the 25th and 26th Dynasties who established their "funerary palaces" in prominent positions near Hatshepsut's temple at Deir el-Bahri.

The two most elaborate structures here were built by Montuemhat, Governor of Upper Egypt, and Pedamenopet, Chief Lector Priest. Other monumental tombs were those of the High Stewards of the God's Wives or the Divine Votaresses (priestesses of Amen), who were princesses holding royal power in the Theban region. The landscape of el-Asasif is dominated by the remains of these huge mudbrick superstructures, while some of the rock-cut substructures surpass in size and complexity other Theban private tombs or the royal tombs in the nearby Valley of the Kings.

The architectural plan of the el-Asasif tombs has five basic elements: (1) the superstructure,

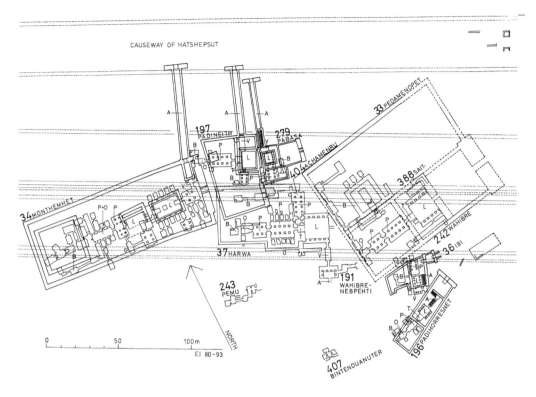

Figure 54 Theban necropolis, western part of the Late period necropolis at el-Asasif
Thick lines indicate superstructures. A=descending stairway; V=vestibule; L=sunken court; T=portal niche; P=pillared hall; O=offering hall; B=burial appartments.

(2) descending staircase with antechamber and vestibule, (3) sunken court, (4) rock-cut subterranean rooms, and (5) burial chambers. As in domestic architecture, a tripartite division forms the design principle for the whole structure (superstructure, rock-cut halls, burial apartments), with increasing secludedness in each section. This general plan, with variations and modifications, is found in all larger tombs, although local traditions from all periods and archaizing tendencies are of considerable influence in details.

The mudbrick superstructures of these tombs, modeled after the royal mortuary temples, usually contain three vast open courts. The inaccessible third court covers the area of the underground halls and chambers. Sometimes a small mudbrick pyramid of the type known from Abydos marks the position of the burial chamber. The entrance pylon is oriented toward the east, or, in the western part of el-Asasif, toward the point where the procession of a ceremony called the "Beautiful Feast of the Valley" first came into sight. On the outside of some superstructures is the archaizing motif of recessed mudbrick paneling, a simplified version of the "palace façade" design, known from the "funerary palaces" of the Early Dynastic period.

In some tombs the descending stairway is entered through a small pylon located along the

434

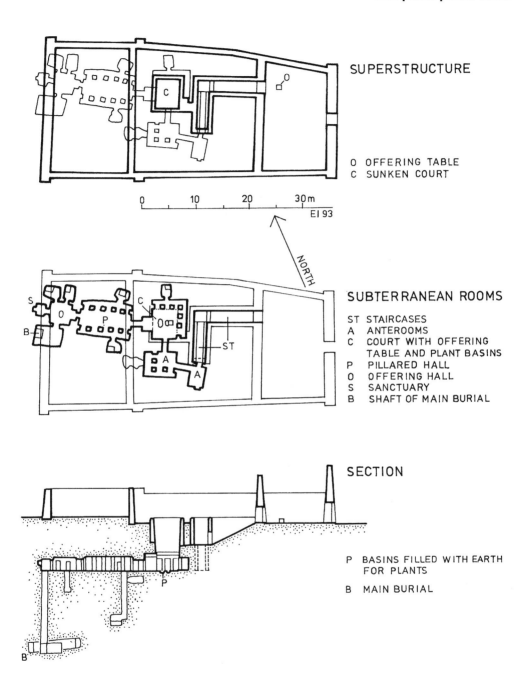

SUPERSTRUCTURE

O OFFERING TABLE
C SUNKEN COURT

0   10   20   30 m

EI 93

NORTH

SUBTERRANEAN ROOMS

ST STAIRCASES
A ANTEROOMS
C COURT WITH OFFERING
   TABLE AND PLANT BASINS
P PILLARED HALL
O OFFERING HALL
S SANCTUARY
B SHAFT OF MAIN BURIAL

SECTION

P BASINS FILLED WITH EARTH
  FOR PLANTS

B MAIN BURIAL

Figure 55 A typical tomb of the 26th Dynasty at el-Asasif (belonging to Ankh-Hor, High Steward of the Divine Votaress)

southern edge of Hatshepsut's causeway. One of the motives for this arrangement was the desire to participate in the "Beautiful Feast of the Valley" as its procession passed by here on the way to Deir el-Bahri. At the foot of the stairway, one or more antechambers or vestibules give access via a bent axis to the sunken court.

The sunken court, on the level of the substructure but open to the sky, is one of the most prominent and innovative features. Here the daily funerary cult was performed at an offering table, located in front of the niche of the entrance to the underground rooms. Plants were grown in a basin filled with earth, which symbolized the tomb of Osiris, with vegetation growing out of the dead god's body.

The subterranean complex, entered only for the performance of special rituals, consists of one or two pillared halls with side chambers, an offering chamber and a sanctuary where Osiris was believed to reside. The arrangement of these rooms, of varying complexity in each tomb, is derived from both domestic and temple architecture. The side chambers of the pillared hall often contain shafts for the burials of relatives of the tomb owner, so that the complex is also a family tomb.

The royal tombs in the Valley of the Kings, with their succession of halls and sloping passages, are the model for the burial chambers of the el-Asasif tombs. From the last hall a shaft descends to the sarcophagus chamber. Sometimes the shaft starts directly from the level of the cult complex.

Executed in fine relief, decorations in the superstructure, descending staircase and sunken court pertain to contact of the dead with the outside world. In the subterranean halls the descent into the underworld is the main theme; in the burial chambers the entire realm of the Egyptian netherworld is represented, as in the royal tombs.

The large tombs at el-Asasif were plundered soon after completion and many secondary burials were deposited here until the Ptolemaic period. Between and around these tombs a maze of smaller structures of the "chapel-and-shaft" type created a veritable "City of the Dead."

In the cemeteries of Memphis local traditions continued (rock-cut tombs, shaft-tombs and tomb chapels), sometimes with very individual solutions. For example, the tomb chapel of Thery at Giza is built of limestone blocks arranged in a cross-shaped plan, with vaulted chambers. The vizier Bakenrenef was the only official to prefer an underground complex of the monumental Theban type, which was carved in the cliff at Saqqara. At Giza, at Abusir and especially at Saqqara, innovative developments are marked by the desire to provide the greatest security for the burial. These tombs belonged to high officials of the 26th Dynasty, but for unknown reasons are called "Persian" tombs. Most of these burials remained untouched until their archaeological investigation in modern times. They were probably inspired by the great pit-tombs in the funerary complex of King Zoser, which were explored in the 26th Dynasty.

The main feature of these 26th Dynasty tombs is a huge rectangular shaft or pit, about 11×8 m, cut about 30 m deep in the bedrock. A subsidiary shaft, about 1.4 m by 1.4 m, is always several meters deeper than the main shaft. A burial chamber built of limestone blocks is located at the bottom of the main shaft. In fact, this "burial chamber," with its vaulted roof and square corner posts, is the outermost of a series of nesting sarcophagi. It has the shape of a sarcophagus known since the 1st Dynasty, imitating an early house form. the chamber fits closely around a huge limestone sarcophagus. Inside the limestone sarcophagus is an anthropoid sarcophagus of slate or basalt, in which is the anthropoid wooden coffin.

After construction the chamber was connected to the subsidiary shaft by a small passage made of limestone slabs or vaulted mudbricks, then the large pit was filled with sand. The actual burial was conducted via the small shaft and corridor, and there is evidence of an ingenious series of devices to insure its security. The basalt sarcophagus was closed and then the lid of the large sarcophagus was lowered. The lid has square projections at the small sides, which fit into grooves in the walls of the chamber, so that the lid could be supported by wooden props resting on sand. The sand was

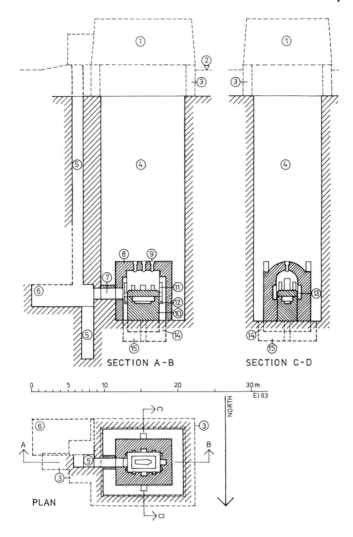

SECTION A-B   SECTION C-D

PLAN

1 superstructure (reconstructed outline)
2 approximate ancient surface level
3 foundations of superstructure
4 main shaft filled with sand
5 subsidiary shaft
6 chamber for storage of building equipment and handling of burial (?)
7 connecting passage between subsidiary shaft and burial chamber
8 vaulted burial chamber built of limestone blocks
9 round openings in vault of burial chamber, temporarily closed with pottery jars
10 monolithic limestone sarcophagus
11 groove holding wooden prop for support of sarcophagus lid
12 opening to release sand under prop
13 niche for canopic jars and *shawabti* boxes
14 small shaft for conveying sand
15 sand-filled chamber under sarcophagus

Figure 56 A typical tomb of the 26th Dynasty at Saqqara (belonging to Amen-Tefnakht, Commander of the Recruits of the Royal Guards)

released to a lower level through small apertures, allowing the lid to descend slowly into place. Then the pottery jars, which had plugged holes in the roof vault of the chamber, were broken and sand streamed in from the fill of the large shaft. In addition, the brick vault of the passage could be broken before the small shaft was filled. Any robbers who wanted to come near the sarcophagus, even via the small shaft, would have had to remove the entire sand fill of about 2000 cubic meters. It has been suggested that the sarcophagus, weighing up to 100 tons, was lowered in place by the sand which was filled into the large shaft. If such an operation actually took place, the downward extension of the subsidiary shaft may have played some part in the gradual removal of the sand.

The interior walls of the burial chamber, and sometimes their outer faces, are decorated with inscriptions in sunken relief, mainly of mortuary texts related to the *Pyramid Texts*. Canopic jars (for the preserved viscera) and *shawabti* (servant figure) boxes were deposited in niches next to the sarcophagus. The superstructures of these tombs are now completely destroyed, except for some remains of foundations following the outline of the pit, with an extension on the eastern side, presumably where a chapel for the mortuary cult was located. The architecture of these superstructures must have been elaborate, as fragments of limestone blocks, and palmiform and composite capitals demonstrate.

More steps to increase security were made in tombs at Abusir and Giza, where the main shaft is surrounded by an even deeper sand-filled trench. Both are connected by large openings through which the sand could flow freely in either direction, and no part could be emptied separately.

With its careful imitation of a contemporary temple building, the tomb chapel of Petosiris at Tuna el-Gebel, erected at the end of the Dynastic period, represents the final development of the Late period private tomb of the chapel-and-shaft type. In western Thebes, the Late period "funerary palaces" are an attempt to insure eternal life for their owners by mobilizing all traditional funerary concepts in religion and architecture, including those of

royal tombs. The results are, despite a general archaizing tendency, original and distinctive monuments. The achievement of ultimate security in the Saqqara tombs, together with the return to an archaic tomb form, can be seen as the final point of development in Egyptian tomb architecture.

See also

Abydos, Early Dynastic funerary enclosures; Deir el-Bahri, Hatshepsut temple; Deir el-Bahri, Tuthmose III temple; funerary texts; Late and Ptolemaic periods, overview; *shawabtis*, servant figures and models; Siwa Oasis, Late period and Graeco-Roman sites; Thebes, el-Asasif; Thebes, Valley of the Kings; Third Intermediate Period, overview; Tuna el-Gebel

Further reading

Eigner, D. 1984. *Die monumentalen Grabbauten der Spätzeit in der thebanischen Nekropole.* Vienna.

Malék, J. 1982. Nekropolen. Late Period. In *LÄ* 4: 440–9.

el-Sadeek, W. 1984. *Twenty-sixth dynasty necropolis at Gizeh.* Vienna.

Thomas, N.K. 1980. *A Typological Study of Saite Tombs at Thebes.* Ann Arbor, MI.

DIETER EIGNER

law

Principles

"The king," explained the vizier Rekhmire, is "the god (on earth) by whose guidance men live." Indeed, Tuthmose III defended his rule as such that "*ma'at* will deserve its place," meaning that order would be perfectly maintained and justice correctly exercised during his reign. The vizier was the chief legal official in ancient Egypt. Yet the office of vizier is described by the king as "bitter as gall" because he is the "hard copper enclosing the gold of his Master's house." Thus, the structure of the legal administration must at the same time shield the king and other important officials and also serve the populace as a whole. For the Egyptians had the concept that justice was the same for everyone, the ultimate goal being "to place everyone in his rights." In his teaching (*sb3yt*), the king expresses two fundamental and compulsory principles: (1) dealing with each case according to the specifications of the law; and (2) handling each case according to its own integrity. As another text shows us, each case was considered "according to its *ma'at*," leading one to conclude that *ma'at* is relative.

In fact, the concept of *ma'at* is much more than that of simple justice. It consists of both practical and ideal justice. It is a model to which one aspires rather than a set of instructions or formalized law code. *Ma'at* requires continuous exertion to achieve the best possible justice, balancing all the particularities of a case. *Ma'at* is a proactive rather than passive concept of justice, which is enlightened by a harmonious application of the rules (*hpw*). Our sources emphasize that a concern for harmony, moral integrity and equilibrium should be the object of the law. Yet neither the rules (*hpw*) themselves nor the rights enjoyed by the populace are ever expressly defined in the Egyptian sources.

The royal instructions end with the decisive recommendation "do not do whatever you desire in cases about which you should have the knowledge of the laws to be applied." Such knowledge presupposes some specialized preparation by judges. This text also indicates that the vizier and his subordinates enjoyed a right of interpretation and that the Egyptians appreciated the situation in which laws were either imprecise, incomplete or even non-existent. Egyptian justice was public and records were available for consultation.

Laws

While there were certainly legal rules (*hpw*), their nature is uncertain. It seems inconceivable that nothing would have been legally codified in such a remarkably centralized country, where everything else was recorded in writing and where according to the classical tradition "written laws" were in existence from the beginning of its history.

Due to King Horemheb of the 18th Dynasty, we know something about how laws were made in ancient Egypt. In a royal edict, Horemheb indicated that current abuses in terms of tax collection were unacceptable and issued decrees in order to reform the situation. These rules (*hpw*) did not exist before Horemheb had taken the initiative; they were not the product of some sort of a common consensus in the country, since the king targeted specific abuses for reform. Neither were they the product of deliberate jurisprudence, since the decrees do not refer specifically to the judgment of legal tribunals. The whole legal system must have relied on similar laws, traces of which are evident in the well-known decrees of immunity from the end of the Old Kingdom. By creating exemptions in a society in principle without privileges, an infringement is made on what may be called the common rights of that time.

Although no actual law code for pharaonic Egypt has yet been discovered, there are some clear pieces of evidence that such a code had existed. For example, during one troubled period it is described how laws were thrown into the street, trod underfoot and ripped to pieces. This means that they must have been written down, although they were not necessarily codified. In addition, the vizier is said to examine legal cases in terms of the law "he keeps in his hand." This must have been a roll of papyrus that the magistrate had at his disposal for consultation during a trial. Furthermore, the discovery of the Hermoplis Code and the publication of Carlsberg Papyrus 302 (the judicial manual of Tebtunis) provide evidence for judicial codes from the end of ancient Egyptian history. According to this tradition, the actual existence of a pharaonic law code may date prior to the reign of Amasis (26th Dynasty), back to the reign of Bocchoris (Bakenrenef) of the 24th Dynasty.

Evidence does exist concerning particular sectors of ancient Egyptian law. For example, in the juridical stela of Karnak we read:

It is in conformity with the stipulations of the law that [the judiciary administration] is concerned with the disputant (even) after he had died (when he could no longer express his will), and when his case was up for renewal every year, as the law prescribes... because it is the vizier's office (in contrast to the local administration) that has the right to proceed in such a case (admitting a delay in implementing a legally registered agreement), conforming to the stipulations of the law.

Such complete information is only given occasionally. From such texts, however, we can deduce evidence for the rules of public law. For example, the contracts of Hepdjefa of Asyut provide evidence that a governor could cancel an administrative decision made unilaterally by one of his predecessors, but he may not cancel or modify, on his own authority, an agreement made with contracting parties.

Concerning penal law, evidence from Papyrus Brooklyn 36.1446 indicates that this formed a separate legal section. In addition to the civil right to compensation of private persons when damage has occurred, Egyptian law also recognized a compensation to society at large for the trouble caused. For example, from the New Kingdom is the case of the Chief Policeman of the Theban Necropolis, Monthumes. The court granted him a month's delay to settle his debt to a worker, with the penalty if it was not paid in this time of a hundred beatings and his debt being doubled. Already during the Old Kingdom, an official boasted about never having been "beaten." Like everybody else, he was subject to the common laws and adds (as if to justify himself) that this was because he did not take anything "by force" from anybody. He avers that he consistently behaved according to the rules with respect for other people and their property.

Centralization in Egypt went hand in hand with judicial individualism. There were no offenses without laws, no retroactivity, no responsibility for others in penal matters, nor any collective or familial responsibilities. The penalties inflicted were in proportion to the offense committed; the pronouncement of a sentence and its execution were the job of the judicial hierarchy. This hierarchy extended up to the king himself, to whom was reserved the final decision and right of approval. Once a serious case had been decided by the appropriate jurisdiction, the verdict was forwarded to the vizier; the vizier himself put the case before the king for the final decision. The king enjoyed some discretionary power about whom to punish. For example, although Sinuhe (the protagonist in a famous Egyptian tale) had committed the double fault of fleeing the country and staying in a foreign land, he was rewarded by the king on his return to Egypt.

Individual rights

Judicial individualism implies the absence of privileged intermediaries and the absence of familial influence. Like men, women in ancient Egypt enjoyed basic civil rights. However, women did not typically study to become scribes or join the ranks of the administrative bureaucracy. Women were also at a disadvantage within the family since within a marriage a man's share of the common property was two-thirds and he served to administer the whole. In practice this gave the husband a superior position in the household, with the wife in an inferior economic position. However, women could possess their own property which they could administer on their own. If a woman were not the legal heir of her husband, she could be made a legatee. To do so, a husband would make out a writ of disposition (*imyt-pr*) with the value of a will. Wives also had the right to dispose of their property by a similar unilateral writ according to the following text of law: "May everybody dispose of his property as he likes." The most ancient known writ dates to the end of the 3rd Dynasty.

From the 12th Dynasty we have evidence of a husband transmitting specific belongings to his wife (via an *imyt-pr*), along with an obligation for her in turn to transmit them to one of their children. If she does not fulfil her obligation (via another *imyt-pr*), then the belongings are to be divided among all the children. Naunakhte, the wife of a worker in the Theban necropolis in the Ramesside period, reproaches three of her eight children (two daughters and a son) for their ungratefulness toward her and takes the radical step of disinheriting them. In her will (a well-balanced writ) she includes several peculiarities; all of the wishes she expresses were sanctioned and authenticated by the local council (*knbt*).

Courts

Local councils (*knbt*) served as courts. In the New Kingdom Theban necropolis, the council was formed by workers and chaired by a "Chief Worker." Scribes acted as clerks and lawyers, being called "magistrate" (*srw*) during the sessions. Such local councils were competent in both litigations and notarial matters. Judging from the boundary stone J.E. 42789 in the Cairo Museum, the case was much the same from the time of the Old Kingdom (although the councils were called *ḏ3ḏ3t* then). Even people of the lowest classes, such as workers of the "Pyramid City" at the Saqqara necropolis, could possess, acquire, sell and make writs, testify in court and take the oath "As the King lives." They could do all this without being put under the tutorship of anyone or assisted by the court.

There were no barristers in ancient Egypt, and instead of a single judge there was always a panel of judges. Everybody had to personally defend themselves and their interests. There may have been some sort of justice auxiliaries giving advice or perhaps members of the council who were not on the panel of judges could participate in this way. There was no official court of appeal in ancient Egypt. However, under the condition of new facts being uncovered or new testimony, a case could be reviewed by the same court in which it was tried.

As an example of the specific procedures, the following case is presented from Papyrus Boulaq 10 (Papyrus Cairo 58.092), completed from Ostracon Petrie 16. During the twelfth century BC a worker in the Theban necropolis inherited a claim from his father. Funerary equipment belonging to the father had been used, with his agreement, to bury a woman whose children then refused to recognize this debt. After the death of the other parent of the debtors, the case went to court. Writs acted as evidence to prove the facts and the right to payment of the debt. The worker supported his claim by appealing to the "law of pharaoh," which prescribed that the goods of the deceased should go to the one who conducted the funeral. One infers that he should be compensated for the expense his father had incurred. He also requested that the court "do what is good" (*nfr*), which indicates that he is seeking a fair solution. He evoked a precedent where during a similar dispute the court had charged the expense to the legacy of the deceased (before it was divided amongst the heirs). This case is, consequently, a decision of justice that gives more precision to the law.

See also

administrative bureaucracy; Deir el-Medina; *ma'at*; social organization

Further reading

Allam, S. 1991. Egyptian law courts in pharaonic and Hellenistic times. *JEA* 77: 109–27.

Lorton, D. 1986. The king and the law. *Varia Aegyptiaca* 2: 55ff.

McDowell, A.G. 1990. *Jurisdiction in the Workmen's Community of Deir el-Medina.* Leiden.

Théodoridès, A. 1971. The concept of law in ancient Egypt. In *The Legacy of Egypt*, 2nd edn. J.R. Harris, ed., 291–322. Oxford.

——. 1995. *Vivre de Maât: Travaux sur le droit égyptien ancien* (Acta Orientalia Belgica I–II). Brussels.

ARISTIDE THÉODORIDÈS

Lepsius, Carl Richard

Most brilliant and productive of the generation of Egyptologists that followed Jean-François

Champollion, Carl Richard Lepsius (1810–84) earned his Ph.D. in classical archaeology at Berlin University in 1833. Lectures in Paris on the history of Egypt awakened his interest in Egyptian hieroglyphs. Lepsius's support for the Champollion system of decipherment of hieroglyphs, expressed in a famous letter to Professor Niccolo Rosellini (Champollion's first student), won general acceptance for that pioneering effort over others. Lepsius advanced understanding of the language by furthering the recognition of syllabic signs and pointing out more similarities to Coptic.

After four years of visiting Egyptian collections in Europe to try out his translation skills, Lepsius organized, with the help of his King and Alexander von Humboldt, the Prussian Expedition (1842–5) that would survey and copy monuments and reliefs throughout Egypt and Nubia and bring back to Europe some 15,000 objects, papyri and casts, plus drawings, maps and plans. The massive epigraphic project, *Denkmäler aus Ägypten und Äthiopien* (Monuments in Egypt and Ethiopia), was published in 1859, in twelve huge folio volumes comprising 894 plates; it is still a valuable resource today. After his death, five more volumes of text were completed from his notes by colleagues, including the Swiss Egyptologist Édouard Naville, and these appeared from 1897 to 1913.

During the Prussian Expedition, Lepsius excavated the "Labyrinth" at Hawara and, with another expedition in 1866, explored the eastern Delta, discovering Tanis, capital of Egypt during the 21st Dynasty. Here he found the important *Decree of Canopus*, a bilingual text that was a valuable means of proving the correctness of Egyptological translations.

Lepsius was appointed Professor at Berlin University in 1846 and soon after Curator at the Egyptian Museum, Berlin, the nucleus of whose collection he had assembled and whose organization he would strongly influence in subsequent years. Besides producing some 142 publications on subjects as diverse as ancient Egyptian chronology, the *Book of the Dead* and Nubian grammar, Lepsius edited for twenty years the German journal, *Zeitschrift für*

ägyptische Sprache und Altertumskunde, which continues today as a major Egyptological publication.

See also

Champollion, Jean-François; funerary texts; Hawara; Tanis (San el-Hagar)

Further reading

Dawson, W.R., and E.P. Uphill. 1995. *Who Was Who in Egyptology*, 3rd edn. M.L. Brierbrier. London.
Encyclopaedia Britannica, 11th edn. "Lepsius, Karl Richard (1810–1884)."

BARBARA S. LESKO

Levantine peoples (Iron Age)

The political and social structure of the Levant changed in the late thirteenth and early twelfth centuries BC. The Canaanite city-state system that predominated during the Bronze Age collapsed, to be replaced in the Iron Age (*circa* 1200–586 BC) by a number of regionally distributed ethnic and political groups, some of indigenous origin, others new to the region. Egypt had only limited relations with the more distant Iron Age polities, such as the Neo-Hittite states and Aramaean kingdoms of Syria, and the Ammonite, Moabite and Edomite kingdoms of Transjordan. The Levantine groups having the greatest impact on Egypt were the Philistines in the Iron Age I period (c. 1,200–1000 BC), and the Israelites and Phoenicians in the Iron Age II period (c. 1000–586 BC).

After their unsuccessful assault on Egypt in the eighth year of the reign of Ramesses III (20th Dynasty), several groups in the confederation known as the "Sea Peoples" settled in Palestine. The most prominent was the Philistines (the "Peleset" in Egyptian texts). Their settlements dotted the coastal plain from just north of Jaffa to the Gaza region. The five major Philistine cities formed a political league (the "Pentapolis"); this encompassed three urban centers along the Mediterranean coast—Gaza, Ashkelon, and Ashdod—as well as two towns inland on the Shephelah: Ekron (identified with Tel Miqne) and Gath (possibly Tell es-Safi). Philistine control over southwest Palestine quickly severed Egypt's links to southwest Asia and was a critical factor in the demise of Egypt's empire in Canaan in the third quarter of the twelfth century BC.

The Philistines prospered in their new homeland through agricultural and commercial activities, as well as through their technological skills (particularly in metal working). Their culture quickly mixed with that of the local Canaanites. The earliest Philistine pottery, though locally made, reflects a Mycenaean tradition in its shapes and decoration. Slightly later, the Philistines began producing a distinctive red-and-black painted pottery; this is found throughout Philistia in tombs and settlements of the late twelfth and eleventh centuries BC and exhibits Canaanite, Aegean, Cypriote, and even some Egyptian influences. The burial practices of the Philistines were also eclectic and may have included the use of anthropoid ceramic coffins, a tradition borrowed from the Egyptians by the Sea Peoples.

Philistine efforts during this period to expand to the north and east of the coastal plain resulted in a series of clashes with the Israelites. The latter people, first mentioned on an Egyptian stela dating to the fifth year of Merenptah's reign (19th Dynasty), lived during the twelfth and eleventh centuries BC in small, unwalled settlements situated primarily in the northern Negev, the central hill country north of Jerusalem, and the hilly areas of Upper and Lower Galilee. They practiced a mixed farming and herding economy. Their cultural forebears seem to have been the Canaanites, though another origin (Shasu) has also been proposed. The pottery at early Israelite sites occurs in a limited repertoire of shapes and is largely undecorated. Unlike Philistine towns, early Israelite settlements reveal few foreign contacts: only a handful of Egyptian artifacts (mostly scarabs) have been discovered in their settlements. The conflict between the Philistines and Israelites ended in the early tenth century BC

with the defeat of the Philistines by King David. Thereafter, the Pentapolis ceased to exist as a formal confederation, and Philistia declined as a military and political power.

The Hebrew kingdom was united under David and Solomon in the tenth century BC (the period known as the "United Monarchy"). Thereafter, the country split into the northern and southern kingdoms of Israel and Judah. Under the "Divided Monarchy," Palestine became a buffer zone between Egypt and the great powers of the Near East, especially the Assyrians and Babylonians. Ultimately, the northern kingdom of Israel perished with the Assyrian destruction of its capital, Samaria, in 721 BC, while the southern kingdom of Judah succumbed to the Babylonians in 586 BC with the capture of Jerusalem.

The Iron Age II period witnessed the growth of urbanization in both northern and southern Palestine. The principal cities in Israel (Dan, Hazor, Megiddo, Samaria, and Gezer) as well as in Judah (Lachish and Jerusalem) were large and well fortified. In addition, a line of fortresses stretched across the northern Negev as far as Kadesh-Barnea in the Sinai; initially constructed in the tenth century BC, the forts continued in use into the Iron Age II period. Israelite tombs, though not nearly as rich as those of the Late Bronze Age Canaanites, have yielded large quantities of pottery, figurines, and other small artifacts. The palaces and temples, especially in the north, were heavily influenced by Phoenician building and decorative techniques. More than 500 fragments of ivory (mostly plaques and inlays) were found on the acropolis at Samaria. These date to the ninth or eighth century BC and are thought to be products of Phoenician art; many of them are decorated with Egyptian motifs. Egypt's influence on Iron Age Palestine was considerably less than that of the Phoenicians, and much of it was probably transmitted through Phoenician intermediaries. Examples of Egyptian influence include the adoption of the scarab form for Israelite seals and the use of hieratic numerals on Hebrew ostraca and shekel weights. Two historically important Egyptian finds from Iron Age Palestine are the fragment of a stela of Sheshonk I (22nd Dynasty), which was found at Megiddo, and part of an alabaster jar inscribed with the name of Osorkon II (22nd Dynasty), which comes from Samaria.

During most of the Iron Age, Egypt was too weak militarily to intervene in the affairs of southwest Asia. In the tenth century BC, however, an unnamed pharaoh—perhaps the 21st Dynasty king Siamen—is reported in I Kings 9:16 to have captured Gezer and given the town as a dowry to his daughter upon her marriage to Solomon. Then, shortly after Solomon's death and the breakup of the United Monarchy, Sheshonk I led an Egyptian army into Palestine. The primary objective of this campaign may have been to prevent Israel and Judah from becoming a threat to Egypt's northern border. The campaign, reported in I Kings 14:25–8 and 2 Chronicles 12:2–12 as well as on a topographical list and fragmentary stela at Karnak, proceeded through the central hill country to the Jezreel and northern Jordan River valleys. The army then returned to Egypt via the coastal plain. Destruction levels found at Megiddo, Gezer, Tel Batash, and many other sites are evidence of this campaign.

For a brief period in the seventh century BC, the Egyptians under Psamtik I (26th Dynasty) reasserted control over the Levantine coast as far north as Phoenicia. A campaign mounted by Neko II (26th Dynasty) against the Assyrians in Syria resulted in the death in 609 BC of the Judean ruler Josiah, who tried to halt the Egyptian advance at Megiddo. Egyptian activity in the Levant during the Iron Age came to an end in 605 BC, when Neko's forces were thoroughly defeated by the Babylonians at Carchemish.

The homeland of the Phoenicians was the northern Levantine coast in the area of modern-day Lebanon. Ancient Phoenicia was not a unified kingdom, but a conglomeration of independent Canaanite city-states—the most important of which were centered at Arvad, Byblos, Sidon and Tyre—which engaged in maritime trade and colonization throughout the Mediterranean world. The Phoenician rulers are mentioned prominently in the Amarna Letters of the mid-fourteenth century

BC, while the report of the Egyptian priest Wenamen (circa 1070 BC) mentions the cities of Tyre, Sidon and Byblos.

The major western expansion of the Phoenicians began in the ninth century BC. Phoenician trading stations and colonies were founded along the northern and southern rims of the Mediterranean coast and as far west as the Iberian peninsula. The transmission of the alphabet to Greece by the Phoenicians may have occurred somewhat earlier, perhaps in the eleventh or tenth century BC (although no examples of Greek writing date before the early eighth century BC). Already in the ninth century BC, the cites of Phoenicia had to pay tribute to the Assyrians. Subsequently, during the eighth and seventh centuries BC, they were incorporated into the Assyrian empire.

Egypt maintained lively commercial and political relations with Phoenicia. The Phoenicians were interested in goods and materials for which Egypt had long been famous, such as ivory, gold and linen, while the Egyptians sought timber, oil and metals in Phoenician ports. The evidence for Egyptian–Phoenician contacts in the tenth–eighth centuries BC is considerable. Fragmentary statues of three 22nd Dynasty kings (Sheshonk I, and Osorkon I and II) come from Byblos, and numerous Egyptian alabaster vases and small finds have turned up at Phoenician sites throughout the Mediterranean. The Phoenicians adopted many features of Egyptian culture, including the use of scarabs as both seals and amulets, while Phoenician art incorporates many Egyptian motifs.

See also

Amarna Letters; Assyrians; Canaanites; Israelites Sea Peoples; Third Intermediate Period, overview; trade, foreign

Further reading

Dothan, T. 1982. *The Philistines and Their Material Culture*. New Haven, CT.
Finkelstein, I. 1988. *The Archaeology of the Israelite Settlement*. Jerusalem.

Kitchen, K.A. 1986. *The Third Intermediate Period in Egypt (1100–650 B.C.)*. Warminster.

Leclant, J. 1968. Les relations entre l'Égypte et la Phénicie du voyage d'Ounamon à l'expedition d'Alexandre. In *The Role of the Phoenicians in the Interaction of Mediterranean Civilizations*, W.A. Ward, ed. 9–31. Beirut.

Levy, T.E., ed. 1995. *The Archaeology of Society in the Holy Land*. New York.

Mazar, A. 1990. *Archaeology of the Land of the Bible: 10,000–586 B.C.E.* New York.

Peckham, B. 1992. Phoenicia, history of. In *The Anchor Bible Dictionary* 5, D.N. Freedman, ed., 349–57. New York.

JAMES WEINSTEIN

Libyans

For the pre-classical world, the term "Libyans" generally refers to all non-Egyptian peoples living in the large and little-known area to the west of Egypt, which makes up the modern country of Libya. These certainly comprised different ethnic groups and there were important changes in population during Dynastic times, but not much is known about the pre-classical archaeology of Libya. The ancient frontiers in this region are also unknown, although Egyptian control of some of the Western Desert oases was already being attempted in the Old Kingdom. The Libyans were not literate in their own languages in antiquity and, until the 26th Dynasty, textual evidence of them comes entirely from scanty Egyptian sources. The first synthetic account was not written until the fifth century BC, when Herodotus, recounting the early history of the Greek colony of Cyrene, also described the city's Libyan hinterland and its people.

Our knowledge of the Libyans is therefore largely confined to their interactions with Egypt. Until the 18th Dynasty, two words, "Tjehenu" and "Tjemehu," were used both for the geographical areas west of Egypt and for the peoples who lived there. The two words originally had specific meanings, but were already generalized and interchangeable by the Middle Kingdom. The term "Tjehenu" tended to describe the area immediately to the west of the Nile Delta, from the Mediterranean coast south to about the latitude of the Fayum. The word "Tjemehu," in contrast, referred to an area which stretched at least as far south as Wadi es-Sebua in Lower Nubia, based on the evidence of a 19th Dynasty stela of the Viceroy of Kush (Nubia), Setjau. The 6th Dynasty inscription of an official named Harkhuf suggests that at that time it may even have extended to the Third Cataract.

Not much is known of this early period. Libya was of relatively little interest to the Egyptians because it lacked rich mineral deposits. There was certainly trade, and more aggressive activity is evident in Egyptian raids for booty, slaves and cattle. The earliest record of this may be the "Libyan" Palette, a ceremonial slate artifact of the late fourth millennium BC carved with a symbolic representation of attacks on settlements. The mortuary temple of Sahure (5th Dynasty) preserves a depiction of a defeated Libyan group, including a chief and his family, and there is a reference in the 12th Dynasty *Tale of Sinuhe* to an expedition in search of captives and cattle.

More is known about Libya later, from the 18th Dynasty onward, when the earlier Egyptian dominance was eventually reversed. Although the old names continue to be used, two new groups, the "Libu" and the "Meshwesh," are found in texts. "Libu" is probably the origin, via Greek, of the word "Libya," while descendants of the "Meshwesh" were possibly a people whom Herodotus calls "Maxyes." These peoples initially occupied the area west of Tjehenu, in Cyrenaica, and gradually moved east along the Mediterranean coast toward the Nile Delta. The appearance of these new ethnic terms marks Egyptian recognition of relatively recent arrivals, perhaps from farther west, who were themselves affected by population upheavals (the Sea Peoples) around the Mediterranean then. Represented differently from their predecessors, these new arrivals were depicted in Egyptian art with pale skin, distinctive hair

445

styles, long pointed beards and extensive body decoration, possibly tattooed or painted. Feathers in the hair are symbols of status.

In the 19th and 20th Dynasties, there was mounting pressure from these newcomers on the western Delta. A very fragmentary papyrus painting from Tell el-Amarna suggests that hostilities had already broken out in the late 18th Dynasty. From the reign of Seti I to at least that of Ramesses III, there was a series of conflicts in which the Libyans slowly gained ascendancy. A chain of forts built by Ramesses II near the Mediterranean coast (for example, at Zawiyet Umm el-Rakham and el-Alamein) ultimately failed to halt them. By the end of the New Kingdom, substantial numbers of Libyans had settled over much of the Delta and the northernmost part of the Nile Valley. Upper Egypt was less affected, although Ramesses III constructed new enclosure walls to protect temples there, and even Thebes suffered raids.

The Libu and the Meshwesh seem to have been essentially nomadic pastoralists. Meshwesh cattle were already known in Egypt in the 18th Dynasty, and sheep and goats were also important to their economy. They possessed bronze weapons, as well as metal vessels, which were probably acquired through trade or battle. Their incursions into Egypt, of whole populations and their livestock, have usually been explained as the result of famine or population displacement, but these can also be interpreted as aggressive expansions into territory occupied by sedentary agriculturalists.

Traditionally, the accession of Sheshonk I, a great chief of the Meshwesh, as the first king of the 22nd Dynasty, has been seen as marking the beginning of "Libyan" rule in Egypt. However, recent research has suggested that the "Libyan period," when many Egyptian rulers were of Libu or Meshwesh stock and Libyan social structure was clearly influential in Egypt, had already begun as early as the late 20th Dynasty. At that point, control of Egypt was divided between a severely weakened king in the north and the high priest of Amen at Thebes. The latter post was attained by Herihor, an army commander who also became Viceroy of Kush and Vizier, an unprecedented accumulation of power for any one individual. Several of Herihor's sons are known to have had Libyan names, as did a later high priest and at least one of the contemporary kings of the 21st Dynasty, Osorkon "the Elder."

It has been assumed that the Libyans assimilated pharaonic culture, but in reality this was a slow process. The retention of Libyan names is seen in a succession of kings called Sheshonk, Osorkon or Takelot. Some elements of dress, especially hair feathers which identified the chiefs, survived for several centuries. Above all, the looser system of government of the Libyan period reflects their tribal structure, under the various chiefs of the Meshwesh and the Libu. Another factor was the use of members of a ruler's family in government, to an extent without precedent in Egypt. Beginning with Sheshonk I, sons of the king were appointed as military commanders at strategically important sites, such as Memphis, Heracleopolis and Thebes, but also as high priests of local cult centers. Hereditary tendencies inevitably led to conflict between collateral branches, and a prolonged power struggle is vividly described in the text, the *Chronicle of Prince Osorkon*.

The best illustration of such divisions is a stela of the 25th Dynasty Kushite king, Piye, which records his defeat of the Libyan rulers in the late eighth century BC. Four Libyan kings and many more chiefs of the Meshwesh, each ruling a different part of Egypt, are named. Although still distinguished by regalia and titulary in the Egyptian record, the kings were really paramount chiefs, who received the allegiance of other chieftains. The principal organizer of opposition to Piye was not a king but a great chief called Tefnakht, who pressed the other chiefs into a coalition.

During this period, traces of the Libyans' cultural background can also be detected in the archaeological record. Coffins, statues and stelae were often provided with lengthy genealogies, whereas in earlier periods only the names of parents had been included. Oral traditions of Libyan families' roots thereby took on a permanent form through Egyptian language and mortuary practices. Reflections of the

Libyan presence may also be seen in changes in burial practices, developments in language and the hieroglyphic script, and in the increased prominence of women in Egypt.

The Kushite kings (25th Dynasty) were content to leave Egypt politically fragmented, but the divisions did not survive the advent of the 26th Dynasty. Although the new kings were also of Libyan descent, and one of them, Apries, is said by Herodotus to have intervened militarily on the side of the Libyans against the Greeks of Cyrene, their reunification of Egypt was accompanied by the disappearance of many of the features which had characterized the Libyan period, including the chiefs of the Meshwesh. With the founding of Cyrene, and the fame which the oracle of Amen in the Siwa Oasis rapidly acquired in the Greek world, a new era in the history of Libya and its relationship with Egypt began.

See also

Apis; Marsa Matruh; Sea Peoples; Siwa Oasis, Late period and Graeco-Roman sites; Third Intermediate Period, overview

Further reading

Hölscher, W. 1955. *Libyer und Ägypter.* Glückstadt.

Leahy, A. 1985. The Libyan Period in Egypt: an essay in interpretation. *Libyan Studies* 16: 51–65.

O'Connor, D. 1990. The nature of Tjemhu (Libyan) society in the later New Kingdom. In *Libya and Egypt c 1300–750 BC*, A. Leahy, ed., 29–113. London.

Osing, J. 1980. Libyen, Libyer. In *LÄ*: 1015–33. Wiesbaden.

ANTHONY LEAHY

el-Lisht

El-Lisht is a small modern village about 65 km south of Cairo and 3 km west of the village of el-Matania on the west bank of the Nile,

probably in the vicinity of the Middle Kingdom capital of Itj-t3wy ("Possessor of the Two Lands"). On the desert plateau west of the village is a cemetery which is dominated by the remains of the pyramids of Amenemhat I and his son Senusret I, the first two kings of the 12th Dynasty. The cemetery was first used in the late Old Kingdom and First Intermediate Period. Burials continued in the Middle Kingdom and well into the 13th Dynasty. The cemetery extends about 3 km north–south and 0.5 km east–west (29°34′ N, 31°13′ E) and includes smaller rock-cut tombs along the ridge of the desert plateau. Large *mastaba* tombs and temple-like tomb chapels of the more important nobility of the early 12th Dynasty are located around the two pyramids.

After Gaston Maspero unsuccessfully attempted to open the blocked entrance corridors of the two pyramids in 1883, Joseph-Étienne Gautier and Gustave Jéquier conducted the first extensive excavations at this site for the French Institute of Archaeology in 1894–5, during which they found a cache of Osiride statues as well as the seated statues of Senusret I now in the Cairo Museum (CG 411–420). In 1906 the most thorough investigations of the site were begun by the Metropolitan Museum of Art under the direction of Albert Lythgoe and Ambrose Lansing. These excavations continued, with brief interruptions, until 1934. In 1984 the Metropolitan Museum resumed work at the site, concentrating on the pyramid complex of Senusret I and the surrounding cemetery. These excavations uncovered the remains of the tomb chapel of the vizier Mentuhotep, with its elaborately painted granite sarcophagus.

Pyramid complex of Amenemhat I

The funerary complex of Amenemhat I was the first since Pepi II (6th Dynasty) to follow the Memphite building tradition of the late Old Kingdom. Like its Old Kingdom prototypes, it has a valley temple, attached to an open causeway, which leads up to the mortuary temple on the east side of the pyramid. A granite false door found near the entrance to the pyramid proves the existence of a northern chapel.

Many building stones from the complex were later robbed. A settlement of the Late period was also built over the temple precinct, destroying the plan, and a reconstruction of the building is not possible now. In the debris a few blocks were found decorated with reliefs of both Amenemhat I and Senusret I. Why both kings appear in the temple decorations has not yet been explained convincingly.

The pyramid was originally 55–60 m high and had a base length of 84 m. Many limestone blocks were reused ones from the Old Kingdom and still retain reliefs from the pyramid complexes at Giza, Saqqara and Abusir. The entrance to the pyramid corridor lies in front of the north face of the pyramid. A slightly sloping corridor with portcullises still in place can only be entered through a robbers' tunnel. Beyond this is a small chamber with a square vertical shaft. Because of the rising ground water, this shaft has never been entered in modern times and it is not possible to investigate the flooded burial apartments of the king.

Although the plan of this complex generally follows Memphite building traditions, there are also elements which seem to reflect Upper Egyptian/Theban traditions employed in the temple of Mentuhotep II at Deir el-Bahri. These include the open causeway, the terrace between the temple area and the pyramid, the row of burial shafts in the western court and the corridor system within the shaft.

Pyramid complex of Senusret I

Only with the much better preserved and better known pyramid complex of Amenemhat I's son and successor, Senusret I, were Upper Egyptian elements abandoned in favor of the Old Kingdom traditions of the Memphite region.

Senusret I's pyramid was surrounded by two walls. The inner stone wall was decorated on both sides with panels of a fecundity figure underneath a palace façade design. The panels were surmounted by Horus falcons elaborately executed in high relief. The destruction of the pyramid, which appears to have begun during the Second Intermediate Period, was already far advanced in the New Kingdom. The destruction, however, has exposed the construction of the core, which consists of a grid of stone walls filled with stones and rubble. This new technique of core construction was used for three generations until the pyramid of Senusret II.

In the eastern court of the pyramid complex a large temple was built abutting the pyramid casing stones, and a small chapel decorated with reliefs and a false door is located to the north of the entrance corridor. Following the examples of the Old Kingdom (and unlike that of his predecessor), Senusret I also built a "ka pyramid" (for the king's ka) in the southeast corner of the inner court.

Remains of a valley temple, which is probably deeply buried beneath floodplain deposits, have never been excavated. A long causeway flanked on either side by Osiris-form statues of the king wearing the Crown of Upper or Lower Egypt connected this building with the mortuary temple. Surrounding the pyramid in the outer court were nine subsidiary pyramids, which were probably built for members of the royal family. Most of these pyramids were finished and had small chapel-like buildings on the east and north sides. The pyramid to the south of the ka pyramid differs in size and construction from the others and may have belonged to Senusret I's queen, Neferu.

The importance of this site is further enhanced by the fact that the remains of several slideways, construction ramps and dressing stations for limestone and granite were found in the area and provide much information about the technology of pyramid construction and the organization of a building site. In addition, many quarry marks copied from the undressed sides of the remaining foundation and sub-foundation blocks provide information on the progress of constructing the monument as well as on the origins of the workmen and how they were organized.

Private cemetery

Both pyramids were surrounded by extensive cemeteries. Besides the large *mastaba*s or tomb chapels of the high officials of Amenemhat I and Senusret I, hundreds of shaft tombs were carved into the ground. The more important of these tombs include the *mastaba* of the vizier Intefiker, southeast of the pyramid of Amenemhat I, and the tomb of the vizier Mentuhotep, in the southeast corner of the enclosure of Senusret I's pyramid complex. The High Priest of the temple of Re-Horakhty at Heliopolis, Imhotep, built his *mastaba* immediately to the north of Senusret I's causeway. To the northeast of this, the remains of the huge *mastaba* complex of the High Priest of the Ptah temple at Memphis was excavated.

See also

Dahshur, Middle Kingdom pyramids; Deir el-Bahri, Mentuhotep II complex; Hawara; Lahun, pyramid complex of Senusret II; Lahun, town; Middle Kingdom, overview; Saqqara, pyramids of the 5th and 6th Dynasties; Thebes, el-Tarif, *saff*-tombs

Further reading

Arnold, D. 1988. *The South Cemeteries of Lisht 1: The Pyramid of Senwosret I*. New York.
——. 1992. *The South Cemeteries of Lisht 3: The Pyramid Complex of Senwosret I*. New York.
Gautier, J.-E., and G. Jévriner. 1902. *Mémoire sur les Fouilles de Licht. Mémoires de l'Institut français d'archéologie orientale du Caire* 6.

CHRISTIAN HÖLZL

Luxor, temple of

Known in ancient times as "the private sanctuary [*opet*] of the south," the temple of Luxor (25°42′ N, 32°38′ E) is located several km south of the state temple of Amen-Re at Karnak. Its god, "Amen of Luxor" (or Amenope), was a fertility figure with strong connections to both Karnak and West Thebes. Neither the cult nor any part of the temple appears to predate the early 18th Dynasty; the few Middle Kingdom fragments found here probably came from another site and were transported to Luxor after the original buildings were dismantled. The present temple is built on a rise (never excavated) that may conceal the original foundations. The most substantial remnant of Luxor temple's Tuthmoside phase is the triple shrine at the northwest corner of the present first court (G). Although rebuilt by Ramesses II, this building preserves many blocks from the structure that was originally built during the joint reign of Hatshepsut and Tuthmose III. During the 18th Dynasty it stood at some distance from the front of the main temple, and it is clearly the last of the bark stations that are mentioned in Hatshepsut's coronation inscription as having stood along the road from Karnak to Luxor.

Although the position of the 18th Dynasty road must have coincided approximately with the avenue visitors see in front of Luxor temple today (A), the latter, along with the sphinxes beside it, date to the reign of Nectanebo I (30th Dynasty). The mudbrick ruins on either side of the road are all that remain of the town of Luxor during the later and post-pharaonic ages. The gate through which the visitor passes from the avenue to the esplanade in front of the temple is also late, for the brick wall around this courtyard is contemporary with the Roman fort (B) built around the temple at the beginning of the fourth century AD. Substantial remains of this camp (mudbrick walls, as well as gates and pillared avenues of stone) can be seen east and west of the temple. Earlier buildings in the forecourt that were sacrificed to this transformation include a chapel (C), erected during the 25th Dynasty and dedicated to Hathor. A modest mudbrick shrine built in honor of Serapis during the reign of Hadrian, and still containing a statue of Isis, survives at the court's northwest corner (D). Later than all of this is the ruined building (E) diagonally across from the Serapis chapel, at the southeast edge of the court, which was one of the several

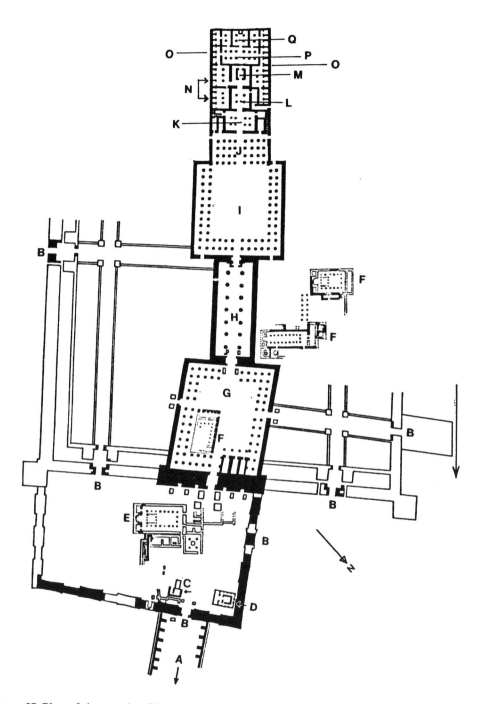

Figure 57 Plan of the temple of Luxor

churches (F) built here during the early Christian era with blocks taken from this and other sites at Thebes.

The pylon and first court of Luxor temple are the work of Ramesses II, who is also responsible for the colossal statues (some of them usurped from earlier pharaohs) in and outside this part of the building. Ramesses II erected two obelisks in front of the pylon, but only one remains in place today: the other was removed to the Place de la Concorde, Paris, in 1835–6. When the first court (G) was built, the porticoes of closed papyrus columns around its sides were broken at the northwest corner by Ramesses II's reconstruction of the 18th Dynasty bark station into a triple shrine. The three rooms of this building briefly lodged the portable shrines of Amen (middle), Mut and Khonsu when they entered Luxor temple once a year for the temple's premier event, the "Beautiful Feast of Opet"; but at other times it also served as a focus for local piety and the delivering of oracles. A false door at the back of Amen's chamber served to evoke the god's presence. Back in the courtyard, a more conspicuous eruption into the Ramesside plan came about early in the Christian era, when a church (F) was built in the court's northeast corner. Its remains can be seen under the mosque that now occupies this space. Dedicated to Luxor's Muslim saint, Abu'l Haggag, the mosque was founded in the thirteenth century AD and has remained in active use down to the present day.

Ramesside influence also extends into the great processional colonnade (H) which lies beyond the first court: the present gateway, in the name of Philip Arrhidaeus, replaced a late 19th Dynasty prototype, and at the same time, Ramesses II's reliefs inside the passage were covered over by his immediate successors. The colonnade itself, with twelve open papyrus columns that are among the largest ever made in Egypt, had already been added by Amenhotep III to the front of the temple he had completely rebuilt earlier in his reign. Carving of the scenes and inscriptions had barely been started when the king's death, and then the disturbances of the Amarna period, brought all work at the site to a halt. Tutankhamen finished most of the carving in the interior, but he had died before reaching the façade, which was executed during the reign of Ay. At some points in the hall (most conspicuously on door jambs and columns) the figure of the deceased Amenhotep III alternates with those of his successors, showing both their piety toward the builder of the colonnade and their eagerness to associate this last orthodox king before the heresy period with their own precarious regimes. In the end, however, a political eclipse befell both Tutankhamen and Ay, whose names can be detected only intermittently under those of their usurper, Horemheb. The few scenes still left in paint at the south end of the hall were finally completed in relief a few years later by Seti I. The walls of the building, which once completely enclosed its great columns, have for the most part been reduced to their lowest register of scenes, which has luckily preserved two extraordinarily detailed sequences depicting the processions north and south during the Opet Feast.

The sun court (I) which lies beyond was virtually identical to the equally grandiose court in front of the inner part of Amenhotep III's funerary temple in West Thebes. As with the Great Colonnade, the original effect of this part of Luxor temple is now compromised by the reduction of its outer walls, which gives undue prominence to the columns. Statues of divinities and the king may have been arranged around the porticoes in ancient times: a number of these images were found buried in the courtyard in 1989.

At the back of the sun court's southern portico (J), a number of chapels that provided lodging for the gods' portable shrines during the Opet Feast flank the entrance to the temple proper. Small rooms off the first hypostyle inside the temple apparently served other participants in the festival procession, but this part of the temple was completely transformed when the Romans changed what had been a columned hall into an open room (K). The doorway leading further on into the temple was blocked up and turned into an apse in which the divine standards of the legion were probably displayed. The stone walls were covered with plaster and painted; the emperor Diocletian and his three partners are displayed inside the apse, while members of the imperial court pay homage on the adjoining walls.

A modern doorway pushed through the masonry of the Roman apse gives access to the temple's second columned hall, sometimes termed the "offering hall" (L) because of the ritual equipment shown being brought into the temple on its walls. A door in the southwest corner leads to a passage that communicated with a "service entrance" into this part of the building on the temple's western side. Back in the offering hall, a wide portal leads into the bark sanctuary of Amen (M). This portal was subsequently adapted to include a small "priest's hole" inside the masonry of the doorway, perhaps to assist in the delivery of oracles. The bark sanctuary includes a freestanding building added by Alexander the Great within the larger chamber created by Amenhotep III. The reliefs, showing Amen's portable bark shrine and other scenes of the king in the presence of the gods, are well preserved, but the focal point of the original room—a colossal false door at the center of the south wall, where now a modern doorway communicates with the back rooms of the temple—has been all but obliterated by changes to this chamber over time.

A doorway at the northeast corner of the bark shrine leads into a two-room "coronation suite" (N) dedicated to the central mystery of the Opet Feast, the annual regeneration of the pharaoh as the son of Amen. In the northern room, after the king's divine birth (east wall), he receives the powers of his office from other divine fathers and mothers (north and south) so that he may appear in triumph at the *sed festival* (E). Other scenes of divine nurturing and recognition are found in the southern room of this suite and at other points inside the temple, for example, inside Amen's bark sanctuary, and on the walls of the first columned hall (the Roman sanctuary), where the king is suckled by one of his divine mothers and presented in public by Amen as his son.

Opening onto the "coronation suite" on the east, and similarly on the west side of the building, are a number of small cult rooms (O) that once served the gods with subsidiary cults in the temple. Most of these chambers on the east were destroyed when the Romans built an alternative southern entrance into the building's interior. More significantly, a narrow doorway at the south end of the "coronation suite" provided the only means of access into the back of the temple, the "southern sanctuary" or *opet* itself. This suite is itself a temple in miniature. A broad columned hall (P) stands in front of the leading cult chambers. In Amenope's sanctuary, there still remains the foundation of the altar on which stood the giant *naos* which contained the god of Luxor's statue (Q). The *opet* functioned on one level as a conventional sanctuary in which its god dwelt. The false door, directly in front of the columned hall, was the medium through which the god was able to "communicate" with his alter ego, Amen of Karnak, in the bark sanctuary, and thence with the triple shrine in the first court by means of its false door. On another level, though, Amenope's sanctuary operated as a mortuary temple, in which the god was regularly brought back to life through the "opening of the mouth" ritual performed by his son, the king. It seems likely that (1) the god's rebirth was also one of the purposes of the Opet Feast, and (2) this aspect of Amenope's nature secured his place in the Feast of the Decade, when the god of Luxor traveled to Medinet Habu every ten days to undergo a further cycle of rebirths.

Luxor temple is one of the few major cult buildings of the New Kingdom that can be studied in detail. Its preservation owes much to the solid construction of Amenhotep III, which was only lightly modified by later pharaohs. Just as important, however, was the site's later history. First, the temple was converted into a Roman military camp (the Latin *castra* was preserved in the Arabic el-Aksar, which became the modern Luxor). Subsequently, its reuse as the core of the medieval and modern town protected large parts of the temple until it was cleared (1880s to 1950s).

See also

cult temples of the New Kingdom; Karnak, temple of Amen-Re; Medinet Habu; New Kingdom, overview; representational evidence, New Kingdom temples; Thebes, royal funerary temples

Further reading

Abd el-Raziq, M. 1984. *Die Darstellungen des Sanktuars Alexanders des Grossen im Tempel von Luxor* (AVDAIK 16). Mainz.

Bell, L. 1985. Luxor Temple and the cult of the royal ka. *JNES* 44: 251–94.

Brunner, H. 1977. *Die südlichen Räume des Tempels von Luxor* (AVDAIK 18). Mainz.

Epigraphic Survey. 1994, 1998. *Reliefs and Inscriptions at Luxor Temple*, I–II. OIP 112, 116. Chicago.

Murnane, W.J. 1985. False doors and cult practices inside Luxor Temple. *Mélanges Gamal Eddin Mokhtar* 2: 135–48. Cairo.

El-Saghir, M. 1991. *The Discovery of the Statuary Cachette of Luxor Temple* (SDAIK 26). Mainz.

WILLIAM J. MURNANE

M

Ma'adi and Wadi Digla

Ma'adi, the type-site for the Lower Egyptian Predynastic culture of the early and mid-fourth millennium BC, lies south of Cairo on the east bank of the Nile (29°58′ N, 31°16′ E). One of the largest excavated settlements in Egypt (40,000 m²), the site has yielded a great quantity of finds, thus providing—together with its nearby cemetery and that of the Wadi Digla— a multi-facetted picture of life in that period.

Excavations at Ma'adi and at Wadi Digla were conducted from 1930 to 1953 by Mustafa Amer, Oswald Menghin and Ibrahim Rizkana on behalf of Cairo University. In 1977, an expedition from the University of Rome resumed research in the area of the Ma'adi settlement.

The Predynastic settlement lay on the summit of a ridge north of the mouth of the valley called Wadi Digla. The area has recently been overrun by the modern community of Ma'adi, a southern suburb of Cairo. The Predynastic remains originally spread over a 100 m wide strip running some 1.3 km from east to west. This extreme scattering of ruins should not be considered as the remains of one large static community; it surely represents the traces of a smaller population with habitation vacillating on the heights of the ridge. Thus, no fixed zones of specific activity (for example, an industrial area or communal storage facilities) could be recognized. The ground was covered with pits and postholes, indicating the one-time existence of simple oval huts constructed of wood and matting. The interpretation of certain rather small, irregular hollows as possible foundation trenches for such dwellings is highly questionable. There was no evidence whatsoever of stone or mud architecture. Many simple hearths were found inside and among the huts; several open-air hearths up to 2 m in diameter had been fashioned within horseshoe-shaped configurations of stone. Quite exceptional were four large structures dug into the earth, probably used as housing. The only known parallels to these are the subterranean dwellings of the Chalcolithic Beersheba culture north of the Negev Desert in Palestine.

Analysis of the animal bones from the site has shown that the people of Ma'adi did little hunting and fishing. They raised their meat: cattle, sheep, goats and pigs. From Ma'adi come the earliest known Egyptian examples of the domesticated donkey, an animal valued for its meat as well as for its services as a beast of burden. Cultivation also enriched the diet. Thanks to the annual flooding of the Nile, the land was very productive, fertile enough— judging from the charred plant remains of Ma'adi—to yield cereal grains much heavier than contemporary equivalents from southeastern Europe.

As in the Predynastic Upper Egyptian Nagada culture, the Ma'adi culture of Lower Egypt buried its dead some distance from the settlements; only stillborns and infants were found buried in pits or vessels within the settlement. The cemetery of Ma'adi, where seventy-six graves were excavated, is some 150 m south of the settlement. The cemetery of Wadi Digla, where 471 graves were located, was about 1 km farther south on a low spur in the mouth of the wadi. This second necropolis must have belonged to another community which outlived that at Ma'adi. In both cemeteries the dead were generally found buried in simple oval graves, lying in a contracted position with the hands in front of the face.

Traces of the matting and cloth used for bedding and shrouds survived.

The orientation of the Ma'adi burials has a chronological significance. In the earlier phase, represented by the Ma'adi necropolis and some of the graves at Wadi Digla, the dead were placed indiscriminately on the right or left side, with only a barely detectable preference for an orientation with the head to the south; graves were found at all angles. In contrast, the later burials at Wadi Digla demonstrate a pronounced conformity; nearly all the dead had been placed on the right side, with the head to the south, facing east. This orientation, predominant as well in the Predynastic cemetery at Heliopolis and the graves at es-Saff, is contrary to that prevailing in burials of the Upper Egyptian Nagada culture, where the dead were placed on the left side with the head to the south, thus facing west, where—according to later pharaonic tradition—the Realm of the Dead was located.

Nearly half the burials at Ma'adi and Wadi Digla had no grave goods. Many burials were accompanied by only one or two utilitarian vessels. The richest grave at Wadi Digla had only eight pots. No special pottery, painted or imported, was encountered, and very rarely were there any other artifacts in the graves. A few geometric stone palettes for mixing cosmetic pigments, one stone vessel, an ivory comb, a few necklaces of snail shells and a number of flint tools (mostly small insignificant blades) comprise the small finds from Wadi Digla.

Animal bones indicative of meat offerings were rare. Of interest in these cemeteries, however, are the animal burials: one dog burial at Ma'adi and the burials of fourteen quadrupeds (a dog and several lambs or kids, not gazelles, as has been erroneously reported) at Wadi Digla. Each animal lay in a separate grave, some accompanied by a pot.

The finds from Ma'adi and Wadi Digla indicate an origin in the Neolithic cultures of Lower Egypt (Fayum A, Merimde Beni-salame, el-Omari); they are in great contrast to the highly conventionalized Nagada inventories of the contemporary period in Upper Egypt. The pottery, made of Nile clay, tends to be in darker tones. The pots were all shaped by hand, although a finishing process carried out on a revolving base quite often left "wheelmarks" apparent near the rims. At the Ma'adi settlement many large storage vessels, some quite impressive in size, were found sunk into the ground. Exceptional finds include vessels in the shape of birds and model boats.

Some elements of the Predynastic Nagada culture of Upper Egypt are evident in the Ma'adi pottery, such as a few vessels of Black-topped Red class and the occasional red-painted bowl. Most of these appear to have been locally manufactured imitations of Nagada wares. However, vessels imported from Palestine, characterized by their pale (usually beige) unburnished surfaces, were also plentiful in the settlement. These must originally have contained goods transported to Ma'adi. Palestinian influence on local production is also apparent in loop-handled jars and in bowls decorated with an impressed line just below the rim. The Palestinian prototypes of the latter, as well as the imported vessels themselves, correspond to the end of the Palestinian Chalcolithic period (Beersheba/Ghassul) and the ensuing Early Bronze Age (EB Ia).

Stone vessels are well represented at Ma'adi. Most characteristic are those of black basalt, barrel-shaped with a ring base or a flat bottom and small lug handles below the rim. Also known from early Nagada contexts in Upper Egypt, these stone vessels developed in Lower Egypt from ceramic prototypes; they were undoubtedly the products of local craftsmen. Other products of the regional stone industry include spindle whorls, beads, palettes, a variety of hammers, whetstones and grinding stones. Some of the stone palettes are rather cursorily shaped ones made of local limestone, but there are also elegant rhomboid examples of slate resembling those found in early Nagada culture contexts, possibly imported into Ma'adi. The few maceheads of stone all display the early, conical form; the pear-shaped form, which became popular by the mid-fourth millennium BC, was not found at the site.

The chipped stone tools from Ma'adi and Wadi Digla represent a typical blade industry,

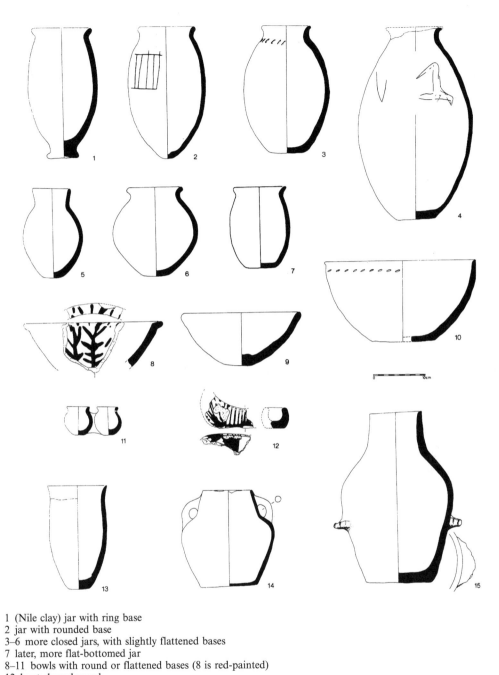

1 (Nile clay) jar with ring base
2 jar with rounded base
3–6 more closed jars, with slightly flattened bases
7 later, more flat-bottomed jar
8–11 bowls with round or flattened bases (8 is red-painted)
12 boat-shaped vessel
13 Black-topped class
14–15 imported Palestinian jars
Figure 58 Ma'adi pottery

in contrast to the core industry of the preceding Neolithic period. There are very few examples of bifacially retouched tools (daggers, "arrowheads"). The blades include end-scrapers, borers, burins and sickles (with various patterns of dorsal and ventral retouch). A few examples of blades typical of the Palestinian Early Bronze Age (Canaanean blades) were found at Ma'adi, as well as hundreds of Palestinian tabular scrapers.

Very significant at Ma'adi is the presence of copper. Three heavy ingots, two adzes and a variety of pins, spatulas and fishhooks, as well as fragments of sheet copper and pieces of wire, were found in the settlement. The adzes in particular are of importance, signifying that an appreciable quantity of copper was already available. Whereas stone adzes were abundant in the Lower Egyptian Neolithic community and in the early Nagada culture of Upper Egypt, not a single one was recovered at Ma'adi or Wadi Digla (nor at any other Predynastic site in Lower Egypt). In this northern region the copper adze, repairable in the forge and recyclable in the crucible, had already replaced its stone counterpart.

Analyses of the copper suggest a Palestinian source, either the mines at Timna or at Fenan in Wadi Arabah. Raw copper may well have been Lower Egypt's major import, carried across the Sinai peninsula by donkey caravan along with other goods: pigments, resin, bitumen, oil, cedar, flint tools, and vases and spindle whorls of basalt. Some of these goods were transported in ceramic vessels. Site H in Wadi Gaza to the east (within the modern Gaza Strip), where many artifacts of Lower Egyptian origin have been found, may represent a trading post along the route to Palestine.

In conclusion, the Lower Egyptian Predynastic culture represented at Ma'adi and Wadi Digla must have developed locally from the preceding Neolithic phase. It is contemporary with the early and middle Predynastic phases of the Nagada culture in Upper Egypt (Nagada I through IIb), as demonstrated by comparable finds in that region. The calibrated radiocarbon dates would indicate a time span from 3,900 to 3,500 BC. There was thriving trade with Palestine, as shown by the various imports mentioned above. Like other known sites of this culture, at the apex of the Delta and farther south (es-Saff, Tura, Giza and Heliopolis), Ma'adi and Wadi Digla were eventually abandoned, which must have occurred as a result of the gradual conquest of Lower Egypt by people from Upper Egypt. Buto and Tell el-Iswid in the Delta, however, were settlements of this Lower Egyptian Predynastic culture which were not deserted but survived into Early Dynastic times, completely absorbing the material culture of Upper Egypt but perhaps still influential in the eventual unification of Egypt into one large territorial state.

See also

Abusir el-Meleq; Buto (Tell el-Fara'in); Canaanites; Fayum, Neolithic and Predynastic sites; Heliopolis, the Predynastic cemetery; Merimde Beni-salame; Minshat Abu Omar; Nagada (Naqada); Neolithic and Predynastic stone tools; el-Omari; pottery, prehistoric; Predynastic period, overview

Further reading

Caneva, I., M. Frangipane and A. Palmieri. 1987. Predynastic Egypt: new data from Maadi. *AAR* 5: 105–14.

Rizkana, I., and J. Seeher. 1987–90. *Maadi* 1–4 Mainz.

Seeher, J. 1990. Maadi – eine prädynastische Kulturgruppe zwischen Oberägypten und Palästina. *Praehistorische Zeitschrift* 65: 123–56.

JÜRGEN SEEHER

ma'at

Ma'at (*m3't*) is the ethical conception of "truth" and the goddess who personifies truth. The goddess Ma'at is, with few exceptions, depicted as a woman wearing a sheath dress with an erect ostrich feather in her hair. The symbolism of the feather is unclear. *Ma'at* as an ethical concept is known from at least the 3rd Dynasty, and the personification of the deity is attested from the middle of the Old Kingdom. *Ma'at* continues to be a feature of Egyptian religion through the Graeco-Roman period.

Ma'at was the daughter of the sun god Re and the sister of the air god Shu, whose feather emblem she shares. She was associated with other gods, primarily Ptah and Tefnut. She had many affinities with Thoth through the ritual of judgment that they both attended, and through Thoth's presentation of the eye of Re, which was equated with Ma'at. By the late New Kingdom, Ma'at entered into a syncretistic relationship with her father Re, and parts of Ma'at's body were equated with his body. Ma'at was referred to as the "food of the gods," because the principles inherent in Ma'at "nourished" them.

Although Ma'at personified one of the most important principles of ancient Egyptian religion, the few temples (Karnak North, Deir el-Medina, Memphis) dedicated to her date only from the New Kingdom onward. There is little information concerning the cult enacted in these temples. However, at least one ruler (Hatshepsut) was crowned at the Ma'at temple at Karnak, and Papyrus BM 10068 (20th Dynasty, in the British Museum) records that tomb robbers were tried there. Both acts are closely associated with the principles inherent in *ma'at*.

Ma'at as an ethical concept incorporates a web of interconnected cosmic and social principles which formed the collective conscious of the Egyptians. Diverse features such as truthfulness in business dealings and personal relationships, as well as the state of the universe, including the most basic events such as the rising of the sun, the inundation of the Nile and rebirth after death, were interrelated aspects of *ma'at*. Since all facets of *ma'at* were intertwined, to transgress against a social aspect of *ma'at* risked upsetting the cosmic balance of the world. Thereby, each member of society was individually responsible for the good of the entire cosmic order, for his own actions and behavior affected other aspects of *ma'at*.

Ma'at ensured the permanence of art, dress and ritual, for artistic styles and socially acceptable behavior were canonized as aspects of *ma'at*. As stated in the *Maxims of Ptahhotep,* dating to the later Old Kingdom, "*ma'at* is great and its appropriateness is lasting; it has not been disturbed since the time of him who made it.... There is punishment for him who passes over its laws." The association of general aspects of culture with *ma'at* contributed to the creation of a conservative society which viewed social change as a potentially dangerous deviation from *ma'at*. The principles of *ma'at* also had a moderating effect upon social behavior, which in turn had implications for the apparently placid response to political change: "Do *ma'at* that you may endure upon earth" (from the Middle Kingdom text, the *Instruction for King Merikare*).

Although each Egyptian bore the responsibility of acting according to the principles of *ma'at*, the ultimate responsibility for maintaining *ma'at* fell to the king, thereby making the head of state the protector of cosmic order. "Do *ma'at* for the king, [for] *ma'at* is what the god loves. Speak *ma'at* to the king, [for] *ma'at* is what the god loves" (from the *Instructions for Kagemni*, dating to the Old Kingdom). *Ma'at* was associated with the legitimacy of the king, as reflected by epithets as early as Seneferu (4th Dynasty), who adopted the Horus name "possessor of *ma'at*" (*nb m3't*). One of the Middle Kingdom *Coffin Texts* (Spell 1105) relates: "I have nurtured *ma'at*...that I might receive the [*wrrt*] crown." With the exceptions of Seti II, Siptah and Sethnakht, all kings of the Ramesside period (19th–20th Dynasties) incorporated "*ma'at*" into their titulary.

From the reign of Tuthmose III through the Roman period, the king is shown on temple walls presenting an image of *ma'at* to a god. This ritual symbolized the king's commitment to uphold the precepts of *ma'at*. Secondarily, it served as a symbol of his royal legitimacy, he being the premier protector of order in the kingdom. In its equation of *ma'at* with all other cult offerings, the Berlin Service Book (20th Dynasty) indicates that *ma'at* was considered to be the supreme offering into which all others were subsumed, just as *ma'at* was the supreme sense of order into which all aspects of behavior and natural order were incorporated. The king, as the donor of *ma'at*, indicated that he alone could ensure those necessities for the gods. Although there are a few examples of a non-royal person presenting *ma'at*, features of the iconography or inscriptions differentiate them from royal scenes.

In the Ramesside period, the king was depicted presenting the gods with a rebus of his prenomen which incorporated the hiero-glyph for *ma'at*. In this ritual, the king not only dedicated himself to the gods, but, as the corporate personality of Egypt, he also offered the people of his kingdom to the gods as a substitute for the usual food offerings that sustained the deity. This ritual also emphasized the direct association of *ma'at* and the king, as stated by King Horemheb: "*Ma'at* has united herself with him."

From the New Kingdom onward, it was thought that upon death, the soul of the deceased was judged by a tribunal of the gods. The heart of the deceased was placed on a balance scale to be weighed against the figure of the goddess Ma'at or her feather emblem, and the deceased recited the "Negative Confession" ("I have not robbed the poor, I have not cheated in the fields, I have not done crimes against people..." [*Book of the Dead*, Spell 125]), swearing to have lived in accordance with *ma'at*. If the confession was accepted and the heart was not heavy with sin, the deceased became "true of voice" (*m3' ḥrw*) and entered an eternity in the afterlife. In the Ramesside period, Ma'at was increasingly associated with mortuary beliefs. She was equated with the personification of the West (*Imntt*, the necro-polis); she was referred to as "Mistress of the West who resides in the Necropolis," and she was credited with the ability to give a good burial.

See also

funerary texts; kingship; mortuary beliefs; religion, state; textual sources, Middle Kingdom; textual sources, Old Kingdom

Further reading

Assmann, J. 1990. *Ma'at: Gerechtigkeit und Unsterblichkeit im Alten Ägypten*. Munich.

Hornung, E. 1982. *Conceptions of God in Ancient Egypt: The One and the Many*, 213–16, 279. Ithaca, NY.

Morenz, S. 1973. *Egyptian Religion*, 110–36. Ithaca, NY.

Teeter, E. 1997. *The Presentation of Maat: Ritual and Legitimacy in Ancient Egypt* (SAOC 57). Chicago.

EMILY TEETER

Macedonians

The Macedonians were originally one of several Greek tribes living on the northern frontier of the Hellenic world. Their most distinguished descendant was Alexander the Great, who conquered Egypt in 331 BC. Alexander inherited from his father, Philip II, an efficient centra-lized kingdom whose expanded territory em-braced Paionia and part of Illyria to the north and extended through Thrace to the Black Sea while exercising control over much of the rest of Greece. It was from this background that Ptolemy, son of Lagos, founder of the Ptole-maic dynasty, came to inherit Egypt in 323 BC as one of Alexander's successors.

The relatively remote geographical situation of the Macedonians contributed to their reten-tion of a social organization different from the rest of the Greeks. Most notable is their monarchic form of government, which survived as a political legacy in the Hellenistic kingdoms. All authority was vested in the king, who was commander-in-chief of military forces, head of religious observances, owner of all resources of the kingdom and issuer of coinage. The king was normally eldest son of the previous king, though custom dictated that final choice rested with the army. He was surrounded by Compa-nions (*hetairoi*) and Friends (*philoi*), who were personal retainers loyal to the king and at his command in war and peace. Thus most of the satrapies, including Egypt, that were created

Drawing by Coleman

Figure 59 King Herihor offering *ma'at* to Khonsu
Courtesy of the Oriental Institute of the University of Chicago

out of Alexander's empire went to one-time Companions. Royal marriages were contracted according to personal and dynastic policies. Polygamy was accepted, but incest involving full siblings, as practiced by certain of the Ptolemies, was not.

Physically, Macedonia consisted of a great fertile plain opening onto the Thermaic Gulf to the east and ringed by rugged mountains to the west. Timber and minerals were the two chief exports and the substantial basis for Macedonia's wealth. Archaeological excavations are beginning to reveal cities, cemeteries and sanctuaries throughout the land. Most important are Aegae (modern Vergina) lying in the foothills of the Pierian mountains, the old capital and traditional burial spot of kings; Pella, then situated near the head of the Thermaic Gulf, the new capital since about 400 BC or so, home of Philip and Alexander and

461

administrative center of their kingdom; and Dion, the great sanctuary sacred to Zeus and the Muses. The Macedonian court had from at least the later fifth century BC promoted cultural activities, attracting artists, writers and thinkers from afar. The refined milieu of scholarly and artistic productivity which later flourished under Ptolemaic patronage in Alexandria surely owes much to the Macedonian heritage of the founding dynasty. Unfortunately, the paucity of Alexandrian physical remains prohibits substantive demonstration of direct artistic linkage in any significant way.

The common folk of Macedonia considered themselves descended from Makedon, according to Hesiod the son of Zeus, while the royal house (the Argead dynasty) traced its ancestry to Temenos, a king of Argos, and through him back to Herakles, also son of Zeus. Religion focused on the orthodox Olympian gods with special emphasis accorded the mystic religions of Dionysos and Orpheus so popular in the north. Noteworthy is the fact that the oracle of Amen-Zeus at Aphytis in the Chalcidice was consulted by the Macedonians long before Alexander's fateful visit to the related shrine at Siwa. It is likely that the variant forms of traditional worship practiced by Alexander's army on the eastern campaign may have influenced religious rituals subsequently adopted by the new Hellenistic kingdoms. The precise origin of the so-called Hellenistic ruler cult, known in Egypt and elsewhere in the Successor kingdoms, is controversial. The tradition which has Alexander playing a role in development of ruler-worship is uncertain, however much he may personally have wished to be the object of worship. In any case, no such cult ever evolved in Macedonia itself. What seems clear is that in Egypt the Hellenistic dynastic cult began with the establishment of a cult of Alexander by the first Ptolemy. Assimilation of the living ruler to that cult began with his son, the second Ptolemy.

In the historical record the Macedonians first entered Egypt in the course of the eastern campaigns of Alexander the Great. In 331 BC Alexander arrived in Egypt, where he visited Memphis, founded the city of Alexandria in the Nile Delta and consulted the oracle of Amea at Siwa in the Libyan desert, which apparently confirmed his divine parentage. After Alexander's sudden death at age 33 in Babylon in 323 BC, his body was craftily claimed by Ptolemy, spirited away and ultimately buried in Alexandria. This event was the initial point of contention in a long history of hostility between the Ptolemies of Egypt and their counterparts in Macedonia, who desired and expected interment of their king at Aegae.

In the struggle for domination following Alexander's death virtually all the contestants (the Successors or *diadochs*) were Macedonian generals. Out of a thoroughly chaotic situation which initially saw Alexander's vast empire divided into numerous satrapies or provinces, three great kingdoms led by Macedonians emerged over the next decades: Macedonia itself, Egypt, and the Seleucid kingdom based in Syria. Of these, Egypt was first the satrapy and subsequently the kingdom of Alexander's trusted Companion and general Ptolemy, also known as an important eyewitness chronicler of Alexander's expedition whose writing was used extensively by the Roman author Arrian in his history of Alexander. Ptolemy (as Ptolemy I Soter) and his descendants controlled Egypt and various outside territories throughout the Hellenistic period until 30 BC, when Cleopatra VII was defeated by the Romans. The Seleucid kingdom, originally a satrapy of Babylonia, grew under the Macedonian general Seleucus (later Seleucus I Nicator) to include most of Asia. Seleucus and his descendants, however, ruled over an unwieldy territory which was quickly reduced by the growth of splinter kingdoms such as that of the Attalids at Pergamon. Macedonia itself was slower to coalesce. Alexander's homeland suffered decades of unrest, caused in no small part by rivalry over issues of regency and legitimate succession in the Argead dynasty. A measure of stability was reached only during the reign of Antigonos Gonatas beginning in 276 BC. The Antigonid dynasty then ruled northern Greece with Thrace and varying parts of southern Greece for the next century down to the Roman defeat of Macedonia at Pydna in 168 BC.

A fundamental problem in the empire left by Alexander was its artificiality; Macedonia, Egypt and the marginally conquered expanses of Asia formed at best a theoretical coalition held together by sheer force of personality. The almost immediate revolt of the Greek cities in the so-called Lamian War of 323 BC, though successfully quashed by the Macedonians, was a foretaste of things to come. The fluctuating balance of power among the Hellenistic kingdoms, not fully understood in detail, is indicative of a volatile situation and symptomatic of the fractious relations among the personally ambitious successors. The last two decades of the fourth century BC saw the Successor Antigonos Monophthalmos (grandfather of Antigonos Gonatas), initially satrap in western Anatolia, attempting to reunite Alexander's empire under his leadership. Opposition to his aims led to repeated conflicts with "separatist" forces led by other Successors: Cassander in Macedonia, Ptolemy in Egypt and Lysimachus in Thrace. Cyprus, for instance, was one area of conflict which saw Ptolemaic domination successfully challenged in battle by Macedonian forces in 306 BC. After only a decade of Macedonian control, however, Cyprus fell once again to the Ptolemies, who ruled it until Roman times. Meanwhile, in Macedonia, Cassander sought to strengthen his own position by eliminating legitimate blood succession. He thus engineered the murders of Alexander's remaining family members: his mentally unstable half-brother Philip III Arrhidaeus (317 BC), his mother Olympias (316 BC) and his underaged posthumous son Alexander IV (310 BC?). Ultimately, hopes of Antigonos's grand scheme were dashed with his defeat and death at the battle of Ipsus (301 BC), waged against the combined forces of Ptolemy, Lysimachus and Seleucus. The next two chaotic and poorly understood decades saw rival power plays within Macedonia by numerous individuals including Demetrius Poliorcetes (son of Antigonos Monophthalmos), Pyrrhus of Epirus, Lysimachus, Seleucus and Ptolemy Ceraunus. The latter, son of Ptolemy I and Eurydice, and thus a full Macedonian of the second Egyptian generation, was disinherited and exiled from Egypt but ruled over Macedonia from 281 to 280 BC. Marriage to his half-sister Arsinoe (married previously to Lysimachus and subsequently to her full brother Ptolemy II Philadelphus of Egypt) was intended to expand and help consolidate a brief rule which ended with his death in the Gaulish invasion of Macedonia. The subsequent defeat of the Gauls at Lysimacheia in 277 BC by Antigonos Gonatas ushered in the relative stablilty of the Antigonid dynasty.

In the Hellenistic period there developed a measure of cultural uniformity or *koine* which tended to blur the lines of certain ethnic and regional characteristics. Mercenaries, merchants and itinerant craftsmen were among those who spread both customs and artifacts over widely disparate areas. Thus, for instance, we see the widespread adoption of the Egyptian gods throughout much of the ancient world. Macedonia itself had major sanctuaries of Serapis at Thessalonica, and Isis and Osiris at Dion, while at Amphipolis there is a remarkable dedication by a private citizen to the gods Serapis, Isis and King Philip V. Historical considerations of Egypto-Macedonian relations, however, make it unlikely that direct Ptolemaic influence lies behind this phenomenon. Rather, like the occasional Egyptian trinket found in Macedonia, it can be attributed to the general receptivity of the age.

The Macedonian background of the Ptolemaic dynasty lived on and was actively promoted by the Ptolemies themselves. They not only founded their dynastic cult on Alexander the Great, but also established from early times a fictitious kinship between the Ptolemies and the Argead dynasty. In a further twist on this bit of propaganda, mythology was rearranged (in a tradition recorded by Diodorus Siculus) so that Makedon, eponymous founder of the Macedonian people, appeared as son of Egyptian Osiris rather than of Greek Zeus.

See also

Alexandria; Late and Ptolemaic periods, overview; Siwa Oasis, Late period and Graeco-Roman sites

Further reading

Ellis, W.M. 1994. *Ptolemy of Egypt.* London.

Hammond, N.G.L., and F.W. Walbank. 1988. *A History of Macedonia III, 336–167 B.C.* Oxford.

Sakellariou, M.B., ed. 1983. *Macedonia: 4000 Years of Greek History and Civilization.* Athens.

Walbank, F.W., A.E. Astin, M.W. Frederiksen and R.M. Ogilvie, eds. 1984. *The Cambridge Ancient History* VII (1), *The Hellenistic World*, 2nd edn. Cambridge.

STELLA G. MILLER

Manetho

An Egyptian high priest born in the Delta city of Sebennytos, Manetho was commissioned by Ptolemy II to write a history of Egypt in Greek from the earliest times down to the end of the 30th Dynasty. He produced a work in three books called the *Aigyptiaka* (History of Egypt), based on an Egyptian tradition which compartmentalized Egypt's past into *dynasteiai*, "ruling families or dynasties." Like the Turin Canon of Kings, Manetho's history began with the gods and demigods. These were followed by thirty dynasties of mortal kings ending with Nectanebo II, the last native Egyptian pharaoh. Subsequently a 31st Dynasty was added by another hand to take account of the Persian rulers of Egypt from Artaxerxes III to Darius III Codomannus, who was deposed as king of Egypt by Alexander the Great in November, 332 BC.

In his account, Manetho appears to have begun by giving each dynasty a number and an origin (e.g. "Sixth Dynasty of six Memphite kings"). He then formulated his chronological information in a manner loosely reminiscent of the Turin Canon, listing the kings in order, giving their reign lengths and concluding with the total length of the dynasty. Where apposite, he added information on the major events within a reign after the manner of the famous account of the Hyksos invasion preserved in

Josephus's *Contra Apionem.* The voluminous original work was supplanted at an unknown date by an *Epitome*, which became widely current and led to the demise of the parent version. This *Epitome* is also lost in its original form and is now only accessible through excerpts made by later chronographers such as Africanus (*circa* AD 160–240) and Eusebius (*circa* AD 260–340). It is almost entirely through these writers that we gain our knowledge of the skeleton of Manetho's work.

Even in its earliest form, the *Aigyptiaka* clearly suffered from major deficiencies: the king list, like earlier Egyptian examples, is in no sense an objective record. The principle on which Manetho divided his kings into dynasties is far from clear and certainly led to error: sometimes a "dynasty" is indubitably a distinct family of kings, sometimes indisputably not. Manetho also assumed a neat linear succession of dynasties running from the beginning to the end of Egyptian history, whereas they are known sometimes to have overlapped (for example, the 10th–11th Dynasties). Furthermore, dynasties can be duplicated (Manetho's 9th and 10th Dynasties are, in fact, identical). In the extant fragments and *testimonia* the problems are aggravated by textual corruption generated by frequent scribal errors which particularly affect the transmission of names and numerals. It is also frequently difficult to determine from these later excerpts what exactly is Manetho and what is later accretion. Our Manethonian material must, therefore, be used with circumspection and always in conjunction with other evidence. For all its deficiencies, however, this tradition has exercised an enormous influence on the development of Egyptology, above all in defining the dynastic framework within which Egyptologists think of Egyptian history and civilization. We must never forget that, though it was written in Greek for Greek and Macedonian consumption, Manetho's work was based on native Egyptian tradition and forms an important index of the nature of that tradition as it was formulated at the beginning of the Ptolemaic period.

See also

dating, pharaonic; Late and Ptolemaic periods, overview

Further reading

Lloyd, A.B. 1988. Manetho and the thirty-first dynasty. *Pyramid Studies and Other Essays Presented to I.E.S. Edwards*, J. Baines *et al.*, eds. 154–60. London.

Málek, J. 1982. The original version of the Royal Canon of Turin. *JEA* 68: 93–106.

Mosshammer, A.A. 1979. *The Chronicle of Eusebius and Greek Chronographic Tradition*. Lewisburg, PA.

Waddell, W.G. 1940. *Manetho* (Loeb Classical Library). Cambridge, MA.

ALAN B. LLOYD

Marea

The ruins of Marea are located approximately 45 km west of Alexandria on the southern shore of Lake Maryut (31°07′ N, 29°55′ E), just west of the Nile Delta. The name of the town, which was used in antiquity to refer to the lake and to the district as well, is a Latin derivative of the Greek "Mareotis," a toponym probably derived from the Egyptian root *mrt* (canal, artificial lake) or *mryt* (bank, shore, quay; plural *mrw*, harbors). The Arabic name of the lake is almost certainly based on that root as well.

The site was identified as the ancient town as early as 1872 by M. Pasha el-Falaki, and was briefly described (with a sketch map) by Anthony de Cosson and others, such as Hermann Kees. Excavations, directed by Fawzi el-Fakharani of the University of Alexandria, were initiated in 1977. A Boston University group participated in three seasons of investigation (1979–81), mapping the lakeside portion of the site and conducting additional excavations.

All of the structures at Marea—some preserved to a height of 1 m or more—identified by survey or exposed by excavation appear to be of Byzantine age (fourth–seventh centuries AD). A town of the same name may have been established there at least as early as the sixth century BC, when, according to Herodotus, Marea was the primary defensive post on Egypt's northwestern frontier, and it continued to be occupied during the Graeco-Roman period. Prior to the establishment of Alexandria, it was the capital of a small kingdom. The Marea/Mareotis area was noted for its agricultural production, especially its wines, which were alluded to by Horace, Virgil, Strabo and other classical writers. To date, no clear archaeological trace of the pre-Byzantine town has been recorded on the main site, in spite of some rather deep soundings, although it should be noted that some sources refer to an "earlier" and a "later" Marea (presumably not necessarily in exactly the same location). Defining the location of the late Dynastic and Graeco-Roman town should be a goal of future investigations.

In 1801, British forces advancing on Napoleon's army deliberately flooded the lake basin, which is separated from the Mediterranean only by a narrow limestone ridge, with sea water. As a result of the substantially lowered water level, the town's harbor facilities have been left exposed along the former shore. Thus the opportunity to examine and reconstruct a 1500-year-old Egyptian lake port lends Marea its greatest significance archaeologically.

Excavated or otherwise visible, limestone-block constructions include three jetties extending out into the lake: a short one (*circa* 40 m) and two longer ones (110–120 m). There are also portions of seawalls, sections of which have ramps down to the water, and a lengthy causeway or breakwater parallel to a promontory on the eastern edge of the site that leads via an ashlar platform to a small offshore island, which contains still-unexcavated structures and a pair of small piers. On top of the middle jetty, at its further end, is an approximately 4 m circle of curvilinear, fitted limestone blocks that has been provisionally interpreted as a basin for a lighted beacon. Between this quay and the short one to the west is a pair of massive runners, supported by large limestone blocks resting on

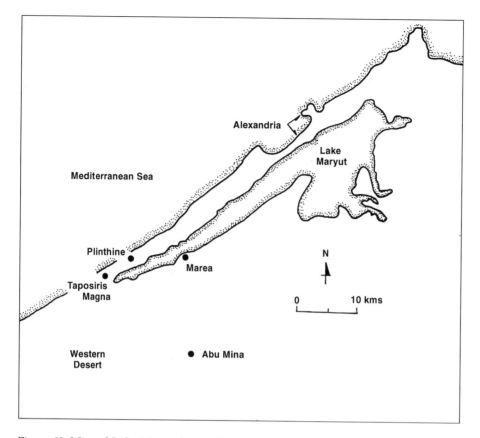

Figure 60 Map of Lake Maryut/Mareotis, showing the location of Marea

bedrock. The runners are about 20 m long and extend down into the former lakebed at a gradient of about 1:16, which should have permitted small vessels to be launched or hauled out, perhaps with the use of rollers. The upper blocks on each side are beveled (or worn down) at an angle of about 15° toward a V-shaped, silted trench in the center. The distal end of the walls probably originally lay about 1 m below the water surface. As on the jetties, the stone courses were bonded with a reddish waterproofing mortar. On the landward end of the runners are several small auxiliary buildings (storerooms?) and water drains. Possibly this structural complex served as a drydock (or, more properly, slipway) for building and/or maintaining the kind of small boats that plied the lake centuries ago.

Along the waterfront, where most of the excavation has been concentrated, is a group of contiguous shops fronting an arcade. These seem to have been divided into commercial and living quarters. Amphorae which once contained oil are found in some shops, and one shop has a feed bin (surrounded by compacted manure) where small stock(?) were kept before being sold. Immediately west of the shops along the same arcade is a pair of apsidal public baths. The base of a staircase at one end of these, as well as in some of the shops, shows that at least some buildings had either second stories or usable flat roofs. Just to the north of the shops, at the base of the promontory, is a curious labyrinthine building foundation of unknown function that was constructed on a slope down into the water, and just beyond that a multi-

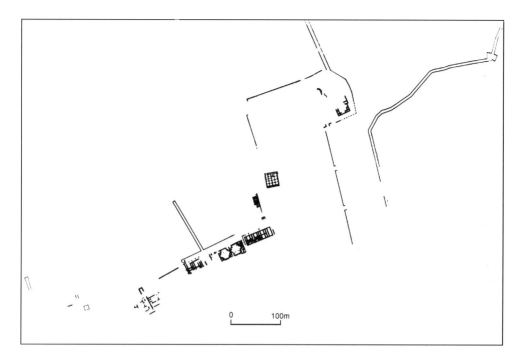

Figure 61 Plan of Marea waterfront (by Thomas Boyd)
Only major excavated or otherwise clearly visible structures are included. From left to right (east to west): the shortest pier; the slipway; partially excavated buildings and the middle pier; the public baths and shop arcade; the "labyrinth" and the mill house; the eastern pier. The flanking causeway is on the far right.

roomed mill house, which seems to have undergone several phases of modification, with two large rotary querns in separate rooms. Out on the end of the promontory is the other larger quay, and near it is the foundation of a basilica church that may have been about 40 m in length (only part of the apse has been excavated, shown on the plan as a short arc).

Other Byzantine as well as Graeco-Roman ruins are common not only around the lake but elsewhere in the immediate area. Several kilometers south of the port are excavated portions of what may be a Byzantine rural estate. Structures here include a villa with an atrium; a well preserved wine press with a lion-head spout leading into a large fermentation vat; and a subterranean rock-cut tomb with descending spiral staircase and cruciform floor plan. On the escarpment overlooking the lake a few kilometers to the west are other tombs, including a rock-cut one of apparent Late Dynastic

date, rock-cut anthropoid (mummiform) pit graves, and a Graeco-Roman shaft grave. One small rock-cut tomb, filled with disarticulated bones and Byzantine sherds, was also found near the Marea basilica at the waterfront. On the shore, more or less below the western tombs and close to Marea, another stone jetty and a three-sided wharf (*circa* 30 × 57 m), enclosing an interior area of water with an opening on the lakeward side, were discovered in 1980. The latter structure may be of Ptolemaic date, but the types of repairs found along the upper courses of blocks, incorporating waterproofing cement or mortar, are known from Roman/ Byzantine construction. Some of the upper blocks on the wharf retain evidence of bollard holes and mooring rings, the latter cut through the blocks from side to top until joining. Just west of these structures is a monolithic, rectangular platform (*circa* 21 × 24 m) with an ascending ramp 20 m long. This seems much more Dynastic in style, and from the existing topography the platform—whatever purpose it served—appears to have been surrounded by water. The exact relationship of these three structures, either to the tombs above or to Marea harbor, is unknown and requires further investigation. All are still some distance east of the Ptolemaic coastal sites of Taposiris Magna at Abusir (with its often-described "watch-tower" or "lighthouse," known as Bourg el-Arab) and Plinthine.

In addition to its role in agricultural production and lake commerce (with access to the Nile via canals, and to the Mediterranean through the Alexandria cross-city canal), Marea may have been a disembarkation point for pilgrims traveling to the shrine and tomb of St Menas (Abu Mina), an early Christian martyr, some 15–18 km south in the desert.

The inventory of artifacts from Marea suggests a fairly simple life for most of the town's inhabitants. The ceramics are dominated by relatively coarse storage, cooking or serving wares, with only occasional sherds of thinner, local Roman pottery. Fragments of blown glass, mostly from small cups, glasses, unguent bottles and the like, and small copper or copper-alloy coins are abundant. Numbers of loose tesserae (small mosaic tiles), apparently fallen from adjacent walls, have been recovered, and there are some remnants of poor quality frescoes, especially in the baths. The rather soft limestone was locally quarried, and imported marble was little used except for some internal flooring and linings for basins within the baths (unless much more of it was robbed out of these or other buildings over the years). No inscriptions have been found beyond occasional graffiti on pots, sherds or building blocks. There is no conclusive evidence of smelting or forging metals, or of ceramic manufacture (although the massive waster dump at Abu Seif Hasan, on the lake east of Marea, may indicate such an activity in the locality). The "glass factory" reported by de Cosson in his 1935 book proved, when excavated, to be a small structure next to the purported drydock that probably had been used as a refuse dump in its final phases.

Analysis of faunal remains from selected loci suggested that pigs, sheep/goats and fish were the primary source of animal protein, although remains of cattle, horses, donkeys, chickens, wild fowl, gazelles and so on were also found. Small rodent and fish bones—even fish scales—were well preserved, as were pollens. Preliminary analysis of the last, however, was not very informative economically, and extremely few macrobotanical specimens have been recovered.

It appears likely that Byzantine Marea was primarily a market and redistribution center for wine, oil, papyrus, vegetables, fruit, grain, livestock and fish. All of these products are attested either archaeologically or historically, or both. In spite of less evidence for the possible role played by manufacturing, so much of the site remains unexcavated that industrial areas within or immediately adjacent to the town may yet be identified. As noted, there was at least one substantial pottery-making site (Abu Seif Hasan) situated nearby, and probable glass-making slag is present on parts of the site. With respect to wine production, the landscape in the vicinity includes many rock-cut and stone-built fermentation vats.

There are no radiocarbon dates for the site, nor any recognizably dated coins (all of which are badly corroded with salts) or dated inscriptions thus far. The cultural and chronological placement of the surface remains and excavated units is based on types of glassware and ceramics, which include decorated oil lamps and small holy-water(?) flasks with the emblem of St Menas impressed on them. Architectural styles, construction techniques and occasional Christian graffiti have also been used to date the remains.

See also

Alexandria; Herodotus; Taposiris Magna

Further reading

el-Fakharani, F. 1983. Recent excavations at Marea in Egypt. *Sonderdruck das Römisch-Byzantinische Ägypten, Ägyptiaca Treverensia, Trierer Studien zum Griechisch-Römischen Ägypten*, 175–86.

Petruso, K., and C. Gabel. 1983. Marea: A Byzantine port on Egypt's northwestern frontier. *Archaeology* 36(5): 62–3, 76.

CREIGHTON GABEL

Mariette, François Auguste Ferdinand

French Egyptologist Auguste Mariette (1821–81) had begun the study of Egyptian hieroglyphs at an early age, inspired by the copious drawings and notes his relative Nestor l'Hôte had made on three expeditions to Egypt. His career took a decisive turn when he arrived in Egypt in 1850, commissioned by the Louvre to collect Coptic and Ethiopic manuscripts. Instead, Mariette explored Saqqara, where he soon recognized an ancient avenue of sphinxes. He followed it to the Serapeum, the huge subterranean gallery where the sacred Apis bulls were buried, which he excavated. At Saqqara he also located the well decorated, 5th Dynasty tomb of Ti.

From 1852 to 53 Mariette sent nearly 6,000 artifacts to France, and in 1855 he was appointed Assistant Conservator in the Louvre's Egyptian Department. Preferring to work in Egypt, he returned, hoping to take measures to keep Egypt's antiquities in the country and protect its monuments from pillagers. In 1858 with the help of Egypt's rulers, Sa'id Pasha and Isma'il Pasha, Mariette founded (at Bulak in Cairo) the first museum for antiquities in the Near East, and was later appointed Director of the Egyptian Antiquities Service (the first anywhere) and supervisor of all excavations.

Mariette excavated some thirty-five sites throughout Egypt in thirty years, finding 300 tombs at Saqqara alone and clearing the temples of Luxor, Medinet Habu, Dendera and Edfu. His efforts enriched the national museum and he managed to raise the international conscience concerning the need to conserve antiquities.

Mariette's publication record is extensive, ranging from five volumes on Dendera (1875), and a catalog of antiquities discovered at Abydos (1880), to collaboration on the libretto for Giuseppe Verdi's opera *Aïda*. He died in January, 1881, leaving his last work to be finished by his successor, Gaston Maspero. He lies buried in a huge sarcophagus outside of the current Egyptian Museum, Cairo.

See also

Dendera; Edfu; Luxor, temple of; Maspero, Sir Gaston Camille Charles; Medinet Habu; Memphite private tombs of the Old Kingdom; Saqqara, Serapeum and animal necropolis

Further reading

Dawson, W.R., and E.P. Uphill. 1995. *Who Was Who in Egyptology*, 3rd edn. M.L. Bierbrier. London.
Wilson, J.A. 1964. *Signs and Wonders upon Pharaoh*. Chicago.

BARBARA S. LESKO

Marsa Matruh

The modern resort city of Marsa Matruh (Graeco-Roman Paraitonion, longitude 31°21' N, 27°14' E) on the northwest Mediterranean coast is situated between Alexandria, 290 km to its east, and the Libyan frontier town of el-Salloum, 210 km to its west. Geographically important in antiquity, Matruh's protected natural harbor and adjacent lagoon systems provided the only reliable haven for mariners between Alexandria and Tobruk (ancient Antipyrgos in eastern Libya), a distance of some 600 km.

Paraitonion was allegedly founded by Alexander the Great at the time of his visit to Siwa Oasis in 331 BC, but there is archaeological evidence of some kind of settlement in trading contact with Greece as early as the eighth century BC. Prior to that, excavation has shown that at least one sector of the Matruh area was utilized in the fourteenth and perhaps into the thirteenth century BC as a way-station for Late Bronze Age (LBA) mariners whose home base was probably Cyprus. Designated "Bates's Island" after the American archaeologist Oric Bates, who surveyed Marsa Matruh for Harvard's Peabody Museum in 1913–14, the settlement occupies a small (135 × 55 m) sandy islet at the east end of the first of the five saltwater lagoons that stretch eastward from Matruh's

harbor. No other sites similar to Bates's Island have come to light in the region, but the island's diminutive size argues that additional foreign settlements may have been established elsewhere here. The presence of a Ramesside fortress at nearby Umm el-Rakham raises the possibility that pharaonic use of the harbor area existed perhaps as early as the 19th Dynasty. The likeliest location for such development would

Figure 62 Plan of structures on Bates's Island, Marsa Matruh

have been in the coastal plain directly south of the harbor, covered today by the modern city and thus inaccessible for excavation.

No early artifacts were retrieved on Bates's Island below 2.5 m above sea level, seemingly because of the rise in water level throughout the lagoon system during the fourteenth century BC, and its Late Bronze Age occupation appears to have been on the island's low sandstone ridge. This implies that the insular setting was substantially smaller than it is today but better protected.

The island's LBA architectural remains are poorly preserved. The upper levels of the rubble walls were entirely demolished for reuse in later Graeco-Roman buildings, as well as in more recent times, when a 12.5 × 12.9 m shelter was built in the late seventeenth or early eighteenth century that eventually housed sponge-divers. Much of the island's imported LBA pottery was found inside or near the "Sponge Divers' House," which today separates clusters of LBA remains to its north and south, suggesting that a single, uninterrupted line of small attached rooms and open enclosures covered much of the island's longitudinal north–south spine during the LBA period.

North of the Sponge Divers' House are structural remains, consisting mostly of sections of isolated walls. Associated pottery, including the island's broadest selection of all classes of LBA pottery (with the exception of Egyptian bowls), suggests that this area was used for storage and domestic activities.

South of the Sponge Divers' House the structural remains are more plentiful, and at least three rooms here are strung out in a stepped-out pattern along the island's spine. A stone oven with a ceramic cover and a stone bin were found inside one domestic structure (S107). Another structure (S119), where traces of two furnaces and bronze scraps were excavated, was probably a bronze casting workshop.

Walls were made of flat, undressed field stones brought from the mainland and laid in rough courses. Some walls were coated on the interiors with white or green plaster. Their superstructures may have been constructed of mudbrick or wattle and daub, but evidence for this is lacking, nor is there evidence for windows or doors. The natural bedrock surface of the island's ridge, later supplanted by layers of trampled sand, provided the only flooring. Paving stones were used for an exterior court. All spacial units were extremely small, which presumably reflects the cramped size of the island.

Apart from animal/bird bones and shells, the principal finds from LBA strata were potsherds, with considerably fewer artifacts in stone, ceramic, faïence and metal. Most of the imported pottery came from Cyprus, including both fine wares (Cypriot White Slip, White Shaved, Base Ring, Monochrome, Black Slip and Red Lustrous) and coarse wares (flat-bottom Plain White and Painted White Wheel-made jars and storage vessels). While Canaanite (Palestinian) jars formed the island's largest class of storage vessels, Egyptian open bowls made up its largest single class of pottery. A small number of contemporary Minoan and Mycenaean sherds also occurred.

Evidence of the bronze workshop suggests that simple bronze tools were cast on the island for local exchange, and bartering of finished craft goods for food and water would have been crucial for the islanders' operations. While the ethnicity of these people cannot be identified, they obviously had close ties with Cyprus. A motivation for short-term profit does not explain the existence of such a remote port, but it can only be understood in the wider framework of Late Bronze Age trade. Ship-borne Cypriot products have been discovered throughout much of the eastern Mediterranean, including Crete, the eastern Nile Delta and along the Levantine coast. Crete, which lies about 420 km northwest of Matruh, was perhaps the final point west for eastern Mediterranean traders. Given the strong north-westerly winds that prevail along this coast, Matruh represented the closest and safest landfall available to mariners leaving Crete to return to the Delta and other points in the eastern Mediterranean.

The local trading partners must have been the Berber Libyans that dominated the coastal plain and desert interior during the second half

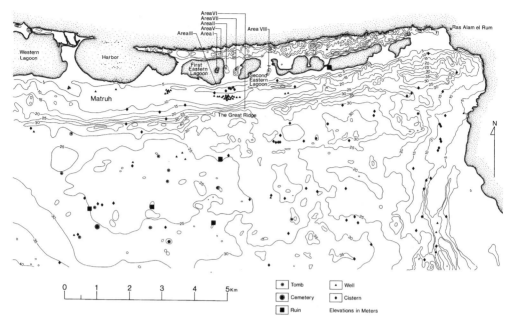

Figure 63 Central Marsa Matruh and the eastern lagoon system as far east as Ras Alam el-Rum

of the second millennium BC. A Libyan presence nearby is reflected in a handmade, coarse ware pottery, a few stone tools, and numerous ostrich eggshell fragments that were recovered from Late Bronze Age strata on the island, as well as five burials found by Oric Bates on the long ridge southeast of the modern town. The burials were in elliptical pits cut into the ridge's soft bedrock. Two were intact, with human remains and grave goods including two small, well-made stone vessels, several handmade ceramic jars, a small stone "mortar" and a number of aquatic shells, three of which were thought to be of Nilotic origin. The ceramics, which were interpreted by Bates and Flinders Petrie to be of early, non-Egyptian origin, are currently awaiting laboratory tests for dating.

During the 18th Dynasty the Matruh area therefore seems to have provided eastern Mediterranean traders with fresh stocks of food and water supplied by the mainland Libyans, and perhaps locally manufactured bronze tools, in exchange for the standard trade goods routinely transported in ships. The island was probably shunned during the stormy

winter months when the Libyans moved their flocks south.

While some form of settlement must have preceded Alexander's visit, the town of Paraitonion is clearly linked with the Ptolemaic, Roman and Byzantine periods. Following the division of Alexander's empire, it was administratively united with Ptolemaic Egypt. Although artifacts and wall remains have been found on Bates's Island dating from the sixth century BC to the fourth/fifth centuries AD, the town's Graeco-Roman development is better attested on the mainland. Bates observed urban remains spreading south of the southeast corner of Matruh's first east lagoon. A set of rock-cut stairs associated with a rock-cut (burial?) chamber leading toward the lagoon's edge may at one time have been associated with a dock. On the mainland west of Bates's Island, the crest of the low outcropping of rock, still littered with Roman period sherds, has traces of some kind of ancient industrial facility (possibly associated with dyeing, given that murex shells turned up in some abundance on the island).

In 1904 the French observer Fourtau saw remains of a large, ancient rock-cut quay or pier at the southeast corner of the deep lagoon west of Matruh's harbor, with a series of stone jetties projecting into the water. The quay's extension was marked by stone towers at both ends, while more than 2 km of urban remains, including a large domestic villa, were said by Fourtau to be visible along the lagoon's south shore. A decade later Bates noted the same kind of development along the southern and eastern shore areas of the west lagoon. Today all traces of Fourtau's and Bates's ancient town and the lagoon quay have been obliterated by military construction and other modern development.

Bates was also aware that an important sector of later Paraitonion occupied the coastal ridge west of the harbor, but, with the exception of a Roman villa excavated by the Egyptian Antiquities Organization, this area has yet to be investigated. Bates observed a defensive wall sealing off the western end of the ridge-top settlement, which he attributed to the sixth century AD (Justinianic period); parts of this are still visible today. Fourtau noted a ridge-top cemetery in the same general area. In the 1930s a well-preserved line of a Roman period(?) aqueduct was surveyed 12 km west of town; it presumably supplied the ridge settlement with sweet water.

Bates was able to record ten cemeteries and eight tombs of mainly Roman–Byzantine date associated either with the "Great Ridge" south of the modern city or with the regions to its west and southwest (i.e. extramural). He also excavated three large rock-cut tombs a short distance inland from the modern harbor. Rock-cut tombs were later reported at Hakfet Abdel–Razek Krim southeast of Matruh. Marble portraits of three local Egypto-Libyan males found in the tombs are in the Alexandria Museum.

Few historical facts are known about Paraitonion following the deaths of Marc Antony and Cleopatra VII, who resided there briefly after their defeat at Actium in 32 BC. Vespasian occupied the town during the civil war (AD 69) that led to his elevation as emperor. Otherwise, prior to the Byzantine period, when the town assumed considerable regional importance as both the seat of the *dux limitis Libyci* and of a bishop, Paraitonion was chiefly remembered as a source for a greasy, soft white mineral coloring agent called *paraetonium*.

See also

Aegean peoples; Apis; Canaanites; Cypriot peoples; Late and Ptolemaic periods, overview; Roman period, overview

Further reading

Bates, O. 1927. Excavations at Marsa Matruh. *Harvard African Studies* 8: 125–97.

Fourtau, R. 1914. La cote de la Marmarique. *BIÉ*: 98–128.

White, D. 1993. Marsa Matruh:the Resurfacing of Ancient Paraetonium and its Ongoing Reburial. *Journal of Roman Archaeology Supplement No. 19: Archaeological Research in Roman Egypt.*

White, D., and L. Hulin. 1989. 1987 Excavations on Bates's Island, Marsa Matruh: Second Preliminary Report; Preliminary Ceramic Report. *JARCE* 26: 87–114.

DONALD WHITE

Maspero, Sir Gaston Camille Charles

Born in Paris of Italian parents, Gaston Maspero (1846–1916) studied Egyptology there and in 1869 became Professor of Egyptology at the École des hautes études. He earned the first Ph.D. in Egyptology in France and joined the faculty of the prestigious Collège de France in 1874.

Maspero's first visit to Egypt in 1880, as head of a mission that would found the French Institute of Archaeology, involved epigraphic work in Thebes in the Valley of the Kings, but soon, with Auguste Mariette's death, he was appointed Director of the Bulak Museum and of the Egyptian Antiquities Service.

Maspero opened late Old Kingdom pyramids and copied and published the funerary texts carved inside them. He also cleared and restored the Luxor and Karnak temples, but his greatest contribution to scholarship was arranging and cataloguing the vast holdings of the new Cairo Museum, resulting in fifty volumes during his lifetime. Not only a gifted philologist but also a brilliant historian, Maspero holds the publication record in Egyptology, with some 1,200 items on his bibliography. A master of the broad view of history, Maspero was one of the great intellects in the history of Egyptology. Perhaps his best known work was his multivolume *Histoire ancienne des peuples de l'orient classique* (Ancient History of the Peoples of the Classical East) (1895–9).

Maspero also effectively reorganized Egypt's Antiquities Service along lines which continue to this day, dividing the country into five inspectorates. Permissions to excavate were granted by a committee on his recommendation, and he did not exclude Egyptians from this, even in the face of criticism. Foreign institutions found him congenial in providing facilities and fair divisions of finds. He hired Howard Carter as Chief Inspector of Upper Egypt and was very supportive during Carter's early career. Maspero was knighted by England in 1909, partly for his generous support of the Egypt Exploration Fund, founded in London in 1882, and he held many honorary degrees and memberships. He retired to France in 1914 at the end of his second long term of service in Egypt, and died suddenly in 1916, not long after his second son, a papyrologist, was lost in battle in the First World War.

See also

Carter, Howard; funerary texts; Karnak, precinct of Montu; Karnak, precinct of Mut; Karnak, temple of Amen-Re; Luxor, temple of; Mariette, François Auguste Ferdinand; Saqqara, pyramids of the 5th–6th Dynasties

Further reading

Dawson, W.R., and E.P. Uphill. 1995. *Who Was Who in Egyptology*, 3rd edn. M.L. Bierbrier. London.
Vercoutter, J. 1992. *The Search for Ancient Egypt*, translated by R. Sharman. New York.

BARBARA S. LESKO

Mazghuna

Mazghuna is the site of two destroyed pyramids of the late Middle Kingdom, on the west bank of the Nile *circa* 35 km south of Cairo and 4 km south of the cemetery of Dahshur (29°46′ N, 31°13′ E). The remains of these pyramids were excavated in 1910–11 by E. Mackay, who assigned them to Amenemhat IV (southern pyramid) and his sister/wife and successor, Neferusobek (Sobekneferu) (northern pyramid), the last two rulers of the 12th Dynasty. There is no textual evidence supporting these identifications and for archaeological reasons several scholars have suggested a 13th Dynasty date, which seems more likely.

The southern pyramid measures *circa* 52.5 m (100 cubits) at the base line and is slightly smaller than its northern neighbor. The superstructure, which was surrounded by a sinuous mudbrick enclosure wall, consists of a mudbrick core with a limestone casing. However, little more than the foundation trench of the casing and one or two layers of the mudbrick core are preserved.

The plan and construction of the burial chamber, with a built-in quartzite sarcophagus and transverse antechamber, aligned in the center of the pyramid, closely resemble the internal arrangement of the pyramid of Amenemhat III at Hawara. The entrance to the interior apartments of Amenemhat IV's pyramid is on the south side of the pyramid, where a staircase with sliding ramps on either side leads down to a small chamber. In the east wall of this chamber a small doorway opens into a corridor, which leads north to the antechamber. To protect the burial from tomb robbers, two sliding portcullises of red granite were built into the entrance staircase.

No remains of a causeway were found.

A small mudbrick structure consisting of an open court and a vaulted sanctuary, which are clearly the remains of the mortuary temple, was excavated in the center of the eastern enclosure.

Apparently the northern pyramid was already abandoned before it was finished. Both portcullises were found in an open position and there were no traces of a burial, which suggest that the pyramid was never used. Only a short section of a causeway-like ramp was found to the east of the complex, but there are no traces of an enclosure wall nor of the superstructure itself. The corridor system, which begins with a flight of steps on the east side of the pyramid, differs considerably from that in the southern pyramid at Mazghuna, but shows a close resemblance to the plan of the pyramid of an unknown king at South Saqqara. The T-shaped plan of the burial chamber and antechamber, which was first introduced in the pyramid of Amenemhat III at Hawara, was abandoned and replaced by a new design consisting of an oblong antechamber followed by a burial chamber with a built-in quartzite sarcophagus. A sliding block, which was intended to separate the two chambers, was found in an open position. This new system shows some resemblance to plans in contemporary private tombs and was probably first introduced in the pyramid of an unknown king at South Saqqara, where the so-called "queen's tomb" adopted a similar plan.

See also

Dahshur, Middle Kingdom pyramids; Hawara; Middle Kingdom, overview; Saqqara, pyramids of the 13th Dynasty

Further reading

Petrie, W.M.F., G.A. Wainwright and E. Mackay. 1912. *The Labyrinth, Gerzeh and Mazghuneh*, 41–55. London.

Stadelmann, R. 1985. *Die ägyptischen Pyramiden*, 247–8. Darmstadt.

CHRISTIAN HÖLZL

Medamud

The site of Medamud (25°44′ N, 32°42′ E) is located about 5 km northeast of Karnak, on the east bank of the Nile. Medamud was part of the Theban nome (Nome IV of Upper Egypt), and is mentioned between Thebes and Kus in the list of nomes and cities carved inside the temple of Ramesses II at Abydos. Its hieroglyphic name is "M3dw" (sometimes "M3tn" in demotic). The site was mainly dedicated to the falcon-headed or bull-shaped god Montu, and to a lesser extent, to his consort Rat-taui and son Harpora. Amen was also worshipped there, but at a later date.

The temple lies at the center of a partly destroyed circular mound and is roughly oriented along an east–west axis. Its ground plan includes the typical features of Graeco-Roman temples: a tribune (platform) overlooking a canal, a *dromos* that leads to a main gate, an open courtyard followed by a portico and a hypostyle hall, and a sanctuary. There was also space behind the sanctuary, which was apparently used as a courtyard for the living sacred bull.

No archaeological investigations took place at the site until Albert Daninos conducted a short survey there at the beginning of the twentieth century. The whole temple area was thoroughly excavated from 1925 to 1932 by the French Institute of Archaeology, Cairo (IFAO) in conjunction with the Louvre Museum, under the direction of Bisson de la Roque. Robichon and Varille, who did not publish a photographic record of their work, took over the fieldwork until 1939. Since then no excavations have been conducted there, but the gate of Tiberius and parts of an early Ptolemaic temple have been restored on paper by D. Valbelle and by C. Sambin and J.-F. Carlotti respectively.

Occupation of the site

Little is known about the necropolis of Medamud or the pharaonic and Graeco-Roman period town, which may have extended toward the unexcavated southwestern part of the site. The oldest structure unearthed at

Medamud is a First Intermediate Period mudbrick sanctuary. Inscriptions on the site begin mainly in the reign of Senusret III (12th Dynasty), and kings of the 13th Dynasty are well attested. In the New Kingdom Tuthmose III and his son Amenhotep II (18th Dynasty) were the most active builders there; however, only a red granite doorway of Amenhotep II is still visible today. The greater part of the present-day temple is of Graeco-Roman date, with some Coptic remains.

The earliest known construction at Medamud is a large, mudbrick polygonal enclosure wall, with a recessed entrance in its northeast section. Two mudbrick structures (later supplemented by two others) were identified as pylons; they led into a rectangular courtyard with vestibules in its western and southern ends. From the two vestibules were narrow, sinuous corridors, each of which ended in a small chamber. The floors of both corridors and chambers were covered with sand.

Unlike the rest of the area within the enclosure wall, two 20 × 15 m oval-shaped areas around the two chambers showed no traces of fire. Robichon and Varille concluded that the site had been burned and that two egg-shaped zones were all that was left from two earlier mounds which had been razed after the fire, to make room for the Middle Kingdom temple. They associated the hillocks with the Osirian cult. Unfortunately, it is exceedingly difficult to know the purpose of this structure because of the lack of any written material from the earliest levels and the fact that Robichon and Varille's interpretation was based solely on much later inscriptions. The ceramic evidence, including bread molds, seems to agree with a First Intermediate Period dating of the complex by the excavators; parallels were later found at the contemporary sites of Dendera and Balat in Dakhla Oasis.

The ground plan of the First Intermediate Period sanctuary appears to have been deliberately integrated into later constructions. The Middle and New Kingdom temples extended south and west, respectively, of the First Intermediate Period entrance, as did the original corridors and mounds.

Before reaching the First Intermediate Period structure, Varille and Robichon found the remains of a mudbrick temple. It was oriented along a north–south axis, with its northern half located under the eastern part of the later Graeco-Roman temple, and its southern half extending in the area east of the Graeco-Roman sacred lake. The better preserved southern half of the complex apparently contained priests' houses and storerooms, mentioned on the Cairo Museum funerary stela from Abydos (CGC 20555) as "the granaries of the temple of Montu in Medamud." The only probable stone architectural feature of the Middle Kingdom found *in situ* by Bisson was an inscribed red granite doorway located near the center of the rear part of the Graeco-Roman temple, from the reign of Senusret III. It was oriented along the same axis as the structure unearthed by Robichon and Varille, and possibly the six foundation deposits found under this temple can also be attributed to Senusret III.

Most of the Middle Kingdom and Second Intermediate Period architectural features at Medamud were discovered as reused material. More than 150 inscribed blocks were removed from the foundations of the later New Kingdom temple, which lies beneath the front part of the Graeco-Roman temple. Many of them were originally from limestone doorways, such as the *heb-sed* (jubilee) portals built by Senusret III and Sobekhotep II (13th Dynasty), now in the Cairo Museum. Another set of limestone blocks that formed a gate, originally leading to the storehouse of divine offerings of Montu, was begun by Senusret III and finished by Sobekemsaf, a ruler of the late Second Intermediate Period. It is now set up in the open-air museum at the temple of Karnak along with another pair of limestone door-posts and a lintel. These doorways were fitted in a mudbrick structure, probably the Middle Kingdom enclosure wall.

Another 13th Dynasty king, Sobekhotep III, usurped many lintels and door jambs. He had his cartouche carved on columns, which seem to have been the only standing sandstone structure at that time at Medamud. A red granite stand, also unearthed from the New

Kingdom foundation platform, contains the names of the otherwise obscure 13th Dynasty kings, Wugaf and Amenemhat-Kay. Late Middle Kingdom and Second Intermediate Period kings give the impression that they merely reproduced or completed monuments of their illustrious predecessor, Senusret III.

Limestone architraves from the reign of Senusret III, along with other reused blocks from the New Kingdom and Late period, were excavated from the thresholds of the Graeco-Roman temple. This demonstrates that part of the Middle Kingdom temple was still standing during the reigns of the first Ptolemies. Lack of

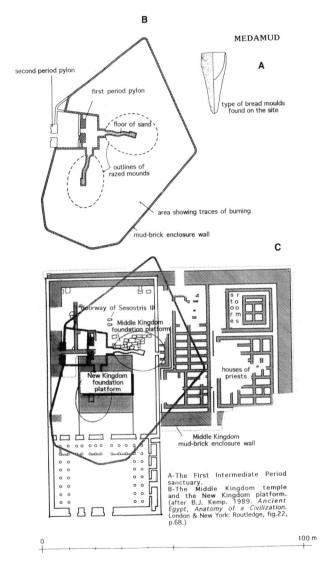

Figure 64 Medamud: A, types of bread molds found at the site; B, plan of the First Intermediate Period temple; C, plan of the Middle Kingdom temple

477

more architectural evidence at Medamud from the Middle Kingdom and Second Intermediate Period can be explained by the destruction of limestone blocks to produce lime.

A number of Middle Kingdom statues are known from Medamud. The earliest written record from the site comes from a seated diorite statue of Senusret II, which was recovered in front of the temple portico. A series of diorite statues of Senusret III were unearthed throughout the temple. With great realism they portray the king at different periods of his life.

New Kingdom

None of the Middle Kingdom and First Intermediate Period blocks removed from the foundations of the New Kingdom temple showed any traces of hacking where the name of Montu was inscribed. This supports the theory that the temple was rebuilt before Akhenaten's time. Most likely, Tuthmose III was the founder of the New Kingdom temple. His name was written on a calcite tablet that was part of a foundation deposit discovered next to the New Kingdom foundation platform, and Minemose, the Overseer of Works, mentions on a statue found in the rear of the Graeco-Roman temple that he attended a grounding ceremony inside the temple of Montu in Medamud under Tuthmose III.

The New Kingdom temple was oriented along an east–west axis. This change is not only demonstrated by the orientation of the New Kingdom foundation platform, but also by the red granite gate erected by Amenhotep II and the rooms in the front part of the Graeco-Roman temple, which comply with the New Kingdom east–west axis. Unfortunately, the plan of the New Kingdom temple cannot be determined. All that is known is that a large mudbrick enclosure wall was erected, and, according to the inscription on the statue of Maanakhtef found at Medamud, a festival hall existed during Amenhotep II's reign. Tuthmose IV probably added a building of his own.

Earlier scholars believed that Akhenaten erected buildings at Medamud, but this is very unlikely. The numerous *talatat* blocks discovered at the site originally came from Akhenaten's temples at East Karnak, as their small size enabled them to be easily transported.

Possibly some of the scanty Ramesside remains at Medamud were likewise brought from another site. William Murnane observed that an unpublished reused block of Seti I's, which was found in the gate of Tiberius at Medamud, refers to a building called "excellent is [Seti] [in] the house of Amen westward of Thebes," the name given to his mortuary temple at Gurna on the west bank of the Nile.

Late period records for Medamud are scarce. According to an inscription in a chapel from the precinct of Mut at Karnak, Montuemhat of the 25th Dynasty restored the temple and erected a statue of Montu.

Two successive structures were built at Medamud during the Ptolemaic period. From the reigns of Ptolemy II Philadelphus to Ptolemy IV Philopator, buildings were set up in the southwestern part of the site. Ptolemy II Philadelphus raised a *heb-sed* gate in honor of Osiris, whose cult at Medamud and the Theban region grew significantly under the Ptolemaic kings. A foundation deposit with the name of Ptolemy III Euergetes came to light under a $27 \times 16 \, \text{m}$ temple extending in a north–south direction. The Theban uprising that occurred during the reign of Ptolemy IV may explain the unfinished state of his gate (now standing along with that of Ptolemy III in Lyons) and ultimately the destruction of the first temple.

From the reigns of Ptolemy V Epiphanes to Ptolemy XII Neos Dionysos, the present-day east–west axial temple was erected. Ptolemy V and Ptolemy VI Philometor possibly built the sanctuary area, of which hardly anything is left. Ptolemy VIII Euergetes II constructed the portico, which was later inscribed by Ptolemy X Alexander and Ptolemy XII. Ptolemy XII also ordered the erection of the three kiosks to the west of the court (of Antoninus Pius). A sharp distinction between the two construction phases is shown by the reuse of the earlier Ptolemaic temple's blocks in the foundations of the latter one, and by the clearcut distribution of cartouches in both temples.

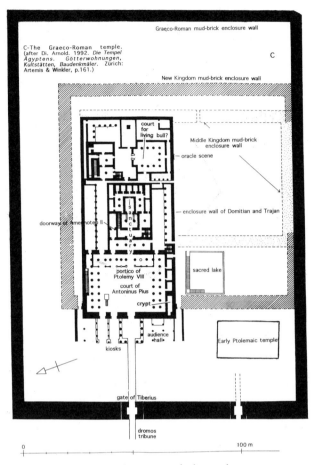

Figure 65 Medamud: plan of the Graeco-Roman period temple

Textual evidence can sometimes throw light on otherwise obscure archaeological data. A commemoration stela (inv. 8668 of the 1935–6 Medamud site book, in the IFAO archives) found 2 m from the gate of Tiberius mentions the construction of the mudbrick enclosure wall under the Roman emperor Augustus. The measurements of the wall given in the stela (176 m long) match very closely those recorded at the site (172 m). Contrary to widespread opinion, Tiberius probably did not build the gate, but merely decorated the monument that had been erected by his predecessor. The gate is named "the door of administering justice," a term which designates the open-air area where local disputes were dealt with. The four-pillared courtyard to the south of the three kiosks may have served a similar purpose under the last Ptolemaic kings. The damage seen on figures on the gate blocks probably occurred in Coptic times.

It is difficult to differentiate the actual construction phase of a building from when it was decorated. This is particularly true for the Graeco-Roman period, and the use of cartouches as a dating criterion can be misleading. However, it seems likely that the last temple of Medamud was near completion under the Ptolemies. Judging from the cartouches of Augustus and Vespasian on the thick north–south wall to the east of the three kiosks, the wall is of Roman date. But the kiosks, which are adorned with Ptolemy XII's name, are of a later date than the wall, as they were clearly built leaning against the wall. Thus, this north–south wall was constructed earlier than Ptolemy XII's reign, but it was decorated in the Roman period.

The Roman contribution may have been mainly of a decorative nature. Vespasian had a hymn to Amen-Re inscribed on part of the wall west of the court where the emperor Antoninus Pius later raised or decorated the double colonnade. The exterior enclosure stone wall of the Graeco-Roman temple was decorated by Trajan, and Domitian had its cornice carved. The famous scene of the bull, engraved on a stone projection on the exterior face of the south enclosure wall, shows the god delivering an oracle before the emperor (probably Trajan). A sacred lake, a well and a crypt were built during the Graeco-Roman period, as well as the *dromos* and tribune, which probably connected Medamud to the precinct of Montu at Karnak. Unfortunately, their exact date of construction is not known. The temple and town were apparently destroyed during the reign of Diocletian, who left his cartouche on a reused block fragment. In Coptic times, two churches were built in the temple area.

Montu, the local god

Middle Kingdom inscriptions refer to Montu as practically the sole god worshipped at Medamud. From the Boulaq Papyrus 18, a procession is described in which the statue of Montu was brought from Medamud and carried for two days to the royal palace in Upper Egypt, during the reign of Sobekhotep II. From the New Kingdom onward, the god also appears in the form of Montu-Re, or later as Amen-Re-Montu, when Montu was gradually superseded by Amen.

The inscriptions at Medamud emphasize Montu's chief role as a warrior god. Senusret III set up a limestone doorway, named "Senusret, who drives the evil away from the Lord of Thebes who lives in Medamud." The temple was also described as a fortress, the so-called "house of fighting." In Graeco-Roman times, reference is often made to an "arena" in which the bull god contended with evil forces.

The quadripartite nature of Montu is another crucial feature of the god: "he is the one with four heads on a single neck." This quadripartite division of the god stresses his ability to control the universe through the domination of its four cardinal points, which materialized in the four cities that embraced and guarded Karnak: Armant, Tod, (North) Karnak and Medamud. Four pairs of Ptolemaic limestone statues of Montu and his consort Rat-taui were discovered in the rear section of the Graeco-Roman temple; each pair carried an inscription which made them the lords of these four cities.

Another important feature of the god described in the Medamud texts is his cosmogonic character. In the first Ptolemaic temple, the gate of Ptolemy IV was oriented toward the holy place of Djeme at Medinet Habu, where the Ogdoad (eight gods) went to rest after having given birth to Ptah and Atum in Memphis and Heliopolis, respectively. Medamud was then believed to be the last stop before Djeme, and Montu, whose statue was probably taken out of the temple on special occasions to face the sacred hill, was thereby associated with the creation myths of the universe.

See also

Armant; Dakhla Oasis, Balat; Dendera; Karnak, Akhenaten temples; Karnak, precinct of Montu; Late and Ptolemaic periods, overview; Medinet Habu; Middle Kingdom, overview; New Kingdom, overview; pantheon; Roman period, overview; Tod

Further reading

Bisson de la Roque, F. 1926–33 Rapport préliminaire des fouilles de Médamoud (1925–1932). *FIFAO* 3–9

——.1946. Les fouilles de l'Institut français à Médamoud de 1925 à 1938. *RdÉ* 5: 25–44.

Drioton, E. 1931. Les quatre Montou de

Médamoud, palladium de Thèbes. *CdÉ* 12: 259–70.

Kemp, B.J. 1989. *Ancient Egypt: Anatomy of a Civilization*. London.

Robichon, C., and A. Varille. 1939. Les fouilles: Médamoud. *CdÉ* 27: 82–7, 28: 265–7.

——. 1940. *Description sommaire du temple primitif de Médamoud* (Recherches d'archéologie, de philologie et d'histoire 11). Cairo.

Sambin, C., and J.-F. Carlotti. 1995. Une porte de fête-sed de Ptolémée II remployée dans le temple de Montou à Médamoud. *BIFAO* 95: 383–457.

Valbelle, D. 1979. La porte de Tibère dans le complexe religieux de Médamoud. *Hommages à la mémoire de Serge Sauneron I, BdÉ* 81: 73–85.

JEAN REVEZ

Medinet Habu

The "city of Habu" designates primarily the town that arose in and around the temple enclosure of Ramesses III on the west bank of the Nile (25°43′ N, 32°36′ E), opposite the ancient city of Thebes (modern Luxor). This modern name probably reflects the settlement's proximity to the temple of a local saint, Amenhotep the son of Hapu, who lived in the fourteenth century BC and was especially revered in the Graeco-Roman period. Modern knowledge of the remains at Medinet Habu itself owes much to the Architectural and Epigraphic Surveys of the Oriental Institute (Chicago), which have worked at the site from the mid-1920s down to the present. This entry covers the following structures: (1) the "Small Temple" of the 18th Dynasty; (2) the mortuary temple of Ramesses II; (3) associated and later chapels; and finally (4) the town of Djeme.

Named "Holy of Place," the small 18th Dynasty temple was begun in the joint reign of Hatshepsut and Thutmose III. Its foundations rest on the remains of an earlier temple, but there is no proof that the cult predates the New Kingdom. The area was known as "the mound of the west" during the 18th Dynasty, but by the eleventh century BC it had been given a more specific name, Iat Tchamuwe, "the mound of the males and mothers," which refers to the eight creator gods and goddesses (ogdoad) who were believed to be buried here. It is from this later cult name that arose the term "Djeme," which was attached to the entire site through late antiquity.

The 18th Dynasty building consisted of two parts, a bark shrine surrounded by pillared porticoes, and the temple proper. The inner chambers of the temple were decorated with reliefs that preserve their paint in almost pristine condition under grime that was removed in the early 1980s by conservators. The interior contains two sets of cult rooms dedicated to different manifestations of Amen; there is also a separate chapel which opens onto the portico at the northeast corner of the building. This chapel (which was devoted to the royal cult), along with the portico and bark shrine, are entirely the work of Tuthmose III, who usurped or erased the figures of his aunt inside the cult rooms of Amen. During the Late period part of the temple's rear wall was temporarily dismantled so that a *naos* could be inserted into the inner sanctuary that lies behind the royal cult chapel. What gave the small temple its longevity was its cult. Unlike the mortuary temples in West Thebes, which could depend neither on their size nor even their owners' posthumous fame for their endurance, this temple was dedicated to a god who embodied the very mysteries of death and resurrection. Amen of Luxor Temple, toward which the small temple was oriented, visited the site every ten days; during this Feast of the Decade he underwent a series of transformations that ended in his own rebirth. The association of the ogdoad with this place heightened its significance, for it became the "underworld" in which the primeval forms of Amen and the eight creator gods rested and yet "lived" mystically within the cycle of nature. Thus this building, which housed processes of such relevance in the city of the dead, not only lasted but grew.

The first structural addition to the small

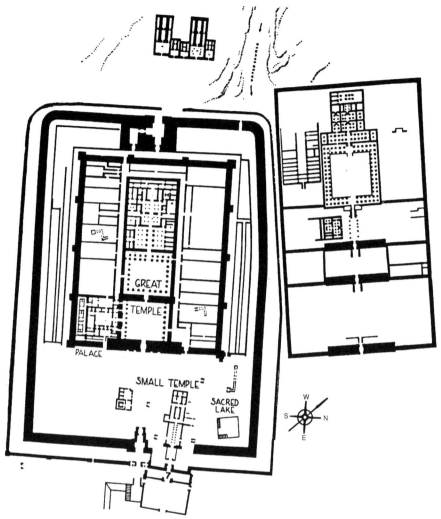

Figure 66 The monuments at Medinet Habu, overall plan
Source: adapted from R. Stadelmann, *LÄ* 3, 1259–60

temple was made during the 25th Dynasty, when the Kushite kings built a pylon connected to the older temple by a gallery which one of the later Ptolemies replaced with a wider columned hall. The small wings attached to either side of Tuthmose III's façade are probably also Ptolemaic in date. Even before this, the sagging roof of Tuthmose III's pillared portico had to be shored up by Hakor (29th Dynasty). At about the same time, a columned

portico was added in front of the "Ethiopian" pylon by a king whose names were usurped by Nectanebo I (30th Dynasty). This served as the temple's front entrance until about 100 BC, when a massive pylon façade was built in front of the precinct's mudbrick enclosure wall. The final, equally impressive addition to the complex was begun under the Roman emperor Antoninus Pius. The plan was to hide the Ptolemaic pylon behind a huge columned porch fronted by a large courtyard, but this project was never completed.

The mortuary temple of Ramesses III, called "The Mansion of Millions of Years of King Ramesses III 'United with Eternity' in the Estate of Amen," was built adjoining Horemheb's temple complex to the north. Its axis represents a compromise between the orientation of its neighbor and that of the small 18th Dynasty temple, which Ramesses III incorporated as a separate precinct inside his mortuary complex.

The ceremonial entrance to the complex was located on the east side, where archaeologists uncovered the remains of a harbor. Visitors entered the temple here, passing first between two "porters' lodges" set into a low crenelated outer enclosure wall, and then through a high gate that pierces the more massive inner enclosure wall of mudbrick. The exterior of this tower is covered with reliefs, most of them depicting the king in triumph over Egypt's enemies. A more intimate tone prevails inside the building, the chambers of which were reached through rooms and passages built into the mudbrick enclosure wall (now destroyed at these connecting points). Scenes on the stone walls of the gate's inner rooms on the second and third stories depict Ramesses III in the company of his daughters and harim women. Another high gate, located on the western side of the complex, probably served as the everyday entrance for members of the temple staff who lived nearby. It was heavily damaged in a siege during the disturbances late in the 20th Dynasty and is a ruin today.

Nothing can be seen today of the walled enclosures and office buildings (all built out of mudbrick) that crowded the space between the eastern high gate and the main temple in Ramesses III's time. The martial tone first seen on the exterior of the high gate is continued on the outer walls of the temple proper: in scenes of war and triumph over wild animals the king is seen as warding off his foes, and by extension, all enemies of Ma'at. Particularly notable are the wild game hunts depicted on the southwest face of the pylon. The triumph scenes inscribed on the pylon's front are more conventional, but the

battle scenes that run along the western and northern walls contain at least three sequences of historical importance (the Libyan wars of years 5 and 11, and the great war against the Sea Peoples, with its naval battle, in year 8). By contrast, most of the building's south wall is inscribed with a liturgical calendar which details the offerings made at the various festivals celebrated in the temple each year. This placement is paralleled in temples of Ramesses II, both at the Ramesseum and at Abydos.

South of the main temple is the ceremonial palace that served both as a rest house for visiting royalty and a mock dwelling for the dead king's spirit. In its original layout Ramesses III's palace bore a close resemblance to its analog at the Ramesseum, but the plan was changed later in the king's reign. It is this later plan that was partially restored by the Chicago expedition. It consists of two sets of public apartments (an audience hall next to a "living room" equipped with a small "window of appearances" for the king) and a corresponding pair of private apartments: one for the king, including a small throne room, bedroom and bath; and four smaller suites, linked by a corridor, along the back of the building. Marks on the south wall of the temple indicate the outline of the missing second story.

Similarities to Ramesses II's mortuary building are not random, but extend also to the layout of the temple proper. Inside, the temple can be divided into three main areas: the first court, the most public part of the building, dominated on the south by the façade of the palace, with its "window of appearances" from which the king presided over public audiences; the second, or "festival" court, with relief sequences illustrating the annual feasts of the gods Min and Sokar; and the main temple beyond, where its resident gods "lived." The basic elements in the plan—courtyards leading to columned halls and thence to inner cult rooms—are typical enough, but it is the decorative program that is the best guide to the way in which the temple functioned in ancient times. Two aspects of the king are reflected throughout. On the south side, many elements are associated with the king's mortality and his apotheosis in the underworld; these themes are evoked by the palace and the "window of appearance" (first court) and the festival of Sokar, a singularly "dead" divinity who resides in the underworld and may represent the potency latent in the earth (second court). The king's innate divinity and his identity are contrastingly represented on the north side of the building, i.e. in the colossal royal statues attached to the piers which hold up the northern portico in the first court, and in the festival scenes (second court) of Min, a fertility god who regularly (re)creates himself and thus exemplifies, like the sun, the eternal cycle of nature.

While the back of the temple has lost its upper parts to later quarrying, the cult rooms at the sides are tolerably well preserved. As before, the king's deified mortal nature dominates on the south side: here we find a ceremonial treasury, chapels of the divine ancestors, Ramesses II and the ancient warrior god Montu, and a suite of rooms dedicated to Osiris, whose identity the dead king regularly assumed. The north side, which accommodates a number of elements necessary to the proper functioning of the building, is less consistently arranged. Following a series of chapels for gods (Ptah, Sokar, Wepwawet) residing in the temple, there is a "slaughterhouse," although it is unequipped for actual use, and must have served merely as a holding area for food offerings prepared elsewhere. The king's innately divine identity is evoked once more, however, in the chapel dedicated to Ramesses III in his identity of the Amen resident in the temple. Further inside, this theme is resumed in the suite of Re-Horakhty, which like the tombs in the Valley of the Kings celebrates the king's grasp of eternity as he joins the solar circuit; and in the chapel of the ennead, the gods who represent the divine pantheon in which the king takes his place. The two halves, human and divine, of both the king and his temple are bound together at the focal point of the building: this suite is dedicated to Amen-Re, King of the Gods, whose identity subsumed not only that of the pharaoh himself, but all other divine forces that prevailed in the Egyptians'

universe. Here, directly behind Amen's bark sanctuary at the center of the building, was the principal false door, through which the dead king manifested himself in his temple. Other false doors were provided in the Osiris suite and the throne room of the first palace. Finally, a series of small rooms (entered through low, hidden doorways at the base of the back wall of Amen's suite) probably represent the crypts in which the temple's more esoteric equipment was stored.

Behind Ramesses III's temple complex is a row of mudbrick funerary chapels, their interiors originally sheathed with stone blocks carved with scenes of their owners' mortuary cults. While they were initially planned for favored contemporaries (including the mayor of Thebes), traces of later burials were found here as well. Toward the end of the 20th Dynasty, when the inhabitants of the workmen's village at Deir el-Medina moved inside the complex for protection, urban sprawl began to engulf the temple: it is to the earliest phase of this occupation that belongs the house (or mortuary chapel) of the necropolis scribe Butehamen, constructed near the temple's southwest corner. Much later are the four chapels of the Divine Votaresses of Amen, which were built over a period of about 200 years, from the last part of the 23rd Dynasty down to the end of the 26th Dynasty and the beginning of the first Persian domination. Only two of these chapels are substantially extant today: they belong to Amenirdis I, daughter of the Nubian king Kashta and to her niece and successor, Shepenwepet II. The latter was eventually converted to include the burials of Psamtik I's daughter Nitocris and her mother, and thus boasts three mortuary chapels in a space originally designed for one. Two other chapels have disappeared: the latest, assigned to Ankhnesneferibre, daughter of Psamtik II, can be inferred only from the traces it left on the west wall of Shepenwepet II's chapel; but the earliest building in the series, built for Amenirdis I's predecessor, Shepenwepet I, still has its substructure, although nearly everything above ground has disappeared.

The process of urban transformation that

began to overtake the site in the later 20th Dynasty continued unabated into the Christian era. Although the cult of Ramesses III lapsed at the end of the New Kingdom, the ongoing cult of Amen at the small temple continued to be a religious focus at the site and maintained its importance in late antiquity. Although the town's inhabitants moved into the small temple when the community became Christian, patterns of occupation continued to favor the preservation of major buildings at Medinet Habu: for example, the "holy church of Djeme," built inside the second court of Ramesses III's temple, reused the space in a fashion that spared it further destruction. The sudden abandonment of the town in the ninth century AD remains unexplained; although the site must have been mined in the centuries that followed—for example, blocks from the great temple made their way to the relatively modern Coptic monastery built on the low desert to the southwest—enough remained *in situ* to have made Medinet Habu uniquely revealing as a cross-section of human occupation over twenty-three centuries in West Thebes.

See also

Deir el-Medina; Luxor, temple of; New Kingdom, overview; representational evidence, New Kingdom temples; Sea Peoples; Thebes, the Ramesseum; Thebes, royal funerary temples

Further reading

Epigraphic Survey. 1930–70. *Medinet Habu*, 8 vols. (OIP 8, 9, 23, 51, 83, 84, 93, 94). Chicago.

Murnane, W. 1980. *United with Eternity: A Concise Guide to the Monuments of Medinet Habu.* Cairo.

Nelson, H.H. 1942. The Identity of Amon-Re of United-with-Eternity. *JNES* 1: 127–55.

Stadelmann, R. 1980. Medinet Habu. In *LÄ* 3, 1255–71.

WILLIAM J. MURNANE

Medjay

Known by the name "Medjay" from the end of the Old Kingdom through the New Kingdom, the peoples of the Nubian Desert, Red Sea Hills and plain to the west (called the "Atbai") served the ancient Egyptians as caravaneers, police and professional soldiers. They were also formidable opponents and historical records frequently refer to clashes with them. Although some of their identifications have been contested, the Medjay probably belonged to the great cultural substratum that appears under various names in all periods of recorded history: as "Meded" in the Kushite records of the first millennium BC, "Belhem" (?) in Egyptian demotic texts, "Blemmyes" in Greek and Roman texts, and "Bedja" in Arabic. Perhaps some were also designated more generically as "Iwntiu" (pillar-folk) by the Egyptians, and "Troglodytes" (cave-dwellers) by the Greeks. The Medjay were an ancient manifestation of one of Africa's great surviving cultural continua which today occupy the desert and coast from Wadi Hammamat in Egypt to Somalia.

Climatic changes in the last four millennia have altered living conditions in the Red Sea Hills and Atbai, but they have always contrasted sharply with the Western Desert. The eroded plateau and mountains cause rain to fall during the monsoon season, and the modest accumulation of water provides pasturage for herds of domestic animals, which in ancient times included sheep, goats and cattle. The limited and seasonal resources stimulated movement at all times, with the inhabitants retreating in the dry months toward the mountains, where they have sometimes escaped the burning heat in caves, or toward the Nile Valley. During the rainy season in late summer, they expanded outward, especially in the Sudanese Butana, an area between the Atbara River, the main Nile and the Blue Nile. This south–north seasonal movement created possibilities for trade and immigration that sustained contact between Egypt and the fringes of Ethiopia (Punt or part of Punt) and ensured that the peoples of the region were never really isolated.

The region of the Red Sea Hills was important even in early times, when its products were imported to Egypt and Lower Nubia in considerable amounts. Because the region had relatively well-traveled trade routes, it has been proposed as the staging area for both Mesopotamian influence and significant early interchange with Sudan. The clearest evidence for peoples from this region in early times is a group of stelae from 2nd Dynasty tombs at Helwan, which show Puntites or (related) people from the Atbai and a small number of related contemporary tombs in Nubia.

Little is known about peoples from the northern Red Sea Hills and adjacent Atbai during the Old Kingdom except for sporadic references to campaigns against them, and possibly similar peoples north of the Wadi Hammamat designated to secure desert routes to the mines and quarries, and port facilities of the Red Sea trade with Punt. The first real mention of the Medjay appears in the 6th Dynasty records at Aswan, both royal inscriptions and tomb biographies of the nomarchs and caravan conductors of Elephantine. There the Medjay are mentioned with the peoples of Nubia, who were consolidating a newly intensified control of the region under the wary eye and sometimes interfering hand of the Egyptians. Although Nubians played a significant role in the turbulence of the First Intermediate Period, little is known about the Medjay in the early Middle Kingdom; they may be first depicted as tall, emaciated cattle herdsmen in the tomb chapels in Middle Egypt dating to the 12th Dynasty.

The Medjay likewise played a more significant role in the records of campaigns against Nubia and Kush that dominated Egypt's attention in those areas and culminated in the erection of huge fortifications in Lower Nubia and near Egypt's southern boundary in the Middle Kingdom. The only records available from the forts indicate that Medjay formed a substantial part of the garrison force, and they were used to prevent infiltration by other Medjay. They even patrolled the desert at the fort of Elephantine, and the fort at Serra East in Lower Nubia was named Khesef-Medjay, i.e.

"repelling the Medjay." At the same time, texts name two major Medjay principalities (Auwshek and Webat-Sepet) among the entities in Nubia as formidable enough to be cursed.

Medjay were active in the disturbances of the Second Intermediate Period, when they have been associated with the archaeological evidence known as the "Pan-grave" culture. In the New Kingdom, after the wars that left Egypt in control of the Nile Valley as far south as the Fourth Cataract, the Medjay are hardly mentioned as a force, but some were employed as a kind of police force. The name became a title for "policeman" and was held by Egyptians in the later New Kingdom.

The term "Medjay" is not known after the New Kingdom and there is very little archaeological evidence for Nubia and Sudan from the end of the New Kingdom to about 900/800 BC. Cemeteries near the Second Cataract dating to that period or shortly after have tombs much like the earlier Pan-graves, and Nubian pottery from them includes types found in the earliest Kushite tumulus graves at el-Kurru, dating to the tenth or ninth century BC. Later Kushite rulers of the fifth and fourth centuries BC fought determined campaigns against a people called the "Meded," who were probably the ancient Medjay, and the "Rehres," who may have been a subgroup operating near Meroe.

The history of the Medjay did not end with these brief mentions, for their location and role were later occupied by peoples known to the Greeks as "Blemmyes," and to the Arabs as "Beja." While the earlier accounts mix mythical or fantastical elements, the resulting descriptions can be reconciled with the often impoverished life near the Red Sea. At times, the Blemmye-Beja groups formed powerful coalitions, controlling trade, operating emerald mines and battling with major powers. In the third through fifth centuries AD they thrust into Upper Egypt and Lower Nubia, raiding as far west as Kharga Oasis and as far north as Sinai.

Although expelled once from Upper Egypt by Roman forces commanded by General Probus, they returned, even setting up a kingdom modeled in part on the late Roman/Byzantine court. They left distinctive archaeological remains in the northern part of Lower Nubia and along the desert edges in southern Upper Egypt. In the end they were only controlled by difficult campaigning and a rivalry with another Nubian group, the Noubadians.

See also

A-Group culture; Aswan; Asyut; Beni Hasan; Elephantine; Helwan; el-Kurru; Meroe, city; Nubian forts; Pan-grave culture; Punt; Wadi Hammamat

Further reading

Bietak, M. 1987. The C-Group and the Pan-Grave culture in Nubia. In *Nubian Culture Past and Present: Main Papers Presented at the Sixth International Conference for Nubian Studies in Uppsala, 11–16 August, 1986*, T. Hägg, ed., 113–28. Stockholm.

Bourriau, J. 1981. Nubians in Egypt during the Second Intermediate Period: an interpretation based on the Egyptian ceramic evidence. In *Studien zur altägyptischen Keramik*, D. Arnold, ed., 25–41. Mainz.

Fattovich, R. 1990. The peopling of the northern Ethiopian-Sudanese borderland between 7000 and 1000 BP: a preliminary model. *Nubica* 1/2: 3–45.

O'Connor, D. 1986. The locations of Yam and Kush and their historical implications. *JARCE* 23: 27–50.

Sadr, Karim. 1987. The territorial expanse of the Pan-Grave culture. *Archéologie du Nil Moyen* 2: 265–91.

——. 1990. The Medjay in southern Atbai. *Archéologie du Nil Moyen* 4: 63–86.

Säve-Söderbergh, T. 1989. *Middle Nubian Sites* (The Scandinavian Joint Expedition to Sudanese Nubia 4). Stockholm.

Török, L. 1988. *Late Antique Nubia: History and Archaeology of the Southern Neighbor of Egypt in the 4th–6th C. A.D.*, Antaeus (Communicationes ex Instituto Archaeologico Academiae Scientarum Hungaricae 16). Budapest.

BRUCE B. WILLIAMS

Meir

The modern village of Meir is situated due west of the town el-Qusiya in Middle Egypt. To the southwest of the village is the archaeological site (27°27' N, 30°43' E), the necropolis of the former capital of Nome XIV of Upper Egypt.

Very little is known about this site, which was extensively pillaged in the nineteenth century and carelessly excavated in the twentieth century. There is not even an accurate site plan, but some of the the Old and Middle Kingdom tombs are nicely recorded in publications. Decorated with exquisite reliefs, these rock-cut tombs were carved in the low hills west of Meir. A First Intermediate Period cemetery possibly existed on the desert plain to the east.

Although finds at the site range in date from the Old Kingdom to Graeco-Roman times, the archaeological record is very poor for most periods except the Old and Middle Kingdom. From these periods are five concentrations of rock-cut tombs, designated A, B, C, D and E, in an order from north to south. The most important Old Kingdom group is A, where the finely decorated and well preserved tombs of the chief priests of the cult of Hathor of Qusiya are located. Tomb A2, of Pepi-ankh, is well known for its unusually detailed representation of the funerary ritual. Groups B and C contain tombs of the 12th Dynasty, with lively and extremely well carved reliefs and paintings, including the famous ancestor list of the governor (nomarch) Ukhhotep III (Tomb B4). Tomb C1, belonging to Ukhhotep IV, is unusual in that, apart from the tomb owner, only females are depicted on its walls. Subsidiary tombs here have also produced a high quantity of Middle Kingdom coffins inscribed with funerary texts known as the *Coffin Texts*.

See also

funerary texts; Middle Kingdom, overview; Old Kingdom provincial tombs

Further reading

Blackman, A.M. 1914–1953. *The Rock Tombs of Meir*, 1–6. London.

Kessler, D., 1982. Meir. In *LÄ* 4: 14–19.

HARCO WILLEMS

Memphis

The city of Memphis (Men-nefer, Inbu-hedj, Hikuptah) is today represented by a large field of ruins, *circa* 600 ha in area, surrounding the modern towns of Mit Rahina and Aziziya, 25 km south of central Cairo on the west bank of the Nile (29°51′ N, 31°15′ E). After the final depopulation of Memphis in the seventh or eighth century AD, the site is often mentioned in medieval Arabic literature (Abd el-Latif, el-Qalqashandi, el-Maqrizi) and by early travelers (William of Tyre, Benjamin of Tudela, Joos van Ghistele); the toponym "Manf" survived into the nineteenth century. One of several names of the city and its temple, Hut-ka-Ptah/Hikuptah, became by extension the Greek name of the whole country, Aigyptos.

The actual location was lost until the late sixteenth century, and remained a question of scholarly debate until the Napoleonic expedition settled the matter at the end of the eighteenth century. From the 1820s the site became the target of archaeologists and antiquities dealers after the discovery by Giovanni Battista Caviglia of a colossal statue of Ramesses II. Major survey and excavations were conducted by Joseph Hekekyan in 1852–4, Auguste Mariette in the 1860s, Flinders Petrie in 1907–13 (for the British School of Archaeology in Egypt), Clarence Fisher in 1914–21 and Rudolph Anthes in 1955–6 (for the University Museum, University of Pennsylvania), and Ahmad Badawi in the 1940s (for Cairo University). Salvage archaeology in advance of building and agricultural development has been undertaken by the Egyptian Antiquities Organization (EAO) during this century, and current archaeological work includes the Apis House Project (American Research Center in Egypt), excavations by the EAO and Cairo University, and the London-based Egypt Exploration Society's Survey of Memphis.

Traditionally the city was founded *circa* 3,100 BC to mark the unification of Upper and Lower Egypt under one rule and to provide a new national capital. Desert-edge cemeteries closest to the settlement site reflect occupation only from this time, although important Predynastic settlements are known on the east bank, at Ma'adi to the north and el-Omari near Helwan to the south. No part of the valley settlement prior to the First Intermediate Period has yet been located with certainty, although current geoarchaeological work is attempting to determine the shifting course of the river and settlement in Early Dynastic and Old Kingdom times.

The city's superb geographical location, commanding the Delta apex and the confluence of desert trade routes, from the Levant and Red Sea to the Sahara and beyond, meant that it was constantly being selected as the administrative center after periods of political instability. After serving as the capital and the center of the royal funerary industry during the Old Kingdom, Memphis ceded power to provincial cities, such as Heracleopolis (Ihnasya el-Medina), Hermopolis (el-Ashmunein) and Thebes, before Amenemhat I revitalized the Memphite region by establishing his new residence at el-Lisht (ancient It-tawy) in the 12th Dynasty. In the 18th Dynasty Memphis became pre-eminent after (and perhaps even before) the move to Akhetaten (Tell el-Amarna) by Amenhotep IV/Akhenaten, and in the Late period it was again the home of royal power: and the chief prize for Assyrian and other invading armies. Ptolemaic kings were still crowned at Memphis and the city was popularly regarded as the Egyptian rival to Alexandria, founded by the Macedonian Greeks. In Roman times texts mention the extent of the palaces and the urban sprawl of Memphis, and it remained a religious center and place of pilgrimage until the eighth or ninth century AD, by which time the Islamic city of el-Fustat (Old Cairo) had effectively replaced it. In medieval times standing monuments at Memphis were systematically dismantled or quarried for building material, particularly at the Cairo citadel of Salah el-Din.

Taken together with its extensive cemeteries (at Dahshur, Saqqara, Abusir and Giza on the west bank, and Helwan, Masara, Tura and Ma'adi on the east bank), Memphis provides an unparalleled body of evidence for the history and material culture of Dynastic and Hellenistic Egypt. The present area of ruins, although often ignored, is one of the largest floodplain sites in Egypt and once stretched along the river for 10 km.

In the following description the site is divided into individual mounds (known as *tell*s or *kom*s), whose local names are subject to some variation. Between these *kom*s are three or more large pools (*birka*s), low-lying areas which usually mark the position of sacred enclosures. The southern half of the site is by far the most extensively explored, although only a tiny part is seen by most visitors to the site today. This summary follows a general south to north, and west to east progression.

Kom el-Rabia, Kom Sabkha

Two small temples built by Ramesses II (19th Dynasty) for Ptah and Hathor have been found at Kom el-Rabia. Both were frequently reused in the Late period and built over by Roman times. Other remains include a building of the 21st Dynasty; part of a Hellenistic temple and *laconicon* (ritual bath), and another bath house on Kom Sabkha to the south. Recent excavations on the west side of el-Rabia have shown a sequence of intensive settlement, from the Middle Kingdom to the Late period, with a notable break in occupation between the 13th and 18th Dynasties. This evidence supports the suggestion that the early phases of the city lie beneath and beyond the western side of the area of ruins, largely buried by the rise of the valley floor.

Kom el-Oala, Kom Helul

A temple and palace complex was laid out here on virgin ground by Ramesses II's successor,

Merenptah, and its boundaries were still respected in Roman times even though the Ramesside structure had long since disappeared under later construction. To the south on Kom Helul, a faïence workshop of the Graeco-Roman period was found by Petrie.

Ptah temple enclosure

This enclosure occupies the central *birka* and was probably also built on a virgin site reclaimed from the river. In its original conception it rivaled in scale the Amen-Re temple at Karnak and colossal statues surrounded the enclosure wall, especially at the four cardinal approaches, with sphinxes at or near the north and south gates. Little is known of the internal design of the temple other than at the west gate, where a hypostyle hall perhaps commemorated a *heb-sed* (jubilee) of Ramesses II. In the southwest corner of the enclosure stood a building of the sixth–first centuries BC associated with the cult of the Apis bull, whose burial place, the Serapeum, was on the desert escarpment at Saqqara. Also at this corner was a small "oratory" of Seti I, perhaps built to mark the ambitious new building program since it contained statues personifying the city and temple walls.

There is no evidence that the Ptah enclosure predates the 19th Dynasty. All earlier inscribed material, such as a lintel of Amenemhat III at the north gate, pyramid casing stones at the west gate, and blocks from the reigns of Amenhotep III and Akhenaten in the interior, is demonstrably reused in the Ramesside construction or otherwise redeposited.

Kom el-Fakhry

A cemetery of the First Intermediate Period and an early Middle Kingdom settlement lay beneath later occupation levels to the south of Mit Rahina, on high ground which almost certainly reflects underlying stratigraphy of the late Old Kingdom. The burials found here were intact but poorly preserved, and probably constitute a family vault. Grave goods and tomb decoration, where preserved, appear closest in style to contemporary tombs at South and North Saqqara. Recent excavations to the east have revealed occupation levels of the 18th Dynasty, including provision for grain storage on a domestic level.

Kom el-Arbain, Kom el-Nawa, Kom el-Qala

Sporadic finds have been made in this eastern area over the past century, but the only concerted archaeological work was by Petrie in the early 1900s. It is now an army camp and therefore inaccessible. On the eastern edge, part of the Roman riverside wall was found in the 1850s, and historical cartography suggests that the celebrated Memphis nilometer, which was used to assess national tax returns in the Hellenistic period, lay nearby. The site of a temple of Mithras was recorded on the north side in the 1840s, and a Late period stone gateway found by Petrie still stands to its full height. The discovery over the years of non-Egyptian (Phoenician, Persian, Archaic Greek) artifacts in this area, and quantities of ceramic heads of foreigners at Kom el-Qala to the south, may signify the whereabouts of the earlier (New Kingdom) port of Perunefer, which attracted the city's ethnic minorities.

Kom Tuman, Kom Dafbaby

At over 20 m above level of the plain, the 26th Dynasty foundations of a royal palace and surrounding military(?) enclosure remain the highest part of the site. Evidence of military occupation in the Persian period was found, including massive column fragments inscribed for Apries and the remains of a pylon thrown into the ditch in front of the palace. The palace would have been a natural focus for the city's defenses and may well have been the citadel known in Hellenistic times as the "White Fortress" (Leukon Teikhos), perhaps a survival or revival of the Egyptian name of Memphis, "Inbu-hedj" (White Walls).

The location of many of the major institutions of the city remains a matter of conjecture or guesswork, a problem compounded by its sheer size and by the fact that contemporary accounts and references rarely distinguish between the metropolitan area and its suburbs and cemeteries. None of the royally endowed temples is known, nor are hardly any of the other cult places for which Memphis was renowned in antiquity. The city center was surrounded on the landward side by river defenses, and several "Islands of Memphis" are recorded, but very few of them can be identified. Horticultural gardens were probably located west of the city, and a possible location for the municipal theater lies north of Kom Dafbaby, just outside the walls of the garrison. Remains of a number of ecclesiastical buildings are known, but again they cannot be identified with any confidence. By Coptic times (seventh century AD) the "Polis-Mempheos" (City of Memphis) had certainly fragmented and shrunk to the size of the neighboring villages, and was outdone in terms of population and resources by the monastic desert communities of Gregorius on the east and Jeremias on the west.

See also

Abusir; Dahshur, Middle Kingdom pyramids; Early Dynastic period, overview; Late and Ptolemaic periods, overview; Mariette, François Auguste Ferdinand; Napoleon Bonaparte and the Napoleonic expedition; New Kingdom, overview; Old Kingdom, overview; Petrie, Sir William Matthew Flinders; Roman period, overview; Saqqara

Further reading

Anthes, R. 1956, 1965. *Mit Rahinah 1955, 1956*. Philadelphia.

Jeffreys, D.G. 1985. *The Survey of Memphis I*. London.

Petrie, W.M.F. 1909–15. *Memphis* I–V. London.

Zivie, A.-P., ed. 1988. *Memphis et ses nécropoles au nouvel empire*. Paris.

Zivie, C. 1982. Memphis: *LÄ* 4: 24–41.

DAVID JEFFREYS

Memphis, Apis bull embalming house

The site known as the embalming house of Apis bulls is located in the southwest corner of the walled enclosure built in the Late period around the Ramesside temple of Ptah in Memphis. It is on the north side of the main road between el-Badrashein and Saqqara, some 180 m west of the great fallen limestone colossus of Ramesses II (Abu'l-Hol) now covered by the local museum.

The earliest recorded discovery in the area was made in the mid-nineteenth century. A group of alabaster blocks was found in what is now the southeast corner of the site. One block bears the names of Ramesses II and the god Living Apis, and another the cartouches of Sheshonk I, figures of the god Anubis and Shedsunefertem (High Priest of Ptah in Memphis) and the names of the gods Osiris, Apis, Atum, Horus. The inscription of Sheshonk I also records the founding of a *w'bt*, possibly an "embalming place" for Osiris-Apis. The first methodically recorded excavations were carried out by the British archaeologist Flinders Petrie in 1908. He found part of a small Late period or Ptolemaic chapel containing an inscribed block with the name of the 25th Dynasty ruler Shabako, probably reused. In about 1914, local farmers digging *sebbakh* (decayed mudbrick used as fertilizer) found six quartzite doorjamb blocks with reliefs of the 26th Dynasty ruler Amasis. Four remain at the site while two have been in Memphis, Tennessee since 1916.

In 1941 Egyptian archaeologists Mustafa el-Amir and Ahmed Badawy began digging into the palm-covered mound east of Petrie's Shabako chapel and the find spot of the Amasis doorjambs. During the course of their work the embalming house of Apis bulls was uncovered. It is a mudbrick building whose walls were originally clad in limestone blocks, many of which were cut from fragments of decorated column bases and capitals. The thickness of the remaining walls, together with the great overburden of collapsed mudbrick debris that filled the long rooms when the site was excavated,

suggest that it may have been roofed with mudbrick barrel vaults similar to those still preserved at the Ramesseum storerooms on the west bank at Luxor. An unusual feature is a carved panel resembling a false door in the center of the south wall; parallels may be found in the mortuary temples of the Old Kingdom, the temples of Seti I and Ramesses II at Abydos and the temple of Osiris Heqa-Djet at Karnak. Amir believed that he had discovered the stall, or *sekos* described by classical writers, in which the Apis bull was housed during its lifetime. He dated the monument to the 26th Dynasty on the basis of inscriptions naming Neko II and Amasis. The reference to Apis came from the same 26th Dynasty inscriptions, those of Ramesses II and Sheshonk I and a basin of Darius I. While the dating was generally accepted, this identification of the site as the Apis stall was not.

It was the American architect John Dimick, working with Rudolph Anthes in 1955, who proposed the name by which the site is known today. Dimick based his identification on the interpretation of limestone and alabaster slabs with lions carved in relief on their longer sides. The largest and most magnificent of the two large alabaster slabs has, in addition to the lions, a revetted upper surface carved to slope down toward a spout beneath which a large circular alabaster tank was found *in situ*. Dimick and others have seen the lion beds as platforms on which the body of the dead Apis bull was embalmed and prepared for its burial in the Serapeum at Saqqara. This view is supported by the *w'bt* inscription of Sheshonk I (in which *w'bt* is translated as "embalming place"), by scenes on the walls of temples and tombs of the New Kingdom and later and on Late period coffins, showing the god Osiris and some royal and non-royal mummies lying on lion-shaped biers frequently attended by Anubis. In addition, the theory draws on the symbolism of the lions as guardians of the dead and sleeping, and their association with rebirth as shown by the lion god Aker, whose form becomes the horizon in which the sun rises at dawn. However, only complete mummies, fully equipped with their masks, are shown on lion biers; the rare representations of the mummification process depict the work taking place on plain boards.

The correct identification of the site and the archaeological interpretation of its remains have therefore been open to dispute. Survey and excavation carried out between 1982 and 1986 by New York University aimed at clarifying these points. As a result, it is now known that the structure found by Amir and Badawy containing the stone lion beds and inscriptions of the 26th Dynasty rulers is the latest in a series of several buildings on the site constructed between the 19th Dynasty and the Ptolemaic or Roman periods. Furthermore, this latest building was fashioned from masonry that had been reused from earlier monuments. The pieces inscribed for Neko II and Amasis, and possibly the basin of Darius I, which bear the only references to the god Apis to have been found at the site, are among these recycled blocks. The alabaster blocks of Ramesses II and Sheshonk I were found to be fragments of a dismantled alabaster building, possibly the *w'bt* itself; probably they had been reused more than once.

John Dimick had already realized in 1955 that the structure was built on a foundation platform whose purpose was to elevate it above the contemporary surrounding ground level. The New York University survey defined the extent of the platform and also ascertained that it was laid out on two levels, creating a terraced structure whose upper level is 1.05 m (two cubits) above the lower. The fill of the foundation compartments provides important evidence for dating the building. In the rubble sealed beneath the floors of the lower terrace, limestone slabs were found inscribed with the names of Psamtik II and the god Osiris-Apis. The names of Psamtik II had been carved in palimpsest over the erased hieroglyphs of the names of Shabako. The fill of the upper terrace contained pottery datable from the Old Kingdom to the Persian period. A hoard of silver coins, locally struck in imitation of Athenian "owls," was discovered within the brickwork of the platform of the upper terrace in a context highly suggestive of a foundation deposit. The coins are datable to the mid-fourth century BC.

No pottery of the Ptolemaic period was found, as would be consistent with a religious building in use at that time. Nevertheless, a scatter of pottery and other objects datable to approximately AD 100, found in the ruins of the building that once stood on the upper terrace, suggests that by then at least a section of the site had been abandoned and partly demolished.

The archaeological evidence for the rebuilding of the site in the fourth century BC is supported by the text of a stela found at Saqqara, dated to the second year of the reign of Nectanebo II (358 BC). It records the inauguration of a new place of Apis in the precinct of Ptah in Memphis. Included as an element of the place of Apis is a *w'bt* to which lavish endowments of property were made by royal decree.

The realization that all the inscribed material found by Amir and Badawy had been reused, none remaining in its original context, cast serious doubt on the identification of the building with the god Apis. However, an inscription on the basin belonging with the largest of the alabaster lion beds states simply "the *w'bt* of the sacred precinct of Apis" (*w'bt [n] ḥwt-ntr n Ḥp*). This basin and lion bed are clearly *in situ*, and archaeologically associated with the latest building into which all the earlier inscriptions had been rebuilt. A continuity in the cult of Apis may therefore be seen in the remains at this site. There is also good reason for supposing that the purpose of the building remained the same from one period to another since lion beds are present both reused in pavement foundations and as a major feature of the latest structure. The two *w'bt* inscriptions, both dedicated to Apis, one of Sheshonk I and the other on the basin which was probably in use during the Ptolemaic period, suggest that this continuity lasted at least from the tenth century BC until the Roman period.

The association with the worship of Apis is further confirmed by the discovery at the site of a number of small limestone plaques bearing carved images of the Apis bull in a shrine conveyed on a wheeled vehicle. Other similar plaques have also been found near the

Serapeum at Saqqara. Similar representations of other sacred animals survive, for example a crocodile from Karanis (Kom Aushim); they are dated to the Late, Ptolemaic or Roman periods. It is not known whether this scene represents the procession in which the preserved remains of the animal were transported from Memphis to the Serapeum, or another ceremony in which the live bull was paraded in a shrine. It may be significant that all the plaques found at the Apis precinct in Memphis with a recorded provenance came from the southern area of the site where they could have been votive objects associated with a processional way leading into the sacred precinct and onto the elevated terraced buildings within.

The extraordinary amount of alabaster present at this site, much of it inscribed for Apis and fashioned into lion beds, implies a highly specific use of the building. Depictions of lion beds, such as those mentioned above, in which color survives, show them painted a golden yellow. By its association with gold, as shown in the name of the quarry at Hatnub ("Mansion of Gold") whence it came, alabaster was associated with the life-giving energy of the sun and the peculiar properties of light. It was used for temple pavements in the pyramid complexes of the Old Kingdom (for example, those of Khafre, Unas and Teti), for offering tables, sarcophagi (such as Queen Hetepheres and Seti I), certain kinds of statues and lamps such as the elaborate examples from the tomb of Tutankhamen. Alabaster was thus identified with the quality of *w'b* "purity," from which the name of the *w'ht* derives. This kind of edifice could have been any of the service buildings, including workshops, attendant on a temple, and in this context mummification may well have been carried on there. In the case of the alabaster lion beds, they may be better understood as the places where the embalmed remains of the Apis bull were placed for purification and revivification ceremonies, prior to the long procession through the Ptah temple and along the Serapeum Way for burial at Saqqara. Libations poured over the mummy would probably have been collected in the basin attached to the bed.

See also

Hatnub; Memphis; mummification; Saqqara, Serapeum and animal necropolis

Further reading

Anthes, R. 1959. *Mit Rahineh 1955*: 75–9. Philadelphia.

Jeffreys, D.G. 1985. *The Survey of Memphis* 1: 65–6, 70. London.

Jones, M. 1990. The Temple of Apis in Memphis. *JEA* 76: 141–7.

Jones, M., and A. Jones. 1983–1988. The Apis House Project at Mit Rahinah: preliminary reports. *JARCE* 20: 33–45; 22: 17–18; 25: 105–16.

MICHAEL JONES

Memphite private tombs of the Old Kingdom

The typical *mastaba* (named after the Arabic word for "bench") private (i.e. non-royal) tomb of the Old Kingdom (3rd–6th Dynasties) contained a rectangular limestone or mudbrick superstructure resembling a box with gently sloping slides. Above ground, the *mastaba* was originally filled solid with mudbrick or rubble, and, later on in its development, with solid masonry. The more elaborate tombs utilized more masonry than their simpler mudbrick counterparts, but both materials continued to be used throughout Egyptian history.

The north and south niches on the exterior of the tomb faced east and were focal points for offerings to the cult of the deceased; they evolved into increasingly elaborate recesses now known as "false doors." The deceased was thought to pass through the false door in order to partake of offerings left by the living to ritually sustain his spirit. The only carved and/or painted decoration on the earliest *mastaba* tombs was either the false door, or a slab stela, with a representation of the deceased seated before a table piled high with bread loaves, and various inscribed spells for the invocation of offerings.

Figure 67 View of the western cemetery at Giza, taken from the top of the Great Pyramid
Courtesy of the Museum of Fine Arts, Boston

The solid core *mastaba* form was eventually enlarged and altered to house a room or series of rooms within the superstructure. Statues of the deceased and his or her family were placed in certain chambers or pits of the tomb, known as *serdab*s, to serve as substitute homes for the spirit should the mummy be damaged. Decoration also expanded from the false door or slab stela to the walls of the interior chambers, and even exterior entrance wall and architrave inscriptions. The chamber walls contained both raised and sunk relief sculpture and painted scenes of daily life on the deceased's estate and beyond (processions of animals, craft work, tax collecting, fishing and fowling, and so on), as well as funerary rites and biographical and religious inscriptions. These mentioned the names and titles of the tomb owner, and included stock laudatory phrases about his career and accomplishments. All of these scenes and texts would be magically recreated in the next world to provide a successful afterlife for the deceased. Stone and ceramic vessels, personal cosmetic implements and servant statuettes were among the various grave goods often deposited in the tomb.

The burial chamber was located underground, usually connected to the *mastaba* by means of a deep shaft through the rubble or debris-filled interior that cut into the bedrock; the shaft was often located behind the false door. The mummified body was placed in a stone or wooden sarcophagus and lowered into the burial chamber, which was then sealed for eternity. In the case of family tombs, several shafts and burial chambers were included. The most complex tombs, occurring later in the Old Kingdom (late 5th–6th Dynasties) contained

494

multiple *serdab*s, multiple burial shafts and on occasion as many as 30–40 decorated chambers housed within the superstructure.

In terms of the economics of the tomb complex, the offerings left in the tomb on specific days for the deceased were part of an arrangement established during life for the provision of the funerary cult. The offerings (bread, beer, cuts of meat, wine, milk, alabaster, clothing and so on) could later be removed from the tomb and redistributed among the priests, administrators and workers responsible for maintaining the cult. This system enhanced the economic relationship between the living and the dead, until the breakdown of the highly centralized Old Kingdom administration at the end of the 6th Dynasty.

The *mastaba* tomb is best preserved in a series of cemeteries stretching along the edge of the desert on the west bank of the Nile in the region of the Old Kingdom capital, Memphis, some 24 km south of modern Cairo. From north to south these sites are: Abu Roash, Giza, Zawiyet el-Aryan, Abusir, Saqqara, Dahshur and Meydum. Although there are numerous private tombs at sites possessing no royal burials, the general trend for the governing classes was to build a tomb at the site chosen by the reigning king. Members of the royal family and court officials closest to pharaoh were granted the honor of tombs in closest proximity to the royal pyramid complex. The largest and best known of these cemetery sites are Giza and Saqqara.

Located on a desert plateau overlooking the floodplain, a few kilometers west of modern Cairo, Giza was the principal royal necropolis of the 4th Dynasty. The early *mastaba*s of the family and court of King Khufu were laid out in rows or streets on the east side of the Great Pyramid. Great double *mastaba*s of princes and princesses, containing exterior chapels and inscribed niches, fill the streets closest to the satellite pyramids southeast of the Great Pyramid. One *mastaba* of a queen contains several rock-cut chambers located beneath the solid *mastaba* superstructure. The largest *mastaba* in the eastern field, and second largest one at Giza, belongs to Prince Ankh-haf, possibly a son of King Seneferu, and the vizier under King Khafre.

On the western side of the Great Pyramid, the cemetery is even larger. The earliest 4th Dynasty tombs were core-filled *mastaba*s laid out in rows with exterior slab stelae added as the only decoration. Many were later altered during Khufu's reign by the addition of casing walls and chapels. Later intrusive *mastaba*s from the 5th and 6th Dynasties complicate the layout. One of the earliest tombs in Egypt to contain a decorated subterranean burial chamber belonged to an official in this area. Other notable *mastaba*s include the largest in the necropolis (G 2000), whose owner remains anonymous, and the (third largest) tomb of Hemiunu, vizier and probable supervisor of the Great Pyramid construction project. A family of successive chief royal architects was buried in a large tomb complex at the northwest corner of the Great Pyramid; this contained copies of letters from a 5th Dynasty king mentioning the length of one *mastaba*'s construction (fifteen months) inscribed on the exterior walls. In addition, numerous rock-cut tombs were carved from the Giza plateau cliffs (East and West Cemeteries, Menkaure Quarry Cemetery), and unusual mudbrick tombs with vaulted ceilings were discovered south of the Sphinx. Excavations to the south have revealed additional cemeteries of construction crew members and overseers, as well as bakeries, fish-processing installations and perhaps even palace buildings. Giza continued to be used as a necropolis during both the New Kingdom and the Late period.

In terms of modern archaeological investigation, Giza was apportioned to different expeditions in an organized and well-defined fashion. At the beginning of the twentieth century the Egyptian antiquities authorities divided the major sections of the necropolis among several international teams, in an effort to put an end to illicit digging. German and Austrian expeditions excavated the central strip of the western cemetery, the street of *mastaba*s south of the Great Pyramid, and the temples associated with the large pyramids of Khufu and Khafre. American teams dug the entire Eastern Cemetery, the two outer thirds of the

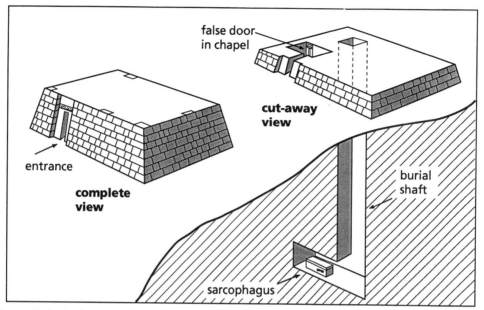

Figure 68 Basic elements of a typical Old Kingdom *mastaba* tomb

Western Cemetery (one-third obtained upon departure of an Italian mission), and the pyramid complex of King Menkaure. Egyptian expeditions excavated the rock-cut tombs south and west of the Great Sphinx and Khafre causeway, and smaller areas at the western edge of the Western Cemetery. Principal finds from these excavations are now at Giza itself, in the Egyptian Museum, Cairo, the Museum of Fine Arts, Boston, the Pelizaeus-Museum, Hildesheim, the Ägyptisches Museum, Leipzig and the Kunsthistorisches Museum, Vienna.

Saqqara is the primary cemetery of the Memphite capital and closest to it geographically. Located high on a desert bluff above the western edge of the cultivation, and measuring some 6 km long and 1.5 km at its widest point, the site first contained cenotaphs of the Early Dynastic period. It was then enlarged with the 3rd Dynasty Step Pyramid complex of King Zoser, probably the world's first monumental structure in stone. The site is larger and less unified than the necropolis at Giza. Limestone and mudbrick sepulchers from a wide range of periods, many of them later than the Old

Kingdom, are in close proximity to each other, and there are far fewer areas with streets of *mastaba*s arrayed in a symmetrical fashion than at Giza. The site was therefore excavated in a less systematic manner. Egyptian, French, British, German, Dutch and Japanese expeditions are just a few of the nations that have worked or continue to work at the site.

South of the Step Pyramid complex lies the pyramid of King Unas, the last pharaoh of the 5th Dynasty, around whose causeway a number of *mastaba*s were constructed, some of them predating and thus underlying Unas's construction. Among the best preserved are those of Ny-ankh-Khnum and Khnum-hotep, Nefer, and the viziers Iy-nofret and Mehu. The largest group of *mastaba* tombs lies north of the Step Pyramid, and includes those of Ti (containing a portico and pillared court), Akhet-hotep and Ptah-hotep (5th Dynasty). Some of the 6th Dynasty tombs surrounding the pyramid of King Teti belonged to the officials Mereruka, Ka-gem-ni, Ankh-ma-hor and Nefer-seshem-Ptah. Excavations continue in these and many other parts of the necropolis.

Private *mastaba* tombs of the Old Kingdom account for some of the largest and best known necropoleis in all of Egyptian archaeology. Rock-cut tombs without superstructures are also known from Giza and Old Kingdom sites in Upper Egypt, such as Sheik Sa'id, Deshasha and Aswan. While these show several different layouts and arrangements of their rock-cut chambers, they include the critical mortuary elements, namely, the false door, inscribed offering formulae, and shafts and burial chambers. It should be remembered that the surviving evidence for Egyptian tomb architecture is skewed in favor of the governing classes and bureaucracy, since their wealth and influence allowed for construction in more permanent materials such as limestone. The great cemeteries of the Memphite area, the largest and most impressive in the country, represent but an elite fraction of the population. The largest proportion of Egyptian society was probably interred in modest graves at the desert's edge.

See also

Abu Roash; Abusir; Early Dynastic private tombs; Giza (all entries); Memphis; Meydum; Old Kingdom provincial tombs; representational evidence, Old Kingdom private tombs; Saqqara, North, Early Dynastic tombs; Saqqara, pyramids of the 3rd Dynasty; Saqqara, pyramids of the 5th and 6th Dynasties; Zawiyet el-Aryan

Further reading

Lauer, J.P. 1976. *Saqqara: The Royal Cemetery of Memphis*. London.

Málek, J. 1986. *In The Shadow of the Pyramids. Egypt during the Old Kingdom*. London.

Reisner, G.A. 1942. *A History of the Giza Necropolis* 1. Cambridge, MA.

Watson, P. 1987. *Egyptian Pyramids and Mastaba Tombs*. Aylesbury.

PETER DER MANUELIAN

Mendes, Dynastic evidence

Mendes, modern Tell Rub'a, is located in the eastern central Delta (30°57′ N, 31°31′ E) in the province of Daqahaliya, roughly midway between the city of el-Mansura and the town of el-Simbillawein.

The mound can be divided into three major areas. The most important area is that in the northwest, which is bounded by massive mudbrick enclosure walls slightly less than 2 km in perimeter. These walls define the sacred temple precinct. The most prominent feature within the enclosure is the *naos* of a Late period temple. Nothing remains of this great temple today except the *naos*, a shrine carved from a single block of stone which bears the cartouches of King Amasis (26th Dynasty). The second major area of the mound is a high rise to the east of the temple precinct. The third major area, the vast southern city, is thought to have been the main residential quarter of Mendes.

A foundation deposit discovered in the northern part of the Amasis temple proper indicates that this area was either originally constructed or rebuilt in the 18th Dynasty and was added to in the 19th Dynasty. The southern part of the temple was built in the 26th Dynasty and contained four monumental granite *naoi*, each over 7 m high, in a courtyard 29.40 × 26.60 m. They were placed on a limestone platform which can be described as a huge floating foundation supported by sand and contained by mudbrick walls. Due to the extreme care of the original architects, who marked the positions of the *naoi* on each course of the limestone foundation, their exact locations are known. Inscriptions on the broken *naoi* remains indicate that they were dedicated by Amasis to Shu, Geb, Osiris and Re. The fact that his name is inscribed while the rest of the text is in relief led some scholars to believe that he had merely usurped a structure built in a previous reign. Discovery of the original foundation deposits at the corners of the limestone foundations, however, demonstrate that this part of the temple had been built by Amasis. Each foundation deposit contained a bovine skull and haunch; a miniature grinding stone and grinder; a number of miniature ceramic cups, jars and bowls; a semicircular limestone model of a loaf of bread; and four plaques each of gold, silver, copper, red stone, greenish stone, faïence, carnelian and lapis lazuli. Each of the plaques have the nomen and prenomen (cartouches) of Amasis, which are incised on the metal plaques and painted on the others.

The temple was built over an Old Kingdom cemetery. Much of the cemetery was completely removed when the deep foundations of the temple were dug. A portion of the cemetery, however, has been preserved to the east and north of the temple.

To the east of the temple were two well preserved mudbrick *mastaba*s, with false door niches at the northern end of their eastern façades and a series of much smaller niches to the south, which probably date to the late Old Kingdom. The one farther north had a false door stela in place with an offering table. The skeleton within the *mastaba* was buried with two pots and two copper razors, and had originally been interred in a wooden coffin. According to the stela, the occupant was named 'Aḥa-pu-Ba, priest of the Ram God of Mendes. A false door stela found associated with the second *mastaba*, to the south, was not *in situ* but was also for 'Aḥa-pu-Ba. As in the first *mastaba*, a single burial was placed within the structure and a series of simple inhumations covered with reeds, of males and females as well as infants, were situated at the bottom. The single burial was of a woman (the wife of 'Aḥa-pu-Ba?); the remains were buried in a badly decomposed wooden coffin and there were no grave goods. According to the stelae inscriptions, both monuments were provided by 'Aḥa-pu-Ba's son, whose own funerary monument did not fare so well; broken fragments of his tomb were found reused in a later tomb farther north.

Over thirty additional burials were recovered in this area. For the most part, these corpses had simply been wrapped in reeds and buried without grave goods. One of these burials, however, of a female in a coffin, was found with beads, a bronze mirror, small alabaster vessels, a stone grinder and over 200 pieces of galena. Above the head and along the sides of the body were small strips as well as large pieces of gold foil. Unfortunately, it was not possible to reconstruct the original configuration of this gold decoration.

Immediately to the east of the *mastaba* area and separated from it by a major north–south mudbrick wall, possibly the precinct wall of the cemetery, were houses which date to the late Old Kingdom and later. To the north of the *naoi*, all the graves were badly damaged. One appears to have been built wholly of limestone. Others were built partly of limestone or wholly of mudbrick. In the debris throughout the area many artifacts were found which came from the destroyed burials; they range in date from the Old Kingdom through the Middle Kingdom. Earlier graves (Early Dynastic) were excavated in a lower level, in deposits that were relatively undisturbed by ancient building activity and modern pillaging of the site. The lower graves were simple interments, usually flexed with the head to the north facing east.

The high rise of the mound to the east, outside of the temple precinct, is aptly called "Kom el-Adham" (Mound of Bones). The top layer is practically a solid mass of bones with many whole and fragmentary faïence *shawabti*s and amulets. Beneath the top layer were several meters of relatively pure sand in which some bones were found, and below the sand was hard packed soil which contained burials and potsherds. A great number of pots which can be dated to the third–second centuries BC were buried within the layer of sand.

See also

Late and Ptolemaic periods, overview

Further reading

De Meulenaere, H., and P. MacKay. 1976. *Mendes* 2. Warminster.
Holz, R., D. Stieglitz, D. Hansen and E. Ochsenschlager. 1980. *Mendes* 1. Cairo.

DONALD HANSEN

Mendes, Predynastic and Early Dynastic

Mendes, which lies in the northeastern Nile Delta (30°57′ N, 31°31′ E), near the modern provincial capital of Mansura, is one of the largest archaeological sites in the Delta, and it is particularly important for research on the origins of the first Egyptian states, as they evolved after about 3,300 BC.

By about 3,300 BC ancient Egypt was beginning a period of fundamental transformation, a process in which the political significance and economic importance of Lower Egypt, including the Nile Delta, greatly increased and both Upper and Lower Egypt became a single political and cultural entity. This process of transformation may have begun as early as 3,500 BC. Northern Egypt gradually grew in importance for two primary reasons: first, Egypt's wars, trade and other interactions with Syro-Palestine and the Mediterranean world were already important by at least 3,100 BC, and in subsequent centuries Egypt's foreign relations became increasingly important economically and politically; second, the Delta has vast agricultural lands and eventually became the farming and stock-raising center of the Egyptian state.

Tell el-Rub'a, which together with the adjacent mound called Tell Timai comprise the archaeological site now known primarily by its Greek name, "Mendes," was one of the major Delta settlements during all or most of this formative era of early Egyptian antiquity. Donald Redford notes that under the name "Npt," which throughout its history was one designation of the city, Mendes is known from the reign of Djer (early 1st Dynasty); but "Ddt," the more common name (from which Mendes is ultimately derived), is attested to not long after, in the 4th Dynasty. By the 6th Dynasty Mendes included a cemetery for local priests. For most of its long history Mendes was the capital of Nome XVI of Lower Egypt, which stretched from just north of Tell Muk-dam to the Mediterranean (i.e. about 129 km north–south). From its beginnings, Mendes appears to have been the cult center of the "Great Buck, Master of Ddt," originally perhaps a ram, and his consort, the "Foremost of Fishes." Through a later Osirian association the pair was augmented to a triad by the addition of the god Harpokrates.

Compared to Hierakonpolis, Abydos, Nagada and other towns in southern Egypt, Tell el-Rub'a was a comparatively small settlement in the third and fourth millennia BC. But the community appears to have been an important element in the regional Delta settlement pattern, and perhaps in a larger national and international context as well, exactly during the period when Egypt was first evolving into a large territorial state. Throughout most of its occupational history, Nile tributaries linked Mendes to the centers of the Egyptian state in the Nile Valley, and also to the southwest Asian shores of Syro-Palestine and to the Mediterranean and Aegean worlds. Thus, Tell el-Rub'a was an important "node" in an evolving pattern of socioeconomic and political interactions that in some ways define this region's complex cultural history.

One of the most important aspects of Tell el-Rub'a is that it is not a typical Early Dynastic cemetery site (as are almost all the other Delta sites of this period that have been located and excavated). The small areas of Tell el Rub'a that have been excavated appear to be entirely residential and occupational, with substantial mudbrick buildings, ovens and other domestic features, and a great deal of refuse typical of early communities, but no burials. Thus, Tell el-Rub'a has the potential to tell us much about changes in the society and economy of the Delta during Egypt's formative era.

Too small an area of Predynastic and Early Dynastic Tell el-Rub'a has been excavated to infer much about this community, but excavations between 1990 and 1993 showed that at least part of this site was probably occupied continuously between about 3,200 and 2,700 BC. A few pieces of pottery known as "Ma'adi blackware" were found in the lower levels of the recent excavations, suggesting that the site was occupied at the same time as Ma'adi, an important Predynastic site located just south of modern Cairo. Along with other northern sites, such as Buto, Tell el-Rub'a was part of the distinctive Lower Egyptian culture of the later Predynastic period. The pottery from the early occupation at Tell el-Rub'a is quite different from that of the contemporaneous Upper Egyptian Nagada culture, yet it is very similar to pottery at the various northern sites, suggesting that until about 3,200 BC the Delta and all of Lower Egypt may have been somewhat culturally isolated from the small states that developed in the south. But the pottery from Tell el-Rub'a from levels dated to the 1st Dynasty and just prior to it—that is, levels that lie directly on those from which the Ma'adi blackware pottery and other distinctive Delta pottery came—is quite similar to contemporaneous Nagada culture pottery found at Hierakonpolis, Abydos, and many other southern sites.

Thus, like several other Delta sites, the evidence from Tell el-Rub'a suggests a fairly rapid transformation of Egypt, from two somewhat separate Predynastic cultures to a single, culturally unified state. It may be that, as in the early Egyptian legends, some southern ruler, such as King Narmer, conquered the Delta and forcibly integrated it into the Egyptian state, but there is little evidence for this.

Despite the limited area of recent excavations, the evidence suggests that the people who lived at Tell el-Rub'a during the period of Egypt's transformation, from about 3,200 to 2,700 BC, subsisted on the traditional ancient Egyptian diet, and, in general, lived lives very similar to the those of later pharaonic eras. Many of the potsherds in the earliest levels were from bread molds, and the plant remains suggest that wheat and barley were staples. The animal remains from the early occupations are poorly preserved, but pig and fish bones are the most numerous, and several fragments of cattle bones have been found, as well as a hippopotamus tooth.

In general, the architecture of the Early Dynastic levels appears to be a complex of mudbrick domestic buildings, but too small an area of the (largely underwater) Predynastic levels has been exposed to determine if they contain remains of the small circular reed huts that have been found in Predynastic levels of at least one nearby site. In a stratum containing standard Early Dynastic ceramics one small clay sealing was found; the hieroglyphs on it seem to refer to a personage of the 1st Dynasty, but the inscription is difficult to decipher.

Mendes was a significant site not only in the Predynastic and Early Dynastic eras, but during most of the later transformational epochs of Egyptian antiquity as well. It was already a significant settlement during the initial formation of the Egyptian state in the late fourth millennium BC, and it increased in size and importance during the maturation of the Egyptian state in the Old and Middle Kingdoms. During the complex imperial dynamics of the New Kingdom and Late period it became one of the greatest Delta cities.

See also

Abydos, Predynastic sites; Dynastic; Early Dynastic period, overview; Hierakonpolis; Ma'adi and the Wadi Digla; Minshat Abu Omar; Nagada (Naqada); pottery, Early Dynastic to Second Intermediate Period; pottery, prehistoric; Predynastic period, overview; subsistence and diet, Tell ed-Dab'a, Second Intermediate Period; trade, foreign

Further reading

Brewer, D.J., J. Isaacson and D. Haag. 1996. Mendes regional archaeological survey and remote sensing analysis. *Sahara* 8: 29–42.

Brewer, D.J., and R.J. Wenke. 1992. Transitional late Predynastic–Early Dynastic occupations at Mendes: a preliminary report. In *The Nile Delta in Transition: 4th–3rd Millennium B.C.*, E.C.M. van den Brink, ed., 175–83. Tel Aviv.

Friedman, R. 1992. The Early Dynastic and transitional pottery of Mendes: the 1990 season. In *The Nile Delta in Transition: 4th–3rd Millennium B.C.*, E.C.M. van den Brink, ed., 199–206. Tel Aviv.

Wenke, R.J., and D. Brewer. 1996. The Archaic–Old Kingdom Delta: the evidence from Mendes and Kom el-Hisn. In *House and Palace in Ancient Egypt*, M. Bietak, ed., 265–85. Vienna.

ROBERT J. WENKE

Merimde Beni-salame

The prehistoric site of Merimde is situated on the western border of the Nile Delta, a few kilometers southwest of the village of Beni-salame (30°19′ N, 30°51′ E). It covers an area of approximately 25 ha on a spur surrounded at the foot of its slopes by a desiccated branch of the Nile. "Merimde" means "the place of the ashes," an allusion to the gray/black deposits of the cultural layers.

Merimde was discovered by Hermann Junker during his West Delta Expedition in 1928. Until then, the Delta was believed to have been uninhabited in prehistoric times. Junker correctly concluded that the cultural dualism of Upper and Lower Egypt dates back to prehistoric times. From 1929 to 1939 he excavated 6400 m^2 of the site. The finds from these excavations are scattered in a number of museums, especially those in Cairo, Stockholm and Heidelberg.

Junker's excavations were never fully published because the documentation was lost during the Second World War. In 1976, excavations were finally resumed by the Egyptian Antiquities Organization (EAO) and, from 1977 to 1982, by the German Institute of Archaeology (DAI) in Cairo. The new excavations have enabled us to reconstruct the stratigraphic sequence of the site, and to fit Junker's many finds into their proper chronological context.

In the course of Merimde's development the settlement often moved about horizontally on the habitable surface of the spur, probably because of changes in the water level of the Nile branch and the height of the annual flood, which were caused by climatic changes. Merimde's inhabitants had to adapt to these circumstances and settled as close as possible

to the river bank, but above the high-water mark.

The stratigraphy of the site as a whole attains a maximum depth of 2.5 m, but can taper off to as little as 0.5 m or less on higher ground bordering the semi-desert. Stratigraphic evidence and numerous surface finds demonstrate that at least 1 m of cultural deposits was lost through deflation (wind erosion) after the abandonment of the Neolithic village. The earliest stratum lies directly on a gravel bed with Middle Palaeolithic stone tools and late handaxes. The scarcity of finds in this stratum would seem to indicate a relatively low density of habitation.

The only structures found were small huts made of wattle and reeds with round or elliptical ground plans. The latter are partly sunken into the ground. The various types of structures in the later strata seem to be grouped in "compounds." Circles of Nile clay and baskets served as storerooms or granaries. Daily activities were pursued outdoors, as abundant remains of open fires, lithic workshops, grinding stones and so on attest.

Burials were found in all of Merimde's strata. There was no separate area for a cemetery, which is characteristic of late prehistoric sites in Lower Egypt. The dead were interred in a contracted position in shallow, oval pits. Children's remains were simply thrown into rubbish pits; apparently, only adults were given a proper burial. In the earliest stratum, they were buried with the head facing the Nile branch; in later strata, there seems to be no obvious orientation of the body. Usually the graves do not contain grave goods; only in the earlier Merimde burials are perforated fresh water mussel shells (*Aspatharia rubens*) relatively common, and were probably sewn on clothing for decoration.

After the abandonment of the Neolithic settlement, parts of the site were used as a cemetery by people of the Predynastic Ma'adi culture. The village associated with this cemetery has not yet been located. Only a few Ma'adi culture burials were richly furnished with pottery. Sporadic surface finds of the Late period are evidence for occasional use of the

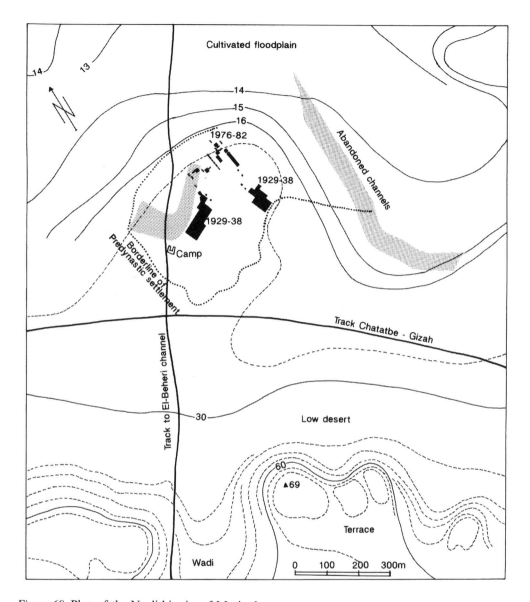

Figure 69 Plan of the Neolithic site of Merimde

area more recently, but probably only for cultivation by inhabitants of the nearby city of Therenutis. It is assumed that the abandonment of the prehistoric settlement was caused by the gradual meandering of the adjacent Nile branch, which now lies buried within the Delta. Stratigraphic observations demonstrate that desertification and deflation of the upper Neolithic layers began as early as the fourth millennium BC.

The exceptionally numerous finds from the large-scale excavations at Merimde are evidence of a fully developed Neolithic culture characterized by sedentary village life, agriculture, animal husbandry, and, to a lesser degree, hunting and fishing. Its material culture was marked by the production of pottery, stone tools of pecked flint and ground hard stone, and various types of bone tools. Anthropomorphic figurines and zoomorphic ones (mostly cattle), modeled in clay or carved in bone, were also found but were not numerous.

In the lowest level at Merimde is evidence of the oldest fully developed Neolithic culture in the Egyptian Nile Valley/Delta. Red pottery, meticulously burnished horizontally, in simple forms (bowls, spherical and ovoid shapes), is typical of this stratum. On some pots, one horizontal band under the rim was left unpolished and was incised with a fish bone pattern. The clay used in the pottery from this stratum, in contrast to that of later strata, is always untempered. Typical features found only on this early pottery are pierced lugs and handles, as well as ring stands for the usually round-bottomed forms.

The flint industry of the earliest stratum is completely different from that of later periods. It is based on blades and flakes which were retouched laterally and terminally. Backed blades as well as tanged projectile points (arrowheads) occur in this stratum, as do borers and several other small, bifacial tools. Other typical finds are beads made of ostrich eggshells and shells of molluscs from the Mediterranean and Red Seas, perforated for use as pendants.

The earliest stratum is separated from later cultural deposits by a sterile layer of eolian sand, evidence that the site had been abandoned for a relatively long time. The oldest Merimde lithic industry shows affinities to that of the preceding Epi-palaeolithic culture in Lower Egypt (known from sites at Helwan), and its pottery is related to that of the early Neolithic of southwest Asia. A specifically Lower Egyptian Neolithic culture developed only in the later strata of the site.

In the second, higher stratum, settlement activity obviously increased. The settlement shifted gradually up the slope of the spur, probably as a consequence of higher Nile floods. Traces of architecture in the form of postholes and various pits are now more common than in the earliest stratum. Elliptical-shaped huts of Nile clay, however, do not yet occur. In comparison to the earliest Neolithic evidence at Merimde, there are radical changes in the second stratum. The pottery is now tempered with chaff, and includes increasingly complex vessel shapes. Rounded bowls and pots are gradually superseded by conical or biconical shapes. Numerous ovoid vessels and large, thick-walled pans or platters (for baking?) are characteristic forms. On all forms, the rim is now abruptly cut off at a sharp right angle, whereas the earliest pottery had tapered rims. The pottery of the second stratum is always undecorated. Light gray burnished vessels are a new type, but the smoothed and the red-burnished wares continue. Burnishing is now applied diagonally, and is irregular.

The flint industry also acquires a new technology: blades and flakes become less common, and are replaced by large, bifacially retouched tools. These include flint knives, celts, long borers and carefully retouched projectile points, with long barbs and deep notches where the shaft was attached. For the first time there is evidence of large, tapering sickle blades with serrated edges showing obvious sheen along the cutting edge, probably from harvesting cereals. The numerous grinding stones and mortars from this stratum would strongly suggest the processing of cereals. Celts for hollowing logs were often hafted as adzes, with an asymmetrical blade set perpendicular to the haft. Notable are projectile points and knives made in a technique combining grinding with retouch. But coarse tools are also found in the second stratum and occur throughout the entire Merimde sequence.

The second stratum is exceedingly rich in small finds, especially bone artifacts. These include tools, such as awls and spatulas, and jewelry, such as pendants, beads and finger rings. Typical artifacts found only in this stratum are large harpoons, probably used for fishing. Ivory bracelets, adzes made from the ribs of large game, and fish hooks of mussel shell are also limited to this stratum.

The deposits of the second stratum also contained small finds in stone, such as alabaster vessels, ceremonial maceheads of slate, limestone and alabaster, and beads of semiprecious stones. Especially notable are some small stone axes made of amphibolite, slate and quartzite (found southeast of the First Cataract). No semi-finished artifacts in these materials were found, and the stone axes were probably acquired through trade as finished craft goods. They were often found grouped in small "hoards" hidden within the settlement: evidence of their great value.

The cultural and geographical orientation of the second (or Middle) Merimde culture known from the second stratum is completely different from that of its predecessor. Significant elements of its material culture were of African origin. These include the harpoons and adzes of bone and flint, fish hooks of mussel shell, and axes of stones from Nubia. The absence of influence from southwest Asia in the artifact assemblages is probably the result of an arid and inhospitable climatic phase, which lasted in Palestine until the middle of the fifth millennium BC.

In the course of its later culture history (Merimde III–V), the settlement grew to cover an area several times its original size, up to 25 ha in strata IV and V. Unfortunately, the later deposits have been exploited by local farmers for fertilizer (*sebbakh*). Finds are plentiful in these strata and Junker's excavations were primarily of this material, which has strongly influenced our scientific definition of the Neolithic culture at Merimde.

Building activity at Merimde was quite intensive during the later periods. Nile clay was used to construct elliptical huts with pisée walls (lumps of mud/clay packed to form a wall), and a floor area of as much as 2×4 m. Large reed baskets (up to 3.0 m in diameter and 1.5 m high), which had been set into pits and reinforced or caulked with Nile clay, were common.

The most obvious changes in the material culture of the later strata are in the ceramics. Conical bowls and biconical pots with flat bases now predominate. Also typical are pots with an "S" profile and flask or bottle shapes. Twin pots also appear in the later strata. In addition to the traditional red- and gray-polished wares, deep black burnished pottery now appears. The development of several new decorative techniques is seen in pots in strata IV and V: applied knobs and ribs are common, followed by various impressed and engraved decorations. A few sherds of painted pottery were also found.

In the lithic industry, large, bifacially retouched tools are perfected, and many types are added to the inventory. Projectile points are especially sensitive to change through time. The characteristic type for stratum II evolves in stratum IV to the classic Merimde point with short, beveled barbs. In stratum V, it is replaced by a type (of arrowhead) known from the Fayum, with pointed barbs.

Further innovations are large burins, tools, tripartite sickles, and several types of celts and knives. Large, carefully retouched and ground ceremonial weapons are typical. Small finds of clay become more diversified and bone artifacts (beads, pendants and belt hooks) are especially common.

Botanical and osteological evidence confirms the classification of Merimde as a fully developed Neolithic settlement. Besides numerous cultivable plants (emmer wheat, barley, lentils and vetches), animal husbandry was also significant. Cattle, sheep, goats, pigs and dogs were kept from the beginning, but the relative economic importance of these species changed through time. Cattle and pig breeding clearly increased in importance, whereas the proportion of sheep and goats decreased correspondingly.

Throughout the history of the settlement, its inhabitants engaged in hunting. Desert game, such as antelopes, gazelles, feline predators, ostriches and so on, were hunted, but the nearby branch of the Nile was also exploited for its game, such as hippopotamus, crocodile, aurochs and many species of water fowl. Fishing played an important role in the economy from the beginning. Fish were caught with nets, fish hooks and harpoons. Bones of more than twenty different species of fish could be identified at Merimde, including specimens more than 1 m in length. Large, edible Nile mussels (*Aspatharia rubens*) were also collected and consumed in great quantities.

Besides foodstuffs, game and fish, the inhabitants of Merimde also brought back various raw materials from their expeditions to other regions. From the terrace immediately to the south of the settlement and from the plateau extending into the Wadi Natrun were sandstone (for grinding stones), petrified wood, flint nodules and pigments (hematite, ocher). Carnelian and other semiprecious stones for jewelry were also collected there.

According to calibrated radiocarbon dates, the Neolithic settlement at Merimde dates to the fifth millennium BC (*circa* 4,750–4,250 BC). Typologically, its later phase corresponds to the Neolithic culture known in the Fayum (Fayum A) and to the earliest Predynastic cultural phase in Middle/Upper Egypt, the Badarian. A gap of at least five centuries, however, separates the evidence at Merimde from the Ma'adi culture of Lower Egypt.

See also

agriculture, introduction of; fauna, domesticated; fauna, wild; Fayum, Neolithic and Predynastic sites; Ma'adi and the Wadi Digla; natural resources; Neolithic and Predynastic stone tools; Neolithic cultures, overview; Paleolithic cultures, overview; Paleolithic tools; pottery, prehistoric; Predynastic period, overview

Further reading

Boessneck, J., and A. von den Driesch. 1985. *Die Tierknochenfunde aus der neolithischen Siedlung von Merimde-Benisalâme am westlichen Nildelta*. Munich.

Eiwanger, J. 1984–92. *Merimde-Benisalâme I, II, III*. Mainz.

Hassan, F.A. 1985. Radiocarbon chronology of Neolithic and Predynastic Sites in Upper Egypt and the Delta. *AAR* 3: 95–115.

JOSEF EIWANGER

Meroe, cemeteries

Several distinct cemeteries lie east of the ancient city of Meroe (16°56′ N, 33°43′ E), near the modern village of Begrawiya in northern Sudan. The distribution of burials and differences in grave styles, ranging from simple pit burials to pyramid capped tombs, as well as the variety of artifacts accompanying the burials, represent complex patterns from which chronological and socioeconomic inferences can be derived.

Four non-royal cemeteries (Northern, Western, Middle and Southern Necropoleis) are located in the area closest to Meroe. They were partly excavated in 1910 by John Garstang of the Institute of Archaeology, University of Liverpool.

The Northern Necropolis is now considered the earliest of these cemeteries and not the latest, *contra* Garstang. These graves are marked by superstructures of low mounds of sand and stones. Narrow steps, neatly cut into the underlying gravel, lead down to small chambers. Grave goods of finely painted "Biscuit" Ware and stamp-decorated pottery provisionally date the cemetery from the first century BC to the second century AD.

Graves of the Middle Necropolis are marked by rings of stone, or white or dark gravel. They consist of two parallel passages which lead westward to a pair of chambers excavated in the gravel. The interred body was placed extended on a wooden bed with the head to the south. Associated pottery is typically a large globular vessel with an upright neck (the so-called "beer jar"). Numerous offering tables, which originally belonged to earlier graves, were found reused to block burial entrances at the end of passages. This group of graves is now considered late or even post-Meroitic (after AD 350).

The Southern Necropolis is distinguished by mounds of sand or stones similar to those in the Northern Necropolis. Entrance passages to the graves are located as usual on the east, but lead down a rough incline of uneven slope with steep steps, reaching a depth of 2–3 m. These graves are similar in form to those of the Middle Necropolis; however, they contained many

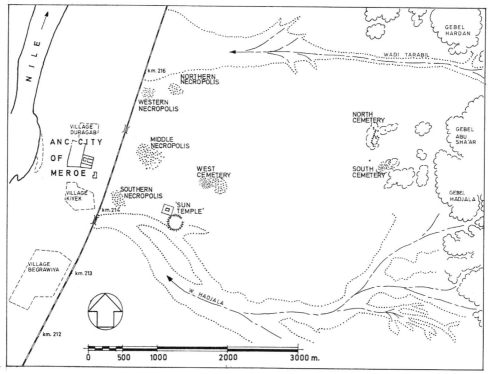

Figure 70 Plan of the site of Meroe and its cemeteries

grave goods and contracted bodies. This necropolis likewise dates to the late or post-Meroitic period.

Very little is known about the smaller Western Necropolis immediately to the west of the Northern Necropolis. Based on pottery from Garstang's excavation, it also seems to be late or even post-Meroitic in date.

Non-royal private burials have also been found farther east in the so-called "Royal Cemeteries" associated with the southern and western pyramid fields (South Group, West Group). Over 200 private pit burials were found in an elevated area west of the South Group pyramids. Similar contemporaneous burials were also found in the western portion of the West Group pyramids and appear to have been used by lesser members of the royal family as well as by commoners. These graves cover the entire period of Napatan/Meroitic culture, from the eighth century BC, beginning with the reign

of Piye, to *circa* AD 350. They range in style from simple pit graves with mound superstructures, to *mastaba*s and pyramids, which are in very ruined states of preservation. Superstructures in the form of a square *mastaba* seem to be contemporaneous with those in the Napatan cemetery at el-Kurru (where they may have been introduced), but apparently continued in sporadic use for some centuries at Meroe.

Royal burials in the Meroe cemeteries are characterized by pyramids, which intentionally replaced the usual mound of sand or stone over the pit or burial chamber of commoners' burials. The prototypical Meroitic pyramid developed at the Napatan site of Nuri. Although differing in size, shape, internal design and structure, it was apparently derived from Egyptian archetypes found in the small pyramids at Deir el-Medina (Thebes) and Aniba (Lower Nubia). With a solidly built interior, the Nuri-type pyramid was succeeded at Meroe by less substantially built ones. The Meroe pyramids were constructed with a core of ferricrete sandstone rubble beneath a fill of soil and sandstone chips, which was encased by only one to three rows of mantle blocks.

Study of the Meroe pyramids began with the visit of the French travelers Frédéric Cailliaud and L.-M.-A. Linant de Bellefonds, who journeyed to Sudan in 1821–2, followed in 1833 by the British traveler George Hoskins. In 1844 the site was visited by Richard Lepsius, director of the Prussian Expedition, which took a number of artifacts to the Berlin Museum. Several pyramids of the North Group were dismantled in 1834 by Giuseppe Ferlini in his search for treasures in burial chambers. While destroying a pyramid (N 6), Ferlini found the jewelry of Queen Amanishakheto (*circa* 15–0 BC), most probably in the burial chamber. In 1903 and 1905 similar exploration of the site was conducted by E.A.W. Budge, who incorrectly assumed that the burial chambers were inside the pyramids.

Under the direction of George Reisner, the joint Harvard University and Museum of Fine Arts, Boston expeditions in 1921–3 excavated subterranean burial chambers in three pyramid cemeteries (the South, North and West Groups, since then known as the Begrawiya cemeteries and referred to by the abbreviation Beg S, Beg N and Beg W). Artifacts found during these excavations are now in the Museum of Fine Arts, Boston and the Sudan National Museum.

The expedition discovered that the South Group (Beg S) was the old family cemetery of the Meroe branch of the Kushite royal family, in use from *circa* 720 to 300 BC. The last tombs built in this cemetery were the first royal ones at Meroe, but by this time the cemetery was becoming too crowded. Excavations here revealed at least ninety superstructures, twenty-four of which were recognized as pyramids, two of them for kings.

The North Group (Beg N) began as the royal cemetery of Meroe, in succession to the South Group. There were forty-one royal tombs with thirty-eight still visible pyramid structures, built between *circa* 270 BC and AD 350. This group of pyramids was reserved for thirty kings, eight reigning queens and at least two princes, who perhaps ruled as coregents.

The West Group (Beg W) was the cemetery of the royal family, as distinguished from that of the sovereigns and acting sovereigns. Besides hundreds of pit burials, excavations revealed evidence of 171 superstructures, including eighty-two pyramids.

One main accomplishment of the excavations was to establish for the first time a chronology of Meroitic rulers (subsequently revised in 1957 by Dows Dunham, and in 1959 by F. Hintze). Even today, however, many of the pyramids at Meroe cannot be definitely associated with known rulers.

Between 1976 and 1987 the Sudan Directorate General of Antiquities and National Museums (Khartoum), in cooperation with the Central Institute of Ancient History and Archaeology of the Academy of Sciences (Berlin), undertook the preservation and restoration work at the North Group (Beg N) pyramids at Meroe. Architectural studies of these monuments were also conducted, and reliefs, inscriptions and graffiti were recorded.

In general, the main architectural and structural elements of the Nuri pyramids were retained in the constructions at Meroe, but with gradual changes over time. Earlier burial chambers of kings generally contained three rooms. The first (offering) chamber was square, probably corresponding to the forecourt of a temple, and often niches and pillars were left standing in the process of hollowing out the chamber. A second chamber extended transversely and may be comparable to a pylon gate. The burial chamber proper may correspond to the sanctuary of a typical one-room Meroitic temple. Burials of queens had only two rooms. Designs of the burial substructures belonging to both kings and queens ultimately degenerated into one or two narrow, low cave-like holes. Most of the tombs contained evidence of sacrificial burials of the harim and servants with the deceased ruler.

Stairways were normally more or less carefully hewn steps leading west down through basal sandstone to the openings to the burial

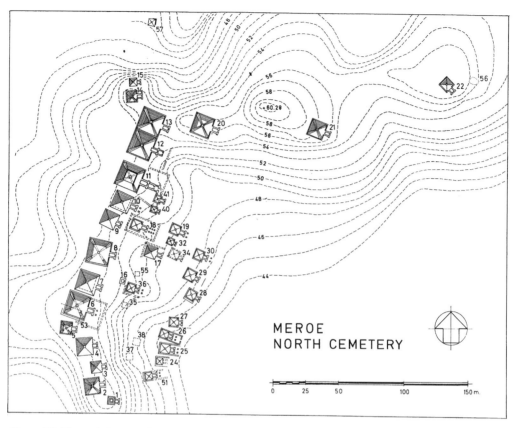

Figure 71 Plan of the Northern "Royal Cemetery" (Beg N) at Meroe

chambers. Originally, during construction of the burial chambers, the staircase was probably a ramp, which was then finished as steps to accommodate the funeral procession.

The pyramids are necessarily truncated as the result of their method of construction. Orientation of pyramids in the North Group (Beg N) varies between 73° (pyramid N 2) and 136° (N 22) from magnetic North. Various materials and surface treatments were used, with a change from solid masonry to brick and rubble construction at the beginning of the second century AD.

An offering chapel with accompanying pylon was added to the eastern side of the pyramid along the central axis. Occasionally, the chapel had a portico. Until *circa* AD 110, chapels were built of sandstone masonry, decorated with funerary scenes in relief. With the introduction

of brick and rubble construction (beginning with pyramid N 32), interior walls of chapels were lined with masonry in order to continue the practice of relief decoration. The exterior chapel walls and pylons of these later constructions were built of fired bricks, which were then plastered. The sacred precinct (*temenos*) was delimited by a low wall, which occasionally surrounded the entire pyramid complex.

The sequence of structural elements described above, based on studies since 1976, corresponds to the succession of building stages. Subterranean structures were built during the lifetime of the ruler. After the burial ceremony, the entrances to the burial chambers were closed and the staircase was filled in. The pyramid superstructure was then built by the successor of the dead king, more or less over the burial chambers. This explanation replaces

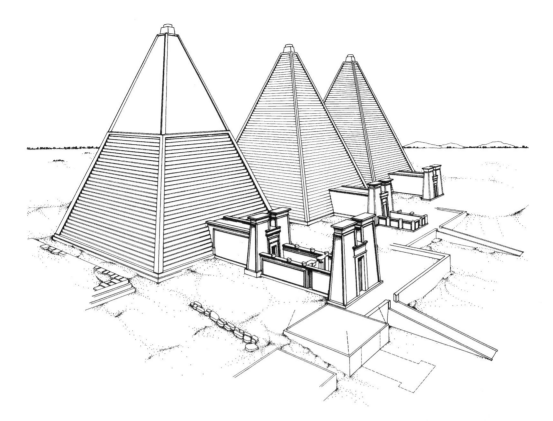

Figure 72 Conjectural restoration of pyramids Beg N 11, Beg N 12 and Beg N 13 at Meroe

Reisner's theory that there were two different burial ceremonies, which was based on the different locations of the pyramid staircases. This new interpretation, together with the evidence from 169 relief scenes (in contrast to the previously known fifty-two scenes), may also alter the Meroitic chronology, especially the succession of rulers during the last centuries of the kingdom.

Evidence from three different sources confirms the necessarily truncated shape of Meroitic pyramids. In 1979 a unique drawing was found engraved on the chapel wall of pyramid N 8, depicting a truncated pyramid. This drawing, done on a scale of 1:10, demonstrates the use of the 8:5 harmonic proportion of the pyramid's height to its base, and also depicts the level of the pyramid's truncation.

The discovery of several pyramid capstones,

which constitute the upper terminus of the pyramid structure, provides the second clue to its truncated form. Thirdly, remnants of cedar poles found in four pyramids suggest the possibility that the *shaduf* was used in pyramid construction. The *shaduf* is a lifting device, consisting of a bucket attached to a weighted lever, that was first used for irrigation in Egypt in the New Kingdom, to lift water to higher levels of ground. The evidence of the cedar poles in the Meroitic pyramids, and the subsequent study and experimental use of the *shaduf* in reconstructing pyramid N 19, confirm that this device is only capable of raising blocks to the level of the truncation and it could not have been used to complete a true pyramid.

All structures were finished with a layer of plaster. Remains of the original plaster, composed of a very rich lime mortar 1–2 cm thick, have been found on the surface of pyramids, chapels, enclosure walls and thresholds. Reliefs were covered by a thinner plaster coat *circa* 1 mm thick. The plaster on all Meroitic buildings served to cover rough masonry and fired brick, protected the weak sandstone, and formed a smooth and coherent surface for the application of paint and painted decoration.

Pyramids in the three "Royal Cemeteries" at Meroe consist of fourteen different types, varying in structure, shape and decoration. Changes in architectural types and degeneration in materials, size, building skill and structural stability of the pyramids is paralleled by changes in the style and contents of reliefs in the offering chapels.

Early decoration of chapels was strongly influenced by Egyptian style. In chapel scenes of the South Group (Beg S) and the earliest chapels in the North Group (Beg N, no later than *circa* 200 BC), a small figure of Isis is carved behind the king, who is seated on a lion throne, and three registers contain figures of gods and servants bringing sacrifices. For the next 200 years members of the royal family were placed behind Isis in reliefs. There are more registers in front of the king, including scenes from the *Book of the Dead*, as well as long rows of stereotyped courtiers and mourners with palm branches. At the end of this period, the high priest (crown prince?), who bears an incense burner, is found in front of the king. Sometimes family members are represented behind the priest. Beginning with chapel N 22 (*circa* AD 30), changes in the relief scenes include an added offering table in front of the king; a simplified representation of registers; replacement of the high priest (crown prince?) by the deities Anubis and Nephthys, who offer libations on the south and west walls; and another composition on the west wall where the deceased makes an offering to Osiris, with Isis behind him.

Reliefs on the north wall of chapels ultimately depict close family relatives as mourners (sometimes life-size in late reliefs), rather than the traditional registers and smaller rows of mourners with palm branches. These changes in relief composition near the end of the Meroitic kingdom may signal an increased importance of the next of kin and a growing individualism within the royal family.

See also

Gebel Barkal; el-Kurru; Kushites; Lepsius, Carl Richard; Meroe, city; Meroe, the "Sun Temple"; Meroitic culture; Nuri; Reisner, George Andrew

Further reading

Adams, W.Y. 1977. *Nubia: Corridor to Africa*, London.

Dunham, D. 1957. *Royal Cemeteries of Kush* 4: *Royal Tombs at Meroe and Barkal*. Boston.

——. 1963. *Royal Cemeteries of Kush* 5: *The West and South Cemeteries at Meroë*. Boston.

Hinkel, F.W. 1981. Pyramide oder Pyramidenstumpf? *ZÄS* 108: 105–24.

——. 1982. Pyramide oder Pyramidenstumpf? *ZÄS* 109: 27–61, 127–48.

——. 1984. Die meroitischen Pyramiden. Formen, Kriterien und Bauweisen. *Meroitica* 7: 310–31.

Hintze, F. 1959. *Studien zur Meroitischen Chronologie und zu den Opfertafeln aus den Pyramiden von Meroe* (Abhandlungen Deutsche Akademie der Wissenschaften zu Berlin 2). Berlin.

F.W. HINKEL

Meroe, city

Meroe was one of the royal and religious capitals of the ancient kingdom of Kush in the middle Nile region (16°54′ N, 33°44′ E). It was known in the ancient world as "Aithiopia," or, from the mid-third century BC, as "Meroe" after the name of this settlement in the Butana grassland, *circa* 120 km north of Khartoum (in the modern district of Shendi on the east bank of the Nile, at the villages Kabushiya and Begrawiya). The ruins of the city and three pyramid cemeteries, at Begrawiya South, West and North, were discovered in 1772 by the English traveler James

Bruce, who correctly identified them with the Meroe of the classical authors. His identification remained unnoticed for well over a century, even though there were expeditions to the site in the nineteenth century, including those of Frédéric Cailliaud and Richard Lepsius, who recorded the site. Pyramid tombs were also opened by Giuseppe Ferlini in 1834, and by E.A.W. Budge in the early twentieth century.

The importance and identification of the city were only recognized in 1909 by A.H. Sayce, who then suggested to John Garstang that the site should be investigated. With his knowledge of important Meroitic cemeteries in Lower Nubia, Garstang began excavating there under the aegis of the University of Liverpool. The fieldwork was directed by Garstang in collaboration with the philologist Sayce and the eminent Egyptologist F.L. Griffith, who was attracted by the chance of discovering monuments that might promote the decipherment of the Meroitic language. With inscribed finds from the first field season at the city of Meroe, and his collection of texts from the entire middle Nile region, Griffith was able to present, between 1910 and 1912, a corpus of Meroitic documents and a decipherment of both the Meroitic hieroglyphic and cursive writing systems (but not the language written in these scripts, which remains undeciphered). The discovery in the first field season of the walls of a monumental temple of Amen also corroborated Bruce's and Sayce's identification and encouraged Garstang's fieldwork there. After five seasons of large-scale fieldwork, however, excavations were interrupted in 1914 by the First World War. The results were only published in brief preliminary reports. The field records and some of the finds are preserved in the School of Archaeology and Oriental Studies, University of Liverpool, and were published by László Török. Other finds are in museums in England, Europe, the United States and Canada.

In the early years of the twentieth century stratigraphic excavations were conducted in the western Mediterranean, and in Egypt by Flinders Petrie. Garstang was aware of these developments, yet he did not realize the significance of stratigraphy and thus failed to investigate Meroe in a contextual sense. While he employed photographic documentation, it was only used to record isolated phenomena. Beyond recording the general building phases, based on the use of different building materials and construction techniques supposedly used in the different periods of the settlement, the only stratigraphic observations were made in the fourth field season by the architect W.S. George. Garstang's analysis of his finds aimed at establishing a chronology that would illustrate Meroitic history, as it was reconstructed from ancient textual evidence, and interpreting this chronology in terms of cultural variation and development. This did not, however, go beyond the limits of descriptive typology.

By the end of the fifth field season Garstang had excavated about one-third of an enclosed area which he named the "Royal Enclosure," the adjacent (late) Amen temple, four other temple buildings and a number of smaller chapels and kiosks outside the Royal Enclosure. He had also identified a number of monumental buildings in the city and at its periphery. Furthermore, three non-royal cemeteries were investigated to the east of the city and Garstang also opened about a dozen pyramid tombs in the Begrawiya West cemetery, dating from the first century BC to the first century AD. Although at several places the sequences of building phases were followed to a depth of 4–5 m beneath the present surface, Garstang only reached settlement levels in isolated places that could be dated before the fifth–fourth centuries BC, and this scarcity of early data further weakened his chronology.

The Begrawiya West, South and North Cemeteries were systematically excavated only in 1921–2 by the Harvard–Boston Expedition led by George Reisner. Reisner's goal was to establish a detailed historical and cultural chronology based on the evidence in the royal necropoleis. In 1923 he published an outline of the royal chronology based on an imposing typological analysis of the burials, placed in absolute dates by a few inscribed finds and historical correlations. After Reisner's death, his finds were published in their entirety by Dows Dunham, in 1957 and 1963.

Excavations at the town site were resumed in 1965 by a joint expedition of the Universities of Khartoum and Calgary, directed by P.L. Shinnie, in order to establish a cultural chronology of the site and to investigate the settlement evidence outside of the Royal and temple enclosures. A summary of the excavations and a catalog of finds of the 1965–72 seasons were published in 1980; a publication of the work of subsequent field seasons and the final results is forthcoming.

During the Egyptian New Kingdom domination of the middle Nile region and the Butana grassland probably belonged to an independent chiefdom named Irame. It is unknown whether a settlement existed at the site of Meroe before the eighth century BC, when the Butana region was united with the chiefdom of Napata, which already ruled over the entire territory of the former Egyptian province. By this time the Napatan chiefdom had adopted elements of Egyptian mortuary customs and the earliest burials in the Begrawiya West and South cemeteries at Meroe attest to an Egyptianization that was obviously a result of political unification with Napata, and based on the establishment of an Egyptian-type cult temple at Meroe. This cult temple not only served the mortuary cults, but was also the center of a temple town and acted as part of the Napatan government and redistributive system.

The early settlement at Meroe was probably built on alluvial islands in a braided channel of the Nile, close to the river, which gradually shifted away from the site in the subsequent centuries. Traces of a temple dedicated to the gods "Amen of Thebes" and "Amen of Napata" were found (but not identified) by Garstang under the later buildings (294 and 98) in the center of the island with the Royal Enclosure. Inscribed finds associated with the temple date from the period between King Senkamanisken (second half of the seventh century BC) and King Amanislo (mid-third century BC), but stray fragments of temple relief in the style of the late eighth/early seventh centuries BC may indicate an earlier building phase. Unprov-

enanced relief blocks in the style of King Taharka's (690–664 BC) Kawa temple perhaps come from the early Amen temple. It may be presumed that there was a royal palace on the western side of the temple.

The orientation of the early structures corresponds with the course of the Nile. The actual connection between the early Amen temple and a later monumental temple (250) erected by King Aspelta (late seventh/early sixth centuries BC) is unknown, but a monumental processional avenue may be presumed. The later temple was situated *circa* 1400 m to the east from the supposed pylons (monumental gateways) of the Amen temple and its main east–west axis was perpendicular to that of the Amen temple. In its preserved form, Temple 250 reflects a late first century BC rebuilding, which, apart from the addition of an outer colonnade, reconstructed the original double-podium structure (i.e. a *cella* on a raised podium within a court with pylons, constructed on a pyloned podium surrounded by a colonnade and approached by a ramp). The carving of the original reliefs was influenced by the war reliefs of King Piye's (*circa* 747–716 BC) Amen temple at Napata.

The island with the temple-palace compound was apparently separated by (temporary?) channels from two settlement areas (North and South Mounds). Under the North Mound excavations of the Khartoum–Calgary expedition revealed traces of a village with mudbrick houses and huts. The early levels were overlaid with a heavy layer of water-borne clay, silt and river cobbles, indicative of an extraordinarily high Nile and probably the great flood reported in year 6 of Taharka's reign.

Isolated finds of artifacts at Meroe indicate an urban character and the existence of workshops of mass-produced craft goods. Royal building activity is evidenced by fragments of high-quality statues and reliefs. The production of a distinctive wheel-turned polychrome pottery, unique in the Nile Valley, is dated to around the early fourth century BC by the context of one of these vessels associated with a fragment of an imported Attic Red Figure vase (from Greece). Probably in connection with the emergence of a

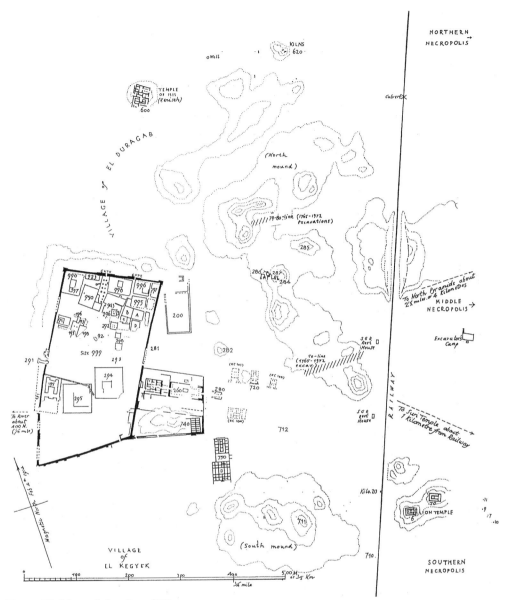

Figure 73 Map of the city of Meroe

new dynasty in the Meroe region, large-scale building activity began there in the third century BC. The island of the early Amen temple was enclosed by a 5 m thick masonry wall. The enclosure, measuring *circa* 400 × 200 m, may have stabilized the soil of the alluvial island, but it was more likely intended to separate the

temple-palace compound in a monumental manner. Its irregular shape was probably determined by the course of the Nile channels, and the position of its gates was determined by the locations of the temple and palace.

By the second half of the third century BC the early Amen temple was, however, abandoned and a new monumental Amen sanctuary adjoining the central portion of the eastern enclosure wall was begun (Temple 260). Its original pylons faced a (temporary?) channel. In the southwest sector of the Royal Enclosure a water sanctuary (Temple 195) was erected. Its basin was filled with water coming directly from the river (or from a channel) during the period of inundation. Such a "sacred lake," symbolic of the Nile, and the associated sculpture, were directly influenced by Alexandrian art and architecture, and the water sanctuary displays the impact of cult beliefs in Egypt in the Late and early Ptolemaic periods, adapting elements of dynastic and ancestor cults of the Ptolemies. This sanctuary stood in its own *temenos* (sacred precinct) and a contemporary royal palace appears to have occupied the area of the abandoned early Amen temple (Building 294). From the second half of the second century BC a processional avenue connected the northern entrance of the water sanctuary with a temple (600, of Isis?) built *circa* 300 m to the north from the northwest gate of the Royal Enclosure. The monumental character of this avenue is indicated by traces of a palm alley discovered south of the gate.

The northern part of the Royal Enclosure was occupied by large houses, which were probably inhabited by the higher status priests of the Amen temple, built along narrow streets with the same orientation as the processional avenue. The houses were probably constructed with two stories and their design was derivative of a known type of Hellenistic house found in urban communities. The ground floor consisted of an entrance corridor leading into the southeast corner of a central courtyard and a single or double room. One of these houses at Meroe (990) shows the influence of a type of Hellenistic palace, such as is found at the city of Ptolemais in Cyrenaica (northern Libya), dating to the second century BC (the "Palazzo delle Colonne"). This suggests direct contact between Meroe and Ptolemaic Alexandria, as this type of house plan was unknown farther south in Egypt.

During the first century BC changes began to occur in Meroe's environment. The gradual silting-up of the channel which supplied water to the basin of the water sanctuary at the time of the New Year, and which probably also supplied ground water during the rest of the year, caused the abandonment of the original aqueduct and the rebuilding of the sanctuary. The late water sanctuary was provided with smaller quantities of water by a mechanical lift device. Remains of the sculpture decorating this new sanctuary indicate an increased importance of native religious concepts and the prominence of the native lion god, Apedemak. The silting up of the channels also made possible an eastern extension of the late Amen temple.

By the first century AD the center of the town was no longer on an island, and it joined the North and South Mounds and the mainland. In front of the new pylons of the Amen temple, chapels and small sanctuaries of different types (such as a "double sanctuary," perhaps influenced by the temple of Kom Ombo in Upper Egypt) were erected along a processional avenue. Thus the city was provided with a monumental east–west axis. In contrast, with the final abandonment of the water sanctuary in the first century AD, the northwest axis was abandoned within the Royal Enclosure and in subsequent centuries the enclosure wall was pulled down and built over in several places. The center of the city shifted entirely to areas outside of the Royal Enclosure. A temple-palace complex was created by the rebuilt double-podium Temple 250 and a monumental residential building within its *temenos*. The rebuilt sanctuary was decorated with monumental reliefs of war scenes faithfully imitating in both iconography and style the original reliefs of the Aspelta building.

Remains of architecture and sculpture dating to the second–first centuries BC indicate the existence of royal workshops. Local traditions and fine ceramics, manufactured in various parts of the Mediterranean and imported from Alexandria, influenced the production of fine pottery. Large kilns provided the entire kingdom with painted wares, which in the late first century BC received a decisive impetus from the discovery of the source of an unusually fine marl clay. The presence of Egyptian vase painters is also attested at Meroe. Fine painted and relief-decorated pottery continued to be traded from Meroe to Lower Nubia as well as to the southern regions of the kingdom in the first to third centuries AD. By the second century AD the town was centered around the late Amen temple, with its processional avenue, the new royal palace (750) and a magazine complex (740). This evidence is also indicative of the continuity of a homogeneous royal/temple redistributive economy. During the second and early third centuries(?) several priestly houses were rebuilt in the northern sector of the Royal Enclosure, but some time in the late third or early fourth century large areas of the Royal Enclosure were destroyed and the ruins were leveled. Poor mudbrick houses were built around the few surviving monumental structures, such as Chapel 98, where the head of a monumental bronze statue of Augustus, which had been taken from Qasr Ibrim in Lower Nubia during the Roman-Meroitic war in the late first century BC, was found buried under the threshold. Garstang recorded clusters of small rooms arranged around open courtyards, which gave the impression of simple, rural architecture. However, the Khartoum–Calgary expedition also found more substantial buildings of the late period outside the Royal Enclosure, indicating a shift of the city center and not a general decline.

The city was briefly occupied around AD 350 by Aksumite invaders (from northern Ethiopia) who left triumphal inscriptions in Greek. Although the Meroitic kingdom survived this invasion for some time, the site seems to have been completely abandoned by the fifth century AD.

See also

Gebel Barkal; Kom Ombo; Kushites; Late and Ptolemaic periods, overview; Meroe, the "Sun Temple"; Meroitic culture; Reisner, George Andrew; Roman period, overview

Further reading

Bradley, R.J. 1982. Varia from the city of Meroe. *Meroitica* 6: 163–70.

——. 1984. Meroitic chronology. *Meroitica* 7: 195–211.

Dunham, D. 1957. *Royal Cemeteries of Kush* 4: *Royal Tombs at Meroe and Barkal*. Boston.

——. 1963. *Royal Cemeteries of Kush* 5: *The West and South Cemeteries at Meroe*. Boston.

Garstang, J. 1911–16. Interim reports. *LAAA* 3: 57–70; 4: 45–71; 5: 73–83; 6: 1–21; 7: 1–24.

Garstang, J., A.H. Sayce and F.L. Griffith. 1911. *Meroë: The City of the Ethiopians*. Oxford.

Shinnie, L.P., and R.J. Bradley. 1980. The capital of Kush I: Meroe excavations 1965–1972. *Meroitica* 4: 1–317.

——. 1981. The murals from the Augustus Temple, Meroe. In *Studies in Ancient Egypt, the Aegean, and the Sudan: Essays in Honor of Dows Dunham*, 167–72. Boston.

Török, L. 1997. *Meroe City, An Ancient African Capital. John Garstang's Excavations in the Sudan*. London.

LÁSZLÓ TÖRÖK

Meroe, the "Sun Temple"

Located on a plain on the east bank of the Nile *circa* 1 km east-southeast of the ancient town of Meroe (16°56′ N, 33°43′ E), the "Sun Temple" is a very ruined complex. Its location, its unique architectural design, the style and subject of its reliefs and the historical events which might have been the reasons for its construction all testify to the importance of this temple in Meroitic times.

The visible structural remains of the temple were first recorded in 1844 by the Prussian Expedition, led by Richard Lepsius. In 1910–11 the site was cleared of rubble by an expedition from the Institute of Archaeology, University of Liverpool, under the direction of John Garstang. The excavator proposed the hypothetical identification of the temple as the "Table of the Sun" mentioned by Herodotus (III, 17–18),

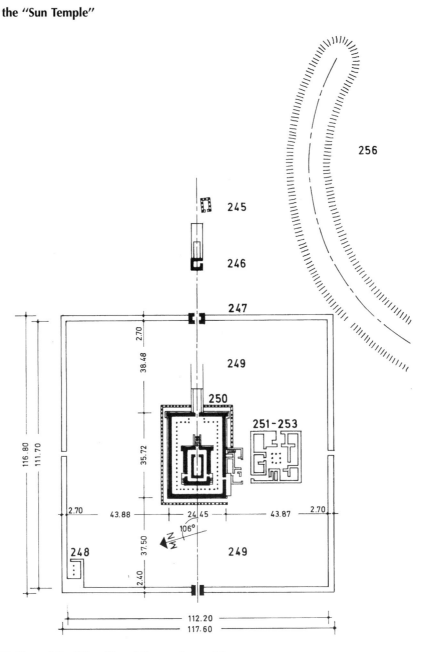

Figure 74 Plan of the "Sun Temple" complex at Meroe

thereby establishing its subsequent name, the "Sun Temple." During these excavations fragments of a stela inscribed in Egyptian hieroglyphs were found in the temple precinct (*temenos*). Part of the name of King Aspelta (593–568 BC) was recognized in the inscription, but it was wrongly taken as evidence for dating the temple.

The site has most recently been examined in 1984 and 1985 by the Central Institute of Ancient History and Archaeology of the Academy of Sciences (Berlin). In 1986 and 1987 conservation work on the very endangered temple structure was begun by the Sudan Directorate General of Antiquities and National Museums.

The temple (Meroe 250) stood in a nearly square *temenos* (Meroe 249) surrounded by a mudbrick wall (Meroe 247), 2.7 m thick, which was faced with fired bricks and a coat of lime plaster. Two of the four entrances, the east and west gates, were constructed in stone masonry. From the east gate, the main entrance, a paved causeway (*dromos*) led to the temple proper. The temple was built in the style of Meroitic one-room temples, with a pylon, fifty cubits wide, in front. Reliefs on the lowest register of the south (exterior) wall depict battle scenes with enemies being slaughtered. On the northern wall reliefs show the triumphal return of soldiers, accompanied by captured men, women and children. These scenes are repeated on many of the 700 relief blocks found scattered at the site, which may have come from the upper faces of the temple's walls.

Most of the temple was surrounded by a type of colonnade (*peridromos*) with an estimated seventy-two columns decorated with open papyrus capitals. An important scene on the west wall includes a southern elevation of the temple showing the colonnade. Archaeological evidence dates the colonnade (and thus the reliefs) to Ptolemaic or Roman times. Iconographic details also demonstrate that the reliefs date to the end of the first century BC/beginning of the first century AD.

From the *dromos* the temple was entered by a ramp through the pylon gateway. An inner court (*hypaethral*), raised 2 m above the ground, was surrounded by fifty-one columns (*peristyle*) with open papyrus capitals. Within this court was a temple with an elevated interior containing a rectangular sanctuary surrounded by a narrow ambulatory. Small stairs provided access from the court to the rear of the inner temple and its ambulatory.

Rooms of a priests' house (?) were also added to the south wall of the outer temple. The function of this house was ultimately transferred to a separate square building (Meroe 251–253), planned on a grand scale and influenced by Roman architecture. Around its Corinthian-style atrium, with an eight-column *peristyle*, were small apartments (*alae*), divided into three separate units of two rooms each and a larger single room. Access to the building was through two entrances, and two staircases led to the roof.

The fragments of the granite stela inscribed in Egyptian hieroglyphics were collected in 1910 from the western part of the *temenos*. More fragments were found in 1984–5. As read by Garstang and A.H. Sayce, the inscription was associated with King Aspelta, whose name is now indicated on several of the 240 fragments. The stela may have been associated with a chapel or small temple in the area where the stela fragments were originally collected, where foundation stones have been found. In constructing the later temple, the chapel may have been dismantled to build the new structure.

In front of the main gate, astride the central temple axis, are the remains of the high altar and its accompanying ramp (Meroe 246). Farther to the east, and south of the temple axis, are the remains of a baldachin (Meroe 245) with nine engaged columns. This was closed on three sides by screen walls, with the fourth side open to the west. Architectural elements of the baldachin exhibit Ptolemaic influence. Part of a column drum was found with sculptured heads of rams, sacred to Amen, the state god of the Meroites. Both the high altar and the baldachin are depicted in the scene on the west wall of the outer temple, thereby providing evidence for the late period in which the whole temple complex was built and decorated.

One of the largest known reservoirs (*hafir*, Meroe 256) is located south of the temple complex at the southeastern corner of the *temenos* wall. Farther south and adjacent to the reservoir, are remains of a heavily damaged square building, approximately 27 m square (Meroe 255). Although similar to Meroitic palaces, its function is not known. It may have been connected with the economic and administrative functions of the temple complex.

All of the temple inscriptions, except those of the Aspelta stela, refer to rulers living at the end of the first century BC/beginning of the first century AD. These include the cartouches of Akinidad, the crown prince and governor in the north, Queen Amanishakheto, and King Natakamani, her son-in-law (on a reused block). Akinidad and his mother Amanirenas are connected with the Meroites' raid on Philae, Syene and Elephantine in 24 BC. At that time the Roman garrison in southern Egypt was reduced because of the engagement of Aelius Gallus in Arabia, and the Meroites hoped to take advantage of the situation. After a counterattack by Petronius, which ended with the destruction of Napata, the Meroites had to send a delegation to Samos to meet the emperor Augustus. The outcome of the negotiations was unexpectedly favorable for Meroe. Even the tribute that was first demanded was rescinded by Augustus under the condition that the Meroites would remain peaceful. From this outcome, the Meroites probably felt that they had become partners of the Romans; this may have been the reason for Amanirenas and Akinidad to give thanks to Amen by erecting this temple. Some years later the complex was finished by Amanishakheto, who built the *temenos* wall.

See also

Gebel Barkal; Kushites; Meroe, city; Meroitic culture; Roman period, overview

Further reading

Garstang, J. 1912–13. Third interim report on the excavations at Meroë in Ethiopia. *LAAA* 5: 73–83.

Garstang, J., et al. 1911. *Meroë, the City of the Ethiopians*. Oxford.

Hinkel, F.W. 1985. Untersuchungen zur Bausubstanz, Architektur und Funktion des Gebäudes Meroe 245. *Alt-orientalische Forschungen* 12: 216–32.

Hinkel, F.W., and M. Hinkel. 1990. Das

Priesterhaus Meroe 251. *Alt-orientalische Forschungen* 17: 18–26.

Török, L. 1997. *Meroe City, An Ancient African Capital. John Garstang's Excavations in the Sudan*. London

Wenig, S. 1975. Propyläen Kunstgeschichte. In *Die Kunst im Reich von Kusch zur Zeit der 25. Dynastie und der Herrscher von Napata*, 400–12. Berlin.

F.W. HINKEL

Meroitic culture

Evidence of Meroitic culture, from the ancient kingdom of Kush, is found in the middle Nile region, from the southern frontier of pharaonic Egypt at the First Cataract (Aswan) to the Khartoum area, and dates from the mid-third century BC, when the royal cemetery shifted from the region of Napata farther south to the city of Meroe, to the end of the kingdom, *circa* AD 350. Meroe was the name of the kingdom in classical literature.

A continuity of traditions of the earlier Napatan period, when the capital of the kingdom of Kush was farther north at Napata, is seen in Meroitic culture and there was an intermittent but intense Egyptian influence. In the initial phase, a re-emphasis of the cults of ancient Kushite deities and their connection with the ideology of kingship is seen. This renaissance of the third century BC coincided with, and was probably partly brought about by, economic and intellectual contacts with early Ptolemaic Egypt, established in *circa* 274 BC after the end of a conflict between the two powers. It may have been a consequence of the conflict with Egypt that in the first half of the third century BC a new dynasty, originating at Meroe, came to the throne. The new dynasty shifted the royal cemetery to Meroe, but this did not mean a shift of the center of power in a multi-centered kingdom. The ensuing development of the settlements in the Butana and the growth of agricultural production and cattle-breeding was part of a general process extending over the entire kingdom. Such activities were supported by large water reservoirs, some measuring *circa* 250 m in diameter, which are probably evidence of state organized labor as well as of the control of the semi-nomadic transhumants.

The expansion of cultivated land and territorial power, the rapid development of specialized industries in urban settlements, and, by the turn of the second and first centuries BC, the emergence of a dense chain of prosperous villages in Lower Nubia inhabited by settlers from the south, was promoted by contacts with Egypt. The main items traded or sent in gift exchange to Egypt were war elephants, Nubian gold, ivory and exotic African wares. In exchange, Meroe received luxury wares and craftsmen, and information from Hellenistic Alexandria and Upper Egyptian temples such as Philae. During the third–second centuries BC a standardized material culture emerged as a result of the presence of a powerful central government, productive royal workshops and a well functioning redistributive system. The principal ethnic groups were Meroitic speakers living in the Butana and Nubian speakers who originally occupied the Napata/Dongola region. Although it may be presumed that there were a number of different ethnic groups that inhabited distinct regional units, cultural differences can be observed only in burial customs. However, these differences may only indicate social differentiation and different levels of initial Egyptianization.

Economic prosperity culminated around the late third/early second centuries BC. After the Upper Egyptian revolt against the Ptolemies (207/6–186 BC), which was supported by Meroe, Meroitic Lower Nubia emerged as a good market for craft goods traded from Upper Egypt and became a region where Egyptian religion and material culture were transmitted among the middle and lower social strata. Another culmination of prosperity and intense contact with Egypt occurred after the Roman occupation of Egypt, following an armed conflict between Meroe and Roman Egypt in 29–21/20 BC.

The Meroitic king, whose power was based on the ideology of the divine son, which was closely related to the New Kingdom Egyptian myth of the state, governed his land through a clericalized territorial administration. The intricacy of civil administration of the territorial units, settlements and temples of the vast kingdom, the management of the interconnected royal and temple economy, and trade and redistribution, brought about and then was promoted by the development of a Meroitic script, with a cursive form as well as a hieroglyphic one. Consisting of twenty-three symbols, the cursive alphabet was a reduction of the Egyptian demotic script system to a simple writing with vowel notations and was used for non-royal and then also for royal funerary texts, administrative purposes, private temple inscriptions and, increasingly in the late Meroitic period, for monumental royal inscriptions. The hieroglyphic script, with signs equivalent to the cursive signs, was used only for royal and temple inscriptions.

The structure of the government, the economy and social stratification are all reflected in settlement patterns. In the southern, central part of the kingdom were the ancient centers of an ambulatory kingship. The temple towns of Meroe, Sanam, Napata and Kawa were built around temple-palace complexes.

In urban settlements monumental architecture along processional avenues (for example, at Meroe and Kawa) and planned streets (at Meroe) have been excavated. While the smaller settlements of the south are unknown, there is more information about the Lower Nubian settlement pattern, as a result of the archaeological surveys connected to the building of the High Dam at Aswan. Provincial centers, such as Faras and Qasr Ibrim, were fortified temple towns. Smaller agricultural villages were built around temple-magazine compounds, such as at Meinarti. In early Meroitic villages nuclear families lived in terraced houses consisting of uniformly arranged two- or three-room units (Gezira Dabarosa, Gaminarti). In late Meroitic times (second–fourth centuries AD) villages of solidly built, two-story mudbrick houses, with barrel-vaulted rooms on the ground floor, have been found.

Multi-chambered temples erected in the major centers, such as the temples of Amen and Isis at Meroe, and the Amen temples at Naga and Amara, closely followed the standard plan of a Ptolemaic cult temple in Egypt. This consisted of pylon gateways, columned court, hypostyle hall, *pronaos* and *naos*, where the sacred bark of the god Amen rested. At Meroe the architecture of the Amen temple *naos* also reflects the traditions of the earlier Napatan period. One-room temples, consisting of a pyloned *cella* within enclosure walls, were erected to the cults of the native deities Apedemak, Arensnuphis and Sebiumeker.

Monumental statues, with squat proportions and massive limbs, attest to the preservation of the style of Napatan monumental art, and the influence of archaizing traits in sculpture in Egypt in the Late period. Contemporaneous Egyptian influence is also prevalent. A synthesis of the tradition of Napatan archaizing with the classicizing tendency of early Ptolemaic sculpture is apparent in the extraordinary late third century BC gilded bronze statue of a Meroitic king from Tabo in Upper Nubia. The same style characterizes the architectural statues of the desert palace at Musawwarat es-Sufra, where, however, non-Egyptian iconographic themes predominated, such as parapet walls ending in carved elephants and elephant column bases. A more direct Hellenistic Egyptian influence is seen in statues of the late second and first centuries BC from the water sanctuary at Meroe, of reclining draped figures, harpists, flute players and philosophers. These belonged to an iconographic program connected to royal ancestor worship and the inundation of the Nile.

Reliefs carved in the soft Nubian sandstone decorated exterior and interior walls of the temples and the royal funerary cult chapels. On the exteriors the reliefs are sunk, while the interior ones are raised. Iconographic and stylistic continuity is indicated by the reliefs of the Apedemak temples at Musawwarat es-Sufra (late third century BC) and Naga (first century AD). Stylistic traits of the Napatan period, derived from Late period Egypt where Old and Middle Kingdom canons and forms were revived, were synthesized with trends arriving from contemporaneous Egypt. But Egyptian themes and forms were adapted and transformed: Meroitic concepts were articulated in Egyptian style, and vice versa. Direct imitation of Egyptian models occurred only exceptionally, such as the first century AD kiosk in front of the Apedemak temple at Naga, which, with its purely Roman-Egyptian structure and details, indicates the importation from Egypt of a plan as well as the presence of Upper Egyptian stonemasons.

In the archaeologically largely unexplored Butana region, the ruins of stone and fired brick temples and palace complexes (at Musawwarat es-Sufra, Naga and Wad ban Naga) indicate the survival of architectural types of the earlier Napatan period as well as the emergence of new types (such as one-room temples and temples or audience halls erected on podia). The presence of Egyptian craftsmen and the influence of both Hellenistic and traditional Egyptian architecture of the Ptolemaic period are also attested.

The rulers were buried in a cemetery at Meroe in the subterranean chambers of pyramid tombs with funerary chapels decorated with reliefs in Egyptianizing style. These reliefs reflect an iconographic development that began in Napatan times under the decisive influence of pharaonic religion and mortuary customs, and was then shaped by Kushite concepts and cult traditions of the temple of Isis at Philae. Mummification of the bodies in royal burials attests to the maintenance of Egyptianized burial customs, yet the abandonment in burials of servant figures (*shawabti*s) and canopic jars (containers for the viscera) shows a re-emphasis of Kushite customs, which are, however, more conspicuous in lower status burials.

The excavated burials of higher status officials and priests in Upper Nubia (Amir Abdalla, third century BC to first/second centuries AD; Sedeinga, third century BC to fourth century AD) and in Lower Nubia (Faras, late second century BC to fourth century AD; Karanog, first century BC to third century AD; Arminna, Qasr Ibrim, Nag Gamus and so on, second to fourth centuries AD) had mudbrick pyramid superstructures complemented with an offering niche, which replaced the earlier royal funerary cult chapel. Beginning in the first century BC, stelae and offering tables inscribed in Meroitic cursive script, and statues of the deceased as an anthropomorphized bird ("*ba*-bird"), were associated with the niches. Burials of commoners and also of Meroitic as well as non-Meroitic groups living at the periphery of the Butana region were covered with earth mounds. In general, the dead were buried with personal ornaments, and royal and aristocratic burials also contained many luxury vessels, mostly of Egyptian origin. In all grave types, vessels connected to water libation are common.

Wheel-made pottery wares, surpassing contemporaneous Egyptian ones in technical quality, and vessel types known from the earlier Napatan period, were produced at Meroe in the third century BC. The large output of the central workshops and the system of redistribution explain the typological and stylistic homogeneity of the pottery assemblage throughout the kingdom. In the first half of the second century BC, the workshops at Meroe began to adopt vessel types and painted decoration patterns of Upper Egyptian (Theban) workshops, which, in turn, were directly influenced by Alexandrian Hellenistic pottery styles. Vessels decorated with simple floral friezes were produced at Meroe in the second half of the second century BC. By the middle of the first century BC, pottery painting reached a high artistic level, and workshop styles and individual painters can be distinguished. Designs of rich floral motifs and religious symbols, and figural motifs, including humans, animals, divine images, caricatures, illustrations of now lost tales and Dionysian scenes, were executed in two colors. The iconographic connections with monumental art are conspicuous.

With the discovery of an extraordinarily fine marl clay in the late first century BC, the Meroe workshops developed a fine, thin-walled "egg-shell" ware. This pottery was inspired by imports: wares of the Augustan period ("Eastern Sigillata"), fine Roman wares and fine Egyptian wares (especially from Memphis) and faïence. A native tradition from pre-Napatan times was also continued in the Butana region with the production of handmade vessels with burnished red or black slip and incised decoration of human figures, ostriches, trees and geometric friezes. The high quality and standard execution of this ware indicate production in central workshops.

While the importance of iron working at Meroe was overestimated by earlier scholars, other industries achieved extraordinary standards by the first century BC. Jewelry from this period discovered in the pyramid of Queen Amanishakheto consists of gold bezel rings decorated with scenes from the cycle of the royal birth legend. Gold working techniques of engraving, embossing, granulation and cloisonné were all employed. The florescence of the royal faïence workshops can be dated to the mid-first century AD, when the walls of temples and palaces were decorated with reliefs of faïence inlays.

The reasons for the economic decline of the kingdom in the third–fourth centuries AD are unknown, but were presumably determined by the decline of the Roman empire and its trade, the growing aggression of nomadic tribes in the area of the Egyptian frontier (the Blemmyes) and along the southern periphery (the Noba), and attacks by the emerging power of Aksum (in northern Ethiopia). Meroe's decline was also aggravated by the social and cultural imbalance caused by the settlement in Meroitic territory of superficially acculturated groups of Noba. The last Meroitic ruler was buried in the royal cemetery at Meroe in *circa* AD 360.

The post-Meroitic rulers were probably of non-Meroitic descent and did not continue to be buried in pyramid graves in the royal cemetery at Meroe. They nevertheless claimed legal continuity by adopting Meroitic symbols of power without, however, maintaining Meroitic administration and institutionalized cults. Territorial unity was preserved until the first third of the fifth century AD, when the former Meroitic kingdom was split up into two kingdoms. By the sixth century there already were three independent kingdoms between the First Cataract (Aswan) and the Butana region.

See also

Alexandria; Gebel Barkal; Kushites; Late and Ptolemaic periods, overview; Meroe, cemeteries; Meroe, city; Meroe, the "Sun Temple"; metallurgy; Philae; Qasr Ibrim; Roman period, overview

Further reading

Adams, W.Y. 1977. *Nubia Corridor to Africa*. London.

Eide, T., T. Hägg, R.H. Pierce and L. Török, eds. 1994, 1996, 1998. *Fontes Historiae Nubiorum* 1, 2, 3. Bergen.

Hochfield, S., and E. Riefstahl, eds. 1978. *Africa in Antiquity: The Arts of Ancient Nubia and the Sudan* 1: *The Essays*. Brooklyn, NY.

Hofmann, I. 1978. *Beiträge zur meroitischen Chronologie*. Bonn.

Shinnie, P.L. 1967. *Meroe, A Civilization of the Sudan*. London.

Török, L. 1988. Geschichte Meroes. Ein Beitrag uber die Quellenlage und den Forschungsstand. In *Aufstieg und Niedergang der Römischen Welt* 2, W. Haase, ed., 107–341. Berlin.

——. 1989. Kush and the external world. *Meroitica* 10: 49–215, 365–79.

——. 1995. *The Birth of an Ancient African Kingdom: Kush and Her Myth of the State in the First Millennium B.C.* Lille.

——. 1997. *The Kingdom of Kush. Handbook of the Napatan–Meroitic Civilization*. Leiden, New York and Cologne.

Trigger, B.G. 1965. *History and Settlement in Lower Nubia*. New Haven, CT.

Wenig, S. 1978. *Africa in Antiquity: The Arts of Ancient Nubia and the Sudan* 2: *The Catalogue*. Brooklyn, NY.

LÁSZLÓ TÖRÖK

metallurgy

Egyptian metalworkers do not seem to have placed a great deal of emphasis upon work in copper, bronze or iron, at least not after the Old Kingdom. Gold was the Egyptian metal *par excellence*; much of our evidence for metal technology in ancient Egypt relates to the acquisition of and work in gold. It is no accident that the most famous Egyptian map relating to mining and metallurgy is the Turin Museum papyrus from the mid-twelfth century BC (reign of Ramesses III of the 20th Dynasty), showing the location of gold mining installations at Bir Umm Fawakhir in the Eastern Desert.

Egyptian silver, which seems to have been even more valuable than gold, at least prior to the New Kingdom, is more accurately identified as "aurian silver," i.e. silver derived from silver-rich alluvial gold rather than extracted from silver-bearing galena by a process known as cupellation, the usual source of silver in the ancient world. This is why the earliest Egyptian texts refer to silver as "white gold" (*nbw ḥḏ*). Egyptian "silver" artifacts therefore have a high gold content, a fact demonstrated by metallurgical analyses. These "silver" artifacts also contain a significant amount of copper (as much as 15 percent).

Since alluvial gold (and aurian silver) almost never contain more than 1 percent copper, the copper in Egyptian aurian silver must have been added intentionally, producing what is technically a silver-gold-copper tertiary alloy. The copper was added to harden the naturally soft silver, just as in modern sterling silver (about 7 percent copper). By the middle of the fourth millennium BC, Egyptian metalworkers had already discovered that copper hardens silver (and gold) and had developed the technology of producing intentional alloys.

Copper (*ḥmty*)

The use of copper itself goes back to the Badarian period (*circa* 4,500–3,800 BC). The four copper beads excavated by Guy Brunton at Mostagedda, in grave 596, remain the earliest copper artifacts known from Egypt. The use of copper increases slightly in the following Nagada I phase (*circa* 4,000–3,500 BC), and more perceptibly during the Nagada II period (*circa* 3,500–3,200 BC). A range of copper tools and implements, including axes, adzes, hoes, saws and knives, can most likely be placed in this period.

One of the axes found by Brunton at Matmar (Tomb 3131) was studied metallurgically in 1932. It proved to have been cast, probably in an open mold, then cold-worked and annealed by heating at low temperature to reduce the strain created by hammering. The ax had been more heavily worked at the edge in order to harden the cutting edge of the tool.

Analysis of early materials is of exceptional importance. It demonstrates that the basic metallurgical techniques of casting, annealing and work-hardening were already in use in Egypt by at least the mid-fourth millennium BC. Egyptian work in copper (and eventually bronze) continued to develop during the Early Dynastic period down to the end of the Old Kingdom. In the Middle and New Kingdoms, gold and hard stones tended to replace copper and bronze in importance. In the Late period, especially the 25th and 26th Dynasties, there was once again a great increase in the use of bronze, chiefly for the manufacture of human and animal figurines.

The fourth millennium BC site of Ma'adi on the east bank of the Nile has often been described as a copper production center, but, given the paucity of metallurgical finds, this interpretation is unlikely. The site has produced some evidence for actual metalworking in the form of about 16 kg of copper ore and some copper fragments that seem to derive from melting operations. Analysis of the ore samples suggests a Palestinian source, either Timna or Fenan, both known centers of ancient copper mining that were being exploited as early as the second half of the fourth millennium BC. This is supported by the presence of Palestinian pottery.

One of the pieces of copper from Ma'adi, possibly a fragment of an ax, had 2.7 percent arsenic and 2.5 percent nickel. This demonstrates that arsenical copper, distinctive of the following phases in Egyptian copper technology, was being used already in Nagada II times. This is almost certainly a fortuitous alloy, since the arsenic came into metallic copper from the

ore. From royal tombs of the 1st Dynasty at Abydos (especially the tomb of Djer) and the 2nd Dynasty (especially that of Khasekhemwy) come a number of copper vessels in a variety of forms, including ewers, basins and bowls, some with spouts and loop handles attached by rivets or wire, used in a washing ceremony. Many of these vessels were made of arsenical copper (with isolated examples of bronze) and were formed by raising a flat sheet of copper. Many other copper artifacts from the Old Kingdom were made of unalloyed copper, as demonstrated by the analysis of eleven of the copper artifacts from the tomb of Impy at Giza.

The use of ewers and other spouted metal vessels continued throughout the Old Kingdom. Much larger vessels of copper were also being produced at this time. One, found in a tomb at Abydos opened by Émile Amélineau in 1896–7 and subsequently lost, had a height of about 66 cm and an estimated diameter of 75 cm.

Probably the most famous copper artifacts from the Old Kingdom are the large copper statue of King Pepi I (6th Dynasty) and the much smaller statue of his son Merenre, both excavated by James Quibell at Hierakonpolis, along with the magnificent gold image of the god Horus. The statues were made by hammering plates of copper over a wooden core. They were found in a poor state of preservation and have never received proper care or scholarly attention. Large-scale metal statues from the Middle and New Kingdoms are quite rare, as hard stone had become the desired medium.

The Old Kingdom has also produced some of the most interesting pictorial evidence relating to ancient Egyptian metalworking technology. Several Old Kingdom tombs are decorated with scenes of a group of men crouched around some sort of furnace, each of them blowing into it through a long hollow tube. At first interpreted as glassblowing scenes, they were soon correctly identified as metallurgical scenes, but the exact nature of the procedure being depicted remains controversial. The best preserved examples come from the Saqqara tombs of Mereruka and Ti.

According to the inscriptions, individuals identified as metalworkers are melting copper.

It has been claimed that human breath, blown onto a fire, could not produce the temperatures necessary for smelting copper ore or for melting metallic copper, which required a higher temperature than smelting, but more recent studies have demonstrated that both processes would be possible, at least on a small scale. These scenes must depict the melting of metallic copper in a crucible; there is very little evidence that the Egyptians themselves were ever engaged in extractive copper metallurgy.

At the Nubian fort of Buhen there is actual evidence of an Old Kingdom copper smelting "factory." This consisted of three furnaces and some quantity of malachite ore. Middle Kingdom copper smelting installations are also reported from the Nubian fort of Kuban, a site that had an estimated 200 metric tons of slag.

The "furnaces" depicted in the Old Kingdom tomb scenes consisted either of a single crucible (tomb of Wepemneferet) or of two crucibles placed back to back (tomb of Mereruka). In the latter scene the crucibles are of the type which provided the model for the hieroglyphic sign that Egyptologist Alan Gardiner identified with an ingot of metal, but which must represent a crucible.

This type of crucible is known from actual examples found in the Sinai (Serabit el-Khadim), in Syria (Tell el-Qitar) and in Mesopotamia (Tell ed-Dhiba'i). Such crucibles tend to be associated not with blowpipes, but with the innovation in smelting/melting technology brought about by the introduction of the pot bellows. With a pair of foot-operated pot bellows, it was possible to reach higher temperatures and to maintain a more controlled atmosphere in the furnace through the use of ambient air rather than human breath. Although known at earlier sites in southwest Asia, the pot bellows does not seem to predate the New Kingdom in Egypt. This has suggested to some scholars that it was introduced into Egypt in the Second Intermediate Period by the Hyksos, but there is no firm basis for this belief.

The revolution in smelting/melting technology is clearly depicted. The old technology, with blowpipes and crucibles, is still found in scenes in the Middle Kingdom tombs at Beni Hasan.

The "bellows," which is thought to be depicted at Beni Hasan in the famous scene showing the caravan of nomadic Asiatics, is not the pot bellows and is probably not any sort of bellows. The new technology, with pot bellows, tuyeres and furnace, is known from a number of New Kingdom tomb paintings, especially those in the Theban tombs of Rekhmire (TT 100) and the Two Sculptors (Nebamen and Ipuky, TT 181).

The best collection of metallurgical paraphernalia associated with the pot bellows actually comes from the metal workshop found in Mine L at Serabit el-Khadim in the Sinai. As this site is now recognized as an area of turquoise rather than copper mining, the excavators propose, following a suggestion first made by Flinders Petrie in 1906, that the metal workshop in Mine L and the smaller one in Mine G produced metal tools used there by the turquoise miners. This would also explain the references to copper workers in the Middle Kingdom inscriptions from the Sinai, especially from the reigns of Amenemhat II, III and IV. The metal workshops there, however, must be of New Kingdom date, roughly contemporary with the time of the vizier Rekhmire (Hatshepsut and Tuthmose III). Copper deposits are also known in the Sinai (Wadi Ba'ba, Wadi Kharig, Bir Nasib, Regeita), and it is now even claimed that the Sinai was the major Egyptian source of copper, as well as turquoise, throughout the pharaonic period. There are major differences of opinion concerning this, however, that have yet to be resolved.

Evidence from the Eastern Desert indicates that the copper deposits there were exploited during pharaonic times, especially at Umm Semiuki (Gebel Abu Hamamid), but also at Gebel el-Atawi and Abu Seyal. At Umm Semiuki the ancient copper workings are said to be some 16 m deep, with the oxidized zone, consisting of the carbonate ores malachite and azurite, comprising the first 7 m followed by sulphide deposits at greater depths. In general, mining during pharaonic times consisted of following a surface exposure along the ore vein until the mineralization petered out. Such shaft mining, known also from the galena mines at Gebel Zeit, never exceeded a depth of some

20 m. This is in contrast to the mines from the Graeco-Roman period, where shafts some 200 m deep were not uncommon.

The Egyptians also derived copper from Timna (now in southern Israel) and Fenan (Jordan), the former actually being an Egyptian-controlled mining operation during the thirteenth–twelfth centuries BC. The Papyrus Harris (dating to the end of the reign of Ramesses III) refers to an expedition by boat and by donkey to the land of "Atike" (most likely the Timna area) in quest of copper. Timna has also produced extensive evidence of the smelting of the copper ore mined there, which was more efficient than smelting it elsewhere. A temple to the goddess Hathor was constructed in the mining area at Timna that was similar to (and presumably contemporary with) the Hathor temple on the acropolis of Serabit el-Khadim.

Egypt, at least during the New Kingdom, also obtained copper from Cyprus, known throughout the second millennium BC as the land of "Alashiya." Some of the Amarna Letters, exchanged between the ruler of Alashiya and various fourteenth century BC pharaohs, contain numerous references to royal presents of copper sent from Cyprus to Egypt.

The Egyptian word for copper, generally read as "*ḥmty*" although some scholars still prefer the reading "*bi3*," appears as early as a year name from the 2nd Dynasty inscribed on the Palermo Stone, a 5th Dynasty king list. Various types or grades of copper are mentioned in texts, including "new" copper, "hard" copper and "glittering" copper. From at least the 6th Dynasty (Coptos Decree), texts refer to the use of "Asiatic" copper. It has been proposed that Asiatic copper was the Egyptian designation for copper from Cyprus, shipped in the form of oxhide ingots. This is most unlikely, as references to such copper in Egyptian texts predate the earliest known oxhide ingot by about a thousand years. Oxhide ingots are shown in the Rekhmire tomb paintings being carried by men from "Keftiu," the Egyptian name for (Minoan) Crete. However, other tomb paintings show such ingots being carried by men from Palestine or Syria.

Other scholars have argued that Asiatic copper was an Egyptian designwation for bronze. This is also most unlikely. Although there is sporadic evidence for the use of bronze (an alloy of copper and tin, normally having 5–10 percent tin) going back to the time of the 2nd Dynasty, as shown by the analysis of some of the ewers from the tomb of King Khasekhemwy, the use of bronze in Egypt really begins only in the New Kingdom. A group of Middle Kingdom artifacts from the University Museum, University of Pennsylvania, were analyzed and proved to be made of arsenical copper, whereas those of New Kingdom date were of bronze.

Bronze (*ḥsmn*)

Egyptian texts use the word *ḥsmn*, usually translated as "bronze," but only during the New Kingdom, after which virtually all copper-based artifacts were of bronze so that the distinction between copper (*ḥmty*) and bronze (*ḥsmn*) was no longer of any interest.

Egyptian texts also refer to *dḥty* (tin), and one late Ramesside letter even mentions adding tin to copper, in order to make a knife and two lamp-pots (?) of bronze. Papyrus Anastasi IV refers to ingots of copper and bars of tin being carried on the necks of the inhabitants of Alashiya. Why tin is here associated with Cyprus, a land that has no local tin deposits, has long been a problem, but the form of the two raw materials designated in the text is exactly that depicted in the metalworking scene from the tomb of the Two Sculptors (reign of Amenhotep III). Ingots of copper and tin were in wide circulation across the Mediterranean during the Late Bronze Age, as clearly demonstrated by the Uluburun shipwreck, excavated off the southern coast of Turkey.

Extensive deposits of alluvial tin (or cassiterite) are known from the Eastern Desert, in contexts often associated with Old Kingdom inscriptions, but there seems to be no evidence attesting to their use in pharaonic times. Sources of tin for pharaonic Egypt still constitute a great enigma.

Iron (*bi3*)

The ancient Egyptians do not seem to have made much use of iron. The earliest Egyptian iron objects are the nine beads found by Gerald Wainwright in two Badarian graves at Gerza in 1911. Analysis by Desch, the leading archaeometallurgist in the 1920s–1930s, revealed that one of these beads had 92.5 percent iron and 7.5 percent nickel, thus establishing beyond reasonable doubt that they were made of meteoritic iron (about 5.0 percent nickel). It is generally assumed that all early iron artifacts from Egypt and elsewhere were made of meteoritic iron. This is not necessarily correct; smelted iron was sometimes inadvertently produced in the course of copper smelting operations. This seems to have been the source of iron used in making the iron artifacts from the New Kingdom Hathor temple at Timna, as none of the eleven analyzed artifacts contained any nickel.

The distinction between terrestrial or smelted iron and meteoritic iron was possibly of interest to Egyptian scribes, so that, when the former became more readily available during the New Kingdom, the latter was further qualified as "iron from heaven" (*bi3 n pt*). The implement (*nttrty*) used in the "Opening of the Mouth" ceremony on mummies seems to have always been made of meteoritic iron. Many examples are known, including a complete set from the tomb of Tutankhamen, but none has been analyzed. The famous iron dagger from Tutankhamen's tomb is also said to have a blade of meteoritic iron, but this cannot be determined on the basis of the existing evidence. This dagger was clearly made to be a companion piece to the one with a blade of gold, a clear demonstration of the value of iron in New Kingdom Egypt.

On the basis of the surviving artifactual evidence it has been argued that Egypt entered the Iron Age (from the technological point of view) about 700 BC. The full technology necessary for turning wrought iron into quenched and tempered steel is not attested in Egypt until then. The best evidence comes from the analytical work carried out on a remarkable collection of twenty-three iron artifacts excavated about a century ago by Petrie at Thebes (and now in the Manchester Museum), which are attributed to the seventh century BC.

Iron working in ancient Egypt has been most closely associated with Meroitic civilization in Upper Nubia, following the discovery of massive slag heaps at the site of Meroe during the initial excavations in 1904–14. Iron working at Meroe seems to date from *circa* 600 BC to the first century AD. A series of five iron-smelting furnaces were excavated in the renewed fieldwork at Meroe (1969–75). Although a controversial issue, it still seems reasonable to assume that knowledge of iron working came to Meroe from Egypt.

See also

Abydos, Umm el-Qa'ab; Amarna Letters; el-Badari district Predynastic sites; Beni Hasan; Cypriot peoples; Gebel Zeit; Hierakonpolis; Hyksos; Ma'adi and the Wadi Digla; Meroe, city; natural resources; Nubian forts; Serabit el-Khadim; Tutankhamen, tomb of

Further reading

Beit-Arieh, I. 1985. Serabit et-Khaddim: new metallurgical and chronological aspects. *Levant* 17: 89–116.

Davey, C.J. 1985. Crucibles in the Petrie Collection and hieroglyphic ideograms for metal. *JEA* 71: 142–8.

Farag, M.M. 1981. Metallurgy in ancient Egypt. Some aspect of technique and materials. *Bulletin of the Metals Museum* (Sendai, Japan) 6: 15–30.

Garenne-Marot, L. 1985. Le travail du cuivre dans l'Égypte pharaonique d'après les peintures et les bas-reliefs. *Paléorient* 11: 85–100.

Leahy, A. 1988. Egypt as a bronzeworking centre (1000–539 B.C.). In *Bronzeworking Centres of Western Asia c. 1000–539 B.C.*, J. Curtis, ed., 297–309. London.

Maddin, R., T. Stech, J.D. Muhly and E. Brovarski. 1984. Old Kingdom models from the Tomb of Impy: metallurgical studies. *JEA* 70: 33–41.

Shaw, I. 1994. Pharaonic quarrying and mining: settlement and procurement in Egypt's marginal regions. *Antiquity* 68: 108–19.

Shinnie. P.L. 1985. Iron working at Meroe. In *African Iron Working—Ancient and Traditional*, R. Haaland and P. Shinnie, eds. 28–35. Oslo.

Weinstein, J. 1974. A Fifth Dynasty reference to annealing. *JARCE* 11: 23–5.

Williams, A.R., and K.R. Maxwell-Hyslop. 1976. Ancient steel from Egypt. *Journal of Archaeological Science* 3: 283–305.

JAMES MUHLY

Meydum

Meydum is the name of a modern village 75 km south of Cairo on the west bank of the Nile where the valley is closest to the Fayum (29°24' N, 31°09' E). The Arabic name of the village is taken from the Greek name "Moithymis," which reproduced the ancient Egyptian name "Mery-Item" (Beloved of Atum), the name of this town as early as the 18th Dynasty. From the 5th Dynasty until the 12th Dynasty the town was called "Djed Seneferu" (Seneferu is steadfast), originally the name of the residential quarter of the priests and staff of Seneferu's pyramid.

The necropolis, in which the earliest of Seneferu's four pyramids was built, lies 3 km west of the village of Meydum. The pyramid resembles a square tower with its base engulfed in sand. Among early explorers who visited it were F.L. Norden (1737), J.S. Perring (1839) and Richard Lepsius (1843), who assigned number LXV to the pyramid. The entrance to the pyramid was found in 1890 by Gaston Maspero when he was Director of the Egyptian Antiquities Service. A year later, Flinders Petrie carried out a clearance of the interior, surveyed the building and undertook considerable excavations in its vicinity. Further explorations were conducted in 1909–10 by Petrie, G.A. Wainwright and Mackay; in 1911–12 by Wainwright; in 1926 by Ludwig Borchardt; and in 1929–30 by Alan Rowe. In 1983 the Egyptian Antiquities Organization under Ali El Khouli removed the sand and debris from the northwest corner of the pyramid.

Seneferu, the first king of the 4th Dynasty, enlarged his pyramid at Meydum twice, and on the second occasion he also altered its shape. In its first form, it had seven steps. In the second form, the steps were increased to eight, and finally it was transformed into a true pyramid. A theory that the nucleus might enshrine an even earlier superstructure was disproved when a tunnel bored by Wainwright from the base of the east face revealed only compact masonry at the center.

The change from a stepped to a true pyramid is unlikely to have occurred if a change had not also taken place in beliefs about the king's afterlife and how to achieve it. This also coincided with the change in the location of the mortuary temple from the north side of the pyramid, where it faced the circumpolar stars, to the east, where it faced the rising sun.

The present form of the pyramid is chiefly a result of the method employed in bonding the eight-stepped pyramid with the pyramid of seven steps. As the former rose to the level of each successive step of the latter, courses of blocks were laid across the two steps to bond them together, but the bonding was not very strong and, in later times, the removal of large parts of the two outermost coverings must have presented few difficulties. A theory that the monument disintegrated because the foundation blocks of the backing stones and the outer casing of the true pyramid were laid in places on sand was disproved when the northwest corner of the pyramid was cleared of sand and debris and no trace of movement was found.

The stones in the two stepped forms of the pyramid and those in the true pyramid were laid in different ways: in the stepped forms the courses inclined inward, but in the true pyramid they were flat. The change of method demonstrates that the transformation to the true pyramid took place at about the same time as the building of Seneferu's Northern Stone Pyramid at Dahshur, where the stones were laid in flat courses. Seneferu's Bent Pyramid at Dahshur, however, has inwardly tilted courses from the base to the level where its incline changes to 43°21′, and consequently it must belong to an earlier stage than either the true pyramid at Meydum or the Northern Stone Pyramid at Dahshur.

In its final form, the Meydum pyramid rose to a height of about 94.5 m, and each side measured about 144 m at the base. Its angle of incline has been variously calculated as 51°52′ and 52°40′. At every stage in its evolution, the entrance was located in the center of the north face, and finally about 18.5 m above ground level. The entrance corridor is 1.55 m high and 82 cm wide, with an angle of about 28°. This corridor ends in a vertical shaft 4.4 m high, which rises through rock to emerge in the northeastern corner of the floor of the corbel-vaulted tomb chamber.

A small mortuary temple, 2.7 m high and 9.18 m wide, is built of Tura limestone and stands against the center of the east face of the pyramid, but is not bonded to it. Visitors in the 18th Dynasty left graffiti expressing their admiration for Seneferu's monument. In the court, backing onto the pyramid, are two large uninscribed stelae in limestone with curved tops, and between them lies a low altar for offerings of food and drink.

Meydum preserves the earliest example of what was to become the standard Old Kingdom pyramid complex. It consisted of five essential elements: the main pyramid, a mortuary temple, a subsidiary pyramid, and a causeway linking the enclosed area of the complex with a temple in the valley on the western fringe of cultivation.

Mudbrick tombs were built in the vicinity of the Meydum pyramid, and at least four of them belonged to Seneferu's sons. The superstructures (mastabas) of the largest ones were excavated in 1871–2 by Auguste Mariette. In 1892 Petrie tried unsuccessfully to locate their tomb chambers. Accompanied by Wainwright and Mackay, he resumed the search in 1909, only to find that ancient robbers had already been there. Most of the mastaba owners were identified by Mariette from inscriptions on lintels and on the symbolic entrances, but the owner of the second largest one (M 17) still remains anonymous. Because of its proximity to

the pyramid and its size, some scholars have suggested that its owner was the heir to the throne but died prematurely. A male skeleton was found in the tomb, completely bandaged in gauze after each bone had been defleshed and wrapped separately. His granite sarcophagus shows a remarkable degree of technical perfection.

Many of the large mastabas had two separate burials for a husband and wife. Each had its own symbolic entrance on the east side of the superstructure, with the husband's to the south and the wife's to the north. Three outstanding works of art were found by Mariette in two of the twin mastabas. In the wife's chapel of the twin mastaba (M 16) belonging to Neferma'at, the "Eldest Son of the King," and his wife Itet, was a wall painting of a line of geese. Another mastaba chapel (M 6) of Prince Rahotep, "Priest of Heliopolis" and "Army General," contained the painted limestone statues of the prince and his wife Nofret, which must rank among the most lifelike sculptures from ancient Egypt. All three works are among the best known treasures in the Cairo Museum.

See also

Dahshur, the Bent Pyramid; Dahshur, the Northern Stone Pyramid; Lepsius, Carl Richard; Old Kingdom, overview

Further reading

Borchardt, L. 1928. *Die Entstehung der Pyramide an der Baugeschichte der Pyramide bei Mejdum nachgewiesen*. Berlin.

Maragioglio, V., and C. Rinaldi. 1964. *L'Architettura delle Piramidi Menfite* 3, 6–53. Rapallo.

Petrie, W.M.F., G.A. Wainwright and E. Mackay. 1912. *The Labyrinth, Gerzeh and Mazghunah*, 24–8. London.

Porter, B., and R.L.B. Moss. 1934. *Topographical Bibliography of Ancient Egyptian Hieroglyphic Texts, Reliefs and Paintings* 4: 84–96. Oxford.

I.E.S. EDWARDS

Minshat Abu Omar

Until recently, many scholars believed that the Nile Delta in late prehistoric times was a broad swampy region and the existence of settlements there would have been impossible. Many of these misconceptions were based not only on the absence of archaeological finds in the Delta, but also on a misinterpretation of the geology. It is now known that settlements in the Delta were possible at all times, especially on levees and *gezira* formations (sandy islands).

The site of Minshat Abu Omar is situated on a *gezira* in the northeastern Delta (30°54′ N, 32°01′ E), *circa* 150 km northeast of Cairo, in a region where the now defunct Pelusiac branch of the Nile was previously flowing. The height of the site is only about 2.5 m above the surrounding cultivated land. It extends from the edge of the modern village of Minshat Abu Omar about 550 m north-northeast. The site was identified in 1966 as part of a survey attempting to locate the place of origin of Predynastic finds being sold in Europe and the USA by an Egyptian art dealer. Excavations began in 1978 and continued yearly until 1991; there were also additional seasons of survey and documentation. Although other ancient sites have been located in the Delta in recent years, Minshat Abu Omar remains the only Predynastic and Early Dynastic site in the Delta that has been extensively excavated, and it provides the best data base for comparison with the material culture of Upper Egypt.

Cemetery

Located in the southern part of the site, the cemetery was almost completely excavated. It dates to the Predynastic/Early Dynastic and the Late and Graeco-Roman periods. Four hundred and twenty graves of the Predynastic/Early Dynastic periods were excavated as well as 2,630 graves of the later periods. A final, six-volume publication of the Predynastic/Early Dynastic cemetery is now being prepared.

Predynastic/Early Dynastic cemetery

The excavated early graves can be divided into two broad, chronologically consecutive groups:

1 late Predynastic graves dating to (the relative phases of) Werner Kaiser's Nagada IIc–d and Flinders Petrie's Sequence Dates 33–78, *circa* 3,300–3,100 BC (MAO I and II).
2 Early Dynastic graves: (a) of the so-called "Dynasty 0," *circa* 3,100–3,000 BC (MAO III); and (b) of the 1st Dynasty, *circa* 3,000–2,850 BC (MAO IV).

The late Predynastic graves (1) consist mainly of pits in which the body was placed in a more or less tightly contracted position on the right side, oriented north–south, with the head to the north facing west. The pits are mostly oval in shape, *circa* 1–1.5 m in length and 1.5–2.0 m deep. Only in rare cases can any elaboration of the pit be noted. Generally, only a few grave goods were included in the burial and consist of small-sized ball- and cone-shaped pots. In a few cases more valuable offerings were found, such as wavy-handled pots (Petrie's W-class), painted vessels, small stone jars, palettes, disc-shaped carnelian beads, ivory spoons and, rarely, a bracelet or harpoon of copper. Of particular interest is a small group of imported pots, which, according to an analysis of form and fabric, were manufactured in Palestine. These also occur in the later group (2a) of graves.

The Dynasty 0 graves (2a) dating to Narmer's reign show an abrupt change in burial tradition. The grave pits are generally rectangular, and are larger and deeper than the earlier ones. Often the walls of the pits (dug in loose fine sand) were reinforced with a kind of mud plastering. Matting was used as roofing and under the burial. The most important change, however, took place in the orientation of the burials. The dead were placed in a contracted position on the left side, with the head to the northeast to east, facing southeast or east. Remains of coffins made of wood, reed and mud were also found in this grave group. Besides a dramatic increase in the number of pots, which are concentrated in a small side chamber, grave goods include a great number of

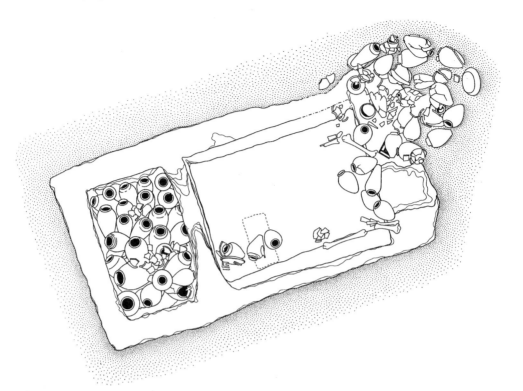

Figure 75 "Elite" burial of the 1st Dynasty at Minshat Abu Omar with two chambers; the larger chamber had been robbed (Tomb 1590)

extremely well made stone vessels, some of which are composite ones made of two different kinds of stone, as well as delicate cosmetic artifacts such as spoons and palettes. Copper axes, harpoons and saws occur more frequently than in the earlier graves, as well as jewelry in different materials. Some of these burials were robbed, another new feature. Especially in the larger graves, robber pits could be clearly observed in the sand before they were excavated.

Graves dating to the 1st Dynasty (2b) have many features similar to those of Dynasty 0 (2a), including the position and orientation of the body, and the number and variety of grave goods. Two ivory boxes are unique finds in this grave group. The largest burials in this group are the so-called tombs of the "elite," represented by eight chamber tombs built of mud or mudbrick. These tombs consist of two or three

underground rooms of unequal size, the largest of which was used as the burial chamber. All of the chambers had been covered with a roof of reed or papyrus mats placed on top of wooden beams. The roof was fastened down with mud and fragments of mudbrick. It was impossible to reconstruct superstructures as no original surface was preserved at the site. The largest of these tombs, with three rooms, had outside dimensions of 4.90 × 3.25 m. It is interesting to note that the main (central) chamber in which the body had been placed was completely robbed, whereas the side chambers were intact. This pattern was repeatedly observed, indicating that the grave robbing probably took place shortly after the burial, when the location of the main chamber containing the most valuable artifacts (probably of copper or gold) was still known to the robbers. Despite having been robbed, four of these chamber tombs represent the richest graves excavated at Minshat Abu Omar, with as many as 125 grave goods. In grave 2275 is the unique occurrence of niches in the tomb interior along the northern side. Although badly preserved, the niches retained evidence that they were originally lined with wood and then covered with plaster painted red and white.

Late period and Graeco-Roman cemetery

The majority of graves at Minshat Abu Omar, which sometimes occur in a density of up to 120 burials per 10 m square, belong to the Graeco-Roman period. Since most of these burials did not contain any grave goods, their dating remains imprecise. Based on their ceramics, some certainly date to the 26th Dynasty, but others are as late as the Coptic period. Generally, these graves are fairly poor, consisting only of a simple pit. In some cases the burial pit was lined with fired or mudbrick, and in rare cases ceramic, wooden or limestone coffins were provided. The most elaborate burials consist of underground chambers, which contained up to twenty-seven burials. Children were often buried in amphorae. Remains of mummies as well as fragments of stucco mummy masks were found. Grave goods consist of amulets and other jewelry (including a gold brooch and earrings), glass bottles and some pots.

Settlements

Only test excavations were conducted in the ancient settlement, located in the northern part of Minshat Abu Omar and known today as Tell Saba Banat. According to the evidence of coins, the settlement dates mostly to the Graeco-Roman period (with a few finds of the Late period occurring in the lower levels). Sondages have shown that the Predynastic/Early Dynastic settlement was not located in the same area.

In 1987 and 1989 testing by augering on a grid system up to 8 m below the present surface was conducted with the intent of locating the earlier settlement. The Predynastic/Early Dynastic settlement was found *circa* 500 m southeast of the cemetery at approximately 4–6 m below the present surface and 3–4 m below the ground water. Another settlement, probably Neolithic, was located somewhat deeper in the deposits, but has not been further investigated.

See also

Early Dynastic period, overview; Late and Ptolemaic periods, overview; pottery, prehistoric; Predynastic period, overview; Roman period, overview

Further reading

Kroeper, K., and D. Wildung. 1985. *Minshat Abu Omar, Münchner Ostdelta Expedition; Vorbericht 1978–1984*. Munich.
——. 1994. *Minshat Abu Omar – Ein vor- und frühgeschichtlicher Friedhof im Nildelta I*. Mainz.
——. 1992. Tombs of the elite in Minshat Abu Omar. In *The Nile Delta in Transition: 4th.–3rd. Millennium B.C.*, E.C.M. van den Brink, ed., 127–50. Jerusalem.
Krzyzaniak, L. 1993. New data on the late prehistoric settlement at Minshat Abu Omar (Eastern Nile Delta). In *Environmental Change and Human Culture in the Nile Basin and Northern Africa until the Second Millennium B.C.*, L. Krzyzaniak, M. Kobusiewicz and J.A. Alexander, eds. 321–5. Poznan.

KARLA KROEPER

Mons Porphyrites

Mons Porphyrites is the only known source of imperial porphyry, a gem-like igneous rock, purple in color, which was prized for sculpture, monolithic columns and other architectural elements in Roman and Byzantine times. The rock was imported in quantity to Rome and Constantinople, but it has a broad distribution and small fragments have been found as far away as Britain. The quarries are located in the

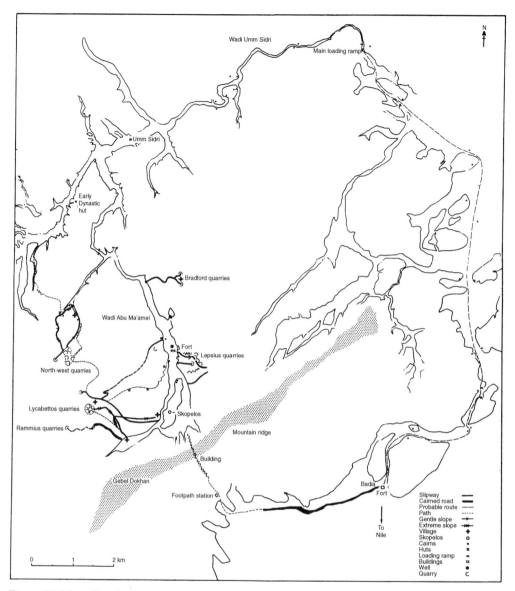

Figure 76 Mons Porphyrites, settlements and quarries

Gebel Dokhan, in the heart of the Red Sea mountains of Egypt (27°15′ N, 33°15′ E). The complex comprises a quarry field, a fortified settlement with a temple of the god Serapis, and smaller settlements believed to be those of quarry workers. The area is of very difficult access and consequently has been little visited.

The archaeology of Mons Porphyrites has been the subject of a number of short contributions, but the first important work was conducted by a German expedition in the 1960s. The team spent five days on the site and produced a plan of the main fortified settlement in Wadi Abu Ma'amel and a related fort at Badia, the first stage on the route to the Nile. They also made a detailed plan and description of the temple of Serapis, and sketch plans of the workers' villages, which was a remarkable achievement in the time available. More recently, an American expedition concentrated on collecting ceramic evidence, which confirmed a first–fourth centuries AD dating. Since 1994 the site has been the subject of detailed examination by a British team working under the aegis of the Egypt Exploration Society.

Mons Porphyrites is a key site in both the study of Roman quarries and in our understanding of Roman Egypt for the following reasons. First, the preservation is excellent, for, apart from some modern extraction, the remote location has ensured little interference since antiquity. It presents an almost pristine Roman landscape, which led earlier explorers to characterize it as perhaps the most remarkable manifestation of Roman activity to be seen anywhere in the world. Second, the rock is important to historians of art and architecture, as it was used for columns as well as decorative elements such as sculpture, baths or basins. Finally, study of inscriptions on potsherds (ostraca) from Mons Claudianus, 50 km to the south, indicates that Mons Porphyrites was the administrative center for military activities and extractive industries in this part of the Eastern Desert. This is also supported by the longer period of operation at Mons Porphyrites, suggested by archaeological evidence on the surface as well as by the textual evidence. The site is clearly the key to understanding Roman operations in this area.

There are two main areas of settlement: a fort in Wadi Abu Ma'amel and another on the south side of the Gebel Dokhan, known as Badia, clearly part of the same system. There are two main wells, both in Wadi Abu Ma'amel. These seem to have been the main sources of water, apart from periodic rock pools which would have acted as reservoirs, retaining water for a short period after flash floods. All food would have had to be imported from the Nile Valley, supplemented by fish from the Red Sea. However, the terrain is so difficult that the workers seem to have been housed in a number of remote villages, which would have to have been supplied with water and food. The villages are approached by footpaths, many of which are still remarkably well preserved.

The quarries are on the tops of mountains, three of which were fancifully named by the German explorer Georg Schweinfurth in the nineteenth century: Lykabettos, Lepsius and Rammius. The northwest quarries seem to have been discovered later, but they may have been a focus of activity as early as the first century AD, while the latest quarrying in the fourth or possibly fifth century seems to have been concentrated on Lykabettos. The slipways down which the partly finished stones would have traveled to the wadi bed are often marked by cairns. Presumably, rollers or sledges would have been used as far as the great loading ramp at the entrance to the Wadi Umm Sidri, where the produce would have been transferred to carts for its 150 km journey to the Nile. Little is known about the types of animal used in traction, but it may be reasonably assumed to be donkeys. There is no animal enclosure at the fort in Wadi Abu Ma'amel, but they exist at Badia and at the halfway station of Umm Sidri.

The most outstanding recent discovery by the British team has been an important inscription found in a small temple high in the mountains and probably unseen by anyone since Roman times. It is a dedication to the gods Pan and Serapis, dominated by an engraving showing the god Pan-Min. The inscription mentions the discovery of the site on July 23, AD 18 by Caius Cominius Leugas. He seems to have been the Roman equivalent of a field geologist, for there is also a list of the rocks he found: porphyry, black porphyry, multi-colored stones and the mysterious "kne-kites." The use of the apparent oxymoron "black porphyry" at this early date is particularly interesting.

Excavations of the rubbish heaps outside the gates of the Badia and Abu Ma'amel forts have also produced new evidence. At Badia the excavated sequence demonstrates that the animal lines were a secondary feature added after the first half of the second century. During the fourth or fifth century there is evidence of industrial activity with dumps of ash, small fragments of charcoal and mudbrick. The excavated area at Abu Ma'amel produced a useful assemblage of artifacts from the second century, filling a notable gap in the ceramic sequence of the Eastern Desert. The rich collection of small finds, both organic and inorganic, suggests a surprisingly sophisticated way of life within the fort.

See also

Bir Umm Fawakhir; natural resources; quarrying; Roman period, overview; Roman ports, Red Sea

Further reading

Klein, M.J. 1988. *Untersuchungen zu den Kaiserlichen Steinbrüchen*. Bonn.

Klemm, R., and D.D. Klemm. 1992. *Steine und Steinbrüche in Alten Ägypten*. Berlin.

Kraus, T., J. Röder and W. Müller-Wiener. 1967. Mons Claudianus — Mons Porphyrites. *MDAIK* 22: 109–207.

Van Rengen, W. 1992. Les Laissez-passer. In *Mons Claudianus. Ostraca Graeca et Latina* 1, J. Bingen *et al.*, eds. 57–74. Cairo.

D.P.S. PEACOCK
V.A. MAXFIELD

mortuary beliefs

In Egypt, mortuary beliefs and customs were undoubtedly influenced initially by the nature of the land and its climate. With inadequate rainfall to support crops and domesticated animals, Egyptians awaited the annual inundation of the Nile to irrigate and cultivate their fields. This cultivated strip on either side of the river was called *Kemet* (the "Black Land"), referring to the rich black silt which the river deposited there and which enabled them to grow excellent crops. Here they lived and farmed, but the bodies were taken and interred in the desert which lay beyond. Feared as a place of death and terror, this desolate area was known as *Deshret* (the "Red Land"), referring to the color of the sand and rocks. Here, the

heat of the sun and the dryness of the sand provided ideal environmental conditions which preserved the bodies (natural mummification) and the artifacts placed in the graves. Later, artificial methods were introduced to achieve long-term preservation of the bodies, making use of chemical dehydrating agents.

The contrast between the cultivation and the desert symbolized the difference between life and death for the Egyptians and probably inspired some of their earliest and most enduring religious concepts. The evidence of grave goods probably indicates that funerary preparations to facilitate the deceased's journey after death were undertaken from earliest times, and that there was an awareness of an individual's continued existence after death. The idea of eternity remained a constant feature of the religion, although the exact state and place of this continued existence were envisaged in several ways.

It was believed that each individual experienced a cycle of life, death, and rebirth, reflecting the annual destruction of the vegetation, due to the parching of the land, and the subsequent resurgence of life which the Nile's inundation brought about. One of Egypt's greatest gods, Osiris, was both vegetation god and king of the underworld; mythology described his annual death as a human king and resurrection as ruler of the underworld. This reflected the natural phenomena and enabled him to offer the chance of resurrection and eternal life to his worshippers. Similarly, Egypt's other great life force, the sun, underwent a daily death but was renewed at dawn, and consequently Re the sun god was regarded as both a great creative force and the sustainer of life. The essential feature of Egyptian mortuary beliefs and customs was the denial of death and the continued affirmation of eternal existence.

The human personality was regarded as a complex entity. The body formed the essential link between the deceased's spirit and his former earthly existence; every attempt was made to preserve it (using mummification techniques for those who could afford them) and to protect it with a tomb and magical spells. It was believed that the spirit returned to the body to partake of the food offerings placed at the tomb, to gain continuing sustenance. Statues of the tomb owner and magical formulas inscribed in the tomb were intended to provide a secondary method of nourishing the spirit, if the mummy should be destroyed.

A person's name was regarded as an integral part of his personality, and knowledge of this could enable others to direct good or evil forces toward him. Also, his body and statue were identified by name inscriptions, as part of the funerary procedure. His shadow, another element of his personality, was believed to incorporate his procreative powers.

Some aspects of this complex personality, however, were only released after death. The most important was the *ka* (often translated as "spirit") which, in its owner's lifetime, was regarded as the embodiment of the life force and the essential "self" or personality, as well as his double. It acted as guide and protector, and after death it was thought to be released as a separate entity which progressed to achieve immortality but retained a continuing and important association with the place of burial, being dependent on the food and other goods placed there for its sustenance. The *ka* is usually shown as a human with upraised arms, or simply as a pair of upraised arms. Another aspect of the human personality, also believed to survive death, was the *ba* (sometimes translated as the "soul"). This force, shown as a human-headed bird, could leave the body and tomb and travel to places which the owner had enjoyed during his lifetime. Another supernatural force known as the *akh* (again depicted as a bird) could be called upon to assist the deceased.

Although royalty, wealthy persons and the poor had different expectations regarding the nature and location of their individual existences after death, all placed great emphasis on the correct procedure of the funerary rituals and on the provision of a properly prepared and equipped burial place. A vital ritual in the burial service was the ceremony of "Opening the Mouth," performed by the deceased's heir. He touched with an adze the deceased's mummy, statues and other representations in the tomb,

to restore the life force to them and to enable the spirit to use the body throughout eternity.

Great consideration was also given to provisioning the tomb with food and drink. This was primarily the duty of a person's heir and descendants, but succeeding generations often neglected this task, threatening the owner's *ka* with starvation, and so other methods were adopted. A *ka* priest could be employed to place the daily provisions at the tomb and to recite the necessary prayers; he and his descendants (to whom the obligation passed) would be paid with provisions from land specially set aside in the dead man's estate. However, even such an endowment could not guarantee that the tomb would be attended in perpetuity, and other measures were introduced. The interior walls of tombs were carved and painted with registers of scenes showing food production and other activities; these could be magically activated for the deceased to enjoy throughout eternity. Also, an offering formula was inscribed on one wall giving details of the food that would be continually available, and model figures of brewers, bakers, butchers and other workers were included to ensure an eternal abundance.

Access to his possessions and to the pleasurable experiences once enjoyed in life was thus obtained for the wealthy commoner. He hoped the afterlife would be a continuation of this existence, but free from danger, illness or worry. He expected to pass time in his tomb, surrounded by the scenes and possessions which reflected the best aspects of his life, and he expended considerable wealth in order to ensure a comfortable eternity.

The king, however, had different expectations. He would ascend to the heavens where he hoped to join his father, the sun god Re, and to sail with him and other deities in the two celestial barks. The earth was envisaged as a flat surface, suspended within a circle. Above the earth's surface, the semicircle formed the sky where the sun sailed throughout the daytime, while at night, it continued its course in another bark, passing through the semicircle beneath the earth (the underworld). Every day, the sun re-emerged at dawn on the earth's surface. Throughout ancient Egypt's history, the major

Figure 77 Wooden model boat with crew, intended for the tomb owner to sail south (upstream) with the wind. There was also a wooden model rowing boat in this tomb, for traveling north (downstream). From the Tomb of Two Brothers, Rifa, 12th Dynasty, *circa.* 1900 BC. *Source*: Manchester Museum, England.

architectural, decorative and inscriptional features of the king's burial place were intended to achieve two main aims: to ensure that the king safely completed his journey after death, overcoming all dangers on his way; and to establish that he would be received as a divine ruler by the gods and allowed to retain this status throughout eternity. During the Old Kingdom, the kings introduced the custom of building pyramids. Each pyramid contained the royal burial and funerary possessions, while other elements of the complex included a mortuary temple, causeway and valley temple, where the burial ceremony and mortuary cult took place. The pyramids were probably closely associated with the sun cult and may have been regarded as "ramps" linking earth and sky, thus enabling the king's spirit to ascend to heaven and return again at will to partake of his earthly food

offerings. Later, in the 5th Dynasty, when royal political power had declined and the construction of the pyramids was less substantial, reliance was placed instead on magic spells. Now, the *Pyramid Texts* were inscribed on walls inside the pyramids, to ensure the king's resurrection by means of magic. In the New Kingdom, when pyramids were abandoned in favor of rock-cut tombs in the Valley of the Kings at Thebes, wall scenes inside the royal tombs depicted the king's journey through the underworld, based on the magical *Books of the Netherworld*. Again, these were intended to ensure the defeat of death.

However, not only royalty and the wealthy were able to claim a chance of eternal life. In the Old Kingdom, only the king could expect an individual immortality and others only hoped to experience this vicariously, as a reward for serving the god-king during life. However, with the political collapse of the Old Kingdom at the end of the 6th Dynasty, the power of the king and his patron deity Re waned considerably, and Osiris emerged with greater popularity. A vegetation god and ruler of the underworld, Osiris received widespread worship and acclaim as a giver of life and fertility, gaining the attributes of a divine judge and symbolizing the victory of good over evil. His annual triumph over death, expressed in the renewal of the vegetation, resulted in his installation as ruler of the dead and of the underworld. The successful outcome of his own trial before the divine judges and his personal resurrection enabled him to promise eternal life to each of his followers. This was not dependent on the king's favor or the performance of the correct rituals and burial procedures, but could now be achieved through devoted worship of Osiris and the pursuance of an exemplary life. At the Day of Judgement, an individual faced the divine tribunal and was required to give an honest account of his deeds. Those worthy enough to achieve immortality now passed to the land of Osiris (situated somewhere in the west), where they were required to till a small piece of land in perpetuity, amidst surroundings that reflected the world of the living. Although this held out the promise of happiness for the poor, wealthier persons did not wish to spend their eternity in agricultural pursuits and took care to provision their tombs with sets of model agricultural workers (*shawabtis*) and overseers, to undertake these labors on their behalf.

The *Pyramid Texts*, the preserve of royalty in the Old Kingdom, were now, as the *Coffin Texts*, changed and used on the coffins of commoners to ensure their resurrection and eternity. There was also a great increase in the number of well-equipped tombs, many of which were now prepared for the middle classes. They were supplied with a variety of model servants, soldiers and animals for use in the next world, some of them based on the subject matter of wall scenes found in Old Kingdom tombs. After the successful outcome of his trial, each deceased person could now place the words "justified" or "true of voice" after his name in

the funerary inscriptions, and the name "Osiris" in front of his own name.

The three main concepts of eternity therefore began to be formulated in the Middle Kingdom: the royal celestial hereafter, continuation of existence within the tomb for the wealthy owner, and, for the poor, an eternity spent tilling the land in the Kingdom of Osiris. To some extent, these concepts were interchangeable and the priests later attempted to rationalize them to some degree. Essentially, however, they remained distinct until the end of the pharaonic period, reflecting the separate aspirations of the country's main social groups.

See also

funerary texts; kingship; mummification; mythology; pantheon; representational evidence, Middle Kingdom private tombs; representational evidence, New Kingdom private tombs; representational evidence, Old Kingdom private tombs

Further reading

Blackman, A.M. 1924. The rite of Opening the Mouth in ancient Egypt and Babylonia. *JEA* 10:47–78.

Edwards, I.E.S. 1985. *The Pyramids of Egypt.* Harmondsworth.

Faulkner, R.0. 1924. The "Cannibal Hymn" from the Pyramid Texts. *JEA* 10: 97–103.

——. 1956. The man who was tired of life. *JEA* 42: 21–40.

Griffiths, J.G. 1970. *Plutarch: De Iside et Osiride.* Cardiff.

A.R. DAVID

mummies, scientific study of

Investigations of Egyptian mummies in many ways reflect the state of the sciences and particularly the focus of the medical sciences at any given time. It is, therefore, no accident that many of the primary investigators are physicians, physical anthropologists, anatomists, bacteriologists, biochemists and others closely related to the health sciences. The great progress in diagnostic procedures, including biochemistry, microscopy, molecular genetics, and radiographic techniques in the medical profession, is mirrored in the diversity of specialists investigating mummies today. Hence, mummy-related investigations are published in every conceivable science journal. Unfortunately, relatively few articles on human remains have appeared in Egyptology journals such as the *Journal of Egyptian Archaeology*. The major sources of scientific interest in Egyptian mummies are reviewed here.

The terms "mummy" and "mummification" have traditionally been applied by most laymen and scholars to human and animal remains that have been preserved by priest specialists in ancient Egypt. The term "mummy" comes from the Persian word *mumia*, meaning "bitumen" or "tar." The coating over the body, which frequently turns black in color with age, was originally a molten resin derived from trees and used during the mummification process. Today, the terms "mummy," "mummification" and "mummified" all refer to any animal or human remains that have been preserved by natural means or through human intervention.

The key to preservation is usually the removal of water from the tissues. In Predynastic times this was accomplished naturally when the remains were placed directly in the sandy floor of a grave pit excavated in the desert, where rapid dehydration or desiccation occurred. Anywhere in the world today where the climate is arid, mummified remains will be found, for example in the African Deserts, the US southwestern deserts, Mexico and Peru.

From the Old Kingdom through the Roman period there was great diversity in the process by which the body was preserved. Two Greek historians, Herodotus (fifth century BC) and Diodorus (first century BC), gave the best known accounts of mummification in antiquity. In recent times, Zaki Iskander, both an Egyptologist and a biochemist with the Egyptian Antiquities Organization, has not only studied the chemistry of mummification but also has successfully mummified animals.

Alfred Lucas, a biochemist, has also analyzed and published the chemistry of techniques used in ancient mummification.

The process was basically dehydration or desiccation utilizing dry natron (sodium carbonate and sodium bicarbonate) for some forty days. Natron was found in ancient lake beds such as the Wadi el-Natrun. Usually, the viscera were removed and preserved separately and only the heart and kidneys remained in the body cavities. The brain was frequently removed through the nasal septum utilizing picks and dissolving chemicals. The body and viscera were washed with palm oils and spices and then sealed with molten resin from the sap of trees. The body was wrapped in many layers of linen and placed inside of one or more coffins. Most coffins were made of wood. In royal burials coffins were sometimes covered with gold leaf or pure gold and were then placed inside of a stone sarcophagus.

Over the 5,000-year history of Egyptian mummification, great variation has been observed. The brain and viscera were not always removed. Sometimes the viscera were placed back into the body. Many different kinds of natron and resins were used to preserve the body. By the late Roman period, the most beautiful mummy cases and wrappings often contain a badly preserved mummy that was essentially only a skeleton.

What preserved the body was principally dehydration. The resin, the linen wrappings and the coffin all helped to protect the body from outside environmental contaminants, especially bacteria and oxygen. However, it is the dehydration of tissues that has caused the major problem to the histologic and pathologic study of the tissues derived from the ancient mummies.

Scientific investigation of mummies may be divided into two major categories: first, the *nondestructive* study of wrapped or unwrapped mummies, and, secondly, the *dissection* or *autopsy* of mummies. The first category includes visual examination, cranial, post-cranial and soft tissue measurements, photographs, full body radiographic surveys, cephalometrics, CAT Scans or CTs (Computed Axial

Tomagraphy) and MRIs (Magnetic Resonance Imaging).

Artists and scientists accompanying Napoleon's expeditionary forces in Egypt at the end of the eighteenth century were the first to observe, describe and record mummies and their tombs. Some tomb paintings indicated disease, nutrition, deformity, trauma and even medical treatment. Since the publication in 1875 of the Ebers papyrus, many other medically related papyri have been published, including the Kahun (1898), the Hearst (1905), the Edwin Smith (1930) and the Chester Beatty papyrus (1935). These papyri have been examined extensively yielding insights not only into the diseases of ancient Egypt, but also the practice of medicine.

In 1834 Thomas Pedigrew wrote the *History of Egyptian Mummies*, the first major publication encompassing historical sources as well as current investigations into mummification at that time. Royal mummies found at Deir el-Bahri by Émile Brugsch in 1881 were later unwrapped by Gaston Maspero before distinguished guests and royalty in the Cairo Museum. In 1895, Maspero published his physical anthropological measurements of height and physical appearance. Also important for these studies, another cache of royal mummies was discovered by Victor Loret in 1898 in the tomb of Amenhotep II.

The building of the first Aswan Dam in 1902 and its enlargement in 1907 resulted in a large-scale archaeological study of the areas to be inundated, especially between the First and Second Cataracts. Archaeological evidence from these areas, including the human remains, was described by George Reisner (1910) and by Warren Dawson (1938). In 1924 Dawson and Elliot Smith published another major work on mummies and mummification, *Egyptian Mummies*.

In his definitive 1912 book, *The Royal Mummies*, Smith gave a detailed, written description (often quoting Maspero) with photographs of the New Kingdom royal mummies in the Cairo Museum. It was Smith who recommended X-ray studies of the royal mummies, and in 1903, at Douglas Derry's request, the mummy of Tuthmose IV was X-rayed by a Dr. Khayet. Beginning in 1968, all of the New Kingdom royal mummies in the Cairo Museum have been examined by James Harris and colleagues utilizing Ytterbium 169, conventional X-rays and cephalometrics. The latter permitted quantification and the biostatistical comparison of the craniofacial skeletons within families and between various populations.

In 1927 Derry published his examination of the mummy of Tutankhamen, whose tomb was discovered by Howard Carter in 1922. A dentist, Filce Leek, with the anatomist R.G. Harrison, X-rayed the skull (utilizing radioactive iodine) and the mummy of Tutankhamen in 1968. Harris secured cephalometric X-rays of Tutankhamen in his tomb in 1978. The later study suggested the similarity of the skull of Tutankhamen to that of Smenkhkare, and suggested that the young pharaoh had died in his early twenties.

Many museums throughout the Americas and Europe have X-rayed their mummy collections over the years. In 1967 Peter Gray utilized radiographs to examine some 133 mummies in Great Britain, France and Holland. Recently, CTs and MRIs have proven to be increasingly popular approaches to non-invasive examination of mummy collections. The Manchester Museum, the University Museum in Philadelphia and the Field Museum in Chicago are examples of museums which have used radiographic techniques to record and examine their mummy collections.

Radiographic studies may yield considerable information about health and disease in the skeleton and soft tissue. Studies of the royal mummies in the Cairo Museum have revealed, for example, antemortem and postmortem trauma, cranial defects, poliomyelitis, arteriosclerosis, rheumatoid and hypertrophic arthritis, ankylosing spondylitis, malocclusion, impacted teeth, dental abscess and so on. In 1971 Walter Whitehouse, a professor of radiology, observed that the most common abnormality in the royal mummies was hypertrophic or degenerative arthritis. The mummy of Amenhotep II showed striking evidence of ankylosing spondylitis (arthritis of the spine). Although Elliot Smith had observed Talipes equinovarus (clubfoot) in the lower extremity of the mummy of Siptah, radiological examination indicated that the deformity strongly resembled a postpoliomyelitis deformity. Arteriosclerosis (extensive vascular calcification) was observed in the mummies of Ramesses II, Seti I, Merenptah and Ramesses III.

Radiographic examination is helpful in confirming the sex and skeletal and dental age of the individual. The open epiphyseal plates in the knee X-rays of Tuthmose I would suggest that the mummy was not yet eighteen years of age.

Cephalometric radiographs, which are taken with a precise orientation to the mid-sagittal plane of the skull, permit the measurements and biostatistical comparisons of one mummy to another, a family or any given population. This approach is particularly helpful in determining the genetic or family background of the individual under study. The University of Michigan teams have recorded over 5,000 cephalograms of Old Kingdom nobles from Aswan and the Giza plateau, New Kingdom royal mummies, New Kingdom elites from Deir el-Bahri, and Nubians (AD 200 to the present).

Multivariate statistical analyses of the computerized tracings and measurements of these cephalograms have revealed the relative homogeneity of the Egyptians, while indicating the great diversity or heterogeneity of the New Kingdom royal mummies. The craniofacial skeleton and dentition of the New Kingdom pharaohs and queens reflect the malocclusions (dental crowding and maxillary prognathism) observed in Western societies today.

Radiographs are also very helpful in discovering and interpreting the funerary artifacts placed inside of the wrappings. Heart scarabs, amulets of the sons of Horus, beads, bracelets, necklaces, rings, arm bands and so on all help to confirm the period in which the individual lived and died. Radiographs have limitations, but they permit non-destructive studies so that the wrapped or unwrapped mummy remains intact for future generations.

The second approach to the study of mummies is to biopsy, dissect or autopsy the mummy, similar in techniques to modern surgery and pathology. Most mummies which have been autopsied are poorly preserved ones in museums or private collections. Many investigators in this area are members of the Paleopathology Association, which holds annual, national and

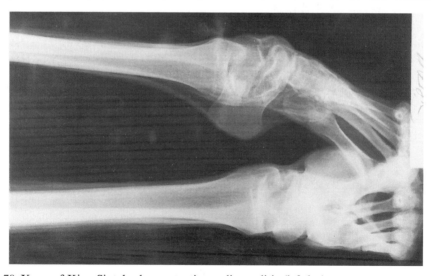

Figure 78 X-ray of King Siptah, demonstrating poliomyelitis (left leg)

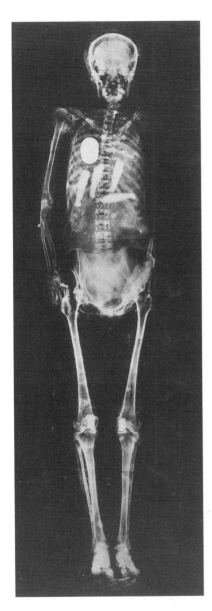

Figure 79 X-ray of Queen Nodjme, revealing a sacred heart scarab and amulets of the four sons of Horus within the mummy

international meetings and publishes the *Paleopathology Newsletter*. The membership consists principally of physicians and physical anthropologists with a special interest in pathology or paleopathology. The Manchester Museum is an example of where both paleopathology and the public exhibition of mummy unwrapping and dissection have been conducted by Rosalie David and associates.

The major problem in utilizing modern pathologic procedures to examine disease in ancient Egyptian mummies has been the rehydration of the tissue since the water was so laboriously removed by the priests of ancient Egypt. Armand Ruffer, a bacteriologist at the School of Medicine in Cairo at the beginning of the First World War, is considered the pioneer in restoring mummified tissue and his techniques, although modified, are frequently utilized today. More recently Sandison has recommended a hydration solution of 95 percent ethyl alcohol, 1 percent aqueous formalin and 5 percent aqueous sodium carbonate.

Once tissue has been rehydrated, is can be treated with care in the conventional setting of a pathology laboratory. Many data published on disease in ancient Egyptian mummies come from this source. Histologists or histopathologists in studies of autopsied mummies in various museums have found evidence of pneumoconiosis, smallpox, pericarditis, intestinal parasites, schistosomiasis and other medical conditions.

Paleobiochemistry has been reviewed by Robin Barraco. The study of proteins, salts and lipids may yield considerable insight into diet, disease, age and sex and general lifestyles. Trace elements, such as lead, zinc, copper, arsenic and mercury, may be utilized to determine the effects of the environment, pollution, nutrition, illness and social differentiation on ancient populations. Methods of measuring elements in mummified tissue include electrochemical, optical spectrometry, X-ray spectrometry, radioisotope and mass spectrometry. Scanning and transmission electron microscopy have been utilized to investigate the microstructure of bone, cartilage, muscle, sclera, blood, teeth, hair, and even ancient textiles. Many of these techniques were applied by French scientists and Egyptologists when they removed the mummy of Ramesses II to the Museum of Man in Paris under the direction of Christine Desroches-Noblecourt and Lionel Balout.

Dental paleopathology, including both the dentition and their supporting structures, has received considerable attention through the years because of the relative indestructibility of teeth through time. Tooth size, shape, number of cusps, root lengths, missing teeth, and supernumerary teeth have been demonstrated to have a strong genetic component. The growth and development of teeth as well as attrition or wear have long been utilized to indicate dental age. Dental caries and periodontal disease, including bone loss and dental calculus (tartar), are often excellent indicators of diet. Enamel or dental hypoplasia may indicate severe onset of disease during the formation of the dentition. Dental caries (tooth decay) were not a major problem in the early Egyptians, compared to the wear or attrition of the dentition which led to pulp exposure and dental abscesses. Ancient Egyptians (as well as modern Egyptians) suffered most severely from dental calculus (heavy tartar) leading to periodontal disease or loss of the supporting bone around the dentition.

Another approach of considerable interest over the past twenty years or so has been serology (the examination of blood groups or blood antigens, usually derived from epithelium or muscle tissue). In an attempt to derive familial relationship between the pharaohs of the late 18th Dynasty, R.G. Harrison compared the mummies of Yuya, Tuya, Amenhotep III, Queen Tiye and Smenkhkare to Tutankhamen's utilizing ABO and MN blood groups. However, other investigators have recently warned about the difficulty in controlling against false positive or false negative results. The latter may occur as the result of contaminating bacterial enzymes. F.W. Rosing has noted that ABO tests were successful from brain tissue, but not from epithelium and muscle tissue.

The latest area of interest has been the DNA fingerprinting or gene sequencing in mummified tissue. One investigator, Svante Paabo, has published the success of DNA sequencing in only one out of twenty specimens examined.

There has been considerable difficulty with DNA amplification in mummified tissue, and the supposition of random mating basic to DNA fingerprinting may be questionable in ancient Egyptian populations.

It should be mentioned that besides the mummy itself, there has been considerable interest in the funerary artifacts. Linen wrappings, plant resins, natron crystals, jewelry, wigs, paint pigments and so on have all been studied for composition and possible derivation. Spectrometry, chromatography and other chemical tests have frequently resulted in discovering the composition of the artifacts, their geographic origins, and subsequently the dating of the burial.

The scientific study of mummies is as varied, then, as the research backgrounds and disciplines of the investigators. In this age of specialization, many articles are placed in medical and scientific journals published for a narrow audience and frequently are not readily known or available to Egyptologists. Those published studies with important implications for Egyptologists should be repeated with technology proven to be reliable in mummified tissue. Finally, the potential contribution of the research scientist will depend not only upon the advancement of science and technology, but even more importantly on greater interaction with Egyptologists and archaeologists.

See also

Deir el-Bahri, royal mummy cache; Egyptians, physical anthropology of; mortuary beliefs; mummification; paleopathology

Further reading

Barraco, R.A. 1980. Paleobiochemistry. In *Mummies, Disease and Ancient Cultures*, A. Cockburn and E. Cockburn, eds. 312–26. Cambridge.

Berg, K., F.W. Rosing, F. Schwarzfischer and H. Wischerath. 1975. Blood groupings of old Egyptian mummies. *Homo* 26: 148–53.

Brothwell, D., and E. Higgs. 1970. *Science in Archaeology*. New York.

Bucaille, M. 1990. *Mummies of the Pharaohs: Modern Medical Investigations*. New York.

Cockburn, A., R. Barraco, T. Reyman, and W. Peck. 1975. Autopsy of an Egyptian mummy. *Science* 187: 1155–60.

Cockburn, A., and E. Cockburn. 1980. *Mummies, Disease and Ancient Cultures*. Cambridge.

Cockburn, E., ed. 1973–92. *The Paleopathology Newsletter*.

David, R. 1978. *Mysteries of the Mummies*. New York.

Harris, J., and E. Wente. 1980. *An X-ray Atlas of the Royal Mummies*. Chicago.

Harrison, R.G. 1966. An anatomical examination of the pharaonic remains purported to be Akhenaten. *JEA* 52: 95–119.

Iscan, M.Y., and K.A. Kennedy. 1989. *Reconstruction of Life from the Skeleton*. New York.

JAMES E. HARRIS

mummification

Examples of mummification (where bodies are preserved by either natural or artificial means) are found in a number of countries, but the ancient Egyptians produced the most advanced techniques and the best results. The word "mummy" may be derived from the Persian or Arabic word *mumia* meaning "pitch" or "bitumen," and was probably originally applied to the artificially preserved bodies of the ancient Egyptians because of their "bituminous" appearance.

In the earliest burials in Egypt from the Predynastic period (*circa* 4,500–3,050 BC), human remains (consisting of the skeleton and remaining body tissue) were preserved by natural circumstances. The bodies were interred in shallow pit-graves on the desert edge, and the combination of the sun's heat and the dry sand desiccated the body tissues before decomposition set in. The result was a remarkable degree of natural preservation of these bodies, which frequently retained substantial amounts of skin, tissue and hair.

However, when more sophisticated tombs were introduced for the elite in late Predynastic times (*circa* 3,400 BC), with underground, brick-lined burial chambers, the bodies, no longer buried in the sand, rapidly decomposed. Nevertheless, well-established religious beliefs demanded that the body should be preserved so that the spirit of the deceased would be able to recognize and take possession of it, in order to obtain nourishment through the body from the food offerings placed at the tomb. A period of experimentation followed, with attempts to find a method of retaining the physical likeness of the deceased and of preserving the body using artificial means. Such methods were unsuccessful, however, because they did not arrest the decay in the body tissues, which continued to deteriorate and disintegrate beneath the linen bandages wrapped around the body. Instead, emphasis was placed on the outward appearance of these "mummies," with the body being encased in resin-soaked linen, which was carefully molded to retain the shape, and details of the face and genitalia were painted on the outermost linen covering.

True (or artificial) mummification, which can be defined as an intentional method of preservation involving various techniques, including the use of chemical and other agents, was already in use at the beginning of the 4th Dynasty. In the burial of Queen Hetepheres (the mother of King Khufu) at Giza, visceral packages were discovered in a chest, and analysis showed that natron had been used to dehydrate these viscera. Natron is a mixture of sodium carbonate and sodium bicarbonate with impurities, including salt and sodium sulphate, found in natural deposits in Egypt.

This type of mummification continued until the Christian era. Originally reserved for the royal family and upper classes, by the Graeco-Roman period it was practiced by a much wider social group, but the majority of the population, never able to afford this process, continued to be buried in simple graves on the desert edge. No extant account of mummification techniques has ever been found in Egyptian literary or representational sources, although there are scattered references to the procedure and its

Figure 80 Anthropoid coffins of the two brothers, Khnum-Nakht (left) and Nekht-Ankh. These finely painted wood coffins are good examples of the geometric style of decoration popular in the Middle Kingdom. The inscription down the front of each gives the funerary menu. From the Tomb of Two Brothers, Rifa, 12th Dynasty
Source: Manchester Museum, England.

associated rituals. Classical sources supply the earliest available descriptions, notably in the writings of the Greek historians Herodotus (fifth century BC) and Diodorus Siculus (first century BC). They are not entirely accurate accounts, written centuries after mummification had passed its peak and probably relying to some extent on hearsay, but they do provide a reasonable description of the procedure.

Diodorus presents a less detailed account than Herodotus, on whose work his own version may be based, but he provides additional information not found in Herodotus. According to Herodotus, three main methods were available according to cost. In the cheapest method, an unspecified liquid was injected into the body *per anum* and it was subsequently treated with natron. In the second method, "cedar oil" (perhaps impure turpentine) was injected into the body *per anum* and then natron was used. The most expensive method, according to recent experiments, has been shown to be the most successful. In this, the brain was removed, partly through mechanical methods and partly through the use of various unspecified substances. An incision was made in the abdominal flank, through which the thoracic and abdominal viscera and contents were removed. The viscera were then cleansed with palm wine and spices, and the body cavities filled with myrrh, cassia and other aromatic substances, before the incision was sewn up. Natron was then used to dehydrate the body, which was finally washed and wrapped in layers of bandages fastened together with gum.

From such literary evidence and from information derived from the mummies themselves, it is evident that there were actually two main stages in mummification. First, the body was eviscerated (although not all mummies underwent this process); only the heart was left *in situ*, because religion dictated that it was the seat of the intellect and of the emotions, and indeed was the essential part of the person. According to Diodorus, the kidneys were also left in place, but there is little physical evidence to support this claim and no known religious explanation. Subsequently, the eviscerated organs were either stored in special containers called canopic jars, or packaged, in which case they were replaced in the body cavities or placed on the legs of the mummy.

The second stage was to desiccate the body and the viscera by dehydrating the tissues with natron. In addition, the body was anointed with oils and unguents, and in some instances it was coated with resin. Perfumed oils and spices may have been regarded as having some insect repellant properties, or they may have partially concealed the unpleasant odors associated with mummification.

In the long history of mummification, only two major innovations were introduced. From perhaps as early as the Middle Kingdom, the brain was removed, and this procedure became widespread from the New Kingdom. The most

Figure 81 Panel portrait of a man, originally placed over the mummy's face, showing the clothing and hairstyle fashionable during the Graeco-Roman period. From Hawara.
Source: Manchester Museum, England.

usual method was to insert a metal hook via a passage chiseled through the left nostril and the ethmoid bone into the cranial cavity or, less commonly, to intervene through the base of the skull or through a trepanned area. Subsequently, the cranial cavity was probably washed out with a fluid, but some brain tissue was often left behind. The other innovation was an attempt to restore the shrunken body, which resulted from mummification, to a plumper, more lifelike appearance. The face, neck and other areas were packed with various materials (linen, sawdust, earth, sand, and butter), which were either inserted through the mouth or through incisions made in the skin surface. This procedure reached its peak in the 21st Dynasty, when mummification techniques in general were at their zenith.

See also

funerary texts; mortuary beliefs; mummies, scientific study of

Further reading

David, A.R., ed. 1979. *Multidisciplinary Research on Egyptian Mummified Remains* (The Manchester Museum Mummy Project). Manchester.

Leek, F.F. 1969. The problem of brain removal during embalming by the ancient Egyptians. *JEA* 55: 112–16.

Lucas, A. 1962. *Ancient Egyptian Materials and Industries.* Revised and enlarged by J.R. Harris, 272–326. London.

A.R. DAVID

musical instruments

Musical instruments from ancient Egyptian tombs have survived in four main categories: idiophones (rattles, clappers), membranophones (drums, tambourines), aerophones (pipes, flute, trumpet, bugle), and chordophones (stringed instruments). In major museum collections, such as those in Cairo, Berlin, London, Paris, Turin, Boston, New York and Philadelphia, idiophones are well represented. Other types are more rare. To supplement the corpus of actual instruments, scenes on temple and tomb walls illustrate music in practice and show how at different periods different ensemble groupings were favored. The absence of any notation implies that musical skills were imparted by word of mouth. This lack is a fundamental impediment to knowledge of how the instruments were played, and theories about rhythms or scales in use can only be conjectural.

The instrument that above all symbolized Egypt for the ancient world was the sistrum. It is the commonest surviving idiophone, and it pervaded the Roman world as an attribute of the goddess Isis. It had two main forms in Egypt, both featuring the goddess Hathor. Essentially a rattle, with sounding plates suspended on metal rods, the sistrum was either arched or in the shape of a miniature rectangular shrine (*naos*). On temple walls the two types might be featured together, as when they appear in the hands of the emperors Augustus and Nero at the temple of Dendera.

Clappers survive from the Early Dynastic period, and sometimes the ends are carved to represent animal or human heads. Later examples are in the form of a human hand, with a head of Hathor carved below the wrist. Bells and cymbals are comparatively late. Bells were often shaped with the features of the household god Bes. The three main sizes of cymbal mostly date to the Graeco-Roman or Coptic periods.

A cylindrical drum from a tomb at Beni Hasan dating to the 12th Dynasty and now in the Cairo Museum is the earliest known Egyptian membranophone. A more common type is the barrel-shaped drum, hung by a cord from the neck of the player. Such drums appear mainly in military scenes, but might also have been used at the dedication of a temple. Tambourines also belong to this group. A rectangular tambourine with concave sides was briefly popular in the 18th Dynasty for use at banquets. The more usual shape was a round tambourine of various sizes. This too was featured in banquet scenes in tombs, but it is also shown in the hands of Bes. Elaborately painted skin coverings for such a tambourine are in the collections of the Cairo Museum, and the Ashmolean Museum, Oxford.

The end-blown flute is the characteristic aerophone of the Old Kingdom, though the earliest surviving example, again from Beni Hasan, dates from the Middle Kingdom. Such flutes were used throughout Egyptian history and have survived into modern times as the *nay*. Parallel pipes played with a single reed, of the clarinet type, were also common in the Old Kingdom, whereas pipes with a double reed were introduced in the New Kingdom. Very slender and easily damaged, these two-pipe instruments were held to make an acute angle between them.

Trumpets and bugles are shown in military scenes, and two such instruments are among the artifacts from Tutankhamen's tomb. One is of silver, and the other is of bronze or copper. Both are decorated with scenes involving Egypt's chief regimental gods. A monkey-shaped ocarina (ceramic pipe) and Graeco-Roman rhytons (drinking horns) used as musical instruments are among the rarer aerophones in the Cairo Museum.

The main Egyptian stringed instrument or chordophone was the harp. It assumed various shapes and sizes during its long history. The type with neck and soundbox making a continuous curve was the characteristic Egyptian harp. It might be as large as the magisterial instruments which tower above the standing players in scenes from the tomb of Ramesses III, or as small as those held on the shoulder in scenes of New Kingdom feasts. The angular harp, usually with horizontal neck at a right angle to the vertical soundbox, may be an import from Asia.

Neither the lyre nor the lute appear to be indigenous instruments. The lyre makes an early appearance in the tomb of Khnumhotep (No. 3) at Beni Hasan in the hands of an Asiatic bedouin from the Eastern Desert, but both instruments achieve popularity in the chamber groups of the New Kingdom. The lyre was either symmetrical like the modern tambour, or asymmetrical and trapezoidal in profile. The lute could have either a long wooden soundbox or a smaller one of tortoise shell. It was played with a plectrum.

A typical ensemble depicted in Old Kingdom tomb scenes consists of an end-blown flute, double parallel pipes and a harp. The player, always male, may be seated opposite a musician who seems to be directing the performance with various hand gestures. In the Middle Kingdom female musicians assume a larger part in tomb scenes, and the parallel pipes tend to disappear. The importance of music in the Middle Kingdom is seen in the presence of harpists and singers among the wooden models made for a nobleman's tomb, his "house of eternity."

Theban tombs of the New Kingdom and later have many musical scenes. Tuthmose III's vizier Rekhmire had three such scenes represented in his tomb. Female players, often scantily clad and probably professional musicians, tend to predominate. The ensemble may contain all three stringed instruments, a pair of angled pipes, and a tambourine, while a female dancer weaves back and forth among the musicians. Final testimony to the popularity of music among the Egyptians is the caricature of such an ensemble, with a lion, crocodile, ass or monkey shown playing the different instruments.

See also

Beni Hasan; representational evidence, Middle Kingdom private tombs; representational evidence, New Kingdom private tombs; Tutankhamen, tomb of

Further reading

Anderson, R.D. 1976. *Catalogue of Egyptian Antiquities in the British Museum 3: Musical Instruments*. London.

Manniche, L. 1975. *Ancient Egyptian Musical Instruments. MÄS* 34.

——. 1991. *Music and Musicians in Ancient Egypt*. London.

ROBERT ANDERSON

mythology

Mythology can be found everywhere and nowhere in ancient Egypt, depending on how rigorously our modern definition of the term is applied. Clearly, the many religious texts that survive include mythological allusions, as do literary, non-literary and historical texts. The same can be said of many artifacts. A single mythology or even a compendium of myths or mythologies has not survived, however, and probably never would have been composed in antiquity. The basics of the myths were learned by children, probably with different emphases in different times and places, and much would have been added to the basics as the children grew older and encountered both variations and modifications that had been proposed by priests or advocated by the king. From what has survived, it is obvious that both the king and some priests of the principal temples of Egypt would have been involved in mythologizing. The myth of "divine kingship" itself became the focal point of Egyptian mythology, and the reason why most other myths were recorded at all was in order to associate them with this myth.

The earliest recorded mythological allusions with any depth of detail are found in the *Pyramid Texts* carved on the walls of the burial chamber in the Saqqara pyramid of King Unas, the last king of the 5th Dynasty. In general, these texts were collected and composed to provide a guide for the king in the afterlife on his way to join the other great gods. The principal tradition upon which the mystery of the king's death is imposed is the great sun cult of Heliopolis, located across the river from Giza on the east bank. Re, who traverses the sky during the day and the area beyond the visible sky at night, is a "father" of the king, who is joined by the king, who is accompanied and guarded by him, and who is glorified by every pyramid, obelisk and sun temple erected by the king on earth. That the king is the "son of Re" is constantly reiterated in his royal titulary as well as being expounded in his *Pyramid Texts*. The complete titulary, that would have been seen by many, included other associations with divinity that are also encountered and elaborated upon in the funerary literature.

First and foremost, the king himself is identified with the god Horus. It is clear that there were several earlier falcon gods whose significance and expansiveness may have varied in their original cult centers, but whose cumulative attributes were sufficient for the divine equation to succeed on a grand scale. The genealogy of this Horus is one of the finest and clearest examples of Egyptian mythology, preserved in allusions from all periods, outlined already in the *Pyramid Texts*, recorded in a Late Egyptian story (New Kingdom), and preserved in classical literature, principally in Plutarch's *De Iside et Osiride* (Concerning Isis and Osiris).

This cosmological, cosmogonical myth places Horus in the fourth generation from the creator god, Atum (meaning the "complete one"), a sky god who himself produced the first pair of chthonic deities, Shu ("air") and Tefnut ("moisture"). Atum's creative force is variously described as his spitting, vomiting or masturbating, but his first generation of a male and female pair leads to their procreation of the second generation, Geb ("earth") and Nut (the "watery sky"). The next generation, anthropomorphic rather than chthonic, consists of two brothers and their two sister-spouses, Osiris and Seth, Isis and Nephthys. The older son Osiris became the god-king of his father's domain, the earth, but his jealous brother Seth connived to assume his throne. Osiris was killed and dismembered. Through his death he became god of the dead and through his dismemberment he became the source (etiology) of numerous shrines and cult temples throughout Egypt, where the parts of his body were buried. His beloved sister-wife, Isis, reassembled the body parts so that Osiris could father her son, Horus, who would avenge the death of his father and become the living god and god of all the living.

The enmity between Osiris and Seth can be seen as the struggle between the older but weaker son and his younger and stronger brother, between the Black Land (*Kemet*, i.e. Egypt) and the Red Land (*Deshret*). Through his death and resurrection, Osiris symbolized the Nile and its fertile black valley (the Black Land), the flood and subsequent harvest, while Seth represented the encroaching, untamed desert (the Red Land), as well as the destructive storm. The conflict of Horus and Seth is likewise symbolic of the triumph of good over evil, the loss (sacrifice, offering) of Horus's eye in the struggle to avenge the wrong done to his father by his uncle, the victory of intellect over brute force, and the resolution of the problem of succession, with that from father to son winning out over that from brother to brother.

The ennead (nine gods) representing the family tree of Horus was a Heliopolitan invention, which at some time prior to the earliest *Pyramid Texts* was identified with Hathor (the House of Horus). This great goddess, who undoubtedly had her own extensive following and clergy, to judge from the surviving titles of her priestesses, thus became another mother of the king along with Isis and Nut (who was really his grandmother). Already in the Old Kingdom the mythology that was central to the divine kingship had been interlaced with old and new ideas, part of a conscious effort to include all the major deities and cults by linking them to the most powerful visible representative they had on earth (the Horus-king).

The Heliopolitan priests who adopted the very old Osiris–Horus myth to their own old (Atum) and new (Re) mythological constructions did not stop there, but also incorporated mythological material from many other cults, especially the creation story from the cult center at Hermopolis in Middle Egypt. This was not difficult since the great god of Hermopolis, Thoth, the god of the moon, wisdom and writing, could be subsumed under the Heliopolitan creator god (Atum), and Thoth's antecedents could be made the real primordial source for Atum himself. At Hermopolis, four male and female pairs of divine beings representing aspects of the cosmos before creation comprised an ogdoad (eight gods), which produced an egg that developed on an island that appeared in the middle of the Nile as the flood receded; from this egg, the creator god was born. The pairs included Amen and

Amaunet (representing "hiddenness"), Huh and Hauhet ("formlessness"), Kuk and Kauket ("darkness"), and Nun and Naunet ("watery abyss"). These deities were represented anthropomorphically at a much later date, but in their original conception seem to have been chthonic at least and perhaps better considered as elements of pre-creation chaos. Unfortunately, the original Hermopolitan myth does not survive. However, the Heliopolitan adaptation in the *Pyramid Texts* would seem to indicate the myth's great antiquity, the fact that it was credited with chronological priority, and the significance of Hermopolis as an early cult center, renowned as the birthplace of the gods and later as a source for important old religious texts: a tradition as old as the Old Kingdom and surviving to the Middle Ages and Renaissance.

The gods of Memphis, Ptah, Sekhmet, Nefertem, Tatenen and Sokar should be the deities most clearly associated with the king of Egypt, since Memphis by tradition was established as the capital by Menes, the first king of the 1st Dynasty, and this king is also supposed to have erected the first great temple there. The Memphite gods are mentioned early enough in texts, but neither as a familial triad plus mortuary god, as they appear later, nor in the context of the creation story credited to Ptah in a much later text. An inscription from the reign of the Kushite king Shabako (25th Dynasty) identifies Ptah with both of the last two deities of the Hermopolitan cosmogony, Nun and Naunet, so that this creator is placed between the ogdoad and the ennead, but while he is somewhat androgynous, he creates by conceiving in his heart and speaking with his tongue. Thus he creates Atum and everything else *ex nihilo*, paralleling one of the creation stories in the Book of Genesis and prefiguring the Logos doctrine of St John's Gospel as well. Ptah's consort, Sekhmet, must have had many of the good characteristics of the other goddesses with whom she is later identified, but she is known as a "powerful one" from her name and hundreds of lioness-headed statues from the New Kingdom. From at least one mythological story she is known as a slayer of men identified with

Hathor. Nefertem, the son of Ptah and Sekhmet, is also encountered separately as the young sun god arising from a lotus. The connection with the sun cult is significant, but the mythological text that links this triad to the Memphite creation story is still lacking. Sokar, the Memphite mortuary god, is found in early texts, but is apparently no competitor for Osiris's position until guidebooks to the after-life are found in New Kingdom royal tombs with Sokar predominant as the god of the domain through which the sun bark passes at night. Somewhat later abbreviated versions of the funerary text called the *Book of Amduat* ("that which is in the Netherworld") are found in papyri belonging to individuals who also had copies of the *Book of the Dead*.

Because Thebes was the power base of the dynasties that founded both the Middle and the New Kingdoms, the Theban gods had to be associated politically as well as mythologically with the other great gods of Egypt. The triad of Amen, Mut and Khonsu was a very fitting group to do all that was necessary to link Thebes both to its allies and to the old religions. The name "Amen" was that of the first of the primordial gods of Hermopolis, but at Thebes the god took on the characteristics of the Theban war god, Montu, as well as the attributes of the ithyphallic fertility god Min from neighboring Coptos (Quft/Qift). The site of Thebes became sacred through the claim that the ogdoad was buried there. Mut "the mother" is easily equated to Isis, Hathor and Sekhmet, and her son Khonsu, a moon god, helps to solidify the link between the two elements of Amen-Re, and at the same time to connect Amen with Thoth, thus enhancing the Theban family's devotion to the moon god. A late mythological text from Thebes has Amen-Re come from Thebes to Hermopolis as Ptah "to open" (*pth*, in Egyptian) Hathor, create the ogdoad, and as Khonsu to travel (*ḥns*) back to Thebes. All of the mythological associations and word play in this Ptolemaic text would not necessarily have been early New Kingdom thinking, but the notion of the Theban site of Medinet Habu (ancient Djeme) as the burial place of the ogdoad apparently was noted already in the reign of Queen Hatshepsut (18th Dynasty).

Clearly, many of the Egyptian myths were elaborated upon and embellished over time, but the sketchy bits that survive in early texts dealing with many other deities could also be merely hints at fuller versions with which the people were familiar. There are, of course, many other partial allusions to powerful local deities, creation stories and etiologies that could be presented here, but since the myths have to be pieced together from disparate sources, they remain for the most part hypothetical.

See also

funerary texts; kingship; mortuary beliefs; pantheon

Further reading

Hornung, E. 1982. *Conceptions of God in Ancient Egypt: The One and the Many*. Ithaca, NY.

Shafer, B., ed. 1991. *Religion in Ancient Egypt: Gods, Myths, and Personal Practice*. Ithaca, NY.

Wilson, J. 1949. Egypt. In *Before Philosophy*, H. Frankfort, ed., 37–133. Harmondsworth.

LEONARD H. LESKO

N

Naga ed-Deir

The cemeteries of Naga ed-Deir (Naga-ed-Dêr; 26°22′ N, 31°54′ E) lie on the east bank of the Nile near Abydos in Upper Egypt. The archaeological remains stretch more than 1.5 km along the limestone cliffs (*gebel*) to the northwest of the modern village and Coptic monastery (Deir) after which the site is named. The cemeteries of Naga ed-Deir cover an almost unbroken sequence from Predynastic times to the present. Inscriptions from Dynastic tombs link the site with the ancient town of Tjeni (Thinis/This).

The Hearst Egyptian Expedition of the University of California worked at Naga ed-Deir between February 1901 and August 1904. Phoebe Apperson Hearst sponsored the Expedition, which was led by George A. Reisner. The Harvard University–Museum of Fine Arts, Boston (MFA) Expedition returned to the site in 1912, 1913 and 1923. The Hearst Expedition numbered cemeteries 100 to 3500 around the three wadis at the southern end of the site, and cemeteries 9000–10,000 which were located farther north. The Harvard–MFA Expedition identified three cemeteries in the area of Sheikh Farag (designated SF 200, SF 500 and SF 5000). Other sites identified in the area of Naga ed-Deir were el-Mesheikh, Mesaeed and Awlad el-Sheikh.

The cemetery identified as N7000 was the oldest at the site, dating primarily to the earlier part of the Predynastic period (Nagada I and II, *circa* 3,800–3,300 BC). There is no known late Predynastic (Nagada III) cemetery from the site comparable to N7000. It may be that during late Predynastic times the cemetery of Mesaeed, located near the town of Naga el-Mesaid (*circa* 4 km south of Naga ed-Deir), became the

primary burial ground for the region. Since a large Early Dynastic cemetery (N1500) is located just 300 m southwest of cemetery N7000 and only a small proportion of the dated graves from Mesaeed belong to the Nagada III phase, it is also possible that there was a Nagada III cemetery at Naga ed-Deir that has been destroyed or remains undiscovered.

The oval and rectangular pit graves from cemetery N7000 held the bodies of one or more individuals in contracted positions, with the head to the south, facing west and wrapped in cloth and reed matting. The graves contained typical Predynastic artifacts, including pottery, cosmetic palettes, stone vessels, and implements and beads of stone, ivory, bone and copper. The rarity of foreign artifacts, such as the cylinder seal from N7304 (possibly of Mesopotamian origin), indicates that any contact between this site and the Mesopotamian region was limited, probably consisting of indirect, long-distance trade. Cemetery N7000 is notable for the extraordinary quality of preservation of perishable materials, such as cloth, wood, baskets, animal skin and human bodies. Grafton Elliot Smith's analysis of the human remains contradicted earlier theories that the Predynastic Egyptians dismembered their dead.

In the Early Dynastic period (1st–2nd Dynasties) burial activity at Naga ed-Deir shifted to the alluvial bank on the west side of Wadi 3 (Cemetery 1500). The Early Dynastic tombs were apparently the first at this site to be built using mudbrick. In Cemetery 1500 large rectangular superstructures (*mastabas*) of mudbrick, with solid mudbrick or rubble interiors and plain or niched exteriors, were built over burial pits sometimes reached by a stairway. These *mastabas* were erected after the interment

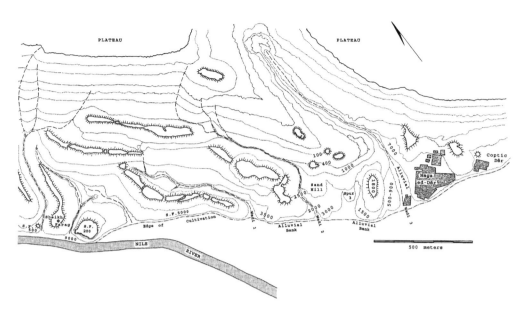

Figure 82 Map of Naga ed-Deir sites, *circa*. 1900
Source: after G.A. Reisner, 1908.

had taken place. The burial pit might be a plain hole or consist of one, two, three or five mudbrick- or wood-lined chambers. The largest chamber contained the body, laid in a contracted position on the left side with head to the south, facing west and placed in a coffin of wood or pottery. The chambers held ceramic storage jars and bowls and plates of pottery or stone. Some tombs contained over forty finely made vessels of Egyptian alabaster, granite, gneiss, slate, and other stones. The largest collection of provenanced cylinder seals from this period was found here. Their distinctively Egyptian designs include hieroglyphic inscriptions. Grave N1532 contained a necklace with repoussé figures of an oryx, a bull and a beetle decorated with the emblem of the Delta goddess Neith, some of the oldest gold jewelry known from Egypt. Other artifacts of note were metal tools, flint blades and knives and decorated cosmetic dishes. Tombs of this period were also found in Cemeteries 500, 3000 and 3500.

Two types of tombs were built in the Old Kingdom. At the base of the *gebel*, *mastaba*s of mudbrick or rough stones plastered with mud, a few with exterior offering niches, were constructed over simple pits or shafts leading to one or more rough chambers. Rock-cut tombs first appeared at this site in the later Old Kingdom in cemeteries 100–400. In some of these, only the burial chamber was rock-cut, while others also had a rock-cut chapel, rarely decorated, which served as the offering area and one or more sealed shafts or corridors leading to burial chambers. Shallow pit graves held the burials of the poorest members of the community. During the 4th Dynasty the predominant orientation of the body changed from head to the south to head to the north. In the early Old Kingdom the body was still placed in a loosely contracted or semi-extended position on the left side, but by the end of the period the fully extended position became the norm in larger graves. Ceramic coffins became less common and wooden coffins, some inscribed with funerary texts, predominated. Headrests and mirrors were often placed within the coffin.

Preservation of perishable materials was better in the rock-cut tombs than in the pits in the gravel and alluvium. Important finds in these upper tombs included statues of stone (N3604) and wood, whole pleated garments (N94) and papyri. The pottery, which was found in both the burial and offering chambers, was generally plain and included bowls, storage jars, pot stands and cosmetic jars. A few fine bowls of Meydum Ware were found. Stone vessels were popular, especially earlier in the period. Hard stones were used less often than in the preceding period. Cylinder seals became rare and may have been replaced by button seals of bone or ivory. Tombs of Old Kingdom date are found in Cemeteries 100–400, 500–900, 1000, 1500, 2000, 2500, 3000, 3200, 3500, SF 200, SF 500 and SF 5000.

In the First Intermediate Period, *mastaba*s and rock-cut tombs were both used for burial. The rock-cut chapels of the more important tombs were decorated with painted and carved reliefs which contained typical Old Kingdom themes. Most of these tombs were reused in later periods and artifacts from different periods are often found in one tomb. Poor burials in the gravel and alluvial deposits held reed, basket or stick coffins. Some scholars believe that the cemeteries of Naga ed-Deir are those reported as being damaged in *The Instructions for King Merikare* (11th Dynasty), although no more specific location than the nome of This/Thinis is mentioned in that text. Tombs of the First Intermediate Period at Naga ed-Deir are found in Cemeteries 100–400, 2000, 2500, 3200, 3500, Sheikh Farag Cemeteries 200, 500 and 5000, and on the west bank of Wadi 3 below the town of Naga ed-Deir.

Painted limestone stelae carved in sunk or raised relief (less common) appeared at the end of the 6th Dynasty and became common in the First Intermediate Period. More than 100 stelae have been attributed to the site. They were placed in the chapels of rock-cut tombs or in small niches in the western face of the *mastabas* and served as the focus of the offering area.

Burial in a wooden coffin painted with the name and titles of the deceased and a short funerary formula was the norm. The body was laid fully extended on its back with head to the north. Where preservation was good, the bodies were wrapped in linen. There were no recorded

examples of evisceration of the body. Lengths of cloth and whole garments were piled over the body and a walking stick, headrest and bronze mirror were often placed in the coffin. Painted funerary masks of cartonnage, made of plaster applied on cloth, appear for the first time at this site (in N3804). A rare ivory statuette (in N3737), wooden models of offering bearers and domestic scenes, and papyri were also found. The unsettled political situation was reflected in the presence of bows and other weapons. The button seals were gradually replaced by seal amulets, the most famous form of which is the scarab. The pottery continues the forms of the Old Kingdom (jars, pot stands, bowls), but the fabric is generally coarser. Stone vessels become very rare.

Burials of the Middle Kingdom were well represented in Cemeteries 100–400, 1000, 1500, 2000, 2500, 3200, 3500, 9000, Sheikh Farag Cemeteries 200, 500 and 5000, and the west bank of Wadi 3 below the town of Naga ed-Deir. Rock-cut tombs, mostly without rock-cut chapels, were common. *Mastaba* tombs, known from elsewhere in Egypt, are not well documented at the site, perhaps due to poor preservation. Burials of poor individuals continue as simple pits in the colluvial and alluvial deposits at the base of the cliffs.

Mortuary stelae were also used during the Middle Kingdom, but they were much less common than earlier, though better made. The extended burial with head to the north, wrapped in cloth and placed in a wooden coffin inscribed with the name and titles of the deceased continued. Clothing was still placed in the coffin, often along with a walking stick, mirror and headrest. Cartonnage masks were also found.

The pottery has new shapes, which reflect the use of the potter's wheel. The largest collections of pots were often found in the offering area. Stone vessels, mostly for cosmetics, reappeared as popular grave goods. Small vessels of anhydrite, sometimes called "blue marble," were typical of the period. The jewelry is renowned for the use of beads of semiprecious stones, such as amethyst, carnelian, garnet and hematite. The legacy of the unrest of the First

Intermediate Period was reflected in the continued presence of weapons in burials.

The Middle Kingdom tombs of Naga ed-Deir also produced a number of artifacts of unusual historical value or rarity. An ivory cosmetic spoon decorated with the figure of a dwarf (in N463) exhibits the finest workmanship. A reed flute was found in the coffin of one individual (in N408/410), perhaps the instrument of a musician. Four papyri, known collectively as the "Reisner papyri," had been left lying on the lid of a coffin in grave N408. They date to the reign of Senusret I and are records of a building project and dockyard workshop in the town of Tjeni (This/Thinis).

Tombs of the Second Intermediate through Roman periods were much less common than earlier graves and were scattered among the older cemeteries of the site. Second Intermediate Period and New Kingdom tombs cut into the gebel and lower gravel slopes are known from Cemeteries 500–900, 1000, 1500, 1800, 3500, 9000, Spur 3, Sheikh Farag 5000, and in cemetery 10,000, near the village of Awlad el-Sheikh. In the New Kingdom tombs, wheel-thrown pottery was the most common type of grave good. Some of these vessels were well made, including 18th Dynasty blue-painted wares and foreign ceramics. A wide variety of other artifacts, from jewelry to game pieces to furniture, was found; some belonging to important individuals. An ebony scribe's palette, inscribed for the Mayor of Tjeni (This/Thinis), Neb-iry, and bearing the cartouche of Tuthmose III, was recovered in grave 10,001. Uninscribed ceramic "funerary cones" were found mixed in among the remains of Middle and New Kingdom graves in Cemetery 1500. None was found *in situ* and their precise function at this site is unknown.

Graves of the Third Intermediate and Late periods were extremely rare, and there was almost no evidence of the construction of new graves, only reuse of older tombs. Artifact remains were almost exclusively limited to ceramics. Graeco-Roman burials were also rare and were found most commonly in Cemeteries 3500 and 9000. Again, ceramics were the most frequently encountered artifacts. Extensive use of Naga ed-Deir as a burial ground resumed in the later Coptic period (*circa* AD 600–900) and continued into recent times. Cemeteries 500, 1500, 2000, 2500 and 3500 contained many Coptic graves, although Coptic burials were found scattered throughout the site.

See also

Early Dynastic period, overview; First Intermediate Period, overview; funerary texts; Middle Kingdom, overview; natural resources; Old Kingdom, overview; Old Kingdom provincial tombs; pantheon; Predynastic period, overview; Reisner, George Andrew

Further reading

Brovarski, E. 1989. "The Inscribed Material of the First Intermediate Period from Naga-ed-Dêr." Ph.D. dissertation, University of Chicago.

Dunham, D. 1937. *Naga-ed-Dêr Stelae of the First Intermediate Period*. Boston.

Lythgoe, A.M. 1965. *The Predynastic Cemetery N 7000. Naga-ed-Dêr, Part IV*, D. Dunham, ed. Berkeley, CA.

Mace, A.C. 1909. *The Early Dynastic Cemeteries of Naga-ed-Dêr* 2. Leipzig.

Podzorski, P.V. 1990. *Their Bones Shall Not Perish. An Examination of Predynastic Skeletal Remains from Naga-ed-Dêr in Egypt*. New Malden.

Reisner, G.A. 1908. *The Early Dynastic Cemeteries of Naga-ed-Dêr* 1. Leipzig.

——. 1932. *A Provincial Cemetery of the Pyramid Age: Naga-ed-Dêr* 3. Oxford.

Simpson, W.K. 1963. *The Records of a Building Project in the Reign of Sesostris I: Papyrus Reisner I*. Boston.

——. 1965. *Accounts of the Dockyard Workshop at This in the Reign of Sesostris I: Papyrus Reisner II*. Boston.

PATRICIA PODZORSKI

Nagada (Naqada)

The Nagada region is on the west bank of the Nile midway between Luxor and Dendera (25°54′ N, 32°43′ E). Investigations during the last decade of the nineteenth century by Jacques de Morgan and Flinders Petrie led to the discovery of several sites from the interval predating the emergence of the first Egyptian dynasties, known as the Predynastic period. Sites from this period show evidence of agriculture and herding and date from *circa* 3,800–3,100/3,000 BC. Nagada was known as "Nubt" (City of Gold) in Dynastic times, and control of gold mines in the Eastern Desert and/or gold trade may have contributed to the center's wealth in later Predynastic times.

De Morgan was the first to work at Nagada, where he excavated two large "royal" tombs with niched mudbrick superstructures, dating to the end of the Predynastic period (Nagada III/Dynasty 0), and a cemetery of lower status burials. In 1894–5 Petrie conducted more thorough excavations at Nagada with J.E. Quibell, who also excavated a Predynastic cemetery with about 1,000 burials to the north at Ballas. A number of Dynastic tombs, a temple and a small step pyramid probably dating to the 3rd Dynasty were also recorded by Petrie in the Nagada region, but most of his fieldwork there concentrated on the Predynastic remains, including three Predynastic cemeteries ("Great New Race" cemetery, and Cemeteries B and T), which contained over 2,200 burials. Two Predynastic settlements, "North Town" and "South Town," were also excavated by Petrie. At South Town Petrie uncovered the remains of a thick mudbrick wall, which he thought was a fortification. South Town was later investigated in the 1970s and early 1980s by an American expedition directed by Fekri Hassan and T.R. Hays, and an Italian one from the Oriental Institute of Naples.

The majority of Predynastic sites in the Nagada region investigated by Hassan and Hays belong to Early Nagada (used here as a local archaeological/stratigraphic subdivision). The sites range in size from a few thousand m^2 to 3 ha. They represent overlapping occupations of many huts in small villages and hamlets. The settlements probably housed 50–250 persons. Evidence of small postholes and the wooden stub of a post suggest architecture of flimsy wickerwork around a frame of wooden posts. The abundance of rubble and mud clumps also indicates that many dwellings were made from mud with rubble, commonly used today in field houses and mud fences. The houses contained hearths and storage pits. In some cases, graves were dug into the floor of houses. Trash areas were interspersed with domestic dwellings. Thick layers of (sheep) dung suggest that animal enclosures (*zeribas*) were common.

The stone tools in Early Nagada sites show a high frequency of burins, scrapers, notches and denticulates, truncations and perforators. They also include grand perçoirs, planes, bifacial tools, concave-based projectile points and axes. The axes are distinctive.

North Town and South Town show evidence of late Nagada occupations (*circa* 3,600–3,300 BC), with a Nagada IIc–d ceramic assemblage. With the exception of sickle blades, the lithic assemblage is very similar to that of early Nagada sites. The pottery, however, is markedly different. South Town and North Town also have high densities of artifacts, which indicates that they could have indeed been small early towns. The sites also show a shift in the location of the main settlement through time.

The rarity of Nagada II sites by comparison to the earlier sites is probably related to a shift of settlement location away from the desert margin, where early Nagada sites are located, closer to the inner Nile floodplain. One reason for this shift is presumably the decline in Nile flood levels at that time, a decline well documented in the Fayum depression. There may also have been a shift in subsistence activities and increased economic interaction and trade via the river.

Faunal and botanical remains, which are abundant and well preserved, clearly indicate that farming and herding were the predominant subsistence activities. People cultivated wheat and barley, as well as other plants, including medicinal plants. They also herded cattle,

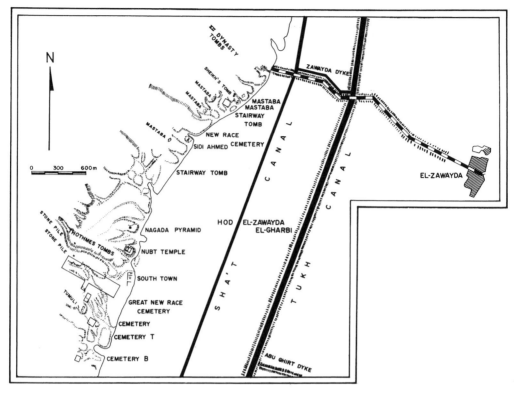

Figure 83 Petrie's Predynastic sites in the Nagada region

sheep/goats and pigs. Hunting was very limited, but fishing was widely practiced.

The cemeteries in the Nagada region were in the low desert adjacent to the settlements. Analysis of the distribution, morphometry, density, clustering and contents of graves shows evidence of gradual, increasing social hierarchy and a shift in sociopolitical organization from a "chiefdom" to a small-scale state society.

Grave goods of figurines, slate palettes and a variety of artifacts (other than pottery) indicate great sophistication, skill and specialization in the production of craft goods. A segment of a rising elite (administrative/religious) was buried with many sumptuary artifacts. Trade was evidently practiced to procure rare minerals, stones and craft goods. The standardization of the placement of the dead suggests that religious burial rites were strictly observed. Scenes on the pottery (Decorated class) may symbolize the duality of death and the notion of resurrection. Figurines of women with raised arms, and representations of such women on pots, towering over men, suggest that female goddesses might have figured highly in the religious discourse at Nagada in late Predynastic times.

See also

dating techniques, prehistory; Neolithic and Predynastic stone tools; pottery, prehistoric; Predynastic period, overview; representational evidence, Predynastic

Further reading

Bard, K.A. 1994. *From Farmers to Pharaohs: Mortuary Evidence for the Rise of Complex Society in Egypt.* Sheffield.

Barocas, C., R. Fattovich and M. Tosi. 1989.

The Oriental Institute of Naples Expedition to Petrie's South Town (Upper Egypt), 1977–1983: an interim report. In *Late Prehistory of the Nile Basin and the Sahara*, L. Krzyzaniak and M. Kobusiewicz, eds. 295–301. Poznan.

Hassan, F.A. 1988. The Predynastic of Egypt. *JWP* 2: 135–85.

Petrie, W.M.F., and J.E. Quibell. 1896. *Naqada and Ballas*. London.

FEKRI A. HASSAN

Napoleon Bonaparte and the Napoleonic expedition

Born into a noble Corsican family, Napoleon Bonaparte (1769–1821) early showed an aptitude for mathematics, a fascination with warfare, and an interest in reading ancient history, particularly the Greek historian Plutarch and Julius Caesar, all of which is reflected in his later career. Trained at French military academies by favor of Louis XVI, Bonaparte nevertheless supported the revolution and with its victory made further advances in command. He won the heart of Josephine de Beauharnais at the same time (1796) that he received command of France's army in Italy. His victories there allowed him to send large amounts of money back to the government in France, and many works of art to the museums of Paris. He wrested the Venetian fleet away from Austrian control, and this allowed him to pursue his plans for conquest beyond Europe. Finding role models in Julius Caesar and Alexander the Great, the young general planned, like them, to conquer Egypt; and to make it a province of France. His justification was to lift Egypt into the modern age and restore it to prosperity after freeing it from the rule of exploitative tyrants, the Mamelukes. However, he also was retaliating for the treatment of French traders there, and he was planning to sever the British hold on India and the East by dominating the Eastern Mediterranean and cutting a canal through the Suez.

Already voted a Member of the Academy of Sciences, as he liked to surround himself with men of science, Napoleon conceived of a scientific and artistic purpose to his great military venture. Along with the army of 25,000 went an impressive company of 165 French scholars, scientists, engineers and students. Commissioned with exploring, studying and publishing as much of the natural and ancient history of Egypt as possible, they landed near Alexandria at the beginning of July, 1798. Among them were the artist Vivant Denon, the mineralogist Deodat Dolomieu and the mathematician Jean-Joseph Fourier, plus zoologists, paleontologists, chemists and engineers. Together they composed the French Commission of Arts and Sciences, and with them they brought a printing press, a library of every work published thus far on Egypt, and crates of scientific instruments. A research center— the Institute of Egypt—was founded in Cairo, and staffed by the most eminent of this band of scholars, but many of them also toured the country, accompanying the army.

Napoleon ordered the exploration of Upper Egypt, and as well as Denon, who followed the French General Desaix for ten months as he pursued the Mamelukes throughout Egypt, three commissions of engineers and scientists also braved enemy fire to carry out their research. A year after landing, many had reached Aswan at the southern border believing that they had measured and drawn every notable monument encountered. The month spent at Luxor by the young engineers Prosper Jollois and Édouard de Villiers du Terrage allowed them to discover the tomb of Amenhotep III in the western Valley of the Kings and make an extensive artistic and architectural record of the ancient temples, which later comprised many of the plates in the monumental work of the Napoleonic expedition, the *Description de l'Égypte* (Description of Egypt). At the temple at Dendera, which dazzled all who saw it, they executed a careful drawing of the zodiac, which had been discovered by Denon on the ceiling of a small room.

As well as producing the first scientific maps of Egypt and collecting and drawing numerous plants, animals and minerals, the expedition collected antiquities, the most notable being the trilingual Rosetta Stone, which would prove to be the key in deciphering the hieroglyphs. The British confiscated this trophy as a result of their successful naval blockade of Egypt, which had trapped the French shortly after their arrival.

Napoleon, taking the senior scientist Gaspard Monge and artist Denon with him, escaped back to a France unaware of his defeat and was made First Consul. Months later the British finally allowed the other hapless French scholars to leave, along with their specimens, drawings and notes. These eventually resulted in the remarkable twenty-four-volume *Description de l'Égypte*, including ten folio volumes with over 3,000 illustrations, five volumes of which were devoted to antiquities and ancient monuments. Due to the magnitude of the writing, editing and printing effort, the massive publication did not begin to appear until 1809 and was not concluded until 1828, long after the Emperor of the French had been defeated and exiled to St Helena, where he died at the age of fifty two.

Through his enlightened interests, Napoleon opened Egypt to the West and started her toward modernity, while he caused Europe to become aware of Egypt's great and rich antiquity and cultural legacy. In this way, he became one of the founders of Egyptology.

See also

Champollion, Jean-François; Dendera; Denon, Dominique Vivant, Baron de; Egyptian (language), decipherment of; Rosetta Stone; Thebes, Valley of the Kings

Further reading

Charles-Roux, F. 1937. *Bonaparte, Governor of Egypt*, trans. E.W. Dickes. London.
Clayton, P.A. 1982. *The Rediscovery of Ancient Egypt*. New York.
Gillispie, C.C., and M. Dewachter. 1987. *Monuments of Egypt: The Napoleonic Edition*. Princeton, NJ.

BARBARA S. LESKO

natural resources

The Nile

Ancient Egypt's greatest natural resource was the Nile River, and the unified kingdom was a navigable stretch of river and floodplain from the First Cataract at Aswan to the Mediterranean shore of the Delta. Without it, large-scale cereal agriculture on the broad fertile floodplains, which was the economic base of the pharaonic state, would not have been possible. The Nile was also the major channel of communication and transportation for this kingdom, facilitating control of a large kingdom and the transport of goods and materials controlled by the state. Not only was transport relatively easy downstream, but prevailing winds from the north also facilitated sailing upstream. Unlike in Nubia, where the Nile is impeded by six cataracts and the floodplain is narrow, the Egyptian Nile was a cohesive and fertile geographic feature.

Most of the waters of the Nile originate in highland Ethiopia, and the floodplain in Egypt was replenished by annual flooding, which deposited new silts and flushed out salts in the soil. In prehistoric times the marshes of the Nile attracted many large mammals which were hunted, as were migratory waterfowl. Papyrus, reeds and lotus pads grew in these marshes. Papyrus was used to make small boats and as a material for writing. Reeds and rushes were used to make matting, and lotus flowers were enjoyed by ancient Egyptians for their beauty and fragrance.

As domesticated animals were introduced into the Nile Valley and as the region became more arid in later prehistoric times, a number of wild animals which had been hunted became scarce or extinct. Cattle, sheep and goats grazed along the margins of the floodplain and, along with fish from the Nile, were the major sources of protein in pharaonic Egypt.

Ceramics

The floodplain in Egypt was also the source of another basic material: clay for ceramics. The brown and black clay which is found in the Nile Valley and the Delta contains much organic matter and iron, and some sand. Some Egyptian pottery was also made of calcareous clay or marl, which is only found in a few locations, notably at Qena and Ballas in Upper Egypt. Marl clay consists mainly of calcium carbonate, and is a light buff color when fired.

Wood

Because Egypt is so arid, many useful species of trees cannot grow there. From early times a species of ebony (*Dalbergia melanoxylon*) was imported for luxury craft goods from regions to the south and southeast. Large timbers were not available, and cedar (*Cedrus Libani*) was imported from Syria by Early Dynastic times. Cedar was used to make coffins, but, perhaps more importantly, it was used to make large ships. Probably the most well-known example of a cedar ship is the (reconstructed) solar bark of Khufu, found in a large pit next to his pyramid at Giza.

The acacia was probably the most common tree that grew in ancient Egypt, and many varieties are found there today. Another common tree was the tamarisk, and again many species are known. Beginning in Predynastic times, two different palm trees, the date palm (*Phoenix dactylifera*) and the dom palm (*Hyphoene thebaica*), were cultivated in Egypt for their wood (domestic uses) and fruit. Leaves of both palms were used for fibers to make baskets and rope. Wood of the persea tree (*Mimusops Schimperi*) was used for making craft goods, and it has an edible fruit. Fruit from the sidder tree (*Zizyphus spina Christi*) has been found in Egyptian tombs, and its hardwood was used by carpenters for dowels.

Two other species of trees found in ancient Egypt were the sycamore fig (*Ficus sycomorus*) and the willow (*Salix safsaf*). The wood of these trees was used for various purposes, and their leaves have been found in funeral garlands. The fruit of the sycamore fig was also eaten.

Because trees were not plentiful in ancient Egypt, animal dung was a major source of fuel, as it is today in farming villages.

Building materials

Much more plentiful in Egypt than wood was the material used to make sun-dried mudbrick. The Nile floodplain provided alluvium for the basic building material for domestic architecture, including royal palaces, and mudbricks were also used for the construction of many cult centers until the New Kingdom. Fired bricks were rare in Egypt until the Roman period. As many species of large trees were not found in Egypt, mudbrick houses were roofed with rafters of palm logs covered with palm branches.

Various stones for monuments were available throughout the Nile Valley and the earliest building in the world built entirely of stone (limestone) is the 3rd Dynasty Step Pyramid at Saqqara. Limestone is found beyond the floodplain from Cairo to Esna in Upper Egypt, south of which the Nubian Sandstone Formation begins, but the quality of this limestone greatly varies. Limestone was quarried locally at pyramid sites, but a finer quality of limestone from Tura on the east bank was used for casing stones. In the north, tomb superstructures constructed in mudbrick and/or limestone were lined with limestone which provided a surface for scenes of the mortuary cult. In other parts of Egypt, limestone cliffs provided the medium for rock-cut tombs. Temple construction in sandstone did not begin until the New Kingdom, and many of the temples in Upper Egypt are built with this material. Granite was used for special constructions, such as obelisks, and the huge blocks that line the King's [burial] Chamber in the Great Pyramid and the five "relieving" chambers above it. Granite was quarried at Aswan and transported by ship downriver.

Alabaster and basalt were used less frequently in the construction of cult centers.

Alabaster was quarried in the Wadi Gerawi in Lower Egypt near Helwan, but there are a number of quarry sites in Middle Egypt, especially at Hatnub, about 25 km east of Tell el-Amarna. Most of the basalt used during the Old Kingdom came from the Fayum region. Gypsum, which was used to make plaster and mortar for stone monuments in the Old Kingdom, was also quarried in the Fayum.

Stone (sculpture and vessels)

Stones used in the construction of monuments were also carved into stelae and sculpture found in cult centers and tombs: limestone, sandstone, granite, alabaster and basalt. Granite was also used for royal sarcophagi and, infrequently, for early stone vessels.

While limestone, sandstone and granite came from quarries near the Nile Valley, other stones used less frequently were found in the Eastern or Western Deserts. According to Lucas, the "diorite-gneiss" used for 4th Dynasty royal statues came from a quarry in Nubia, about 60 km northwest of Abu Simbel. Marble used for stone vessels and statues was found at sites in the Eastern Desert. Quartzite, which was mainly used for royal sarcophagi and statues, was probably quarried in the Gebel Ahmar northeast of Cairo, or north of Aswan.

Red and white breccia used for Predynastic and Early Dynastic stone vessels can be found at several sites in Middle and Upper Egypt. Green breccia was quarried in the Wadi Hammamat (Eastern Desert) and exported by the Romans. "Imperial" porphyry, which is purple in color, was also exported by the Romans, and came from quarries in the Eastern Desert, as did other varieties of porphyry used for early stone vessels. Diorite, probably from a quarry near Aswan, and dolomite from the Eastern Desert were also used for these vessels. Graywacke (sometimes called schist) and slate from the Wadi Hammamat were used for various artifacts, such as palettes, bracelets and stone vessels in the Predynastic and Early Dynastic periods, and later for statues. Serpentine, which is green to black in color, came from sites in the Eastern Desert.

With the exception of flint, stone quarrying in Egypt and the (state organized) quarrying at sites in the Sinai and Eastern and Western Deserts were conducted to obtain materials used for luxury craft goods of elites and monuments constructed by the crown.

Stone (tools)

Flint is found in many parts of Egypt, in limestone deposits and as nodules on the surface of the desert. Not only was it used for stone tools in prehistoric times but, because copper was rare in Egypt, flint was a locally available material used for tools in Dynastic times as well.

Obsidian is not found in Egypt, and the obsidian used for tools, beads and eye inlays in statues was imported from Ethiopia or southern Arabia.

Stone (jewelry)

Various stones used for beads, such as agate, carnelian and chalcedony, were plentiful in Egypt where they were found as pebbles. Amethyst and garnet are found at mines in the Eastern and Western Deserts. Beryl, green feldspar, red and yellow jasper come from mines in the Eastern Desert. Quartz of different colors and rock crystal are found in veins of rock in the Eastern Desert and near Aswan.

The most common kind of scarab was made of glazed steatite from the Eastern Desert, near Aswan. Beads were also made of (glazed) steatite.

Although lapis lazuli was used for jewelry and small objects beginning in the Predynastic period, it was not found in Egypt and was imported from Afghanistan. Turquoise came from two mines in the Sinai which were worked in Dynastic times.

Metals

Cast metal artifacts in ancient Egypt could be considered luxury goods, as metals had to be brought into the Nile Valley from elsewhere. Copper ore was found in small mines in the

Eastern Desert, and it was mined in the Sinai in the Wadi Maghara and in the vicinity of Serabit el-Khadim. In the New Kingdom, copper ingots were imported from Cyprus and Syria. Bronze, an alloy of copper and a small proportion of tin which is much harder and stronger than pure copper, was not found in Egypt in any great quantity until the New Kingdom, when tin would have been imported from southwest Asia.

Malachite, a copper ore which occurs in the Eastern Desert and Sinai, was ground to make pigment for eye paint. Galena, the ore of lead, was also used for eye paint, and came from mines in the Eastern Desert near the Red Sea.

Iron minerals occur in Egypt, and hematite was made into beads as early as the Predynastic period. Red and yellow ochers, compounds of iron used as pigments, are found in the Eastern Desert and Sinai, and in the oases of the Western Desert. Although a few iron artifacts were found in Tutankhamen's tomb and isolated iron artifacts are known earlier, iron working and tool production did not develop on any large scale in Egypt until the first millennium BC, during the 25th–26th Dynasties.

Ancient Egypt was best known for its gold, and in the New Kingdom it may have been the major supplier of gold to other states in the Near East. The main gold deposits are in the Eastern Desert, from the Qena region south. The Eastern Desert was even richer in gold deposits in Nubia than in Egypt, and this was a major reason for Egypt's motivation to control parts of Nubia during the Old, Middle and New Kingdoms.

Egyptian gold contains varying proportions of silver, but high grade silver ores do not occur in Egypt. The light-colored gold found in some Egyptian artifacts was a naturally occurring alloy of gold and silver, called electrum by the Romans. Silver was rare in Egypt, and most silver in artifacts is thought to have been imported from countries in southwest Asia.

See also

agriculture, introduction of; Aswan; Dynastic stone tools; faïence technology and production;fauna, domesticated; fauna, wild; Gebel Zeit; Giza, Khufu pyramid complex; jewelry; metallurgy; Mons Porphyrites; mummification; Neolithic and Predynastic stone tools; obelisks; Paleolithic tools; papyrus; plants, wild; pyramids (Old Kingdom), construction of; quarrying; Saqqara, pyramids of the 3rd Dynasty; sculpture (stone), production techniques; Serabit el-Khadim; ships; stone vessels and bead making; Wadi Maghara

Further reading

Gale, G.A., and Stos-Grale, Z.A. 1981. Ancient Egyptian silver. *JEA* 67: 103–15.

Lucas, A. 1989. *Ancient Egyptian Materials and Industries*, revised by J.R. Harris. London.

KATHRYN A. BARD, WITH
REFERENCE TO A. LUCAS
(AND HARRIS), 1989

Naukratis

The ancient city of Naukratis (modern Kom Ge'if) is located in the Behera province about 80 km southeast of Alexandria and about 5 km west of the modern junction town of Ityai el-Barud (30°54′ N, 30°35′ E). In antiquity, this important Graeco-Egyptian trading post lay to the west of the Canopic branch of the Nile, connected to it by a canal. It was Pharaoh Amasis of the 26th Dynasty, according to Herodotus (II.178–9), who first allowed Greek merchants to settle and trade at the site, and who granted land so that they could erect altars and temples to their gods. However, earlier Greek imports (Early Corinthian aryballoi, East Greek bird-bowls and Middle Wild Goat style pottery) indicate a Hellenic presence at the site in the second half of the seventh century BC, perhaps during the reign of Psamtik I, who had utilized the services of Greek mercenaries ("men of bronze from the sea") in his struggles to consolidate his newly reunified Egypt. This early group of Greek settlers may have come from Miletus, as Strabo (17.I.18) believed.

In his *Life of Solon*, Plutarch (26.1) records

that when the famous Greek lawmaker left Athens after instituting his reforms, he stopped first in Egypt and spent time "where the Nile pours forth its waters by the shore of Canopus." Given the political situation at the time, and the mercantile nature of Solon's mind, this description must refer to Naukratis. Further evidence that Naukratis was a thriving entrepôt in the early sixth century BC is the fact that Sappho's brother Charaxus, a wine dealer, made frequent visits to the site where he tempered the rigors of his business with the pleasures of the courtesan Rhodopis, against whom his sister reviled (see also Herodotus II.135, Strabo XVII.I.33, and Athenaeus *Deipnosophistae*, XIII: 596b). Perhaps Amasis had simply codified a *de facto* situation, for it was he who made Naukratis the only legal outlet for Greek wares in all of Egypt, an exclusivity that was strickly enforced by local Egyptian regulations (Herodotus II.179). Throughout his long reign the city flourished, and the famous Hellenion was built, the product of a combined effort of nine East Greek cities (the Ionian cities of Chios, Teos, Phocaea and Clazomenae, the Dorian cities of Rhodes, Cnidus, Halicarnassus and Phaselis, and one Aeolian city, Mytilene). This building was said by Herodotus (II.178) to have been the "best known . . . most used . . . and . . . largest of all of the *temene* at Naukratis."

It is difficult to determine the degree to which the merchants of Naukratis were affected by the politics of the 27th Dynasty. Excavation has shown that a significant quantity of imported goods continued to arrive at the site during this period. The loss of access to Black Sea markets through Persian control of the Hellespont, however, as well as the growing size and importance of both the Athenian and Phoenician fleets, must have caused the merchants of Naukratis some financial hardship. The threat to Naukratite exclusivity that was posed by a decade of Athenian military intervention in local Delta affairs (Papremis, Memphis, Amyrtaeus) was brought to an end by the "Peace of Callias" (449/8 BC) between Athens and Persia. It was not long after this event that Herodotus was supposed to have visited Egypt; his description of Naukratis as a town dotted with temples hardly conjures up the image of a cultural backwater.

Although little material at Naukratis can be assigned with any certainty to the local rulers of the 28th and 29th Dynasties, Naukratis continued to be an important manufacturing center. It was the foremost commercial city in the Delta throughout the 30th Dynasty. In the first year of his reign, Nectanebo I built a temple to the goddess Neith in the local Egyptian section (Piemro) of Naukratis. In the precinct of this temple he erected a black granite stela that decreed that 10 percent of the existing levies on "gold, silver, timber, worked wood, and everything coming from the Sea of the Greeks" as well as 10 percent of the existing tax on similar luxury goods manufactured "at Piemro called Naukratis" would be used to provide for its upkeep.

The brief reimposition of Persian rule (31st Dynasty) was brought to an end by Alexander the Great when he conquered Egypt in 332/1 BC. Although victory celebrations at Memphis were made more festive by entertainers brought from Naukratis, Alexander did not visit the site. Situated on the coast with the Mediterraean world before it, Alexandria rapidly eclipsed the centuries-old emporium at Naukratis, but the transition could not have occurred so quickly if it were not for native sons such as Cleomenes and the rich pool of trained administrators and bureaucrats that were available at Naukratis, just a few kilometers south of Alexandria.

Naukratis did not wither and fade after the foundation of Alexandria. To the contrary, the old city seems to have witnessed a period of rebirth functioning as a trans-shipment depot for goods coming from the Mediterranean to the capital at Memphis, or eastward to Pelusium and beyond. Pottery and other artifacts excavated at Naukratis indicate that life and business continued as usual under the Ptolemies. Although it could no longer boast of its status as the sole gateway to Egypt for foreign products, it did remain (with Alexandria and Ptolemais) one of the three major Greek cities in Egypt. Perhaps the most significant indication of its importance was the program of restoration carried out in the city by Ptolemy II, for example, his addition of a monumental entryway to the massive structure referred to by Petrie as the "Great Temenos." The picture is less clear during the later Ptolemaic period as Egypt fell steadily under Roman control, culminating in the installation of a Roman governor in 30 BC.

The events that surrounded the final incorporation of Egypt into the Roman Empire by Octavian do not seem to have left their mark on Naukratis. The old trading center continued as it had for centuries, governing itself through the elected members of its own council (*boule*), a privilege that was not restored to the residents of Alexandria for over 200 years. That the laws of Naukratis were well known and well respected is evident in the fact that the emperor Hadrian chose them as a model for those to be used in the city of Antinoopolis, founded in AD 130. Naukratis continued to be a place of learning and culture, and was still able to inspire the sophist and grammarian Julius Pollux (who wrote the *Onomastikon*) as well as to stimulate the many and varied interests of the young Athenaeus (who wrote the *Deipnosophistae*) as he came of age there early in the third century AD. Subsequent documentation for Naukratis is slight; the date and cause of the city's final demise is unknown. Coptic records sporadically mention bishops from Naukratis at least through the fourteenth century AD, but by that time the name Naukratis may have been transferred to the neighboring village of Neqrash, where some late artifacts have been recovered.

In 1884, Flinders Petrie identifed the ancient city of Naukratis with the group of mounds near the village of Kom Ge'if. Even in the nineteenth century, almost one-third of the 950 × 580 m area represented by the "mounds" had been dug away by local farmers for use as a high-phosphate fertilizer (*sebbakh*) in their fields. His excavations there in 1884–5 were continued by E.A. Gardner in 1886 and by D.H. Hogarth in 1899 and 1903. Their work combined to uncover the remains of sanctuaries dedicated to Apollo and Aphrodite (each probably founded in the seventh century BC), and the slightly later buildings dedicated to the Dioskouroi and to Hera (sixth century BC).

These early excavators concentrated almost exclusively on religious structures and materials that were contemporary with the Archaic period in Greece (sixth century BC); they had paid very little attention to the domestic and mercantile character of the ancient city. In addition, the Hellenistic and Roman periods were almost completely ignored. In an attempt to rectify this situation, renewed investigation of ancient Naukratis was begun in 1978 by W.D.E. Coulson and Albert Leonard, Jr. The high water table in the Delta had transformed the entire area of the early excavations into a lake, thus precluding any reinvestigation of the structures unearthed in the early part of the century. However, to the south of the lake, a small (*circa* 100 × 50 m) mound in the area of Petrie's "Great Temenos" remained. This "South Mound" offered the only opportunity for recovering what remained of the original stratigraphy. Between 1980 and 1983, excavation in the South Mound (directed by Leonard) uncovered 6 m of vertical stratigraphy that indicated ten phases of (apparently domestic) occupation, all of which dated to the Ptolemaic period. Excavation was also conducted at neighboring Kom Hadid, originally part of the Naukratis mounds, where Petrie had recorded "slag heaps" and "large structures of red baked Roman brick [and] painted frescoes." This area had been severely damaged by the *sebbakhin*, and contiguous architecture was rare. The artifactual material (almost all from secondary deposits) ranged from Ptolemaic times into the Roman period.

Pedestrian survey of the fields surrounding the modern lake (directed by Coulson) recorded an artifact scatter that extended 2 km to the north and to the south of the area of the early excavations. Although this material dated from the fourth century BC to the seventh century AD, the greatest amount of pottery dated to the Ptolemaic and Roman periods. The distribution of the finds suggests that, between the fourth and first centuries BC, the city expanded to the north and east while, during the Roman period, expansion and growth was to the west.

The regional survey in the vicinity of Naukratis/Kom Ge'if produced a gazeteer of twenty-nine ancient sites. Extensive mapping, sherding and soundings conducted at four sites (Kom Firin, Kom Dahab, Kom Barud and Kom Kortas) demonstrated that the area was widely settled during the Ptolemaic and Roman Periods. At all of these sites, excavation was hampered by the high water table. The Naukratis Project also included an epigraphic survey which concentrated on the recording of the Egyptian material, especially the tomb of Khesu-wer at Kom el-Hisn (conducted by David Silverman), as well as hieroglyphic inscriptions from other sites in the survey area.

See also

Alexandria; Herodotus; Kom el-Hisn; Late and Ptolemaic periods, overview; Roman period, overviewtrade, foreign

Further reading

Coulson, W.D.E. 1996. *Ancient Naucratis II, 1: The Survey on Naukratis*. Oxford.

Coulson, W.D.E., and A. Leonard, Jr. 1981. *Cities of the Delta* 1: *Naukratis: Preliminary Report on the 1977–1978 and 1980 Seasons*. Malibu, CA.

——. 1982. Investigations at Naukratis and Environs, 1980 and 1981. *AJA* 86: 361–80.

Coulson, W.D.E., A. Leonard, Jr. and N. Wilkie. 1982. Three seasons of excavations and survey at Naukratis and environs. *JARCE* 19: 73–109.

Venit, M.S. 1988. *Greek Painted Pottery from Naukratis in Egyptian Museums*. Winona Lake, IN.

ALBERT LEONARD, JR.

Neolithic and Predynastic stone tools

Despite the richness of material, the chipped stone artifacts of Neolithic and Predynastic Egypt have, until recently, been greatly neglected. Earlier Egyptologists seldom had any detailed knowledge of lithic artifacts, so they tended to collect and describe only the more elaborate pieces. Moreover, they found stone tools to be less useful for dating purposes than pottery, so they only briefly discussed lithic finds. There were a few exceptions, notably Gertrude Caton Thompson who described the lithic finds from her excavations in the Fayum, Kharga Oasis and at Hemamieh, and S.A. Huzayyin, who wrote a detailed report on the flint artifacts from the Predynastic settlement at Armant.

A proper understanding of the stone artifacts from a site can only be achieved by studying all chipped stone, from recognizable tools to small waste chips. Statistical representativeness is very important. The tools and other pieces of chipped stone found at a site reveal information about how the occupants processed and used the stone, how they were related to other communities, whether they traded with other areas, and various other aspects.

Neolithic and Predynastic lithic assemblages vary both spatially and temporally. Each group had its own lithic tradition (or "industry"). Nevertheless, there is a certain progression, and a peak of technological excellence was attained in the late Predynastic and 1st Dynasty.

The known Neolithic sites of the Nile Valley occur in northern Egypt. Stone artifacts of the Fayum Neolithic are based on two main technologies: the production of flakes from simple cores with some of the flakes subsequently being shaped into tools, and the manufacture of tools by bifacial flaking. Modern excavations have shown that the tools consist primarily of simple flake tools, such as side-scrapers, notches, denticulates, and other flakes with *ad hoc* retouch ("retouched pieces"). Bifacial implements occur in much smaller numbers. Earlier researchers collected large numbers of bifacial tools, the main classes of which are polished and flaked axes, bifacial sickle blades, knife and symmetrical leaf-shaped implements, and an enormous diversity of concave-base projectile points ("arrowheads"). Other tool types characteristic of the Fayum

Neolithic are scrapers on side-blow flakes, planes and ground celts.

The Neolithic settlement of Merimde Beni-salame on the western margin of the Delta has a stratigraphy which modern excavators have divided into five phases. The lithic artifacts of the first phase represent a flake-blade industry with flake and blade tools (mainly end-scrapers and side-scrapers, small perforators and various retouched pieces). The blades, however, are irregular specimens that are not the result of a separate blade technology. A few flake tools have bifacial edge retouch (i.e. retouch along one edge on both sides), while there are also some small nodules with bifacial retouch. One of these seems to have been shaped into an axe. True bifacial tools (with retouch entirely covering both sides) are rare, and consist of small leaf-shaped implements. One distinctive projectile point was found: it is a stemmed and barbed piece with lateral notches.

The lithic industry of Phases II–V at Merimde is very different. While there are some flake and blade tools (e.g. side-scrapers and elongate perforators), bifacial tools predominate. Particularly numerous are concave-base projectile points, bifacial sickles and axes with polished edges. Also present are bifacial drills and triangles.

The lithic industry represented at the Neolithic site of el-Omari, to the south of Cairo, is based primarily on flake technology. Tools, such as end-scrapers, notches, denticulates, perforators and retouched pieces, are common. Also present are a few tools made on fairly regular blades. These include handled knives (a type apparently unique to el-Omari), sickle blades and double-backed perforators. The fairly numerous bifacial tools are mainly flaked and polished axes, concave-base points, bifacial triangles and bifacial sickles.

The stone tool industries of the Fayum, Merimde and el-Omari span a period of more than a thousand years (*circa* 5,200–4,100 BC). Their chronological relationship to each other, however, has not been precisely determined. The Fayum Neolithic and the Merimde sequence are certainly early, while that of el-Omari seems younger, at least in part. Although each has its own distinctive lithic tradition, there are also clear points of similarity, particularly among the bifacial tools. The el-Omari industry shares similarities with both Merimde industries (Phase I, and Phases II–V). Despite a careful recent analysis of the finds from el-Omari, the site was excavated about fifty years ago and its chronological development is poorly understood. It may indeed span a period of several centuries, as a series of recently obtained radiocarbon dates suggests.

In the early fourth millennium BC, a new lithic tradition appeared in Lower Egypt: the Buto–Ma'adi industry. It is dominated by well-developed blade and bladelet technologies (the resulting blades and bladelets often showing a twisting around the long axis). The blades are large and fairly regular, and many were retouched into perforators, end-scrapers and backed pieces. The bladelets are also fairly regular, and they were frequently made into perforators and backed tools, though many were retouched into micro-end-scrapers. The industry, particularly at the site of Ma'adi, also contains a variety of well-made flake scrapers, including circular scrapers as well as a series of large scrapers of tabular form, which probably represent imports from the southern Levant. Bifacial technology is very rare in the Buto–Ma'adi industry, and many of the bifacial tools found at the site of Ma'adi may represent imports from Upper Egypt. There are a few concave-base points, knives and bifacial sickles. Axes are notable for their absence.

The oldest distinct Predynastic lithic industry in Upper Egypt is the Badarian of the el-Badari region. Unfortunately, it is still essentially only known from the work of Guy Brunton and Gertrude Caton Thompson, and studies of the collections from their excavations. The Badarian is a generalized flake-blade industry, which in many ways recalls the lithic traditions of Lower Egypt. The main non-bifacial tools appear to be end-scrapers, perforators and retouched pieces. Worked tabular slabs of raw material also seem to be characteristic. The industry has a bifacial component comprising concave-base projectile points, bifacial sickles, bifacial triangles, small ovate axes and various

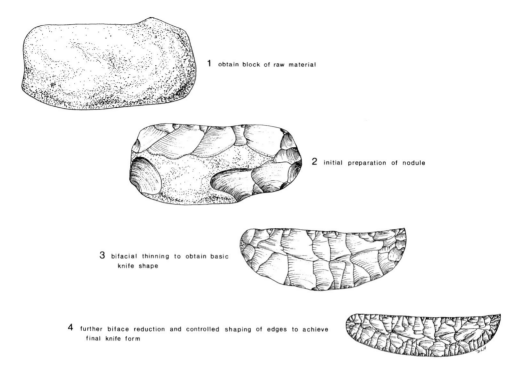

1 obtain block of raw material

2 initial preparation of nodule

3 bifacial thinning to obtain basic
  knife shape

4 further biface reduction and controlled shaping of edges to achieve
  final knife form

Figure 84 Stages in the manufacture of a Predynastic bifacial knife

other nonstandardized forms. While the basic classes overlap with those of the Neolithic of Lower Egypt, the Badarian tools display their own distinctive variations of form and flaking style. The concave-base points, for example, are generally much more refined in shape, with delicate narrow barbs and very flat, regular retouch.

In the el-Badari region, the Badarian industry is succeeded by the Mostagedda industry, which dates primarily to the Nagada II phase of the Upper Egyptian Predynastic sequence. In contrast to the continuum of small flakes and blades of the Badarian, the Mostagedda industry is characterized by large, regular blades, many of which were used for tool manufacture. The predominant blade tool categories are end-scrapers, truncations, backed pieces, sickle blades and retouched pieces. Also present are burins, perforators, blade knives and truncation knives, as well as large circular scrapers (made on cortex flakes and natural

spalls). Additionally, there are distinctive heat-treated bladelets which were retouched into micro-end-scrapers and other simple tool forms. Bifacial tools occur, including bifacial knives, "fishtail"-shaped implements, bifacial sickles and concave-base points.

Moving southward, the next distinct lithic industry is in the area from Nag Hammadi to Armant. This industry is typified by assemblages from the Nagada region. It is predominantly a simple flake industry with the main tool types consisting of end-scrapers, burins, notches and retouched pieces. (Other tools include perforators, truncations, grand perçoirs and planes.) There is a small percentage of bifacial tools, which consist mostly of small axes with a distinctive (tranchet) preparation of the axe edge. A small proportion of regular blades and blade tools is added to the Nagada industry during the Nagada II phase.

The lithic industry of the Hierakonpolis region during the Nagada I phase is based on

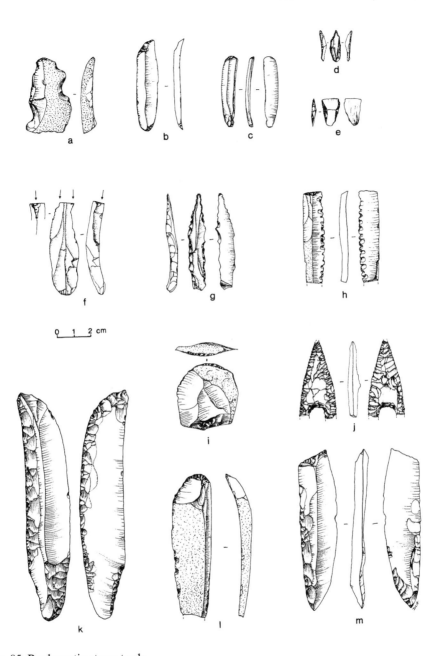

Figure 85 Predynastic stone tools
(a) notch; (b) truncation knife; (c) micro-end-scraper (on bladelet of heat-treated flint); (d) microdrill; (e) transverse arrowhead; (f) burin; (g) perforator; (h) sickle blade; (i) end-scraper on flake; (j) concave-base projectile point; (k) blade knife; (l) end-scraper on blade; (m) truncation with backing retouch

two major blank technologies: the production of flakes and a blade–bladelet technology yielding small blades and bladelets of moderate regularity. Both flakes and blades were retouched into burins, end-scrapers, notches and other tools (including a few truncations, denticulates, backed pieces and transverse arrowheads). Bifacial tools are rare, but include knife-like implements and winged drills. Also present is a heat-treated bladelet technology. Another technology which seems to appear in the late Nagada I is the limited production of bladelets of a slightly coarse gray variety of flint for conversion into small drill bits or "micro-drills." As in the Nagada industry, regular blades and tools on such blades are added to the inventory of the Hierakonpolis industry in the Nagada II phase.

The adoption of a regular blade technology in Nagada II times is a phenomenon observed throughout the Upper Egyptian Nile Valley. It may represent a technology derived from the Buto–Ma'adi industry of Lower Egypt, and there seem to be similarities between the Buto–Ma'adi blade and bladelet technologies and those of the Mostagedda industry of the el-Badari region. By the end of the Predynastic period, the Lower Egyptian blade technology had developed further to become even more standardized and regular than that of the earlier Buto–Ma'adi industry. Thus by the beginning of the 1st Dynasty (*circa* 3,100–3,000 BC), very regular blades and blade tools were being produced in both Upper and Lower Egypt.

The production of regular blades represents only one of several stone-working technologies that were practiced by craft specialists. The elaboration of stone tool techniques seen in the later Predynastic undoubtedly reflects a concomitant increase in the number of lithic artisans as Predynastic society became more differentiated.

The above discussion is based primarily on artifacts recovered from settlements. The spectacular implements, such as the fishtails and ripple-flaked knives that are generally regarded as so characteristic of the Predynastic, are in fact very rare and virtually all come from graves. Compared with the settlements, Predynastic cemeteries have yielded a more restricted number and range of stone artifacts. Among them is a relatively high proportion of bifacial tools, on which earlier excavators focused their attention, consequently biasing our view of Predynastic stone tools.

See also

Armant; el-Badari district Predynastic sites; Buto (Tell el-Fara'in); Fayum, Neolithic and Predynastic sites; Hierakonpolis; Kharga Oasis, prehistoric sites; Ma'adi and the Wadi Digla; Merimde Beni-salame; Nagada (Naqada); Neolithic cultures, overview; el-Omari; Paleolithic tools; Predynastic period, overview

Suggested readings:

Debono, F., and B. Mortensen. 1990. *El Omari, A Neolithic Settlement and Other Sites in the Vicinity of Wadi Hof, Helwan* (AVDAIK 82). Cairo.

Eiwanger, J. 1988. *Merimde Benisalame 2: Die Funde der mittleren Merimdekultur* (AVDAIK 51). Cairo.

Holmes, D.L. 1989. *The Predynastic Lithic Industries of Upper Eqypt: A Comparative Study of the Lithic Traditions of Badari, Nagada and Hierakonpolis* 1, 2. BAR, Int. Ser. 469. Oxford.

Inizan, M.-L., H. Roche and J. Tixier. 1992. *Technology of Knapped Stone*. Meudon.

Rizkana, I., and J. Seeher. 1988. *Maadi 2: The Lithic Industries of the Predynastic Settlement* (AVDAIK 65). Cairo.

DIANE L. HOLMES

Nile, flood history

Unusually high or low Nile floods are not directly related to climatic changes in the Egyptian deserts, but to the monsoonal rains over Ethiopia and, to a lesser degree, the White Nile Basin. "Good" Nile floods were critical for agricultural productivity, while indifferent floods could lead to food shortfalls and unusually low ones might result in disastrous famines. Exceptionally high floods could be disastrous as well, by destroying irrigation works or natural levees and by keeping water on the fields too long, delaying planting and hence harvesting until early in the hot season, parching the crops and reducing yields. During the planting season, waterlogged soils teemed with parasites that attacked the sown seed.

The unpredictable rhythms of the Nile also affected hunting, fishing and gathering peoples during earlier times. The primary fish taken by prehistoric fishers all spawn on the flooded plain, so that good inundations assure plenty of fish, which become stranded in isolated pools as the floodwaters recede. Poor floods, on the other hand, spell a poor catch; with a few decades of declining floods, the Nile channel begins to entrench, eventually carving out a lower and narrower floodplain, that spawns even fewer fish. Other food resources also suffer with poor floods, as primary productivity declines and grazing animals find less grass, that also withers earlier, on a floodplain that has been incompletely inundated. The impact of unusually high floods must be inferential, but protracted flooding would probably allow predatory, juvenile Nile perch unusual opportunity to reduce fish stocks; increasingly stagnant waters would also be deleterious, while reducing nutritive grasses in favor of high cellulose plants, so providing poorer pasturage for game returning to the floodplain.

The prehistoric record of Nile behavior remains encoded in the concepts and nomenclature of geomorphology, which identifies dunes sands, channel beds, shore zones and, above all, the overbank silts that build up on an aggrading floodplain after each flood. A valley-margin lake fed primarily by the Nile seepage water and supporting rich diatom blooms may seem a good resource environment, but the chances are that the alkaline waters are barely potable and support little vegetation, much like the wave spill-over ponds behind the beaches of modern Lake Turkana. Active accretion of overbank silts most probably signals abundant resources tied to good floods, while advancing valley-margin dunes may be symptomatic of indifferent floods, unable to support seepage vegetation or to rework wind-borne sand by undercutting and erosion. Silt encroachment high on the desert edge may or may not record unusually severe flooding, while evidence for even temporary channel entrenchment may reflect a run of particularly poor floods. The geological record must therefore be decoded in order to appreciate its geoarchaeological implications.

The Nilotic environment during the profusion of Late Paleolithic stone tool industries about 20,000–12,500 BP (years "before present") was unstable in terms of human ecology, with suites of good floods allowing fish, mammal and human populations to grow, but a few decades of Nile entrenchment provoking crises for all three. An incisive period of entrenchment perhaps 16,000 BP, coincident with a marked turnover of Late Paleolithic industries, possibly provoked social realignments and adaptive readjustments. A similar process may also have been underway toward 12,500 BP, when the Nile had begun to entrench, only to be overwhelmed by some 500 years of catastrophic flood events (the "Wild Nile"), 5–10 m higher than usual. Then, after 12,000 BP, the configuration of the Nile floodplain was radically changed, as the Nile channel cut down by 25 m or more, a crisis probably more serious than that of the Wild Nile. The subsequent Epi-paleolithic industries suggest some simplification and a redirection of subsistence patterns.

The semi-continuous, late prehistoric archaeological record of the Fayum offers an unusual opportunity to move beyond typological identification and simple models, contrasting the Qarunian stone tool industry with those of the Fayumian or Moerian, to examining elements that may be more sensitive to severe, periodic subsistence crises, as the lake level rose and fell in response to changing Nile flood volumes. Of interest is the first appearance of Predynastic materials, following a surge of Nile floods and then a spate of low floods *circa* 4,200–4,000 BC.

Information on flood history during the

Dynastic period comes mainly, but not only, from textual sources. Nile flood levels declined markedly between the 1st and 4th Dynasties, especially at the end of the 1st and the beginning of the 2nd Dynasty. Here the records are supported by floodplain entrenchment in Nubia. During the 5th and 6th Dynasties, a rock causeway was built in the Fayum desert to bring quarried rock to a boat-loading ramp usable between 12 and 22 m, implying a moderately high lake. The available physical evidence does not support a Nile flood crisis at the end of the 6th Dynasty, and the breakdown of the First Intermediate Period is better explained by the collapse of trading networks in the Near East, reinforcing the impacts of decentralization within Egypt.

During the 12th–13th Dynasties, the Fayum lake rose to unusually high levels on at least three occasions, confirming phenomenal floods recorded by late 12th Dynasty inscriptions at the Second Cataract. During the second half of the Ramesside period (circa 1,170–1,100 BC), the Nubian floodplain was again entrenched, at a time of spiraling food prices in Egypt. During the ninth century BC, flood levels were normal or high, as they were at the time of Herodotus. The food crisis of the twelfth century BC may have contributed to the destabilization of the New Kingdom.

See also

climatic history; Epi-paleolithic cultures, overview; Fayum, Neolithic and Predynastic sites; Nile, modern hydrology; Paleolithic cultures, overview; subsistence and diet, Dynastic

Further reading

Bell, B. 1970. The oldest records of the Nile floods. *Geographical Journal* 136: 569–73.
——. 1975. Climate and the history of Egypt: The Middle Kingdom. *AJA* 79: 223–69.
Butzer, K.W. 1976. *Early Hydraulic Civilization in Egypt*. Chicago.
——. 1984. Long-term Nile flood variation and political discontinuities in Pharaonic Egypt. In *From Hunters to Farmers: Causes and Consequences of Food Production in Africa*, J.D. Clark and S.A. Brandt, eds. 102–12. Berkeley, CA.
——. 1997. Sociopolitical discontinuity in the Near East c. 2200 B.C.E.: Scenarios from Palestine and Egypt. In *Third Millennium B.C. Climate Change and Old World Collapse*, H.N. Dalfes, G. Kukla and H. Weiss, eds. 245–96. Berlin.
——. 1998. Late Quaternary problems of the Egyptian Nile Valley. *Paléorient* 23(2): 151–73.
Kozlowski, J.K., and B. Ginter. 1989. The Fayum Neolithic in the light of new discoveries. In *Late Prehistory of the Nile Basin and the Sahara*, L. Krzyzaniak and M. Kobusiewicz, eds. 157–80. Poznan.

KARL W. BUTZER

Nile, modern hydrology

Statistics on Nile discharge at Aswan begin in 1871, and by 1912 for the major tributaries in Sudan. Despite a trajectory across nine modern countries, 83 percent of the waters reaching Egypt come from Ethiopia: 55.8 percent from the Blue Nile, 13.8 percent from the Atbara, and 13.3 percent from the Sobat rivers, which respectively drain the center, north and west of that mountainous nation. Only 16.5 percent of the Nile waters entering Egypt come from the equatorial lakes, and about 50 percent of that discharge is evaporated in the Sudd swamps of southern Sudan that filter out half of the year-to-year variability, delay the seasonal maximum by two months, and trap most of the sediment coming from Uganda, Zaire, Tanzania and Kenya. The Bahr el-Ghazal of southwestern Sudan contributes only 0.6 percent of the discharge reaching Egypt. Apart from modern water use for irrigation, there are substantial losses due to evaporation and net percolation to subsurface aquifers as the Nile flows across the Sahara, including 4.5 percent between the Atbara confluence and Aswan.

Despite the valid reputation of the Nile as a dependable water source, reflecting runoff derived from different climatic regions, variability is significant. Mean discharge at Aswan was 15 percent higher for the years 1871–1905 than for 1905–65, and that for 1840–1900 (using less reliable earlier measures) probably was 30 percent greater than during the twentieth century. The lowest annual volume (in 1913) was 45.5, the highest (in 1978), 150, compared with a mean of 84 milliard m^3; or a range from −46 percent to +79 percent. These deviations tell only part of the story: the coefficient of variation of the annual Nile volume at Aswan 1912–73 was low at 18.5 percent, but that for Nile flow during the peak month of September was 32.8 percent, reflecting (a) the less predictable date of the flood crest, between 20 August and 19 October, (b) the concentration of discharge in a single, short but high peak, of as little as twelve days, or a series of longer but lower crests (spanning up to fifty days), and (c) the maximum flood elevation attained (within a range of 2.75 m).

There are other important complications. For the period 1902–63 (prior to the impact of the High Dam), the Blue Nile provided 68 percent of the flood discharge and 72 percent of the critical increment of sediment for Egypt. However, these proportions vary with climatic trends. Southwestern Ethiopia was unusually wet in 1962–81, as was the basin of the Victoria Nile, while central Ethiopia experienced an attenuated drought in 1965–86. Consequently, the annual contribution of the Blue Nile declined by 15.4 percent for 1962–86, while that of the White Nile increased by 19.8 percent (with respect to the mean for 1912–86). The proportion of White Nile waters thereby increased from 30.4 percent to 36.4 percent. But in Egypt, White Nile discharge dominates during the low-water stage, from December to June, and adds no fertile sediment to the fields. The Atbara, representing trends in northern Ethiopia, was in phase with the Blue Nile during the first half of the drought years, 1963–74, but during 1975–83 its discharge was well above average.

An excessively dry or wet year is far more likely to be felt throughout Ethiopia than is a trend that lasts a decade or more. Nonetheless, the last decades of the nineteenth century were evidently wet in both central and southwestern Ethiopia. In general, the several contributions of the main affluents of the Nile do not covary, and their relative influx during historical and prehistoric times will have fluctuated considerably.

See also

irrigation; Nile Valley, geological evolution

Further reading

Abu-Zeid, M.A., and A.K. Biswas, eds. 1992. *Climatic Fluctuations and Water Management*. Oxford and Boston.
Hurst, H.E. 1957. *The Nile*. London.
Shahin, M. 1985. *Hydrology of the Nile Basin*. Amsterdam.
Willcocks, W., and J.I. Craig. 1913. *Egyptian Irrigation*. London.

KARL W. BUTZER

Nile Valley, geological evolution

One of the world's longest rivers (6670 km), the Nile spans some 34 degrees of latitude, from 2° south of the equator to 32° north, at the tip of its delta. It draws its waters from the Ethiopian Plateau (Lake Tana at 1830 m elevation) and the lake district of equatorial East Africa (Lake Victoria, 1134 m). Yet its drainage basin is only of moderate size (2.87 million km^2), about half of which contributes next to no runoff, and its volume is less than half that of the Danube.

The irregular watershed of the Nile cuts across several tectonic provinces, with a complex geological history that remains imperfectly understood. A river did run northwards, near the course of the western Egyptian Nile, since at least Oligocene times (some 40 million years ago), but it did not yet tap into the sub-Saharan basins of the Blue and White Nile. The updoming of Ethiopia began 30 million years ago, with the capping basalt flows in place 24 million years ago. That would have directed much of the Ethiopian drainage toward the older sedimentary basin in southern Sudan. Uplift and initial erosion of the Red Sea Hills 20 to 17 million years ago began to define the axis of the Saharan Nile, connecting the Blue Nile drainage by 5 million years ago.

The landscape of Egypt consists of three main components: (1) the Eastern Desert, (2) the Western Desert and (3) the Nile Valley.

(1) The eastern perimeter is formed by a spine of ancient igneous and metamorphic rocks, upfaulted from the African Shield to form the Red Sea Hills of the Eastern Desert. Rough and jagged in profile, these low ranges are interrupted by small basins and cut by west–east drainage lines that facilitate travel from the Nile Valley to the Red Sea.

(2) The bleak plains and plateaus of the Western Desert stretch westward from the valley, and are level and tabular. They are formed by multiple horizons of sedimentary rocks, exposed to erosion for more than 100 million years in the south (Cretaceous: Nubia Sandstone) and 20 million years in the north (Miocene limestones). At great intervals there are steep escarpments or shallow depressions, partly excavated by wind action, that intersect aquifers to provide springs that sustain oases such as Dakhla and Kharga.

(3) The Nile Valley is incised into the erosional surface of the eastern Sahara, running roughly parallel to the axis of the Red Sea Hills on its northward course to the Mediterranean Sea. Through Nubia, the valley is shallow and cut into Nubia Sandstone, with local thresholds of hard, igneous rocks that form six cataracts between Khartoum and Aswan. A tectonic basin intersects the valley at Kom Ombo. Near Esna, high cliffs (200–500 m) of Eocene limestone (some 50 million years old) close in on the valley, remaining prominent downstream to Minya. From there the margins of the valley open up, with sand-swept plains to the west, and open hill country to the east. The Fayum Depression, its bedrock floor 50 m below sea level, has overland and subsurface links to the Nile, with a more shallow counterpart in the Wadi Natrun.

Deep entrenchment of the Nile Valley and its delta is dated to the Messenian (6 to 4 million years ago), when the Mediterranean Sea dried up and a remarkable canyon was cut by river action, facilitated by crustal movements, to 2000 m below modern sea level near Cairo, and 175 m below sea level even as far upstream as Aswan. During the subsequent 2 or 3 million years, this over-deepened canyon was filled with marine, estuarine and fluvial beds, remnants of which remain visible along the valley margins. But the weight of accumulating sediment in the Delta continued to depress the underlying crust, now as much as 4 km below the surface.

During the last 1–2 million years, sweeps of river gravel were washed together as river terraces, at progressively lower levels below the desert cliffs, fragmentarily preserved at elevations of 60 to 15 m above the modern floodplain of the Nile. These gravel "terraces" contain a small fraction of sands derived from the Upper Nile Basin, and at least the younger units show evidence of early Paleolithic occupation, such as Acheulian handaxes. Distinctive Ethiopian flood silts first appear as interbeds within Acheulian terrace gravels, and after about 75,000 years ago the Nile ceased to accumulate gravels and switched to its modern regime of summer, flood silts. This change was not the result of a shift in behavior of the Upper Nile, but of the tributary wadis in the Egyptian deserts; their channels became almost defunct, with only sporadic activity since that time.

An archaeological record for continuous human settlement in the Egyptian Nile Valley only begins roughly 20,000 years ago, represented by Late Paleolithic industries, some of which evolved into the Epi-paleolithic hunting-fishing-gathering economies of the early Holocene.

See also

Nile, flood history; Nile, modern hydrology

Further reading

Burke, K., and G.L. Wells. 1989. Trans-African drainage system of the Sahara: was it the Nile? *Geology* 17: 743–7.

Butzer, K.W., and C.L. Hansen. 1968. *Desert and River in Nubia*. Madison, WI.

Paulissen, E., and P.M. Vermeersch. 1987. Earth, man and climate in the Egyptian Nile Valley during the Pleistocene. In *Prehistory of Arid North Africa*, A.E. Close, ed., 29–68. Dallas, TX.

Said, R., 1981. *The Geological Evolution of the River Nile*. New York.

KARL W. BUTZER

nome structure

Egypt was divided into a series of districts or provinces, called nomes, from an early point in its history. The problem of when and how the nomes were created in Egypt for administrative purposes has not yet been definitely resolved. Certainly they existed at the beginning of the Old Kingdom; inscriptions giving names and titles of nome administrators (nomarchs) were discovered inside the Step Pyramid of King Zoser at Saqqara.

The nomes were characterized either by an emblematic sign mounted on a standard designating a particular district, by the hieroglyphic sign for nome as a general term for a district, or by a combination of the two. The expression "nome" derives from the Greek word *nomos*, denoting a local or more accurately a regional administrative unit of the country during the Graeco-Roman period. Therefore, the term "nome" may be applied to any administrative subdivision at the regional level; it is not important whether or not the name of the nome is written with the canonical nome sign and whether or not its area coincides with that of the traditional nomes symbolized by a nome emblem.

The traditional nomes written with nome emblem or canonical nome sign were administrative entities only during the Old Kingdom.

These original nomes lost their importance as administrative subdivisions during the First Intermediate Period, at least in the southern part of the country. In the Middle Kingdom they were replaced by other administrative units, the town districts consisting of towns and their surrounding area. The name of the town was used to designate both the town and its district, the new "nome."

In spite of having lost their functional importance, the original nome symbols were still used in later times in geographical and especially in religious contexts. Thus, the most complete lists of the traditional nomes are preserved in temples of the Graeco-Roman period, where processions of nome personifications are depicted bringing offerings. Only in this context are the traditional forty-two nomes of Egypt mentioned: twenty-two in Upper Egypt and twenty in Lower Egypt. These geographical lists use traditional forms and names common in the remote past—a phenomenon not uncommon in the religious sphere—but they do not represent the contemporary administrative division of the country. Administrative documents of the same time did not use these designations, even if they were written down on the walls of Egyptian temples like the donation text of Edfu. The twenty-two Upper Egyptian nomes mentioned in these lists coincide with those known from the Old Kingdom. Some of the twenty Lower Egyptian nomes seem to have been artificially created during the Late period for religious reasons, and reflect in their own way the changes within the nome structure in the Delta.

The nomarchs, or nome administrators, were responsible for civil administration in their nomes. The hieroglyphic sign for "nome" (*sp3t*), used to designate the administrative unit during the Old Kingdom, shows a grid of lines at right angles. According to Egyptological tradition, this indicates a plot of land furrowed with irrigation channels. The importance of irrigation during the Old Kingdom is seriously debated today, and this explanation can no longer be accepted. The sign represents land with clearly defined subdivisions or fields, divided and registered for cadastral purposes.

The registration of the land was the basis of all administrative activities in the country. The most important duty of the nome administrators was to levy and collect taxes, mainly agricultural products but also the corvée of people attached to the land for temporary work for the state. Officials of the nome administration are explicitly mentioned as being responsible for this work in royal decrees from the Old Kingdom exempting temples from various kinds of service and taxes. In their tombs in Beni Hasan and Elkab, nomarchs of the Middle Kingdom and of the New Kingdom, respectively, are depicted collecting taxes in their districts.

In the late Old Kingdom nomarchs were called "great overlord of a nome." Later this became an honorific title; from the Middle Kingdom onward a new title was introduced to designate the chief administrator of a nome. This title is normally translated as "mayor." This translation can give the false impression that this official held responsibility only over the nome capital, which is incorrect. The whole district in its entirety was under this official's jurisdiction. This title was also used to designate district administrators in Nubia particularly during the New Kingdom, when Nubia was part of the Egyptian empire.

See also

administrative bureaucracy; taxation and conscription; urbanism

Further reading

Helck, W. 1974. *Die altägyptischen Gaue* (Tübinger Atlas des Vorderen Orients, Beih. B. 5). Weisbaden.

Kees, H. 1961. *Ancient Egypt: A Cultural Topography.* London.

Martin-Pardey, E. 1976. *Untersuchungen zur ägyptischen Provinzialverwaltung bis zum Ende des Alten Reiches* (Hildesheimer Ägyptologische Beiträge 1). Hildesheim.

EVA MARTIN-PARDEY

Nubian forts

The art of fortification reached its highest point before the Romans in the strongholds built in Nubia by kings of the Egyptian 12th Dynasty, in a chain that extended from Aswan (Elephantine) to the southern end of the Second Cataract at Semna (21°30′ N, 30°57′ E).

From very early times, the Egyptian government was concerned with frontier security, especially in Nubia, and the first actual fortification discovered there was on the island of Elephantine, dating at least as early as the 1st Dynasty, *circa* 3,000 BC. Its location on the newly established southern frontier of Egypt is significant, for Egyptian power had demolished concentrated occupation (of the local A-Group peoples) in the Nile Valley south of the First Cataract.

The centralized Egyptian monarchy viewed fortifications as belonging either to the state or to rebels, and the storming and destruction of forts was a standard theme of official art. The construction of strong points was also commemorated, in inscriptions and in the aggressive names sometimes given to fortresses on the frontier. The true fortresses erected at the frontiers, especially in the Middle Kingdom, controlled access to Egypt, secured bases for mining and quarrying expeditions, and provided forward positions for military campaigns.

Although usually attributed to economic motives, the 12th Dynasty military occupation of Nubia had its background in the extended wars, disturbances and instability of the preceding period. The Nubian Nile Valley had been intensively resettled before the end of the Old Kingdom, *circa* 2,400 BC, and during the First Intermediate Period Nubians entered Egypt in sufficient numbers to play an important role in the military establishments of local and regional rulers as far north as Asyut. They established their own settlement north of Aswan and even acquired important positions in the 11th Dynasty court at Thebes. For a brief time, there was even an independent dynasty in Nubia that included one ruler with a Nubian name who fought against forces from the north. It was probably this dynasty that erected an administrative and possibly fortified complex near Amada. The Amada "fort" consisted of two rectangular mudbrick structures with irregular additions of enclosures and pens, all linked into a single walled complex. Although the 11th Dynasty campaigned in Nubia, it was not until the 12th Dynasty, during the reign of Senusret I, that the first real conquest of Lower Nubia was accomplished. While economic interests may have played a role in Senusret's conquest, he probably undertook this conquest, along with the establishment of fortresses and the stabilization of the frontiers, to increase the security of the borders and to reduce or eliminate the numbers of foreign soldiers in the private armies of his governors (nomarchs).

The 12th Dynasty rulers reversed the anti-settlement policy of the Early Dynastic period and Old Kingdom, when only a fortified industrial site near Buhen (21°55′ N, 31°17′ E) is known. Instead, the 12th Dynasty government maintained a chain of mudbrick fortresses to protect its interests among a population that retained its own culture, and became, if anything, more prosperous and numerous under Egyptian rule.

The exact date when each of the seventeen fortresses of the Nubian complex was founded is not always clear, but the first part of a system was almost certainly put in place by Senusret I. Forts at the Egyptian frontier probably already existed, at Elephantine and Biga (in Egyptian, "Senmet") islands, and possibly as far north as Gebel Silsila. New were the round-bastioned structures at Ikkur and Kuban ("Baki," 23°10′ N, 32°46′ E) on the west and east banks of the Nile at the entrance to the Wadi Alaqi, Aniba ("Miam," 22°40′ N, 32°01′ E), at the largest center of the local C-Group culture, and Buhen, at the southern end of C-Group settlement in Lower Nubia. A fortified industrial site was established at Kor (21°52′ N, 31°14′ E) near Buhen, which grew into a large administrative and trading (?) center.

Although these fortresses provided security and possibly some logistical support for wide-ranging renewal and expansion of mining and quarrying activities as well as trade, they were not nuclei for Egyptian settlers. The necessary evidence of permanent settlement, Egyptian townsites and burials, rarely occur in Nubia during the 12th Dynasty. Egyptians in Nubia at this time were transitory garrison soldiers, workmen and administrators. Evidence of the fortresses' function is preserved only from the New Kingdom, but the archaeological evidence of the C-Group in Lower Nubia suggests that this occupation was stabilized, with little of the cultural change or diversity that marks their remains south of Egyptian control. It is noteworthy that the forts of Ikkur and Kuban are located where the Wadi Allaqi enters the Nile Valley. This wadi was the main route to the Nubian gold mines and the most important route for infiltration from the Nubian Desert. For a century or so, the peoples of Lower Nubia were controlled by the Egyptians.

The threatening rise of the Nubian kingdom of Kush, centered at Kerma, and allied powers in the south, and possibly worsening conditions in the Eastern Desert, made this policy obsolete by the time of Senusret III. He repeatedly campaigned against Kush, which was part of a greater political agenda also evident in his campaign in Palestine, his suppression of the powerful nomarchs in Middle Egypt, and a new bureaucratic state apparatus. This new policy was strongly evident in the military administration of Nubia.

For all Senusret III's boasting in his texts carved on the Semna Stelae, the campaigns must have been hard fought and may have been inconclusive. The older fortresses were rebuilt and a new frontier was established at Semna, the narrowest point on the northern Nile, where the largest and most complex system of fortifications known to precede the Roman military frontier (*limes*) are found. The complex of fortifications he completed in Nubia was the greatest secular construction to survive from ancient Egypt. It is one of the ancient world's most impressive feats of military planning, architecture and engineering. In terms of organized state projects, it represents the effort that might have been required to build several Middle Kingdom pyramids. The fortresses and the boundary they protected were administered with a rigorous detail hardly seen before the rise of modern police states.

The old forts in Lower Nubia proper, Ikkur, Kuban and Aniba, and presumably also Elephantine and Biga, were expanded and enhanced. The other older fortresses near the frontier, Buhen and the fortified center at Kor, were greatly expanded, but otherwise the forts were new.

The Nubian frontier was concentrated in the region of Heh (21°30′ N, 31° E), comprising the forts of Kumma ("Itnuw-Pdjut," 21°30′ N, 30°57′ E) on the east bank, and Semna ("Sekhem-Khakaura' Ma'-kheru'") and Semna South ("Dair-Seti," 21°29′ N, 30°57′ E) on the west bank, and the island fortress of Uronarti ("Khesef-Iunuw," 21°32′ N, 30°57′ E). The two west bank fortresses were linked together by a low wall that isolated an area where vessels could be beached. Here at the large granite outcrop of the Semna Cataract, the main channel of the Nile was less than 50 m wide at low water. At the northern end, this complex of forts was anchored by the fortress of Uronarti, which was located on a large island with a palatial administrative complex.

The distance between the Semna complex and the Second Cataract proper (circa 40 km to the north) was secured by two fortresses, Shalfak ("Wa'f-Khasut," 21°33′ N, 31°02′ E) on the west bank, and Askut ("Djer-Setiu," 21°38′ N, 31°06′ E), on an island farther north. Beyond Askut, the Nile is broken entirely into a cataract of braided channels and is impassable to shipping, particularly at low water. The large fortress of Mirgissa (21°49′ N, 31°10′ E) was located at its upstream end. The cataract was bypassed below Mirgissa by a mud-paved slipway along which boats were dragged, apparently on low runners. This slipway extended in a straight line some 8 km to a point above the rock of Abusir, almost to the great fortified center of Kor (ancient name unknown), now greatly expanded and given elaborate fortifications to accommodate large official complexes. Just to the north was Buhen, also greatly expanded and with fortifications of considerable sophistication. The cataract region complex was completed by the establishment of two smaller fortresses, at Faras West ("Inktawy," 22°13′ N, 31°29′ E) and Serra East ("Khesef-Medjay," 22°07′ N, 31°24′ E), not far to the north.

The fortresses dating to the reign of Senusret III have various plans, adapted to controlling their situation and keeping ready access to the river. Most were rectangular, with one wall fronting the Nile, but others had shapes adapted to the available high ground: Semna was L-shaped, while Uronarti and Askut were roughly triangular. The smallest (Kumma, Semna South) were about 50 m sq., while the larger ones (Buhen) were about 200 m sq. The great outer wall at Buhen extended some 700 × 250–300 m.

The details of construction varied somewhat, but can be summarized as follows. First, the ground was cleared and leveled to bedrock as far as was practicable. The outer perimeter of the fortress was surrounded by a ditch with sloping sides and a flat bottom. Where bedrock and space allowed, the ditch was cut from stone, but otherwise lined with stone masonry or even mudbrick. The surface inside the ditch was paved, either with stone or mudbrick, up to the platform of the inner curtain. At most of the forts on the river banks, the parapet of the ditch was crowned with a low mudbrick wall of variable elaboration. For example, at Serra East this was a simple straight wall, while that of the inner citadel of Buhen had convex bastions, shield-shaped crenellations, and complex groups of loopholes that would allow an archer to shoot arrows in several directions with a minimum of exposure. At Buhen the outer parapet of the ditch was also walled, but it is difficult to understand the purpose of such a construction except as a low barrier to keep animals from sliding into the ditch. The curtain was located about 2 m (sometimes more) behind the edge of the ditch. At Serra East, this was built on a shallow layer of sand laid on the subsurface. The core of the curtain was a wall of mudbrick courses, of alternating headers and stretchers about 5 m (or more) thick. Thick mats of local halfa grass were laid at intervals, especially in the lower courses where the wall was thickest.

In some forts, notably those built on rocky hills or bluffs (Askut, Shalfak, Semna, Kumma, Uronarti, Serra East), the mudbrick was reinforced, sometimes heavily, with timber, including both longitudinal and transverse beams, while Mirgissa had only transverse logs. Rectangular piers (some 2 m deep by 3 m wide) were built against the outer face, generally with mud plaster making sloping lower faces, but were much wider at the corners. In some cases, such as Mirgissa, the walls had flat pier-like bastions, but most of the forts were also equipped with spur-walls or towers which were connected to the main wall only by a passage on the wall parapet, and barbicans, pairs of spur-towers guarding an important gate. Sometimes, as at Uronarti and Askut, the spur-walls were long and elaborate, and were used to occupy ground that could not be effectively enclosed but which could be used by an enemy to threaten the fort. The great permanent gates were protected by the barbicans, and others by smaller spurs, but some gates were simply breaks in the wall, presumably closed up during a siege. Fortresses without direct access to the river were often equipped with a stone-covered stairway to the water.

The interior of the fortress proper was almost completely filled with buildings, with only narrow passageways around the inside of the wall and streets providing communication. At Buhen, these streets were equipped with covered drains. Open squares were permitted to occupy only a small space. The plans of the buildings were rectilinear, even when the curtain had an irregular shape; only the buildings next to the outer wall were fitted to the shape of the wall. On irregular or sloping surfaces, the buildings might be terraced and the streets given rock-cut steps, as at Serra East, and some of the rooms were partly rock-cut. Magazines, some kind of headquarters building and granaries seem to have been the most common internal structures, but some may have been residences or offices. Military equipment, such as flint-tipped spears and leather shields, was manufactured in some of the forts. Evidence is incomplete because only the ground floors of the buildings are preserved.

A number of simple or exposed forts may have had no outbuildings, but the larger ones, such as Buhen and Mirgissa, and island forts, such as Uronarti and Askut, had residences, magazines and even substantial official buildings located close to the walls. These were sometimes protected by very strong outer fortifications, which at Aniba and Buhen greatly enlarged the protected area. Such outer fortifications, not tightly packed with buildings, were probably used as refuges in times of disturbance, or as staging areas for campaign operations. Simple, non-fortified enclosure walls found at Mirgissa and Semna South were probably for staging areas, trading camps or pens. The fortress complexes were not complete with these structures, for there were more distant residences and official buildings, such as the great slipway for transporting ships at Mirgissa, and even pottery kilns.

Two other types of structures associated with the forts remain enigmatic. The first consists of a circular basin sloped to a sunken pot or round depression in the center. Draining into the basin are four rectangular slabs, each sloped to a channel. The second structure at Serra East consists of a roughly rectangular basin, *circa* 30×20 m. Walls of irregular stones were sloped very much like an outer ditch built against a smooth, sloping surface of mudbrick, which continued over the parapet. No entry existed on the west side of this rectangular structure, so it was not a harbor, as was once thought. It was certainly important, for it occupies the fortress's center, and it may have been used to confine captives.

The fortresses represent an immense allocation of resources. The walls of Serra East contained some 15,000 m^3 of mudbrick alone. For the entire complex, a truly major logistical effort must have been mounted, including the acquisition of large amounts of imported (?) timber, which was unavailable in the region. Each fort was built to sustain a siege by a well-organized opponent, and ritual architecture, consisting of small temples, was minimal. The great dry ditches were designed to obstruct tunneling, prevent combustibles from being piled against the walls, and fend off tanks, such as those shown in scenes in Middle Kingdom tombs at Beni Hasan, which covered sappers using poles to pry mudbricks from forts.

Administrative routine in the forts is reflected in the shreds of accounts, memoranda and dispatches that have been excavated, and there are numerous sealings for documents, chests and what were probably door-bolts. The door-bolt seals identify the main offices, most commonly the fort itself, the fortress granary, treasury, magazines and "Upper Fort" (Headquarters?). They were impressed in conical or shield-shaped mud lumps, placed over the bolt and cord which secured the door, and counter-stamped with the personal (scarab) seal of the officer on duty. Most of these stamps have no names or titles, with the audit trail assured by conical sample sealings kept on a string for reference. Where named, these officers were men of very moderate rank, mostly simple retainers. Only occasionally is there evidence of a seal of a high-ranking official, such as the southern vizier, usually from a document sent to the fortress. Seals from royal documents are rare and found only in a few fortresses.

Senusret III gave a general order for the southern frontier forts, to let no valley Nubian ("Nḥsy") pass on land or on the river except to trade at Mirgissa. They might be fed, and "every good thing" done for them, but they had to leave the region. From the reign of Amenemhat III or slightly later, comes a papyrus, the *Semna Dispatches*, that vividly illustrates the measures taken to enforce this order, both against the valley Nubians and against the Medjay people of the Eastern Desert. It preserves eight somewhat fragmentary reports of contacts presented in a style familiar in modern military and police organizations, including the source of the report (Egyptians named, with forces described), persons encountered, their purpose, date and time, and action taken. The reports are signed by the reporting officer, with persons who received copies indicated, where appropriate. They were collected at Semna and forwarded to the office of the southern vizier at Thebes. Most of the contacts consisted of small parties (up to nine persons) of valley Nubians, including women,

who arrived at Semna to trade. Their goods (not specified) were traded, and they returned southward by river the next morning. Three reports mention contacts with the Medjay. The dispatches reveal a policy of complete border control and careful reporting of all contacts, which contrasts with the relatively free access depicted in the tomb chapels of Middle Egypt less than a century earlier. Lower Nubia and Egypt were to be protected with a curtain of mudbrick fortresses, aggressive patrols and relentless administrators.

In the mid- and later eighteenth century BC, tombs and monuments of Egyptian officials and residents became common at some of the forts, especially Buhen. Other forts show signs of haphazard internal alterations, which reinforce the impression that those in the garrisons were becoming settlers, and an Egyptian village was built at Askut. Dating somewhat later, tombs and small cemeteries of the "Pan-grave" culture are found in Nubia and Upper Egypt, belonging to people from the Atbai region to the southeast, which demonstrate that the frontier no longer held back the Medjay. Still later, the fortress-populations fell under the control of the Kushite ruler, who was recognized as a pharaonic overlord by a commandant of Buhen. At Wadi es-Sebua on the east bank, Nubians themselves constructed a fort, a roughly circular enclosure of field stones, with the edge of the cliff forming its western side. Equipped with loopholes and three low, narrow gates, one of which was fortified, the entire structure was filled with huts and pens (?).

Most of the Egyptian fortresses were destroyed by fire some time after the Middle Kingdom. There is little stratigraphic evidence now to date this, but it seems unlikely that this destruction occurred when Lower Nubia came under Kushite control during the Second Intermediate Period. The forts were probably destroyed by the resurgent New Kingdom rulers, who followed an entirely different policy in Nubia by conquering it at least as far upriver as the Fourth Cataract, and perhaps even established posts beyond this point.

The New Kingdom was not the last time that

forts in Nubia were built or renewed, for during the Napatan, Saite and Persian periods (beginning with the reign of the Kushite King Piye, *circa* 753 BC, to the conquest of Alexander, 332 BC), the frontier in Lower Nubia was again active. Although Roman forts built in northernmost Lower Nubia were part of the far-flung boundary complex of their empire, and the castles and fortified towns of later times (including Dabenarti near Mirgissa) were sometimes elaborate, none approached the systematic organization of the Egyptian Middle Kingdom boundary fortresses or the New Kingdom fortified towns.

See also

C-Group; Elephantine; Kushites; Medjay; Middle Kingdom, overview; Nubian towns and temples; Pan-grave culture

Further reading

Dunham, D. 1967. *Second Cataract Forts* 2: *Uronarti Shalfak Mirgissa*. Boston.

Dunham, D., and J.M.A. Janssen. 1960. *Second Cataract Forts* 1: *Semna Kumma*. Boston.

Emery, W.B., H.S. Smith, and A. Millard. 1979. *Excavations at Buhen* 1: The Fortress of Buhen: The Archaeological Report. London.

Knudstad, James E. 1966. Serra East and Dorginarti; a preliminary report on the 1963–64 excavations of the University of Chicago Oriental Institute Sudan Expedition. *Kush* 14: 165–86.

Smith, H.S. 1976. *Excavations at Buhen* 2: The Fortress of Buhen: the Inscriptions. London.

Smith, S.T. 1990. Administration at the Egyptian Middle Kingdom frontier: sealings from Uronarti and Askut. In *Aegean Seals, Sealings and Administration; Proceedings of the NEH-Dickson Conference of the Program in Aegean Scripts and Prehistory of the Department of Classics, University of Texas at Austin January 11–13, 1989*, T.G. Palaima, ed. *Aegaeum* 5: 197–216.

——. 1991. Askut and the role of the Second Cataract forts. *JARCE* 28: 107–32.

Smither, Paul C. 1945. The Semnah dispatches. *JEA* 31: 3–10.

Steindorff, Georg. 1937. *Aniba* 2. Glückstadt.

Trigger, Bruce G. 1976. *Nubia under the Pharaohs*. London.

Vercoutter, Jean. 1970. *Mirgissa* 1. Paris.

Zabkar, L.V., and J.J. Zabkar. 1982. Semna South. A preliminary report on the 1966–68 excavations of the University of Chicago Oriental Institute Expedition to Sudanese Nubia. *JARCE* 19: 7–50.

Zibellius-Chen, K. 1988. *Die ägyptische Expansion nach Nubien*. Wiesbaden.

Ziermann, M. 1993. *Elephantine* 16: *Befestigungsanlagen und Stadtentwicklung in der Frühzeit und im frühen Alten Reich*. Mainz.

BRUCE B. WILLIAMS

Nubian towns and temples

Temples were major features of the towns of Egypt during the New Kingdom, and the temple town was also a primary form of settlement in Nubia. These monumental temples served as symbols of Egyptian power after the conquest of the region by the pharaohs of the New Kingdom, and their consequent right to exploit the region's resources.

Although Middle Kingdom fortifications in Lower Nubia were renovated during the New Kingdom, the Egyptian colonies were apparently not strongly fortified. However, the enclosures controlled movements into and out of the towns and temple storage areas, and therefore facilitated security.

The labor force used in the construction of these monuments sometimes included prisoners of war. Both Ramesses I and his successor, Seti I, claim to have endowed the temple at Buhen with captives, and they were reportedly used to build the Great Temple at Abu Simbel. These slaves may have been skilled artisans intended for the temple workshops, or peasants destined for settlement on the temple estates.

The temples seem to have functioned as a branch of the Egyptian state, serving as centers for the administration and economic exploitation of Nubia. Temples and temple towns were often strategically located near mines, quarries or agricultural land, or where land routes converged on the river. The temples collected local produce and foreign goods in order to maintain themselves and to provision the temple establishments back in Egypt, to which land and trading rights in Nubia had been donated by royal edict. Temple and palace establishments in New Kingdom Egypt were related symbiotically, but it is unclear whether temple personnel in Nubia ever acted as agents of the state.

Archaeologists have also located many temples in Nubia for which no associated settlement remains were found (possibly a function of poor preservation). However, the military control or political administration of the region was the responsibility of soldiers and government officials who were undoubtedly settled in or near temple towns. These ritual centers also functioned as administrative, economic and cultural centers. It has been noted that the distribution of New Kingdom temples and temple towns mirrors the pattern of primary settlement found during earlier and later periods. Although temple towns continued to be important in later periods in Nubia, the following discussion will deal only with those known from the New Kingdom. These centers were not all contemporaneous, and detailed evidence for their dating cannot be given here.

New Kingdom settlements in Nubia

The Egyptian administration of Nubia was conducted from numerous outposts, but the residences of the high officials who helped administer the northern (Wawat) and southern (Kush) districts of Nubia were located at Aniba (22°40′ N, 32°01′ E) and Amara (20°48′ N, 30°23′ E). Faras (22°13′ N, 31°29′ E) and Soleb (20°27′ N, 30°20′ E) briefly usurped this function during the reign of Tutankhamen. All four of these sites were major towns throughout the period. The Middle Kingdom forts at Kuban (23°10′ N, 32°46′ E), Ikkur (23°13′ N, 32°48′ E), Aniba, Serra (22°07′ N,

31°24′ E) and Buhen (21°55′ N, 31°17′ E), which were located in the most fertile regions of Lower Nubia, as well as the Second Cataract forts at Mirgissa (21°49′ N, 31°10′ E), Semna (21°30′ N, 30°57′ E), Uronarti (21°32′ N, 30°57′ E), Kumma/Semna East (21°30′ N, 30°57′ E) and Shelfak (21°33′ N, 31°02′ E), were all renovated and reoccupied during the New Kingdom. Some of these centers were active only at the beginning of the 18th Dynasty, and were abandoned after the Egyptians consolidated their power down to the Fourth Cataract. All had at least one New Kingdom temple.

There were no apparent settlement remains found in association with the New Kingdom temples or chapels at Beit el-Wali (23°33′ N, 32°52′ E), Gerf Hussein (23°17′ N, 32°54′ E), Wadi es-Sebua (22°45′ N, 32°34′ E), Derr (22°44′ N, 32°12′ E), Ellesiya (22°42′ N, 32°03′ E), Qasr Ibrim (22°39′ N, 32°00′ E), Abu Simbel (22°21′ N, 31°38′ E), or Abu Hoda/Gebel Adda (22°18′ N, 31°37′ E). Most of these temples were built by Ramesses II. The presence of New Kingdom graves near a few of these sites, and the inscriptional evidence which mentions a fort or town in the area (as at Derr), may point to contemporary settlements which were never found by modern surveys.

After the military campaigns of Tuthmose I, the Egyptians had advanced beyond the Fourth Cataract. The forts in Lower Nubia became less important for military security, and some of them were apparently abandoned by the mid-18th Dynasty. Those that continued to exist were eventually expanded beyond the perimeters of the earlier fortifications.

The Middle Kingdom fortress of Kuban, which was situated at the entrance to the gold-mining region of the Wadi Allaqi, was reoccupied during the New Kingdom and a temple built therein. New Kingdom remains were also found across the river at the reoccupied fortress of Ikkur, which eventually lost its importance to an unfortified town that developed at nearby Dakka.

The Middle Kingdom fortress at Aniba was reoccupied early in the 18th Dynasty, and cemeteries in the area continued to be used.

The town later expanded beyond the fortification walls of the earlier settlement, and another wall was constructed. The town was never thoroughly investigated, but a New Kingdom temple was discovered in the northwest corner of the new enclosure, and this was surrounded by residential, administrative and storage buildings. Eventually, buildings were constructed outside Aniba's walls.

There is still no conclusive evidence of New Kingdom occupation across the river at Qasr Ibrim, but a number of New Kingdom rock-cut shrines, built by officials of Tuthmose III, Amenhotep II and Ramesses II, were found in the vicinity. Temples were discovered to the north at Ellesiya, Derr and Amada (22°43′ N, 32°15′ E). The latter was originally built during the reign of Tuthmose III, but the nearby settlement was never thoroughly investigated. An inscription from a New Kingdom grave at Aniba also mentions a settlement at Derr, and there are New Kingdom graves nearby.

An inscription from the reign of Tutankhamen mentions the town of Ibshek, the ancient name of Faras and numerous New Kingdom temples were built in the vicinity. However, no contemporary settlement remains were found at Faras, and the Middle Kingdom fortress was apparently not reoccupied. (The area was extensively used during later periods, and possibly an earlier settlement existed below the Christian citadel). At nearby Aksha the enclosure walls of the Ramesside temple were partly utilized as the main wall of a later town, which formed south of the temple and outside the walls; it was not extensively investigated.

The New Kingdom temples and graves at Faras are spread over a large area, which has led scholars to assume that the administrative, religious and residential buildings of Faras were dispersed (like those of Thebes in Egypt). The mortuary evidence may indicate that the main administrative center was surrounded by small settlements of the indigenous population. However, none of these local centers was ever identified.

The Middle Kingdom fortifications and buildings at Buhen and Mirgissa were extensively renovated and resettled at the beginning of the New Kingdom. New temples were also constructed. The town area of Buhen eventually spread beyond the old walls and the expanded enclosure. The fortified site at nearby Kor (21°52′ N, 31°14′ E) may have also been partially reused during the New Kingdom, but no Middle or New Kingdom temples were found in the enclosure.

Although the Middle Kingdom fortresses south of Mirgissa received some attention during the New Kingdom, their strategic importance decreased after Egyptian expansion to the Fourth Cataract. The fortresses of Semna and Uronarti, however, were renovated during the New Kingdom, and new temples were also built at these sites, as well as at Kumma.

No New Kingdom remains were found between the southern end of the Second Cataract and the southern end of the Batn el-Hagar, but temples and settlements were built in the fertile region between the Third Cataract and the Dongola Reach. Evidence from both archaeological surveys and inscriptions show that towns existed contemporaneously with the temples at Amara, Sai, Soleb, Sesebi, Tabo/Argo Island (19°30′ N, 30°28′ E), and perhaps also at Kawa (19°07′ N, 30°30′ E). No New Kingdom settlement was found at the temple site of Seddenga (20°33′ N, 30°17′ E).

The New Kingdom levels at the partially excavated town of Amara date from the Ramesside period. This walled temple town was a major Egyptian administrative center located in an agriculturally fertile area capable of supporting a settled population. It was also strategically located within view of the desert and river routes and was near a gold-mining region.

The fortified settlement at Soleb, located south of the temple built by Amenhotep III, was one of the major Egyptian administrative towns in Nubia under Tutankhamen (the center was later moved to Amara). The nearby temple at Seddenga was built for Amenhotep III's wife, Tiye, but no settlement remains were found there. A rock-chapel of Tuthmose III was built on the west bank at Gebel Dosha (20°30′ N, 30°18′ E), south of Seddenga.

At Sesebi, the entire circuit of the late 18th Dynasty enclosure wall is known. Its streets, which were constructed on a grid pattern, divided the settlement into residential and administrative, religious and storage sectors. After the reign of Akhenaten, it began to grow in a more haphazard manner. Akhenaten founded all four of the temples located along the northwest wall of the town. A roadway connected this site with the temple town at Soleb.

According to an inscription from Tumbus (19°42′ N, 30°24′ E), which is situated at the south end of the Third Cataract, a fortress was constructed at the site under Tuthmose I. Little is known about New Kingdom remains from the site, but inscriptions found in the vicinity mention Tuthmose III, Amenhotep II and Amenhotep III.

It was once believed that Kerma, to the south of Tumbus, was abandoned during much of this period, but New Kingdom remains have recently been found there, including a cemetery and some houses in the settlement. New Kingdom pottery and inscribed stone blocks were found west and north of the earlier town. A religious complex with associated New Kingdom (and later) remains have also been found (at the "Kom of the Bodegas").

The town of Kawa is believed to be identical with the ancient town of Gempaten, which was established by either Amenhotep III or Akhenaten. The unexcavated settlement stretching north and south of the 25th Dynasty temple at Kawa may be contemporaneous with a New Kingdom temple, lying beneath the later one.

No New Kingdom remains have been found in the area along the river between Kawa and Napata, which perhaps suggests that an overland route was in use at this time. Located at the southern terminus of this route is Napata/Gebel Barkal, where a victory stela of Tuthmose III was found. It mentions a fort called "Death to the Foreigners" in which there was a chapel dedicated to Amen. An inscription of Tutankhamen also refers to a fort in this area. The remains of a New Kingdom temple and inscribed artifacts dating from the 18th to 20th Dynasties have also been found in the region, but evidence for a contemporary fortress, settlement or cemeteries is still lacking.

Finally, inscriptions of Tuthmose I and III have been found near modern Kurgus (19°12′ N, 33°30′ E), south of Abu Hamed, between the Fourth and Fifth Cataracts. Although there is an unexcavated fortress on the nearby island of Mograt, none of the surface remains has been dated to the New Kingdom.

Conclusion

Egypt's occupation of Nubia required administrative, religious and social centers, both for the Egyptian colonizers and the Nubian officials, and for the local people working for them. However, because of past emphasis on excavating temples and cemeteries in Nubia, and because of the abbreviated nature of salvage excavations (preceding the flooding of Lower Nubia by Lake Nasser), information concerning the administrative, residential and service areas of these towns is lacking. Contemporary settlements of the indigenous population are also unknown. The occupation of Nubia during the New Kingdom allowed the Egyptian state and temple establishments to have direct access to the produce of the region, sources of gold and precious stones, and to the markets for luxury products from the south (ebony, ivory, electrum, myrrh trees and myrrh, other types of wood, incense, fruits, cosmetics, throw-sticks, ostrich eggs and feathers, and exotic animals and skins). The inhabitants of temple-centered fortress towns and newly established temple towns in Nubia not only regulated the flow of local goods for the support of the settled population in these centers, but they also facilitated the flow of luxury products northwards into Egypt.

See also

Gebel Barkal; Kerma; Kushites; natural resources; New Kingdom, overview; Nubian forts; Qasr Ibrim; urbanism

Further reading

Adams, W.Y. 1984. *Nubia: Corridor to Africa*. Princeton, NJ.

Emery, W.B. *Egypt in Nubia*. London.

Kemp, B.J. 1978. Imperialism and empire in New Kingdom Egypt. In *Imperialism in the Ancient World*, P.D.A. Garnsey and C.R. Whittaker, eds. 7–57. Cambridge.

Trigger, B.G. 1976. *Nubia Under the Pharaohs*. London.

LISA A. HEIDORN

Nuri

Nuri, whose ancient name is unknown, is a modern Sudanese village, 10 km upstream from Gebel Barkal on the opposite bank of the Nile, approximately 28 km downstream from the Fourth Cataract (18°33′ N, 31°55′ E). It is the site of the royal necropolis of Kush during the three centuries following the end of the 25th Dynasty and the abandonment of el-Kurru. Founded by the Kushite king Taharka (*circa* 690–664 BC), the Nuri cemetery was used by all but two of his twenty-one known successors to the time of Nastasen (*circa* 335–315 BC), and fifty-three queens. Nuri was explored and described by George Waddington and Barnard Hanbury, Frédéric Cailliaud and Louis Linant de Bellefonds in 1820–2, by George Hoskins in 1833, and by Carl Richard Lepsius in 1844, among others. It was excavated by George Reisner and the Harvard University–Museum of Fine Arts, Boston Expedition between 1916 and 1918.

Why Taharka chose to abandon the dynastic cemetery of el-Kurru and to choose for his pyramid the novel site of Nuri is unclear, but Timothy Kendall has proposed a mythological explanation. Nuri lies on the left bank of the Nile, the traditional place of burial in Egypt, which was associated with the west. As the place of sunset, the west was identified as the realm of the dead and the entrance to the underworld. Here, paradoxically, due to the reverse curve in the river, Nuri actually lies in the east, which, as the place of sunrise, was identified with rebirth and new life. From the summit of Gebel Barkal, the Nuri pyramids can be seen to the northeast, 68–70° from true north. When sunrise is observed from the summit of Gebel Barkal at the summer solstice, the sun appears to rise at 65°, just to the right of the Nuri pyramids. Several weeks later, when the sun rises at 68–70°, directly behind the pyramids, the period coincides with the heliacal rising of Sirius, which marked the start of the ancient Egyptian New Year, coinciding with the annual Nile flood. Since the New Year symbolized renewal and re-creation, the site of Nuri would appear to have been deliberately chosen to create the most favorable metaphorical environment for the king's assumed rebirth and resurrection.

The Nuri pyramids were erected on a pair of parallel ridges running northeast to southwest about 1.5 km from the Nile. Taharka was the first king to use the site, but his tomb (Nu. 1) is such an aberration from those built before and immediately after his reign that it is not clear whether it was entirely constructed in his lifetime or whether it was built in different stages after his death by his successors. The subterranean rock-cut tomb, 13 m deep and accessed by a stairway with fifty-one steps, is unique among all the Kushite royal mausolea in that it is closely related in plan to the Osireion of Seti I at Abydos, the cenotaph of Osiris. Taharka's tomb consists of a room with six massive square pillars and vaulted aisles, once plastered and brightly painted, and encircled by a corridor joining the room at its front and rear axis. The coffin had been raised on a dais in the center of the room, which, being cut below the level of the water table, remained flooded, thus symbolically creating for the king's mummy the environment of rebirth on the primeval mound emerging from the waters of Nun.

The pyramid itself, with a base length of 51.75 m (approximately 100 cubits), is four times larger than the those of his two immediate successors and twice as large as any built later at the site. Degradation of the outer surface of this pyramid, however, revealed that an earlier, smaller pyramid with a base length of 28.5 m (approximately 50 cubits), a size identical to those built by most of his successors, had originally marked the tomb. No trace of a chapel has ever been found, leading to speculation that the original chapel might have been encased in the masonry of later additions.

Taharka's tomb was located between the two ridges; the tombs of two of his queens were sited just to the north of this. Although his successor, Tanwetameni, chose to be buried at el-Kurru, four queens of his generation preferred burial at Nuri. Subsequently, all kings' tombs were built in a row to the southeast of Taharka's tomb, while all the royal women were buried to the north or northeast of Taharka's pyramid. According to Dows Dunham, each tomb was built on the most favorable spot remaining vacant on the site at the time it was constructed.

Following the burial of Atlanersa, whose tomb (Nu. 20) was similar in scale to that of Tanwetameni at el-Kurru, the kings established an entirely new, more grandiose tomb and pyramid type, with an average base length of 28 m (50 cubits), which remained the standard for three more centuries. Chapels with pylons were built against the southeast façades of the pyramids. The subterranean tombs, 8–9 m below ground, now consisted of three interconnecting rock-cut chambers accessed by a deep stairway. When well finished, the walls of each of these rooms were completely carved or painted with Egyptian funerary texts and scenes.

The Napatan kings were mummified according to Egyptian fashion; their bodies were wrapped holding gold crooks and flails, and green stone heart scarabs and gold pectorals were placed over their chests. Their fingers and toes were capped with gold, and their faces were covered with gold masks (although the only existing examples were found in queens' tombs). The viscera were placed in large canopic jars. The royal mummies were encased within wooden anthropoid coffins covered with gold foil and adorned with inlaid eyes of bronze, calcite and obsidian. These coffins were then placed within larger coffins, covered with gold leaf and inlays of colored stones in designs of falcons or vultures with outstretched wings. In two cases (Nu. 6 and 8), the kings' outer coffins were placed within

huge, fully decorated granite sarcophagi. Around the walls of the burial chambers *shawabti* (servant) figures of stone or faïence, numbering between several hundred to over a thousand, would be arranged standing. Although the tombs were all badly plundered, evidence suggests that the kings were buried with chests of valuable jewelry, vessels, toilet articles and other personal possessions. Typically, the first chamber probably contained large numbers of jars of food and drink.

The queens' tombs and burials shared much in common with those of the kings', but they were less elaborate and the materials used were less costly. The most developed queens' tombs contained two interconnecting rock-cut chambers, 4–8 m deep, surmounted by pyramids about half the size of those of the kings. A lesser type contained only a single rock-cut chamber with an even smaller pyramid. Still another contained only a single chamber without any evident superstructure. These were the same types of queens' tombs that had been manifested at el-Kurru. As preserved, the walls exhibited little decoration, but one tomb (Nu. 24) was extensively carved with texts from the *Book of the Dead*, and others (e.g. Nu. 53) bore traces of plastered and painted decoration. Some tombs contained niches in their walls, either for lamps or for statues. In the center of the floor, or slightly off-axis to the south, a low bench, either rock-cut or of masonry, appeared on which the queen's coffin was laid. Each tomb was marked on the surface by a pyramid ranging in base length from 6.3–7.5 m for the earliest, to 10–11 m for those in mid-sequence, to 12–13 m toward the end of the sequence. This increase in size would seem to correspond to the increasing political importance of the great queens in the Meroitic period, when the capital of the Kushite state was farther south at Meroe. None of the queens' pyramids preserved a chapel with a pylon.

Nuri was abandoned as a royal cemetery in the late fourth century BC. Subsequent kings initially built their tombs at Gebel Barkal, but by the mid-third century BC the royal cemetery was moved to Meroe.

See also

funerary texts; Gebel Barkal; el-Kurru; Kushites; Meroe, cemeteries; Meroitic culture; Reisner, George Andrew; Sanam; Third Intermediate Period, overview

Further reading

Dunham, D. 1955. *The Royal Cemeteries of Kush* 2: *Nuri*. Boston.

Kendall, T. 1982. Kush: *Lost Kingdom of the Nile*. Brockton, MA.

——. 1997. Kings of the Sacred Mountain: Napata and the Kushite Twenty-fifth Dynasty of Egypt. In *Sudan: Ancient Kingdoms of the Nile*, D. Wildung, ed., 161–71. Paris.

Reisner, G.A. 1918. Known and unknown kings of Ethiopia. *Museum of Fine Arts Bulletin* 16: 67–81.

TIMOTHY KENDALL

O

obelisks: quarrying, transporting and erecting

There are scarcely any original sources for the quarrying, transport and erection of the tall temple obelisks of ancient Egypt. We can only examine the results and try to discern the technical steps by investigating the possibilities using the resources that were at the disposal of the ancient Egyptians. Egyptian obelisks are well known from examples such as the obelisk now in Central Park in New York, originally erected by Tuthmose III in Heliopolis, or the obelisk in front of the Lateran in Rome, originally erected by Tuthmose IV at Karnak. Only such large-scale obelisks will be dealt with here. At least until the end of the New Kingdom, they were shaped from hard stone, reddish-brown quartzite or red granite, a stone which is found in Egypt only in the region of Aswan. Due to their color, both types of stone have a symbolic connection with the rising sun. In the quarries near Aswan are found many traces of the extraction of granite, some of quite recent date but others also reaching back to pharaonic times. This evidence allows us to see how the stone was extracted. One unfinished obelisk measuring nearly 42 m in length still lies in the quarry. When finished, it would have weighed nearly 1,200 tons. This is the largest obelisk known; its unfinished condition, showing certain stages of the work, helps us to reconstruct the quarrying methods used by the ancient Egyptians.

Only great experience enabled the Egyptians to select a place likely to include a flawless piece of stone long enough for an obelisk. Once a section of rock was chosen, the outer weathered layers would be removed, partly by burning

fires on the surface of the rock and cooling it suddenly with water while it was still hot, and partly by pounding with stone hammers. Then the surface of the block was more or less smoothed. During or before smoothing, the masons hammered vertical hollows round the shaft in order to test for any weaknesses which would make further work senseless. After successful testing, they began to dig trenches round the perimeter of the desired shaft.

In pharaonic times, Egyptians working on hard stones had to use tools made of still harder stone, because metal implements of iron were not in use until very late in pharaonic history. Many finds from the quarries are sharp-edged dolorite hammers which were used for working on granite. During the process of hammering, pieces of stone were burst with each blow until the hammers gradually got round and could only be used for pounding, i.e. bruising off small flakes of granite. On the trench walls one can still clearly see slightly concave vertical grooves about 30 cm wide. One man worked on two such grooves. More than 100 men were able to work on the unfinished obelisk at the same time, all in the same position, either to the right or to the left of the grooves. One man would squat in front of the shaft and the next would squat with his back to it. Remains of ocher-colored lines marking the working sections and control marks for the efficiency of the laborers may still be seen.

An especially difficult task was detaching the obelisk, rough-worked on three sides, from the parent rock. Where it was possible, the masons tried to use natural bedding planes. These, however, only very seldom ran as wanted, especially when huge blocks were required. Only in such cases was it possible to first hack out the lower side in the same way as the lateral surfaces. The Egyptians probably tried to squeeze off the block by beginning to bash out the lower side and then employing huge levers at the top of one of the trenches, so the block was broken from the bedrock by leverage. Next, the front wall of the hole in which the obelisk lay had to be removed so that it could be transported out of the quarry. All this toil would have been facilitated enormously by the technique of wedging with iron chisels. This method was not used in Egypt before post-pharaonic times, however.

As a rule the blocks were shaped as much as possible while still in the quarry in order to save weight in transporting the block; several unfinished but extensively worked and partly decorated objects prove this. Anomalies in the monuments occasionally show us evidence of slight carelessness among the stoneworkers. For instance, the slight longitudinal curves of the Luxor obelisks may be the result of the sagging of the measuring cord when the stone was still lying in the quarry, and the slight convexity in section seems to have come from the system of polishing, which produced a more intensive rubbing along the edges than at the center.

The transport of the monuments from the quarry to the banks of the Nile took place by means of sledges or rollers (used for the bigger and heavier objects) on tracks beaten for that purpose. Further transport was by river on vessels known by the term *wsht*. However, we have no exact descriptions or representations of them. Probably the most famous depiction of the transport of obelisks occurs in the temple of Hatshepsut at Deir el-Bahri. One of the four obelisks erected by this queen is still standing at Karnak. Although the vessels and sledges on which the obelisks are transported are shown in great detail, we should not take this representation as being completely accurate; diverse stages of an action are projected in a hieroglyphic manner, that is, condensed into one picture to demonstrate the aim or intention of the action. Thus, although the obelisks are shown fixed on a sledge, this does not mean that they were actually transported on sledges. The sledge is used here as a pictogram for forwarding weighty cargoes: the actual transport could

have been done by rollers. The same holds true for the obelisk-vessels represented with many details in the same temple. They must not be interpreted literally; the depiction does not indicate whether the obelisks were stored on the vessel one behind another—as represented—or side by side. Neither can the type of vessel on which the obelisks were shipped be deduced with any certainity; shipping by means of a raft remains a possibility. Hatshepsut's relief indicates only the transportation of an obelisk by water.

The most vexing problem involves how the obelisks were actually erected. We know of officials responsible for the erecting of obelisks or other labors concerning them from tomb inscriptions or rock graffiti; these are high-ranking functionaries of the temple-administration, but the inscriptions give no technical details. There are also papyri (such as Papyrus Anastasi I, a satiric model letter) including arithmetical problems about the work needed to build embankments (for obelisks) and the like. However, such papyri contain a number of unique words or phrases which make interpretation difficult. Some of the data presented may in fact have been fanciful; for instance, the length of an obelisk relative to its thinness on Papyrus Anastasi I would not have been possible to transport and erect because of the dead weight. With all known obelisks, this ratio is always within a range where sound stone would not break.

Ritual representations in temples show the king erecting obelisks by means of ropes. However, again we should not interpret these illustrations as technical drawings. The erection of obelisks seems to have been possible by lifting up with levers and ropes and simultaneous gradual underpinning. More probably, as generally supposed, the obelisk was slid off an embankment. First, sufficiently strong foundation layers were built and pedestals raised. Horizontal grooves on their upper sides served as construction elements for the erection, especially during the final stage, in order not to damage the lower edges of the shaft through the weight pressing heavily upon them. Grooves at right angles to the ones mentioned above were probably of use for fixing a crossbeam buttressing the obelisk during erection. According to current opinion, it seems most probable that two facing embankments were built parallel to the front of the pylon, enclosing conical pits of masonry at the bottom and ending at the upper side of the pedestal, with drains for sand at right angles to the axis of the forward ramp. The obelisk was slid into the shaft filled with sand by discharging the sand from the drains. It was then pulled into its final position by means of ropes. For all these tasks, it was necessary to calculate the center of gravity and to take precautions that the obelisk did not rock and twist too much after passing over dead center.

See also

Aswan; cult temples of the New Kingdom; Deir el-Bahri, Hatshepsut temple; quarrying

Further reading

Arnold, D. 1991. *Building in Egypt: Pharaonic Stone Masonry*. New York.
Clarke, S., and R. Engelbach. 1990. *Ancient Egyptian Construction and Architecture*. New York.
Habachi, L. 1977. *The Obelisks of Egypt: Skyscrapers of the Past*. New York.
Isler, M. 1987. The curious Luxor obelisks. *JEA* 73: 137–47.

KARL MARTIN

Old Kingdom provincial tombs

The Nile Valley in Upper Egypt is only 1.5–20.0 km wide. Because of the narrowness of the arable land in most places, the great men of the provinces and their lesser contemporaries cut their tombs in the steep cliffs that border the valley. The earliest rock-cut tombs were not located in Upper Egypt, but were actually made for the family of Khafre in an abandoned quarry west of the second pyramid at Giza. The traditional *mastaba* form (a low, rectangular superstructure with a flat roof and sloping sides

containing an offering chapel with false door(s) and constructed above a rock-cut shaft and burial chamber) was not easily abandoned, however. In a number of the early rock-cut tombs at Giza, the external façade was treated as the face of a *mastaba* and cut to a batter.

The early rock-cut tombs in the Nile Valley likewise imitated a *mastaba* in form. One of the first is situated at Tihna el-Gebel, on the east bank of the Nile just north of the modern town of Minya. The tomb probably dates to the early 5th Dynasty and belongs to an important local personage named Ny-ka-ankh. In form, it is a freestanding, rock-cut *mastaba*, a rectangular mass of rock that was detached from the surrounding cliff. Three narrow, open passages were thus formed on its north, south and east sides. In the long north–south chapel are fifteen statues of Ny-ka-ankh and of his wife and children cut in the four walls. Two false doors, for Ny-ka-ankh and his wife, are sculpted in the rear (west) wall opposite the entrance of the chapel. As in a stone-built *mastaba*, the square, vertical burial shafts were located behind the false doors.

The true rock-cut tombs of Upper Egypt belong to the end of the 5th Dynasty or later exhibit a greater appreciation for the potential of tombs hewn in solid rock. The rooms are generally larger and cut deeper into the cliff, and the wall area available for decoration is thereby greatly increased. No two of the tombs are exactly alike, but, excepting those at Akhmim which exhibit marked local characteristics, a number of features commonly recur:

1 The façades continue to be cut on a sloping line and are provided with a lintel set on recessed jambs with a drum between, on the pattern of the entrance of *mastaba* tombs.
2 The basic plan for rock-cut tombs of all sizes consists of a north–south offering room whose long axis is parallel to the façade.
3 The plan of the tomb-chapel tends to be symmetrical or nearly so on either side of a central axis passing through the entrance doorway.
4 In larger tombs with two transverse chambers, the outer one serves as the offering room

and the inner one is usually uninscribed. The principal false door is located in the west wall of the offering room whether that wall is a rear wall (west bank tombs) or entrance wall (east bank tombs).

5 In the middle of the rear wall of the offering room or of the inner room a cult niche or statue chamber often appears.

6 Rows of square pillars, only rarely columns, support the roofs of the offering room or divide a chapel into two or more rooms. They may join the ceiling directly, but frequently a transverse architrave connects them with each other and the side walls.

7 Rock-cut statues in wall niches figure prominently in the decoration of the chapels.

8 Additional rooms, such as antechambers, side chambers, shaft rooms, storerooms and *serdab*s (statue chambers), are not uncommon.

The façades of the majority of rock-cut tombs are usually quite plain. In larger tombs, however, the lintel may be inscribed with a prayer for the benefit of the tomb owner, and the recessed jambs often bear large-scale figures of the owner and his family. At Aswan and Meir, in addition, the jambs of several tombs are incised with biographical texts, but at other Upper Egyptian sites biographical inscriptions are relatively rare. On the drum of the entrance, the titles and name of the owner may be inscribed, and the thicknesses of the doorway may have figures of the owner or of the owner and his family or personal attendants. Occasionally, younger and older portrayals of the owner appear on opposite sides of the doorway. All of the façade sculptures tend to be in sunk relief. Rarely, as at Akhmim and Deshasha, a pillared portico runs in front of the façade.

From the end of the 5th Dynasty, the offering room or main hall (at Akhmim) is frequently divided transversely by a row of square rock-cut pillars. One face or more of the pillars may be decorated in relief or paint with figures of the owner or his wife or family. The transverse architrave may be inscribed with a prayer for the soul of the owner. The ceiling in most of the true rock-cut tombs is flat and may be painted to imitate red granite, but low vaults

appear in a few cases at Qasr es-Sayyad, Deshasha and Tihna.

Statues in niches seem to represent an alternative to pillars in the decoration of the offering room. But statues are fewer in number and more randomly placed than pillars or appear in a separate statue chamber in the middle of the rear wall opposite the entrance. At Zawiyet el-Amwat in the tomb of Khunes, three walls of this axial room are occupied by a niche with a rock-cut statue of the tomb owner, while in one tomb at Sheikh Sa'id a deep niche at the back of the room contains life-sized seated group statues of the owner and his wife. Elsewhere, the statue chamber is either plain and undecorated, or irregular and unfinished.

In keeping with Memphite usage, Upper Egyptian tombs located on the west bank were generally entered from the east, and the false door was located on the rear (west) wall of the offering room. Over much of the 300 km south of Cairo, however, the Nile flows closer to the east side of the valley, and the cultivation is mainly on the west bank. For this reason, the majority of rock tombs in this stretch are cut in the eastern cliffs. To preserve the traditional orientation, the false door (or doors) in east bank tombs appear mostly on the entrance (west) wall. Alternatively, the back of the cult niche may feature the owner or the owner and his wife at a table, like the scene on the panel of false doors, whose function the cult niches seem to usurp.

With the exception of Akhmim, where paint was the preferred medium for wall scenes throughout the period in question, most of the provincial rock-cut tombs of Upper Egypt in the Old Kingdom are decorated in raised relief. Only at the end of the 6th Dynasty does carved decoration largely give way to paint (for example, in the Deir el-Gebrawi tombs of Ibi, Djau Shemai and Djau).

To a considerable extent, the style, composition and content of the reliefs reflect trends current in the cemeteries of the capital of Memphis. The increased wall areas of the true rock-cut tombs resulted in an expansion of the repertoire used in the earlier chapels, especially scenes from daily life—agricultural scenes, marsh scenes, the owner sallying forth in his carrying chair, craftsmen at work, and so forth—a development which is also seen in 5th and 6th Dynasty tombs at the capital.

Many rock-cut tombs show the direct influence of the Memphis workshops in their decorative scheme. An early example is the siege scene in the tomb of Inti at Deshasha, which closely resembles a scene in the chapel of Ka-em-heset at Saqqara. It is possible that these scenes were copied by local artists from Memphite originals or were executed by artists who were trained at the capital. Resemblances in composition or in detail among certain other provincial tombs may be explained by craftsmen who directly copied scenes in tombs at neighboring sites, or possibly by provincial workshops operating at more than one site.

The service equipment of the rock-cut tombs includes offering stones with a loaf-on-mat symbol in relief or plain platforms in front of the false doors for the deposit of offerings. Between two columns of the central aisle of the tomb of Mekhu at Aswan is a flat table on three upright stone slabs, undoubtedly intended for the paraphernalia of the mortuary priests who conducted the periodic funeral services for the dead owner. In front of one false door at Meir, a pierced tethering stone for tying up a sacrificial ox is cut in the rock, and beside it is a basin to catch the blood.

Access to the burial chamber in the rock-cut tombs is usually from within the chapel through a vertical shaft or sloping passage in the floor of the offering room or an adjacent chamber. The mouth of the shaft or sloping passage alternatively may be located in the floor or at the back of the cult niche, or even in a separate shaft room. More rarely, a small door in one of the walls may lead to a burial chamber.

The burial chambers are most often roughly finished and undecorated. However, at Meir the burial chambers of Pepi-ankh the Middle, his wife Het-y'ah, and their son Hepi the Black are painted with food offerings, cloth and ornaments, rows of granaries with their contents, a list of offerings, and palace-façade false doors in a manner similar to burial chambers of the 6th Dynasty at Saqqara.

Officials of middle rank constructed simpler tombs, usually one-chambered, adjacent to or nearby the tombs of the provincial governors (nomarchs). Their walls are sculptured with table scenes or, more rarely, scenes from life, and show that decorated tombs were not entirely the monopoly of provincial governors. At certain sites relatives or favored retainers of the local governors excavated small subsidiary tombs or dug burial pits in the forecourts of the great tombs, or on occasion within the chapels themselves. Small false doors are sometimes sculpted in the wall above the pits. At many places, lower ranking officials hewed out small undecorated chapels in the cliffs with deep pits or chambers with sloping passages just large enough to hold a wooden coffin.

Because the rock-cut tomb is the predominant form of sepulcher in Middle and Upper Egypt, it is easy to forget that *mastaba* tombs were built in the course of the Old Kingdom at places like Aswan, Edfu, Elkab, Nagada, Dendera, Gozeriya, Abadiya, Abydos, Reqaqna and Naga ed-Deir in Nomes I–VIII of Upper Egypt, and at Deshasha in Nome XX. The Dendera cemetery extended at least 1 km in the low desert south of the ancient town and contained more than 100 mudbrick *mastaba*s of the Old Kingdom, First Intermediate Period and Middle Kingdom. At least twelve mudbrick *mastaba*s in the center of the cemetery go back to the 5th Dynasty or earlier. The largest have two niches on the eastern façade, and one of these has an interior cruciform chapel in place of the southernmost niche.

Characteristic of the Dendera *mastaba*s of the second half of the 6th Dynasty and the First Intermediate Period is a long row of niches of the same size down the entire length of the façade with a rectangular stela placed atop each niche displaying a standing figure of the owner and a funerary formula. The *mastaba*s were also provided with a segmented limestone frieze inscribed with a single line of text, often biographical in content, which ran along the length of the façade near the top. The offering chamber consists of a long corridor parallel to the façade which is sometimes divided into rooms. The *mastaba* of Idu I, in fact, has a row of four such chambers with a niche in the southernmost for a false door. The tomb was the largest and most important in the cemetery. A T-shaped burial chamber was lined with stone slabs and carved with inscriptions and representations of food and funerary equipment. It was probably decorated around the middle of the long reign of Pepi II.

In the wide, flat expanses of the Nile Delta, *mastaba* tombs of stone or mudbrick had of necessity to be built. Due to the deep deposits of Nile mud and surface sand, however, Old Kingdom *mastaba* tombs have only been unearthed at a few sites, notably at Tell-el Rub'a. Large mudbrick *mastaba*s with stone elements of the later Old Kingdom have also been found at Balat in Dakhla Oasis.

See also

Akhmim; el-Ashmunein; Aswan; Gebelein; Mendes, Dynastic evidence; Naga ed-Deir; Old Kingdom, overview; representational evidence, Old Kingdom private tombs

Further reading

Badawy, A. 1954. *A History of Egyptian Architecture 1: From the Earliest Times to the End of the Old Kingdom*. Cairo.
——. 1966. *A History of Egyptian Architecture 2: The First Intermediate Period, the Middle Kingdom, and the Second Intermediate Period*. Berkeley, CA.
Fischer, H.G. 1968. *Dendera in the Third Millennium B.C. down to the Theban Domination of Upper Egypt*. Locust Valley, NY.
Harpur, Y. 1987. *Decoration in Egyptian Tombs of the Old Kingdom*. London and New York.
Kanawati, N. 1980–9. *The Rock Tombs of El-Hawawish*. Sydney.
Kessler, D. 1980. Nekropolen, Frühzeit und AR. 1.-6. Dyn. *LÄ* 4: 395–414.
Reisner, G.A. 1936. *The Development of the Egyptian Tomb down to the Accession of Cheops*. Cambridge, MA.
——. 1942. *A History of the Giza Necropolis 1*. Cambridge, MA.
Smith, W.S. 1949. *A History of Egyptian Sculpture and Painting in the Old Kingdom*. Boston.

EDWARD BROVARSKI

el-Omari

El-Omari is the site of a Neolithic settlement in the Cairo region (29°53′ N, 31°20′ E). It is located 5 km north of Helwan at the northern end of the Helwan plateau, immediately to the south of Wadi Hof. The plateau is well-known for its many springs, and sites of hunters and gatherers were also located there in Paleolithic and Epi-paleolithic times.

The site of el-Omari was first discovered in 1924 by an Egyptian mineralogist, Amin El-Omari, in collaboration with Paul Bovier-Lapierre, a French archaeologist and priest. Unfortunately, El-Omari died shortly thereafter, and the site was named after him. Bovier-Lapierre excavated parts of the site during two weeks in 1925. In 1943 Fernand Debono, an archaeologist living in Egypt, continued the excavation. At first the excavation was interrupted by the Second World War, and then in 1951 by the Egyptian military, who wanted to build a factory beside the site. Today the site is covered by the Helwan–Heliopolis highway.

A contemporary site is located on Gebel Hof, the mountain just at the mouth of Wadi Hof, more than 100 m above the wadi floor. It was partly excavated in 1952 by the Egyptian Antiquities Organization (EAO); since then it has been a military zone and is off-limits to archaeologists.

On the basis of six radiocarbon dates, the settlement at el-Omari was occupied for about 200 years, from approximately 4,600 to 4,400 BC. It is contemporary with the early culture at the site of Merimde Beni-salame in the southern Delta and the Neolithic settlements in the Fayum. The earliest settlement at el-Omari had a simple economy based mainly on fishing and perhaps hunting. Later there was a shift to farming, which was probably the result of a moister climate than when the site was first occupied, and was conducive for the adoption of agriculture.

Remains of the settlement covered an area about 750 m in length and 500 m in maximum width, but the total area was never inhabited at one time. Through time the living area shifted horizontally, as new houses were constructed and others were abandoned.

The only evidence of domestic structures at el-Omari are pits and postholes. Houses would have been made of wattle and daub, which consisted of wooden frames placed in the postholes and then covered with mud. Possibly the small pits and the larger ones, which were used for storage, formed a kind of residential unit. Remains of baskets, which had been closed with lids, were found at the bottom of some pits (1–2.5 m in diameter). Some pits were lined with clay or lime/clay plaster and matting, and sometimes large, coarse ceramic basins had been placed in them for storage. A few hearths were found in abandoned pits. Through time the pits had been filled with debris and all the artifacts were found in them. No settlement debris was found on the site surface between the pits.

Most of the pots from the settlement were made with local clay (a calcareous clay or marl, and a gray clay). Nile clay was used only rarely. The clay was tempered with straw, sometimes very profusely. The surface was wet-smoothed or covered with a ferruginous slip, for a red or brown color. The predominant forms are open and half-closed shapes, which were used to store food and artifacts, as well as for eating. Cooking may have been done in vessels with knob handles.

The stone tools were dominated by small flakes, and (bifacially worked) tools such as axes, sickles and points. Unique at el-Omari are the large-handled knives made of a gray, non-local flint (with steeply retouched backs and notching to facilitate hafting).

Craft activities at el-Omari included the preparation of animal skins, wood working, basket making, textile weaving, bead making and the manufacture of simple stone vases. Bone tools, and stone axes, scrapers, perforators and borers, were used for these activities

and have been found at the site. Stone knives, scrapers and sickle blades were used in food production and preparation. For fishing, fowling and hunting, there is evidence of stone points, arrowheads and net sinkers. Ornaments include beads of ostrich eggshell, stone and bone, as well as pendants of shell (nummulites), mother-of-pearl and limestone. Artifacts that might point to social inequality do not seem to have been produced.

The farmers at el-Omari cultivated cereals. Emmer wheat, an early species of domesticated wheat, was the most important cultigen, but there is also evidence of barley, club wheat and einkorn wheat. Flax was cultivated for textile production and the wild halfa grass was used for basket making. Remains of tamarisk and acacia trees, which grew at the site, have also been identified. Wild shrubs that grew in nearby wadis were used for fuel. Most of the excavated animal bones are those of fish. Pigs and cattle were the most common domesticated animals, but there were also a few sheep and goats.

Long-distance trade is demonstrated at the site by shells from both the Mediterranean and the Red Sea. Some small pieces of galena wrapped in leather, perhaps from the Sinai or Eastern Desert, were found in one pot. The gray flint used for the large knives was possibly from the western Negev Desert in southern Palestine.

The dead were either buried in abandoned storage pits or in shallow pits near the houses. It is doubtful whether the notion of a cemetery separated from the residential area existed. As a rule, the body was placed in the pits on the left side, with the head to the south and facing west. Forty-three of the excavated burials were wrapped in matting, and a few were in animal skins. Two or three small blocks of limestone were placed at the back of the body or sometimes on it. Grave goods in the burials were relatively poor. Many burials contained a small pot placed either in front of the head or arms, or between the arms and legs. These pots always contained yellow sand, mixed with some charcoal or gravel. In one grave, flowers were found on the chest of the deceased.

One burial of an adult male was exceptional. In front of his hands was a wooden stick, which perhaps symbolized his authority or had some association with magic. Around the grave were the remains of wooden posts, which had originally formed a hut or fence with an opening to the west. The same kind of posts were found around the grave of an old woman. Similar burials with small tumuli marking their position were found by Bovier-Lapierre in a nearby wadi (Wadi Nagb el-Agel).

See also

Fayum, Neolithic and Predynastic sites; Helwan; Ma'adi and the Wadi Digla; Merimde Beni-salame; Neolithic and Predynastic stone tools; Neolithic cultures, overview; Paleolithic tools; pottery, prehistoric; Predynastic period, overview; Tura, Predynastic cemetery

Further reading:

Debono, F., and B. Mortensen. 1990. *El Omari: A Neolithic Settlement and Other Sites in the Vicinity of Wadi Hof, Helwan.* Mainz.

BODIL MORTENSEN

Oxyrhynchus (el-Bahnasa)

Oxyrhynchus is the Greek name commonly used for the pharaonic town of Per-medjed, which means "the meeting house." During the Ptolemaic period the Greeks adopted the name *Pempte* for the town. Because of the sacred fish worshipped there named "oxyrhynchus" (a fish with a pointed head, which was also known as "mormyrus"), the town would also become known as Oxyrhynchus, and the nome was called Oxyrhynchites. Its Coptic name is *Pemdje*, and today it is known as el-Bahnasa. The site is located on the west bank of the Bahr Yusuf channel of the Nile (28°32′ N, 30°40′ E), approximately 14 km northwest of Bani Mazar in the Middle Egyptian province of Minya.

Nothing is really known about the town until the New Kingdom and only then toward the end. The first reference to the town appears in an inscription from the Kushite (Nubian) king, Piye (25th Dynasty). According to the inscription found on the adoption stela of Nitocris, who was the daughter of King Psamtik I (26th Dynasty), the city is described as the capital of Nome XIX of Upper Egypt, replacing Sepermeru, which had been the nome capital since the New Kingdom.

The most important god of the town was Seth, whose temple at Seper-meru received great gifts from Ramesses III (20th Dynasty). Not much is known about his temple at Oxyrhynchus, even from the Graeco-Roman period. Yet the town was the site of one of the largest known finds of Greek papyri, discovered by B.P. Grenfell and A.S. Hunt at the end of the nineteenth century. The so-called "Oxyrhynchus Papyri" include a large number of literary, historical and biographical texts, as well as many official records, private documents and letters.

According to the various documents, after Seth, the next most important deity was the hippopotamus goddess Taweret. The Greeks identified her with Athena and she had many places of worship in the town. Other deities also had shrines at Oxyrhynchus, including Asch, Thermutis, Osiris-Serapis, Isis, Harpokrates and Asklepios. Strabo (XVII, 812) discusses a shrine for the sacred oxyrhynchus fish, and Plutarch reports battles between the townsmen of Oxyrhynchus and Kynopolis.

In the Roman period and under the Byzantines, Oxyrhynchus was an important town in Middle Egypt. Economically, it was associated with Baharia Oasis. Under the Byzantines the town first belonged to the province of Aegyptus and was later the major town in the province of Arkadia. At the beginning of the fourth century AD it was a bishop's residence. By the end of that century so many churches and monasteries had been built around the outside of the town that they formed a secondary town. These as well as others of the town and its nome are named in Greek papyri of the Byzantine period.

Still considered one of the most important archaeological sites in Middle Egypt, the ancient town of Oxyrhynchus extends under and west of the modern village of el-Bahnasa. Two column pedestals from a Roman theater and an old mosque are found there now, and the town's cemetery is situated 300 m west of the Roman theater. In 1982 a large tomb dating to the Saite period (26th Dynasty) was uncovered by the Egyptian Antiquities Organization, and inscriptions were found on the walls of the main burial chamber and on the sarcophagus. Other graves and a burial chapel from the Late period were also discovered near this tomb.

See also

Late and Ptolemaic periods, overview; Roman period, overview; Third Intermediate Period, overview

Further reading

Gomaà, F. 1982. Oxyrhynchos. In *LÄ* 4: 638–9.
Petrie, W.M.F. 1925. *Tombs of the Courtiers and Oxyrhynkhos*. London.
Turner, E.G. 1952. Oxyrhynchos and its papyri. *Greece and Rome* 21: 127–30.

FAROUK GOMAÀ

P

Paleolithic tools

The word "Paleolithic" means "Old Stone Age," and most of the remains from that period are stone artifacts. (Any materials that have been shaped or modified by human beings are artifacts, which may or may not have been used as "tools." Thus, both stone tools and the waste products from their manufacture are artifacts.) However, this is in large part a result of differential preservation: stone artifacts are much more durable than those in other raw materials. It is likely that, throughout the Paleolithic, people made use of all the raw materials known in later prehistory, with the exceptions of such "artificial" materials as ceramics and metal. The stone artifacts that we have must have been accompanied by a range of tools made of plant materials (wooden digging-sticks, spears, perhaps handles and hafts, and fiber baskets), and animal materials (leather bags and containers, perhaps ropes of sinew), but there is no direct evidence for this in Egypt. Bone is not preserved in most Egyptian Paleolithic sites, but even when it is present, there are no bone tools until the Late Paleolithic (after 20,000 BP, or years "before present").

The development of tools during the Paleolithic was cumulative. New techniques were invented and new tool forms were created, but these were almost always additions to what was already known and used, rather than replacements. Some of the simpler and earlier types of artifacts were made throughout the Paleolithic (and continued in use afterwards), and we can determine whether they are early or late only by their association with other, more time-sensitive artifacts.

Paleolithic stone tools may be divided into three major groups: unmodified, ground or pecked, and flaked. Unmodified tools are stones that could be used without being shaped, such as rounded pebbles, which might be used for throwing or as bola stones. They can be very difficult to recognize unless they were very heavily used, such as a cobble with visibly battered ends from its use as a hammerstone. Ground or pecked stone tools do not appear in Egypt (or anywhere else) until the Middle Paleolithic, about 130,000 years ago. Flaked stone artifacts are the one consistent component of the Paleolithic record; from the earliest to the latest, there is no Paleolithic site in Egypt which lacks flaked stone tools, and many sites have nothing else.

Shaping stone by flaking is based on the principle that it is possible (and not very difficult) to strike a stone and make it break in the way the striker, or knapper, desires. This is particularly true of fine-grained, homogeneous (cryptocrystalline) types of rock, such as flint or chert, which also produce the best and sharpest edges; it also true, although less so, of coarser-grained or crystalline rocks, such as sandstone or quartz. The fundamental distinction in flaked stone artifacts is between cores and flakes. Conventionally, a core is a block of stone identifiable by the concave scars of the flakes removed from it. A flake is (usually) the smaller piece struck from the core; it tends to be thin (compared with the core), but may be wide and long, and has a slightly convex (ventral) surface, which matches the concave scar left on the core after the flake has been removed.

Obviously, removing flakes from a block of stone is a way of shaping that block. Tools shaped by this method are called core-tools, and one type of core-tool, the handax, is the characteristic implement of the Lower Paleolithic in Egypt. Handaxes are rather flat pieces of rock, or sometimes large flakes, from which many smaller flakes have been removed across the whole of both faces (bifacial flaking), and all around the edge, to make them more or less lentil-shaped in cross-section. In plan, most are rounded at one end and pointed at the other, but they occur in a variety of shapes ranging from triangular to oval. Handaxes are known from much of the Nile Valley and the Western Desert of Egypt. They are always referred to as "Acheulean," a subdivision of the Lower Paleolithic. However, manufacture and use of handaxes are not indicators of a self-conscious social group. Handaxes are ubiquitous in Africa, and occur through most of the western half of the Old World. Their specific functions as tools also remain unknown, although their ubiquity may suggest that they were rather general, or multi-purpose, tools.

Many of the flakes struck during the shaping of a handax could have been tools in their own right. Archaeologists have traditionally paid little attention to such flakes, concentrating instead on the most modified pieces (in this case, handaxes). However, it seems likely that one of the most common needs in everyday life would be for a fresh, sharp cutting-edge—and the best such edges are those of simple flakes.

In addition to core-tools and simple flakes, Lower Paleolithic people also used flake-tools. Flake-tools are flakes which, after being struck, were worked to the desired shape by trimming (removing very small pieces from) the edges—a process called retouching, or secondary retouching. Flake-tools are more important, and highly varied, later in the Paleolithic. In the Lower Paleolithic, they are given a variety of formal names, but they are very unstandardized and are usually recognizable as Lower Paleolithic only because of their association with handaxes.

Flake-tools are most characteristic of the Middle Paleolithic, which may have begun by about 200,000 years ago; core-tools continued to be made, but are less important and less typical. In some Middle Paleolithic sites, the Levallois technique was intensively used for the production of tools. This technique involved very careful preparation and shaping of the

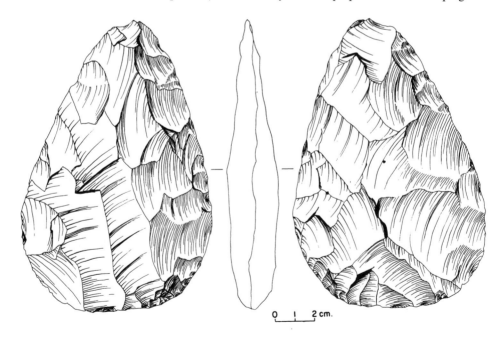

Figure 86 Lower Paleolithic handax (from Bir Tarfawi, Western Desert)

surface of the core, so as to permit the striking of one flake of predetermined shape. (The core could then be—and often was—reshaped for the production of another flake.) Since the shape of the Levallois flake was predetermined, there was often no need for secondary retouching.

Other Middle Paleolithic flake-tools were retouched to shape and archaeologists classify them into a wide variety of types: the standard list used for Middle Paleolithic tools defines over sixty types. Flake-tools are now more standardized than they were in the Lower

Paleolithic and there is some repetition of forms. However, as in the earlier period, no particular effort was made to obtain good quality stone for tool-making, and the use of coarse-grained quartzites, sandstones or quartz means that consistency of manufacture often resides largely in the eye of the archaeologist rather than in the tools themselves.

In the Egyptian Middle Paleolithic as a whole, the commonest types of flake-tools are denticulates and side-scrapers. Denticulates, ideally, have a serrated edge, while side-scrapers

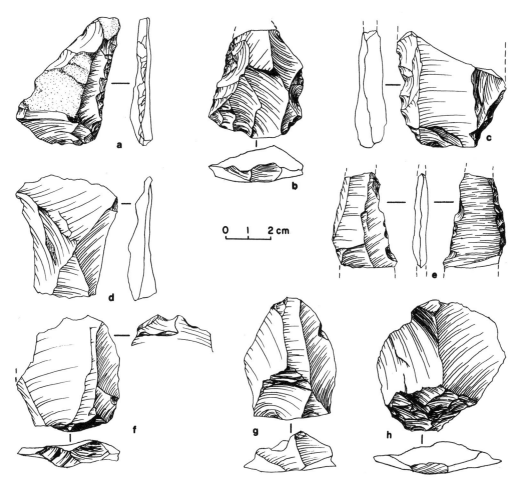

Figure 87 Middle Paleolithic flake-tools (a, c, e) and Levallois flakes (b, d, f–h) (from Bir Tarfawi, Western Desert)

have a rather thick, steep edge (both formed by retouch); the two can grade into each other. These, and other tools, are given names which seem to imply that we know what they were used for: scrapers, knives, perforators and so on. However, by convention these names refer solely to the method of manufacture or final morphology of the tools, and their actual functions remain unknown.

Techniques are now available that can reveal the uses to which individual tools were put. These involve microscopic examination of the edges of the tools and identification of the scars (use-wear) left there by working particular raw materials in particular ways, such as cutting meat, scraping hide or sawing wood. These techniques have not yet been applied to any Egyptian Middle Paleolithic tools (and cannot be used on most, since they require fine-grained stone). As with Lower Paleolithic handaxes, many of the Middle Paleolithic flake-tools could be multi-purpose. The only thing of which we are sure is that secondary retouching was an important part of their manufacture.

Apparently late in the Middle Paleolithic, a few tools begin to have tangs (pedunculates). The use of tangs implies that the tools were hafted, but there is no direct evidence of this. Surprisingly, tangs were made on tools of any type, and are not confined to points, as might be expected; this may mean that we do not understand what they are.

Ground and pecked stone tools first appear early in the Middle Paleolithic of the Western Desert. They include small (*circa* 10 cm in diameter) stone spheres, which could be bola stones, and a series of blocks of quartzitic sandstone, each with one flat or slightly concave face smoothed by pecking and grinding. The blocks are otherwise unshaped and resemble Late Paleolithic grinding stones from the Nile Valley. Some of the Middle Paleolithic examples may be anvils, used for breaking bone, hard plant parts (nuts?), or possibly stone. Others are grinding stones (both small handstones and large lower grinding stones occur). They bear no traces of ocher (although ocher also makes its first appearance at this time), and were presumably used on perishable materials, most

probably food; we know that their Late Paleolithic counterparts were used to grind plant foods. The appearance of grinding stones in the Middle Paleolithic suggests either that new foods had been added to the diet which required processing (as do some wetland tubers), or that there was a new, culturally defined need to process foods which previously had been acceptable in less processed forms.

The Upper Paleolithic, which began after 40,000 BP in Egypt, is characterized by blade-tools. A blade is a flake that is at least twice as long as it is wide, so that blade-tools are, in effect, elongated flake-tools. The elongation and narrowness of blades means that they have more edge per unit volume of stone than the flakes have, which means in turn, since the edge is the working part of the tool, that they represent a more efficient use of raw material. Upper Paleolithic tools are considerably more standardized than were Middle Paleolithic tools, with the same forms being unmistakably repeated over and over; they are also much better made. Flake-tools continued to be made in the Upper Paleolithic, and some blade-tools are simply elongated versions of types previously made on flakes, such as denticulated blades. However, many new forms appear and there is also considerable emphasis on end-of-blade tools, as opposed to lateral working edges. This may mean that hafting was becoming common.

Upper Paleolithic blade-tools are comparable in size, if not in shape, to the flake-tools of the Middle Paleolithic. However, starting somewhat before 20,000 years ago, in the Late Paleolithic, there was a marked diminution of stone tools, which are now classed as microliths. Tools were often made on very small blades, 25–30 mm long, called bladelets, and the commonest form almost throughout the Late Paleolithic was the parallel-sided bladelet, of which one edge had been retouched to make it blunt (backed bladelets). Most of these are so small that they must have been hafted, either as cutting edges or as points but, again, we lack direct evidence.

Bladelet-tools, or microliths, are even more efficient in terms of raw material than are

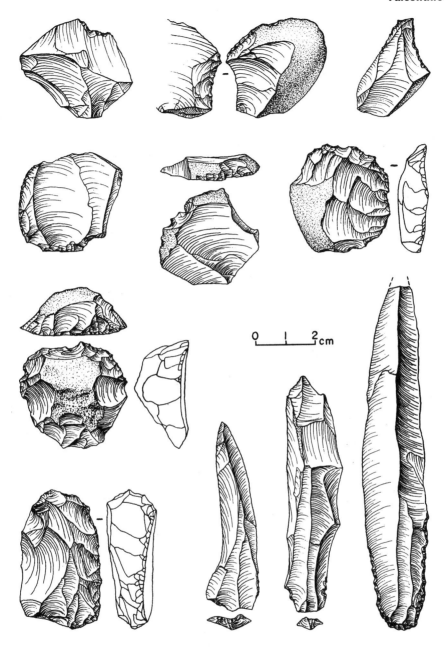

Figure 88 Upper Paleolithic blade-tools and and flake-tools (from a site near Edfu)

blade-tools, and their small size made raw material quality a more important consideration that it had been. In the Late Paleolithic, we thus begin to see high quality stone regularly transported for up to 150 km along the Nile Valley. This is a pattern which continued later in prehistory (particularly in the Neolithic, when the Western Desert again became habitable),

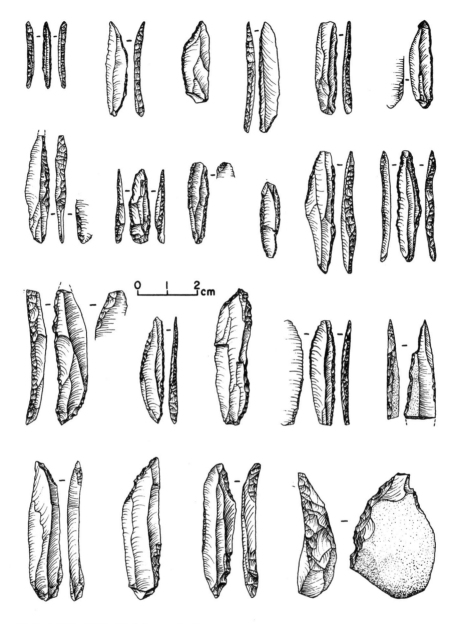

Figure 89 Late Paleolithic bladelet-tools (from a site near Esna)

and which could free tool-making from the constraints of locally available raw materials. For example, the only fine-grained stone available in Nubia was in the form of small pebbles, so only very small artifacts could be made. At Wadi Kubbaniya, in Lower Nubia, the problem was circumvented by importing large pieces (often as Levallois flakes) of flint from the Esna

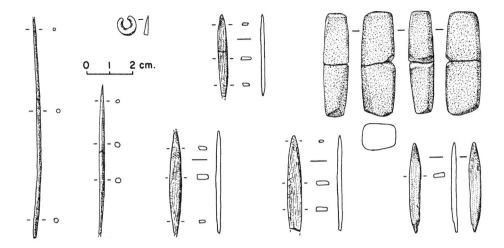

Figure 90 Late Paleolithic ostrich eggshell, ground stone and bone tools (from Wadi Kubbaniya)

area. The movement of stone over long distances may also tell us something about group mobility, or long-distance trade, or boundaries to mobility or trade (that is, areas to which stone was not transported). Its transport must surely mean that there was an appreciation of, and active desire for, better quality stone.

Although more numerous, the ground stone tools of the Late Paleolithic are little different from those of the Middle Paleolithic. They are somewhat better made, but are still large blocks smoothed on one or two faces; mortars and pestles are new forms. We now know that, at least at Wadi Kubbaniya, they were being used to process plant tubers. Kubbaniya also yielded a small ground, grooved stone, which resembles a net-sinker; this piece is unique and not a sufficient basis on which to postulate the existence of nets.

The earliest known bone-tools in Egypt are Late Paleolithic. Some are simply split long bone shafts, of which the edges have been partially smoothed to form tapered blades rather like letter openers. Others are extremely long, thin, polished points, which seem too fragile for use and thus might be decorative items. The third group are small, double-pointed pieces, flat (or almost so) in cross-

section and lentil-shaped in plan. They are called "fish-gorges" and could have served to hook some of the numerous fish with whose bones they are found.

The working of ostrich eggshell is also first attested in the Late Paleolithic, in the form of eggshell beads which are very rare but are indistinguishable from those of the Neolithic. There is no evidence for the use of eggshells as water bottles at this time, such as are found with the Neolithic of the Western Desert; this may be because water was less critical in the Valley, where there was a permanently flowing river.

See also

Dakhla Oasis, prehistoric sites; dating techniques, prehistory; Kharga Oasis, prehistoric sites; Neolithic cultures, overview; Paleolithic cultures, overview; stone tools, Neolithic and Predynastic; Wadi Kubbaniya

Further reading

Bordes, F. 1961. *Typologie du Paléolithique ancien et moyen* (Mémoires de l'Institut de Préhistoire de l'Université de Bordeaux 1). Bordeaux.

Tixier, J. 1963. *Typologie de l'Epipaléolithique du Maghreb* (Mémoires du Centre de Recherches Anthropologiques, Préhistoriques et Ethnographiques 2). Paris.

ANGELA E. CLOSE

paleopathology

Egyptology and paleopathology

Although it did not emerge as a science until recently, paleopathology as a discipline was stimulated by discoveries made working with ancient Egyptian materials. Even before Napoleon's expedition to Egypt at the end of the eighteenth century (1798–1801), which stimulated interest in Egypt, mummified remains had been traded into Europe as medical preparations called 'mumia'. Autopsies on mummies were performed as early as 1825 and the preservation of soft tissue provided a wealth of material for anatomical and histological analysis. Arteriosclerosis was soon diagnosed by histological analysis. Mummified remains were beginning to be used to systematically answer scientific questions, especially regarding the methods and process of mummification and its historical and religious significance.

The objective of early studies was the diagnosis of disease from dried tissue and skeletal remains. Paleopathologists developed a remarkable ability for diagnosis and correctly identified many pathological conditions. Unfortunately, diagnosis became an end in itself and paleopathology remained descriptive: it was not used as a tool to understand how people lived.

From 1890 to 1930, paleopathologists were unraveling the history of specific infectious diseases, such as syphilis, tuberculosis and leprosy. Historical perspective (determining the chronology and geography of specific diseases and medical practices) consumed the attention of paleopathologists and few attempted to generalize.

During this period, archaeology in general and Egyptology specifically became professionally instituted in Europe and the United States and regular expeditions began to be sent to Egypt. Monumental architecture and art, and many large cemeteries, were excavated between 1880 and 1930. The recovery of artifacts was the objective, and skeletal remains were often ignored and frequently not even collected. Pathological studies were limited to the most extreme examples of pathological abnormalities and other remains were not recovered or curated.

The completion of the Archeological Survey of Nubia, however, was a key to the development of paleopathology. In 1902, the Egyptian government finished the great (low) dam at Aswan. The reservoir created in 1903 inundated many monuments, such as the temple of Philae, and thousands of burials. Public outrage was so great that when the government planned to heighten the dam they also decided to record all antiquities and examine, describe, photograph and recover all burials that could be found. This represents the largest sample of burials that has ever been excavated. The examination of 10,000 burials revealed many interesting diseases and the methods that were developed to examine these remains changed the course of paleopathology.

Thus, from 1890 to 1930 researchers began applying new technology from medical science to the study of ancient disease. Soon after Wilhelm Roentgen discovered the X-ray in 1895, radiographs were used to study mummies. In 1898 X-ray technology was used to study material from Deshasha and to identify bone abnormality in the hand of a mummy. The pioneering use of radiographic techniques on Egyptian materials waned, however, and was not aggressively re-employed until the 1960s.

The application of advanced medical technology without attempting to solve a problem is a theme that is replayed throughout the history of paleopathology. However, it was during this same period that some of the most impressive research in paleopathology was undertaken using Egyptian material. M.A. Ruffer, who played a key role in the definition and development of paleopathology, undertook histological analysis of mummified tissue and was able to demonstrate the preservation of normal tissue as well as pathological changes. With colleagues, Ruffer identified histological evidence of schistosomes, tuberculosis, pneumonia, arteriosclerosis and variola. Other researchers reported arteriosclerotic changes in coronary and renal arteries. Appendicular adhesions in a Graeco-Roman period mummy and unilateral shortening of the femur suggesting poliomyelitis (a diagnosis that is still being debated) were also reported.

Gallstones, gout, scrotal hernia, rectal and vaginal prolapse were diagnosed in mummified remains. Achondroplasia and hydrocephaly and associated paralysis were diagnosed in dry bone. A number of cases of carcinoma were also reported and recent studies support the diagnosis. Other pathologies that were being recognized and discussed include osteoarthritis, mastoid infection, and patterns and occurrences of dental wear, caries and abscesses.

Although diagnosis of infectious disease is always problematic, researchers at the beginning of the century were able to successfully develop methods of diagnosis. The difficulty in diagnosing a specific infectious disease is that the pathogen does not always leave a distinctive lesion on the skin or bones. Many pathogens will cause change on the periosteum (the outer layer of bone), which is a general indicator of inflammation and infection. However, there are diagnostic features (the pattern of skeletal involvement) which provide indisputable evidence of specific diseases, such as syphilis, leprosy and tuberculosis. Leprosy, tuberculosis, schistosomiasis and smallpox were discovered in Egyptian and Nubian remains. Although over 10,000 mummies were examined, no evidence of syphilis was ever found.

The several known medical papyri and numerous depictions in art provide important insights into ancient Egyptian recognition and conceptions of diseases, and their causation, treatment and prevention. Such information is generally not available to paleopathologists, but it is vital to a fuller understanding of biocultural processes, especially concerning the repertoire of existing diseases and the nature of cultural buffering of environmental stresses. The medical papyri list a great number of symptoms and diseases. There is, however, considerable disagreement about which diseases were being described, and the degree of understanding the ancient Egyptians had of human physiology, disease etiology and pathogen ecology. There is also disagreement about the nature and extent of the medical profession and its effectiveness in altering the course of disease.

While these are intriguing questions from a biocultural perspective, the texts do not provide information as to the frequency or prevalence of specific diseases. Such information could, however, be derived from the study of skeletal populations. A number of studies have made correlations between skeletal evidence of pathologies and the diseases described in medical papyri, but in most cases the goal has been to verify or refute interpretations of the texts, rather than to better understand the effects of disease within the population and its biocultural context. Effectively excluded are more holistic theoretical considerations which have been developed in the sciences.

Dental studies reveal the limited scope of historical questions. A common theme has been to determine the antiquity of dentistry in Egypt. This question bespeaks an underlying fascination with and delight in demonstrating the precociousness of Egyptian civilization. There has also been an emphasis on royal descent, and on the diet and dental health of the elite. These biases are in part due to the nature of available data, but are ultimately symptomatic of the historical and elite-centered emphases of traditional Egyptology.

Rise of modern paleopathology

The 1930s are usually considered to herald the modern era of paleopathology. Pivotal to this was E.A. Hooton's *The Indians of Pecos Pueblo* in 1930, which described a population from the American Southwest. In this monograph Hooton introduces the paleoepidemiological approach, which analyzes the relationship between the host, pathogen and the environment. Hooton's major contribution was his use of statistics in presenting his data, since few publications of the era provide information on the observations made or the frequency of a pathology.

A number of theoretical developments also set the stage for the modern era of paleopathology. The first factor was the acceptance of a population perspective. While the individual may be the unit of diagnosis, the population is the unit of analysis and an understanding of the disease process requires a consideration of its existence within the context of a population. The second factor was the realization that culture is an environmental variable which can affect the disease process. From this perspective, a group's technology, social organization and ideology may all play a major role in inhibiting or creating an environment for disease. This consideration of culture has led to a more thorough analysis of human/disease interaction. Third, the concept of pathogen was expanded to include other insults which cause disease. Rather than consider pathogens as the sole source of disease, other factors, such as trauma, pollutants, psychological and social stress, are seen as potential agents of disease. The full impact of these changes was not realized in paleopathological studies until the 1950s.

Three major objectives of modern paleopathology have emerged from these historical developments. The first objective of paleopathology remains historical and spatial. Defining the chronology and geography of disease was, and is, the primary objective of most paleopathological research. The second objective of paleopathology is determining the biocultural interactions which occur as a population adapts to its environment. Therefore, the analysis of disease can provide important information about the success or failure of their adaptation. The biocultural approach not only considers the effect that culture has on the pattern of disease, but also attempts to understand the impact that disease has on the culture. The third objective of paleopathology is concern for understanding the processes (production of change) involved in prehistoric disease. In living organisms, we can often study the biological system as it is actually undergoing transformation in order to unravel the underlying process. In dead populations, the understanding of process is much more difficult. The factors which bring about change are inferred from the examination of many individuals in various stages of this transformation, or by studying the histological basis underlying this change.

In paleopathology, the study of process can focus on the change that occurs at a number of levels. The analysis can be studied at the cellular level, tissue level, organ level, organism or population level. For example, biological changes which occur in the skeleton as the result of disease insult may be studied. In fact, the examination of various stages in the development of treponemal infection has helped us understand this disease process in prehistory. Process can also be analyzed within the context of the biocultural system. Change in demographic structure of a population can be studied with respect to this response to infectious disease.

Recent reviews clearly demonstrate that the historical/descriptive themes which guided paleopathological work in Egypt during the early decades of the twentieth century are giving way to more processual analysis. The exceptional state of preservation of Egyptian remains continues to allow the application of new technologies and clinical methods to enhance diagnosis and expand and confirm the listing of recognized pathologies. For example, a technique (ELISA) has been modified to determine individuals that carry evidence of schistosomal infection. This methodology provides prevalence rates for the infection. It has even been established that ancient populations from Egypt and Sudan were using tetracycline 1,500 years before the modern discovery. Nubian populations were used to establish evidence of osteoporosis in prehistory and models for measuring obstetric problems in ancient populations.

The wedding of new methods to an approach that will test hypotheses will once again establish Egyptian paleopathology in a role that it once held. By incorporating a scientific perspective that tests alternative hypotheses, paleopathology can advance our understanding of Egyptology and the biology of ancient populations.

See also

Egyptians, physical anthropology of; mummies, scientific study of; mummification

Further reading

Brothwell, D.R., and B. Chiarelli. 1973. *Population Biology of the Ancient Egyptians.* New York.

Cockburn, T.A., and E. Cockburn. 1980. *Mummies, Disease and Ancient Culture.* Cambridge.

David, R. 1986. *Science in Egyptology.* Manchester.

Davies, W.V., and R. Walker. 1993. *Biological Anthropology and the Study of Ancient Egypt.* London.

Greene, D.L., D.P. Van Gerven and G.J. Armelagos. 1986. Life and death in ancient populations: bones of contention in paleodemography. *Human Evolution* 1(3): 193–207.

GEORGE J. ARMELAGOS
JAMES O. MILLS

Pan-grave culture

About the end of the eighteenth century BC, tombs generally known as "Pan-graves" appeared in Lower Nubia and Upper Egypt. The graves of this culture consist of circular pits with low rubble-ringed tumuli, shallow offering pits and trenches with painted goat skulls. The contracted burials were associated with distinctive incised bowls and thin black-topped bowls. Identified with peoples known in texts as the "Medjay," these burials gradually acquired Egyptian characteristics until those of the early 18th Dynasty are indistinguishable from Egyptian ones.

The peoples of this culture played a role in both Nubia and Egypt as far north as Memphis. Their simple pottery, often indistinguishable from the ordinary pots of the Kerma culture in Upper Nubia, is found widespread in both Egypt and Nubia.

The most notable installation of this culture is a fortified stone village, compact and circular in design, at Wadi es-Sebua across the river from an earlier (C-Group) Nubian structure at Amada. Both were probably used as defenses against the increasing threat of the Egyptian 17th Dynasty centered at Thebes. At about this time, and possibly extending into the New Kingdom, Pan-grave type pottery is found in the southern Atbai (near Kassala in eastern Sudan), indicating that the Medjay had a radius of action that closely resembles that of the modern Bedja peoples, who live in the Red Sea Hills.

See also

C-Group culture; Kerma; Medjay

Further reading

Bietak, M. 1987. The C-Group and the Pan-Grave Culture in Nubia. In *Nubian Culture Past and Present: Main Papers Presented at the Sixth International Conference for Nubian Studies in Uppsala, 11–16 August, 1986,* T. Hägg, ed., 113–28. Stockholm.

Bourriau, J. 1981. Nubians in Egypt during the Second Intermediate Period: An interpretation based on the Egyptian ceramic evidence. In *Studien zur altägyptischen Keramik,* D. Arnold, ed., 25–41. Mainz.

Gratien, B. 1985. Le village fortifié du groupe C à Ouadi es-Sebua Est, typologie de la céramique. *CRIPEL* 7: 39–69.

Sadr, Karim. 1987. The territorial expanse of the Pan-Grave culture. *Archéologie du Nil Moyen* 2: 265–91.

BRUCE B. WILLIAMS

pantheon

One of the most daunting aspects of the study of ancient Egyptian religion is the sheer number of Egyptian gods. It has been estimated that over 2,000 gods and goddesses are attested in the remains of 3,000 years of Egyptian civilization. Of course, not all of these gods were worshipped simultaneously, and over the course of Egyptian history one can observe the rise and decline of individual deities. Also, not all 2,000 deities were the recipient of a cult, meaning that not all gods had temples dedicated to them in which priests made daily offerings on their behalf, nor were all of these deities the subject of prayers by pious Egyptians. Many gods were largely unknown outside of the world of the scholar-priests of the temples.

The Egyptians themselves recognized different categories of gods, and in a stela of Ramesses IV (20th Dynasty) he states that he "studied" the great gods more than the small ones. Unfortunately, the Egyptians failed to indicate what criteria were used to designate a god as major or minor. John Baines has suggested that important gods are frequently depicted enthroned and holding scepters representing the attributes of life (*'nh*) and power (*w3s*). He has also suggested that the Egyptian phrase *ntr '3* should be understood to mean "major god." Membership in this category is indicated by the fact that the god is depicted in the major areas of the temple as the recipient of a cult, and that the king is described as being beloved of the god, since in Egyptian "love" is directed from the superior to the inferior being. Regardless of how one defines major as compared to minor gods, membership in a particular category was not fixed, and a particular deity could move from one category to another depending on the context in which he was worshipped. The notion of ranking Egyptian gods must therefore be seen as somewhat subjective and fluid.

Under the term *ntr*, which we translate as "god," a number of beings were classed whose common factor seems to be that they possessed superhuman powers. Beings which we would describe as ghosts, spirits, or demons were all referred to by the term *ntr*. Dimitri Meeks (1971) has described *ntr* as being "any entity which, because it transcended ordinary human reality, received a cult and became the object of a ritual." The characteristics of an Egyptian

god also differ from those of the god encountered in the Judaeo-Christian tradition. An Egyptian god was neither omniscient nor omnipotent. Most Egyptian gods were thought to have power only within a defined geographic area, such as a particular town or nome. Beyond these boundaries, a god's powers were considerably reduced. An Egyptian god experienced ageing and death in the same manner as humans, and the tombs of various deities were at times listed in papyri.

The Egyptians employed several different methods to bring some sort of order to the plethora of deities they worshipped. One method of organizing deities into groups was based on a numerical schema. Deities could be grouped in pairs, usually consisting of a god and a goddess, although pairs of the same sex did exist (for example, Isis and Nephthys, or Horus and Seth). The most common method of organizing deities was based on the triad, consisting of a god, a goddess and their offspring. Examples of this type of organization are Osiris, Isis and Horus, and Amen, Mut and Khonsu. There are, however, exceptions to this type of grouping. In the triad of Qadesh, Resheph and Min, we find a goddess (Qadesh) represented with two male companions. Triads consisting of a god with a pair of goddesses are also known to exist, for example, Osiris, Isis and Nephthys. Larger numerical groupings of deities were the ogdoad (group of eight gods, consisting of four pairs of matched male and female deities) and the ennead. The ennead also involved the genealogical classification of gods, in which a god or gods were seen as resposible for the creation of the succeeding generation of gods. The Heliopolitan Ennead, discussed below, is an example of such a geneaological associaiton of gods. The ennead became a popular method of organizing and relating gods, and in fact during the New Kingdom the number of gods in an ennead was not limited to nine, but grew as high as fifteen, or as few as seven.

The Egyptian pantheon knew of a number of creator gods, and even a creator goddess. In the Heliopolitan ennead, the primeval god Atum created the god Shu (air) and the goddess

Tefnut (moisture), who in turn begat Geb (male, earth) and Nut (female, sky). Geb and Nut produced Osiris, Isis, Seth and Nephthys. The sun god Re was also seen as a creator god. He first appeared on the primeval waters (the god Nun) as a child floating on a lotus. He then set about creating the four winds and the inundation of the Nile. From his sweat he created the gods, and from his tears he created mankind (there is a wordplay between *rmt*, "man," and *rm.t*, "to weep"). The Memphite god Ptah, the patron of craftsmen, was said to have created Atum and the rest of the ennead through pronouncing their names. Khnum, a god worshipped primarily in the First Cataract region, was thought to have created the gods and men on his potter's wheel. The goddess Neith, in a Roman period cosmogonic text recorded at Esna, is said to have taken the form of a cow while floating in the primeval waters of Nun. She then proceeds to create thirty divine assistants to aid her in her work of creation, as well as creating the sun god (called Amen) who then continues the work of creation.

Another group of gods closely associated with the idea of creation is the Hermopolitan ogdoad, a group of four male deities and their feminine doublets representing the primordial forces of creation. Nun and Naunet represent the primordial waters in which creation begins, Heh and Hauhet embodied spaciousness, Kuk and Kauket darkness, and Amen and Amaunet hiddenness. The last two members of the ogdoad were not fixed, and at times one finds Tenem and Tenemet (disappearance) or Gereh and Gerehet (restraining) instead of Amen and Amaunet. These eight gods unite on a primeval hill, called the "isle of flame," and create the sun god.

A number of the major gods of the pantheon played a role in the funerary beliefs of the ancient Egyptians. Foremost among these was Osiris, who was the ruler of the underworld, before whom each Egyptian expected to be judged after death. Osiris was said to have suffered death and dismemberment at the hands of his brother Seth, who seems to have represented chaotic and destructive forces. Isis, wife and sister of Osiris, and their sister Nephthys collected the parts of Osiris and revivified him long enough for Isis to conceive his son Horus (originally an ancient sky-god closely linked to kingship), who grew up to challenge and unseat Seth. Thoth, a god who is associated with wisdom, writing and the moon, also played a role in aiding Isis in her search for Osiris, as well as acting as mediator between Horus and Seth. The jackal-god Anubis was considered as the guardian of the necropolis and as the god of embalming who prepared the corpse of Osiris, and therefore was the patron god of embalmers. Wepwawet (literally "Opener of Ways"), also a jackal-god, was thought to lead the dead along the paths of the underworld, and at Abydos he served to protect Osiris from attacks by his enemies.

A number of the major gods of Egypt are not so easily grouped into categories. Hathor, thought of as the daughter of the sun god Re, was a goddess of sexual love, music and dance. She was thought of as guarding the Theban necropolis, and possessed a destructive nature, as evinced by the so-called "Myth of the Heavenly Cow." The lion-headed goddess Sekhmet is another feminine deity known for her destructive capability and her ability to cause and cure disease. Min was a god of fertility and procreation. Montu was a warrior god of Thebes who rose to prominence during the 11th Dynasty, but was supplanted by Amen during the 12th Dynasty.

One category of gods which played a considerable role in Egyptian religion was that of personifications. Foremost among this type of deity is the goddess Ma'at, who personified the order of the world first established at creation, including the notions of truth and justice. Other significant personifications include Hu, who embodied the authoritative utterance of the sun god Re through which he called all of creation into existence, and Sia, who personified the planning which took place before creation. Hike personified magic, the force which makes it possible for the spoken word to become actual. The goddess Seshat embodied the arts of writing and learning, and was frequently associated with Thoth. The god Hapy personified the inundating waters of the Nile, on which Egyptian prosperity depended.

Various aspects of the king could be personified as deities. For example, the god Dua-wer personified the royal beard, Tjety the table on which the king was served his meals, and Membit the royal couch. It was the Egyptian capacity to create personifications which contributed a significant number of the 2,000 deities known throughout Egyptian history.

There were also a number of foreign gods worshipped in Egypt. The Syrian god Resheph was introduced into Egypt during the 18th Dynasty, and his warlike nature made him popular with the warrior-kings of this period as well as with the common people who turned to him for relief from diseases. The Canaanite goddess Astarte was another warrior deity associated with chariots and horsemanship. Anat is a Canaanite warrior goddess introduced into Egypt who was known for her sexual prowess, as was the goddess Qadesh. From an earlier period, the Nubian god Dedwen is found in the *Pyramid Texts* and he was thought to be responsible for the desirable products which Egypt appropriated from his native land.

A number of minor gods were popular among the rank and file Egyptians. The bandy-legged dwarf god Bes was thought to protect women during childbirth. In this endeavor he was aided by the goddess Taweret, who had the head of a hippopotamus, the arms and legs of a lion, the tail of a crocodile and human breasts. The god Shed was solely a popular deity who never seems to have had an official cult or temple. He was looked on as a savior god who could deliver his worshippers from illness, misfortune or danger. The cobra goddess Meretseger was popular with the inhabitants of the village of Deir el-Medina, and was thought to punish those guilty of crimes, but to have mercy and heal the truly repentant.

It was also possible for humans to reach the status of *nṯr*. The first recorded individual to have done so was Imhotep, who served as a vizier under King Zoser of the 3rd Dynasty, and who is credited with being the architect who designed that king's Step Pyramid complex at Saqqara. In the Graeco-Roman period Imhotep was said to be the son of Khreduankh, his real

mother, and the god Ptah; he was looked on as a god of wisdom and a healer. The vizier Isi, who served during the 6th Dynasty, was worshipped as a god from the 13th Dynasty until the eighteenth century BC. Hekaib, a nomarach of the late Old Kingdom, was worshipped during the Middle Kingdom, and there was a chapel built in his honor on the island of Elephantine. Amenhotep, son of Hapu, an official of some influence under Amenhotep III of the 18th Dynasty, was deified in the Ptolemaic period as a god of wisdom and healing.

See also

mortuary beliefs; religion, state

Further reading

Baines, J. 1983. "Greatest god" or category of gods? *GM* 67: 13–28.

Hart, G. 1986. *Egyptian Gods and Goddesses*. New York.

Hornung, E. 1982. *Conceptions of God in Ancient Egypt*, trans. J. Baines. Ithaca, NY.

Meeks, D. 1971. Génies, anges, démons en Égypte. In *Génies, anges et démons* (Sources Orientales 8), 17–84. Paris.

Meeks, D., and C. Favard-Meeks. 1996. *Daily Life of the Egyptian Gods*, trans. G.M. Goshagarian. Ithaca, NY.

Schafer, B., ed. 1991. *Religion in Ancient Egypt*. Ithaca, NY.

Watterson, B. 1984. *The Gods of Ancient Egypt*. New York.

STEPHEN E. THOMPSON

papyrus

The papyrus plant (*Cyperus papyrus L.*) was widespread in ancient times in the lands of the eastern Mediterranean, and was common in the Nile Valley, especially in the marshes of the Delta. In the wild, the plant could attain a height of 3–4 m, and grew in thick swamps near the river. It could also be cultivated in gardens.

From the earliest times it was put to a variety of industrial purposes, notably rope and fiber manufacture, shoes and matting, even sizable constructions such as boats. The strong stems of the plant could also be used in architecture (buildings of this kind survive today in marshes of southern Iraq). Several styles of Egyptian column show their origin in reed construction of this type. However, the principal and best-known use was as a writing medium, in which it survived until superseded by paper in modern times.

The earliest papyrus roll, unfortunately un-inscribed, was found in the tomb of the official Hemaka at Saqqara (reign of the 1st Dynasty King Den), and it is clear from this that papyrus manufacture was already highly skilled. No Egyptian accounts of the process survive, but the essentials are known from classical sources, especially the elder Pliny, and the finished products themselves. The thinner parts of the stem, which are triangular in section, were split along the corners and opened out flat; these fibers could then be hammered, releasing the natural sap, and so joined to other strips, until a sizable sheet was formed. A second sheet would be produced and pasted onto the first, probably with the aid of river water. The fibers of the second sheet would be laid at right angles over the first; the final product was a rectangular sheet some 40 cm high, with fibers running horizontal on one side and vertical on the other. The horizontal side, known to modern scholars as the recto, was normally preferred for writing, since the pen was less likely to snag against the fibers. The verso was normally left blank, although small pieces of a verso could easily be used for short messages, especially when turned at right angles. Sheets were normally pasted together to form a roll; rolls of twenty sheets seem to have been regarded as normal. In classical times the first sheet of a roll would be pasted upside down (this was known as the *protokollon*); when the roll was wound tight, the outermost surface would then consist of horizontal fibers, which would not split under tension.

Papyrus rolls formed the medium for most of Egyptian literature, and for the administration of what was always a bureaucratic state; later the use of papyrus was extended to the Hellenic world, and to much of the Roman empire. Ancient papyrus texts survive in arid conditions (Egypt, the Dead Sea), or in unusual circumstances (for example, carbonized at Herculaneum). Papyrus manufacture may have been a royal monopoly, and court records in particular were written on material which is far superior to any modern imitation.

See also

cult temples of the New Kingdom; representational evidence, papyri and ostraca; writing, reading and schooling

Further reading

Černý, J. 1947. *Paper and Books in Ancient Egypt*. London.

Drenkhahn, R. 1982. Papyrus, -herstellung. In *LÄ* 4: 667–70.

Lewis, N. 1974. *Papyrus in Classical Antiquity*. Oxford.

Parkinson, R., and S. Quirke. 1995. *Papyrus*. London.

JOHN D. RAY

Persians

The Persians were a group of people who migrated to the Iranian plateau some time during the second half of the second millennium BC. Assyrian records of the ninth century BC attest to the presence of Medes and Persians in the central western Zagros region. By the mid-sixth century BC, the homeland of the Persians was established in the region of Parsa in the southwestern Zagros and the Achaemenid dynasty had emerged as the rulers of Persia. Cyrus II was the Achaemenid king who united the Persian tribes, assimilated the Medes and began the rapid expansion of Persian power. His conquests began with the rest of Iran and Afghanistan, parts of Central Asia and the region of Anatolia. The conquest of Babylon in

539 BC meant that the Persian empire instantly acquired all lands belonging to the Babylonian Empire, including Assyria, Syria and Palestine. Cyrus died in 530 BC leaving his son Cambyses as successor to the throne, fully aware that Egypt was the only power left in the Near East that was independent of Persia.

The death of the 26th Dynasty pharaoh Amasis early in 525 BC left his son Psamtik III to defend Egypt against the approaching Persian king Cambyses. The Persian army crossed the desert from Gaza with the assistance of camel trains bearing water-skins provided by the Arabian king. They engaged the Egyptian army at the Pelusiac branch of the Nile. The battle led to the retreat of Psamtik III to Memphis. When that city was besieged, Psamtik III was forced to surrender to the Persians and became the prisoner of Cambyses. Herodotus (who visited Egypt about seventy-five years later) relates a colorful account of the subsequent deeds of Cambyses. Cambyses is accused of burning the body of Amasis, an action which would run counter to Persian religious beliefs concerning the sanctity of fire. He is also accused of killing the sacred Apis bull, which was said to have been secretly buried by Egyptian priests. This story is disproved by a stela from the Serapeum, the burial ground of the sacred bulls at Saqqara, which records the ceremonial burial in the 6th year of Cambyses of the Apis bull born in the 27th year of Amasis. The Serapeum also houses the splendid stone sarcophagus, donated by Cambyses himself, which contained the animal's remains. The successor to this bull died a natural death in the 4th year of Darius I. In fact, Cambyses seems to have taken care to follow religious observances and to present himself to the Egyptian people as the grandson of the 26th Dynasty king Apries, and therefore the legitimate successor to the throne of Egypt.

A contemporary account of the early years of the First Persian Domination of Egypt comes from the naophoros statue of Udjahorresne, an Egyptian official who had served the Saite kings and was given new honors by Cambyses and his successor Darius I. The statue, now located in the Vatican Museum,

was originally set up in the temple of Neith at Sais in the 3rd or 4th year of Darius I. It was Udjahorresne who composed the proper titulary for Cambyses to use as pharaoh of Egypt. Udjahorresne reports that although Persian troops had damaged temples, Cambyses himself was not personally responsible and he repaired the damage inflicted by the disruption to normal life.

Cambyses stayed in Egypt until 522 BC, functioning as an Egyptian pharaoh. He led campaigns into Libya and Nubia, both of which

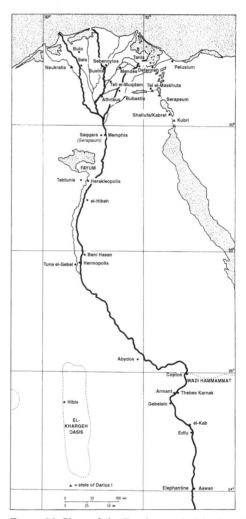

Figure 91 Sites of the Persian period in Egypt

ended in failure. While he was at the southern borders of Egypt, Cambyses strengthened the Jewish settlement at Elephantine which thereafter became a solid enclave of support for the Persians. The prolonged absence of Cambyses from the center of the Persian empire provided opportunity for a usurper to claim the throne of Persia by posing as Smerdis, the brother of Cambyses. Cambyses died in 522 BC on his journey home to Persia, having left Aryandes as Satrap in charge of Egypt. It was left to his successor Darius I to defeat the false Smerdis and restore order to the empire.

Darius I respected the customs and traditions of the provinces under his rule while using his talent for organization to streamline the administration of his empire. In his 3rd year, Darius directed his satrap in Egypt to codify the existing legal system of Egypt up to the 44th year of Amasis, a move designed to restore the old laws and gain the support of the priests. A copy of the collection of laws dated to the 27th year was transcribed in Aramaic for the guidance of non-Egyptian administrators; a Demotic copy also exists. Like Cambyses before him, Darius came to Egypt to establish himself on the throne of the pharaohs. This visit may have been the occasion for the beginning of the great engineering work which connected the Nile to the Red Sea by means of a navigable canal running from Bubastis eastward along the Wadi Tumilat to Lake Timsah, then turning south to the Red Sea. This work completed the canal which had been started by Neko II (26th Dynasty) about a hundred years previously.

The reign of Darius I is the best documented of the Persian period in Egypt. Over half of the datable buildings, inscriptions and objects ascribed to the Persian kings belong to Darius I. Darius I set up four large commemorative stelae along the route of the Red Sea canal: the first stela, found near Tell el-Maskhuta, is now in the Cairo Museum; pieces from a second stela found at a site called Serapeum, between Lake Timsah and Lake Amer, were sent to the Louvre in 1886, but could not be found two years later; the third was the Kabret (or Shallufa) stela found near Lake Amer and now located in Ismailia; and two fragments of

the fourth "Suez" stela were left in place near Kubri, 6 km north of Suez. The stelae were inscribed in hieroglyphs on one side and cuneiform on the other. Although the inscriptions are badly damaged, the cuneiform text informs us that "ships went from Egypt through this canal to Persia thus as was my desire".

The Egyptians revolted during the last year of the reign of Darius I (486 BC), killing the satrap Pherendates. By January 484 BC, the rule of the Persians was re-established by Xerxes, son of Darl; who appointed his brother Achaemenes as satrap in Egypt. The number of datable inscriptions and Aramaic papyri decrease, suggesting Xerxes's attention was elsewhere; in fact, we know he was preparing to invade Greece and that his brother Achaemenes was put in command of the Persian fleet. Meanwhile, Egyptian resistance against the Persians continued. Xerxes's successor, Artaxerxes I, had to deal with an Egyptian rebellion in which Inaros, a descendant of Psamtik, was placed on the throne. He drove out the tax collectors, collected mercenaries, and requested aid from Pericles of Athens, who sent 200 ships. With the death of Darius II, Egypt rebelled again, successfully this time, and the First Persian Domination of Egypt was over in 401 BC. Artaxerxes II had lost control of Egypt, although he was destined to enjoy a long reign as ruler of Persia. He did attempt to regain control of Egypt by armed invasion during the reign of Hakor (29th Dynasty), but Hakor had hired 20,000 Greek mercenaries to help defend his kingdom and was able to drive back the Persian invaders. Egypt managed to remain independent of the Persian empire as long as the attention of the Persians remained elsewhere.

The Persians under Artaxerxes III Ochus returned to Egypt in 343 BC, overcoming the defense mounted by Nectanebo II of the 30th Dynasty. The Second Persian Domination was a harsher regime than the first. Artaxerxes III demolished the walls of the most important cities, plundered shrines to obtain silver and gold, carried off temple records and sent Greek mercenaries back to their native lands with lavish rewards. After installing Pherendates as satrap, Artaxerxes returned with his army to Babylon. There he was poisoned by orders of the eunuch Bagoas, who placed Arses, son of Ochus, on the throne. During Arses's reign, a certain Khababasha, whose name suggests Kushite origin, assumed the title of pharaoh in Egypt. He is not mentioned in Manetho's dynastic lists, but his name was used to date a marriage contract at Thebes, a slingshot at Memphis and, in his second year, a sarcophagus of the Apis calf in the Serapeum at Saqqara.

Arses did not last long on the Persian throne and was succeeded by Darius III, a grandson of Artaxerxes II. Darius III soon set out to reconquer Egypt. Khababasha tried to guard the Delta against the invading fleet, but failed, and Darius was accepted as king of Egypt in early 334 BC. He appointed Sabaces as satrap, but the conquest of Asia by Alexander was under way and Sabaces was killed at the Battle of Issus. The new satrap, Mazaces, surrendered Egypt to Alexander. By that time Darius III had fled and Phoenicia, Syria and most of Arabia were in Alexander's hands. Thus ended the Second Persian Domination of Egypt.

Persian period settlement remains have been uncovered at Tell Defenneh, Tell el-Maskhuta, Tell el-Muqdam and Mendes in the eastern Nile Delta region. The burial place of the sacred Apis bulls in the Serapeum at Saqqara contains the sarcophagi of bulls buried during the reigns of Persian kings as well as stelae erected to commemorate the births and deaths of those bulls. Many private stelae from this period also have been found at Memphis. There is very little inscribed material from Thebes for either the First or Second Persian Domination, but inscriptions left by work crews in the Wadi Hammamat provide evidence for extensive quarrying in the area to obtain stone for buildings and monuments. Cartouches of Darius I are inscribed on blocks in the temple of Amen at Hibis in the Kharga Oasis, at Elkab in Upper Egypt, and at Busiris in the Delta. The statue of Udjahorresne also testifies that Darius gave orders for the restoration of the "House of Life" at Sais. Cartouches of Darius I, Hakor and Nectanebo II were carved on stone used for rebuilding in the temple of Tuthmose III at Elkab.

Several categories of small objects can be dated to the Persian period, either by inscriptions or by their context. Among these are the stone (variously described as alabaster or aragonite) vases found at sites both inside and outside Egypt. These vases are all dated to the reigns of Darius I, Xerxes I and Artaxerxes I, with a single example belonging to Khababasha. Many are inscribed with Persian cuneiform script as well as the hieroglyphic cartouche of the Persian king. Datable metal objects are relatively rare and include the silver bowls and the silver coin hoard from Tell el-Maskhuta, a silver bowl from Mendes, and the silver hoards from Athribis and Naukratis. Most of the silver objects seem to come from the end of the fifth century BC, the end of the First Persian Domination. The majority of inscribed bronze objects are dated to the reign of Darius I: door hinges from Kharga Oasis, a knife from Memphis, and a plaque made of bronze from Karnak. One bronze cube without provenance was inscribed with the cartouche of Xerxes I. Non-inscribed objects which have been dated to the Persian period by their stratified context at Tell el-Maskhuta include small cuboidal limestone incense altars similar to those found at sites in Arabia and at sites associated with the incense trade. Figurines of fired clay depicting a horse and rider were similar to those commonly found at Palestinian sites during the Persian period.

Large numbers of papyrus documents from the Persian period record leases and contracts of all kinds. Those written in the demotic script are mainly dated to the reign of Darius I. The discovery of the Aramaic papyri from Elephantine provides a written record of the activities of the settlement until 395 BC. Jews at Elephantine provided the garrison which protected the interests of the Persians on the southern borders of Egypt. The best published plans of a Persian period settlement are those of the German excavations at Elephantine, which have uncovered the houses occupied by the Jewish colony. The names and history of these inhabitants can be traced through the Aramaic papyri of the fifth and fourth centuries and the documents have been used to identify some of the topography of the area. The publication of recent archaeological work at Tell el-Maskhuta, Tell el-Muqdam and Mendes should further increase our knowledge of the archaeology of the Persian period in Egypt.

See also

Elephantine; Herodotus; Kharga Oasis, Late period and Graeco-Roman sites; Late and Ptolemaic periods, overview; Mendes, Dynastic evidence; Saqqara, Serapeum and animal necropolis; Tell el-Maskhuta; Tell el-Muqdam; Wadi Hammamat; Wadi Tumilat

Further reading

Bresciani, E. 1985. The Persian occupation of Egypt. In *The Cambridge History of Iran* 2. Cambridge.
Cook, J.M. 1983. *The Persian Empire*. London.
Cruz-Uribe, E. 1986. The Hibis Temple Project, 1984–85. *JARCE* 23: 157–66.
Posener, G. 1936. *La première domination Perse en Égypte* (BdÉ 11). Cairo.

PATRICIA PAICE

Petrie, Sir William Matthew Flinders

The British archaeologist and Egyptologist Sir William Matthew Flinders Petrie (1853–1942) is noted for almost sixty years of fieldwork in Egypt (and Palestine), his important publications of this fieldwork, and major contributions to archaeological method and theory resulting from this fieldwork.

Flinders Petrie was educated at home by his mother, the daughter of the explorer Matthew Flinders, and his father, a civil engineer. From an early age he showed unusual scientific ability and collected coins. In his teens he started surveying earthworks and ancient monuments, and with his father he made plans of Stonehenge. His first work in Egypt was a detailed survey of the pyramids of Giza, undertaken in 1881–3 to test the theories of those who

believed that the Great Pyramid had been built under divine inspiration and foretold the future of mankind; his meticulous measurements proved the theory false.

Employed by the newly formed Egypt Exploration Fund (EEF, later the Egypt Exploration Society, EES) to excavate Tanis in the Delta, Petrie set new standards for archaeological work in Egypt: whereas excavators had hitherto left the supervision of their workgangs to overseers, and disregarded all finds but marketable antiquities, Petrie watched the work carefully and kept records of everything found, demonstrating the value of pottery and small domestic artifacts for dating. After finding and excavating the site of ancient Naukratis in the Delta, he left to excavate in the Fayum, opening the pyramids of Illahun (Lahun) and Hawara and, in the tombs of Roman date, finding mummies with painted portraits which caused a sensation when they were exhibited in London. In 1890, at the invitation of the Palestine Exploration Fund, he excavated Tell el-Hesy, drawing the first section through a *tell* (an artificial mound formed by many centuries of human occupation). He dated the levels by pottery with which he was already familiar in Egypt. Returning to the Fayum, he worked for a season at Meydum, excavating *mastaba* tombs and finding the pyramid's temple. In 1891–2 he was at Tell el-Amarna, uncovering part of the palace with its painted pavement and surveying the wide domain of Akhenaten's city. The Mycenaean pottery he found in this closely dated context enabled the discoveries of Heinrich Schliemann and his successors in the Aegean to be fixed in time.

In 1892 Petrie was appointed to the chair of Egyptology at University College London, which was endowed by the will of his patron Miss Amelia Edwards. With academic status and a small salary, he was to train students and, in winter months, excavate in Egypt. Many of his finds went to enrich the collection of antiquities formed by Miss Edwards and himself, now called the Petrie Museum. At Quft (ancient Coptos) in 1893–4, he found puzzling early statues unlike those familiar from the Dynastic period. In the following year, at Nagada, graves he excavated yielded pottery and grave goods of an unfamiliar type. His first hasty conclusion that these were the burials of foreign invaders was later corrected when he realized that they were those of Predynastic Egyptians. Two years later, by an ingenious and painstaking method of arranging his tomb records, he was able to put them into chronological sequence, which he called "Sequence Dating." His division of artifacts into the Amratian and Gerzean periods is still, with some modifications, valid.

In 1896 Petrie married. For the next forty-five years his wife Hilda was to be a devoted partner in his work, helping with recording and copying, surveying and measuring, paying and doctoring the workmen and, above all, after Petrie had broken with the EES, raising funds for the work of the Egyptian Research Account. Their camp was run in a Spartan manner, and the privations of a "Petrie dig" became legendary. But students were encouraged to work on their own and given credit in the publications; many of them became Inspectors of Antiquities or excavators on their own account.

At Abydos (Umm el-Qa'ab) between 1899 and 1903, Petrie re-excavated the royal tombs of the 1st Dynasty, which had been badly disturbed by earlier diggers. From fragments of stone and ivory he recovered the names of kings of the 1st–2nd Dynasties. His subsequent work, at Giza, Rifa, Meydum, Tarkhan, Hawara and other sites, added each year to archaeological knowledge and enriched museums all over the world. From 1908 onward, for part of each season, he excavated in the ruins of Memphis. During the First World War he remained in London, organizing his museum and publishing a series of catalogs which are still of value to Egyptologists. He edited his own journal, *Ancient Egypt*, and popularized the subject in lectures and a series of books for the general public.

In 1920 he returned to Egypt for a few years of excavating, but in a different political climate he could obtain less favorable terms in the division of finds, so that museums were less inclined to support his work. In 1926 he moved his work to southern Palestine, excavating mounds in what he called "Egypt over the Border," frontier forts in the days of the New Kingdom. At Tell el-'Ajjul, the largest of these sites, he found burials which he believed to be of Hyksos rulers. Retiring from his academic chair at the age of 82, he settled in Jerusalem; he is buried on Mount Zion.

Petrie was no philologist and his ideas were not always acceptable to his colleagues. Few scholars followed his long chronology for ancient Egyptian history, and some of his theories were more ingenious than plausible, but as an excavator he had no rivals. Gifted with a remarkable visual memory, he was an able surveyor and photographer, a practical craftsman who made his own packing cases and, if necessary, built his own house. In the early days he excavated almost single-handed. Workmen trained by Petrie at Quft (called "Quftis") were summoned in subsequent seasons to wherever he was working; their descendants are still employed as professional overseers in Egypt.

Petrie published his results promptly every year; he wrote over a hundred books and more than a thousand articles and reviews. Though in his later years his methods were overtaken by more modern techniques, the basic principles of excavation laid down by Petrie have been followed by archaeologists all over the world. With all due respect he was known among his Egyptian workmen as "Father of Pots."

See also

Abydos, Early Dynastic funerary enclosures; Abydos, Umm el-Qa'ab; Aegean peoples; Early Dynastic period, overview; Fayum, Graeco-Roman sites; Hu Hiw (Diospolis Parva); Hyksos; Lahun, town; Memphis; Nagada (Naqada); Naukratis; pottery, prehistoric; Predynastic period, overview; Quft/Qift (Coptos); Tanis (San el-Hagar); Tell el-Amarna

Further reading

Drower, M.S. 1995. *Flinders Petrie, A Life in Archaeology*, reprint. Madison, WI.

Petrie, W.M.F. 1995. *Methods and Aims in Archaeology.* Madison, WI.

——. 1931. *Seventy Years in Archaeology.* London.

Uphill, E.P. 1972. A bibliography of Sir William Matthew Flinders Petrie (1853–1942). *JNES* 31: 356–79.

MARGARET S. DROWER

Philae

The island of Philae (24°01′ N, 32°53′ E) in the Nile River is now submerged in the reservoir between the Aswan High Dam and the older dam 8 km south of Aswan. The island (120–150 × 350 m) was famous in Graeco-Roman times as the site of an important sanctuary of Isis. It was also connected with a tomb of Osiris, the "Abaton" situated on the neighboring island of Biggeh. The name "Philae" is an approximate Greek rendering of the local name "Pilak" known from hieroglyphic texts, itself possibly of Nubian origin.

Few studies were devoted to Philae after the first decade of the twentieth century until the late 1960s, when the construction of the Aswan High Dam to the south created the danger that the monuments of Philae would disappear forever. To prevent this, several proposals were presented to the Egyptian Antiquities Organization and studied together with the counsels of UNESCO. The solution acted upon was to dismantle and to remove all major monuments and to rebuild them at a higher level on the neighboring island of Agilkyia, maintaining the orientation and relative position of the buildings. This was successfully done from 1974 to 1980, so that current visitors hardly notice that the whole site has been shifted. The dismantling of the monuments permitted an attentive study of their construction and excavations disclosed reused remnants of earlier ones, even parts of structures that had been covered.

A few sherds of Middle Kingdom date are the first trace of human activity on the original island, which was so low that most of its surface was alluvial soil covering the base of granitic rock. Some blocks with New Kingdom inscriptions have been found; these may have been brought as material for repairs from elsewhere, and cannot be accepted as proof of a New Kingdom occupation at the site. Also doubtful is the origin of eighteen blocks from a monument of the Kushite king Taharka. An altar was also dedicated by him to Amen of Takompso, of a town whose location remains unknown. There exists nevertheless the possibility that the Kushites, on invading Egypt, established a stronghold on Philae. Traces of mudbrick houses disclosed in trenches between the stone foundations of the later temples and the early nilometer west of the *mammisi* may date to this period.

The earliest building definitely belonging to Philae is a modest 26th Dynasty kiosk, with columns inscribed in the name of Psamtik II. Its erection may have been connected with the king's visit to the cataract when he launched his mercenary armies on an expedition in Sudan. Amasis then built a small temple on an outcrop of rocks on the west side of the island. It consisted of only three rooms in line, its main door opening toward the south. Its existence has been known from reused blocks since the nineteenth century; more reused blocks showing sections of wall relief were recovered on dismantling the floor slabs of the *pronaos* and the inner pylon of the Isis temple. The number of reliefs is too small to determine whether the temple of Amasis was dedicated to Isis, to Hathor, or to both divinities.

Other uncertainties exist with two buildings of Nectanebo I, the gateway between the towers of the great pylon and the large kiosk standing at the southwest point of the island. Both were previously known as the oldest buildings at Philae, and they have been re-erected on the new site. The Nectanebo I gate is not accurately placed in alignment with the temple of Amasis, yet it once formed the entrance of the mudbrick enclosure that surrounded the early sanctuary. Older publications still present the hypothesis that the kiosk of Nectanebo I was the only preserved part of the porch of a small temple that had once existed farther to the south and had been washed away. This erroneous interpretation was largely based on the correct observation that the kiosk above the high embankment lacks a proper back side, a fact that was anciently concealed by two obelisks set on the parapet. Recent investigation of the foundations, however, has shown that the kiosk was built on an artificial extension of the *dromos* (processional way) that could not be older than the second century BC. After knowledge of structural details underground had been lost, the kiosk was moved and rebuilt in ancient times. Graffiti on the remaining obelisk may indicate that this was done either in the reign of Ptolemy XII Neos Dionysos or shortly before.

The great promotion of the cult of Isis is due to the early Ptolemies. A splendid new house for the goddess was built behind the modest temple of Amasis. There the sloping surface of the live rock permitted the inclusion of three crypts in the temple's substructure. The wall scenes and inscriptions of the interior are all carved in the name of Ptolemy II Philadelphus. The first addition to the sanctuary of Isis was the construction of her birth-house or *mammisi*. It was built on the low ground south of the rock and to the west of the main axis. It originally consisted of only two rooms enclosed around the back by a peristyle of columns with Hathor capitals and preceded by a wide porch. The oldest parts of the interior decoration present the cartouches of Ptolemy III. Ptolemy V had his report on the suppression of a serious revolt in Upper Egypt engraved on the east side of the porch. In the reign of Ptolemy VIII, the *mammisi* was enlarged by the addition of a new sanctuary at its back. The decoration of the exterior surfaces, however, lasted from the years of Ptolemy XII Neos Dionysos down to Roman times.

When the decision to build the *mammisi* was taken, the temple of Isis was still without a *pronaos*, a forecourt and a pylon, major elements of Egyptian temples of the time. After the dismantling of the temple of Amasis, the rock surface available to build these elements was very restricted. Therefore, the masterbuilders had to adopt an exceptional solution: the *pronaos* was limited to two rows of columns,

with screen walls in the front row, and the peristyle of the open court was reduced to a single column on each side, the roof above them being level with the roof of the *pronaos*, which extended to the second or inner pylon. Without regard to the architectural form, this part of the temple is often erroneously designated as "the hypostyle." When this building project was inaugurated is uncertain. It is not likely that the construction began in the reigns of Ptolemies IV and V because of the disturbances then prevailing in Upper Egypt. The stela visible on the rock under the east tower of the pylon inscribed in the name of Ptolemy VI Philometor may well refer to the real founder, although the interior walls of the *pronaos* were first inscribed for Ptolemy VIII.

The replacement of the mudbrick enclosure on both sides of the Nectanebo I gate by the two towers of the great pylon may also be ascribed to Ptolemy VI. A passage had to be provided through the west tower so that it would not block access to the *mammisi*. The frame of the front gate and the walls of the passage were inscribed in the name of Ptolemy VI, just as the central part of the porch of the *mammisi* immediately behind it. In the years of Ptolemy VIII, when the *mammisi* was extended, its length closed almost completely the west side of the area between the two pylons. In order to close the space on the opposite side, the east corners of both pylons were linked by a colonnade backed by a series of chambers. The northernmost of these chambers became a passage leading to a gate opening east through the earlier brick enclosure wall. The area between the two pylons was thus transformed into a courtyard of festive appearance.

Outside the enclosure along the approach to the temple from the south, later kings founded a series of minor temples, starting near the temple with a gate of Ptolemy II and a temple dedicated by Ptolemy V Epiphanes to Asklepios or Imhotep. A small temple of undetermined date is often erroneously attributed to Mandulis, whose late Ptolemaic stela was found close to it in a single room of mudbrick. The largest of these buildings is the temple of Arensnuphis at the southern end of the sequence. The earliest inscriptions from this temple date from the reign of Ptolemy IV Philopator, but irregularities in its foundations indicate that it was founded even before, and blocks with the name of Ergamenes I prove that these activities were not interrupted by the Upper Egyptian revolt; they were immediately continued by Ptolemy V. A platform that included a stairway leading down to the edge of the water was built west of the temple; the scales of a nilometer were marked on its wall at an unknown later date. In the time of Ptolemy VIII, a new room was added at the back, and the earlier granite shrine of the image moved back into the new sanctuary. The whole building, except the porch, was then surrounded by a high wall, the interior surface of which was covered by reliefs as late as the reign of Tiberius. In Christian times, the Arsenuphis temple was reconstructed as a church. When the site was excavated at the end of the nineteenth century, the temple was partly reassembled from blocks that had been reused.

The existence of minor sanctuaries along the causeway south of the Isis temple necessitated first an enlargement, and when this proved insufficient to accommodate the crowds of pilgrims, a very ambitious construction of a causeway was started. In the time of low water, high embankment walls were built on rocks at the foot of the mud banks; these embankments were strengthened by equidistant stabilizing walls, then the intermediate space was bridged over with huge stone slabs on which the pavement was spread. In this way, the area between the great pylon of the Isis temple and the temple of Arensnuphis, and a wide stretch along the west and the south side of the island, was transformed into a wide terrace. The date of this great enterprise cannot be established with certainty. The reigns of Ptolemy V or VI seem to be the best possible guess.

The kiosk of Nectanebo I, moved from an unknown original location, was re-erected at the southern end of the terrace. It was intended there as a way-station for processions, also as a look-out onto the river that could be watched for a considerable distance.

The somewhat irregular western edge of the terrace was hidden by a straight colonnade during the reign of Augustus. A similar colonnade was built on the opposite side, only much shorter, extending from the temple of Arensnuphis to the temple of Imhotep and hiding the irregular forms of the buildings in between. In spite of the fact that the eastern colonnade was left unfinished, both have to be seen as part of a single project to change the open terrace into a trapezoidal courtyard, widening toward the pylon and with its axis directed to the gate in the west tower, the passage to the *mammisi*. Thus, the importance attached to the rites performed there is stressed by architectural means. The windows that open in the back wall of the west colonnade deserve special mention. Inscriptions say that they were intended to permit the pilgrims to view the "Abaton," the tomb of Osiris on Biggeh across the west channel.

The activities of the Philae temples were not interrupted by the AD 392 decree of Theodosius, closing the pagan temples of Egypt. As late as AD 451–2, the Byzantine general Maximinus had to conclude a contract with the Blemmyes and the Nobadae confirming their ancient right of free access to the sanctuary of Isis at Philae. These Nubian tribes were even allowed to take the image of Isis upstream to their homelands in festive seasons. An end to the cult was made around AD 535 by the emperor Justinian, who ordered its suppression by force. Yet it took forty years longer until the temple was desecrated by crosses on its doors and the *pronaos* changed into a church. Only about a century later, Philae became a Moslem stronghold against the Christian kingdoms of Sudan.

See also

Aswan; Kushites; late and Ptolemaic periods, overview; pantheon; Roman period, overview

Further reading

Giammarusti, A., and A. Roccati. 1980. File. *Storia e vita di un santuario egizio.* Novara.

Haeny, G. 1985. A short architectural history of Philae. *BIFAO* 85: 197–233.

Vassilika, E. 1989. *Ptolemaic Philae* (Orientalia Lovaniensia Analecta 34). Leuven.

Winter, E. 1982. Philae. In *LÄ* 4: 1022–7.

GERHARD HAENY

plants, wild

The linear pattern of the Nile and the concentration of resources along its main course encouraged the establishment of numerous sites of hunter-gatherers throughout Paleolithic times. In the late Pleistocene, 22,000–14,000 BP (years before present), archaeological sites show a remarkable decrease in the faunal remains accompanied by a gradual shift toward the utilization of plants.

The natural vegetation is believed to have been of the scrub type where acacias, tamarisks or palms were the main woody species growing among dense cover of "halfa" grasses and other herbaceous species. Closer to the watercourses, sycamore and sidder became more important, while silty embankments were encircled by thickets of reeds and other moisture-loving plants.

With the introduction of agriculture and the adaptation of domesticates in Egypt during the Neolithic and Predynastic periods (after 6,000 to *circa* 3,100 BC), an estimated 170 species were introduced and naturalized. With other native species, these constituted the early weed assemblages associated with cultivated field plots. Following the introduction of other crop plants during pharaonic times, the number of adventive species is believed to have reached between 225 and 250.

A reconstruction of the prevailing plant life during Predynastic and Dynastic Egypt would suggest a vegetation which is similar in most of its features to that of parts of the Sohag–Qena governorates in Upper Egypt, where an ancient pattern of agriculture is still being practiced today. Field plots of limited area and palm groves grew among thickets of acacias and tamarisks. Seasonal swamps and water runnels provided favorable conditions for the growth of a variety of reeds and moisture-loving plants.

The oldest known evidence for the flora of the Nile Valley is probably that of the Late Paleolithic Kubbaniyan culture (sites E-78-3, E-78-4, E 81-1, E 81-6), dating to 19,000–17,000 BP. The sites lie in areas reached by seasonal floods at the mouth of the Wadi Kubbaniya, a few kilometers north of Aswan. The recovered plant remains consist mostly of charcoal of tamarisks and acacias. Other identified plant remains include charred tubers of purple nutgrass, stones of the dom palm and achenes of several species of camomile.

At Hierakonpolis, a Predynastic site (11C) dating to *circa* 3,800–3,500 BC has yielded the richest known material. The identified plants comprise five crop plants and 47 species of wild plants which were of potential value. Among these are fodder plants for herding livestock and species of medical utility as well as firewood plants. The identified species include farmland weeds (21 species), plants of moist habitats (11 species) and plants of dry habitats (15 species).

A total of 115 species are listed below, which comprise the wild plants which were recovered and identified from contexts in the Nile Valley during the period extending from Late Paleolithic to Graeco-Roman times. Among these, 75 species (65 percent) belong to the native flora of Egypt by the beginning of the Holocene. The other 40 species (35 percent) are believed to have been introduced during Dynastic and Graeco-Roman times.

Farmland weeds (79 species; 69 percent) constitute the bulk of the recorded species, among which 36 species are foreign and were likely to have been associated with domesticates introduced into Egypt from southwest Asia. Aquatics, reeds, rushes and plants of moist habitats are represented by 26 species, or 23 percent of the recorded species; only four of these species are of foreign origin. Ten species are native trees or plants of dry habitats.

The following list of species of wild plants includes the valid Latin name followed by the English name (if known). Dates/periods of the known evidence are also given with information about the plant's habitat, and possible uses.

Salix subserrata Willd., Palestine willow
Predynastic/Dynastic, (native) tree along water courses
Uses: timber, charcoal, medicinal

Ficus sycomorus L., sycamore
Predynastic/Dynastic, (native) tree along water courses
Uses: timber, edible fruits, medicinal

Thesuim humile Vahl, toad flax
Predynastic, (native) winter weed

Emex spinosa (L.) Campd., prickly dock
Predynastic, (native) winter weed

Persicaria lapathifolia (L.) Gray, willow weed
1st–3rd Dynasties, (introduced) weed in moist habitat

Persica salicifolia (Willd.) Assenov, willow-leaved knotweed
Predynastic, (native) plant on canal banks

Polygonum aviculare L., knot grass
19th Dynasty, (introduced) ruderal weed

Polygonum plebejum R.Br.
1st Dynasty, (introduced) agrestal and ruderal weed

Rumex dentatus L., dentated dock
Predynastic, (native) weed on canal banks/moist habitat
Uses: vegetable, medicinal

Rumex pulcher L., purple dock
Predynastic, (native) weed on canal banks/moist habitat
Uses: vegetable, medicinal

Rumex simpliciflorus Murb., yellow dock
1st–3rd Dynasties, (native) weed in moist habitat
Uses: vegetable, medicinal

Portulaca oleracea L., purslane
Predynastic, (native) weed
Uses: vegetable, medicinal

Beta vulgaris L., sea beet
1st Dynasty, (native) winter weed
Uses: vegetable

Chenopodium murale L., nettle leaved goosefoot
1st–3rd Dynasties, (introduced) winter weed

Uses: salad herb

Chenopodium album L., white goosefoot
1st–3rd Dynasties, (introduced) winter weed, herb
Uses: salad plant, medicinal

Amaranthus graecizans L., white pigweed
Predynastic, (native) summer weed
Uses: seed crop

Brassica nigra (L.) Koch, black mustard
1st–3rd Dynasties, (introduced) winter weed
Uses: ornamental, oil and medicinal

Sinapis allionii Jacq., wild mustard
12th Dynasty, (native) winter weed
Uses: medicinal

Didesmus aegyptius (L.) Desv.
Late period, (introduced) weed in moist habitat
Uses: medicinal

Enarathrocarpus lyratus (Forssk.) DC.
Graeco-Roman, (introduced) winter weed

Raphanus raphanistrum L., wild radish
Middle Kingdom, (introduced) weed
Uses: medicinal

Lepidium sativum L., garden cress
Predynastic, (introduced) agrestal and ruderal weed
Uses: vegetable, medicinal

Coronopus niloticus (Del.) Spreng., Nile cress
Predynastic, (native) weed on Nile banks and moist habitat
Uses: salad plant

Eruca sativa Miller, rocket
Predynastic, (native) weed
Uses: salad plant, medicinal

Ranunculus asiaticus L., Asiatic crowfoot
Middle Kingdom, (introduced) weed in moist habitat
Uses: ornamental, medicinal

Nymphaea lotus L., Egyptian lotus, sacred lotus
Predynastic, (native) aquatic flower
Uses: ornamental, food plant

Nymphaea coerulea Savigny, blue water lily
Predynastic, (native) aquatic flower

Uses: ornamental, food plant

Papaver rhoeas L., corn poppy
4th–22nd Dynasties, (introduced) winter weed
Uses: ornamental, medicinal

Capparis spinosa L., common caper-bush
Middle Kingdom, (native) rock plant, shrub
Uses: medicinal

Potentilla supina L., cinquefoil
Predynastic, (native) weed on canal banks and
moist habitat
Uses: medicinal

Lupinus digitatus Forssk., wild lupine
5th Dynasty, (introduced) weed, herb
Uses: medicinal

Trigonella hamosa L., Egyptian fenugreek
3rd Dynasty, (introduced) winter weed, herb

Medicago polymorpha L., toothed medik
Old Kingdom–Graeco-Roman, (native) winter
weed, herb

Melilotus indicus (L.) All., Indian melilot
Middle Kingdom, (introduced) winter weed,
herb
Uses: fodder

Trifolium resupinatum L., reversed clover
12th Dynasty, (introduced) winter weed, herb
Uses: fodder

Trifolium alexandrinum L., Egyptian clover
12th Dynasty, (introduced) winter weed, herb
Uses: fodder, medicinal

Lotus corniculatus L., bird's foot trefoil
12th Dynasty, (introduced) winter weed, herb
Uses: medicinal

Scorpiurus muricatus L., scorpiontail
3rd Dynasty, (introduced) winter weed, herb

Vicia narbonensis L.
3rd Dynasty, (introduced) winter weed, herb
Uses: fodder

Vicia lutea L.
Predynastic, (native) winter weed, herb
Uses: fodder, edible seeds

Vicia sativa L., common vetch
Predynastic, (native) winter weed, herb

Uses: fodder, edible seeds

Vicia monantha Retz., Syrian vetch
12th Dynasty, (introduced) winter weed, herb
Uses: fodder

Lathyrus aphaca L., yellow vetchling
Predynastic, (native) agrestal and ruderal weed
Uses: fodder

Lathyrus hirsutus L., rough-podded vetchling
Predynastic, (native) agrestal and ruderal weed
Uses: fodder

Lathyrus sativus L., bitter vetch
Predynastic, (native) weed, herb
Uses: food, medicinal

Lathyrus marmoratus Boiss.
3rd Dynasty, (introduced) weed, herb
Uses: fodder

Vigna unguiculata (L.), Walp.
5th Dynasty, (native) weed, herb
Uses: food plant

Senna alexandrina Miller, true senna
Predynastic, (native) desert shrub
Uses: medicinal

Acacia nilotica (L.) Delile, Nile acacia
Predynastic, (native) tree along water courses
Uses: timber, medicinal

Ricinus communis L., castor oil plant
Predynastic-Dynastic, (native) shrub in moist
places
Uses: oil, medicinal

Euphorbia helioscopia L., sun spurge
Middle Kingdom, (introduced) winter weed,
herb

Ziziphus spina-christi (L.) Desf., sidder
Late Paleolithic, (native) tree along water
courses
Uses: edible fruits, medicinal

Corchorus olitorius L., Jew's- mallow
Predynastic, (native) summer weed, herb
Uses: vegetable, medicinal

Malva parviflora L., small-flowered mallow
3rd Dynasty, (native) winter weed, herb
Uses: vegetable, medicinal

Hibiscus trionum L., bladder hibiscus
Middle Kingdom, (introduced) weed, herb

Tamarix nilotica (Ehrenb.) Bunge, Nile tamarisk
Late Paleolithic, (native) shrub or small tree in moist places
Uses: timber, charcoal

Tamarix aphylla (L.) H. Karst., athel tamarisk
Late Paleolithic, (native) tree in dry habitats and desert outskirts
Uses: timber, charcoal

Epilobium hirsutum L., large flowered willow-herb
20th–26th Dynasties, (introduced) herb in moist places

Bryonia cretica L., snake bryony
Old Kingdom, (native) herb in moist shady places
Uses: medicinal

Citrullus colocynthis (L.) Schrader, colocynth
Old Kingdom, (native) creeping herb in desert outskirts
Uses: medicinal

Coriandrum sativum L., coriander
Old Kingdom, (native) aromatic herb
Uses: spice, medicinal

Cuminum cyminum L., cumin
Predynastic, (native) aromatic herb
Uses: spice, medicinal

Apium graveolens L., celery
Old Kingdom, (native) aromatic herb
Uses: spice, medicinal

Pimpinella anisum L., anise
Middle Kingdom, (introduced) aromatic herb
Uses: medicinal

Foeniculum vulgare Miller, common fennel
Middle Kingdom, (introduced) aromatic herb
Uses: spice, medicinal

Galuim tricornutum Dandy
Graeco-Roman, (introduced) weed in moist shady places

Cuscuta pedicellata Ledeb., dodder

Graeco-Roman, (introduced) parasitic herb
Uses: medicinal

Echuim rauwolfii Del., viper's bugloss
Predynastic, (native) ruderal weed in desert outskirts

Solanum nigrum L., black nightshade
Predynastic, (native) ruderal and agrestal weed
Uses: medicinal

Withania somnifera (L.) Dunal., clustered withania
18th Dynasty–Roman period, (introduced) shrub in waste ground
Uses: medicinal

Centaurea depressa M.B., cornflower
Middle Kingdom, (introduced) weed(?), herb
Uses: ornamental

Ceruana pratensis Forssk., ceruana
Predynastic, (native) herb on canal and river banks
Uses: baskets and brooms

Pluchea dioscorides (L.) DC, plowman's spike-nard
Predynastic, (native) shrub along irrigation canal
Uses: medicinal

Sphaeranthus suaveolens (Forssk.) DC
18th–19th Dynasties, (native) undershrub along irrigation canals

Pseudognaphaluim luteo-album (L.) Hilliard & B.L. Burtt
Middle Kingdom, (native) weed along irrigation canals
Uses: medicinal

Ambrosia maritima L., sea ambrosia
Graeco-Roman, (introduced) weed along Nile and canal banks
Uses: medicinal

Anthemis retusa Del.
5th Dynasty, (introduced) winter weed, herb

Anthemis pseudocotula Boiss., stinking camomile
3rd Dynasty, (introduced) aromatic weed
Uses: medicinal

Chrysanthemum coronarium L., crown daisy
Predynastic, (native) winter weed, herb
Uses: ornamental, medicinal

Cotula anthemoides L.
Predynastic, (native) weed in moist places and canal banks

Senecio glaucus L.
Graeco-Roman, (introduced) weed in moist shady places
Uses: ornamental

Senecio aegyptius L.
Predynastic, (native) weed along canal banks

Calendula arvensis L., field marigold
Predynastic, (native) winter weed, herb

Cichorium endivia L., wild chicory
Middle Kingdom, (introduced) winter weed, herb
Uses: salad plant, medicinal

Picris asplenioides L.
Middle Kingdom, (introduced) winter weed, herb

Sonchus oleraceus L., snow thistle
Predynastic, (native) agrestal and ruderal weed
Uses: salad plant, medicinal

Asphodelus fistulosus L., asphodel herb
Predynastic, (native) weed in moist places

Juncus acutus L., sharp rush
Predynastic, (native) shrublet in salt marshes and moist places
Uses: baskets, medicinal

Juncus rigidus Desf., common rush
Predynastic, (native) shrublet in salt marshes
Uses: baskets, matting

Sphenopus divaricatus (Gouan) Reichb.
Predynastic, (native) tiny grass in moist habitats

Desmostachya bipinnata (L.) Stapf., halfa grass
Predynastic, (native) grass in uncultivated ground, roadsides and canal banks
Uses: baskets, matting, fodder

ragrostis barrelieri (Willd.) Del., tickle grass
Predynastic, (native) weed in moist places

Phragmites australis (Cav.) Trin. ex Steud., common reed
Predynastic, (native) reed found in ditches, irrigation canals and drains, moist places
Uses: baskets, matting

Lolium temulentum L., bearded rye-grass
Predynastic, (native) winter weed especially in wheat fields
Uses: medicinal

Lolium perenne L., perennial rye-grass
Predynastic, (native) weed in fields, orchards and moist places
Uses: medicinal

Rostraria cristata (L.) Tzvelev
20th–26th Dynasties, (introduced) weed in moist places

Avena fatua L., wild oat
Graeco-Roman, (introduced) winter weed
Uses: fodder

Crypsis schoenoides (L.) Lam., crypside
Predynastic, (introduced) winter weed in moist places

Cynodon dactylon (L.) Pers., Bermuda grass
Roman period, (introduced) agrestal and ruderal weed
Uses: medicinal, fodder

Phalaris minor Retz., lesser Canary grass
Predynastic, (native) agrestal and ruderal weed
Uses: fodder grass with edible grains

Phalaris paradoxa L.
3rd Dynasty, (introduced) winter weed
Uses: fodder

Digitaria sanguinalis (L.) Scop., crab grass
Predynastic, (native) winter weed
Uses: fodder

Paspalidium geminatum (Forssk.) Stapf, millet grass
Predynastic, (native) grass in moist ground

Echinochloa colona (L.) Link, deccan grass
Predynastic, (native) summer weed in fields, orchards and waste ground
Uses: fodder, edible grains

Setaria verticellata (L.) Beauv., rough bristle grass
Predynastic, (native) agrestal and ruderal weed

Imperata cylindrica Raeusch., cogon grass
6th Dynasty, (introduced) grass in waste ground, roadsides and canal banks
Uses: baskets, ropes, matting

Typha domingensis Pers., cat's tail
Predynastic, (native) tall reed in moist places
Uses: baskets, matting

Fimbristylis bisumbellata (Forssk.) Bubani
Predynastic, (native) weed on Nile and canal banks, herb

Scirpus tuberosus/maritimus?, sea club-rush
Late Paleolithic, (native) weed in marshes and moist ground
Uses: edible tubers

Eleocharis palustris (L.) Roem. & Schult., marsh club-rush
Predynastic, (native) weed in moist places
Uses: edible tubers

Cyperus rotundus L., purple nut-grass
Late Paleolithic, (native) weed in moist places
Uses: edible tubers, medicinal

Cyperus articulatus L., articulated rush
Old Kingdom, (native) stout herb on canal banks
Uses: matting, fragrant tubers

Cyperus alopecuroides Rottb., mat sedge
Predynastic, (native) stout herb on canal banks
Uses: matting, ropes

Cyperus esculentus L,, rush nut
Predynastic, (native) herb in moist places
Uses: edible tubers, medicinal

Cyperus papyrus L., papyrus
Predynastic, (native) stout reed in water and moist places
Uses: food, medicinal, bouquets, garlands, boats, cordage, sandals, matting, boxes, writing material, etc.

See also

agriculture, introduction of; Hierakonpolis; Neolithic cultures, overview; Predynastic period, overview; Wadi Kubbaniya

Further reading

El Hadidi, M.N. 1985. Food plants of prehistoric and Predynastic Egypt. In *Plants for Arid Lands*, G.E. Wickens, J.R. Goodin and D.V. Field, eds. 87–91. London.
——. 1993. A historical flora of Egypt, a preliminary survey. In *Biological Anthropology and the Study of Ancient Egypt*, W.V. Davies and R. Walker, eds. 144–54. London.
El Hadidi, M.N., and A.A. Fayed. 1995. Materials for excursion flora of Egypt. *Taekholmia* 15: i–x, 1–223.
Fahmy, A.G., and U. Willerding. 1996. The Palaeœthnobotany of Locality 11C; Hieraknopolis (3800–3500 cal. BC); Egypt. 1. Cultivated crops and wild plants of potential value. *Taeckholmia* 16: 45–60.
Germer, R. 1985. *Flora des pharaonisches Ägypten*. Mainz.
Manniche, L. 1989. *An Ancient Egyptian Herbal*. London.
Täckholm, V.-G., and M. Drar. 1954. *Flora of Egypt* 3. *Bulletin of the Faculty of Science, Cairo University* 30.

M. NABIL EL HADIDI

Porter, Bertha, and Rosalind Moss

Among Egyptologists, the names Porter and Moss are "shorthand" for the indispensable research tool to which these women dedicated their careers as editors. The *Topographical Bibliography of Ancient Egyptian Hieroglyphic Texts, Reliefs, and Paintings* was conceived by Egyptologist Adolf Erman of Berlin University, but Professor F. Llewellyn Griffith of Oxford University actually set the project in motion by financing it and hiring Bertha Porter

(1852–1941), a professional bibliographer with the *Dictionary of National Biography*, who studied with Griffith and Kurt Sethe, Erman's successor. Never visiting Egypt herself, Porter depended wholly on publications, photographs and drawings, and verifications by others in the field.

In 1924 she took on as assistant another of Griffith's students, Rosalind Moss (1890–1990), an energetic woman of independent means and a published anthropologist, who was willing to travel to Egypt to undertake verification of the information to be published in their first volume, *The Theban Necropolis* (1927). Their fruitful collaboration continued until Porter's retirement in 1929, with Moss continuing and producing seven volumes, including largely augmented and revised editions of the original three volumes. Moss took on as her editorial assistant a widow, Ethel W. Burney, and together they maintained a huge file at the Griffith Institute at Oxford where, by 1938, the *Bibliography*'s records had been transferred. A small staff of part-time salaried assistants was installed.

Whereas originally the *Topographical Bibliography* aimed at covering all monuments in Egypt, efforts now expanded to inscribed objects in museums worldwide. Sites in Sudan and the Egyptian oases were also included in the *Bibliography*. The constant appearance of new publications called for continual updating of the files. Moss dedicated over fifty years to her enterprise, worked six days a week and never drew a salary. She was granted an Hon.D.Litt from Oxford in 1961 and retired in 1972, having provided a unique and profoundly useful research tool, which continues to be updated and published.

Further reading

Dawson, W.R., and E.P. Uphill. 1995. *Who Was Who in Egyptology*, 3rd edn. M.L. Bierbrier, ed. London.

Griffith, F.L. 1927. Preface. In *Topographical Bibliography of Ancient Egyptian Hieroglyphic Texts, Reliefs and Paintings* 1. Oxford.

James, T.G.H., and J. Málek, eds. 1990. *A Dedicated Life: Tributes Offered in Memory of Rosalind Moss*. Oxford.

BARBARA S. LESKO

pottery, Early Dynastic to Second Intermediate Period

Much of the information given here is currently in a state of change. New excavations, especially of settlement sites, are altering our knowledge about Egyptian ceramics almost daily. There is a clear contrast between pottery found in tombs and that of settlements, and it should be remembered that much information is still based on evidence from tombs and may not reflect the situation within settlements.

Early Dynastic period

Much of what is known about pottery of this period is based on excavations at the cemeteries of Saqqara and Abydos, although some sites in the Delta, such as Minshat Abu Omar and Buto, have recently shed new light on the end of the Predynastic period and the beginning of Dynastic times. The pottery was a continuation of that found in the late Predynastic (Nagada III phase). The shapes are largely similar, as is the decoration. The huge storage jars of the 1st Dynasty developed from torpedo-shaped jars, and began to have a characteristic ridge around the body. They were also made in stone. Rough pottery made from Nile silt clays resembled that of the Predynastic. Manufacturing techniques continued much as in the Predynastic, with an emphasis on coiling and pinching. A slow wheel continued to be used for finishing vessels.

Old Kingdom

Old Kingdom pottery is quite distinct from earlier pottery. Coarse wares include bread molds. These are in a distinctive bell shape, made in a wide range of sizes from a gritty, coarse clay. Other vessels include the characteristic beer jars. Oval bodied and with a pointed base and small mouth, they were made from Nile silt clay tempered with straw. Dishes and bowls, often with a small foot, were also made from this clay. Coarse pottery is undecorated and unburnished. It was mainly handmade, but some bowls show evidence of turning on a slow wheel.

The fine wares of the Old Kingdom are of very good quality. Both marl and silt clays were used to make the body. The clay was often coated with a slip of red or black, which was burnished. Some of the clays are much finer and harder than anything which had been used previously. A new set of shapes developed which included some copies of shapes in metal and stone. Ewers and basins were especially important in this respect. Tall vessels with flared rims and slim bodies (including the *hes* vase shape) were made during the Old Kingdom. Perhaps the most typical form from this period was the series of carinated bowls, known as "Meydum bowls" (from the important Old Kingdom site of Meydum). These bowls, which have sharply angled walls, were handmade, with wheel-made rims. They were usually made from marl clays, but some silt examples are known. The paste was very fine and the surface was coated with a red slip and polished to a high burnish. Some examples have applied or modeled spouts (as do other types of vessels).

By the 5th Dynasty, a faster wheel had come into use. This was used to produce turned vessels, including Meydum bowls. Although the wheel was used to make whole vessels and not just sections, the potter had to turn the wheel himself using one hand. This resulted in the production of wheel-shaped pots which were smoothed and finished by hand. This practice continued into the Second Intermediate Period.

Painted decoration of any type is extremely rare, although a few examples from the late Old Kingdom at Aswan do have post-firing painted decoration.

First Intermediate Period

With the collapse of the centralized state of the Old Kingdom, standards in pottery manufacturing declined. Although wheel technology remained local, ceramic styles flourished as a result of the breakdown in centralized control. For this reason, the pottery of this period is very diverse. Important sites include Sedment, Gurob, Tarkhan, Haraga, Abydos, Memphis and Qau.

Carinated profiles disappeared and vessel shapes became more rounded and smoother. A very common type of vessel in Middle and Lower Egypt was the water jar. This has a long, oval tapering body with a rounded or pointed base and a long, wide funnel neck.

Silt clays were most commonly used, but some marl clay vessels have been found in Upper Egypt. Very little decoration is known from this period.

Middle Kingdom

During the Middle Kingdom the clear division between domestic and fine pottery was maintained. Dorothea Arnold has divided the pottery of the Middle Kingdom into three clear phases. From the late 11th to early 12th Dynasty, pottery continued to preserve its regional variations. During the mid-12th Dynasty and from the late 12th to 13th Dynasty, a higher degree of uniformity developed, until, at the end of the period, pottery was very similar all over Egypt, including Nubia.

Much Middle Kingdom pottery was made of extremely fine clays, of both marl and silt types, although marl clays were comparatively rare and were distinctly different in Upper and Lower Egypt. Common characteristics include black and red line decoration, wavy rims, vessels with quatrefoil mouths, and incised decoration, often featuring fish and other animals on the inner surface of dishes.

The characteristic vessel of the Middle Kingdom is the hemispherical bowl. These are found in profusion at sites of Middle Kingdom date, and were used as drinking vessels. They progress from being red and completely burnished to having a red rim band. Over time they also became deeper. They were made from a particularly fine, sandy silt clay. This fine clay was also used in the last ceramic phase for small, carinated cups that were red burnished or decorated in red. Wheel technology continued to develop.

Domestic pottery continued to be made in coarse Nile silt clay, and a range of shapes was used, one of the most common being an oval, rather bulbous jar form with a slightly curved neck and a straight rim. Huge storage jars with wide rims were also used, as were smaller, bag-shaped cooking pots of both marl and silt clays. The lower part of these jars was often less well finished than the upper part, which was smoothed to neaten the finish. It was probably felt that a careful finish was superfluous, as the lower section would be concealed by rows of jars stacked together.

Two of the most notable forms of domestic pottery from the Middle Kingdom are flat and conical bread molds. The long conical type was handmade, and pinched and stroked to shape with the fingers. The large, oval platter-type mold was often incised with deep lines on the inside. Bread molds (of this and earlier date) were probably formed over a core of wood or rough clay, before being finished with the fingers. Pottery was also used to make domestic articles, such as a rat trap from the site of Lahun.

Fine marl clays were used to make small cosmetic jars which imitated those made of alabaster. Imported pottery includes jars from Palestine, Cypriot Base-ring Ware, and Pan-grave pottery from Nubia.

Second Intermediate Period

As the society of the Middle Kingdom collapsed, Egyptian pottery again began to show strong regional diversification. Trade with Palestine and Cyprus influenced styles and designs of pottery and brought foreign pottery to Egypt. Changes in the Second Intermediate Period included the introduction of more elaborate painted decoration. Bulbous "drop pots" began to appear. These vessels were long, with slightly tapering sides and a rounded bottom. Deep carinated bowls with a small foot also became popular. These two shapes were often patterned with a shallow, incised decoration of wavy lines.

Tell el-Yahudiya Ware, named after the site where it is most commonly found, first appeared in the 13th Dynasty, but continued into this period. It was a distinctive style of burnished pottery, usually black in color, in the form of a small jug. A design was pecked out on the surface in punctate indentations, which were filled with a white pigment. This ware originated somewhere in the Levant. Early examples in Egypt were imported, but the style was adopted and copied in local clay by the Egyptians. At first, the common shape for this style of pottery was a single-handled juglet, but more shapes were developed when the style became absorbed into Egypt.

From the 13th Dynasty on, vessels began to be wholly wheel-made and finished. Before this, bases were often hand-finished. The clay used during this period was still predominantly Nile silt, although marl clays were also in use. As the period progressed, the fine paste of the Middle Kingdom gradually disappeared, and the clay became coarser and more sandy.

See also

Abydos, North; Abydos, Umm el-Qa'ab; Aswan; Buto (Tell el-Fara'in); Canaanites; Cypriot peoples; Lahun, town; Meydum; Minshat Abu Omar; Saqqara, North, Early Dynastic tombs; Tell el-Yahudiya

Further reading

Bourriau, J.D. 1981. *Umm El Ga'ab. Pottery from the Nile Valley Before the Arab Conquest.* Cambridge.

Bourriau, J.D., and D.E. Arnold. 1993. *Introduction to Ancient Egyptian Pottery.* Mainz.

SALLY SWAIN

pottery, New Kingdom through the Ptolemaic period

Early to mid-18th Dynasty

During the early part of the 18th Dynasty, the black painted style which first appeared at the end of the Second Intermediate Period continued, but the type of vessels to which this decorative style was applied increased. In addition to the squat carinated jars, linear decorative styles were added to a series of bowls and jugs. At some point in mid-18th Dynasty, true bichrome pottery had developed in Egypt. Bearing little resemblance to the Cypriot ware from which the Egyptian ware ultimately derived, the Egyptian bichrome ware continued the traditions established during the early 18th Dynasty, but with the addition of red bands. At the same time a marked difference is found in the types of pots selected for burials. Storage vessels are found less often, and small cosmetic vessels, often double pots, become common. Also at this time, perhaps as a result of Tuthmose III's growing contacts with the Levant, lentoid-shaped "pilgrim flasks" first appear. At first these are all imported, but they were soon copied in Egypt, and the type remained popular at least into the 26th Dynasty.

During the reigns of Amenhotep II and Tuthmose IV, new experiments began to be made by the painters of Egyptian pottery. A development of the bichrome black and red ware resulted in the addition of scenes, most often on tall necked jars, of birds (generally storks and pintail ducks), fish, shrubs, palm trees, lotuses, gazelles, horses and oxen. Additionally, *ankh* signs, usually grasping a scepter shaped like the hieroglyph *w3s*, are also common.

One of the most significant developments was the addition of blue decoration. At first this was confined to simple bands, often flanked by red and black ones. When used in the main scenes, it was used sparingly, in contrast to the predominant blue of the later blue-painted pottery. Pre-fired yellow paint also appears at this time.

From the same time (the reigns of Tuthmose III, Amenhotep II and Tuthmose IV) comes the first evidence for the reuse of polychrome (post-fired) painting since the early Middle Kingdom. For example, two amphorae, found in the tomb of Tjanuni at Thebes and dating to the reign of Amenhotep II, show scenes of a vineyard and representations of grapes: appropriate symbols for vessels made to hold wine. The colors employed, all on a white ground, are red, black, yellow, light green and dark green.

Late 18th Dynasty to mid-20th Dynasty

Although true blue-painted pottery, where the blue predominates over all the other colors, first appears during the reign of Tuthmose IV, it only began to appear in quantity during the reign of Amenhotep III. This type of pottery, perhaps the most notable and characteristic type of Egyptian painted pottery, enjoyed a brief but brilliant period of production reaching its peak at the end of the 18th Dynasty (reigns of Tutankhamen and Horemheb), fading away during the Ramesside period. After the reign of Ramesses IV it ceased to be produced.

During the height of this pottery's production the typical motifs were primarily floral, based mainly on the blue and white lotus flowers, though cornflowers, poppies, mandrakes and papyrus are not uncommon. More rarely, faunal motifs (pintail ducks, falcons, bulls, gazelles, ibexes, horses) and humans are also encountered. Although most blue-painted vessels are typically found in the contemporary shapes, some of them are extremely elaborate and have modeled representations of gazelles, cows, heads of the goddess Hathor and faces of the god Bes. The blue painted designs are usually found on a white or cream/pink slip, though some are on a red slip, and others, yet rarer, are painted onto an uncoated surface. Restricted almost entirely to Memphis, Gurob, Tell el-Amarna, Malkata and Qantir, the distribution pattern shows that the production of blue-painted pottery was almost certainly centered at cities with royal residences.

By the early 19th Dynasty fashions changed, and although blue-painted pottery continued to be produced in quantity, the use of floral and faunal motifs gradually fell out of favor. Pottery of this period is characterized by simple linear bands with the lotus the only floral motif retained. One innovation of the Ramesside potters, however, seems to be the introduction of a vessel type best described as "fluted funnel-necked jars." Modeled grooves are found on goblets of the late 18th Dynasty, but under the Ramesside kings, this decorative motif is applied to the belly, and sometimes to the neck of funnel-necked jars. The best example of this type of pot is undoubtedly in the Museum of Fine Arts, Boston (64.9).

During the early 20th Dynasty, blue-painted decoration differed little from that of the 19th Dynasty, though the introduction of decorated carinated bowls seems to have developed then. After the reign of Ramesses IV, however, no more blue-painted pottery appears to have been produced.

Contemporary with the main phases of blue-painted pottery, the use of polychrome (post-fired) painted pottery also developed. This does not have the tenacity of prefired colors, and can be readily washed off. Both the colors used and the styles of this decoration differ from contemporary blue-painted pottery. In the late 18th Dynasty this style of decoration seems confined to fine marl clay vessels with handles, and is rare. To this phase, however, may be attributed the amphora and large jug (*oenichos*) from Gurob, a jar from Abydos, the jugs and squat two-handled jar from the tomb of Kha at Deir el-Medina, a number of unpublished amphorae from the Memphite tomb of Horemheb, and a few sherds from Malkata and Tell el-Amarna. At first the decoration runs around the pot, but the designs on those from Tell el-Amarna and the Memphite tomb of Horemheb are clearly intended to represent floral collars tied onto the "front" of the vase, anticipating the decorated collars found on the polychrome vessels of the 19th Dynasty. At that time, polychrome painting seems confined to, or at least was most popular on, a series of small amphorae with tall necks and horizontal handles, known principally from Gurob and Deir el-Medina. The main decorative motif

used on these vessels is a floral collar on the upper belly with the representation of string ties on the back, while the neck can be decorated in various geometrical and floral patterns.

Painted pottery, while clearly the most spectacular pottery of the New Kingdom, accounts for only a small proportion of the New Kingdom corpus. The reign of Amenhotep III also saw a new range of shapes, most familiar from the excavations at Tell el-Amarna, and a marked increase in the use of marl (D) clays. Slight changes are noticeable between the ordinary pottery of the reigns of Akhenaten and Ramesses II, which suggests that such shapes continued to evolve. Some time between the reigns of Siptah and Ramesses III, however, a marked change in pottery forms is clearly noticeable. The bases of amphorae made from marl (D) clays lose their pronounced carination in favor of rounded bases, while the necks tend to be taller. This tendency is also found in the lentoid-shaped pilgrim flasks (with taller necks), while mugs tend to be taller and thinner than earlier examples. Handles on both pilgrim flasks and mugs tend to start from lower down the neck and are more ring-shaped than before. At the same time, new forms, represented in deposits dating to the 20th Dynasty at Gurob and Tell el-Yahudiya, are found.

Mid-20th Dynasty and Third Intermediate Period

With the cessation in production of blue-painted pottery, the use of paint to decorate pottery vessels went into decline. During the late 20th and 21st Dynasties, decoration seems confined almost entirely to red and black bands, though a small number of pilgrim flasks occasionally have black stars under the handles. Amphorae from the tomb of Ramesses VI have black prefired decoration, which seems to represent a stylized collar at the shoulder. Usually, however, the black paint is confined to rim bands on both open and closed forms, and on the shoulders of globular jars. Red bands are also found on the rims of both open and closed forms, and are very common at this time, as are red circles on pilgrim flasks. The use of more than one color on the same pot becomes rare, though the use of black and red is found on a small number of jars from Memphis.

Pottery development during the Third Intermediate and Late periods is still far from clear, and, paradoxically, pottery of the first millennium BC is less well known than that from either the second or third millennium BC. The shapes and decorative styles that developed in the late 20th Dynasty clearly continued into the 21st Dynasty, but pottery of the tenth and ninth centuries BC is much more difficult to define. The pottery of this age is, in some ways, transitional, with many forms harking back to the twelfth and eleventh centuries BC, but a few forms, more common in the 25th Dynasty, begin to appear. What appears certain, however, is that, in contrast to the earlier phase, typical New Kingdom shapes are no longer found, and, with the possible exception of the Memphite area, clays of one type of marl (A4) replace the marl (D) clays used earlier. During the tenth and ninth centuries BC, almost no painted pottery is known, but a number of vessels from the "22nd Dynasty" settlement at Medinet Habu are decorated with red bands on the shoulder and lower body. The use of a red rim band on open forms continues, though it is less common than in earlier times. The latter may continue through the 25th–26th Dynasties since red rim bands are also found on platters at Saqqara dating to the period of Persian rule in Egypt.

Some time during the late eighth century BC, a new ceramic corpus appears in the south and is characterized by the introduction of a thin walled marl (A4) clay used for a wide range of shapes, particularly closed forms. Such vessels are invariably thin walled, and often show distinct signs of ribbing on the walls. Vessels of Nile silt clay, however, still retain the same characteristics as such wares of the Third Intermediate Period, though during the 25th Dynasty a new decorative scheme came into fashion. Dating to this period are a number of closed vessels with a white spiral pattern painted on them.

Late period

Studies on Delta pottery of the Late period show that it can be divided into three phases. The first, represented by material from Buto, Saft el-Henna and Suwa, can be dated to the middle of the seventh century BC. A second phase, characterized by the introduction of ring-based, wide-mouthed jars, can be dated to the sixth century BC, and is represented at Buto, Mendes and Memphis. Thinner walled, more graceful forms of this date are also found at Buto, Shaganba, Tell el-Maskhuta and Lahun, the latter showing that, at this date, northern pottery forms had spread into the Fayum. Finally a third phase, dating to the fifth–fourth centuries BC (hence termed "Persian"), is also well known in the north, particularly in the Memphis/Saqqara region, and elsewhere at Tell Nebesha, Tell ed-Dab'a and Tell el-Sab'a Benat, though for the most part, this remains unpublished. It is characterized by thick red slips, many of them fugitive. A series of thin walled, better made vessels also appears at this time, and is connected to the introduction of a new, improved fast wheel during the period of Persian domination. During the 26th Dynasty and Persian times, pottery deposits are often characterized by a number of imported amphorae, particularly of Aegean and Phoenician origin. Late period pottery development in the south is even more poorly understood, but the discovery of stratified deposits at Elephantine in recent years should help to remedy this situation.

As with the Third Intermediate Period, painted pottery of the Late period is somewhat rare. Perhaps the best known are a series of small flasks, usually of marl clay, with representations of faces of the god Bes on their bodies. They often have neck bands of black or red, which are also found above and below the Bes face. They would appear to date to Persian times. Dating from the sixth–fourth centuries BC are a series of amphorae which appear to be modeled on contemporary vessels from Chios in the Aegean. The decoration on these vessels is usually in a red to brown to black color. At Gurna a few bowls made of the same clay have black rim bands.

During the Persian period a number of large, handmade platters were produced with broad, red-slipped rim bands applied to the interior. Some of the most spectacular painted pottery of the Late period, however, was produced in the early part of the fourth century BC. Such vessels, known only from Elephantine and Thebes, were formerly dated to the Ptolemaic period, though stratigraphic excavations at Elephantine show that the painted vessels there first appear in pre-Ptolemaic levels. They are decorated in red, which is often burnished, and yellow and black. All Elephantine examples so far discovered are decorated in simple linear bands, while those from Thebes also have floral and cross-hatched patterns.

Ptolemaic period

During the Ptolemaic period there appear to have been two main artistic trends in pottery. The first comprises the addition of a number of black bands to a series of small flasks and juglets, and the other consists of a series of floral motifs which seem to have been ultimately derived from Hellenistic Greek ones. The latter form of decoration is found most often on open forms, sometimes with added white, and, if a vessel from Gurna has been dated correctly, a few large jars as well. At this time the use of a deeply burnished black ware also became popular, but the corpus of forms begins to owe much more to Hellenistic influences than to native Egyptian ones.

See also

Late and Ptolemaic periods, overview; New Kingdom, overview; pottery, Early Dynastic to Second Intermediate Period; pottery, prehistoric; Third Intermediate Period, overview

Further reading

Aston, D.A. 1996. *Egyptian Pottery of the Twelfth–Seventh Centuries B.C.* Heidelberg.
——. 1998. *Elephantine xx. Pottery from the Late New Kingdom to the Early Ptolemaic Period.* Mainz.
Bourriau, J., and D. Arnold, eds. 1993. *An Introduction to Ancient Egyptian Pottery.* Mainz.
1987. *Cahiers de la Céramique égyptienne* 1. Cairo.

D.A. ASTON

pottery, prehistoric

Since the discovery of the remains of late prehistoric cultures in Upper Egypt at the turn of the century, ceramics have been used to date, define and chart the social and technological development and interaction of the earliest settled inhabitants along the banks of the Nile. As no inscriptional evidence is available to date the remains, pottery is the primary tool for constructing relative chronological sequences. Because it was relatively easy and inexpensive to produce and had a limited span of use, pottery is considered to represent accurately the prevailing style at the time of its abandonment. Once placed in an order, these stylistic trends reflect a relative chronology of the culture that created them.

In addition to chronological concerns, consistent differences in the handmade pottery of prehistoric Egypt, in the choice of clay, temper, shape, surface treatment and decoration, reflect cultural and regional traditions in pottery making. These are important for understanding trade and social or political interaction in this formative period of Egyptian culture. The most notable and widespread traditions are those of the Nagada culture of Upper Egypt and the contemporary Ma'adi–Buto culture of Lower Egypt. Several earlier and probably related traditions are known, however, and a variety of distinct ceramic traditions are also found in the Western Desert, Nubia, Sinai and southern Palestine.

Upper Egypt

The earliest known culture in Upper Egypt

which used ceramics is the Tarifian, found at el-Tarif (Theban region) and Armant on the west bank of the Nile. Sherds of simple bowls and collared jars made of Nile silts most often mixed with plant material and sand, with a rough or more rarely polished surface, were found in association with distinctive stone tools and hearths. This pottery appears to belong to a pre-agricultural nomadic population related to Epi-paleolithic cultures known farther south in Nubia, and has no demonstrable link to the later cultural sequence (Nagada culture) in Upper Egypt.

Another locally restricted early tradition may be the Tasian culture, named after the site of Deir Tasa in Middle Egypt. The pottery is generally restricted to deep biconical vessels with small flattened bases made of poorly cleaned silts taken from the Nile banks. The surface is either rough brown or coated with a gray slip. Black polished flaring lipped beakers decorated with incised geometric designs filled with white pigment are also characteristic of this ceramic assemblage. The Tasian culture is now generally believed to be an early phase of the Badarian culture, but may represent a separate but contemporary population with origins in the Eastern Desert. On the basis of three vessels which are blackened at the rim, Tasian pottery has been placed at the beginning of the Upper Egyptian pottery sequence, but the evidence is too meager for such an attribution.

The earliest major phase in the Predynastic period of Upper Egypt is called the "Badarian," after the modern town of el-Badari in Middle Egypt on the east bank of the Nile. Badarian pottery has been divided into six classes based on the color and quality of the surface treatment. Most Badarian pottery is made from fine Nile silt. The finest and most characteristic classes are the Black-topped Brown class (abbreviated BB) and Black-topped Red class (BR). The blackened rim and interior were produced by placing the rim of the vessel down in smoke-producing fuel, probably during firing. Distinctive of the period are extremely fine, thin-walled bowls, often carinated, and bag-shaped vessels of BB and

BR with a "rippled" surface. This rippling effect was produced by dragging a comb across the surface of the wet clay and then using a smooth stone to polish or burnish the surface after the clay had dried but before firing. Also considered characteristic of Badarian pottery are designs made by the polishing stone against the matte black surface on the interior of bowls. Motifs produced by pattern burnishing include cross-hatching, chevrons, crosses and floral designs. Similar pottery without the black top was also produced, although less frequently (Polished Red, All Black, and Smooth Brown classes). For general domestic purposes, there were thick-walled bowls, either shallow or deep, and hole-mouth jars of Rough Brown pottery (RB), tempered with chopped grass stems.

Because extensive evidence of Badarian remains appears limited to the Badari region in Middle Egypt, the ancestral relationship of Badarian ceramics to the repertoire of the Nagada culture has been questioned despite the continued appearance of Black-topped Red pottery and carinated vessel forms. Badarian ceramic assemblages (albeit composed of less fine clay) have been found in the Dendera region and as far south as Armant and Hierakonpolis. The pottery found in settlements of the early Nagada culture (Nagada I or Amratian) is morphologically similar to Badarian ceramics. Thus, there seems to be little doubt that the beginning of the ceramic sequence of Upper Egypt can be found within the Badarian assemblage.

The best evidence for the chronology of the Nagada culture ceramics comes from the numerous cemeteries found along the desert's edge. Flinders Petrie, the first to uncover these remains, was also the first to realize the chronological potential of the ceramics from these cemeteries. He called his pioneering effort "Sequence Dating," which was the first example of pottery seriation in archaeology.

Petrie developed the sequence by first creating a corpus of shapes divided into nine classes, five of which are made from Nile silts:

1 Black-topped Red (B-) class, red slipped and polished with a blackened area at the rim;

2 Red polish (P-) class, the same as B but without the black top;

3 White Cross-line (C-) class, polished red with the addition of white painted decorations;

4 Incised (N-) class, which was fired entirely black and incised with geometric designs filled in with white pigment, now recognized to be an import from Nubia;

5 Rough (R-) class, made of Nile silt tempered with straw which burned away during firing leaving a rough pitted exterior surface.

A fine, calcareous clay (marl) often made from shales found in desert wadis was used for the following two classes:

6 Decorated (D-) class, fired to a light orange to buff and decorated with red painted designs;

7 Wavy-handled (W-) class, jars with applied handles.

In addition, Petrie created two classes which are no longer used in classification:

8 Late (L-) class, the majority of which is composed of marl clay, but also includes what Petrie considered to be decadent forms of other classes;

9 Fancy (F-) class, consisting of oval, theriomorphic and otherwise oddly shaped vessels of various classes.

Petrie then listed the contents of a selected number of graves from the cemeteries at Nagada and Hu (Diospolis Parva) and ordered or seriated the graves according to their ceramics, the frequency of certain pottery classes and developments in form. Petrie's Sequence Dating system and corpus continue to be used today, although certain inaccuracies have been noted in both. As a result, a revised dating system based on the clustering of ceramic types within cemeteries was developed in the 1950s by Werner Kaiser. Both systems divide the ceramic material (and thus the Nagada culture) into three main chronological phases (although the points of division in the two systems differ somewhat): Amratian or Nagada I, Gerzean or Nagada II, and Semainean, now called the Protodynastic or Nagada

III (equivalent in part to the earliest historical period).

The Nagada I phase is typified by the high frequency of B-class bowls and beakers with flat bases and simple rims. Jars with modeled rims develop at the end of the period. Bowls, occasionally carinated, and bottles of P-class and C-class vessels, with white painted figures and geometric designs, are also characteristic. The painted figures on C-class indicate certain regional artistic distinctions as well as evidence of different symbolic expression. A clearer indication of regionalism is seen in the coarse utilitarian pottery from Nagada I settlements. Such pottery is not found in graves of the period, and as a result little is known about it. Thick bowls and cooking and storage pots from the early settlements at Hierakonpolis, Nagada, and Hemamieh in the Badari region, demonstrate at least three different regional traditions of pot making based on the temper added to the local Nile clay: coarse shale, crushed potsherds or chopped grass. These rough and crudely made vessels were homemade for domestic use, while evidence such as the kilns at Hierakonpolis, which produced B-, P-, and C-class pottery, suggests that the fine, polished and more standardized pottery found in graves and settlements was made by at least part-time specialists.

By the middle of the Nagada II phase, the utilitarian straw-tempered Rough class jars, bottles and bowls become frequent in graves. Large conical jars containing ashes from the funerary feast or substitutes for real food offerings are particularly numerous. Distinctive of this phase is the use of light colored marl clay, either pure or mixed with Nile silts, to produce W- and D-class jars and some L-class vessels. The gradual transformation of Wavy-handled jars from their original globular shape, adapted from jars imported from Early Bronze Age Palestine, into an increasingly slender form with abbreviated handles was a key element for Petrie's seriation. Although Petrie's proposed Wavy-handled sequence is inaccurate for the beginning of the Nagada II phase, it works well later.

Decorated class pots are the hallmark of the

Nagada II phase and replace the earlier C-class. Designs of spirals, wavy lines and riverine scenes, featuring boats, ostriches, ibex and occasionally stylized human figures, were applied in red to brown ocherous paint on globular and ovoid D-class jars with a distinctive flattened rim and barrel handles which imitate the shapes of stone vessels. The interest in boats, and the appearance and influence of imported pottery from Palestine and Nubia (N-class), attest to wide-ranging trade connections in this phase. By the middle of the Nagada II phase there is a notable decrease in the labor-intensive B-class pots, but fine P-class bottles and jars continue to be made, although P-class bowls tend to be polished only on the interior. For the first time there is evidence for the use of a slow wheel or tournette to produce the finely modeled rims and necks on these handmade jars. Regional diversity is no longer apparent by the middle of Nagada II, and by the very end of the phase, the mass-produced and standardized ceramics of Upper Egypt are also found in Lower Egypt.

The chronological construct called Late class characterizes the Nagada III (which includes Dynasty 0) or Protodynastic period. "Late ware" is the name given by Petrie to necked jars and bowls of marl clay, conical jars of straw-tempered R-class, and orange slipped and roughly polished P-class bowls, all of which were manifestly changed in style and have a direct connection to pottery styles found in the 1st Dynasty royal graves at Abydos. Wavy-handled pots become slender cylinders with a decorative band running entirely around the vessel rather than a handle. Decoration on D-class pots degenerates to series of wavy lines, splashes and dots. The general trend in all classes is toward narrower forms with well formed necks and rims.

Lower Egypt

Unlike Upper Egypt, where ceramics in burials are frequent, most of the Lower Egyptian ceramics have been found in the scattered remains of settlements. Although there are many similarities in the ceramic repertoire of the relatively few known Lower Egyptian prehistoric sites, it has not been entirely resolved whether they represent several contemporary regional variants or successive typological phases.

Some of the earliest pottery known in Egypt (first half of the fifth millennium BC) is found at the site of Merimde Beni-salame, located on the southwestern border of the Delta. The limited repertoire consists of simple bowls and hole-mouth jars made of untempered Nile silt, smoothed or coated with a red slip and polished. A connection with the Neolithic culture of the Jordan Valley has been suggested by the incised herringbone patterns that appear on some of the red polished pottery, but this association is questionable. Like the Tarifian ceramics of Upper Egypt, the pottery of level I at Merimde has no apparent connection to later developments.

At about the same time, the pottery of the fishers and farmers in the Fayum, although quite different from that of the earliest phase of occupation at Merimde, can be placed at the beginning of what may be considered the main line of ceramic development in Lower Egypt. The early ceramics in the Fayum are followed by the pottery found in the upper levels (II–V) at Merimde and at el-Omari, located in the Cairo region, which later develop into the Ma'adi–Buto cultural assemblage. The pottery tradition at all sites generally involves tempering local clays with "straw" actually derived from papyrus heads and grasses. The surface is either roughly smoothed or coated with a slip and polished. A preference for a red to brown slip gradually gives way to entirely black polished pottery (at Merimde and Ma'adi). This trend, along with increasing sophistication in shape, is considered to have chronological significance. The early pottery in the Fayum is characterized by plain or red-slipped bag shape vessels and rectangular basins. At the later sites, oval bowls, beakers and globular jars with and without necks are characteristic. The surfaces on these ceramics are wet-smoothed, or slipped in red or grey, but later black-slipped surfaces appear. Certain similarities with the nearly contemporary Badarian repertoire of shapes perhaps suggest some connection.

Approximately contemporary with the Nagada I–mid-Nagada II period in Upper Egypt, the settlements at Ma'adi and other sites in the Cairo region provided most of what was known about the Ma'adi–Buto culture when this entry was written in 1992. Distinctive are red- or more often black-polished, narrow jars of "straw"-tempered Nile silt, with everted rims and added ring bases. Providing a synchronism with the Upper Egyptian sequence are imitation and imported Black-topped beakers, and jars and bowls coated with yellow wash and decorated with red painted designs. Imported ceramics from Palestine are also numerous at Ma'adi. Although this cultural complex is widely distributed throughout Lower Egypt, regional diversity is apparent, and new discoveries at Buto are changing our view of its chronology and character.

The end of the settlement at Ma'adi is attributed to intruders from Upper Egypt. The best evidence for this is found in the burials at Minshat Abu Omar in the east Delta, which include typical late Nagada II pottery. Soon thereafter Upper Egyptian Nagada III pottery and shapes become dominant in Lower Egyptian sites, and this transformation appears to be an archaeological reflection of the process of unification of Egypt into one large territorial state with a unified material culture.

See also

Abydos, Umm el-Qa'ab; Armant; el-Badari district Predynastic sites; Buto (Tell el-Fara'in); Fayum, Neolithic and Predynastic sites; Hierakonpolis; Hu/Hiw (Diospolis Parva); Ma'adi and the Wadi Digla; Merimde Beni-salame; Minshat Abu Omar; Nagada (Naqada); natural resources; el-Omari; Predynastic period, overview; representational evidence, Predynastic; Thebes, el-Tarif, prehistoric sites

Further reading

Adams, B. 1988. *Predynastic Egypt*. Aylesbury.

Bourriau, J. 1981. *Umm el-Ga'ab: Pottery from the Nile Valley Before the Arab Conquest.* Cambridge.

Finkenstaedt, E. 1985. Cognitive vs. ecological niches in prehistoric Egypt. *JARCE* 22: 143–7.

Hendrickx, S. 1996. The Relative Chronology of the Nagada Culture. Problems and Possibilities. In *Aspects of Early Egypt*, J. Spencer, ed., 36–69. London.

Kantor, H.J. 1992. The relative chronology of Egypt and its foreign correlations before the First Intermediate Period. In *Chronologies in Old World Archaeology*, R. Ehrich, ed., 3–21. Chicago.

Köhler, E.C. 1992. The Pre- and Early Dynastic pottery of Tell el-Fara'in/Buto. In *The Nile Delta in Transition: 4th.–3rd Millennium B.C.*, E.C.M. van den Brink, ed., 11–22. Tel Aviv.

Needler, W. 1984. *Predynastic and Archaic Egypt in the Brooklyn Museum*. New York.

Petrie, W.M.F. 1901. *Diospolis Parva*. London.

——. 1920. *Prehistoric Egypt*. London.

——. 1921. *Corpus of Prehistoric Pottery and Palettes*. London.

Rizkana, I., and J. Seeher. 1987. *Maadi I. The Pottery of the Predynastic Settlement* (AVDAIK 64). Mainz.

RENÉE FRIEDMAN

Punt

Punt was a region to the south of Egypt where many exotic goods and materials were obtained in Dynastic times. Typical products of Punt were frankincense and others resins, gums, electrum and, during the New Kingdom, ebony, ivory, leopard skins, baboons, monkeys, dogs and perhaps slaves.

Contact with Punt was first recorded in the late Old Kingdom (5th–6th Dynasties). In the Middle and New Kingdoms contact was frequent, and there is textual evidence of a shrine or temple in Punt dedicated to the Egyptian goddess Hathor. The most extensive evidence is found in the reliefs of a naval expedition to Punt in the mortuary temple of

Queen Hatshepsut (18th Dynasty) at Deir el-Bahri. Contact apparently ceased in the 20th Dynasty. Some attempts to resume contact were probably made during the 26th Dynasty and the Persian period (27th–31st Dynasties), but there is no definite evidence that any contact took place. In Graeco-Roman times only mythological references to Punt are reported.

Information about Punt in Egyptian sources is vague. It is depicted as a tropical region with dom palms and baboons, accessible from both the coast and the interior. Punt was divided into different districts, suggesting that its territory was fairly large. Breeders of short-horned cattle lived in round houses elevated above the ground on piles. In the hinterland were herders of long-horned cattle. Some form of control and exploitation of frankincense trees was practiced. Puntites had some knowledge of metallurgy and were able to sail along the Red Sea as far as the Egyptian coast. A "king" and a "queen" of equal status ruled there. In the Deir el-Bahri reliefs the "king" is depicted as personally supervising the trade with the Egyptians.

From Egypt Punt was reached by both land and sea. The products of this region were usually obtained through intermediaries along caravan routes, but (donkey) caravans were probably sent to Punt from Egypt in the 6th Dynasty. In the Middle and New Kingdoms, trade with Punt was mostly conducted along the Red Sea route by Egyptian expeditions going southward and Puntite merchants sailing northward. In the Middle Kingdom Egyptian ships left for Punt from a port at Gasus, to the north of Quseir.

The exact location of Punt is still uncertain. A number of scholars now agree that Punt was located in eastern Sudan and Eritrea, from Port Sudan to the Gulf of Zula, with a hinterland in the Ethio-Sudanese lowlands possibly as far as the middle Atbara valley. Archaeological evidence confirms that an interchange circuit between Egypt, the Horn of Africa and southern Arabia existed in the third–second millennia BC. In a level dating to the mid-second millennium BC at the site of Mahal Teglinos, near Kassala (eastern Sudan), a fragment of an alabaster vessel and about 100 early New

Kingdom potsherds were excavated. At Agordat in the middle Barka valley (Eritrea), an Egyptian-style, ceramic ear-plug and some stone celts which imitate bronze prototypes of the 17th–18th Dynasties have been excavated in sites dating to the mid-second millennium BC. On the Eritrean coast at Adulis, two fragments of glass vessels typical of the New Kingdom have been found in a level dating to the late second millennium BC. In southern Somalia some cylindrical beads of blue faïence, of a type made in the 18th Dynasty, have been discovered in an ancient cemetery of uncertain age. A cylindrical bead of Egyptian faïence has also been found in a second millennium BC site at Nakuru, Kenya. Although scarce, the archaeological evidence at least points to indirect contacts between Egypt and the Horn of Africa, especially the northern Ethio-Sudanese lowlands, in the second millennium BC.

See also

Deir el-Bahri, Hatshepsut temple; trade, foreign

Further reading

Herzog, P. 1968. *Punt*. Glückstadt.
Kitchen, K.A. 1992. The land of Punt. In *The Archaeology of Africa: Food, Metals and Towns*, T. Shaw, P. Sinclair, B. Andah and A. Okpoko, eds. 587–608. London.

RODOLFO FATTOVICH

pyramid tombs of the New Kingdom

Abandoned by the pharaohs of the 18th Dynasty, the pyramid as an architectural element was taken over by the nobles. The idea of combining pyramid and *mastaba* developed in the course of the New Kingdom, and the pyramid tomb was used in several parts of Egypt and Nubia, such as Saqqara, Thebes, Aniba and Soleb. After its growing significance in the private tombs of the Old and Middle

Kingdoms, the funerary chapel became the most important part of the tomb superstructure in the New Kingdom. The chapel may be preceded by an open court. The substructure consisted mainly of a shaft leading to the burial chambers. The pyramid tombs varied in form from one region to another, due to different topographical conditions at each site, different materials used in construction, and other local and religious factors.

Many of the New Kingdom chapels at Saqqara had a small pyramid capped with a stone pyramidion built above the cult room. The existence of such a pyramid is confirmed both by the ancient representations of Memphite chapels and by their pyramidal capstones, which have been found in the area. Regarding the general layout of the tomb, two categories of New Kingdom chapels have been revealed at Saqqara: (1) the more royal type that imitates the plan of a temple, such as the tomb of Horemheb and the tomb of Tia and Tia; (2) the simpler and much smaller *mastaba*-chapel type, such as the tomb of Apuia. In the first group, an isolated pyramid stood behind the cult room on a base or podium, while in the second, the pyramid may have stood above the cult room.

Existing pyramid tombs at Thebes can be found mainly in two areas: at Dra' Abu el-Naga and at Deir el-Medina. These tombs are better preserved than those at Saqqara and offer various types of plans; the method of construction adopted often depended on the location chosen for the erection of the tomb. At Dra' Abu el-Naga, the offering chamber and all the succeeding parts of the chapel were wholly cut in the rock cliff and the general form of the plan resembles a reversed letter "T." The pyramid of the Dra' Abu el-Naga tombs was their most prominent exterior feature. These pyramids were built high up the slope of the natural rock, after the surface was leveled by constructing a narrow platform which served as the pyramid base. The pyramid was pushed back from the chapel's façade in order to be placed above the cult room. The pyramid itself contained a single small chapel which was probably dedicated to Hathor (Theban tombs nos. 35, 158, 282–3). This feature suggested a

particular Theban symbolism, whereby the great peak of Gurna was considered as a natural huge pyramid dedicated to Hathor as Mistress of the West.

At Deir el-Medina, on the upper levels of the necropolis where the chapel could be wholly cut in the rock, a reversed "T" shaped plan was adopted, as in the tomb of Neferhotep (no. 216). Lower down the slope, the chapels were partially built against the face of the hill, with the inner parts of the tomb being hewn into the rock. The earlier Deir el-Medina tombs, dating mostly from the second half of the 18th Dynasty, have chapels consisting of a single small room, its longer axis perpendicular to the façade, with a niche sometimes cut in the rear end of it. This chapel is either encased in a brick pyramid reaching to the ground, or topped with one also in brick resting on a cubic *mastaba*-like edifice (no. 291). In both types, the pyramid was capped with a stone pyramidion. The pyramids at Deir el-Medina were smaller than those at Dra' Abu el-Naga and did not have podiums. The free-standing type of pyramids at Deir el-Medina were not totally isolated structures, except for the tomb of Kha (no. 8); they were always attached from the rear to the cliff. This attachment symbolized the veneration of the inhabitants of this particular locality towards the peak of the western mountain.

The New Kingdom chapels at Aniba in Nubia may be divided into two groups: (1) the earlier tombs of the 18th Dynasty built in the shape of vaulted houses; and (2) the Ramesside tombs (19th–20th Dynasties), taking the form of pyramids. In the second group, most examples have the cult room encased in a brick pyramid with the summit of the latter right above the center of the former. Two representations of a typical tomb at Aniba could be found in the tomb of Pennut, on the west part of the north wall of the chapel, showing many similarities to contemporaneous tomb representations from the Theban necropolis.

The first step in constructing a pyramid tomb at Soleb was to prepare an oval tumulus on top of which the superstructure was erected. The pyramid stood on the west part of this tumulus; the chapel also stood on it, immediately to the east of the pyramid. This feature might have inspired the builders of later monuments at the cemetery of el-Kurru, which contains the tombs of ancestors and early rulers of the kingdom of Kush.

It has been suggested that the royal pyramid tombs of the 17th Dynasty at Thebes were behind the popularity of the private pyramid tomb during the Ramesside period in the vicinity of Thebes. However, the diffusion of this type in the Memphite region, as well as being simultaneously adopted in the southernmost regions of Egyptian control (i.e. Aniba and Soleb), suggests that this propagation was not the result of simple copying of a royal form or simply due to the tendency of royal customs to descend the social scale. More likely, the New Kingdom private pyramid tombs were inspired by the renewed zeal and support of the solar cult attested during the Ramesside period.

See also

Deir el-Medina; pyramids (Old Kingdom), construction of; Saqqara, New Kingdom private tombs; Thebes, Dra' Abu el-Naga

Further reading

Bruyère, B. 1923–51. *Rapports sur les fouilles de Deir el-Medineh*, 19 vols. Cairo.

Marcks, D. 1937. In *Aniba II*, G. Steindorff, ed., 51ff. Glückstadt.

Martin, G.T. 1982–4. The tomb of Tia and Tia: preliminary report on the Saqqara excavations. *JEA* 69: 25–69; 70: 5–12.

Giorgini, M., C. Robichon and J. Leclant. 1965. *Soleb II*, 81ff. Florence.

Kitchen, K.A. 1979. Memphite tomb-chapels in the New Kingdom and later. In *Festschrift E. Edel*, 272–84. Bamberg.

DOHA MAHMOUD MOSTAFA

pyramids (Old Kingdom), construction of

The Old Kingdom Egyptians built pyramids for their kings and queens in a 72 km span of the Western Desert from Abu Roash to Meydum. Excluding the pyramids of Djedefre at Abu Roash and Seneferu at Meydum as outliers, the twenty-one other Old Kingdom pyramids are found in a 20 km stretch west of Memphis at Giza, Zawiyet el-Aryan, Abusir, Saqqara and Dahshur.

Egyptian pyramids are composed of a *core* comprising the bulk of the structure formed from limestone quarried nearby on the west bank, a fine outer *casing* of fine limestone quarried on the east bank (often called Tura after the site of one of the principal quarries), and *backing* stone between the core and the casing. When pyramids are formed of an inner step pyramid, *packing stone* fills in the steps or tiers.

Origin and development

The first pyramid, Zoser's Step Pyramid, began as a *mastaba*, built with small, gray "one-man" limestone blocks (of a size that one man could carry) set along roughly horizontal courses in gravel and desert clay (*tafla*), and encased with fine white limestone. The builders twice expanded the *mastaba* before they conceived the idea of a pyramid, built in six steps from roughly shaped, larger core stones, directly over the fine Tura limestone casing of the earlier *mastaba*. They built the core as a series of accretions that lean inward about 74°, an effect achieved by tilting each course toward the core of the pyramid. This kind of core masonry is found in all later step pyramids: Sekhemkhet's; the Zawiyet el-Aryan Layer Pyramid; seven small "provincial" pyramids located at or near Abydos (Sinki), Elephantine, Edfu, Hierakonpolis (el-Kula), Nagada, Seila and Zawiyet el-Amwat (Hebenu); and the two step-pyramid building stages (E1 and E2) inside the Meydum pyramid.

The true pyramid was developed during the

reign of Seneferu, who built the Meydum pyramid in seven steps and began to increase it to eight steps. Around the 15th year of his rule he founded a new pyramid necropolis at Dahshur, where he began what was intended as the first true pyramid at a steep slope of 60°. The builders still set core blocks at a tilt toward the center of the pyramid rather than on horizontal beds. As at Meydum, they built upon the desert gravel and clay, but here at Dahshur the softer surface soon threatened the steep pyramid with settling and collapse. They added a girdle around the base of the pyramid, reducing its slope to 54°31'13", but more settling and cracking prompted the builders to reduce the pyramid slope to 43°21' at about half its height, creating the Bent Pyramid. At this point they began to lay core blocks along horizontal, rather than tilted, beds.

The Northern Stone Pyramid at Dahshur was built at a uniform 43° slope. A casing fragment that can only have belonged to the southeast corner was inscribed "bringing to earth...the fifteenth time of Counting," the 28th or 30th year of his reign. During his last years, Seneferu's builders filled out the steps of his Meydum pyramid with packing stones and Tura casing, laid on horizontal beds, to create a true pyramid (E3) of 51°50'35", practically the same slope as Khufu's pyramid and within the 52–53° range of the classic Old Kingdom pyramid.

The gigantic stone pyramids, the classic pyramids of popular imagination, were built in only three generations. All other king's pyramids combined, including those of the Middle Kingdom (but excluding queens' and other satellite pyramids), contain only 54 percent of the total mass of the pyramids of Seneferu, his son Khufu and his grandson Khafre. The size of stone blocks and the quantity of gypsum mortar, as opposed to *tafla*, increased from the Dahshur to Giza pyramids. Khufu's was the largest and most accurately built and aligned of all Egyptian pyramids, rising more than 146 m from a base 230 m sq. and containing about 2.3 million blocks. Menkaure still used multi-toned stone blocks for his (the third) pyramid at Giza, but

the total mass was less than that of Zoser's Step Pyramid.

The pyramid complex

With the exceptions of Seneferu and Khufu, who had some of their chambers moved up into the very body of the pyramid, Old Kingdom rulers had their burial chambers built or carved out of bedrock below the pyramid beyond a sloping entrance corridor which pointed generally toward the northern circumpolar stars. As the superstructure of the royal tomb, the pyramid was the central element in what Egyptologists call the "pyramid complex," a standard east–west axial layout that first appeared in simple form with Seneferu's Meydum pyramid: temple or chapel at the eastern base of the pyramid, causeway, and entrance or valley temple.

Since Khafre, pyramid temples included an entrance hall that connected to the causeway, a colonnaded court, five statue niches, magazines and an inner offering hall that, certainly from the end of the 4th Dynasty, included a "false door." Walls were decorated with painted relief carving. The causeway, often walled, roofed and covered inside with painted relief, ran down the plateau to the valley temple, the entrance to the complex. The valley temples were probably accessible by a canal or a channel that held water at least during the six- to eight-week inundation season, and possibly after the flood receded. The pyramid was surrounded by one or two walls of stone or mudbrick, forming enclosures that often included a small satellite pyramid. Nearby were often smaller pyramids for principal queens. Several pyramids are flanked by pits for the burial of boats, either real or stone-built imitations.

Pyramid building

Construction theories often assume a generic pyramid on a flat level surface. However, any account of how the pyramids were built must include the composition and setting specific to each pyramid. Building 5th and 6th Dynasty pyramids, or the Middle Kingdom pyramids with a mudbrick core, were very different tasks than composing the stone-block pyramids of the early Old Kingdom to which the questions and answers about pyramid building are most often addressed. The generations who built these pyramids developed and honed the necessary skills in masonry and labor organization selectively utilized by later pyramid builders.

Laying out the pyramid base

Most of the Egyptian pyramids show a careful orientation to the cardinal directions. The sides of Khufu's pyramid, the largest (230 m to a side) and most accurately aligned, show an average deviation less than 4' of arc. Khufu's and Khafre's builders incorporated an irregular patch of natural bedrock protruding as high as 7–10 m in the middle of the pyramid base. Khufu's builders did their finest leveling, off by only 2.5 cm in the entire circumference, on a platform built of fine limestone slabs. The baseline of the Khafre pyramid was simply a vertical cut in the foot of the bottom casing course of granite, where the slope of the pyramid would meet the top surface of the pavement of the pyramid court. These builders achieved their final results with a method of successive approximation, first drawing their lines on the sloping natural surface 7–10 m higher, then successively refining their squares as they quarried away the rock to the level of the final baseline.

The builders could have determined true north by marking the rising and setting positions of northern stars over an artificially leveled horizon, or by measuring the length and angle of the shadow of a vertical pole at the same time interval before and after noon. Next, the north line had to be extended for the length of the pyramid base, without developing an increasing angle of error. During this operation, the ancient surveyors could have "checked in" to true north with a series of observation points along the line. Extending the line great distances probably required pounding stakes in the ground. Lines of regularly spaced holes around the bases of the Khufu and Khafre pyramids

may have been for staking an outside reference line, accurately marked by a taut cord from which the surveyors could establish the parallel lines of the pyramid base and its length using rods marked in cubits for incremental measurements.

Right-angled corners could have been established with the Pythagorean triangle, three of any unit on one side, four on the other and five on the hypotenuse (such triangles are found in the proportions of the Old Kingdom mortuary temples attached to pyramids); or the Egyptian set square, an A-shaped tool with perpendicular legs set at right angles and a cross brace; or by pulling two intersecting arcs of the same radius from two different center points spaced along the same line. A line connecting the points of intersection will be at a right angle to the original line. Once again, the perpendicular line had to be extended without developing an increasing angle of error.

Quarries

The core stone for the Zoser complex may have been quarried from a large trench or "moat" that surrounds the enclosure. At Dahshur and Abusir, quarries for core stone are located west of the pyramids. Most of the core limestone for the three Giza pyramids came from quarries along the low southeast part of the Mokkatam Formation, where thick layers that alternate soft–hard were advantageous for extracting large blocks. Farther south, the Ma'adi Formation's thin crumbly layers of clay and limestone provided material to build ramps. The broad wadi between the two plateaus probably served as a conduit for deliveries from outside Giza.

Casing stone was extracted from east bank quarries along terraces or banks in deep galleries that followed the best layers of stone, beginning with a "lead" shelf that would become the ceiling of the gallery. Granite was extracted from Aswan, either as natural boulders that were shaped into blocks, or quarried by means of separation channels pounded out with dolerite hammer stones.

Cutting stone

Modern Egyptian masons split very large blocks by simply etching a line with a corner of a heavy flat-headed hammer, then pounding the surface directly until the stone falls away to the desired cleavage. They also use the flat end of smaller hammers to dress the surface of a block by hitting it directly, which causes thin flakes to pop off the surface. Ancient masons did the same, albeit with dolerite hammers of diverse sizes and forms, hand-held and hafted, as we know from fragments recovered in excavations. The diversity of Old Kingdom hammer stones has yet to be cataloged.

Metal for tools was limited to copper. Use of a metal point, or "nail" for rough work, is evidenced by long, thin and deep strokes in unfinished jobs such as the subterranean chamber underneath Khufu's pyramid. The chisels used for fine dressing masonry as extensive as the pyramid casings were all the width of a thumb or less, as evidenced by chisel marks on unpolished stone. Copper chisels needed to be sharpened and reworked often.

There are numerous saw marks and drill holes on hard stone such as granite and basalt at several pyramid sites. Copper blades and cylinders guided an abrasive wet slurry of quartz sand, which did the cutting, possibly mixed with gypsum. Some ancient cuts still retain a dried mixture of quartz sand and gypsum tinted green from the copper blade.

Hauling

Rope, perhaps the most important tool in pyramid building, certainly of all block moving operations, had to be thick enough to withstand the strain of pulling multi-ton loads, yet thin enough that the haulers could get a good grip. About a dozen men could have tumbled blocks weighing two tons or more short horizontal distances by pulling on ropes tied around the top of the block while others pushed and levered from behind. Today's Egyptian quarrymen maneuver heavy blocks by tipping and turning them on a small hard fulcrum or pivot, such as a stone cobble. The ancient Egyptians used round dolerite balls like ball bearings to maneuver into position heavy sarcophagi in tombs at Giza.

Rollers, small cylindrical pieces of hard wood, could have been used for block moving, with the requirement that the underside of the load and the track must be smooth and hard. As few as ten men on two lines could pull a two-ton block up a grade that matched the lower parts of the pyramid construction ramps. To move blocks from the harbor or quarry to the pyramid exclusively by this method would have required an enormous supply of rollers, which were probably labor-intensive to produce in a country lacking the modern lathe and short on trees.

Wooden sleds and hard lubricated surfaces were most probably used for transporting blocks overland. Tomb scenes show funerary statues dragged on sleds, as a man pours water from a jar onto the surface just in front of the runners of the sled. Near the 12th Dynasty pyramids of Amenemhat I and Senusret I at el-Lisht, archaeologists have found hauling tracks composed of limestone chips, mortar and wooden beams spaced like railroad ties.

Lifting

Pyramid builders probably used ramps to raise most of the building material. Mudbrick ramps have been found near the Middle Kingdom pyramids of el-Lisht, including ramps that must have been used to raise stone up onto the pyramid of Senusret I. Construction ramps for the 4th Dynasty stone-block pyramids must have been large enough that we should expect to find sizable deposits of the material from which they were composed. At Giza, the quarries south of the pyramids are filled with millions of cubic meters of *tafla*, gypsum, and limestone chips. Remains of ancient ramps and construction embankments associated with structures other than pyramids at Giza are composed of such material.

Ideas about the form of pyramid construction ramps can be reduced to two major proposals: (1) a sloping straight ramp that ascends one face of the pyramid, and (2) one or more ramps that begin near the base and wrap around the pyramid as it rises during construction. Straight ramps have been found at the unfinished step pyramids at Sinki (South Abydos) and Saqqara (that of Sekhemkhet). Serious problems result in using a straight ramp for the higher reaches of the large 4th Dynasty pyramids. In order to maintain a low functional slope (e.g. about 1 unit of rise in 10 units of length), the straight-on ramp must be lengthened each time its height against the pyramid is increased. Either work stops during these enlargements, or the ramp is built in halves and one side serves for builder traffic while the ramp crew raises and lengthens the other half. In order to maintain a functional slope up to the highest part of the pyramid, the ramp would need to be extremely long. At Giza, this slope would take the ramp for the Khufu pyramid far to the south beyond the quarry where Khufu's builders took most of the stone for the core of his pyramid.

The wrap-around ramp has been proposed in two major forms, either supported on the slope of the pyramid or supported on the ground and leaning against the faces of the pyramid like a giant envelope with a rising roadbed on top. Since it cloaks most of the pyramid, such a ramp makes it difficult to control the squareness and slope as the pyramid rises by checking back to the part already built. A ramp founded on the 52–53° sloping faces requires extra stock of stone on the casing blocks in wide enough steps to support it, a requirement that is not met by the unfinished granite casing on the lower part of the Menkaure pyramid. Near the top, the faces of the pyramid become too narrow to support any large ramp which would anyway become increasingly steep.

The form of the supply ramps probably changed as the pyramid rose. Near the base, the builders could have delivered stone over many short ramps. As the largest pyramids rose about 30 m above ground, it is plausible that a principal ramp ran to one corner and along one side, leaning against the pyramid and gaining rise with the run. To complete the top of the pyramid, very small ramps, or levers, could have been used on steps left on the pyramid faces. Once the top was complete, the masons could have trimmed away the steps.

It has been speculated that many or most of the stones were raised by using levers to "see-saw" a block upward, raising one side at a time and placing supports underneath, then raising and supporting the opposite side, for which stepped supporting platforms would have been needed. Except for the uppermost blocks, which become smaller, it is inconceivable that such lever-lifting was used on the stepped courses of the core stone or the undressed casing stone to lift most of the blocks. Lever-lifting requires the use of well-planed wood cribbage, or stacked supports, as the blocks are raised, vastly increasing the wood requirement.

Evidence of ancient levering indicates it was mostly used for side movements and final adjustments. It is possible that levering was the only means to raise the last few blocks of the highest courses, near the apex, once the builders had brought them as far as they could on ramps.

Setting stones, rise and run

When pyramid core masonry consists of stone blocks they are loosely set with considerable mortar and debris fill, even in the Khufu pyramid, which may have the most regular core. Casing stones, however, were custom cut one to another and placed with the finest joins ever seen in any masonry.

The builders probably began by setting the corner casing stones and several stones in between to establish the "lead lines" of the four sides of the pyramid. The stonecutters in the work yard had only dressed one side— which would be the bottom—of each casing block. At or near their final places, adjacent casing blocks had their joining sides cut to fit before they were set down off rollers, wedges or other supports. The "flat-bedding" of each stone had to wait until its join face had been custom cut to fit with the next stone down the line of each course. The masons left a good amount of extra rough stone protruding on the front face of each block. As they joined one block to another, the masons drew on each block the lines where the sloping plane of the pyramid face intersected the extra stock. Then they chamfered or beveled the extra stock of stone on the outer face away from the pyramid facial lines. This beveling was a lead, created block by block, for the final dressing of the pyramid casing, starting from the top and working down to the baseline as they removed the construction ramps and embankments. As the masons cut away the extra stock to free the four faces, the beveled spaces between the blocks would come together. When the spaces between adjacent blocks closed to a fine join, the masons knew that they should not cut any deeper. They were at the desired plane of the pyramid face.

To avoid twist as the pyramid rose, the builders could have used wooden poles down on the ground as back sights aligned with the center axes and diagonals. In the rock floor around the large Giza pyramids, there are holes and notches that appear to align with the major lines of the pyramids. These have yet to be mapped.

Inner step pyramid

If the core masonry was built ahead of the fine outer casing, perhaps as a rough inner step pyramid, the masons could have transferred reference points and lines from the ground up onto the core for measuring out to the facial lines of the pyramid.

The Meydum pyramid has an inner step pyramid because it was first planned as such. The steps of the inner seven- (E1) or eight-step pyramid (E3) have fine sharp corners and faces that could have served as references for measuring set amounts out to the slope of the enlarged true pyramid. We do not know if the largest pyramids of the 4th Dynasty were built with an inner step pyramid. The cores of Menkaure's pyramid and of the pyramids of his queens and Khufu's queens are composed of great rectangular blocks of crude masonry which must have been built ahead of the casing. On the southernmost pyramid of Khufu's queens (GI-c), there are small holes, about

5 cm in diameter, near the corners of the tiers of the inner three-step pyramid. Some of these align with the casing corners near the base. The holes might have held wooden pegs that carried temporary reference lines in cord for measuring out to mark the line of the outer pyramid face in the casing blocks.

Middle to late Old Kingdom

Pyramid building changed radically following the Giza group. The last pharaoh of the 4th Dynasty, Shepseskaf, built a large *mastaba* at South Saqqara, composed of large blocks like those in the Giza pyramids. Kings of the 5th and 6th Dynasties built classic "Meydum-type" complexes, but with smaller pyramids composed of clay, rubble and smaller stones. Weserkaf, the first king of the 5th Dynasty, built a pyramid only one-thirtieth the volume of Khufu's pyramid. The core of debris and small stones may reflect the thin geological layering of the Saqqara Formation. The core of Sahure's pyramid was built of five or six steps of mud mortar and broken stone with a wide "construction gap" in the center north side that allowed the builders to work on the inner corridor and chamber while they proceeded to raise the pyramid core. Such gaps, later filled, may have been used to build internal chambers and passages for earlier pyramids such as Khufu's, where the gap might be masked by backing stones. Neferirkare built a six-tier step pyramid of well-laid, locally quarried limestone retaining walls. A single course of red granite casing was laid but never smoothed.

The cores of the 5th Dynasty pyramids are often illustrated, following Richard Lepsius and Ludwig Borchardt, as stepped accretions around a tall and narrow central tower, like pyramids of the 3rd Dynasty, but without the inward tilted beds. However, when the Czech Abusir Mission excavated the unfinished pyramid of Reneferef in the 1980s, they found no accretions in the single completed step, only an outer retaining wall of four or five courses of well-laid gray limestone blocks and an inner line of smaller blocks that framed the trench of the burial chamber and construction gap. The fill between the two frames consisted of poor quality limestone, mortar and sand.

Although his reign was triple those of his longest reigning predecessors, Pepi II's pyramid, the last of the Old Kingdom, was no larger than 150 cubits (78.60 m) square, 100 cubits (52.50 m) high, with a slope of 53°13′, the 6th Dynasty standard. The five-step core was formed by retaining walls of small irregular stones bonded in *tafla* and Nile alluvial mud, then encased with heavy blocks of Tura limestone set without mortar. The retaining walls of the core are reminiscent of retaining walls in construction ramps and embankments at Giza. In effect, the descendants of the Giza builders dispensed with heavy stone blocks and simply built the pyramid core with the material, far easier to mold and manipulate, from which their predecessors formed temporary ramps.

As the pyramid core decreased in size and quality, the fine craftsmanship, complexity and standardization of the temples was increased. The German excavators estimated Sahure's complex was adorned originally with 10,000 m^2 of painted fine relief. The highly standard pyramid temple of the 6th Dynasty included more extensive magazines than early Old Kingdom temples, a clear separation by means of a transverse hallway between an outer temple (entrance hall, court, magazines) and inner temple (five-statue niche, single-pillar antechamber, offering hall). The pyramid interior, consisting of a standard three-part magazine, antechamber and burial chamber, included, since Unas, *Pyramid Texts* for the royal afterlife. The decrease in pyramid size and durability probably reflects a decrease in social and political centralization during the half-millennium of the Old Kingdom.

See also

Abu Roash; Abusir; Dahshur, Middle Kingdom pyramids; funerary texts; Giza, Khafre pyramid complex; Giza, Khufu pyramid complex; Giza, Menakure pyramid complex; el-Lisht; Meydum; Old Kingdom, overview; quarrying; Saqqara, pyramids of the 3rd Dynasty; Saqqara, pyramids of the 5th and 6th Dynasties; Seila/Silah; Zawiyet el-Aryan

Further reading

General surveys

Edwards, I.E.S. 1993. *The Pyramids of Egypt.* London.

Labrousse, A. 1996. *L'Architecture des Pyramides à Textes* 1: *Saqqara Nord* (IFAO, Mission archéologique de Saqqara III). Cairo.

Lauer, J.-P. 1962. *Histoire monumentale des Pyramides d'Egypte. Tomb I. Les Pyramides à Degrés (IIIe Dynastie)* (IFAO, BdÉ 39). Cairo.

Lehner, M. 1997. *Complete Pyramids.* London.

Maragioglio, V., and C.A. Rinaldi. 1963–77. *L'Architettura delle Piramidi Menfite,* 8 vols. Turin and Rapallo.

Stadelmann, R. 1985. *Die Ägyptischen Pyramiden: von Ziegelbau zum Weltwunder.* Mainz.

Pyramid building

Arnold, D. 1991. *Building in Egypt: Pharaonic Stone Masonry.* New York.

Clarke, S., and R. Engelbach. 1930. *Ancient Egyptian Masonry.* London.

Quarries

Harrell, J.A., and V.M. Brown. 1995. *Topographical and Petrological Survey of Ancient Egyptian Quarries.* Toledo, OH.

Klemm, D., and R. Klemm. 1981. *Steine der Pharaonen.* Munich.

Röder, J. 1965. Steinbruchgeschichte des Rosengranits von Assuan. *Archäologischer Anzeiger* 3: 461–551.

Survey and alignment

Borchardt, L. 1926. *Längen und Richtungen der vier Grundkanten der grossen Pyramide bie Gise.* Berlin.

Dorner, J. 1981. *Die Absteckung und*

astronomische Orientierung ägyptischer Pyramiden. Innsbruck.

Lehner, M. 1983. Some observations on the layout of the pyramids of Khufu and Khafre. *JARCE* 20: 7–25.

Ramps, levers, lifting theories

Arnold, D. 1981. Uberlegungenzum Problem des Pyramidenbaues. *MDAIK* 37: 15–28.

Dunham, D. 1956. Building an Egyptian pyramid. *Archaeology* 9(3): 159–65.

Rise and run, casing

Lally, M. 1989. Engineering a pyramid. *JARCE* 26: 207–18.

Building a late Old Kingdom pyramid

Pfirsch, L. 1990. Les Bâtisseurs des pyramides de Saqqara. In *Saqqara*, C. Berger, ed., 32–5. Dijon.

MARK LEHNER

Q

Qantir/Pi-Ramesses

The site of Pi-Ramesses (the "City of Ramesses"), the Delta residence of the Ramesside kings (19th–20th Dynasties), is situated in the eastern Nile Delta, about 100 km northeast of Cairo and 80 km west of Ismailia on the Suez Canal (30°48′ N, 31°50′ E). The modern name of the site is Qantir, a village north of Faqus.

The Pelizaeus-Museum Hildesheim, Germany, has been excavating this settlement in order to reconstruct the architecture and living conditions of the Ramesside capital. Evidence for relations between Egypt and the eastern Mediterranean is of special interest. This includes not only political relations, but also the introduction of new technologies. Two major results of the work at this site are: (1) the discovery of a vast, quasi-industrial metalworking area for bronze covering at least 30,000 m^2; and (2) evidence for the presence of Hittites and Mycenaeans, as represented by their tools and artifacts, in a large complex of chariot workshops and stables—unique for the eastern Mediterranean. These discoveries illuminate the foreign relations of Ramesside Egypt, which up to this time have been known mainly from the cuneiform archives at Hattusa/Boghazköy in Anatolia.

The location of Pi-Ramesses at Qantir has been greatly disputed by Egyptologists. The first attempts to locate Pi-Ramesses concentrated on the northern and middle parts of the eastern Nile Delta. Heinrich Brugsch identified Pi-Ramesses with Tanis/San el-Hagar; Alan Gardiner looked for it at Pelusium; Édouard Naville considered the fortress of Zaru or Sile, which has now been located at the site of the modern city of el-Qantara, near the Suez Canal. The most convincing of these theories was the identification of Pi-Ramesses with Tanis, because the latter site contained enormous quantities of Ramesside monuments. The French excavator of Tanis, Pierre Montet, then identified Tanis with the residence of Ramesses II, which was accepted by most scholars.

The main credit for establishing the location of Pi-Ramesses at Qantir goes to two Egyptian scholars, Labib Habachi and Mahmond Hamza. It was Habachi who first connected the ancient site of Pi-Ramesses geographically with the capital of the Hyksos, Avaris, situated at the site of Tell ed-Dab'a, about 1 km south of Qantir. Fifty years later, Habachi's theory was confirmed by Manfred Bietak of the University of Vienna, the excavator of Avaris/Tell ed-Dab'a and the southern parts of Pi-Ramesses, and by the Pelizaeus-Museum mission working in the northern parts.

The area of ancient Pi-Ramesses, stretching over more than 30 km^2 within the region of Qantir/Tell ed-Dab'a, is now covered by a number of small settlements surrounded by agricultural land and divided by numerous, small irrigation canals. One of the archaeological mission's goals is to uncover not only palaces and temples, but also evidence from everyday life. Because most of the settlement is now cultivated and is privately owned, only small parts of the ancient city can be investigated, but the results of these excavations are extremely valuable.

The site of Pi-Ramesses includes stratigraphy dating from the beginning of the 18th Dynasty through the Ramesside era up to the Third Intermediate Period. Thus, the city came into existence much earlier and lasted longer than has been estimated from the textual evidence. It is now clear that the capital continued to be occupied after the end of the 20th Dynasty.

The first fully preserved stratum (B2) at Qantir, in area Q I, contains remains of the first chariot garrison excavated in the Near East, with associated multi-functional workshops, including evidence for the presence of foreigners. Pottery and inscribed artifacts from this stratum can be dated to the reigns of Seti I and Ramesses II. The existence of a chariot garrison had already been postulated on the basis of textual evidence (the "Praise of the Delta Residence Pi-Ramesses"). The chariotry complex contains a wide, pillared exercise court, which had been modified several times. Within the court and nearby workshops some 400 artifacts were found which can be associated with chariots. The well-preserved chariots from Tutankhamen's tomb have helped to identify these artifacts as the stone finials of chariots, attached at the yoke, pole and the rear end of the chariot body. Also found here were several kinds of daggers, lances and arrowheads, metal scales of body armor, a complete pair of horse-bits, a navehub and a linchpin. The navehub is unique, not only in Egypt, but in the entire ancient world. These finds, combined with the discovery of hoofprints in the corresponding layers, clearly identify the court and surrounding workshops as the chariot garrison of Pi-Ramesses known from textual sources.

The most interesting finds of the multi-functional workshops were stone molds for the manufacture of metal applications for shield rims, such as those carried by Hittite troops in the Battle of Qadesh in Syria. They prove that Hittite workmen and soldiers were present at Pi-Ramesses, living and interacting with Egyptians after the peace treaty between the Hittite king Ḥattusili III and Ramesses II, which had been consolidated through the first diplomatic marriage of Ramesses II with a daughter of Ḥattusili III (*M3't-nfrw-R'*). This treaty not only exists on an Egyptian stela from Karnak and on a cuneiform tablet from Ḥattusa, but also in the reality of peaceful cooperation between Hittites and Egyptians within the chariotry garrison of Ramesses II.

There is even more evidence for the presence of foreigners at Pi-Ramesses; Mycenaeans are represented by large quantities of their pottery and a scale of a Mycenaean boar's tusk helmet, of the type carried exclusively by high-ranking Mycenaean officials. Pottery from Cyprus, the Levant and Hittite Anatolia has also been excavated. From this evidence, there is little doubt that real ambassadors stayed and lived at Pi-Ramesses.

Stratum B3 at Qantir (in area Q I), which dates to the late 18th to early 19th Dynasties, contains a huge workshop for bronze production which covers an area of at least $30,000 \text{ m}^2$. This evidence corrects the widely held assumption that Egyptians were working only in small-scale metal workshops. In total, the mission uncovered seven "melting channels," approximately 15 m long and built of parallel rows of mudbricks about 20 cm apart, into which blast pipes were inserted. These blast pipes were worked by pot bellows, as is depicted on many paintings in private Theban tombs of the New Kingdom. Adhesive slags and embedded remains of bronze, as well as crucibles with the same features, define these installations as a bronze-melting factory in which several hundred people worked. Huge quantities of melted bronze could be produced in a single day for large-scale artifacts, such as doors and statues, which were needed during the enlargement of the capital.

In the same stratum a series of at least three furnaces of a new type were excavated north of the melting channels. These were called "cross-furnaces" because of their cross-like design, measuring 9 m north–south and 8 m east–west. The highest temperature was achieved from top to bottom and from the center to the outer regions of the cross-furnace, judging from the oxidation of the originally unburnt mudbricks. Since the slag adhering to the furnaces is similar to that discovered in the melting channels, the cross-furnaces may also be connected with bronze processing. Possibly these were casting devices of a previously unknown type from this period, but this hypothesis will have to be confirmed by further studies.

In another excavation area at Qantir (Q IV), about 250 m east of Q I, totally different structures have been uncovered. This area contains a single monumental structure that covers an area of at least 15,000 m². Its plan is something of a novelty, and consists of five architectural units repeated from north to south. Each unit is made up of a mudbrick pylon with a west–east entrance and a large open court, off which is a pillared hall with ten palmiform columns and eleven or more rooms. To date only the western side of this structure has been found. This structure can be identified as stables, each of which has six *in situ* tethering stones associated with six limestone "drains." Animal urine was directed to the drain openings in the center of the room through an incline in the whitewashed floors away from the walls. In addition to these installations, each stable room has an area, mostly in the south, where domestic pottery, tools and other artifacts of daily life (e.g. game pieces and game boards) were found. Other finds, such as stone chariot finials, weapons and door lintels with representations of horses, suggest that chariot horses were kept in these stables. A minimum of 460 horses could have been housed in the stables, as well as the personnel attending them. As the stables of area Q IV belong stratigraphically and chronologically to the chariot garrison of area Q I, together they represent the infrastructure for a chariotry complex with horse stables, exercise court and repair works.

Recently evidence was discovered at the site for a sanctuary dedicated to Astarte, the Syrian goddess of love and war, and protectress of the royal horse team, the first evidence in Egypt for such a sanctuary. Her name is preserved in hieroglyphs on a portico column from the stables. In addition, a relief from area Q IV is of the lower part of an offering scene, with the king in front of the cult statue of Astarte on horseback. This closely coincides with the description in Papyrus Anastasi II 4–5 identifying different districts of the city with four deities: "Her west is the House of Amen, the south is the House of Seth, Astarte is situated in her east and Wadjet is in her north." The temple of Seth has been found by Bietak at Tell ed-Dab'a to the south. Shehata Adam excavated a temple in the north, which may be attributed to the snake goddess Wadjet. The stables are located to the east of the axis between these two temples.

See also

Aegean peoples; army; chariots; Cypriot peoples; metallurgy; Tanis (San el-Hagar); Tell ed-Dab'a, Second Intermediate Period

Further reading

Bietak, M. 1984. Ramsesstadt. In *LÄ* 5: 128–46. Wiesbaden.

Gore, R. 1991. Ramses the Great. *National Geographic* 179(4): 2–31.

Pusch, E.B. 1996. "Pi-Ramesses-Beloved-of-Amun, Headquarters of thy Chariotry." Egyptians and Hittites in the Delta Residence of the Ramessides. In *Pelizaeus-Museum Hildesheim Guidebook: The Egyptian Collection*, A. Eggebracht, ed., 126–44. Mainz.

EDGAR B. PUSCH
ANJA HEROLD

Qasr Ibrim

Qasr Ibrim is located on a high bluff on the east bank of the Nile, some 116 km north of the Egyptian–Sudanese border and 238 km south of Aswan (22°39′ N, 32°00′ E). Its occupation spans *circa* 1000 BC to AD 1813. It is the only substantial ancient site to have survived the flooding of Lower Nubia with the construction of the Aswan High Dam. At the highest lake levels (which were recorded in 1979–80) around 70 percent of the walled town remained unflooded. The hyperarid conditions of Lower Nubia, combined with the elevated position of the site above the Nile, have resulted in the exceptional preservation of organic materials. Numerous textiles, baskets, leather and wooden artifacts have been recovered. Biological residues include seeds, coprolites and lipids, as well as soft animal tissues. Texts are preserved on papyrus, parchment and paper as well as on stone, pottery and wood and as grafitti. The main languages or scripts found on the site are hieroglyphic, hieratic, Demotic, Meroitic, Greek, Latin, Coptic, Old Nubian, Arabic and Turkish.

The area was known in medieval and modern times as Ibrim, with the place-name of Qal'at or Qasr Ibrim applied to the fortress. Ibrim is probably a corruption of Primis, Prima and Premnis, names given by classical authors, which themselves are probably versions of the Meroitic Pedeme. The Egyptian version of the name is not known; as the site lay within the pharaonic locality of Mi'am, this may have been applied to both sides of the river.

The earliest remains come not from the hilltop, but cut into the side of the rock-face at river level. Six shrines were recorded by Ricardo Caminos in 1961, before they were removed to Wadi es-Sebua with the flooding of the lake; four commemorate viceroys of Kush and range in date from Tuthmose III to Ramesses II. On another headland to the south, there was a rock-cut inscription of Seti I and his viceroy, Amenemope, as well as a series of New Kingdom grafitti. These most probably relate to the important site of Aniba, the residency of the viceroy, located on the west bank, almost opposite to Ibrim, but now completely flooded.

New Kingdom occupation on the hilltop itself remains unproven. Several pieces of carved stone of New Kingdom date have been excavated from the site; none is from early contexts, and it must be assumed that they have been brought from elsewhere during post-pharaonic times. Among notable finds is a small granite obelisk of Hatshepsut, laid in a stairway of Christian date, a door lintel of Amenhotep II, set at the entrance to the Meroitic temple and a stela of Amenhotep I, found in the Cathedral.

Stratified deposits belong to the early first millennium BC, on the basis of radiocarbon dates. A fortification was built around the cliff, with an entrance facing to the southeast. The wall was built with outer and inner faces of mudbrick and a core of pitched stones; an internal stair suggests that there was also a walkway at an upper level. The entrance was subsequently modified, then encased in a large stone tower, which was in turn surrounded by a mudbrick bastion. A stone terrace, which was built against this bastion, contains a mudbrick temple with sandstone column drums bearing the cartouche of Taharka. Within the fortress, a number of mudbrick structures of a domestic and administrative nature have been found with associated deposits containing mainly Napatan (25th Dynasty) pottery. This sequence contradicts the received interpretation that Lower Nubia was abandoned at the end of the New Kingdom; at Ibrim, it seems that fortifications were maintained in good order until the 25th Dynasty. These levels have also provided evidence for the early use of domestic camel.

There was considerable building activity at the site between the 25th Dynasty and the Roman occupation; this may be Ptolemaic or very early Meroitic. Remains include the construction of the South Gate, the Podium, a large stone temple and a further phase of defensive wall. The Podium is a notable structure, similar in plan to temple quays, known from Karnak, Kalabsha and Philae. The Ibrim example, however, is located 70 m above the Nile and faced a dry wadi rather than the Nile. It remains undated except through its stratigraphic association, although it does contain a Greek inscription (unread).

The Roman military occupation at Ibrim is documented both by classical sources (notably Strabo and Cassius Dio) and by archaeological evidence. The campaign against the Meroites concluded with a peace treaty in 21 BC, which established the southern frontier of Egypt at Maharraqa, north of Ibrim. In the intervening period, Gaius Petronius, the Roman prefect, fortified and garrisoned Ibrim, with sufficient food for 400 men for two years and "made the place thoroughly secure by sundry devices." The existing walls were heightened, and a large bastion was constructed facing upriver. Military artifacts have been found, notably by the southern defensive wall. Here textiles, baskets, leather, including sandals, imported amphorae and *terra sigillata* and a small number of coins were dumped around 21 BC, when the garrison moved out. Manuscripts have also been found, including a papyrus containing nine lines of elegaic verse, which have been attributed to Petronius's predecessor as prefect, Cornelius Gallus. Excavation within the fortress has revealed scant remains of buildings associated with the military occupation, although survey of an adjacent area of desert plateau identified two Roman siege camps.

Nubian people seem to have moved in after the Roman evacuation. The main evidence comes from the eastern terraces of the site, which have produced sizable assemblages of first century BC/AD Meroitic pottery. The survey of the desert to the rear of the site has yielded further examples of this pottery, often associated with robbed burial sites and dry stone-walled structures. This area seems to have been a cemetery and possibly a festival ground. By AD 250, Ibrim was a major Meroitic center. A new stone temple was constructed with extensive magazines on one side. A further unexcavated temple may also belong to this period, with a processional way cut through the rock to link the two structures. On the south and east sides of the site, mudbrick buildings suggest a permanent population. Considerable numbers of Meroitic papyri have been excavated, which, while remaining largely unread, point to the importance of the site as an administrative as well as a religious center. A number of significant innovations can be noted in the late Meroitic period, including the cultivation of summer crops, the use of the *saqqiya* irrigation and the local use of cotton cloth.

The transition to the X-Group period around AD 400 resulted in few changes in the use of the fortress. Houses were now built on a more extensive scale; the storage areas incorporated within them have produced a wealth of sealed artifacts, environmental material as well as pottery. The population remained strongly pagan; at least one more temple was constructed in stone, and possibly a second in mudbrick, making a total of six on the site. The extensive barrow cemeteries in the valleys below excavated by Walter Emery in 1961 date to this period. Texts, including correspondence between kings of the Nobatae and the Blemmyes, suggest that Ibrim remained an important administrative center.

Christianity seems to have been introduced relatively peacefully during the latter part of the sixth century, and it is just possible that Ibrim was chosen by the early monophysite missionary Longinus as his residence in Nobatae during *circa* 569–75; an ostracon apparently bearing his name has been found at the site. There is some evidence for a transitional phase between paganism and Christianity at Ibrim, including a richly furnished X-Group tomb, decorated with a single rock-cut cross, and a tomb within the Cathedral containing X-Group grave goods. One pagan temple was clearly ransacked at the conversion, with a few objects safely buried in nearby storage pits. The Taharka temple, however, was converted to a church, on ceramic evidence during the late sixth century. Two other surviving churches, the Period One Cathedral and the Church on the Point, may also date to the late sixth or seventh century. From the latter church, possible sixth-century liturgical objects, including a book cover, have been found. The Cathedral was largely constructed from stones taken from the Meroitic temples nearby; the nave was flanked by granite columns and capitals brought from Aswan, which are stylistically very close to those used in the sixth-century church at Philae.

The Cathedral was later rebuilt on an even grander scale, and repaired again, possibly after an Ayyubid raid of 1172–3. Outside the Cathedral, the robbed tombs of bishops have also been found, containing their stelae in Coptic as well as the remains of shrouds made from tiraz cloth of Fatimid date. The only intact burial of a bishop found on the site was that of Timouthias, buried inside the Cathedral, with his testimonial letters, dating to shortly after 1378. The last bishop of Ibrim is noted in a document from Gebel Adda dated 1484; it is likely that around this time the Christian occupation ceased. Apart from the Cathedral and its bishop, Ibrim was also the residence of the Eparch, the Christian official appointed by the king of Makurra, to regulate trade with the Muslim north as was set out in the *bagt* treaty. Official correspondence has been found documenting this trade, including an Arabic letter, dated AD 759, listing violations. Later correspondence dates to the Fatimid period and notes such places as Aidhab on the Red Sea and Soba to the south at the confluence of the Blue and White Niles. Artifacts from long-distance trade include glass, ceramics (including luster wares) and cloth. The archaeological sequence has been divided into the Early (600–850), Classic (850–1170) and Late Christian periods (1170–1500) on the basis of Nubian ceramics; numerous houses, with associated occupation deposits containing both artifacts and documents, have been found. The main languages in use were Old Nubian, Coptic and Arabic.

The final occupation was as a military fortress, forming part of the southern frontier of the Ottoman empire, established *circa* 1560–70, by the creation of a *sanjak* between the First and Second Cataracts; Ibrim was a supply point with Sai, to the south, acting as the forward base. In 1589 there were around seventy soldiers in the garrison and these numbers seem to have been maintained until 1650, largely on a hereditary basis. The earliest Turkish document from Ibrim dates to 1576; in the decades thereafter, numerous documents have been found representing vouchers, pay chits, letters and legal documents written in both Arabic and Turkish. The Ottoman levels have also produced the widest range of artifactual material, including textiles, leather, basketry and wooden objects. Along with the documentary evidence, these permit a minute reconstruction of daily life during this period.

Biennial excavations have taken place at Qasr Ibrim, under the aegis of the Egypt Exploration Society of London, since 1961. Results have been reported in the *Journal of Egyptian Archaeology*, as well as in specialist monographs published by the Society.

See also

Meroitic culture; Nubian forts; Nubian towns and temples

Further reading

Adams, W.Y. 1982. Qasr Ibrim: an archaeological conspectus. In *Nubian Studies: Proceedings of the Symposium for Nubian Studies, 1978*, J. Plumley, ed., 25–33. Warminster.

Caminos, R.A. 1968. *The Shrines and Rock Inscriptions of Ibrim*. London.

Horton, M. 1991. Africa and Egypt: new evidence from Qasr Ibrim. In *Egypt and Africa*, W.V. Davies, ed., 264–77. London.

Mills, A.J. 1982. *The Cemeteries of Qasr Ibrim*. London.

MARK HORTON

Qau el-Kebir (Antaeopolis), Dynastic sites

Archaeological sites at Qau el-Kebir (26°54′ N, 31°31′ E) dating to pharaonic times are in the following locations:

1 An area to the east of the village of Qau with a 6th Dynasty *mastaba* (tomb superstructure), which is now destroyed. To the south of this *mastaba* are two cemeteries. The northern cemetery, Cemetery 400, is near the modern village. The southern one is known as the "Southern Cemetery."

2 An area on the slopes of the local limestone cliffs to the south of the prehistoric site at Hemamieh, with rock-cut tombs of Middle Kingdom nomarchs and other less important officials.

3 Two areas with burials dating to the Late and Graeco-Roman periods. Cemetery A-H is located near the rock-cut tombs of Ibu and Wahka II. The other cemetery (1450) is at the base of the limestone cliffs. There is also some archaeological evidence here from the Middle and New Kingdoms.

4 A quarrying area northeast of the rock-cut tombs with evidence of use during the New Kingdom and Graeco-Roman times.

5 An area to the southwest of the village of Qau with a Ptolemaic period temple that was recorded in 1820 but is now destroyed.

There is very little archaeological evidence at Qau el-Kebir from the Old Kingdom. A few hieratic inscriptions on potsherds, including two with the name of Pepi II (6th Dynasty), can be dated from the 4th to 11th Dynasties.

During the Middle Kingdom the region was particularly important, which can be inferred from the large tombs belonging to three nomarchs: Wahka I, Ibu and Wahka II (Ibu's brother). These three tombs are located in the western sector of the Middle Kingdom cemetery. The tomb of Ibu is about 50 m to the east of that of Wahka I, and the tomb of Wahka II is about 130 m from that of Ibu. A small tomb belonging to Sobekhotep is near the tomb of Wahka II.

The Qau el-Kebir tombs were excavated in the first half of this century by the Italian Archaeological Mission (1905–6), the Ernst von Sieglin Expedition (1913–14), and the British School of Archaeology in Egypt (1923–4). The well equipped tombs contained large, inscribed limestone sarcophagi, and statues in limestone, granite and diorite. Tomb scenes of great artistic skill were painted or carved in relief. Such evidence confirms the high status of these Middle Kingdom nomarchs (governors), and they have been compared in quality to contemporaneous ones belonging to Khnumhotep (Beni Hasan), Djehutyhotep (Deir el-Bersha) and Sarenput (Aswan).

Artifacts from the three nomarchs' tombs at Qau el-Kebir are now in the Egyptian collections in Turin, Leipzig and London (University College). Unfortunately, a comprehensive study of these tombs has yet to be published.

There are many problems concerning the dating of the three tombs. Flinders Petrie noted that the name "Wahka" appears 197 times in inscriptions from the 6th through the 12th Dynasties (including the owner of Cairo stela 20549). Petrie suggested that the name "Wahka" is derived from the name of King Khetj (Wah-ka-Re) of the 9th Dynasty. This could be supported by the epithet "Wah-ka-nefer" ("the good *ka* endures"), which appears on many scarabs before the 12th Dynasty.

The earliest of the three nomarchs' tombs at Qau el-Kebir (Tomb 7) belonged to Wahka I. A stela in the Drovetti Collection, and a life-size statue from the tomb now in the Egyptian Museum, Turin, record the names of his father

(Sobek-djjw), mother (Neferhotep) and wife (Sobek-djjt). Georg Steindorff suggested that the tomb dates to the reign of Amenemhat II (12th Dynasty). While the inscriptions could date to the 11th or early 12th Dynasty, the sculptures seem to be later in style.

A 12th Dynasty date could be supported by the name of Wahka II's son, Senusret-ankh, suggesting a direct link with the Theban royal family of this dynasty. A stela in Stockholm, from the reign of Amenemhat III, mentions the nomarch Wahka, who was the son of the nomarch Nakht. A fragment of Nakht's wooden coffin was found by the Italian Archaeological Mission in the tomb of Wahka II. On the basis of this evidence the tombs of Ibu and Wahka II have been dated to mid-12th Dynasty. The earlier tomb of Ibu dates to the reign of Senusret III.

The architecture of the three nomarchs' tombs includes a lower courtyard entered by a covered passageway carved at the foot of the cliffs. Stairs connect the courtyard with an upper porch, with columns or pilasters, connected to a hall with pilasters. To the right of this hall is a small room, probably for storage. An outer chapel with a barrel vault was located beyond the pilastered hall. Beyond this is an inner chapel with a central niche for the statue of the tomb owner. In a hall around this chapel are shafts to burial chambers. The plan of the tomb of Wahka I is the simplest one, with the burial chambers aligned parallel to the main axis of the tomb. The plans of the tombs of Ibu and Wahka II are more complex.

Polychrome paintings on the ceiling of the tomb of Wahka II, of geometric and vegetal motifs, are remarkable, as are the reliefs and statues in the three tombs. Reliefs include offering scenes, and scenes of hunting and fishing in the marshes. The statues, usually life-size, were carved in granite or limestone and painted. Unfortunately, only a statue of Wahka I in the Egyptian Museum, Turin, and another one still *in situ* in his tomb, beneath the stairs from the lower court to the porch, are completely preserved.

Other tomb furnishings include sarcophagi, offering tables and the base of an altar. The sarcophagi are rectangular in section with lids that are arched inside. Tomb goods include canopic jars, which contained the viscera, and pottery with a red slip. Inscriptions on the walls of a small burial chamber in the tomb of Wahka II, belonging to a man named Henib, are particularly interesting. They record some chapters of the *Theology of [the god] Shu*, the *Heliopolitan Cosmology* and some excerpts from the *Pyramid Texts*. An inscribed stela and pots of scented unguent for the deceased are painted on one wall of this chamber.

Near the tomb of Wahka II is Tomb 14, which belonged to Sobekhotep. This tomb is certainly less impressive than those of Wahka I, Ibu and Wahka II. It includes a hall that leads to a chapel with a niche for the deceased's statue, and a shaft to the burial chamber, which contained a limestone sarcophagus. Other tombs recorded here by Petrie (2–6, 9–12, 15 and 17) are even more simple in design than that of Sobekhotep.

Some evidence suggests that this cemetery was also used sporadically after the Middle Kingdom. In a tomb near Tomb 12 were some fragments of reliefs and inscriptions with the name Nubkhaes, and alabaster vessels dating to the 17th Dynasty, now in University College London. Some fragments of a sarcophagus with the name Mai, dating to the 19th Dynasty, were discovered to the southeast of the tomb of Wahka II. In the area of the quarries, to the northwest of the Middle Kingdom tombs, a passageway was excavated with mudbrick walls and the cartouches of Amenhotep III (18th Dynasty).

Most burials between the tombs of Wahka II and Ibu, and at the base of the limestone cliffs, date to the Graeco-Roman period. They consist of simple pits, often coffin-shaped, and shaft tombs with a plastered and painted burial chamber. Sometimes they are decorated with vine motifs. Rectangular or square funerary chapels in mudbrick are also found here. Some chapels have barrel vaults and niches, usually on the west side, but less frequently on the east. Coffins from these tombs are made of clay or stone, and less frequently of wood. A sarcophagus belonging to an "overseer of the [scented] unguents," Petosiris, is particularly notable.

Other artifacts dating to the early first millennium AD, from robbed tombs, have also been collected here. These include potsherds, amulets, fragments of plaster mummy masks and ornaments, vessels of faïence or bronze, and ceramic lamps decorated with the figure of a frog. The frog was a propitious symbol for the continued existence of the deceased in the afterlife. Graeco-Roman period evidence was also found in the area of the quarries, to the east of the rock-cut tombs. An image here of the local god Antaeus, from which the Greek name of the town (Antaeopolis) is derived, is particularly remarkable.

See also

Asyut; Beni Hasan; Deir el-Bersha; Meir; Middle Kingdom, overview; representational evidence, Middle Kingdom private tombs

Further reading

D'Amicone, E. 1990. Qaw el-Kebir. In *Beyond the Pyramids. Egyptian Regional Art from the Museo Egizio, Turin*, G. Robbins, ed. Atlanta, GA.

Petrie, W.M.F. 1930. *Antaeopolis, The Tombs of Qau*. London.

Steckeweh, H. 1936. *Die Fürstengräber von Qaw*. Leipzig.

ELVIRA D'AMICONE

quarrying

The land of Egypt is rich with a readily available variety of hard and soft stones which lend themselves to exploitation by the inhabitants of the Nile Valley, in contrast to ancient Mesopotamia, where stone of any kind is scarce. The principal stones native to Egypt are alabaster (Egyptian alabaster is calcite, not gypsum alabaster), limestone, sandstone, diorite, granite and quartzite.

The two types of quarrying carried out in

Egypt can be classified as open and covered cutting. Where the stone was of good quality and consistent density on or near the surface, it could be exposed from the top and sides of cliffs, but occasionally it was necessary to cut tunnels and galleries to follow the veins of material of best quality. The open method was obviously the most efficient and least complicated procedure, whereas the tunneling method was complicated by problems of lighting, dust and safety. The extensive galleries in the limestone quarries of Tura, east of Cairo, provide considerable evidence of the techniques of covered cutting.

The earliest utilization of stone was restricted to the crude adaptation and alteration of material found loose, or pieces which had naturally become detached from a matrix, such as large pebbles, stones and boulders. Early in the Dynastic period, with the wider availability of copper tools, the possibility of separating and removing large pieces of stone from the natural rock formations became more practical and could be accomplished with a higher degree of efficiency. The discovery of the technique of hardening copper by hammering and tempering it by annealing made it possible to use metal even more efficiently in the quarrying process. Hammering increased the hardness of copper by about one-third, thus making it a much more useful cutting material.

The only evidence preserved as to the actual methods employed to remove stone from a quarry are the traces left in the ancient beds and on the surfaces of unfinished blocks, where the characteristic marks of picks, saws and chisels can be recognized. With the more common use of metal at the beginning of pharaonic history, it became possible to deal with soft stones such as limestone and alabaster with greater ease. Whereas soft-stone quarrying apparently employed metal as well as stone tools, it is likely that the process of hard-stone quarrying always employed a system of pounding and pecking with balls of yet harder stone, such as dolerite. Until recently it was usually assumed that stones such as granite and diorite were detached from the quarry bed through a process which involved cutting rows of slots, inserting wooden wedges into the slots and

wetting the wood to cause it to swell, thus forcing the stone to crack along the predetermined lines. It is now considered by many scholars that the work was done by pounding with stone tools and with the use of large levers, rather than the inserted wedges, to detach the block which had been undercut. The use of fire and water for alternate heating and quenching has also been suggested for the splitting or detaching of hard stones and it seems possible that fire heating was used for the removal of a surface layer of lesser quality stone in order to reveal the more solid and consistent material below.

Hard stones such as flint, chert and crystalline limestone were fashioned with wooden handles into picks or mauls; these were employed in the working of softer stones. It is entirely possible that small points of flint and chert were used in the production of inscriptions and reliefs in soft stone. The ready availability of flint and chert as inclusions in limestone beds, taken together with the fact that representations of stone workers using stone tools are known and actual examples of such tools have been found, all suggest that stone was used as a tool material long after the introduction of metal.

The basic method for quarrying all kinds of stone began with the identification of an unflawed area of material. The desired block was then isolated by cutting small trenches around it. It was detached from its bed with the use of levers. These techniques have been ascertained by the inspection of the remains of ancient quarries, particularly where the outline of the blocks have not been completely removed, as in the limestone quarries north of the Khafre pyramid at Giza or where the block itself is still in place, as is the famous unfinished obelisk preserved in the granite quarry at Aswan.

In most cases, building blocks were partially dressed in the quarry and material intended for use as objects such as sarcophagi or sculpture was partly carved to reduce weight in transportation. In construction the stone was generally cut and fit on the building site, thus reducing the time that would have been needed for the care involved in producing standardized units at the quarry. Readily available stone in nearby derelict buildings, already cut to cubic units, could be re-employed at great saving of time and labor, but even irregular blocks and statue parts were often used as fill material. There is some indication that the reuse of stone from monuments of predecessors might have political or religious significance as well. This tactic, typically used in ancient Egyptian construction, was employed time and time again, to obvious economy in the building process.

See also

cult temples, construction techniques; metallurgy; sculpture (stone), production techniques

Further reading

Arnold, D. 1991. *Building in Egypt: Pharaonic Stone Masonry.* London.

Clarke, S., and R. Englebach. 1930. *Ancient Egyptian Masonry.* Oxford.

Lucas, A. 1962. *Ancient Egyptian Materials and Industries.* 4th edn. revised and enlarged by J.R. Harris. London.

Reisner, G.A. 1931. *Mycerinus: The Temples of the Third Pyramid at Giza.* Cambridge, MA.

WILLIAM H. PECK

Quft/Qift (Coptos)

Ancient Coptos is on the east bank of the Nile, 38 km northeast of Luxor (26°00′ N, 32°49′ E). Inhabited from at least Early Dynastic to modern times, it was the capital of Nome V of Upper Egypt. Located at a point of the Nile closest to the Red Sea, it was an important trade center and gateway to the mineral resources of the Eastern Desert from earliest times. In Graeco-Roman times, with the opening of trade routes from the Mediterranean to India by way of the Eastern Desert and the Red Sea, it became a major trans-shipment point. Today the greater part of the site lies under the modern village of Quft/Qift.

Large-scale excavations at the site were conducted by Flinders Petrie in 1893–4, and by Adolf Reinach and Raymond Weill in 1910 and 1911. Both expeditions focused on the ruins in the southeast sector of the modern town, where Petrie found remains of a sacred enclosure (*temenos*) dominated by a temple to Min, Isis and Horus. According to Petrie, this temple was built by Tuthmose III and was probably rebuilt and enlarged by Ptolemy II, with numerous dedications by later Ptolemies and Roman emperors through Caracalla. Although Petrie found no architecture earlier than the 18th Dynasty, artifacts excavated under and around the temple, including torsos of three colossal statues, indicate cultic use of the area by the Early Dynastic period, and probably earlier.

For the most part, Reinach and Weill worked to the southwest of the temple, where they found several small temples, shrines and dedications ranging in date from Nectanebo II (26th Dynasty) to Ptolemy XIV, and Roman emperors from Augustus through Claudius. The earliest temple here was dedicated to the god Geb, who appears to be the principal deity worshipped in this sector. Houses attributed to the reign of Diocletian were built over the temple wall and signal the end of the cultic use of the area. Reinach and Weill also explored an area of Christian churches to the west of Petrie's temple. The size and architectural quality of this complex convinced Reinach that Coptos must have been one of the metropoleis of the Coptic church. The French team also explored some Roman houses outside the east wall of the *temenos* (Kom el-Ahmar) and a temple in the northern suburb of el-Qal'a, built during the reign of Tiberius.

From 1987 to 1992 a University of Michigan– University of Asyut team, led by Sharon Herbert and Henry Wright and overseen by Ahmad El-Sawy, excavated in Ptolemaic– Roman levels to the north and east of the Min temple. The primary goal of this expedition was to produce a datable stratified sequence of local ceramics, which, analyzed in conjunction with finds from the fortified stations in the Eastern Desert, would allow close dating and better understanding of the Graeco-Roman trade routes to the Red Sea. Stratified deposits ranging in date from the Middle Kingdom to the fifth century AD were recovered and are currently under study. Evidence which dates the eastern *temenos* wall to the reign of Nectanebo I or II was discovered, as well as a sequence of early Ptolemaic houses within the *temenos*. Remains of a later (mid-second century BC) *temenos* wall, supplanting that of Nectanebo, were found to the north of the temple. Interestingly, the room in the northeast angle of this wall was decorated by painted stucco in Macedonian style imitating carved stone blocks.

Due to Coptos's continuous occupation and strategic position, excavations there have produced a rich array of epigraphic, architectural and artistic remains. Early finds include three fragmentary colossal stone cult statues of the fertility god Min, discovered by Petrie. As restored, these would have stood 4.1 m high and weighed almost two tons. Although there is some debate about the precise date of these statues, it is clear that they are some of the earliest colossal images from Egypt.

From the Graeco-Roman period come the numerous royal dedications to the Egyptian gods of the city, testifying to the rich religious syncretism of the era and complementing the Roman geographer Strabo's description of the site as a cosmopolitan trade center (*Geography* 17.1.45 10). Most interesting in this respect is the so-called tariff inscription found midway between the city and the desert. Dated to the reign of Domitian (AD 90), the inscription lists the fees levied on travelers over the route between Coptos and the Red Sea ports, the highest fee being placed on prostitutes.

Oddly, the bulk of the excavated remains from the city somewhat contradict the image of the thriving and cosmopolitan trade center. The most striking aspect of the Coptos classical period ceramic corpus (as documented by the 6,000 kg found in the Michigan/Asyut Expedition) is its poverty. There is a restricted range of forms: innovation was infrequent, decoration rare, tablewares crude and visually dull and, perhaps most interestingly, there were very few

imports. Similarly, there are few coins and no glass. The residents of this quarter of the site, at least, seem to have shared very little, if at all, in the luxury products passing through their city.

Today, the growing market village of Quft encircles ancient Coptos and is encroaching upon the numerous but yearly diminishing exposed archaeological remains, and the site is clearly in danger of disappearing entirely.

See also

Roman forts in Egypt; Roman period, overview; Roman ports, Red Sea; trade, foreign

Further reading

Adams, B. 1986. *Sculptured Pottery from Koptos in the Petrie Collection*. Warminster.
Petrie, W.M.F. 1896. *Koptos*. London.
Reinach, A. 1912. Rapport sur les fouilles de Koptos. *Bulletin de la Société française des Fouilles archéologiques* 3(1): 47–82.
Traunecker, C. 1992. *Coptos: Hommes et Dieux sur le Parvis de Geb* (Orientalia Lovaniensa Analecta 43). Louvain.

SHARON HERBERT

Qus

The town of Qus (25°56' N, 32°46' E)—Geza or Gesy in ancient Egyptian and Apollinopolis Parva in Greek—is located in Upper Egypt, 10 km south of Coptos on the east bank of the Nile. It is situated across the Nile 5 km south of Nagada, and was presumably the Predynastic town site associated with the Nagada cemeteries. If so, its early prominence may have been due to its use as a starting point for expeditions to the Eastern Desert via the Wadi Hammamat, both for mining and to gain access to the Red Sea. A number of funerary monuments—ranging from the 6th Dynasty through the Heracleopolitan period (9th–10th Dynasties)—are attributed to the cemetery on the west bank. The modest status of an overseer of priests represented on one of these monuments is adduced as evidence of the secondary status of the local temple in this period. The capital of Nome V of Upper Egypt, which included Qus, is thought to have been at Coptos during the Old Kingdom.

Aside from the cemetery evidence, some pharaonic monuments have been found in the town of Qus. Among the more interesting are the red granite *naos* of the 8th Dynasty vizier Shemai, sandstone blocks with cartouches of the Aten (the sun-disc deity) and Nefertiti found near a sheikh's tomb west of town, and a gray granite stela depicting Ramesses III leading prisoners, with a text dating to year 16 of his reign. Qus is also represented in the taxation lists in the 18th Dynasty Theban tomb of Rekhmire.

The principal deity of Qus during the New Kingdom and later was Haroeris, mainly alluded to by the epithet "Horus the Elder, Lord of Qus in Upper Egypt." In earlier times, the Qusite divinity was known simply as "Lord of Upper Egypt." Gardiner posits that it was this god who, together with Seth of Ombos (a town almost opposite on the west bank of the Nile), gave rise to the emblem of the Ptolemaic "Nome of the two falcon deities." Thus, the gods of Qus and Ombos may be recognized in this pair of falcons and Qus was no longer part of the same administrative district as Coptos. During the Ptolemaic period, Qus belonged to a district separate from Coptos with an emblem which may be read as *Bnbn* or *Brbr*.

As Apollinopolis Parva, the town enjoyed a time of prosperity during the Ptolemaic period, as shown by the remains of the temple of that era. In 1898, Ahmed Kamal uncovered the lower portions of two pylons dating to Ptolemy XI. Texts from the scenes in these ruins show Ptolemy XI harpooning hippopotamus, presenting offerings to Haroeris and slaying enemies, as well as slaying gazelle on an altar. In the third century AD the town was known in Latin as Diocletianopolis. Later, in Coptic, it came to be called Kos Berbir, from which the modern name is derived.

During the Middle Ages, according to the historian Abu'l Feda (1273–1331), Qus became the center of eastern trade in Upper Egypt and, among all cities of Egypt, second only to Fostat in importance and size. Once again access to the Red Sea and the Wadi Hammamat via Higaza, some 8 km to the southeast, were essential to the city's prosperity. The discovery of new sea routes by the Europeans in the fifteenth–sixteenth centuries AD led to the city's decline in the Ottoman period.

See also

Nagada (Naqada); Quft/Qift (Coptos); Wadi Hammamat

Further reading

Fischer, H. 1986. Qus. In *LÄ* 5: 71–3.

Gardiner, A. 1947. *Ancient Egyptian Onomastica* 1. London.

Kamal, A.B. 1902. Le pylone de Qous. *ASAE* 3: 215–35.

DEMETRA MAKRIS

Quseir el-Qadim

Quseir el-Qadim (26°06′ N, 34°17′ E), a small port on the Egyptian coast of the Red Sea, lies about 8 km north of the modern town of Quseir. The port attracted early archaeological interest due to its location at the end of the Wadi Hammamat, the shortest route in Upper Egypt between the Nile Valley and the Red Sea. The ruins lie at the head of a small bay on the northern arm of a raised coral reef. In historical times the *sabkha* (mud-flats) to the east and south may have been a shallow lagoon. The desert conditions (*circa* 4 mm annual rainfall) and the distance to the nearest potable water (*circa* 10 km inland at Bir Karim) explain the intermittent and limited settlement in this coastal region.

The site of Quseir el-Qadim is approximately 10 ha in area. It was excavated by the University of Chicago in 1978–82. These excavations confirmed occupation in two historically attested periods: Roman (first–second centuries AD); and Ayyubid and Bahri Mamluk (thirteenth and early fourteenth centuries). A break of a millennium between these two periods is indicated by an absence of Byzantine (Coptic), early Islamic and Abbasid/Fatimid materials. Furthermore, there is no archaeological evidence at this site of pre-classical Egyptian occupation.

Roman period

Most of the site is an early Roman settlement of the first and early second centuries AD. This dating is confirmed by the excavated papyri, ostraca and coins. An impressive number of languages has been found written/inscribed on artifacts in or near this settlement, including Latin, Greek, demotic Egyptian, Tamil, Nabataean and South Arabian. The Tamil texts are the most interesting, attesting to trade with India. One Tamil personal name recorded at Quseir also occurs at Arikamedu, a Roman period site on the eastern coast of India. Other evidence for connections with India include ceramic assemblages (*terra sigillata* and amphorae) and coinage recovered at Quseir which precisely duplicate those at Arikamedu. The site of Quseir now seems to be identifiable as "Myos Hormos," which, according to textual evidence (Strabo and the *Periplus of the Erythrian Sea*), was the most important Egyptian port for the Roman trade with India. The architectural remains at Quseir include a large *horreum* (warehouse) identical to one excavated at Ostia, the port of Rome, and a row of shops fronting a nearby street. Nevertheless, structural details and construction techniques have close parallels at Karanis and other sites in Roman Egypt. Another building, less fully excavated, seems analogous to the *castellum* (fort) excavated at contemporary Mons Claudianus and, like that building, has a large stable nearby. Planned surface remains and topography at Quseir give indications of an orthogonal city plan, with a series of *insulae* (blocks) along a *cardo*, the principal north–south street. This idealized plan was soon altered as the economic fortunes of the port faltered (or failed to increase).

The harbor area is marked by an "island" created by dredging, in an ancient effort to keep the harbor clear. This was a large lagoon suggestive of a *cothon*-type of harbor (with an enclosed inner basin). Strabo reports a fleet of 120 ships engaged in the India trade from Myos Hormos after AD 25. He also states that this port was the principal point, from Coptos in the Nile Valley, crossing an isthmus. Strabo probably thought of this route as connecting the Indian Ocean with the Nile and Mediterranean, rather like the Corinthian isthmus which connected Asia and Italy.

Islamic period

The site of Quseir el-Qadim was abandoned for almost a millennium; there is no trace of Byzantine (Coptic, fourth–sixth centuries), Umayyad or Abbasid (seventh–tenth centuries) occupation there. Numismatic and other artifactual evidence points to the resettlement of this port in the late eleventh or beginning of the twelfth century. Fatimid occupation (tenth–twelfth centuries) is unlikely. The period of greatest prosperity was the Bahri Mamluk period, when there is evidence of traded artifacts from India, China, Syria and even Tekrur (West Africa). Numismatics and the large corpus of letters found in the excavations confirm this conclusion. The settlement of the fifteenth century may have shifted to the site of the modern port. Soundings within the town, inspection of the fort and study of the oldest shrines confirm only an Ottoman occupation (sixteenth to early twentieth centuries). The fort is not mentioned by Portuguese accounts, suggesting construction during the reign of Selim I, after 1517.

The middle Islamic settlement forms a crescent around the silted-up Roman harbor. There were a series of modular residential units and a large house in the center of this area (called the "Sheikh's house"). These well-constructed residences lack architectural embellishments and seem similar to contemporary urban architecture of the Nile Valley. Settlement in the Eastern area, immediately above the beach, was very different. This consisted of a housing complex made of reeds and matting, with minimal foundations, not unlike contemporary villages along the Red Sea littoral. The Eastern area presents the paradox of "rich" artifacts in a "poor" architectural setting.

Both of the Islamic settlement areas at Quseir, around the Sheikh's house and in the Eastern area, produced evidence of Indian Ocean trade, including Far Eastern ceramics (celadons and porcelains, but early blue and white Ming wares were found only in the Eastern area). Other eastern imports excavated at Quseir are the resist-dyed textiles, which, along with other organic materials, were remarkably well preserved. These brightly patterned textiles were made in India for Islamic markets; the majority were found in the Eastern area. Differences of artifacts and coinage demonstrate two distinct periods of occupation: the Sheikh's house belongs to the thirteenth century and the Eastern area to the late thirteenth and fourteenth centuries.

The commercial patterns in the Indian Ocean have usually been characterized as the "spice trade." Records from Cairo (the Cairo *Geniza*) and studies of mercantile organizations, such as the Karimi, indicate that the vast majority of the wealth was tied up in spices (cinnamon, ginger and so on), aromatics (sandalwood, etc., and perfumes), drugs (medicines) and varnishing plants. The majority of these products have left no traces in the archaeological record, even at Quseir. The plant remains recovered (usually by dry sieving) present an interesting picture of imports and probably consumption. A sample of these foodstuffs includes coriander, garlic, peppercorns, coconut and fenugreek, as well as hazelnut, walnut, almond, pinenut and pistachio. Preliminary study of distribution of these products suggests that imports from India (and southeast Asia) were probably constant for both periods. On the other hand, there seems to have been a decline in imports from the Mediterranean region in the Mamluk period (during the fourteenth century).

The excavations at Quseir have produced a corpus of documents similar to those of the Cairo *Geniza*. Like the *Geniza*, this is a random preservation rather than an archive; the Quseir letters were not gathered together for storage, but were found as a random part of normal trash accumulation. These letters, about 200 of which are fairly complete, provide details of the daily life of the community, ranging from discussion of crops and trade to love letters. A comprehensive analysis of these documents, however, has yet to be done.

Conclusion

The port of Myos Hormos has been traditionally associated with a foundation under Ptolemy II Philadelphus. While Quseir el-Qadim produced no artifacts of this period, four blocks with hieroglyphic inscriptions from a Ptolemaic temple were discovered by Arthur Weigall in the modern town of Quseir. One inscription was thought to contain the name of the town, Duau, a reading now consistently rejected by Egyptologists. However, the inscriptions do seem to indicate the existence of a temple to Hathor, a goddess who was identified with Aphrodite. This association strengthens the tradition of Aphrodite's harbor and may suggest that modern Quseir overlies the Ptolemaic harbor. Clearly, further archaeological investigation will be necessary to complete the history of ancient ports in this region.

See also

Quft/Qift (Coptos); Roman ports, Red Sea

Further reading

Meyer, C. 1992. *Glass from Quseir al-Qadim and the Indian Ocean Trade*. Chicago.

Vogelsang-Eastwood, G.M. 1989. *Resist-dyed Textiles from Quseir al-Qadim, Egypt*. Paris.

Whitcomb, D. 1995. Quseir al-Qadim, Egypt: text and context in the Indian Ocean spice trade. *al-'Usur al-Wusta* 7: 25–7.

——. 1996. Quseir al-Qadim and the location of Myos Hormos. *Topoi* 6: 747–72.

Whitcomb, D., and J.H. Johnson. 1979. *Quseir al-Qadim 1978, Preliminary Report*. Cairo.

——. 1982. *Quseir al-Qadim 1980, Preliminary Report*. Malibu, CA.

DONALD WHITCOMB

R

Reisner, George Andrew

Born in Indianapolis on November 5, 1867 to a German-American family, Reisner made his way east to Harvard University for his BA, MA and Ph.D. degrees. In 1893, one year after his marriage to Mary Bronson, he became a Traveling Fellow of Harvard and left for Berlin to study first Semitics and then ancient Egypt. After his years in Germany, Reisner returned to Harvard, where he obtained a post as Instructor in Semitics. He served as Assistant Professor of Semitic Archaeology at Harvard from 1905 to 1910. Research and fieldwork, however, appealed to him more than classroom teaching. He obtained funding for excavation in 1899 from the California-based Mrs Phoebe Apperson Hearst, mother of the well-known newspaper publisher.

Reisner concentrated on the great cemeteries of Naga ed-Deir, as well as the sites of Quft and Deir el-Ballas. He applied a methodical approach far ahead of his time in his excavation techniques, and began to develop a unique working system. He delegated different aspects of the excavation, and emphasized field photography as a fundamental element of the archaeological process. In addition, he maintained a variety of expedition record books and numbering systems.

Reisner attained his most important site concession in 1905, the Old Kingdom cemeteries surrounding the three great pyramids of Giza. His expedition was now supported by Harvard University and the Museum of Fine Arts, Boston. Reisner became curator of the Boston Museum's Egyptian Department soon thereafter. He was in succession Archaeological Director of the Nubian Archaeological Survey by the Egyptian Government (1907–9), Director of the Harvard Excavations at Samaria, Palestine (1909–10), Director of the Harvard–Boston Egyptian Expedition, Professor of Egyptology, and Curator of the Egyptian Department of the Museum of Fine Arts, Boston (1910–42).

Some of Reisner's most spectacular Old Kingdom discoveries at Giza include the subterranean burial chamber of Queen Hetepheres, wife of King Seneferu and mother of King Khufu; the painted tomb chapel of Queen Meresankh III, granddaughter of King Khufu; the excavation of the third Giza pyramid and funerary temples of King Menkaure; and important inscriptional material on a range of subjects.

Reisner's second towering achievement in archaeology was the opening of an entirely new chapter in ancient African history. After directing the Archaeological Survey of Nubia (1907–9), intended to record sites prior to construction of the original Aswan High Dam, Reisner explored the cultures of Nubia (modern Sudan) to the south of Egypt more extensively. His work at sites along the upper Nile such as Gebel Barkal, Kerma, el-Kurru, Nuri and Meroe opened up a new field of Nubian studies.

Reisner died at Giza in the Harvard Camp on June 6, 1942. In his final years, despite near total blindness, he continued working, dictating manuscripts to a secretary. By the end of his career, he had explored the most famous archaeological site in the world (the Giza pyramids), discovered hundreds of artistic masterpieces, rewritten the history of Nubia and three millennia of Egypto-Nubian relations, and permanently altered the course of modern archaeology. He was buried in the Christian cemetery in Cairo.

Aswan; Deir el-Ballas; Gebel Barkal; Giza, Hetepheres tomb; Kerma; el-Kurru; Memphite private tombs of the Old Kingdom; Nuri

Further reading

Dunham, D. 1942. George Andrew Reisner. *AJA* 46: 410–12.
——. 1972. *Recollections of an Egyptologist.* Boston.
Manuelian, P.D. 1990–1 (Winter). Boston at Giza. *KMT* 1(4): 10–21.
——. 1996 (Summer). March 1912: A Month in the Life of George A. Reisner. *KMT* 7(2): 60–75.

PETER DER MANUELIAN

religion, state

In the earliest communities of Predynastic Egypt (*circa* 4,500–3,050 BC), local tribal gods were probably worshipped. This resulted in an apparent multiplicity of deities throughout the country, and as the unified state emerged at the end of the fourth millennium BC, the gods were also amalgamated into a confusing pantheon, with identities and characteristics that sometimes overlapped. During the Old Kingdom, there was a clear attempt by the priests of the various gods to rationalize and centralize these cults, and in certain cities, great religious centers were established where the deities were grouped into families, ogdoads (groups of eight gods), or enneads (groups of nine gods).

Eventually, two main religious systems emerged in Egypt. First, the state cults were organized, with temples and priesthood, to ensure the survival of the gods, Egypt and the king. These included "local gods" whose cults were limited to particular geographical districts, and the great "state gods," who were frequently elevated from the ranks of the local gods to have national importance and influence. When a family of rulers succeeded in gaining the throne, they would often raise the deity whom

they had worshipped in their own locality to become the supreme state god and royal patron. Some of the state gods, however, had never had simply local origins; rather, as firmly established members of the supreme league of deities, they had always been regarded as universal.

The term "household gods" is applied today to the second category of deities. They were worshipped at small, domestic shrines, and had neither temples, divine cults, nor priesthood, but were approached by people at all levels of society for help and guidance in everyday matters. The state gods probably had only a remote effect on people's lives, since their contact with these deities was minimal, whereas household gods were always approachable.

During the Old Kingdom, the most important priesthoods associated with the foremost religious centers developed separate theologies. These included mythologies about the lives of the gods, some of the most important of which centered around the creation of the universe and of other gods and mankind. In these cosmogonies (creation myths), each priesthood sought to advance the claims of its own god and to assert his or her primary role in creation. The most famous and influential cosmogony grew up at Heliopolis, where the sun god Re had taken over the cult of an earlier god, Atum. This myth underlines Re's association with nature deities—the sky, earth, wind, moon and stars— and with other gods, and is mainly preserved in the *Pyramid Texts*, which decorated interior walls in some of the later pyramids. It tells how Re-Atum, the first god of Heliopolis, emerged from a great primeval ocean, Nun, and created a mound on which to stand (his priesthood claimed that their temple was built on this "Island of Creation"). Dispeling the gloom by bringing light, he then took the form of the mythical *bennu* bird and alighted on the *benben* (the pillar associated with Re's cult at Heliopolis). He brought into existence the god of air and the goddess of moisture, who in turn produced the earth and sky deities, who became the parents of Osiris, Isis, Seth and Nephthys. This family was known as the Great Ennead. Other Old Kingdom priesthoods attempted to rival Heliopolis; the greatest threat came from

Memphis where the priests of Ptah, the creator-god and patron of craftsmen, sought to prove that Ptah had preceded Re-Atum. They claimed that Ptah was in fact Nun (the primeval ocean) and that he had produced a daughter, Naunet; together they became the parents of Re-Atum, the Heliopolitan creator. Another center developed at Hermopolis (Khnumu). Here, the mythology centered around an ogdoad, consisting of four male and four female gods. They created the world and then ruled on earth for a time before they died and continued to exist in the underworld, where they ensured that the Nile flowed and the sun rose each day, so that life would flourish on earth.

Other myths emerged, including the later cosmogony at Thebes, which established the supremacy of Amen, the god of air, as the great state god and universal deity, ruler of all lands, when Thebes became capital of Egypt and its empire during the New Kingdom. In Amen's temple at Karnak, temple architecture can be seen at its greatest and the influence of the priesthood on the state and the community can be most clearly appreciated. This temple, like the tombs, was intended to endure for eternity and was therefore built of stone.

Cult and mortuary temples had distinct uses, but their architecture and rituals were closely associated. The cult temple housed the god's statue and provided a location where the king or priest could approach the god through regular rituals and establish a mutually beneficial relationship. The mortuary temple, originally attached to the pyramid, was the place where the burial ceremonies were performed, and where offerings continued to be brought to ensure the king's survival after death. In the New Kingdom, the kings were no longer buried in pyramids but had rock-cut tombs in the Valley of the Kings at Thebes. Here there was no space to build attached mortuary temples or chapels, so these kings built separate temples, mostly situated on the flat plain between the Valley and the river. Such temples were also dedicated to the cults of the gods and had provision for the rituals of both the dead king and the deity.

Cult temples and mortuary temples all had the same basic architectural plan, with only minor variations, although they were dedicated to different gods and kings. The shape and arrangement of the building were dictated by the mythology of the temple and its ritual requirements. A series of inscriptions at the temple of Horus at Edfu (known as the "Building Texts") give a full account of the mythological explanation of the temple and relate how each temple was regarded as the "Island of Creation" on which the first bird-god had alighted and found refuge, and where the creation of the universe and of society had occurred. The architectural features of the stone temples—the ceiling painted to resemble the sky, the plant-form columns and capitals, and the plants carved on the bases of the walls—all recreated the physical environment of the Island of Creation and provided a place of great spiritual sanctity and potency where mankind could approach the gods. The temple was also the "Mansion of the God," where the resident deity was given shelter, protection and worship, in the same way as the bird-god had found refuge on the Island of Creation. The temple was regarded as the deity's residence, in the way that the tomb was the "house" for a dead person's spirit, and provision was made for the dead and the gods which followed the pattern of accommodation for the living.

The gods and the dead were believed to have the same physical needs as the living: food, drink, washing, clothing, rest and recreation. Food was supplied for the dead by means of the funerary cult, and the gods' needs were met by the performance of the divine rituals. In the cult temple, there were two main types of ritual. The most important ritual (known as the "Daily Temple Ritual") was carried out three times a day for the resident god in every temple, and dramatized the commonplace events of everyday existence, providing food, clothing, washing and regular attendance for the god's cult-statue in his sanctuary. The second type of ritual, the festivals, varied in content from one temple to another, each being based on the mythology of the particular resident deity. They were celebrated at regular, often yearly, intervals and marked special events in the god's life, such as marriage, death and resurrection. A main feature of most festivals was the procession of the god's statue outside the temple, giving the crowds their only opportunity to see the deity and to participate in his worship.

In the mortuary temples, from the New Kingdom onward, provision was made for the daily food offerings to revert from the god's table and to be presented to all the legitimate former kings of Egypt (represented in the temple in the form of a king list). In this way, the king who had built the temple could gain their support for his reign and their acceptance of him after his death. This was known as the "Ritual of the Royal Ancestors," and was performed by the king during his own lifetime and by the high priest after his death. As in the cult temple, the food eventually reverted to the priests as their daily payment, once the ritual was completed.

The rituals once performed in the temples are still preserved in scenes, carved and painted on many of the walls in the enclosed areas of the buildings. In the same way that tomb scenes could be "brought to life" by means of magic, following the performance of the Opening of the Mouth ceremony, the temple scenes were believed to be similarly activated and charged so that the rituals depicted on the walls would become eternally effective.

These scenes all show the king performing the rituals for the gods. As the incarnation of Horus and the son of Re, and as the divine heir, the king alone could act as representative of mankind in approaching the gods. In return for his performance of the rituals, he asked the gods for eternal life, victory over his enemies, an abundance of crops for Egypt, and the well-being of his subjects. However, in reality, although he may have performed the daily rituals in the main temple of the chief state god, in all other temples his duties would have been delegated to the high priest.

Each sizable town possessed a temple, and there would have been a number of temples in the capital city and in the other great religious centers. Each temple had its own priesthood; some of the priests were permanent temple personnel, but most held their posts secondary to their main professions, such as doctors and scribes. They pursued these duties in the community for nine months of each year, only entering the temple for three months, on a rotating basis, where they were engaged in religious, liturgical and sometimes teaching commitments. They were not required to be celibate, and indeed, access to the priesthood was often on a hereditary basis, although there were other means of entry by selection.

The main function of the priests was to act as "god's servants," ministering to the deity's ritual needs. They were expected to understand the divine liturgy, and to study and teach their specializations in the temple, but they were not required to give counseling or religious instruction to the community at large and the temple never became a center of community worship. Nevertheless, the temple's role was essential in society. Not only did it ensure that the gods continued their beneficence toward Egypt, but every temple also owned estates where the food was produced for the god's altar; some also had mines and workshops to provide the materials and labor to manufacture the cultic and divine possessions. Revenue was collected in kind from many parts of the country, sometimes in the temple's own fleet of ships, and was kept in storehouses in the temple precinct, where it was recorded and redistributed as payment to the temple personnel. The temples were the largest employers in Egypt, since they required an extensive work force to administer and operate the vast estates. Although the religious duties were reserved for the priests, a wealthy and elite group drawn mainly from the privileged sections of society, many of the temple employees were menials, engaged in a variety of mundane tasks. The temples had further influence on the community at large because they were places of teaching and learning, and some acquired reputations as centers for medical knowledge and healing.

The role of the god-king was crucial in terms of the state religion. Deemed to be the physical son of the country's chief god through his union with the previous king's "Great Royal Wife," each ruler had a unique relationship with the gods and with mankind. However, the supposed absolute powers of the king were controlled by the dictates of Ma'at, the goddess who personified the divine order and the equilibrium of the universe, and his actions were largely limited by precedents set by former rulers. Nevertheless, when a king wished to revolutionize religious concepts, to some extent he could achieve his aims. The so-called Amarna period, when Akhenaten (*circa* 1360 BC) attempted to introduce and impose an exclusive sun cult based on the worship of the god Aten, was a short-lived experiment when the king was able to demonstrate this ability.

See also

Abu Gurab; cult temples of the New Kingdom; cult temples prior to the New Kingdom; Edfu; Karnak, temple of Amen-Re; kingship; *ma'at*; mythology; pantheon; representational evidence, New Kingdom temples; taxation and conscription; Tell el-Amarna, cult temples; Thebes, royal funerary temples; Thebes, Valley of the Kings

Further reading

David, A.R. 1981. *A Guide to Religious Ritual at Abydos, ca. 1300 B.C.* Warminster.

Fairman, H.W. 1954. Worship and festivals in an Egyptian temple. *Bulletin of the John Rylands Library* 37: 165–202.

Gardiner, A.H. 1950. The baptism of Pharaoh. *JEA* 36: 3–12.

A.R. DAVID

representational evidence, Early Dynastic

Several types of representational evidence are known for the earliest culture in Dynastic Egypt. First, ceremonial palettes, stone palettes for grinding eye paint, and maceheads, decorated with various representations, date to the transitional period from the late/final Predynastic to the 1st Dynasty, at the end of the

fourth millennium BC. The scenes on the palettes shift from clashes with wild animals (such as ostrich and lion hunts, and taming animals with music) to battles with human enemies (with the king as a lion ripping apart the enemy, or as a bull trampling the foe underfoot). On one side of the famous Narmer Palette, excavated at Hierakonpolis, the king in lion form breaches enemy settlements. The Macehead of King Scorpion, also excavated at Hierakonpolis, depicts the king and an unknown figure allied with him in a ritual seed sowing.

Second, there are hippopotamus ivory knife handles decorated with repeated rows of animals, also found on the so-called ivory "magic staffs." These cannot be accurately dated, but they probably belong to this transitional phase. The Gebel el-Araq knife handle also belongs here, although its authenticity has been questioned. In addition to representations of the hunt, the decoration on this knife handle also includes a water and land battle.

Third, there are inscribed square tags of hippopotamus ivory or wood. Excavated in the royal tombs at Abydos, these tags have been known for some time and date from Dynasty 0 to the end of the 1st Dynasty. While the oldest examples are still unreadable, it may yet be established that they contain information about the origins of the goods to which they were affixed. The 1st Dynasty tags on oil jars are dated annually by "year names." Since these years were named for important events, the labels contain information for reconstructing the history of this period. Some labels appear to have been reused, as occasionally on the reverse there are details of other objects to which they were originally attached (such as game-boards or sandals).

Finally, there are seal impressions, rolled onto the large mud sealings on (wine) jars. These contain information about various administrative units and their organizational changes. Their use begins at the end of the Predynastic period and continues until the end of the Old Kingdom.

See also

Abydos, Umm el-Qa'ab; Early Dynastic period, overview; Hierakonpolis; Predynastic period, overview; representational evidence, Predynastic; writing, invention and early development

Further reading

Emery, W.B. 1967. *Archaic Egypt*. Baltimore, MD.

Helck, W. 1987. *Untersuchungen zur Thinitenzeit*. Wiesbaden.

WOLFGANG HELCK

representational evidence, Middle Kingdom private tombs

One of our richest sources of information about the way the ancient Egyptians of the Middle Kingdom lived, worked and conceptualized the universe is the representational art with which the walls of private tombs of the elite were decorated. The most impressive and significant of these tombs were built for nomarchs and other high officials of the country's provincial nomes. Some of the more important sites at which decorated tombs, especially from the early Middle Kingdom, have been found are Kom el-Hisn in the Delta, Dahshur in the Memphite area, el-Lisht in the Fayum, Beni Hasan, Deir el-Bersha, Meir, Asyut and Qau el-Kebir in Middle Egypt, and Thebes and Aswan in the south. After the reign of Senusret III, large provincial tombs are found only at Qau el-Kebir; other high-ranking nobles were buried in the cemeteries associated with the royal pyramids.

Before examining the representational art in these tombs, it is useful to look briefly at the architectural contexts in which this art is found. Although some of the important decorated tombs are free-standing *mastabas* (tombs with rectangular mudbrick superstructures), the majority were cut into the limestone cliffs that border the Nile Valley. The most usual form for these tombs was a single or multiple-roomed chapel, which often included a small shrine containing rock-cut statues and burial shafts leading to the chambers in which the mummies and their equipment were buried. The principal area of figurative decoration within these structures was the chapel, which could be adorned with painted relief or with flat painting. These chapels are sometimes so richly decorated that the walls appear to be covered with ornate tapestries in vibrant colors. Some tombs contained, instead of two-dimensional decoration, three-dimensional models of many of the objects or scenes that appear in the decoration; this is a carry-over from a practice common in the First Intermediate Period, and enhances our understanding of the pictorial representations.

Many of the tomb scenes illustrate activities connected with the production and processing of food, such as plowing fields, baking bread, brewing beer, fowling and fishing. Other scenes depict the manufacture of objects such as chairs, beds, coffins, jewelry, pottery and cloth. These depictions are usually quite lively, full of detail, and often lend insight into the activities represented. For example, in a fishing scene from the 12th Dynasty tomb of Ukhhotep at Meir (Tomb B4), the net used is clearly delineated, down to the lead weights on the bottom and the wooden floaters on the top. Each of the fish within the net is drawn so carefully that its species can be identified.

Associated with many of the tomb scenes are labels which describe the activities being carried out, identify the individuals depicted by name (thus enabling them to share in the eternal life of their masters), or record conversations between the workers. These descriptive labels can help us to understand the processes of food production and manufacture which are represented, and the conversations give us glimpses into the comradery between the workers and sometimes hint at the ancient Egyptian sense of humor. We even see wrongdoers being judged, scolded and punished for their transgressions.

Due to the exactness with which the workers are drawn and the fact that many are identified by name, scholars are able to draw some conclusions about the ethnic composition of the Egyptian population. For instance, the armies which fight in battles illustrated in some tombs are composed of a mixture of Egyptians, Nubians, Asiatics and Libyans. Nubians can also be found among the personal servants of at least one noble. The tombs provide us with information about the division of labor between the sexes; men do most of the hunting, fishing and manufacturing, while women are shown spinning and weaving, baking and brewing, and working in the fields.

Tomb decoration of the Middle Kingdom also offers us a considerable amount of information about Egyptian religion, especially as it relates to the mortuary cults of the nobles. All of the scenes of manufacture and food production discussed above can be linked in some way to the funerary cult of the deceased person, as each of the items produced can be shown to have a function within the context of the funerary meal and/or the burial equipment of the noble. For example, cloth shown being woven in a tomb painting would be magically destined for the cult, to be used in wrapping the mummy, or to be placed within the tomb as part of the burial equipment. Wine, which is often shown being made and stored, would have been offered to the deceased noble at his funerary and daily cult meals. In many cases, the tomb owner is shown supervising such manufacturing activities, or being presented with the resultant materials.

One of the most important religious celebrations depicted in tomb chapels of the Middle Kingdom is the funerary meal. In scenes representing this ritual, the tomb owner (always male in these cases), often accompanied by his wife, sits at a table heaped with food and drink, while processions of offering bearers bring additional items to add to the feast or objects to include with the burial equipment. As in the scenes of manufacture and food production, the individual items of food and equipment are shown in some detail and are often quite specifically identifiable. Priests, including the eldest son of the tomb owner, perform rituals designed to insure the effective worship of the deceased. For example, libations are poured and sacrificial animals are slaughtered. By

depicting such offerings and rites, the deceased nobles were guaranteed that they would be supplied with the necessary nourishment and ritual attention that they needed for eternity.

Other aspects of the celebration of the mortuary cult are also represented in these tombs. For example, processions involving the transport of statues and their associated rites of dancing and singing are portrayed, and Hathoric celebrations are shown. Pilgrimages to holy sites such as Abydos, often involving the mummy of the deceased, are depicted. The original purpose of such scenes was to insure magically that the appropriate rites were carried out properly, but they can now be read as elaborate manuals which tell us how to bury an ancient Egyptian properly.

There is another very prominent category of scenes which show the tomb owner hunting in the desert or fishing and fowling in the marshes. These depictions cannot be easily explained. They are often described as portrayals of sporting events that the noble enjoyed during his lifetime and wished to repeat for eternity. However, many aspects of these scenes suggest that their importance lay in the the realm of ritual and myth; they serve primarily to identify the noble with the king as the repeller of the forces of chaos. It is significant that such scenes appear first in the royal repertoire, and then are found in non-royal contexts.

Each of the scenes within a particular tomb chapel, in addition to its individual meaning, can be seen in the context of the chapel as a coherent entity. The individual tomb chapels can, like later temples, be read on several levels as miniature models of the Egyptian cosmos. This can be demonstrated in the 12th Dynasty tomb of Khnumhotep II at Beni Hasan (Tomb 3), in which this concept is brought to fruition. Each of the scenes within Khnumhotep II's chapel can be interpreted on a number of different levels, and then analyzed in the context of the chapel as a whole.

In this particular tomb, the decoration can be shown to function on three levels, each correlating with a different but interrelated cosmos. On one level, the scenes tell of Khnumhotep II's life on earth, his funeral and his life in the hereafter within his own personal cosmos, in which he functions and is worshipped as a god. This same narrative can be read again as the life cycle of Egypt, complete with all the features of the Egyptian landscape and all the seasons of the Egyptian year. At this level, Khnumhotep II acts as the king within the royal cosmos. The third level illustrates the life of the larger cosmos, complete with a reiterated cosmogony, wherein Khnumhotep II embodies the sun god and therefore the god of creation.

The decoration of Middle Kingdom private tombs provides us with information about many aspects of the daily life of the average Egyptian, and we see the environment in which they lived in some detail. Our knowledge of religious beliefs of the ancient Egyptian elite, especially as they relate to private mortuary cults, is greatly enhanced by these illustrations. Finally, we can ascertain a great deal about the overall culture and social structure of the Middle Kingdom, and the ways in which the deceased noble and his mortuary monument functioned within the Egyptian cosmos.

See also

Beni Hasan; brewing and baking; Deir el-Bahri, Meket-Re tomb; Deir el-Bersha; Kom el-Hisn; el-Lisht; Meir; Middle Kingdom, overview; Qau el-Kebir (Antaeopolis), Dynastic sites; wine making

Further reading

Aldred, C. 1950. *Middle Kingdom Art in Egypt, 2300–1590 B.C.* London.
Guglielmi, W. 1973. *Reden, Rufe und Lieder... auf altägyptischen Darstellungen der Landwirtshaft, Viehzucht, des Fisch- und Vogelfangs vom Mittleren Reich bis zur Spätzeit.* Bonn.
Kamrin, J. 1997. *The Cosmos of Khnumhotep II.* London.
Klebs, L. 1922. *Die Reliefs und Malereien des Mittleren Reiches.* Heidelberg.

JANICE KAMRIN

representational evidence, New Kingdom private tombs

Representations in New Kingdom private tombs can be divided into four basic types: (1) illustrations of religious ritual, including representations of rulers and the gods, certain ritual architectural features of the tomb such as the false door, and the ceremonies at the entombment; (2) representations of activities in which the deceased took part or supervised or for which he was responsible; (3) representations of activities for the benefit of the spirit of the deceased in the next life; and (4) representations of activities of a pleasing nature intended for the enjoyment of the deceased in eternity. The knowledge to be gleaned from these varied types of representations provides us with considerable information which might not otherwise be preserved about ritual and daily life.

Illustrations of religious ritual provide us with information on the worship of the gods and deified rulers, participation in festivals, the funeral process, the procession to the tomb, the types of objects considered necessary to furnish the tomb and the ritual of the funerary banquet with family, retainers and entertainment. The procession of the mummy and the funerary accessories to the tomb is often illustrated; the mummy is shown on its bier and sled being transported to the tomb, then standing upright at the entrance to the tomb, lustrated and incensed, culminating with a depiction of the ritual of the "Opening of the Mouth" which enabled the faculties of the spirit to function in the next life, performed at the door of the tomb as the last act before interment.

Observations such as the makeup of the funerary procession, with all of its participants enumerated, or the inclusion of the mourners who greet and interrupt the funeral procession, give us a vivid picture of the process. The funerary banquet, with family members and friends or associates, is usually represented in some detail. Attendants serve food and drink and minister to the needs of the guests. Music and dance are an integral part of the celebration, with detailed representations of dancers, musicians and their musical instruments. The representation of the tomb façade gives us additional information about tomb architecture, often illustrating details of architectural decoration (pyramidion above the entrance, rows of funerary cones set into the façade) otherwise badly preserved or lost.

An additional type of representation associated with the funerary rite is the depiction of the two-part ritual voyage of the deceased to and from Abydos. This pilgrimage to the ancient cult center of the god Osiris was a pious act believed necessary for the protection and reward of the spirit. The inclusion of this scene has not only added to our knowledge of the importance of this religious belief, but also incidentally provided information on boat construction, rigging and boat management. The reigning king and his queen, and on occasion deified rulers, may be represented. In some instances the deceased is shown receiving decorations or awards from the hands of his ruler. Deified rulers are also represented as a part of the pious activity of the deceased or as part of his official duties in the service of a cult or of a particular temple.

The activities supervised by the tomb owner in life which were represented in the tomb are as varied and diverse as position and responsibilities entailed. An excellent example of this variety is exhibited in the tomb of Rekhmire of Thebes. Rekhmire held the rank of Vizier and was also Mayor of Thebes. His official duties included receiving tribute offered to the king by foreign emissaries and the overseeing of a wide variety of royal and temple workshops. The illustrations of the procession of foreigners from Africa to the south, western Asia and the islands of the Aegean carry with them a great deal of visual information about exotic peoples (Africans, Asiatics, Aegean islanders), animals (bears, giraffes, elephant, monkeys, baboons) and desirable and imported commodities (ostrich feathers, ivory, ebony, gold). The representations of workshop activities contain considerable detail about handicrafts and manufacturing techniques (brick making, furniture crafting, rope twisting, metal smelting and casting, jewelry craftsmanship, leather work

and so on). The representation of the production of sculpture in its various forms provides a virtual inventory of sculptural types, many of which can be associated with actual examples.

In many tombs the complete agricultural cycle is shown from the breaking of the ground to the harvesting and processing of the foodstuffs; the process of viticulture from the picking of grapes to the bottling (potting) and labeling of the vintage; animal husbandry from the birth of the calf to the butchering of the mature animal. The significance of such representations on tomb walls may be twofold. They certainly provided tangible representation of the activities in which the tomb owner may have participated and which may have been intended for the benefit of the spirit in the life to come. They also represented the cycle of life through the depiction of seasonal activities: sowing, reaping, processing of foodstuffs or the life of animals from birth to death. The cyclical nature of these representations is considered by some scholars to be the most important reason for their inclusion in the tomb in that they would magically ensure the continuation of life for the spirit of the deceased by ensuring his participation in the unfolding of the seasons.

The deceased is also represented in activities which are clearly intended to provide amusement and diversion in the next life. A dual depiction of the tomb owner, often accompanied by wife and children, in the act of hunting birds in a papyrus thicket and spearing fish in its waters, is a standard element in tombs from the Old Kingdom onward. This representation becomes elaborated with considerable attention to the incidental details of the milieu and the wildlife during the 18th Dynasty. That this standard piece of tomb iconography was meant to provide comfort for the deceased is certainly suggested by a labeling text which indicates that the deceased is "taking recreation and seeing what is good in the place of eternity." The sporting nature of the activity is suggested as the deceased is depicted using a throwing stick to hunt birds and a harpoon for spearing fish, since the more productive techniques for each activity involve various kinds of nets and traps. A comparable activity involving the deceased is depicted in "the hunt in the desert" where a wide variety of wild life is pursued, usually with bow and arrow, in a landscape suggesting wilderness at the desert's edge and in the foothills bordering the Nile. Hare, ostrich, jackal and various horned animals such as the ibex and gazelle are included, giving us some idea of the indigenous wildlife available for this sport.

In contrast to the paintings of the 18th Dynasty, in the Ramesside period (19th–20th Dynasties) there is considerably more emphasis on representations of the deceased carrying out ritual activities in the "Land of the Blessed" (plowing, sowing and reaping, drinking from the blessed waters of life). These are of a much more stylized nature and are treated with less attention to detail than scenes of "daily life" and ordinary activities.

See also

Aegean peoples; mortuary beliefs; Saqqara, New Kingdom private tombs; Thebes, New Kingdom private tombs

Further reading

James, T.G.H. 1986. *Egyptian Painting*. Cambridge, MA.

Mekhitarian, A. 1978. *Egyptian Painting*. Geneva.

Peck, W.H., and J.G. Ross. 1978. *Drawings from Ancient Egypt*. London.

Smith, W.S. 1981. *The Art and Architecture of Ancient Egypt*, revised with additions by W.K. Simpson. Harmondsworth.

WILLIAM H. PECK

representational evidence, New Kingdom royal tombs

Beginning with Tuthmose I, it became the custom to inter the bodies of the deceased New Kingdom kings in complex tombs cut into the rock cliffs on the west bank of the Nile. The symbolic representations carved and painted on the walls and ceilings of the royal tombs of this period were created to magically provide for the guidance, protection and sustenance of the spirit of the ruler after death. In contrast, the painted and carved representations in non-royal tombs have as their main content the depictions of scenes associated with the duties of the deceased during life and the funerary procedures after death. The royal representations include five major themes: (1) the major religious texts current in the New Kingdom; (2) representations of the dead king in the company of the gods; (3) the judgment of the dead king after death; (4) representations of offerings and tomb equipment for the use of the spirit of the king; and (5) astrological representations of the sky, stars and constellations.

The representations of religious texts, such as *The Litany of Re*, *The Book of Gates*, *The Book of Caverns*, *The Book of What is in the Underworld* and *The Books of Night and Day*, give us an insight into the concerns of the monarch for his spirit after death. They illustrate the tests and trials, the obstacles and barriers to be met on the journey into the "Land of the Blessed." A considerable portion of such illustrations depict the voyage of the sun god through the day and night sky, protected by a wide variety of deities and often accompanied by the spirit of the king. The religious texts which form the basis for these designs evolved in the New Kingdom and are most thoroughly developed by the Ramesside period (19th and 20th Dynasties).

Images of the dead king in the company of the gods are common in New Kingdom royal tombs. The king is shown offering to the gods or simply in their company, embraced by or embracing them and being nurtured and "given life" by them. Osiris as god of the dead is prominent, as are Isis and Nephthys, in their roles as protectors of the dead. Anubis as the god of the mortuary establishment and the necropolis is also often shown with the king, but other gods and goddesses are depicted in the role of familiar of the king as well.

Though not as frequently encountered in royal tombs as the other descriptions of what is to be expected in the next life, the scene of the "weighing of the heart" with attendant deities occurs in some tombs, beginning with the tomb of Horemheb, at the start of the 19th Dynasty.

Representations of offerings and tomb equipment include depictions of statues, furniture, tools and weapons as well as storage vessels and boxes. Astrological representations of stars and constellations primarily show the night sky through which the sun god and the deceased must pass.

During the 18th Dynasty, the range of religious texts and attendant illustrations were somewhat limited, generally restricted to *The Book of Gates*, *The Book of What is in the Underworld* and *The Litany of Re* as well as depictions of gods and the king in the company of gods. The small tomb of Tutankhamen was something of an exception in that it also includes paintings of the funeral procession and the "Opening of the Mouth" ritual. With Seti I at the beginning of the 19th Dynasty, the increased size and complexity of the tombs is accompanied by an expanded range of texts and illustrations.

The principal representations encountered in the royal tombs are: maps and diagrams of the route taken by the sun god in his boat; the doors and attendant door keepers who must be satisfied or placated; images of deities, including many that are obscure or grotesque; ritual scenes such as the weighing of the heart; depictions of provisions for the deceased; and diagrams or maps of the sky. The predominant theme is the victory of the sun god over the spirit of chaos, with the attendant advantages for the spirit of the deceased king. Obstacles overcome and trials endured, he would accompany Re through the endless cycle of day and night, of birth and rebirth, throughout eternity. Equipped with the correct responses and guides to the proper ritual, he would overcome obstacles and gain admittance to the realms of the blessed. Thus, these representations are concerned with the process of becoming one with the gods and participating in the cycle of rebirth.

See also

funerary texts; New Kingdom, overview; Thebes, Valley of the Kings

Further reading

Hornung, E. 1990. *The Valley of the Kings: Horizon of Eternity*. New York.

Reeves, N., and R.H. Wilkinson. 1996. *The Complete Valley of the Kings*. London.

Romer, J. 1981. *Valley of the Kings*. New York.

WILLIAM H. PECK

representational evidence, New Kingdom temples

The relief decoration of New Kingdom temples can be divided broadly into two phases: (1) the 17th and 18th Dynasties up to the reign of Amenhotep III, and (2) Akhenaten's reign through the Ramesside rulers. Earlier stone temples were decorated mostly with scenes of religious ritual concerned with the deities, cults and rituals celebrated in the temples. Scenes were included from the daily cult ritual, from major religious festivals, and from events within a pharaoh's reign. Some of the earliest representations of the Opet festival are found on blocks originally used for the red quartzite sanctuary built by Queen Hatshepsut for the Amen bark at Karnak, recovered from the filling of Pylon III.

Military victories and annal records often were depicted on pylon towers at temple entrances, such as on Pylons VII and VIII at Karnak. Other records were carved on commemorative stelae in temples, or on obelisks erected in front of temple pylons. The famous "Dream Stela" of Tuthmose IV, in which he dreams of becoming king if he restores the Great Sphinx at Giza, was set between the stone paws of the monument.

More unusual scenes are found in specialized temples connected with the pharaoh. The so-called "Botanical Garden" scenes in the festival hall (*Akh-Menu*) of Tuthmose III at Karnak depict plants and animals recorded during the king's seventeen military campaigns in south-west Asia. Scenes of the king's donations to the temple of Amen at Karnak are depicted on the same wall as his royal annals.

Reliefs in the funerary temple of Queen Hatshepsut were very innovative; besides religious scenes in the temple's chapels, the earliest known examples of narrative relief were carved on the walls of the temple's colonnades. Scenes from the queen's political career are found here, including the earliest attested scenes of divine birth. Important events during her reign are depicted, such as the transport of two giant obelisks by barge from the Aswan quarries to Karnak, and the expedition the queen sent to the land of Punt on the Red Sea. The Punt reliefs show the dispatch of the expedition, its voyage south in the Red Sea, the arrival at Punt and the expedition's reception there by the "king" of Punt. Scenes of Punt are also depicted, including ones in which the products of Punt, especially incense and incense trees, are obtained and loaded onto Egyptian ships. The return voyage to Egypt includes faithful renderings of the marine life in the Red Sea. Other more fragmentary scenes in Hatshepsut's temple include her military expeditions against the Kushites in Nubia.

Funerary temples of mid-18th Dynasty are too poorly preserved to indicate what was depicted in their reliefs, but in the main cult temples, religious and offering scenes continue to dominate. A fragment of a red granite shrine of Tuthmose III shows priests carrying the divine bark of Amen, possibly a scene from the Opet festival, in narrative style. The next major evidence comes from Amenhotep III's reign. Major parts of the Luxor temple were built during this reign and contain reliefs of offerings and rituals; in a suite of rooms on the eastern side are scenes of Amenhotep III's divine birth in narrative style. Here the god Amen is shown coming to the queen mother in the guise of the king, followed by scenes of the child's conception, the pregnant queen, the delivery of the divinely conceived child with the Hathor goddesses who pronounce the child's fate, and the god Khnum fashioning the child and his *ka*, or soul, on his potter's wheel.

The second phase of reliefs in New Kingdom temples begins with innovations undertaken during the reign of Akhenaten. In the six temples that he built at Karnak for the god Aten, his *heb-sed* (jubilee) festival is depicted in narrative style, including processions and festivities in great detail. Akhenaten's other temples at Karnak and at Tell el-Amarna show narrative style scenes of the royal couple adoring the Aten.

The next example of fully narrative temple relief is of the Opet festival in the processional colonnade of the Luxor temple, which formed the temple's entrance during Tutankhamen's reign. The Opet festival, with the procession's journey downstream from Karnak to Luxor and back, is fully depicted. On the western side of the colonnade, the procession exits from Pylon III of the temple of Karnak, and priests carrying the divine barks of the sun god proceed to the river and embark on barges. Accompanied by dancers, musicians, drummers, and priestly and police escorts, the barges are then towed by boat to Luxor. Next, the divine barks are unloaded from the barges and carried into Luxor, where they are taken to the sanctuaries. Priests and workers are shown preparing offerings of food for the gods, and the pharaoh makes offerings to the gods in their shrines. Reliefs on the eastern wall of the colonnade show the procession's return to Karnak from Luxor. Many of these scenes replicate earlier ones of Queen Hatshepsut's. Tutankhamen also commissioned narrative battle reliefs, as Ray Johnson has now demonstrated. In the Luxor temple were scenes of his campaign to Carchemish in Syria, led by Horemheb, who was later to become pharaoh.

During the 19th and 20th Dynasties the narrative relief of the late 18th Dynasty was developed to a new level. Reliefs on the outer walls of the Hypostyle Hall at Karnak enumerate all the major military campaigns of Seti I in full narrative style. On the northern wall is the campaign against the Shasu people (bedouin), through Sinai to the city of Pa-Kanaan along the "Way of Horus," the royal road from Egypt across Sinai to southwest Asia. Forts and wells are depicted, as is a canal separating Sinai from Egypt. Other reliefs here show the Lebanese chiefs felling cedars, and Egyptian attacks on their fortified towns. Prisoners are rounded up and brought to Egypt, where they are presented to the gods of the Theban triad. At the central door is the traditional scene of the king smiting prisoners, with a topographical list of the conquered lands. Seti I's other military campaigns, against the Amurru in southwest Asia, the Libyans, the Hittites, and the city of Qadesh in western Syria, are depicted on the eastern and western walls. This was the first time that such reliefs were displayed on the outer walls of large cult temples. Seti I's other major temples, at Abydos and Gurna, both remained unfinished when he died, and many of these reliefs were completed by his son Ramesses II. At Abydos are scenes showing the education of the crown prince, and a series of reliefs about the Osiris drama. Reliefs in chapels of this temple show rituals performed for the divine images. The Gurna funerary temple includes reliefs of Ramesses II's coronation by Amen before the other Theban deities and a deified Seti I.

Ramesses II carried narrative relief to new heights in his depiction of his battle with the Hittites at Qadesh. At the Luxor temple and the Ramesseum, his mortuary temple across the river at Thebes, scenes of the Battle of Qadesh cover the entire surface of the pylon towers. Even the registers, which were an artistic device to divide scenes, were eliminated. Reliefs of this battle are also found at Abydos and Abu Simbel. Ramesses II continued his father's tradition of narrative battle scenes with reliefs of his later wars in Syro-Palestine and Jordan. These are found on the outer walls of the Hypostyle Hall at Karnak, exterior walls of the Luxor temple, and interior walls of the first court of the Abydos temple. In the Ramesseum, battle reliefs were continued on interior walls, in the second court, and even on an inner wall of the temple's hypostyle hall. Ramesses II also made use of other narrative scenes on the walls of his temples. In the First Court of the Luxor temple his sons and daughters are depicted marching toward the temple's Pylon I. Reli-

gious festivals, such as the festival of the god Min, were carved in narrative style, as found on the inner face of the eastern tower of the pylon at Luxor and in the Ramesseum. At Abydos and Karnak Ramesses II is shown subjugating the forces of chaos, symbolized by netted birds.

Merenptah, who followed his father Ramesses II on the throne, continued the tradition of narrative battle scenes with reliefs of his Canaanite campaign in the temple of Karnak on the walls of the transverse axis. But wall space was limited, and his great victory over the Libyans and Sea Peoples is represented only in a text version at Karnak. At Abydos Merenptah decorated a corridor with reliefs of the Osiris myth, including scenes of the sun's passage through the night and the punishment of Osiris's foes.

Ramesses III was the last major builder of temples in the New Kingdom, and narrative reliefs of the great naval battle against the Sea Peoples are found in his funerary temple at Medinet Habu. The superb scene of a bull hunt on the rear of the pylon's south tower represents the culmination of the narrative relief style. The small Karnak temple of Ramesses III contains an interesting scene of a river procession during the Opet festival.

With a decline of temple construction in the Third Intermediate Period, there are only a few examples of post-Ramesside building in Upper Egypt. In the Khonsu temple at Karnak is a fine depiction of the cult center's Pylon II together with a relief of the Opet festival procession on the river, dating to the reign of Herihor, circa 1,080–1,070 BC. The reliefs of Sheshonk I at Karnak, showing victory over Judea and Israel during Rehoboam's reign, continue the tradition of the prisoner-smiting scenes accompanied by place names.

The Ramesside kings built sizable temples in the Delta cities, but these were disassembled and moved by the kings of the 21st and 22nd Dynasties to furnish material for later temples at Tanis and Bubastis. These rebuilt temples are now in ruins, but one surviving scene, of the pharaoh Siamen smiting his enemies, demonstrates his victory over Gezer, a Philistine city in Palestine. Other Third Intermediate Period reliefs, such as at the small temple of Amen at Medinet Habu, only contain scenes of religious rituals and offerings. When the Kushite king Piye of the 25th Dynasty depicted his victory over the kings of Libyan descent ruling in northern Egypt, he chose to do so on a large stela.

The reliefs and inscriptions of the New Kingdom, when stone temples were built on a large scale, are a major source of information about ancient Egypt at this time, from foreign relations to religious cults. While many of the claims of kings in these inscriptions are exaggerated, the reliefs depict an age in which Egypt was a major force controlling an empire beyond the lower Nile Valley. Central to the New Kingdom reliefs is the role of the pharaoh, who was an absolute ruler and god-king at home, and a military commander controlling great resources abroad.

See also

Abydos, North, *ka* chapels and cenotaphs; cult temples of the New Kingdom; Deir el-Bahri, Hatshepsut temple; Deir el-Bahri, Tuthmose III temple; Karnak, Akhenaten temples; Karnak, temple of Amen-Re; Luxor, temple of; Medinet Habu; Punt; Tell el-Amarna, cult temples; Thebes, royal funerary temples

Further reading

Arnold, D. 1962. *Wandrelief und Raumfunktion in ägyptischen Tempeln des Neuen Reiches* (MÄS 2). Berlin.

——. 1992. *Die Tempel Ägyptens: Götterwohnungen, Kultstätten, Baudenkmäler.* Zürich.

Gaballa, G.A. 1976. *Narrative in Egyptian Art.* Mainz.

Groenewegen-Frankfort, H.A. 1987. *Arrest and Movement: An Essay on Space and Time in the Representational Art of the Ancient Near East.* Cambridge, MA.

Myśliwiec, K. 1976. *Le portrait royal dans le bas-relief du nouvel empire.* Warsaw.

FRANK J. YURCO

representational evidence, Old Kingdom private tombs

Private (i.e. non-royal) tombs of the Old Kingdom originally bore a very simple wall decoration scheme that evolved into an elaborate and highly accomplished repertoire of painting and relief sculpture. Most of our evidence comes from such sites as Saqqara, Helwan, Meydum, Dahshur, Giza and Abusir. The earliest decorated tombs contained little more than simple niches, or a slab stela set into the exterior of a solid *mastaba* (from the Arabic word for "bench") superstructure. The niches evolved into the so-called "false door," or cult center of the tomb. The slab stela usually held a scene of the deceased seated before a table of offering loaves, along with accompanying inscriptions bearing his name and titles and listing additional invocation offerings.

From these simple beginnings, the *mastaba* decoration scheme expanded along with the architectural development of the private tomb itself. Solid *mastaba* superstructures were eventually given interior chambers, and decoration was moved from the exterior to the interior of the tomb, possibly to protect it from the elements. The artists drew and then carved the decoration directly on the walls themselves, either in raised or sunk relief, or carved them after an initial coat of plaster had been applied to the stone. Paint was usually applied to the figures, inscriptions and often even the background, resulting in a highly polychromed surface. The repertoire of wall scenes and inscriptions grew to include pictures of daily life, of religious events such as the funeral and presentation of offerings, and a host of inscriptions, from simple captions explaining events depicted to full biographical statements of the career and accomplishments of the tombowner. All of these elements were added, not as the artistic self-expression of individual painters and sculptors, but rather to fulfill the functional need for such events in the next world. The activities, provisions and offering spells shown on the tomb walls served the deceased in the afterlife, just as their actual counterparts had done during his or her lifetime.

These wall paintings and carvings provide one of the key elements for the study of all aspects of ancient Egyptian society. The dry climate on the desert's edge, away from the arable lands of the Nile Valley, helped preserve thousands of decorated Egyptian tombs intact, often including even the ancient color scheme. Since so many facets of Egyptian life were recorded on the tomb walls, archaeologists today have a glimpse into ancient Egyptian society, a primary source unavailable for most other dead civilizations. Just how far this "encyclopedia" of ancient Egyptian culture extends is illustrated by the brief comments on selected aspects of Egyptian society provided below.

Daily life

Perhaps the greatest amount of wall space is covered by scenes of daily life. These included representations of fishing and fowling, boating and boat-jousting matches, fieldwork and food production (sowing, harvesting, storage and presentation of crops, brewing, baking), craftsmanship (wood and metal working, ceramic production), and tax collection. The members of the deceased's estate are usually the ones engaged in the labor, but in some ritual scenes, such as fowling in the marshes or the supervision of fieldwork, the deceased himself is portrayed in the scene, usually at a much larger scale to denote his importance.

Language

Private tombs of the Old Kingdom are pivotal for the study of the earliest phase of the language, known as Old Egyptian. For the first time, long narrative texts and biographical accounts appear, facilitating the study of textual composition and grammatical forms. The tomb reliefs and paintings are indispensable to the study of early palaeography, as well as the evolution of the language from Old Egyptian into its classical phase (Middle Egyptian) during the Middle Kingdom.

Literature

Literary genres occurring in Old Kingdom private tombs are fairly limited compared to later phases of the language, but nevertheless contain as many as three loosely defined types. Stock religious invocations beginning with the familiar *hetep di nisut* formula ("A gift that the king gives...") abound, followed by wishes for a good burial in the necropolis and offerings provided on the days of certain festivals. Menu lists, arranged in compartments somewhat resembling a modern crossword puzzle, list offering provisions of bread, beer, milk, wine, cuts of meat and fowl, fruits and vegetables and linen, and their respective amounts.

A second literary genre gives the deceased's names and titles repeatedly throughout the tomb, listing all his promotions and duties. These passages are part of the biogaphy genre, often including praiseworthy statements of the deceased's conduct and awards granted by the king. Lengthier narratives describing actual historical events, such as trading expeditions to the south, or military campaigns, are rare but do occur on occasion. These give us some of the more informative impressions of Old Kingdom political and social history.

A third literary category is that of the captions accompanying representational scenes. Along with simple captions explaining the process of winnowing, or assisting in the birth of a calf, there are often quotations by the workers involved, calling for assistance or criticizing each other's laziness. These inscriptions afford a glimpse into the "local color" of fieldwork, and the slang of the craftsmen, as they go about their tasks.

Music

Certain festivals and holidays are listed in inscriptions and/or portrayed in representations. Musical instruments, such as harps and flutes, are depicted in such scenes, but no system of musical notation seems to have existed; or at least it is absent from the tomb wall decoration.

Figure 92 Subterranean chambers showing wall paintings and engaged statuary, tomb of Queen
　　　　　Meresankh III at Giza (G 7530-7540)
Courtesy of the Museum of Fine Arts, Boston

Religion

All of the tomb's decoration served the mortuary function of providing for the deceased in the next world. For this reason, all of the categories listed here could be cited as part of the religious culture of the Egyptians. Nevertheless, the scrutiny of specific scenes and inscriptions reveals much about the ancient systems or festivals and their calendrical cycles, and about offering ceremonies and which family members perform them. Offering spells list specific deities with specific protective functions. Even certain articles of clothing,

such as the leopard skin worn by the *sem*-priest during offering rituals, are accurately reproduced in tomb wall scenes.

State/social organization

The lists of functional titles held by the deceased are a primary source for the study of the highly structured and hierarchical nature of the Egyptian administration. Often, particular institutions, such as a temple complex, are mentioned, lending insights into the operation of large administrative centers. However, deciphering the precise meaning of the titles, many of which must have been honorary, is often a difficult task. In addition to listing the role of the deceased, tomb wall inscriptions and representations also contain several social strata of the ancient population. Among the individuals represented in the tomb are priests and other religious functionaries, tax gatherers, scribes and other administrators, craftsmen and artisans, fowlers and fishermen. Some of these groups do not mix with others, and are never represented together.

Legal decrees inscribed on tomb walls also provide assistance in understanding the administration of goods and services. Usually, these "wills" or decrees designate certain individuals or institutions with the task of maintaining the cult of the tomb-owner, and append various provisions for protection from external interference.

Architecture

Numerous structures are portrayed in scenes from Old Kingdom tombs. Buildings, canopies, boats, workshops, granaries and other structures are often represented with attention to detail.

History

The Egyptians were more concerned with providing the correct funerary formulae and stock phrases and scenes in the tomb than they were with depicting historical events in the modern sense. Thus history must be largely reconstructed indirectly from a variety of sources, some of which come from private tomb decoration. The listings of various kings and construction projects help to answer chronological questions, and occasionally a biographical text will go into some detail about a specific expedition or royal decree.

Art

A wide range of styles is evident from even the most cursory of comparative studies of Old Kingdom private tombs. As more tomb decoration is published, scholars are able to study chronological developments, regional art styles, the work of specific workshops, and varying painting and carving techniques. The proportional canon of Egyptian art, the system of laying out a grid on the wall for the placement of figures, is also a feature that evolved over time and may be studied on tomb walls.

Other aspects of Egyptian culture revealed by the wall scenes are costume, including dress, jewelry, hair and wig styles, and footwear. In addition, diet and nutrition are represented by the types of food offerings preferred by the Egyptians.

See also

Giza, workmen's community; Memphite private tombs of the Old Kingdom; Old Kingdom provincial tombs; textual sources, Old Kingdom

Further reading

Bolshakov, A. 1997. *Man and His Double in Egyptian Ideology of the Old Kingdom* (Ägypten und Altes Testament 37). Wiesbaden.

Cherpion, N. 1989. *Mastabas et hypogées d'Ancien Empire: Le problème de la datation.* Brussels.

Harpur, Y. 1987. *Decoration in Egyptian Tombs of the Old Kingdom.* London.

Málek, J. 1986. *In The Shadow of the Pyramids: Egypt during the Old Kingdom.* London.

Smith, W.S. 1949. *A History of Egyptian Sculpture and Painting in the Old Kingdom,* 2nd edn. Boston.

PETER DER MANUELIAN

representational evidence, papyri and ostraca

The ancient Egyptians employed two basic types of material as a surface for writing and drawing. The easily available and relatively economical papyrus was used for official documents, dockets, letters, memoranda, religious texts and literary compositions, but it could also be employed for plans, maps, construction drawings and other illustrative material. An alternative surface for writing and drawing of various kinds was early recognized in the abundance and easy availability of broken pottery and limestone chips from quarries and tomb excavation (both termed "ostraca" in Egyptological literature, although the term more properly describes only the pottery fragments). Slightly curved potsherds and neatly fractured limestone flakes provided nearly flat surfaces that required no preparation and had the advantage of being virtually permanent as well as without cost. Other materials used for drawing and writing included leather, parchment and prepared boards.

By far the most common illustrations found on papyrus are the so-called "vignettes" in the New Kingdom *Book of the Dead*, with a rich imagery describing the activities of the spirit after death. These include standardized subjects such as the "weighing of the heart," the personal judgment of the individual before the gods, the "plowing of the fields in the land of the blessed," the participation of the deceased in activities pleasing to the gods and for the sustenance of the spirit in the next world, and a wide variety of encounters and rituals carried out by the spirit. All of these contribute to our knowledge of what the Egyptians believed or expected in the life after death.

In addition to those that contain illustrations from the *Book of the Dead* there exists a class of papyrus rolls which have been called "Mythological Papyri." They contain very little text but are principally representations related to other religious works such as the *Book of Gates* and *The Book of What is in the Underworld*. They were made to aid and accompany the spirit of the deceased and they provide a wealth of religious and mythic images, some of which are difficult or impossible to interpret without accompanying texts.

Architectural drawings on papyrus, and occasionally on ostraca, have been preserved in a limited but sufficient quantity to suggest that these were common vehicles for the presentation of plans and elevations of construction projects and designs. Notable among them are a plan for the royal tomb of Ramesses IV in the Valley of the Kings at Thebes, and the front and side elevation designs for an elaborate shrine from Gurob. These show that careful and detailed drawings were committed to papyrus to be used much as modern construction drawings and blueprints in the process of the actual work.

A very rare papyrus in the Brooklyn Museum actually depicts a historic event which can be precisely dated to year 14 of King Psamtik I in 651 BC, recording the granting of a petition by the god Amen. The rarity of this single example emphasizes the fact that almost all representations on papyrus are of a religious, ritual or simple practical (architecture and design) nature and that the ancient Egyptian concept of history did not include committing representations of an ephemeral nature to ink on papyrus.

The types of evidence to be found on ostraca are considerably different, however. This may be ascribed to the fact that the waste material of stone and broken pottery may have been used for less important work or records or the same material was less perishable than papyrus. Ostraca were used for literary texts, letters and accounts, but they were also used as the practice pads for scribes or artists in training and the sketch book pages and pattern drawings for accomplished craftsmen. From the quantity of such sketches, trials and finished drawings preserved, we can deduce information concerning the training of the artist and some of the technical steps in the execution of large-scale works on the walls of temples and tombs. It is evident that some designs were more difficult to execute than others because many more examples of them exist, either as models or copies. Some drawings clearly show the work of two artistic hands, one skillful and practiced while the second is less so, probably illustrating the work of a student or apprentice copying the master. Other drawings incorporate elements such as hands or clenched fists, which seem to have been used as standards of measure or proportion.

One distinct class of drawings, occurring both on papyri and ostraca, represents a series of animals engaged in human activities. A cat standing on its hind legs might herd geese as a man would herd cattle. A baby mouse is attended to by a cat nurse-maid. These and other examples like them have been interpreted as illustration for animal fables which were probably only conveyed through the spoken word and not through writing. They seem to suggest a body of fable in which animals deport themselves with human attitudes, a type of folk tale common in many cultures.

More typical of the type of drawings preserved on ostraca are the many studies of figures and heads, particularly the heads of kings, which were intended as practice or model pieces to be reproduced on tomb walls. Such drawings are often overlaid with a network of proportioned squares as an aid in the transfer of the small design to a larger format. Working drawings also exist of complicated subjects such as the king in a chariot or combatants in various games. Animal forms, both as used in hieroglyphic writing and as used in scenes of domestication or of hunting and fishing, are abundantly illustrated, probably because the types were difficult to render and required working out or practice. It is to these randomly preserved trials and sketches that we must turn in an effort to understand the education of the Egyptian draughtsman-artist, for from them we gain an impression of the stages of training and practice necessary to the production of the strict canonical art of ancient Egypt.

See also

funerary texts; papyrus

Further reading

Kischkewitz, H. 1972. *Egyptian Drawings*. London.
Peck, W.H., and J.G. Ross. 1978. *Drawings from Ancient Egypt*. London.

WILLIAM H. PECK

representational evidence, Predynastic

This entry deals only with painted or incised designs and not with three-dimensional artifacts. Painted and incised representations played a considerable role in Predynastic culture, both in a purely decorative way and as an important part of ritual practices. All the material discussed relates to the Predynastic Nagada culture of Upper Egypt. This kind of art is represented by four categories: (1) decorated pottery, (2) incised rock drawings known as petroglyphs, (3) tomb paintings (only known from one example), and (4) slate palettes.

Predynastic painted pottery is divided into two classes. The early material, dating to the Nagada I phase (*circa* 4,000–3,500 BC) is known as White Cross-lined class. It consists of a plum to reddish-brown body with a burnished surface and designs in white, pale yellow or pale pink paint.

The decorated pottery of the Nagada II and III phases (*circa* 3,500–3,100 BC) is quite different, in a pale buff colored clay with designs painted in red-brown. It is known as Decorated class. Both types of pottery have been known since the late nineteenth century when Flinders Petrie first worked at the important Predynastic site of Nagada on the west bank of the Nile north of Luxor.

The painted designs of White Cross-lined class most commonly consist of geometrical patterns, especially with triangles and rhombuses. Shapes are filled in with cross-hatching, diagonal lines, chevrons, wavy lines and plain bands of paint. Some rare examples depict animals, such as scorpions, antelopes or gazelles, giraffes, hippopotami, and horned sheep or goats. Plants are also occasionally shown, but very few vessels have depictions of humans. Many of these latter scenes are interpreted as having some kind of ritual significance.

Decorated class may be divided into three groups. The first group consists of abstract designs which are purely decorative. The motifs used include wavy lines, geometric figures, irregular splashes, and lines and "comma" shapes. The second group uses motifs which imitate stone. The variegated surface of stones, such as diorite and breccia, are represented by spiral patterns and irregular shapes. These pots may have been intended as substitutes for real stone vessels, which must have been more costly.

The third group of Decorated class has more complex designs showing many-oared boats, often with cabins, steering oars, sails and so-called "nome standards," referring to the later emblems of the Dynastic districts (nomes) of Egypt. Each Dynastic nome had an emblem or standard by which the nome was recognized. It is impossible to ascertain whether these Pre-dynastic standards represented particular regions or had other significance, but during this period it seems that the standards probably had a social and politico-religious meaning. Some of the signs also appear to be early forms which later became hieroglyphs.

The boats are often accompanied by several varieties of plants, wading birds and geometric figures, such as bands of triangles and lines of "Z" shapes, which have been interpreted as flying birds. Less commonly, some boats have human and/or animal passengers.

The purpose and meaning of these scenes is obscure. Attempts have been made to interpret the boats as temple buildings, but this is not generally accepted. The identity of the frondy plant, known as the "Nagada plant," has also been debated: it has been identified as an aloe and as a type of tree known as the "false banana" (ensete). Neither of these interpretations is wholly acceptable, however. What is significant is its importance as a sacred tree. The importance of boat scenes is also borne out by petroglyphs. These rock drawings are found in the caves and wadis of the Eastern Desert, and to a lesser extent in the Western Desert, in Upper Egypt. They were hammered out of the rock, and were sometimes neatened or elaborated with incisions. They often depict boats, men and animals in scenes which are strikingly similar to those on Predynastic pottery. The animals depicted include all those mentioned above in connection with pottery, along with elephants, wild cattle, wild felines, crocodiles

and dogs. The people depicted in association with boats often have upraised arms. This pose is commonly shown on Decorated class pottery and was probably associated with ritual activity. The pose is also found in association with hunting scenes. A number of petroglyphs show hunting activities, including the use of throw-sticks and the pursuit with harpoons of hippopotami.

Both boat and hunting scenes seem to have been accompanied by people performing ritual activities, and this suggests that both painted pottery and petroglyphs had some greater symbolic significance. One site (Site 18, north-east of Luxor between Wadi el-Qash and Wadi Zeidun) notable for its petroglyphs was so thickly covered with boat drawings that no single outline remained clear and unobscured. This cannot have been done with artistic intent, but suggests that the site and the drawings had special meaning for the Predynastic Egyptians; especially since the drawings were sited at such a distance from the Nile Valley.

The theme of boats is continued in the only known painted tomb from Predynastic Egypt, Tomb 100 at Hierakonpolis. This mudbrick-lined tomb was decorated with painted designs on walls with a background of either white or buff-yellow. The designs seem to have been sketched out in red ocher before being completed, and then they were filled in with red, green, blue-black and white paint.

The Tomb 100 drawings, which are very similar to both petroglyphs and Decorated pottery motifs, show quite complex boat scenes. The ships are without banks of oars, but they do have steering oars and cabins. Some also have human occupants and show standards. Interspersed with the boats are hunting scenes and the trapping of animals. The tomb was in very bad repair when it was discovered and presents great difficulties of interpretation.

The wide range of representational art known from Predynastic Egypt is often the only key to understanding Predynastic society. There are no texts to read, therefore attempts must be made to "read" the scenes which were painted and carved by the Predynastic Egyptians. This is difficult, and often dangerous, since it is likely that scenes will be misinterpreted or endowed with more significance than they merit.

The ownership of painted pottery or a painted tomb certainly demonstrates that the owner was of a high rank in society. Some of the scenes may have indicated a specific status of the owner, and it is possible that the so-called nome standards were particularly important in this respect.

It is clear that boat scenes were of great importance in Nagada II times. This might well imply the importance of some kind of nautical festival as early as the Predynastic period. The ritual importance of ships is well attested in Dynastic Egyptian religion, and it seems clear that such importance developed early in Egyptian history. The "cabins" on the boats may have been some kind of shrine, and it is possible that figures depicted above the cabins were intended to be understood as being inside the cabins. The human figures may, therefore, have had a priest-like role, with the animals intended for sacrifice.

The Nagada plant was also of considerable importance in association with boat scenes, and may have been regarded as a kind of sacred tree. This seems especially likely since the design which is often displayed at the prow of boats is the same as that shown sprouting from the Nagada plant. The importance of animals and birds, both on White Cross-lined class and Decorated class pottery, implies that there may also have been an early origin for some of the animal cults favored by the Dynastic Egyptians. Animals also had considerable significance within the context of hunting scenes. These occurred not only in Tomb 100 at Hierakonpolis, but also as petroglyphs and on White Cross-lined class pottery.

Boats were probably also considered important because they were a means by which goods could be traded up and down the Nile Valley, both regionally and over long distances. This economic interaction was of great importance in Predynastic Egypt because it encouraged the growth of an extended trade in luxury items, such as stone vases and elaborate pottery. Such trade had a major role to play in the emergence of complex society. Exotic craft goods were in

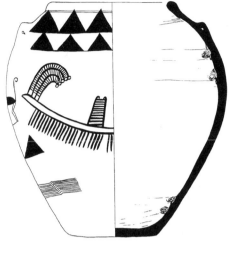

Figure 93 Decorated class pot with scenes of boats, ostriches and the "Nagada plant"
Source: Manchester Museum 7755, drawing by Sally Swain

demand in Nagada II times by elite groups wishing to express their social status. Boats were vital to trade, and this almost certainly bolstered their religious significance.

Representational art was of great importance to the Predynastic Egyptians, not only for decorative purposes, but also because it played an important role in enhancing the ritual of their beliefs. A variety of techniques was used to create several artistic styles in different media. It seems possible that some of the conventions which became important in Dynastic times were already present during the Predynastic era, including the importance of animal and boat scenes, the use of painted substitutes in graves, the emphasis on tomb painting and the importance of representing religious ritual.

See also

Hierakonpolis; Nagada (Naqada); pottery, prehistoric; Predynastic period, overview; representational evidence, Early Dynastic; ships

Further reading

Adams, B. 1988. *Predynastic Egypt*. Aylesbury.

Hoffman, M.A. 1991. *Egypt Before the Pharaohs*. Austin, TX.

Monet Saleh, J. 1987. Remarques sur les representations de la peinture d'Hierakonpolis (Tombe No. 100). *JEA* 73: 51–8.

Petrie, W.M.F. 1921. *Corpus of Predynastic Pottery and Slate Palettes*. London.

——. 1953. *Corpus of Protodynastic Pottery and Ceremonial Slate Palettes*. London.

Winkler, H.A. 1938–9. *The Rock Drawings of Southern Upper Egypt* 1 and 2. London.

SALLY SWAIN

Roman forts in Egypt

More than 100 Roman forts exist throughout Egypt with construction and occupation dates spanning the late first century BC to the sixth or early seventh century AD. The major role of these forts and of the Roman army in Egypt was maintenance of internal security; there was little threat of invasion by major forces from outside the province throughout most of the Roman period. The forts and their garrisons performed multiple functions, including monitoring activities (commercial, official-governmental, security) of peoples living in and passing through regions where they were located. They also protected vital trans-desert routes or key locations on the Nile and in the Delta from hostile peoples, mainly bandits and, from the third/fourth century AD on, bedouin marauders like the Nobatae and Blemmyes. Larger forts on the Nile and in the Delta were often support bases for smaller outlying desert garrisons.

Forts in Lower Egypt tend to be poorly preserved, as do those in Upper Egypt along the Nile, due mainly to human depredations. Those at Luxor, Qal'at el-Baben *circa* 20 km south of Edfu and Babylon south of Cairo have been studied to some extent. Those in the desert regions vary greatly in size, but tend to be better preserved than their counterparts in the Nile Valley. Damage to and destruction of the desert forts has been caused by floods and, more recently, human activity.

The Eastern Desert installations guarded key roads leading to ports, mines or quarries or protected the more important quarries and mines themselves, such as Mons Porphyrites, Mons Claudianus, Semna, Barrimiya, Samut and Nakheil. Those in the Western Desert guarded trade/invasion routes coming from Sudan to the south especially along the Darb el-Arba'ein, the key oases (Fayum, Baharia, Farafra, Dakhla, Kharga) and routes leading thence to the Nile. In the Fayum (e.g. Qasr Qarun) these forts monitored more densely populated areas. Those in Sinai, such as the one at Pelusium, guarded key urban centers or transportation arteries, while others protected mines and quarries.

Few of the forts in the deserts have been excavated. The French have been working at sites in the Western Desert. An international team led by L'Institut français d'archéologie orientale excavated at the Eastern Desert quarry site and fort at Mons Claudianus (first to early fourth(?) centuries AD), at Zerkah (Maximianon) and el-Muwayḥ (Krokodilo) on the ancient route between Quseir and the Nile. American teams have excavated at the late Roman (late third(?) to sixth or seventh century) fort at Abu Sha'ar *circa* 20 km north of Hurghada on the Red Sea coast (University of Delaware) and at Didyme (Khasm el-Menih/ Zeydun) toward the northern end of the Berenike–Coptos road (University of Michigan). Other Eastern Desert forts along the Abu Sha'ar–Kainopolis (Qena) road, the Quseir (Myos Hormos?)–Coptos (Quft) road, the Berenike–Apollinopolis Magna and Berenike–Coptos/Edfu roads (Strabo, *Geography* 17.1.45 and Pliny, *Natural History* 6.26.102–3) and the Marsa Nakari (Nechesia?)–Edfu route have been plotted on a map using the Global Positioning System, examined, drawn in plan and dated through surface (mainly ceramic and numismatic) artifact analysis. Several roads noted by earlier scholars in the Eastern Desert and along the Red Sea coast no longer exist, such as that at Qwei *circa* 30 km north of Quseir and Clysma (near Suez) (Claudius Ptolemy, *Geography* 4.5). Others, both known and unknown to earlier scholars, survive in only very poor condition (e.g. Abu Sha'ar *circa* 40 km southwest of Ras Gharib, Gedami, Abu Gerida, Compasi). The ancient names of these forts are unknown, except for a number along the routes between Berenike and Coptos and Quseir el-Qadim and Coptos.

Generally, regular Roman units were stationed in major legionary camps in the Nile Valley; auxiliaries, mostly mounted cavalry and dromedary units, corvée and "police" were posted in more outlying desert regions, no doubt assisted by local scouts. The legionary units were not permanently stationed in Egypt and were occasionally transferred out of the province. There is growing knowledge of garrison sizes, specific names of units stationed in the outlying desert forts, along desert roads, in mines and quarries, and the regional/ethnic origins of the troops. Roman troops, probably supervising local labor, repaired installations in the Eastern Desert in the first century AD.

Shapes of the forts varied in plan; rectilinear shapes were the most popular. Less numerous are oval or circular plans or a combination of oval/circular and rectilinear, such as the forts at Qal'at el-Baben on the Nile and el-Kanaïs, at Wadi Abu Greiya (Vetus Hydreuma), Semna and Wadi Belih in the Eastern Desert; these shapes seem to fall in the Ptolemaic or earlier period of Roman occupation rather than the later. An unusual semicircular fort exists at Wadi Umm Gariya (previously and erroneously located at Umm 'Ushra) in the Eastern Desert along the Berenike–Nile road. Nile forts were built of stone with some brick; those in the desert were built mainly of locally acquired dry laid stones and mudbrick, with fired brick used sparingly in hydraulic contexts.

Larger forts had either rectilinear or circular/oval shaped towers at the corners, flanking the gates and midway along the walls; the smaller forts had fewer towers or lacked them altogether. Fort wall bases were usually of stone with superstructures in stone or mudbrick. Walls often tapered toward the top and frequently had a batter. The interiors of the Eastern Desert *hydreumata* (fortified water installations) generally had large cisterns or wells surrounded by rooms abutting the interiors of the main fort walls. Occasionally the cisterns/wells for desert installations lay outside the defensive walls (e.g. Wadi Belih, Abu Sha'ar on the Red Sea coast, Mons Claudianus, Mons Porphyrites). In some instances the forts are too ruined to determine cistern/well location; some forts stored water channeled into their interior cisterns from nearby mountains (e.g. Abu Hegilig North and South). Animal tethering lines (providing rest and revictualing points for draught animals hauling quarry stone) lay outside and adjacent to many of the forts in the Eastern Desert along the Abu Sha'ar–Nile road in that segment between the quarries at Mons Porphyrites and Kainopolis and the trunk routes leading westward to the Nile from the quarries at Mons Claudianus.

Most of the desert forts were set along routes of varying widths, cleared of surface boulders and cobbles. These "roads" were generally unpaved though a few paved sections of questionable date survive on the Abu Sha'ar–Kainopolis road. Cairns defined most or all of the courses of some of these desert highways (Via Hadriana, Abu Sha'ar–Kainopolis road, Mersa Nakari–Edfu route, Quseir el-Qadim–Coptos road, Berenike–Edfu and Berenike–Coptos roads). Signal and watch towers also appear regularly and in great numbers on some (Abu Sha'ar–Kainopolis and Quseir el-Qadim–Coptos) roads, more sporadically on the Berenike–Nile routes. Provisions of water for travelers might also be found next to some of the cairns and towers (e.g. the Abu Sha'ar–Kainopolis and Berenike–Coptos roads).

In the later period of Roman occupation (early fourth century AD onward), the region east of the Nile was styled a *limes* (frontier administrative zone). This may have been the case prior to the fourth century as well. Some of these forts continued in sporadic, non-military use later in the Roman period as monasteries (such as Abu Sha'ar on the Red Sea coast) or stopping points for Christian travelers. In the Islamic era forts along some of the main thoroughfares between the Nile and the Red Sea (Coptos–Quseir and Quft/Edfu–Berenike south to 'Aidhab) were convenient overnight stops for pilgrims making the *hajj* (pilgrimage to Mecca).

See also

Abu Sha'ar; Mons Porphyrites; Roman period, overview; Roman ports, Red Sea

Further reading

Sidebotham, S.E., and R.E. Zitterkopf. 1995. Eastern Desert of Egypt: survey of the Berenice–Nile roads. *Expedition* 37(2): 39–52.

Sidebotham, S.E., R.E. Zitterkopf and J.A. Riley. 1991. Survey of the Abu Sha'ar–Nile Road. *AJA* 95(4): 571–622.

Zitterkopf, R.E., and S.E. Sidebotham. 1989. Stations and towers on the Quseir–Nile road. *JEA* 75: 155–89.

STEVEN E. SIDEBOTHAM

Roman ports, Red Sea

The second century AD geographer Claudius Ptolemy (*Geography* 4.5) indicates six ports on the Red Sea coast of Egypt. They were, from north to south: Clysma-Qolzoum-Arsinoë-Cleopatris (near Suez), Philoteras, Myos Hormos (Quseir?), Leukos Limen/Albus Portus, Nechesia (Mersa Nakari?) and Berenike. Ptolemy's locations are only approximate; he does not indicate when these were founded nor whether all were operating in his day.

Confusion in the location and identification of the classical Red Sea Egyptian ports stems from Claudius Ptolemy's imprecise coordinates and from differing accounts in other ancient authors. Strabo (*Geography* 16.4.5) lists four

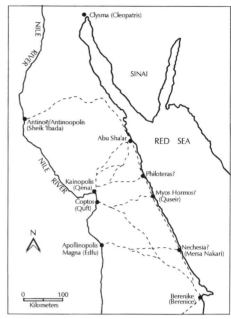

Figure 94 Map of the Eastern Desert with principal routes and emporia, on both the Nile and the Red Sea

ports from north to south: Philoteras, Arsinoë, Myos Hormos and Berenike. Later in the first century AD, Pliny the Elder (*Natural History* 6.33.167–8) gives the order of Egypt's Red Sea ports from north to south as: Arsinoë, Philoteras (Aenum), Myos Hormos and Berenike. The *Periplus Maris Erythraei* 1 (approximately contemporary with Pliny) mentions that Myos Hormos was 1,800 stades from Berenike. No ancient author except Claudius Ptolemy mentions Leukos Limen and Nechesia. Other classical references spanning the third/second centuries BC to the sixth century AD refer to the Egyptian ports of Clysma-Qolzoum-Arsinoë-Cleopatris (29°58′ N, 32°33′ E), founded on or near the pharaonic settlement of Kemouer; Philoteras; Myos Hormos; and Berenike (23°55′ N, 35°28′ E).

Literary accounts and/or etymology of port names indicate that most "classical" Egyptian Red Sea emporia seem to have been founded during the Ptolemaic period. Some, such as Clysma-Qolzoum-Arsinoë-Cleopatris (named after Arsinoë II, queen-wife-sister of Ptolemy II in *circa* 270/269 BC), Philoteras (named after the sister of Ptolemy II) and Berenike (named after the mother of Ptolemy II, in *circa* 275 BC), were official Ptolemaic foundations; others founded in the Ptolemaic period, such as Myos Hormos (Mussel Harbor, less likely Mouse Harbor) and Nechesia, may have been unofficial creations. Excavations at Quseir el-Qadim (26°10′ N, 34°17′ E) suggest that it was founded only in the Roman period (first century AD). There is scholarly debate on the identification of Quseir el-Qadim; recent arguments associate it with Myos Hormos. Perhaps the ruins of an earlier Ptolemaic site lay under modern Quseir.

All the ports appear to have functioned at some point in Roman times, but there is no extant evidence that any of the ports—with the possible exception of Arsinoë and Berenike—operated throughout most of the Roman occupation of Egypt. Berenike was important enough in the Roman era to lend its name to the region governed for a time in the first and early second centuries AD by a military prefect. Papyrus Hamburg 7, of AD 132, indicates that Berenike was part of a nome of that name by the reign of Hadrian. Archaeological surveys and excavations have investigated Clysma-Qolzoum-Arsinoë-Cleopatris, Quseir el-Qadim and Berenike; Myos Hormos may be at modern Quseir or at Quseir el-Qadim. The identifications of Philoteras (in the Wadi Safaga or Wadi Gawasis?) and Nechesia (Mersa Tundaba, Mersa Nakari or Wadi Mubarak?) are uncertain.

There was commercial activity at some of the ports in the Ptolemaic era. At that time trade seems to have been mainly within the Red Sea with the establishment of a number of elephant-hunting stations down the African coast to the Bab el-Mandeb and perhaps beyond, along the Indian Ocean coast of Africa (Strabo, *Geography* 16.4.7ff; Pliny, *Natural History* 6.34.170–5). Major items of import from this region in this period were elephants and gold for the Ptolemaic military. Evidence of limited Ptolemaic contact with India indicates occasional forays beyond the Red Sea to lands bordering the Indian Ocean.

Literary evidence and archaeological excavations in Egypt and elsewhere in the Red Sea–Indian Ocean region suggest that in the early Roman era (30 BC–second century AD) maritime commerce with South Arabia, India, Sri Lanka and coastal sub-Saharan Africa reached its zenith. This trade was of a greater volume, involved a larger variety of goods and ranged farther afield in the Roman than in the Ptolemaic period. Roman trade in the Red Sea–Indian Ocean was more commercially motivated than that of the Ptolemies. Despite the generally held scholarly view that Rome suffered a balance of trade deficit in this eastern trade, there are no ancient statistics to support this assumption; the few disparaging references to it by ancient sources are hyperbolic (Pliny, *Natural History* 6.26.101; 12.41.84, whose figures are suspicious; Tacitus, *Annals* 3.53; Dio Chrysostom, *Discourse* 79.5.6).

From excavations undertaken at Clysma-Qolzoum-Arsinoë-Cleopatris, Quseir el-Qadim and Berenike, it is clear that most buildings at these emporia were quickly and poorly constructed of mudbrick, locally acquired stone and coral. This kept overhead costs minimal in order to maximize profits from the commerce. Evidence at Quseir el-Qadim and Berenike suggests that those ports were laid out on a grid pattern, implying some organizing central power at work (the Ptolemaic/Roman governments of Egypt).

Roads connected these ports to emporia on the Nile. All the major trans-desert Red Sea–Nile roads had way-stations, many of which were fortified watering points (*hydreumata*). Cairns and signal towers dotted the lengths of the major roads linking Abu Sha'ar with Kainopolis (Qena), Myos Hormos with Kainopolis or Coptos (Qift), Berenike with Apollinopolis Magna (Edfu) and Coptos, Nechesia (Mersa Nakari?) with Edfu. In addition, cairns marked the course of the Via Hadriana which began at Antinoë/Antinoopolis (Sheikh 'Ibada) on the Nile in Middle Egypt, ran east to the Red Sea coast and proceeded south where it terminated at Berenike.

The Berenike–Edfu route was popular in the Ptolemaic and early Roman period, but was little used in the later Roman and Islamic eras.

In Roman times the preferred route from Berenike to the Nile went to Coptos. The latest of the major highways was the Via Hadriana, built and named in honor of the emperor Hadrian in the second century AD. The Eastern Desert highway linking the late Roman fort at Abu Sha'ar to the Nile emporium of Kainopolis also acted as part of the *limes* (administrative frontier zone) in the region from the early fourth century AD on. This may also have been the case with the other major highways linking key Red Sea ports to the Nile in Roman times, if not earlier in the Ptolemaic period.

See also

Abu Sha'ar; Berenike Panchrysos; Quseir el-Qadim; Roman forts in Egypt; Roman period, overview; trade, foreign; Wadi Hammamat

Further reading

Begley, V., and R.D. De Puma. 1991. *Rome and India: The Ancient Sea Trade.* Madison, WI.

Sidebotham, S.E. 1986. *Roman Economic Policy in the Erythra Thalassa 30 B.C.–A.D. 217* (Mnemosyne supplement no. 91). Leiden.

Sidebotham, S.E. and Wendrich, W.Z. 1996. Berenike: Roman Egypt's maritime gateway to Arabia and India. *Egyptian Archaeology* 8: 15–18.

STEVEN E. SIDEBOTHAM

Rosetta Stone

The Rosetta Stone, one of the most famous monuments from ancient Egypt, is a slab of black basalt containing a single text in Greek and Egyptian versions. The stone, now in the British Museum in London, played a crucial role in the decipherment of hieroglyphic writing.

Rosetta is a small modern Egyptian town, founded in the second half of the ninth century AD. Once a flourishing seaport, it is located on the Mediterranean coast about 50 km east of Alexandria. Its actual Arabic name is Rashid;

"Rosetta" is an anglicized version. About 7 km northwest of Rashid, at a strategic location on a branch of the Nile, are the remains of a medieval fort, partially built of stones hauled from ancient Egyptian monuments both nearby and far away. It is one of these stones that became known as the Rosetta Stone.

The stone was found in the summer of 1799 by French army engineers engaged in the restoration and expansion of the Arab fort during Napoleon's Egyptian expedition (1798–1801). The slab was transported to Cairo and, upon Napoleon's defeat, surrendered to the British in Alexandria under the terms of capitulation. It reached London in early 1802 and was deposited later that year in the British Museum.

The stone is about 118 cm high, 77 cm wide, and 30 cm thick, and weighs 726 kg. Its top portion is now missing, but it must originally have been about 180 cm in height.

The flat front of the Rosetta Stone bears a single text in three versions. The version inscribed on the bottom third is Greek. The other two versions are in two different scripts of Egyptian. The text may be characterized as bilingual, not trilingual, if the two Egyptian versions are counted as a single language.

The fragmentary version at the top is written in Middle Egyptian, an earlier phase of the language which died out many centuries before the stone was inscribed and which remained in use only as an official language for academic and religious purposes. The Middle Egyptian version of the text is written in hieroglyphs.

The version in the center of the stone is Demotic, the (Egyptian) language spoken at the time when the stone was inscribed. This version is written in the Demotic script, a cursive variant of hieroglyphic writing used exclusively to write the Demotic stage of Egyptian.

It was realized immediately upon discovery of the stone that its text offered the best chances yet to decipher hieroglyphic writing. The Greek version stated that the undeciphered Egyptian texts were but versions of the translatable Greek text. Copies of the text were made available to scholars throughout Europe in an exemplary spirit of cooperation, and for about two decades the text of the Rosetta Stone formed the focus of all efforts at decipherment by European scholars. Although, in the end, the Rosetta Stone was not the exclusive provider of clues for the decipherment of the Egyptian language by Jean-François Champollion in 1822, it has rightly emerged as the symbol of one of the great intellectual achievements of mankind.

The extraordinary history of the stone and its crucial role in the decipherment have tended to overshadow its value as a historical document. The slab records a royal decree dating to 196 BC during the Ptolemaic period, when Egypt was governed by rulers of Greek descent who had come into power at the death of the Macedonian conqueror Alexander the Great. This explains the bilingual character of the stone.

The text commemorates the accession to the throne of Ptolemy V and was composed in the ninth year of his reign. Ptolemy V promises various benefits such as gifts and reduction of taxes to the temple domains of Egypt. In return, the priests pledge to promote the cult of the young king by erecting stone slabs exactly like the Rosetta Stone next to a statue of the pharaoh in temples throughout the land. It is interesting to note that, since the discovery of the Rosetta Stone, fragmentary duplicates have emerged elsewhere in Egypt.

See also

Egyptian (language), decipherment of; Late and Ptolemaic periods, overview; Napoleon Bonaparte and the Napoleonic expedition

Further reading

Andrews, C. 1981. *The Rosetta Stone*. London.
Quirke, S., and C. Andrews. 1988. *The Rosetta Stone: Facsimile Drawing with an Introduction and Translations*. New York.

LEO DEPUYDT

S

el-Salaam Canal

The el-Salaam (Peace) Canal is the largest irrigation project undertaken by the Egyptian government in recent years. It is certainly the most significant in terms of impact on archaeological sites since the building of the High Dam at Aswan and the subsequent Nubian Salvage campaign. The canal, begun early in the 1990s, is designed to run eastward across to the northern Sinai, close to and broadly parallel with the Mediterranean coast, from just north of Qantara to el-Arish. The direct course of the el-Salaam Canal brings it close to, or across, archaeological sites in a region which, unlike southwestern Sinai, has not been intensively explored archaeologically apart from work early this century by Jean Clédat and more recently by Eliezer Oren. Current work, predating the canal project, has been carried on in the Qantara region by Mohammed Abdel Maksoud at Tell Hebua (New Kingdom) and by Dominique Valbelle at Tell el-Herr (late Dynastic and Graeco-Roman). In addition, the subsidiary canalization, which represents the secondary phase of the irrigation project, with the intention of turning desert into cultivated fields, also poses an immediate threat to archaeological sites.

The North Sinai Salvage Project is an international collaborative effort, bringing together teams from the Egyptian Supreme Council for Antiquities (formerly the Egyptian Antiquities Organization) with teams from a variety of foreign countries. To date, most work has been focused on the western part of the sector, where canal digging has proceeded most rapidly. Particular attention has been placed on survey and excavation of sites in the vicinity of Pelusium, an important ancient city, especially in the Graeco-Roman period. Pelusium was once located at the mouth of the Pelusiac branch of the Nile and thus it was the effective eastern border town of the Delta in antiquity. The city is now represented by the significant (over 2 km from east to west) mound of Tell Farama, with an array of visible and/or recently excavated public buildings of the Graeco-Roman period, including a large theater and an impressive, well-preserved red-brick fortress which dominates the center of the tell. There are also a number of satellite sites around Tell Farama which came within the environs of the ancient city, including a substantial series of early Christian buildings at Tell Makhzan, immediately to the east of Tell Farama. To the south of Tell Farama is a low-lying salt plain, which is an area of mixed agricultural/cemetery usage at least as early as late Roman times; this area is bisected by the el-Salaam Canal running east–west through it.

Sites which have been partially destroyed by the progress of the canal include Tell el-Fadda and Tell el-Louly, both on or close to its direct line and both less than 10 km from the Suez Canal. Both these sites seem to be of post-New Kingdom date, the latter at least probably on the Pelusiac branch as it existed in the Late and Graeco-Roman periods. Farther south, a line roughly from Qantara to Tell Farama marks the edge of the Flandrian coast (probably the coastline in the New Kingdom and earlier). Located here are a number of archaeological sites whose importance for the Late period and earlier has been demonstrated by pre-Canal investigations, which continue (Tell Hebua, Tell el-Herr). Some newer investigations here have been stimulated by the Salvage Project (Tell el-Kedua, Tell el-Mufariq).

See also

Serabit el-Khadim; Sinai, North, late prehistoric and Dynastic sites; Tell el-Herr; Wadi Maghara

Further reading

Clédat, J. 1913. Le temple de Zeus Cassios à Peluse. *ASAE* 13: 79–85.
CRIPEL 14 (1992), 15 (1993), 16 (1994).
Oren, E. 1987. The "Ways of Horus" in North Sinai. In *Egypt, Israel, Sinai: Archaeological and Historical Relationships in the Biblical Period*, A.F. Rainey, ed., 69–119. Jerusalem.

STEVEN SNAPE

Sanam

Sanam is an ancient town site about 7 km downstream from Gebel Barkal on the east bank of the Nile (18°27′ N, 31°48′ E), within the bounds of the modern town of Merowe, Sudan. First noted by Carl Richard Lepsius in 1844, it consists of a settlement (still unexcavated), an extensive cemetery, a "treasury," and a temple built by the Kushite king Taharka (*circa* 690–664 BC) to a local form of the god Amen. The site's modern Arabic name means "idol," attesting to the large numbers of antiquities found here, but its ancient name was probably that of the epithet of the local Amen, "Bull of the Bow-Land [Nubia]," (*Ka-ta-seti*). In ancient times Sanam must have been the northern terminus of the Bayuda Desert road connecting Napata (Gebel Barkal) and Meroe, as well as the site of the primary river ferry in the district, as Merowe still is today.

The site was excavated in 1912–13 by an Oxford University expedition directed by Francis L. Griffith. The excavated remains can be dated with certainty only from the reign of Piye (*circa* 747–716 BC) to the reign of Aspelta (*circa* 600–580 BC). In the time of the latter king the town was evidently destroyed and the site remained abandoned until after the first century AD. The evidence of widespread burning and destruction appears to be the result of the well-known military raid on Kush by the 26th Dynasty Egyptian king Psamtik II in 593 BC. However, the important geographical location of this site at the northern end of the Bayuda Road belies its abandonment after the Egyptian attack. The settlement must have been rebuilt in another nearby location, as yet unidentified, and its important function as a caravan transfer point must have continued after the capital of the Kushite state moved farther south to Meroe. Later Meroitic material is indeed manifested on the Sanam site.

The major monument at Sanam is the Amen temple, which lay on the southeastern edge of the settlement. It was a near duplicate of the temples built by Taharka at Tabo and Kawa: 68.5 m in length and fronted by a pylon 41.5 m wide. Inside the first pylon was a colonnaded court, a second pylon, a hypostyle hall (4 × 4 columns), followed by a *pronaos* and a sanctuary of various chambers. The walls and foundation deposits were inscribed for Taharka, who added a small chapel in the northern half of the *pronaos*. Texts of Senkamenisken (*circa* 643–623 BC) were present, as was a chapel of Aspelta in the southern half of the *pronaos*. Shortly after the construction of the latter shrine, the temple was then damaged by fire. It does not appear to have been restored. Curiously, prior to the temple's destruction, *shawabti*s (servant figurines) and other small ornaments were manufactured in shops built in the outer courts, whose mudbrick walls had been constructed between the columns.

Although the temple ruins were much denuded by wind and blowing sand, the recovered blocks of relief are of great interest. If the interior scenes depicted ritual processions involving the royal family and the bark of Amen, as well as subject rulers(?) prostrating themselves before the king, the exterior reliefs illustrated unusual four- and six-wheeled vehicles, chariots, mounted donkeys and pack animals—perhaps desert caravans from Meroe—arriving at cult buildings surrounded by gardens. Other reliefs depicted ships on the river and hilly landscapes. Large fragmentary granite statues of a cobra and vulture, undoubtedly representing the royal goddesses Wadjet and Nekhbet, respectively, were recovered in a chamber to the left (northeast) of the sanctuary.

Sanam's second important structure, termed the "treasury" by Griffith, seems actually to have been a warehouse either for the semi-permanent storage of goods or for their stockpiling prior to being shipped from Sanam by overland caravans or river craft. Located about 1 km from the Nile, and 500 m east of the temple, this severely denuded structure was at least 256 m long and 45 m wide, orientated perpendicular to the river. At its east end it was isolated in the desert, but at its west end it was separated by a road from another colonnaded mudbrick building, as yet unexcavated. It consisted of a double series of seventeen store-rooms, each 13.4 × 20.5 m in area, the roofs of each of which were supported by twelve stout sandstone columns in three rows and by seven rows of thinner columns, forming seventy-six columns in each chamber. This perhaps suggests that the structure was multi-storied. On the floors of each of these cells were found many small artifacts inscribed with royal names from Piye to Aspelta, and one contained heaps of charred elephants' tusks. Like the temple, the "treasury" was burned.

Over 1,500 graves were excavated in the cemetery at Sanam; these provide the primary evidence for the burial customs of the commoners of the early Napatan period (eighth–early seventh centuries BC). Dug into a silt bank rather than bedrock, the graves have suffered severe erosion, and thus little evidence has survived of enclosures or superstructures. Below ground they were universally plain and exhibited no expensive or elaborate construction. Three types of burials were noted: (a) Egyptian-style interments in chamber graves, accessed by stairways, containing mummified bodies placed in wooden or cartonnage coffins, accompanied by wheel-made pottery and ornaments of Egyptian type, (b) much more simple burials, in which the dead were merely laid extended on their backs in rectangular pits, yet accompanied by the same kinds of wheel-made pottery, and (c) contracted burials of traditional Nubian type laid in rectangular or oval pits, accompanied both by wheel-made and local handmade pottery. These different burial types suggest that the population of ancient Sanam consisted of several different social classes and/or tribal groups living together simultaneously.

See also

Gebel Barkal; el-Kurru; Kushites; Meroe, city; Nuri; Third Intermediate Period, overview

Further reading

Griffith, F.L. 1923. Oxford excavations in Nubia. *LAAA* 10: 73–171.

TIMOTHY KENDALL

Saqqara, Late period and Graeco-Roman tombs

Although the royal family of the 26th Dynasty originated in Sais and maintained its religious links with this city, the administrative, religious and economic pull of Memphis was impossible to resist. It was therefore inevitable, as in previous dynasties, that the necropolis of Saqqara (29°50–53′ N, 31°13′ E) would be the site for some of the most important burials in the land, even if the kings themselves were buried in the Delta. Unfortunately, many of the finest tombs of the period were ransacked during the early years of the nineteenth century, and detailed records of their decoration and plans, even sometimes of their very location, are missing. Similarly, the period has not attracted the attention from archaeologists that the earlier Dynasties have done, and lack of historical and art historical studies means that chronology is often subjective. Nevertheless, enough remains to give rise to a whole category of Egyptian art: neo-Memphite reliefs are increasingly recognized as an important chapter in the history of that art, even if most of the surviving pieces are no longer in their architectural context. It is also possible that many of the Late period anthropoid sarcophagi in museum collections originate from Saqqara. A royal atelier somewhere in Memphis is made likely by the chance discovery in the falcon galleries at Saqqara of a canopic jar originally intended for the burial of Pharaoh Apries. It is clear that much remains to be discovered.

To the visitor, the best-known Late period monuments at Saqqara are the so-called "Persian" tombs, whose deep shafts are clearly visible to the south of the pyramid of Unas. In fact, these burials seem to date to the reign of Amasis; the Unas causeway was chosen for the site because it was readily accessible from Memphis and the Valley. The site includes the tombs of Tjannehebu, Overseer of the Royal navy, the Chief Physician Psamtik, and the Overseer of Confidential Documents Peteniese. The latter may account for the discovery of important Demotic records at the nearby pyramid of Sekhemkhet; these are unpublished, but are apparently part of the official records of the court of Amasis. The better-known Aramaic letter of Adon, ruler of one of the Philistine cities, was also found in this neighborhood, and may even be connected with these documents. The size and depth of the tomb shafts (over 20 m), and the austere decoration of the burial chambers with funerary texts in hieroglyphs, are impressive features of these burials. Such tombs must have been expensive, and this may explain why so many of them are shared. There are other sizable tombs east of the Step Pyramid and south of Weserkaf's pyramid, which may or may not be contemporary with the Unas shafts. One of these belongs to Hor-neferibre-emakhet, who was born, to judge from his name, about the time of the death of Psamtik II (589 BC), and may therefore have survived into the reign of Amasis or a little beyond.

Farther east, in the escarpment overlooking the valley and the modern road, is the important tomb of Bokenrinef (Bocchoris), vizier of Psamtik I. This tomb has been excavated and published by an Italian team led by Edda Bresciani. It is not a shaft-tomb, but is rock-cut, rather on the lines of Ramesside models, and the interior is elaborate in the extreme. The prestige of the site is further confirmed by the fact that it was later modified to include the burial of Petineith, vizier under Nectanebo I of the 30th Dynasty and possibly a descendant of Bokenrinef; this too has been published by the Italian expedition. The entire eastern bluff north of the Unas causeway, near the temple sites of the Anubieion and Bubastieion, contains deep shafts, many of which must date from the Late period; these probably yielded some of their contents, unrecorded, early in the nineteenth century, but the area would nonetheless repay exploration.

Another area of importance lies west of the later monastery of Apa Jeremias, some way south of the New Kingdom necropolis, but situated by a wadi which gave natural access to and from Memphis. Here lies the complex of the two Psamtiks, exotic characters who were respectively High Steward and Overseer of Scribes of the Royal Repast. They are in august company, since they share their tomb with Khetbeneithyerboni II, daughter of one king (either Psamtik II or Apries) and wife of another (either Apries or Amasis), and at any rate one of the principal queens of the 26th Dynasty. This tomb has yielded some notable statuary. It is most unlikely that this is the only such burial in the neighborhood, and it is clear that the area behind the monastery merits a thorough survey.

The area around the Serapeum was ransacked, probably in the 1830s, and was then dug summarily by Auguste Mariette. Much information is therefore lost, or buried under deep sand drifts, but it is probably in this area that we should locate the Ptolemaic tombs of the high priests of Memphis. These must have been discovered at some point, since we possess a whole series of hieroglyphic and demotic biographies of this family which was without doubt one of the most important in Egypt, particularly after the foundation of Alexandria had removed the Ptolemaic court from Memphis and left them in sole religious authority in the old capital. This series of inscriptions includes the famous elegiac stela of Taimhotep, now in the British Museum. One would expect that the chapels which housed these stelae would have been equally imposing, and there is a need to relocate these monuments. If they were not near the Serapeum, an alternative site is the area near Abusir, a place-name which features prominently in these inscriptions. Late period tomb shafts are now known from Abusir, including that of Udjahorresne, admiral of the fleet of Psamtik III and arch-collaborator in the Persian conquest of 525 BC.

Important burials also lined the processional way which ran through central Saqqara starting from the Anubieion in the east (this is the site termed the Greek Serapeum by Mariette). Tombs situated here would overlook, and in a sense participate in, the great processions from Memphis to the Serapeum. A satellite area of the Serapeum Way is probably the cluster of Late period tombs southwest of the pyramid of Teti, which includes an individual called Petipep, a royal scribe named Hor, and Psamtik-nebpahti, a commander of the Saite army (26th Dynasty). The Serapeum Way is also the site of the tomb of the royal statue-priest Onnofri son of Painmou, who informs us in a fragmentary inscription that he accompanied the Phoenician campaign of Teos (361–360 BC) and was falsely accused of treachery, only to be later vindicated.

Most Mediterranean and Near Eastern nationalities are attested in written sources from Memphis or its necropolis, and it is natural to expect that immigrants would increasingly be buried in Egypt and in the Egyptian fashion. Evidence for this has come from an unusual setting, the catacombs of the baboons situated in the sacred animal necropolis to the north of the Saqqara plateau. Here were found a series of funerary stelae written partially in hieroglyphs and partially in Carian, a language from southwest Turkey. The Carians came to Egypt as mercenaries, later settling in Memphis where they shared a quarter with their cousins, the Ionians. The degree to which they adopted Egyptian customs and beliefs is well illustrated in their funerary stelae. The whereabouts of their cemetery is unknown, but it must have been near the sacred animal necropolis where the stelae were found, and may have been in the wadi between Saqqara

and Abusir. A few Ionian burials were found in the latter place, one of which contained the well-known dramatic papyrus of Timotheos. Memphis also had large Phoenician and Aramaic communities, and traces of their burials have been reported, in one case from Abusir, but especially from the area immediately south of the causeway of Unas. The existence of regional quarters at Memphis may well have been paralleled in the use of distinct cemeteries at Saqqara, or at least this is what the scanty evidence at present suggests.

Memphis, however, remained an Egyptian city. As in all periods, the mass of the populace were in no position to afford luxurious burials, and resorted to the usual substitutes: reused tombs, poor individual burials and mass catacombs. This aspect of Saqqara has been little studied. Some lower-class burials were discovered by Macramallah in his excavations directly north of the Serapeum proper, and others came to light at the eastern end of the Serapeum Way in the neighborhood of the mortuary temple of Teti. Other evidence has been found in the excavations of the Egypt Exploration Society at the sacred animal necropolis, and in the Anubieion complex. In addition, it is known that there were extensive catacombs in the neighborhood of the Unas causeway, and in particular in the subterranean galleries near the pyramid which have been attributed to kings of the 2nd Dynasty. In all, the necropolis at Saqqara was in use for thirty-five centuries until the arrival of Christianity, and even then its importance was not finished.

The tombs of Late period Saqqara exhibit all the variety and ingenuity known from other periods of Egyptian architecture. The depth of their sand-filled shafts, and their massive stone sarcophagi, sometimes separate, at other times carved from the bedrock, make them among the most impressive burials ever found in Egypt. However, little is known about their contents beyond some statuary and the abundant use of amulets. As these tombs come to be better studied, they will increasingly be seen as an architectural achievement, and it is certain that this is a neglected field where important discoveries are still to be made.

See also

Abusir; Late and Ptolemaic periods, overview; Late period private tombs; Memphis

Further reading

Bresciani, E., *et al.* 1980. *Saqqara 1: Tomba di Boccori: La Galleria di Padineit.* Pisa.

Kaenel, F. von. 1980. Les mésaventures du conjurateur de Serket, Onnophris, et de son tombeau. *BSFE* 87–8: 31–45.

Reymond, E.A.E. 1981. *From the Records of a Priestly Family from Memphis* (ÄA 38). Wiesbaden.

Smith, H.S. 1984. Saqqara, Late Period. In *LÄ* 5: 412–28.

JOHN D. RAY

Saqqara, New Kingdom private tombs

Large parts of the Saqqara plateau were occupied with private tombs from the New Kingdom. Most of the original occupants of these tombs lived and worked in Memphis during the 18th and 19th Dynasties. The transferal of the royal residence and administrative center of the country from Thebes to Memphis by Tuthmose III (*circa* 1,475 BC) gave the city an important status until Amenhotep IV/Akhenaten founded a new capital at the modern village of Tell el-Amarna in Middle Egypt. Under Tutankhamen, however, the old situation was restored. Memphis remained the capital of Egypt until the second half of the reign of Ramesses II (*circa* 1,250 BC), when the government was moved to his newly founded residential city in the Delta, Pi-Ramesses ("Ramesses-City").

The first New Kingdom tombs at Saqqara date from the beginning of the 18th Dynasty, probably shortly after Tuthmose III had moved the royal residence to Memphis. Documents on papyrus indicate that the last tombs may date from the 20th Dynasty; 20th Dynasty tombs have not yet been discovered. The three main areas or concentrations of New Kingdom tombs at Saqqara are in three areas.

Area I: tombs in and around the mortuary temple of the pyramid of Teti

The particular interest in this area may be explained by the revival which the cult of the 6th Dynasty King Teti enjoyed in the New Kingdom. The superstructures and precise locations of almost all these tombs are now practically lost, since they are covered with debris and sand. North of the pyramid of Teti the tombs of the following officials are situated: Amenemone, Overseer of Craftsmen and Head of Goldworkers of the Lord of the Two Lands; Tjay, Overseer of the Horses of the Lord of the Two Lands; Ipuia, Overseer of the Workshop and Head of Goldworkers of the Lord of the Two Lands; Huy, Scribe of the Troops of the Lord of the Two Lands, all dating from the late 18th Dynasty; and Mosi, Scribe of the Treasury of Ptah; Meryre, Head of Custodians; and Mahu, Custodian of the Treasury, from the 19th Dynasty. East of the pyramid, above the mortuary temple, the tomb of Heka-Ma'at-Re-neheh, First Royal Butler of the Lord of the Two Lands, was situated and, east of the temple, the tomb of 'Akhpet, Chief Lector-priest in the Two Houses of Mummification, both from the 19th Dynasty.

Area II: rock-cut tombs in the escarpment above the Bubasteion

The second concentration of New Kingdom tombs is located southeast of the pyramid of Teti, where the edge of the escarpment of the Saqqara plateau turns sharply west. They are cut in the south and east sides of the limestone rock-face, above the later Cemetery of the Cats (the Bubasteion) and just below the terrace on which the resthouse of the Egyptian Antiquities Department is built. The chambers and passages are on two or three levels and the walls are partly covered with inscriptions and scenes in relief, on some of which remains of the original coloring is still partly preserved. These rock-cut tombs are among the earliest New Kingdom tombs at Saqqara. They date from the early 18th Dynasty up to (and including) the reign of Akhenaten. The oldest tomb is that of the chancellor Nehesy, a contemporary of Queen Hatshepsut and Tuthmose III. Other tombs are in the names of Resh, Overseer of Ships under Tuthmose IV and Amenhotep III; Meryre, "Minister of Finance" of Amenhotep III; Merysakhmet, Overseer of the Granaries; and, last but not least, the vizier Aperia (or 'Aper-El, a foreign name), his wife Taweret and their son, the Overseer of the Chariotry Huy. Aperia served under Amenhotep III and probably also under Akhenaten. Great parts of his rich burial equipment and that of his family as well, such as coffins, canopic jars, *shawabti*s, alabaster vessels and jewelry have been found in the debris of the tomb chambers. Several of the tomb owners seem to have been attached to the cult of the goddess Bastet.

Area III: south of the Unas Causeway and west of the Monastery of Apa Jeremias

The third and largest concentration of New Kingdom tombs at Saqqara can be found on the desert plateau south of the Step Pyramid of Zoser. This vast terrain is bounded on the north by the causeway of the pyramid of Unas and on the east by the Coptic monastery of Apa Jeremias, which separates it from the southern part of the escarpment mentioned above. To the west, it probably extends as far as the pyramid enclosure of Sekhemkhet and to the south, to the vast shallow stretch of desert between central Saqqara and the pyramid complexes of the 6th Dynasty in South Saqqara. Like the major tombs in the Teti pyramid area, the tombs in this largest section of the New Kingdom necropolis consist of a superstructure with one or two open courtyards with chapels, and a substructure cut into the bedrock and containing several burial chambers. The oldest tombs discovered so far are the impressive temple-like buildings with subterranean chamber complexes of General Horemheb and the Overseer of the Treasury Maya, both contem-

poraries of Tutankhamen. They are located in the center of the whole area. Horemheb later became pharaoh himself and was eventually buried in the Valley of the Kings at Thebes. However, his Memphite tomb was not given up, but used for the interments of his first and second (Queen Mutnodjemet) wives, and the chapels and courtyards above ground served as a sanctuary where a mortuary cult for King Horemheb, and possibly also for his queen, was celebrated.

The clustering of tombs of many important persons—not only officials, but also people of royal blood—around the mortuary buildings of Horemheb and Maya can be explained by the fact that both men, restorers of orthodox kingship and of the traditional cults of Egypt, were worshipped as the saintly initiators of a new era, qualities which must have imbued their tombs and the adjacent area with an aura of sanctity. To date the tombs of the following officials and their families have been excavated here: Tia, Overseer of the Treasury in the Temple of User-Ma't-Re'-Setep-en-Re' (Ramesses II) in the Domain of Amen (Ramesseum), and his wife Princess Tia (a sister of Ramesses II); Iurudef, Scribe of the Treasury, and secretary of Tia; Ra'ia, Chief Musician of Ptah Lord of Truth; Paser, Royal Scribe and Overseer of the Buildingworks; Khay, Goldwasher of the Lord of the Two Lands; Khay's son Pabasa, Head of the Bowmen of the Tradesmen; Ramose, Head of the Bowmen of the Army; Pay and Ra'ia, father and son, both Overseers of the Royal Apartments; and Iniuia, Chief Steward and Overseer of the Cattle of Amen, a contemporary of Tutankhamen.

The northeast sector of this huge area is covered with tombs of high officials of the Ramesside period. The most prominent examples are the tombs of Amenemone and Neferrenpet, a vizier under Ramesses II. This sector of the necropolis undoubtedly extends farther south to where parts of the tomb of another vizier, Parahotep, have been found.

Figure 95 Wall reliefs in the tomb of General Horemheb in the New Kingdom necropolis at
    Saqqara
Courtesy EES–RMO

Archaeological investigations: from exploitation to exploration

Like other parts of the Memphite necropolis, the New Kingdom cemeteries at Saqqara have in the past been plundered, reused by later generations for mass interments, used as stone quarries or otherwise exploited. Long before real scientific research had started, hundreds of monuments and objects from the New Kingdom tombs at Saqqara had already been brought to light and had disappeared into collections, both in Egypt and abroad. Objects belonging to the contents of the same tombs often ended up in many different museums. When the Prussian Egyptologist Carl Richard Lepsius appeared in Saqqara in 1843, the location of most of the tombs exploited by the art collectors was already known. Lepsius was the first archaeologist to make a proper map of the largest sector of New Kingdom tombs, and to relocate and investigate, albeit only partially, the tombs of Maya, Iurokhy (Royal Scribe and General), Raia and Harmin (both Overseers of the Royal Apartments of the King's Wife). In the 1860s the French Egyptologist Auguste Mariette worked in the same area and entered parts of the tombs of General Horemheb and Tjuneroy (Overseer of Works of All the Monuments of the King). From the tomb of the latter comes the famous "King List of Saqqara," now in the Cairo Museum.

It was only in the 1970s that archaeological research in the New Kingdom cemeteries of Saqqara commenced on a grand scale. In 1975

Figure 96 The tomb of Iniuia in the New Kingdom cemetery, Saqqara
Courtesy EES–RMO

"The Memphite New Kingdom Necropolis Project" was started, a joint venture of the British Egypt Exploration Society and the National Museum of Antiquities at Leiden (Netherlands) under the directorship of Geoffrey T. Martin, assisted by Hans D. Schneider. The objectives of this project are the relocation, investigation and publication of the tombs which were partly explored by Lepsius in 1843, as well as the other tombs opened or seen in the nineteenth century in the same area (Area III).

Among the tomb complexes discovered so far are the tombs of Horemheb and Maya of the late 18th Dynasty, and the tomb of the Ramesside Princess Tia and her husband of the same name. Since 1977 a mission of the University of Cairo has been working in the northeast sector of the same site. Initiated by Soad Maher, this project was directed by the late Sayed Tawfik, whose team has excavated the group of Ramesside tombs of which mention has been made above. The third project of major importance is

697

that of the Mission archéologique française du Bubasteion, directed by Alain-Pierre Zivie. The objective of this expedition, which started in 1980, is the clearance and publication of the rock-tombs in the north escarpment above the Bubasteion (Cemetery of Cats), the second concentration of New Kingdom tombs listed above (Area II).

Architecture and iconography

From the architectural point of view the New Kingdom tombs at Saqqara can be divided into two main categories: rock-cut tombs and free-standing tombs with subterranean, rock-cut substructures. The rock-cut tombs consist of an entrance room or vestibule, presumably acting as a cult place or chapel, leading to a complex of passages and chambers on various levels, which are linked by one or more inner shafts. As a rule, the walls of these vestibules are decorated in relief with scenes showing the tomb owner and with inscriptions mentioning his name and titles. In some cases, such as the tomb of Meryre in the cemetery at the Bubasteion, the rough walls had a revetment of relief-decorated limestone slabs. The rock-cut tomb is the common type of New Kingdom tomb up to and including the reigns of Amenhotep III and Akhenaten.

By the time Tutankhamen came to the throne and the residence was moved again to Memphis, so that there was a considerable demand for tombs in the Memphite necropolis, there may have been little or no space left for new tombs in the cliffs of the eastern escarpment. Hence the architects were led to open up another area, the vast terrain south of the Unas causeway. They designed a new type of tomb, the free-standing tomb with rock-cut substructure. To make room for the new tombs, most of the superstructures of the Old Kingdom *mastaba*s which were then occupying this site were removed. The shafts and burial chambers of these old buildings were partly reused and recut to create the substructures of the new tombs and limestone blocks of the *mastaba* chapels—many of which still covered with fine reliefs—were used as building material in the superstructures.

The standard layout of the free-standing tomb shows an open courtyard, with or without columns, in front of three chapels, the central one being the main cult room with a stela where the funerary offerings for the tomb owner could be placed. The roof of this chapel has the shape of a pyramid crowned with a pyramid-shaped capstone (pyramidion). In the court, a shaft gives access to a subterranean complex of chambers; in the bigger tombs, there are two or more levels which are linked by inner shafts. Small tombs may only have one or two rooms above ground and no courtyard. In large tombs, such as for Horemheb and Maya, the standard design is extended through the addition of a second court and three more chapels, and an impressive entrance gateway (pylon) in the east. The length of the bigger structures could be 50 m.

These large tombs are in fact mortuary temples, where not only the cult of the deceased took place but also the rites for the gods (especially Osiris) were celebrated. An inscription in the tomb of Tia and Tia says that this tomb was built under the supervision of Ramesses II (Tia's brother-in-law) himself, who "made it as a monument for his father Osiris." All buildings were oriented east–west in accordance with the orbit of the sun. Thus, the architecture expresses the theology of Atum and Osiris, who are in fact manifestations of one and the same god.

The tombs of the late 18th and early 19th Dynasties were built of mudbrick. The walls of the cult chapel had limestone revetments decorated in relief, which in the luxurious tombs of the greatest officials was also applied on the walls of other parts of the building. In the later Ramesside period, the walls were entirely made of limestone. In the 19th Dynasty the miniature pyramid with pyramidion, which formerly crowned the main chapel, is sometimes found as a separate free-standing construction (tomb of Tia and Tia). The walls of chapels and courtyards are decorated with limestone reliefs, usually carved in sunk relief and painted. Representations painted on layers of mud-plaster have also been found, such as in the tombs of Iniuia and Pay.

Late 18th Dynasty tombs have reliefs of a superb quality. The following themes and subjects can be distinguished in the decoration: events and inscriptions dealing with the life, career and family of the deceased; burial rites such as the Ritual of the Breaking of the Red Pots; funerary processions with bearers of grave goods and the carrying or leading of cattle; the tomb owner worshipping gods; inscriptions of prayers and hymns, specifically to Osiris; and scenes and texts related to the *Book of the Dead*, such as the Ritual of the Opening of the Mouth or the deceased in the Fields of Ialu. Typical for Saqqara is the presence of king lists, an expression of the worship bestowed on the divine ancestors of the king (tomb of Tjuneroy).

Of the freestanding tombs discovered so far at Saqqara, the tomb of Maya is the only one having tomb chambers decorated with reliefs. These chambers are located at a depth of 22 m below the pavement of the courtyard; their walls have a revetment of limestone slabs decorated with reliefs painted in yellow showing large figures of Maya and his wife Meryt before Osiris and other gods as well as scenes of the burial chamber with Anubis bending over the mummy on a bier, similar to the vignette of Spell 151 of the *Book of the Dead*. As a rule, the central or cult chapel of the tomb contained a stela; this was standing against the west wall and showed the deceased and members of his family praying and offering to Osiris, Atum and other gods related to the afterlife or to the city of the dead. The courtyards seem to have been reserved for statues of the deceased and his family, as well for statues of gods.

In large temple tombs, such as the ones of Maya and Horemheb, special statue rooms can be found. The number of statues and the variety of types occurring were exceptionally large, which is traditionally characteristic for the Memphite region. There were statues representing the deceased seated on a chair, sometimes accompanied by his wife (in statue groups), or kneeling while supporting an offering table, or holding a *naos* with the image of a god (Osiris, Ptah or Hathor) in front of him. Statues of gods

were common, for example of Osiris (tomb of Mose), of the Anubis jackal (tomb of Horemheb) or the Hathor cow "Lady of the Southern Sycamore" protecting the tomb owner and his wife (tomb of Pabasa). These statues were sometimes placed and hidden in special shrines erected in the courtyards.

Again typical for the Memphite New Kingdom tombs are the square pillars in the courtyards with representations in relief of the deceased supporting the *djed* pillar. These are an expression of the Ritual of Erecting *Djed-Shepsy*. During the New Kingdom this ritual was part of the Osirian rites in the mortuary temples of the kings, and the theme itself is related with the vignette of Chapters 15 and 16 of the *Book of the Dead*.

The results of modern archaeological research on the New Kingdom tombs at Saqqara are rich and abundant. Only limited parts of these sites have been investigated so far. On stylistic and other grounds, however, it is known that numerous objects in many Egyptian collections were once part of the rich contents of the Memphite cemeteries. Hence, it stands to reason that abundant information still remains hidden under the sands of Saqqara.

See also

Lepsius, Carl Richard; Mariette, François Auguste Ferdinand; Memphis; New Kingdom, overview; pyramid tombs of the New Kingdom; representational evidence, New Kingdom private tombs; Tell el-Amarna, nobles' tombs; Thebes, New Kingdom private tombs

Further reading

Martin, G.T. 1989. *The Memphite Tomb of Horemheb, Commander-in-chief of Tut'ankhamun I*. London.

——. 1991. *The Hidden Tombs of Memphis: New Discoveries from the Time of Tutankhamun and Ramesses the Great*. London.

Schneider, H.D. 1996. *The Memphite Tomb of Horemheb, Commander-in-chief of Tut'ankhamun II*. Leiden.

Zivie, A.-P., ed. 1988. *Memphis et ses nécropoles*

au Nouvel Empire: nouvelles données, nouvelles questions (Actes du colloque international CNRS). Paris.

——. 1990. *Découverte à Saqqarah, Le vizier oublié.* Paris.

HANS D. SCHNEIDER

Saqqara, North, Early Dynastic tombs

The Saqqara necropolis is situated in the Western Desert approximately 24 km south of Cairo and immediately southwest of the modern village of Abusir (29°53′ N, 31°13′ E). The Early Dynastic tombs excavated at Saqqara/Abusir can be divided into three groups: (1) the large 1st and 2nd Dynasty *mastaba* tombs occupying the eastern edge of the North Saqqara plateau; (2) two areas of smaller tombs in the Abusir Valley; and (3) a series of underground galleries of the 2nd Dynasty (but no surviving super-structures) in the area of the Unas pyramid and pyramid temple (5th Dynasty). Excavations at North Saqqara by English archaeologists J.E. Quibell, C.M. Firth and W.B. Emery have exposed a series of large 1st and 2nd Dynasty tombs along the 55 m contour line on the eastern edge of the desert plateau, a location which would have made such structures highly visible from the cultivation.

The 1st Dynasty tombs at North Saqqara are large imposing structures often surrounded by single or double enclosure walls and rows of subsidiary tombs. Various other structures are associated with individual tombs.

Architectural development

Roughly three broad stages of tomb develop-ment can be discerned within each Dynasty (early, middle and late). The tomb type of the early 1st Dynasty is well represented by Tomb 3357, dated to the reign of Aḥa. It consists of a rectangular pit cut in the gravel and rock, subdivided by mudbrick walls into five rooms, with the larger, central one as the burial place.

At ground level, a rectangular mudbrick super-structure (called a *mastaba*) was built. It was subdivided into magazines and had a rubble core. As there is no recognizable method of entry to the burial chamber, it is assumed that the structure was finished after the burial had taken place. The exterior façade had recessed paneling ("palace façade") on all four sides. Tomb 3357 had a double enclosure wall (overall measurement 48 × 22 m), but no subsidiary burials. To the north of Tomb 3357 is a series of low buildings described by the excavator as a "model estate." Two of the buildings at the east and west have arched roofs and three rounded structures may represent granaries. To the north of the "estate" a boat grave was excavated.

Another example of the "pre-stairway" tomb type is the large Tomb 3503, attributed to Queen Merneith. It also has an enclosure wall, a boat and twenty subsidiary (human) burials.

The tomb of the official Sekhemka (3504) shows a transitional design. It is also the earliest example of a superstructure surrounded by a low bench on which were placed 300 bulls' heads modeled in clay and fitted with real horns. Tombs 3507 and 3505, respectively, dating to the reigns of Den and Qa'a, also have this feature.

The mid-1st Dynasty is a period of innova-tion, with a large number of tombs built at Saqqara during the reign of Den. There is also an increase in size and elaboration of tombs leading to the introduction of the stairway. These are from the east, beginning outside the superstructure and leading directly to the burial chamber. The design of the substructure remained unchanged, although these were cut at a deeper level (earlier tombs were usually cut no deeper than 4 m). Tomb 3038 is situated at the northern apex of the plateau and is dated to the time of Anedjib. Originally, it had a rectangular earthen tumulus with mudbrick casing over the burial pit. The tumulus was later changed into a stepped form. Similar tumuli are attested in Tombs 3507, 3111 and 3471. These were considered to be the proto-type of Zoser's Step Pyramid (3rd Dynasty) and later pyramid structures. However, they are more likely to be a device incorporating the

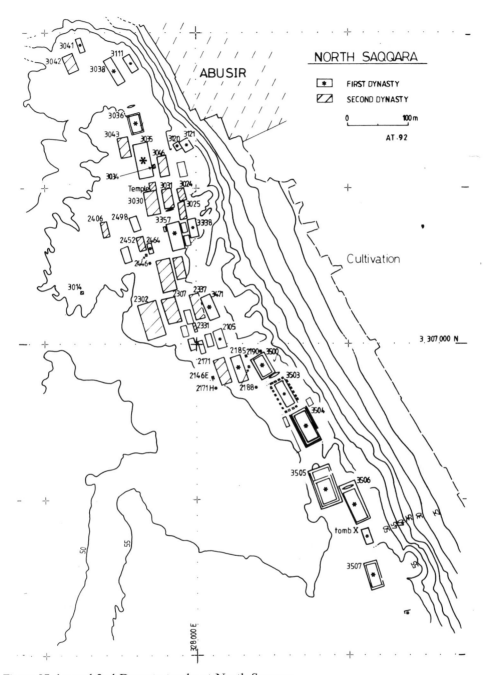

Figure 97 1st and 2nd Dynasty tombs at North Saqqara

early Upper Egyptian tomb type into Saqqara *mastaba* tombs.

During the late 1st Dynasty, the paneled façade was abandoned in favor of plain façades with two "false doors" at the north and south ends of the east wall. The superstructure now has a solid core of rubble or mudbrick and the stairway is L-shaped, starting from the east and entering the burial room from the north. Subsidiary rooms within the substructure are not adjacent to the burial chamber but placed to either side of the stairway. This tomb type is exemplified by Tomb 3338. Tomb 3500 retains the east–west axis of the burial chamber (a north–south axis is more common at this time) and the stairway approach is from the east. This tomb also has the latest subsidiary burials, which differ in form and construction from early examples.

The largest Early Dynastic *mastaba* tomb at North Saqqara is Tomb 3505, dating to the reign of Qa'a. This tomb retained the paneled façade and had a double enclosure wall and a funerary temple to the north. Access to the burial chamber was via a north–south ramp, which turns and enters the chamber from the east. At the end of the 1st Dynasty the system of open working of the substructure was abandoned. Tombs 3120 and 3121, dating to Qa'a's reign, already have the burial chamber excavated in the bedrock. The superstructure is then as a conventional mudbrick *mastaba*.

In the early 2nd Dynasty the tomb design of the late 1st Dynasty was retained, but the L-shaped stairs, the magazines and the burial chamber are all rock-cut. Mudbrick walls were used to divide the underground chamber into different rooms, with the burial chamber on the west side. The practice of burying provisions within the superstructure had not quite died out, as is attested by the large amounts of pots found buried in groups within the core of some tombs.

By the mid-2nd Dynasty, the standard tomb design is of the "house" type, where the various rooms are cut separately and may represent the plan of contemporary houses. This is well represented by Tomb 2302, dated to the reign of Nynetjer. Tombs 2307 and 2337 even have

areas identified as a bathroom and lavatory. The superstructures are of mudbrick covering a solid core of rubble or liquid mud, and the plain façade has two false doors. At the close of the 2nd Dynasty examples of shaft tombs of the "dummy-stairway" type appear at North Saqqara.

Although the area was systematically excavated between 1910 and 1959, some of the results have not been fully published. For example, built against the north enclosure wall of Tomb 3505 is a semicircular or horseshoe-shaped, whitewashed mudbrick wall, of unknown purpose.

At North Saqqara some new tomb features appear during the reign of Qa'a, including a funerary temple to the north of Tomb 3505, and statue niches in Tombs 3120 and 3121. A transitional design is found later in Tomb 2464, and, dating to the end of the 2nd Dynasty, Tomb 2407 has a statue annex which, together with the temple to the north of Tomb 3030, shows a close resemblance in plan to the temple of 3505.

Boat graves from the time of Aḥa to Den have been excavated at Saqqara. Each was on an east–west axis roughly parallel to the north side of their associated *mastaba*. The boat grave of Tomb 3506 is placed within an enclosure wall, immediately north of the *mastaba*, while the boat grave of Tomb 3357 was over 25 m to the north of the model estate. The boats of Tombs 3357 and 3036 were sunk below ground level, then lined with mudbrick and plastered, while those of Tombs 3503 and 3506 had the mudbrick superstructure built directly on the desert surface. The excavator noted that all showed signs of the enclosure wall having been built after the boat was in position. Unlike examples at Helwan, where hardly any traces of the superstructures survive, the Saqqara boat graves were preserved up to 1 m high. Traces of wood, rope and pottery were found *in situ*.

Topographic distribution

A pattern can be seen in the distribution of large 1st Dynasty tombs on the Saqqara escarpment: the earliest tomb (3357), dated to

Aha's reign, has a prominent and central position, near an indentation in the escarpment, which probably served as an access route to the plateau. *Mastaba*s dated to the reigns of Djer and Djet spread southward from Tomb 3357. During the reign of Den tombs continued to spread south along the escarpment edge, as well as north from Tomb 3357. This development in both directions continued until the end of the dynasty. The large *mastaba*s of the 2nd Dynasty were generally built behind those of the 1st Dynasty, also following the alignment of the escarpment. Again, the area around Tomb 3357 functions as a focal point with tombs dated to the reign of Nynetjer spreading north and south from a point just behind it (i.e. to the west). At present, the southern limit of the necropolis is unknown: the large tombs extend for approximately 300 m along the escarpment edge, and were generally assumed to end in the south at Tomb 3507. However, traces of an Early Dynastic structure, almost certainly a tomb, have been found during excavations halfway down the rock face in the Anubieion temple area and in 1987 the niched northern façade of an early 1st Dynasty *mastaba* was exposed during construction of a water tower immediately north of the Egyptian Antiquities Organization Inspectorate office.

The North Saqqara cemeteries show an absence of medium-sized tombs of the 1st Dynasty: the escarpment was dominated by large *mastaba* tombs and their subsidiary burials, with the much smaller tombs in the cemeteries of the Abusir Wadi. A different pattern of use seems to emerge during the 2nd Dynasty, with greater variety in tomb sizes, including very small burials, more intensive use of space, with small tombs wedged between larger ones, and spreading further toward the eastern edge. This is evident in the area south-southeast of Tomb 2302, and to the north and east of Tomb 3038, where Emery excavated various small 2nd Dynasty tombs.

The early tombs at North Saqqara follow the line of the escarpment, with the axis on a northwest–southeast alignment, in contrast to the alignment of the long axes of most 3rd Dynasty *mastaba*s, which are only a few degrees off true north. The position of the Early Dynastic tombs is clearly related to the topography of the Saqqara plateau. Unlike *mastaba*s of the 3rd Dynasty, which have a fairly consistent line of approach, earlier tombs show greater variation, although there is a general preference for an east-facing approach. Tomb 3505 has the entrance to its superstructure at the north end of the east wall. This, however, is related to the position of the funerary temple and the fact that access farther south was hampered by the proximity of Tomb 3506. Tomb 3500, although retaining a niche on the east wall and access to the substructure from the east, has an entrance at the southwest of the enclosure wall. This unconventional arrangement is perhaps due to the proximity to the desert edge and the fact that the boat grave of Tomb 3503 was just to the south, limiting access even further. Access to Tomb 3038 was via north and south stairways, which relate to the unusual tomb design.

Royal or private cemetery?

Current research suggests that North Saqqara was a private cemetery during the Early Dynastic period, and not a royal one. Evidence for this is based on the following:

1 The small size of Saqqara tombs when compared with the "funerary enclosures" at Abydos.
2 The number, size and absence of stelae in subsidiary burials at Saqqara.
3 The attribution of more than one *mastaba* per king at Saqqara.
4 Lack of differentiation in layout or location between presumed "royal" tombs and other *mastaba*s at North Saqqara. Size alone is not sufficient evidence for royal attribution.
5 The presence of tumuli within the superstructures of some Saqqara tombs is not an indication of royal ownership but an attempt to incorporate the early Upper Egyptian tomb type within these Saqqara *mastaba*s.
6 The funerary temple of Tomb 3505 is not a royal feature but does fit into evidence of private tomb development.

7 The mix of large and small tombs and the reuse of the area from the early 2nd Dynasty suggest that this is unlikely to be a royal site.

8 Royal and private cemeteries remain quite distinctive at Saqqara until the 5th Dynasty.

As the main cemetery for the newly founded capital, the North Saqqara cemetery is also crucial in providing an indication of the whereabouts of Early Dynastic Memphis.

See also

Abydos, Early Dynastic funerary enclosures; Abydos, Umm el-Qa'ab; Early Dynastic period, overview; Early Dynastic private tombs; Helwan; Saqqara, pyramids of the 3rd Dynasty

Further reading

Emery, W.B. 1939. *Excavations at Saqqara 1937–38. Hor Aha.* Cairo.

——. 1949. *Great Tombs of the First Dynasty* 1. Cairo.

——. 1954–8. *Great Tombs of the First Dynasty* 2 and 3. London.

——. 1967. *Archaic Egypt.* Baltimore, MD.

Firth, C.M. 1931. Excavations of the Department of Antiquities at Saqqara, 1930–1931. *ASAE* 31: 45–8.

Helck, W. 1983. Saqqara. *LÄ* 5: 386–400.

Kemp, B.J. 1967. The Egyptian First Dynasty Royal Cemetery. *Antiquity* 41: 22–32.

Lauer, J.-P. 1976. *Saqqara: The Royal Cemetery of Memphis.* London.

Quibell, J.E. 1923. *Excavations at Saqqara (1912–1914).* Cairo.

Smith, W.S. 1936. Topography of the Archaic cemetery at Saqqarah. In *The Development of the Egyptian Tomb down to the Accession of Cheops*, G.A. Reisner, ed. Cambridge, MA.

ANA TAVARES

Saqqara, pyramids of the 3rd Dynasty

On the west bank of the Nile on the edge of the desert at Saqqara (29°50′ N, 31°13′ E) is the Step Pyramid complex of Horus Neterikhet, known as King Zoser (or Djoser), probably the second pharaoh of the 3rd Dynasty. The buildings of the complex are remarkable because they are the first ones made of quarried stone, in regular courses.

The third century BC historian Manetho confirms the Zoser complex's originality when he reports that Imhotep, whom the Greeks called "Asclepios" for his medical talents, invented the art of stone masonry during the reign of Tosorthros (Zoser). Excavation of the colonnade at the enclosure's entrance led to the discovery of one of the statues of the king, on which are engraved the names "Horus Neterikhet" and "Imhotep," with the titles "Chancellor of the King of Lower Egypt, first under the King of Upper Egypt, administrator of the grand palace, noble heir, high priest of Heliopolis, Imhotep, the builder, the sculptor...."

The first modern exploration of the Step Pyramid was made by the Prussian general Baron von Minutoli, who entered it with the Italian engineer Geronimo Segato in 1821. They discovered two chambers, decorated with blue faïence panels, and the granite vault, which had already been plundered in antiquity. In the corner of a hallway they found what was left of a mummy with a heavily gilded skull and a pair of sandals, also gilded. These were removed by von Minutoli, but then lost at sea.

In 1924, Pierre Lacau and Cecil M. Firth began excavating the complex. The first places they explored were two mounds, situated at the northeast corner of the main pyramid. They were greatly surprised to find two façades with fluted columns almost in the Greek Doric style. Firth at first thought he was excavating a Ptolemaic structure, but some New Kingdom hieratic writing on the walls of the entrance corridors soon proved the building to date to the 3rd Dynasty. It was in these inscriptions that the name "Zoser" was first found; contemporary

Figure 98 Model of Zoser's Step Pyramid complex at Saqqara

texts all use the name "Neterikhet," sometimes followed by the epithet "golden sun."

During study for the restoration of the structure, it was recognized that the design of a wooden building was reproduced in stone. The façade is composed of fluted, slender columns, up to 12 m high and in the shape of pine tree trunks. These columns, together with perpendicular beams, appear to support an arched roof modeled after the reed structures of the festival pavilions and primitive sanctuaries that are represented by the hieroglyph *sh*.

Firth discovered the enclosure's only entrance, a narrow passage (1.05 m wide and 6 m long) cut into the outer wall's most prominent niching. Only the first two or three courses of the wall remained, but the original size can be reconstructed. The entrance leads to a second, wider passage and a magnificent corridor of forty columns, in a previously unknown style of reeds. These once supported a heavy ceiling made of stone blocks, which were rounded below to represent logs of palm trees trunks. Each column is engaged to a protruding wall,

perpendicular to the direction of the corridor. These walls are intended both as a supplementary, strengthening precaution, and as a means to compensate for the excessive segmentation of the columns.

Near the middle of the colonnade a passage leads to a small sanctuary, which must have contained Zoser's statue and its pedestal, inscribed with the king's name and Imhotep's titles. The passage opens on its west side into a perpendicular room, its ceiling supported by eight columns. It has been possible to restore these columns to their original height, using many of the original stones.

Beyond the colonnade is a vast open space bounded on the north by the pyramid and on the other three sides by mounds of rock with a few vestiges of what once was a magnificent paneled wall of fine Tura limestone. In the southwest corner is a sanctuary that must have been Zoser's second tomb, a kind of cenotaph built at the base of the south wall, with a frieze of *uraei* (sacred cobras) at the top. Several meters of this wall have been restored.

At the north end of the large court is a structure shaped like a pair of D. A twin structure facing in the other direction, 55 m farther south, has almost disappeared. These were markers staking out a course for the king's *ka* to run symbolically the races of the *heb-sed* (jubilee) festival. About 50 m north of the better preserved double-D is an altar with an access ramp, almost touching the base of the pyramid. To the east a false door opens into the rest house of the king's *ka*, the waiting place for the *heb-sed* ceremony of the afterlife, which is depicted in the complex. Beyond this is the sanctuary where the king's statue must have been situated in the central niche, flanked by two others, above which are lintels decorated with symbols of rebirth (*djed* pillars). A few meters to the south, and then east, following an unusual, curved wall, is the *heb-sed* court.

All the main deities have sanctuaries in the *heb-sed* court, along 80 m of the west and east walls, and north of the king's dais. On the better preserved west side, chapels of two types have been reconstituted: the first has torus molding along the external corners, and a horizontal roof, with a slight overhang that suggests the later cavetto cornice. The other type has narrow, decorative, fluted columns, placed on pedestals more than 2 m high and topped by capitals with fluted leaves, which support an arched roof. Two restored chapels have stairways of inclined steps leading to a very large niche, which probably held a larger than life-size statue of Zoser, a few fragments of which were found. The chamber with a horizontal roof in the southwest corner of the court has been restored to its original size.

On the east side of the *heb-sed* court is a row of twelve chapels with vaulted roofs, narrower than the others and without columns. Two of them have been restored, partly with original blocks. To the south of these chapels fragments of three caryatid statues of King Zoser were found on the ground. All of these chapels are accessible from the court through roofless, zigzagging corridors, formed by low walls four cubits high. A small niche with a vaulted roof is the only accessible chamber in these chapels; the main edifice is solid stone.

Leaving the *heb-sed* court by the north side, one comes to the base of a pavilion with torus moldings. Inside it are the surviving feet of four statues, two of adults and two of children. They are probably from statues of Zoser, as King of Upper and Lower Egypt, and the two king's daughters, Hetephernebti and Inkaes.

The pyramid was first designed as a *mastaba* (M1), a long low superstructure that was later expanded in two stages (M2, M3). Only in its fourth and fifth building stages was it enlarged to a stepped form.

Along the east face of the original *mastaba* are eleven shafts, about 30 m deep, for members of the royal family. At the entrance of one shaft thick logs are still preserved which once helped to lower the alabaster sarcophagus, funerary equipment and furniture, and the coffin of an eight year-old child. At the same location what is left of the casings of three structures can be seen: the third and latest *mastaba* (M3), the first, four-step pyramid (P1), and the second, six-step one (P2). At the northeast corner of *mastaba* M3 the horizontally laid stones of *mastaba* M3 and stones of pyramid P1, with courses sloping down inward, can both be seen.

Along the east side of the Step Pyramid are the two "Houses of the South and North," where the king's *ka* was meant to receive delegations from Upper and Lower Egypt. Columns with lily capitals (identifying the South building) and papyrus capitals (for the North one) once decorated the walls.

Around the northeast corner of the pyramid, one comes to the statue chamber (*serdab*), which lies directly against the pyramid. This chamber contained the remarkable painted limestone statue of Zoser that is in the Egyptian Museum in Cairo. In its place in the *serdab* is a replica that can be viewed through two cylindrical holes, which allowed the *ka* statue to receive incense smoke from the mortuary temple.

Immediately to the west of the *serdab* is the east wall of the mortuary temple, preserved to a height of approximately 2 m, which meets the north side of the pyramid. Through the temple's entrance is a corridor which turns around the temple, and ends at two rectangular inner

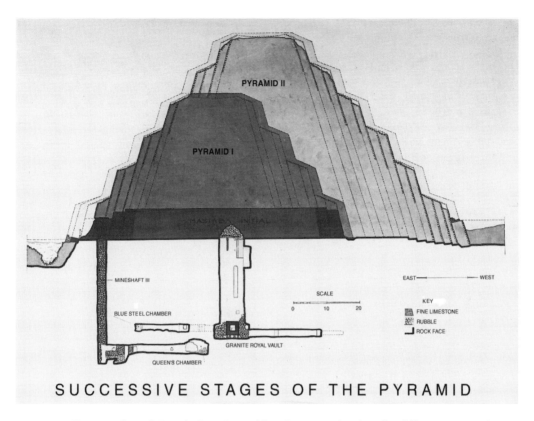

SUCCESSIVE STAGES OF THE PYRAMID

Figure 99 Cross-section of Zoser's Step Pyramid at Saqqara, showing the different stages of construction

courts. These are bounded on the pyramid side by a portico of four fluted columns, engaged in the corners of two rectangular pillars. Remains of two rooms with basins and water channels were found here. Beyond several rectangular chambers is space for a statue facing the pyramid, and another space, probably for an offering table perhaps flanked by two stelae, as at Meydum.

Finally, in the western porticoed court, is the entrance of the descending gallery to the king's granite vault, where one of Zoser's feet was found, mummified in the Old Kingdom manner. The shaft also gives access to some adjoining galleries and storerooms, and to the chambers reserved for the king's *ka*. Two of these, containing blue faïence, were already known when Firth and Lauer found two new

ones: one with three false door stelae depicting the king, the other with three panels of blue faïence topped by ornamental arcades of *djed* pillars. There were also fragments of a fourth panel, which has been rebuilt by Lauer in the Egyptian Museum in Cairo.

Inside the south enclosure, near the "wall of *uraei*," is the great shaft of the so-called South Tomb, of the same size as the one in the pyramid (7 m on a side and 28 m deep). The granite vault at the bottom of this shaft is in the same style as the pyramid's, but smaller, and square (approximately 1.60 m on a side) instead of rectangular. Except for a part of the granite plug, nothing was left in this section of the tomb when, in 1927, Firth and Lauer became the first persons to enter it since the tomb robbers, 4,000 years before. Toward the east, the bottom of the shaft leads to rooms laid out like the ones under the pyramid, with the same decoration (stelae, and blue faïence tiles in panels topped by arches with *djed* pillars).

The existence of the tomb is marked by a rectangular superstructure (84 × 12 m), with transverse arches indicating a roof. On this roof was a casing of fine limestone, of which only a few blocks remain on the south face. The outside paneled wall is particularly well preserved along the length of the tomb, still rising in some places as high as 4.80 m.

Another superstructure, similar, but twice as wide and 400 m long, occupies a large part of the complex's west terrace. Beneath it are two very long, shallow, subterranean galleries, which give access to a large number of rectangular chambers. The extremely bad condition of the rock prevented Firth from excavating these chambers. Numerous fragments of 3rd Dynasty stone vases were found at the south end. The clay from here was used as mortar for the pyramid and the complex's other large masses of masonry. According to Firth, the presence in this area of hard-stone plates and dishes indicates the presence nearby of secondary tombs.

Finally, in the obviously unfinished northern part of the complex, there is a gigantic altar carved into the rock, with the remains of a limestone casing. Offerings must have been exposed on the altar before being taken, through a shaft 60 m away, down into storerooms that branch from a gallery running east–west. These chambers contained mostly wheat and barley, as well as sycamore figs, bunches of grapes and what were probably loaves of bread. Above the passageway, the mass of rock against the outer wall is oddly divided into rectangular chambers, each one having two outside openings one above the other, as in granaries. They apparently represent storehouses.

Tomb complex of Horus Sekhemkhet

Horus Sekhemkhet, probably the son of Zoser (or Horus Neterikhet), seems to have been Zoser's immediate successor. He planned an even bigger step pyramid, square in design with each side about the length of one of the long sides of Zoser's rectangular pyramid. Such a pyramid might have had seven tiers, had Horus Sekhemkhet not disappeared. A beautiful alabaster sarcophagus, which had been placed there for him, remained empty. Nevertheless, he had enough time to begin the enlargement of the paneled enclosure wall, similar in appearance to Zoser's but initially intended to cover a much smaller area. A planned *mastaba* was only partially built, between the pyramid and the first wall on the south side. Like that of the pyramid, its underground chamber was barely begun and was used, no doubt after Sekhemkhet's disappearance, as the tomb of a two-year-old child.

See also

Lepsius, Carl Richard; Manetho; Memphis; Old Kingdom, overview; pyramids (Old Kingdom), construction of

Further reading

Firth, C.M., and J.E. Quibell. 1935–1936. *Excavations at Saqqara: The Step Pyramid*, 2 vols. Cairo.

Friedman, F.D. 1995. The underground relief panels of King Djoser at the Step Pyramid Complex. *JARCE* 32: 1–42.

Lauer, J.-P. 1936–65. *Fouilles à Saqqara: La pyramide à degrés*, 6 vols. (volume 3 in collaboration with P. Lacau). Cairo.

——. 1962. *Histoire monumentale des pyramides d'Égypte* 1: *Les pyramides à degrés*, 2 vols. (BdÉ 39). Cairo.

——. 1976. *Saqqara, the Royal Cemetery of Memphis: Excavations and Discoveries since 1850*. New York.

——. 1991. *Les pyramides de Sakkarah*, 6th edn. Cairo.

JEAN-PHILIPPE LAUER

Saqqara, pyramids of the 5th and 6th Dynasties

Like their predecessors in the 4th Dynasty, the kings of the 5th Dynasty espoused the solar theology, symbolized in the form of the pyramid. For their burials, they too built pyramids on the limestone plateau to the west of the Nile but south of Giza. The pyramid of Weserkaf, the first king of the 5th Dynasty, is at Saqqara (29°50′ N, 31°13′ E), near the famous Step Pyramid of Zoser (beginning of the 3rd Dynasty) that inaugurated large-scale building in stone. However, Weserkaf's successors, Sa- hure, Neferirkare, Neferefre and Nyusserre, built their funerary monuments at Abusir, halfway between Giza and Saqqara and not far from their sun temples. Today their pyr- amids are in ruin, having lost most of their limestone casing stones. It was not until late in the 5th Dynasty that Djedkare-Isesi and Unas, the last king of this dynasty, brought royal tomb building back to Saqqara.

Djedkare-Isesi's pyramid is in the middle of the necropolis. Its ruins were given the name "Haram el-Shawwaf" ("the watchman's pyra- mid") because they are located at the edge of the valley. After the Second World War, the Egyptian Antiquities Organization (EAO) be- gan but unfortunately never finished or pub- lished the excavations of this pyramid complex.

"Complex" is the correct term because each of the pyramids is only a part of a group of structures, including a "valley temple," a walled causeway ascending the plateau, and a mortuary temple, just to the east of the pyramid, with outer and inner areas. The outer temple included a vast court, paved with alabaster and surrounded by pillars with granite bases, and large storerooms for the temple's provisions and equipment. A stairway led to an upper story.

Two cubits (slightly longer than 1 m) above the level of the outer temple was the inner one, with the chamber of the "five niches," or small chapels, each containing a statue. Behind these was a complex passage of corridors and chambers which led to the "offering chamber," just in front of the pyramid. Next to the

pyramid's base was an enormous, upright, granite stela. To the north and south of the offering room were narrow deep storerooms, each with a second story. At the southeast corner of the pyramid, and inside a thick wall that surrounded it and the mortuary temple, was a much smaller pyramid, the function of which is greatly disputed. The existence of two pyramids is perhaps a vestige of the double burial, symbolic of the double nature of the king, who was Lord of Upper and Lower Egypt.

Such an arrangement is seen in the pattern- setting design of Unas's pyramid complex, and the later complexes of a sequence of kings of the 6th Dynasty: Teti, Pepi I, Merenre and Pepi II. Since antiquity all of these pyramids and their mortuary temples have suffered intense damage and their designs have only been determined after long and difficult investiga- tions. In the early nineteenth century, when the French Egyptologist Jean-François Champol- lion was working at Saqqara, the entire plateau was nothing but a great expanse of sand, stones and pebbles. The temples had been a source of building blocks for the stone masons who built Islamic Cairo across the river and the pyramids were barely recognizable as mounds.

The French Archaeological Mission at Saq- qara has only recently begun to study the mortuary temples of Unas and Teti. The French also oversaw the excavation of the vast temple of Pepi I, which took twenty years of fieldwork and is still being published, and the temple of Merenre, which still requires more investiga- tions. In the 1930s, the Swiss archaeologist Gustave Jéquier explored and published the mortuary temple of Pepi II, the last ruler of the 6th Dynasty, to the south of Saqqara.

Near the kings' pyramids are the tombs of their principal queens. The rectangular super- structures (*mastaba*s) under which Unas's queens, Nebet and Khenut, are buried, although simple, contain chambers richly deco- rated in relief. They were discovered long ago, but their publications are only appearing now. King Teti's two queens, Khuit and Apuit I, each had a small tomb complex. The outlines of these were uncovered at the beginning of the nineteenth century, and they are now being investigated by a joint Franco-Egyptian mission (directed by A. Labrousse). In the area of Pepi I's complex, excavations on the south side of the king's pyramid have been in progress for a decade, and five other pyramids have been located. These have revealed the names of two queens, Nubunet and Inenek/Inti, who were previously unknown. In the course of his research in the 1930s, Jéquier discovered the tombs of three of Pepi II's wives: Neith, Apuit II and Udjebten.

Beginning with the pyramid of Unas and those of the kings of the 6th Dynasty, funerary texts known as the *Pyramid Texts* are inscribed on the walls of the royal burial chambers. The discovery of these texts, and the recognition of their fundamental interest to the study of Egyptian religion, are the accomplishments of the French Egyptologist Gaston Maspero. When he had just arrived in Egypt in 1882, bedouin showed him some fragmentary inscriptions, which he believed were hieroglyphs from the royal pyramids. The severely ailing Director of the Egyptian Antiquities Service, Auguste Mariette, proclaimed that such finds were impossible, but a few hours before his death he finally admitted that this discovery was genuine.

Because of the destruction of the burial chambers in the pyramids with texts, Maspero could proceed only by hasty and incomplete excavations. In spite of the difficulties, he copied the accessible inscriptions of Unas, Teti, Pepi I, Merenre and Pepi II. He then quickly edited the texts, published them in one volume in 1894, and fearlessly offered a translation. Considering that he was without any of the references that now facilitate translation, his performance was amazing. With Maspero's rubbings, Kurt Sethe, a major German Egyptologist, was then able in 1908 to publish the *Pyramid Texts*. Within a system of chapters grouping sequences of paragraphs, he arranged in parallel the versions of texts from the five pyramids then known and produced a translation with copious commentary. Sethe's publication of the *Pyramid Texts* is still used today.

During his research in the 1930s, Jéquier

excavated Pepi II's burial chamber and passageway, and discovered many additional texts. He also found the nearby tombs of three queens, which contained still more. As a result Pierre Lacau, who was Director of the Egyptian Antiquities Service for many years, decided in the 1950s to reopen the excavations of Teti's pyramid. Jean-Philippe Lauer and J. Sainte-Fare Garnot found more fragmentary texts, but the political difficulties of the period hindered their work.

In 1963 Jean Leclant resumed the work at Saqqara, with the help of the newly formed French Archaeological Mission to Saqqara. In 1966, the systematic unearthing of Pepi I's burial chamber and passageway was undertaken. During five excavation seasons, thousands of blocks were discovered which yielded new texts. The same kind of fieldwork was conducted inside the pyramid of Merenre. In all the pyramids it was necessary to fortify the enormous blocks, especially those covering the burial chambers. The fragmentary texts had to be catalogued, copied and photographed, and then pieced together. The publication of this epigraphic material is now in progress.

The results considerably advance our knowledge of Egyptian writing. On the whole the signs are very clearly engraved, particularly the ones from the pyramid of Pepi I, which are painted in a striking green made of ground malachite and gum arabic. This is the color known in Egyptian as *wadj*, symbolic of renewal and germination.

The *Pyramid Texts* are concerned with the king's survival in the afterlife. In all of these inscriptions, however, there is no historical information about any of the kings. The auspicious formula of resurrection, "No, you were not dead when you departed, O King; you were alive when you departed," is systematically found engraved on the feet of the kings' sarcophagi. The king could be reborn like the god Osiris, but he could also follow the sun's daily course, or perhaps join the movements of the circumpolar stars which turn forever around the world's axis.

Because of the recent studies of these 6th Dynasty kings and queens, their mortuary temples and the interiors of their tombs, we now have a better understanding of the religion of the late Old Kingdom.

See also

Abu Gurab; Abusir; Champollion, Jean-François; funerary texts; Mariette, François Auguste Ferdinand; Maspero, Sir Gaston Camille Charles; Old Kingdom, overview

Further reading

Edwards, I.E.S. 1993. *The Pyramids of Egypt.* Harmondsworth.

Lauer, J.-P. 1991. *The Pyramids of Sakkara.* Cairo.

Leclant, J. 1979. *Recherches dans la pyramide et au temple haut du Pharaon Pépi Ier à Saqqarah. Scholae Adriani De Buck memoriae dicatae* 6. Leiden.

——. 1984. Recent recherches in the pyramids with text at Saqqarah. In *Monarchies and Socio-religious Traditions in the Ancient Near East*, H.I.P. Prince Takahito Mikasa, ed., 51–4. Wiesbaden.

JEAN LECLANT

Saqqara, pyramids of the 13th Dynasty

Only a few funerary complexes are known for the many kings of the 13th Dynasty, most of whom seem to have been ephemeral. Apart from the royal tombs at Mazghuna and two smaller structures in the Dahshur region, the most important pyramid complexes of that time are found at South Saqqara (29°50′ N, 31°13′ E), approximately 1 km southeast of the 4th Dynasty tomb of King Shepseskaf, known as the "*Mastaba* Faraun." When Richard Lepsius visited the site during his expedition in the early 1840s, he already suspected that the mounds of limestone chips covering the desert surface might be the remains of pyramids, but it was not until 1929 that Gustave Jéquier began excavations, which continued until 1931.

Jéquier uncovered the remains of two royal funerary complexes some 80 m apart. The smaller northern one belonged to the seventeenth king of the 13th Dynasty, Weserkare Khendjer. His name appears on several fragments of relief from the pyramid's mortuary temple as well as on the pyramidion, which was found smashed in the debris on the north side of the pyramid and is now displayed in the Cairo Museum.

Despite the deplorable state of Khendjer's pyramid complex, Jéquier was able to determine its plan, which generally follows the traditions of the 12th Dynasty pyramids. The pyramid measures *circa* 52 m (100 cubits) square at the base and consists of a mudbrick core in a limestone casing. It is at the center of the precinct, surrounded by two enclosure walls. A causeway, which seems to have remained unfinished, connected the precinct with a valley temple. The temple should be located at the edge of the cultivation, but it has not yet been found. A reconstruction of the plan of the mortuary temple is not possible as only parts of the sub-foundations and some fragments of relief have been found. Fragments of papyri-form columns found in the debris, however, indicate the existence of a pillared hall or court. In the center of the northern court, a foundation trench and some fragments of reliefs and a false door are evidence of a northern chapel. The entrance to the burial apartment is hidden beneath the casing of the pyramid's western side. Apart from the fact that the sarcophagus is cut from a single block of quartzite, which entirely occupies the burial chamber as in other 13th Dynasty pyramids, the general plan is similar to the innovative design of the burial apartment of Amenemhat III's pyramid at Hawara (12th Dynasty).

The function of the small pyramid found in the northeastern corner of the outer court remains obscure. It contains two burial chambers with quartzite sarcophagi which were found open and apparently unused, although the blocking stones (portcullises) of the corridor were in place. It is not possible to determine whether the pyramid was intended for burials of members of the royal family or as the *ka* pyramid (for the king's *ka*).

With a base length of more than 90 m, the southern pyramid at South Saqqara is almost double the size of its northern neighbor and closely corresponds in size to the 12th Dynasty pyramids. Unfortunately, the whole complex remained unfinished and the owner is unknown. The complex is generally dated to the 13th Dynasty, but there is no evidence to ascribe it to a certain king. No remains of a causeway, mortuary temple or northern chapel were found. The pyramid consists of the usual mudbrick core with limestone casing, but it was only surrounded by a single sinuous wall, which was probably intended to be replaced by another enclosure. Apart from slight differences in the arrangement of the corridor, the burial apartment differs only slightly from that in the pyramid of Khendjer. The most surprising change is the existence of a second burial chamber, which opens from the north wall of the antechamber. This secondary burial chamber was probably intended for a member of the royal family, but its sarcophagus was found open and apparently was never used.

See also

Dahshur, Middle Kingdom pyramids; Hawara; Lepsius, Carl Richard; Mazghuna; Middle Kingdom, overview; Second Intermediate Period, overview

Further reading

Edwards, I.E.S. 1993. *The Pyramids of Egypt.* Harmondsworth.

Jéquier, G. 1933. *Deux pyramides du Moyen Empire.* Cairo.

CHRISTIAN HÖLZL

Saqqara, Serapeum and animal necropolis

The sacred animal necropolis at Saqqara comprises several separate sites, the best documented of which lie in two groups: (1) north of the Step Pyramid of Zoser, and (2) east of the pyramids of Teti and Weserkaf. The first group includes the Serapeum (burials of the Apis bulls), the tombs of the Isis cows (mothers of Apis bulls) with the adjacent catacombs of ibises and baboons of Thoth, and falcons of Horus. The second group contains the burials of cats of Bastet and dogs/jackals of Anubis in the escarpment overlooking the Nile Valley at the site of the city of Memphis. Each of these burial sites was an important element in a temple complex dedicated to the deity for whom the particular creature was a symbol. Papyri and ostraca speak of a Memphite cult of the Ram of Mendes, whose undiscovered burials must be at Saqqara; rams' horns found north of the Serapeum and at the unfinished funerary complex of Sekhemkhet may indicate the site. A cemetery of lions is also mentioned in a papyrus from the same area. At South Saqqara, snake burials found near the pyramid of Djedkare-Isesi remain an isolated discovery in that area, indicating that animal cemeteries are not restricted to the most thoroughly explored region of the Memphite necropolis.

In 1851, Auguste Mariette began digging at Saqqara with the express purpose of finding the Serapeum, known at that time only from the classical writers. Inspired by Strabo's description of the *dromos* lined with sphinxes buried in sand, Mariette proceeded to uncover the processional way leading from Memphis, across the desert from the east, to the entrance of the underground burial vaults of the Apis bulls. The importance of Mariette's discovery of the Serapeum was immediately recognized and continues to influence research. He had found a monument that had played a major role in the religious life not only of Memphis, but of all Egypt and much of the Hellenistic world. The quantity of portable finds retrieved, statues, inscribed stonework, bronzes and stelae was

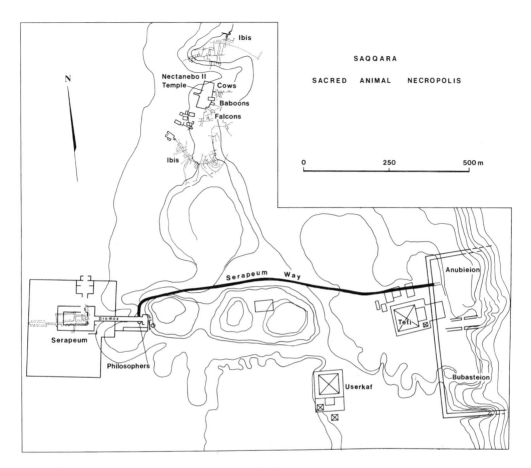

Figure 100 Map of the sacred animal necropolis, Saqqara

extraordinary. Most went to the Louvre in two ships sent from France specifically to transport them; much of this important material still remains unpublished.

Of the objects Mariette recovered, the Serapeum stelae comprise the single most important group. Many are simple, humble petitions from workmen and minor officials involved with the burial procedures for the bulls, while others are royal monuments dated by the contemporary rulers' names. The latter frequently provide a dated account of a bull's birth, installation in the temple of Ptah at Memphis, its life, death and burial. The stelae attest to deep personal devotion, to royal patronage and to the scale of the funerary rites

observed for the Apis bulls, especially from the Late period onward, when the god was laid to rest accompanied by national mourning. Together, the stelae form one of the most important archives of historical and social documents recovered from Egypt, being an almost continuous literary record from one place spanning over a millennium from the reign of Ramesses II to the end of the Ptolemaic period.

In 1965 Walter B. Emery, working among the Archaic and Old Kingdom *mastaba*s of North Saqqara, found the catacombs containing the remains of the cows (mothers of Apis bulls), the ibises, falcons and baboons, together with the 30th Dynasty temple terraces and shrines that stood before them. More recently Alain Zivie, investigating New Kingdom rock tombs in the escarpment facing the remains of the Bubasteion (temple of Bastet) on the east edge of the Saqqara plateau, found thousands of mummified cats which had been buried there in later times.

The underground burial chambers of the Apis bulls developed in three stages: (1) individual tombs; (2) galleries known as the Lesser Vaults; and then (3) the Greater Vaults. The earliest burials were in isolated tombs with decorated chapels above. Eight burials are known from the reign of Amenhotep III to year 30 of Ramesses II. The last was a double interment with the previously deceased bull which had died in year 16 of Ramesses II. This tomb contained the only Apis burial to have survived unplundered from antiquity. In it, Mariette found two massive black wooden sarcophagi with gilded designs. Inside each was a bituminous lump containing fragmentary bones without any trace of a head. Gold jewelry among the contents bearing the names of Ramesses II and his son Prince Khaemwaset attest to their integrity.

In year 55 of Ramesses II the Lesser Vaults were begun, remaining in use until the reign of Psamtik I. This was a subterranean gallery which grew in size as burials were made in specially cut niches on either side of the corridor. They contained wooden sarcophagi datable mainly from the stelae found in the niches and carved on the walls, from Ramesses II to Ramesses IX, and from Osorkon II to Psamtik I. No burials of the 21st and early 22nd Dynasties have been identified. In the center of the Lesser Vaults, the ceiling collapsed in antiquity. Beneath the rock blocking the corridor lay the burial of Prince Khaemwaset comprising the lower part of his gilded coffin containing an intact mummy wearing a gold mask and various items of jewelry, with *shawabti*s and a collection of human-headed statuettes inscribed for Osiris-Apis. The presence of the prince's burial inside the Serapeum vault has never been satisfactorily explained. It is possible, however, that as the gallery was progressively enlarged, laborers accidentally

broke into the burial chamber of Khaemwaset's tomb. The resulting weakness of the already brittle rock could have caused the roof to fall. Nevertheless, there was a special association between Khaemwaset and Apis. A large granite stela of Khaemwaset was found at the entrance to the Serapeum.

The Greater Vaults of the Serapeum were inaugurated with an Apis burial in year 52 of Psamtik I (612 BC), possibly coinciding with new buildings at the precinct of Apis in Memphis. These galleries lead off the Lesser Vaults, but are executed on a grander scale; this is the part of the Serapeum now accessible to visitors. On either side of a long corridor a total of twenty-eight burial niches were excavated, of which twenty-four contain a granite or basalt sarcophagus. All had been opened and their contents destroyed in antiquity. One sarcophagus remains today in a side passage where it was abandoned during its installation; a lid, from burial 41, inscribed for an Apis bull under Amasis, was found just inside the entrance corridor. Only two sarcophagi bear datable inscriptions, that of Amasis and another of year 2 of Khababash (*circa* 336 BC), which by its small size appears to have contained a calf. According to the stelae, the Greater Vaults were in use until the end of the Ptolemaic period, probably the reign of Cleopatra VII.

The Serapeum Way did not come into use until about the 26th Dynasty. It scaled the desert escarpment overlooking the Nile Valley, perhaps by means of stairs or a causeway, and passed by the earlier tombs north of the pyramids of Teti and Weserkaf, arriving finally at the Serapeum. In the 30th Dynasty this route was lined with the 134 limestone sphinxes found by Mariette. Under both Nectanebo I and II an impressive new funerary temple was built in an enclosure around the entrance to the underground Serapeum vaults, now known as Ka-Kome, possibly replacing a 26th Dynasty structure. The temple pylon was guarded by a pair of limestone lions. A quartzite stela of Nectanebo II, found reused in the monastery of Apa Jeremias, records his official generosity to Apis.

Under the Ptolemies the final stretch of the Serapeum Way contained a hemicycle of eleven

Hellenistic statues of Greek philosophers and writers. The avenue led thence directly to the temple enclosure between statues of Dionysos riding a lion, Dionysos riding a Cerberus, peacocks draped with bunches of grapes and Hellenistic female sphinxes. A similar temple *dromos* was found at Medinet Madi in the Fayum. Explicit imagery of Dionysos demonstrates the European identification of the Egyptian Osiris cult, with whom Apis had become closely connected, with the mysteries of Dionysos, as recorded by Herodotus.

The sacred animal cults enjoyed their greatest popularity in the Saite period (26th Dynasty) and later. There is evidence that during the second Persian period the sacred animal cults may have suffered from neglect or even aggression. The extensive building program of Ptolemy I and II in the Serapeum area and Anubieion suggests that the 30th Dynasty structures had either been left unfinished or had been damaged. No burial of a mother of Apis is recorded between year 9 of Nectanebo II (351 BC) and year 3 of Alexander the Great (329 BC). Furthermore, a cache of broken and burnt temple equipment dating from the 18th to 30th Dynasties discovered outside the north wall of the sacred animal necropolis temple precinct may indicate the ravages of this period.

With the Ptolemaic revival burials resumed. The mothers of Apis bulls were interred continuously down to year 11 of Cleopatra VII (40 BC); the smaller animals and bird burials numbered millions. An important deposit of Demotic ostraca known as the "Archive of Hor [a priest of Sebennytos]" was found in front of the new ibis galleries. Hor addresses Ptolemy VI about the mismanagement of the ibis cult. In order to establish his credentials, Hor relates his gift for interpreting dreams, including one foretelling the withdrawal from Egypt of the Seleucid Antiochus IV on July 30, 168 BC. Other valuable historical information includes the embassy of Noumenios to Rome and the proclamation of Philometor's son, Ptolemy Eupator, as crown prince in October, 158 BC.

The sacred precincts supported a vast community of workers and attendants. These included the shrine openers *(pastophoroi)* and dream interpreters *(oneirokritai)*, and the writers of oracle petitions, astrologers and magicians, for which Egypt became increasingly famous. Others were the *katochoi*, people who were summoned by Apis to remain in his

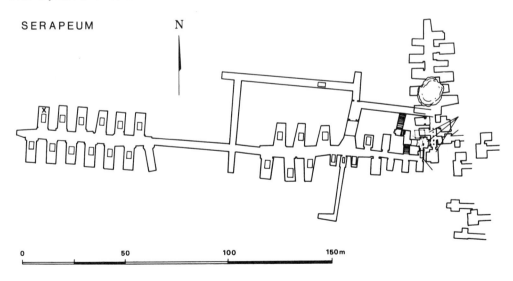

Figure 101 Plan of the Serapeum, Saqqara

service within the temple where they would dedicate themselves to divine contemplation in seclusion, often for many years, until they experienced the god's release. There were also facilities for housing pilgrims *(katalumata)*, possibly represented by mudbrick buildings unearthed north of the Serapeum.

For the devotees who came in such numbers to dedicate mummified creatures, the significance of the sacred animal cults may be partly reconstructed from the discovery of numerous votive phallic figurines, which combine representations of Bes and Harpocrates. Large numbers came from the courts of the sacred animal necropolis. They may be associated with a procession in which a phallic image of Osiris was paraded. A close connection emerges between the animal cults (really animal burial cults) and concerns about procreation, generation and regeneration in which funerary rituals played a major part. Chambers lined with figures of Bes molded in plaster on the walls were found in the Anubis enclosure, adjacent to the mortuary temple of the pyramid of Teti. They may have been incubation cells where pilgrims would spend the night hoping to experience healing dreams; numerous phallic figurines were also found there.

Archaeological excavation has revealed only part of the complex remains of this phase of the history of Saqqara. It is known, for example, that the Serapeum Way entered the temple area through the Anubieion. However, it has so far proved impossible to trace its course farther east, to link the necropolis with the temple of Ptah and the Apis precinct in Memphis, which lie a considerable distance south of the Anubieion. Furthermore, Apis burials predating the reign of Amenhotep III may await discovery near the Serapeum. Other animal cemeteries may even be present beneath the unexplored sands between the New Kingdom necropolis south of the pyramid of Unas and the pyramids of South Saqqara.

See also

Mariette, François Auguste Ferdinand; Memphis; mortuary beliefs; mummification;

Saqqara, Late period and Graeco-Roman tombs

Further reading

Jeffreys, D.G., and H.S. Smith. 1988. *The Anubieion at Saqqara* 1. London.
Martin, G.T. 1981. *The Sacred Animal Necropolis at North Saqqara, The Southern Dependencies of The Main Temple* (Excavation memoir 50). London.
Smith, H.S. 1974. *A Visit to Ancient Egypt.* Warminster.

MICHAEL JONES

sculpture, production techniques

The visual impression generated by Egyptian stone sculpture of all periods is both cubic and frontal. Sculpture in stone seems to have been conceived in terms of the cubic block as it was removed from the quarry, unlike sculpture in other materials such as clay, bone, ivory or metal. As the techniques for quarrying stone developed, it seemed to have been practical or economical to detach units of the material from the quarry bed in regular cubes. These regular shapes perhaps first suggested and later dictated an approach to the production of sculpture, which was visualized from the four sides of the block.

The particular stone employed dictated some of the technical requirements of tools and technique. Limestone, soft when recently quarried, required cutting tools which could be of hardened copper or sharp stone such as flint or chert. The harder stones, including granite, diorite, quartzite and sandstone, required the use of a variety of techniques based on battering, pecking, sawing, drilling and abrading.

George Reisner lists eight stages in the production of stone sculpture based on observations made on a number of contemporary unfinished statues of the pharaoh Menkaure found at Giza:

1 The rough blocking of the stone, with figure vaguely indicated without delineating face, arms or legs, but with some smoothing of surfaces, probably by rubbing with stone and some kind of abrasive paste.

2 Continued blocking with some differentiation of parts—face, arms, legs, seat—and red paint outlines of areas of stone to be removed.

3 Face, beard, wig, arms and hands take on more definite outlines.

4 Planes of the face are developed and areas of decoration, such as the *uraeus* at the forehead, are defined. The definition of limbs is advanced, the groove between the two legs (in seated statues) is deepened.

5 Details of facial anatomy begin to emerge; less evidence of bruising of the entire surface is visible, suggesting use of smaller and more delicate tools.

6 The entire surface appears to be the product of fine bruising and rough polishing; the statue is recognizable as a representation of a king.

7 Fine details have been added, such as the separate definition of fingers, lines around the eyes and so on. Polishing could continue for greater or lesser time, determining the quality of the piece.

8 Fully finished and inscribed piece.

From Reisner's description it is clear that he saw the process as having employed carving, pecking or bruising, and grinding, used together at all stages. The reduction of planes as the finish of the piece progressed was accomplished by a combination of all these techniques.

The eight steps or stages are not always clearly demarcated and cannot always be observed or defined as they were by Reisner. The sculptural process can be summarized in four more general steps: (1) roughing out of general shape, (2) rounding of forms, (3) carving of detail, and (4) finishing (polish and carving of inscription).

The outline of front, sides and back of the desired image were drawn on the appropriate faces of the block in ink or paint. The initial carving followed those outlines to eliminate the excess stone leaving a broad and still square figure with no rounded corners. The contours were then modeled to provide the transitions from one cubic plane to another. This was followed by a series of general reductions to refine and better describe the image, ending with the careful carving of detail of anatomy and decoration, and in the case of hard stone, the final polishing.

Egyptian sculpture, regardless of the stone employed, was always solidly designed. To ensure the permanence of the piece the sculptor usually included a back pillar, a buttress-like pilaster of attached stone which strengthened the figure from behind. The spaces between the body and arms and the space between the legs were connected by areas of uncarved stone. There was little undercutting where to do so would have weakened the statue, even if the remaining stone made the form hard to visualize. Such connectives were often painted black and treated as if they were invisible. The craftsmen were generally very conservative in their treatment of stone, rarely taking chances by removing too much of the supporting material and thus risking the weakening of the statue.

Egyptian sculpture was generally completed by painting and sometimes gilding. The vivid colors used, where they have been preserved, present to the modern observer a vastly different impression from the large majority of pieces which have lost their polychrome surface. A further embellishment, particularly in the Old Kingdom, was the use of inlaid eyes. They were often made of several different colors and types of stone to define the anatomical parts of the eye; rock crystal was regularly employed to suggest depth and transparency.

Sculpture in metal has been little preserved from early periods in Egyptian history and as a result we know little about its manufacture. Copper statues of Pepi I and his son Merenre from the 6th Dynasty demonstrate that metal sculpture existed. These examples, at least, were formed over a wooden core rather than being cast. From the Third Intermediate Period on there is considerable evidence for the process of "lost wax" casting in the thousands of small images of deities and sacred animals which abound.

The other major materials used for sculpture were wood, clay and Egyptian faïence. The conventions employed in stone sculpture could be considerably modified in the treatment of wood. Wood could be carved more freely with less concern for its weight and, as a consequence, there was no necessity for back pillars and connective areas of material to support limbs. Examples such as the famous Sheikh el-Baled found at Saqqara demonstrate the ability of the Egyptian artist to carve in wood. Wooden statues, such as this one, were finished with a coat of gesso plaster and painted color. The eyes could also be inlaid in other materials. Clay or ceramic sculpture as well as sculpture made from Egyptian faïence was either modeled freely or cast in a mold. Both materials were frequently employed for small figurines and decorative objects. The fired clay might be painted as a final decoration, again after a coating of gesso. Faïence was made in a range of colors by adding various minerals to the quartzite body material before firing.

It can be seen that the form of ancient Egyptian sculpture of all kinds was dictated by the materials employed. Works in stone are quite different from those in wood or the plastic materials of clay and faïence. The canonical rules so often discussed in histories of Egyptian art apply most particularly to works in stone. In other materials, the artist or craftsman had somewhat more freedom in the development of sculptural form.

See also

quarrying

Further reading

Lucas, A. 1962. *Ancient Egyptian Materials and Industries*, revised and enlarged by J.R. Harris, 4th edn. London.
Reisner, G.A. 1931. *Mycerinus: The Temples of the Third Pyramid at Giza*. Cambridge, MA.
Smith, W.S. 1949. *A History of Egyptian Sculpture and Painting in the Old Kingdom*. Boston.
——. 1981. *The Art and Architecture of Ancient Egypt*, revised with additions by W.K. Simpson. Harmondsworth.

WILLIAM H. PECK

Sea Peoples

"Sea Peoples" is the generic name for an array of peoples from the Mediterranean northern lands who attacked the Near East and Egypt, initially in piratical raids but later in major population movements that brought the Late Bronze Age to a close. They are attested from the Amarna period into the reign of Ramesses III (20th Dynasty). The raiders were identified by various names in the Egyptian scenes and inscriptions documenting their activities. Shardana, Lukka, Tursha, Akawasha/Ekwesh, Shekelesh, Peleset, Tjekker, Denyen and Wesesh all are names recorded for them. Some have been identified with historic peoples and places. The Lukka often are identified with Lycia, the Tursha with the Etruscans, Akawasha/Ekwesh with Achaeans, and Denyen with Danaoi (Mycenaean Greeks). Shardana have been linked with Sardinia and Shekelesh with Sicily, though these may be places they settled in their later wanderings.

In the Egyptian sources, the Sea Peoples came in three successive phases. Initially, from the Amarna period into the reign of Ramesses II (19th Dynasty), they appeared as pirates, harassing shipping and raiding isolated, unprotected coastal settlements. Such were the Lukka mentioned in the Amarna Letters, and also the Shardana who attacked Egypt's Delta in regnal year 2 of Ramesses II. Ramesses did trap and capture the raiders in year 2, and he impressed the captives into the Egyptian army. At the Battle of Qadesh in Syria, in regnal year 5, they formed part of the pharaoh's bodyguard, distinctive in their horned helmets and with long swords. Ramesses II was concerned sufficiently by these raids that he built a series of coastal fortresses from Rosetta to Marsa

Matruh to protect the coasts. He also built another line of fortresses along the western Delta edge, to guard against Libyan raids.

The Egyptians were right to be concerned about the Libyans; in regnal year 5 of Merenptah, the Sea Peoples came in a new wave, probably landing in Cyrenaica. They armed the Libyans with bronze armor and weapons, and then jointly attempted to invade Egypt. They stirred up the southern Libyans and Nubians to revolt against Egyptian suzerainty. Merenptah was ready for the challenge; he crushed the Nubian–southern Libyan revolt, and then met the allied Libyan and Sea Peoples forces north of Memphis, defeating them roundly in a pitched battle. The Libyan chief slunk away, humiliated, and Merenptah's forces slew and captured 9,300 prisoners, of which some 2,700 were Sea Peoples, including Akawasha, Shardana, Shekelesh, Lukka and Teresh. Merenptah, like Ramesses II before him, impressed captives from his Canaanite and Sea Peoples–Libyan wars into his armed forces. As the Sea Peoples fought in new ways, with thrusting and striking swords as infantry, Egypt gained an advantage by incorporating these in her armies. Merenptah also supplied grain and arms to his Hittite allies, as they suffered from drought and Sea Peoples raids. At Ugarit, one of the long bronze Sea Peoples' swords, stamped with Merenptah's cartouche, was excavated, probably part of the arms aid.

The final and heaviest raids of the Sea Peoples came against Ramesses III, in regnal year 8, and are recorded in scenes on the walls of his funerary temple at Medinet Habu. This Sea Peoples campaign came between two Libyan wars, of regnal years 5 and 11. Those Libyans though had no Sea Peoples help this time, for the Sea Peoples attack came from the Levant. From Ramesses III's documents we are told that the Sea Peoples had hatched a conspiracy in their isles and had started their attack on the Hittites, Ugarit and northern Syria, all of which they overwhelmed. They seized Cyprus also, and advanced on Amurru, where they set up a camp. Another contingent came in ships by sea, wiping out local navies. From there they set out for Egypt. The Egyptian navy drew the sea raiders into the Delta. With archers stationed along the river banks, the Egyptians overwhelmed the Sea Peoples with many drowning and others being taken captive. Ramesses III marched armies into Syro-Palestine to halt the Sea Peoples land contingent. These land units were depicted not just as raiders but as migrants, complete with women and children in wagons. Ramesses III also defeated and deflected these Sea Peoples from Egypt, though he had to allow them to settle along the coasts of Palestine and Lebanon. Initially they were under loose Egyptian control, but by the mid-20th Dynasty they became independent and ruled in the coastal cities.

Known as Philistines to the early Israelites, these Sea Peoples sorely troubled the early Israelite settlements in the hill country in the twelfth century BC. From the Egyptian sources, this group of Sea Peoples were Peleset, Tjekker, Shekelesh, Weshesh and Denyen. The Peleset were the biblical Philistines. The Sea Peoples are mentioned in Papyrus Wilbour, where Shardana feature among the Egyptian veterans holding plots of land in Middle Egypt. These Sea Peoples had done well, earning settlement in Egypt and land grants as veterans.

Another Egyptian document mentioning the Sea Peoples is the tale of Wenamen. Around 1075 BC, Wenamen was sent to Lebanon to buy cedar for Amen's divine bark. He boarded a ship in the Delta, and found the Tjekker controlling the coastal cities of Palestine. A Tjekker aboard his ship robbed him in Dor, and, failing to gain satisfaction from the ruler, Wenamen in turn plundered a Tjekker ship that came into Dor. Proceeding to Byblos, he eventually met the ruler, Tjekker-Baal. After much sarcasm from the prince and some haggling, the prince agreed to fell the cedar, but only after receiving promise of full payment from Smendes and Tanutamen, ruling in Tanis in Egypt. The prince also mentioned that the settled Sea Peoples now had a lively trade going with Tanis in Egypt. After receiving full payment he allowed Wenamen to sail. The Tjekker lay waiting for Wenamen just outside Byblos, in retribution for his plundering of them in Dor. The prince of Byblos did not allow them to touch Wenamen in his port, but he permitted them pursuit on the open sea. Luckily for Wenamen, a storm arose at sea and he outwitted the Tjekker but was blown off course and landed on Cyprus. There a mob descended, ready to kill him, but he glibly talked himself out of this predicament. Thus, he survived the adventure to tell his story. It is clear that by now the Sea Peoples were independent rulers from Gaza to Byblos, and they were totally free of Egyptian dominion.

Whence, and why, did the Sea Peoples appear? Some have suggested locales including Lycia and other parts of coastal Anatolia. Still others may have originated from Mycenaean lands, Achaea and elsewhere. Still others may have come from lands north of the Aegean Sea. It is clear that the Sea Peoples were excellent seafarers and that they possessed a strong bronze culture. Other factors that led to their appearing in the Late Bronze Age may include the collapse of the Minoan navy and the decline of the Egyptian navy, both of which had dominated the Mediterranean earlier. The Mycenaeans had invaded and seized Crete, and during Akhenaten's reign the Egyptians lost naval supremacy in the Levant. It is just then that the Lukka are first attested as raiders. It is a truism in the Mediterranean that when strong navies exist, piracy and freebooting are reduced, but whenever such navies decline, the peoples of Lycia, Caria and Illyria ever have been ready to start piratical raiding. That could well account for the initial Sea Peoples raids.

During Merenptah's reign and the late Hittite imperial age, larger freebooting raids were attempted. Now certain coastal areas could be menaced, and even city-states could succumb. To this stage may belong the Homeric raids on Troy. Still later, under Ramesses III, whole populations were on the move. What provoked such migrations? Drought has been implicated and Herodotus's account about the Etruscans/Teresh, and Merenptah's shipments of grain to Hatti, might denote climatic problems. New methods of warfare by the Sea Peoples emphasizing infantry have been suggested as a factor, and the use by Egypt of captive Sea Peoples lends to this credence. Finally, a mega-volcanic event, the eruption of

Hekla III in Iceland in 1159 BC, may have played a role. That eruption is dated by ice cores and tree rings. It coincides with Ramesses III's last years, during which the pharaoh had trouble supplying grain rations to Deir el-Medina's work force. Also in the mid-20th Dynasty, wheat and barley prices rose dramatically in Egypt. Thus massive crop failures may have set whole populations migrating.

The Homeric poems and other Bronze Age Greek epics may record traces of Sea Peoples' activities. In one epic, Odysseus raids Egypt and is captured, but spared. After serving Pharaoh seven years, he leaves Egypt wealthy. This echoes the experiences of captured Sea Peoples who went on to serve in Egypt's armies and ended up with land grants. Another Greek epic recounts how Menelaus pursued his wife Helen to Egypt, where she had fled with Paris. Excavations in Palestine and Lebanon have confirmed Sea Peoples settlement in the coastal areas and are revealing the sophisticated Philistine civilization that emerged, confirming Wenamen's account. This Philistine civilization has many traits in common with Mycenaean culture, from pottery types to architecture and political organization. Along the way the Philistines also acquired iron-working technology that allowed them to dominate the early Israelites. As Lawrence Stager, excavator of Ashkelon, has remarked, all that lacks now is a Philistine text in Linear B from Palestine. Ultimately the Sea Peoples transformed the Near East, ending the Bronze Age and ushering in the Iron Age that followed.

See also

Aegean peoples; Amarna Letters; army; Cypriot peoples; Israelites; Libyans; Medinet Habu; New Kingdom, overview; ships; textual sources, Late period; Third Intermediate Period, overview

Further reading

Dothan, T.K., and M. Dothan. 1992. *People of the Sea*. New York.

Drews, R. 1993. *The End of the Bronze Age.* Princeton, NJ.

Sandars, N.K. 1985. *The Sea Peoples,* rev. edn. London.

Ward, W.A., and M. Joukowsky, eds. 1992. *The Crisis Years: The 12th Century B.C.* Dubuque, IA.

Yurco, F.J. 1986. Merenptah's Canaanite campaign. *JARCE* 23: 189–215.

——. In press. The end of the Late Bronze Age and other crisis periods: a volcanic cause. In *Gold of Praise: Studies on Ancient Egypt in Honor of Edward F. Wente*, E. Teeter and J.A. Larson, eds. (SAOC) Chicago.

FRANK J. YURCO

Seila/Silah

Seila is the name of a site (29°23′ N, 31°03′ E) with the largest pyramid of a group of seven small step pyramids in which no chambers or corridors have yet been found (they probably never existed). The pyramid stands on a high peak in the chain of hills called the Gebel el-Rus which overlook the fertile plain of the Fayum to the west and the desert and the Nile Valley to the east. The pyramid of Meydum, about 18.5 km to the east, can be clearly seen from the pyramid of Seila.

In 1898, Ludwig Borchardt visited Seila and identified the inner core of a small step pyramid that Flinders Petrie (in 1889–90) had concluded represented the remains of a *mastaba*. In 1961 J.-P. Lauer published a short report confirming that the building was a pyramid, probably with four steps. A joint expedition of the University of California, Berkeley, and Brigham Young University, directed by Leonard Lesko and C.W. Griggs, began a detailed survey of the monument in 1981. Six years later the work was resumed by Griggs.

The exact dimensions of the pyramid have not yet been ascertained. Its base is approximately 35.5 m sq. and its height is calculated to have been about 10 m. It probably had six steps, but very little of the two lowest steps has been preserved. Its special importance lies in the fact that its builder is known beyond doubt to have been Seneferu, the first king of the 4th Dynasty. In 1987, two round-topped stelae were found on the east side of the pyramid; one of these was inscribed with the names of Seneferu. The other stela was uninscribed.

Seven pyramids in the chamberless group have been identified. The second largest of these was built at Zawiyet el-Mayitin (Zawiyet el-Amwat); each of its sides measures 22.48 m at the base. The base dimensions of the chamberless pyramids, at Abydos (Sinki), Edfu (el-Ghenimiya), Elephantine, el-Kula and Nagada, average about 20 m square. Only the pyramid of Zawiyet el-Mayitin has preserved a substantial part of its fine limestone casing. The visible cores of all these pyramids consist of local stone which, in the case of the Elephantine pyramid, is granite. It is the only pyramid in the group, apart from that of Seila, for which written evidence of its builder's name seems to have been preserved. A large granite cone, excavated near the pyramid, bore on its base the name of Huni, Seneferu's predecessor and the last king of the 3rd Dynasty.

While there is no reason to doubt that all the pyramids in the chamberless group date from about the same time as those which can be ascribed to the reigns of Huni and Seneferu, nothing is known with certainty about their function. One suggestion is that they were cenotaphs for queens, which were erected at their places of birth while their real tombs would be near those of their husbands. Another suggestion is that they were cenotaphs erected near a king's provincial residences as emblems of his power. Yet another theory is that the pyramids were representations of the primeval mound, the hieroglyphic sign for which depicted a step pyramid. Two discoveries by the Brigham Young University expedition at Seila in 1990–1 may indicate that rituals were conducted there. An alabaster (travertine) altar was found on the north side of the pyramid, as were fragments of a seated human figure, also in alabaster. There is, however, no positive evidence of these pyramids' use, but it seems certain that they are not tombs.

See also

Meydum; Saqqara, pyramids of the 3rd Dynasty

Further reading

Edwards, I.E.S. 1993. *The Pyramids of Egypt*, 65–70. Harmondsworth.
Lauer, J.-P. 1962. *Histoire monumentale des pyramides de l'Égypte*, 221–30. Cairo.
Lesko, L. 1988. Seila, 1981. *JARCE* 25: 216–35.

I.E.S. EDWARDS

Serabit el-Khadim

Serabit el-Khadim ($29°02'$ N, $33°28'$ E) in South Sinai is located *circa* 29 km east of the Gulf of Suez, and lies 735 m above sea level on a sandstone plateau. During the 12th Dynasty and New Kingdom periods Egyptian expeditions mined and smelted copper at Wadi Nasb (*circa* 6 km to the west of Serabit el-Khadim), mined turquoise from at least twenty mines at Serabit el-Khadim, and established a Hathor temple on the plateau. The Middle and New Kingdom inscriptions from this site record the use of sea transport and overland caravans consisting of 50 to 500 donkeys and 200 to over 700 men, often led by treasury officials.

Since Niebuhr's rediscovery of Serabit el-Khadim in 1762, many travelers have visited this site. The first significant investigations at Serabit el-Khadim include the 1845 expedition of Richard Lepsius, mostly unpublished excavations by Major C.K. Macdonald in 1845–6 and 1867, and an ordnance survey by Wilson and Palmer in 1868–9. Captain Weill published two volumes concerning pharaonic activity in South Sinai, and later accompanied Flinders Petrie's expedition to South Sinai in 1904–5, during which Petrie copied inscriptions and excavated the Hathor temple and surrounding mines. Lake directed Harvard University's 1927 survey at Serabit el-Khadim. Professor Hjelt led a Finnish expedition to this site in 1929. Lake continued investigating Serabit el-Khadim in

1930 and 1935, excavating parts of the temple, five quarries and Mine M. W.F. Albright explored Serabit el-Khadim during a 1947–8 survey of the Sinai peninsula. This site was examined more thoroughly between 1967 and 1982, when numerous Israeli archaeological surveys and excavations were conducted in the Sinai peninsula by Rothenberg (1956–7 and 1967–73) and Beit-Arieh. Beit-Arieh excavated parts of the Hathor temple and Mines G and L in 1978–9. Lastly, Dominic Valbelle surveyed South Sinai in 1992, and in 1993 began an ongoing program of excavation and restoration in the Hathor temple.

The earliest, albeit probably indirect, Egyptian contact with South Sinai dates to the Predynastic and Early Dynastic periods; during these periods, turquoise is found in Egypt. The South Sinai contains 1st Dynasty Egyptian pottery amounting to 1 percent of the pottery assemblages at a Chalcolithic settlement (*circa* 3,500 BC) near Serabit el-Khadim and some Early Bronze I–II sites (3,200–2,650 BC) in South Sinai. Despite the presence at Serabit el-Khadim of a hawk statuette bearing the name of the 4th Dynasty ruler Seneferu, this statuette likely dates to the Middle and New Kingdom periods, when many Sinai inscriptions contain dedications to Seneferu.

Expeditions during the 12th Dynasty initiated turquoise mining at Serabit el-Khadim and concentrated on this site in contrast to other South Sinai sites, such as Maghara, Wadi Kharig and Wadi Nasb. The 12th Dynasty inscriptions indicate the presence of at least one expedition during the reigns of Amenemhat I, Senusret I, Amenemhat II, Senusret II and Senusret III, 18–20 expeditions during Amenemhat III's reign, and four expeditions during the rule of Amenemhat IV. These expeditions began the temple at Serabit el-Khadim by cutting northern (Room T) and southern (Room U) shrines within a rock outcrop. Giveon has suggested that prior to becoming a Hathor Shrine, Room T began as a tomb chapel with funerary-style inscriptions and scenes, but remained unfinished. Giveon also proposed that Room U began as a shrine to Hathor rather than to Sopdu. The presence of

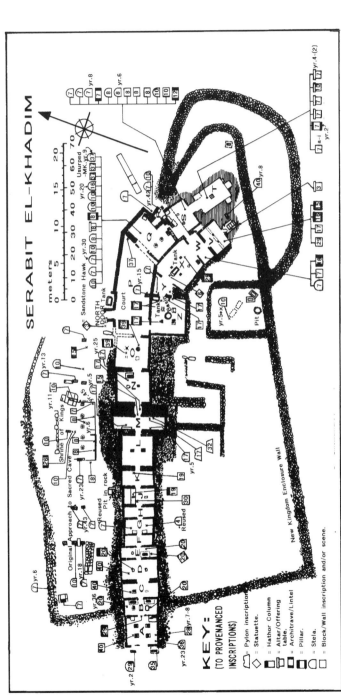

SERABIT EL-KHADIM

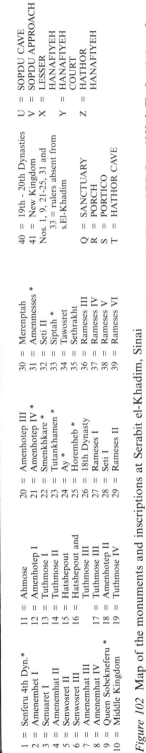

KEY:
(TO PROVENANCED INSCRIPTIONS)

◇ = Pylon inscription.*

△◇ = Statuette.

◻▭□◻ = Hathor Column

▭ = Altar/Offering table.

□ = Architrave/Lintel

◻ = Pillar.

◯ = Stela.

□□ = Block/Wall inscription and/or scene.

1 = Senferu 4th Dyn.*	11 = Ahmose
2 = Amenemhet I	12 = Amenhotep I
3 = Senuaret I	13 = Tuthmose I
4 = Amenemhat II	14 = Tuthmose II
5 = Senwosret II	15 = Hatshepout
6 = Senwosret III	16 = Hatshepout and
7 = Amenemhat III	Tuthmose III
8 = Amenemhat IV	17 = Tuthmose III
9 = Queen Sobekneferu *	18 = Amenhotep II
10 = Middle Kingdom	19 = Tuthmose IV

20 = Amenhotep III	30 = Merenptah
21 = Amenhotep IV *	31 = Amenmesses *
22 = Smenkhkare *	32 = Seti II
23 = Tutankhamen *	33 = Siptah *
24 = Ay *	34 = Tawosret
25 = Horemheb *	35 = Sethrakht
26 = 18th Dynasty	36 = Rameses III
27 = Rameses I	37 = Rameses IV
28 = Seti I	38 = Rameses V
29 = Rameses II	39 = Rameses VI

40 = 19th - 20th Dynasties	U = SOPDU CAVE
41 = New Kingdom	V = SOPDU APPROACH
Nos. 1, 9, 21-25, 31 and	X = LESSER
33 = rulers absent from	HANAFIYEH
s.El-Khadim	Y = HANAFIYEH
	COURT
Q = SANCTUARY	Z = HATHOR
R = PORCH	HANAFIYEH
S = PORTICO	
T = HATHOR CAVE	

Figure 102 Map of the monuments and inscriptions at Serabit el-Khadim, Sinai

Source: Adapted from W.M.F. Petrie, 1905, *Researches in Sinai*, London, John Murray, Map 4, and from A.H. Gardiner and T.E. Peet, 1952–5, *The Inscriptions of Sinai*, Parts I–II.

12th Dynasty-style beads indicate that these expeditions likely brought votive jewelry to the temple. Other Middle Kingdom activity on the plateau includes twenty-three graffiti (boats, people and animals) and a rock stela at Rod el-'Air (Valley of Donkeys), which provided access to the plateau and a nearby fortified settlement ("the camp of the Egyptians") with circular structures, ore-processing basins and a 12th Dynasty stela, as well as a series of circular enclosures (bethels) with a central stela en route to the temple.

From the Second Intermediate Period, Serabit el-Khadim and Bir en-Nasb have produced seven Hyksos-style scarabs, several sherds from Tell el-Yahudiya juglets (noted by Giveon), and twenty-nine or more Proto-Sinaitic inscriptions. The Proto-Sinaitic script is assigned to either the 12th Dynasty or the 18th Dynasty. Sass has concluded that a palaeographic comparison between it and related Northwest Semitic languages allows a date range from 1,800–1,000 BC. Proto-Sinaitic is a Semitic language containing 27–29 consonantal, pictographic signs with 23–26 identified forms derived largely from Egyptian hieroglyphs. Proto-Sinaitic inscriptions occur on two statue busts, a block statuette and a sphinx (recently redated from the 18th Dynasty to the 12th Dynasty), a stone slab from the "camp of the Egyptians," five slabs from stone enclosures (near Mines K and L), fourteen to sixteen slabs beside and in Mines L and M, and five to six rock inscriptions at Mines L, M, N and an undesignated mine. Some Proto-Sinaitic inscriptions accompany depictions of the Egyptian deity Ptah, who occurs more frequently in Middle Kingdom inscriptions and scenes than on New Kingdom monuments from the Hathor temple. Although the Asiatic character of this script is best reflected in Middle Kingdom texts which mention the presence of Asiatics at Serabit el-Khadim, New Kingdom texts from the site usually lack detailed personnel lists. Two New Kingdom stelae bear Semitic names (Aperba'al and Shalim-Shema') for officials with Egyptian titles.

New Kingdom expeditions utilized two routes to South Sinai. One route traversed the Eastern Desert, then crossed the Red Sea to el-Merkha Bay (18th Dynasty coastal site no. 345), and subsequently followed Wadi Baba inland to Wadi Nasb, Rod el-'Air, Serabit el-Khadim and possibly Wadi Reqeita in southeast Sinai. The Wadi Tumilat and Isthmus of Suez provided an alternative maritime and/or overland route to el-Merkha Bay, and included Ramesside sites at Tell er-Retabeh, Serapeum(?), Gebel Abu Hassa, Gebel Mourr, Kom el-Qulzoum at Port Suez (where a "Ramesside" fort lies below Ptolemaic Clysma), and possibly at Ain Moussa (Moses's Well) where Major Macdonald found a fragmentary *shawabti*.

Egyptian activity at Serabit el-Khadim and its environs intensified during the New Kingdom. Wadi Nasb contained a well (Bir en-Nasb), a copper mine, two furnaces, slag heaps with New Kingdom faïence, clay tuyères and an inscription of Ramesses II. New Kingdom expeditions carved three inscriptions and a graffito (boats, an axe and a giraffe) at Rod el-'Air, and dedicated an inscription and three stelae to Hathor and Ptah at Rock-Shrine Q which lay on the plateau en route to the Hathor temple. Mine M contained a few stone containers, a hammerstone, a disk and sherds from two bowls. Mine L produced forty-seven stone molds for axes, adzes, knives, chisels, mirrors and ingots, forty crucible fragments, five clay tuyères, a stone foot-bellows, an arrowhead, bronze lumps, stone tools and vessels, and a New Kingdom potsherd. Mine G yielded a New Kingdom faïence bowl, while a fragmentary stone foot-bellows, five tuyères, seven clay crucibles and two mortars lay above this mine.

The Hathor temple contains inscribed monuments and votive artifacts dating from the reigns of Ahmose to Ramesses VI, including the prenomen of Horemheb on an unpublished ring-stand (in the Royal Ontario Museum), but the names of Akhenaten, Smenkhkare, Tutankhamen, Ay and Amenmesses are lacking. The votives encompassed plain and inscribed objects from the sanctuary (Q) and portico (S): faïence vases, bowls, cups, jar-stands, beads and pendants, *menat*-necklace counterpoises, "wands" (throw-sticks), sistra, bracelets, cat-figure and Hathor-head plaques, a Bes-head, female figurines, a clay ear, scarabs, fragmentary alabaster vessels, several alabaster statuettes, 1,045 pieces of late 18th–19th Dynasty Egyptian core glass vessels (bowls, *krateriskoi* and pomegranate vessels), Egyptian pottery, and some Cypriot and Mycenaean sherds. The Hathor shrine (T), the Sopdu shrine (U) and the Shrine of Kings yielded ten stone "altars." In addition, a 10–45 cm deep layer of white wood ash lay below the walls and surface of Rooms E/F to O (which were built during the reigns of Hatshepsut to Amenhotep III); this has been interpreted as waste from camp fires or burnt offerings.

New Kingdom expeditions repaired, embellished and/or added new rooms onto existing structures within the Hathor temple in addition to erecting private and royal monuments. Amenhotep I repaired the 12th Dynasty Hathor shrine. Queen Hatshepsut and Tuthmose III embellished and added several rooms with Hathor-headed columns: the Sopdu hall (V), the sanctuary (Q), the Hathor Hanafiyah (Z), the pylon (M/N), and Rooms L, M and N. Amenhotep II added Room K. Tuthmose IV constructed Room J, inscribed parts of Room K, and appears on rock stelae beside two mines. Amenhotep III built Rooms C–G and may have built the temple's outer enclosure wall. Seti I probably constructed Room B, and appears on a reused block in Room A which was built by Ramesses II. Merenptah inscribed a door jamb between Rooms H and J, while Setnakhte and Ramesses III each added a stela before Room A. Ramesses IV constructed the porch (R), and embellished the sanctuary (Q) and Room O. Ramesses VI conducted modifications to the temple, inscribing a wall and two pillars in Room O.

See also

Sinai, North, late prehistoric and Dynastic sites; trade, foreign; Wadi Maghara; Wadi Tumilat

Further reading

Beit-Arieh, I. 1985. Serabit el-Khadim: new metallurgical and chronological aspects. *Levant* 17: 89–116.

Chartier-Raymond, M., B. Gratien, C. Traunecker and J.-M. Vinçon. 1994. Les sites miniers pharaoniques du Sud-Sinaï: quelques notes et observations de terrain. *CRIPEL* 6: 31–77.

Pinch, G. 1993. *Votive Offerings to Hathor.* Oxford.

Sass, B. 1988. *The Genesis of the Alphabet and Its Development in the Second Millenium B.C.* (Ägypten und Altes Testament 13). Wiesbaden.

G.D. MUMFORD

shawabtis, servant figures and models

Servant figures

Servant statues are customarily interpreted as representations of the workers on a nobleman's estate. The models recreate a rich illustration of ancient Egyptian domestic life. They were placed in tombs with the belief that they would magically be recreated in the next world, where they would continue their work in the same capacity that they had in this world.

Servant statues are in many ways three-dimensional versions of the two-dimensional relief scenes depicted on tomb walls. Parallels for all the activities performed by the statuettes can be found in the reliefs, illustrating that the statuettes were not meant to be a replacement for the relief scenes, but rather supplemental to the reliefs. Just like the two-dimensional representations, they were placed in the tombs of non-royal officials but were not found in royal tombs.

In a few instances, names and titles were inscribed on servant statues. They suggest a more complex interpretation of their function. Those which carry more than the personal name bear titles which name the statuette as son, daughter or "soul-priest" of the deceased. Therefore, some Egyptologists suggest that the inscriptions indicate that the statuettes represent the relatives or priests who were responsible for bringing the funerary offerings to the deceased. The inscribed pieces never bear the title or the actual profession of the person represented.

A type of servant statue possibly appeared in Predynastic burials, in the form of crudely made human figures of ivory or clay. These figures give way to limestone statues in the 4th Dynasty. At this time they are depicted in the form of servants engaged in their daily tasks. They mainly occur in the non-royal tombs in the cemeteries of Giza and Saqqara. At the end of the 6th Dynasty wooden statuettes become more common. Their provenance is no longer confined to the Memphite cemeteries. A further development near the end of the Old Kingdom was for separate statues to be mounted together on a single wooden base. These groups display different aspects of a single task.

In the First Intermediate Period group figures predominate, and individual servant figures now exist only when they are carrying offerings for the deceased. Workshops are represented in much greater detail at this time.

The Middle Kingdom marks the high point in the servant figure tradition. The number and variety of the models from this period are far greater than the combined total for the Old Kingdom and First Intermediate Period. The material used was usually wood. In the Old Kingdom these statues are primarily concerned with food preparation, but in the Middle Kingdom agriculture, fishing and other activities are added to the themes represented. Animated models represent the whole household of the tomb owner, including brewers, millers, dough kneaders, bakers, butchers, cooks, potters, brick makers, farmers, sailors, artisans, musicians and sometimes even military personnel. A miniature world of the whole community, including gardens, workshops, storehouses and even fleets of ships, was recreated.

One of the largest collections of Middle Kingdom wooden models ever found comes from the tomb of Djhuty-Nakht from Deir el-Bersha, now housed in the Museum of Fine Arts, Boston and the Cairo Museum. Djhuty-Nakht's burial chamber contained more than fifty-five boats, at least thirty-three workshops, and a dozen or more individual figures carrying offerings. The majority of the scenes represent some aspect of food production, from plowing the fields to preparing bread and beer.

During the Middle Kingdom, these models have mainly been located at sites in Middle and Upper Egypt. Very few servant statuettes are seen after the first half of the 12th Dynasty. It is noteworthy that at this very time the first *shawabti*s (servant figures in mummiform) appear in tombs.

Statuettes were commonly placed in the *serdab* (statue chamber) of the tomb's superstructure (*mastaba*). However, throughout the First Intermediate Period and Middle Kingdom, when *serdab*s were less popular, the servant figures were situated in or near the burial chamber. In one known instance they were placed in the fill of the burial shaft along with statues of the tomb owner. In their final development, the servant figures were placed in the burial chamber itself. One exception is the famous 11th Dynasty tomb of Meket-Re at Deir el-Bahri, where the servant figures were found in a small *serdab* chamber. Within the burial chamber, they were placed either in or adjacent to the sarcophagus. Sometimes servant figures were placed in a niche in the wall of the burial chamber, or even in a hole in the floor of the chamber.

Shawabtis

It is no coincidence that when funerary statuettes disappear, *shawabti*s appear. Both types of statuettes were supposed to perform menial tasks of labor, and often occupy the same position in the tomb. As the ancient Egyptians were loath to eliminate any essential part of their funerary symbolism, these two types of funerary figures probably share a common origin or function. This link is further demonstrated by the rare occurrences of New Kingdom servant statues inscribed with the

"*Shawabti* Spell" from Chapter 6 of the *Book of the Dead*.

There are major differences, however, between servant figures and *shawabti*s, in both form and function. The *shawabti* figure is mummiform and does not depict an active, living person. The type of work which is requested to be done by the *shawabti* is not domestic and has no relation to food preparation. Furthermore, the tasks which the *shawabti* perform are curiously not depicted on tomb walls.

Initially, the *shawabti* was a substitute for the deceased. Later it evolved into a servant of the deceased. The earliest *shawabti*s appear at the beginning of the Middle Kingdom. They are mummiform figures made of wax, clay or wood. Often they were placed in miniature coffins. Later *shawabti*s were made of wood, faïence or stone. Those that were inscribed carried only the name of the deceased and occasionally also the offering formula. In the second part of the 12th Dynasty these mummiform figures begin to appear in graves, which is also when mummiform figures first appear on stelae, and coffins take an anthropoid form—reflecting changes that were taking place in the funerary ritual.

A longer text appears on *shawabti*s for the first time at the end of the 12th Dynasty, and the offering formula continues to be used in various longer and shorter versions until Ptolemaic times. This text is found in Chapter 6 of the *Book of the Dead*. The tasks were "to do all the works which are required in the god's domain." In particular, they were to plow the fields, irrigate the arable land and generally maintain the irrigation system in the netherworld, a physical realm believed to be exactly like Egypt.

Royal *shawabti*s do not appear until the early 18th Dynasty. Prior to this they were made only for private individuals. Numerable iconographic and stylistic developments of the *shawabti* occurred at this time. They were now made of a wide variety of materials: wood, faïence, terracotta, unbaked clay, stone, bronze and even with inlays of glass. During the reign of Tuthmose IV the agricultural implements carried by the *shawabti* evolved, consisting primarily of both a narrow and a broad-bladed hoe, baskets, bags, molds for brick making, whips and pots for carrying water. These model tools could be painted on, shaped in relief, or added separately.

New *shawabti* types developed which are unconventional and mainly seen only in the New Kingdom, such as the double *shawabti*, the *shawabti* lying on a bier and the *shawabti* milling grain. Some of colossal size also appear. After the Amarna period (late 18th Dynasty) *shawabti*s in the dress of the living are found. Instead of being mummiform, they wear elaborate, pleated linen clothing that was the fashion of the day, and some seem to be copies of full-scale statues.

In the 19th Dynasty the "overseer" figure evolves, and the dress of daily life was reserved for these *shawabti*s, which are modeled holding a whip. In tombs there is one *shawabti* overseer for every ten worker figures, based on the actual division of labor.

The number of *shawabti*s made for the deceased appears to vary, and most likely depended on the tomb owner's economic status. During the late Middle Kingdom and early New Kingdom the number of *shawabti*s for private individuals usually did not exceed five, and in the early 19th Dynasty, ten was the maximum. Toward the end of the 18th Dynasty the ideal number of *shawabti*s in royal tombs was 365, one for every day in the year, plus one overseer for every ten figures (401 *shawabti*s total). However, a wide variety of numbers have been found in tombs, and diverse types and sizes could belong to one tomb owner. Tutankhamen's tomb contained 417 *shawabti*s.

*Shawabti*s were stored in the tomb in a variety of ways. They could be placed in the burial chamber or in the coffin itself. In the 18th and 19th Dynasties they were kept in model coffins and shrine-shaped containers. Later in the New Kingdom, ceramic jars were also used for *shawabti* storage. During the Third Intermediate Period complete gangs of *shawabti*s were placed in large wooden boxes, which were used until the 30th Dynasty.

Great numbers of *shawabti*s have been found from the Third Intermediate Period, when they were mass-produced, primarily in faïence with a blue-green glaze. In general, the features of these *shawabti*s were summarily treated and the details were enhanced with black paint.

In the 25th and and early 26th Dynasties the *shawabti* underwent another major transformation. A new arrangement of tools is found consisting of a pick, hoe and small seed bag suspended from a cord slung over the left shoulder. The figure takes on a new shape with a back pillar and base. *Shawabti*s from this period are customarily made of faïence with a distinctive pale-green or blue-green glaze.

Kushite *shawabti*s from the first millennium BC kingdoms in Nubia have an entirely different iconography than Egyptian ones, with different tools and hairstyles. *Shawabti*s continue to be used in burials in the Late and Ptolemaic periods, but disappear with the onset of Roman times.

See also

Deir el-Bahri, Meket-Re tomb; Deir el-Bersha; domestic architecture, evidence from tomb scenes; funerary texts; mortuary beliefs; representational evidence, Old Kingdom private tombs

Further reading

Aubert, J. F. and L. 1974. *Statuettes égyptiennes, chaouabtis, ouchebitis*. Paris.

Breasted, J.H., Jr. 1948. *Egyptian Servant Statues*. The Bollingen Series XIII. Pantheon Books. Washington, DC.

Schneider, H.D. 1977. *Shabtis*, 3 vols. Leiden.

Winlock, H.E. 1955. *Models of Daily Life In Ancient Egypt From the Tomb of Meket Re at Thebes*. Boston.

JOYCE HAYNES

ships

There is much evidence in ancient Egypt for the study of ships. Models of boats were made in clay, metal, ivory and wood, and the remains of real boats have been excavated. Boats are depicted in rock-art and numerous pictorial representations are found on pottery, papyri, textiles, stelae, and the walls of tombs and temples. Reliefs and wall paintings provide information about all kinds of shipbuilding and life on the Nile. There are scenes of wharfs, sailing, overseas expeditions and funeral voyages. Information is also provided by texts.

Most of what is known about ships in ancient Egypt concerns river craft, whereas information about sea-going ships is limited. Since traveling overland in Egypt was difficult, an elaborate nautical transport technology developed which used the available natural resources, such as wood and papyrus reeds. Pictorial evidence and models show both simple dug-out canoes and a great variety of rafts (or boats) made of papyrus bundles—which may also have been used for maritime shipping. In scenes, rafts of all kinds were often painted green and with the bindings typical of papyrus reed constructions. Since hunting and fowling in the marshes were favorite activities of upper class Egyptians, the archaic reed-bundle craft was used until Roman times.

The evolution of wooden plank boats is too complicated to be discussed here and is not very well understood. Many boat depictions look like wooden replicas of reed boats and indeed this may have been the process of development. Possibly wooden boats developed from dug-out constructions with added planks. The two most famous wooden boats are the "royal barks" of Khufu. One of these boats is now reconstructed in a museum next to the Great Pyramid; it is 43.3 m long and is made of 1,214 pieces of wood, including planks, tenons, battens, pillars, stanchions and frames. The boat was constructed by transversely binding the planks of the hull. It may have carried the king's mummy in the funeral procession, but there is no evidence for any other use.

Six wooden boats dating to the 12th Dynasty were found at Dahshur and are now in museums in Cairo, Chicago (Field Museum of Natural History) and Pittsburgh (Carnegie Museum). Although their exact purpose is not known, they are excellent examples of working boats and provide first-hand information about "tenon and dowel" plank construction. These boats are *circa* 10 m long and 2.2 m in beam, with planks up to 6 m long. To secure the boats' internal strength, the shipwrights used additional lashings; the three pieces of the keel plank are pieced together by dovetailed wooden clamps. Numerous funerary and cult ships were of this type, but most such boats were for ordinary travel on the Nile and on canals—to transport passengers, soldiers, officials, animals, stones, wood, craft goods and so on. Such boats were used as ferries, kitchen boats and pleasure craft; they were also used for fishing and recreational activities.

A model fleet from the tomb of Meket-Re, who was a vizier in the 11th Dynasty, consists of traveling and kitchen boats, fishing and fowling skiffs, a pair of fishing canoes, sporting boats and funerary barks. The models are with oars or sails (for traveling up or down the Nile), and lively figures of crew members have been placed in them. These models are now in Cairo and New York (Metropolitan Museum). In Tutankhamen's tomb, a royal flotilla of thirty-five model boats of nine different types was found which represents both ceremonial boats and ones actually used on the Nile. These models, which rank among the finest ever made in antiquity, are on display in museums in Cairo and Luxor.

Many boats must have been multi-purpose crafts, but there were also many highly specialized ships or barges, such as for obelisk transport. The reconstruction of these barges presents tremendous structural problems. The Karnak obelisks are nearly 23 m high and each weighs *circa* 186 tons. Barges used to transport them must have been about 63 m long with a beam of 21 m—which implies a tonnage of perhaps 1,500 tons. How these barges were built, launched and maneuvered, how the obelisks were loaded, and how the boats were towed, sailed or rowed can only be hypothesized.

Other huge ships are reported from Ptolemaic times. The writer Athenaios gives a detailed description of the *thalamegos* of Ptolemy IV. This ship, which was really a floating palace, must have been *circa* 100 m long, with staircases for a two-story construction consisting of a large hall, kitchen, bedrooms, dining rooms and even a temple. Precious materials were used to make it a truly magnificent court on the Nile and it probably was never moved from its permanent mooring place.

There is much less information about Egyptian sea-going ships than for river craft. One of the earliest sources is the reliefs from the 5th Dynasty pyramid complex of Sahure at Abusir, with scenes of the return of an overseas military expedition. The hulls of these ships are long, slender and spoon-shaped; they are built of edge-joined planks with a minimum of framework. An important feature of the construction is the rope truss (or hogging) running from stem to bow, which prevented the ship, with greatly overhanging bow and stern, from breaking apart. Such a feature resembles the function of the hogging trusses on Mississippi river boats. Other sea-going ships, such as the Punt ships of Hatshepsut depicted in her temple at Deir el-Bahri, show the same rope truss to support overhanging ends. Many other details are seen in these reliefs, including foredecks and afterdecks with screens and straight stem posts decorated with carved lotus buds. These ships could be rowed by thirty rowers or sailed with one low, wide sail on a pole mast.

The so-called Sea Peoples were groups of different tribes which came to Egypt in the middle of the fourteenth century BC. Some of them worked as mercenaries, but during the reign of Ramesses III others tried to invade the country. They were defeated in a combined sea and land battle in the Nile Delta, which is depicted on the outer walls of the temple of Medinet Habu. In the reliefs two kinds of ships are seen: Egyptian and foreign (northern?). The latter are sickle-shaped and their stems are carved with heads of an Asiatic and a lion. All vessels are equipped with both oars and sails. On the pole masts there are lookout platforms which could possibly also hold a bowman. Between the fore- and aftercastles there are parapets to protect the oarsmen, which number between six and eleven on each side. This number was hardly sufficient to row a war

Figure 103 Relief of a ship from a pyramid temple of Sahure, 5th Dynasty
Source: Ägyptisches Museum, Berlin

galley, and probably represents artistic license in the details that could be depicted.

The Egyptians clearly loved elaborate ship decorations. Their ships are depicted with all kinds of elements, of floral, animal or human motifs, which were painted, carved or cast. A prominent feature is the *"wadjet* eye," a symbol of the god Horus's eye, which represented his protective powers. It is found on the bows of many (model) ships, especially those for cult or funerary use. The "magic eye" on boats is a common symbol found on many boats in different cultures, and can be seen, for example, in China, Sri Lanka, Portugal, the Adriatic and Malta.

Another motif of great importance was the bud of the *cyperus papyrus*, which was used as an architectural element (for columns) as well as for nautical decoration. Many stems are shaped like papyrus buds, which give the ship an elegant and papyriform appearance. Motifs of animals, such as hedgehogs, falcons, hawks,

ibex and bull heads, decorated ships. Various cult emblems and standards, and ornaments of all kinds decorated sails, oars, cabins and hulls, and emblems of the gods and the sun were used as figureheads. "Floating temples" were built for priests and royalty; one belonging to Ramesses III was supposedly 63.5 m long. As houses of the gods and goddesses, these barks were lavishly carved, painted and decorated with precious stones and metals.

The great works of Egyptian shipbuilding must be regarded as part of the national identity. There are some ninety terms for ships in Egyptian (hieroglyphs). *Br* was a boat used for transport (also a galley, scow or freighter), and became a loanword in German (*Barke*) and English (*bark*). The names of 175 ships are known (actual ships and symbolic ones, as well as portable barks in temples). There are 126 verbs relating to naval activities—which demonstrate the rich nautical vocabulary in Egyptian.

The historical, political, economic, military

and communications uses of ships are too complex to discuss here. Problems of timber supply (cedar from Lebanon, native acacia), wharf and harbor organization, administration, logistics, recruiting and wages of personnel, trade and exchange, exploration, and the types of ships used for overseas trade to Punt and Byblos, require longer studies. Nile shipping certainly dominated Egyptian mythology and religion, and funeral and cult practices; and reflects the Egyptians' love of their water craft.

See also

Abusir; Dahshur, Middle Kingdom pyramids; Deir el-Bahri, Hatshepsut temple; Deir el-Bahri, Meket-Re tomb; funerary texts; Giza, Khufu pyramid complex; Giza, Khufu pyramid sun barks and boat pit; Levantine peoples (Iron Age); Medinet Habu; natural resources; obelisks; Punt; Sea Peoples; Tutankhamen, tomb of

Further reading

Göttlicher, A. 1992. *Kultschiffe und Schiffskulte im Altertum*. Berlin.
Jones, D. 1988. *A Glossary of Ancient Egyptian Nautical Titles and Terms*. London.
Landström, B. 1970. *Ships of the Pharaohs*. London.
Lipke, P. 1984. *The Royal Ship of Cheops*. Greenwich Archaeological Series 9 (BAR Int. Ser. 225). Greenwich.
Vinson, S. 1994. *Egyptian Boats and Ships*. Princes Risborough.

ARVID GÖTTLICHER

Sikait-Zubara

Sikait-Zubara was an emerald mining region in the southeastern desert of Egypt, centered on Gebel Sikait (24°40′ N, 34°49′ E) and Gebel Zubara (24°45′ N, 34°48′ E). In ancient times, the two principal sources of emeralds were located at Sikait-Zubara in Egypt and in the Salzburg region of Austria. In the Eastern Desert, the combination of schist and granitic fluids provided the necessary chemistry for the formation of beryl during metamorphism. The faulting that formed the Red Sea also produced the uplift of the metamorphic basement along the eastern margin of Egypt, thus creating the mountains of the Eastern Desert and revealing the emerald deposits within them.

The Sikait-Zubara mines, worked from at least the beginning of the Ptolemaic period, were the only source of emeralds for Europe, Asia and Africa then, and they continued to be exploited until at least the Middle Ages, when Arab writers document the appearance of larger, heavier stones from the Indian subcontinent. The preliminary examination of pottery from the region suggests that the mining activity covers an extremely wide chronological range, extending at the very least from the late Roman period at Wadi Gimal to the sixteenth century at Gebel Zubara. Since the rock temples at Gebel Sikait are usually assigned to the Ptolemaic period, the full period of exploitation at Sikait-Zubara must have spanned more than 1,500 years.

Several geologists and archaeologists have published accounts of their visits to the Sikait-Zubara region, particularly during the first three decades of the twentieth century. In 1994, a geological survey undertaken by Shaw, Jameson and Bunbury examined four emerald mining sites in the region in order to gain a better understanding of the changing patterns of procurement from the Ptolemaic period to the Middle Ages.

Emeralds do not appear to have been used regularly in Egyptian jewelry until the Roman period, when techniques for polishing the stones were probably introduced. However, in lists of gemstones dating to the Late period, the phrase "eastern green (stone)" (*wadj n Bakhw*) appears; if this term refers to beryl or emerald, it may possibly indicate that the stone was being exploited before the end of the pharaonic period. There is some tenuous support for pharaonic mining of emeralds in Sir John Gardner Wilkinson's assertion in 1878 that the Sikait-Zubara mines were worked as early as the reign of Amenhotep III (18th Dynasty). He does not, however, give any specific evidence for this early date, and in any case, none of the surviving archaeological remains associated with the mines appears to date any earlier than the Ptolemaic period.

There is clear documentary evidence for emerald mining in the southeastern desert in 24 BC, when Strabo (*Geography* XVII, I: 45) writes: "Then follows the isthmus, extending to the Red Sea near Berenike. . . . On this isthmus are mines in which emeralds and other precious stones are found by the Arabians, who dig deep subterranean passages." The Sikait-Zubara mines had fallen out of use by the seventeenth century, and by the time James Bruce undertook his expedition through Egypt in 1768, even the location of the mines seems to have been temporarily forgotten. As a result, Bruce misinterpreted Pliny's description of Egyptian emerald mining as a reference to the procurement of peridot on St John's Island.

In 1816, the French goldsmith Frédéric Cailliaud, searching for mines on behalf of the Egyptian ruler Muhammad Ali Pasha, rediscovered the Sikait-Zubara mining region. He first stumbled on the Ptolemaic rock temples at Gebel Sikait, and later entered one of the deep mine shafts at Gebel Zubara. He is said to have found an emerald after descending through a winding passage for a distance of about 100 m, reaching a depth of 30 m below the ground surface. In the nineteenth century the principal mining sites in the region were also visited by Giovanni Belzoni, John Gardner Wilkinson and Nestor l'Hôte, and the general geology has been described by Oskar Schneider and W.F. Hume. During the early 1900s the archaeological remains were also explored by Donald MacAlister, E.S. Thomas and Gilbert Murray.

Because of the presence of three Ptolemaic rock-cut temples, the Gebel Sikait mining area has tended to attract more Egyptological attention than the Wadi Nuqrus and Gebel Zubara. One of the most impressive sites in the Sikait region is a settlement located on the northeastern side of the Wadi Nuqrus, close to Gebel Sikait itself, where the miners created substantial buildings incorporating roofing slabs and lintels. All the structures are square

or rectangular in plan, and they would originally have had walls reaching at least to head height. Some of the buildings are high enough to have originally had two stories. There were also a number of structures consisting of rows of deep narrow rectangular niches, presumably used for storage; some of these were incorporated into level podiums of dry stone on which the houses are built. The houses often have small square recesses built into the interior walls, which were presumably used for storage.

The mines at Gebel Zubara, at the northern end of the Sikait-Zubara region, are the largest and probably also chronologically the most recent. The ancient pre-eminence of the site, even in comparison with the extensive works farther south at Wadi Nuqrus/Gebel Sikait, is reflected in its classical name, Mons Smaragdus: the "emerald mountain." The settlement at Zubara is contained within a narrow wadi floor, spectacularly situated at the foot of the mountain. The essential differences from the hillside settlements at Wadis Nuqrus and Sikait arise from the curvilinear character of many of the building plans at Zubara. In many cases the walls of the huts or hut "compounds" are circular or spiral, and even the more angular plans lack the precise 90° corners of many of the buildings at Wadi Nuqrus. The best preserved and most "formal" building at Zubara consists of two adjoining perfectly circular enclosures (arranged in a sort of dumbbell shape) near the mouth of the wadi. Two carefully corbelled beehive-shaped ovens are built into its walls, and it may have functioned as a sort of communal cooking and eating place.

The sides of the wadi are lined with large heaps composed almost entirely of fragments of schist. The gangue has been extracted from a large number of shafts piercing the wadi sides. Although there is evidence of some comparatively recent attempts to reopen the mines, a number of the shafts bear clear chisel marks, demonstrating that they were created by ancient mining activity. These shafts broadly follow the contact of the schists with the granite, and the shape of the tunnels suggests that adits were cut along the sub-horizontal emerald-bearing lodes until the deposit gave out, whereupon shafts were sunk from the original galleries until a new lode was struck. While many of the excavations are shallow pits or tunnels undermining specific quartz veins, a few of the entrances appear to lead to more extensive tunnel systems.

The Sikait-Zubara emerald mines seem to form a continuum of types of exploitation from adventitious to structured mining. The more "opportunist" mines are found in areas such as the Wadi Nuqrus, where the emerald deposits are relatively poor and widely distributed, whereas the more structured mines appear to have developed in areas where emeralds were both abundant and localized, as at Gebel Zubara, where the geological context was relatively straightforward.

See also

jewelry; Late and Ptolemaic periods, overview; natural resources; quarrying; Roman period, overview; Wadi el-Hudi; Wadi Maghara

Further reading

MacAlister, D.A. 1900. The emerald mines of northern Etbai. *Geographical Journal, London* 16: 537–49.

Schneider, O., and A. Azruni. 1892. Der ägyptische Smaragd nebst einer vergleichenden mineralogischen Untersuchung der Smaragd von Alexandrien, vom Gebel Sabara und vom Ural. *Zeitschrift für Ethnologie* 24: 41–100.

Shaw, I., J. Bunbury, and R. Jameson. *Journal of Roman Archaeology*. The emerald mines of ancient Egypt: a preliminary survey of four sites in the Sikait-Zubara region.

IAN SHAW

Sinai, North, late prehistoric and Dynastic sites

The Mediterranean coast of North Sinai, between the Suez Canal and Gaza, served as a land bridge connecting Egypt and Asia. Its early history is documented in Egyptian and Assyrian sources. Later detailed information is found in Graeco-Roman, Byzantine and Islamic records, maps and itineraries by historians, geographers and church fathers. From 1910 to 1924, French archaeologist Jean Clédat investigated a few sites in northern Sinai, almost all of which date to the Roman and Byzantine periods. During 1972–82, the North Sinai Expedition of Ben Gurion University, under the direction of Eliezer Oren, conducted a systematic archaeological survey and excavations in an area of approximately 2,000 square km. Investigations in North Sinai since 1985, by Egyptian, Franco-Egyptian and other expeditions doing salvage archaeology where the el-Salamm canal is being constructed, have focused on the region between Baluza and Qantara in northwestern Sinai.

The Ben Gurion expedition recorded some 1,300 sites, including large towns and villages, forts and road stations, camp sites and cemeteries, which range in date from the Paleolithic to the Ottoman period. As a result, it is now possible to reconstruct in detail the history of settlement in northern Sinai and its role as the principal corridor between Egypt and Asia.

Prehistoric assemblages along the coastal strip of Sinai between el-Arish and Gaza indicate human activity, mainly seasonal camp sites, from Paleolithic times. About 190 late prehistoric settlement sites (Pottery Neolithic and Chalcolithic, dating to the sixth–fourth millennia BC) were recorded in northeastern Sinai and as far afield as the region of the Suez Canal.

Excavations at Site Y-3 (terminal Pottery Neolithic) unearthed various installations and a child burial in a jar. Faunal evidence, including many pig bones, implies that this was a permanent settlement of an agricultural/pastoral subsistence. Some Chalcolithic sites (R-48, Y-79) yielded stratified occupational remains, including mudbrick structures and violin-shaped figurines, that exhibit close affinities with the contemporaneous material culture of the western Negev. A few examples of Predynastic ceramics (Nagada I) imported from

Upper Egypt, and a locally manufactured palette in an Egyptian style, indicate the earliest trade contacts with Predynastic Egypt (early fourth millennium BC).

Between Qantara and Raphia, some 250 settlements were investigated with material remains of the Canaanite Early Bronze Age (EBI) and the later Egyptian Predynastic phases (Nagada II–III). One such site was discovered in 1910 by Clédat at el-Beda. The settlement pattern was characterized by site clusters, organized in a two- or three-tiered settlement hierarchy of seasonal encampments alongside core sites and way-stations. The rich and diverse ceramic assemblages included both Canaanite (EBIa–c) and Predynastic (Nagada II–III/Dynasty 0) wares. The latter comprised nearly 80 percent of the entire ensemble and represent the full spectrum of domestic classes. Finely worked stone vessels, sandstone copper ore and copper artifacts have also been found. These sites represent the eastward extension of the Egyptian state-organized sphere of interest into Canaan that resulted in Egypt's domination and administration of the entire territory of northern Sinai and southern Canaan in the late fourth and early third millennia BC.

Nearly 300 sites, both base settlements and seasonal encampments, of the late third millennium BC (EBIV period) were recorded between the Suez Canal and Raphia. The bulk of pottery is southern Canaanite (EBIV), but there are also late variants of Egyptian "Meydum Ware." The clusters of EBIV sites belonged to pastoralist groups that maintained limited exchanges with the farming villages in the Egyptian Delta.

Beginning about 2,000 BC, the Middle Bronze Age in northern Sinai is represented by about 300 localities, mostly small seasonal encampments, for essentially transhumant pastoralists with limited trading activity. In contrast, in the vicinity of the Suez Canal the expedition recorded the remains of extensive sedentary settlements from the Middle Kingdom and Second Intermediate Period. Egyptian excavations at one of these sites (Tell Hebua) since 1988 by M. Abdel Maksoud on behalf of the Supreme Council for Antiquities in Egypt have revealed the remains of well-organized fortified settlements, including limestone blocks carved with royal names of the Second Intermediate Period and New Kingdom. The ceramics from the campsites exhibit a rich variety of Egyptian Middle Kingdom/Second Intermediate Period (35 percent) and Canaanite Middle Bronze Age (MBI–III, 32 percent) wares. The rural aspect of the ceramics is best manifested in the crude, handmade cooking vessels (33 percent). The archaeological evidence suggests that regular trade of bulk commodities was conducted between the Egyptian Nile Delta and Canaan via the state-run maritime traffic. At the same time, the ceramics clearly reflect close socio-economic interaction on a lower level between the terminal regions, southern Canaan and the eastern Delta.

Repeated military campaigns into Asia by the Egyptian army in the early New Kingdom (beginning *circa* 1,550 BC) marked the establishment of the "Ways of Horus" network, Egypt's principal artery of communication to, and a key for the administration of, its provinces in Canaan and Syria. The first campaign of Tuthmose III from the border fortress of Zeru (known in Graeco-Roman times as Sile) to Gaza, about 250 km away, in nine to ten days demonstrates the effectiveness of the Egyptian organization of the "Ways of Horus." The North Sinai Expedition recorded 231 New Kingdom settlements between Qantara and Raphia. Additional base sites of this period were excavated between Raphia and Gaza: Tell Abu-Salima (excavated by Flinders Petrie), Tell Ridan (Vitto) and Deir el-Bala (Dothan).

The distribution pattern is characterized by clusters of base sites (usually forts or way-stations), 15–20 km apart, surrounded by campsites and seasonal encampments. The close proximity to several New Kingdom sites in northwestern Sinai of the recently discovered ancient frontier canal may indicate a New Kingdom construction of the canal. Architecture and site organization, as well as the size of mudbricks and method of construction and bonding, are all characteristic of mudbrick architecture in New Kingdom Egypt.

The large (4–5 square km) cluster at Haruba in northeastern Sinai is represented by twenty-odd sites, including two settlements: a fort (A-289) and an administrative center (A-345). Fort A-289 is *circa* 2,500 sq.m in area, comprising a 4 m wide enclosure wall, a massive, 13 × 20 m gate house and a complex of rooms for storage and various domestic activities. A number of child and adult burials were found under the floors and mudbrick debris. One chamber contained two huge Egyptian pithoi jars bearing large cartouches of Seti II. Floor and refuse deposits included Canaanite (LBIII), Egyptian (19th–20th Dynasties) and many Mycenaean and Cypriot wares; seals and scarabs; ceramic *uraeus* (the sacred cobra) heads; and stone vessels. The archaeological evidence dates the building of the fort (Phase III) to the early 19th Dynasty, most likely as part of the reorganization of the "Ways of Horus" by Seti I. There are also some remains (Phase IV) of earlier, perhaps unfortified, structures of the 18th Dynasty. Building remains of Phase II mark extensive repairs of the original structure, probably after it no longer served as a fortress. Following the destruction by fire of Phase II, some time in the late twelfth century BC, parts of the fort were reoccupied (Phase I) as a campsite in late Iron Age I, *circa* 1,050–1,000 BC.

North of the fort a section (2,000 sq.m) of an extensive administrative complex (A-345) of the 18th Dynasty was investigated. In the center of the site was a spacious magazine unit with long, mudbrick-floored halls opening onto a central courtyard and enclosed by a wall. Archaeological soundings yielded evidence of earlier walls, storage and refuse installations. The site was abandoned peacefully. To the east of the magazine was a large industrial quarter, including a potters' workshop that manufactured a specific line of Egyptian-type vessels. Cypriot imports were numerous compared to fewer Mycenaean vessels. Similarly, the number of Canaanite vessels was relatively small and was mostly limited to storage jars.

The central site (BEA-10) in the cluster of Bir el-Abd is represented by the badly eroded remains of a fort with a 4 m wide enclosure wall and a variety of rooms and domestic installations. South of it was a magazine with long parallel rooms fronted by an enclosed courtyard. Nearby a well preserved granary was excavated with four cylindrical silos, each *circa* 4 m in diameter. The granary could have held up to 44,600 liters (about 40 tons) of grain or legumes. Following the collapse of the silo domes, the granary became the fort's refuse installation and much pottery, alabaster, faïence, and animal and fish bones were excavated here. About 200 m northwest of the fort, the remains of an artificial, rectangular depression measuring *circa* 10 × 15 m and bordered by a kind of clay plastered embankment were surveyed. The thick layer of silt that lined the depression suggests that it served as the fortress's water reservoir.

The rich assemblages of artifacts from these sites, including scarabs and seal impressions, reflect in detail the history of occupation in North Sinai, beginning in the early 18th Dynasty up to the withdrawal of Egyptians from their Asiatic provinces toward the end of the 20th Dynasty, *circa* 1,130 BC.

By the early first millennium BC (Iron Age II), North Sinai resumed its role as a vital link between Egypt and Canaan. The survey map is represented by 233 settlement sites from the late eleventh to the late sixth centuries BC (Iron Age II–III). A cluster of some thirty Iron Age sites between Wadi el-'Arish and Wadi Gaza provided evidence of Assyrian control in this region during the eighth–seventh centuries BC. The largest site, Tell Ruqeish, near Deir el-Balah, yielded domestic and public architecture of a well-organized town enclosed by a massive defensive wall. Earlier excavations outside the walled area revealed a cemetery with Phoenician-type cremation burials. Tell Ruqeish, probably the "sealed *Karu(m)* of Egypt" (mentioned on the Calah prism of the Assyrian king Sargon II) served as the major Assyrian commercial headquarters. It also figured prominently in the maritime traffic and coordinated trade with Egypt. Additional Assyrian-style architecture was recovered at Sheikh Zuweid by Flinders Petrie in 1935–6, providing evidence for Assyrian-administered territory as far as the "Brook of Egypt" (Wadi el-'Arish) in the eighth–seventh centuries BC.

Of the numerous sites from the Saite period

Figure 104 North Sinai, granary at New Kingdom site BEA-10

(26th Dynasty) in the sixth century BC, the larger cluster was investigated in the Canal zone, a region which, according to textual sources, was occupied by border garrisons and inhabited by foreign merchants and mercenaries. Near Tell el-Herr, on the ancient frontier canal, a sizable (*circa* 10 ha) garrison (Tell Qedua) was investigated, probably to be identified with ancient Migdol. The center of this site was occupied by a massive fortified compound with a 15–20 m wide enclosure wall. The large ceramic corpus is represented by Egyptian, Phoenician, Greek and Cypriot wares, and there are also many metal artifacts, copper ore and slag. The fortress was subsequently destroyed by fire in the late sixth century BC, apparently as a direct result of the invasion of Egypt by the Persian king Cambyses in 525 BC.

The annexation of Egypt into the Persian empire brought about the establishment of a well-organized road system along the coast of northern Sinai, including the building of forts, way stations, fishing villages and landing facilities. Subsequently, these became the nuclei for the network of towns and stations that characterized the coast of northern Sinai in Graeco-Roman and Byzantine times. The North Sinai Expedition recorded 235 settlement sites of the Persian period, *circa* fifth–fourth centuries BC. Their distribution indicates large concentrations in northwestern Sinai, on the shores of the Bardawil lagoon and along the coast between el-'Arish and Gaza. At almost every site much Greek pottery was recorded, testifying to the major role that Greek trade played in the economy of North Sinai.

The impressive remains of the Persian period at the coastal site of Tell Ruqeish support its identification as one of Herodotus' coastal emporia south of Gaza. Nearby at Tell Qatif, a massive mudbrick fort was investigated which was enclosed by a 5 m wide wall with a tower overlooking the sea. The fort belonged to a network of Persian military installations along the coastal highway, between Gaza and Pelusium. Remains of such forts were encountered near Sheikh Zuweid, Ras Qasrun, Rumani and Tell el-Herr. Stratified remains of a large settlement were uncovered at Sheikh Zuweid by Petrie in 1935–6, while nearby excavations in 1976 uncovered a large fortified structure of the courtyard type. Settlement strata of the Persian period were found in a limited salvage investigation at Tell Raphia, and some 1,200 m west of the site the expedition uncovered the badly damaged remains of a small cult site with a two-room structure and courtyards. The larger of the courtyards had a plastered basin and pits full of ash, animal bones and many fragments of ceramic and faïence figurines, in Greek, Phoenician, Cypriot and Egyptian styles. In the center of the Bardawil sandbar at Katib el-Gals, identified as the site of Kasion, 22 of the 43 surveyed sites included material remains of the Persian period. Limited soundings at Ras Qasrun (M36), traditionally equated with Mons Kasius and the location of the Phoenician cult site of Baal Zephon, yielded scanty domestic remains of the Persian period. The settlement of Kasion and the cult site of Zeus Kasion/Baal Zephon are probably buried somewhere under the el-Gals sand dune ridge.

In the vicinity of Tell el-Herr, the North Sinai Expedition explored extensive cemeteries from the Persian and Graeco-Roman periods. Many badly preserved burials, complete with plaster funerary masks, were recorded. The masks were fashioned in a mixed Greek and Cypriot style, with Egyptian mythological motifs. Finally, the coastal strip between Pelusium and Tell Mahmadiya is represented by a dense cluster of more than 30 sites dating to the fifth–fourth centuries BC. These sites have yielded unusually large deposits of imported Greek amphorae and black-glazed fine wares, as well as Phoenician-type transport jars, and they may represent trading depots for consignments of wine and oil for redistribution and consumption by the foreign population in the eastern Nile Delta.

The North Sinai Expedition also investigated hundreds of settlement sites of the Graeco-Roman, Byzantine, early Islamic and medieval periods, including large-scale excavations at town sites such as Rhinocolura, Qasrawet and Ostrakine. Explorations since 1985, specifically in the northwestern Sinai at the large town sites of Tell el-Farama (Pelusium) and Tell el-Herr, have also produced rich material remains of public, domestic and industrial quarters of the Graeco-Roman and Byzantine periods.

See also

Aegean peoples; Assyrians; Canaanites; Early Dynastic period, overview; Herodotus; Israelites; Levantine peoples (Iron Age); Persians; Predynastic period, overview; el-Salaam canal; Tell el-Herr; trade, foreign

Further reading

Clédat, J. 1913. Les vases de el-Béda. *ASAE* 13: 115–24.

——. 1916. Fouilles à Khirbet el-Flousiyeh. *ASAE* 16: 6–32.

——. 1923. Notes sur l'isthme de Suez. *BIFAO* 21: 135–89.

Gardiner, A. 1920. The ancient military road between Egypt and Palestine. *JEA* 6: 99–116.

——. 1993. Northern Sinai. *The New Encyclopedia of Archaeological Excavations in the Holy Land*, E. Stern, ed., 1386–96. Jerusalem.

Oren, E.D., and J. Shereshevski. 1989. Military architecture along the Ways of Horus—Egyptian reliefs and archaeological evidence. *Eretz Israel* 20: 8–22.

Oren, E.D., and Y. Yekutieli. 1992a. North Sinai in the Middle Bronze Age—pastoral nomadism and sedentary settlement. *Eretz Israel* 21: 6–21.

——. 1992b. Taur Ikhbeineh in Wadi Gaza—earliest evidence for Egyptian interconnections. In *The Nile Delta in Transition: 4th–3rd Millennium B.C.*, E.C.M. van den Brink, ed., 361–84. Tell Aviv.

ELIEZER D. OREN

Siwa Oasis, Late period and Graeco-Roman sites

Siwa Oasis (29°12′ N, 25°31′ E) is located some 300 km south of the Mediterranean port of Marsa Matruh, close to the modern border between Egypt and Libya. The Oasis is the economic and cultural center of a large depression in the far corner of the Egyptian Western Desert, lying an average of 13 m below sea level. Siwa Oasis enjoys, and at the same time is threatened by, an overabundance of water. Date palms and olive trees set among large lakes have traditionally formed the basis of the Oasis's economic life. The salt of the Oasis (*sal ammoniacum*) was coveted abroad in classical times (Arrian, *Anabasis* III.4; Athenaeus, *Deipnosoph.* II.67b). Archaeological evidence suggests that oil production was a major industry in Roman times; papyrological evidence indicates that oil from the Siwa Oasis cost more than oil from other oases.

Nothing is known yet of Siwa Oasis during the pharaonic periods of Egyptian history until the 26th Dynasty. At this time, Siwa was an independent state ruled by a tribal Libyan chieftain.

These chieftains were referred to as "king and (great) chief of foreign lands" (*nsw-bity wr ['3] h3swt*) in hieroglyphic inscriptions from the Oasis and as "king" (*basileus*) in Greek sources. The Oasis was called *T3(j)* in the Libyan-Egyptian language (Herodotus II.24), Ammon by the Graeco-Roman world and Santariya according to medieval Arab sources. During these periods, Siwa Oasis was a melting pot of the indigenous Libyan civilization and the adopted Egyptian and Hellenistic cultures.

Two events mainly have kept the memory of Siwa alive. One is the tragic fate of an army of allegedly 50,000 Persian soldiers. Supposedly sent by King Cambyses (524 BC) to sack the oasis, the army is said to have perished in a sandstorm while on its way there (Herodotus III.25–6). The other is the journey made to

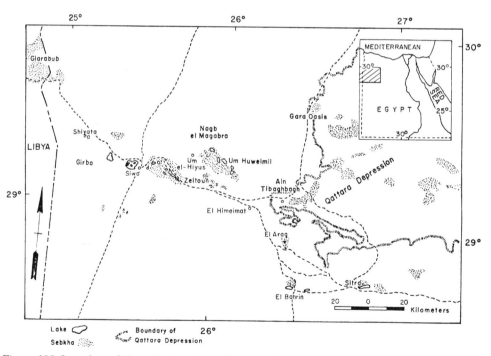

Figure 105 Location of Siwa Oasis and the Qattara Depression in the Western Desert

Siwa by Alexander the Great (332/331 BC). In 1899 the Egyptologist Georg Steindorff definitely identified the site of the famous Temple of the Oracle with the rocky acropolis of Aghurmi. Some thirty-five years later Steindorff, accompanied by the architects Ricke and Aubin, conducted the first detailed archaeological exploration of the temple, publishing accurate plans and epigraphic material. Subsequently, it was the distinguished Egyptian archaeologist Ahmed Fakhry who contributed immensely to our knowledge of Siwan archaeological sites in general and who studied the Ammoneion in particular detail.

We have the following detailed description of the oracular complex in central Siwa by the first century BC historian Diodorus (XVII 50–1):

All the people of Ammon live together as in a village. In the midst of their country there is an acropolis secured by triple walls. The first wall encloses the palace of the ancient rulers; the second one encompasses the women's court, the dwellings of the children, women and relatives, and the guard rooms of the scouts, as well as the sanctuary of the god and the sacred spring, from the waters of which offerings addressed to the god take on holiness; the third wall surrounds the barrack of the king's guards and the guard rooms of those who protect the person of the ruler. Outside the fortress at no great distance there is another temple of Ammon shaded by many large trees, and near this is the spring which is called the Spring of the Sun because of its behaviour.

The acropolis of Diodorus's account has been correctly recognized by Steindorff as the hill of modern Aghurmi (Berber: "village"), approximately 1.7 km east of Shali (Berber: "town") and the surrounding urban center of Siwa.

The temple is unmistakably Egyptian in style, but rather small (*circa* 14 × 22 m) and unassuming in appearance. On the basis of controversial epigraphic evidence, it would seem to date from the reign of Pharaoh Amasis (26th Dynasty). Its pseudo-isodomic masonry of local limestone is an exceedingly rare feature of Egyptian architecture; free standing walls with the larger

courses made up of casing blocks enclosing a fill of stone and mortar, as at Aghurmi, have no Egyptian parallel. Technical details, such as the use of the claw chisel, the use of pulleys to hoist up blocks and a high degree of finish along the edge of blocks (*anathyrosis*), indicate that a non-Egyptian workforce built the oracle temple. The evidence points to Greeks (from Cyrenaica?) constructing the monumental architecture of the Siwa acropolis.

The "other temple of Ammon" referred to by Diodorus can be identified with the large site (*circa* 50 × 120 m) of Umm 'Ubaydah some 400 m south of Aghurmi, where scant remains on a small hillock tell of the existence of a once splendidly adorned sanctuary. It was richly decorated with reliefs and hieroglyphic texts in raised relief; the masonry was partially of locally quarried alabaster. Excavations have uncovered the remains of palmiform columns and architraves, suggesting the existence of a colonnaded forecourt to the temple. On the eastern slope were found the remains of a large platform-like structure of limestone masonry and a cistern, both probably dating to the Hellenistic or Roman era. Hieroglyphic inscriptions associate the temple with a Siwan kinglet called Wenamen and Pharaoh Nectanebo II, the last indigenous Egyptian ruler before the Macedonian conquest. Still surrounded by dense groves of palm trees like "in the shade of many large trees," Diodorus's mention of Umm 'Ubaydah indicates that the oracle once comprised two major sanctuaries. This is supported by the fact that the Umm 'Ubaydah temple faced the entrance to Aghurmi and was aligned along a common axis with the latter temple. Analogies from the Nile Valley would lead one to expect that, originally, both temples should have been linked by a processional causeway (*dromos*).

The "Spring of the Sun" was most probably a well forming part of the Ammoneion precinct of Amen-Re; the popular identification of this "spring" with a large well formerly called 'Ain al-Hammam (now 'Ain al-Gubba or "Cleopatra's bath") some 750 m farther south remains speculative. Water welling up from within the limestone and shale layers of the hill made

Figure 106 Archaeological plan of the area from Aghurmi to Ubayada

Figure 107 Relief in the Umm 'Ubaydah temple, Siwa Oasis: processions of gods and King Wenamen wearing the Libyan chief's ostrich feather headdress and kneeling in front of the shrine of Amen (top right)

Aghurmi an ideal choice for the location of the temple and residence of the kings of Siwa. Curbed in a hollow at the foot of the temple, the ancient well is still visible and still contains water. Undoubtedly, it is Diodorus's sacred spring "from the waters of which offerings addressed to the god take on holiness."

The Aghurmi temple faces south and is aligned north-northwest. It consists of an open forecourt, a first and second hall lit by light-shafts high up in the western walls, followed by the holy of holies or sanctuary proper which to the west is flanked by another big hall and a small niche-like vestry to the east. Only the holy of holies carries some conventional scenes and hieroglyphic inscriptions in sunk relief. They show Pharaoh Amasis on the east (Nile) side and the Ammonian ruler Sutekh-irdes on the west (Libyan) side offering to a row of gods headed by Amen. Architecturally striking features are a thinner wall which surrounds the sanctuary to the north and west (forming a blind passage 52–67 cm wide) as well as two curved ledges protruding from the lateral walls of the sanctuary *circa* 3.00 m above floor level. Evidently, these ledges carried a ceiling which took the appearance of the hieroglyphic sign for "sky" (*pt*); this ceiling created another room above the sanctuary. Originally, this chamber was accessible from the roof of the building only. There is no evidence either for doors or a staircase leading toward it. Access could have been gained by means of a ladder, indicating that for all intents and purposes this room was a secret feature. The outer walls surrounding the sanctuary would have shielded from view whoever climbed into the hidden chamber above the holy of holies. A window in the sanctuary's western wall aligns with another window in the opposite wall in the big hall allowing a shaft of light to penetrate toward the god's barge *naos* in the center of the sanctuary. The fact that Onuris and Tefnut are represented right next to this window and the mythology connected with these two gods suggest the occurrence of this event to have coincided with the winter solstice.

Recent investigations have revealed the presence of two undecorated tombs extending under the northern part of the temple. They are accessible by means of vertical shafts partly covered by the temple's masonry, are undecorated and were robbed. They are either contemporary with the temple or of earlier date. Another tomb extends under the forecourt; it has a mummy-shaped pit sunk in the floor of the burial chamber. In the light of this new evidence, similar features which were partly destroyed and exposed when erosion caused the loss of considerable masses of rock immediately to the northwest and behind the temple are likely to have been tombs as well. Such temple burials recall similar practices in Third Intermediate Period and Late Period Egypt at such sites as Tanis (royalty) and Medinet Habu (high priests).

Much speculation surrounds the mystery of the Siwan oracle and the *omphalos* worshipped there. In the Late Period, Amen may be iconographically represented as a human head (with feathered crown) resting on a globular shape that shows an *omphalos*-like protrusion emerging from it. It represents the god in his common ithyphallic form (Min-Amen) shrouded by an amulet-studded cloak, the raised arm with the flagellum creating the umbilical shape commented upon by classical authors (Curtius Rufus IV.7,23; Diodorus XVII.50,6).

Accounts relating Alexander's journey to Siwa show that the oracular procedure was clearly the same as that practiced in the Nile Valley, where the underlying principle of bark oracles was based on presenting questions in such a way that they could be answered either yes or no. Divine advice would never be heard (priests imitating the voice of gods), but only be seen. Oracles performed in public would usually take the form of a procession, the god being carried out of the temple on his sacred bark in order to visit neighboring shrines. As most Egyptian people were barred from entering the temples, this was the only occasion on which deities could be approached by the masses. Delivering a positive statement, the bow of the bark (taking the ram-headed shape of Amen's sacred animal) would nod approval as the bearers in front would "involuntarily" bend and straighten up again several times. A verdict of no was indicated by the bark retreating or not moving at all. As there is practically no room for such a procession to deploy on Aghurmi hill it seems a reasonable assumption that the bark oracles would have taken place along the processional way (*dromos*) linking the Aghurmi and Umm 'Ubaydah temples. Some archaeological evidence for this processional way together with the remains of a third, new temple, has been uncovered some 50 m south of the foot of Aghurmi Hill.

Different rules applied to oracles delivered to royalty. Egyptian pharaohs attended bark processions inside temples, but could also seek detailed advice by talking to the divine images resting in their sanctuaries. The example of Alexander's visit to Siwa reveals that even foreign kings were accorded the privilege of calling upon Amen in the privacy of his sacred quarters. There was no possibility of manipulating the statue into giving answers by significant movements or gestures and answers would sometimes necessitate research and detailed instructions; for example, Queen Hatshepsut's inquiry about the routes leading to the land of Punt. Thus, the *modus operandi* devised by the Egyptian priests was communication via letter. Composed in "the writing of Thoth" (hieroglyphs), the letter allegedly arrived from heaven and would be announced by the high priest. In the same vein, books were believed to have fallen miraculously from heaven. For the priests to be able to contrive an answer, it meant that, somehow, they had to gain knowledge of the questions. This could explain the function of the hidden chamber above the sanctuary at Aghurmi where one or more of them would hide and secretly overhear the private "conversations" taking place right below them.

Of the numerous cemeteries, only the rock-cut tombs of the "Mountain of the Dead" (Jabal al-Mawta) north of Shali have attracted scholarly attention. Stylistic (e.g. *loculi*) and archaeological evidence (surface pottery) indicate a Hellenistic to Roman period date. The beautifully painted tomb of a wealthy Ammonian called Si-Amen is well-known; exclusively Egyptian in appearance and subject matter,

much of the decoration was destroyed by intrusive *loculi*-style burials. A painted wooden beam divides the ceiling of the tomb into a mythological half (showing the sky goddess Nut, stars and the journey of the solar bark) and a ceiling covered by a gobelin with an intricate pattern of flying hawks and vultures as well as stars.

Stunning portraits depict Si-Amen at two different stages of his life: on the east wall he is shown standing in profile as a youthful man with full, curly hair and beard; on the west wall, Si-Amen is depicted sitting, visibly aged, with his hairline receding and the beard sparse. The latter scene conveys a notion of unusual intimacy in Egyptian art: the deceased is touched by a little boy (son or slave) as though to bid him farewell. Although Egyptian in style, the composition looks uninspired by iconographical patterns found in the Nile Valley and is more reminiscent of Greek funerary art. Experiments with rendering the human body in profile (rather than the normal Egyptian way), the artistic verve behind the drawings and details like the shape of Si-Amen's beard or the *chlamys*-like garment of the little boy suggest that the Si-Amen painter entertained close contacts with Greek art or artists, maybe in Alexandria.

Quite possibly, Si-Amen himself could have been in touch with Greeks, notably merchants, but there is nothing tangible to suggest that he was of Greek origin. Nothing specific points to where else, besides on Aghurmi, the Ammonian nobility might have buried their dead. However, the scene showing the youthful Si-Amen protected by the vulture goddess Nekhbet, protectress of the Egyptian king, might imply royal Ammonian ancestry. Attributing to the tomb any other than a vague late Hellenistic/early Roman date remains a problem. However, the types of storage jars (amphorae) depicted in the murals would seem to compare to wares which are known from the second to first centuries BC, with the latest possible date early in the second century AD.

During the first century AD the Ammonian kingdom came under Roman rule (Pliny, *Natural History* 49). At the beginning of the fourth century AD, Siwa formed part of the diocese of Alexandria and served as a place of banishment for Theban heretics. Christianity seems to have made little inroad into Siwan society; in the seventh century AD, when Samuel of Kalamun was abducted to the oasis by marauding tribesmen, the population were still worshipping the sun. Possibly the old tradition of the pagan cults of Ammon (sun) and Parammon (moon/Thoth) had continued to this period. During the Middle Ages, a Berber tribe from Cyrenaica (the Swa or Suwa) settled in the oasis, giving it its present name. According to al-Idrisi, a small Muslim community had come into existence there by the mid-twelfth century.

See also

cult temples, construction techniques; Kharga Oasis, Late period and Graeco-Roman sites; Late and Ptolemaic periods, overview; Libyans; Macedonians; Persians

Further reading

Fakhry, A. 1971. Recent excavations at the Temple of the Oracle at Siwa Oasis. *Beiträge Bf* 12: 17–33.

——. 1973. *The Oases of Egypt* 1: Siwa Oasis. Cairo.

Hassan, F. 1978. Archaeological exploration of the Siwa region. *CA* 19: 146–8.

Kuhlmann, K.-P. 1988. *Das Ammoneion: Archäologie, Geschichte und Kultpraxis des Orakels von Siwa* (AVDAIK 75). Mainz.

KLAUS-PETER KUHLMANN

Siwa Oasis, prehistoric sites

Siwa Oasis (29°12′ N, 25°31′ E) lies in the northwestern corner of the Western Desert, close to the Libyan border, and is the northernmost oasis in the Egyptian Sahara. It is approximately 560 km west of the Nile Valley and 274 km south of the Mediterranean coast. There are several small oases in the neighborhood of Siwa, including Gara, el-Areg, Bahrin

and Sitra, situated in a depression in the Marmarica plateau. Today, water from springs and wells in the oases irrigates orchards and agricultural fields characterized by lush groves of palm trees.

Sites in the Siwa region consist of scatters of lithic artifacts and fragments of ostrich eggshell. The raw materials utilized consist mostly of local chert and silicified limestone. The most common tool classes are backed bladelets and burins. Other less common tool classes include perforators, end-scrapers, notched and denticulated pieces, and points. The points include a variety of stemmed arrowheads and points, and leaf-shaped bifacial points. Fragments of grinding stones and ostrich eggshell beads are present. Although a few potsherds were found at two sites, their association with lithic artifacts cannot be conclusively established.

Assemblages from different parts of Siwa are similar. They date to an interval from the ninth to seventh millennia BP. In general, the assemblages of the Siwan industry are in the same tradition as the Epi-paleolithic assemblages of the Libyco-Capsian (Libya) and the Qarunian (Fayum). Lack of faunal and plant remains, as well as pottery, does not permit a valid interpretation of the subsistence regime of the Holocene inhabitants of the Siwa region. However, considering the presence of arrowheads and grinding stones, it seems that they were at least in part, if not exclusively, hunters and gatherers. The lack of permanent settlements also suggests that there were no "Neolithic" villages. Climatic conditions during the occupation were fairly moist to sustain a few pools, and sediments suggest that at times rain was torrential.

There is no indication that the Holocene Siwa dwellers were cattle herders or pastoralists. It is possible that Siwa, which received some winter rain and may also have received some summer rain during episodes when the monsoonal rains advanced much farther north than their current limit, never sustained permanent lakes or even large ephemeral freshwater lakes. Under such conditions, cattle might have been difficult to raise. Perhaps some of the inhabitants of Siwa kept a few goats and sheep, but it seems they probably depended heavily on wild resources.

See also

dating techniques, prehistory; Epi-paleolithic cultures, overview; Paleolithic cultures, overview; Paleolithic tools

FEKRI A. HASSAN

social organization

For most of ancient Egypt's history the king held pre-eminent temporal power. He was also considered divine and able magically to insure the desired annual inundation and subsequent good harvests. However, it is not until the Old Kingdom's 5th Dynasty that Egyptian sources—written and artistic—begin to reflect commoners with any clarity. For information about Old Kingdom social organization, we are more dependent on artifacts and monuments than the sparse written texts which have survived.

The hierarchical Egyptian society of the 4th Dynasty is expressed in the layout of the royal necropolis around the Great Pyramid at Giza, with the gigantic pyramid tomb of the king surrounded by the tombs of his immediate family (on the east) and those of the courtiers and officials (on the west). These *mastaba* tombs, with flat-topped superstructures and underground tomb chambers, were laid out in many rows. Only the mother and wives of the king shared with him the pyramid-style tomb. Thus courtiers and high officials—including male relatives of the king—were not originally as privileged in the afterlife as the king and the royal women. Tombs in the so-called workmen's cemetery at Giza are very small in scale, but the designs imitated certain features of their superiors' tombs and reflect hopes for an afterlife.

In this life, however, the most powerful positions of the realm in the 4th Dynasty were filled by the royal princes: the king's brothers, cousins and sons, who controlled the office of the vizier, the treasuries and all royal construc-

tion works. Royal succession was from father to son, with the offspring of the marriage to the daughter of the previous king given priority. Both royal men and women held positions in the cults of many deities.

The sheer size of the royal pyramid complexes required large numbers of unskilled as well as skilled laborers. In the absence of large-scale slavery in the Old Kingdom, a system of corvée labor developed in which all citizens could be conscripted for part of the year. Ancient Egypt was an agrarian society and peasant farmers, who made up the bulk of its population, were the majority of the conscripted laborers. During the Nile's annual inundation when no farming could be done, farmers were put to work. Housing, clothing and feeding of the work teams was provided by the state, perhaps utilizing women as weavers and food preparers, as later records show that women could also be conscripted. Hardly anyone seems to have been exempt from the corvée system, including priests and high officials, who might be pressed to act as overseers of those repairing dikes, building fortifications, or moving colossal stone blocks and carved monuments. Well-to-do Egyptians were buried with so-called servant statues, which provided proxies to do the work. Possibly this indicates that many rich Egyptians bought out of the corvée by hiring a substitute, or giving a bribe.

In the New Kingdom when a permanent army was established, its members were often put to work in quarries and on construction projects, and many foreign captives were also utilized. However, since the origin of the corvée system was long before the rise of a professional military, it has been suggested that the corvée was an early form of the welfare state.

With the 5th Dynasty, radical change in the government is obvious. Princes were now excluded from the kingdom's administration, and even the highest ranking official next to the king, the vizier, was no longer a member of the royal family. Evidence throughout Egypt indicates the growth and ascendancy of a common-born managerial class. While strong centralized rule from the capital at Memphis continued, provincial tombs and private statues are now in evidence and reflect the growth in wealth of a literate class which could run the government efficiently, overseeing tax collection and redistribution and mustering work teams for royal building projects, mining and trade.

Inscriptions of the ever-expanding managerial class of the late Old Kingdom, while scarcely autobiographical, contain titles which provide hints of the structure of rank and official positions for both sexes. From the 5th and 6th Dynasties are titles reflecting positions of authority held by women, such as "Overseer of the Weavers' House" (weaving was largely a female activity then) and "Overseer of Female Physicians." Some titles may have been merely honorific, but the use in the 5th Dynasty of titles previously held by royalty still reflected rank.

Among more ordinary people depicted in scenes of "daily life," which are more frequent in late Old Kingdom private tombs, are women in diverse activities outside the home, such as piloting boats, overseeing flax harvesting, and joining men in harvesting cereal. Young children, however, are portrayed playing separately with members of their own sex. Not only the elite but also a larger cross-section of society is represented by the participants in temple and funerary rituals. During the late Old Kingdom the cult of the goddess Hathor was dominated by women in its middle and upper administrative positions. Sons, however, appear more prominently in private funerary contexts and family tombs stress the importance of the male head of the family.

As there was no true separation of state and temple in ancient Egypt, it is difficult to evaluate the relative power and social prestige of religious and secular title holders. However, running the government depended upon the scribal class, which was exclusively male because of the many years of education required to master reading, composition and mathematics. Such training would have prevented women from learning what for many were the basic skills of survival: the myriad tasks of food and clothing production. Women are assumed to have been wed during their early teens, and surely would have spent most of their lives pregnant or nursing children. Marriage among commoners seems to have been overwhelmingly monogamous. Young couples founded their own households and did not join an extended family of a *pater familias*.

It is clear that many successful bureaucrats were utilized in a wide variety of capacities during their careers, perhaps to prevent them from concentrating too much power in one position or place. Typically, a man trained to compose letters, do surveying and compute geometrical problems could be sent by the king to organize mining operations, put down insurrections and oversee the construction of temples.

During the 6th Dynasty the use of high-ranking honorific titles became even more common, indicating a progressive cheapening of titles as they became prerogatives of office and as they grew in number (almost 2,000 are known). Later literary texts hint at a period of social upheaval, and certainly political disruption marked the First Intermediate Period, which followed the Old Kingdom. Occurring simultaneously and in the early Middle Kingdom was the added autonomy claimed by provincial governors. The titles of women in the Middle Kingdom, however, seldom reflect positions of authority and seem to have been associated with service industries.

The independence and wealth of the provincial governors (nomarchs) is reflected in the series of imposing tombs in the provinces (as at Meir, Deir el-Bersha and Beni Hasan) during the early 12th Dynasty. Under Senusret III, these suddenly cease and stronger centralized authority was re-exerted. Already under Senusret II, a strictly regulated society can be observed, as evidenced by the organization of a planned town at Lahun near the royal pyramid complex in the Fayum, with the obvious separation in the town of officials' houses and those of the workers.

Records of the Middle Kingdom increasingly reflect the incursion of foreign peoples into the Nile Valley. Some household records reveal dozens of foreigners on their staffs, but these may well have been itinerant craftspeople, rather than true slaves. The influence of foreigners from the Aegean, southwest Asia and Nubia in Egypt during the Second Intermediate Period helped to create the more pluralistic society of the New Kingdom.

In the wars of the 18th Dynasty, when an empire developed and was exploited, large groups of foreigners taken captive by the Egyptian army were brought as war booty to Egypt, where they were put to work on the ambitious royal construction projects. Female captives were probably put to work in temple and royal weaving workshops. Due to their experience and language capabilities, a number of foreign captives were possibly utilized in trade. Traders do not show up in scenes or texts on the monuments, and seem to have had little social prestige (many are known to have been slaves); yet they served not only institutions such as the palace and temple, which produced excesses in commodities and craft goods, but also private individuals who wished to trade surpluses for luxury goods or metals. Judging from some names among the civil service, royal artisans, police force and military, it also seems likely that foreigners with previous bureaucratic, military or palace experience abroad were utilized by the Egyptians in similar capacities.

At this time the upper echelons of society consisted of the royal family, the viziers, the viceroy of Kush (Nubia), royal butlers, stewards of the royal estates and, following closely behind, the military generals and high priests and stewards of the most important temples. The first families of the provinces could probably have a claim to the top ranks of society, too, as mayors of towns are known who had much property in land, cattle and slaves.

A large professional army developed for the first time in the New Kingdom. An elite military class arose, on which the king depended for officers who would lead troops into battle in foreign lands. Also utilized internally in peacetime, the officer class was enlisted to control many aspects of Egyptian life, including the civil bureaucracy and the temple hierarchy. By the later 18th Dynasty an elite military class of charioteers had developed who rode into battle aligned closest to the king. This was, in effect, an aristocracy based on wealth (needed to maintain a team, a chariot, a stable and a groom). Its members might live in the provinces, where they owned much property, but they were not permitted to keep their own weapons, which were stored by the government.

Already recorded in the reign of Tuthmose IV was the promotion of a chariotry officer to the high religious rank of "Overseer of Prophets of All the Gods of the Two Lands [Egypt]." This seems to indicate that the king was taking a more direct control over the priestly hierarchies, which may have become hereditary and too independent. Before the New Kingdom, priestly families had been supported by the land holdings of their temples and the food which was first offered to the gods on the temple altars. However, during the 18th Dynasty, the temples had become rich from the generous gifts of booty donated by Tuthmose III and Amenhotep II as a result of their foreign victories. Wealth and prestige may have propelled segments of the priesthood to grow into a power that might challenge the king, especially when no clear line was drawn to separate the political from the ecclesiastical institutions of the state. For whatever reason, during the second half of the Dynasty a royal policy increasingly placed officials with military backgrounds in charge of the country's religious institutions. The priestly class undoubtedly suffered more severely during Akhenaten's reign. When his eventual successor, Horemheb, reopened the temples which had been closed during most of Akhenaten's reign, he filled them with "ordinary priests and lectors from the pick of the army." This policy, which furthered the militarization of the state, continued under the rulers of the 19th Dynasty. For the ambitious peasant, the army might provide a more adventurous life with chances for promotion into leadership positions and even wealth from rewards of gold and captives. Land grants were also made to army veterans. However, the increasing numbers of foreigners in the army from the late 18th Dynasty onward seem to indicate that the average Egyptian preferred to stay home.

Certainly every aspect of Egyptian life depended upon the farmers and their harvest.

The large labor force that served the state and the gods in their temples was fed by what the government obtained from the farmers. Taxes were collected on all types of commodities, but especially on grain, fruit, honey, oil, cattle, firewood and linen. Hereditary ownership of land was possible, and extant records trace ownership of even small plots over centuries. The official class was among the landowners, but a man could always rent plots from an institutional landowner. Women and foreign mercenaries show up in a late New Kingdom tax roll as cultivators, but one town in western Thebes listed only one-third of its householders as farmers; the others were herders, policemen, administrators or craftsmen.

New Kingdom records reveal an involvement, perhaps even an increase in activities, for women outside the home, in the marketplace and in cult centers. There are scenes of women both selling and buying in the market, which demonstrates that they handled the family's purchasing power and were not a segregated element of society. Their roles in the hierarchies of local temples, and some major ones, seem to have depended mainly upon the social ranking of their husbands. Economic and legal documents, which increase in number beginning in the late New Kingdom, show women as independent, needing no legal guardians and bearing the full obligations of taxpayers and citizens.

In statues for their tomb chapels or temple display, and in tomb paintings, warriors were never portrayed with their arms and armor. Only the king was shown on monuments as a victor on the battlefield. The general, the priest and the courtier alike were frequently portrayed as seated scribes, heads bent over their papyrus roll, thus stressing their education, which set them apart from everyone else. No one rose in this society without some literacy and without being part of the bureaucracy of the state. To be an official was to have true prestige.

The site of Deir el-Medina, a village built to house the families of workers in royal tombs in the Valley of the Kings, has yielded the most documentation for social relations in the late New Kingdom. The village was administered by the government's scribe and foremen, who received more pay than their underling laborers. The artisans, however, were permitted to produce salable items in their free time for their neighbors and other private customers, which considerably enhanced their incomes. (They worked eight-hour days and had their weekends and frequent holidays off.) The women of this and other communities were also earners, selling cloth and the produce they raised. From the Deir el-Medina textual archive, it is even possible to detect some social mobility. Some of the scribes who became community leaders there had been promoted through the bureaucracy. Some were the sons of the community's scribes, but others were the sons of men of the work crews. Thus even the son of a manual laborer, through ambition and years of study, could advance to a highly respected and lucrative position in the civil service.

It has been argued that the tenant farmer may have enjoyed more actual independence than those whose livelihoods depended directly on decisions of the crown. The royal artisans could be shifted around the country from job to job, or be given extra jobs to complete for their immediate supervisors. The civil servant could be promoted or demoted at will without much recourse, just as a woman of the royal harim might be sent off to a foreign land as a royal gift. The tenant farmer, however, had to fear the tax collectors, who visited each cultivator with armed police. These police would thrash any farmer who could not give the government its quota of his harvest. The "free citizen" of Egypt was definitely at the mercy of his superiors, and perhaps that is why education, which could set some men above the dependency of most others, was so valued.

See also

administrative bureaucracy; army; Beni Hasan; Deir el-Bersha; Deir el-Medina; funerary texts; Giza, Khufu pyramid complex; Giza, workmen's community; Lahun, town; law; *ma'at*; Meir; quarrying; taxation and conscription; Tell el-Amarna; textual sources, New

Kingdom; Thebes, Valley of the Kings; trade, foreign; writing, reading and schooling

Further reading

Baer, K. 1960. *Rank and Title in the Old Kingdom*. Chicago.

James, T.G.H. 1984. *Pharaoh's People: Scenes from Life in Imperial Egypt*. London.

Kemp, B.J. 1989. *Ancient Egypt: Anatomy of a Civilization*. London.

Lesko, B.S., ed. 1989. *Women's Earliest Records from Ancient Egypt and Western Asia*. Atlanta, GA.

Lesko, L.H., ed. 1993. *Pharaoh's Workers: the Village of Deir el Medina*. Ithaca, NY.

Trigger, B.G., B.J. Kemp, D. O'Connor and A.B. Lloyd. 1983. *Ancient Egypt: A Social History*. Cambridge.

Ward, W.A. 1986. *Essays on Feminine Titles*. Beirut.

Wente, E.F. 1990. *Letters from Ancient Egypt*. Atlanta, GA.

BARBARA S. LESKO

stone vessels and bead making

In every period the shaping of all hard stone vessels, including those manufactured from basalt, diorite, porphyry, breccia, granite and Egyptian alabaster (calcite), was completed by flint chisels, punches and scrapers. Flint was the only abundantly available tool-making material which was satisfactory for the exterior shaping of hard stone vessels. After 3,600 BC, Egyptian craftsmen learned to cast copper tools, but tests with hardened and sharpened copper chisels have demonstrated their inability to effectively cut any stone used for vessels, other than soft limestone and gypsum. Even these stone vessels needed awkward places to be shaped by flint scrapers; necks, rims and the undercutting of vessels' shoulders all required skilled carving techniques. After preliminary shaping, coarse and smooth sandstone rubbers were utilized to complete this process and initiate surface polishing, which was probably finished by a sand/stone/copper powder used wet, followed by clay/mud, both applied by leather laps.

The technology for hollowing vessels was fully established in the Predynastic period. During the early Predynastic phases (Badarian and Nagada I) hard stone vessels would have been laboriously hollowed by hand-held stone borers, used in conjunction with desert sand abrasive; hand-held flint borers would have been used for very soft stone, without the benefit of sand abrasive. However, before the advent of copper tubes by the mid-fourth millennium BC (Nagada II), craftsmen possibly employed a reed tube, also in use with sand abrasive. This tube could have been spun between the hands, twisted by wrist action or driven by a bow. Reed drills will efficiently cut limestone and calcite, but not the harder stones, such as granite and porphyry.

After the introduction of cast copper, the stone vessel craftsman was able to imitate the hollow reed by beating thick sheets of cast copper into thin sheets and rolling them around wooden, cylindrical formers. Larger diameter copper tubes may have been directly cast by making tubular-shaped molds in damp sand. A wooden shaft was then forcibly driven, partway, into the tubular drill. This allowed the drill to be rotated by a bow, the upper part of the shaft turning in a hand-held, stone bearing-cap.

The tubular drill produces a tubular-shaped slot, which surrounds a central core. This technology allows the removal of a small amount of stone by drilling, but achieves the full-sized hole on removal of the core. The bow-driven copper tubular drill was certainly used to drill the holes in tubular lugs carved into vessels in Nagada II times. However, holes and cores produced by bow-driven tubes are tapered, caused by a motion actuated by the push and pull of the bow, and, as vessels were always shaped before drilling of the interior commenced, there was a severe risk of damaging them. Additionally, experiments have demonstrated that bow drilling also causes quartz sand crystals, trapped between the outer wall of the tube and the wall of the hole, to elongate the originally circular hole, thereby meeting the external wall of a shaped vessel.

Clearly the stone vessel craftsman needed a special tool to drive his tubular drills and stone borers which did not suffer from these drawbacks. During Nagada II times, a combined vessel-drilling and boring tool was developed by craftsmen. The tool, which is illustrated in several Egyptian tombs dating from the 5th to 26th Dynasties, generally consisted of a straight wooden shaft that inclined at an angle near the top to form a handle. The shaft and handle were created from a forked tree branch, adapted by cutting away the main stem just above the point where it branched into a lesser stem, which in turn was cut to length and carved into a distinctly tapered handle. The tool's main shaft was fitted with two stone weights, fastened under the handle. These weights placed a load upon a tubular drill or stone borer and, consequently, upon the sand abrasive under the drill and borer. A single, circular weight was introduced during the 12th Dynasty.

Although tubular drills were fitted directly to the tool's main shaft, borers were driven by a forked shaft lashed to the bottom of the main shaft. The principal borer for enlarging the initial cylindrical hole was shaped like a figure-of-eight when viewed from the top. The fork engaged on each side of the borer, which was deliberately fashioned from an oval pebble. Other types of borers were circular and conical, the latter shape being in use to enlarge vessels' mouths. Cylindrical vessels of soft stone, such as gypsum, would have been completely excavated by crescent-shaped flint borers. Worn forked shafts could be replaced when necessary, and this stratagem ensured the continued use of the main tool.

In order to operate the tool, one hand firmly gripped the handle while the other hand gripped the shaft under the weights. The tool's shaft was then twisted and reverse-twisted by a continuous wrist action. Extensive tests have established that wet sand abrasive is not conducive to the efficient drilling and boring of stone, and it is highly likely that dry sand was used. Different diameter drill tubes, on the same axis, were probably used to weaken a large core, and a vessel with a large mouth had a series of adjacent holes drilled around the

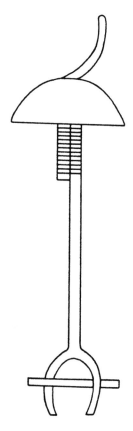

Figure 108 An 18th Dynasty representation of the stone vessel drilling and boring tool

perimeter to isolate the central mass. After drilling, figure-of-eight shaped borers of ever-increasing lengths were utilized to bore out bulbous vessels. Hand-held, hook-shaped flint and other stone borers were employed to complete the undercutting of vessel shoulders.

Experiments have determined that tubes and borers ground the sand abrasive and stone into a finely powdered material, which must have caused lung damage to ancient craftsmen. Powder produced by copper tubes also contained fine particles of copper. Significantly, the by-product powder produced from drilling granite contains approximately twelve times the amount of copper in powder obtained from drilling soft limestone, and this enabled other ancient craftsmen to use different powders for stone polishing, bead drilling and, possibly, faïence manufacture.

Bead making began in Epi-paleolithic times (*circa* 10,000–5,500 BC). At first craftsmen utilized natural objects, such as pebbles, shells and teeth. In the Predynastic period, beads were also made from copper, gold, silver, greenish-blue glazed quartz and stones (agate, calcite, carnelian, diorite, garnet, limestone and serpentine). The Egyptians' most favored bead shapes were rings, barrels, cylinders, convex bicones and spheroids, but amulets and pendants were also threaded into strings. Glass beads were introduced during the Dynastic period, and they were made by winding a thin thread of drawn-out glass around a wire.

Experiments have demonstrated that the powdered by-product material, when mixed with sodium bicarbonate (natron in ancient times) and water, creates faïence cores and glazes after firing. Ancient faïence bead, amulet and pendant cores could have been manufactured from powders derived from drilling soft stone with copper tubes. In ancient times a stiff paste, with a thread, wire or awl initially inserted to make the perforation, was molded or modeled into shape, and then glazed with a runny paste probably manufactured from powders derived from drilling hard stone. After firing, cores turned into a hard, whitish material that was sometimes tinted blue, green, yellow, brown or gray, while glazes turned mainly blue or green due to an increase in copper content.

Metals can be shaped by hammering, but hard stone beads were first formed by breaking up pebbles, then roughly shaping the pieces by chipping with flint tools, followed by grinding on harsh and smoother grades of sandstone. Final polishing was achieved by rubbing along grooves in wooden benches coated with a runny polishing abrasive, possibly made by mixing by-product powder with muddy water.

Perforation of stone beads was accomplished by flint borers from the earliest periods, but the use of bow-driven copper drills first appeared in early Predynastic (Badarian) times. Even so, flint borers were concurrently in use with copper drills and were also needed to make initial depressions in beads to center these drills. A thin abrasive paste, probably made from the by-product powder, was used with copper and bronze bead drills. At Kerma, in Nubia near the Third Cataract, small bronze drills were force-fitted into waisted wooden handles which were individually driven by a bow string, but by the 18th Dynasty at Thebes, craftsmen evolved mass-production drilling technology. The bow's length was increased to approximately 1.2 m; its 2 mm diameter string simultaneously turned two, three, four, or even five bronze drill rods, each 5 mm in diameter. These rotated in bearing holes drilled into the bottom ends of vertical sticks, held in line by the craftsman's free hand. The drills revolved at high speed in stone beads secured in the top of a three-legged table. Mass production of bead perforation considerably reduced the time, and cost, of bead making.

See also

Dynastic stone tools; faïence technology and production; jewelry; metallurgy; Neolithic and Predynastic stone tools

Further reading

Aldred, C. 1971. *Jewels of the Pharaohs*. London.

Lucas, A., and J.R. Harris. 1962. *Ancient Egyptian Materials and Industries*. London.

Stocks, D.A. 1989. Ancient factory mass-production techniques: indications of large-scale stone bead manufacture during the Egyptian New Kingdom Period. *Antiquity* 63: 526–31.

——. 1993. Making stone vessels in ancient Mesopotamia and Egypt. *Antiquity* 67: 596–603.

——. 1997. Derivation of ancient Egyptian faience core and glaze materials. *Antiquity* 71: 179–82.

DENYS A. STOCKS

subsistence and diet in Dynastic Egypt

As in other parts of the Near East, the transition from prehistoric to historical times in Egypt was accompanied by a fundamental shift of subsistence strategies that led to dietary change. About 7,500–6,000 BC (calibrated dates), sites along the Fayum lake shore and in southern Egypt indicate that fishing and hunting were both prominent, presumably in conjunction with wild plant processing. During the same time range, and even earlier, small mobile groups in the eastern Sahara followed game from one water hole to another, probably driving some domesticated cattle to take advantage of ephemeral pastures, and possibly planting a little sorghum or millet on an opportunistic basis. In each case, animal protein was a prominent dietary component.

When agriculture became a viable economy in the Nile Valley, after perhaps 5,500 BC, wheat and barley soon became important. However, even in late Neolithic and early Predynastic times (circa 4,500–3,500 BC), livestock remained important, and fishing or hunting provided important complementary foods. There is some evidence that cattle, for example, were stalled and fed with fodder, at least on a seasonal basis; but by the end of that millennium, the population was presumably expanding rapidly. By then, given the evidence for a hierarchical society, a system of land tenure was probably introduced, that would have begun to increasingly restrict access to resources for common people.

There is little information on the diet of rural or urban populations for either Old or Middle Kingdom times, because everything is skewed toward the lifestyle of the elites, as shown for example in the 5th and early 6th Dynasty tomb reliefs. The well-to-do evidently had sumptuous diets, including a variety of meats (with different cuts), several fowl, cooked in different kinds of oil, many types of breads and cakes, honey, a range of fruits and fresh plants, milk, and various kinds of beer and wine. The most common meat was beef, with that of sheep, goats and pigs enjoying less prestige. Hunting had become a prestigious sport for the elite, with more adventure linked to stalking wild cattle or boar in the marshlands than shooting at antelopes or gazelles in game enclosures. Geese and ducks, as well as cranes, were raised on estates or hunted in the wetlands. In short, elite diets remained diversified, including as much animal protein as did their prehistoric counterparts. Any dietary problems encountered would mainly have involved overindulgence and obesity.

For simpler folk, there is the New Kingdom evidence from Deir el-Medina, supplemented by other information on workmen's rations and the comments of Herodotus. These diets were little varied, with an allocation of wheat and barley, complemented by fish, domesticated doves or pigeons, and beer, perhaps brewed mainly from barley. In sufficient quantities, that represented a balanced if monotonous diet. Any hunting was limited to catching hares or migratory birds. The limited skeletal materials that have been properly studied suggest a life expectancy of thirty years, which, if representative, implies a reasonably long and healthy life for the period.

The subsistence economy was increasingly based on irrigated agriculture. Despite some genetic roots and ritual survivals of North African origin, the agrosystem was of Mediterranean–Near Eastern origin, rather than African. That applies firstly to the essential crops, including wheat, barley and legumes planted in the autumn and harvested in late winter or early spring. Second, meat, labor and special products were provided by the standard Near Eastern herd animals. Oxen pulled the basic "scratch" plow, and although wooly strains of sheep were introduced during the Middle Kingdom, flax was woven into linen as the most common cloth. There is next to no information on the secondary dairy products potentially derived from cow's, ewe's or goat's milk, although it is improbable that they were not used. In so far as small stock were owned and eaten, that probably was in times of shortfall. Third, fruit trees brought variety and vitamins to the diet, while also reducing subsistence risk. Indigenous tree crops such as dates, dom nuts and sycamore figs came first.

Over time, pomegranates, sebesten "plums," persea fruits, Mediterranean figs, apples and grapes were added to the orchard component; but they were not deep-rooted and thus required irrigation as they matured during the spring and early summer.

Fortuitously, the Nile flood regime mimicked the seasonality of winter rainfall experienced in Greece, Syro-Palestine or the Zagros Mountains. That Mediterranean pattern begins with October showers that germinate the plowed and seeded fields, with the rainy season ending during the early spring months when the crop is about ready to harvest. The Nile floods crest over a six-week period, beginning in mid-August at Aswan and ending in early October at the head of the Delta. Four to six weeks later the fields emerge and can be seeded. Given the higher growing season temperatures, the grains and legumes can be harvested in late winter, drawing their moisture from the saturated clayey soils. Summer crops are another matter, requiring constant irrigation at a time when the river and ground-water level are down. Until an economical irrigation technology became available, this precluded green vegetables and non-indigenous fruit trees except in gardens or on commercial estates.

Grapes and olives had a special status in ancient Egypt. Wine and olive oil acquired ritual status in Early Bronze Age Syro-Palestine, to become a hallmark of Mediterranean civilization. They were being produced on a commercial scale by the late third millennium BC, and were an integral part of the exchange economy that supported urban growth in southwest Asia. Palestinian wine jars are found in quantity in the Abydos tombs (Umm el-Qa'ab) of late Dynasty 0 monarchs (immediately preceding the 1st Dynasty), suggesting that imported wines were a critical part of elite banquets. Vintages were distinguished by special marks. By Old Kingdom times, all aspects of wine production are documented in tomb reliefs and leave no doubt that irrigated viticulture was common on estates in Egypt. The role of olive oil is more obscure, although it too was imported since late Predynastic times. Olive cultivation is not depicted in Dynastic art, and a hieroglyphic designation, if current, was ambiguous even in New Kingdom times. Unlike grapes, irrigated olive trees produce much foliage but few fruits, so that efforts to acclimatize them in Egypt have been unsuccessful in regard to oil production.

See also

Abydos, Umm el-Qa'ab; agriculture, introduction of; brewing and baking; fauna, domesticated; fauna, wild; Nile, modern hydrology; wine making

Further reading

Boessneck, J. 1988. *Die Tierwelt des alten Ägypten*. Munich.

Brewer, D.J., and R. Friedman. 1989. *Fish and Fishing in Ancient Egypt*. Warminster.

Butzer, K.W. 1996. Ecology in the long view: settlement histories, agrosystemic strategies, and ecological performance. *JFA* 23: 141–50.

——. 1997. Sociopolitical discontinuity in the Near East *c.* 2200 B.C.E.: scenarios from Palestine and Egypt. In *Third Millennium BC Climate Change and Old World Collapse*, H.N. Dalfes, G. Kukla and H. Weiss, eds. 245–96. Berlin.

Darby, W.I., P. Ghalioungi and L. Grivetti. 1977. *The Gift of Osiris*. London.

Masali, M., and B. Chiarelli. 1992. Demographic data on the remains of ancient Egyptians. *Journal of Human Evolution* 1: 161–9.

Moens, M.F., and W. Wetterstrom. 1985. The agricultural economy of an Old Kingdom town in Egypt's West Delta: insights from the plant remains. *JNES* 46: 159–73.

Wetterstrom, W. 1993. Foraging and farming in Egypt: the transition from hunting and gathering to horticulture in the Nile Valley. In *The Archaeology of Africa*, T. Shaw, P. Sinclair, B. Andah and A. Okpoko, eds. 165–226. London.

Zohary, D., and M. Hopf. 1993. *Domestication of Plants in the Old World: The Origin and Spread of Cultivated Plants in West Asia, Europe and the Nile Valley*. Oxford.

KARL W. BUTZER

T

Tanis (San el-Hagar)

Tanis lies in the eastern Nile Delta (30°59′ N, 31°53′ E), east of the Tanitic branch. It was a royal residence during the Third Intermediate Period, and the nome capital in the Late and Ptolemaic periods. Its ancient Egyptian name, "Ḏ'nt" (in Greek, Tanis), first appears in the *Onomasticon of Amenemope* (*circa* end of the 20th Dynasty) and the *Report of Wenamen*, but a "Field of Tanis" is mentioned on the walls of a Memphite temple dating to the reign of Ramesses II. Although the earliest datable building phase is from the reign of Psusennes I (21st Dynasty), Tanis must have begun to have a prominent role at least as early as the end of the 19th Dynasty, for in the *Wenamen* text it is the capital of Smendes and Tentamen.

The monumental remains of Tanis were first investigated by the scholars accompanying Napoleon's expedition to Egypt, and drawings and descriptions of the site appeared in the *Description de l'Égypte.* In 1825, Jean-Jacques Rifaud explored the site to procure statues for the antiquities market (which eventually ended up in museums in Paris, St Petersburg and Berlin). The first archaeological exploration of the city was undertaken by Auguste Mariette in 1860. Flinders Petrie excavated at the site and published some of the results of his work in 1884. In 1903–4, Alexandre Barsanti took most of the uncovered artifacts to the Cairo Museum. A systematic investigation of the site was undertaken by Pierre Montet (1928–56), and has been continued, first under the direction of Jean Yoyotte (1965–86) and later by Philippe Brissaud (from 1987 onward).

Initially, the great number of architectural elements and statues inscribed with the cartouches of Ramesses II and Merenptah found at Tanis prompted its identification with Pi-Ramesses, the capital of the Ramesside state. The discovery of the famous "Stela of the Year 400" also suggested an identification with the Hyksos capital, Avaris. It eventually became clear that no datable buildings were earlier than the Third Intermediate Period, and all of the Ramesside monuments, which included a number of Middle Kingdom sculptures, must have been usurped by later kings. The discovery at the neighboring sites of Qantir and Tell ed-Dab'a of the remains of a city identified as the actual Pi-Ramesses/Avaris led to the conclusion that the Ramesside monuments were brought from there to Tanis. Manfred Bietak has indicated that the probable reason for moving the capital from Pi-Ramesses to Tanis was that at the end of the New Kingdom the Pelusiac branch of the Nile was silted up, thus cutting off the Ramesside capital from access to the river and the sea. Labib Habachi has also suggested that the Third Intermediate Period loathing for the god Seth could have been reason enough to forsake Pi-Ramesses.

The most conspicuous archaeological features of Tanis are the remains of its temples and the royal necropolis. Temples of the Theban triad, consisting of the main temple of Amen, a temple of Khonsu, a temple of Mut and Khonsu Pachered, and a sacred lake, were evidently patterned on analogous monuments in Thebes. The Theban prototype is also stressed by the absence of local connotations in the inscriptions: Amen, Mut and Khonsu bear their typical Theban epithets, and Theban place-names occur more frequently than the name Tanis itself. The parallel is further enhanced by the moving of the seat of the royal necropolis from Thebes to Tanis in the 21st and 22nd Dynasties.

Tanis was the main royal residence during the 21st Dynasty, and remained a royal residence alongside Bubastis during the 22nd Dynasty. Evidence from the end of the 22nd Dynasty to the beginning of the 26th Dynasty, however, is scarce. In the Late and Ptolemaic periods, the city was the capital of Nome XIX of Lower Egypt. A phase of intense building activity began with the 30th Dynasty and extended well into the Ptolemaic period.

The limestone structures of the Tanis temples have suffered greatly from lime-making activities and robbing of the stones for use elsewhere. In general, only the granite parts of the above-ground structures have survived. However, the practice of building underground mudbrick retaining walls, to prevent the sand foundations for the buildings from sliding, has made it possible to recognize the ground plans of many of the structures. The foundation deposits associated with them, when preserved and not anonymous, have provided the most important source of information on the names of individual builders. The decrease in size of mudbricks from the 21st Dynasty to Ptolemaic times provides yet another criterion for dating, though not an error-proof one.

Three temple enclosures have been located. The best known and best investigated area comprises a northern precinct occupied by several temples, and a southern precinct, the so-called temple of Anat. In 1988, the remains of another temple precinct were unearthed at the south end of the tell (Tulûl el-Bêd).

The northern precinct is surrounded by two mudbrick enclosure walls. The inner one dates to the reign of Psusennes I, which is demonstrated by stamps on the mudbricks. The roughly rectangular outer enclosure wall, intersecting the inner one to the north and west, has been dated to the 30th Dynasty on the basis of the size of its mudbricks. The monumental pylon gateway of Sheshonk III (22nd Dynasty), the only one of granite, led into Psusennes I's enclosure. It was largely made of reused blocks from monuments of Ramesses II, as well as from Old and Middle Kingdom ones. The lower reliefs depict Sheshonk III before the Theban triad and other deities. To the east, in the outer enclosure wall, is the pylon of Ptolemy I Soter, on the axis of the temple of Horus. Two more pylons of uncertain date are located in the east and north walls of Psusennes I's enclosure.

The ground plan of the main temple (220 × 72 m), which was dedicated to the god Amen, is still recognizable. A limestone wall of Nectanebo I (30th Dynasty) delimits it to the east, and two foundation deposits of Osorkon II (22nd Dynasty) mark its northwest and southwest corners. Four pairs of large obelisks of Ramesses II marked the position of three pylons. In what was presumably the second courtyard, the remains of four sandstone colossi of Ramesses II were found, as well as maned sphinxes of Amenemhat III (12th Dynasty). A total of twenty-six obelisks, all but one of Ramesses II, were found in the temple. The central area of the temple, lying behind the large obelisks marking the pylons, has yielded thirteen stelae of Ramesses II, including the "Stela of the Year 400," as well as most of the 12th and 13th Dynasty sculptures and the remains of pillars, columns and lintels bearing inscriptions of King Siamen (21st Dynasty).

At right angles to the main temple, along a north–south axis, lies another temple whose ground plan is perceivable in the mudbrick retaining walls of the foundation. The temple was dedicated to Khonsu, and was built by Nectanebo I and his successor Teos over an earlier building, which is evidenced here by baboon statues with dedications to Khonsu by Psusennes I. Numerous blocks of Sheshonk V from the earlier temple were reused in the masonry of the sacred lake, along with blocks from a jubilee (*heb-sed*) hall of this king.

The walls of the basin of the sacred lake, in the northeast corner of the inner enclosure, also contained numerous limestone blocks from older buildings at Tanis dating from the Middle Kingdom (i.e. reused for the second time) to the 26th Dynasty (fragments of a relief depicting a procession of the nomes of Upper and Lower Egypt led by King Psamtik I).

In the outer enclosure, outside of the southeast corner of the inner enclosure wall on the axis of the east portal of Ptolemy I Soter, is a

Ptolemaic temple whose ground-plan is still recognizable. It was apparently dedicated to Horus of Mesen, whose cult was on the island of Sile. Just east of the temple of Amen, between the two enclosure walls, are the remains of the so-called "east temple." Its only vestiges are the fragments of ten granite columns with palm capitals, originally from an Old Kingdom temple usurped by Ramesses II and then again by Osorkon II.

Other constructions in the northern enclosure include a large mudbrick building of uncertain purpose to the north of the main temple, a bronze workshop, a pottery kiln, pools, the royal tombs, and mudbrick structures of several phases of the Ptolemaic period, to the south of the temple and extending west over the royal tombs. In one of these structures, a remarkable statue of the falcon god Hauron protecting Ramesses II as a child was found. Hauron, like Anat, was one of several Canaanite gods worshipped in Pi-Ramesses. Northwest of the tomb of Sheshonk III, under the remains of Graeco-Roman mudbrick structures, a building erected in the 30th Dynasty has yielded amulets and dozens of Demotic papyri dating to the 30th Dynasty and early Ptolemaic period. Some of these are unreadable, but others contain accounts and lists of persons.

The southern precinct is delimited by a rectangular enclosure, and consists of a single building, called the "temple of Anat" because of the reused statue groups of Ramesses II with the goddess Anat, as well as the goddesses Uto and Sachmis. The post-Ramesside remains, however, indicate that it must have been a temple of Mut and Khonsu Pachered (Khonsu the Child). The main entrance to the enclosure was through the north pylon built by Siamen, on the axis of the temple. Between the pylon and the temple lie the remains of a Ptolemaic kiosk. The only visible above-ground structures of the temple are the ruins of its hypostyle hall, consisting of six reused Old Kingdom columns with palm capitals of the same type as those of the "east temple." Under these columns, foundation deposits of Apries (26th Dynasty)

were found. The southern structures of the temple were built by Ptolemy IV.

The temple remains, which were discovered in the southern sector of the tell (Tulûl el-Bêd) in 1988, were surrounded by massive mudbrick walls. This temple was completely dismantled at the beginning of the Ptolemaic period, and was presumably replaced by another building which has yet to be found. Statues of private persons found here, including two of musicians, indicate that it was the site of a temple of Amenemope, dating to the 21st Dynasty and still in use in the Late and Ptolemaic periods.

See also

New Kingdom, overview; Qantir/Pi-Ramesses; Tell Basta; Tell ed-Dab'a, Second Intermediate Period; Third Intermediate Period, overview

Further reading

Brissaud, P., ed. 1987. *Cahiers de Tanis* 1 (Éditions Recherche sur les Civilisations, Mémoire 75). Paris.
Montet, P. 1952. *Les énigmes de Tanis*. Paris.
Römer, M. 1986. Tanis. In *LÄ* 6: 194–209.
For an up-to-date bibliography of the ongoing excavations at Tanis, see the *Bullétin périodique de la Société française des Fouilles de Tanis*, 1988–.

FEDERICO POOLE

Tanis, royal tombs

The royal tombs of the 21st and 22nd Dynasties lie at the southwest corner of the great temple of Amen at Tanis, within the inner enclosure wall built by Psusennes I (21st Dynasty), inaugurating the practice in the Third Intermediate and Late periods of burials inside temple precincts. They were discovered in 1939 by Pierre Montet under the remains of mudbrick houses of the Late and Ptolemaic periods, and their exploration has continued to the present, under the direction of Montet, followed by Jean Yoyotte

(1965–86) and Philippe Brissaud (from 1987 onward). The area was already used as a necropolis in earlier times, as simple inhumations with poor grave goods (some arbitrarily interpreted by Montet as human sacrifices), stratigraphically earlier than the royal tombs, have also been recovered.

The royal tombs (nine have been recorded to date) consist of subterranean buildings of limestone and granite, much of which was taken from monuments at Pi-Ramesses made of reused blocks, both Ramesside and earlier. The majority of the sarcophagi show evidence of usurpation. The use of heavy stone beams for the ceilings of burial chambers, as well as the discovery of an offering table of Psusennes I, indicate that the tombs originally had superstructures, of which there are few traces.

Tomb 3 (the numbers refer to the order of discovery), which belonged to Psusennes I, was found intact after the last secondary burial. It consisted of a limestone antechamber, two granite burial chambers enclosed by a limestone wall, and two limestone chambers. The remains of the king were in the northern granite chamber (which was decorated with funerary texts and reliefs, including a hymn to Re-Horakhty), in a usurped, hawk-headed granite sarcophagus originally made for King Merenptah (19th Dynasty). In the sarcophagus was a black granite coffin and a silver inner coffin holding the mummy of the king with its rich jewelry. The chamber was closed by a granite plug and remained undisturbed until its discovery, although humidity damaged or destroyed some of the grave goods. Near the coffin lay an animal skeleton, vessels, the king's *shawabti*s (servant figures), canopic jars for his viscera, and other grave goods. The contents of the burial chamber are now in the Cairo Museum.

The southern granite chamber, also inscribed and decorated with reliefs, was made for Queen Mutnedjemet, the mother of Psusennes I, but was appropriated by the latter's successor, King Amenemope, whose remains were in a silver inner coffin. Amenemope's gilt wooden coffin remained in the front part of the chamber because it was too large to fit in a usurped granite sarcophagus. This burial and its grave

goods were also undisturbed. A limestone burial chamber was added for the prince and high official, Ankhefenmut, a son of Psusennes I. There was apparently a project to usurp his chamber as well, as his name was deleted from the walls and the sarcophagus was found empty. A fourth chamber within the limestone walls, but unconnected to the antechamber, was the burial place of a high official of Psusennes I, Wendjebawendjedet. It was decorated with funerary reliefs depicting the deceased with several gods and contained his canopic jars and a usurped granite anthropoid coffin of the New Kingdom, which was coated with plaster and gold leaf (badly preserved) for the added funerary texts and figures of the new owner. In this chamber were the remains of a gilt wooden coffin and a silver inner coffin, artifacts in gold and silver, various ornaments and weapons, and the mummy with its sumptuous coverings and jewelry. The rest of Wendjebawendjedet's grave goods were in the tomb's antechamber. Those bearing his name included a vase, small bronze artifacts and *circa* 360 faïence *shawabti*s and some of bronze, as well as their model tools.

The mummy of Sheshonk II (22nd Dynasty), also richly ornamented, lay in the antechamber, in a falcon-headed coffin of electrum, to the sides of which were the scanty remains of two mummies in gilt wooden coffins. In the antechamber were piles of artifacts: gilt bronze necklaces, vessels, canopic jars, small artifacts of faïence and bronze (including model implements for *shawabti*s), and *shawabti*s of Wendjebawendjedet (see previous paragraph) and Sheshonk II. There were also two groups of statuettes (360 and 400 in number) of Siamen and a different Psusennes (probably Psusennes II), the last two kings of the 21st Dynasty.

Tomb 1 consists of three limestone rooms (an anteroom and two chambers) decorated with funerary reliefs (notably some extracts from the *Book of Amduat*) executed for Osorkon II (22nd Dynasty), and a large granite burial chamber, also decorated. The asymmetrical plan of the adjoining Tomb 3 of Psusennes I indicates that Tomb 1, later appropriated and renovated by Osorkon II, was built before the later modifications of Tomb 3, still under Psusennes I, and might be earlier than Tomb 3 altogether. Hence, it has tentatively been identified as the tomb of Smendes, the founder of the 21st Dynasty. The tomb had been broken into and partially plundered in antiquity. The huge uninscribed granite sarcophagus in the granite chamber contained the badly preserved remains of three mummies with some of their jewelry and amulets, including Osorkon II's heart scarab, while his *shawabti*s and canopic jars were in the chamber. Fragments of more of the king's *shawabti*s, presumably intentionally broken, were found in a deposit in front of the tomb entrance. The chamber was reopened and enlarged to accommodate the richly decorated mummy of Osorkon II's nine/ten-year-old son, the High Priest of Amen-Re-sonter, Hornakht, in a granite sarcophagus and silver inner coffin (destroyed by humidity), and accompanied by canopic jars and *shawabti*s. The walls of this chamber are decorated with funerary scenes, some carved and others painted on plaster, which are now nearly destroyed.

Much later, King Takelot II of the 22nd Dynasty was buried in the southernmost limestone chamber. Inscriptions and scenes painted on plaster (of which nothing remains) were added for him over Osorkon II's original reliefs. The chamber and coffin, which still contained bones and the remains of the mummy coverings, were plundered in antiquity. Grave goods, including Takelot's *shawabti*s, canopic jars and vessels, still lay near the coffin.

Tomb 2, which consists of a limestone chamber preceded by a shaft, is anonymous and undecorated. It contained a large limestone sarcophagus, canopic jars and other remains of grave goods. The tomb was built in two phases, before and after the adjacent tomb of Osorkon II was constructed.

Tomb 4, also a single limestone chamber, contained a granite sarcophagus and some thirty *shawabti*s inscribed with the name of King Amenemope, whose remains were moved to the tomb of Psusennes I, presumably after having been buried first in this tomb. In the outer coffin was an unidentified mummy in a wooden coffin. Very little remains of this secondary burial, as the tomb was plundered in antiquity and remained open.

Tomb 5, consisting of a burial chamber preceded by a shaft, was for the burial of Sheshonk III, but contained a canopic jar and a heart scarab of Sheshonk I, who was possibly buried here. The chamber is decorated with funerary reliefs (extracts of the *Book of the Night*). Some of the masonry consisted of reused blocks from tombs built for a family of officials of Psusennes I.

Tomb 6 is of very uncertain date, possibly the beginning of the 22nd Dynasty. It now consists of a single chamber, but there is evidence suggesting that it once may have had more. Tomb 7 is an anonymous limestone chamber, later in date than that of Psusennes I, as evidenced by a reused lintel with the king's name. It was destroyed when construction was undertaken for Osorkon II's tomb.

See also

funerary texts; jewelry; Libyans; mortuary beliefs; New Kingdom, overview; Qantir/Pi-Ramesses; Third Intermediate Period, overview

Further reading

Arnold, D., and E. Hornung. 1980. Königsgrab. In *LÄ* 3: 495–514.

Brissaud, P., ed. 1987. *Cahiers de Tanis* 1 (Éditions Recherche sur les Civilisations, Mémoire 75). Paris.

Montet, P. 1947–1960. *La nécropole royale de Tanis, Fouilles de Tanis dirigées par Pierre Montet*, 3 vols. Paris.

Römer, M. 1986. Tanis. *LÄ* 6: 194–209.

For an up-to-date bibliography of the ongoing excavations at Tanis, see the *Bullétin périodique de la Société française des Fouilles de Tanis*, 1988–.

FEDERICO POOLE

Taposiris Magna

The ruins of the ancient Hellenistic and Roman

city of Taposiris Magna, modern Abusir (30°57′ N, 29°31′ E), are situated 45 km west of Alexandria and about 0.5 km south of the Mediterranean shore in the modern province of Matruh. The city stood at the navigable limit of the now dried-out bed (over a meter below sea level) of the western arm of ancient Lake Mareotis. Through the lake, Taposiris could communicate directly with the Nile via the Canopic branch, with the Red Sea through the canal of Darius and with the Mediterranean Sea by a short overland haul. Since Callisthenes tells us that Alexander the Great visited Taposiris on his way to the Oasis of Siwa, there must have been a town here before the Hellenistic period. Unfortunately, the few excavations that have taken place on the site have not penetrated to the earlier levels.

The size of the lake harbor lends credence to Taposiris Magna's presumed role in the trade between Egypt and Libya. Merchandise and travelers heading west from Egypt would make use of the easier water transportation as far as Taposiris and then go on by caravan trail, while merchandise and travelers from Libya and western parts of the nome would be shipped aboard boats at Taposiris, headed for towns in the interior of Egypt. From a military point of view, it was the westernmost harbor facility of sufficient size to handle a fleet; war ships were stationed on the lake, at least in Ptolemaic times.

Traces of an extensive irrigation system and findings of carbonized seeds in stratified levels during the excavations in 1975 indicate the lushness of the surrounding grain fields and orchards. The entire region was famous for its wines, while the lake supported a wide variety of freshwater fish. The bird population was great enough to make fowling a popular sport. Lake Mareotis was a popular resort area during the Graeco-Roman period.

Atop the Taenia Ridge, an outcropping of limestone which separates the sea from the ancient bed of Lake Mareotis, stand two ancient monuments which were partly restored in the 1930s and early 1940s. One is a tower that has been used as a model in the reconstruction of the Pharos lighthouse of Alexandria, and the other is the remains of a temple generally

believed to have been dedicated to Osiris. These two monuments dominate the horizon for several kilometers in every direction and, like most buildings at Taposiris Magna, are constructed of limestone quarried from the ridge.

The Taposiris Magna tower rises in three dissimilar stages to a preserved height of 127 m on the ridge. A solid podium 10.75 m sq. provides a level surface for an octagonal stage, which in turn supports a cylinder on a low socle. A narrow stairway on the north side of the octagon, in combination with a spiral staircase in the cylinder, gave access to the top. The tower is built over a rock-cut underground chamber in the middle of a cemetery; for this reason, the monument has been called by some a funerary monument even though the contemporaneity of the the tower and subterranean apartment is not certain. Others prefer to see the structure as a lighthouse built atop the ridge to warn mariners of the rocky headland, or as the one extant link in a hypothetical chain of signal towers extending across the North African coast as far west as Cyrene. The remains of the "temple of Osiris" crown the ridge about 400 m to the west of the tower and consist today of a massive enclosure wall 4 m thick at the base, forming a rectangle measuring 92 × 86 m. The enclosure has three entrances: two narrow doorways placed opposite one another in the north and south walls, and a wider opening between two large pylon towers fronting the structure on the east. A small doorway in the back of each tower leads to a series of chambers on two levels connected by a stairway to the top. No trace remains of the temple proper that presumably stood inside the enclosure. In the early Christian period a church was built inside the enclosure at the east, almost blocking the main gate. The original plan of the church was T-shaped and included an apse and small sacristy flanked by rectangular side chapels. At a later date a narthex was added to the west end, which extended around both sides of the nave. The church and rows of cells built up against three sides of the Ptolemaic enclosure may have served the monastic community that is known to have existed at Taposiris Magna.

In the one place where the area at the foot of the Taenia Ridge on the lake side was explored in 1975, it was clear that its smooth, vertical face had been purposely and sharply cut back in antiquity. Monuments, probably of funerary character, were built on artificially leveled terraces at the end of the third or first half of the second century BC. Four rock-cut chamber tombs were excavated between the tower and nearby Kom el-Nagus by Raschid Anwar in the 1930s, but the results have never been published and the tomb inventories have disappeared. Some of the burial niches are decorated with extremely fine painting or architectural detail; several can be dated stylistically to the early Christian period.

South of the ridge, the land falls away to a more gently inclined area where the remains of numerous buildings comprising the major portion of the ancient town are easily discernable. The town, whose eastern edge is not clearly defined, is delimited on the west by a wall about 2 m thick. This wall originally extended from the sea to Lake Mareotis, providing the inhabitants with a barrier against attack and a means of controlling traffic along the ridge. Constructed of small blocks of locally quarried limestone, it is preserved only in its lower courses. A section of a broad street originating perhaps from a gate at the wall's southern end can still be traced. Preliminary investigations suggest that it belonged to a system of streets and avenues in a grid plan whose orientation was apparently determined by the direction of the ridge, and the slope of the ground below. A narrow embankment is joined to the southern-most projecting spit of habitation by a bridge or causeway. It stretches east for several hundred meters parallel to the shore and separates what may have been a narrow, artificially deepened channel from the larger part of the lake to the south. A shorter embankment projecting from the spur of land to the north of the bridge forms the northern bank of the channel. Both embankments contain remains of warehouses and other harbor installations.

The 1975 excavations revealed part of the drainage system that carried water from the higher slopes into the lake, a platform near the shore which may have supported a small temple and, north of the "deepened channel" at the western end of a finger-like projection of the ancient lake bed, a secular basilica built of blocks of local limestone. The fourth century AD basilica was fronted by a forecourt, originally with colonnades on two sides which led to the basilica's façade. The basilica with its forecourt is approximately 25 m long × 16.5 m wide. Somewhat later, the structure was enlarged by the addition of a large courtyard at the back, approximately 14 m long × 18 m wide.

See also

Marsa Matruh; Siwa Oasis, Late period and Graeco-Roman sites

Further reading

De Cosson, A. 1935. *Mareotis: Being a Short Account of the History and Ancient Monuments of the North-western Desert of Egypt and of Lake Mareotis*, esp. 109–14, 201 ff. London.

——. 1941. Notes on the Coast Road between Alexandria and Mersa Matruh. *Bulletin de la Société royale d'archéologie d'Alexandrie* 34: 48–61.

Ochsenschlager, E. 1979. Taposiris Magna: 1975 Season. *First International Congress of Egyptology, Acts* (Schriften zur Geschichte und Kultur des alten Orients 14), 503–6. Berlin.

Oliver, F.W., and A. de Cosson. 1938. Note on the Taenia Ridge. *Bulletin de la Société royale d'archéologie d'Alexandrie* 32: 162–75.

EDWARD L. OCHSENSCHLAGER

taxation and conscription

The ancient Egyptian government met its needs for food, raw materials, manufactured goods and labor through taxation and conscription. The pre-market, essentially moneyless Egyptian economy was structured so that the residents of the Nile Valley provided support for the king and other government institutions while at the same time the king redistributed these essential commodities to each class on the basis of rank and status in the society. Tax is the name that modern scholars give to deliveries of these items to the government. There is no single word in ancient Egyptian for "tax." Instead there are specific names of levies based on modes of delivery of goods. Typical names of taxes include: "that which is carried" (f3i), "that which is brought" (inw), "that which is given" (rdy), and "that which is taken" (sdy). Taxation and conscription were thus an essential element of a redistributive economy in which, according to Egyptian ideology, the king owned "everything which the sun-disc encircles." The redistribution of goods and services which had been collected by the central government was the glue which held society together. When the central government lost the strength to maintain this system, there was a tendency to recreate it on a smaller scale in the nomes.

Information about taxation and conscription can be gleaned concerning government estimates of its resources, collection of taxes through the nomarchs, and tax exemptions. Some classes of individuals were exempt from taxation, as were those who lived in certain tax havens such as pyramid towns, where priests, administrators and workers attached to the cults of the royal funerary monuments lived. The system of labor conscription and the punishments for avoiding it are also revealed in government records, exemption decrees, temple records, and depictions of tax collection in temples and tombs. The evidence for reconstructing the system of conscription includes inscriptions about the phyle system of labor (rotating periods of service), and documents which record criminal prosecution of those who avoided or escaped from service.

From earliest times, the government conducted an inventory on the wealth of Egypt, presumably to set taxation goals and estimate its wealth. Wealth was counted primarily in terms of the number of cattle, but there is evidence for counts of land, other objects of value and people. Inscriptions on the Palermo Stone refer to biannual cattle counts as early as the 2nd Dynasty, and also a count of "gold and the fields." The 6th Dynasty tomb biography of Weni refers to a count of "everything which can be counted," probably including people for conscription.

The nomarchs (local governors) were responsible for actual delivery of taxes to the central government. The nomarch Ameny of the Gazelle Nome (Beni Hasan), who lived in the late 11th or early 12th Dynasty, succinctly described the process in his tomb biography:

I spent years as Lord of the Gazelle Nome; all levies for the Palace were made through me. The Overseer of the Cattle House of the Gazelle Nome gave to me 3,000 steers as their Cattle levy. I was praised because of it in the Palace. I took the entire levy to the palace and there were no arrears against me in any of its departments.

Residents of Old Kingdom pyramid towns were exempted from many taxes as well as conscription. A series of decrees found at Dahshur, Giza and Quft (Coptos) all exempt various classes of priests and other workers at the royal funeral monuments from paying specific kinds of taxes and from conscription for other kinds of work. This must have been an incentive to remain at work in the pyramid towns, though why such an incentive was needed is not clear. Perhaps kings wanted to insure against removal of those charged with maintaining the funeral cult which was to keep them alive forever in the afterlife. Exemption from the cattle levy, however, is notably absent from these exemption decrees. This may point to the importance of this particular type of levy to maintaining the central government.

Labor was provided to the government though a system of conscription, which may have originated in late prehistoric times. This was the chief source of labor for construction projects, maintenance of the irrigation system, agricultural work on crown administered lands, and expeditions outside of Egypt for raw materials. To some extent, this labor was organized by the phyle system. During the Old Kingdom, this system divided at least some Egyptians into five groups of workers. Each group had a name: the "Great Phyle," the "Eastern Phyle," the "Green Phyle," the "Little Phyle," and the "Perfection Phyle." Each phyle name probably made reference to its protective deity. In the Middle Kingdom there were only four phyles, each known by number. The numbers might refer to the season of the year when the phyle served. The evidence for phyles in the New Kingdom is much less specific. A different system of gangs, as seen at Deir el-Medina, may indicate a reorganization of the labor force at this time. Workers were initiated into a phyle, possibly at puberty. There is some evidence that circumcision marked entrance into a phyle. Each phyle did government service for a specific amount of time each year. The amount of time seems to have varied with the kind of labor performed. Many of the phyle rotations seem to have been monthly. During this period, workers received rations and lodging, possibly generous enough to help support their families for part of the year.

The ancient Egyptians identified two major crimes associated with avoiding conscription: failure to arrive at work and flight from a place of work. The punishments for these crimes were very severe. The family of the offender was sometimes forced to work in his place while he performed state labor for an indefinite period of time. Each prisoner's case seems to have been reviewed after ten years of servitude. In seventy-eight of eighty cases known from the late Middle Kingdom, the prisoner was then released.

The Egyptian capacity to organize people and materials for a common goal is clearly revealed in their taxation and conscription system. It provided a stable means of providing food, raw materials and finished goods to much of the population. Though modern viewers must avoid romanticizing the notion of redistribution, it is clear that long-lasting social solidarity could be built out of a system that emphasized reciprocal responsibilities of the government and the governed.

See also

administrative bureaucracy; Deir el-Medina

Further reading

Helck, H.W. 1972. Abgaben und Steuern. In *LÄ* 1: 3–12.

Quirke, S. 1990. *The Administration of Egypt in the Late Middle Kingdom: The Hieratic Documents*. New Malden.

Roth, A.M. 1991. *Egyptian phyles in the Old Kingdom: the evolution of a system of social organization*. Chicago.

EDWARD BLEIBERG

Tell el-Amarna, city

The site of Tell el-Amarna (27°38′ N, 30°53′ E) is on the east bank of the Nile 312 km south of Cairo, in what was Nome XV of Upper Egypt. The modern name, correctly el-Amarna, as there is no prominent tell or mound, is a compound formed from the name of the village of et-Till and the name of the Beni Amran tribe that had settled in the area. The name possibly is influenced by the name of another village, el-Amariya. The ancient name of the site is Akhetaten, "Horizon of the Aten [sun-disc]" denoting the whole district, and probably Per Aten ("House of the Aten") for the city itself, as well as the principal temple.

The remains were briefly visited by the French expedition under Napoleon, but the first serious survey was by J.G. Wilkinson in 1824. Richard Lepsius and Wilkinson also mapped the city ruins. Flinders Petrie excavated at Tell el-Amarna in the 1890s, followed by Urbain Bouriant and Alexandre Barsanti, after which Norman de Garis Davies recorded the tomb inscriptions and boundary stelae texts for the Egypt Exploration Fund in 1901–7. A German expedition under Ludwig Borchardt did further work on the town in 1911–14, and the Egypt Exploration Society a great deal more, 1921–36. Finally in the 1960s the Egyptian Antiquities Organization worked at Kom el-Nana and the Egypt Exploration Society under Barry Kemp has been excavating and surveying at the site since 1977.

There is little evidence for occupation at the

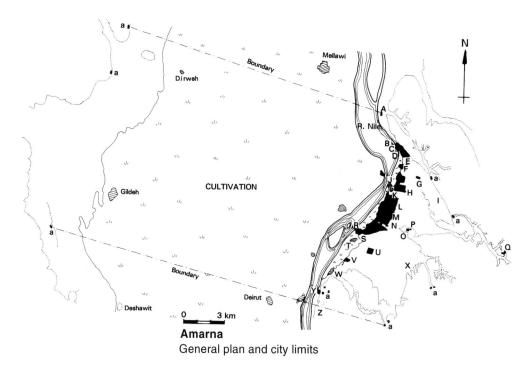

Amarna
General plan and city limits

Amarna

A, north city limits; B, customs house; C, great wall; D, east palace; E, north city;
F, north palace; G, altars; H, north suburbs; I, northern tombs; J, et Till; K, Esbi;
L, great temple area; M, palace; N, main city; O, tomb chapels; P, workmen's village;
Q, royal wadi; R, river temple;   S, Hagg Qandil; T, El Amarea; U, royal enclosure;
V, Maru-Aten; W, Hawata; X, southern tombs; Y, southern entrance; Z, south city limits.

Figure 109 Tell el-Amarna, general plan and city limits

site before Akhenaten chose it as the site for his new capital. Akhetaten was essentially a royal residence and religious center, rather than a capital in the modern sense like Memphis or Thebes. To understand its purpose, it is necessary to recall the great new city foundation of Amenhotep III in western Thebes, Tehen Aten (Splendor of the Aten). Both had an official central area called Per Hai (House of Rejoicing), with temples and palaces used for the royal jubilees (*heb-sed*), and other features such as the Maru Amen and Maru Aten pleasure complexes.

The city of Akhetaten seems to have been partially occupied from at least year 5 of Akhenaten's reign and endured until the mid-

dle, if not the end, of Tutankhamen's reign. A reused stone block and a statue base indicate a temple still existed at Tell el-Amarna under Horemheb, and possibly later, as a jar inscription of Seti I attests. Reused *talatat* blocks in the pylons and buildings of Ramesses II at el-Ashmunein, and possibly at Antinoopolis, show when the city was probably dismantled. Finally, a few 22nd and 23rd Dynasty burials in the workmen's village suggest a slight reoccupation in the later pharaonic period, while Roman houses and a large cemetery in the North Suburb were followed by a late Roman fort and the conversion of Tomb 6 into a church by Christians.

The foundation ceremonies for Akhetaten

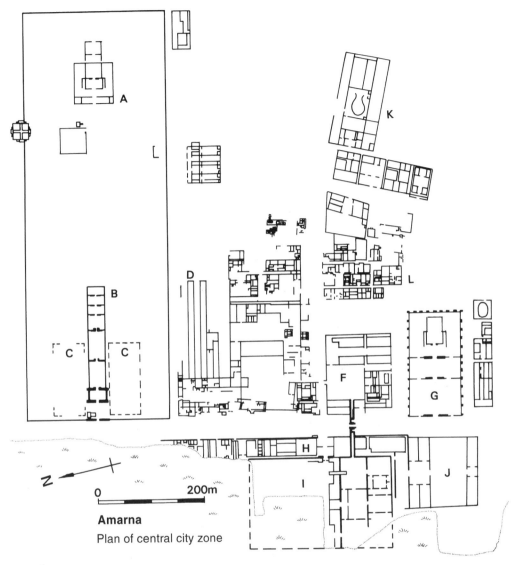

Amarna

Plan of central city zone

Amarna

A, Sanctuary; B, Gem Aten; C, offering tables; D, stores; E, High Priest's house;
F, private palace; G, Hwt Aten temple; H, harim , I, major temple complex;
J, coronation hall; K, military & police headquarters; L, records office.

Figure 110 Tell el-Amarna, plan of the central city zone

are recorded on fourteen great boundary stelae (2.5–8.0 m in height) that define the city and surrounding district. These have two main texts, dated to years 4 and 6, and an added one of year 8 of Akhenaten; in some cases, additional sculptured figures appear at the sides. Six of them defined an area of mainly agricultural land approximately 19 km east–west by 12.5 km north–south, that was intended to supply the city. The actual city remains occupy the eastern edge of this zone measuring about 9–10 km north–south by an average of 1 km east–west, rising to 1.5 km in the central area. While this area is broken up by wadis (valleys) and areas without construction, the built-up portions were on an imperial scale, covering up to 1,200 ha. This was divided into sectors by three great parallel roads running north–south, the Sikhet es-Sultan or King's Road (up to 40 m wide) being the most important. Other east–west streets crossed the north–south thoroughfares to create a rough grid plan.

Going from north to south, the first sector of the city near the northern boundary hills contained an important administrative building blocking the access road. This building has been called the "customs house" by its excavators. The northern sector also contained some large houses and the Great North Palace. This palace was guarded by double walls stretching for hundreds of meters along the west of the road and entered by a ceremonial gate. A great ramp on the east side of the road might have led to a bridge across the highway or

0   1 m

Figure 111 Tell el-Amarna, Stela N

simply served the associated granaries. To the south lay the North Palace (145 × 115 m), containing an aviary court and animal pens for the royal pets, as well as ceremonial halls, a large central pool and a shrine to the Aten. The north suburb contained 298 houses of all sizes and classes. As usual, the better ones had outbuildings and a garden set within an outer walled enclosure.

The central city was the only fully planned part of Akhetaten, being laid out on a grid system that covered about 1100 × 900 m. This sector may have been called "The Island of the Aten" or, more likely, Per Hai ("House of Rejoicing"). East of the King's Road lay the Great Temple composed of two stone buildings in a vast 800 m long mudbrick-walled enclosure. The western building, called Gem Aten ("Finding the Aten," 180 × 30 m) consisted of a series of open courts and sanctuaries behind the entrance pylon and first columned hall. Hundreds of offering tables were placed within or to either side of it, apparently for mass open air worship by the court. Some distance to the east lay the Ḥwt Benben ("House of the Benben," about 30–35 m²), a solar shrine containing a cult pillar (benben). It stood on a gypsum plaster or concrete platform whose embankments average 1 m above ground level and 6 m wide, with a gentle sloping angle to the mudbrick pavement.

To the south lay many storerooms and temple adjuncts, then a smaller more private palace of the king, followed by a more compact temple, the Ḥwt Aten (House of the Aten). This again consisted of a stone building round an open court (about 35 m²) set in a 200 m long enclosure surrounded by a heavily buttressed mudbrick wall, approached through a series of mudbrick pylon gateways. It was the nearest thing to a royal funerary temple at Akhetaten. Behind were the official administrative buildings, including the so-called Foreign Office where the famous Amarna Letters on cuneiform tablets were found, the "House of Life" or scribal department, military police quarters and stables, as well as the official house of the High Priest. The trash dumps in this area yielded many interesting smaller artifacts.

The whole area to the west of the road as far as the river bank was originally occupied by the so-called Great Palace (450 × 200 m). Of this complex, 4 ha was taken up by the most monumental group of stone buildings and courts in the city, which were mainly decorated with religious scenes and royal statuary like a temple. Great emphasis was placed on plant and vegetable decoration in the architectural ornamentation, and incredibly rich colored materials were used on a far greater scale than in previous reigns. The main court had a great portico with columns over 10 m high occupying the center of the south side, this being decorated with colored glass and faïence inlays set in gilded cloisons like gigantic jewelry, an innovative feature found in other royal buildings at Akhetaten.

The palace and harim buildings proper were alongside on the east by the road, with garden courts and halls decorated with rich plaster work and more inlaid columns. The Tell el-Amarna artists brought outdoors within, floors being painted to resemble flower gardens and pools of water with fish in them and birds hovering above, while columns were covered with green faïence tilework imitating bundles of reed stalks. Ceilings would have shown skies with birds flying across. The ceremonial routes followed by visitors to the king's throne dais were decorated with captive figures of foreign peoples and bows symbolizing the traditional Nine Bows, or peoples of the world. The king's feet thus stepped over them as a sign of universal rule. Domestic scenes of the inhabitants of the palace were also featured, servants being shown sweeping up or about other household duties. A bridge over a triple archway gate spanned the royal road and connected this harim to the private palace on the east. To the south a huge new hall complex (150 m long) was added, possibly for the coronation of King Smenkhkare, although some scholars would rather see it as a pleasure unit, judging from its painted vine decorations. The main hall (126 × 73 m) had 510 mudbrick pillars arranged in thirty rows, being ornamented with gaily colored ceramic tiles with daisy flower inlays.

The south quarter of the main city was the

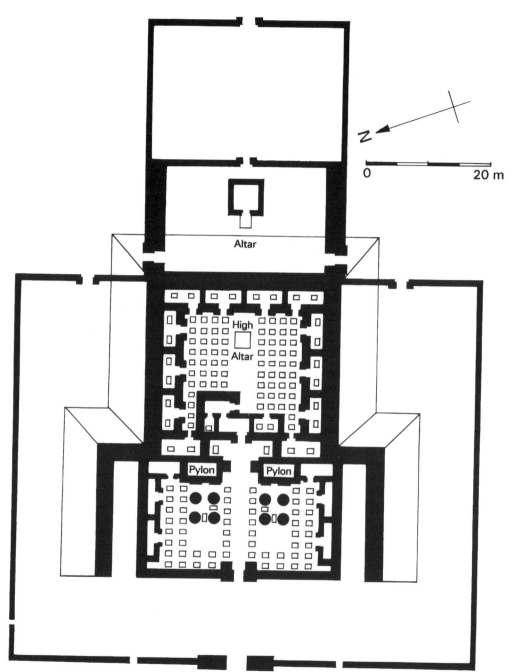

Figure 112 Tell el-Amarna, restored plan of the Great Temple sanctuary

chief occupational area containing administrative buildings, workshop areas like that of the sculptor Tuthmose who produced the famous head of Nefertiti, and innumerable houses. A typical house is that of the vizier Nakht (35 × 26 m) with thirty rooms on the ground floor arranged round a lofty central hall. The more southern sectors are not fully known, but the "River Temple," possibly a palace, was inhabited after the city's decline, possibly under Ramesses III or even later. The Maru Aten (Viewing Place of the Aten), sited further from the river, was both a pleasure and religious complex arranged in two adjoining enclosures (215 × 110 m and 156 × 85 m). The larger northern enclosure had a series of pavilions scattered round a large lake (120 × 60 m) with a group of stone kiosk temples on an island in a smaller pool. One of these kiosks is called the "Sunshade" of Meritaten, the king's eldest daughter, although originally it may have been built for the king's wife Kiya.

To the east of the city is the workmen's village (70 m square), surrounded by a thin wall only 75–80 cm thick. It was laid out in two separate quarters with seventy-three houses, including that of the overseer. Like their prototypes at Deir el-Medina, these units are tripartite in plan and built in blocks. In the vicinity are a number of mudbrick-built tomb chapels and animal pens. Another village built of rough stone housed the men when they were actually working on the tombs. Finally, there are three cemeteries in the eastern hills, the north and south groups. These are generally incomplete and few were used before the city was abandoned by the majority of its inhabitants. The tombs contain columns and statues in standard Theban form, but their scenes only depict daily life, and that mainly at court and in the temples.

See also

Amarna Letters; Antinoopolis; el-Ashmunein; Deir el-Medina; New Kingdom, overview; Tuna el-Gebel

Further reading

Borchardt, L., and H. Ricke. 1980. *Die Wöhnhäuser in Tell el-Amarna* (Wissenschaftliche Veröffentlichung der Deutschen Orient-Gesellschaft 91). Berlin.

Frankfort, H., J.D.S. Pendlebury and H.W. Fairman. 1933. *The City of Akhenaten* II. London.

Kemp, B.J., *et al.* 1984–9. *Amarna Reports* 2–5. London.

Murnane, W.J., and C.C. Van Siclen III. 1993. *The Boundary Stelae of Akhenaten*. London.

Peet, T.E., G.B. Woolley, G.B. Gunn and F.G. Newton. 1923. *The City of Akhenaten* 1. London.

ERIC P. UPHILL

Tell el-Amarna, cult temples

Around the fifth year of his reign Akhenaten created a new city, Akhetaten (known today as Tell el-Amarna), replete with palaces, mansions, workshops and temples. Two major temples have been uncovered at Tell el-Amarna: the Per Aten (Great Temple) at the northern end of the central city and the similar, albeit smaller, Ḥwt Aten (House of the Aten) farther south along the Royal Road. The latter appears to have contained one of the first monuments erected at Tell el-Amarna: a massive mudbrick altar. Probably the earliest cultic structure erected by Akhenaten (then Amenhotep IV) is the Gem-pa-Aten at East Karnak; other shrines arose in Heliopolis, Memphis, Nubia and perhaps Sam-Behdet in the Delta.

Great Temple

The Great Temple consisted of at least two composite sanctuaries surrounded by a *temenos* wall of 300 × 800 m. In addition, other structures—including the Hall of Foreign Tribute and the butchers' yard—formed part of the complex. To the south of the Great Temple lay the official residence of the Superintendent of the Cattle of the Aten, Panehsy, and the

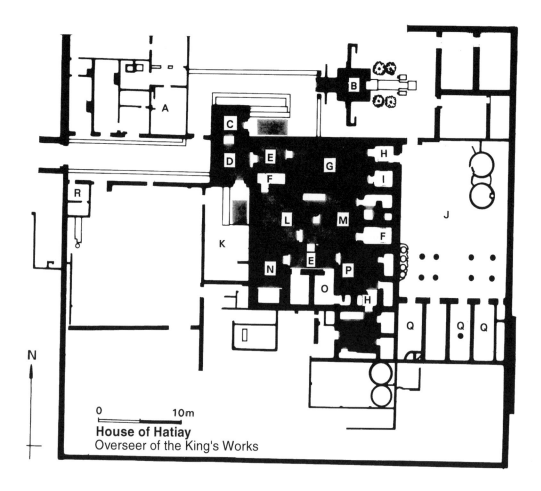

A, servants' quarters; B, chapel; C, later porch; D, earlier porch; E, vestibule;
F, store; G, north loggia; H, ante-room; I, pantry; J, kitchen court;
K, earlier entrance; L, west loggia; M, central room; N, master's bedroom;
O, anointing room; P, inner sitting room; Q, magazines;
R, gatekeeper.

Figure 113 Tell el-Amarna, plan of the house of Hatiay, Overseer of the King's Works

temple magazines, which yielded large quantities of broken bread molds. Immediately to the west of the Great Temple was the Great Palace complex.

The daily ritual celebrated in the Great Temple by the king and queen was probably very simple. A few expressions of adoration and thanksgiving were spoken to the Aten, the text of which may have been mirrored in the tomb representations of the period. The main altar was reserved for worship by the royal family, while the sea of miniature, secondary altars were used by individuals and communities to make offerings to the king and the Aten.

In the eastern part of the enclosure of the Great Temple lay the site of the oldest sanctuary, known by the excavator J.D.S. Pendlebury simply as "the Sanctuary." New work by the Egypt Exploration Society under the direction of Barry Kemp has altered our reconstructed view of the Sanctuary (and Amarna religious structures generally) from being a closed, private area to an elevated, open-air structure suited to the king's semi-public worship of the sun-disc, a scene familiar from tomb decorations. The Sanctuary was constructed on a low, elevated gypsum concrete platform and consisted of two open courts—the outer containing priests' houses—followed by two walled areas bisected by a central causeway. The walled part of the temple may have been higher and appears to have had an unconventional entrance with free-standing flag poles, rather than the usual type attached to pylons. The rear part of the Sanctuary was surrounded by a low casemate wall and contained the high altar of the Great Temple and more small offering tables.

Elusive references to the "the Mansion of the Benben in the House of the Aten" (*Hwt-Bnbn-n-Pr-Aten*) do not definitively identify the location of this structure, but Pendlebury has identified it with the Sanctuary. In this case, the *benben* stone was not the obelisk of the Heliopolitan solar cult, but rather a great stela of the king and queen worshipping the Aten.

The second composite sanctuary in the Great Temple, comprised of the Per Hai (House of Rejoicing) and the Gem Aten (Finding the Aten), may have superseded the Sanctuary in the later years at Tell el-Amarna. The Per Hai preceded the Gem Aten in a linear progression of courtyards and sanctuaries along a central axis. The Per Hai consisted of a platform with two rows of four columns on either side of the central axis. Passing through the Per Hai to the Gem Aten, there were three courtyards of similar style, but varying size, separated by pylons. Each courtyard contained numerous offering tables and to the north and south of the Per Hai and Gem Aten also lay "a forest of offering tables," approximately 1,800 in total. Following the third court there were two inner sanctuary courts reminiscent of the rear part of the Sanctuary. These sanctuary courts were surrounded by small chambers, each of which contained an offering table. At the back of each of the inner sanctuaries there was a great altar, surrounded again by many smaller offering tables.

Small Temple

The House of the Aten, or Ḥwt Aten, lay to the south of the Great Temple in a conspicuous place beside the Royal Road. Although it was built on a similar plan to the Great Temple, one key difference was the heavily buttressed wall on three sides. The House of the Aten consisted of two courtyards separated by pylons, the first of which contained the great altar, believed to date to Akhenaten's earliest days at Tell el-Amarna. The great altar was leveled during a subsequent phase of the temple's use. Following the third pylon, there was a sanctuary on a plan very similar to the Sanctuary of the Great Temple, albeit less elaborate. In the final phase, the temple had an interesting gateway consisting of a central square limestone platform, accessed on the inside by a ramp and on the outside possibly by steps. The platform may have carried a canopy or wooden doors and would have served the double function of a ceremonial entrance and a presentation place to the Royal Road outside.

Maru Aten

The Maru Aten was a religious structure intended as a "viewing place" for the Aten. Prior to the Amarna period, *maru* were known in connection with other solar gods such as Amen-Re and Horus at Thebes, Dendera, Edfu and Philae. The Maru Aten has been interpreted as an embodiment of the powers of the god, as celebrated at monthly festivals (*mswt Itn*). The two contiguous rectangular enclosure walls contained houses for officials and priests, a royal palace, a lake and a front temple. In addition, there was a so-called "Sunshade" kiosk, which may have formed part of a larger complex dedicated to the monthly festivals. Each of the eleven T-shaped contiguous flora-filled tanks, interlocking about thirteen square bases, may have represented the bounty of one month in the Aten's cultic calendar, with the kiosk representing the initial festival month. Hieratic dockets suggest that the monthly festivals may have been for the Aten's birthday.

Kom el-Nana

Another sunshade or solar shrine lay south of the main city at Tell el-Amarna on the line of the Royal Road. This structure has been identified by excavator Barry Kemp as the last unexcavated royal and ceremonial building known at Tell el-Amarna. Kom el-Nana consisted of an enclosure, surrounded by a mudbrick wall braced by square buttresses and cut by entrances flanked by pylons. The north side of the enclosure was dominated by substantial bakery–brewery facilities, while the rest consisted of religious and ceremonial buildings of stone and mudbrick. Two stone shrines contained a series of rooms behind a columned area. In addition, two sets of chambers and a columned hall containing three daises were supported by a mudbrick platform reached by ramps. Kemp has suggested that this area may have been a Window of Appearances within a sunshade dedicated to Queen Nefertiti.

Desert altars

To the northeast of the North Suburb were several altars and pavilions. The more substantial Northern and Central Altars may have had some funerary connection with the Northern Tombs, while the Southern "Altar" or pavilion may have been erected for a ceremony connected with the dedication of the northern boundary stelae.

Main Chapel, walled village

The Main Chapel is the most representative of a series of chapels found in the area of the walled (eastern) village. Perched on a shelf cut into the hillside, the Main Chapel was a sheltered cultic area with low walls, approximately 1.4 m high. The *temenos* wall enclosed a chapel proper of standard design, and an annex. The chapel consisted of two halls followed by a sanctuary with three shrines, the whole arranged symme-

trically on a central axis. The floors of the inner hall and sanctuary were taken up by low square mudbrick offering tables. All of the walls, floors and ceilings of the chapel proper were plastered and decorated with geometric friezes and elaborate floral groups. Benches lined the two principal walls of the outer hall and were commonly occupied by people eating and engaged in simple craft activities. In addition to this ordinary arrangement, there was a side chapel on the north, provided with a single shrine and two rooms containing benches.

Interesting features of the Main Chapel include the remains of possible flag poles set in gypsum at the principal entrance to the chapel and the screen walls topped by windows, which divided the chapel from east to west while allowing continuous communication between the "outer hall" and the sanctuary. Also interesting are the many narrow scratches or grooves on the floors and benches of the sanctuary, suggesting "sacred dust" may have been harvested for secondary use. The Main Chapel stands in notable contrast to the private shrines of the inhabitants of the walled village, which were dedicated mainly to Bes. Evidence of other gods is also found in the village, including Amen, Hathor, Taweret and the common eye of Horus ring-bezels.

The corpus of religious architecture of the Amarna period is comprised of a variety of different structures, including temples, "sunshades," shrines and altars. Certain features distinguish many of these buildings from the traditional ancient Egyptian religious architecture, including the fully open-air concept, the lack of cult statues and bark niches, and the presence of numerous offering tables. One of the essential elements of Amarna ceremonial architecture is the use of gypsum concrete, found, for example, in the Sanctuary, the Per Hai and the Maru Aten. The construction of cult temples at Tell el-Amarna was solid, well-designed and intended to be durable: even offering tables had foundations to desert subsoil. The obliteration of these structures required intentional and thorough activity.

See also

cult temples of the New Kingdom; cult temples, construction techniques; Karnak, Akhenaten temples; Tell el-Amarna, city

Further reading

Badawy, A. 1956. Maru-Aten: pleasure resort or temple? *JEA* 42: 58–64.

Kemp, B.J. 1987. The Amarna workmen's village in retrospect. *JEA* 73: 21–50.

——. 1991. Discovery and renewal at Amarna. *Egyptian Archaeology:* 19–22.

Pendlebury, J.D.S. 1951. *The City of Akhenaten. Part III: The Central City and the Official Quarters*, 2 vols. London.

Redford, D.B. 1984. *Akhenaten: the Heretic King*, 102 ff. Princeton, NJ.

ELSBETH WILLIAMS

Tell el-Amarna, nobles' tombs

The tombs at Tell el-Amarna are among the best known in Egypt, despite their relative inaccessibility in the eastern cliffs which enclose the Amarna plain about 3–5 km from the Nile. They were surveyed and their reliefs were copied by J.G. Wilkinson in 1824; Wilkinson and James Burton in 1826; Nestor l'Hôte, Hay and Laver in 1833; and Richard Lepsius in 1843–5. They were known to tourists and travelers from at least the mid-19th century. After Lepsius's initial survey some of the tombs were published by Urbain Bouriant and his colleagues in 1883, for the French Institute of Archaeology in Cairo. This publication includes photographs and copies of reliefs from the Royal Tomb, and the tombs of Ay and Mahu. The most complete publications are the six volumes prepared by Norman de Garis Davies for the Archaeological Survey of Egypt early in this century. Even at this time, Davies was forced to depend upon the work of earlier scholars such as Lepsius to restore missing fragments of relief. The deplorable condition of the tombs is due to several factors. The lime-

stone of the Amarna cliffs is of inferior quality and desecration occurred during Dynastic times. Coptic monks who later occupied the tombs altered and vandalized them. More recently, activity in the nearby alabaster quarry at Hatnub has also contributed to their decay.

Originally the tombs of at least forty-three officials were planned at Tell el-Amarna. Only officials of Akhenaten's regime began tombs there, and nearly all were unfinished at the time the city was abandoned, *circa* 1350 BC. There are two groups of tombs, both cut into the eastern cliffs. The northern group is situated high on the cliff face to the north of the modern village of et-Till and the desert altars of the ancient city, about 2.5 km from the river. The six officials who were buried in the most finished northern tombs were: Huya, "Steward of the Household of Queen Tiye" (Tomb 1); Meryre (called Meryre II), who was Nefertiti's steward (Tomb 2); Ahmose, the "King's Fan-Bearer" (Tomb 3); another Meryre, the High Priest (called Meryre I, in Tomb 4); Pentu, the "Royal Physician" (Tomb 5); and Panehesy, called "Chief Servitor of the Aten" (Tomb 6). Internal textual evidence shows that the tombs of Huya and Meryre were built later and are somewhat isolated, to the north of the others, which are to the south of Boundary Stela V.

Most of the tombs from the northern group are relatively simple in design, consisting of a very short entry-way, a larger hall (usually with two columns) and an inner chamber which may have contained a statue of the deceased. The columned hall is generally the most lavishly decorated area. The innermost rooms, however, are undecorated and largely unfinished. The coffin and intimate funerary equipment would have been deposited in a shaft descending from one of these inner rooms. The tomb of Panehesy is the best preserved of these six, and some its decorated external façade is still visible. Inside there are two chambers, with four columns each instead of the usual two. Two stairways lead to burial chambers and a small shrine with a vandalized statue of the owner.

Considerably to the south of the first group of tombs is a second group consisting of five tombs. These are located a short distance to the south of the "Royal Wadi" and to the southeast of the modern villages of Hagg-Qandil and Hawata. Today the doors of most of these tombs are blocked by blown sand piled up against the metal gates that are intended to protect the tombs from thieves and vandals. The future pharaoh Ay originally planned a tomb there (Tomb 25). Maya, "Fan Bearer at King's Right Hand" (Tomb 14), and Tutu, who was in charge of protocol (Tomb 8), had two of the larger tombs. The southern tombs are more architecturally elaborate than those of the northern group. Their plans include a small outside façade, a short vestibule and usually a large inner room, which was meant to contain a dozen or more columns. The final resting place of Tutu also had a number of small alcoves, but, like so many of the chapels of nobles at Amarna, it is unfinished. Although badly weathered, traces of the external decoration of these tombs can still be seen. Scenes from these façades were mostly representations of the royal family at worship.

All the nobles' tombs are notable for the prominence given to the royal family in the decorative scheme. Throughout each tomb, representations and references to the owners take second place to those of the royal family. This has been interpreted as the outcome of the semi-divine status of the royal family. The tomb of Kheruef at Thebes (TT90), however, provides an interesting parallel. The owner, a high-ranking official in Queen Tiye's household who was responsible for the organization of Amenhotep III's jubilee (*heb-sed*), had the artists devote most of the wall space in his tomb to recording this event. Perhaps the officials of Akhenaten were similarly motivated by the desire to record their careers; in some respects these reliefs could be regarded as pictorial versions of the traditional Egyptian autobiographies seen in tombs.

Another hypothesis has been proposed by Barry Kemp. The tombs at Amarna are too few to have accommodated more than a fraction of the officials associated with the royal court. Kemp has suggested that these tombs were symbolic of special privileges, granted as a sign of the owners' closeness to the king and their

devotion to the new order. Notables who were not part of this clique would have made plans for their tombs to be constructed in their native provinces. (The recently discovered tomb of Aper-'el at Saqqara is the perfect example of the latter group.)

See also

Lepsius, Carl Richard; New Kingdom, overview; Saqqara, New Kingdom private tombs

Further reading

Davies, N. de G. 1903–08. *The Rock Tombs of el-Amarna*, 6 vols. London.

Kemp, B.J. 1989. *Ancient Egypt: Anatomy of a Civilization*. London.

LYNDA GREEN

Tell el-Amarna, royal tombs

In addition to the rock-cut tombs of the nobles in the cliffs at Tell el-Amarna, there are also a number of lesser known burial places in the Wadi Abu Hasah el-Bahri (also known as the "Royal Wadi"). The tomb of Akhenaten (the "Royal Tomb") is the best known of these, but there are four other unfinished tombs (27, 28, 29 and 30) along the wadi. Little was known about them until the early 1980s, when Geoffrey Martin led an expedition to the area.

According to Flinders Petrie, local villagers probably rediscovered the Royal Tomb in the 1880s, when some jewelry which was claimed to be from there appeared on the antiquities market. The first European visitors to the Royal Tomb were Wallis Budge in 1887–8, and Alexandre Barsanti in 1891 and 1892. Barsanti investigated the tomb for the Egyptian Antiquities Service, and removed fragments of a royal sarcophagus or sarcophagi. In 1894, Bouriant, Legrain and Jéquier conducted an epigraphic survey for the French Institute of Archaeology in Cairo. The Egypt Exploration Society (EES) expedition to Tell el-Amarna under J.D.S. Pendlebury made forays to the Royal Tomb in 1931–2 and again in 1935. The first expedition was to assess the condition of the tomb and the possibility of future EES work there, while members of the later one looked for other tombs. Between these visits, the Egyptian Antiquities Service briefly investigated the wadi in 1934 and found a number of fragments of royal *shawabti*s (servant figures).

The Royal Tomb (Tomb 26) is unfinished but still impressive. After the entrance hall, which has steps and a slide for bringing in the sarcophagus, there is a long corridor which leads to a stairway, shaft room and pillared hall. Possibly other doorways were intended to open off the long corridor: three preliminary cuts were made in both the south and north walls, but abandoned. To the north of the long corridor are a series of six long chambers. The sixth chamber is the largest; the walls are dressed but undecorated. Martin suggests that this complex was intended as a tomb within a tomb, perhaps for Nefertiti.

Three rooms open off the tomb stairway. The reliefs in these chambers have been extensively published and are justly famous. Besides the usual representations of the worship of the Aten, the scenes on these walls record the death, perhaps in childbirth, of a royal woman and the participation of the royal family in her funerary rites. The shaft room was also decorated, but only traces of relief remain.

The so-called pillared hall has two roughly finished square pillars. It probably was where Akhenaten was buried, as indicated by the presence of a sarcophagus plinth. The sarcophagus was smashed to pieces, but many of the fragments have been pieced together in a reconstruction in the Cairo Museum. Very little remains of the wall decoration of this room, which was vandalized in ancient times, and further destruction has been caused by salts in the rock. Throughout the tomb the decorations have suffered because of the poor quality of the stone and the hurried techniques used by the artists (usually the reliefs were cut in plaster over the bedrock). The tomb also suffered from the intentional destruction in the post-Amarna period by those who wished to obliterate all traces of Akhenaten.

Virtually all the artifacts that have come from the Royal Tomb are in fragmentary condition. The sarcophagus may be the only large-scale find in the tomb, and it is difficult to determine whether the tomb was ever actually occupied. Georges Daressy mentioned the discovery of shreds of mummy wrappings and fragments of a destroyed mummy in the tomb, but his testimony is the only evidence that human remains were ever found there.

Of the other burial places in the Royal Wadi, Tombs 27 and 30 are the smallest. Tomb 30 is located on the north side, at the level of the wadi floor. Although unfinished, it was clearly intended to be simple in design, consisting only of an entrance passage and one room. Tomb 27 consists of an entrance with stairway and slide for the sarcophagus, and a corridor. This tomb is unfinished, and was undoubtedly intended to be much bigger. Noting the presence of the slide, usually found only in kings' tombs, the excavators have suggested that it may been intended for use by Tutankhamen or another successor of Akhenaten. In contrast, Tomb 29 is much larger and more elaborate, with four consecutive corridors. Traces of plaster indicate that the walls of the first two corridors had at least been finished and prepared for decoration. The plan of Tomb 28 differs from that of the other minor tombs in the Royal Wadi in that it consists of an entrance-way and three rooms connected by doorways and stairways.

In 1934 Pendlebury cleared the tombs in the Royal Wadi for the Egyptian Antiquities Service, and although no records of these excavations are known, it seems likely that any larger finds were removed then. In the most recent work many sherds, ostraca and other fragmentary artifacts were found in dumps outside the entrances to these tombs. Burials may have taken place in Tombs 28 and 29, based on the evidence of the debris. One inscription found there mentions Nefernefrure, the fourth daughter of Akhenaten, and either of these tombs may have been used by her.

In texts on some of the Amarna boundary stelae, Akhenaten mentions preparing a tomb for a (Mnevis) bull in the "eastern mountain" and Martin has proposed that one of the royal tombs may have been used for this burial. Recently, in a discussion of a Theban tomb in the Valley of the Kings (KV 55), Aidan Dodson has suggested that either Tutankhamen or the coregent Smenkhkare was originally intended to be buried in the Royal Wadi at Amarna.

See also

New Kingdom, overview; Tell el-Amarna, city; Tell el-Amarna, nobles' tombs; Thebes, Valley of the Kings; Tutankhamen, tomb of

Further reading

El-Khouly, A., and G.T. Martin. 1987. *Excavations in the Royal Necropolis at el-'Amarna, 1984.* Supp. aux *ASAE 33.*

Martin, G.T. 1974. *The Royal Tomb at el-'Amarna I: the objects.* In *The Rock Tombs of el-'Amarna* 7. London.

——. 1989. *The Royal Tomb at el-'Amarna II: the reliefs, inscriptions and architecture.* In *The Rock Tombs of el-'Amarna* 7. London.

LYNDA GREEN

Tell Basta

The ancient city of Basta is located some 77 km northeast of Cairo at the mound of Tell Basta (30°34′ N, 31°31′ E), on the southeastern edge of the modern city of Zagazig. Its Greek name, "Bubastis," is derived from the ancient Egyptian *per-basta*, meaning "house/estate of the goddess Bastet." In antiquity the city was located on the most easterly, Pelusiac branch of the Nile (known to the geographer Ptolemy as the "Bubastic" river), and its position was accurately recorded on older maps. It was re-identified in 1798 by Malus de Mitry and the engineer Fevre, members of the Napoleonic expedition to Egypt. The general topography of the site was first recorded by the Greek historian Herodotus (Book II, 138) in the fifth century BC, and the rough outlines of the city's monuments were still visible in the mid-nineteenth century, when, according to the map of John Gardner Wilkinson, the ruins covered *circa* 200 ha.

Scientific excavations at Tell Basta have been sporadic. From 1887 to 1889 excavations were conducted by Édouard Naville for the Egypt Exploration Fund/Society. Occasional excavations were undertaken by the Egyptian Antiquities Service, often in connection with the removal of organic material (*sebbakh*) for fertilizer. In the 1940s, excavations by Labib Habachi uncovered the temple of Pepi I. In the 1960s, Shafik Farid and Ahmed es-Sawi excavated a Middle Kingdom palace complex and cemetery, and the cat cemetery. Since 1977 the University of Zagazig, in cooperation with German archaeologists, has been excavating in the late Old Kingdom cemetery and the temple of Bastet.

The city of Bubastis, or Basta as it was known to the ancient Egyptians, was occupied from the Early Dynastic period (1st–2nd Dynasties) until its abandonment some time after the Arab conquest of Egypt (AD 642). During the Graeco-Roman period, tradition held that the city was founded by the goddess Isis, a view probably based upon a pseudo-etymology of the hieroglyphic writing of the name of Basta as the "*ba* [soul] of Isis" (*ba-iset*). The earliest recorded historical event, cited by the Egyptian historian Manetho (third century BC), was a destructive earthquake there during the reign of a king "Boethos" (Hotepsekhemwy?), the first king of the 2nd Dynasty. A roughly contemporary grave excavated at the site suggests occupation at this early date.

Basta's titular goddess was a lion-headed or cat-headed female deity called Bastet, "She-of-Basta." The goddess's cult became prominent in Egypt by the 4th Dynasty, when her name appeared on the valley temple of the pyramid complex of Khafre at Giza, and the city may also have achieved a similar importance then. By the end of the Old Kingdom, Basta was a major center in the eastern Delta. It was the site of temples to the 6th Dynasty kings Teti and Pepi I. There must have been a temple to the goddess Bastet then as well, but no certain remains have been discovered. To the east of the present ruins of the temple of Bastet is an extensive cemetery dating to the late Old Kingdom/First Intermediate Period.

During the Middle Kingdom, building activities resumed at Basta. The city was not a nome or district capital then, but it was still an important regional center because of its prime location and religious importance. Evidence of structures of the Bastet cult have been dated to the reigns of 12th Dynasty kings Amenemhat I, his son Senusret I and his great-grandson Senusret III. This latter king also may have been responsible for the rebuilding (or expansion) of the supposed earlier temple of Bastet. A vast administrative palace complex, which served as residence and office for a series of mayors during the Middle Kingdom, and an associated cemetery have been excavated. The palace complex included administrative offices and storerooms, rooms of state and private apartments. The structure was probably in use throughout the 12th Dynasty, although the only datable relief discovered in it contains the name of Amenemhat III. In the 13th Dynasty, the palace complex was destroyed by fire and it was not rebuilt. This destruction seems to coincide with the takeover of the Delta by the Hyksos, invaders/settlers from Palestine who ruled during the Second Intermediate Period.

During the New Kingdom the historical record for Basta is patchy. Under Amenhotep III a small temple was constructed there. In Ramesside times (19th–20th Dynasties), the city produced high officials of state, including the vizier Iuty and two Viceroys of Kush, Hory II and his son Hory III, all of whose tombs have been excavated there. Much—if not all—of the Ramesside evidence found at the site is clearly reused and could come from other places in the Delta, and it is unclear whether monuments were constructed at Basta then.

During the 22nd Dynasty, Basta was the family seat of a series of Libyan rulers of Egypt. Two of these "Bubastite" pharaohs, Osorkon I and his grandson Osorkon II, were responsible for the rebuilding of the great temple of Bastet. Rebuilding the front part of the temple proper, Osorkon I added a portico with Hathor-headed column capitals and erected a monumental pylon gateway for the temple enclosure. He also built a small temple (traditionally said to be dedicated to Thoth) about 750 m from the Bastet temple. Osorkon II added a pylon gateway adorned with scenes celebrating his jubilee (*heb-sed*) to the temple of Bastet. This king apparently usurped the Hathor-headed capitals which Osorkon I had added to the temple, putting his own name in place of that of his grandfather. Next to the temple of Bastet, Osorkon II also built a small temple to Bastet's son, the lion-headed god Mihos. In *circa* 718 BC the last king of the 22nd Dynasty, Osorkon IV, surrendered his much reduced Delta kingdom (including Basta) to the Kushite pharaoh Piye, who conquered the petty kingdoms of northern Egypt. From then onward Basta ceased to take any major political role in Egyptian history.

During the 26th Dynasty, many vaulted mudbrick structures were built to the northwest of the temple of Bastet. These "catacombs" were used to house the mummified bodies of cats sacred to the goddess Bastet. The devotees of this cult apparently offered these mummies as a symbol of their piety. Near the cat cemetery structures were industrial areas where votive artifacts in bronze and faïence were produced for the faithful. While Basta was no longer of any real political importance, its reputation was still such that the biblical prophet Ezekiel (30:17) foretold of the city's fall when he railed against Egypt (*circa* 550 BC).

During the first Persian conquest of Egypt, Herodotus may have visited the city known to him as Bubastis, and his description (in Book II, 138) of the great temple, as rebuilt in the 22nd Dynasty, remains the best description of the ancient city.

Under Nectanebo II (30th Dynasty), a large number of free-standing, small shrines to various deities were placed within chambers at the rear of the temple of Bastet, and the statue of his chancellor, Ankh-hap, probably comes from the city as well. In 342 BC, a Persian army reconquered Egypt and plundered the Delta cities, including Bubastis, which was the site of fighting over booty between Persian troops and their Greek mercenaries. From this point on,

Bubastis was part of an Egypt ruled by foreigners.

Remains from later periods at Bubastis are fragmentary. A royal statue of Ptolemy II may come from the site. The well-known estate manager Zenon, whose extensive archive has survived and who lived during the reign of Ptolemy II, wrote several of his letters from Bubastis, which he visited on business. During the reign of Ptolemy V, two statues were erected in the temple of Bastet by his officials, Apollonios, son of Theon, and Apollonios's "brother" Ptolemy, son of Apollonios. The last major identifiable structure at Bubastis was probably a large late Roman or Byzantine fortress, which once stood atop the mound of the city. When Egypt became Christian during the fourth century AD, the temple of Bastet would have been closed.

Bubastis functioned as a trading and religious center during the Graeco-Roman period, when it became a wealthy city. The lavish house at Bubastis of the lady Tabubu is mentioned in the Egyptian tale, *The Story of Setne Khaemwas and Naneferkaptah*, written early in the Ptolemaic period. It is described as being filled with objects of gold, lapis lazuli, turquoise, ivory and ebony.

The city's wealth was based in part on its geographic position. Located on the eastern-most branch of Nile, Bubastis provided good communication between the northern Delta and regions to the south. It was also on a route of canals which crossed the Delta from west to east, connecting the city of Alexandria to the Red Sea. A Ptolemaic blue glass pendant, probably manufactured in Alexandria, was found at Tell Basta, and a duplicate pendant, probably from the same mold, was excavated at Aksum in northern Ethiopia, suggesting Bubastis's position in an extensive trade route from northern Egypt to the Red Sea coast and the Horn of Africa.

The city's wealth was also based on its religious importance. Bastet, the titular goddess of Bubastis, was somewhat frightening in her original leonine aspect. In later periods, Bastet (associated by the Greeks with the goddess Artemis) was symbolized by the cat. In this form she more benign and was associated with pleasure, music and dance. Herodotus reported that one of the great Egyptian festivals took place annually at Bubastis when thousands of pilgrims visited the city to worship the goddess, make great offerings and drink much wine.

The visible monuments at Tell Basta are now greatly diminished. By 1949, the site's remains covered only some 84 ha (including 14 ha used for a sewage system drainage farm), and at present the accessible ruins cover only 20 ha, with an army camp on an additional 30 ha. The ruins of the temples of Bastet and Mihos still exist, as does a part of the temple of Pepi I. The Middle Kingdom palace complex and cemetery survive, as do parts of the late Old Kingdom cemetery.

See also

Giza, Khafre pyramid complex; Herodotus; Late and Ptolemaic periods, overview; Libyans; Manetho; Napoleon Bonaparte and the Napoleonic expedition; Roman period, overview; Third Intermediate Period, overview; trade, foreign

Further reading

Bakr, M.I. 1992. *Tell Basta* 1: *Tombs and Burial Customs at Bubastis*. Cairo.

Habachi, L. 1957. *Tell Basta*. Cairo.

Naville, É. 1892. *The Festival Hall of Osorkon II in the Great Temple of Bubastis (1887–1889)*. London.

El-Sawi, A. 1979. *Excavations at Tell Basta. Report of Seasons 1967–1971 and Catalogue of Finds*. Prague.

CHARLES VAN SICLEN

Tell ed-Dab'a, Second Intermediate Period

Tell ed-Dab'a in the northeastern Nile Delta (30°47′ N, 31°50′ E) is the site of ancient Avaris, the capital of the Hyksos and, together with Qantir (2 km north), the site of Pi-Ramesses, the capital of the 19th Dynasty. Excavations were conducted there by Édouard Naville (1895), Labib Habachi (1937, 1941–2), S. Adam (at 'Ezbet Rushdy, 1955), and the Austrian Archaeological Institute, Cairo (1966–9 and annually since 1975).

The settlement was probably founded during the First Intermediate Period by one of the Heracleopolitan kings named Khety (*circa* 2040 BC) as a royal estate. The first king of the 12th Dynasty, Amenemhat I, who was very active in settlement politics, re-established the site as a crown estate. A temple of his was excavated at 'Ezbet Rushdy es-Saghira. It was, however, only constructed by Senusret III, according to new excavations by the Austrian Institute. Senusret III also rebuilt a pillared hall, probably a reception hall of an administrative palace of Amenemhat I. Its doorway was removed during the Hyksos period (15th–16th Dynasties), and was found reused in the citadel of the Hyksos at 'Ezbet Helmy. The 12th Dynasty town is situated to the southeast of a deviation of the Pelusiac branch of the Nile, and, except for a large villa-like building, is mostly unexplored. But a large orthogonally planned workmen's village from the early 12th Dynasty was found some 100 m southwest of the Middle Kingdom town by the Austrian excavations. The village's inhabitants were probably the builders of this town.

Beginning in the late 12th Dynasty new settlers from Syro-Palestine occupied the land south of the Middle Kingdom town. Their material culture is a highly Egyptianized one of the Middle Bronze Age (MB) of Syria Palestine. A north Syrian "Middle Hall-House" in this village demonstrates the Syro-Palestinian origin of the settlers. Burials are located within the settlement, a custom characteristic of Syro-Palestinian cultures. Despite looting, 50 percent of all male burials have MBIIA type copper weapons. One of the male burials had a duckbill-shaped ax and a copper belt with embossed engravings. Pits with pairs of donkey burials are also found in the cemeteries. The people who lived in this village were employed by the Egyptian crown as soldiers and possibly in other specialized professions, such as caravan leaders and traders.

In the early 13th Dynasty, part of the new settlement was covered by a palace, *circa* 90 × 60 m in area (excavated 1979–89). From the north, a broad portico led to two groups of flats (offices?). The architecture of this palace is purely Egyptian, and in plan it resembles the large houses at the Middle Kingdom workmen's town of El-Lahun.

North of the palace's eastern entrance hall and the new reception hall was a garden with formal flower beds. A garden with trees in a rectangular plan was found south of the palace. The garden was soon occupied by a series of tombs, which probably belonged to the resident palace officials. Each tomb has a subterranean chamber and there are remains of a chapel for each on the surface. One tomb, located separately in the south of the garden, seems to have a pyramid superstructure of mudbrick.

These tombs are Egyptian in design, but donkey burials in front of each entrance are a tradition from southwest Asia. Weapons excavated in a less looted tomb are of Syro-Palestinian types. This evidence suggests that these officials were probably of Levantine origin, in service in Egypt. A very corrupt inscription on a magnificent amethyst scarab demonstrates that its owner was probably an "overseer(?) of the foreign countries" and a "caravan leader" (*metjen*?). In the early 13th Dynasty the settlement at Tell ed-Dab'a was possibly the center for launching expeditions to foreign countries, such as mining expeditions to the Sinai and seaborne expeditions to the Levant.

Contacts at this time with Ebla (Tell Mardikh) in Syria can be demonstrated by a scepter of King Hotepibre (early 13th Dynasty) found in an Ebla royal tomb. A statue of the same king was found by Labib Habachi at Tell ed-Dab'a, together with statues of the last monarch of the 12th Dynasty, Queen Sobekneferu. It is not improbable that Tell ed-Dab'a, which was inhabited then mainly by Asiatics, played an important role in this king's foreign relations.

A statue of the Asiatic dignitary found in the tomb which probably had a pyramid superstructure had been deliberately smashed, especially in its face, which demonstrates that the political turmoil of the late Middle Kingdom did not spare this town. A project to enlarge the palace stopped, and artifacts, such as plumb bobs, paint pots and tools for smoothing the walls, were left on the spot. Prepared door frames of stone were not installed.

The settlement continued to be used during the second half of the eighteenth century BC and actually increased in size (Stratum G). Its plan suggests an egalitarian social organization of ordinary citizens. The material culture is less Egyptianized and more Syro-Palestinian in character than earlier. The production of bronze tools in open molds played an important part in the economy now. However, there is also evidence of epidemics (probably bubonic plague, referred to in an early 18th Dynasty medical papyri as the "Asiatic disease"): there were multiple burials with the dead thrown into pits, and random burials in house middens. The eastern part of the town was abandoned, but in the center settlement continued.

A sacred precinct was constructed on top of the deserted eastern part of the town (Stratum F, circa 1,710–1,680 BC), with a typical Middle Bronze Age temple in the center and a "Breithaus" temple on the western edge of the district. In front of the main temple was a rectangular altar surrounded by pits, probably for trees. Deep pits were later excavated for offering remains, such as calcinated animal bones and broken pottery from ritual meals and drinking ceremonies. Before circa 1,600 BC, such remains were scattered on the ground in front of the main temple or in the adjoining courtyard.

Around the sacred precinct, burials with Egyptian-type mortuary chapels appeared. This precinct remained intact until the end of the Second Intermediate Period, but the burials were covered by the expanding settlement. Tombs consist of mudbrick chambers within pits. Burials of soldiers continued until the middle Hyksos period, when weapons were no longer placed in burials. Donkey burials in front of tomb entrances were also discontinued at about the same time. For a short period

around 1,700 BC (Stratum F) bodies of young females were deposited in front of some tomb chamber entrances and they must have been interred (sacrificially) at the same time as their masters.

From this time onward a differentiation of houses can be observed in the central part of the town. Besides more spacious houses with three central rooms, smaller houses were built in the peripheral eastern part of the town or clustered around the residences of their masters. During the Hyksos period the town expanded considerably to circa 2.5 km^2 in area. The semi-Egyptian material culture of the inhabitants would suggest that they had lived for some time in Egypt, possibly in the Memphis area, and were resettled by the crown on a strip of land going east from the Pelusiac branch of the Nile. An influx from the Tell el-'Ajjul region in southern Palestine, however, cannot be excluded.

The settlement became more densely occupied and there was no available space for burials. Consequently, they were placed under house floors or sometimes in large single or double chambers constructed on the ground floor. Some of the burial chambers had more than fifteen individuals; most of them, however, were robbed. Although the vault construction of burials of the early Hyksos period has affinities with techniques known from Mesopotamia, in the later burials the tomb architecture is purely Egyptian, with the exception that these burials were not set apart from the settlement in discrete cemeteries.

Small children were normally buried in amphorae, which continued to be imported from southern Palestine in large quantities. Other types of Middle Bronze Age pottery, such as Tell el-Yahudiya Ware, was imported in the first half of the 13th Dynasty, but later it was also produced in Egypt. During the Hyksos period, MB pottery was made locally and exported to Cyprus, Lower Nubia and Kerma, the capital of the Kingdom of Kush. From Cyprus, Avaris received imports, especially during the Hyksos period.

In 1991, at the western edge of Avaris and east of the Pelusiac branch, the citadel of the late Hyksos period was discovered. It is surrounded by a fortification wall with angular buttresses.

Inside were found gardens and some monumental architectural remains. Of particular importance are burials of many young men, obviously victims of the conquest of Avaris. For finds of Hyksos royal inscriptions see 'Hyksos' above.

From tomb inscriptions at Elkab (Ahmose, son of Ibana) we know that Avaris was taken by the Upper Egyptian king Ahmose, the founder of the 18th Dynasty. Evidence of destruction is only present in the area of the citadel. Around the platform construction, architectural elements were found lying scattered on top of the garden in a layer formed by conflagration. In other parts of the citadel there are multiple burials thrown into pits, which were cut in the mudbrick architecture of the Hyksos period. There are also skeletons of equids, possibly horses, interred in pits nearby. Possibly this is evidence of victims of the final assault on Avaris.

The rest of Avaris shows no evidence of conflagration or destruction; however, all tombs of the late Hyksos period were thoroughly looted. According to Josephus (*Contra Apionem* I.14 § 88), the inhabitants of Avaris negotiated a retreat to Palestine after the siege of the city. The archaeological evidence seems to support this much later account.

The town remained deserted until the 19th Dynasty, with the exception of two areas. The temple, dedicated to Seth (i.e. the northern Syrian storm god identified with the Egyptian god Seth), continued to be used, as was the former citadel of the Hyksos. The palace was razed to the ground and rebuilt during the (early) 18th Dynasty. The Egyptian army needed a headquarters near the northeastern border, and possibly this included a royal residence. There is even evidence for troops stationed in the former citadel of Avaris: numerous arrowheads of bone and flint, as well as household pottery of the Nubian Kerma culture, demonstrate that Nubian archers were there. Other arrowheads in copper have Aegean parallels. A workshop for slingshot stones of calcite and various other stones was also excavated.

Set into the Hyksos fortification system is a huge platform (*circa* 72 × 45 m), which can be reconstructed as a palatial fortress. To the south of it a huge palatial compound was partly uncovered. So far magazines with big quantities of Cypriot and Syropalestinian date Bronze Age pottery were investigated. They give an insight into the intensive trade between Egypt and the eastern Mediterranean world.

Scattered east of the platform, and in the same context as the large palace compound, numerous fragments of wall plaster with Minoan wall paintings were excavated. This was a major surprise. Besides floor paintings of maze patterns, there are fragments from scenes of humans engaged in bull leaping and bull grappling. The bull leaping scene is set against the background of a maze pattern. There are also scenes of lions and leopards hunting deer and ibexes, and human hunters with dogs chasing ungulates. Bearded men suggest priests in scenes of rituals. The iconography and style are close to those of frescoes found on the island of Thera in the Aegean (Late Minoan IA, *circa* 1,580–1,500 BC). Some elements, however, such as the maze pattern, a frieze of half-rosettes and the bull leaping scene, are derived directly from the palace of Knossos on Crete, although such scenes are only later represented there. Unquestionably, these scenes and design elements were exclusive royal symbols at Knossos. Fragments of full-scale representations of bulls and humans in plaster relief excavated in the Tell ed-Dab'a palace also resemble decoration at Knossos.

A door of the 18th Dynasty palace painted with Minoan motifs was in a more decorative style, with ivy and loop-patterns.

There is also evidence of a more humble settlement of the early 18th Dynasty to the north of the Hyksos platform construction. Numerous scarabs with royal names found in the excavated strata document occupation from the reigns of Ahmose to Amenhotep II.

At present it is unclear how long occupation at Tell ed-Dab'a continued. Within the precinct of the temple of Seth at Avaris there is evidence of continued use: a seal of Amenhotep III, and a lintel of a door from a shrine of Seth inscribed with the cartouches of Horemheb. In the 19th Dynasty Seti I and Ramesses II constructed a splendid new residence, Pi-Ramesses, at Qantir (2 km north of Avaris). The temple of Seth was rebuilt by Seti I in order to honor the god from which the kings of the 19th Dynasty claimed descent (in the "Stela of 400 Years"). Building activity during the Ramesside period (19th–20th Dynasties) has also been verified by limited excavations at Tell ed-Dab'a.

Similar to the plan of the old capital of Memphis, Pi-Ramesses had the royal residence in the north of the city, while the temple of the main god, Seth of Avaris, was in the south. Both buildings formed the original poles for the new planned capital, which was still called Avaris during Seti I's reign. Ramesses II later put his personal imprint on this new royal center and changed its name to Pi-Ramesses.

See also

Aegean peoples; Canaanites; Cypriot peoples; Hyksos; Kerma; Lahun, town; New Kingdom, overview; Qantir/Pi-Ramesses; Second Intermediate Period, overview

Further reading

Adam, S. 1959. Report on the excavation of the Department of Antiquities at Ezbet Rushdi. *ASAE* 56: 207–26.

Bietak, M. 1975. *Tell el-Dab'a 2* (Untersuchungen der Zweigstelle Kairo 1). Vienna.

——. 1986. Avaris und Piramesse, Archaeological Exploration in the Eastern Nile Delta. *Proceedings of the British Academy* 65: 225–90.

——. 1991a. Der Friedhof in einem Palastgarten aus der Zeit des späten Mittleren Reiches und andere Forschungsergebnisse aus dem östlichen Nildelta Tell el-Dab'a (1984–1987). *Ägypten und Levante* 2: 47–109.

——. 1991b. Egypt und Canaan during the Middle Bronze Age. *BASOR* 281: 27–72.

——. 1996. *Avaris, Capital of the Hyksos: New Excavation Results*. London.

Bietak, M., J. Dorner, I. Hein and P. Janosi.

1993. Neue Grabungsergebnisse aus Tell el-Dab'a und Ezbet Helmi im östlichen Nildelta (1989–1991). *Ägypten und Levante* 4: 9–80.

Boessneck, J., and A. von den Driesch. 1992. *Tell el-Dab'a 7. Tiere und historische Umwelt im Nordost-Delta im 2. Jahrtausend anhand der Knochenfunde der Ausgrabungen 1975–1986* (Untersuchungen der Zweigstelle Kairo 10). Vienna.

Habachi, L. 1974. Khata'na-Qantir: Importance. *ASAE* 52: 443–559.

Winkler, E.M., and H. Wilfing. 1991. *Tell el-Dab'a 6. Die menschlichen Skelettfunde aus dem Bereich des Tells A* (Untersuchungen der Zweigstelle Kairo 9). Vienna.

MANFRED BIETAK

Tell el-Farkha

Tell el-Farkha is located immediately to the north of the modern village of Ghazala in the eastern Nile Delta (30°56′ N, 31°36′ E). The site was first recorded in 1987 by the Italian Archaeological Expedition in the Eastern Nile Delta, of the *Centro Studi e Ricerche Ligabue*, Venice. Excavations were conducted there from 1988 to 1990.

The excavations have revealed a stratigraphic sequence with four main occupational phases. The earliest one (phase I) dates to the Predynastic period (fourth millennium BC) and appears to be contemporary to the Nagada II b–c phases in Upper Egypt. The later phases at Tell el-Farkha (phases II, III, IV) date to Dynasty 0, the Early Dynastic period and the early Old Kingdom (3rd–4th Dynasties). In the Predynastic phase (I), the only evidence of architecture consists of light clay structures associated with pits. Mudbrick buildings appear in all the later phases.

The Predynastic evidence at Tell el-Farkha can be ascribed to a local cultural horizon that is different from the contemporary Predynastic (Nagada) culture in the Nile Valley. In the phase I strata a very distinctive pottery with incised decorations, mainly vertical bands of zig-zags, was excavated. At present, this type of decoration is known only from Tell el-Iswid South and Tell Ibrahim Awad, two sites in the vicinity of Tell el-Farkha, and the late Predynastic strata at Tell el-Fara'in (Buto). The lithic industry from the phase I strata at Tell el-Farkha is similar to the lithic industry from the Early Bronze (I) site of En Shadud in Palestine.

A clear stratigraphic break between phases I and II suggests that the site was abandoned for some time. The stratigraphic break also marks an abrupt change in the material culture.

Phase II (Dynasty 0) ceramics are characterized by sherds of bread molds, frequently with traces of potmarks. Bowls, plates and jars of rough and fine wares are common. Phase III (1st–2nd Dynasties) ceramics are also characterized by many sherds of bread molds. Potmarks are sometimes found. Plates, and thick bowls and jars with roll rims, are frequent. Sherds of bread molds are also common in the Old Kingdom (Phase IV) strata. Many fragments of clay sealings, sometimes with the impression of the seal, have also been excavated in these strata.

The frequency of blades with sickle sheen is indicative of increased agricultural activity in the early historical periods, especially in the Old Kingdom phase, where they are associated with many grinding stones.

The archaeological evidence from Tell el-Farkha fits well with what is known about the Predynastic period from other sites in the eastern and central Delta. This evidence demonstrates the occurrence of a different Predynastic culture in the eastern Delta than that found in Upper Egypt (Nagada culture), but related to the late phase of the Lower Egyptian Buto/Ma'adi (Chalcolithic) culture. Thus the present data point to the development of a Predynastic culture in the Delta, with regional variants, different from the Nagada culture in the Nile Valley. The origins of this culture are still obscure, as practically nothing is known about its earlier stages.

The occurrence of Nagada II c–d artifacts in the Delta, as well as the occurrence of Nagada III/Dynasty 0 artifacts in southern Palestine, demonstrate a progressive expansion northward of peoples of the Upper Egyptian Nagada culture, beginning in the mid-fourth millennium BC. The archaeological evidence suggests that starting in Nagada II times the eastern Nile Delta was progressively included in the Upper Egyptian cultural and economic sphere, but this was not by military conquest. The evidence, however, does not exclude a possible conflict between southern and northern forces in late Predynastic times with the subsequent unification of the whole country by a southern royal dynasty (Dynasty 0). In Early Dynastic times the Delta was firmly incorporated in the Egyptian state.

See also

Buto (Tell el-Fara'in); Ma'adi and the Wadi Digla; Nagada (Naqada); pottery, prehistoric; Predynastic period, overview

Further reading

Chlodnicki, M., R. Fattovich and S. Salvatori. 1992. The Nile Delta in transition: a view from Tell el-Farkha. In *The Nile Delta in Transition: 4th–3rd Millennium B.C.*, E. C. M. van den Brink, ed., 171–90. Jerusalem.

RODOLFO FATTOVICH

Tell el-Herr

Tell el-Herr is located in northwest Sinai (30°58′ N, 32°30′ E), in the vicinity of Gilbana, a bedouin village on the road joining el-Qantara to el-Arish. In antiquity, this area was the eastern limit of Nome XIV of Lower Egypt. Tell el-Herr lay south of the Pelusiac branch of the Nile, 7 km from Tell el-Farama (Pelusium). This northern part of the Egyptian border was characterized by lagoons along the Mediterranean coast, and the slow evolution of the shore and the situation of the two southern lagoons determined the distribution of the fortifications and settlements in the region.

Tell el-Herr has often been identified with the site of Migdol, shown on the Karnak relief depicting the campaign of Seti I into Palestine. However, no remains from the Ramesside period (19th–20th Dynasties) have yet been discovered at Tell el-Herr. Therefore, it is still difficult to locate the "Migdol of Menma're" (Karnak temple), the "Migdol of Seti-Merenptah" (P. Anastasi V, 20:2), or the "Migdol of Ramesses-Prince-of-Heliopolis" (Ramesses III at Medinet Habu). In the first millennium BC Tell el-Herr was one of the principal garrisons of Egypt, as would be expected of Migdol (Jeremiah 44:1; 46:14; Ezekiel 29:10; 30:6). During the Roman period, the "Itinerary of Antoninus" confirms the identification of Tell el-Herr with Migdol.

Jean Clédat was the first to undertake serious archaeological work at Tell el-Herr. In 1905 he excavated at the request of the Suez Canal Company; his notes, kept in the Louvre Museum, are still unpublished. During the Israeli occupation of Sinai, Tell el-Herr was used as a military position and suffered some damage on the top of the tell (mound) as well as in the settlement areas. Eliezer Oren, who was directing the Ben Gurion University excavations at another site (T.21) north of Tell el-Herr, was able to excavate some trenches on the tell and in the cemeteries. In 1984–5, the Egyptian Antiquities Organization (EAO) began extensive excavations, directed by Mohamed Abd el-Maksoud, on the tell and in the settlement where a Ptolemaic bath was discovered. Since 1985 a joint mission (EAO–Lille III) has proceeded with this work, under the direction of Dominique Valbelle.

The area covered by the whole site is about 30 ha. It is composed of a tell, occupied by successive fortresses, an extensive settlement and cemeteries. Both the tell and the settlement lie in the western part of the site, on the edge of the eastern lagoon. Farther east, the cemeteries are distributed from north to south. Several categories of burials have been found, some without visible substructures, and others with a rectangular lining of mudbrick. The richer burials were covered by small domes of baked bricks. Several tombs were excavated by Jean Clédat, while others were uncovered by the Ben Gurion expedition. The most ancient remains

at Tell el-Herr have been observed on the tell itself, dating back to at least the fifth century BC. Nothing earlier than the Graeco-Roman period has been discovered in either the settlement or the cemeteries.

Four principal stages of construction have been recognized in the tell at Tell el-Herr, which is 200 m in diameter and 10 m high. The most recent one is a fort erected during the late Roman empire. Its external wall destroyed some monumental remains from the end of the Ptolemaic period. The largest stronghold at the site was built during the Persian occupation of Egypt; it continued in use during much of the Ptolemaic period. A smaller, earlier fortress was destroyed and used as a foundation for it. This older fortress is only known from its enclosure wall in the south and at the northeast corner, and by some buildings uncovered in this corner. This enclosure wall (*circa* 124 m on a side) with square bastions on each side is made of mudbrick. The buildings include a sanctuary and several rooms connected with it, such as kitchens.

The remains of the 2d Persian stronghold (140 m square) are the most important of the tell. The enclosure wall, also with square bastions on each side, was entirely made of cylindrical mudbricks, which are unknown elsewhere. The entrance on the west side was protected by two bastions similar to the others. Four principal levels of construction and occupation have been noted. In the buildings, square and cylindrical bricks were used alternately. The three earlier levels are contemporary with the Persian occupation. The third one is the most complete, and the Attic ceramics found date it to the end of the fourth century BC. The fourth level is composed of early Ptolemaic reconstructions or additions to the previous levels. In the area excavated so far, the general plan is regular, with parallel streets oriented east–west.

After the destruction of the 2d Persian fortress, at least two large buildings were erected over the ruins. The cellar of a tower (17 × 17 m) has been located near the northeast corner of the preceding fortress, and the foundations of a temple (20 × 25 m) exist near

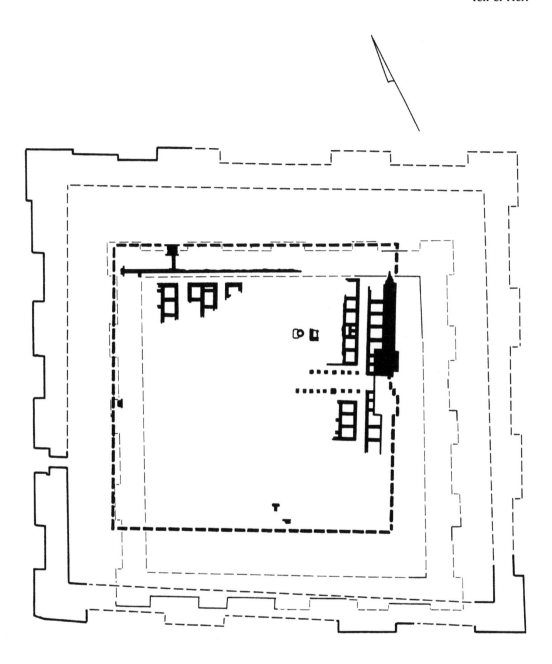

Figure 114 Sketch of the three successive fortresses at Tell el-Herr (1988)

the western entrance to this Persian stronghold. A fort (90 × 90 m) was erected at the site at the end of the third century AD; it remained in active use until the seventh century AD. Made of baked and mudbrick, its plan is rather similar to that of Qasr Qarun in the Fayum or the fort of Abu Sha'ar on the Red Sea. The northern doorjamb of the entrance is still preserved in the middle of the east side, as are the bases of sixteen pillars along the main street, dividing the internal space into two equal halves. The northern half was occupied by casemates. The walls of a large building may be traced in the southern half of the fort. In many places Byzantine alterations are visible.

Jean Clédat made some excavations in the settlement areas, but kept only small sketches of structures without a precise localization and description of objects. A bath dating from the time of the earlier Ptolemies was excavated in 1985 and 1986. It lies near the edge of the eastern lagoon, 500 m from the tell. In 1989 the Franco-Egyptian expedition surveyed the whole area, covering 15 ha, with the help of three excavated trenches. The surface remains, as well as the ceramics collected in the trenches, are exclusively of Ptolemaic and Roman date.

Much uncertainty remains concerning the history of Tell el-Herr, as well as the broader history of the eastern border of Lower Egypt. Recent archaeological work in this region, however, has already filled in some gaps in our knowledge and promises to do more of the same in the future.

See also

Abu Sha'ar; Persians; Roman forts in Egypt; el-Salaam canal

Further reading

Gratien, B. 1996. Tell el-Herr: étude stratigraphique de la céramique. *CRIPEL* 18: 51–105.

Louis, E., and D. Valbelle. 1988. Les trois dernières forteresses de Tell el-Herr. *CRIPEL* 10: 61–71.

Oren, E. 1984. Migdol: A new fortress on the edge of the eastern Nile Delta. *BASOR* 256: 7–44.

Valbelle, D., and C. Defernez. 1995. Les sites de la frontière égypto-palestinienne à l'époque perse. *Transeuphratène* 9: 93–100.

DOMINIQUE VALBELLE

Tell el-Maskhuta

Tell el-Maskhuta (30°33′ N, 32°06′ E) is a stratified townsite in the Wadi Tumilat region of the eastern Nile delta, *circa* 16 km west of modern Ismailia. The site was occupied in the Second Intermediate Period and again from the reign of Neko II until the early Roman period, with a possible break in the later fourth century BC and a definite break *circa* 100 BC to AD 100.

The name of the site in the Second Intermediate Period is unknown. Inscriptions found by Édouard Naville and J.S. Holladay, as well as Egyptian literary references interpreted in light of the site's chronology, indicate that the Egyptian name of the settlement established by Neko II, *circa* 610 BC, was Per-Atum Tjeku (the "Estate of Atum in Ṯkw"). In biblical Hebrew this name appears as Pitom (or Pithom, as in Exodus 1:11). This Per-Atum is not to be confused with earlier instances of the name. Thus, the Per-Atum mentioned in the 22nd Dynasty statue of Ankh-renep-nefer relates to the cult of Atum at Heliopolis and 'An (the region of Tura); although found by Naville at Tell el-Maskhuta, this statue must have been relocated to the new Per-Atum some time after 610 BC.

It seems that the biblical references to Pithom were anachronistic, inserted during the fifth or sixth century BC editing of the Exodus account. In classical times, the site still retained its ancient name, as seen in the Pithom Stela and Herodotus II.158 ("the Arabian town of Patumus"). The town was generally known by its Hellenized name of "Heroon polis" (variously Heroonpolis, Eroopolis, Heroon, Hero and so on). Under the Romans, this was shortened to Ero.

Tell el-Maskhuta was first excavated in 1883

by Édouard Naville for the Egypt Exploration Society. Lacking control of the pottery and small finds, his major contributions were the identification of the site, the discovery of an important series of inscribed objects and the general plan of the site. Naville's storehouses "built by the Children of Israel" were dated 1,000 years too early. Jean Clédat conducted explorations for the Antiquities Service, yielding further museum objects. More recently, the Egyptian Antiquities Organization has conducted a number of excavations at the site, including work in the northern cemetery area, along the Ismailia canal, in the Persian period necropolis south of the temple precincts, and in the area of the present village. The "Wadi Tumilat Project" excavations were undertaken by a team directed by John S. Holladay, Jr., of the University of Toronto.

Tell el-Maskhuta was a short-lived Hyksos outpost, an unfortified village, probably only 2–3 ha in extent, founded in the later part of the Second Intermediate Period. Its archaeology closely parallels strata E1 through D3 at Tell ed-Dab'a, the ancient site of Avaris. As at Tell ed-Dab'a, this phase at Tell el-Maskhuta is characterized by sinuous boundary walls, a steady progression in area use from above-ground circular silos and burials to an increasingly dense pattern of houses and associated features, mostly related to agriculture, animal husbandry, cooking and industrial processes.

Wheat and barley farming coupled with herding (cattle, sheep, goats and pigs) dominated the local economy during the Second Intermediate Period. The horse was known; hartebeest and gazelle, together with a wide variety of small game and bird life, were hunted. Craft specialization included pottery making, secondary bronze smelting and tool or weapon making, textile production, utilizing the warp-weighted loom, and production of sickles using preformed blades. One long-lived but enigmatic workshop, possibly for the manufacture of leather with metal fittings, utilized a bank of high-temperature hearths in conjunction with industrial processes involving multiple stakes driven into the floor, red and yellow ocher, cobble-sized grinders, palettes and hammer stones.

Second Intermediate Period burials included "warrior's" tombs marked by donkey burials and weapons, such as daggers and a chisel-shaped Asiatic ax. Other tombs, including small mudbrick tombs for infants and youth, had rich tomb offerings including gold and silver headbands, armbands, earrings, silver torques and hair rings, scarabs in gold or silver mountings, bronze toggle pins, tools such as knives and awls, beads of semiprecious stones such as amethyst, amulets and food offerings. Infant jar burials and inhumations in disused silos produced few or no grave goods.

Although the village exhibits all the signs of an urbanized settlement, paleobotanical analysis demonstrates conclusively that occupation in the excavated portions of the site was purely seasonal, from autumn through the spring wheat harvest. The site's main purpose, probably as an outpost facilitating long-distance caravan trade, was met during its winter occupation. During the summer months, the population presumably relocated elsewhere, possibly at the Middle Bronze Age encampments near Tell er-Retabah.

With the advent of Neko II and the construction of the sea-level canal connecting the Pelusiac branch of the Nile with the Red Sea via the Wadi Tumilat (Herodotus II.158), the site's exposed frontier position became an asset. Following a brief phase of use as a work camp for canal construction, a large number of bulls were sacrificed and buried in individual rectangular graves; these may have been foundation sacrifices for the building of the large temple to Atum. North of the temple, a number of houses, granaries and outdoor bread ovens were constructed. Shortly thereafter, plans changed radically, probably based upon Neko's defeat at Carchemish and expulsion from Asia in 605 BC. The original town plan was overridden by an 8–9 m wide defensive wall, enclosing an area roughly 200 m on a side. At no time in the Saite period did the settlement fill the entire 4 ha site. Two destruction phases followed, one in 601 BC, the second in 568 BC; both may be ascribed to Nebuchadnezzar II of

Babylon. Two pieces of Judaean domestic pottery associated with a house destroyed in 568 BC may attest to the presence of Jeremianic refugees of 582 BC. Similar Judaean wares in larger quantities are attested at Daphnae and Oren's western Sinai site T.21, provisionally identified as Migdol.

During the Saite period the expanded trade enabled by the sea-level canal was evidenced by massive quantities of Phoenician Crisp Ware amphorae (storage jars), a less massive presence of East Greek amphorae (notably from Thassos and Chios), and imported mortaria, heavy bowls with thick rims probably of Anatolian origin. A Phoenician terracotta statuette of a seated goddess, probably Asherah or Tanit, was found in the ruins of a small limestone shrine; it may attest to the presence of Phoenician traders at the site (see Herodotus II.112 for a Phoenician "camp" at Memphis). The Red Sea and Indian Ocean aspect of the trade must be inferred from the evidence of widespread trade connections at a small provincial town at the midpoint of the long canal terminating near Suez.

Another destruction marked the Persian conquest of Egypt in 525 BC. In the Persian period the townsite expanded to fill the entire enclosure area and may have expanded to the southwest as well. The four great quadrilingual stelae of Darius the Great, beginning at Tell el-Maskhuta, attest to this king's successful completion of the sea-level canal to the Red Sea and hence to Persia. Outside of the enclosure wall there was a stone-built well, which was deliberately blocked up with garbage, including quantities of pottery, in the rebellion against the Persians in 487 BC. Industrial and warehouse activities at the site are concentrated near the enclosure and the presumed gateway on the eastern, or canal, side of the town.

Monuments from the 30th Dynasty, found only as small fragments in Naville's dump, may attest to continued Nectanebid administration of the canal, or may be Ptolemaic period imports to the site. During the 30th Dynasty there was an increase in the importation of goods in Phoenician trade amphorae, as well as in Thassian and Chian amphorae. These amphorae probably contained mostly wine, but possibly also olive oil, fish sauce and other preserved products. Ink inscriptions on jar fragments are mostly in demotic Egyptian, with a few being in Phoenician script. Mortaria continue to be imported. Small cuboidal limestone altars, ultimately of South Arabian inspiration, witness to the use of incense in domestic cult installations at the site. The chance discovery of a cache of thousands of Athenian tetradrachms points to a trade gift to the Atum temple, as do the "Tell el-Maskhuta bowls." These bowls are Persian in style and probably in origin, but most likely arrived at Tell el-Maskhuta by way of South Arabia. They are inscribed "to the Lady" (presumably Hathor) from Gashmu, a princely Arabian name, attested in the Bible (Nehemiah 2:19, 6:1–6). Hymarytic silver coins, bearing the owl of Athena on the reverse, further attest to trade relations with South Arabia.

Following an apparent gap in occupation, the site's fortunes revived under Ptolemy II, who rebuilt the canal, celebrating some of his southern imports on the stela found at the site by Naville. A large six-roomed granary with an attached bank of bread ovens, scattered sculptors' "trial pieces," many scraps of non-local limestone and evidence for secondary bronze smelting give indirect evidence for a major renewal of the Atum temple. A smaller two-room storehouse or granary from the late Persian period was renewed; during its declining years it provided space for a potter's workshop. It is probable that the series of large storehouses discovered by Naville began as a result of Ptolemy II's renewal of the canal. A number of massive storehouses, the latest being *circa* 75 m long, were uncovered by the Wadi Tumilat Project and even more storehouses remain to be investigated. The series of storehouses explored so far are provisionally dated from the second half of the third century BC to *circa* 150–125 BC.

Following a break in occupation covering some or most of the first century BC through the first century AD, the site witnessed its greatest period of expansion. This reoccupation is associated with Trajan's reconstruction of the canal. Except for two small excavations in the Roman cemetery, remains from this period were not purposively investigated by the University of Toronto team. However, quantities of pottery of this period characterized most of the largely disturbed uppermost layers at the site.

The Roman cemetery occupied the location of a former Hellenistic period suburban village, filling it with squarish, mostly subterranean, mudbrick tombs with vaulted roofs. The tombs were entered from a walled *dromos* or entrance-way, centered on the eastern side. An arched tomb entrance was bricked in after each burial, while the *dromos* was backfilled with sand. The tombs were looted during their period of active use, and afterwards by the use of pits. Traces remained of the rich burial goods, such as gold foil, an earring, glass vessels and carved bone hairpins. Simple inhumations without grave goods were cut in open spaces between the tombs. The area also contained a children's cemetery of amphora burials. Noteworthy among the latter was a Christian burial, marked by a Coptic epitaph and two *chi-rho* symbols on the upper portions of a "Gaza" amphora covering the burial amphora. This burial was oriented toward Jerusalem. A very few other inhumations shared this orientation, and may be tentatively classified as Christian. The majority of the burials were oriented in a westerly fashion, consistent with the orientation of the built tombs.

A relatively early date for the end of the site is suggested by the absence of figured lamps, African Red Slip Ware and other late indicators; occupation may have ceased by the later third to early fourth centuries AD. The Christian pilgrim Egira mentions a Roman military post at Hero *circa* AD 381; however, by this date the military garrison may have been relocated further northwest, where a modern military airbase and the town of Abu Suweir preclude survey activities.

See also

Hyksos; Persians; Roman ports, Red Sea; Tell ed-Dab'a, Second Intermediate Period; trade, foreign; Wadi Tumilat

Further reading

Holladay, J.S., Jr. 1982. *Cities of the Delta, Part III. Tell el-Maskhuta: Preliminary Report on the Wadi Tumilat Project 1978–1979.* Malibu, CA.

MacDonald, B. 1980. Excavations at Tell el-Maskhuta. *Biblical Archaeologist* 43: 49–58.

Oren, E. 1984. Migdol: a new fortress on the edge of the eastern Nile Delta. *BASOR* 256: 7–44.

Paice, P. 1987. A preliminary analysis of some elements of the Saite and Persian period pottery at Tell el-Maskhuta. *BES* 8: 95–107.

JOHN S. HOLLADAY, JR.

Tell el-Muqdam

Tell el-Muqdam (Leontopolis, or "T3-rmw(?)") lies in Daqaliya Governorate in the south central Nile Delta, approximately 80 km northeast of Cairo and about 10 km southeast of the modern town of Mit Ghamr (30°41′ N, 31°21′ E). Just 100 years ago the site boasted some of the largest manmade earthworks in the Delta. Today it is sadly diminished, comprising approximately 0.25 km^2 of preserved, but disturbed tell area within maximum dimensions of some 1 km east–west by 0.75 km north–south. A large and malodorous shallow water body now dominates the northwestern quadrant of the tell, and fields and an adjacent village have encroached on all sides.

The name Muqdam apparently derives from that of an Islamic saint. The ancient city is identified with Strabo's Leontopolis (City of the Lions), known from early Ptolemaic times as the capital of Nome XI of Lower Egypt. The traditional Egyptian geographical lists unfortunately are silent on this nome, although other attestations of the nome occur, beginning in Old Kingdom times. The city's chief deity was the lion god Mihos. Theophoric names compounded with Mihos occur on Late period and

Ptolemaic coffins found at Muqdam, as well as on Late period statuary attributed to the site. Mihos himself appears on Ptolemaic donation stelae attributed to Muqdam; one stela, now in the Allard Pierson Museum, has a Greek graffito reading "The Sacred House of the Tomb of the Lions." The Egyptian name of the site was probably "T3-rmw" (Land of the Fish), although this attribution is not accepted universally. "T3-rmw," or a variant, occurs on a statue of Ramesses II from Muqdam; in a *Coffin Text* etiological spell (Spell 158); and on the Victory Stela of King Piye of the 25th Dynasty, where it is identified as the residence of King Iuput II.

Little is known of early archaeological work at Muqdam. Rifaud's publication of his 1823 excavations included one plan and section, both idealized, and some statuary. Mariette worked at Muqdam in the mid-1800s; typically, he seems to have left no notes and published only three inscribed finds. In 1892, Naville investigated the site for the Egypt Exploration Fund, but published only two short paragraphs on his fieldwork. A salvage operation in 1915 uncovered a tomb with two vaulted stone chambers, one looted, the other intact. The intact chamber contained a coffin of red granite with royal-quality jewelry and a scarab bearing the name of Kama, possibly a 23rd Dynasty queen or a shortened form of Karomama, mother of Osorkon III. The coffin lid, today visible in fields north of the tell, was a reworked red granite dyad or triad statue of Ramesses II.

Over the years Muqdam has proved itself a rich source of illicit antiquities. The "Fouquet Collection," purchased in 1885, may have originated from a Mihos temple *favissa* or burial place for sacred objects. The bronzes with lion motifs may be dated stylistically to the Persian period. The earliest material known from the site comprises three 12th Dynasty statue bases. One was usurped by Nehesy of the Second Intermediate Period and Merenptah of the 19th Dynasty; another was usurped by Osorkon II. Other inscribed finds included statues of Ramesses II, a statue of Osorkon II, a door jamb of Ramesses III, and a door hinge of Iuput II.

From 1992 to 1996, archaeologists from the University of California at Berkeley carried out four seasons of archaeological research at Muqdam. Investigations focused on four major activities: (1) a regional survey; (2) non-destructive surface and sub-surface survey; (3) test excavations; and (4) a geoarchaeological auger program.

The regional survey has documented rapid site destruction in the area: of twenty-four sites recorded at the turn of the century within a 16 km radius of Muqdam, only nine still exist in varied states of preservation. Surface survey at Muqdam produced material dating predominantly to the Late and Graeco-Roman periods, but including an occasional Third Intermediate Period find. Fragments of statuary and architectural elements, some inscribed (mostly by Ramesses II; one limestone jamb belonged to an Overseer of the Stables of Ramesses III), still lay scattered over the site. The northwest and southeast quadrants of the tell are badly disturbed. The southern portion of the tell evidently comprised the more limited Roman period town. To the southwest, test trenches revealed a badly damaged fired brick structure with an apse, probably dating to late Roman times.

Soundings in the central and eastern portions of the tell indicate an extensive Persian period occupation, comprising both industrial and habitation zones, the latter apparently violently destroyed at least once. A substantial Saite occupation lay below the Persian, also with at least one major destruction. The earliest occupation, just above the water table, dated to the late Third Intermediate Period. Geoarchaeological augering identified cultural deposits at least 6 m below the current water table, dating predominately to the Third Intermediate Period. Augering also located a probable river channel on the eastern portion of the tell that migrated eastward over time; this was most likely the Mendesian branch of the Nile.

Muqdam was a large and prosperous city throughout much of the first millennium BC. Fieldwork to date has revealed nothing predating the first millennium BC and it is likely that the site was first founded in late Ramesside times or early in the Third Intermediate Period.

The site has well preserved archaeological deposits from the mid-first millennium BC. To date, Muqdam has produced no decisive evidence regarding the seat of the 23rd Dynasty; Kitchen locates this dynasty at Tell el-Muqdam, but others have located the Dynasty at Thebes. Further work at Muqdam should help resolve this issue.

See also

Late and Ptolemaic periods, overview; Libyans; nome structure; Third Intermediate Period, overview

Further reading

Gomaà, F. 1985. Tell el-Moqdam. In *LÄ* 6: 351–2.

Leahy, A., ed. 1990. *Libya and Egypt c1300–750 BC* (A Publication of the SOAS Centre of Near and Middle Eastern Studies and the Society for Libyan Studies). London.

Redmount, C.A., and R. Friedman. 1993. Tell el-Muqdam: City of the Lions. *Bulletin of the Egypt Exploration Society* 3: 37–8.

——. 1994. The 1993 field season of the Berkeley Tell el-Muqdam Project: preliminary report. *NARCE* 164: 1–10.

Spencer, P.A., and A.J. Spencer. 1986. Notes on Late Libyan Egypt. *JEA* 72: 198–201.

CAROL REDMOUNT

Tell el-Yahudiya

Tell el-Yahudiya is the name of several archaeological sites in Egypt, but the most important one is located near Shebin el-Qanater (Qaliubiya province) in the eastern Delta, *circa* 20 km northeast of Cairo (30°17′ N, 31°20′ E). The origin of this name is a temple of Yhwh which was constructed there *circa* 160 BC by Onias (III), the ousted high priest of the temple in Jerusalem, with the permission of Ptolemy VI Philometor. The temple was closed in AD 71 during the pogroms under Vespasian, but it was still mentioned by the geographer Ptolemy in

the second century AD. Ptolemy places the site east of the Pelusiac branch of the Nile and gives it the toponym "Oniou," after "Onias" rather than "On" (the ancient Egyptian name of Heliopolis, which is mentioned separately).

Onias's temple was situated on a high artificial mound of sand just outside the northeastern corner of a square embankment of sand with rounded corners. The outer slopes of this embankment had a gradient of about 30° and were covered with a layer of plaster. The inner slopes were steeper and were originally lined with a mudbrick wall.

Herbert Ricke considered this embankment a sacred construction—an artificial "primeval mound" like the one supposedly at the cult center of Heliopolis. Flinders Petrie, one of the site's early excavators, recognized a rampart that was characteristic of Syro-Palestinian fortifications of the Middle Bronze Age (MB). It can be expected that a mudbrick fortification wall was originally built on top of this rampart, which had a base diameter of about 100 cubits. The sloping rampart was a precaution to keep siege machinery from the foot of the fortification walls. Such a design can be reconstructed from the remains of an access ramp that once led to a tower on the east. The foundations for this tower are recognizable on Petrie's excavation plans. Middle Bronze Age remains within the fortification walls, however, have been largely destroyed by later constructions.

Typical MB graves have been found within the site, but also some distance from it. They consist of narrow mudbrick chambers covered by vaults. Grave goods are of the same types as those excavated in strata D/3 and D/2 at Tell ed-Dab'a. Black burnished juglets with incised white patterns, named "Tell el-Yahudiya Ware" after the site, are typically found in these graves. Such pottery is frequent in the MB culture in Palestine, but these juglets were produced in the Delta, which was controlled during the Second Intermediate Period by Hyksos, rulers of Syro-Palestinian origin.

The location of a Hyksos military fortification at Tell el-Yahudiya can be explained because of its strategic position controlling access to the Memphis area from Sinai through the Wadi Tumilat in the eastern Delta. From this location, the land route from the eastern edge of the Delta to the north and the river traffic on the Pelusiac branch could also be controlled.

In Ramesside times (19th–20th Dynasties) the site was a ruin, but it was probably regarded as a deserted sacred place, a primeval mound. A temple was built there, possibly in the 19th Dynasty. A (later) temple built by Ramesses III (20th Dynasty) is named in the Harris Papyrus I (35.5, 32a.8): "the estate of the temple of Ramesses III, living, prospering, in health, in the abode of Re, north of Heliopolis" (*N3y-[n-]t3-ḥwt-Rʿmssw-ḥḳ3-Iwnw-'nḫ-wḏ3-snb-m-pr Rʿ-[ḥr-]mḥt-Iwnw*). The name suggests an estate of the mortuary temple of Ramesses III, and it is probably also found in abbreviated form in the Wilbour Papyrus. A palace was also connected to this temple, and beautifully painted faïence tiles from it are in a number of museum collections.

The temple name is also preserved in texts from Assyria as the second princedom of Nathû, and in Greek texts as Natho. In Graeco-Roman times, Tell el-Yahudiya was also called Leontopolis, also the name of another town in the central Delta (modern Tell el-Muqdam). To identify the southern Delta town more accurately, it was named "Leontopolis of the Heliopolites," after the name of its nome, as mentioned by the historian Josephus (*Antiqua Judaica* XIII.3, 1–3). The association of the name Leontopolis with Tell el-Yahudiya comes from the primeval gods of Heliopolis, Shu and Tefnut, who were venerated as a pair of lions.

Today the site of Tell el-Yahudiya is encroached on by agricultural development all around it. Only parts of its former rampart are now visible, but it would still be an interesting place to conduct archaeological investigations.

See also

Hyksos; Second Intermediate Period, overview; Tell ed-Dabʿa, Second Intermediate Period; Tell el-Maskhuta; Tell el-Muqdam; Wadi Tumilat

Further reading

Naville, É. 1890. *The Mound of the Jew and the City of Onias.* London.
Petrie, W.M.F. 1906. *Hyksos and Israelite Cities.* London.
Tufnell, O. 1978. Graves at Tell el-Yahudiyeh: reviewed after a life-time. In *Archaeology in the Levant. Essays for Kathleen Kenyon*, R. Moorey and P. Parr, eds. 76–101. Warminster.
Zivie, A.-P. 1986. Tell el-Jahudiya. In *LÄ* 6: 331–5.

MANFRED BIETAK

textual sources, Early Dynastic

The Early Dynastic period has left behind a somewhat limited but nevertheless abundant textual record. There are several monumental hieroglyphic stelae from royal tombs at Abydos which record the name of the kings buried there. Surrounding these royal tombs are found the graves of retainers and servants which were indicated by stelae containing the names and titles of their owners. The earliest substantial hieroglyphic inscription from this period is a stela belonging to the nobleman Merka, found at Saqqara, and dating to the First Dynasty, under the reign of Qa'a.

Texts from this period also occur on labels which were attached to items deposited in tombs. These labels, sometimes engraved, sometimes painted in black and red ink, preserve the name of the deceased and the type of the commodity to which they were attached. At times these labels are dated by referring to an important event in the reign of a particular king. Similar in purpose to these labels are jar-sealings, which were lumps of clay which covered the mouths of jars of wine and other foodstuffs. These sealings were impressed with the names and titles of the deceased by means of engraved cylinders of wood or stone.

There are also a number of inscriptions found on stone and pottery vessels. These texts could be incised either before or after firing, or painted on the vessels in black ink. The oldest datable hieratic inscription, the Horus-name of King Scorpion, was found on a jar at Tarkhan. These texts preserve the names and titles of the recipients of the vessels, the names of the places for which the vessels were intended, or the place of manufacture of the objects.

As can be seen from the above description, the information content of the Early Dynastic material is not great and consists mainly of names and titles. It has been noted that the longest connected sentence from this period reads: "The Golden [God], he has given the two lands to his son, the king of Upper and Lower Egypt, Peribsen," which is nothing more than an expansion of the king's name.

See also

Abydos, Early Dynastic funerary enclosures; Early Dynastic period, overview; representational evidence, Early Dynastic; writing, invention and early development

Further reading

Emery, W. 1961. *Archaic Egypt*. Harmondsworth.

Kaplony, P. 1963. *Die Inschriften der ägyptische Frühzeit*. Wiesbaden.

——. 1973. Die ältesten Texte. In *Textes et langages de l'Égypte pharaonique*. BdÉ 64(2): 3–13.

STEPHEN E. THOMPSON

textual sources, Late period

Extensive textual sources, literary and non-literary, official and private, exist to aid the study of Egypt during the Late period. Hieroglyphs continued to be used for formal monumental inscriptions, whether private biographical inscriptions, formal royal inscriptions and decrees, or religious texts carved on temple walls. Private individuals with the necessary resources built and decorated for themselves monumental tombs. Especially fine examples are those of Saite (26th Dynasty) officials in Thebes (for example, Montuemhat (TT 34), 'Ankh-Hor (TT 414) and 'Ibi (TT 36)), and a tomb near Hermopolis of the high priest Petosiris, who probably lived during the fourth century BC, just prior to Egypt's conquest by Alexander the Great. A very interesting example of a private stela is that of Ta-'Imyhotep, wife of the last Ptolemaic High Priest of Ptah during the reign of Cleopatra VII. Private individuals also dedicated statues of themselves in major temples; these statues frequently bore important biographical inscriptions. Excellent examples include those of Peftjawawy-Neith (Saite), Udja-Hor-resnet (Persian period) and Sematawytefnakht (time of Alexander the Great). Private religious dedications also included large numbers of stelae dedicated to and recording the lives and deaths of various of the increasingly important sacred animals, such as the Apis bulls and Mothers of the Apis, of whom extensive records have been found at Saqqara. Private stelae also include major magico-religious texts, such as the Metternich Stela, covered with texts intended to protect the individual against snake bite and other potential dangers.

Formal royal inscriptions from the Late period include Saite stelae commemorating historical events (for example, the Adoption Stela of Nitocris set up by her father Psamtik I, and the stela erected by Psamtik II recording his campaign in Nubia) and recording temple dedications (Mit Rahina stela of Apries). Similar stelae were established by or on behalf of various Ptolemaic rulers (for example, the "Satrap Stela" of Ptolemy [I], the Pithom Stela of Ptolemy II, and the so-called "trilingual decrees" issued on behalf of Ptolemies III, IV and V). The Persian king Darius I had carved a series of multilingual stelae recording his excavation of the canal connecting the Nile Valley with the Red Sea. Nectanebo I (30th Dynasty) set up the Naukratis Stela recording major contributions to the temple of Neith of Sais. With the apparent exception of the Persian kings who succeeded Darius I, all kings of the Late period contributed to Egyptian temples, whether enhancing existing temples or building new ones. Temple decoration included both dedicatory inscriptions recording the actions of the rulers and extensive presentations of (non-mortuary) religious texts, including hymns, temple ritual and cultic information not preserved from earlier periods. Occasional texts of economic and geographic importance, such as those at Edfu, are also preserved.

An extensive corpus of non-monumental religious texts, especially hymns and a very wide range of mortuary literature, some known earlier but much of it new, has been preserved from the Late period. Much is written in hieratic, in which there are also rare secular literary compositions. However, most secular literature, and some religious texts, were written in demotic, a very cursive script and late stage of the Egyptian language, which was developed during the Saite period and quickly replaced both hieratic (for literary materials) and abnormal hieratic (which had been developed in the Theban area for private documents). New compositions in several literary genres have been preserved in demotic, including narrative stories, didactic or wisdom texts, epic cycles and moralizing animal stories. Some reflect familiarity with foreign literary traditions, especially Greek and Aramaic, while remaining basically Egyptian compositions. Scientific texts, prophetic texts, myths, dreams and dream interpretation are all found.

Large numbers of personal documents have been preserved from the Late period. In the course of the Saite dynasty, demotic replaced abnormal hieratic for such documents and from then until the end of the Late period, private documents written in Egyptian were written in demotic on either papyrus or ostraca. Well attested are private letters, contracts for sale, lease, mortgage (and foreclosure) of private property (real and personal), surety bonds, and oaths sworn before a specified god concerning accusations of broken contracts, theft and so on. Although made between husband and wife, the so-called "marriage contracts" are perhaps better called "annuity contracts," since they are economic documents establishing lines of economic responsibility and inheritance and have nothing to do with the "legality" of the institution of marriage itself. Many demotic

documents directly or indirectly reflect administrative concerns (such as the so-called Hermopolis law "code"), lists of people or goods or amounts of money (owed or paid), contracts to supply goods or services, tax receipts, rules of conduct for members of cult guilds, and even letters or petitions addressed to the king or his senior representatives. One of the most informative of the latter is the "Petition of Petiese" (also known as Papyrus Rylands IX), written during the reign of Darius I but covering several generations spanning the Saite and early Persian periods. More informal, but frequently quite informative, are graffiti left in temples, tombs, quarries, mining regions and along major roads.

When Egypt was ruled by non-Egyptian speakers, the official administrative language was no longer Egyptian. From the Persian period, important documents written in Aramaic have been preserved. Some are official or semi-official documents, such as the letters written to the satrap Arsames. Others are private letters or contracts (many come from the Jewish community living at Elephantine in the Saite and Persian periods). Ptolemaic Egypt is especially rich in Greek materials, formal administrative decrees, private letters and contracts, and a vast collection of Greek literature. Egypt in the Late period was home to a number of non-Egyptian speaking populations, many of whom have left behind at least occasional written records. For instance, private stelae and graffiti are attested in Phoenician and Carian (the language of one of the provinces of Asia Minor).

Egypt was part of a much larger world during the Late period, and some of the cultures with which it came into contact left records of that contact. Thus, mention of Egypt occasionally occurs in the annals of Assyrian kings, in writings preserved in the Hebrew Bible, in records of the Roman Republic and, more frequently, in the writings of classical authors from various periods. Among the most famous of the classical authors are Herodotus, who lived during the Persian empire and thus was a contemporary or near contemporary of some of what he wrote about, and Diodorus Siculus, who lived during the Roman empire and compiled his history from earlier classical sources.

Excavation has turned up extensive written material, including inscribed architectural fragments, ostraca and papyri, both Egyptian and non-Egyptian. Although many early excavations treated inscribed materials as separate from the rest of the excavation, many recent excavators have made major contributions to our understanding of Egypt during the Late period by fully incorporating excavated textual information with the other archaeological results. The importance of inscribed materials found in controlled archaeological excavation is underscored by the Egypt Exploration Society's publication series entitled "Texts from Excavations," several of which stem from their excavations at portions of North Saqqara occupied during the Late period.

See also

Egyptian (language), decipherment of; Herodotus; Late and Ptolemaic periods, overview; Late period private tombs; Saqqara, Serapeum and animal necropolis

Further reading

Fitzmyer, J.A., and S.A. Kautman. 1992. *An Aramaic Bibliography* 1: Old, Official, and Biblical Aramaic. Baltimore, MD.

Lichtheim, M. 1980. *Ancient Egyptian Literature* 3. Berkeley, CA.

Pestman, P.W. 1990. *The New Papyrological Primer*, 5th edn. Leiden.

Porter, B., and R.L.B. Moss. 1960. *Topographical Bibliography of Ancient Egyptian Hieroglyphic Texts, Reliefs and Paintings*, 7 vols. Oxford.

Posener, G. 1936. *La première domination perse en Égypte, Recueil d'inscriptions hiéroglyphiques* (BdÉ 11). Cairo.

Turner, E.G. 1980. *Greek Papyri: An Introduction*. Oxford.

JANET H. JOHNSON

textual sources, Middle Kingdom

Though limited in quantity, there is considerable variety in the textual sources surviving from Middle Kingdom Egypt. Royal and temple records are scarce, while autobiographical texts are fewer than in either the Old or the New Kingdoms. Pedagogic texts constitute a cohesive group that is small in number and survive mainly through later copies, including hundreds of excerpts on New Kingdom ostraca (potsherds and flakes of limestone which provided an inexpensive surface for writing and drawing). Contemporary papyri include some legal and medical texts (veterinary and gynecological) from the pyramid town of Lahun, the Semna dispatches from the fort in Nubia, and letters of a farmer named Hekanakhte. Graffiti from the period found at the quarries in the Wadi Hammamat, at Hatnub and in the Sinai provide interesting insights, while execration texts written in ink on bowls or figurines are among the most significant historical documents of this period. For religious literature, there are numerous examples of coffins and related funerary artifacts inscribed with funerary texts that bridge the gap between the *Pyramid Texts* (inscribed in the burial chambers of late Old Kingdom pyramids) and the New Kingdom *Book(s) of the Dead*. There are also votive stelae that attest to the religiosity of the common man.

The Middle Kingdom is perhaps best known from the literary texts that survive from that period. The names of the authors of several of these pieces are known, and they account for half of the eight individual great authors listed on a much later New Kingdom papyrus. Unlike the listed authors of the Old Kingdom, who were princes or highest officials, the Middle Kingdom authors seem to have been scribes who were teachers in the palace or temple schools. Khety, called the greatest of the scribes on a later, well-known papyrus (Chester Beatty IV), wrote what is now known as a *Satire on the Trades*, that pointed out all the dangers, difficulties and disadvantages associated with the various professions a young man might pursue. Khety argues humorously and emphatically that the scribe's position is the finest possible goal in life. This type of propaganda for the profession was obviously a school textbook since it survived in hundreds of partial copies.

According to papyrus Chester Beatty IV, this Khety was also known as the author of the *Instruction of King Amenemhat I*, a propaganda text of a different kind. Written after Amenemhat I had been assassinated (probably as the result of a harim conspiracy), the text was obviously composed for the benefit of his son and successor, Senusret I. It provides some historical information about a difficult transition, albeit from the perspective of one who had to re-establish order after several successive dynastic crises. This popular work is closely attuned with the famous *Story of Sinuhe*, whose author is unknown, but whose purpose is also to demonstrate both the legitimacy and the goodness of Senusret I. Perhaps related as well is the so-called *Prophecy of Neferti*, who was another of the famous scribes listed in papyrus Chester Beatty IV. Set in the Old Kingdom court of Seneferu, the text provides some description of the chaos of the First Intermediate Period and foretells *ex-post facto* the coming of Amenemhat I as a savior. Neferti's work also shows affinities with the anonymous *Story of the Miracles in the Reign of King Khufu*. This work was also a prophecy of dynastic change from Khufu's 4th Dynasty to a 5th Dynasty heavily influenced by the cult of the sun god Re. From details and language this also appears to be a Middle Kingdom work. It is likely that the Khufu setting would have influenced Neferti's even earlier setting in the reign of Seneferu.

Certainly the most pious text in the well documented genre of instruction literature is the royal "confession" known as the *Instruction for King Merikare*. The setting for this text is the impending collapse of a dynasty centered at Heracleopolis at the end of the First Intermediate Period. Candidly admitting his own mistakes, the unnamed king advises his son, warning of the omniscience and justice of Re.

This essentially religious text obviously has its historical dimension and, whether an original Heracleopolitan text or another 12th Dynasty composition, it fits well with the rest of these texts, that, when taken together, seem to exemplify a different type of historiography which combined explanations of past events as related to their present and as applicable to their future.

Another text with a Heracleopolitan setting that was at least copied, if not written, in the Middle Kingdom is the story of the *Eloquent Peasant*. The subject is justice; the message is patience. The unseen king is shown to be provident, generous and eventually responsive, and a temperate, deferential and persistent approach with regard to his apparently unresponsive bureaucracy is shown to be the best course. The fanciful story of the *Shipwrecked Sailor* does not seem to have a historical setting nor does it have any propaganda value, though it may have served as a lesson in how not to explain one's failure on a royal mission. The instructions of *Sehotepibre* and *Father to Son* are gross propaganda pieces that most likely date to the second half of the 12th Dynasty. These works offer little more than exaggerated, fulsome praise of the king, and were probably intended to benefit Senusret III, who had difficulties with local nomarchs (governors) that led to his suppressing them. The *Instruction from Father to Son* may have been written by a man named Ptahemdjedhuty, from the list in the papyrus Chester Beatty IV. The last of the great named authors on this papyrus, Khakheperresonb, complains that he wants new words to express himself since everything had already been said, but he also criticizes those who wrote *ex-post facto* prophesies as well as those who plagiarized; things that all the other great Middle Kingdom authors certainly were guilty of doing.

Among the literary texts, the *Admonitions of Ipuwer*, whether describing fictitious or real happenings in the First or Second Intermediate Periods or even in the Middle Kingdom, is an elaborate lamentation addressed either to the king or to the sun god Re. The descriptions are poignant and complete enough that the author may have witnessed the events described, and the text is often used to describe the effects of Egyptian civil war. *The Dispute of a Man with His Ba* (soul) is the most difficult to understand of the literary texts (both because of its incomplete state and the lack of a clear unifying structure), but it is most intriguing for its psychological debate about suicide as a response to guilt for a heinous crime.

Literary texts such as the *Instruction of King Amenemhat I* and the *Story of Sinuhe* are always cited in histories of ancient Egypt because of the information they offer concerning the internal and external affairs at the time, but they are not properly historical texts. The remaining Middle Kingdom texts are classified as non-literary, ranging from tomb inscriptions (religious and autobiographical), stelae (personal and political), to letters, graffiti, contracts and miscellaneous items. The texts on tomb walls in provincial cemeteries, such as Beni Hasan, Deir el-Bersha and Asyut, reveal something about the changes that took place in the First Intermediate Period, the growing independence of the nomarchs, their local administration, and their expeditions undertaken at royal behest. Some stelae of individuals also record expeditions (for example, to Nubia and Syria), but most merely list their owners' titles and record their personal piety. The texts in the tomb of Hapidjefa at Asyut record in detail the owner's contracts with priests to provide for his offerings after he died.

The major collections of graffiti from the Middle Kingdom tend to be rather long, formal texts that record quarrying expeditions by dates and leaders, and sometimes give information about the size, specific purpose and noteworthy events. One long inscription from the Wadi Hammamat gives an elaborate explanation of the portent that led to their choice of a stone slab for a sarcophagus lid, something that was thought to have accounted for the success of this expedition. The inscriptions in Sinai are not as lengthy or formal. Based on seamen's titles, it can be surmised that some part of the route to the quarries was on the Red Sea.

The letters that survive from this period are very limited but interesting. Those from the fort at Semna, in the region of the Second Cataract

in Nubia, are reports and generally very fragmentary. The Hekanakhte letters are much more informative about the administration of agricultural land and allow us to get much closer to an Egyptian family (in Thebes) through the eyes of the absent head of the household. Hekanakhte's letters to his sons instruct them in dealing with his tenants, who work fields that he rents from others, as well as in how to deal with his wives and other children. Another rare papyrus now in the Brooklyn Museum lists the staff members of a large estate in Middle Egypt, both field hands and household staff, including a very high percentage of Asiatics.

Execration texts from the 12th and 13th Dynasties survive from several sites (Saqqara, Thebes and Nubia). Found on either bowls or figurines, these formulaic texts were written to eliminate magically whatever or whomever was considered inimical by deliberately smashing the artifact. Foreign cities and their rulers are listed at length, particularly from the western Asiatic littoral, but Libyan and Nubian enemies of Egypt are also included, as are a few Egyptians whose names and titles indicate probable involvement in a harim conspiracy. Through such ritual these particular enemies could be repeatedly damned.

The large body of funerary literature from the Middle Kingdom is known as *Coffin Texts*, even though these texts were copied on tomb walls, papyri, stelae, statues, masks, biers and canopic chests (containers for the viscera of a mummy), as well as on wooden coffins of all sizes. The texts include hymns, prayers and spells of all kinds, plus identifications of deities, demons and places of the afterlife. These collections of texts were essentially "guidebooks" to the afterlife similar to the *Pyramid Texts* of the Old Kingdom. Although the surviving monuments of the Old and New Kingdoms are much more impressive than those of the Middle Kingdom, the texts that survive from this period are generally of the greatest significance, the broadest range and the highest quality, fully justifying the study of Middle Egyptian as the best introduction to this ancient language.

See also

Asyut; Beni Hasan; Deir el-Bersha; Egyptian (language), decipherment of; First Intermediate Period, overview; funerary texts; Hatnub; Lahun, town; Middle Kingdom, overview; Nubian forts; papyrus; textual sources, New Kingdom; Wadi Hammamat; writing, reading and schooling

Further reading

Breasted, J.H. 1906. *Ancient Records of Egypt: Historical Documents* 1. Chicago.
Faulkner, R.O. 1973–8. *The Ancient Egyptian Coffin Texts*, 3 vols. Warminster.
Lichtheim, M. 1973. *Ancient Egyptian Literature* 1. Berkeley, CA.
Pritchard, J.B. 1969. *Ancient Near Eastern Texts Relating to the Old Testament.* Princeton, NJ.
Simpson, W.K. 1973. *The Literature of Ancient Egypt.* New Haven, CT.

LEONARD H. LESKO

textual sources, New Kingdom

Only a fraction of the textual output of the New Kingdom (*circa* 1,550–1,070 BC) has been preserved, but from what remains it is obvious that most traditions established in the Old and Middle Kingdoms were carried on. As before, a sizable portion of the texts pertains to the mortuary cult, as texts have survived in much greater numbers in the dry desert where cemeteries and mortuary temples are located. In what follows, a survey of New Kingdom textual traditions precedes a list of some innovations of the period. As in other epochs of pharaonic history, texts appear mostly on stone walls, papyrus rolls or potsherds.

If distinguished by social function, texts are either public or private. Public or communal texts are not written for any specific individuals, though access may be restricted to certain classes. Public texts encompass those that are intended for display, and those that are not.

Private or personal texts are in principle aimed at one or more specific persons. When we speak of ancient Egyptian literature, we usually mean public texts. Literature as a product of the creative and imaginative use of language is a concept born in the nineteenth century. If it were applied to ancient Egyptian texts, the body of texts that could be called literature would be very limited.

Public texts meant for display are mainly historical (that is, autobiographical or biographical) or religious. They typically appear on stone and are as a rule promulgated by political or religious authorities. Like their forebears in the Old and Middle Kingdoms, New Kingdom pharaohs and nobles adorned the walls of their temples and tombs with historical and biographical records of their deeds. Some typical examples are as follows.

In the royal sphere, Tuthmose III had the annals of his sixteen campaigns into southwest Asia inscribed on the walls of the temple at Karnak. On a stela found near the sphinx at Giza, Amenhotep II recounts his love of horses and the many athletic exploits of his youth. At Thebes and elsewhere, multiple copies have been found of a text narrating the battle of Ramesses II against the Hittites at Qadesh in Syria; the king describes with poetic hyperbole how he trounced the enemy all by himself when his troops had deserted him. In the private sphere, the inscriptions in the tomb of Ahmose son of Ibana at Elkab describe the tomb owner's brilliant military career in the service of the kings Ahmose, Amenhotep I and Tuthmose I. They also provide unique historical information about the end of Hyksos rule in Egypt. The Theban tomb inscriptions of the vizier Rekhmire (TT 100), who served under Tuthmose III, provide, in addition to information about the tomb owner's life, valuable juridical data about the duties of the vizier, the highest ranking official in the ancient Egyptian administration.

Temples and tombs are also lavishly ornamented with religious texts, including hymns and prayers to gods and kings and ritual texts. These texts are found not only on walls but also on stelae. For example, a hymn on a stela now in the Louvre Museum narrates the myth of Osiris.

Public texts not for display are typically written on papyrus. Among those texts whose imaginative use of language makes them the most akin to what one thinks of as literature in modern times are tales, love poems and wisdom literature. These texts are for entertainment and moral instruction. Among the best preserved tales are the following: the *Doomed Prince* narrates the adventures of a young Egyptian crown prince abroad; the *Two Brothers* is a tale of conflict and reconciliation between two brothers, perhaps as an allegory of the strife and unification of two Egyptian cities; the *Contendings of Horus and Seth* describes the fierce contest between two arch-rivals, the son and the brother of Osiris, and the superiority of Horus; the *Report of Wenamen* portrays the mission of an Egyptian royal envoy who sails out to buy Lebanese timber for his lord. Two great wisdom texts, the *Instruction of Amenemope* and the *Instruction of Any*, continue a tradition inaugurated by such famous Old and Middle Kingdom works as the *Maxims of Ptahhotep* and the *Teaching for the Vizier Kagemni*.

Public texts not for display also include religious and magical works. The *Book of the Dead* is a collection of spells inscribed on papyrus, placed next to the deceased in the tomb. The spells, which differ in number and selection from copy to copy, were thought to protect the deceased against evils in the netherworld. *Guides to the Hereafter*, a genre exclusive to the New Kingdom, are found on the walls of royal tombs in the Valley of the Kings; there they are at least potentially on display, but they have been classified here because they were perhaps originally not so intended. Such *Guides* (for example, the *Book of Caves* and the *Book of Gates*) teach the deceased about the geography and other aspects of the netherworld.

Private texts from the New Kingdom abound, pertaining to every aspect of daily life and commerce, official and casual, such as letters, deeds of sale, accounts, and court documents. What follows is a list of eight

characteristics of the New Kingdom textual corpus, as compared to Old and Middle Kingdom texts.

(1) *Size of the corpus.* New Kingdom texts vastly outnumber those of the Old and Middle Kingdoms. This difference does not seem entirely due to accidents of survival. To what extent increased literacy or population growth played a role remains a matter of conjecture.

(2) *Emergence of a "classical" literature.* Many literary texts of the Middle Kingdom continued to be copied and read and thus acquired the status of a classical literature. At the same time, Middle Egyptian, the language of the Middle Kingdom, remained in use as an artificial language for religious and literary purposes. The continuation of things Middle Egyptian lends a certain complexity to New Kingdom texts. Among literary texts of the New Kingdom, it is necessary to distinguish between those written in the New Kingdom in Late Egyptian, the contemporary language (e.g. the *Report of Wenamen*), those written in the New Kingdom in the language of the Middle Kingdom (e.g. the many 18th Dynasty biographical inscriptions), and those written in the Middle Kingdom but copied and read also in the New Kingdom (e.g. the *Story of Sinuhe* on the Ashmolean Ostracon dating to the Ramesside period (19th–20th Dynasties)). The sense of a classical literature is supported by a text in papyrus Chester Beatty IV which describes the immortality of writers of the past, stating, "A man has perished, and his corpse has become dust.... But writings cause him to be remembered in the mouth of the story-teller."

(3) *Variety of linguistic expression.* New Kingdom textual sources are characterized by an almost bewildering assortment of idioms. First, there are texts written in the language spoken at the time. This idiom is found as a rule in texts serving a practical function in daily life, be it as official documents of the royal chancellory or as letters between private individuals, hence the name "non-literary Late Egyptian." It is generally assumed that the *Report of Wenamen* is also a specimen of non-literary Egyptian, as it seems based on actual events.

Most texts with literary pretensions seem

influenced by older stages of the language. Their idioms are probably different mixtures of the spoken language and archaizing features. Differences of dialect may also have played a role. For example, the idiom of the literary stories on papyrus is different from that of the monumental inscriptions of the Ramesside era. Both in turn differ from the idiom of the school texts.

Linguistically speaking, the reign of Amenhotep IV/Akhenaten was a watershed. In the early New Kingdom, the colloquial language spoken by the average Egyptian had been for some time Late Egyptian, while Middle Egyptian persisted as the written language. One of the many revolutions that took place during the reign of the heretic king was the promotion of Late Egyptian from a vernacular to the standard *Hochsprache*.

(4) *Cosmopolitan character.* The New Kingdom was a period of imperial expansion eastward into Asia and southward into Nubia. This is reflected in the texts, thematically in the historical texts such as the Annals of the Asian campaigns of Tuthmose III and in fictional narratives such as the tale of the *Doomed Prince*, and linguistically in the many Semitic loanwords. As evidence of textual traffic, one might also mention the cuneiform texts inscribed on tablets found at Tell el-Amarna, Akhenaten's capital, containing correspondence between the pharaoh and foreign rulers.

Another striking point of contact between Egypt and southwest Asia is that the *Instruction of Amenemope* served as a source for the biblical book of Proverbs 22:17–23:10, as Adolf Erman established. Already before Erman's discovery, it was assumed that Proverbs 22:17–24:22 was once a separate unit. Compare, for example, *Amenemope* Chapter 9 (column 11, lines 13–14), "Do not befriend the heated man, nor approach him for conversation," with Proverbs 22:24, "Make no friendship with a man given to anger, nor go with a wrathful man." Proverbs 22:20 indirectly acknowledges the Egyptian source: "Have I not written for you thirty sayings of admonition and knowledge?" The *Instruction of Amenemope* contains exactly 30 chapters (27, 7–8: "Look to these thirty chapters; they inform, they educate").

(5) *Rise of individualism.* This aspect is all-pervasive of life in the New Kingdom. For example, the *Book of the Dead*, which was inscribed on papyrus, was accessible to a far larger class of people than its Old Kingdom predecessor, the *Pyramid Texts*, which were the privilege of kings and queens, or than its Middle Kingdom predecessor, the *Coffin Texts*, which were restricted to high-ranking and wealthy nobles. New Kingdom hymns and prayers give more expression to personal piety than their antecedents. Humility first clearly emerges as a virtue.

No love poetry is attested before the New Kingdom. Perhaps it is a creation of this period. The following verses sound quite modern, and their tone is unlike any Old or Middle Kingdom text: "With graceful step she treads the ground, captures my heart by her movements. She causes all men's necks to turn about to see her; joy has he whom she embraces, he is like the first of men!"

(6) *School texts.* A large number of surviving school texts is characteristic of the New Kingdom. Hardly any such Old or Middle Kingdom texts are known, but this may be an accident of survival.

(7) *Illuminations in manuscripts.* These are also an innovation of the New Kingdom.

(8) *Amarna period.* As mentioned above, the New Kingdom also encompasses the single most remarkable interval in Egyptian history, Akhenaten's reign. His theology is explained on boundary stelae erected around the capital at Amarna and in the tombs of his courtiers located there.

See also

Amarna Letters; Egyptian language and writing; funerary texts; representational evidence, New Kingdom private tombs; representational evidence, New Kingdom royal tombs; textual sources, Middle Kingdom; textual sources, Old Kingdom

Further reading

Altenmüller, H., *et al.* 1970. *Literatur.*
Handbuch der Orientalistik I, 1. Leiden and
Cologne.

Faulkner, R.O., W.K. Simpson and E.F. Wente,
Jr. 1972. *The Literature of Ancient Egypt: An*
Anthology of Stories, Instructions, and Poetry,
W.K. Simpson, ed. New Haven, CT.

Lichtheim, M. 1976. *Ancient Egyptian*
Literature: A Book of Readings 2: *The New*
Kingdom. Berkeley, CA.

LEO DEPUYDT

textual sources, Old Kingdom

The first substantial hieroglyphic inscription is
the early 4th Dynasty text from the tomb of an
official named Metjen, who served the last kings
of the 3rd Dynasty. This text is the first example
of what are called tomb biographies. At first
these texts consisted only of the titles which the
official held, and copies of legal documents
which had been of particular significance to the
deceased, such as decrees establishing his
funerary foundation and estates. Around the
middle of the 5th Dynasty, the information
found in these texts becomes more varied, and
includes events which occurred throughout the
career of the deceased. Beginning with the
inscriptions of the 6th Dynasty official Weni,
we have the first lengthy narrative texts describing several events and accomplishments of the
deceased. These events are centered around the
king, however, and describe tasks which the
officials performed for the king, such as the
successful completion of military expeditions,
the judging of important matters and so on. The
main purpose of these biographies was to
impress passers-by sufficiently that they would
be moved to recite the offering formula, and
thereby ensure that the deceased would be well-
provisioned in the afterlife.

In connection with tomb biographies, copies
of letters from the king to various officials are
found carved on the walls of the tombs of their
recipients. The majority of these letters date to
the reign of Djedkare-Isesi and deal with
expressions of royal favor and praise for the
tomb owner. The one such text dating from the
6th Dynasty is a copy of a letter from Pepi II to
an official named Harkhuf, which instructed
him to take good care of a dwarf that he was
bringing from Nubia.

A number of legal texts have also been
preserved in stone copies. There are numerous
examples of royal decrees which were issued by
the king on behalf of particular temples or
statue-cults, and which granted immunity to
their beneficiaries from royal imposts and taxes.
The extent to which such institutions were
exempt, however, has been debated. Copies of
private legal documents usually deal with
matters related to the funerary needs of an
individual, such as the organization of his
funerary cult.

The *Pyramid Texts*, which are first found on
the interior walls of the pyramid of Unas (the
last king of the 5th Dynasty), and later in the
pyramids of the 6th Dynasty kings (and some
queens), are a major source of texts from this
period. These texts are probably to be dated no
earlier than roughly one hundred years before
the earliest preserved copy, and many of the
texts are contemporary with the pyramids in
which they are found. These texts were intended
to aid the deceased king in his transition to and
continued well-being in the hereafter. They
include magical spells, whose purpose is to
protect the deceased from various dangers (for
example, snakes and scorpions), texts which are
related to various funerary rituals, and spells
designed to allow the deceased to overcome any
obstacles that he might encounter in the next
life.

There are several examples of administrative
texts preserved on papyri. An archive discovered at Abusir, believed to date to the reign of
Djedkare-Isesi, contains records from a royal
funerary temple which cover a period of
twenty-four years. The Gebelein Papyri, also
dated to the end of the 5th Dynasty, contain
accounts of the production of grain and cloth.

In addition to these administrative texts, a
number of letters have been preserved on
papyri, the earliest dating again to the reign

of Djedkare-Isesi. Most of these texts date to the 6th Dynasty; they deal with both affairs of the administration and purely private matters. There are also several examples of what are called "Letters to the Dead" preserved on linen and pottery. In these texts, Egyptians would write to their dead relatives in order to gain their help in righting wrongs which they felt they were suffering on earth. Frequently the deceased individual is asked to take another deceased person before the court of the afterworld to obtain satisfaction for a living relative.

Several inscribed potsherds, known as ostraca, are preserved from the Old Kingdom. The eight so far published all seem to have functioned as labels which accompanied the body of an individual during transfer to its place of burial. There are also several examples of what are known as "execration texts" preserved from this period. The names of enemies of the king were recorded on clay figurines which were then smashed in a ritual intended to render the enemy powerless. Old Kingdom Egyptian officials who visited remote or foreign locations left graffiti at places like the Sinai, the quarries of Hatnub, the Wadi Hammamat and Abu Simbel. These texts usually contain the names of officials, the dates of their visits and the nature of their business for the king.

There are several texts, not preserved in copies dating to the Old Kingdom, which are thought to have originated at that time. The Palermo Stone, a fragmentary text which is thought to date to the 25th Dynasty, contains what appears to be a copy of an Old Kingdom document which recorded a list of kings from the Predynastic period to the end of the 5th Dynasty; it lists important events in each year of their reign. There are several "Instruction" texts preserved in later copies that have been traditionally dated to the Old Kingdom. These texts preserve aphoristic sayings which offer advice on the proper behavior essential to achieving success and prosperity in this life and the next. One text, attested no earlier than the New Kingdom, is attributed to Hardjedef, a son of Khufu. The author of the *Instructions of Ptahhotep* was thought to be a vizier who served under King Djedkare-Isesi of the 5th Dynasty,

and the *Instructions for Kagemni* appears to have been addressed to a vizier who served under Huni and Seneferu. It should be noted that these last two works are preserved in the stage of the Egyptian language known as Middle Egyptian, rather than in the language of the Old Kingdom. Some scholars date these texts to periods considerably later than the authors to whom they are attributed, and their actual composition in the Old Kingdom is doubtful.

See also

Abusir; Egyptian language and writing; Old Kingdom, overview; Old Kingdom provincial tombs; representational evidence, Old Kingdom private tombs; Saqqara, pyramids of the 5th and 6th Dynasties

Further reading

Faulkner, R. 1969. *The Ancient Egyptian Pyramid Texts*, 2 vols. Oxford.

Posener-Kriéger, P. 1973. Les papyrus de l'ancien empire. In *Textes et langages de l'Égypte pharaonique*. BdÉ 64.2: 25–35.

Roccati, A. 1982. *La littérature historique sous l'ancient empire égyptien*. Paris.

Simpson, W.K., ed. 1973. *The Literature of Ancient Egypt*. New Haven, CT.

Wente, E. 1990. *Letters from Ancient Egypt*, E. Meltzer, ed. Atlanta, GA.

STEPHEN E. THOMPSON

Thebes, el-Asasif

There are two regions in the Theban necropolis called el-Asasif. Both are plains at the beginning of wadis (valleys) leading to the west. Commonly, the northern site (25°44′ N, 32°37′ E), east of Deir el-Bahri between the regions of Dra' Abu el-Naga and el-Khokha, is connected with the name el-Asasif. The southern counterpart at the end of the valley leading to one of the unfinished royal tombs of the early Middle Kingdom and next to the southern slope of Sheikh Abd el-Qurna, is almost neglected. As far as the southern Asasif has been investigated, only six tombs of the Late period are known. Their architecture, plans and sections have been published by Dieter Eigner.

The history of the cemetery in the northern Asasif starts with the second half of the 11th Dynasty, when some *saff*-tombs were hewn out at the bottom and on the southern side of the valley (for example, the tombs of Antef and Zar). In connection with the construction of the causeway leading to the royal tomb and mortuary temple of King Nebhepetre Mentuhotep II at Deir el-Bahri, the plain of the Asasif was no longer used for private tombs of that period. Most of the contemporary corridor-shaped Middle Kingdom tombs were situated on the upper parts of the hillsides surrounding Deir el-Bahri. The position of those tombs, namely of the cemeteries 500, 600 and 800 (numbers after H.E. Winlock), underlines in an impressive way the importance of orientation and the connection between private tombs and royal mortuary buildings.

The same tradition and purpose is again to be realized in the position of the tomb of Puiemre, which is oriented to the causeways of Hatshepsut and Tuthmose III. Although this tomb is hewn out in the northern slope of the hillock of el-Khokha, the context assigns it to the Asasif. The same connection must be attributed to the tomb of Parennefer, dating from the period of Amenhotep III and Akhenaten. During the time of Amenhotep III the northern Asasif again becomes popular. A new type of huge private tomb, reminiscent of temples rather than of private tomb-chapels, was begun but never finished in the plain of the Asasif. The tomb of Kheruef is one of these tombs, consisting of an entrance building, a pathway leading to a sunken courtyard surrounded by a colonnade, followed by an enlarged inner room scheme with a long sloping passage leading down to the sarcophagus chamber.

In Ramesside times, by the reign of Ramesses II, the walls and colonnades of the courtyards of the 18th Dynasty tombs served as new places for many small tombs, mostly belonging to middle-rank employees of the temple of Amen

at Karnak. With the beginning of the 21st Dynasty the earlier rock-cut tombs frequently were reused for simple burials, consisting only of the sarcophagus and the absolutely essential funeral equipment.

During the Late period, the Asasif achieved for the last time an era of great importance. The chief stewards of the Divine Votaresses and the prophets of Amen began to erect their huge tombs, or mortuary palaces, in this region. As Manfried Bietak has pointed out in the publication of the tomb of Ankh-Hor, several of these buildings are radially oriented by their main pylons to one of the bark shrines along the causeway of Queen Hatshepsut. Their main entrances, framed by smaller pylons, are directly and at right angles connected to this causeway. An exhaustive investigation of the tombs of the Late period with an excellent map of the region has been published by Eigner.

The most important tombs of the el-Asasif are listed below in chronological order, according to their numbers (TT = Theban Tomb), their owners and their professions.

11th Dynasty:

TT 366 Zar, Custodian of the King's Harim
TT 386 Antef, Chancellor of the King of Lower Egypt, Overseer of Soldiers,

Hatshepsut/Tuthmose III:

TT 39 Puiemre, Second Prophet of Amen

Amenhotep III/Akhenaten:

TT 188 Parennefer, Royal Butler and Steward
TT 192 Kheruef, Steward of the Great Royal Wife Tiye

Ramesses II:

TT 194 Dehutemhab, Overseer of the Marshland-dwellers of the Estate of Amen
TT 409 Samut, called Kyky, Scribe, Counter of the Cattle of the Estate of Amen

Late period:

TT 27 Sheshonk, Chief Steward of the Divine Votaress
TT 33 Pedamenopet, Prophet, Chief Lector Priest

TT 34 Mentuemhet, Fourth Prophet of Amen

TT 36 Ibi, Chief Steward of the Divine Votaress

TT 37 Harwa, Chief Steward of the God's Wife

See also

Late and Ptolemaic periods, overview; Late period private tombs; Middle Kingdom, overview; New Kingdom, overview

Further reading

Arnold, D. 1971. *Das Grab des Inj-jtj.f: Die Architektur* (AVDAIK 4). Mainz.

Bietak, M., and E. Reiser-Haslauer. 1978–82. *Das Grab des Anch-Hor* (Untersuchungen der Zweigstelle Kairo des Österreichischen Archäologischen Institutes 4–5). Vienna.

Eigner, D. 1984. *Die monumentalen Grabbauten der Spätzeit in der thebanischen Nekropole* (Untersuchungen der Zweigstelle Kairo des Österreichischen Archäologischen Institutes 6). Vienna.

Kampp, F. 1996. *Die Thebanische Nekropole— Zum Wandel des Grabgedankens von der XVIII. bis zur XX. Dynastie* (Theben 13). Mainz.

FRIEDERIKE KAMPP-SEYFRIED

Thebes, Dra' Abu el-Naga

One of the most important parts of the Theban necropolis, called Dra' Abu el-Naga (25°44′ N, 32°27′ E), stretches from the mouth of the Valley of the Kings on the north to the entrance of the valley leading to el-Asasif and Deir el-Bahri in the south. In general, the area is divided into Dra' Abu el-Naga North and South, with a transitional area between the two. More detailed and precise designations of specific points are as follows from north to south: (1) Khawi el-Alamat, a wadi (or valley) leading to one of the supposed early royal 18th Dynasty tombs; (2) the so-called "main hill"; (3) the region around and below the Coptic monastery of Deir el-Bakhit; (4) the wadi called "Shig el-Ateyat"; and (5) the hillside and plain of "el-Mandara."

The history of Dra' Abu el-Naga starts with the beginning of the 17th Dynasty. Since the excavations of Auguste Mariette, Giuseppe Passalaqua, Flinders Petrie, the Marquis of Northampton and Howard Carter and Lord Carnarvon beginning in the nineteenth century, it has been known that royal and private cemeteries of the 17th Dynasty were situated at Dra' Abu el-Naga. Numerous and important artifacts of private and royal burials went to various museums, but the unpublished notes and manuscripts of the excavators gave no precise description of the location of the important royal tombs. Studying these notes in comparison with the pharaonic description of the site in the famous Tomb Robbery Papyri of the 20th Dynasty, H.E. Winlock published a noteworthy article in 1924. His results suggest that the royal tombs were situated more or less at the foot of the Dra' Abu el-Naga hills, in the close vicinity of the private tombs and arranged like the itinerary order of the ancient papyri.

After conducting a survey of the area in 1989, Friederike Kampp pointed out that the royal tombs would be likely located in the upper regions of the site. She offers the following reasons for this: (1) there should be some distance between the royal and the private cemeteries, and it is unlikely that private tombs would be situated "behind" royal tombs of the same period, which would be the case in Winlock's proposal; (2) in the regions of Khawi el-Alamat and the "main hill" rock-cut tombs resembling the corridor *saff*-tombs of the Middle Kingdom were recorded, but show such architectural modifications as to be interpreted as a consequent development of the former shape of the Middle Kingdom type; and (3) almost at the top of the "main hill," near the Coptic monastery of Deir el-Bakhit, there are three extraordinary huge tombs, which most likely are 17th Dynasty royal tombs. These latter consist of a large courtyard with a boundary wall at the front, followed by a kind of vestibule, and then by one single-pillared room, in whose middle opens an enormous deep shaft. At about the same time as Kampp, Daniel Polz came to similar conclusions; he now hopes to find further proof from excavations at the site.

Polz has excavated part of a cemetery in front of Khawi el-Alamat, where he discovered tomb structures comparable to the lost tomb of Tetiky (TT 15) in the plain of el-Mandara. The basic layout of these tombs consists of a trapezoidal courtyard, surrounded by a mudbrick wall, with a shaft in the middle of the court and a mudbrick building serving as cult chapel west of the shaft, but inside the courtyard.

The cemeteries of Dra' Abu el-Naga lost most of their importance from the reign of Hatshepsut until the end of the 18th Dynasty. Nevertheless, some officials were buried in Dra' Abu el-Naga and hundreds of minor tombs have been constructed so that this part of the necroplis shows one of the densest concentrations of tombs in the whole Theban area. Recent excavations on the "main hill" proved that beside the tomb of Huy (TT 40) and the one of Nay (TT 271) at Qurnet Murai, one of the earliest tombs after the Amarna interim was erected in Dra' Abu el-Naga. This tomb, belonging to a high priest of Amen called Parennefer, lies within a small group of tombs dating to the end of the 18th and the beginning of the 19th Dynasty.

Important Rammesside tombs (19th–20th Dynasties) are to be found in the upper regions of Dra' Abu el-Naga South at the hill of el-Mandara. Here most of the high priests of Amen, a viceroy of Nubia and high military officials mostly connected to the southern territories of Egypt constructed their large, elaborate tombs. Most of these tombs have mudbrick pyramids as superstructures and courtyards with pylons in front. Smaller Ramesside tombs are scattered all over Dra' Abu el-Naga as in the other parts of the Theban necropolis. After the 20th Dynasty, a time of usurpation and reusing of tombs flourished in Dra' Abu el-Naga as well as in the other regions of the necropolis.

In the Late period, only one tomb was hewn out of the hillside at el-Mandara; the owner of this tomb used the already existing courtyard and façade of the famous tomb of Bakenkhonsu (TT 35). In Ptolemaic times some tombs in the plain at the foot of the "main hill" were used to house ibis burials. From Coptic times on, the region of Dra' Abu el-Naga was populated and the impressive ruins of the monastery at Deir el-Bakhit demonstrate its prosperity.

A selection of the most important tombs of Dra' Abu el-Naga are listed below in chronological order, according to their numbers (TT = Theban Tomb), giving the name and title of the tomb owners.

Late 17th–early 18th Dynasty:

TT 12 Ḥray, Overseer of the Granary of the King's Wife and King's Mother AḢhotep

TT 15 Tetiky, King's son, Mayor of the Southern City

Hatshepsut–Tuthmose III:

TT 11 Djehuty, Overseer of the Treasury

TT 155 Antef, Great Herald of the King

Tutankhamen–Horemheb:

No official TT no.
        Parennefer, High Priest of Amen

TT 255 Roy, Royal Scribe and Steward of the Estates of Horemheb and of Amen

Ramesses II:

TT 35 Bekenkhonsu, High Priest of Amen

TT 156 Pennesuttaui, Captain of Troops, Governor of the Southern Lands

TT 157 Nebwenenef, High Priest of Amen

TT 288 and TT 289
        Setau, Viceroy of Kush, Overseer of the Southern Lands

Late 19th Dynasty–Ramesses III:

TT 148 Amenemopet, Prophet of Amen

TT 158 Thonefer, Third Prophet of Amen

Late period:

TT 160 Besenmut, True Royal Acquaintance

TT 11 and TT 12
        Ibis burials

See also

New Kingdom, overview; pyramid tombs of the New Kingdom

Further reading

Fisher, C. 1924. A group of Theban tombs. *The Museum Journal, University of Pennsylvania* 15: 28–49.

Kampp, F. 1996. *Die Thebanische Nekropole— Zum Wandel des Grabgedankens von XVIII. bis zur XX. Dynastie* (Theben 13). Mainz.

Polz, D. 1992. Bericht über die erste Grabungskampagne in der Nekropole Dra Abu el-Naga/Theben West. *MDAIK* 48: 109–30.

Winlock, H.E. 1924. The tombs of the kings of the Seventeenth Dynasty at Thebes. *JEA* 10: 217–77.

FRIEDERIKE KAMPP-SEYFRIED

Thebes, el-Khokha

One of the minor parts of the Theban necropolis, called el-Khokha (25°44′ N, 32°37′ E), consists of a hillock and an adjacent little valley to the south, which separates the region of el-Asasif in the north from Sheikh Abd el-Qurna in the south. This location, next to the causeways leading to the mortuary temples of Deir el-Bahri, seems to be one of the main reasons for the popularity of this part of the necropolis, especially for persons of middle rank in the New Kingdom. Other reasons may be its proximity to the funerary temple of Tuthmose III and the fact that one of the two access roads leading to the hillside of Sheikh Abd el-Qurna runs along the southern slope of the hillock of el-Khokha. In all parts of the necropolis, easy access and orientation to processional roads are basic motives for the position of tombs. The honeycombed hill of el-Khokha should be counted among the most intensively occupied parts of the Theban necropolis, along with the northern region of Dra' Abu el-Naga.

The earliest rock-cut tombs of Thebes are situated at el-Khokha. The area had such prestige at the end of the Old Kingdom and the First Intermediate Period that even nomarchs erected their tombs in this part of the necropolis; the reason for this is still unknown. In addition to the four decorated and officially numbered tombs of this period, there may be a number of undecorated and unexcavated tombs, likewise dating to the First Intermediate Period or the Middle Kingdom.

Most of the tombs at el-Khokha date from the New Kingdom, both to the 18th Dynasty and the Ramesside period (19th–20th Dynasties). New results of a survey done by Friederike Kampp in 1989 and 1990 indicate that numerous undecorated or little-decorated tombs exist in the area. Sketch maps of her work show how dense the original tomb occupation of the area had been. Aside from two tombs, one usurped from a Ramesside tomb and the other inaccessible, the Late period is not represented at el-Khokha.

The most important tombs of el-Khokha are listed below in chronological order, according to their numbers (TT = Theban Tomb), their owners and their professions.

Old Kingdom and First Intermediate Period:

TT 185 Seni-iker, Hereditary Prince
TT 186 Ihy, Nomarch
TT 405 Khenty, Nomarch
TT 413 Unas-ankh, Nomarch, Overseer of Upper Egypt

Hatshepsut–Tuthmose III:

TT 294 Amenhotep, Overseer of the Granary of Amen

Tuthmose III–Amenhotep II:

TT 200 Dedi, Governor of the Desert on the West of Thebes

Amenhotep III:

TT 47 Userhat, Overseer of the Royal Harim
TT 48 Amenemhat, Chief Steward, Overseer of the Cattle of Amen

TT 181 Nebamen and Ipuky, Head Sculptor and Sculptor of the Lord of the Two Lands

Tutankhamen–Ay:

TT 49 Neferhotep, Chief Scribe of Amen
TT 254 Mosi, Scribe of the Treasury

Ramesses II:

TT 32 Tuthmose, Chief Steward of Amen
TT 183 Nebsumenu, Chief Steward, Steward in the House of Ramesses II

Late period:

TT 392 Usurped Ramesside tomb, name unknown
B.3 Hauf, Head of the Kitchen of the Estate of Amen (inaccessible)

See also

Deir el-Bahri, Hatshepsut temple; New Kingdom, overview

Further reading

Kampp, F. 1996. *Die Thebanische Nekropole— Zum Wandel des Grabgedankens von der XVIII. bis zur XX. Dynastie* (Theben 13). Mainz.
Saleh, M. 1977. *Three Old Kingdom Tombs at Thebes* (AVDAIK 14). Mainz.

FRIEDERIKE KAMPP-SEYFRIED

Thebes, Malkata

Malkata is the modern Arabic name for a royal ceremonial and palace site at the southern end of the line of royal funerary temples on the west bank of Thebes (25°43′ N, 32°36′ E). The site was established about year 29/30 of the reign of Amenhotep III (18th Dynasty) in connection with that king's first *heb-sed* (jubilee) festival. Foundation of the new royal settlement was a symbolic act of creation, reflecting the renewal of both monarch and royal power. At the center of the site is the main palace, built of mudbrick

with colorful designs painted on the walls, floors and ceilings. The main palace was flanked by at least three subsidiary palaces for different members of the royal family. Oriented at a right angle to the main palace is a temple to the god Amen. The house of the king corresponded to the house of the god in terms of such architectural elements as restricted inner chambers, a series of colonnaded courts set along a single axis and in a massive enclosure wall surrounding the complex. Situated around the royal complex are the villas of the palace officials and other nobles, as well as more modest structures serving as dwellings and workshops for palace functionaries and artisans. Large earth mounds mark out a vast (originally 1.5 km^2) T-shaped artificial basin, the Birket Habu, southwest of the main palace. Although it could have served as a functional harbor, the enormous size of the basin indicates ceremonial significance.

Malkata was identified as the site of a palace of Amenhotep III in 1888 by Georges Daressy, who did exploratory work while working at nearby Medinet Habu. Systematic excavations were begun in 1900 by Percy E. Newberry under the auspices of the American Robb de Peyster Tytus. Excavations at the site were carried out intermittently by the Egyptian Expedition of the Metropolitan Museum of Art from 1910 to 1921. In the 1970s, the palace site and harbor were investigated by a team led by David O'Connor of the University Museum, Philadelphia and Barry Kemp of the University of Cambridge.

Concurrently in the 1970s, a Japanese expedition from Waseda University, Tokyo investigated Malkata South, uncovering an unusual desert altar or ceremonial kiosk. The modern name of the site, Kom el-Samak (Hill of Fish), refers to mummified fish buried there in late Roman/Coptic times. The underlying structure, however, was clearly built and renovated for the celebration of the *heb-sed*s of Amenhotep III. It consists of a kiosk set on a platform with a ramp to the south and a staircase to the north. The thirty stairs were decorated with alternating painted depictions of bows and bound prisoners. In the 1980s the

Japanese expedition began working at the palace of Malkata, emphasizing the study of the mural paintings.

The many fragments of decorative painting help indicate the different functions of the rooms in the Malkata palace. The small audience hall uncovered by Daressy had a painted pavement consisting of a papyrus marsh scene with ducks, birds and fish. The ceiling of the chamber was decorated with blue and red rosettes alternating with yellow spirals. The steps of the throne base were decorated with bound prisoners and bows, similar to those found at Kom el-Samak. As the king mounted the kiosk or throne he would symbolically "trample" upon Egypt's enemies. The great central hall of the palace preserves sixteen limestone column bases which would have supported two rows of wooden columns. On the south wall of the hall, a figure of the enthroned king was depicted, no doubt imaging the scene in the throne room beyond; no decoration from the throne room itself has been reported.

Even the areas of the palace not meant for public display were lavishly decorated. The "king's bedchamber" was decorated with painted panels of spirals, bulls' heads and rosettes. On the ceiling was a pattern of vultures with outspread wings. In addition to the bedroom, a bathroom, robing rooms, retiring rooms and private dining halls completed the royal suite. Eight smaller suites including a hall with two columns and a raised dais against one wall, an antechamber, a bedroom and a bathroom are thought to belong to the ladies of the royal harim. They are decorated with painted grape arbors and have ceilings covered with flying ducks and pigeons. Other parts of the palace included storerooms, work rooms and courts, offices and quarters for royal officials and kitchens. Even the storage magazines contained frescoes depicting stands heaped with food, fattened cows and leaping calves. Motifs such as the spiral and the "flying gallop" in the Malkata paintings (along with a Mycenaean sherd from the site) indicate some connection with the Aegean world.

Amenhotep III created at Malkata a new royal zone in the southern area of the west bank of Thebes, stretching from his funerary temple at Kom el-Hetan some 5 km southwest to Kom el-Abd. Interpretations vary as to whether this monumental royal establishment was purely ceremonial in nature (Kemp) or was intended to function as an urban administrative center (O'Connor). At some point after the initial construction of the palace and its enclosure wall, the complex (including the Kom el-Samak structure) was renovated on a different alignment. The different stages of rebuilding are usually connected with the various *heb-sed* celebrations (in years 34 and 37, as well as 30) held at the site. Large quantities of small finds, including many inscribed pieces of jar labels, sealings, glass and faïence, as well as decorated (blue-painted) ceramics have been recovered from Malkata. They indicate that the palace was occupied through to the reign of Horemheb, but cannot prove that either Akhenaten or Tutankhamen actually resided at Malkata. The spacious linear plan of Malkata with palaces, temples, villas and so on strung out along the edge of the cultivation at a previous unoccupied site serves as an obvious precursor to Akhenaten's establishment of a new city at Tell el-Amarna.

See also

Gurob; Tell el-Amarna, city

Further reading

Iida, K. *et al.* 1993. *Studies on the Palace of Malqata 1985–1988: Papers in Honor of Professor Watanabe Yasutada on the Occasion of his 70th Birthday.* Tokyo.

Kemp, B.J. 1989. *Ancient Egypt: Anatomy of a Civilization.* London.

Lacovara, P. 1997. *The New Kingdom Royal City.* London.

O'Connor, D. 1980. Malqata. In *LÄ* 3: 1173–8.

STEVEN BLAKE SHUBERT

Thebes, New Kingdom private tombs

The area which is commonly called the "Theban necropolis" lies opposite the modern upper Egyptian town of Luxor (25°44′ N, 32°38′ E) on the west bank of the Nile along the western foothills of the Western Desert. Private tombs are located in the following private cemeteries, geographically from north to south (1) el-Tarif, (2) Dra' Abu el-Naga, (3) el-Asasif and the valley of Deir el-Bahri, (4) el-Khokha, (5) Sheikh Abd el-Qurna, and (6) Qurnet Murai and the cemetery belonging to the village of Deir el-Medina.

The modern names designate the villages built within the pharaonic cemeteries. The ancient term for the whole region opposite the capital of Thebes was *imntt W3st* or *imntt niwt*, meaning "West of Wose" or "West of the City." This designation comprises all the cemeteries and the village of Deir el-Medina, as well as the royal mortuary temples of the New Kingdom along the edge of the cultivation. The name for the pyramid-shaped hill surmounting the whole area was *t3 dhnt*, "The Peak," which is today called el-Qurn (The Horn). The cemeteries today called el-Tarif, Dra' Abu el-Naga, el-Asasif, el-Khokha, Sheik Abd el-Qurna and Qurnet Murai were designated as *Ḥft-ḥr nb.s* ("She, who is in front of her lord").

Serving as the capital cemetery during several dynasties, it is not surprising that from the time of Napoleon's expedition to Egypt in 1789–99 the interest of scholars, plunderers, adventurers and excavators has been concentrated on this site. With the beginning of the nineteenth century, more and more scientifically oriented missions visited the Theban necropolis, starting in 1815 with Belzoni, who discovered the tomb of Seti I in 1817. Nevertheless, the results of the archaeological enterprises during the nineteenth century were basically concentrated on the "export" of valuable finds to museums all over the world. It is to the credit of Flinders Petrie that we owe a new kind of field archaeology at the site of the Theban necropolis. About the same time the Carter–Carnarvon expedition, the crew of the Marquis of Northampton, Gauthier and Chassinat excavated several sites in the Theban necropolis, followed a little later by the Metropolitan Museum expedition under the supervision of H.E. Winlock and the Pennsylvania Museum expedition with Clarence Fisher. Those various activities called for a final systematic numbering of the rock tombs, which was done by Alan Gardiner and Arthur Weigall in 1913, supplemented by Reginald Engelbach in 1924 and finally summarized in the bibliography of Porter and Moss, published in 1927 (revised and augmented in 1960) and mapped by the Survey of Egypt in 1924.

In the twentieth century more and more efforts have been undertaken to publish the texts and decoration of the most important private tombs in an adequate and scientific manner. It is due to the patience, perseverance and talent of Nina and Norman de Garis Davies that the epigraphic work gained such remarkable and impressive results up to the 1950s. After the Second World War, Torgny Säve-Söderbergh published many of Davies's notes and drawings, but neglected the archaeological findings and objects. Apart from a general overview by Steindorff and Wolf, a classificatory attempt by Abdul Qader Muhammed, a short article concerning the occupation of the cemeteries by Wolfgang Helck, art historical publications by Wegner and Baud and several guidebooks, the history and development of the New Kingdom necropolis has not been scientifically investigated. A new approach in this direction dealing with the architectural development of the Theban private cemeteries during the New Kingdom has been commenced by Friederike Kampp.

The history of the Theban necropolis started with the occupation of the site in the late Old Kingdom and the First Intermediate Period, when a few rock-cut tombs were carved in the hillock of el-Khokha, belonging to local nomarchs and their officials. Furthermore, some ruined *mastaba*s (mudbrick tombs) of this period on the plain of el-Tarif have been recorded by Dieter Arnold. The necropolis reached its first heyday in the 11th Dynasty, when the region of el-Tarif was occupied. Here the huge royal *saff*-tombs of the Intef kings had been constructed, with the tombs of their officials in close proximity.

In the second half of the 11th Dynasty under King Mentuhotep Nebhepetre, the cemeteries were transferred to the Asasif, Deir el-Bahri, the hill of Sheikh Abd el-Qurna and the northern slope of Qurnet Murai. Lining the various valleys, the private tombs were usually situated on the hillsides and were oriented toward the causeways of the royal funerary temples. In front of these 11th Dynasty tombs were large walled courtyards. The tomb façades were constructed with either plain slightly sloping walls or with a pillared portico. The general interior scheme of these tombs consists of a long corridor leading to a chapel with a statue niche and the entrance to burial shafts or sloping passages. In the 12th Dynasty, the Theban necropolis lost its importance until the 17th Dynasty, when Thebes again became the center of political power.

While the kings of the 17th Dynasty built their tombs in all probability near the top of the Dra' Abu el-Naga hills, the private tombs were situated in front of them along the slope of the hills and on the plain to the east. The rock-cut tombs of the higher ranking officials of this period and of the very beginning of the 18th Dynasty were constructed in nearly the same manner as those of the 11th Dynasty, continuing as corridor and *saff*-shaped tombs. There are changes in the shape of the portico pillars, the shortening of the corridor and the enlarging of the chapel to a kind of broad hall, as well as a preference for deep vertical shafts rather than sloping passages. The tombs of the middle high-ranking officials were built on the plain, consisting of a shaft in the middle of a somewhat trapezoid courtyard, which was surrounded by a brick wall. A cult chapel, also built of mudbrick, was placed within this court. Both Dra' Abu el-Naga and Sheikh Abd el-Qurna served as cemetery sites at the end of the 17th Dynasty.

Following the geographical direction of the 18th Dynasty royal funerary temples along the edge of the cultivated land, the occupation of Sheikh Abd el-Qurna began in the north during the time of Hatshepsut and Tuthmose III and ended up in the southern part of this region about the time of Amenhotep II and Tuthmose IV. From then on the tombs were distributed more or less evenly in the different parts of the necropolis. The typical 18th Dynasty tomb of the Theban necropolis is the so-called "inverse T-shaped tomb," whose inner rooms consist of a broad hall followed by a longitudinal corridor. This scheme can be enlarged by constructing additional pillared halls or by adding rooms and cult chapels according to the individual needs and taste of the tomb owner, his social rank and financial resources. The courtyards of these tombs, when situated on the hillslopes, seem to be open terraces, protected and lined by side walls with a rounded top. The tomb façades were likewise protected by a plastered wall of limestone rubble above the entrance. Within these walls, above the tomb entrances, there were sometimes little niches for stelophorus statues of the tomb owner, praising the rising sun. The top of the façade walls was built with a different type of molded bricks, containing the so-called rows of "funerary cones" which contained the name and titles of the tomb owner.

With the era of Amenhotep III a new kind of private tomb layout appears, which resembles for the first time that of a funerary temple rather than the usual private tomb plan. Such large tombs could only be realized in the best rock strata, which caused the tomb owners to construct their sepulchers on the plains of Sheikh Abd el-Qurna, el-Khokha and el-Asasif. Though none of these colossal tombs was ever finished, they were conceived following a similar scheme, with a large sunken courtyard and a ramp or staircase leading down, framed at the entrance by a kind of pylon. The courtyard has colonnades on all sides and the inner halls were planned to be pillared halls with several rows of columns or pillars in various shapes. For the first time since the 11th Dynasty, sloping passages seem to be the obligatory type of access to the burial chambers, but they are now elaborate bending tunnels. After the interim of the Amarna period, the reoccupation of the Theban necropolis took place mainly in the region of Qurnet Murai, but there are a few tombs of the time of Tutankhamen until Horemheb on the plain of Sheikh Abd el-Qurna, el-Khokha and on the "main hill" of Dra' Abu el-Naga.

In Ramesside times, the majority of the tomb owners belong to the clergy of the temple of Amen at Karnak and to the military administration of Upper Egypt and Nubia. While the small tombs of lower rank Ramesside priests are scattered all over the necropolis, the hill of el-Mandara at Dra' Abu el-Naga seems to be the favorite place for the high priests of Amen and viceroys of Nubia. The plans of the larger Ramesside tombs resemble those of the large tombs from the era of Amenhotep III, having one or two courtyards surrounded by colonnades with pylon gateways. The entrance to these tombs is usually framed with funerary stelae on both sides. Elaborate sloping passages with a sequence of subterranean chambers and a brick pyramid as superstructure complete the plan.

With the 20th Dynasty, when only a few rock-cut tombs were constructed, the period of reusing older tombs began to flourish. Some of the usurped tombs received decoration and inscriptions, mostly on still undecorated walls, but the majority of the tombs received only numerous intrusive burials until the end of the Third Intermediate Period. During the 25th and 26th Dynasties the Theban necropolis had its last peak period of construction. The region of el-Asasif in particular was dominated by the enormous mudbrick pylons, walls and superstructures of the huge tombs of the Late period. These buildings represent the last stage of Theban tomb development, following the tradition of the Ramesside period, but are even more connected with the idea of the netherworld, which is realized in the subterranean chambers and tunnels.

Aside from more intrusive burials, including those of animals during Ptolemaic times, the Theban necropolis lost its importance until the advent of Christianity. Several monasteries were then built in nearly every part of the necropolis and numerous tombs served as houses or churches. In many cases the decoration of the tombs suffered much from the vandalism of the monks and the soot of fires. Except for the northern region of Dra' Abu el-Naga, the Asasif and the hill of Sheikh Abd el-Qurna, all the other parts of the necropolis are covered by modern villages. Unless the plans of the Egyptian government to transfer the villages to other locations are successful, and tomb robberies cease, the absolute destruction of the Theban necropolis will occur within the next few decades.

See also

Deir el-Medina; mortuary beliefs; New Kingdom, overview; pyramid tombs of the New Kingdom; representational evidence, New Kingdom private tombs; Tell el-Amarna, nobles' tombs; tomb furnishings

Further reading

Abdul-Qader, Muhammed. 1966. *The Development of the Funerary Beliefs and Practices Displayed in the Private Tombs of the New Kingdom at Thebes*. Cairo.

Kampp, F. 1996. *Die Thebanische Nekropole—Zum Wandel des Grabgedankens von der XVIII. bis zur XX. Dynastie* (Theben 13). Mainz.

Porter, B., and R.L.B. Moss. 1970–3. *Topographical Bibliography of Ancient Egyptian Hieroglyphic Texts, Reliefs, and Paintings* 1: *The Theban Necropolis*, 2 vols, 2nd revised edn. Oxford.

Wegner, M. 1933. Stilentwickelung der thebanischen Beamtengraber. *MDAIK* 4: 35f.

FRIEDERIKE KAMPP-SEYFRIED

Thebes, Qurnet Murai

A small hill called Qurnet Murai (25°44′ N, 32°36′ E) forms the southernmost part of the private necropolis at Thebes. It is situated directly behind Kom el-Hetan, the great funerary temple of Amenhotep III. As with Sheikh Abd el-Qurna, the occupation of the site began during the second half of the 11th Dynasty. Several huge *saff*-tombs dating back to this epoch are nowadays hidden behind modern houses. The presence and expansion of the present village has caused the permanent destruction and disappearance of numerous tombs in this area. Although the whole hillside is honeycombed with rock-cut tombs (mostly undecorated), only seventeen have been placed on the official list of numbered tombs. During the last decade, even some of these tombs have vanished.

Apart from a few tombs dating either to the first half of the 18th Dynasty or to the Ramesside era (19th–20th Dynasties), the majority of Qurnet Murai tombs date to the reigns of Amenhotep III, Ay and Tutankhamen. The vicinity of the royal funerary temples of these kings and the neighborhood of Amenhotep's city of Malkata are the main reasons for the popularity of Qurnet Murai during the late 18th Dynasty. High-ranking officials of this era were buried at Qurnet Murai. Examples include the Viceroy of Nubia Merimose and the famous architect Amenhotep, son of Hapu, if Dino Bidoli's 1969 identification is accepted. In Coptic times the northern part of the hillock was dominated by the monastery of St Mark, one of the best preserved ancient Coptic buildings on the west bank of Thebes.

The most important tombs at Qurnet Murai are listed below in chronological order, according to their numbers (TT = Theban Tomb), the name and title of the tomb owners.

Amenhotep III:

TT 383 Merimose, Viceroy of Nubia

Amenhotep IV/Tutankhamen:

TT 40 Amenhotep (called Huy), Viceroy of Nubia

Ay:

TT 271 Nay, Chief Physican and Royal Scribe

Ramesses III–IV:

TT 222 Heqamaatrenakht, High Priest of Monthu

Further investigations of Qurnet Murai are to be expected by the French, especially by Luc Gabolde, who is entrusted with the publication of tombs in this area.

See also

New Kingdom, overview

Further reading

Bidoli, D. 1970. Zur Lage des Grabes des Amenophis, Sohn des Hapu. *MDAIK* 26: 11–14.

Gabolde, L. 1995. Autour de la tombe 276: Pourquoi va-t-on se faire enterrer à Gournet Mourrai au début du Nouvel Empire. In *Studien zur Archäologie und Geschichte Altägyptens* 12. Heidelberg.

Habachi, L., and P. Anus. 1977. Le Tombeau de Naÿ à Gournet Mareï (MIFAO 97). Cairo.

FRIEDERIKE KAMPP-SEYFRIED

Thebes, the Ramesseum

The Ramesseum, the funerary temple of Ramesses II, is located on the west bank of the Nile at Thebes in Upper Egypt, not far from Deir el-Bahri. It was built on the edge of the cultivated land, and is oriented east–west. Together with its support buildings and enclosure wall, the temple complex covers an area of about 37,380 sq. m. The temple proper, constructed mostly of sandstone, is not quite rectangular in plan but forms a parallelogram, due to the presence of an earlier temple. A foundation deposit with the earliest form of the king's prenomen provides evidence that construction on the temple began very early in his reign. Other inscriptions refer to Ramesses II's first jubilee (*heb-sed*), celebrated in the thirtieth year of his reign. Thus the temple's construction occupied some three decades.

The Ramesseum's ancient name was "Mansion of Millions of Years, United with Thebes" (*Ḥwt nt Ḥḥ m rnpwt ḫnmt W3st*). The architect who designed and built the temple was named

Penre. Its plan is of the standard funerary type, and most closely resembles that of Ramesses II's father Seti I at Qurna. An entrance pylon forms the front of the temple, opening onto two unroofed courts. On the inner face of the entrance and second pylons are reliefs of the Battle of Qadesh, fought in northwest Syria during the fifth year of Ramesses II's reign. Later battles are depicted in the reliefs of the northern, first pylon tower. Beyond the courts is a hypostyle hall, similar to the one at the temple of Karnak, with a raised central clerestory. To the west are three smaller columned halls, the westernmost one of which opens into the sanctuary, now in ruins.

Porticoes surrounded the first court of the temple, and at the north end on piers was a row of Osiride statues of Ramesses II, carved in the mummiform position characteristic of the god Osiris. Only two of these statues survive. The court was dominated by a huge granite statue of the seated pharaoh, located on the western side south of the processional axis. Named "Re of the Rulers," the colossus had its own chapel, as shown by a row of four small column bases at its feet. Now broken, this statue was the inspiration for the poem "Ozymandias" by Percy Bysshe Shelley. Opposite the colossus was another statue of the queen mother Tuya, also with its own cult chapel. On the south side of the court was an entrance to a small palace of the king, adjacent to the temple. This palace is similar in design to a palace attached to Seti I's temple at Abydos, also completed by Ramesses II.

Slightly higher in elevation, the second court was originally surrounded on all sides by porticoes, with Osiride statues of the king on piers on the eastern and western sides. Only the northeastern corner of this court still stands, along with a section of the second pylon's inner face. Carved on this face is a version of the Battle of Qadesh, and above that, a portion of relief of the festival of the god Min. In the early nineteenth century Giovanni Belzoni removed the upper torso and head of one of the two colossi that stood in the second court; a drawing of this scene has been much reproduced. What remains of this colossus is now in the British Museum, but the head of the companion statue still rests in the Ramesseum's second court.

To the west of the second court, the front wall of the hypostyle hall still stands. Reliefs on the outer side of this wall show Ramesses II being given scepters by the Theban triad, the deities Amen, Mut and Khonsu. Carved below this is a procession of Ramesses II's sons, moving toward the central aisle of the temple. Battle reliefs of the king and his sons attacking the town of Dapur in Syria are on the wall's inner side. Three staircases led into the hypostyle hall from the second court. Originally there were forty-eight columns in this hall, with the central taller columns supporting the clerestory. The hall's side walls are now destroyed, but the central part with its roofing is well preserved. Three small halls were located to the west of the hypostyle hall, and to the north and south of these were two small temples. The southern one is a small processional-style temple, possibly dedicated to Ramesses I, with a room for the bark of Amen and a triple shrine.

North of the hypostyle hall was a small double shrine, probably dedicated to Seti I and Tuya, the queen mother. The shrine's façade had a columned portico that opened onto a court, with columned porticoes on all sides. Two small columned halls led to a double shrine with a storeroom in the center. Most of this shrine is now badly ruined. The small columned hall immediately to the west of the hypostyle hall is noted for the astronomical scenes carved on its ceiling. On one wall is a relief of Amen and the goddess Seshat recording the length of Ramesses II's reign on leaves of a persea tree. As Seshat is associated with numbers and writing, some scholars have speculated that the temple library was in this hall, but more likely it would have been in one of the smaller side rooms. Other reliefs in this hall show the divine barks of the Theban triad. On the walls of a second columned hall to the west are offering lists for the gods Ptah and Re. A third columned hall, now ruined, led to the bark shrine, a square room with four piers on which the portable bark with divine images was placed. Rooms to the south were probably storerooms for temple equipment, while rooms to the north included a hall open to the sky, a small temple to Re, and possibly areas for food preparation of the cult offerings. Beyond the bark shrine to the west was the rearmost room of the temple, the sanctuary for the images of the gods.

The stone temple of the Ramesseum is surrounded on three sides by a great number of storerooms, mostly built of mudbrick. These storerooms were where the temple's wealth, in grain and other commodities, was stored. Best preserved are the storerooms on the northwest side of the temple, including a central columned hall. Impressive barrel vaults of mudbrick formed the ceilings of these storerooms, which were originally coated inside with gypsum plaster. Reused blocks of limestone from Hatshepsut's funerary temple have been found in some storerooms, usurped by Ramesses II with his deeply cut reliefs over the delicate, raised ones of Hatshepsut's. The entire complex was surrounded on three sides by a thick wall of mudbrick, enclosing an area of 210 × 178 m. On the east side the enclosure wall joined the temple's first pylon. Inside the north tower of this pylon was a staircase leading to the roof, which temple astronomers used for celestial observation or measurement. Part of the pylon has collapsed, and its foundations were probably undermined by the waters that inundated agricultural fields outside the temple.

During the 20th Dynasty, the Ramesseum served as an administrative center on the west bank. In Ramesses III's reign, the work crew that lived at the village of Deir el-Medina marched on the Ramesseum during a labor strike, prompted by arrears in pay, and demanded that officials release some of the grain stored there. Toward the end of the 20th Dynasty there is textual evidence of renegade priests stripping gold, silver and bronze ornaments from the temple. The demolition of the temple began in part during the reign of Ramesses III, who reused some blocks on his own funerary temple at Medinet Habu. In the Graeco-Roman period the Ramesseum was known as the "Tomb of Ozymandias," a corruption of Ramesses II's prenomen, *User-ma'at Re.*

Excavations at the Ramesseum by J.E. Quibell indicate that it was partly built over Middle Kingdom tombs. Quibell also found later burials from the 21st–23rd Dynasties in the temple's storerooms. In the 1970s, French and Egyptian archaeologists made further investigations in the temple. Uvo Hölscher's studies demonstrate that the later funerary temple of Ramesses III at Medinet Habu closely follows the Ramesseum in design. Hieroglyphic texts from the temple have been studied and published by Kenneth Kitchen in his magisterial corpus of Ramesside inscriptions. Today, despite its ruined state, the Ramesseum is among the most picturesque sites in Egypt, a fitting memorial for its larger-than-life owner.

See also

Belzoni, Giovanni Baptista; Deir el-Medina; Medinet Habu; New Kingdom, overview; representational evidence, New Kingdom temples; Thebes, royal funerary temples

Further reading

Centre d'Études et de Documentation sur l'ancienne Égypte. 1973–1980. *Le Ramesseum*, 11 vols. Cairo.

Habachi, L. 1966. The Qantir Stela of the Vizier Rahotep and the statue "Ruler of Rulers." In *Festgabe für Dr. Walter Will*, 67–77. Cologne.

Helck, W. 1972. *Die Ritualdarstellungen des Ramesseum*. Wiesbaden.

Stadelmann, R. 1984. Ramesseum. In *LÄ* 5: 91–8. Wiesbaden.

FRANK J. YURCO

Thebes, royal funerary temples

During the New Kingdom royal funerary temples were built apart from the kings' tombs in the Theban hills and erected on the strip of low desert that separated those hills from the cultivation on the west bank of the Nile opposite the city of Thebes (modern Luxor). There were roughly twenty royal funerary foundations built in West Thebes during the approximately 500 years of the New Kingdom. These were formally described as "the mansion of millions of years of King *X*" followed by an epithet, for example, "United with Eternity." More often, this lengthy name was shortened to "the mansion" followed by the king's name and/or the temple's distinctive epithet or a local nickname. It is thus not always possible to discern whether such a name describes a true mortuary temple. Temples for a number of rulers during this period remain unattested: some may have never been built, while others were either destroyed, usurped by later rulers or remain to be discovered. In the following checklist, letters in parentheses refer to locations on the map.

18th Dynasty

Ahmose: not preserved.

Amenhotep I: identity uncertain. A temple (A), named "Most Established of Place," was dedicated to the king and his mother, Ahmose-Nofretari. It was found in front of the Dra' Abu el-Naga hills, but it is not clear that this structure must be the king's mortuary temple (as opposed to that of his mother).

Tuthmose I: the building, attested in contemporary sources and named "United with Life," is not preserved. It must have been located at the south end of the site, near Medinet Habu.

Tuthmose II (B): named "Receiver of Life," and located between the hill of Qurnet Murai and Medinet Habu.

Hatshepsut (C): named "Holiest of Holies" and located inside the bay of Deir el-Bahri beside the 11th Dynasty temple of Mentuhotep I, which may have influenced its unusual terraced design. A causeway led to a valley temple, now poorly preserved.

Tuthmose III (D): named "Gifted with [?] Life," located opposite the northern end of the Sheikh Abd el-Qurna hill. The pylon in front of the temple, along with parts of the enclosure wall (both made out of mudbrick), can still be seen, but the stone temple inside has been

reduced to fragments, although the ground plan has been traced.

Amenhotep II (F): located between the Ramesseum and Tuthmose III's mortuary temple; given the same name as Tuthmose II's mortuary temple, "Receiver of Life." The ruins, poorly preserved, are now covered by modern debris.

Tuthmose IV (G): located south of the Ramesseum. The ground plan has been reconstructed, but the building itself is destroyed.

Amenhotep III (H): located east of Qurnet Murai and known locally as Kom el-Hetan. Named "[Mansion] which Receives Amen and Elevates his Beauty," the complex was set apart by the great size of its original grounds and the vast number of statues, representing both the king and numerous divinities, which it once housed. Along with the misnamed "colossi of Memnon" that still mark the now vanished entrance to the temple, remains of a number of other statues can still be seen above ground. The only architectural remnant of any size is near the back of the temple, where a great "sun court" was surrounded with columned porticos (like those of Luxor temple) adorned with statues of the king. The excavation of the site is still only partly reported in print. South of Amenhotep III's foundation was the much smaller mortuary temple (I) which the king had built as an extraordinary honor for his most favored contemporary, the scribe Amenhotep son of Hapu, who by late antiquity would be revered as a local saint.

Amenhotep IV (Akhenaten): built no mortuary temple at Thebes, but the "Mansion of the Solar Disc" at el-Amarna is believed by some scholars to be the mortuary temple that would be expected to accompany the tomb which the king built for himself at this site. Structures called "sunshades," which the king had built for his wives, daughters and mother, appear to have functioned as mortuary chapels for them.

Smenkhkare and/or Nefernefruaten: neither preserved nor clearly attested. A "Mansion of Ankh-kheprure in Thebes" mentioned in a contemporary graffito has been assumed to be a royal mortuary temple, but the name might as well belong to a foundation that was planned within the Karnak temple on the east bank.

Tutankhamen: a mortuary temple was surely planned for this king, but neither the building's name nor its location is known. It may have lain in the area of Medinet Habu, perhaps on (or near) the site used by his successors.

Ay (J): began his mortuary temple (named "Most Established of Monuments") north of the 18th Dynasty temple to Amen at Medinet Habu, but the building remained unfinished at his death.

Horemheb (J): took over his predecessor's mortuary temple site and redesigned its plan. The building is ruined, but a careful excavation of the site yielded much that sheds light on both phases of its history.

19th Dynasty

Ramesses I: see below.

Seti I (K): the so-called "Qurna temple" is located opposite the north end of the hills at Dra' Abu el-Naga and was named "Effective is Seti Merneptah in the Estate of Amen." It included a cult chapel for Ramesses I, who reigned too short a time to build a temple for himself, and it was finished by Seti's successor, Ramesses II.

Ramesses II (L): named "United with Thebes," but popularly known as the "Rames-seum," Ramesses II's funerary temple is located opposite Sheikh Abd el-Qurna. It was the most ambitious building of its type since Amenhotep III. Like the latter's temple, the Ramesseum was a tourist attraction during late antiquity (Diodorus I 47–9) but it was less extensively quarried. The central part of the building is substantially intact.

Merenptah (M): located between the Rames-seum and Amenhotep III's mortuary temple, it was reduced to its foundations before modern times. Excavations have revealed that much of the stone used in its construction derived from the adjoining complex of Amenhotep III. The remains are currently being studied for publication by the Swiss Archaeological Institute.

Amenmesse: not preserved. His successor may well have destroyed or usurped it.

Seti II: although mentioned on wine jar dockets found at the temple of Siptah, the building itself has not been rediscovered.

Siptah (N): located between the temples of Tuthmose III and Amenhotep II, the building is now reduced to its foundation trenches.

Tawosret (O): located between the temples of Merenptah and Tuthmose IV, the building was larger than Siptah's but was just as completely destroyed.

20th Dynasty

Sethnakht: since no cult rooms for this short-reigning king were included in his son's mortuary temple, Sethnakht probably owned a foundation of his own; but no trace of the building has been found.

Ramesses III (P): named "United with Eternity," but commonly known as Medinet Habu, this is the southernmost, and best preserved, of the New Kingdom mortuary temples.

Ramesses IV: this king began construction on three temples in West Thebes: two (Q, R) respectively north and south of the entrance to the bay of Deir el-Bahri (only foundation deposits of this king, with many blocks reused from earlier temples); and another, smaller temple (S) north of Medinet Habu. Since work on the very large temple near the hill of Asasif (R) was continued by Ramesses V and VI, a reasonable if not conclusive case can be made that Ramesses IV began this structure as his own mortuary temple but abandoned it in favor of the smaller building near Medinet Habu.

Ramesses V and Ramesses VI: it is assumed that Ramesses V continued his predecessor's Asasif temple (R), and that it was usurped from him by Ramesses VI, who also took over the tomb Ramesses V had begun for himself in the Valley of the Kings.

Ramesses VII–XI: no mortuary temples are attested even though all but the ephemeral Ramesses VIII had tombs in the royal valley. Hard economic times and the increasing withdrawal of royal patronage from southern Egypt during the late 20th Dynasty may both have inhibited temple building, but it seems incredible that no provision was made for the cults of these kings at Thebes. A possible candidate for one of these "lost" temples might be the small building to the north of Tuthmose II's temple near Medinet Habu (T); but although it was constructed later than the adjoining 18th Dynasty temple of Amenhotep son of Hapu on which it encroached, there is no solid evidence for its date or purpose.

Design and function

The earliest mortuary temples of the New Kingdom were small buildings that seem to follow the layout of contemporary cult temples in West Thebes. The plan of Tuthmose II's temple, for example, is strikingly similar to that of the 18th Dynasty temple at Medinet Habu. In both the chapel of the royal cult is isolated at the northeast corner of the building, separate from the other, larger suite(s) which, at Medinet Habu, were dedicated to various forms of the god Amen. By analogy, we may speculate that the predominant divine presence in Tuthmose II's mortuary temple was also that of Amen, as it would be in all later mortuary temples of the New Kingdom.

What would become the classic plan is first revealed in the temple of Hatshepsut, where the chambers of the Osiride mortuary cult are shifted to the south side of the inner temple, balanced by a suite dedicated to the solar resurrection on the north side, while Amen's cult chambers lie between these two units along the center of the building's axis.

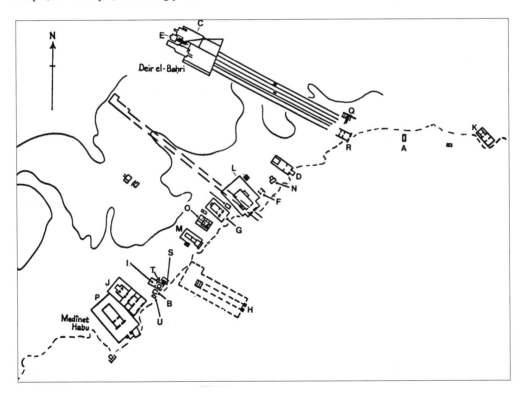

Figure 115 Royal funerary temples in West Thebes
Source: adapted from Porter and Moss 2, 2nd edn. pl. 33.

With slight variations, this layout was continued throughout the New Kingdom: compare the temples of Tuthmose III, Ramesses II, Merenptah and Tawosret. The most variable elements of the plan were the solar suite (which may have been omitted or located elsewhere, as in Horemheb's temple); and the cult room(s) of the royal ancestors, which nonetheless always lay somewhere in the Osiride region along the south side of the building (e.g. Seti I and Ramesses III).

These arrangements reflect the complex divine identity of the pharaoh. The solar suite reflects the afterlife as portrayed in the royal tombs, where the king joined the circuit of nature by joining the sun god Re on his eternal rounds. This celestial identity was balanced by the pharaoh's transformation into Osiris, the god who had conquered death and ruled as king of the underworld. At Thebes, moreover, the fusion of royal ideology with the theology of Amen (who had also acquired a solar identity as Amen-Re) made the pharaoh both the son of and a manifestation of this deity: in this mortuary temple, each king was recognized as the resident form of the god (e.g. at Medinet Habu the divine Ramesses III was "Amen-Re United with Eternity," while his ancestor Ramesses II was "Amen-Re United with Thebes"). In fully developed temples of the later New Kingdom, the king's ceremonial presence under his various forms was maintained by a series of "false doors," which communicated symbolically with the king's tomb and with other parts of the temple. At Medinet Habu, for example, false doors are found not only at focal points in the suites dedicated to Osiris and Amen, but also in the palace, a small building attached to the south wall of the temple, which served both as a rest house during royal visits to the site and as an eternal dwelling for the king's spirit.

The royal mortuary and cult temples must have formed an imposing "kings' row" at the edge of the Theban necropolis during the New Kingdom. Few are substantially extant today. Some remained unfinished, functioned for only a short time before the ruler's cult lapsed or suffered natural damage. Most of the damage is manmade, however, and resulted when blocks were quarried from these buildings for use in projects by later rulers. Such depredations, continued as sporadic pilferage by the inhabitants of West Thebes, have reduced most of the New Kingdom mortuary temples to the barest foundations. Those that survived best were reused by later generations for their own purposes. Buildings inside the complex of Ramesses III, for example, were integrated into the town of Djeme that grew up around them and thus survive in remarkably good condition. Hatshepsut's temple at Deir el-Bahari, which was not as badly damaged by falling rock as its neighbor just to the south, served as the foundation for a Christian monastery. A combination of local celebrity and reuse seems also to have rescued large parts of Seti I's and Ramesses II's temples from destruction; although Amenhotep III's temple was on the whole less fortunate, the great size, hardness and mystique of its quartzite colossi have conspired to preserve them, battered but still largely intact, into the present day.

See also

Deir el-Bahri, Hatshepsut temple; Deir el-Bahri, Tuthmose III temple; Medinet Habu; mortuary beliefs; New Kingdom, overview; Thebes, the Ramesseum; Thebes, Valley of the King

Further reading

Eaton-Kraus, M. 1988. Tutankhamun at Karnak. *MDAIK* 44: 1–11.

Haeny, G., ed. 1981. *Untersuchungen im Totentempel Amenophis' III* (Beiträge Bf 11). Wiesbaden.

Kemp, B.J. 1989. *Ancient Egypt: Anatomy of a Civilization*. London.

Osing, J. 1977. *Der Tempel Sethos' I. in Gurna. Die Reliefs und Inschriften 1* (AVDAIK 20). Mainz.

Stadelmann, R. 1985. Totentempel III. In *LÄ* 6: 706–11.

WILLIAM J. MURNANE

Thebes, Senenmut monuments

The Theban monuments of Senenmut, Great Steward of Amen during the coregency of Hatshepsut and Tuthmose III, are not only large in number but significant for the cultural and historical light they shed on the early 18th Dynasty. In addition to an impressive tomb split into two architecturally separate components, Senenmut dedicated no fewer than eighteen statues and a land donation stela in the area of ancient Thebes. As a group, these monuments provide crucial information on the meteoric career of Senenmut, the history of the coregency of Hatshepsut and Tuthmose III and its aftermath, the nature of contemporary private tomb architecture, and the development of statue types during the early 18th Dynasty. Despite this wealth of documentation, however, the circumstances surrounding the death of Senenmut and the posthumous persecution of his name have never been satisfactorily explained.

West bank monuments

Because of its unusual architecture and the circumstances of its discovery, Senenmut's tomb possesses two numbers in the catalog of the Theban necropolis. The funerary chapel of Senenmut was built near the summit of the Sheikh Abd el-Qurna hill and was well known in both antiquity and in recent times, when it was assigned number 71 and assumed to comprise his tomb *in toto*. The wall paintings were copied in the 1920s by Norman de Garis Davies and clearance was carried out in 1930–1 by Herbert Winlock, both of the Metropolitan Museum's Egyptian Expedition. Carved for the most part in layers of loose shale, Senenmut's funerary chapel is the largest of its kind prior to the reign of Amenhotep III, but is otherwise typical, in both its architecture and decoration, of contemporary Theban chapels. The transverse passage was lit by eight rectangular windows set into the façade, and its roof was supported by a row of eight pillars. The separate aisles formed by the pillars were distinguished by different ceilings: flat, curved,

gabled and shrine-shaped. The long axial corridor leading directly into the hill ended in a false door stela (now in Berlin, no. 2066) and a rough-cut niche above, originally lined with carved and painted relief blocks.

Because of the poor quality of the bedrock, the decoration was executed almost entirely in paint on a plaster ground, supported by thousands of small limestone chips embedded in structural plaster. Much of this delicate painted layer has now collapsed, leaving only hints of the magnificence of the original decoration. A number of scenes can still be recognized: a tribute scene featuring a procession of Aegean men carrying their foreign wares; a depiction of the "Abydos pilgrimage," showing the deceased en route to visit the mythical tomb of Osiris; the funeral procession, in which the sarcophagus and personal belongings of the deceased are carried to his tomb; the funeral banquet and a long menu list of offerings; and the hauling of statues sheltered under canopied shrines.

On the hillside above the niched façade of the tomb, a rock-cut statue of Senenmut was begun but never finished, perhaps because of a fissure in the rock. In front of the façade, a large artificial terrace was built to provide a wide entrance forecourt. Under this terrace William Hayes and Ambrose Lansing of the Metropolitan Museum's Egyptian Expedition excavated in 1935–6 the intact burials of Senenmut's parents, Ramose and Hatnefer, interred with six other poorly wrapped mummies, apparently all family members. Six other burials, all of the early 18th Dynasty, were found in the loose scree of the hillside, as well as deposits of hunting weapons and the coffins of a horse and an ape.

In January 1927, Herbert Winlock discovered a descending passage in the floor of the Asasif Valley northeast of the mortuary temple of Hatshepsut at Deir el-Bahri, leading to a chamber decorated with funeral texts and vignettes depicting Senenmut. This "second" tomb, never finished in antiquity, was given number 353 and was initially assumed to be a separate tomb that Senenmut began late in his life but which was abandoned before its completion. In fact, Tomb 353 is simply the

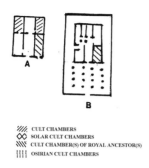

//// CULT CHAMBERS
◇◇ SOLAR CULT CHAMBERS
\\\\ CULT CHAMBER(S) OF ROYAL ANCESTOR(S)
|||| OSIRIAN CULT CHAMBERS

Figure 116 A, Medinet Habu, 18th Dynasty temple; B, Funerary temple of Tuthmose II
Source: by William Murnane.

burial apartment that complements the separate funerary chapel (Tomb 71) on Sheikh Abd el-Gurna. Arranged around a carved false door stela, several chapters from the *Book of the Dead* adorn the western side of the chamber, most pertaining to the specific topography of the netherworld. The eastern side of the room is decorated with the texts of two long funerary liturgies, unique for the New Kingdom. The ceiling bears the earliest known astronomical representation of the night sky, comprising a star clock, the northern constellations, and the twelve lunar months and their associated

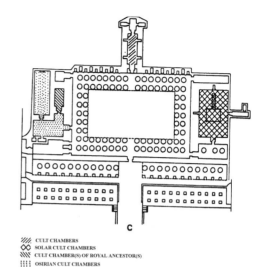

//// CULT CHAMBERS
◇◇ SOLAR CULT CHAMBERS
\\\\ CULT CHAMBER(S) OF ROYAL ANCESTOR(S)
|||| OSIRIAN CULT CHAMBERS

Figure 117 Funerary temple of Hatshepsut
Source: adapted by R. Stadelmann in *LÄ* 4: 707–9.

deities. Situated near the tomb were five foundation deposits containing model tools and objects, some of which bear the names of Senenmut or Hatshepsut. Sealed at the time of its abandonment, the tomb was initially buried by broken statuary and debris from Hatshepsut's temple at the time of her posthumous persecution. The area was later used as a dump for votive offerings discarded from the several temples at Deir el-Bahri and as a repository for Late period embalming caches.

Senenmut's quartzite sarcophagus was dis-

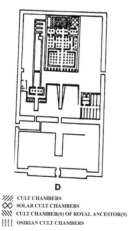

//// CULT CHAMBERS
◇◇ SOLAR CULT CHAMBERS
\\\\ CULT CHAMBER(S) OF ROYAL ANCESTOR(S)
|||| OSIRIAN CULT CHAMBERS

Figure 118 Funerary temple of Tuthmose III
Source: adapted by R. Stadelmann in *LÄ* 4: 707–9.

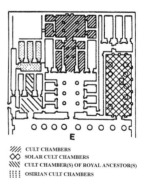

//// CULT CHAMBERS
◇◇ SOLAR CULT CHAMBERS
\\\\ CULT CHAMBER(S) OF ROYAL ANCESTOR(S)
|||| OSIRIAN CULT CHAMBERS

Figure 119 Funerary temple of Seti I
Source: adapted by R. Stadelmann in *LÄ* 4: 707–9.

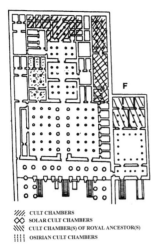

Figure 120 Funerary temple of Ramesses II
Source: adapted from Porter and Moss, 2nd edn. pl. 41.

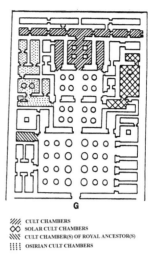

Figure 121 Funerary temple of Ramesses III
Source: adapted by R. Stadelmann in *LÄ* 4: 707–9.

covered in the vicinity of his funerary chapel, Tomb 71, smashed into more than a thousand fragments. Reconstruction reveals that in its material, its oval shape and its choice of texts the sarcophagus is roughly similar to contemporary royal sarcophagi, although its interior decoration consists largely of a version of Chapter 125 of the *Book of the Dead*. The sarcophagus was unfinished and never used.

Two statues of Senenmut have been found at Deir el-Bahri, a fragmentary one by Édouard Naville in 1894 during his clearance of Hatshepsut's temple (*Ḏsr-ḏsrw*), and a sistrophorous sculpture (the owner, kneeling, presents a large votive sistrum) by the Polish–Egyptian Mission in 1963 at the adjacent temple of Tuthmose III (*Ḏsr-3ht*).

Unusually for a private official, Senenmut appears in several places in the formal reliefs of Hatshepsut's mortuary temple. As the inscriptions state, this signal favor was granted by the queen.

East bank monuments

In the precinct of the Montu temple at North Karnak, a stela of Senenmut was found by Louis Christophe in the late 1940s. The text describes a donation of land made by Senenmut to establish endowments for certain institutions within the domain of Amen at Thebes, the land in question having been given to Senenmut earlier by the young Tuthmose III.

The thirteen statues of Senenmut from the east bank of Thebes represent several of the earliest types of sculpture that are later attested throughout much of the 18th Dynasty and even into the New Kingdom, including sistrophorous, naophorous (a votive *naos*, or shrine, is presented), "tutor" statues (the owner is shown with his or her royal ward) and rebus statues (a hieroglyphic rebus of a royal name or emblem is presented). Four statues of Senenmut were unearthed in the great cachette at Karnak that was found by Georges Daressy in 1904 (Cairo CG 42114, 42115, 42116, 42117). The body of a fifth (Cairo JdE 47278), a block statue of Senenmut and Neferure, Hatshepsut's only daughter, was discovered by Maurice Pillet in 1922 to the south of Pylon 9. This statue was reused as a building block in Late period foundations; the head and other fragments, however, came to light in 1970–1 in an ancient tree enclosure near the temple of Montu in North Karnak, where it was probably erected originally.

The temple of Mut at Karnak has also yielded a block statue of Senenmut (Cairo CG 579), which recounts the construction projects he undertook there; it was discovered by Margaret Benson and Janet Gourlay in 1896 in the southwest corner of the temple enclosure. A quartzite rebus statue of Senenmut (Cairo JdE 34582) was found in 1900 at the temple of Luxor. Two other sculptures, presently housed in the Sheikh Labib and Karakol magazines at Karnak, were apparently dedicated in the precinct of the temple of Amen.

Other monuments

Several noteworthy monuments belonging to Senenmut have been identified outside the Theban area. The largest is a rock-cut shrine carved into the sandstone bluffs of the western Gebel el-Silsila quarries, from which so much stone was extracted for the construction of the temples of Thebes. Like many of his contemporaries who supervised work there, Senenmut dedicated a small chapel in honor of himself, the gods of the First Cataract region, and the reigning king; in this case, Queen Hatshepsut, prior to her assumption of kingly titles but nonetheless portrayed here as a man. At Aswan, a graffito commemorates Senenmut's efforts in quarrying two granite obelisks during the period Hatshepsut was acting as regent for the young Tuthmose III. Finally, another commemorative stela at the temple of Hathor at Serabit el-Khadim in southern Sinai, dated to year 11 of Tuthmose III and Hatshepsut, depicts Senenmut standing behind his former ward, the princess Neferure.

See also

Deir el-Bahri, Hatshepsut temple; Deir el-Bahri, Tuthmose III temple; funerary texts; Karnak, precinct of Montu; Karnak, precinct of Mut; Karnak, temple of Amen-Re; Luxor, temple of; New Kingdom, overview; obelisks; Serabit el-Khadim

Further reading

Dorman, P.F. 1988. *The Monuments of Senenmut: Problems in Historical Methodology.* London.
——. 1991. *The Tombs of Senenmut: the Architecture and Decoration of Tombs 71 and 353.* New York.
Simpson, W.K. 1984. Senenmut. In *LÄ* 5: 849–51.

PETER F. DORMAN

Thebes, Sheikh Abd el-Qurna

The best known region of the Theban necropolis is Sheikh Abd el-Qurna (25°44′ N, 32°36′ E), named after the little shrine of a local saint on top of the hill. The ancient cemetery designated by this modern name consists of three parts: (1) the main hill, surrounded by the "upper enclosure wall," erected by Sir Robert Mond at the beginning of the twentieth century; (2) the plain at the foot of the hill, directly west of the Ramesseum; and (3) a small region, topographically better assigned to el-Khokha, called the "lower enclosure," named after a surrounding wall built under Mond's supervision. The "lower enclosure" forms the end of the northern access road to the main hill of Sheikh Abd el-Qurna and is a natural continuation of el-Khokha. Many tombs of the 18th Dynasty line the sides of this road. After the Amarna period, the road seems to have had no further use; three important tombs of the 19th Dynasty were constructed at the end and directly in the middle of the former road.

The earliest tombs in the region of Sheikh Abd el-Qurna date from the second half of the 11th Dynasty and from the very beginning of the 12th Dynasty. In contrast to the New Kingdom, when only the eastern half of the hill was in use as a cemetery, during the Middle Kingdom all slopes of the hill were occupied by tombs. Every side of Sheikh Abd el-Qurna afforded a view of the royal mortuary temples and their causeways. Unfortunately, only two of the numerous *saff* and corridor-shaped tombs, belonging to Herbert Winlock's cemeteries no. 800 and 1100, have been entered into the official numbered list of Theban tombs (nos. 60 and 103 according to the bibliography of Porter and Moss). The architectural development of these Middle Kingdom tombs has been investigated by Dieter Arnold in his publication of the tomb of Intef.

Although there are no decorated tombs of the 17th Dynasty at Sheikh Abd el-Qurna, Friederike Kampp has pointed out that there can be no doubt about an occupation of the site during this period, because of some significant architectural features, visible in otherwise undated constructions. The first decorated tombs from the beginning of the New Kingdom at Sheikh Abd el-Qurna can be dated to the reigns of Ahmose, Amenhotep I and Tuthmose I. From this period until the reign of Amenhotep III, Sheikh Abd el-Qurna became the most popular part of the Theban necropolis. All the highest ranking officials and priests built their tombs in this region, following geographically the order of the royal mortuary buildings from north to south. The connection with the position of the tombs, the social rank of their owners and the orientation to the mortuary temples has been worked out by Wolfgang Helck and had already been mentioned by Georg Steindorff and Walther Wolf.

As most of the upper parts of Sheikh Abd el-Qurna had been occupied at the end of the reign of Amenhotep II, the majority of the tombs dating to the time of Tuthmose IV and Amenhotep III are situated in the lower regions of this site. However, it was not only the density of occupation which caused the high rank officials of Amenhotep III to erect their tombs in the plain. As in el-Asasif, the new type of enlarged tombs reminiscent of funerary temples needed not only sufficient space for constructing the sunken courtyards and the huge inner halls, but also a good quality of rock, which is not to be found in the upper parts of the hill.

In the first half of the Ramesside period (19th–20th Dynasties) the lower regions of Sheikh Abd el-Qurna were used as a cemetery of some importance. Aside from three major tombs in the area of the "lower enclosure," most of the minor Ramesside tombs were cut into the side walls of the already existing courtyards of 18th Dynasty tombs. With the 20th Dynasty a new era of tomb usurpation began; many tombs at Sheikh Abd el-Qurna were reused in this period, some of them receiving new decoration or architectural modifications. During the Third Intermediate Period most of the tombs at Sheikh Abd el-Qurna, as in the other parts of the Necropolis, served as places for simple burials, and until the end of Dynastic Egypt there were no further rock-cut tombs constructed at Sheikh Abd el-Qurna.

The most important tombs of Sheikh Abd el-Qurna are listed below in chronological order, according to their numbers (TT = Theban Tomb), giving the name and title of the tomb owners.

Middle Kingdom:

TT 60   Antefoker, Governor of the Town and Vizier

TT 103 Dagi, Governor of the Town and Vizier

Ahmose–Tuthmose I:

C.2   Amenemhat, Noble at the Head of the People

TT 21   User, Scribe and Steward of Tuthmose I

TT 81   Ineni, Overseer of the Granary of Amen

Hatshepsut–Tuthmose III:

TT 71   Senenmut, Chief Steward and Steward of Amen

TT 83   Amethu, Governor of the Town and Vizier

TT 61 and TT 131
        User, Governor of the Town and Vizier

TT 86 and TT 112
        Menkheperrasoneb, First Prophet of Amen

Tuthmose III–Amenhotep II:

TT 85   Amenemhab, Lieutenant-Commander of Soldiers

TT 100 Rekhmire, Governor of the Town and Vizier

Amenhotep II:

TT 72   Re, First Prophet of Amen in the Mortuary Temple of Tuthmose III
TT 93   Kenamen, Chief Steward of the King
TT 96   Sennefer, Mayor of the Southern City

Tuthmose IV:

TT 52   Nakht, Scribe and Astronomer of Amen
TT 64   Heqerneheh, Nurse of the King's Son Amenhotep

Amenhotep III:

TT 55   Ramose, Governor of the Town and Vizier
TT 120 Anen, Second Prophet of Amen

Horemhab–Seti I:

TT 41   Amenemopet, Chief Steward of Amen in the Southern City
TT 50   Neferhotep, Divine Father of Amen-Re

Seti I–Ramesses II:

TT 106 Paser, Governor of the Town and Vizier

Merenptah:

TT 23   Thay, Royal Scribe of the Dispatches of the Lord of the Two Lands

See also

Middle Kingdom, overview; New Kingdom, overview

Further reading

Arnold, D. 1971. *Das Grab des Jnj-jtj.f* (AVDAIK 4). Mainz.
Helck, W. 1962. Soziale Stellung und Grablage. *Journal of the Economic and Social History of the Orient* 5: 225–43.
Steindorff, G., and W. Wolf. 1936. *Die Thebanische Gräberwelt* (Leipziger Ägyptologische Studien 4). Glückstadt.

FRIEDERIKE KAMPP-SEYFRIED

Thebes, el-Tarif, prehistoric sites

El-Tarif is a prehistoric site situated on the west bank of the Nile (25°44′ N, 32°38′ E), about 5 km north of Sheikh Abd el-Gurna, at the foot of the Theban cliffs. It has been known for a long time as part of a Theban cemetery from the Old and Middle Kingdoms, and since the 1970s it has also been identified as an important Predynastic site.

The site was first mentioned in the years 1826–30, and is indicated on the map made by the English Egyptologist Sir John Gardner Wilkinson, and a Scottish traveler and collector, Robert Hay. Later it was investigated by the Italian Egyptologist Ernesto Schiaparelli and Flinders Petrie (in 1908–9), after which it became covered by the contemporary village of el-Tarif. Exploration of the site was again taken up by Dieter Arnold (1970–4), and its Predynastic evidence was later investigated by a Polish team, Bolesltaw Ginter, Janusz Koztlowski and Joachim Sliwa (1978–82).

The cemetery of el-Tarif is very large. It covers an area *circa* 1200 m (north–south) by 600 m (east–west), which corresponds to what Petrie called cemeteries "A" and "B." According to Petrie, these cemeteries date to the 11th and 12th Dynasties; however, their precise location is not known. The most important part of the cemetery consisted of the graves of the first three kings of the 11th Dynasty, described by Arnold as the so-called *saff* (row) tombs. The best archaeological stratigraphy was found in the area between two 4th Dynasty tombs (*mastaba*s) excavated by Arnold. The bedrock in that area consisted of sediments of the younger gravel pediment on which the two *mastaba*s were built. In the top part of the gravel pediment, Late Paleolithic stone tools were discovered. This stone tool industry shows affiliations with the Late Paleolithic units found in Nubia (such as the Qadan).

The sediments of the younger gravel pediment are overlain by a soil formed by eolian activity, which contains stone tools now known as the "Tarifian," dating to the early Holocene. In the course of systematic excavations of the area in between the two *mastaba*s, a concentration of about 3,200 flint artifacts was discovered around a hearth. This is primarily a stone tool industry of flakes dominated by retouched flakes and atypical scrapers, followed by end-scrapers, perforators and denticulated-notched tools. Burins and microliths are few in number.

The closest stone tool industry to that of the Tarifian is the Post-Shamarkian industry, known in Nubia. It is also characterized by the development of flakes, the gradual disappearance of microliths and the appearance of Neolithic elements, such as the bifacial tools and axes made from cores.

In the immediate vicinity of the hearth, the concentration of Tarifian lithics also yielded several dozen potsherds. These are almost entirely without decoration, but occasionally have a pattern of slanting impressions. Forms are of vessels with cylindrical necks, hemispherical bowls and plates of a type later known as "bread molds." Technologically, the sherds belong to three groups:

1 sherds of medium thickness, with straw, fiber and mineral (sand) temper;
2 thin-walled sherds with a smoothed surface, sand temper;
3 sherds of medium-thickness vessels, straw tempered, with mineral inclusions (crushed stone).

Although the Tarifian layer did not contain organic remains, the character of the camp, with no habitation structures and absence of wear on stone tools which would point to their use as sickles, suggests a hunting-gathering-fishing subsistence. The data from the sediments suggest that the Tarifian developed in a dry period when there was eolian activity, possibly in the sixth millennium BC. This preceded another wet event when rain channels formed, associated with a Predynastic Nagada culture settlement (fourth millennium BC). With the discovery of more Tarifian sites in the Theban region south of Gurna, the first radiocarbon date for the Tarifian site of MA 2/83 was obtained (calibrated, *circa* 5,200 BC). The

Tarifian was probably derived from local Epipaleolithic cultures with microlithic and geometric stone tool industries. Its foraging economy is accompanied by the first ceramics in the Nile Valley. At the site of Hamamieh in Middle Egypt, in the lowermost layers of the trial trench, a similar stone tool industry of flakes was excavated with ceramics which included sherds like those of the Tarifian as well as the characteristic rippled ware of the Badarian culture.

Above the Tarifian layer at el-Tarif was a sterile layer with materials washed from the slopes of cliff. Here the site yielded distinct traces of Nagada culture occupation, with two dwellings with stone foundations and four hearths. The hearths formed a semicircle around the stone dwellings. One hearth was made in a shallow basin, which prior to firing had been coated with Nile silt. Dwelling 1 was rectangular, with slightly rounded corners (approximately 3.5 × 2.0 × 5.0 m). The foundation was built of two rows of large stones, in between which was fill of gravel and small stones. Dwelling 2 was also rectangular (3.0 × 1.5 m), but no double foundation was visible. The two dwellings from el-Tarif are the first well-documented construction of stone foundations for the Predynastic culture of Upper Egypt.

The Nagada culture layer at el-Tarif consisted of three phases of occupation which yielded more than 3,400 potsherds, predominantly (more than 80 percent) of a ware with much organic temper. This ware most closely resembles the ceramics from the el-Khattara sites in the Nagada region, excavated in the 1970s by Fekri Hassan and T.R. Hayes, where "rough brown" ceramics are predominant. The el-Tarif sherds mostly come from flat-bottomed, hole-mouthed pots and various bowls, grayish-brown in color, but some with a reddish-brown slip. Less numerous was red-polished pottery (*circa* 10 percent), and black-topped pottery (*circa* 20 percent). A group of pottery specific to this site was decorated with carefully spaced impressions, in round, triangular or fish-scale shapes.

The very rich stone tool industry from the

Nagada layer is characterized by the manufacture of blades. A new tool type consists of rectangular sickle blades. Tools with bifacial retouch were also used as sickles. Chipped stone axes occur occasionally. In general, this industry differs from other known Nagada culture stone tool assemblages.

The Nagada culture evidence at el-Tarif also included plant remains, such as grains of emmer wheat and barley, but the faunal remains (domesticated sheep and goats) were poorly preserved. One of the hearths from the Nagadan layer yielded a (calibrated) radiocarbon date of 3,715 BC (Gd-689). Another dating technique, thermoluminescence, was used in the 1970s on samples of the Nagada culture pottery from this site, yielding slightly older dates of 3,810 BC and 4,340 BC.

See also

el-Badari district Predynastic sites; dating techniques, prehistory; Epi-paleolithic cultures, overview; Nagada (Naqada); Neolithic and Predynastic stone tools; Paleolithic tools; pottery, prehistoric; Predynastic period, overview; Thebes, el-Tarif, *saff*-tombs

Further reading

Ginter, B., and J.K. Kozlowski. 1984. The Tarifian and the Origin of Naqadian. In *Origin and Early Development of Food-Producing Cultures in North-Eastern Africa*, L. Krzyzaniak and M. Kobusiewicz, eds. 247–60. Poznán.

Ginter, B., J.K. Kozlowski, M. Pawlikowski and J. Sliwa. 1997. *Frühe Keramik und Kleinfunde aus el-Tarif* (AVDAIK 40). Mainz.

JANUSZ K. KOZLOWSKI

Thebes, el-Tarif, *saff*-tombs

The term "*saff*-tomb" applies to an important provincial type of tomb which developed locally in the Theban area during the First Intermediate Period and found its monumental expression in the tombs of the Theban kings of the early 11th Dynasty. This type of tomb, which probably derives from earlier types built during the late Old Kingdom, consists of a large court and comparatively small interior rooms. The *saff*-tomb's main feature is a single or double row of pillars cut out of the hard gravel along the rear end of the courts. The Arabic term "*saff*" ("row") refers to the row of openings between the pillars, which have been misunderstood as entrances into separate, aligned burial chambers.

With few exceptions (such as the tomb of Intefiker and Intef at Dendera), this type of tomb is restricted to the Theban site of el-Tarif, an extensive cemetery which stretches in the low desert northeast of the mortuary temple of Seti I, and just opposite the temple of Karnak on the west bank of the Nile. The cemetery covers an area approximately 1.2 km north–south and 0.6 km east–west, and comprises an estimated 300–400 *saff*-tombs.

The cemetery of el-Tarif has never been systematically investigated. Between 1860 and 1889 several sondages were carried out by Auguste Mariette, Gaston Maspero and Georges Daressy, who found parts of a stela (CG 20512) of the Theban king Wahankh Intef II. Flinders Petrie excavated some of the smaller tombs in 1908–9, but did not mention the royal tombs in his publication. Between 1966 and 1974 Dieter Arnold conducted systematic excavations in the royal tombs, which provided new insights into their structure, arrangement and sequence. In addition, a survey map of the whole cemetery was prepared on a scale 1:1000, including all *saff*-tombs which were visible on the ground.

The cemetery centers around three monumental royal tombs which are known under their local names: *Saff* el-Dawaba, *Saff* el-Kisasija and *Saff* el-Baqar (in early maps "Ssaft-el-leben"). The courts of the tombs, 65–80 m wide and 100–300 m long, were sunk about 5 m deep into the low desert with the gravel of their excavations piled up high on either side and originally retained by mudbrick walls. With the exception of the *Saff* el-Kisasija, where the remains of a chapel-like mudbrick structure and wall were found at the eastern end, the front part of these courts seems to have remained open. Two rows of 20–24 pillars are cut out of the hard gravel along the rear end of the courts and form the actual front of the tombs. Behind the pillars in the center of the back wall, a short narrow corridor leads into the royal cult chamber, with two pillars supporting the ceiling. From the cult chamber, either a sloping passage or a vertical shaft gives access to the burial chamber, where the king was buried in a stone sarcophagus. More corridors and chambers of similar plan but smaller, which served as tombs for members of the royal family and other courtiers, are cut in the back wall on either side of the royal chambers, as well as along the side walls of the court. With the exception of small stelae, the narrow corridors and chambers of the *saff*-tombs probably remained undecorated, although the walls seem to have been plastered. More elaborately furnished was the *Saff* el-Baqar, where the floor of the central corridor was covered with sandstone

slabs and the walls were lined with limestone. No evidence has been found for pyramids associated with the royal tombs of el-Tarif, as postulated by Mariette and others.

According to the fragments of a stela (CG 20512) found in the eastern end of the *Saff* el-Kisasija's chapel, this tomb belonged to Wahankh Intef II. Carved on the stela are figures of the king and his five dogs, who are all named. No textual evidence was found concerning the owners of the other two royal tombs, but archaeological evidence proved that the *Saff* el-Baqar was built later than the *Saff* el-Kisasija, while the *Saff* el-Dawaba was the earliest of the group. Based upon this sequence, the *Saff* el-Dawaba has been attributed to Sehertawi Intef I and the *Saff* el-Baqar to Nakhtnebtepnefer Intef III.

Little is known about the private tombs, which have never been systematically explored. They are of the same type but much smaller than the royal monuments. The survey of the accessible tombs has shown that there are two

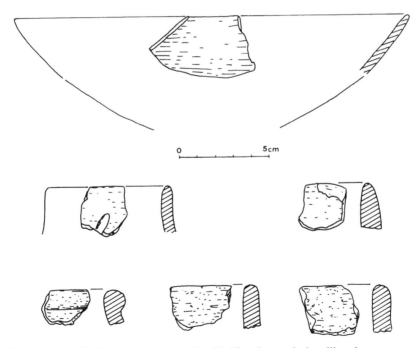

Figure 122 Thebes, el-Tarif, potsherds from the Tarifian layer, sixth millennium BC
Source: after B. Ginter and J.K. Kozlowski.

groups. A probably earlier group of tombs has just a single pillar supporting the ceiling of the cult chamber, while later tombs seem to have adopted two pillars. Deprived of their stelae and otherwise undecorated, their owners remain unknown.

See also

First Intermediate Period, overview; Middle Kingdom, overview

Further reading

Arnold, D. 1976. *Gräber des Alten und Mittleren Reiches in El-Tarif.* Mainz.

Winlock, H.E. 1915. The Theban Necropolis in the Middle Kingdom. *American Journal of Semitic Languages and Literatures* 32: 13–24.

CHRISTIAN HÖLZL

Thebes, Valley of the Kings

The Valley of the Kings, called in Arabic the Wadi el-Biban el-Muluk (Valley of the Gates of the Kings), and in ancient Egyptian, "The Great, Noble Necropolis of Millions of Years of Pharaoh," or, more simply, "The Great Place," was the burial place of pharaohs and many others in Egypt's New Kingdom (18th–20th Dynasties). The Valley of the Kings lies on the west bank of the Nile (25°45′ N, 32°36′ E), across from modern Luxor.

There are many valleys (wadis in Arabic) in the rugged Theban hills adjacent to the Nile, and there are several reasons why the Valley of the Kings was selected from among them as the site of the royal burials. Three reasons are geographical:

1 a stratum of particularly fine limestone, into which the tombs could be hewn, is exposed there;
2 the wadi is less than 1 km from the Nile Valley, where the mortuary temples (which, together with the tombs, form the principal parts of a royal funerary complex) are located;
3 the wadi is easily guarded because of the sheer cliffs and high hills that surround it.

Two further reasons are religious:

4 the goddess Hathor, who was closely allied with ideas of rejuvenation, was associated with the Theban landscape;
5 the Qurn, a mountain that rises above the wadi, and which has given its name to the entire area (Qurna), appears from the Valley of the Kings, and only from there, to have the shape of a pyramid, a form long associated with the god Re.

Actually, there are two Valleys of the Kings: the West Valley (WV), which is by far the larger of the two, in which were cut at least three royal tombs; and, immediately beside it, the much smaller East Valley (KV), in which over sixty tomb entrances were dug. The East Valley is the better known of the two.

During the New Kingdom, the Valley of the Kings was considered a sacred precinct, regularly guarded and, presumably, off limits to all but certain priests and officials and the royal family. After it ceased to be used for royal burials, after the end of the 20th Dynasty, tourists came to the Valley frequently. Graffiti left by post-Dynastic visitors, especially by Graeco-Roman travelers, are found throughout the Valley of the Kings and on the walls of fourteen or so tombs or parts of tombs that were accessible then. Such visits continued well into the seventh century AD, when Coptic Christians visited the Valley of the Kings and used several tombs as hermitages or churches. After the Arab invasion of Upper Egypt, such visits apparently stopped; no later graffiti have been found dating before 1739, when the first European visitors left their mark. By the nineteenth century, the Valley of the Kings had become a required stop on every European's Nile tour, and today nearly a million persons visit it annually.

Not everyone who visited merely looked. Tomb robbery in the Valley of the Kings is attested as early as the New Kingdom; we have ancient transcripts of the interrogations and trials of thieves who broke in almost as soon as a tomb was sealed. The thieves seem usually to have taken objects whose source could be disguised—metals, unguents, perfumes or oils, for example—which could be melted down or repackaged and easily disposed of. In the 20th Dynasty, such looting may have been sanctioned by various governmental and priestly officials anxious to replenish their dwindling economic resources while ostensibly opening tombs in order to rewrap and safeguard royal mummies.

Illicit digging has continued—fortunately with much less frequency—into recent times. During the nineteenth century, even while scenes in some tombs were being recorded by Jean-François Champollion, Richard Lepsius and other early Egyptologists, tomb robbing was occurring nearby. Artifacts from the Valley of the Kings are occasionally still found on the international market.

The KV tomb numbers used today are part of a system established by Sir John Gardner Wilkinson in 1827. At that time, twenty-one tombs were known in the Valley of the Kings, and Wilkinson numbered them in geographical order, north to south and west to east. Since then, many other tombs have been found in both the East and West Valleys: numbering has now reached 62, plus an additional 20 pits and unfinished shafts which have been given letter designations (KV A through KV T). Numbers from 22 onward have been assigned to tombs more or less in order of discovery, KV 62 (Tutankhamen's tomb) being the most recent.

The first clearing and recording of a whole tomb for which there is contemporary data was undertaken in 1816 by Giovanni Belzoni and his sponsor, Henry Salt; they opened Tombs 16, 17, 19, 21, 23 and 25. Belzoni's discovery of KV 17 (the huge and spectacularly decorated tomb of Seti I) made the Valley of the Kings one of the world's best known archaeological sites, and copies of its scenes and inscriptions, which Belzoni exhibited in London, greatly stimulated European interest.

Sixty-seven years later, in 1883, Egyptologist Eugène Lefébure began copying inscriptions in KV tombs. In 1898, Victor Loret, Director of the French-controlled Egyptian Antiquities Service, began the clearing of KV 33–8. (It was Loret who discovered, in KV 35, one of the two caches of royal mummies hidden by 20th Dynasty priests.) Lefébure's copies were not precise facsimiles, and Loret's clearing was little more than hacking through stratified sand and rubble in search of doors and pits. But both kept notes, both published their results, and their work is considered by some to mark the beginning of modern research in the Valley.

The most extensive archaeological work in the Valley of the Kings was that conducted by the English archaeologist Howard Carter. His work there had begun in 1900 when, as an Inspector of Antiquities, he supervised the introduction of electricity. Carter first excavated in the Valley in 1902 (working on a project of the American millionaire Theodore Davis), and continued to dig (supported after 1907 by Lord Carnarvon) until 1922, when he discovered KV 62, Tutankhamen's tomb.

None of the work done in the Valley of the Kings prior to the 1970s involved much more than moving debris in search of artifacts. There were only a few exceptions: among these, Alexandre Piankoff's epigraphic work stands out. Since the 1970s, however, more controlled fieldwork has been undertaken, including the epigraphic work of Eric Hornung, the geological studies of the Brooklyn Museum, and the mapping, stratigraphic excavation and conservation projects of the Theban Mapping Project of the American University in Cairo. All of these have been guided by the masterful history of the Valley of the Kings published by Elizabeth Thomas.

The first pharaoh to have been buried in the Valley of the Kings seems to have been Tuthmose I. An official in his court, Ineni, claimed to have supervised digging his tomb. Some have argued that this tomb was KV 38; more likely, it was KV 20, later usurped by Queen Hatshepsut. Even today, there is disagreement about the correct attribution of some tombs. Egyptologists believe that every New Kingdom pharaoh from Tuthmose I to Ramesses XI began work on at least one tomb in the Valley. But neither the texts in these tombs nor the elements of their design always guarantee certain knowledge of the owner.

A great deal is known, however, about how tombs were carved and decorated, thanks to the vast number of documents found at Deir el-Medina, the New Kingdom village in which lived the quarrymen and artisans responsible for their cutting and painting. We are also beginning to understand more fully the reasons for the tombs' frequently changing plans. These changes reflect evolving theological views of a king's journey to the afterlife, but they also indicate that rulers sought to outdo their predecessors in the size of their burial place. From one New Kingdom pharaoh to the next, doors and corridors usually become wider, chambers larger and more numerous.

Royal tombs may be arranged roughly into three categories according to their plan. Type 1 tombs have a corridor (sometimes level, sometimes sloping, sometimes with stairs) that often turns to the right. These are tombs of the 18th Dynasty, with entrances cut at the base of steep cliffs. Type 2 tombs are similar, but often turn to the left. Their plan sometimes jogs just beyond a shaft now thought to represent the burial place of Osiris (rather than simply being a precaution against thieves or floods). Their entrances are dug in a variety of topographical positions. They date from the 18th and 19th Dynasties.

Tombs Egyptologists call Type 3 were called by the Greeks "syringes," meaning "shepherd's pipes," and their long succession of corridors and chambers, sometimes descending deep into bedrock, do indeed look like long rectangular tubes. These tombs are of the 19th and 20th Dynasties. Their entrances lie at the bottom of sloping hillsides.

The following list includes royal (or thought to be royal) tombs, plus a few others of special interest. (Most of the tombs omitted from this list are little more than small, crudely cut, single chambers or unfinished pits, or tombs "lost" in modern times.)

KV 1, Ramesses VII: Type 3, 40 m long; open since antiquity.

KV 2, Ramesses IV: Type 3, 66 m long; an ancient plan of this tomb is found on a papyrus now in Turin; never completely cleared, but accessible in Graeco-Roman times.

KV 3, a son of Ramesses III: non-royal, 37 m long; cleared by Harry Burton (1912).

KV 4, Ramesses XI: Type 3, 93 m long; open since antiquity, cleared by the Brooklyn Museum expedition (1979).

KV 5, originally a late 18th Dynasty tomb, reused by Ramesses II for at least three of his sons: largely inaccessible since then; unique, complex plan; clearance by the Theban Mapping Project began in 1989.

KV 6, Ramesses IX: Type 3, 86 m long; open since antiquity, cleared by Georges Daressy (1888).

KV 7, Ramesses II: Type 3, over 100 m long; one of KV's largest tombs, partly dug in 1913, but still largely uncleared.

KV 8, Merenptah and perhaps Isinefret, his wife: Type 3, 115 m long; open since antiquity, dug by Howard Carter (1903).

KV 9, double tomb of Ramesses V and Ramesses VI: Type 3, 104 m long; open since antiquity, cleared by Daressy (1898).

KV 10, Amenmesse and family members: Type 3; open since antiquity, currently being cleared.

KV 11, Sethnakhte, completed by Ramesses III: Type 3, 125 m long; open in antiquity, but never fully cleared.

KV 13, perhaps tomb of Bay (under Tawosret): seriously damaged by flooding in 1994.

KV 14, Tawosret and her husband Seti II, then usurped by Sethnakhte: Type 3, 110 m long; some digging in 1909.

KV 15, Seti II: Type 3, 72 m long; perhaps the digging of this tomb was started, abandoned, then hastily resumed but never completed; open in antiquity, cleared in modern times.

KV 16, Ramesses I: 29 m long; dug by Giovanni Belzoni (1817).

KV 17, Seti I: Type 2, one of the largest and longest KV tombs (over 230 m, including an enigmatic passageway extending 90 m beyond the burial chamber); dug by Belzoni (1817).

KV 18, Ramesses X: never cleared.

KV 19: Mentuherkhepshef, a son of Ramesses IX, was perhaps hastily buried in this hardly begun (20 m long) and never finished tomb; found by Belzoni, cleared by Edward Ayrton (1905).

KV 20, Tuthmose I: Type 1, 200 m long; perhaps the first tomb dug in the Valley of the Kings, later usurped and enlarged by Hatshepshut; first dug by James Burton (1824), later by Carter (1903).

WV 22, begun by Tuthmose IV, the tomb was used by Amenhotep III (but probably not by others of his family): Type 1, 100 m long; discovered in 1799, cleared by Carter in 1915.

WV 23, Ay: 55 m long; discovered by Belzoni (1816), but not cleared until 1972.

WV 25, possibly begun for Amenhotep IV, although Tuthmose IV or one of his sons, Amenhotep III, Smenkhkare or Tutankhamen have also been suggested: unfinished; found by Belzoni (1817) and only recently cleared.

KV 34, Tuthmose III: Type 1, 55 m long; cleared by Loret (1898).

KV 35, Amenhotep II: Type 1, 60 m long; reused as one of the two caches in which priests of the 20th Dynasty reburied royal mummies; opened by Loret in 1898.

KV 38, perhaps dug by Tuthmose III for the re-burial of Tuthmose I (moved from KV 20): Type 1; cleared by Loret (1899).

KV 42, perhaps intended for Hatshepsut, but never used by her; may have been used by the mayor of Thebes, Sennefer, and his family: Type 1; cleared by Carter (1900).

KV 43, Tuthmose IV: Type 1, 90 m long; cleared by Carter (1903).

KV 46, Yuya and Tuya, parents of Amenhotep III's wife, Tiye: they were buried at different times (Yuya first), and shortly after the last interment the tomb was plundered of valuable items, later robbed again, resealed in the reign of Ramesses III, robbed yet again and finally resealed by Ramesses XI; when found by Theodore Davis (1905), it still contained numerous artifacts.

KV 47, Siptah and his mother: Type 3, 89 m long; dug by Ayrton (1905), Harry Burton (1912) and Carter (1922).

KV 54, a small pit, in which embalming materials of Tutankhamen were buried: opened in 1907.

KV 55, this small unfinished tomb is late 18th Dynasty, but its attribution (to Tiye or Akhenaten or Smenkhkare) and true purpose remain hotly debated: cleared by Ayrton for Davis (1907).

KV 57, Horemheb: Type 2, 114 m long; elegant examples of wall decoration in various stages of completion; dug by Ayrton for Davis (1908).

KV 62, Tutankhamen: the most famous (and most carefully recorded) tomb in the Valley of the Kings; twice robbed, but nevertheless found almost perfectly intact by Carter in November, 1922; still largely unpublished.

See also

Deir el-Medina; funerary texts; New Kingdom, overview; Thebes, royal funerary temples; Thebes, Valley of the Kings, Tomb KV 5; Tutankhamen, tomb of

Further reading

Helck, W. 1980. Königsgräbertal. In *LÄ* 3: 514–26.

Hornung, E. 1990. *The Valley of the Kings: Horizon of Eternity*, trans. by D. Warburton. New York.

Reeves, C.N., and R. Wilkinson. 1996. *The Complete Valley of the Kings*. London.

Romer, J. 1981. *Valley of the Kings*. New York.

Weeks, K.R. 1992. The Theban Mapping Project and Work in Valley of the Kings Tomb Five. In *After Tutankhamun*, C.N. Reeves, ed., 99–121. London.

KENT R. WEEKS

Thebes, Valley of the Kings, Tomb KV 5

In 1800, savants accompanying Napoleon Bonaparte's expedition to Egypt prepared a map of the Valley of the Kings and noted the presence of a tomb entrance at the head of the path leading into the Valley. During the nineteenth century, several other visitors acknowledged the presence of this tomb entrance on sketch plans or in their notes, but only Richard Burton, in 1825, attempted to breech the rubble-filled door and explore the tomb's interior. Burton dug a narrow channel through the fill in the first three debris-choked chambers, but, able to see only the ceiling of the tomb and none of its walls, he decided that the tomb was undecorated and of no importance. Similarly, early in the twentieth century, Howard Carter's workmen dug through the first 50 cm of debris at the tomb's entrance, then abandoned their work, convinced that the tomb was simply a small, undecorated pit. Carter's men proceeded to use the hillside above the tomb entrance as a dumping ground for debris from their other excavations. This tomb is called KV 5, the number given it on the survey of John Gardner Wilkinson (1827), and it has lain since Carter's days hidden beneath several meters of rubble.

In 1987, the Theban Mapping Project (TMP) sought to relocate KV 5. The general area in which it was believed to lie was to be cleared by the Egyptian Antiquities Organization (EAO) to create a large bus park and the TMP wanted to prevent that work from doing any inadvertent damage to the tomb. After only a few weeks of work, KV 5's entrance was found. Over the next seven years, the TMP cleared the tomb's first two chambers and discovered not only that their walls were extensively decorated, but that there were large quantities of artifacts lying on the chamber floors.

Both artifacts and inscriptions indicated that KV 5 was a tomb used for the burial of several sons of Ramesses II: the names of three sons were found in chamber 1 alone. It was clear that KV 5 could be a tomb of considerable historical interest.

In the spring of 1995, the TMP explored a doorway in the rear wall of chamber 3, a huge sixteen-pillared hall. The doorway was sealed by debris, and it subsequently became clear that no one had gone beyond it in the last 3,000 years. We expected to find that the door

led into nothing more than a small chamber. Instead, we found a 30 m corridor at the end of which were two 20 m transverse corridors. At their junction stood a 1.5 m tall statue of Osiris, and in their walls were cut forty-eight doorways leading into 3 × 3 m rooms, or suites of rooms. The walls of both corridors and rooms were decorated in relief or painted plaster and showed scenes of Ramesses II presenting various of his sons to deities in the afterlife.

In the autumn of 1996, two additional corridors were found in the front wall of the sixteen-pillared hall. These lead steeply down at a 35° angle and are also lined with side chambers. Only one of these two corridors has so far been explored—we have dug 20 m, exposing twelve rooms—but work has not yet revealed the end of the corridor, or its destination. The walls here are also decorated.

Artifacts from KV 5 include thousands of potsherds, hundreds of pieces of jewelry, scores of red granite, alabaster, basalt, and breccia sarcophagus fragments, broken canopic jars (where the internal organs of a mummy were separately embalmed), servant statuettes (*shawabtis*), stone statues, wooden coffins, bird and animal bones, and bits of three fragmentary and one nearly complete adult male mummy. This evidence makes it clear that KV 5 was not only intended to be a tomb but was in fact used as the burial place of a number of Ramesses II's many sons.

The TMP is continuing its work in KV 5 and, given the size of the tomb, work is likely to continue for at least another decade. But it is already possible to make several observations. First, KV 5 is the largest tomb ever found in Egypt. To date, 108 chambers and corridors have been identified. Second, the plan of KV 5 is unique; there are few tombs of any period that bear even a superficial resemblance to it, and few temples that show even remote similarity. Third, KV 5 was the burial place of many of the sons of Ramesses II and was used as such. We have so far found the names of four sons associated with the tomb, but there are at least twenty-five representations of sons on chamber and corridor walls (the accompanying

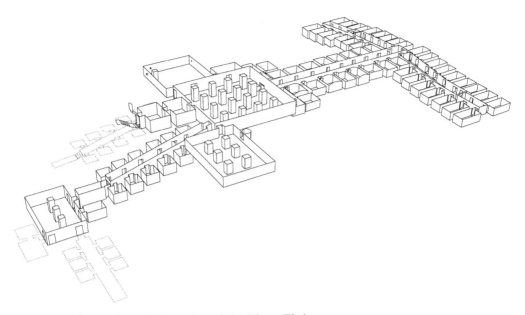

Figure 123 Plan of Tomb KV5, Valley of the Kings, Thebes

names either missing or not yet cleared of debris). Fourth, KV 5 is unique in Egyptian history: no other family mausoleum has ever been identified. Fifth, the many chambers found so far seem unlikely to have served as the actual burial chambers of the sons (unlikely in part because their narrow doorways could not have accommodated a stone sarcophagus), and we are assuming that the burial chambers lie elsewhere in the tomb, perhaps to be reached via the steeply sloping corridors at the front of the sixteen-pillared hall. If this assumption is correct, then the number of chambers in KV 5 will increase substantially before the TMP completes its clearing.

See also

mummification; Napoleon Bonaparte and the Napoleonic expedition; New Kingdom, overview; *shawabti*s, servant figures and models; Thebes, Valley of the Kings

KENT R. WEEKS

Thebes, Valley of the Queens

The Valley of the Queens, a necropolis for the wives and children of New Kingdom pharaohs, is located in the southern part of West Thebes (25°43′ N, 32°36′ E), southwest of the village and temple of Medinet Habu. The valley forms a large asymmetrical indentation in the western cliffs, with a waterfall, preceded by a dam which still receives the waters of torrential rains that occasionally fall in the desert. The ancient Egyptians considered the valley as a place where this "water of heaven" (*mw n pt*) had left significant traces. The pharaonic name for the valley, "Place of the Royal Children" (*t3 st nfrw*), means in a wider sense "of the Royal Harim." It is attested in a series of documents (papyri, ostraca, stelae and so on) of the Ramesside period (19th–20th Dynasties), though the site was used for burials from the 18th Dynasty onward.

In Arabic, the valley has been designated by various toponyms: Biban el-Hajj Ahmed (Doors of the Pilgrim Ahmed), Biban el-Banat (Doors of the Daughters), Biban el-Harim (Doors of the Women), and Biban el-Melekat or Wadi el-Melekat, the "Doors or Valley of the Queens," the latter of which is now commonly used. About ninety tombs, including unfinished ones, have been numbered in the main valley. In addition, on the northern side of the main valley is the Valley of the Dolmen, with a rock-cut sanctuary dedicated to Ptah and Meretseger by the Deir el-Medina workmen. Also in this area are the Valley of the Three Pits, with tombs dating back to the Tuthmosid period, and the Valley of the Rope, located near the ruins of Deir er-Rumi. Deir er-Rumi was a small monastery during the Byzantine period built on top of a Roman sanctuary from the time of Antoninus Pius. On the southern side of the main valley is the Valley of Prince Ahmose, with funerary pits dating back to the beginning of the New Kingdom and, on its heights, traces of cells used by Coptic anchorites and hermits.

In 1903–5, the valley became the subject of systematic investigation by the Italian archaeological mission under the direction of Ernesto Schiaparelli and Francesco Ballerini (succeeded by Giulio Farina). This work led to the discovery of the tomb of Nefertari, wife of Ramesses II (QV 66), as well as of the tombs of the princes Amenherkhopshef (QV 55), Khaemwaset (QV 44) and Sethherkhopshef (QV 43), all sons of Ramesses III. The Italian mission also cleared the 18th Dynasty pit tombs of the Vizier Imhotep (QV 46), Princess Ahmose (QV 47), Chief of the Stables Nebiri (QV 30), and Prince Ahmose (QV 88). Investigation was renewed in the valley in 1970 with a Franco-Egyptian team; intensive work began in 1984.

The first remains from the Valley of the Queens date to the beginning of the 18th Dynasty. Pit tombs dug into the mountain are attested from the reigns of Tuthmose I, Tuthmose II, Hatshepsut, Tuthmose III, Amenhotep II, Amenhotep III and even Akhenaten. These tombs have one or several burial chambers with finished, but undecorated walls; the absence of any traces of a superstructure suggests that these sepulchers did not possess funerary chapels. Only the remains of the tomb furnishings (e.g. canopic jars, *shawabti*s, pottery, papyri and the linen clothes used for mummification) have enabled the burials of this period to be identified by name.

In the Ramesside period more care was given to the development of the Valley of the Queens, considered now as a pendant to the Valley of the Kings. Tombs from this period were prepared by the Deir el-Medina workmen. In contrast with the simplicity of the 18th Dynasty tombs, those of the 19th Dynasty have real rooms with decorated walls. The iconographical themes and texts are mainly inspired by the *Book of the Dead*. Ramesses I had a tomb prepared for his wife, Satre (QV 38). Seti I had several tombs prepared in advance, without being intended for a specific person. Attributed to this reign are tombs QV 31 (unnamed great royal wife), QV 33 (royal wife Tanedjemy), QV 34 and QV 36 (unnamed princesses), and QV 40 (unnamed princess and great royal wife). These tombs were all conceived on a similar plan and are all grouped together along the southern lateral branch of the valley.

Ramesses II chose the northern slope of the main valley for the "houses of eternity" for his mother, Queen Tuy (QV 80), his wife, Queen Nefertari (QV 66) and some of his daughters, namely Nebettawy (QV 60), Merytamen (QV 68), Bentanta (QV 71), Henutmire (QV 75), Hennuttawy (QV 73) and an unnamed princess (QV 74). This latter tomb (QV 74) was later converted into the burial place of Duatentipet, the great royal wife of Ramesses IV. In the reign of Ramesses II, a village (*whjt*) was built in the middle of the valley. Material found in the ruins of the houses indicate that workmen from Deir el-Medina lived there while working on the royal and princely tombs.

In the reign of Ramesses III, tombs were dug in the lower parts of the southwestern slope of the main valley and at the far end of the southern lateral branch. From this reign date princely sepulchers for Amenherkhopshef (QV 55), Ramesses-Meriamen (QV 53), Khaemwaset (QV 44), Sethherkhopshef (QV 43) and Pareherwenemef (QV 42). Tombs were made for two of the great wives of Ramesses III: QV 51 for Isis, mother of Ramesses IV, and QV 52 for Tity, presumably mother of the princes Khaemwaset, Amenherkhopshef and Ramesses-

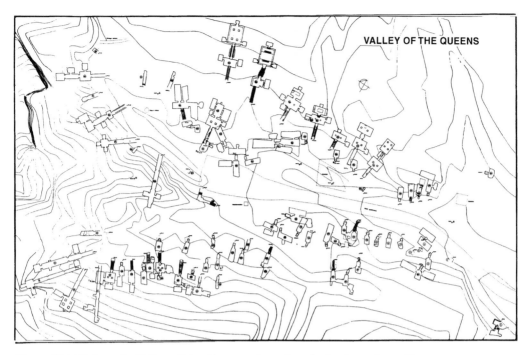

Figure 124 Thebes, the Valley of the Queens, plan of tombs in the main wadi
Source: drawing by Y. Laurent, Centre national de la Recherche scientifique.

Meriamen. Two other unfinished tombs (QV 41 and QV 45) may be placed in the reign of Ramesses III.

The Turin Papyrus mentions six tombs being prepared in the valley during the reign of Ramesses VI, but no trace of them has yet been identified. From the second half of the reign of Ramesses III on, economic confusion and social disorder led to strikes by the royal workmen and even to desecration of the royal tombs. Tomb robbery papyri (Papyrus Abbott, Papyrus Meyer and Papyrus Ambras) show that some of the tombs in the Valley of the Queens had been looted, including the tomb of Queen Isis (QV 51). Possibly after these robbings, the priests transferred the mummies of the Ramesside queens and royal children to a "cachette" or hiding place, probably outside of the valley, just as they had done for the pharaohs of the New Kingdom. This would explain why none of the remains of those buried in the Valley of the Queens during the 19th and 20th Dynasties have been found during archaeological excavations.

The Third Intermediate Period marks a transition in the history of the necropolis. Most of the plundered tombs were reused from the 22nd Dynasty into Saite-Persian times (26–27th Dynasties). Changed into family concessions and enlarged according to need, they now received members of the Theban minor clergy (priests, purifiers, singers and songstresses of Amen) and, above all, the personnel in charge of the agricultural estate or laboratories for perfumes for the God of Thebes (overseers of the estate, gardeners, flower cultivators, florists and perfumers).

Even more extensive is the reuse that occured in the Roman period, about the second century AD. The tombs of the 18th Dynasty as well as those of the Ramesside reigns were systematically reoccupied. Some tombs (QV 15, QV 16, QV 34 and QV 39) contained more than 100 Roman mummies. They were piled in a labyrinth of corridors and rooms, resembling the burial system of the catacombs. In addition to serving as a popular cemetery for the inhabitants of Thebes, a few sepulchers were also used for mummified animal remains; ibis and falcon mummies were found in QV 3 and 4, QV 9 and 10, QV 11 and 12, and QV 53. The sanctification of the Theban mountain and the presence of sanctuaries in the Valley of the Queens or nearby, such as those of Antoninus Pius at Deir er-Rumi and Qasr el-Aguz at Medinet Habu, are reason enough to explain the renewal of funerary activities in the necropolis.

Toward the second half of the fourth century AD, the Valley of the Queens became a place of refuge and meditation for anchorites and hermits. Tombs, cells and natural shelters were fitted up and occupied. Some of the first Christian monasteries, about ten in total, appeared on the slopes of the western mountains of Thebes. The monastery at Deir er-Rumi is considered to be the center of the group of hermitages (*laura*) established in the Valley of the Queens between the sixth and seventh centuries AD.

See also

Deir el-Bahri, royal mummy cache; Deir el-Medina; New Kingdom, overview; Thebes, Valley of the Kings

Further reading

Helck, W. 1980. Königinnengrabertal. In *LÄ* 3: 468–73.

Leblanc, C. 1989a. Architecture et évolution chronologique des tombes de la Vallée des Reines. *BIFAO* 89: 227–47.

——. 1989b. *Ta set neferou: une nécropole de Thèbes-Ouest et son histoire* 1. Cairo. Vols 2–5 in preparation.

——. 1990. L'archéologie et l'histoire de la Vallée des Reines. *Les Dossiers d'archéologie* 149–150: 22–9.

——. 1993. The Valley of the Queens and Royal Children: history and resurrection of an archaeological site. In *Art and Eternity: the Nofretari Wall Paintings Conservation Project (1986–1992)*, 19–29. Santa Monica, CA.

CHRISTIAN LEBLANC

Thmuis

Tell Timai (30°56′ N, 31°31′ E), in antiquity a Graeco-Roman city known by the Greek name Thmuis, is located in the Delta province of Daqahliya roughly midway between the city of el-Mansura and the town of el-Simbillawein. The tell is about 7 km in perimeter and lies about 0.5 km south of the smaller mound of Tell el-Rub'a, ancient Mendes. There is some evidence to suggest that the Mendesian branch of the Nile originally flowed between the two mounds. To the northeast stands the modern village of Timai el-Amdid, and on the northwest the modern village of Kafr el-Amir Abdallah Ibn as-Salam encroaches on the mound itself.

Reference by ancient authors indicates that Thmuis was a very important city. Although Herodotus (2.166) includes a Thumuite Nome among the nomes of the Calasirians, the first mention of the town of Thmuis appears in Josephus' *A History of the Jewish Wars* (4.659), where we learn that Titus disembarked his army here for the long march overland to Jerusalem. Like the city of Mendes, therefore, it must have been an important port city located on the Mendesian branch of the Nile. By the second century AD, Thmuis had become the capital of the Mendesian Nome and was presumably in control of the manufacture and distribution of the exotic *unguentum mendesium*, an extremely popular perfume in antiquity, according to Pliny. Ammianus Marcellinus (22.16) informs us that Thmuis was one of the four most important towns in Egypt in the fourth century AD, Hierocles tells us it was one of the cities of the eparchy of Prima Augusta in the sixth century, and George of Cyprus (*circa* AD 606) includes it among the dioceses of the eparchy of Augustamica A. Thmuis became an episcopal see at the end of the third or the beginning of the fourth century AD. Several bishops of Thmuis are known, from Phileas, who was martyred in Alexandria in *circa* AD 305, to the saintly Anba Mennas, who participated in the council that elected the patriarch Michael I of Alexandria in AD 744.

Aside from Tanis, Thmuis is the only site in the Delta where readable papyri have been found. These papyri give a number of insights into the economic organization of the northern nomes during the first three centuries of this era. The descriptions of Naville's excavations in the "library" in January 1892 and Chaban's excavations of 1906 and their inability to preserve much of the papyri, which apparently filled several rooms, cause one to wonder how much information has been lost. From what fragments of papyri have survived, one learns that religious organization was closely associated with the government, probably in the form of a state religion. Government functions included the maintenance of a navy and a guard. A government-controlled education system did not exist; one must imagine that most of the people were at best semi-literate. Grain, wheat and grapes were raised, and linen and probably wine were exported. There are indications that trade, as with many port cities, may have been substantially more important to the area economically than agriculture.

Other discoveries made here in the past accentuate the importance of the city. Quantities of reliefs, marble statues and bronze statuettes, including ten fine heads in a hoard of sixty-two late Hellenistic pieces, and some of the finest Hellenistic and Roman mosaics in the Alexandria Museum, assure us of the city's wealth. Most of these finds were accidental. Over the years the central section of the mound has been despoiled by the surrounding villagers, who used it as the source of materials for the construction of their houses, as well as by the *sebbakhin* who used the sifted soil for their fields. At present mudbrick walls and portions of walls from buildings of the Ptolemaic period stand to considerable heights alongside mounds of pottery sherds mixed with pieces of stone architectural members, small fragments of painted plaster and mosaic tesserae. Some of these walls are foundations, but others have openings for roof beams, windows and doors; portions of staircases and upper stories also are preserved. Within this chaotic context, some evidence of ancient streets has survived. Georges Daressy tells us that up until 1887 the structures of brick on the mound were quite well preserved. When he returned again in 1890 he was confronted with much the same devastation that we see today.

During the 1965, 1966 and 1976 seasons of the Mendes excavations, small soundings were conducted at Thmuis, and in 1965 a pottery survey was made of the tell. The survey sherds recovered range in date from fragments of fourth century BC kraters to Islamic sherds as late as the ninth century AD. One of the soundings, conducted at the west side of the central part of the mound, proved productive enough to become an area excavation. A series of rooms produced sealed floor levels dating from the end of the third to the first part of the first centuries BC. Nine Ptolemaic bronze coins dating from the third and second centuries BC were found in sealed contexts in Level I. Four identifiable bronze coins were found in Level II, immediately below the rooms. These included an Athenian tetradrachm datable to the first quarter of the fourth century BC and three bronze coins dating from the reign of Ptolemy I. The discovery of late Hellenistic strata in the highest part of the central section of the mound makes one wonder if the mound is not considerably older than the Ptolemaic period.

See also

Late and Ptolemaic periods, overview; Mendes, Dynastic evidence; Roman period, overview

Further reading

Holz, R., D. Stieglitz, D. Hansen and E. Ochsenschlager. 1980. *Mendes* 1. Cairo.

De Meulenaere, H., and P. MacKay 1976. *Mendes* 2. Warminster.

Ochsenschlager, E. 1967. The excavations at Tell Timai. *JARCE* 6: 32–51.

——. 1971. Excavation of the Graeco-Roman

city Thmuis in the Nile Delta. *Annales archéologiques Arabes Syriennes* 21: 185–91.

EDWARD L. OCHSENSCHLAGER

Tod

Tod is a town located on the east bank of the Nile (25°35′ N, 32°32′ E), 20 km south of Luxor. In ancient Egypt it was known as "the city of the Falcon" (*Djarty*), located in the southern part of the Theban nome (Nome IV of Upper Egypt). Its Greek name is unknown, but the Coptic name was *Tu(u)t*, which is derived from *Du(u)t*, an earlier version of the name. Today it is known as el-Tod.

Tod is primarily known for its temple of Montu, excavated by Fernand Bisson de la Roque in 1934–6. Some column fragments found on the site were inscribed with the name of King Weserkaf (5th Dynasty), and the oldest parts of this building are believed to have been constructed in the Old Kingdom.

The most important part of the temple is inscribed with the names of King Mentuhotep II and his successor, Mentuhotep III, both from the 11th Dynasty. Amenemhat I and Senusret I of the early 12th Dynasty built a new temple, and it was under this temple's foundation deposit that several bronze chests inscribed with the name of Amenemhat II were found. Their contents include gold and silver vessels from the Aegean and cylinder seals from Mesopotamia, of the Third Dynasty of Ur.

The temple was expanded during the 13th Dynasty and the New Kingdom. Several blocks and fragments from the temple are inscribed with the names of Tuthmose III, Amenhotep II, Seti I, Ramesses II and Ramesses III. In the 29th–30th Dynasties the temple was restored by Hakor and Nectanebo I. Later the Ptolemies built a larger temple, which was enlarged during the Roman period, as evidenced by blocks inscribed with the name of Emperor Antoninus Pius. The stone kiosk located on the steep eastern bank of the temple's sacred lake also dates to the Roman period.

Tod continued to be inhabited during By-zantine and Islamic times, and the remains of two churches have been uncovered in the area of the Ptolemaic temple. Archeological investigations of the Tod temple, including the surrounding buildings, have not yet been completed. Besides the falcon god Montu, his companion, the goddess Tjenenet, was also honored there. Eventually Rat-taui, the "(female) sun of the two countries," became the most revered goddess of the Tod cult. The sacred animal of the god Montu was the bull, which became known as the "bull from Tod" and was also referred to as "that which descended from," or "that which came out of" the town of Tod. For this reason, Tod became known as the home of Montu's animal, and in the New Kingdom a sacred "bull house" was built in its honor. Other deities, such as Sekhmet, Astarte and Amun, also had cults at Tod.

The town's cemetery is located east of the modern village. An unmarked grave dating to the 18th Dynasty and other burial shafts were discovered there. Perhaps the unexcavated cemetery located near the village of el-Salamiya is also associated with the ancient town of Tod. Artifacts, including a shell with the cartouches of Amenemhat II and some stelae dating to the 12th–13th Dynasties, were found in this cemetery.

See also

Late and Ptolemaic periods, overview; Middle Kingdom, overview; New Kingdom, overview; Roman period, overview

Further reading

Gomaà, F. 1986. Tôd. In *LÄ* 6: 615–16.
Vercoutter, J. 1952. Tod (1946–949): Rapport succinct de fouilles. *BIFAO* 50: 69–87.
Weill, R. 1938. Le trésor de Tôd. *Rd'É* 3: 168–9.

FAROUK GOMAÀ

tomb furnishings

A characteristic feature of ancient Egyptian

burials was that they regularly contained the personal possessions and other artifacts of the deceased. Such items in any grave assemblage could be numerous and elaborately made, or they might be few in number and simple in style, depending upon the wealth and circumstances of the deceased. They might also be manufactured specifically for the tomb, or they could be the actual belongings used by the deceased when alive. The Egyptians believed that in many aspects life after death mirrored life on earth. The dead could enjoy a happy afterlife if certain physical and spiritual conditions were fulfilled, i.e. maintaining the corpse intact in a proper burial, providing the deceased with regular food offerings to sustain it in the hereafter, and furnishing the dead with the artifacts of daily use needed to exist in comfort and safety.

To the Egyptians, the tomb was a house for the deceased. The *ba*, one of the spiritual essences of the dead, was thought to fly up to heaven during the day and return to the tomb at night to reinhabit its corpse. This daily joining of the *ba* and the body was essential to the spiritual life of the dead person. In keeping with these beliefs, the Egyptians furnished their burials with two types of artifacts: household items of personal use and religious items for ritual use. The purpose of the household goods was to serve the physical needs of the deceased in the hereafter. They included artifacts of daily life, food and drink.

The purposes of the religious items were to protect the soul of the deceased from any spiritual harm in the hereafter and to guarantee for the latter a verdict of "innocence" during the judgment of the dead. Inside the tomb various magical amulets on the mummy would protect it from evil spirits. Papyri inscribed with the *Book of the Dead* would safeguard the soul and enable it to achieve immortality. Statues of the deceased would act as replacements for the mummy in case it was damaged. Ritual equipment, offering tables, and statues and stelae portraying the deceased performing rituals would magically garner the spiritual benefits of those rites.

The earliest burials in which artifacts are found in Egypt are Badarian from the early Predynastic period. These are plain oval graves containing simple furnishings, pottery jars, ivory spoons and combs, and stone palettes for grinding eye-paint. Thereafter in the Nagada I (Amratian) phase, the assemblages of grave goods become more complex, as the burials become richer. Long-toothed ivory combs, jewelry and funerary figurines are features of this period. Large jars made of stone occur alongside the characteristic pottery, which is often in the shape of a human figure or with human appendages.

Beginning in the Nagada II (Gerzean) phase, upper Egyptian graves increase in size and evolve into a large rectangular shape. Commensurately, the quantity of artifacts in these tombs increases over earlier graves. Typical grave goods of this period and the following Nagada III (Semainean) era include painted pottery of Nagada II type, finely wrought flint knives, animal-shaped cosmetic palettes, maceheads, copper and ivory tools and implements, and jars with wavy handles of Palestinian manufacture or inspiration. Significantly, it is in the Nagada III phase that the disposition and contents of tombs, especially at Hierakonpolis and Nagada, first indicate the emergence of a class of social elite. Their tombs are larger than most and contain significant numbers of fine quality goods. From this time onward, the number and nature of the artifacts in tombs are indications of stratification in Egyptian society.

At Saqqara in the cemetery of the Early Dynastic period, tombs can be grouped according to four social categories based on their size and content: (1) *mastaba*s of royalty and the greater nobility; (2) those of the lesser nobility; (3) subsidiary burials of servants and craftsmen; and (4) simple commoners' graves. Despite the fact that the burial chambers of most of the *mastaba*s had been plundered in antiquity, they still contained significant numbers of artifacts important for the archaeologist. Among its many contents, the *mastaba* of King Djer included an impressive array of flint knives, sickles, weapons, copper chisels, awls, needles, saws and sets of copper vessels and dishes. Other tombs similarly contained copper-bladed knives, hoes and adzes. Gameboards and pieces of games are very common at this time and are a characteristic feature of Early Dynastic period burials. Significantly, the earliest roll of papyrus ever discovered was found uninscribed here in a *mastaba* contemporary with King Den.

A large *mastaba* typical of the Early Dynastic period at Saqqara enclosed many magazines in its superstructure, as well as storerooms and a burial chamber underground. The burial chamber contained the coffin, around which was often set a funerary meal. Here, food was placed on dishes set on the floor. Nearby jars held reserves of more food and drink. The burial chamber also contained chests of garments, jewelry, games and furniture (inlaid ivory chairs, tables and beds). The adjacent subterranean rooms contained still more furniture and tools and weapons. Often, one room was set aside as a food storehouse with great joints of meat, bread and cheese, and many large jars of wine. A great quantity of empty jars, bowls and dishes was also placed here in reserve. In the superstructure above, each of the many magazines could be designated for a specific class of artifacts, such as tools and weapons, games, food and drink, and so on.

*Mastaba*s of the lesser nobility were smaller in size and contained fewer tomb furnishings than those of higher officials. All of the Early Dynastic period royal tombs at Saqqara and Abydos, as well as many of those of the high nobility, were surrounded by the smaller tombs of their servants and artisans. Some of these persons might have been sacrificed for burial with their lords in order to serve them in the next world. While the servants' burials were not elaborate, their tomb furnishings were sometimes suited to their specific occupations, such as copper and flint tools for the craftsman, pots of paint for the artist, model boats for the sailor, knives and meat for the butcher, and cosmetics and toilet utensils for the servant-woman. In contrast to the burials of the elite, a commoner's grave at this time consisted merely of an oval pit covered with a small mound of rubble. Its simple furnishings might include some pottery, stone vessels, copper and flint

tools, and toilet utensils. What is clear is that the customs involving the deposit of tomb furnishings in the Early Dynastic period set the pattern for burials, rich and poor, in all subsequent periods of Egyptian history.

From the Old Kingdom onward, the evidence for tomb furnishings is no longer limited to the actual artifacts found in burials, but also includes the representations of those artifacts depicted on the walls of tombs for religious purposes. One of the best examples of this phenomenon is found in the 3rd Dynasty *mastaba* of Hesyre at Saqqara. While very few artifacts from this tomb have survived, murals painted on the wall depict in extreme detail a wide assortment of Hesyre's tomb furnishings. These include furniture (beds, headrests, chairs, stools, standing chests and tables), disassembled tents, assorted tubs and strikers (for measuring grain), boxes and trays, staves, games, tools, scales, model storehouses, jars of food and so on.

Also from the Old Kingdom onward, Egyptian tombs regularly contained a statue of the deceased as a repository for the *ka*, another of the spiritual essences of the dead. This *ka* statue was often placed in an inaccessible chamber of the *mastaba*, called the *serdab*, from which it looked out and observed the world; or else the statue was located in the offering chamber of the tomb. Reserve heads occur in *mastaba*s of the 4th and 5th Dynasties at Dahshur, Giza and Abusir. These were portrait heads of the deceased, finely sculpted in stone, that were placed inside the burial chamber on or near the sarcophagus. While the purpose of the reserve heads is obscure, they might have functioned as substitutes for the mummy in case it was destroyed, to preserve the identity and personality of the deceased.

Clay models of houses, towns or storehouses occur in Egyptian burials as early as the Nagada I phase and continue sporadically through at least the 3rd Dynasty. However, it is later in the First Intermediate Period that funerary models become widespread in Egyptian burials. Initially, these took the form of serving trays on which the house of the deceased was crudely modeled in clay along with various foods. These miniatures, called "soul-houses," magically provided home, protection and sustenance to the deceased. In the First Intermediate Period, the Egyptians also began making models of estate workshops that were conceived along the lines of the earlier servant statues. By the Middle Kingdom, these models were elaborate dioramas composed of individual figurines performing specific tasks. Even earlier in the 6th Dynasty, the custom of interring model boats and sailing craft became widespread. These boats represented various utility vessels and pleasure craft to serve the deceased in the next life.

The necropolis of Western Thebes is an important source of tomb furnishings from the Middle Kingdom through the Late period. The Theban tombs contained all manner of items of daily use and cult objects buried with their owners. Unfortunately, almost no tomb has escaped plundering by robbers or survived intact. However, two remarkable exceptions give us some insight into the lives of both commoners and royalty. The tomb of Khay and Meryt at Deir el-Medina was discovered intact in 1906. Khay was a royal architect in the Theban necropolis, and his burial contained stools, tables, decorated chests, wigs, cloth and clothing, cosmetic kits, utensils, staves, a gameboard, baskets, jars, situlae and food supplies. The cult-items included sarcophagi, a *shawabti*-coffin, statuary and a *Book of the Dead* papyrus. Significantly, a portion of these grave goods originally belonged to other persons, who may have donated them to the burial, or else Khay acquired them through other means. Two other artifacts in this assemblage clearly came as gifts from King Amenhotep II. Similarly, the tomb of Tutankhamen contained a number of artifacts which were presented as gifts to the burial by other individuals. While no systematic study of such presentations has yet been made, it is possible that in Egypt bereaved relatives and friends customarily gave tomb furnishings as gifts during the funerals of friends and loved ones.

The artifacts found inside Egyptian tombs are evidence of the material culture of the ancient Egyptian civilization. They are impor-

tant for revealing the Egyptian way of life, their natural resources and technological abilities at any given period. The number and quality of the tomb furnishings in association with other factors (tomb size, location, etc.) can also be used to make determinations about Egyptian social development and the stratification of Egyptian society.

See also

Deir el-Bahri, Meket-Re tomb; Giza, Hetepheres tomb; mortuary beliefs; Saqqara, North, Early Dynastic tombs; *shawabtis*, servant figures and models; ships; Tutankhamen, tomb of

Further reading

D'Auria, S., P. Lacovara and C. Roehrig. 1988. *Mummies and Magic: The Funerary Arts of Ancient Egypt*. Boston.

Donadoni, A.M. 1987. *Egyptian Civilization: Daily Life*. Milan.

Killen, G. 1980. *Ancient Egyptian Furniture*. Warminster.

——. 1994. *Egyptian Woodworking and Furniture*. Princes Risborough.

PETER A. PICCIONE

towns, planned

The excavation of ancient settlements in Egypt is still in its infancy. At present, moreover, most ancient settlements in Egypt are badly preserved, which prevents archaeologists from obtaining needed information about settlement patterns. The little evidence of ancient Egyptian settlements suggests that towns were developing in middle to late Predynastic times (fourth millennium BC). These "towns" probably developed around cult centers with temples or shrines made of light, organic materials, which are difficult to detect archaeologically. To date, the best preserved remains of a Predynastic proto-urban site have been excavated at Hierakonpolis (Kom el-Ahmar).

Proper towns appeared in late Predynastic

and Early Dynastic times, when the pharaonic state arose. Most likely, typical towns consisted of houses clustered around a central planned area with a temple and, in the capital city, the residence of the king. Ancient Egyptian towns were probably internally differentiated and surrounded by a wall. A good example of this is the late Old Kingdom town at Elephantine. The plan of this town included the residential quarters of officials and elites to the northwest and two temple areas to the southeast.

True planned towns were built in Dynastic times, at least beginning in the Old Kingdom. Two main types of planned towns are known archaeologically: workmen's towns and fortified towns. Although planned state towns are the best preserved evidence of ancient Egyptian settlements, most Egyptian towns were probably not as rigidly organized spatially, but would have developed more organically through time.

Workmen's towns were built to house the workmen, officials and priests (and their families) involved in the construction of royal tombs and their funerary cults. Remains of such towns have been excavated at Lahun, near the pyramid of Senusret II (Middle Kingdom), and at Deir el-Medina, near the Valley of the Kings (New Kingdom). A workmen's town, dating to the Old Kingdom, has recently been discovered near the pyramids at Giza. Both towns at Lahun and Deir el-Medina were surrounded by an enclosure wall. The houses at Lahun formed regularly spaced blocks, and were divided into quarters for the workmen and the officials of the town. The houses at Deir el-Medina were compactly organized with narrow streets dividing the main blocks of houses.

Fortified towns were built as military and colonial outposts along the Nile in Lower Nubia, in the Old, Middle and New Kingdoms. Archaeological evidence of these settlements has been found at Amara West, Aniba, Askut, Bigga, Buhen, Dabenarti, Faras, Ikkur, Kor, Kumma, Mirgissa, Quban, Semna, Semna South, Serra, Shalfak, Sesebi and Uronarti.

The Old Kingdom evidence from Buhen, and possibly Aniba, Ikkur and Quban, is scarce. The Middle Kingdom fortresses were always surrounded by a massive mudbrick enclosure wall, roughly rectangular in area. Sometimes the enclosure wall was reinforced with a second wall and a ditch. The buildings in the fortresses were arranged in a grid plan. They included houses of the governor and officials, military barracks, workshops and storerooms. Fortified towns of the New Kingdom included a temple and administrative buildings.

See also

Deir el-Medina; Dorginarti; Elephantine; Lahun, town; Nubian forts; Nubian towns and temples; ships

Further reading

Bietak, M. 1979. Urban archaeology and the "town problem" in ancient Egypt. In *Egyptology and the Social Sciences*, K. Weeks, ed., 97–144. Cairo.
Kemp, B.J. 1989. *Ancient Egypt: Anatomy of a Civilization*. London.
Trigger, B.G. 1976. *Nubia under the Pharaohs*. London.

RODOLFO FATTOVICH

trade, foreign

It is possible to trace Egypt's participation in trade with other regions in western Asia and Africa from the later fourth millennium BC and onward. This involved both direct commercial contacts with Egypt's immediate neighbors— Canaan to the north, Nubia to the south—and, through them, indirect trade contacts with areas farther afield. It is generally believed that trade with foreign places was carried on by the central government. Individuals involved in international commercial ventures were usually agents of the crown or temples, or government administrators. Buying and selling on this scale was a prerogative of officialdom and there is no convincing evidence of private enterprise in foreign trade contacts.

The land of Egypt was blessed with ample

resources of the basic materials used for construction and for the manufacture of objects of all sizes, but there was a great deal more available in the mountains along the Red Sea coast and down the Nile River into Nubia. Both regions were considered Egyptian spheres of influence, not part of their own land but theirs by right of exploitation. Rich mineral, stone and gold deposits lay in these areas, and royal expeditions regularly went there to bring back these natural resources on behalf of the state. To the southeast were the extensive gold mines of Nubia from which Egypt derived much of its internal wealth. In the eastern mountains there were deposits of jasper, feldspar, dolerite and other minerals. Tin, copper and lead were also to be found here, though it is not possible to determine how early these metal ores were mined. The copper deposits seem to have been exploited first in the 12th Dynasty, those of tin and lead not until the later periods. Farther north lay the peninsula of Sinai, the source for turquoise, used extensively throughout Egyptian history in the jewelry industry.

The major land route northward was across northern Sinai, then up to Gaza and the coastal plains that lay beyond. This route served as a trade artery to the inland towns of Palestine and connected with other routes moving eastward into Jordan and Syria. Parallel to this lay a coastal sea lane to the harbors of Phoenicia. This sea route was vital to Egypt since it offered easier transportation for the timber and other products Egypt obtained from the coniferous forests of the Lebanese mountains. While trees such as the acacia and sycamore grew in Egypt, they were not suitable for the finer coffins and furniture the Egyptian upper classes desired, nor for the stronger timbers needed in construction and shipbuilding. Lebanon supplied the more durable cedar, pine and fir, the resins and oils of which were in great demand in Egypt for use in perfumes, medicines and mummification. This trade in coniferous woods and their products created a special tie between Egypt and Byblos, the center for the timber trade in the Levant, which lasted almost two thousand years. It is unknown how early this

trade began, though it was well-established at least by the beginning of the 3rd Dynasty.

The regions closest to the Nile Valley were the gateways to other places. The trade route that followed the river south brought Egyptians into indirect contact with the exotica of central Africa. The routes from the Theban district to the mines and quarries of the eastern mountains eventually ended at ports on the Red Sea. From here, Egyptian ships sailed down the coast to fabled Punt, in the region of modern Somalia or Eritrea, where they had direct access to the resources of sub-Saharan Africa. The products from sub-Saharan Africa are listed in Hatshepsut's reliefs describing her Punt expedition: processed myrrh and live myrrh trees, incense, throw-sticks, ebony and other rare woods, ivory, eye paint, baboons and apes, panther skins, electrum and gold. Elsewhere, other exotic items such as giraffe tails and ostrich feathers are noted.

Commercial contacts beyond Egypt's northern neighbors were indirect, or at least not as a result of Egyptian initiative. Minoan pottery in Middle Kingdom contexts undoubtedly arrived in Egypt through the intermediary of the Levantine ports. The later Mycenaean pottery and other Aegean products found in New Kingdom Egypt came the same way, or on Mycenaean ships and the Levantine coastal freighters now known from several ancient shipwrecks.

From Canaan, New Kingdom Egypt imported horses, coniferous woods and resins, silver, copper, tin, wine, various animal and vegetable oils, and manufactured items such as metal vases and jewelry. The frequent assumption that olive oil and wine were major imports from Canaan is misleading. The few references to olive oil in Egyptian texts make it obvious this was a luxury product for royalty, and wine was produced in Egyptian vineyards throughout Dynastic history, though some imported wine is mentioned in the texts.

Egyptian exports are partially summed up in the well known *Report of Wenamen* of about 1,100 BC, whose payment to the king of Byblos for cedar included gold, silver, various kinds of cloth, ox hides, ropes, linen mats and foodstuffs.

There is every reason to suppose that papyrus was exported already in New Kingdom times, though no actual proof is available. Egyptian alabaster vessels were a constant trade item from the early third millennium. From the early second millennium BC are found the ubiquitous Egyptian scarabs, amulets and other small objects wherever excavations have taken place. The fine linen cloth manufactured in Egypt must also be added to this list. Certainly, grain and other foodstuffs were a major export as Egypt had a dependable surplus each year. While such items as linen and foodstuffs fall under the rubric of "invisible" exports which leave no physical trace, literary allusions to them as exports are frequent.

A significant by-product of trade was the transfer of manufacturing processes and techniques. One of the most important of these was metallurgy, brought into Egypt from southern Canaan toward the end of the fourth millennium BC. The Beer Sheva Valley in the northern Negev was an early center for mining and smelting copper ore from the Wadi Arabah below the Dead Sea. At the same time, the Egyptian town of Ma'adi near Cairo was a flourishing mercantile center with substantial storage areas in which some of the trade goods were found intact. Here were also found the first traces in Egypt of casting molten copper in molds, Canaanite pottery like that of the Beer Sheva region, and, most significant, underground dwellings which are totally un-Egyptian but characteristic of the Beer Sheva sites.

In between Beer Sheva and Ma'adi, recent archaeological work has discovered Egyptian colonies at sites near Beer Sheva, and over a hundred settlements of varying sizes all along coastal Sinai. Many of the latter show both Egyptian and Canaanite artifacts, but several are more like Egyptian colonies. There is nothing in all this material which hints at military domination by either group and the Egyptian levels clearly indicate peaceful occupation, so there is no question of Egyptian expansion into Canaan as sometimes suggested. The reason for all this must be the transport of copper ore and the techniques of metallurgy from Canaan to Egypt with Egyptian food-stuffs being sent to Canaan in return. Other contemporary sites in the eastern Egyptian Delta now under excavation continue to yield Canaanite pottery and locally made copper tools. At the beginning of Egyptian history there was thus a very strong trade contact, based on the copper industry, between Egypt and Canaan. This soon evaporated as Egypt turned to more lucrative markets, but Egyptians had learned how to deal with metals as a direct result of trade contacts.

The search for raw materials was one motivation for establishing an Egyptian presence in foreign places. This was not necessarily political. There is evidence of a small Egyptian mercantile colony at Byblos in Old Kingdom times as a result of the timber trade with that city. The Hathor temple at Serabit el-Khadim in Sinai, the source for turquoise, was first built in the Middle Kingdom. A Hathor temple of the New Kingdom was constructed at Timna in the Wadi Arabah, a major source of copper ore. Such structures assume a resident Egyptian community during at least part of the year.

Similar activity was carried on in the south, especially at the Second Cataract of the Nile. The principal site here is Buhen, which already boasted a resident Egyptian commercial colony in the early Old Kingdom. By the Middle Kingdom, Buhen and several neighboring sites were fortified, although these fortresses served also as trade centers. In the New Kingdom, when Egyptian political domination of Nubia was at its height, the entire Nile Valley from Aswan to far below the Third Cataract was liberally sprinkled with Egyptian temples. As in Sinai and the Wadi Arabah, Egyptian temples served Egyptian communities. Even during the New Kingdom, when Egypt controlled an empire from northern Canaan to Upper Nubia, large segments of these communities were involved in commercial rather than political enterprises. The moving force behind establishing an empire in the first place was to assure economic stability and growth by controlling the sources of the needed raw materials and opening foreign markets to Egyptian products.

International trade fostered cultural developments far beyond the importing of raw materials and technologies. Canaanite craftsmen were strongly influenced by Egyptian prototypes, especially in the minor arts which drew heavily on Egyptian designs and symbolism. This is already seen in jewelry from Middle Bronze Age Byblos and the contemporary Syrian glyptic art. At the same time, Canaanite artisans had begun the process of adapting the Egyptian scarab tradition, which had meaning only in an Egyptian religious context, to their own needs and beliefs. Egyptian artistic influence reached its height in the Iron Age, when Phoenician artisans created their own scarab tradition and produced the Egyptianizing metal bowls and ivories which they sold throughout the ancient world. The same process occurred to the south of Egypt, in the kingdoms of Napata and Meroe. Here too Egyptian artistic influence, especially in the minor arts, remained prominent into Hellenistic and Roman times.

Trade also meant the movement of people for other than commercial reasons. As new markets were opened up, new opportunities arose for those free to move to foreign places, a group which has been termed the mobile middle class. The aristocracy was tied to government and administration in the cities; peasants were tied to the land they worked. But there was that group of artisans, poets, musicians and the like, that was free of permanent ties to either government or the land and thus more easily able to move where they wished. Foreigners lived everywhere, and their imprint on the art, language, literature and even religion is obvious in all societies of the ancient world. International commerce brought people of many cultures together and, human curiosity being what it is, the result was a free and open exchange of the cultural heritage each person took with him wherever he traveled. This personal meeting of individuals was as much the cause of the appearance of internationalism as was the more forced integration of political empires; if not more so.

See also

Aegean peoples; C-Group culture; Canaanites;
Deir el-Bahri, Hatshepsut temple; Hyksos; Israelites; Kushites; Levantine peoples (Iron Age); Ma'adi and the Wadi Digla; Medjay; Meroitic culture; metallurgy; natural resources; Nubian forts; Nubian towns and temples; Punt; Qantir/Pi-Ramesses; Qasr Ibrim; Serabit el-Khadim; Sinai, North, late prehistoric and Dynastic sites; Wadi Maghara; Wadi Tumilat

Further reading

Adams, W.Y. 1977. *Nubia, Corridor to Africa.* London.

Moscati, S., ed. 1988. *The Phoenicians.* New York.

Vercoutter, J. 1956. *L'Égypte et le monde égéen préhellénique.* Cairo.

Ward, W.A. 1991. Early contacts between Egypt, Canaan, and Sinai. *BASOR* 281: 11–26.

WILLIAM A. WARD

Tukh el-Qaramus

The site of Tukh el-Qaramus is located in the eastern Delta to the north of Tell Basta and Zagazig and to the south of the modern village of Tukh el-Qaramus; it was originally located between the Tanitic and the Pelusiac branches of the Nile and within Nome XIX of Lower Egypt. Two ancient names for the site are "*Bḥn*" and "Dqit," and its sacred area is referred to as "Pr-B3w," the "House of the Spirits." The site is best known for its large collection of gold jewelry and temple silver plate which is now held in the Cairo, Ashmolean, British and Metropolitan Museums.

Tukh el-Qaramus has been the subject of two excavations and a survey. The first excavation occurred in 1887 under the direction of Édouard Naville and Francis Llewellyn Griffith. Their work resulted in an identification of a basic site plan. The second series of excavations took place in 1905–6 under the direction of Campbell Cowan Edgar. It was during these excavations that the valuable collection of gold jewelry, coinage and temple silver plate was discovered within the temple precinct. In 1986 Stephen Snape conducted a survey of Tukh el-Qaramus.

The work of Naville and Griffith, and Edgar has provided us with the principal sources of archaeological evidence for the site. Naville and Griffith's work described an area of about 34 ha enclosed by thick fortification walls. The enclosed area was subdivided into secular and sacred areas. The sacred section was further divided by an additional set of *temenos* walls. Within the *temenos* walls, Naville and Griffith discovered the remains of a limestone temple and an upper temple. They noticed a curious mudbrick cellular structure that consisted of a large number of independent rooms. Naville and Griffith believed that these had originally served as storerooms. Throughout the site Naville and Griffith also noticed large deposits of limestone chips. In their opinion, these chips indicated that monumental structures, such as temples and pylons, had once existed but had since been burnt down deliberately.

In addition to establishing a layout for the site, Naville and Griffith discovered part of the foundation deposit. Their find included a faïence foundation plaque of Philip Arrhidaeus, enabling them to date the site to the early Ptolemaic period. Naville and Griffith also found a faïence vase datable to the Third Intermediate Period, with a hieratic inscription, fragments of ceramic figurines, potsherds and a pair of bronze tongs. In his 1905–6 excavations, Edgar discovered three types of objects: coinage, gold jewelry in Roman, Hellenistic and traditional Egyptian styles, and temple silver plate. The coinage included 108 gold *trichrysa*, and a large quantity of *pentadrachms* and *tetradrachms*. All of these coins were minted during the reigns of the first two Ptolemies. A small number of these coins had been minted in Phoenicia (Tyre and Sidon) and Cyprus.

The silver plate consisted of over thirty pieces, eight of which were inscribed in demotic. Stylistically, many of these vessels have Near Eastern, Achaemenid or traditional Egyptian prototypes; many similar examples may be found in Egypt from the fifth century BC onward, particularly from Tell el-Maskhuta

and Tell Timai. Three of the demotic inscriptions are from women and represent life wishes to Isis, Amen and Imhotep; the other five are the product of temple administration.

The jewelry included seven gold bracelets, nine earrings with three different forms of animal terminals, a long gold chain with lion-griffin terminals, three gold crescents and a number of additional small gold artifacts. Many of these pieces combine both Greek and Achaemenid influences, and are datable to the Hellenistic and Roman periods. The hoard also contained a number of pieces of ritual equipment and jewelry in Egyptian style. These included two miniature broad collars designed for statuary use, a number of gold amulets representing not only members of the Egyptian pantheon but also traditional Egyptian symbols such as *wadjet*-eyes and a papyrus scepter, seven gold cowrie shells, and a silver and gilded (*hmhm*) crown. There was also a bronze and gold aegis depicting the head of a pharaoh; the facial features strongly resemble those of Ptolemy II Philadelphus.

There can be little doubt that Tukh el-Qaramus functioned primarily as a military fortification protecting Egypt's northeast frontier. A stela of Sheshonk III refers to Tukh el-Qaramus as a "fortified place" (*bhn*). Not only does the site have thick fortification walls, but many of the cellular constructions, located throughout the site, probably acted as watch-towers as well as storage facilities. There is, however, evidence to suggest that Tukh el-Qaramus developed into a fortified town rather than simply remaining a fortress. Women figured prominently amongst the population, suggesting that Tukh el-Qaramus had a social infrastructure that was more developed than that of a mere fortress. Not only were women responsible for three personalized demotic inscriptions, but much of the gold jewelry was originally intended for female wear. Furthermore, the presence of spinning whorls probably indicates that women were engaged there in the manufacture of textiles.

There is controversy about two aspects of the site's history: the ethnic composition of its inhabitants, and the length of its occupation.

Most archaeologists have assumed that Tukh el-Qaramus was inhabited by Greek mercenaries. There is some evidence to suggest, however, that Egyptians rather than Greeks inhabited the site. In fact, the motifs and forms of much of the jewelry and temple plate may be traced to Near Eastern and Egyptian rather than to Greek prototypes. Moreover, Naville and Griffith found fragments of limestone sculpture in traditional Egyptian style. Late period foundation pits throughout the site indicate that traditional Egyptian temples and pylons originally existed. Two stelae indicate that the inhabitants originally worshipped the traditional Egyptian triad, Amen, Mut and Khonsu. There is also evidence that Isis was worshipped at the site. Much of the treasure is unmistakably Egyptian: several gold amulets depict gods common to the Egyptian pantheon, while the temple plate was inscribed in demotic. There is, by contrast, a remarkable absence of Greek luxury objects. Together, this evidence strongly suggests that the population of Tukh el-Qaramus was primarily Egyptian rather than Greek.

The second area of debate concerns the length of site occupation. The earliest evidence from Tukh el-Qaramus indicates that it was inhabited during the New Kingdom. During his work, Edgar uncovered tombs which he dated to the 18th Dynasty. Further evidence suggests that the site was inhabited during the Third Intermediate Period. In conjunction with the stela of Sheshonk III, some of the pottery found by Naville and Griffith, such as the faïence inscribed vase, indicates site occupation during this time. It is clear that the site was then refounded during the Late period/early Ptolemaic period; in addition to the cartouche of Philip Arrhidaeus, the foundation pits throughout the site are characteristic of Late period Egyptian architecture. Scholars disagree as to when the site was abandoned. Most academics believe that this occurred during the early Ptolemaic period, i.e., at the end of the reign of Ptolemy II Philadelphus or the beginning of the reign of Ptolemy III Evergetes. However, there is some evidence to indicate that the site was not abandoned until the Roman period.

Some of the jewelry found at Tukh el-Qaramus can clearly be dated to the Roman period. Moreover, the large quantities of limestone chips throughout the site suggest that Tukh el-Qaramus may have been a victim of Roman campaigns to destroy pagan religious shrines, including Egyptian temples. Furthermore, the drying-up of the Pelusiac branch of the Nile during the early Roman period, and with it the destruction of a major thoroughfare for both men and goods, might help to explain why the site was eventually abandoned.

See also

jewelry; Late and Ptolemaic periods, overview

Further reading

Edgar, C.C. 1906. Report on an excavation at Toukh el Qaramous. *ASAE* 7: 205–12.

Milne, J.G. 1941. The Tukh el Qaramus Gold Hoard. *JEA* 27: 135–7.

Pfrommer, M. 1987. *Studien zu alexandrinischer und grossgriechischer Toreutik frühhellenistischer Zeit.* Berlin.

Snape, S. 1986. *Six Archaeological Sites in the Sharqiyeh Province.* Liverpool.

SARAH QUIE

Tuna el-Gebel

Tuna el-Gebel is a modern village lying on the west bank of the Nile in the Minya Governorate of Middle Egypt (27°46′ N, 30°44′ E) that has given its name to a group of neighboring archaeological remains of varied character and date. This composite site occupies a narrow strip of land running along the desert edge 7 km long and 7 km to the west of the major ancient city of Hermopolis Magna (el-Ashmunein). Tuna el-Gebel is also known as Hermopolis West (Ptolemaic, Ḥmnw-p3-mk). The site falls naturally into three major areas: (1) to the south, a Graeco-Roman necropolis and sacred animal catacombs; (2) to the north, a substantial town of the second–sixth centuries AD;

and (3) in the central region cemeteries of varying dates. In addition, Paleolithic artifacts have been recovered from the local gravel terraces.

The earliest of the major archaeological remains are the New Kingdom cemeteries lying in the central region in an area now known as Gabbanet Ghereifa. These remains include material from the tombs of high-ranking officials of the 18th and 19th Dynasties, the period when Tuna was first used as a necropolis for Hermopolis. This central region continued to serve as the major regional cemetery well into the Late period. There was a sudden change in burial patterns at the beginning of the Graeco-Roman period, when these cemeteries were abandoned and burials recommenced to the south of the site.

The southern part of the site, an area sometimes called el-Fasagi, is the best-known part of Tuna el-Gebel. Here burials of ibises and baboons, animals particularly associated with the god Thoth, patron deity of Hermopolis Magna, started as early as the reign of Ramesses II. Substantial underground galleries were built to house these mummified animals from the 26th Dynasty onward. These galleries were greatly expanded under the early Ptolemies, an activity perhaps associated with an expansion of the Thoth cult at Hermopolis Magna. The underground complex eventually included galleries for the interment of many thousands of mummified ibises and baboons, specific cult rooms, and the burials of eminent Hermopolite officials including the High Priest Ankh-Hor. An important temple built close to the entrance to the catacombs ("The Temple of the Superior Spirits") now survives only in a destroyed condition.

The tomb chapel built by the High Priest of Thoth, Petosiris, is justifiably the best known and also probably the earliest of a cluster of tombs with imposing superstructures at the southern end of the site. The tomb of Petosiris, chiefly excavated by Gustave Lefebvre in 1920, eventually housed three generations of this family of high priests. It consists of a roughly square chapel preceded by a transverse hall (*pronaos*) with colonnaded façade. Its resemblance to a Ptolemaic temple is probably no coincidence since, in his autobiographical inscription within the tomb, Petosiris speaks of his principal involvement in a major building project at Hermopolis Magna which was designed to refurbish the temples of the city after neglect during foreign occupation of Egypt. This suggests that Petosiris was active after the second Persian occupation had been ended by the beginning of the Macedonian domination of Egypt, as does the curious mix of traditional Egyptian and innovative Hellenistic styles in the decoration of the *pronaos* of his tomb chapel. This mix of artistic styles continued in later tombs at Tuna. Like the sacred animal galleries, these tombs were chiefly excavated by Gabra between the two World Wars.

During the Roman period the northern part of Tuna el-Gebel, an area known as Nazlet Tuna, was the site of a substantial settlement. This is almost certainly the town referred to in administrative papyri of the second–seventh centuries AD as θῦυις. The site now consists largely of dumps of potsherds (dated to *circa* AD 350–650), but includes a building identified as a church in recent excavations by the Egyptian Antiquities Organization. The town was primarily an agricultural community; its presence indicates that the cultivable land was far more extensive in classical times than it is now, a fact which is also attested by the enormous Roman *saqqiya* (water-wheel and well-shaft) sunk into the southern part of the site. Burials of the late Roman period are common at Tuna el-Gebel, in both the central and northern parts of the site; the most substantial of these tombs consist of chambers built into rocky overhangs in the limestone cliffs which form a natural western limit to Tuna el-Gebel as an archaeological site. These cliffs also served as an occasional source of low-quality stone for buildings at Hermopolis Magna.

Boundary Stela A, the most northerly of the Amarna boundary stelae, was set up on the west bank of the Nile at Tuna el-Gebel. The stela, cut from the living rock of the cliff face a short distance to the north of the sacred animal catacombs, dates from year 6 of Akhenaten and is surmounted by a scene showing the king adoring the Aten, accompanied by Queen Nefertiti and his daughters, Meritaten and Meketaten. Immediately to the south of the stela are two more than life-size statue groups, also cut from the cliff face, each showing the king, queen and princesses in offering/adoring poses; the figure of Princess Ankhesenpa-aten was added in carved relief to the northern group.

See also

el-Ashmunein; Macedonians; Persians; Tell el-Amarna

Further reading

Gabra, S. 1939. Rapport sur les fouilles d'Hermopolis Ouest, Tounah el-Gebel. *ASAE* 39: 483–96.

Kessler, D. 1986. Tuna el-Gebel. In *LÄ* 6: 797–804.

Lefebvre, G. 1923–24. *Le Tombeau de Petosiris* 1–3. Cairo.

Tyldesley, J.A., and S.R. Snape. 1988. *Nazlet Tuna: an Archaeological Survey in Middle Egypt*. Oxford.

JOYCE A. TYLDESLEY

Tura, Dynastic burials and quarries

The site of Tura (ancient T-r3w; in Greek, Troe/ Troia) is located on the east bank of the Nile (29°56′N, 31°17′E) 14 km south-southeast of central Cairo. It consists today of three main residential clusters (from north to south): Tura el-Haggara, Tura el-Hait and Tura el-Ismant, on a westward bend of the river caused by the paleofan of the Wadi Digla to the north.

Like Ma'sara and Helwan to the south, Tura was associated throughout antiquity with the important limestone and calcite quarries of Gebel Tura, where rock strata exposed by fluvial downcutting through sedimentary formations, which sloped down from east to west and are thus higher on the eastern (Arabian) side, were

exploited. Processing of high-grade limestone began during the 3rd Dynasty or earlier and still continues today, and modern activity is responsible for the destruction of much of the evidence for the Dynastic period. The quarries certainly serviced the pyramid building activities of the Egyptian kings from the 4th Dynasty, which is when references to the "fine stone" of "R-3w" and "Ainu" appear for the first time.

In addition to the importance of the region as a source of building stone, the marginal zone from Helwan to Tura, and even as far north as el-Fustat (Old Cairo), served as burial fields. In contrast to the west bank cemeteries, almost none of the larger tombs on the east side are rock-cut. Rather, they consist of chambers excavated in the flat low desert gravels and revetted by walls of mudbrick or upright limestone slabs. The vast majority of burials date to the Late or Graeco-Roman periods and probably belong to laborers or craftsmen employed in the quarries. A few tombs of the Middle Kingdom and Second Intermediate Period are known, but these occur in uncertain contexts: an unused 12th Dynasty tomb is recorded at the most northerly of Saad's "Helwan" (Ezbet el-Walda) cemeteries, and at least two pottery "slipper" coffins were found between Ma'sara and Tura. No Old Kingdom tombs have been found with the exception of tomb H6 287 (3rd Dynasty) at Helwan, the assumption being that most tombs of this period were located on the west bank, and there is little evidence for Predynastic occupation between the wadi-based cultures of Ma'adi and el-Omari. The Early Dynastic period (1st–2nd Dynasties), however, is well represented, although many tombs of this date await full publication.

The centers of Early Dynastic funerary activity were at the important site of Helwan and at the Tura–Ma'adi sites described by Hermann Junker and Guy Brunton. It is less well known that the area between these two groups also contained extensive burial fields, principally in and around the perimeter of the modern Tura cement factory (Tura el-Ismant). From the short published accounts of the excavation (from the 1950s to the 1970s) of these tombs, it appears that they were similar on the whole to the smaller Helwan tombs in having rectangular burial chambers cut through the marginal desert gravels, which were retained by sand/marl-mudbrick or limestone slab walls. The stone-lined tombs recorded by Holroyd and Perring in the 1830s are neither precisely located nor internally dated, but probably belong to this group: one such tomb contained a later or intrusive multiple burial, the corpses being laid side by side, heads to the north, not mummified but treated with bitumen. Burials of all periods in this 3 km stretch of desert were said to have been made in a "bank of sand," probably a former terrace of river gravels undisturbed by the seasonal watercourses to the north and south (the Wadis Digla and Hof, respectively), but exploited in much the same way as the lower slopes of the Hof and Digla paleofans.

Little use seems to have been made of the cemeteries in the New Kingdom, however intensively the quarries were used at that time, and for the Late and Graeco-Roman periods only individual sarcophagi and coffins, not built tombs, are recorded. Both quarries and cemeteries were in at least a partial state of neglect during late Roman and Coptic times (third–sixth centuries AD), since a monastery (Deir el-Quseir) was built over the uneven ground of one abandoned quarry. An alternative name of this monastery, Deir Arsaniyus, preserves the memory of St Arsenius, the fifth-century monk who lived and was supposedly buried at Tura (Trohen). Rufinus says that the area was noteworthy at this time for its large numbers of monks. Although many of them would have been accommodated in the large west bank and valley communities, such as Jeremias and Apollonius, a large number, perhaps like Arsenius, would have used the abandoned quarries as heremetical desert cells in the same way as the Dynastic tombs on the west bank were reoccupied.

The ancient quarries themselves extend for some 2.5 km along the eastern cliffs above Tura and Ma'sara, and consisted of galleried mines in the rock face (similar in technique to most rock-cut tombs and to the subterranean cata-

combs of the sacred animal necropoleis at North Saqqara), which contrast with the open method of quarrying used in recent times. The administration of the industry was probably based at Saqqara or Memphis, since a group of papyri mentioning the pyramids of Kings Merenre and Pepi II, including a letter from the commander of workmen to the vizier(?), was found within the Zoser pyramid enclosure. Even though the suburb of "East Memphis" (ancient Inb-ḥd i3btt; in Greek, Arabias tou Memphitou) continued into Roman times, the responsibility for the quarries rested with officials of the city on the west bank, as indeed it did until the Ottoman period.

Documentary evidence also comes from the Tura and Ma'sara quarries themselves, where a series of stelae and rock inscriptions attest to the opening of new galleries from the 12th Dynasty (reign of Amenemhat III) to late in the Ptolemaic period. There may well have been earlier records which were removed or obliterated as the quarries expanded; several of the stelae are uninscribed and therefore undatable. The earliest local use of limestone in tomb architecture dates to the 1st Dynasty (at North Saqqara and Helwan), but these are only rough-cut slabs used for tomb chamber linings and door jambs/portcullises, which would hardly require deep mining methods.

The later tradition (e.g. Strabo XVII I.34) that the quarries were once manned by "Trojans" (hence, by false etymology, the name) is comparable to the association of Roman Babylon (Old Cairo) with an original Persian garrison, and appears to have no historical basis. The legend, however, may preserve some folk memory of the use of foreign (Carian or Lycian?) mercenaries or prisoners-of-war as quarrymen.

In medieval times there were several important monasteries and convents situated on this part of the east bank, notably Deir el-Adhra, Deir Barsum el-'Aryan and Deir Shahran, as well as the hospice and monastery of Gregorius at Helwan. Today the area is part of the almost unbroken conurbation that stretches from Cairo to Helwan, containing not only the vital quarries but also other related light and heavy industries and large power stations, with only occasional pockets of local agriculture.

See also

Helwan; quarrying

Further reading

Brunton, G. 1939. A First Dynasty cemetery at Maadi. *ASAE* 39: 419–24.

Junker, H. 1912. Bericht über die Grabungen der kaiserlichen Akademie der Wissenschaften in Wien auf dem Friedhof in Turah. *DÖAW* 55. Vienna.

el-Khouli, A. 1968. A preliminary note on the excavations at Tura, 1963–64. *ASAE* 60: 73–6.

Meyer, C. 1986. Tura. In *LÄ* 6: 807–10.

DAVID JEFFREYS

Tura, Predynastic cemeteries

Tura is the name of a village 14 km south-southeast of Cairo on the east bank of the Nile (29°56′ N, 31°17′ E). Although known primarily for its limestone and calcite quarries, it was also the site of some important early cemeteries.

In 1910 the Austrian archaeologist Hermann Junker excavated a late prehistoric cemetery north of the village of Tura. At the same time some graves of the Predynastic Ma'adi culture, named after the site of Ma'adi located 2 km west of Tura, were found near the Tura railway station.

Cemeteries S, N and O

The late Predynastic cemetery where Junker worked was revealed by well digging in 1903. He excavated about 600 graves in three areas, which he named S, N and O. Areas S and N are middle and late Predynastic in date (Nagada II–III) while the graves in Area O may date to the 3rd Dynasty.

Most of the graves that Junker excavated were simple pits, but some were covered with wooden beams. More rare were graves lined with mud-bricks with one chamber. A few graves had several chambers for the grave goods. These larger graves were covered with wooden beams on top of which were stones covered with Nile mud.

Most of the bodies were covered or wrapped with reed mats. Some of the bodies were placed in oval coffins made of Nile clay, burned or unburned. Remains of wooden coffins were also found. Children were buried in baskets.

About 80 percent of the bodies were in contracted positions lying on the left side, half of these with the head to the south facing west, and half with the head to the north facing east. Grave goods were placed in the corners of the grave, or in the available space. A small jar was often placed near the head (mostly behind it) and was perhaps symbolic for mortuary ritual.

Grave goods consisted mainly of pottery typical of late Predynastic burials: large and smaller jars with round bases, cylindrical jars (some painted with a net pattern), and small jars and bowls. Some of these pots were inscribed with the names of early kings.

Stone vessels of the same shapes as the pottery, made of limestone, schist and granite, were found in some graves. Other craft goods included round or rectangular schist palettes. Jewelry consisted of ivory or stone bracelets, and necklaces in beads of carnelian, faïence, lapis lazuli, amethyst and ivory.

Cemetery near the railway station

This cemetery was found by workmen building a road, and no excavation of the graves was conducted. The workmen at least collected the pots from these graves, which were subsequently identified as belonging to the Ma'adi culture, the fourth millennium BC Predynastic culture found in northern Egypt.

The cemetery is very close to the three cemetery areas excavated by Junker, and they may all have been used by the same village. Possibly in the beginning of the Dynastic period, later inhabitants of this village moved a short distance south to Ezbet el-Walda, where the largest known cemetery of the Early

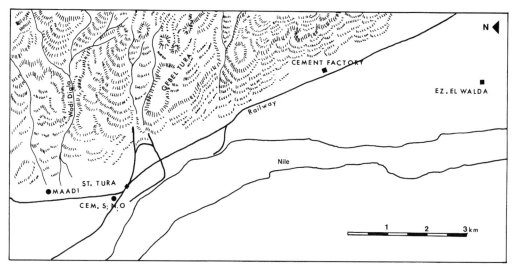

Figure 125 Predynastic and Early Dynastic cemeteries in the Ma'adi–Tura region

Dynastic period, with about 10,000 graves, is located.

Settlement(s)

No settlements were found belonging to any of the Tura cemeteries and they have probably been destroyed. Over the past 5,000 years the Nile has changed its course, and now the distance between the Tura limestone cliffs and the Nile is only 2–3 km. In Dynastic times the Nile was father to the west, and any evidence of an early settlement(s) has probably been washed away by the river.

The settlement(s) at Tura no doubt played an important role in the development that culminated in the formation of the Early Dynastic state in Egypt. They were located at one of the most important centers of the Early Dynastic period, exemplified by the tombs of high government officials across the river at North Saqqara.

See also

Early Dynastic period, overview; Early Dynastic private tombs; Ma'adi and the Wadi Digla; Predynastic period, overview; Saqqara, North, Early Dynastic tombs; Tura, Dynastic burials and quarries

Further reading

Junker, H. 1912. Bericht über die Grabungen der kaiserlichen Akademie der Wissenschaften in Wien auf dem Friedhof in Turah. *DÖAW* 55. Vienna.

Kaiser, W., and A. Zaugg. 1988. Zum Fundplatz der Maadikultur bei Tura. *MDAIK* 44: 121–4.

BODIL MORTENSEN

Tutankhamen, tomb of

Tutankhamen was probably the younger son of the "heretic" pharaoh Akhenaten, and was his ultimate successor. For the first few years of his reign he lived at Tell el-Amarna under his birthname of Tutankhaten, and almost certainly began a huge tomb there, now numbered 29. When abandoned, this had been cut 45 m into the mountain, without yet reaching the intended location of its first chamber.

When he returned to the ancestral capital of

Thebes under the name Tutankhamen, by now in his early teens and the figurehead for the restoration of the ancient religion, a new tomb was begun for him in the Valley of the Kings in western Thebes. It should probably be identified with WV 23, which was later used for the burial of his successor, Ay.

This tomb was unfinished at Tutankhamen's death while the latter was still in his late teens, perhaps as the result of a head injury. Accordingly, he was interred in a modified private tomb in the eastern branch of the Valley of the Kings (KV 62): the putative original tomb was located in the western section of the valley. A number of highly placed private individuals had been buried in that area during the 18th Dynasty, particularly since Amenhotep III had moved the site of his tomb (WV 22) to the remoter western branch. It seems very likely that KV 62 had been intended for General Ay, Tutankhamen's probable great-uncle, and possible maternal grandfather, who had shared effective control of the country during Tutankhamen's minority with another army commander, Horemheb.

The tomb, as designed for Ay, seems to have comprised a passageway leading to a main chamber, off of which opened one or two storerooms. When adapted for the young king's burial, the right-hand wall of the principal chamber was cut away to provide access to a large room, running at right angles to the original apartment, its floor lying around 1 m below that of what was now to be the antechamber. The new space was employed as the royal burial chamber, with the king's sarcophagus installed there.

The quartzite sarcophagus followed the late 18th Dynasty practice of being rectangular, with a cavetto cornice and torus molding. This contrasts with the cartouche-form employed by kings from the time of Hatshepsut to Tuthmose IV, and again from Ramesses I onward, but corresponds to the form of private wooden examples. The four corners of Tutankhamen's sarcophagus are embraced by the four winged tutelary goddesses, Isis, Nephthys, Neith and Selket. The whole coffer shows extensive signs of reworking, which probably accompanied the change of the king's second cartouche from "Tutankhaten" to "Tutankhamen." Possibly, however, the sarcophagus might have been taken from the king's elder brother and Akhenaten's coregent, Smenkhkare/Neferneferuaten, pieces of whose unused funerary equipment were adapted for use in Tutankhamen's tomb.

The sarcophagus was closed by a granite lid, apparently broken while being lowered into place. The occasion for this accident was probably the discovery that the toes of the outermost coffin were higher than the rim of the sarcophagus, and needed adzing down. This coffin, which depicts the king wearing the *ḫ3t*-headdress, is part of a set of three, and is made of wood covered with carved gesso and then gilded. The middle coffin is again of wood, elaborately inlaid as well as gilded, and bearing a cloth (*nms*) headdress. It had been made for the burial of Smenkhkare/Neferneferuaten in traditional style, but had not been to the revolutionary taste of Akhenaten, who was responsible for his coregent's burial following his premature death. Smenkhkare/Neferneferuaten had been interred in an adapted coffin, leaving his original one in storage along with other pieces, to be employed for his brother's burial a decade later.

Tutankhamen's innermost coffin, which contained the king's mummy, is made of solid gold and, like the outer examples, is covered with a feathered (*rishi*) pattern that represents the king as a human-headed bird. Wearing the *nms*-headdress, it also has inlaid representations of the vulture goddesses, Nekhbet and Edjo, added at a late stage in the coffin's manufacture.

The mummy was found adorned with a gold portrait mask, gold hands and inlaid golden bands, containing religious formulae. Some additional trappings had been made from odd pieces of unused scrap originally belonging to Smenkhkare/Neferneferuaten. Tutankhamen's mummy wrappings contained huge quantities of jewelry, but the cloth was in a very poor state, having carbonized through the chemical reaction of the unguents with which the royal body had been drenched at the funeral. The unguents had also badly damaged the flesh of the mummy itself, which was stuck to the bottom of the gold coffin. This led to the necessity of dismembering the body in order to extract it for examination by Douglas Derry.

The sarcophagus was surrounded by a series of four gilded wooden shrines, each covered with representations from the various funerary compositions of the Egyptians. At least one had originally been made for a predecessor of Tutankhamen, either Smenkhkare/Neferneferuaten, or Akhenaten while still the nominally orthodox Amenhotep IV. A linen pall was also incorporated into the nest, supported on a frame and embellished with gilded rosettes. Such shines were usual in Egyptian royal tombs from at least the reign of Amenhotep II to that of Ramesses IV; the height of the outer shrine accounts for the low floor of the area containing the sarcophagus, a feature also found in royal sepulchers from Amenhotep II onward.

The walls of the burial chamber are the only ones of the tomb to be decorated, with scenes painted on a yellow background. One wall shows, uniquely, the king's mummy receiving the last rites from Tutankhamen's successor, King Ay. The appearance of this motif may relate to the known difficulties concerning the succession that occurred after Tutankhamen's death, and seem to have delayed his burial until eight months after his demise. The other elements of the decoration include the king before various deities, vignettes from the *Book of Imyduat*, and the king's catafalque, drawn by his officials. Like the scene with Ay, this latter depiction seems to be unique for a royal sepulcher, although of a type common in private tomb chapels.

A doorway opposite the foot of the sarcophagus leads into a small room, dubbed the "Treasury." A large shrine-shaped chest, upon which rested a canine image of the god Anubis, originally lay at the threshold of the chamber. The most important item in the room was Tutankhamen's square canopic shrine, of wood, guarded on each side by an image of a tutelary goddess, each apparently adapted from the gilded wooden figure of an Amarna period queen. Within the shrine was the calcite canopic chest, with a goddess carved at each corner and

adorned with texts containing formulae associated with the protection of the embalmed internal organs.

The interior of the chest is sculpted in such a manner as to suggest four compartments each holding a canopic jar, but in fact they are all carved as one within the body of the chest. Each "jar" was stopped with a calcite head of the king, and contained a miniature coffin of inlaid solid gold. Each of these is of identical design to the full-size middle coffin, and, like it, all had been made for Smenkhkare/Neferneferuaten, traces of whose names can be seen in their interior texts. These coffinettes each held a linen-wrapped bundle of embalmed viscera, and had been heavily anointed with unguents.

The Treasury also held a large number of resin-varnished shrines containing wooden figures of the king and deities, overlaid with gold leaf; some of these were also leftovers from earlier reigns, including possibly the early years of Amenhotep IV. Similar figures have been recovered from other royal tombs, but they were less rich, being merely covered with black varnish. Other containers in the room held a large number of *shawabti* figures, while also present were a model granary, two chariots, model boats and various other items, including three miniature nests of coffins.

The largest set of coffins, comprising what may have been intended as *shawabti* coffins of Tutankhamen, contained a gold figure of a king and a lock of the hair of Queen Tiye, Tutankhamen's grandmother. This has been matched with the hair of a mummy found in the tomb of Amenhotep II, which was thus proclaimed that of the queen. Unfortunately, the archaeological context of this mummy contradicts this identification, and the scientific analysis has been suggested as being possibly flawed. The other two nests of coffins, of designs appropriate to private persons of the later 18th Dynasty, contained the mummies of two premature infants; both were female, and one had suffered from spina bifida. They almost certainly are the remains of offspring of Tutankhamen and his (half?-)sister and wife, Queen Ankhesenamen.

The burial chamber was separated from the

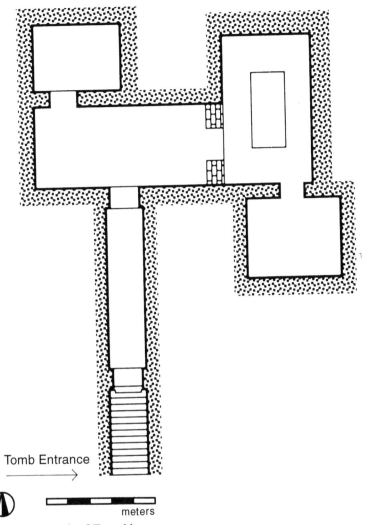

Tomb Entrance

meters

Figure 126 Plan of the tomb of Tutankhamen

antechamber by a false wall and sealed door-way, which was guarded by a pair of wooden, gilded and varnished statues; these are of a type familiar from royal tombs of the Ramesside period. One wall of the antechamber was taken up by three gilded wooden couches, each with a different pair of animal heads, under and on top of which were piled all kinds of food containers and furniture including a richly gilded and inlaid throne. Half of the other side

of the room was taken up by four dismantled chariots.

A door under one of the couches gave access to the so-called "Annex," a storeroom crowded with all kinds of funerary equipment, badly disturbed by tomb robbers and those who had cleared up after them. The tomb had been entered by robbers on two occasions, not long after the funeral and perhaps in the reign of Horemheb, when the tomb of Tuthmose IV was certainly plundered. A considerable amount of damage had been done, but the innermost shrines and sarcophagus remained intact, suggesting that the thieves were perhaps caught in the act.

After the last robbery and subsequent resealing of the sepulcher, the tomb, which lies in the very bottom of the valley, was progressively covered by debris, in part from the construction of neighboring tombs, until the huts of the artisans working on the tomb begun by Ramesses V (and continued by Ramesses VI (KV 9)), were erected directly above its entrance. Because of this, the tomb was passed by and missed in the orgy of tomb robbing which accompanied the troubles of the late 20th Dynasty.

Through its deep burial and its position near the entrance to the much visited tomb of Ramesses VI, the tomb escaped discovery by the early diggers in the Valley of the Kings, although a number came fairly close. Its entrance was only revealed during the systematic clearance of hitherto uninvestigated parts of the valley by Howard Carter and Lord Carnarvon. The first step of the access stairway was uncovered on November 4, 1922, and work on the tomb and its contents continued until the spring of 1932 when the last artifacts were removed to the Egyptian Museum in Cairo. The royal mummy, the outer coffin and the sarcophagus remain in the tomb.

The importance of the discovery of the tomb of Tutankhamen is the fact that, alone of all New Kingdom royal tombs, it was essentially intact, thus providing key detailed evidence on the kind of equipment that accompanied a king of that era to the grave. It also allows the reconstruction of some of the fragmentary items recovered from the badly robbed tombs of the period, and provides useful comparison with the burials found in the intact 21st Dynasty tomb of King Psusennes I at Tanis, and the only partly robbed tomb of the 13th Dynasty King Hor at Dahshur.

See also

Carnarvon, George Edward Stanhope Molyneux Herbert, Earl of; Carter, Howard; New Kingdom, overview; Tell el-Amarna, royal tombs; Thebes, Valley of the Kings

Further reading

Beinlich, H., and M. Saleh. 1989. *Corpus der Hieroglyphischen Inschriften aus dem Grab des Tutanchamun*. Oxford.

Carter, H., and A.C. Mace. 1923–33. *The Tomb of Tut-ankh-Amen* 1–3. London.

Reeves, C.N. 1990a. *The Complete Tutankhamun*. London.

——. 1990b. *Valley of the Kings: the Decline of a Royal Necropolis*. London.

Tut'ankhamūn's Tomb Series 1–7. 1966–. Oxford.

AIDAN DODSON

U

urbanism

The process of urban development in Egypt is not well understood. Many ancient urban sites are buried under modern towns and villages, and thus cannot be excavated. Frequently settlements were occupied from late prehistoric to Roman times, forming large mounds which cannot be completely excavated. Riverine settlements have probably been destroyed by lateral shifts in the channels of the Nile. In rural areas, development is systematically destroying archaeological sites to expand villages and arable land. Thus, any attempt to outline the development of urbanism in ancient Egypt must be regarded as largely hypothetical.

The landscape and culture history of Egypt greatly affected this process. The lower Nile Valley is a complex habitat with different ecosystems and resources, distributed along an east–west axis on both sides of the river. These include the river, riverine marshes, alluvial plains and the savanna of the low desert. Since Predynastic times this landscape probably generated a division of the population of the Valley into a sequence of territorial units aligned north–south and connected to each other by the river. These units exploited resources along an east–west transect, and formed distinct polities. Such divisions may be detected in the regularly spaced clusters of Predynastic (Nagada culture) sites in Upper Egypt. The distinctive hierarchy of settlements within each territorial unit set the stage for the later emergence of towns, and in Dynastic times these units survived as an administrative division of the country into "nomes."

The pharaonic state arose with the progressive incorporation of small-scale polities into a large territorial state with highly centralized control. In this process a hierarchy of settlements developed with a capital (such as Memphis), and large towns and small towns which served as administrative and commercial centers of the nomes and villages. Some settlements developed into towns because of their location as nodes in the regional trade network, and a number of cult centers became towns. Sometimes towns were deliberately planned and constructed for a specific function, such as royal residences, nome centers and the fortresses in Nubia. The history of ancient Egypt is marked by periods with a strong centralized government (Old, Middle and New Kingdoms), when planned towns were founded, and decentralized periods (First, Second and Third Intermediate Periods), when many (unplanned) towns and settlements were fortified for protection.

Ancient Egyptian towns were found in three different topographical locations: on the relics of Nile sediments which form a natural mound (*gezira*) above the floodplain (especially in the Delta); on high levees along the river; and along the desert edge, such as the pyramid towns.

The development of urbanism in Egypt surely began in Predynastic times. Archaeological evidence from Upper Egypt suggests the following sequence of development:

1 Small egalitarian communities were scattered along the Valley in the late fifth millennium BC. They occupied temporary camps at the margins of the floodplain, on levees and in the low desert (Badarian culture/period).
2 Centers for specialized production (pottery and craft goods) involved in an increasing regional trade network appeared in the early fourth millennium BC. Incipient social

differentiation can probably be inferred from the burials. These settlements were located along the edge of the floodplain and on levees (Nagada I phase).

3 Hierarchical society involved in long-distance trade arose by the mid-fourth millennium BC. Villages were located at the edge of the floodplain, and probably on high ground in the floodplain and next to the river. Specialized centers with manufacturing activities increased in number. At least one town which arose at this time was at Hierakonpolis. Another possible town was located near Nagada (Flinders Petrie's "South Town") (Nagada II phase).

4 Complex society, probably small-scale early states, emerged at the end of the fourth millennium BC. These polities were centered at Hierakonpolis, Nagada and Abydos, which developed as administrative and cult centers.

Archaeological evidence dating to the fifth–fourth millennia BC from the Delta and Lower Egypt is scarce. A large settlement arose in the Delta at Merimde Beni-salame. Towns were probably located at Tell el-Fara'in in the Delta and Ma'adi, near Cairo. They occupied strategic nodes in the trade network between Palestine and the Nile Valley.

New towns were probably built after the rise of the large territorial state in Egypt, in the early third millennium BC (Early Dynastic period). Evidence for this, however, is still scarce. At Hierakonpolis and Abydos there were walled towns not exceeding 10 ha in area. Dense urban communities on the scale of the huge city-states which had developed in southern Mesopotamia by this time, however, were unknown in Egypt.

An urban society was definitely established by the mid-third millennium BC (Old Kingdom), as a consequence of the sophisticated administrative system. Walled towns were internally divided with areas for a temple, administrative building(s), houses and craft production. Remains of such a town have been excavated at Elephantine. Temporary towns were also built near the pyramid construction

sites to house officials, supervisors, craftsmen and workmen (and their families). The royal palace was probably located near these temporary towns. The textual evidence, however, suggests that in the Old Kingdom the Egyptians distinguished only two main types of settlements, indicated by the hieroglyphic signs *hwt* and *niwt*. The *hwt* sign depicts a rectangular structure, which designates the centers of royal administration. The *niwt* sign, a circle with lines (streets?) crossing through it, indicates any other type of settlement, from a small rural village to a proper town.

In the early second millennium BC (Middle Kingdom) the settlement pattern was dominated by major towns which functioned to exploit the nome resources, as suggested by textual evidence for a highly organized state bureaucracy. Yet there is very little archaeological evidence for such towns, except at the pyramid town at Lahun, which might suggest an increasing size of towns at this time.

A mature urban society appeared by the mid-second millennium BC (New Kingdom). Textual evidence suggests that three main types of settlements were distinguished then: "city" (*niwt*), "town" (*dmi*) and "village" (*whyt*). Capitals were built at different locations (Thebes, Memphis, Tell el-Amarna and Tell ed-Dab'a/Pi-Ramesses), and were the most impressive cities in the country. Excavations at Tell el-Amarna have revealed the city's sprawling complex plan, with a central area where the (ceremonial) palace of the king, administrative buildings and large temples were located, with suburbs to the north and south.

See also

Further reading

Bietak, M. 1979. Urban archaeology and the "town problem" in Ancient Egypt. In *Egyptology and the Social Sciences*, K. Weeks, ed., 97–144. Cairo.

Butzer, K.W. 1976. *Early Hydraulic Civilization in Egypt*. Chicago.

Kemp, B.J. 1989. *Ancient Egypt: Anatomy of a Civilization*. London.

Trigger, B.G., B.J. Kemp, D. O'Connor and A.B. Lloyd. 1983. *Ancient Egypt: A Social History*. Cambridge.

RODOLFO FATTOVICH

W

Wadi Abu Had/Wadi Dib

Wadi Abu Had and Wadi Dib are located in the Eastern Desert approximately 70 km north of Hurghada and 25 km west of Gebel Zeit where the Gulf of Suez joins the Red Sea. Archaeological sites are located in a part of the two wadis, in an area 30 × 20 km (27°36′–27°50′ N, 33°08′–33°23′ E). To the east, the area is bordered by a granite and dolerite mountain range reaching 448 m above sea level. The plain of Wadi Abu Had is 25 km wide and is bisected longitudinally by a limestone range, Gebel Safr Abu Had. The western edge of the plain is delineated by the andesite mountains of Gebel Ladid el-Gidan, with peaks reaching 1,131 m above sea level.

The Wadi Abu Had plain forms a natural crossroad in the desert with the lateral-running Wadi Dib in the north. This in turn links with the longitudinal Wadi Usum, which provides access to copper and gold mines at Gebel Darah West, el-Urf and Mongul, about 50 km to the north. In the south, Wadi Abu Had merges with the Wadi Mellaha where, 50 km beyond, the Roman quarries of Mons Porphyrites are located. Both Wadis Abu Had and Dib join the great Wadi Qena, leading to the Nile Valley to the west, and in the east emerge onto the coastal plain opposite Zeit Bay, a potential harbor. The two wadis form secondary routes in the middle Eastern Desert.

The present archaeological investigations are the first to be done in this area. John Gardner Wilkinson passed through Wadis Abu Had and Dib in 1823, but never recorded any detailed information. Only geological work has been done in the Wadi Abu Had area. Among the earliest investigations were those by Schweinfurth in the nineteenth century and Barron and Hume in the early twentieth century. The most recent investigations have been conducted by Egyptian geological surveys.

Wadi Abu Had/Wadi Dib is a transit area with both semi-nomadic and sedentary settlements. Evidence for human presence is derived from installations, lithics, potsherds and other artifacts, from both prehistoric and historical periods. These include the Lower, Middle and Late Paleolithic, Neolithic, Predynastic, Early Dynastic and late Roman periods.

Survey work began in 1992 and was conducted in part of the eastern and western plains of Wadi Abu Had and around Gebel Safr Abu Had. During this time a major Paleolithic flint quarry with associated artifacts was located. Other flint-working sites and stray finds were noted near the foothills of Gebel Safr Abu Had. The survey continued in Wadi Abu Had in 1993 with the discovery of an Early Dynastic site, WAH 29, a small late Roman installation and more flint-working sites. In the same year the survey moved into Wadi Dib where two Predynastic camp sites, several small late Roman installations and flint-working sites were located. In 1994 the work concentrated in Wadi Abu Had with the initial excavation of WAH 29 and the detailed analysis of the Paleolithic quarry at Gebel Safr Abu Had and its environs. Excavation of WAH 29 continued in 1995, and a survey concentrated within a 5 km^2 area in the western plain of the wadi located a series of prehistoric sites. At present, dating of the sites is based on artifact typologies, and radiocarbon dates are in the process of being organized. Work is expected to continue within the concession in future field seasons.

Main sites

The main sources for flint are found in nodules stratified in seams in Gebel Safr Abu Had. This type of flint predominates, although the tabular variety is also present. The main quarry is 0.5 km long, and about thirteen sites were located on the limestone ridges. These show evidence of the *in situ* extraction and working of weathered flint nodules to produce (lamellar) flake blanks from which stone tools were made. In the quarry itself, within a square of 5 × 5 m, an average of 400 examples lie on the surface, excluding the number in the subsurface. In general, the artifacts of this region range from late Middle Paleolithic to Late Paleolithic and are found in the context of ephemeral hunting camps and flint-processing camps.

The site of an ancient lake, which is demonstrated by land forms and tufa deposits (a calcareous, siliceous rock deposit of lakes, springs and ground water), lies in the western plain and in the region of Gebel Safr Abu Had. The presence of raw materials for stone tools and standing water holes suggests a relationship between the lake and quarry—and the reason so many sites are located in such a small area. Twenty-seven new localities were located within a 5 km^2 area in the western plain of Abu Had, and provide evidence of prehistoric use. These range from hunting camps to more intensely occupied living sites. The first group is largely exemplified by flint-knapping scatters across different tracts of the landscape, from a raw material source to a probable water source. The second group, the "living sites," take the form of oval and sub-oval clusters of stone, mostly of fine-grained igneous rocks which show a marked desert varnish, in small mounds up to 40 cm high and 4 m in diameter. These stone clusters are usually in groups of three or four.

Possible chronological comparisons of technology, typology and location indicate a strong Middle and Late Paleolithic presence in the area. The stone clusters are more characteristic of living sites of a highly organized, possibly early Neolithic hunter-gatherer population.

The site of WAH 29 is situated in a depression within one of the terraces in the eastern branch of Wadi Abu Had. It covers an area of *circa* 18.6 m north–south, and 12.5 m east–west. Within the site are the remains of a building, spatially defined by a series of curvilinear enclosure walls, which is cellular in plan. It consists of a forecourt, outer enclosure, inner enclosure and possibly three annexes. The walls are substantially constructed with stones from three to five courses high and two wide. Stones of different sizes, from cobbles to boulders, were sunk in a matrix of carbonated sand and small basalt chips, which act as a mortar. Numerous boulders were selected with flat surfaces, as a facing for the interior of the enclosure walls. Materials used include dolerite/basalt, sandstone, limestone, tufa, conglomerate, andesite, granite, flint, quartz and hematite. Doorways are usually marked by two opposing monoliths, a threshold stone, remains of possible limestone lintels and sandstone bricks, *circa* 35 × 15 × 10 cm. The walls of one enclosure were made entirely of sandstone, much of it brick-shaped. A centrally placed posthole is located in most enclosures thus excavated – three of which still retain fragments of timber. A series of poles were probably lashed to the central post to support a cover of cloth, skin or reeds.

The site appears to have served as a processing center for three different raw materials: malachite, clear quartz and amethystine quartz. Deposits of ash, some carbonated and up to 12 cm in depth, appeared in various areas of the excavated enclosures. These hearths were used mainly for stone processing. Malachite was extracted by fracturing the rock with heat and then breaking it into smaller fragments with stone tools, which exposed the thin veins of green stone. The malachite is powdery rather than solid. If solid pieces were present, they were probably transported elsewhere. Only small fragments of solid pieces appeared sporadically. The same method was applied to the amethystine quartz, which usually fractured into microliths. The clear quartz, however, was knapped in the same way as flint. To date, 110 stone tools have been recovered from the site. These include sandstone abraders (the most frequent tool), hammerstones of coarse-grained igneous rock, grinders, anvils, flint tools and one pick. Among this assemblage is a porphyritic, disk-shaped macehead in the first stages of production.

The site has yielded pottery which can be divided into four main types:

1 jars of marl fabrics;
2 polished bowls in fabrics of alluvial silts, and alluvial silts and marls;
3 vessels for food preparation in fabrics which appear to be unique to the area;
4 small jars and bottles in fabrics of alluvial silts and marls.

The most numerous vessel type is a variety of necked jars with folded-over rims and mouth diameters of 8–13 cm. Some have globular bodies, while others are slimmer in shape with a higher shoulder tapering to a small rounded or flattened base. The majority of urns were turned on a slow wheel and applied separately to hand-built bodies. Bodies were trimmed vertically with a sharp tool, as typical of Early Dynastic pottery. Red washes on the exterior are frequent: some have a degenerate design characteristic of the end of the Predynastic period. Almost all jars are of marl or a marl/silt mixture, which came from various places in the Nile Valley, and served as transport vessels. Some of the pots have potmarks.

Among the assemblage is a unique pottery type in a fabric composed of a friable, light brown, non-Nilotic silt tempered with various quantities of crushed white quartz and/or grit (possibly water-worn pieces of shell). This pottery type may represent a local industry. Other potential locally made wares are composed of silt with basalt tempering, dung, and dung and sand tempering. This pottery is quite unlike other wares recovered to date from settlements and cemeteries in the Nile Valley and Delta. On the basis of the material recovered so far, WAH 29 can be dated to the end of the Predynastic period (Nagada IIIc2) and early 1st Dynasty, from the reigns of Narmer to Djet.

The excavated evidence suggests that WAH 29 functioned as a permanent processing center for malachite, clear quartz and amethystine quartz in a remote part of the Eastern Desert. These stones may have been traded between the Nile Valley, and possibly Sinai and southwest Asia, using Wadi Abu Had as a route.

Along the main wadi track about 1 km west of WAH 29, a small late Roman installation (WAH 30) was located. The complex includes two oval enclosures, two hearths and a silt-filled accumulation well. Amphora sherds were scattered near it, and a rim of African Red Slip Ware was also found there. The assemblage dates to the late fourth century AD.

The survey in Wadi Dib located two Predynastic camping sites. One is situated on a terrace near Wadi Usum (WUS 1). Surface finds include granite grinders, an anvil, a flint hammerstone similar to those at el-Badari in Middle Egypt and a shell (*tridacna sp.*). Such shells were used mainly for making bracelets, a practice known from the Predynastic period. Other surface finds, probably intrusive to the site, are sherds from an Antioch-type amphora of the fourth century AD. The second site (WD 5) is within the mountain range on a terrace. Traces of hut circles and surface finds of weathered flint artifacts, including an ax typical of the Predynastic Nagada culture, were found at this site.

Finds dating to the Roman period in Wadi Dib include small cairns (road markers, WD 6) situated on hilltops overlooking the plain, a collapsed lookout structure (*skopeloi*, WD 7) and a series of five dry stone huts (GSD 2) situated on escarpments farther west. These may be *laurae*, small huts used by hermits living in the desert in early Christian times. Structures like these are situated in Wadi Umm Diqal near Mons Claudianus.

The numerous deposits of tufa together with the accumulation wells point to the fact that humans could adapt to a changing climate within this part of the Eastern Desert. The wetter conditions which prevailed during the Mousterian Pluvial, *circa* 50,000–30,000 BP (years before present), and the Neolithic Subpluvial, *circa* 9,000–5,000 BP, provided long-term supplies of water in some parts of the desert. The time range suspected for the archaeological remains and the relative density of remains point to long-term adaptations to local conditions, as well as successful adjustments by various hunting, gathering and herding peoples.

The project has opened a new area for prehistoric and historical research in the middle Eastern Desert, which was previously unknown and thought to be devoid of human activity.

See also

Early Dynastic period, overview; Epipaleolithic cultures, overview; Gebel Zeit; metallurgy; Mons Porphyrites; natural resources; Neolithic and Predynastic stone tools; Paleolithic cultures, overview; Paleolithic tools; pottery, prehistoric; Predynastic period, overview; Roman period, overview; Wadi Hammamat

Further reading

Bomann, A. 1995. Third season 1994: Wadi Abu Had-Wadi Dib, Eastern Desert, Egypt. *JEA* 81: 14–17.

Meredith, D. 1958. *Tabula Imperii Romani, Coptos, Sheet N.G. 36*. London.

Nordström, H.-Å. 1972. *Neolithic and A-Group Sites*. The Scandinavian Joint Expedition to Sudanese Nubia 3:1, 4–6, 8–9. Stockholm.

ANN BOMANN

Wadi Garawi dam

The ancient Sadd el-Kafara dam is situated in the Wadi Garawi (29°46′ N, 31°19′ E), one of the numerous wadis in the desert east of the Nile Valley, some 30 km south of Cairo and 11 km southeast of Helwan. The dam was originally 113 m long and 14 m high, but now there are only the remains of construction on both sides of the wadi. The northern wall extends about 24 m into the wadi, and the southern one is about 27 m long. Between the two preserved walls is a breach, *circa* 50–60 m wide, which has been formed by the numerous floods of the past 4,500 years.

In cross-section, the Sadd el-Kafara dam consists of three construction elements, 98.0 m total in width, which differ in composition and function:

1 a central core of rubble, gravel and weathered material;
2 two sections of rock fill on either side (upstream and downstream) of the core;
3 layers of ashlars placed in steps on the slopes of the rock fill.

The central, impervious core of the dam is essentially calcareous silty sand and gravel. As this core material was mostly brought from the wadi terraces, it can be assumed that the filling progressed from the terrace edges toward the middle of the wadi.

On both the upstream and downstream sides, the core is faced by sections of rock fill which support and protect it. The core and rock fill were placed directly on the stripped bottom and cleared slopes of the wadi. The fill consists of rocks, usually 30 cm thick, but these also range in thickness (10–60 cm). The color and the mineralogical composition of these rocks show that they were quarried from the wadi banks in the vicinity of the dam. The quarried fill material was thrown down haphazardly and the cavities between these rocks were not filled with gravel or debris.

The outside facing of the rock fill is without doubt one of the most remarkable construction features of the Sadd el-Kafara dam. On the upstream side, parts of the facing are still well preserved. On the downstream side, isolated stone blocks indicate that facing corresponding to that on the upstream side was planned and at least partially constructed.

On the upstream side of the southern wall, only thirteen courses of stone near the crest are still partially preserved. The facing of the upstream side of the northern wall is much better preserved, with thirty-one courses still in place. The ashlars are of slightly differing sizes (30 × 45 × 80 cm, on average), and were quarried from the wadi slopes directly upstream and downstream from the dam. The coarsely hewn blocks are placed flat, forming terraced steps 30 cm in height. While the downstream face has a slope of 30°, the northern remains of the dam on the upstream side clearly show different slope angles: 43–45° in the lower section and 35° in the middle section. The shallow slope of the upper steps, *circa* 25°, was probably not intentional and may be the result of much erosion.

There are no traces of operational devices, such as outlets or a spillway. If they existed at all, which is doubtful, they would have been placed in the destroyed center portion of the dam. In any case, it appears that a spillway was not required. A rough calculation shows that, in the case of overtopping, the discharge critical for the stability of the stepped downstream facing is of the order of 120–140 m³/s, which corresponds to an upstream water level of 126 m. Under these conditions, more than 200 m³/s would bypass the dam by flowing over the wadi terraces. The completed dam would have had a safe "spillway capacity" of more than 300 m³/s and might therefore have withstood all floods that could reasonably be expected.

Considering the construction methods and technology available, and taking into account the volume of fill that had to be transported from the wadi terrace to the dam core, and the amount of rock fill to be transported from the wadi edges to the supporting structure, the construction can be estimated to have taken 10–12 years.

Assessments of the dam's stability by modern methods lead to the conclusion that the design was basically correct, though very conservative. This probably indicates that no experience with structures of this kind was available when it was built (Old Kingdom).

The total volume of the reservoir when fully impounded to an elevation of 125 m is *circa* 620,000 m³. Below an elevation of 123.5 m, about 465,000 m³ can be stored. Basically, a large-scale reservoir was needed either to fulfill a heavy demand, such as for irrigation and/or drinking water, or to protect a large area from excessive flooding. It is unlikely, however, that the Sadd el-Kafara dam was built to supply drinking water or water for irrigation. The dam is too distant from the alabaster quarries situated upstream to have supplied the labor force with drinking water, and vast stretches of fertile arable land with an abundant supply of water were available in the nearby Nile Valley.

Due to the geographical and geological conditions prevailing in the catchment area of the Sadd el-Kafara dam, sudden and heavy rainfalls lead to flash floods with disastrous effects in narrow valleys like the Wadi Garawi. Inhabitants in the region have reported the recent occurrence of floods several meters high which have destroyed villages and claimed lives. It can therefore be assumed that the Sadd el-Kafara dam was built to protect the lower Wadi Garawi from floods (and possibly to safeguard buildings situated around the Ain Fisha spring), and to protect the stretch of the Nile Valley at the mouth of the wadi where settlements were probably located.

Since the rediscovery of the Sadd el-Kafara by Georg Schweinfurth in 1885, there has been no doubt that the dam is a very old structure. Analyses of pottery and radiocarbon dates obtained from samples of charcoal and textiles found in the remains of buildings northwest of the dam (probably a workers' camp during the construction of the dam) indicate that the dam was constructed in the early Old Kingdom, *circa* 2,700–2,600 BC. This dating makes the Sadd el-Kafara dam one of the oldest in the world, and certainly the world's oldest large-scale dam.

Investigations demonstrate, however, that the dam was never completed. There is evidence that the upstream rock fill was almost (or fully) completed, but a gap still remained in the middle section of the downstream rock fill, and perhaps also in the core, when the structure was destroyed by a flood overtopping the upstream rock fill. The dam collapsed, which must have resulted in a catastrophic flood in the lower wadi. The impression left by the disaster, which was not caused by faulty design but by a natural phenomenon that could not have been foreseen, must have been so terrible that the damaged structure was abandoned.

See also

climate; pyramids (Old Kingdom), construction of; quarrying

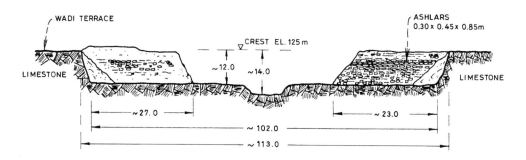

Figure 127 Remains of the Sadd el-Kafara dam in the Wadi Garawi in 1982 (view from upstream)

Further reading

Garbrecht, G. 1983. Der Sadd el-Kafara. *Bulletin 81 of the Leichtweiss Institute for Water Research, Technical University, Braunschweig.*

Hellström, B. 1951. The oldest dam in the world. *Bulletin 28 of the Institution of Hydraulics at the Royal Institute of Technology, Stockholm.*

Mackay, E. 1912. Old Kingdom dam in Wadi Gerrawi. In *Heliopolis, Kafr Ammar and Shurufa*, E. Mackay and W.M.F. Petrie, 38–40. London.

GÜNTHER GARBRECHT

Wadi Gasus

Wadi Gasus (26°33′ N, 34°02′ E) is a valley opening out from the Eastern Desert to the Red Sea coast, about 80 km south of Hurgada and 60 km north of Quseir. About 2 km south of the wadi on the coast is Mersa Gawasis, a Red Sea harbor. Mersa Gawasis, which lies at the mouth of the Wadi Gawasis, was formerly thought to be the site of the 12th Dynasty port of Saww. "Mersa" indicates a harbor and "Gasus" is a medieval term for a "spy" boat, with "Gawasis" being its plural. In 1976, the true site of the port of Saww was discovered at Mersa Gawasis by an archaeological expedition of the History Department, Faculty of Arts, University of Alexandria, under the direction of Abdel Monem A.H. Sayed.

Pharaonic evidence is scattered throughout the Wadi Gasus. At Bir Abu Gowa, Psamtik I (26th Dynasty) is seen in a rock drawing pouring libations to the gods Amen-Re and Min, god of the Eastern Desert. Behind the king stand his daughter Nitocris and Shepenwepet II, daughter of the Nubian pharaoh Piye (25th Dynasty); these two are the actual and former "Divine Votaresses" of Amen, respectively. The inscription also names two other Divine Votaresses: Shepenwepet I, daughter of the Libyan king Osorkon III (23rd Dynasty), and Amenirdis, sister of Piye. In a small valley which branches off the south of the Wadi Gasus, about 6 km from the sea, is an inscription carved at the entrance to a lead mine. Another inscription is found on a nearby granite block recording expeditions sent by the Governor of the South, Monthuemhat, in the time of Psamtik I.

About 7 km from the sea on the south side of the Wadi Gasus are the remains of a Graeco-Roman water station (*hydreuma*). Among these remains, two hieroglyphic stelae were found at the beginning of the nineteenth century by James Burton and Sir John Gardner Wilkinson. One records the erecting of the stela by an official named Khnumhotep in the first year of Senusret II (12th Dynasty). The other stela records the expedition of a ship's captain called Khentkhtaywer in the twenty-eighth year of Amenemhat II. It mentions how his ships landed at the port of Saww, after a safe return from the land of Punt (on the African coast of the Red Sea). The 1976 University of Alexandria expedition began work in the Wadi Gasus at the Graeco-Roman water station. After excavating this to its foundations, no pharaonic monuments were found. Consequently, the 12th Dynasty stela of Khentkhtaywer must have been transferred to the station in Roman times from the Red Sea port of Saww. Work was then shifted to two sites on the Red Sea shore: (1) Mersa Gasus at the mouth of the Wadi Gasus, where no pharaonic remains were found by the expedition; and (2) Mersa Gawasis, a small dhow harbor at the mouth of the Wadi Gawasis, thought to be the site of the Ptolemaic port of Philoteras. At Mersa Gawasis, however, the expedition discovered some small stelae and fragmentary inscriptions, including the cartouche of Senusret I and the geographical name "Bia-n-Punt." This evidence suggests that Mersa Gawasis is, in fact, the site of the 12th Dynasty port of Saww.

About 250 m west of the port, on the northern edge of Wadi Gawasis, a small shrine was discovered. Its façade is inscribed in hieroglyphs with the name and titles of a man called Ankhow, who was a chamberlain of Senusret I. The shrine and pedestal are made of limestone anchors, after cutting off their upper holes. The name of the port of Saww occurs in the shrine's inscriptions (but in a somewhat different form, "Sww"), which confirms the port of Saww at Mersa Gawasis.

Some 200 m west of the shrine of Ankhow, the expedition unearthed a small limestone stela, inscribed with a hieroglyphic text recording an order of Senusret I to the Vizier Antefoker, to build ships to be sent to the region of "Bia-Punt." The stela stood on a limestone anchor which formed its base. During excavations in 1977, the expedition uncovered some potsherds inscribed in hieratic. They record the contents, source and destination of food contained in the original jars. Among these names are a temple of Senusret II, the

Figure 128 Upstream face of the northern wall (right bank of the wadi)

geographical term "Punt," and the name of an official who lived at the time of Senusret III.

The results of these studies suggest the following conclusions:

1 The 12th Dynasty port of Saww or Sww is decisively identified with Mersa Gawasis rather than with Mersa Gasus.
2 The use of the port began in the reign of Senusret I and continued during the reigns of his successors at least until the reign of Senusret III.
3 The ships which the Egyptians used in the Red Sea were built on the banks of the Nile, then dismantled and carried in sections to the Red Sea where they were reassembled (Stela of Antefoker, lines 3–7).
4 No canal from the Nile to the Red Sea existed during the use of Mersa Gawasis, despite the attribution by classical writers of the first digging of a Nile–Red Sea canal to a pharaoh called "Sesostris" (Senusret). Evidence for this conclusion is found in the anchors used in the shrine of Ankhow and to support the stela of Antefoker. This means that the ships ended their journey at Mersa Gawasis and did not continue on to the Gulf of Suez to the presumed location of the canal of "Sesostris." A dismantling operation was probably again performed and the ships were returned to the Nile Valley to be used again. The heavy stone anchors (*circa* 250 kg each) were made at Mersa Gawasis, as two unfinished anchors found in the second season attest. They were left behind at the site when the expeditions returned to the Nile Valley and used in various construction projects such as the shrine of Ankhow and the pedestal for the Stela of Antefoker.
5 The port at Mersa Gawasis was also used as a transfer point for journeys to the mines in Sinai. Evidence for this conclusion is found in a comparison of the Stela of Khnumhotep found at Wadi Gasus and the scene depicting thirty-seven Asiatics in the tomb of Khnumhotep at Beni Hasan. In addition, leaders of the expeditions to Sinai often held naval titles.
6 The triangular objects represented on ships in Egyptian maritime scenes are stone anchors. An upper hole holds a thick rope for lowering and lifting the anchor. There is also a lower hole for inserting another rope to help disengage the anchor from the sea bottom.

See also

Beni Hasan; Middle Kingdom, overview; Punt; Roman ports, Red Sea; Serabit el-Khadim; ships; trade, foreign; Wadi Hammamat

Further reading

Nibbi, A. 1976. The two stelae of the Wadi Gasus. *JEA* 62: 45–56.

Sayed, A.M.A.H. 1977. Discovery of the site of the 12th Dynasty port at Wâdi Gawâsîs on the Red Sea shore. *RdÉ* 29: 139–78.

——. 1980. Observations of the Gawâsîs discoveries: I The stone anchors, II. The mortised blocks. *JEA* 66: 154–7.

——. 1983. New light on the recently discovered port on the Red Sea shore. *CdE* 58: 23–37.

ABDEL MONEM A.H. SAYED

Wadi Hammamat

One of many wadis or dry canyons in the rugged mountains of the Eastern Desert, the Wadi Hammamat constitutes the central section of one of the most important routes between the Nile and the Red Sea. The Wadi Hammamat itself lies halfway between the Nile and the Red Sea, or about 60 km either from Quft (ancient Coptos) on the Nile or from Quseir (near ancient Myos Hormos). The Hammamat route is one of the shortest Nile–Red Sea tracks, and for this reason it has been utilized for millennia and is now marked by scores of ancient ruins and resting places and hundreds of rock inscriptions or graffiti. In addition, extensive mining and quarrying have been carried out in or near the Wadi Hammamat.

Although there is some variation in the usage of the geographical label, "Wadi Hammamat" here refers to the stretch from the well and

Roman way station at Bir Hammamat, through the Wadi Hammamat proper, up to the natural gate in the mountains at Bir Umm Fawakhir (25°58′–26°35′ N, 33°32′–33°35′ E). Within the Wadi Hammamat itself lie quarries for both breccia verde antica, a variegated green stone and for *bekhen*-stone, highly prized by the ancient Egyptians. *Bekhen*-stone, which occurs nowhere else in Egypt, is a Precambrian graywacke that has a fine-grained, tough texture. The stone is dark gray when freshly cut but weathers to a reddish cast. Most of the more than 400 hieroglyphic and hieratic rock inscriptions in the Wadi Hammamat record the activities of the expeditions sent to obtain the precious *bekhen*-stone for the statues, sarcophagi and building projects of the pharaohs.

The history, or rather the prehistory, of the Wadi Hammamat extends much farther back than pharaonic times. Although there are Paleolithic sites in the Eastern Desert, the oldest readily accessible relics in the Wadi Hammamat are the late Predynastic petroglyphs immediately northeast of the *bekhen*-stone quarries. Like thousands of other prehistoric rock carvings in the Eastern Desert, these depict hunters, animal traps, ostriches, gazelles and other game in a style datable to the late fourth millennium BC by the similarity to designs painted on Gerzean pottery. The richness of the wildlife represented, which elsewhere includes elephants, is one indication that in late prehistory the Eastern Desert was more abundantly watered and vegetated than it is today.

Most of the hieroglyphic inscriptions are carved on the smooth southeast cliffs facing the main *bekhen*-stone quarries. The other side of the wadi is littered with quarrying debris, including a split, abandoned sarcophagus. The inscriptions typically include a dedication to Min, the god of Coptos and the desert, or to the Coptos divine triad of Isis, Horus and Harpocrates, and the block of hieroglyphic text may be surmounted by an offering scene or image of the god(s). The name of the expedition leader and his titles are generally given, often along with the name of his pharaoh, and sometimes details of the expedition. In New Kingdom times emphasis shifted to Amen-Re, and in Roman times Isis/Hathor, Horus/Harpocrates and Amen/Pan became the most commonly depicted deities. The great importance of the Wadi Hammamat graffiti is that they may be considered historical records of royal activities in a given year, in contrast to other writings such as temple inscriptions which were intended for another function, i.e. recording the king's unvarying duties to the gods and vice versa.

Hieroglyphic inscriptions recording quarrying expeditions date back to the great pyramid builders of the Old Kingdom, Khafre, Menkaure, Djedefre, Sahure and Unas. Pepi I of the 6th Dynasty is especially well represented with about eighty graffiti. Graffiti from the First Intermediate Period exist, but their chronology is not yet clear. The Middle Kingdom inscriptions, however, are among the fullest and most informative in the Wadi Hammamat. Mentuhotep II, III and IV of the 11th Dynasty are named in about thirty texts, as are Amenemhat and Senusret of the 12th Dynasty. Mentuhotep III's expedition with 3,000 men actually had as its goal the dispatch of a ship to Punt, located in what is now Eritrea, to procure incense and other exotic goods, but on the return through the Wadi Hammamat the expedition quarried *bekhen*-stone for statues. The lengthy inscriptions of Mentuhotep IV are the most important records of his brief reign; they tell of his dispatch of 10,000 men and ample provisions for them to bring back a sarcophagus and lid for the king. No fewer than two "miracles" distinguished the expedition. A fleeing gazelle, exhausted, gave birth to her young on the very block chosen for the king. The second "miracle" was a rare flash flood that revealed a well of clean water, all-important in a hyperarid desert. The leader of the expedition, who boasted of accomplishing everything without the loss of a single life, was the vizier Amenemhat, in all likelihood the same man who usurped the throne as Amenemhat I. A less spectacular graffito records a quarrying expedition on his behalf, and another inscription carved during the reign of his son, Senusret I, tells of 17,000 men sent to obtain stone for sixty sphinxes and 150 statues.

The Second Intermediate Period is represented by Sobekhotep IV and Sobekemsaef, but what is more surprising is that the New Kingdom pharaohs are poorly attested before the Ramesside period. The few inscriptions that there are provide little more than the names and titles of Ahmose, Amenhotep II, Amenhotep IV, Seti I, Ramesses II and Seti II. Queen Hatshepsut's famous expedition to Punt is believed to have taken a more northerly route via the Wadi Gasus. The most striking New Kingdom reference to the Wadi Hammamat is the Turin Papyrus, a papyrus roll recovered from Deir el-Medina and dating to the reign of Ramesses IV of the 20th Dynasty. The papyrus is a map that may reasonably be read as showing the route to the *bekhen*-stone quarries in the Wadi Hammamat and the gold and silver mines a little farther east.

Only one inscription can be attributed to the Third Intermediate Period and not many to the Late period, but these do include some of the most famous names of the age: Shabako, Amenirdis, Taharka, Psamtik I and II, Neko II, Amasis, Cambyses, Darius, Xerxes and Artaxerxes. The last hieroglyphic inscriptions date to the reign of Nectanebo II of the 30th Dynasty, but at that point the record is continued by a series of demotic texts in the nearby Paneion. The latter is a sheltered bay in the cliffs apparently utilized as a shrine to Pan, patron god of the desert. The walls are now covered by graffiti, the oldest dating to the 23rd Dynasty, but the majority are demotic or Greek texts of the Ptolemaic and Roman periods.

The Ptolemaic period saw a sudden resurgence of interest in the desert routes to the Red Sea and thence to East Africa. The increased activity was at least partly motivated by the need for elephants, the equivalent of tanks in their day, to be employed in the wars with the Seleucid kings in Syria. Though exploitation of the quarries may have diminished, Ptolemy II at least is named in one graffito, and the desert routes, including the Wadi Hammamat and Berenike tracks, were developed and provided with new wells or cisterns and way-stations.

Building on the Ptolemaic infrastructure, the Romans expanded the desert trade even farther.

Their camel caravans, large study ships, and recently acquired knowledge of the monsoons permitted them to sail to Africa perhaps as far as Dar es-Salaam, to Aden and the Spice Coast, and on to the tip of India on a regular basis. The remains of a fortified watering station at Bir Hammamat, the well-preserved (and partly rebuilt) circular well, and the intervisible signal towers on mountain peaks along the Hammamat route are all part of the Roman road system. Although the *bekhen*-stone may not have been so intensively quarried, the breccia verde antica outcrop probably was, as indicated by large, rough-hewn, abandoned blocks. In the nearby *bekhen*-stone quarries themselves, however, a carefully constructed temple with a series of side rooms can be dated to the time of Tiberius by an inscribed *naos*. In addition to Tiberius's inscription, graffiti record activity under Augustus, Nero, Titus, Domitian, Antoninus, Maximinus and perhaps Hadrian. At the end of the second century AD the Roman empire faced so many internal difficulties that the costly, far-flung Red Sea trade and its desert routes became too difficult to maintain and records became correspondingly sparse thereafter.

Later activity in the Eastern Desert is certainly attested, including Byzantine towns and forts at Abu Sha'ar, Berenike and Bir Umm Fawakhir, the medieval trade and pilgrimage routes through the Wadi Qena to the north or the Wadi Qash just south of the Wadi Hammamat, and the thirteenth–fourteenth-century Mamluk port at Quseir el-Qadim. Still, the ancient quarries in the Wadi Hammamat were finally abandoned about the end of the second century AD, and with them the associated houses, temples and shrines. Three millennia of quarrying, traffic and cutting rock inscriptions—some of the latter already ancient to the Romans—all but ceased.

See also

Berenike; Panchrysos; Bir Umm Fawakhir; Punt; quarrying; Quft/Qift (Coptos); Quseir el-Qadim; Roman ports, Red Sea; trade, foreign

Further reading

Bernand, A. 1972. *De Koptos à Kosseir.* Leiden.

Gundlach, R. 1986. Wadi Hammamat. In *LÄ* 6: 1099–1113.

Harrell, J.A., and V.M. Brown. 1992. The World's Oldest Surviving Geological Map: The 1150 B.C. Turin Papyrus from Egypt. *Journal of Geology* 100: 3–18.

CAROL MEYER

Wadi el-Hudi

The Wadi el-Hudi is a mining and quarrying region covering an area of some 300 square kilometers in the Eastern Desert, approximately 35 km southeast of Aswan (23°50′ N, 33°10′ E). It was the primary location for amethyst procurement in Egypt from the 11th Dynasty until the end of the Middle Kingdom, during which time the use of amethysts in jewelry reached a peak of popularity. Like many other parts of the Eastern Desert, the Wadi el-Hudi region includes deposits of auriferous quartz; it has been exploited for its minerals (including mica, barytes, gold and amethyst) since at least the early second millennium BC, and modern miners and quarriers are still extracting hematite and building stone from the immediate area.

The ancient remains at Wadi el-Hudi were first discovered by the geologist Labib Nassim in 1923, and the earliest archaeological examination of the site took place in 1939, when it was visited by G.W. Murray and Ibrahim Abdel 'Al of the Egyptian Topographical Survey. At this time three stelae (WH143–5) were transferred from the Middle Kingdom area of Wadi el-Hudi to the Cairo Museum, and numerous other inscriptions were transported to the Aswan Museum, but as many as twenty inscribed objects appear to have been stolen from the unguarded site over the next five years. Ahmed Fakhry undertook three brief seasons of archaeological and epigraphic survey in the region in 1944–9, recording most of the inscriptions and graffiti and providing the first general description of the pharaonic and Graeco-Roman remains, numbering the individual ancient "sites" from 1 to 14. In 1975 the inscriptions and graffiti were examined by Ashraf Sadek, who published a more exhaustive epigraphic study of the site. A survey undertaken by Ian Shaw and Robert Jameson in November 1992 concentrated on the examination of the archaeological aspects of the site.

The region is dominated by the Gebel el-Hudi, a large hill located about halfway along the floor of the Wadi el-Hudi, which extends for about 12 km from northwest to southeast, surrounded by a network of ridges and smaller wadis to the west and the east. The traces of ancient mining and quarrying expeditions are scattered throughout this adjacent region of smaller valleys rather than in the main wadi itself.

There are five ancient sites in the eastern part of the region, and probably all of these date to the Roman period or later. From north to south they comprise a barytes mine (site 1), a small hill fort dating to the Roman period (site 2) and, at the southeastern end of the main wadi, a gold mine and associated encampment (sites 13–14). The latter consists of an unusual combination of stone huts and shelters partly formed by caves in the rock face, surrounded by numerous remains of basalt grinding stones similar to those found in the vicinity of the gold mines in the Wadi Hammamat.

On the western side of the Wadi el-Hudi there are a number of areas of archaeological interest, clustering together amid a succession of high rocky ridges and valleys. These include five mining sites, two of which (sites 5 and 9) are amethyst mining settlements dated both by inscriptions and pottery to the Middle Kingdom, while the other four sites (3, 4, 11 and 12) appear to be amethyst and gold mining areas dating primarily to the Roman period. The other two areas of interest to the west of the main wadi are sites 8 and 10. Site 8 consists of an ancient well and associated stone structures, probably dating to the Roman period. Site 10 is a deep tunnel penetrating horizontally into the hillside for a distance of at least 20 m. This was identified as a mica mine by Fakhry, who argued that both the mine and a small stone hut at the foot of the hillside must have been contemporary with sites 11 and 12. The 1992 survey, however, suggested that the "mica mine" and the associated stone hut may be much more recent in date.

Sites 5, 6 and 9—a hilltop settlement, a peak carved with inscriptions and drawings, and a fortress, respectively—constitute an area of intense Middle Kingdom amethyst mining activity. Site 5 consists of a hilltop settlement and adjacent amethyst mine. Incorporated into the walls of the settlement are numerous rock drawings and inscriptions. The three earliest inscriptions (WH2–4) date to the first two years of the reign of the last ruler of the 11th Dynasty, Mentuhotep IV, while three others (WH14 and 144–5) date to the reign of Senusret I. It therefore seems likely that the amethyst mine at site 5 was in use for at least the period between year 1 of Mentuhotep IV and year 29 of Senusret I. The large quantities of pottery also date mainly to the early Middle Kingdom.

Site 9 is a large rectangular stone fort, the architectural style of which (together with the presence of Middle Kingdom sherds) suggests that it was constructed in the 12th Dynasty and that it may be contemporary with the string of mudbrick fortresses built between the reigns of Senusret I and Senusret III in Lower Nubia, between the First and Third Cataracts. To the northeast of the fort are two amethyst mines, while to the northwest there is a short, well preserved section of ancient road.

The fortress appears to be a unique structure, in which the familiar features of the mudbrick fortresses of Lower Nubia have been transformed into a purely dry stone complex, scaled down and adapted to the needs of a 12th Dynasty mining expedition. Apart from the interest of the fortress as an unusual method of accommodating mining expeditions, it is perhaps the only surviving example of a type of basic fortification which may once have been more common in the Egyptian Nile Valley (and would perhaps usually have been built in mudbrick). The preservation of the Wadi el-Hudi fortress is particularly fortunate, in that most of the Second Cataract fortresses have vanished under the waters of Lake Nasser.

Roughly midway between sites 5 and 9 is a conical hill, the summit of which is decorated with numerous inscriptions and rock drawings, mainly dating to the Middle Kingdom (site 6). There were once considerably more inscriptions and rock drawings on the peak, but large numbers have been stolen or removed to the museums at Cairo and Aswan. It was here that Murray found a large, finely carved limestone stela inscribed by a man named Hor, a high official in the reign of Senusret I (WH143, Cairo JE 71901). Since the stone used for the Hor stela is not local, it has been suggested that it may have been specially brought to the site to mark the resumption of mining in year 17 of Senusret I's reign (or perhaps earlier), although Hor's text includes no year date. The only other dated inscription definitely assigned to site 6 is WH1, which was carved in the first year of the reign of Mentuhotep IV.

While there is some evidence for amethyst mining at Wadi el-Hudi *after* the Middle Kingdom (sites 11–12), the principal mines of the Roman period appear to have been located in the Safaga region.

See also

Hatnub; jewelry; Middle Kingdom, overview; natural resources; Nubian forts; Sikait-Zubara; Wadi Hammamat

Further reading

Fakhry, A. 1952. *The Inscriptions of the Amethyst Quarries at Wadi el-Hudi*. Cairo.

Sadek, A.I. 1980–1985. *The Amethyst-mining Inscriptions of Wadi el-Hudi*, 2 vols. Warminster.

Shaw, I. 1994. Pharaonic quarrying and mining: settlement and procurement in Egypt's marginal areas. *Antiquity* 68/258: 108–19.

Shaw, I., and R. Jameson. 1993. Amethyst mining in the Eastern Desert: a preliminary survey at Wadi el-Hudi. *JEA* 79: 81–97.

IAN SHAW

Wadi Kubbaniya

About 10 km north of Aswan, Wadi Kubbaniya (24°12′ N, 32°52′ E) is one of three major wadis that reach the Nile from the southwestern desert, draining most of the area between the river and the Eocene scarp on the west. On each side of the wadi are steep sandstone scarps, 30–40 m above the wadi floor. Near the mouth of Wadi Kubbaniya is one of the densest and most extensively studied groups of Late Paleolithic sites in Egypt.

Throughout the Late Paleolithic, Egypt was probably drier than today and human habitation was confined to the Valley. The river then was much smaller than now, with perhaps less than 20 percent of the modern flow, and was confined to a network of braided channels. Each summer, rain in the central African mountain headwaters of the Nile caused floods downstream in Egypt. The floodwaters were laden with silt, which was deposited over the floodplain. The accumulation of silt caused the floodplain to gradually build up until the Valley was choked with sediment. By 21,000 years ago, the floodplain at Aswan was some 16 m higher than today, and still rising. When the Valley fill became higher than the mouth of Wadi Kubbaniya, the seasonal flooding would invade the wadi and, at its maximum, would extend up the wadi for several kilometers, so that the lower part of the wadi became a large embayment of the floodplain.

The water permitted vegetation to grow along the edge of the floodplain, and this vegetation began to trap the sand blowing into the wadi from the north, which formed dunes. The level of the Nile continued to rise, and each year the summer floods covered the dunes, leaving silty sediments on their surfaces. Thus began a process of simultaneous dune and silt accumulation that resulted in the formation of an extensive dune field close to the northern scarp of the wadi, while the center of the wadi remained a floodplain where only silts were deposited.

The dune and silt accumulation continued throughout the Late Paleolithic, advancing southward across the wadi floor. By 13,000 BP (years before present), a barrier had been created near the wadi mouth, preventing the Nile floods from reaching up-wadi. Seepage from the floods, however, formed extensive ponds behind the barrier and occasionally floods were also able to overflow the barrier.

During this period, the first Late Paleolithic occupants of Wadi Kubbaniya settled on the dunes and on the seasonally dry floodplain. The settlements in both areas are large and were used repeatedly. There are also a few sites near the mouth of the wadi, several meters higher than the other sites. Most of the Late Paleolithic sites in Wadi Kubbaniya are assigned to the same taxonomic unit, the Kubbaniyan. The stone tools are characterized by numerous (backed) bladelets with light retouch along one edge (known as "Ouchtata" bladelets) and a few other tools (mostly truncations, scaled pieces and burins). There are also grinding stones, hand stones and mortars. Numerous radiocarbon dates indicate an age between *circa* 19,000 and 17,000 BP.

The actual surfaces upon which people lived in the dune field have all been removed by deflation. However, some of the debris from each occupation, including organic remains, have been preserved at the front of the dunes, covered by seasonal silting and wind-blown sand, which occurred repeatedly in a stratigraphic order.

The identified floral remains (besides wood charcoal, all of which is tamarisk) include ten varieties of tubers and soft vegetable tissues. Tubers of purple nut-grass and club-rush are by far the most common. There are also eleven varieties of fruiting structures, which, like the tubers, still grow on the wetlands and swampy areas near the Nile. Plants identified from human coprolites include club-rush and camomile seeds, and possibly grass-stem fragments. All of these plants are edible and are believed to have been part of the diet of the Kubbaniyan people. Radiocarbon dates on twelve specimens from three different sites confirm that the plant remains were contemporaneous with the Kubbaniyan occupations.

When mature, nut-grass tubers are rich in complex carbohydrates but also contain toxins and must be processed, by grinding and boiling or roasting. The grinding stones in the dune sites were probably used primarily for this purpose, and for grinding other fibrous foods such as reed rhizomes and fruits.

The Kubbaniyan sites yielded many fish bones and various large mammal bones, particularly wild cattle, hartebeest and gazelle. The fish are mostly adult catfish, together with tilapia and eels. A massive harvest of catfish probably occurred during the spawn, which begins with the onset of the flood (early July) and ends just before the water recedes (early September). The quantities of fish taken were so large (over 100,000 fish bones in one site) that some of them may have been dried or smoked for later consumption. The dune sites also yielded a few shells of an edible freshwater mussel, and bird bones, many of which are of species which still spend winters in Egypt.

These faunal and floral collections provide a glimpse of what must have been a very complex and seasonally diverse diet during the Late Paleolithic in the Nile Valley. The yearly round in the Nile Valley was governed by the flood, and in Late Paleolithic times the main channels of the river were several meters higher than today; and the seasonal rise was at least as great. At peak flooding, the area under water extended several kilometers up Wadi Kubbaniya and the known Kubbaniyan sites were probably under water. Sites that might have been occupied then are unknown and have probably been destroyed by deflation. There may also have been some large mammal hunting at this time; the rising water would have forced the animals from the lowland areas to the edge of the floodplain where there was less cover. As the floodwaters began to recede, fishing probably continued in the swales and cutoff ponds on the floodplain.

After the seasonal flooding, plants were also important components of the diet. Among the first may have been seeds of annuals, including camomile, which are available in October. The gathering of immature nut-grass and club-rush tubers could have begun then; they would have required only rubbing and roasting to be edible. However, tubers reach their maximum food value only at maturity in December and

January, when they require processing; thus, the presence of grinding stones and carbonized tubers in the dune sites suggests winter occupation. Purple nut-grass probably grew as a dense carpet over much of the wadi, including the dune areas, and a surplus could have been gathered and stored for later consumption. Once dried, the tubers retain their food value for several months.

Use of the dunes later in the year is indicated by dom palm fruits, which mature in February and March, and by occasional shells of the freshwater mussel (*Unio abyssinicus*), which probably could be gathered only in the period of lowest water, between February and the end of June. However, there is no other evidence that these sites were much used in the driest part of the year and it seems likely that most of the settlements at that time were closer to the deeper Nile channels.

Large mammals were probably hunted all year round, but they were not as important as fish. Despite the greater size and density (and hence survivability) of mammal bones, they represent only about 1 percent of the bones in the dune sites.

At Kubbaniya, key areas were probably reused to exploit a variety of seasonal resources, but there was no semi-permanent or permanent occupation. This may correlate with the appearance of a new subsistence system in the Nile Valley, based on the intensive use of seasonally available foods which could be processed and stored for later consumption. Such intensive use is evident during two periods of the year: in the summer when large quantities of spawning catfish were taken; and in the autumn, winter and spring when wetland tubers were gathered. Together, these two foods could have provided the basis of a balanced diet: catfish are rich in protein and fat, and wetland tubers contribute carbohydrates and dietary fiber.

The earliest Late Paleolithic in Wadi Kubbaniya is called "Fakhurian-related," because of its resemblances in stone artifacts to sites at Deir el-Fakhuri, near Esna in Upper Egypt. Characteristic stone tools include backed bladelets, elegant perforators, retouched pieces, notches and denticulates. There are three Fakhurian-related sites at Kubbaniya, with radiocarbon dates between 21,000 and 19,500 years ago.

A highly fossilized human skeleton was found near the Fakhurian-related sites, and is probably around 21,000 years old. In physical type, the skeleton is similar to a robust but fully modern population (called the Mechtoids) associated with Late Paleolithic sites throughout North Africa. In the Kubbaniya skeleton there is evidence of violence, including several healed wounds and a presumably fatal wound inflicted by two bladelets found in the pelvic cavity. Wadi Kubbaniya continued to be used by Late Paleolithic groups long after the period of the Kubbaniyan. The stone tool industries include some of those already known both farther south in Egyptian and Sudanese Nubia and farther north in Upper Egypt. After 12,500 BP a dune barrier formed across the mouth of the wadi, which would have destroyed the conditions favoring the wetland plants and made impossible the massive seasonal fish harvests. The series of exceptional floods around 12,500 BP and the subsequent down-cutting of the Nile would also have contributed to the changes in the economic system. Elsewhere in the Nile Valley, however, the system based on intensive exploitation of seasonally available foods may have persisted throughout the Late Paleolithic.

See also

climatic history; Paleolithic cultures, overview; Paleolithic tools

Further reading

Wendorf, F., R. Schild, and A.E. Close. 1989. *The Prehistory of Wadi Kubbaniya* 2, 3. Dallas, TX.

Wendorf, F., *et al.* 1984. New radiocarbon dates on the cereals from Wadi Kubbaniya. *Science* 225: 645–6.

Wendorf, F., *et al.* 1988. New radiocarbon dates and Late Palaeolithic diet at Wadi Kubbaniya, Egypt. *Antiquity* 62: 279–83.

FRED WENDORF

Wadi Maghara

Wadi Maghara ("Valley of the Caves" in Arabic) is located in South Sinai (28°54′ N, 33°22′ E), about 19 km east of the Gulf of Suez; it lies in a mountainous sandstone region containing ancient and modern turquoise mines. During the Old, Middle and New Kingdom periods, Egyptian expeditions either crossed the Eastern Desert and the Red Sea, or traversed the Wadi Tumilat, the Isthmus of Suez and the coastline of West Sinai to reach el-Merkha Bay, and then followed Wadi Sidri and its tributary Wadi Iqneh to arrive at Maghara. Egyptian texts at Maghara refer to this region as the "Terraces of the Turquoise" (ḫtyw mfk3t).

Since Seetzen's rediscovery of Maghara in 1809 many travelers have visited this region. The first significant explorations at Maghara include Richard Lepsius's 1845 expedition to Sinai, the residence of Major C.K. Macdonald at Maghara between 1854 and 1866, mining turquoise and making squeezes of Egyptian rock inscriptions, and the British Ordnance Survey in 1868–9. Captain Weill published two volumes concerning pharaonic activity in South Sinai, and accompanied Flinders Petrie's 1904–5 Sinai expedition, during which Petrie excavated settlement areas and mines and recorded inscriptions at Maghara. The Harvard University Expedition visited Maghara in 1932, noting numerous Nabataean graffiti in Wadi Qena. Many Israeli archaeological surveys of the Sinai peninsula occurred between 1967 and 1982, including one in 1968 by Rothenberg who explored Maghara; a Tel Aviv University expedition in 1970 which planned the mining camps at Maghara; and visits by Giveon, who rediscovered the second inscription of Sekhemkhet in 1973 and found two new Old Kingdom texts in 1978. In 1978, Stone recorded many Greek and Nabataean inscriptions in the region, including an Armenian pilgrim inscription at Maghara. Valbelle directed a survey of South Sinai in 1987, during which J.M. Vinçon and M. Chartier-Raymond mapped the hilltop settlement at Maghara and excavated one structure.

The first evidence for a direct Egyptian presence in South Sinai occurs during the Old Kingdom at Maghara and consists of two settlement areas and twenty-five hieroglyphic rock inscriptions near the turquoise mines. The 3rd Dynasty rock tablets include two of Sanakht, who is depicted smiting an enemy before the jackal god Wepwawet, one of Zoser, who appears beside a goddess, and two virtually identical rock tablets of Sekhemkhet. The 4th Dynasty rock tablets include two of Seneferu, who is depicted striking enemies, and one of Khufu, who is described as "smiting the tribesmen" as he accompanies the deities Wepwawet and Thoth. The 5th Dynasty rock tablets include two of Sahure, who is described as "smiting the Mentju of/and all foreign lands" (and who also appears on a rock tablet at Wadi Kharig to the north); two of Nyusserre, who accompanies a libation vase, Horus of Beḥdet, Thoth and a caption ("Thoth, lord of the foreign countries, may he give cool water"); one of Menkauhor; and three of Djedkare-Isesi. One of Djedkare-Isesi's texts records an expedition's arrival at the "Terraces of the Turquoise" during the year after the third cattle census (which usually occurred every second year), while another tablet depicts the king "smiting the chief of the foreign land" during the ninth year of the cattle census. The 6th Dynasty rock tablets contain a text of Pepi I which dates to the year after the eighteenth cattle census, and an inscription of Pepi II which dates to the year of the second cattle census. The remaining eight Old Kingdom rock tablets encompass three graffiti (including two of Administrators of a Foreign Land discovered by Giveon in 1978), a fragmentary text listing an expedition of 1,400(?) men, a 5th(?) Dynasty graffito of a controller of officials, and three 5th/6th Dynasty graffiti.

The main Old Kingdom settlement at Maghara lay on the summit of a 59 m high hill in Wadi Iqneh. It contained 125 rough stone structures with large amounts of wood ash, Old Kingdom potsherds and a copper borer. Chartier-Raymond's 1987 excavation of a six-chambered house (Building A) and its exterior passage produced some vessel sherds (of Nile Valley clays) which date from the Old Kingdom and the late Middle Kingdom to the Second Intermediate Period. This settlement was accessed by a stone staircase on the hill's northern edge, while a stone wall extending westward across the wadi from the hill's northern end probably formed a defense against hostile bedouins (who are depicted in the smiting scenes).

The rock ledges at the western foot of the hill fort yielded numerous Old Kingdom potsherds, while a wide shoal further to the west produced well-built stone structures. These structures had straight walls with smoothed faces, and contained some turquoise, large quantities of copper slag and smelting waste, copper ore chips, numerous crucible fragments, hammerstones (for crushing ores), a broken ingot mold, numerous Old Kingdom potsherds and some Middle Kingdom pottery. Two nearby large refuse heaps produced hundreds of flint tools such as flakes, blades, awls and scrapers. The slag heaps and vicinity of the mines yielded hundreds of turquoise fragments, many stone pounders, picks, mauls and hammerstones, but lacked copper ore and flint tools. The use of stone tools and copper chisels is attested by marks on the walls of the turquoise mine galleries.

Egyptian mining expeditions returned to South Sinai during the Middle Kingdom, leaving at least twenty rock inscriptions at Maghara. One of three inscriptions dating to year 2 of Amenemhat III depicts this king before Hathor and Thoth and mentions the dispatch of 734 men to collect "copper and turquoise" under the command of the Chief Chamberlain of the Treasury, Khentekhtayhotep-Khenomsu. Other texts dating to years 20+, 30, 41, 42 and 43 of Amenemhat III mention the opening of turquoise galleries, list expedition members and titles, request invocation offerings for the *kas* of expedition members, and refer to Hathor ("Lady of the Turquoise Country"), Sopdu ("Lord of the East"), Ptah ("South of his Wall") and a deified King Seneferu. Three texts date to year 6 of Amenemhat IV. The remaining Middle Kingdom inscriptions include five hieroglyphic texts and two graffiti in hieratic, a 12th Dynasty stela (no. 500) to the north of Maghara. A Middle

KEY TO MAGHARA:
* = Exact location unknown

DYNASTY III (2705-2630 BC)
1 = Sanakht (inscr. no. 3)
2 = Sanakht (inscr. no. 4)
* = Zoser (Inscr. no. 2)
3 = Sekhemkhet (Inscr. no. 1)
23 = Sekhemkhet (2nd Inscr.)
Absent kings: Khaba and Huni

DYNASTY IV (2630-2524 BC)
4 = Seneferu (Inscr. no. 5)
5 = Seneferu (Inscr. no. 6)
6 = Khufu (Inscr. no. 7)
Absent kings: Radjedef, Khafre, Menkaure and
    Shepseskaf

DYNASTY V (2524-2400 BC)
Absent king: Userkaf
7 = Sahure (Inscr. no. 8)
* = Sahure (Inscr. no. 9)
Absent kings: Meferirkare-Kakai, Shepseskare-Isi and
    Meferefre
8 = Nyussere-Ini (Inscr. no. 10)
* = Nyussere-Ini (Inscr. no. 11) South of Old Kingdom
    tablets
9 = Menkauhor-Ikauhor (no. 12)
* = Djedkare-Isesi (Inscr. no. 13) North of point 8
* = Djedkare-Isesi (Inscr. no. 14)
* = Djedkare-Isesi (Inscr. no. 15) South of point 9
Absent king: Unas

DYNASTY VI (2400-2250 BC)
Absent kings: Tety and Userkare
* = Pepi I Meryre (Inscr. no. 16) South of point 9
Absent king: Merenre I Antyemsaf
* = Pepi II (Inscr. no. 17)
Absent kings: Merenre II Antymsaf and Queen
    Mitocris

OLD KINGDOM (2705-2250 BC)
* = Rock Inscriptions nos. 18-22, and two new ones
    south of point 9
10 = 125 huts/settlement on hill (200 feet above wadi)
11 = Occupation debris: Old Kingdom pottery sherds
    at foot of hill
12 = Stone structures with traces of copper processing
13 = Waste heap A (contained flint tools)
14 = Waste heap B (contained flint tools)
15 = "Old Kingdom" Wall across wadi
* = Mine waste heaps (Contained mining tools, and
    lacked the tool types found within the settlement
    debris)

DYNASTY XII (1991-1783 BC)
Absent kings: Amenemhet I, Senwosret I, Senwosret II,
    Amenemhet II and Senwosret III
16 = Amenemhat III (Inscr. no. 23): Location?
17 = Amenemhat III (Inscr. no. 24-5): year 2
* = Amenemhat III (Inscr. no. 26): year 30
18 = Amenemhat III (Inscr. no. 27): year 41
18 = Amenemhat III (Inscr. no. 28-9): year 42
18 = Amenemhat III (Inscr. no. 30): year 43
* = Amenemhat III (Inscr. no. 31-2): year 20

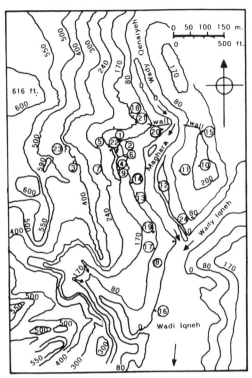

MAGHARA

18 = Amenemhat IV (Inscr. no. 33-35): year 6
Absent ruler: Queen Sobekneferu

MIDDLE KINGDOM (1991-1787 BC)
19 = Middle Kingdom (Inscr. nos. 38-41)
* = Middle Kingdom (Inscr. nos. 37, 42 and 43)
* = Middle Kingdom (Stela no. 500)
20 = Structure with five rooms and a central pit (in
    which pottery jars and bowls were found)
21 = Dynasty 12 mine ("XII" on Petrie's 1906 Map)

PROTO-SINAITIC INSCRIPTION:
* = One Proto-Sinaitic Inscription discovered by
    H. Palmer 1868-9 (Inscr. no. 348: now lost)

DYNASTY XVIII-XIX (1552-1188 BC)
22 = Hatshepsut and Tuthmose III (Inscr. no. 44)
    found near a New Kingdom mine
* = Ramesses II stela (Inscr. no. 45) Reported by Ebers

NEW INSCRIPTIONS:
23 = Sekhemkhet inscription (rediscovered 1973) 35
    metres north of Inscription no. 1
24 = Old Kingdom inscription (R. Giveon: 1978)
* = Old Kingdom inscription (R. Giveon: 1978) 500
    metres north of Old Kingdom Wadi Wall
* = Armenian Pilgrim inscription (M. Stone: 1979)
    c. 7th to 10th Century AD

Figure 129 Location of recorded scripts at Wadi Maghara, Sinai
Source: adapted from A.H. Gardiner and T.E. Peet, 1952, The Inscriptions of Sinai, Part I, 2nd edn., revised and
    augmented by J. Černy London, Geoffrey Cumberlage, pl. XV.

Kingdom stone structure lay to the west of the hilltop settlement; it contains five chambers with a storage pit in the center of each room. Three pits contained a lining of grinding stones and Middle Kingdom storejars and small bowls. The rooms yielded large amounts of copper slag, smelting scraps, crucible fragments, crushed ore in a crucible, charcoal, two tips from copper chisels/picks, many hammerstones, and numerous shells and echini (sea-urchin) spines.

An inscription that may date to either the Middle Kingdom or the 18th Dynasty requests future travelers to this "mining region" to give invocation offerings and libations and burn incense for the kas of three officials, in exchange for a safe return home and rewards from Hathor and Thoth. Evidence for New Kingdom activity at Maghara is limited. One rock stela dates to year 16 of Hatshepsut and Tuthmose III, and depicts Tuthmose III offering bread to Hathor, "Lady of the Turquoise," while Hatshepsut presents wine to Sopdu, "Lord of the East." Eber's report of a stela of Ramesses II remains unconfirmed.

See also

metallurgy; Serabit el-Khadim; Sinai, North, late prehistoric and Dynastic sites; trade, foreign

Further reading

Chartier-Raymond, M. 1988. Notes sur Maghara (Sinai). *CRIPEL* 10: 13–22.

Cooney, J.D. 1972. Major Macdonald, a Victorian romantic. *JEA* 58: 280–5.

Gardiner, A.H., and T.E. Peet. 1952–5. *The Inscriptions of Sinai, Parts I–II*, 2nd edn. revised and augmented by J. Černý. London.

Giveon, R. 1978. *The Stones of Sinai Speak*. Tokyo.

Ward, W. 1991. Early contacts between Egypt, Canaan, and Sinai: Remarks on the paper by Amnon Ben-Tor. *BASOR* 281: 11–26.

G.D. MUMFORD

Wadi Tumilat

The Wadi Tumilat today is a narrow, intensively cultivated valley, some 52 km long, but only 2–6 km wide, leading eastward from the town of Abassa to Ismailia and the shores of Lake Timsah. It is one of the two main overland routes leading from the Nile Delta to the Sinai and western Asia, and is heavily traversed today. Geologically, it is the ancient bed of a large Pleistocene river down-cutting through earlier Plio-Pleistocene deltaic sands and gravels, which today form the northern portions of the Eastern Desert. The Wadi is bounded on the north by the Tell el-Kebir island, a turtle-back of deltaic sands and gravels, and on the south by a line of sand dunes bounding the northern edge of flat level desert.

Rainfall in the Wadi Tumilat is sparse and erratic, insufficient to sustain settled occupation. Ordinary Nile floods regularly reached the western section of the Wadi, which was bounded by a large natural dike, the Ras el-Wadi, in the region of Tell er-Retabah and the modern Qassassin. Only exceptionally high Niles reached the central and eastern sections of the Wadi, replenishing Lake Timsah to the east and the many small lakes in the central section of the Wadi. As a consequence, the western end of the Wadi (about 24 km) was more heavily alluviated, and had more arable land. The depressed central region of the Wadi probably contained a perennial marshy lake sustained by the yearly Nile flood. Economic activities may have included farming, grazing, hunting and fishing in and around the lake.

During much of antiquity, the Wadi Tumilat appears to have been largely deserted. Settled occupation from the Middle Kingdom (?) onward is attested only at Tell er-Retabah, located on high ground at roughly the Wadi's midpoint; this site may have been the "Walls of the Ruler" mentioned in the texts *Sinuhe* and the *Prophecy of Neferti*. The only two periods in which the Wadi was intensively occupied were the Second Intermediate Period, when there was a considerable Asiatic (Hyksos) presence in the middle section of the Wadi, and the Late period, i.e. the later Saite through early Roman periods. Neko II of the 26th Dynasty initiated the great sea-level canal linking the Mediterranean to the Red Sea, a project successively given renewed effort by Darius the Great, Ptolemy II and Trajan.

In the New Kingdom, the written evidence indicates that the Wadi Tumilat belonged to a military zone, known as Tjeku (Ṯkw). Both the orthography of the word and the context of the references imply that Tjeku was a district rather than a town, although its specific boundaries cannot be determined. The early occurrences of Tjeku all carry the throw-stick and hill country determinatives, rather than the city determinative. Identification of particular fortifications mentioned in the New Kingdom texts with archaeological sites is difficult. The one exception is the "Fortress of Merneptah-Content-with-Truth" of Papyrus Anastasi VI, which Redford has equated with Tell er-Retabah. The archaeological data indicate the presence of a major stronghold at Retabah during late New Kingdom times, and little or no occupation elsewhere in the Wadi. Inscribed blocks from an Atum temple were found by Flinders Petrie at Tell er-Retabah virtually at the surface of a site known to be deeply stratified. It is almost certain that, like other Atum-related Ramesside material found in the Wadi, these blocks were imported following the building of the transit canal, possibly even as late as the Ptolemaic period.

With the founding of the transit canal and of Tell el-Maskhuta in the reign of Neko II, it appears that the designation "Per-Atum Tjeku" was simply moved eastward from Retabah, which underwent a severe reduction in size and influence at this time. Thus, the monumental Pithom Stela of Ptolemy II, found by Naville at Tell el-Maskhuta, records the building (more accurately the rebuilding) of a temple to Atum in Tjeku; this claim has been borne out by modern excavation. The stela identifies the region as belonging to Nome VIII of Lower Egypt.

Possible connections with the biblical narrative of the sojourn in Egypt (Genesis 45 to Exodus 15), traditions of an early sea-level canal linking the Mediterranean and the Red Sea by way of the Pelusiac branch of the Nile and the Wadi Tumilat, and the striking visual evidence of the remains of an ancient canal running the length of the Wadi early attracted the attention of the French Expedition and subsequent engineers, scholars, explorers and excavators. Captivated by the dream of building a canal joining the Mediterranean and the Red Sea, Napoleon Bonaparte rode through the Wadi and the Isthmus of Suez during the winter of 1798–9 to see for himself the spoilbanks of this ancient achievement. Faulty calculations of sea levels forced the cancellation of these plans, but when de Lessups and the Suez Canal Company began work a half century later, the first order of business was the construction of a sweet-water canal carrying the water of the Nile through the Wadi Tumilat and down to the Red Sea. This canal provided fresh water for the work effort and for the towns of Ismailia and Suez, as well as revivifying the large-scale agricultural reclamation projects initiated by Mohammed Ali in the Wadi Tumilat some fifteen years after the French Expedition. This sweet-water canal today forms the basis for the agricultural wealth of the region.

Inspired by the goal of providing a firm archaeological grounding for the biblical traditions, the newly-formed (1882) Egypt Exploration Society commissioned the Swiss philologist Édouard Naville to undertake excavations at Tell el-Maskhuta (1883). Tell el-Maskhuta lies some 15 km west of Ismailia and was the site of significant discoveries of Ramesside statuary and other antiquities by the engineers of the Suez Canal Company. These excavations uncovered the remains of massive, deeply-founded storehouses, "said by a visitor to have been made with bricks without straw." Not unnaturally, given the large number of Ramesside monuments found at the site, these storehouses were attributed to the Ramesside period. Also found were a large enclosure wall, an immediately adjacent Roman town, a badly ruined temple, the Pithom Stela of Ptolemy II, and two Latin inscriptions mentioning Ero, which Naville equated with Heroonopolis. The connection between these ruins and the biblical text was apparently assured by the Septuagintal substitution of "Heroonopolis in the land of

Ramesses" for the Hebrew Goshen, as the place where Joseph goes to meet his father (Genesis 46:28).

In 1905 W.M. Flinders Petrie excavated at Tell er-Retabah, discovering additional Ramesside material, including an architectural façade of Ramesses II with an inscription to Atum, Lord of Tjeku, and a reused portion of the doorjamb of a tomb, also mentioning Tjeku. On this evidence, Petrie suggested the identification of Tell er-Retabah with the biblical city of Ramesses, and the identification of Tell el-Maskhuta with Pithom. Sir Alan Gardiner contested Petrie's identifications, maintaining that Retabah must be Pithom/Heroonopolis, and that Tell el-Maskhuta must be the fortress of Tjeku, standing in the midst of the district of Tjeku. In the absence of further evidence, scholars largely chose sides based on personal inclination.

In 1930, a team from the German Institute in Cairo conducted a survey of the Wadi Tumilat, still remembered in 1981 by some residents of the Wadi. This expedition's expertise centered on the classical remains, and the results were both error-prone and of little lasting interest. A number of occupation sites were identified and mapped, and a limited number of surface materials were published. Recent work has not sustained their identification of Old Kingdom pottery at Tell er-Retabah and Tell Samud. With the exception of Inspector Abed el-Haq's discovery of a series of Hyksos tombs at Tell es-Sahaba, and some exploratory work by the Egyptian Antiquities Organization at Tell el-Maskhuta, interest in the Wadi prior to 1977 continued to be focused around its possible biblical connections.

In 1977, the team of John S. Holladay, Jr., Michael Coogan and Edward Campbell conducted a one week survey in the Wadi Tumilat. Military security limited this survey to the sites of Tell el-Maskhuta, Tell es-Sahaba (a natural formation), Tell er-Retabah and Tell el-Gebel. On the basis of surface collections of diagnostic sherds, the team quickly established (a) that there were no significant New Kingdom remains at Tell el-Maskhuta, and (b) that major occupational remains at Maskhuta began with the late Saite period and continued until some time in the early Roman period. Tell el-Gebel appeared to be largely of the Roman period. Of the four sites, only Tell er-Retabah had occupational remains from the later New Kingdom. Subsequent discoveries confirmed initial tentative identification of Second Intermediate Period (Hyksos) material in surface collections from both Tell el-Maskhuta and Tell er-Retabah.

Multi-disciplinary stratigraphic excavations at Tell el-Maskhuta by a team headed by John S. Holladay of the University of Toronto (1978–85) confirmed and extended the conclusions of the initial site survey. They established the framework of a locally based ceramic chronology encompassing part of the Second Intermediate Period, and the period *circa* 610 BC to the third or fourth century AD, with a possible gap in the fourth century BC and a longer gap spanning the first century BC through the first century AD. This stratigraphically based chronology made practicable a systematic survey of the entire Wadi Tumilat, co-directed by Carol A. Redmount and John S. Holladay, in which thirty-five sites of archaeological significance within the Wadi were identified.

Three large tells or occupation mounds exist in the Wadi Tumilat at the sites of Tell el-Maskhuta, Tell er-Retabah and Tell Shaqafiya. Aside from the University of Toronto excavations at Tell el-Maskhuta, the Egyptian Antiquities Organization has worked at this site. Tell er-Retabah has been investigated by Hans Goedicke of Johns Hopkins University and by the Egyptian Antiquities Organization. Philip Hammond of the University of Utah has conducted excavations at Tell el-Shaqafiya in the western portion of the Wadi. Tell el-Shaqafiya and the later occupation levels at Tell el-Maskhuta were intimately bound up with the operation of the sea-level canal. Tell er-Ratabah was a major government outpost in the Middle Kingdom and Second Intermediate Period, and again in the late 29th–30th Dynasties and later.

Nine of the ten medium or small tells in the Wadi Tumilat are in the western division of the Wadi. These are the sites of Tell el-Kebir, Tell el-Ku'a, Tell el-Niweiri, Tell Samud, Tell el-Hatab, Saiyid el-Shafi'i, Tell el-Gebel, el-Abbasa and el-Ahawashma". A number of other sites consisting of large and small sherd scatters may be non-sedentary campsite locations. Most of these are located in the central division of the Wadi, probably because of the small lakes in this region. Only Tell el-Niweiri, now destroyed by development, yielded some Predynastic material.

The results of the 1983 Wadi Tumilat Survey are summarized in Table 4, giving site distribution by Wadi division and major archaeological periods. Most sites had archaeological remains from several archaeological periods. Given that the western portion of the western division was the agriculturally favored part of the Wadi, it is undoubtedly significant that few Second Intermediate Period sites were located there. For the Saite period, the distribution is related to servicing the needs of the sea-level transit canal. Large-scale agricultural development of the area started in the Persian period and peaked in the Ptolemaic and early Roman eras.

See also

Tell el-Maskhuta

Further reading

Holladay, J.S., Jr., and C.A. Redmount. Forthcoming. *The Wadi Tumilat Project* 1: *Surveys in the Wadi Tumilat, 1977 and 1983, Results and Archaeological Interpretation.* Toronto.

JOHN S. HOLLADAY, JR.

wine making

Wine was far more a luxury in ancient Egypt than the staple beer. In tomb and temple scenes it was offered to the gods and kings. At bacchanals of both religious and secular nature wine (or beer) was consumed, while the sober scribes made admonitions against excess.

Wine was made from grapes, figs, dates, pomegranates or other fruits. Grapes in particular require more water and care than do the grains from which beer and bread were made. The earliest evidence of grapes are pips from Predynastic features at el-Omari and Hierakonpolis. This evidence is roughly contemporary with grape pips found at Huma (Syria), and somewhat earlier than a residue from wine in a jar from Godin Tepe (Iran). An Egyptian generic term for wine was *irp*.

Named vineyards (such as "The Enclosure of the Beverage of the Body of Horus") and vintages are known from 1st Dynasty records. Sealed wine jars were recovered from the Early Dynastic tombs at Saqqara as well as from later contexts. Details of wine making are depicted in tomb scenes from the Old Kingdom onward.

Grapes were trodden in great vats, from which the juice flowed through a spout. The lees that remained were squeezed in cloth bags tied to poles and twisted to extract any remaining juice. The juice was filtered through cloth into large fermentation jars and eventually siphoned or decanted into wine jars of various sizes and shapes for storage or consumption. These were stoppered with clay, which was impressed with indications of vintage, quality and ownership. Fermentation was

Table 4 Site distribution in the Wadi Tumilat by wadi division

Wadi Division	II Int. Period	New Kingdom	Saite	Saite/- Persian	Persian	Ptolemaic/ Roman	Roman/ Coptic	Islamic
Isthmus	-	-	-	-	1	2	1	1
Eastern	-	-	-	-	-	5	2	3
Central	14	1	2	2	1	19	11	4
Western	7	-	2	2	5	15	8	6

still active by the time of this transfer, as wine jars were often vented through small holes.

Some wines were blended to taste at the time of consumption. Only the best vintages were exported beyond the region in which they were made. By Graeco-Roman times it appears that a taste for wine had trickled down to the masses, and cheap vintages were available.

See also

brewing and baking

Further reading

Darby, W.J., P. Ghaliounghui and L. Grivetti. 1977. *Food: The Gift of Osiris* 2. London.

Lutz, H.F. 1922. *Viticulture and Brewing in the Ancient Orient*. New York.

Wilson, H. 1988. *Egyptian Food and Drink*. Aylesbury.

JEREMY GELLER

writing, invention and early development

Egyptian writing appeared first in the late fourth millennium BC, and evolved until the earliest continuous written language was recorded in the late 2nd or early 3rd Dynasty. During this long period, writing was a very limited instrument. It was used both for administration and in artistic display, but it may not even have been considered that it could provide a medium for writing down communications in full linguistic form. This restricted form of writing was a vital means for communication and display within the elite, but probably not beyond it. Administration, writing and representational art were three central and interlinked resources of the newly formed state.

Origins

The precise date of origin of Egyptian writing is uncertain. The earliest recognizable writing from a secure archaeological context is on tags originally attached to grave goods in the royal Tomb U-j at Abydos and on pottery from the same tomb. This material may be up to two centuries earlier than the 1st Dynasty, and is significantly older than the nearby tombs of kings of Dynasty 0 in Cemetery B, which lead directly into the 1st Dynasty. Tomb U-j is unlikely to contain the earliest writing that existed, which will probably never be recovered. Its system, although very limited, appears well formed and its repertoire of signs includes the royal throne and palace façade, symbols of kingship that come into their own later.

The Tomb U-j material is not a simple precursor of the notations of royal names preserved on potsherds, fragments of stone vases, and decorated schist palettes which are known from Dynasty 0. Most of these take the form of the Horus name, a falcon surmounting a rectangle representing the royal palace compound, within which was inscribed a variable element that was the name adopted by a king when he came to the throne. At least four pre-1st Dynasty kings can be identified from Horus names, and probably more. Although the readings of their names are uncertain, the script was quite developed; words were encoded both in logographic form—with a single sign writing a complete word—and phonetically, with several signs recording individual phonemes or pairs of phonemes. By the early 1st Dynasty, almost all the uniconsonantal signs are attested, as well as the use of classifiers or determinatives, so that the writing system was in essence fully formed even though a very limited range of material was written. The language of the script was always Egyptian.

It is often assumed that Egyptian writing was invented under a stimulus of the Mesopotamian writing system, developed in the late fourth millennium BC, that might have come at the time of the short-lived Uruk Culture expansion into Syria. A variety of artistic and architectural evidence for contact between Mesopotamia and late Predynastic Egypt has been found, but none of it can be dated precisely in relation to Tomb U-j. Moreover, the Egyptian writing system is different from the Mesopotamian and must have been developed independently. The possibility of "stimulus diffusion" from Mesopotamia remains, but the influence cannot have gone beyond the transmission of an idea.

A second point of contrast with Mesopotamia is in uses of writing. The earliest Egyptian writing consists of inscribed tags, ink notations on pottery, again principally from the royal cemetery at Abydos, and hieroglyphs incorporated into artistic compositions, of which the chief clear examples are such pieces as the Narmer Palette, which is probably more than a century later than Tomb U-j. Thus, while administrative uses of writing appear to have come at the beginning—examples from the Abydos tombs include such notations as "produce of Lower Egypt"—the system was integrated fully into pictorial representation. An intermediate, emblematic mode of representation in which symbols, including hieroglyphs, were shown in action also evolved before the 1st Dynasty. These three modes together formed a powerful artistic complex that endured as long as Egyptian civilization.

Egyptian writing does not seem to have been invented in order to record "history," but was used both for administration and more generally for display. Very soon after its invention, the ideological aspect of writing had become extremely important, and early evidence is all from royal contexts and usages. With its limited capacity to convey linguistic messages but great symbolic potential, writing was vital in the administrative and ideological consolidation of the unified polity of Egypt. Whereas many scholars have sought historical information in the hieroglyphs on such monuments as the Narmer Palette, these may not record specific exploits as much as expressing general aspirations and conformity to norms of rulership through apparently specific references.

Usage in the 1st–2nd Dynasties

Representation and writing crystalized and drew together around the beginning of the 1st Dynasty, when the artistic principles of register composition were also elaborated, the whole forming a stable system which changed little for two centuries, and whose maintenance must have absorbed a large amount of resources. Writing already divided into hieroglyphs, used in artistic compositions, and cursive forms used for administration and mostly written in ink; these latter are the forerunners of the hieratic script.

Many inscribed artifacts are preserved from the first two Dynasties, the most numerous categories being cylinder seals and sealings, cursive annotations on pottery, and tags originally attached to tomb equipment, especially of the 1st Dynasty kings. Continuous language was still not recorded, but the verb form of the narrative infinitive appears and may well represent a semi-linguistic construct devised for notation in a limited writing system, rather than a form transferred from the spoken language.

The tags attest indirectly to a related reform around the beginning of the 1st Dynasty in which year names of kings were introduced for dating purposes. Years were named after salient events and a record kept of their order and identification. This record, often termed the annals, survived into the 5th Dynasty (and probably beyond into the Middle Kingdom). It is known from the fragmentary basalt slab called the Palermo Stone, and is probably an ancestor of the modern counting of dynasties. Together with the tags, the Palermo Stone attests both to the year names themselves and to an expanding record of events that went beyond the narrowly functional. Many years are named after rituals.

The tags give a fuller record of year names than the Palermo Stone and exhibit a different principle of organization. Until the Middle Kingdom, most writing was arranged either in vertical columns or in tabular form, but the tags are organized in horizontal lines. The lines are essentially pictorial in layout, and hieroglyphs are sometimes present at a miniature scale or only partially integrated into the design. This linear organization shows that the tags are elaborate semi-pictorial equivalents for the vertically written notations on the Palermo Stone, rather than identical records; they are probably ceremonial in intent, and so do not indicate how year names were used on normal administrative documents. Necropolis sealings found at Abydos contain enumerations of rulers from Narmer to the end of the 1st Dynasty and thus show the use of writing for a condensation of "history" as well as for the "annals."

How extensively writing was used for administration is uncertain. Papyrus rolls were invented by the middle of the 1st Dynasty and possibly earlier, so that a suitable surface for large documents was available, but the only papyrus preserved from the period is a small uninscribed roll found in a fine inlaid box in the mid-1st Dynasty tomb of a high official. This attests to the prestige of papyrus, but the material may or may not have been in everyday use at that date. The earliest preserved inscribed papyri are administrative rolls perhaps of the late 4th Dynasty from Gebelein. These clearly belong to a long-standing tradition.

Early administrative documents were probably tables, ledgers, and lists accompanying deliveries. Because continuous language was not written, letters may not have existed. Documents would have needed an oral context to be fully comprehensible. Writing was therefore an aid to personal contact rather than an impersonal replacement for it. Evidence for the use of writing in administration derives more from the titles of officials and the naming of government institutions on sealings and tags than from documents written in those institutions, which do not survive. The administration was quite well developed, with separate departments for different categories of materials and activities. Most sealings were applied to jars and probably to other types of containers, and thus were guarantees of the integrity and ownership of what was delivered. At the same time they no doubt marked the prestige of the owner and of the product.

Writing in early Egypt was integrated with the ruling group. Almost all preserved material comes from cemeteries and relates to the small elite of high officials and their subordinates. It does not allow us to say whether writing was widespread in the whole country, but it is safe to assume that literacy was extremely limited. As in later times, the leading members of society held administrative office. Their seals, which disseminated one of the main uses of writing, were important badges of office marking delegated royal power, often through royal names inscribed on them. By the 3rd Dynasty, the connections between administrative power and the status of scribes were depicted explicitly in the pictorial representations and titularies of such high officials as Hesire. Another usage of writing that points to its significance is on small artifacts, such as metal vases and ivories, dedicated as votive offerings in temples or deposited in tombs. Inscribed stone vases of the first two Dynasties, many of which appear to have been used in the cult of the gods, were deposited in large quantities beneath the Step Pyramid of Zoser in the 3rd Dynasty.

Despite writing's very high status, most larger inscribed monuments of the first two Dynasties are unimpressive. Non-royal stelae with figures of the deceased are known from Abydos, where those from subsidiary tombs surrounding the royal monuments are particularly poorly worked, and from Helwan and Saqqara. A few have elaborate titularies and some include offering lists, which were the essential focus of interest in a mortuary context. The lists, which became vastly extended in the Old Kingdom, are in a sense the original form of Egyptian "literature," a written form conveying culturally significant material in the form writing could then record. Contrasting with the non-royal stelae are the royal stelae from Abydos and probably Saqqara, whose sole decoration is the king's Horus name. The finest monuments may have been temple reliefs, of which fragments are known from Hierakonpolis (reign of Khasekhem; end of the 2nd Dynasty), and from Gebelein.

Further development of the system

Around the late 2nd Dynasty and lasting into the 3rd, there was a reform of writing which regularized sign forms, reduced the number of different signs, and led to a greatly increased use of writing in works of art (and probably in administration). The most important change appears to have been the encoding of continuous language. Perhaps the earliest preserved full sentence in Egyptian is on a seal of the reign of peribson late in the 2nd Dynasty. Within a generation or two, the design of temple reliefs was perfected to include speeches of deities to the king in which they vouchsafed to him gifts of life, long duration on the throne, and power. The presentation of titularies on early 3rd Dynasty non-royal monuments approaches the standard and style of classical Old Kingdom writing. Thus, available evidence suggests that the hieroglyphic writing system was improved for purposes of high culture and display rather than for administration; but the latter no doubt also exploited such developments.

See also

Abydos, Umm el-Qa'ab; Early Dynastic period, overview; Egyptian language and writing; Gebelein; Hierakonpolis; Old Kingdom, overview; papyrus; representational evidence, Early Dynastic; textual sources, Old Kingdom; writing, reading and schooling

Further reading

Baines, J. 1989. Communication and display: the integration of early Egyptian art and writing. *Antiquity* 63: 471–82.

Dreyer, G. *et al.* 1993. Umm el-Qaab: Nachuntersuchungen im frühzeitlichen Königsfriedhof, 5./6. Vorbericht. *MDAIK* 49:23–62.

Helck, W. 1990. *Thinitische Topfmarken* (ÄA 50). Wiesbaden.

Kahl, J. 1994. *Das System der ägyptischen Hieroglyphenschrift in der 0.–3. Dynastie.* GOF IV: 29.

Kaplony, P. 1963. *Die Inschriften der ägyptischen Frühzeit*, 3 vols (ÄA 8). Wiesbaden.

Schott, S. 1950. *Hieroglyphen: Untersuchungen zum Ursprung der Schrift*. Wiesbaden.

JOHN BAINES

writing, reading and schooling

What is known about reading, writing and schooling in ancient Egypt comes primarily from copies of texts on papyri and ostraca (potsherds and flakes or pieces of limestone which provided an inexpensive surface for writing and drawing). These texts were used in schools as exercises with the double purpose of providing examples of writing to be copied while also including instructional or edifying contents. Already in the Old Kingdom Egypt had a very large bureaucracy with many positions that required scribal training. Who was chosen for schooling is not clear, though presumably a father's position frequently had influence on that of his son, so many would have learned from their fathers or followed the same course of training. Instructions from father to son perhaps developed out of auto-biographical texts, often inscribed on funerary stelae. This genre of instructional literature provided guidance in social behavior, ranging from good manners or etiquette to clearly moral pronouncements, from very general rules for success to specific behavior to be copied or avoided. While some of these instructions were put in the mouths of famous men, they evidently were most frequently collected from different sources and could have been valuable regardless of the bureaucratic level. Although surviving copies are in Middle Egyptian and from the Middle Kingdom and later, several texts are attributed to Old Kingdom viziers (such as Ptahhotep and Kagemni) and a priestly prince named Hordedef.

A significant variation in the traditional instruction seems to have originated in the Heracleopolitan period (9th–10th Dynasties), or at least it was attributed to an unfortunate king from Heracleopolis who lived during the First Intermediate Period, following the collapse of the Old Kingdom. In this *Instruction for King Merikare*, the father advises his son not only concerning those things that he should do but also about what he should not do, with himself as a bad example of a man, even a king, facing divine retribution for allowing his soldiers to sack an ancient cemetery. The text is elegant with a high moral tone stressing fear of god (Re), who is described as being omniscient and just, who discerns between those righteous of heart and hypocrites. It is indeed an edifying work based on an authentic historical event, and would certainly have made an impression on the young scribes copying it in school. Another "royal" instruction, this one known to have been composed by a scribe named Khety, also has a historical setting, and is actually used to explain the assassination of King Amenemhat I, the supposed author. Here the tone is not so moral or ethical, but the young heir apparent is warned that even a king must be on guard at all times. Senusret I, the son and successor of the assassinated king, likely had this *ex-post facto* last will and testament composed to enhance his own reputation and provide at least a partial account of what must have been a serious dynastic crisis. This poorly written propaganda piece obviously was successful, as it remained one of the most popular school texts for at least 700 years.

In addition to the many other school texts of instructions, stories, lamentations and complaints, copied formerly or as actual school writing exercises (and numerous copies, often abbreviated from memory), there are also a number of texts with a purely pedagogic purpose. The so-called *Satire on the Trades* by the same scribe, Khety, was written to make any other occupation than the scribal profession appear absolutely revolting and obviously undesirable. Besides avoiding all the dangers of the other professions satirized, the student who becomes a scribe is told that he will be his own boss. This work also survives in hundreds of partial copies, but apparently needed reinforcing by other texts warning school boys to avoid beer "halls," and threatening beatings with aphorisms like "a boy's ears are on his back." Some of the texts were even used to lure students to become teachers, describing the rewards of the profession as having a fine villa on the river with an abundance of fowl and cattle at hand.

Another type of classroom text that was instructive was the sample letter. All of these demonstrate the formal aspects of letter writing, some to superiors and others to inferiors, but some of these were also descriptive of situations likely to be encountered or were accounting procedures that would be useful in the students' future professions. One specific example by a supposed manure shoveler goes on for twenty-eight pages telling the addressee how stupid he is, incapable of dealing with all the problems and identities the writer lists. Obviously, there is much here that the young scribes had to absorb to avoid such ridicule. This satirical letter also contained mathematical problems involving logistics and geography.

One final type of school text has a wonderful introduction that presents it as an encyclopedia of knowledge. What follows, however, is a list of names—sun, moon, planets, stars, types of land and waterways, geographical locations, and occupations. This list of common and proper nouns has considerable logic in its arrangement, but, unless the students or teacher had some elaboration in mind, however brief, it would be far from complete in itself.

While the principal deity associated with wisdom and writing is the moon god, Thoth, there is also a goddess, Seshat, whose patronage is more clearly limited to writing. Generally those who had learned to read and write included officials, priests, physicians, teachers, some military scribes, butlers, draftsmen and ordinary workmen. Some workmen clearly wrote letters to their wives without going through the intermediary step of employing professional scribes for writing and reading them. Some women were proud enough of their literacy that they had scribal equipment included in their tomb portraits, and the title "scribess" is known. Graffiti left in many out of the way places presupposed that their finders would be able to read them, and numerous inscribed temples, tombs and stelae would indicate that more than a few people would have understood at least some of what was written. Letters to the dead may have been optimistic, but are so intimate and non-professional in appearance that they had to be authentic jottings of those who considered this the best way to express themselves.

There were certainly both palace and temple schools in ancient Egypt, but how many and how large or precisely where they were located is not known. There may have been village schools, but local scribes could also have taught apprentices or others eager to learn. An early reference to a scribe who took his own son "to the Residence [palace] to place him in the school of writings among the children of the magistrates, the most eminent men of the Residence" occurs at the beginning of Khety's *Satire on the Trades*. A high priest of Amen in the Ramesside period (19th–20th Dynasties), Bakenkhonsu, recorded going to school at age five and studying for twelve years in the writing school of the temple of the goddess, "Lady of Heaven."

There are references to show that in the schools students read aloud as well as copied texts to practice writing, and also did calculations. For their practice pieces they used wooden tablets covered with gesso or limestone pieces cut in a similar shape, and they worked with reed brushes and ink made from soot. The types of errors encountered in manuscripts would indicate that some scribes copied from texts that they occasionally misread, and others may have misunderstood what they heard dictated to them. Corrections found in manuscripts indicate that they were sometimes collated either by the copyist himself or by a teacher.

A bureaucracy the size of Egypt's required a core of educated people. Whether high ranking or not, those who were schooled were among the elite and had potential for advancement. The schools do not seem to have changed much over the historically well-known periods, and even the texts used were remarkably consistent for probably a millennium. This means that when their spoken language had changed markedly, the texts they were using in school in the later periods were practically in a foreign language.

See also

administrative bureaucracy; Egyptian (language), decipherment of; First Intermediate Period, overview; Middle Kingdom, overview; New Kingdom, overview; Old Kingdom, overview; papyrus; textual sources, Middle Kingdom; textual sources, New Kingdom; textual sources, Old Kingdom

Further reading

Brunner, H. 1957. *Altägyptische Erziehung*. Wiesbaden.
Janssen, R.M., and J.J. Janssen. 1990. *Growing Up in Ancient Egypt*. London.
Montet, P. 1958. *Everyday Life in Egypt in the Days of Ramesses the Great*. London.

LEONARD H. LESKO

Z

Zawiyet el-Aryan

Zawiyet el-Aryan is a village on the west bank of the Nile about 6 km south of the Giza pyramids (29°57′ N, 31°09′ E). In its vicinity are the remains of tombs dating from the 1st Dynasty, the New Kingdom, and Roman times. Its principal monuments are two pyramids, generally known as the Layer Pyramid and the Unfinished Pyramid.

The Layer Pyramid dates to the 3rd Dynasty, and is the more southerly of the two pyramids. It was explored by J.S. Perring in 1837, Gaston Maspero in 1885, Jacques de Morgan in 1896, and Alessandro Barsanti in 1900. In 1842 Richard Lepsius assigned number XIV to this pyramid. More thorough studies were done by G.A. Reisner and C.S. Fisher in 1910–1 for Harvard University and the Museum of Fine Arts, Boston.

The Layer Pyramid is a stepped pyramid measuring 83.8 m sq. at the base, and its present height is about 18 m. This pyramid was probably never finished. If completed, it would have consisted of five or six steps about 40 m high. Its thirteen or possibly fourteen upright layers of small stone blocks, quarried locally, slope inward at an angle of 68–70° toward a square brick nucleus. Each layer is about 2.6 m thick.

Steep stairs, excavated in the bedrock 12 m outside of the northeast corner of the pyramid, end in a tunnel 36 m in length, which leads to a square pit 20 m deep. At the bottom of the pit are two entrances to corridors, the one to the south having a second flight of stairs and ending at the burial chamber 24 m below ground and under the center of the pyramid. The burial chamber measures 3.6 m north–south, 2.65 m east–west, and is 3 m high. The second entrance opens northward onto a short passage which connects it with a gallery 120 m long, 1.4 m wide and 1.8 m high. At its eastern and western ends are extensions, both about 38 m long, leading southward. Thirty-two cells, all about 5 m in length and 1.6 m in width, were hollowed at equal intervals apart in the rock of the inner wall of the gallery; they are all oriented toward the pyramid. Like the burial chamber, all these cells were empty when Barsanti first entered the pyramid.

Excavation has not yielded any evidence that the pyramid had a fine limestone casing, and this seems unlikely. A suggestion that some mudbricks found on the superstructure were remnants of a brick casing is not convincing, and the bricks were probably relics of a construction ramp. Reisner's search for a mortuary temple on the east side was unsuccessful, perhaps because it may lie on the north side, like the mortuary temples of Zoser and Sekhemkhet. Reisner found a mudbrick building in the expected position north of the pyramid with stone bowls bearing the name of Khaba, the successor of Sekhemkhet. Khaba, better known by the name of Huni, was probably the king for whom the pyramid was built.

The Unfinished Pyramid is 1.5 km north of the Layer Pyramid. Commonly called "Shughul Iskandar" (the "Work of Alexander"), this pyramid probably dates to the late 4th Dynasty. The builder's name was written in ink on some of the stone blocks, but it is uncertain whether it is to be read Nebka or Bikka. (Manetho includes a king named Bicheris, the Greek form of Bikka, in the second half of the 4th Dynasty.) He may have been a son of Djedefre, and his short reign probably fell between the reigns of Djedefre and Khafre.

Barsanti excavated at the Unfinished

Pyramid for the Egyptian Antiquities Service intermittently between 1904 and 1912, and G.A. Reisner excavated there for the Museum of Fine Arts, Boston, in 1910–11. V. Maragioglio and C. Rinaldi published a survey of the pyramid in 1970.

Except for some huge limestone blocks, which formed part of what was possibly the only course laid, nothing of the superstructure has been preserved. Barsanti estimated that the base of the pyramid measured 200 m north–south and 180 m east–west. It seems unlikely, however, that it would not have had a square base, and the estimate of Maragioglio and Rinaldi that its dimensions were between 209 m (400 cubits) sq. and 213.2 m (410 cubits) sq. is more probable. Traces of an enclosure wall 2.1 m thick have been found.

What can now be seen is a rectangular shaft, 21 m deep, 25 m east–west and 11.7 m north–south, and an open trench 6.35 m wide, which slopes down from the north, joining the base of the shaft at a point just east of the middle of its north side. Both the shaft and the trench were hewn in the rock. The slope of the trench is broken by two almost flat stretches, one about halfway from the top and the other at the bottom. Between the level sections are two parallel flights of stairs which were cut in the rock. They are separated by a raised, flat-topped ramp, 0.9 m wide, and are bounded at the outer sides by two similar but narrower ramps also cut in the rock.

Owing to the poor quality of the rock at the intended level for the base of the shaft, it was deepened by 4.5 m and refilled with four layers of granite and limestone blocks, with the top layer entirely of granite except for a limestone skirting. One block of granite on the west side was hollowed to become the form of an oval sarcophagus, 2.5 m long and 1.05 m deep, on which a granite lid was laid and fastened with mortar. When it was opened, there was nothing inside except traces of a black deposit which had left a stain about 2 cm deep.

The very wide trench was designed to provide enough space for dragging the massive floor blocks—some weighing 8,000 kg—and the sarcophagus lid to the shaft. The steps in the steeper part of the trench gave the workmen a firmer foothold. A similar trench, in which an inner corridor had been built, was cut for the pyramid of Djedefre at Abu Roash. No doubt it was intended to construct such an inner corridor in this trench.

See also

Abu Roash; Lepsius, Carl Richard; Manetho; Old Kingdom, overview

Further reading

Edwards, I.E.S. 1993. *The Pyramids of Egypt*, 63–4, 146–7. Harmondsworth.

Maragioglio, V., and C. Rinaldi. 1967. *L'Architettura delle Piramide Menfite* 6: 16–29. Rapallo.

Porter, B., and R.L.B. Moss, revised by J. Málek. 1974. *Topographical Bibliography of Ancient Egyptian Hieroglyphic Texts, Reliefs and Paintings* 3: *Memphis*, 312–14. Oxford.

Stadelmann, R. 1982. Pyramiden AR. In *LÄ* 4: 1218–19.

I.E.S. EDWARDS

Glossary

alae	Latin, small rooms/apartments within a larger building.
amphora	large pottery jar with two handles and a narrow neck, most often used for the transport of liquids such as wine and olive oil.
atef	a special crown worn by the king and the god Osiris, or other associated divinities. It is shaped like the White Crown of Upper Egypt, but is surmounted by a round disc and flanked by two plumes.
Aten	the sun-disc deity worshipped by the heretical king Akhenaten (18th Dynasty) during what is called the Amarna period.
ba	sometimes translated as "soul," but more the embodiment of the "personality" of the deceased, often depicted in the form of a human-headed bird.
ballas	type of ceramic water jar, made in the region of Deir el-Ballas.
benben	sacred stone/pillar originally associated with the cult of Re of Heliopolis; as a hieroglyph it is shaped like a short, squat obelisk.
birka	Arabic, low-lying area/pool which often marks ancient monuments.
bp	"before present" in radiocarbon years.
canopic chest/jar	vessels used to store the viscera of the deceased after mummification.
cartouche	oval formed by a rope design in which the name of a ruler is inscribed in hieroglyphs.
castellum	Latin, fortress.
cella	central cult room of a temple.
core	in stone tool making, a block of stone from which flakes or blades are removed.
djed	a hieroglyph of a type of pillar, symbolizing stability.
dromos	processional street/causeway.
ennead	the nine (Heliopolitan) gods of the family of Horus
faïence	type of glazed Egyptian artifact, often blue-green in color, frequently used for beads, amulets and small artifacts.
false door	a niched design of a door in stone in the interior of a mastaba, through which the *ba* was to communicate with the deceased in the tomb and the outer world, usually carved with titles of the deceased.
favissa	burial place for sacred objects.
flake	stone tool created by striking off a small, thin sharp-edged piece of stone from a core.
gebel	Arabic, mountain/cliffs.
gezira	Arabic, sand or gravel island/mound in the Nile floodplain or Delta.
ḥ3t	a bag wig or kerchief worn by Egyptian royalty, such as Hatshepsut and Akhenaten.
handax	a large, bifacially chipped stone tool used in the Lower Paleolithic, of unknown use.
ḥeb-sed	royal jubilee, supposedly celebrated in the thirtieth year of a king's reign, but frequently celebrated earlier.
hemhem	an elaborate crown that first appears in the New Kingdom, formed by three *atef* crowns set in a row on top of horizontal ram's horns.

Glossary

hemispeos	rock-cut temple/shrine.
hes	a spouted vessel, water jar.
horreum	Latin, a warehouse.
ḥotep/ḥetep	a hieroglyph meaning "to be pleased"; also an offering table, altar, offerings.
hypostyle	a large columned hall.
ka	often translated as "spirit"; the life-force, an aspect of all living peoples, which separates from the body at death.
kohl	Arabic, black eye paint.
Levallois	stone tool making technology involving the intentional preparation of a core which would then be struck producing flake tools of a predetermined shape, first used in the Middle Paleolithic.
ma'at	meaning "justice" or "truth," but also more generally the earthly and cosmic order that the king was believed to ensure through the proper propitiation of the gods and good government, sometimes personified by the goddess Ma'at.
mammisi	literally "birth house," a temple celebrating the divine birth of a ruler.
mastaba	Arabic "bench"; a mudbrick superstructure built over a subterranean burial chamber, frequently cut in the bedrock at the bottom of a deep shaft.
menat	ceremonial beaded necklace with a weighted end worn by priestesses associated with the Hathor cult.
naos	(pl. *naoi*) sanctuary, chamber containing a cult statue/shrine.
nemes	the royal headcloth.
nome	administrative district/province in Egypt governed by a nomarch.
obelisk	tall four-sided monolithic monument tapering to a point with hieroglyphic texts which was placed in temple courtyards.
ogdoad	the (Hermopolitan) group of eight gods, consisting of four males and four females, that existed before creation.
Opet festival	the annual ceremony validating Egyptian kingship held in New Kingdom Thebes, when the cult images of Amen, Mut and Khonsu traveled in portable barks from Karnak to Luxor and back.
ostraca	(sing. ostracon) stone chips or potsherds used as a writing or drawing surface, often an inexpensive alternative to papyrus.
papyri	plural of papyrus, referring to texts written on papyrus.
peridromos	colonnade.
peristyle	courtyard surrounded by columns.
phyle	rotating system of part-time service, particularly in the priesthood.
pronaos	room/hall in front of a *naos*, usually with a columned façade.
pylon	a large temple gateway, found on temples of the New Kingdom and later.
sabbakhin	farmers who dig for *sebbakh* (see below).
saff-tomb	Arabic, "row"; a type of royal tomb (early 11th Dynasty) carved out of the hard gravel of West Thebes, with a number of subsidiary burial chambers in a row along a pillared courtyard.
saqqiya	Arabic, water-wheel used for irrigation.
scarab	amulet made in the shape of a scarab beetle.
sebbakh	Arabic, organic material and decomposed mudbrick from ancient settlements, frequently used by Egyptian farmers for fertilizer.
serdab	statue chamber/pit in a tomb.
serekh	earliest format of the royal name, within a "palace façade" design surmounted by the Horus falcon.

shawabti	a servant figure (in mummiform) placed in tombs, to serve the deceased in the afterlife.
speos	rock-cut temple.
stela	(pl. stelae) an upright stone slab, carved or painted with inscriptions and sometimes scenes.
step pyramid	the earliest form of a pyramid monument, with stepped sides rather than the true four-sided pyramidal form.
tafla	Arabic, desert clay, sometimes used as mortar.
talatat	small, stone blocks of standardized size used for temple reliefs during the reign of Akhenaten.
tell (also kom)	Arabic, mound of occupational debris formed from the successive rebuilding of structures within settlements over many (hundreds of) years.
temanos	sacred precinct of a temple, surrounded by a wall.
uraeus	the sacred cobra, a symbol of kingship.
wadi	Arabic, a seasonal stream bed formed by erosion and runoff, and in Egypt usually dry.
wadjet	an amulet, symbol of the (uninjured) eye of the god Horus.

INDEX

Index

Index

Index

Index

900

Index

Index

Index

Index

flake: bifacial, 597–603; blank, 6–14, 861–4; heat-treated, 374–6; retouched, 501–5, 824–6; side-blow, 226–9; truncated, 15–16

flask, 465–8

Flavius Abinnaeus archive, 308–12

flax, 121–4, 592–4, 745–8, 752–3

flint: knapping, 262–5, 861–4; mining, 262–5, 861–4; sources, 501–5, 558–61; tools, 6–14, 91–3, 875–8

flooding, *see* Nile River

floors, scratched or grooved, 769–72

Florence: Archaeological Museum, 194

flotation, 353–6

flowers in burial, 592–4

flute, 546–7, 551–4

fodder, 415–18, 620–5, 752–3

foliate, bifacial, 6–14, 408–11

folklore, 135–8

Followers of Horus, 371

food, 178–9, 842–5; offerings, 100–2; preparation techniques, 121–4; storage, Paleolithic, 6–14; tomb, 389–90, 852–6

foragers, 121–4

foreigners in Egypt, 66–72, 745–8, 842–5

foreshortening, 124–8

fortifications, 115–18, 129–33, 152–7, 649–52, 783–6, 791–2, 845–7

forts: coastal, 718–20; defensive chain, 141–2; North Sinai, 733–7; Palestinian, 259–61; Roman, 531–4, 682–4, 763–9; Syrian, 87–90

Foucart, G., 338

foundations, 199–201; deposits, 199–201, 475–80, 491–3, 497–8, 755–7, 812–14, 845–7; platform, 491–3; sacrifices, 786–9; trenches, 199–201

Fouquet Collection, 789–91

Fourier, Jean-Joseph, 192, 557

Fourtau, R., 473

Fourth Cataract, 283–9, 325–8, 423–7, 485–7, 574–9, 579–82, 583–4

fowl, 305, 752–3

fowling, 15–16, 306–8, 592–4, 728–31, 759–61; scenes, 124–8, 493–7, 666–8, 668–70

Frankfort, Henri, 95–7, 137, 293–4

frankincense, 636–7

Fraser, George W., 169–70, 338–9, 363

Frazer, James G., 137

French Academy of Sciences, 557–8

French Archaeological Mission at Saqqara, 709–11

French Commission of Arts and Sciences (in Egypt), 557–8

French Institute of Archaeology, Cairo (IFAO), 82–4, 114–15, 216–19, 252–4, 334–8, 397–9, 406–8, 447–9, 473–4, 475–80, 773–4, 774–6

Friedman, Ren e, 26, 374, 632–6

frit, 357–8

frontier: eastern, 783–6; southern, 574–9

fruit, 752–3

Fundacion Clos, Barcelona, 325

funeral: artifacts, 795–7; banquets, 668–70, 819–22; chapels, 331–4; cones, 551–4, 668–70, 809–11; cult, 36–41, 801–2; enclosures, 95–7, 109–13, 432–8, 700–4; equipment, 255–9; meal, 366–7, 666–8; processions, 668–70, 819–22; rites, 487, 493–7, 505–10

funerary temple, *see* tomb

funerary texts, 42–6, 93–5, 319–21, 321–4, 518–21, 583–4, 795–7, 798–800, 819–22

furnaces, 647–9

furniture, 838–41; replicas, 340–1; *see also* temple and tomb

el-Fustat (Old Cairo), 488–90, 849–51

Gabel, Creighton, 465–9

Gabolde, Luc, 394–7, 812

Gabra, Sami, 848

Gaillard, C., 338

Gaius Petronius, Roman prefect, 650

galena, 143–5, 334–8, 522–6, 558–61, 592–4

Galerius, Emperor, 86

Galilee, 189, 443

gallstones, 604–6

game board, 665

game enclosure, 752–3

games, 267–9, 430, 838–41

Gaminarti, 518–21

Gara Oasis, 744–5

Garbrecht, Gunther, 864–6

garden, 381–2, 752–3, 763–9, 778–82; *see also* models

Gardiner, Sir Alan H., 524, 647, 809, 880

Gardner, E. A., 562

Gardner, E. W., 19, 26, 191, 408, 411

garlic, 658–60

garnet, 143–5, 385–7, 551–4, 558–61, 749–51

garrisons, 66–72, 647–9, 783–6

Garstang, John, 23–9, 95–7, 97–100, 104–6, 169–70, 371–4, 505–10, 510–15, 515–18

Gasus, 637

gate, 84–7

gathering, 6–14, 15–16, 752–3

Gauls, 463

Gauthier, Henri, 809

Gautier, Achilles, 300–6

Gautier, Joseph-tienne, 447

Gayet, Albert Jean, 140

Gaza, 54–6, 133–5, 186–9, 377–9, 442–4, 455–8, 733–7

gazelle: dorcas, 306; Red-fronted, 15–16

Gazelle Nome, *see* Beni Hasan

Geb, 497–8, 548–50, 607–10, 656–7

Gebel Abu Hamamid, 522–6

Gebel Abusir, 91–3

Gebel Adda, 579–82

Gebel Barkal, 325–8; Amen temple, 325–8; cemeteries, 325–8; Hillet el-Arab tombs, 325–8; Napatan palace, 325–8; Napatan temples, 326–8; *see also* Napata

Gebel Darah West, 861–4

Gebel Dokhan, 531–4

Gebel el-Araq, 665

Gebel el-Atawi, 522–6

Gebel el-Haridi, 328–31

Gebel el-Hudi, 871–2

Gebel el-Rus, 721

Gebel el-Silsila, 204–6, 331–4, 391–4, 574–9, 819–22

Gebel el-Teir, 204–6

Gebel Hof, 592–4

Gebel Ladid el-Gidan, 861–4

Gebel Safr Abu Had, 861–4

Gebel Sheikh Suleiman, 79–80

Gebel Sikait, 731–3

Gebel Tingar, 152–7

Gebel Uweinat, 195, 195

Gebel Zeit, 334–8, 522–6, 861–4

Gebel Zubara, 731–3

Gebelein, 316–19, 338–40, 882–5

Gebelein Papyri, 801–2

Geertz, Clifford, 136

geese, 6, 302, 528

Geller, Jeremy, 178–9, 373, 881–2

Gem-Aten (Tell el-Amarna), 769–72

Gempaten, *see* Kawa

Index

Index

Index

Index

Index

Index

Index

Index

Index

Index

Ramesses X, King: tomb (Thebes, Valley of the Kings, KV 18), 828–31
Ramesses XI, King, 186–9, 247–9, 394–7, 828–31
Ramesses-meriamen, son of Ramesses III, 834–5
Ramesseum, *see* Thebes
Ramesside period, 868–71, 878–81
Rammius, 531–4
Ramose and Hatnefer (parents of Senenmut), 819–22
Ramose, 293–4, 822–4
rampart, 404–5
ramps, 394–7, 639–45, 769–72
Raneb, King, 31–5
Raphia (Sinai), 733–7
Ras Gharib, 334–8
Ras Qasrun, 733–7
Ras Shamra, 207–9
Ras Umm el-Rakham, 141–2
Rashid, *see* Rosetta
Rat-taui, 475–80, 838
rations, 752–3
Ray, John D., 610–11, 691–4
Rayt, 165–7
Re, 40, 42, 47, 80, 143–5, 204–6, 294–5, 342–6, 368–70, 400–4, 497–8, 607–10, 795–7, 812–14, 885–7; Litany, 65, 323, 670, 671
Re, Son of, 412
Re-Atum, 325–8
Re-Horakhty, 87–90, 234–7, 252–4, 289–93, 481–5, 757–9
reading, 745–8, 885–7
realm of the dead, 583–4
rebirth, 458–60
rebus, 274–6
recarving, 394–7
reconstructions, 243–4
recording process (archaeology), 340–1
Red Crown of Lower Egypt, 239–41
Red Land, *see* Deshret
Red Sea: canals, 878–81; coast, 842–5; ports, 168–9, 485–7, 684–6; scenes of marine life in, 671–4; trade, 259–61, 488–90, 636–7; watersheds, 195–8
Red Sea Hills, *see* Eastern Desert
Redford, Donald B., 57–61, 201–4, 391–4, 499–500, 878–81
redistributive system, 66–72, 97–100, 465–8, 510–15, 518–21, 745–8
Redjedef, *see* Djedefre, King
Redmount, Carol A., 789–91, 878–81
reduction sequences, 597–603
reed matting, 551–4
Regeita, 522–6
regiments (army), 145–7
regional survey, 104–6
Rehkmire, 546–7
Rehres, 485–7
Rehu, 124–8
Reisner, George Andrew, 152–7, 244–6, 282, 325–8, 340–1, 347–50, 351, 352, 353–6, 421–3, 423–7, 505–10, 510–15, 539, 551–4, 583–4, 661–2, 716–18, 889, 890
Rekhmire, Vizier, 243–4, 438–41; tomb, 115–18, 118–21, 157–9, 522–6, 657–8, 668–70, 798–800, 822–4
relative chronology, 233–4
relief decoration, 694–9
relief sculpture, 674–7
reliefs, Meroitic, 518–21
'relieving' chambers, of Khufu's pyramid (Giza), 347–50
religion: state, 662–5; Egyptian, 518–21; Roman period, 73–6; ritual, scenes of, 671–4; texts, 66–72, 793–5, 798–800
remote sensing (in archaeology), 350–1

Reneferef, *see* Neferefre
Renenutet, shrine of, 47–52
Renni, 289–93
Renseneb, 289–93
Report of Wenamen, 755, 799, 843
representational evidence: Early Dynastic, 665–6; Predynastic, 679–82; Middle Kingdom private tombs, 666–8; New Kingdom private tombs, 668–70; New Kingdom royal tombs, 670–1; New Kingdom temples, 671–4; Old Kingdom private tombs, 674–7; papyri and ostraca, 677–9
Reqaqna, 589–92
Res Gestae Divi Augusti, 73–6
reserve head, 353–6, 838–41
Resh, Overseer of Ships, 694–9
Resheph, 186–9, 607–10
resins, 143–5, 455–8, 636–7, 842–5
resist-dyed textiles, 658–60
resurrection/rebirth of the king, 583–4
Retjenu (part of Syria), 186–9
retouching, 6–14, 408–11, 597–603, 824–6
reunification of Egypt (11th Dynasty), 42–6
Revez, Jean, 475–81
Rhind Papyrus, 54–6, 377–9
rhinoceros, 6–14
Rhinocolura, 733–7
Rhodes, 118–21
rhyton, 118–21, 546–7
Rib-Adda, 133–5
Richards, Janet, 95–7
Ricke, Herbert, 211, 791
Rifa, 544, 615–16
Rifaud, Jean Jacques, 755, 789
Rinaldi, C., 211–12, 347, 890
rings, 297–8, 385–7
Rizkana, Ibrahim, 455
Ro, King, 109–13
roads, 246–7, 363–4, 682–4, 684–6, 871–2
Robichon, C., 475–80
rock art, 226–9, 306–8
rock crystal, 716–18, 558–61
rock drawings, 289–93, 331–4, 871–2
rock inscriptions, 152–7, 283–9, 289–93
rock slides, 243–4
rock tablet, 875–8
rock temple, 731–3
rock-cut tomb, 152–7, 589–92
Rod el-'Air, 724
Roeder, Gunther, 147, 149
Roehrig, Catharine H., 242
Roentgen, Wilhem, 604
Rohlfs, G., 298, 408
Rome: administration of Egypt, 73–6; baths, 414–15; citizenship, 73–6; court, 485–7; garrisons, 73–6, 485–7, 515–18; Isis and Serapis temple, 165–7; legions, 73–6; Roman period overview, 73–7; records, 793–5; texts, 485–7; *see also* forts
Rome University, 298–300, 325–8
Rondot, Vincent, 394–7
rope, 610–11, 639–45
Rosellini, Ippolito, 169, 281
Rosellini, Niccolo, 192, 331, 423, 441
Rosetta Stone, 66–72, 192, 271–2, 273, 281, 557–8, 686–7
Rosher, Charles, 252–4
Rosing, F. W., 542
Rothenberg, B., 722
routes, caravan, 423–7
Roveri, A. M. Donadoni, 338–40

927

Index

928

Index

Seth, 220–2, 222–6, 247–9, 269–71, 328–31, 411–13, 548–50, 594–5, 607–10, 647–9, 657–8, 755–7, 778–82, 798–800
Seth of Avaris, 377–9
Sethe, Kurt, 625–6, 709–11
Sethherkhopshef, son of Ramesses III, 834–5
Sethnakht, King, 57–61, 458–60, 814–18, 828–31
Seti I, King: cenotaph, 321–4; mortuary temple, 475–80, 826–8; mummy, 537–42; sarcophagus, 168–9, 321–4; tomb, 168–9, 321–4, 828–31
Seti I Papyrus, 172–4
Seti II, King, 147–50, 247–9, 331–4, 394–7, 400–4, 458–60, 733–7, 814–18, 828–31, 868–71
Setjau, Viceroy of Kush, 445–7
Setka, nomarch, 316–19
Setne Khaemwas and Naneferkaptah, The Story of, 776–8
settlement: Badarian, 161–3; desert, 195–8; foreign, 469–73; Predynastic, 114–15, 143–5, 455–8, 555–6; preservation of, 841–2
settlement archaeology, 191, 262–5
settlement hierarchy, 733–7
settlement patterns: Delta, 499–500; Meroitic, 518–21; pre-historic, 408–11
Severus Alexander, Emperor, 139–41
Seyala, 79–80, 185–6
Seyene, see Elephantine
Shabaka, King, 62–5, 150–2, 252–4, 394–7, 421–3, 423–7, 491–3, 548–50, 868–71
Shabataka, King, 394–7
shaduf, 381, 509
shaft tomb, see tomb
Shalek, King, 377–9
Shalfak, 576, 842
el-Shalla, 207–9
Shalmaneser V of Assyria, 150–2
Shamarkian assemblage, 15–16
Shamash-shum-ukin, Assyrian ruler of Babylon, 150–2
Shapur I, 73–6
Shaqanba, 629–32
Shardana (Sea People), 718–20
shards (pottery), 677–9
Sharuhen, see Tell el-Ajjul
Shasu, 442–4
Shaw, Ian, 363–5, 731–3, 871–2
shawabti, see temple
She-resy, see Fayum lake
Shebin el-Qanater (Qaliubiya province), 791–2
Shebitku, King, 150–2, 252–4, 421–3
Shechem, 133–5
Shed, 607–10
Shedyet, 47–52
sheep: Barbary, 306, 306–8; domestic, 15–16, 303–4; fat-tailed, 300–6; hair or screw-horned hair, 300–6; horned, 679–81; wild, 17–21; wool or 'amen', 300–6; woolly, 752–3
Sheikh 'Ibada, see Antinoopolis
Sheikh Abd el-Qurna, see Thebes
Sheikh el-Baled (statue), 716–18
Sheikh el-Haridi, 328–31
Sheikh 'Esa, 161–3
Sheikh Muftah culture, 220–2
Sheikh Sa'id, 246–7, 493–7, 589–92
Sheikh Zuweid, 733–7
shekel, 442–4
Shekelesh (Sea People), 718–20
Shelfak, 579–82
Shellal (plain south of Aswan), 152–7, 185–6
Shelley, Percy Bysshe, 813
shellfish, 6–14

shells: bracelet, 143–5, 161–3, 226–9, 592–4
Shemai, Vizier, 42–6, 657–8
Shemanefer, 294–5
Shendi, 510–15
Shepenwepet II, divine adoratrix, 394–7, 481–5, 866–8
Shephelah (Israel), 442–4
Shepseskaf, King, 351–3, 711–12
Shepseskare, King, 90–1
Shepsi-pu-Mim, Governor, 124–8
Sheshat, 607–10, 812–14, 885–7
Sheshonk I, King, 62–5, 368–70, 442–4, 445–7, 671–4
Sheshonk III, King, 62–5
Sheshy, King, see Maaibre Sheshy, King
shields, Hittite, 647–9
Shig el-Ateyat (Thebes), 804–5 XR?
Shinnie, P. L., 510
ship building (or dismantling), 866–8
ships/boats, 728–31; decorative motifs, 728–31; Egyptian terms for, 728–31; foreign, 728–31; funerary, 350–1; piloting, 745–8; pit (of pyramid complex), 342–6, 347–50; ritual importance of, 679–81; river craft, 728–31
ships/boats, royal, 106–8; Sahure temple relief, 730; scenes of, 90–1, 106–8, 679–81, 745–8; sea-going, 728–31; wooden plank, 728–31; see also burials: boat; models; barks
shipwreck, 207–9, 842–5
Shipwrecked Sailor, The, 206
shoes, 610–11
Shoshenk I, King, 331–4, 491–3
Shoshenk II, King, 757–9
Shoshenk III, King, 757–9, 845–7
Shoshenk V, King, 755–7
shrew, sacred animal of Heracleopolis, 368–70
shrines, 704–8; private, 769–72; workmen's, 244–6, 363–4
Shu, 179–80, 458–60, 497–8, 548–50, 607–10, 791–2; Theology, 654
Shubert, Steven Blake, 103–4, 807–8
Shut (in trans-Jordan?), 186–9
Shuwikhat-1, 6–14
Si-Amen, 738–44
Si-Iset, 321–4
Sia (diety), 607–10
Siamen, King, 62–5, 382–4, 442–4, 671–4, 755–7, 757–9
Sicard, Claude, 281
Sicily, 718–20
sickle, 17–21, 298–300, 313–15, 455–8, 501–5, 592–4, 786–9, 824–6
sidder tree, 558–61, 620–5
Sidebotham, Steven E., 84–7, 170–2, 682–4, 684–6
sidereal year, 229–32
sidescraper, 6–14
Sidmant el-Gabel, see Heracleopolis
Sidon, 150–2, 442–4
siege scene, 589–92
signal towers, 759–61, 868–71
Sihathor, King, 54–6
Sikait-Zubara, 731–3
Sikru Haddu, see Seker Her, King
Silah, see Seila
Sile, 54–6, 150–2, 755–7
silica, 297–8, 357–8
silos, grain, 244–6, 313–15, 786–9
siltation, 195–8
silver, 62–5, 252–4, 385–7, 522–6, 558–61, 749–51, 757–9, 786–9, 845–7, 868–71
Silverman, David, 561–4
el-Simbillawein, 497–8
Simmons, A. H., 408–11

Index

Index

Index

Index